# The Forbes® Book of Business Quotations

# The Forbes® Book of Business Quotations

*14,266 Thoughts on the Business of Life*

EDITED BY TED GOODMAN

BLACK DOG
& LEVENTHAL
PUBLISHERS

Published by
Black Dog & Leventhal Publishers, Inc.
151 West 19th Street
New York, NY 10011

Distributed by
Workman Publishing Company
708 Broadway
New York, NY 10003

Designed by Martin Lubin Graphic Design
Typesetting by Angela Taormina

Manufactured in the United States of America

h g f e d c b a

**Library of Congress Cataloging-in-Publication Data**
The Forbes book of business quotations / edited by Tom Goodman.
p. cm.
Includes index.
Jacketed Trade Edition: ISBN 1-884822-62-2
Deluxe Edition: ISBN 1-884822-94-0
1. Business—Quotations, maxims, etc. I. Goodman, Ted, 1952–
II. Forbes.
PN6084.P87F66 1997
650—dc21 96-52600
CIP

# CONTENTS

# FOREWORD

Many things about *Forbes* Magazine have changed since its first issue appeared in 1917. One that has not is "Thoughts on the Business of Life." This last page of the magazine, which collects wisdom new and old, consistently has been among the most read in the magazine.

It was almost half-a-century ago that our grandfather, B.C. Forbes, first collected "Thoughts" between hard covers. With each edition, the selection has expanded and changed, but the animating idea has not. His introduction to the original volume follows. It eloquently explains the underlying purpose of "Thoughts" and, indeed of *Forbes* Magazine itself.

Undoubtedly, B.C. would be delighted and proud that continued demand led to the current volume. So are we!

Steve Forbes

# INTRODUCTION

The moving motive in establishing *Forbes* Magazine, in 1917, was ardent desire to promulgate humaneness in business, then woefully lacking.

Too many individual and corporate employers were merely mercenarily—minded, obsessed only with determination to roll up profits regardless of the suicidal consequences of their shortsighted conduct.

They were without consciousness of their civic, social, patriotic responsibilities.

This writer warned, a third-of-a-century ago, that unless employers altered their tactics, unless they exhibited more consideration for their workers, the time would come when "Politicians will step in and do the job in a way that employers will not like."

That had happened with a vengeance!

Every issue of *Forbes,* since its inception, has appeared under the masthead: "With all thy getting, get understanding."

Not only so, but we have devoted, all through the years, a full page to "Thoughts on the Business of Life," reflections by ancient and modern sages calculated to inspire a philosophic mode of life, broad sympathies, charity towards all.

Having assiduously sought all these years to pursue this objective, I would—having already passed the Biblical span of three-score-years-and-ten—pass on contented if I could conscientiously feel that we have rendered at least a little service to our day and generation, that we have done something towards bequeathing a better world for my four sons and an increasing number of grandchildren.

This volume is a humble contribution to furthering human, humane Understanding.

I'm convinced, despite all the woes, wars, strife, bloodshed afflicting mankind at this moment, that Robert Burns was truly prophetic when he wrote:

> "It's comin' yet for a' that,
> That Man to Man, the world o'er.
> Shall be brothers for a' that."

I have faith that the time will eventually come when employees and employers, as well as humankind, will realize that they serve themselves best when they serve others most.

B.C. Forbes

# A

## Ability

Because your own strength is unequal to the task, do not assume that it is beyond the powers of man; but if anything is within the powers and province of man, believe that it is within your own compass also.
MARCUS AURELIUS ANTONINUS

Ability has nothing to do with opportunity.
NAPOLEON BONAPARTE

Is it in destroying and pulling down that skill is displayed? The shallowest understanding, the rudest hand, is more than equal to the task.
EDMUND BURKE

Men who undertake considerable things, even in a regular way, ought to give us ground to presume ability.
EDMUND BURKE

Behind an able man there are always other able men.
CHINESE PROVERB

Natural ability without education has more often raised a man to glory and virtue than education without natural ability.
CICERO

Capacity never lacks opportunity. It cannot remain undiscovered because it is sought by too many anxious to use it.
BOURKE COCKRAN

I will not be concerned at other men's not knowing me; I will be concerned at my own want of ability.
CONFUCIUS

The superior man is distressed by the limitations of his ability; he is not distressed by the fact that men do not recognize the ability that he has.
CONFUCIUS

People are always ready to admit a man's ability after he gets there.
BOB EDWARDS

What I need is someone who will make me do what I can.
RALPH WALDO EMERSON

A smooth sea never made a skilled mariner.
ENGLISH PROVERB

Almost any idea is good if a man has ability and is willing to work hard. The best idea is worthless if the creator is a loafer and ineffective.
WILLIAM FEATHER

The ultimate high: A man's abilities equaling his opinion of 'em.
MALCOLM FORBES

The tools to him who has the ability to handle them.
FRENCH PROVERB

There are few, if any, jobs in which ability alone is sufficient. Needed, also, are loyalty, sincerity, enthusiasm and team play.
WILLIAM B. GIVEN, JR.

The man who occupies the first place seldom plays the principal part.
JOHANN WOLFGANG VON GOETHE

If I accept you as you are, I will make you worse; however, if I treat you as though you are what you are capable of becoming, I help you become that.
JOHANN WOLFGANG VON GOETHE

When ability exceeds ambition, or ambition exceeds ability, the likelihood of success is limited.
RALPH HALF

Ability is useless unless it's used.
ROBERT HALF

Skill and confidence are an unconquered army.
GEORGE HERBERT

It is a fine thing to have ability, but the ability to discover ability in others is the true test.
ELBERT HUBBARD

A human being feels able and competent only so long as he is permitted to contribute as much as, or more, than he has contributed to him.
L. RON HUBBARD

There is nothing of permanent value (putting aside a few human affections), nothing that satisfies quiet reflection, except the sense of having worked according to one's capacity and light to make things clear and get rid of cant and shams of all sorts.
THOMAS H. HUXLEY

A man with ability and the desire to accomplish something can do anything.
DONALD KIRCHER

Abilities wither under faultfinding, blossom under encouragement.
DONALD A. LAIRD

Latent abilities are like clay. It can be mud on shoes, brick in a building or a statue that will inspire all who see it. The clay is the same. The result is dependent on how it is used.
JAMES F. LINCOLN

We should be on our guard against the temptation to argue directly from skill to capacity, and to assume when a man displays skill in some feat, his capacity is therefore considerable.
TOM H. PEAR

In private matters everyone is equal before the law. In public matters, when it is a question of putting power and responsibility into the hands of one man rather than another, what counts is not rank or money, but the ability to do the job well.
PERICLES

Executive ability is deciding quickly and getting somebody else to do the work.
JOHN G. POLLARD

Ability and necessity dwell near each other.
PYTHAGORAS

Ability wins us the esteem of the true men; luck that of the people.
FRANÇOIS DE LA ROCHEFOUCAULD

The art of using moderate abilities to advantage often brings greater results than actual brilliance.
FRANÇOIS DE LA ROCHEFOUCAULD

It is a great ability to be able to conceal one's ability.
FRANÇOIS DE LA ROCHEFOUCAULD

It is always pleasant to be urged to do something on the ground that one can do it well.
GEORGE SANTAYANA

A man's ability cannot possibly be of one sort and his soul of another. If his soul be well-ordered, serious and restrained, his ability also is sound and sober. Conversely, when the one degenerates, the other is contaminated.
SENECA

The young man of native ability, (with) the will to work and good personality will, in the long run, get the equivalent of a college education in the tasks he will set for himself. If he has ability and determination, he will find ways to learn and to get ahead.
EDWARD G. SEUBERT

To think we are able is almost to be so; to determine upon attainment is frequently attainment itself; earnest resolution has often seemed to have about it almost a savor of omnipotence.
SAMUEL SMILES

To be what we are, and to become what we are capable of becoming, is the only end of life.
BARUCH SPINOZA

The fine points that are uncovered in our work as a result of close study, diligent care, constant application and always trying to improve our methods represent the best and most valuable knowledge we get in business—and the sum total of that attentive attitude is what we call skill.
RODERICK STEVENS

Anyone can hold the helm when the sea is calm.
PUBLILIUS SYRUS

Not because of an extraordinary talent did he succeed, but because he had a capacity of a level for business and not above it.
TACITUS

The abilities of man must fall short on one side or the other, like too scanty a blanket when you are abed.
WILLIAM J. TEMPLE

Forget yourself in your work. If your employer sees that you are more concerned about your own interests than about his, that you are fussy about getting credit of every little or big thing you do, then you are apt to be passed by when a responsible job has to be filled.... Don't worry about how big an increase in your salary you can contrive to get. Don't let your mind dwell on money at all, if you can help it. Throw yourself, body, soul, and spirit, into whatever you are doing.... The truth is that in every organization, no matter how large or how small, someone is taking notice of any employee who shows special ability.
HARRY B. THAYER

They are able because they think they are able.
VIRGIL

Men are often capable of greater things than they perform. They are sent into the world with bills of credit, and seldom draw to their full extent.
HORACE WALPOLE

Ability is a poor man's wealth.
MATTHEW WREN

## *Absurdity*

To tax and to please, no more than to love and be wise, is not given to men.
EDMUND BURKE

The absurd is sin without God.
ALBERT CAMUS

In a world where everything is ridiculous, nothing can be ridiculed. You cannot unmask a mask.
G. K. CHESTERTON

No folly is more costly than the folly of intolerant idealism.
WINSTON CHURCHILL

There is no opinion so absurd but that some philosopher will express it.
CICERO

He who hath not a dram of folly in his mixture hath pounds of much worse matter.
CHARLES CALEB COLTON

There is no fact that cannot be vulgarized and presented in a ludicrous light.
FYODOR DOSTOYEVSKY

No man is quite sane. Each has a vein of folly in his composition—a slight determination of blood to the head, to make sure of holding him hard to some one point which he has taken to heart.
RALPH WALDO EMERSON

The magnificent and the ridiculous are so close that they touch.
LE BOVIER DE FONTENELLE

Life is a jest, and
All things show it;
I thought so once,
But now I know it.
JOHN GAY

Modern man must descend the spiral of his own absurdity to the lowest point; only then can he look beyond it. It is obviously impossible to get around it, jump over it, or simply avoid it.
VACLAV HAVEL

The privilege of absurdity, to which no other living creature is subject, but man only.
THOMAS HOBBES

It is not in the world of ideas that life is *lived.* Life is lived for better or worse *in* life, and to a man *in* life, his life can be no more absurd than it can be the opposite of absurd, whatever that opposite may be.
ARCHIBALD MACLEISH

Oh, life is a glorious cycle of song,
A medley of extemporanea;
And love is a thing that can never go wrong;
And I am Marie of Roumania.
DOROTHY PARKER

Life is full of infinite absurdities, which, strangely enough, do not even need to appear plausible, because they are true.
LUIGI PIRANDELLO

To pardon those absurdities in ourselves which we cannot suffer in others, is neither better nor worse than to be more willing to be fools ourselves than to have others so.
ALEXANDER POPE

One step above the sublime makes the ridiculous, and one step above the ridiculous makes the sublime again.
**THOMAS PAINE**

Look for the ridiculous in everything, and you will find it.
**JULES RENARD**

He who lives without folly is not so wise as he thinks.
**FRANÇOIS DE LA ROCHEFOUCAULD**

Much of the wisdom of one age is the folly of the next.
**ARTHUR SCHOPENHAUER**

Ridicule: The weapon of all others most feared by enthusiasts of every description, and which from its predominance over such minds, often checks what is absurd, and fully as often smothers that which is noble.
**SIR WALTER SCOTT**

In the sphere of thought, absurdity and perversity remain the masters of the world, and their dominion is suspended only for brief periods.
**CHARLES SIMMONS**

The ultimate result of shielding men from the effects of folly is to fill the world with fools.
**HERBERT SPENCER**

The *reductio ad absurdum* is God's favorite argument.
**GEORGE TYRRELL**

## *Accomplishments*

We can accomplish almost anything within our ability if we but think that we can! Every great achievement in this world was first carefully thought out. . . . Think—but to a purpose. Think constructively. Think as you read. Think as you listen. Think as you travel and your eyes reveal new situations. Think as you work daily at your desk, or in the field, or while strolling. Think to rise and improve your place in life. There can be no advancement or success without serious thought.
**GEORGE MATTHEW ADAMS**

Financial rewards follow accomplishment, they don't precede it.
**HARRY F. BANKS**

There is nothing that God has judged good for us that He has not given us the means to accomplish, both in the natural and moral world. If we cry, like children, for the moon, like children we must cry on.
**EDMUND BURKE**

"I can't do it" never yet accomplished anything; "I will try" has performed wonders.
**GEORGE P. BURNHAM**

Life is the art of drawing sufficient conclusions from insufficient premises.
**SAMUEL BUTLER**

Knowledge may give weight, but accomplishments give lustre, and many more people see than weigh.
**LORD CHESTERFIELD**

Always there will be, along the sidelines of life, inferior souls who throw mud at those whose attainments they do not quite understand. The man who really accomplishes doesn't pay attention to such detractors. If he did, he'd be on their level. He keeps an eye singled on the higher goal—and the mud never touches him.
**JEROME P. FLEISHMAN**

Too few accomplish twice as much as too many.
**MALCOLM FORBES**

It's more fun to arrive at a conclusion than to justify it.
**MALCOLM FORBES**

In the long run, a short cut seldom is.
**MALCOLM FORBES**

Too many of us, when we accomplish what we set out to do, exclaim, "See what I have done!" instead of saying, "See where I have been led."
**HENRY FORD**

In the United States, to an unprecedented degree, the individual's social role has come to be determined not by who he is but by what he can accomplish.
**JOHN W. GARDNER**

Everyone has his superstitions. One of mine has always been when I started to go anywhere, or to do anything, never to turn back or to stop until the thing intended was accomplished.
**ULYSSES S. GRANT**

If well thou hast begun, go on; it is the end that crowns us, not the fight.
**ROBERT HERRICK**

You can do what you want to do, accomplish what you want to accomplish, attain any reasonable objective you may have in mind.... Not all of a sudden, perhaps, not in one swift and sweeping act of achievement.... But you can do it gradually—day by day and play by play—if you want to do it, if you will to do it, if you work to do it, over a sufficiently long period of time.
**WILLIAM E. HOLLER**

The most agreeable thing in life is worthy accomplishment. It is not possible that the idle tramp is as contented as the farmers along the road who own their own farms, and whose credit is good at the bank in town. When the tramps get together at night, they abuse the farmers, but do not get as much satisfaction out of it as do the farmers who abuse the tramps. The sounder your argument, the more satisfaction you get out of it.
**EDGAR WATSON HOWE**

It's amazing what ordinary people can do if they set out without preconceived notions.
**CHARLES F. KETTERING**

For truth and duty it is ever the fitting time; who waits until circumstances completely favor his undertaking, will never accomplish anything.
**MARTIN LUTHER**

In our own days we have seen no princes accomplish great results save those who have been accounted miserly.
**NICCOLÒ MACHIAVELLI**

We would accomplish many more things if we did not think of them as impossible.
**C. MALESHERBES**

No institution which does not continually test its ideals, techniques and measure of accomplishment can claim real vitality.
**JOHN MILTON**

If you have known how to compose your life, you have accomplished a great deal more than the man who knows how to compose a book. Have you been able to make your stride? You have done more than man who has taken cities and empires.
**MICHEL DE MONTAIGNE**

I wonder if there is anyone in the world who can really direct the affairs of the world, or of his country, with any assurance of the result his actions would have.
MONTAGU C. NORMAN

The man who has accomplished all that he thinks worth while, has begun to die.
E. T. TRIGG

The great accomplishments of man have resulted from the transmission of ideas and enthusiasm.
THOMAS J. WATSON

It is by what we ourselves have done, and not by what others have done for us, that we shall be remembered in after ages.
FRANCIS WAYLAND

The secret of the true love of work is the hope of success in that work; not for the money reward, for the time spent, or for the skill exercised, but for the successful result in the accomplishment of the work itself.
SIDNEY A. WELTMER

I am an acme of things accomplished, and I am an encloser of things to be.
WALT WHITMAN

## *Achievements*

It is a favorite belief of mine that no student ever attains very eminent success by simply doing what is required of him; it is the amount and excellence of what is over and above the required, that determines the greatness of ultimate distinction.
CHARLES KENDALL ADAMS

The only worthwhile achievements of man are those which are socially useful.
ALFRED ADLER

Our prayers are answered not when we are given what we ask, but when we are challenged to be what we can be.
MORRIS ADLER

Who works achieves and who sows reaps.
ARABIAN PROVERB

Nothing splendid has ever been achieved except by those who dared believe that something inside them was superior to circumstance.
BRUCE BARTON

We shall never have more time. We have, and have always had, all the time there is. No object is served in waiting until next week or even until to-morrow. Keep going day in and out. Concentrate on something useful. Having decided to achieve a task, achieve it at all costs.
ARNOLD BENNETT

Achievement is the death of endeavor and the birth of disgust.
AMBROSE BIERCE

The only conquests which are permanent and leave no regrets are our conquests over ourselves.
NAPOLEON BONAPARTE

The full-grown modern human being who seeks but refuge finds instead boredom and mental dissolution, unless he can be, even in his withdrawal, creative. He can find the quality of happiness in the strain and travail only of achievement and growth. And he is conscious of touching the highest pinnacle of fulfillment which his life-urges demand

when his is consumed in the service of an idea, in the conquest of the goal pursued.
**R. BRIFFAULT**

When a great man has some one object in view to be achieved in a given time, it may be absolutely necessary for him to walk out of all the common roads.
**EDMUND BURKE**

Every attempt, by whatever authority, to fix a maximum of productive labor by a given worker in a given time is an unjust restriction upon his freedom and a limitation of his right to make the most of himself in order that he may rise in the scale of the social and economic order in which he lives. The notion that all human beings born into this world enter at birth into a definite social and economic classification, in which classification they must remain permanently through life, is wholly false and fatal to a progressive civilization.
**NICHOLAS MURRAY BUTLER**

The great law of culture:
Let each become all that he was created capable of being.
**THOMAS CARLYLE**

The thorough man of business knows that only by years of patient, unremitting attention to affairs can he earn his reward, which is the result, not of chance, but of well-devised means for the attainment to ends.
**ANDREW CARNEGIE**

Think of yourself as on the threshold of unparalleled success. A whole clear, glorious life lies before you. Achieve! Achieve!
**ANDREW CARNEGIE**

Instead of being concerned that you have no office, be concerned to think how you may fit yourself for office. Instead of being concerned that you are not known, see to the worthy of being known.
**CONFUCIUS**

It is not the ship so much as the skillful sailing that assures the prosperous voyage.
**GEORGE WILLIAM CURTIS**

I have always admired the ability to bite off more than one can chew and then chew it.
**WILLIAM DEMILLE**

A dark horse, which had never been thought of, rushed past the grandstand in sweeping triumph.
**BENJAMIN DISRAELI**

They can conquer who believe they can.
**WILLIAM DRYDEN**

You can't achieve anything without getting in someone's way. You can't be detached and effective.
**ABBA EBAN**

The devotion of thought to an honest achievement makes the achievement possible.
**MARY BAKER EDDY**

The three great essentials to achieve anything worth while are, first, hard work; second, stick-to-itiveness; third, common sense.
**THOMAS EDISON**

What is the recipe for successful achievement? To my mind there are just four essential ingredients: Choose a career you love.... Give it the best there is in you.... Seize your opportunities.... And be a member of the team. In no country but America, I believe, is it possible to fulfill all four of these requirements.
**BENJAMIN F. FAIRLESS**

We all know that the nation can't divide more than the people produce, but as individuals we try to get more than our share and that's how we get ahead.
**WILLIAM FEATHER**

It is well for civilization that human beings constantly strive to gain greater and greater rewards, for it is this urge, this ambition, this aspiration that moves men and women to bestir themselves to rise to higher and higher achievement. Individual success is to be won in most instances by studying and diagnosing the kind of rewards human hearts seek today and are likely to seek tomorrow.
**B. C. FORBES**

Always fall in with what you're asked to accept. Take what is given, and make it over your way. My aim in life has always been to hold my own with whatever's going. Not against: with.
**ROBERT FROST**

The significance of man is not what he attains, but rather in what he longs to attain.
**KAHLIL GIBRAN**

If you think you're tops, you won't do much climbing.
**ARNOLD GLASOW**

It is only after an unknown number of unrecorded labors, after a host of noble hearts have succumbed in discouragement, convinced that their cause is lost; it is only then that the cause triumphs.
**FRANÇOIS GUIZOT**

A fellow doesn't last long on what he has done. He's got to keep on delivering as he goes along.
**CARL HUBBELL**

The rung of a ladder was never meant to rest upon, but only to hold a man's foot long enough to enable him to put the other somewhat higher.
**THOMAS H. HUXLEY**

Our business in life is not to get ahead of others but to get ahead of ourselves—to break our own records, to outstrip our yesterdays by our today, to do our work with more force than ever before.
**STEWART B. JOHNSON**

Spurts don't count. The final score makes no mention of a splendid start if the finish proves that you were an also ran.
**HERBERT KAUFMAN**

The great scientists, as all great men, have not been concerned with fame. The joy of achievement that comes from finding something new in the universe is by far their greatest joy. A great research scientist is constantly discovering new things in his field. This is his reward. He knows how to spend long years in preparation and long hours in investigation, with no thought of public honor or reward.
**WILLIAM P. KING**

Keep a definite goal of achievement constantly in view. Realize that work well and worthily done makes life truly worth living.
**GRENVILLE KLEISER**

Nothing worthwhile ever happens quickly and easily. You achieve only as you are determined to achieve . . . and as you keep at it until you have achieved.
**ROBERT H. LAUER**

I have done what I could do in life, and if I could not do better, I did not deserve it. In vain have I tried to step beyond what bound me. Despite my years, I am still trying!
**MAURICE MAETERLINCK**

In time of difficulties, we must not lose sight of our achievements.
MAO TSE-TUNG

It is more important to know where you are going than to get there quickly. Do not mistake activity for achievement.
MABEL NEWCOMBER

The balance between price in past achievements and consciousness of present shortcomings is difficult to strike.
JOHN O'REN

Take a look at those two open hands of yours. They are tools with which to serve, make friends, and reach out for the best in life. Open hands open the way to achievement. Put them to work today.
WILFRED A. PETERSON

Five minutes, just before going to sleep, given to a bit of directed imagination regarding achievement possibilities of the morrow, will steadily and increasingly bear fruit, particularly if all ideas of difficulty, worry or fear are resolutely ruled out and replaced by those of accomplishment and smiling courage.
FREDERICK PIERCE

The great achievements have always been individualistic. Indeed, any original achievement implies separation from the majority. Though society may honor achievement, it can never produce it.
GEORGE CHARLES ROCHE

There's a lot more in each of us than any of us suspects. Undoubtedly many former athletes had the power to run the four-minute mile. It was a barrier only until one man achieved it!
CHARLES K. RUDMAN

Many things which cannot be overcome when they stand together yield themselves up when taken little by little.
SERTORIUS

How my achievements mock me!
WILLIAM SHAKESPEARE

There's no thrill in easy sailing when the skies are clear and blue, there's no joy in merely doing things which any one can do. But there is some satisfaction that is mighty sweet to take, when you reach a destination that you thought you'd never make.
SPIRELLA

Is there anything in life so disenchanting as achievement?
ROBERT LOUIS STEVENSON

If one advances confidently in the direction of his dreams, and endeavors to live the life which he has imagined, he will meet with a success unexpected in common hours.
HENRY DAVID THOREAU

The awareness of the ambiguity of one's highest achievements (as well as one's deepest failures) is a definite symptom of maturity.
PAUL TILLICH

In every triumph there's a lot of try.
FRANK TYGER

Within us all there are wells of thought and dynamos of energy which are not suspected until emergencies arise. Then oftentimes we find that it is comparatively simple to double or treble our former capacities and to amaze ourselves by the results achieved. Quotas, when set up for us by others, are challenges which goad us on to surpass ourselves. The outstanding leaders of every age are those who

set up their own quotas and constantly exceed them.
**THOMAS J. WATSON**

There's a man in the world who is never turned down, wherever he chances to stray; he gets the glad hand in the populous town, or out where the farmers make hay; he's greeted with pleasure on deserts of sand, and deep in the aisles of the woods; wherever he goes there's a welcoming hand—he's the man who delivers the goods.
**WALT WHITMAN**

He who finds diamonds must grapple in mud and mire because diamonds are not found in polished stones. They are made.
**HENRY B. WILSON**

Capital which overreaches for profits, labor which overreaches for wages, or a public which overreaches for bargains will all destroy each other. There is no salvation for us on that road.
**OWEN D. YOUNG**

## *Acting*

Generally speaking, success brings out the actors' worst qualities and failure the best.
**GEORGE ABBOTT**

The trouble with plays these days is that they're too easy to understand.
**ROBERT ALLEN ARTHUR**

It's one of the tragic ironies of the theatre that only one man in it can count on steady work—the night watchman.
**TALLULAH BANKHEAD**

One of my chief regrets during my years in the theater is that I couldn't sit in the audience and watch me.
**JOHN BARRYMORE**

There is an audience for every play; it's just that sometimes it can't wait long enough to find it.
**SHIRLEY BOOTH**

After my screen test, the director clapped his hands gleefully and yelled: "She can't talk! She can't act! She's wonderful!"
**AVA GARDNER**

When I first went into the movies Lionel Barrymore played my grandfather. Later he played my father and finally my husband. If he had lived, I'm sure I would have played his mother. That's the way it is in Hollywood. The men get younger and the women get older.
**LILLIAN GISH**

Too caustic? To hell with the cost. If it's a good picture, we'll make it anyway.
**SAMUEL GOLDWYN**

I believe that God felt sorry for actors so he created Hollywood to give them a place in the sun and a swimming pool. The price they had to pay was to surrender their talent.
**SIR CEDRIC HARDWICKE**

Actors are the only honest hypocrites. Their life is a voluntary dream; and the height of their ambition is to be beside themselves.
**WILLIAM HAZLITT**

Acting is the most minor of gifts and not a very high-class way to earn a living. After all, Shirley Temple could do it at age four.
**KATHARINE HEPBURN**

I think there are probably more closet conservatives in Hollywood than there are closet homosexuals.
**CHARLTON HESTON**

Is it a stale remark to say that I have constantly found the interest excited at a playhouse to bear an exact inverse proportion to the price paid for admission?
**CHARLES LAMB**

The audience is not the least important actor in the play, and if it will not do its allotted share the play falls to pieces.
**SOMERSET MAUGHAM**

Some of the greatest love affairs I've known have involved one actor—unassisted.
**WILSON MIZNER**

One half of the pleasure experienced at a theatre arises from the spectator's sympathy with the rest of the audience, and, especially from his belief in their sympathy with him.
**EDGAR ALLAN POE**

The stage is actor's country. You have to get your passport stamped every so often or they take away your citizenship.
**VANESSA REDGRAVE**

[In the theater] you've got to perform in a role hundreds of times. In keeping it fresh one can become a large, madly humming, demented refrigerator.
**RALPH RICHARDSON**

Acting is standing up naked and turning around very slowly.
**ROSALIND RUSSELL**

It is with life as with a play—it matters not how long the action is spun out, but how good the acting is.
**SENECA**

I do not want actors and actresses to understand my plays. That is not necessary. If they will only pronounce the correct sounds I can guarantee the results.
**GEORGE BERNARD SHAW**

Heaven never helps the man who will not act.
**SOPHOCLES**

You can pick out actors by the glazed look that comes into their eyes when the conversation wanders away from themselves.
**MICHAEL WILDING**

Every now and then, when you're on the stage, you hear the best sound a player can hear. It's a sound you can't get in movies or in television. It is the sound of a wonderful, deep silence that means you've hit them where they live.
**SHELLEY WINTERS**

Acting is a child's prerogative. Children are born to act. Usually, people grow up and out of it. Actors always seem to me to be people who never quite did grow out of it.
**JOANNE WOODWARD**

## *Action*

Trust only movement.
**ALFRED ADLER**

Action is only coarsened thought—thought become concrete, obscure and unconscious.
**HENRI FRÉDÉRIC AMIEL**

For purposes of action, nothing is more useful than narrowness of thought combined with energy of will.
HENRI FRÉDÉRIC AMIEL

Effective action is always unjust.
JEAN ANOUILH

To live well is to work well, to show a good activity.
THOMAS AQUINAS

In the arena of human life the honors and rewards fall to those who show their good qualities in action.
ARISTOTLE

Use your gifts faithfully, and they shall be enlarged; practice what you know, and you shall attain to higher knowledge.
MATTHEW ARNOLD

All our actions take their hue from the complexion of the heart, as landscapes their variety from light.
FRANCIS BACON

We live in deeds, not years; in thoughts, not figures on a dial. We should count time by heart throbs. He most lives who thinks most, feels the noblest, acts the best.
PHILIP JAMES BAILEY

The secret of success is the consistency to pursue.
HARRY F. BANKS

Action without study is fatal. Study without action is futile.
MARY BEARD

Consistency requires you to be as ignorant today as you were a year ago.
BERNARD BERENSON

Think like a man of action, act like a man of thought.
HENRI BERGSON

A thought that does not result in action is nothing much, and an action that does not proceed from a thought is nothing at all.
GEORGES BERNANOS

The greatest felony in the news business today is to be behind, or to miss a big story. So speed and quantity substitute for thoroughness and quality, for accuracy and context.
CARL BERNSTEIN

The wise man never initiates any action.
BHAGAVAD GITA

The individual activity of one man with backbone will do more than a thousand men with a mere wishbone.
WILLIAM J. H. BOETCKER

Active natures are rarely melancholy. Activity and sadness are incompatible.
CHRISTIAN BOVÉE

The noblest deeds are well enough set forth in simple language; emphasis spoils them.
JEAN DE LA BRUYÈRE

Though good may come of practice,
this primal truth endures:
The first time anything is done,
It's done by amateurs.
ART BUCK

Every person has some splendid traits and if we confine our contacts so as to bring those traits into

action, there is no need of ever being bored or irritated or indignant.
GELETT BURGESS

No men can act with effect who do not act in concert; no men can act in concert who do not act with confidence; no men can act with confidence who are not bound together with common opinions, common affections, and common interests.
EDMUND BURKE

It is not what a lawyer tells me I may do, but what humanity, reason and justice tell me I ought to do.
EDMUND BURKE

The most drastic and usually the most effective remedy for fear is direct action.
WILLIAM BURNHAM

Every noble work is at first impossible.
THOMAS CARLYLE

The end of man is action, and not thought, though it be of the noblest.
THOMAS CARLYLE

He that has done nothing has known nothing.
THOMAS CARLYLE

There is no Fate that plans men's lives. Whatever comes to us, good or bad, is usually the result of our own action or lack of action.
HERBERT N. CASSON

Good actions ennoble us, and we are the sons of our own deeds.
MIGUEL DE CERVANTES

We inherit nothing truly, but what our actions make us worthy of.
JOHN CHAPMAN

Dispatch is the soul of business.
LORD CHESTERFIELD

A man of sense may be in haste, but can never be in a hurry.
LORD CHESTERFIELD

Whoever is in a hurry shows that the thing he is about is too big for him.
LORD CHESTERFIELD

An adventure is only an inconvenience rightly considered. An inconvenience is only an adventure wrongly considered.
G. K. CHESTERTON

I am myself so exceedingly Nordic, as far as physical constitution is concerned, that I can enjoy almost any weather except what is called glorious weather. At the end of a few days, I am left wondering how the men of the Mediterranean ever managed to do almost all the most active and astonishing things that have been done.
G. K. CHESTERTON

I never worry about action, but only about inaction.
WINSTON CHURCHILL

A nation's character is the sum of its splendid deeds; they constitute one common patrimony, the nation's inheritance. They awe foreign powers, they arouse and animate our own people.
HENRY CLAY

No two things differ more than hurry and dispatch. Hurry is the mark of a weak mind, dispatch of a strong one. A weak man in office, like a squirrel in a cage, is laboring eternally, but to no purpose, and is in constant motion without getting on a job; like a turnstile, he is in everybody's way, but stops nobody; he talks a great deal, but says very little;

looks into everything but sees nothing; and has a hundred irons in the fire, but very few of them are hot, and with those few that are, he only burns his fingers.
CHARLES CALEB COLTON

The only things in which we can be said to have any property are our actions. Our thoughts may be bad, yet produce no poison; they may be good, yet produce no fruit. Our riches may be taken away by misfortune, our reputation by malice, our spirits by calamity, our health by disease, our friends by death. But our actions must follow us beyond the grave; with respect to them alone, we cannot say that we shall carry nothing with us when we die, neither that we shall go naked out of the world.
CHARLES CALEB COLTON

The most important part of every business is to know what ought to be done.
LUCIUS COLUMELLA

Each honest calling, each walk of life, has its own elite, its own aristocracy based on excellence of performance.
JAMES BRYANT CONANT

A true history of human events would show that a far larger proportion of our acts are the results of sudden impulses and accident, than of that reason of which we so much boast.
MYERS Y. COOPER

Unless a capacity for thinking be accompanied by a capacity for action, a superior mind exists in torture.
BENEDETTO CROCE

You cannot be buried in obscurity: you are exposed upon a grand theater to the view of the world. If your actions are upright and benevolent, be assured they will augment your power and happiness.
CYRUS

This is a world of action, and nor for moping and droning in.
CHARLES DICKENS

Action may not always bring happiness; but there is no happiness without action.
BENJAMIN DISRAELI

Those who do the most for the world's advancement are the ones who demand the least.
HENRY L. DOHERTY

Through unity of action we can be a veritable colossus in support of peace. No one can defeat us unless we first defeat ourselves. Every one of us must be guided by this truth.
DWIGHT D. EISENHOWER

We must not sit down and wait for miracles. Up and be going!
JOHN ELIOT

Act as though everything you do, rightly or wrongly, accurately or carelessly, may tip the scale of the bigger things of tomorrow for all of us, as indeed every act, potentially, can. Remember: Enemies try to break through at the weakest point. Don't let it be on your sector.
L. G. ELLIOTT

A little consideration of what takes place around us every day would show us that a higher law than that of our will regulates events; that only in our easy, simple spontaneous action are we strong, and by contenting ourselves with obedience we become divine.
RALPH WALDO EMERSON

Congratulate yourselves if you have done something strange and extravagant and broken the monotony of a decorous age.
**RALPH WALDO EMERSON**

What you do speaks so loudly that I cannot hear what you say.
**RALPH WALDO EMERSON**

There is no strong performance without a little fascination in the performer.
**RALPH WALDO EMERSON**

He who does a good deed is instantly ennobled. He who does a mean deed is by the action itself contracted.
**RALPH WALDO EMERSON**

Unnecessary hustle is one of the American follies. We hustle at both work and play, and consequently enjoy neither to the utmost.
**WILLIAM FEATHER**

The sweaty players in the game of life always have more fun than the supercilious spectators.
**WILLIAM FEATHER**

Contemplation is necessary to generate an object, but action must propagate it.
**OWEN FELTHAM**

All worthwhile men have good thoughts, good ideas and good intentions—but precious few of them ever translate those into action.
**JOHN HANCOCK FIELD**

Pressure is on us by the nature of the job. Performance releases pressure.
**J. T. FISHER**

The victors of the battles of tomorrow will be those who can best harness thought to action. From office boy to statesman, the prizes will be for those who most effectively exert their brains, who take deep, earnest and studious counsel of their minds, who stamp themselves as thinkers.
**B. C. FORBES**

The hardest time to tell: when to stop.
**MALCOLM FORBES**

If you do what you should not, you must bear what you would not.
**BENJAMIN FRANKLIN**

Up, sluggard, and waste not life; in the grave will be sleeping enough.
**BENJAMIN FRANKLIN**

When confronted with two courses of action I jot down on a piece of paper all the arguments in favor of each one—then on the opposite side I write the arguments against each one. Then by weighing the arguments pro and con and canceling them out, one against the other, I take the course indicated by what remains.
**BENJAMIN FRANKLIN**

Words may show a man's wit but actions his meaning.
**BENJAMIN FRANKLIN**

It seems to me that man is made to act rather than to know. The principles of things escape our most persevering researches.
**FREDERICK THE GREAT**

Haste and rashness are storms and tempests, breaking and wrecking business; but nimbleness is a full, fair wind, blowing it with speed to the haven.
**THOMAS FULLER**

It is good to dream, but it is better to dream and work. Faith is mighty, but action with faith is mightier. Desiring is helpful, but work and desire are invincible.
**THOMAS ROBERT GAINES**

The fundamental principle of human action . . . is that men seek to gratify their desires with the least exertion.
**HENRY GEORGE**

Unless there be correct thought, there cannot be any action, and when there is correct thought, right action will follow.
**HENRY GEORGE**

The deed is everything, the glory naught.
**JOHANN WOLFGANG VON GOETHE**

Noble blood is an accident of fortune; noble actions are the chief mark of greatness.
**CARLO GOLDONI**

Hurry is the weakness of fools.
**BALTASAR GRACIÁN**

Act quickly, think slowly.
**GREEK PROVERB**

The greatest ability in business is to get along with others and influence their actions. A chip on the shoulder is too heavy a piece of baggage to carry through life.
**JOHN HANCOCK**

Great thoughts reduced to practice become great acts.
**WILLIAM HAZLITT**

Indolence is a delightful but distressing state; we must be doing something to be happy. Action is no less necessary than thought to the instinctive tendencies of the human frame.
**WILLIAM HAZLITT**

We must be doing something to be happy. Action is no less necessary to us than thought.
**WILLIAM HAZLITT**

The men of action are, after all, only the unconscious instruments of the men of thought.
**HEINRICH HEINE**

Who hath no haste in his business, mountains to him seem valleys.
**GEORGE HERBERT**

Pleasure and pain are the only springs of action in man, and always will be.
**CLAUDE-ADRIEN HELVÉTIUS**

Since life is action and passion, a man must share the passion and action of his time at peril of being judged not to have lived.
**OLIVER WENDELL HOLMES**

An acre of performance is worth a whole world of promise.
**WILLIAM DEAN HOWELLS**

Action is thought tempered by illusion.
**ELBERT HUBBARD**

The world is moving so fast these days that the man who says it can't be done is generally interrupted by someone doing it.
**ELBERT HUBBARD**

A fellow doesn't last long on what he has done. He has to keep on delivering.
**CARL HUBBELL**

For man's greatest actions are performed in minor struggles. Life, misfortune, isolation, abandonment and poverty are battlefields which have their heroes—obscure heroes who are at times greater than illustrious heroes.
VICTOR HUGO

Logical consequences are the scarecrows of fools and the beacons of wise men.
THOMAS H. HUXLEY

The world belongs to those who think and act with it, who keep a finger on its pulse.
WILLIAM RALPH INGE

Man has been called the representative product of the universe; and we will do well to remember that in this position his actions represent the worst of which nature is capable as well as the best.
L. V. JACKS

Action and feeling go together and by regulating the action which is under the more direct control of the will, we can regulate the feeling, which is not.
WILLIAM JAMES

We are all ready to be savage in some cause. The difference between a good man and a bad one is the choice of the cause.
WILLIAM JAMES

None so little enjoy themselves, and are such burdens to themselves, as those who have nothing to do. Only the active have the true relish of life.
WILLIAM JAY

It is happily and kindly provided that in every life there are certain pauses, and interruptions which force consideration upon the careless, and seriousness upon the light; points of time where one course of action ends and another begins.
SAMUEL JOHNSON

Sorrow is the mere rust of the soul. Activity will cleanse and brighten it.
SAMUEL JOHNSON

Many persons wonder why they don't amount to more than they do, have good stuff in them, energetic, persevering, and have ample opportunities. It is all a case of trimming the useless branches and throwing the whole force of power into the development of something that counts.
WALTER J. JOHNSTON

Life is the faculty of spontaneous activity, the awareness that we have powers.
IMMANUEL KANT

Act in such a way that you always treat humanity, whether in your own person or in the person of any other, never simply as a means but always also as an end.
IMMANUEL KANT

Act so that the maxim of your act could be made the principle of a universal law.
IMMANUEL KANT

You will never stub your toe standing still. The faster you go, the more chance there is of stubbing your toe, but the more chance you have of getting somewhere.
CHARLES F. KETTERING

You cannot antagonize and influence at the same time.
J. S. KNOX

Act well at the moment, and you have performed a good action to all eternity.
**JOHANN LAVATER**

He is incapable of a truly good action who finds not a pleasure in contemplating the good actions of others.
**JOHANN LAVATER**

Iron rusts from disuse, stagnant water loses its purity, and in cold weather becomes frozen; even so does inaction sap the vigors of the mind.
**LEONARDO DA VINCI**

A word that has been said may be unsaid—it is but air. But when a deed is done, it cannot be undone, nor can our thoughts reach out to all the mischiefs that may follow.
**HENRY WADSWORTH LONGFELLOW**

All the beautiful sentiments in the world weigh less than a single lovely action.
**JAMES RUSSELL LOWELL**

The man who saves time by galloping loses it by missing his way; the shepherd who hurries his flock to get them home spends the night on the mountain looking for the lost; economy does not consist in haste, but in certainty.
**RAMSAY MACDONALD**

It is well to think well; it is divine to act well.
**HORACE MANN**

We live in an age of haste. Some people look at an egg and expect it to crow.
**ORISON S. MARDEN**

It is the direct man who strikes sledgehammer blows, who penetrates the very marrow of a subject at every stroke and gets the meat out of a proposition, who does things.
**ORISON S. MARDEN**

So much one man can do that does both act and know.
**ANDREW MARVELL**

Give a good deed the credit of a good motive; and give an evil deed the benefit of the doubt.
**BRANDER MATTHEWS**

There is a sort of man who pays no attention to his good actions, but is tormented by his bad ones. This is the type that most often writes about himself.
**SOMERSET MAUGHAM**

We cannot live only for ourselves. A thousand fibers connect us with our fellow-men; and along those fibers, as sympathetic threads, our actions run as causes, and they come back to us as effects.
**HERMAN MELVILLE**

Every duty brings its peculiar delight, every denial its appropriate compensation, every thought its recompense, every cross its crown; pay goes with performance as effect with cause.
**CHARLES MILDMAY**

Life is a short day; but it is a working day. Activity may lead to evil, but inactivity cannot lead to good.
**HANNAH MORE**

And the deeds that ye do upon this earth, it is for fellowship's sake that ye do them.
**WILLIAM MORRIS**

Nothing is unthinkable, nothing impossible to the balanced person, provided it comes out of the needs of life and is dedicated to life's further developments.
**LEWIS MUMFORD**

One will not go far wrong if one attributes extreme actions to vanity, average ones to habit, and petty ones to fear.
FRIEDRICH WILHELM NIETZSCHE

The very essence of all power to influence lies in getting the other person to participate. The mind that can do that has a powerful leverage on his human world.
HARRY A. OVERSTREET

Without consistency there is no moral strength.
ROBERT OWEN

It is our individual performances, no matter how humble our place in life may be, that will in the long run determine how well ordered the world may become.
PAUL C. PACKER

Never tell people how to do things. Tell them what to do and they will surprise you with their ingenuity.
GEN. GEORGE S. PATTON

What we have done for ourselves alone dies with us. What we have done for others and the world remains and is immortal.
ALBERT PINE

American business men must learn human nature to the point of accepting as necessary the Rabble Rouser of the Right. . . . To get fast action somebody must stir millions to genuine anger over conditions which are adversely affecting their lives.
WALTER B. PITKIN

Let deeds match words.
PLAUTUS

Necessity of action takes away the fear of the act, and makes bold resolution the favorite of fortune.
FRANCIS QUARLES

Only actions give life strength; only moderation gives it charm.
JEAN PAUL RICHTER

However brilliant an action may be, it ought not to pass for great when it is not the result of a great design.
FRANÇOIS DE LA ROCHEFOUCAULD

We would often be ashamed of our best actions if the world knew the motives behind them.
FRANÇOIS DE LA ROCHEFOUCAULD

In modern times, it is only by the power of association that men of any calling exercise their due influence in the community.
ELIHU ROOT

In my opinion, he only may be truly said to live and enjoy his being who is engaged in some laudable pursuit, and acquires a name by some illustrious action, or useful art.
SALLUST

We like to think it is enough if we keep our own lives straight. Quite plainly it is not. If we talk cynically or encourage a lowering of standards, even though we still control our own actions, we become responsible for the failure of those who, weakened by our influence, fail to stand upright.
GEORGE P. T. SARGENT

We are not forced into unpleasant activities. We either allow them to come about or we encourage them to come about.
WILLIAM SAROYAN

The most important single influence in the life of a person is another person. We may say to our children: Here is art, science, philosophy, mathematics, music, psychology, history, religion—and we may

open innumerable doors along the corridors of living so that they will have a broad and even a minute acquaintance with the segments of life; but these introductions are not as important as knowing people whose characters and actions, personalities and words have grown after similar introductions and have become worthy of emulation.
**PAUL D. SHAFER**

Suit the action to the word, the word to the action; with this special observation, that you overstep not the modesty of nature.
**WILLIAM SHAKESPEARE**

If our impulses were confined to hunger, thirst and desire, we might be nearly free, but now we are moved by every wind that blows, and a chance word or scene that that word may convey to us.
**MARY SHELLEY**

Stagnation is something worse than death; it is corruption also.
**WILLIAM SIMMS**

When you cannot make up your mind which of two evenly balanced courses of action you should take—choose the bolder.
**W. J. SLIM**

Rightness expresses of actions, what straightness does of lines; and there can no more be two kinds of right action than there can be two kinds of straight lines.
**HERBERT SPENCER**

Allow time and moderate delay; haste manages all things badly.
**PUBLIUS PAPINIUS STATIUS**

It is the mark of a good action that it appears inevitable in retrospect.
**ROBERT LOUIS STEVENSON**

The end of all knowledge should be in virtuous action.
**PHILIP SYDNEY**

What is done hastily cannot be done prudently.
**PUBLILIUS SYRUS**

What we do best or most perfectly is what we have most thoroughly learned by the longest practice, and at length it falls from us without our notice, as a leaf from a tree.
**HENRY DAVID THOREAU**

Why should we live with such hurry and waste of life? We are determined to be starved before we are hungry. Men say that a stitch in time saves nine, and so they take a thousand stitches today to save nine tomorrow.
**HENRY DAVID THOREAU**

There hath grown no grass on my heels since I went hence.
**NICHOLAS UDALL**

Activity makes more men's fortunes than cautiousness.
**MARQUIS DE VAUVENARGUES**

A slender acquaintance with the world must convince every man that actions, not words, are the true criterion of the attachment of friends.
**GEORGE WASHINGTON**

The chiefest action for a man of spirit is never to be out of action; the soul was never put into the body to stand still.
**JOHN WEBSTER**

Nothing is impossible for the man who doesn't have to do it himself.
A. H. WELLER

Actions lie louder than words.
CAROLYN WELLS

No man doth think others will be better to him than he is to them.
BENJAMIN WHICHCOTE

A race preserves its vigor so long as it harbors a real contrast between what has been and what may be; and so long as it is nerved by the vigor to adventure beyond the safeties of the past. Without adventure civilization is in full decay.
ALFRED NORTH WHITEHEAD

Any use of a human being in which less is demanded of him and less is attributed to him than his full status is a degradation and a waste.
NORBERT WIENER

Consistency is the last refuge of the unimaginative.
OSCAR WILDE

Action is the last resource of those who know not how to dream.
OSCAR WILDE

We should not only master questions, but also act upon them, and act definitely.
WOODROW WILSON

Thought and theory must precede all salutary action; yet action is nobler in itself than either thought or theory.
WILLIAM WORDSWORTH

Activity back of a very small idea will produce more than inactivity and the planning of genius.
JAMES A. WORSHAM

The effects of our actions may be postponed but they are never lost. There is an inevitable reward for good deeds and an inescapable punishment for bad. Meditate upon this truth, and seek always to earn good wages from Destiny.
WU MING FU

Influence is like a savings account. The less you use it, the more you've got.
ANDREW YOUNG

In an active life is sown the seed of wisdom; but he who reflects not, never reaps; has no harvest from it, but carries the burden of age without the wages of experience; nor knows himself old, but from his infirmities, the parish register, and the contempt of mankind. And age, if it has not esteem, has nothing.
EDWARD YOUNG

I really believe that more harm is done by old men who cling to their influence than by young men who anticipate that influence.
OWEN D. YOUNG

We protract the career of time by employment, we lengthen the duration of our lives by wise thoughts and useful actions. Life to him who wishes not to have lived in vain is thought and action.
JOHANN ZIMMERMANN

## *Adversity*

Adversity introduces a man to himself.
ANONYMOUS

You never will be the person you can be if pressure, tension and discipline are taken out of your life.
**JAMES G. BILKEY**

In every kind of adversity, the bitterest part of a man's affliction is to remember that he once was happy.
**BOETHIUS**

'Tis looking downward makes one dizzy.
**ROBERT BROWNING**

Adversity is a severe instructor, set over us by one who knows us better than we do ourselves, as he loves us better too. He that wrestles with us strengthens our nerves and sharpens our skill. Our antagonist is our helper. This conflict with difficulty makes us acquainted with our object, and compels us to consider it in all its relations. It will not suffer us to be superficial.
**EDMUND BURKE**

Adversity is sometimes hard upon a man, but for one man who can stand prosperity, there are a hundred that will stand adversity.
**THOMAS CARLYLE**

Don't be disquieted in time of adversity. Be firm with dignity and self-reliant with vigor.
**CHIANG KAI-SHEK**

It is the character of a brave and resolute man not to be ruffled by adversity and not to desert his post.
**CICERO**

All adverse and depressing influences can be overcome, not by fighting, but by rising above them.
**CHARLES CALEB COLTON**

Adversity is the trial of principle. Without it, a man hardly knows whether he is honest or not.
**HENRY FIELDING**

He that can heroically endure adversity will bear prosperity with equal greatness of soul; for the mind that cannot be dejected by the former is not likely to be transported with the later.
**HENRY FIELDING**

Some people as a result of adversity are sadder, wiser, kinder, more human. Most of us are better, though, when things go better.

Knowing when to keep your mouth shut is invariably more important than opening it at the right time.

Always listen to a man when he describes the faults of others. Ofttimes, most times, he's describing his own, revealing himself.
**MALCOLM FORBES**

Adversity makes men; good fortune makes monsters.
**FRENCH PROVERB**

A leaf that is destined to grow large is full of grooves and wrinkles at the start. Now if one has no patience and wants it smooth offhand like a willow leaf, there is trouble ahead.
**JOHANN WOLFGANG VON GOETHE**

The greatest object in the universe, says a certain philosopher, is a good man struggling with adversity; yet there is still a greater, which is the good man that comes to relieve it.
**OLIVER GOLDSMITH**

Adversity has the effect of eliciting talents which in prosperous circumstances would have lain dormant.
**HORACE**

In time of prosperity friends will be plenty;
In time of adversity not one in twenty.
**James Howell**

Adversity has ever been considered the state in which a man most easily becomes acquainted with himself, then, especially, being free from flatterers.
**Samuel Johnson**

Sometimes what a man escapes to is worse than what he escapes from.
**Stan Lynde**

Kites rise against, not with the wind. No man has ever worked his passage anywhere in a dead calm.
**John Neal**

Often when economic pressure is lifted, a man must pump back into himself a feeling of must.
**A. F. Osborn**

Adversity makes a man wise, not rich.
**John Ray**

If adversity purifies, why not nations?
**Jean Paul Richter**

In the adversity of our best friends we often find something that is not wholly displeasing to us.
**François de la Rochefoucauld**

Genuine morality is preserved only in the school of adversity; a state of continuous prosperity may easily prove a quicksand to virtue.
**Johann Friedrich von Schiller**

In prosperous times I have sometimes felt my fancy and powers of language flag, but adversity is to me at least a tonic and bracer.
**Sir Walter Scott**

Great men rejoice in adversity, just as brave soldiers triumph in war.
**Seneca**

The good things of prosperity are to be wished; but the good things that belong to adversity are to be admired.
**Seneca**

It is not every calamity that is a curse, and early adversity is often a blessing. Surmounted difficulties not only teach, but hearten us in our future struggles.
**James Sharp**

Adversity has made many a man great who, had he remained prosperous, would only have been rich.
**Maurice Switzer**

By trying we can easily learn to endure adversity. Another man's, I mean.
**Mark Twain**

You can't hold a man down without staying down with him.
**Booker T. Washington**

People seldom want to walk over you until you lie down.
**Elmer Wheeler**

## *Advertising*

Doing business without advertising is like winking at a girl in the dark. You know what you are doing, but nobody else does.
**Stuart H. Britt**

There are different ways of saying "It pays to advertise." It pays, too, to have a quality product, ade-

quate distribution, good salesmen. Advertising is just one factor in the balance mechanism that leads to a sale: product, quality, distribution, advertising and selling. Advertising is really salesmanship in print. Although capacity may be oversold, you can never oversell the product. You can always continue to sell the goodwill and the assurance of quality and service that make buyers seek out your brand beyond all others.
PAUL B. BUCKWALTER

The business that considers itself immune to the necessity for advertising sooner or later finds itself immune to business.
DERBY BROWN

Advertising is the principle of mass production applied to selling.
JOHN T. DORRANCE

You can tell the ideals of a nation by its advertisements.
NORMAN DOUGLAS

The advertising man is a liaison between the products of business and the mind of the nation. He must know both before he can serve either.
GLENN FRANK

There is nothing in the way of amelioration of the conditions of life, of politics, of social and ethical matters, that may not be affected through the skilful application of those principles of advertising that, in business, have proved to be so wonderfully effective.
GEORGE FRENCH

Promise, large promise, is the soul of an advertisement.
SAMUEL JOHNSON

The product that will not sell without advertising, will not sell profitably with advertising.
ALBERT LASKER

Advertising may be the only business in the world where the clients with the most money can make demands until they get the agency's worst product, while the small client with little to spend must meekly accept the agency's best.
THOMAS D. MURRAY

Advertising is one of the few callings in which it is advisable to pay attention to some one else's business.
HOWARD W. NEWTON

Advertising helps everybody: by showing comparative values and new products, thus increasing sales, resulting in greater production and lower prices.
JOHN HENRY PATTERSON

Advertising gives industry an opportunity to keep its clean hands before the public. If industry is clean and has no dirty hands to hide, it should be proud to display its purity.
ROBERT W. SPARKS

When someone stops advertising, someone stops buying. When someone stops buying, someone stops selling. When someone stops selling, someone stops making. When someone stops making, someone stops earning. When someone stops earning, someone stops buying. (Think it over.)
EDWIN H. STUART

## *Advice*

There is nothing which we receive with so much reluctance as advice.
JOSEPH ADDISON

It is an easy thing for one whose foot is on the outside of calamity to give advice and to rebuke the sufferer.
AESCHYLUS

He that gives good advice builds with one hand; he that gives good counsel and example builds with both; but he that gives good admonition and bad example builds with one hand and pulls down with the other.
FRANCIS BACON

The light that a man receiveth by counsel from another is drier and purer than that which cometh from his own understanding and judgment, which is ever infused and drenched in his affections and customs.
FRANCIS BACON

Listen to everything a man has to say about what he knows, but don't let him advise you about what he doesn't know. And usually he doesn't know too much about what's best for you.
BARNEY BALABAN

Advice: The suggestions you give someone else which you hope will work for your benefit.
AMBROSE BIERCE

Advice is like castor oil, easy enough to give but dreadful uneasy to take.
JOSH BILLINGS

What you do not use yourself, do not give to others. For example: advice.
SRI CHINMOY

In those days he was wiser than he is now; he used frequently to take my advice.
WINSTON CHURCHILL

Advice; it's more fun to give than to receive.
PAT H. COIL

Advice is like snow; the softer it falls, the longer it dwells upon, and the deeper it sinks into the mind.
SAMUEL TAYLOR COLERIDGE

To profit from good advice requires more wisdom than to give it.
JOHN CHURTON COLLINS

We ask advice, but we mean approbation.
CHARLES CALEB COLTON

When we feel a strong desire to thrust our advice upon others, it is usually because we suspect their weakness; but we ought rather to suspect our own.
CHARLES CALEB COLTON

Advice after injury is like medicine after death.
DANISH PROVERB

In every society some men are born to rule, and some to advise.
RALPH WALDO EMERSON

It is better to advise than upbraid, for the one corrects the erring; the other only convicts them.
EPICTETUS

The best advice I can give to any young man or young woman upon graduation from school can be summed up in exactly eight words, and they are—be honest with yourself and tell the truth.
JAMES A. FARLEY

Families break up when people take hints you don't intend and miss hints you do intend.
ROBERT FROST

Advice: It's more fun to give than to receive.
**MALCOLM FORBES**

How can you avoid people who say, "Let me tell you," and then do?
**MALCOLM FORBES**

Listening to advice often accomplishes far more than heeding it.
**MALCOLM FORBES**

Once you've given advice to someone, you're obligated.
**MALCOLM FORBES**

If a man knows where to get good advice, it is as though he could supply it himself.
**JOHANN WOLFGANG VON GOETHE**

To accept good advice is but to increase one's own ability.
**JOHANN WOLFGANG VON GOETHE**

Do not be inaccessible. None is so perfect that he does not need at times the advice of others. He is an incorrigible ass who will never listen to any one. Even the most surpassing intellect should find a place for friendly counsel. Sovereignty itself must learn to lean. There are some that are incorrigible simply because they are inaccessible: They fall to ruin because none dares to extricate them. The highest should have the door open for friendship; it may prove the gate of help. A friend must be free to advise, and even to upbraid, without feeling embarrassed.
**BALTASAR GRACIÁN**

When you counsel someone, you should appear to be reminding him of something he had forgotten, not of the light he was unable to see.
**BALTASAR GRACIÁN**

Facts are worthless to a man if he has to keep running to somebody else for advice on how to use them.
**SVEN HALLA**

By the time a man asks you for advice, he has generally made up his mind what he wants to do, and is looking for confirmation rather than counseling.
**SYDNEY J. HARRIS**

Harsh counsels have no effect; they are like hammers which are always repulsed by the anvil.
**CLAUDE-ADRIEN HELVÉTIUS**

It is expedient to have an acquaintance with those who have looked into the world; who know men, understand business, and can give you good intelligence and good advice when they are wanted.
**B. HORNE**

A bad cold wouldn't be so annoying if it weren't for the advice of our friends.
**KIN HUBBARD**

Teeth placed before the tongue give good advice.
**ITALIAN PROVERB**

No man is so foolish but he may sometimes give another good counsel, and no man so wise that he may not easily err if he takes no other counsel than his own. He that is taught only by himself has a fool for a master.
**BEN JONSON**

Advice is what we ask for when we already know the answer but wish we didn't.
**ERICA JONG**

He who can take advice is sometimes superior to him who can give it.
**KARL LUDWIG VON KNEBEL**

The toad beneath the harrow knows
Exactly where each tooth point goes;
The butterfly upon the road
Preaches contentment to that toad.
RUDYARD KIPLING

You will always find some Eskimos willing to instruct the Congolese on how to cope with heat waves.
STANISLAUS LEC

We are so happy to advise others that occasionally we even do it in their interest.
JULES RENARD

Men give away nothing so liberally as advice.
FRANÇOIS DE LA ROCHEFOUCAULD

Old men are fond of giving good advice to console themselves for their inability to give bad examples.
FRANÇOIS DE LA ROCHEFOUCAULD

Don't follow any advice, no matter how good, until you feel as deeply in your spirit as you think in your mind that the counsel is wise.
DAVID SEABURY

One can advise comfortably from a safe port.
JOHANN FRIEDRICH VON SCHILLER

How is it possible to expect that mankind will take advice when they will not so much as take warning?
JONATHAN SWIFT

Many receive advice, only the wise profit by it.
PUBLILIUS SYRUS

I have found the best way to give advice to your children is to find out what they want and then advise them to do it.
HARRY S TRUMAN

I am, at heart, a tiresome nag complacently positive that there is no human problem which could not be solved if people would simply do as I advise.
GORE VIDAL

The only thing to do with good advice is to pass it on; it is never of any use to oneself.
OSCAR WILDE

I've learned that you can't expect your children to listen to your advice and ignore your example.
51-YEAR-OLD'S DISCOVERY

## *Aging*

The Indian summer of life should be a little sunny and sad, like the season, and infinite in wealth and depth of tone—but never hustled.
HENRY BROOKS ADAMS

He who would pass the declining years of his life with honor and comfort should, when young, consider that he may one day become old, and remember, when he is old, that he has once been young.
JOSEPH ADDISON

While one finds company in himself and his pursuits, he cannot feel old, no matter what his years may be.
AMOS BRONSON ALCOTT

To know how to grow old is the master-work of wisdom, and one of the most difficult chapters in the great art of living.
HENRI FRÉDÉRIC AMIEL

That judges of important causes should hold office for life is not a good thing, for the mind grows old as well as the body.
ARISTOTLE

Middle age is a time of life
That a man first notices in his wife.
**RICHARD ARMOUR**

I refuse to admit that I am more than 52, even if that does make my sons illegitimate.
**NANCY ASTOR**

Discern of the coming on of years, and think not to do the same things still, for age will not be defied.
**FRANCIS BACON**

Men of age object too much, consult too long, adventure too little, repeat too soon, and seldom drive business home to the full period, but content themselves with a mediocrity of success.
**FRANCIS BACON**

The secret of staying young is to live honestly, eat slowly, and lie about your age.
**LUCILLE BALL**

A man is not old until regrets take the place of dreams.
**JOHN BARRYMORE**

With maturity comes the wish to economize—to be more simple. Maturity is the period when one finds the just measure.
**BÉLA BARTÓK**

To me—old age is 15 years older than I am.
**BERNARD M. BARUCH**

The essence of any plan for financing old age is saving—to put aside some part of today's earnings for the future. Anything that saps the value of savings—and inflation is the worst single threat—is the enemy of the aged and of those who expect to grow old.
**BERNARD M. BARUCH**

I entered my Seventies
A decade ago.
My span here on earth
Has been quite a good show.
I owe a great deal
To my relative peace,
And I'm terribly grateful
For such a long lease.
**CECIL BAXTER**

We grow neither better nor worse as we get old, but more like ourselves.
**MAY LAMBERTON BECKER**

The war years count double. Things and people not actively in use age twice as fast.
**ARNOLD BENNETT**

When I was 40, my doctor advised me that a man in his forties shouldn't play tennis. I heeded his advice carefully and could hardly wait until I reached 50 to start again.
**HUGO L. BLACK**

The child's toys and the old man's reasons are the fruits of two seasons.
**WILLIAM BLAKE**

Grow old along with me! The best is yet to be, the last of life, for which the first was made.
**ROBERT BROWNING**

I'm finding, as I've thrived and aged,
That much I'd thought was good was bad.
I doubt I'd want to age again
Without the harmful fun I had.
**ART BUCK**

The toll of time brings few delights
In facing age's deadly spike;
Atop the list
Perhaps is this:
Outliving those we didn't like.
ART BUCK

If you wish to be positive, which means youthful, never speak of the past any more than you can help.
GELETT BURGESS

The old say, "I remember when." The young say, "What's the news?"
GELETT BURGESS

As the fruit ripens, so does man mature; after many rains, suns and blows.
JOSÉ DE LA LUZ Y CABALLERO

Given three requisites—means of existence, reasonable health, and an absorbing interest—those years beyond sixty can be the happiest and most satisfying of a lifetime.
EARNEST ELMO CALKINS

Those who enjoy the large pleasures of advanced age are those who have sacrificed the small pleasures of youth.
CHARLES E. CARPENTER

We are but older children, dear,
Who fret to find our bedtime near.
LEWIS CARROLL

Sure I'm for helping the elderly. I'm going to be old myself some day.
LILLIAN CARTER (IN HER 80S)

The dead might as well try to speak to the living as the old to the young.
WILLA CATHER

The greatest comfort of my old age, and that which gives me the highest satisfaction, is the pleasing remembrance of the many benefits and friendly offices I have done to others.
MARCUS CATO

Middle age is when your classmates are so gray and wrinkled and bald they don't recognize you.
BENNETT CERF

I would not say that old men grow wise, for men never grow wise; and many old men retain a very attractive childishness and cheerful innocence. Elderly people are often much more romantic than younger people, and sometimes even more adventurous, having begun to realize how many things they do not know.
G. K. CHESTERTON

One pleasure attached to growing older is that many things seem to be growing younger; growing fresher and more lively than we once supposed them to be.
G. K. CHESTERTON

Growing old isn't so bad when you consider the alternative.
MAURICE CHEVALIER

As I approve of a youth that has something of the old man in him, so I am no less pleased with an old man that has something of the youth. He that follows this rule may be old in body, but can never be so in mind.
CICERO

Short as life is, some find it long enough to outlive their characters, their constitutions and their estates.
CHARLES CALEB COLTON

It is better to wear out than to rust out.
RICHARD CUMBERLAND

I think that to have known one good, old man . . . one man who, through the chances and mischances of a long life, has carried his heart in his hand, like a palm branch waving all discords into peace . . . helps our faith in God, in ourselves and in each other more than many sermons.
GEORGE WILLIAM CURTIS

Growing old is not for sissies.
BETTE DAVIS

The really frightening thing about middle age is that you know you'll grow out of it.
DORIS DAY

These are the effects of doting age: vain doubts, idle cares and overcaution.
JOHN DRYDEN

Old men's eyes are like old men's memories, they are strongest for things a long way off.
GEORGE ELIOT

A man's years should not be counted until he has something else to count.
RALPH WALDO EMERSON

Life is eating us up. We shall be fables presently. Keep cool: It will all be one a hundred years hence.
RALPH WALDO EMERSON

It is time to be old, to take in sail.
RALPH WALDO EMERSON

The years teach much which the days never know.
RALPH WALDO EMERSON

To a longer and worse life, a shorter and better is by all means to be preferred.
EPICTETUS

If youth knew; if age could.
HENRI ESTIENNE

If we could be twice young and twice old we could correct all our mistakes.
EURIPIDES

One of the many things nobody ever tells you about middle age is that it's such a nice change from being young.
DOROTHY CANFIELD FISHER

It can be set down as a broad, general principle that we cannot indulge in idleness and abundance during both the first and second half of our life. Study, application, industry, enthusiasm while we are young usually enable us to enjoy life when we grow older. But unless we toil and strive and earn all we can in the first half, the second half of our life is liable to bring disappointment, discomfort, distress. The time to put forth effort is when we are most able to do it, namely, in the years of our greatest strength. The law of compensation hasn't ceased to function.
B. C. FORBES

After 40, one's face begins to tell more than one's tongue.
MALCOLM FORBES

As you get older there shouldn't be anything you won't try. The payoff is that you open up whole new avenues that are fun. It's a misinterpretation of life to live it only in preparation for the next one. To subordinate the one you've got to an indefinite next round is foolish. It's a waste of this life not to live this life. What's next is anybody's guess.
MALCOLM FORBES

That everyone earning should contribute to Social Security is indisputable; that everyone, regardless of how he's financially fixed at retirement age, should collect Social Security is indisputably wrong. As it was well put in *Washington Monthly,* Social Security's a device for taking money from present workers to support retired ones. Fair enough. But by what standard can we justify a system that taxes a $14,000-a-year secretary with two kids and gives that money to a Malcolm Forbes?

At what to set the cap should be, can be, debated. But there should not be any debate as to whether a cap should be.

**MALCOLM FORBES (1985)**

If you take all the experience and judgment of men over fifty out of the world, there wouldn't be enough left to run it.

**HENRY FORD**

The better part of maturity is knowing your goals.

**ARNOLD GLASOW**

No one can avoid aging, but aging productively is something else.

**KATHARINE GRAHAM**

There's only one way to avoid getting old, and that is to die young.

**GEORGIA PHYSICIAN**

Gray hair is a sign of age, not wisdom.

**GREEK PROVERB**

The old age of an eagle is better than the youth of a sparrow.

**GREEK PROVERB**

Most people say that as you get old, you have to give up things. I think you get old because you give up things.

**THEODORE FRANCIS GREEN**

So then the year is repeating its old story again. We are come once more to its most charming chapter.

**JOHANN WOLFGANG VON GOETHE**

Age that lessens the enjoyment of life, increases our desire of living.

**OLIVER GOLDSMITH**

It's hard to believe that some day I'll be an ancestor.

**ROBERT HALF**

Old age, believe me, is a good and pleasant time. It is true that you are quietly shouldered off the stage, but then you are given such a comfortable front seat as spectator, and if you have really played your part you are more content to sit down and watch.

**JANE ELLEN HARRISON**

There's worse ways to get old than rummaging around in your memories.

**JON HASSLER**

A snow year, a rich year.

**GEORGE HERBERT**

Old people have fewer diseases than the young, but their diseases never leave them.

**HIPPOCRATES**

Age, like distance lends a double charm.

**OLIVER WENDELL HOLMES**

I credit my youthfulness at 80 to the fact of a cheerful disposition and contentment in every period of my life with what I was.

**OLIVER WENDELL HOLMES**

Men, like peaches and pears, grow sweet a little while before they begin to decay.

**OLIVER WENDELL HOLMES**

To be seventy years young is sometimes far more cheerful and hopeful than to be forty years old.
**OLIVER WENDELL HOLMES**

Geriatric Logic:
Take one good breath while still in bed,
One cautious stretch from toe to head.
If nothing hurts—I must be dead!
**HOSPITAL RHYME**

You'll find as you grow older that you weren't born such a very great while ago after all. The time shortens up.
**WILLIAM DEAN HOWELLS**

Forty is the old age of youth; fifty is the youth of old age.
**VICTOR HUGO**

Young people think they know it all, but a lot of old salts around know they don't.
**RICHARD JACKSON**

Let us not look at ourselves but onwards, onwards to the ideal life of man, and take strength from the leaf and the signs of the field. Let us labor to make the heart grow larger as we become older, as the spreading oak gives more shelter.
**RICHARD JEFFRIES**

It is the height of absurdity to sow little but weeds in the first half of one's lifetime and expect to harvest a valuable crop in the second half.
**PERCY H. JOHNSTON**

This evening of a well-spent life brings its lamps with it.
**JOSEPH JOUBERT**

If you wish to live long, you must be willing to grow old.
**GEORGE LAWTON**

Aging is not simply decay; it is an accumulation of choices and consequences which, if there is any education at all, consists also of alternatives, an experience of strangeness, a sense of other possibilities, an appreciation of might-have-been.
**JOHN LEONARD**

How do you know when you're old? When you double your current age and realize you're not going to live that long.
**MICHAEL J. LEYDEN II**

Maturity is achieved when a person accepts life as full of tension; when he does not torment himself with childish guilt feelings, but avoids tragic adult sins; when he postpones immediate pleasures for the sake of long-term values.... Our generation must be inspired to search for that maturity which will manifest itself in the qualities of tenacity, dependability, co-operativeness and the inner drive to work and sacrifice for a nobler future of mankind.
**JOSHUA L. LIEBMAN**

Psychologically I should say that a person becomes an adult at the point when he produces more than he consumes or earns more than he spends. This may be at the age of eighteen, twenty-five, or thirty-five. Some people remain unproductive and dependent children forever and therefore intellectually and emotionally immature.
**HENRY C. LINK**

Nobody grows old by merely living a number of years. People grow old only by deserting their ideals. Years wrinkle the face, but to give up enthusiasm wrinkles the soul. Worry, doubt, self-interest, fear,

despair—these are the long, long years that bow the head and turn the growing spirit back to dust.
WATTERSON LOWE

At sixty a man has passed most of the reefs and whirlpools. Excepting only death, he has no enemies left to meet.... That man has awakened to a new youth.... Ergo, he is young.
GEORGE LUKS

From the earliest time the old have rubbed it into the young that they are wiser, and before the young had discovered what nonsense this was they were old too, and it profited them to carry on the imposture.
SOMERSET MAUGHAM

Growing old is no more than a bad habit which a busy man has no time to form.
ANDRÉ MAUROIS

I wish it were O.K. in this country to look one's age, whatever it is. Maturity has a lot going for it, even in terms of esthetics. For example, you no longer get bubblegum stuck in your braces.
CYRA MCFADDEN

The best years are the forties; after 50 a man begins to deteriorate, but in his forties he is at the maximum of his villainy.
H. L. MENCKEN

The older I grow, the more I distrust the familiar doctrine that age brings wisdom.
H. L. MENCKEN

It is 11 years since I have seen my figure in a glass [mirror]. The last reflection I saw there was so disagreeable I resolved to spare myself such mortification in the future.
MARY WORTLEY MONTAGU

Every period of life has its peculiar prejudices; whoever saw old age that did not applaud the past and condemn the present time?
MICHEL DE MONTAIGNE

If each of us can be helped by science to live a hundred years, what will it profit us if our hates and fears, our loneliness and our remorse will not permit us to enjoy them?
DAVID NEISWANGER

You can judge your age by the amount of pain you feel when you come in contact with a new idea.
JOHN NUVEEN

A man is sane morally at thirty, rich mentally at forty, wise spiritually at fifty—or never!
SIR WILLIAM OSLER

Even under a harsh God—and I do not believe in a harsh God—one is entitled to serenity in old age.
ALBERT OUTLER

How old would you be if you didn't know how old you was?
SATCHEL PAIGE

A comfortable old age is the reward of a well-spent youth. Instead of its bringing sad and melancholy prospects of decay, it should give us hopes of eternal youth in a better world.
R. PALMER

We are all prisoners of cell biology.
H. B. PEARL

We get too soon old, und too late schmart.
PENNSYLVANIA DUTCH PROVERB

Youth is not a time of life; it is a state of mind. People grow old only by deserting their ideals and

by outgrowing the consciousness of youth. Years wrinkle the skin, but to give up enthusiasm wrinkles the soul. . . . You are as old as your doubt, your fear, your despair. The way to keep young is to keep your faith young. Keep your self-confidence young. Keep your hope young.
LUELLA F. PHELAN

The belief that youth is the happiest time of life is founded on a fallacy. The happiest person is the person who thinks the most interesting thoughts, and we grow happier as we grow older.
WILLIAM LYON PHELPS

Old age: A great sense of calm and freedom. When the passions have relaxed their hold, you have escaped, not from one master but from many.
PLATO

Our youth and manhood are due to our country, but our declining years are due to ourselves.
PLINY

The years that a woman subtracts from her age are not lost. They are added to other women's.
DIANE DE POITIERS

Years following years steal something every day;
At last they steal us from ourselves away.
ALEXANDER POPE

When we are young, we are slavishly employed in procuring something whereby we may live comfortably when we grow old; and when we are old, we perceive it is too late to live as we proposed.
ALEXANDER POPE

If by the time we are 60 we haven't learned what a knot of paradox and contradiction life is, and how exquisitely the good and bad are mingled in every action we take, and what a compromising hostess Our Lady of Truth is, we haven't grown old to much purpose.
JOHN COWPER POWYS

No one grows old by living—only by losing interest in living.
MARIE BEYNON RAY

As a man grows older it is harder and harder to frighten him.
JEAN PAUL RICHTER

As winter strips the leaves from around us, so that we may see the distant regions they formerly concealed, so old age takes away our enjoyments only to enlarge the prospect of the coming eternity.
JEAN PAUL RICHTER

Memory, wit, fancy, acuteness, cannot grow young again in old age, but the heart can.
JEAN PAUL RICHTER

What can a man do to move along in some kind of grace through his days and years?
WILLIAM SAROYAN

Nothing is more disgraceful than that an old man should have nothing to show to prove that he has lived long, except his years.
SENECA

My age is as a lusty winter Frosty, but kindly.
WILLIAM SHAKESPEARE

It's all that the young can do for the old, to shock them and keep them up to date.
GEORGE BERNARD SHAW

I know not whether increasing years do not cause us to esteem fewer people and to bear with more.
WILLIAM SHENSTONE

When you have lived longer in this world and outlived the enthusiastic and pleasing illusions of youth, you will find your love and pity for the race increase tenfold, your admiration and attachment to a particular party or opinion fall away altogether.
**JOSEPH HENRY SHORTHOUSE**

The greatest danger to an adequate old-age security plan is rising prices. A rise of 2 per cent a year in prices would cut the purchasing power of pensions about 45 per cent in thirty years. The greatest danger of rising prices is from wages rising faster than output per man-hour.... Whether the nation succeeds in providing adequate security for retired workers depends in large measure upon the wage policies of trade unions.
**SUMNER H. SLICHTER**

### As A Man Grows Older

He values the voice of experience more and the voice of prophecy less.

He finds more of life's wealth in the common pleasures—home, health, children.

He thinks more about worth of men and less about their wealth.

He begins to appreciate his own father a little more.

He boasts less and boosts more.

He hurries less, and usually makes more progress.

He esteems the friendship of God a little higher.
**ROY L. SMITH**

Emotional maturity is ability to stick to a job and to struggle through until it is finished; to endure unpleasantness, discomfort and frustration; to give more than is asked for or required; to size things up and make independent decisions; to work under authority and to cooperate with others; to defer to time, other persons, and to circumstances.
**EDWARD A. STRECKER**

The mark of the immature man is that he wants to die nobly for a cause, while the mark of the mature man is that he wants to live humbly for one.
**WILHELM STEKEL**

Years do not make sages; they only make old men.
**ANNE SWETCHINE**

Everyone desires long life, not one old age.
**JONATHAN SWIFT**

There cannot live a more unhappy creature than an ill-natured old man, who is neither capable of receiving pleasures, nor sensible of conferring them on others.
**WILLIAM J. TEMPLE**

If one would understand older people, one should first forget age. Oldness is not so much passing a certain birthday as it is the rearrangement of a complicated set of physical, mental, social and economic circumstances. One must not label a man who has lived a lot of years as an old person. For an individual who has early formed good habits of living, picked up the important techniques of adjustment and acquired a good attitude or philosophy, life continues to be an ever-increasing adventure in development. Development can continue at sixty, seventy and eighty as surely as it did in youth.
**WILLIAM B. TERHUNE**

We have no simple problems or easy decisions after kindergarten.
**JOHN W. TURK**

The first half of life consists of the capacity to enjoy without the chance; the last half consists of the chance without the capacity.
**MARK TWAIN**

Last spring I stopped frolicking with the mince pie after midnight. Up to then I had always believed it wasn't loaded.
**MARK TWAIN**

Whatever a man's age, he can reduce it several years by putting a bright-colored flower in his buttonhole.
**MARK TWAIN**

Youth is a silly, vapid state;
Old age with fears and ills is rife;
This simple boon I beg of Fate—
A thousand years of Middle Life!
**CAROLYN WELLS**

A man's liberal and conservative phases seem to follow each other in a succession of waves from the time he is born. Children are radicals. Youths are conservatives, with a dash of criminal negligence. Men in their prime are liberals (as long as their digestion keeps pace with their intellect).
**E. B. WHITE**

Old age: The estuary that enlarges and spreads itself grandly as it pours into the Great Sea.
**WALT WHITMAN**

The tragedy of old age is not that one is old, but that one is young.
**OSCAR WILDE**

More women grow old nowadays through the faithfulness of their admirers than through anything else.
**OSCAR WILDE**

Young men want to be faithful and are not; old men want to be faithless and cannot.
**OSCAR WILDE**

In masks outrageous and austere,
The years go by in single file;
But none has merited my fear,
And none has quite escaped my smile.
**ELINOR WYLIE**

I really believe that more harm is done by old men who cling to their influence than by young men who anticipate it.
**OWEN D. YOUNG**

## *Alcohol*

Bronze is the mirror of the form; wine, of the heart.
**AESCHYLUS**

The vine bears three kinds of grapes: the first of pleasure, the next of intoxication, and the third of disgust.
**ANARCHIS**

The driver is safer when the roads are dry, and vice versa.
**ANONYMOUS**

When the cock is drunk, he forgets about the hawk.
**ASHANTI PROVERB**

Drinking makes such fools of people, and people are such fools to begin with, that it's compounding a felony.
**ROBERT BENCHLEY**

If the headache would only precede the intoxication, alcoholism would be a virtue.
**SAMUEL BUTLER**

Most Americans are born drunk, and really require a little wine or beer to sober them. They have a sort

of permanent intoxication from within, a sort of invisible champagne.
**G. K. CHESTERTON**

I have taken more out of alcohol than alcohol has taken out of me.
**WINSTON CHURCHILL**

When I was younger I made it a rule never to take a strong drink before lunch. Now it is my rule never to do so before breakfast.
**WINSTON CHURCHILL**

Wine, to a gifted bard, is a
Mount that merrily races;
From watered wits,
No good has ever grown.
**CRATINUS**

Drink never made a man better, but it made many a man think he was better.
**FINLEY PETER DUNNE**

He talked with more claret than clarity.
**SUSAN ERTZ**

A man's got to believe in something. I believe I'll have another drink.
**W. C. FIELDS**

I feel sorry for people who don't drink, because when they get up in the morning, it's as good as they'll feel all day.
**W. C. FIELDS**

What a man says drunk he has thought sober.
**FLEMISH PROVERB**

Would you have suspected drunk or drugged train drivers couldn't be checked by the railroads to see if they were until now? This, despite the fact that in the past ten years there have been dozens of railroad accidents, deaths and injuries, plus tens of millions in property damage directly attributed (after the fact) to alcohol or drug consumption by the trainmen. It was not until a couple of weeks ago that the Department of Transportation gave the railroads the power to test suspected employees. Only in December will it become for the first time illegal for train operators to be drunk on duty.
**MALCOLM FORBES (1985)**

Wine is constant proof that God loves us and loves to see us happy.
**BENJAMIN FRANKLIN**

Some people spend the day in complaining of a headache, and the night in drinking the wine that gives it.
**JOHANN WOLFGANG VON GOETHE**

Wine makes a man more pleased with himself; I do not say that it makes him more pleasing to others.
**SAMUEL JOHNSON**

I have drunk since I was 15, and few things have given me more pleasure. When you work hard all day with your head and you must work again the next day, what else can change your ideas and make them run on a different plane like whiskey?
**ERNEST HEMINGWAY**

Malt does more than Milton can,
To justify God's ways to man.
**A. E. HOUSMAN**

The sway of alcohol over mankind is unquestionably due to its power to stimulate the mystical faculties of human nature, usually crushed to earth by the cold facts and dry criticisms of the sober hour. Sobriety diminishes, discriminates, and says no; drunkenness expands, unites and says yes.
**WILLIAM JAMES**

The habit of intemperance by men in office has occasioned more injury to the public, and more trouble to me, than all other causes; and, were I to commence my administration again, the first question I would ask respecting a candidate for office, would be, "Does he use ardent spirits?"
THOMAS JEFFERSON

One of the disadvantages of wine is that it makes a man mistake words for thoughts.
SAMUEL JOHNSON

Even though a number of people have tried, no one has yet found a way to drink for a living.
JEAN KERR

I often wonder what the vintners buy
One half so precious as the stuff they sell.
OMAR KHAYYAM

Wine is like rain: when it falls on the mire it but makes it fouler, but when it strikes the good soil wakes it to beauty and bloom.
JOHN MAY

I drank at every vine.
The last was like the first.
I came upon no wine
So wonderful as thirst.
EDNA ST. VINCENT MILLAY

In wine there is truth.
PLINY THE ELDER

It is all nonsense about not being able to work without ale, and gin, and cider, and fermented liquors. Do lions and cart-horses drink ale?
SYDNEY SMITH

An alcoholic is someone you don't like who drinks as much as you do.
DYLAN THOMAS

Water taken in moderation cannot hurt anybody.
MARK TWAIN

I must get out of these wet clothes and into a dry martini.
ALEXANDER WOOLLCOTT

## *Ambition*

Ambition is the subtlest beast of the intellectual and moral field. It is wonderfully adroit in concealing itself from its owner.
JOHN ADAMS

The ambitious climbs up high and perilous stairs and never cares how to come down; the desire of rising hath swallowed up his fear of a fall.
THOMAS ADAMS

A man's worth is no greater than the worth of his ambitions.
MARCUS AURELIUS ANTONINUS

In this country, every man is the architect of his own ambitions.
HORTON BAIN

The slave has but one master; the man of ambition has as many as there are people useful to his fortune.
JEAN DE LA BRUYÈRE

Say what we will, we may be sure that ambition is an error. Its wear and tear on the heart are never recompensed.
EDWARD BULWER-LYTTON

The same sun which gilds all nature, and exhilirates the whole creation, does not shine upon disappointed ambition.
EDMUND BURKE

He who would rise in the world should veil his ambitions with the forms of humanity.
CHINESE PROVERB

It is by attempting to reach the top at a single leap that so much misery is caused in the world.
WILLIAM COBBETT

Ambition is to the mind what the cap is to the falcon; it blinds us first, and then compels us to tower by reason of our blindness.
CHARLES CALEB COLTON

All ambitions are lawful except those which climb upward on the miseries or credulities of mankind.
JOSEPH CONRAD

Ambition, having reached the summit, longs to descend.
PIERRE CORNEILLE

Without ambition one starts nothing. Without work one finishes nothing. The prize will not be sent to you. You have to win it. The man who knows how will always have a job. The man who also knows why will always be his boss. As to methods there may be a million and then some, but principles are few. The man who grasps principles can successfully select his own methods. The man who tries methods, ignoring principles, is sure to have trouble.
RALPH WALDO EMERSON

Ambition is the germ from which all growth of nobleness proceeds.
THOMAS D. ENGLISH

For the spear was a desert physician,
That cured not a few of ambition,
And drave not a few to perdition,
With medicine bitter and strong.
JAMES ELROY FLECKER

Ambition and the belly are the two worst counselors.
GERMAN PROVERB

Ambition is most aroused by the trumpet-clang of another's fame.
BALTASAR GRACIÁN

From its very beginnings ambition was a political word, born of the Latin *ambitus,* the walking around that a Roman politician did when buttering up the voters.
JOHN P. GRIER

What is my loftiest ambition? I've always wanted to throw an egg into an electric fan.
OLIVER HERFORD

Ambition is not a weakness unless it be disproportioned to the capacity. To have more ambition than ability is to be at once weak and unhappy.
GEORGE S. HILLARD

God gives every bird its food, but he does not throw it into the nest.
JOSIAH G. HOLLAND

Men are more often bribed by their loyalties and ambitions than by money.
ROBERT H. JACKSON

To be unhappy at home is the ultimate result of all ambition.
SAMUEL JOHNSON

The thrust of ambition is, and always has been, great, but among the bright-eyed it had once a more adventurous and individualistic air, a much more bracing rivalry.
**LOUIS KRONENBERGER**

Ambition does not see the earth she treads on: The rock and the herbage are of one substance to her.
**WALTER SAVAGE LANDOR**

Ambition and suspicion always go together.
**GEORG CHRISTOPH LICHTENBERG**

Most people would succeed in small things if they were not troubled by great ambitions.
**HENRY WADSWORTH LONGFELLOW**

Ambition is so powerful a passion in the human breast, that however high we reach, we are never satisfied.
**NICCOLÒ MACHIAVELLI**

It is a psychological law that whatever we desire to accomplish we must impress upon the subjective or subconscious mind; that is, we must register a vow with ourselves, we must make our resolution with vigor, with faith that we can do the thing we want to do; we must register our conviction with such intensity that the great creative forces within us will tend to realize them. Our impressions will become expressions just in proportion to the vigor with which we register our vows to accomplish our ambitions, to make our visions realities.
**ORISON S. MARDEN**

If you have a great ambition, take as big a step as possible in the direction of fulfilling it, but if the step is only a tiny one, don't worry if it is the largest one now possible.
**MILDRED MCAFEE**

Ambition is the spur that makes men struggle with destiny. It is heaven's own incentive to make purpose great and achievement greater.
**DONALD G. MITCHELL**

Ambition is a lust that is never quenched, but grows more inflamed and madder by enjoyment.
**THOMAS OTWAY**

The tallest trees are most in the power of the winds, and ambitious men of the blasts of fortune.
**WILLIAM PENN**

The same ambition can destroy or save,
And makes a patriot as it makes a knave.
**ALEXANDER POPE**

Though ambition may be a fault in itself, it is often the mother of virtues.
**QUINTILIAN**

We often pass from love to ambition, but we hardly ever return from ambition to love.
**FRANÇOIS DE LA ROCHEFOUCAULD**

It is the constant fault and inseparable evil quality of ambition, that it never looks behind it.
**SENECA**

The very substance of the ambitious is merely the shadow of a dream.
**WILLIAM SHAKESPEARE**

Ambition is an idol on whose wings great minds are carried to extremes, to be sublimely great, or to be nothing.
**THOMAS SOUTHERN**

Many people have the ambition to succeed; they may even have special aptitude for their job. And yet they do not move ahead. Why? Perhaps they

think that since they can master the job, there is no need to master themselves.
**JOHN STEVENSON**

In private enterprises men may advance or recede, whereas they who aim at empire have no alternative between the highest success and utter downfall.
**TACITUS**

How like a mounting devil in the heart rules the unreined ambition.
**NATHANIEL P. WILLIS**

They build too low who build beneath the skies.
**EDWARD YOUNG**

## *America*

The whole of the American Dream has been based on the chance to get ahead, for one's self or one's children. Would this country have ever reached the point it has if the individual had always been refused the rewards of his labors and dangers?
**JAMES TRUSLOW ADAMS**

Yesterday the greatest question was decided which was ever debated in America; and a greater perhaps never was, nor will be, decided upon men. A resolution was passed without one dissenting colony, that those United Colonies are, and of right ought to be, free and independent states.
**JOHN ADAMS (JULY 3, 1776)**

America's future will be determined by the home and the school. The child becomes largely what it is taught, hence we must watch what we teach it, how we live before it.
**JANE ADDAMS**

The American Republic and American business are Siamese twins; they came out of the same womb at the same time; they are born in the same principles and when American business dies, the American Republic will die, and when the American Republic dies, American business will die.
**JOSIAH W. BAILEY**

The making of an American begins at that point where he himself rejects all other ties, any other history, and himself adopts the vesture of his adopted land.
**JAMES BALDWIN**

America is the country where you buy a lifetime supply of aspirin for one dollar, and use it up in two weeks.
**JOHN BARRYMORE**

Alligator: The crocodile of America, superior in every detail to the crocodile of the effete monarchies of the Old World.
**AMBROSE BIERCE**

Despite whatever agreement there may be between some of us, let us never forget that we are all working whole-heartedly and humbly for the same goal—a country of peace, abundance and prosperity—for all of our people of all races, of all groups—whoever they may be, wherever they may live.
**CHESTER BOWLES**

If you will help run our government in the American way, then there will never be any danger of our government running America in the wrong way.
**GEN. OMAR NELSON BRADLEY**

It is to the United States that all freemen look for the light and the hope of the world. Unless we dedicate ourselves completely to this struggle, unless we combat hunger with food, fear with trust, suspicion with faith, fraud with justice—and threats with

power, nations will surrender to the futility, the hopelessness, the panic on which wars feed.
**GEN. OMAR NELSON BRADLEY**

America has believed that in differentiation, not in uniformity, lies the path of progress. It acted on this belief; it has advanced human happiness, and it has prospered.
**LOUIS D. BRANDEIS**

No one in this country has any roots anywhere; we don't live in America, we board here, we are like spiders that run over the surface of the water.
**VAN WYCK BROOKS**

Americans are a broad-minded people. They'll accept the fact that a person can be an alcoholic, a dope fiend, a wife beater, and even a newspaperman; but if a man doesn't drive there's something wrong with him.
**ART BUCHWALD**

The history of the building of the American nation may justly be described as a laboratory experiment in understanding and in solving the problems that will confront the world tomorrow.
**NICHOLAS MURRAY BUTLER**

It's a scientific fact that if you stay in California you lose one point of your IQ every year.
**TRUMAN CAPOTE**

Americans are a backward people, with all the very real virtues of a backward people; the patriarchal simplicity and human dignity of a democracy, and a respect for labor uncorrupted by cynicism.
**G. K. CHESTERTON**

I like the Americans for a great many reasons. I like them because even the modern thing called industrialism has not entirely destroyed in them the very ancient thing called democracy. I like them because they have a respect for work which really curbs the human tendency to snobbishness.
**G. K. CHESTERTON**

The historic glory of America lies in the fact that it is the one nation that was founded like a church. That is, it was founded on a faith that was not merely summed up after it had existed; it was defined before it existed.
**G. K. CHESTERTON**

There is nothing the matter with Americans except their ideals. The real American is all right: It is the ideal American who is all wrong.
**G. K. CHESTERTON**

America is the only nation in history which miraculously has gone directly from barbarism to degeneration without the usual interval of civilization.
**GEORGES CLEMENCEAU**

When the Pilgrims landed they fell on their knees and then they fell on the aborigines.
**PRESCOTT C. CLEVELAND**

More material progress has been made during the past one hundred and fifty years under the American system of business enterprise than during all the preceeding centuries in world history. This record of achievement is a challenge to those who would radically change that system.
**KARL T. COMPTON**

It is a great advantage to a President, and a major source of safety to the country, for him to know that he is not a great man.
**CALVIN COOLIDGE**

The government of the United States is a device for maintaining in perpetuity the rights of the people, with the ultimate extinction of all privileged classes.
**CALVIN COOLIDGE**

America grew great from the seed of the will to do and dare; the will to get up and go on and not to quit after we had erred and fallen; the will to struggle to our feet and plod along and not to give up and lie down when we wavered and stumbled from fatigue. It grew not from the seed of slumping down and giving in when laden with apparent discouragement and seeming defeat, but from the seed of the will to rise to the occasion, shake it off, stand firm and resolute, and challenge defeat. Yes, it seems what we in America need is to get back to the planting and cultivating of that good old American seed.
ARNOLD W. CRAFT

There are certain fundamental requisites for wise and resolute democratic leadership. It must build on hope, not on fear; on honesty, not on falsehood; on justice, not on injustice; on public tranquility, not on violence; on freedom, not on enslavement. It must weave a social fabric in which the most important strands are a devotion to truth and a commitment to righteousness. These are essential ingredients of the American way of life. They are the necessary conditions for the achievement of freedom and human progress the world over.
EDMUND EZRA DAY

A vision of the future has been one of the sustaining marks of the American experience. Without that vision and without the men who devote themselves to realizing that vision, there can be no true American way of life. We must beware of the thoughtless men who proclaim that a particular stage of our social development, or any special set of conditions, is the best that progress can offer. These men would immobilize us in the great stream of history. They would let its great challenges and chances pass us by, . . . forgetting that the American way of life is a way of acting, not a state of inactivity.
CORNELIS W. DE KIEWIET

By patience and determination, rather than by a harsh upsetting of tradition, we move toward our national aspirations. . . . This is the way we get things done in America. One man tells another, does what he can, till the sum of these efforts grows into a national aspiration—a precious goal. Then occurs our miracle of democracy: because the groundwork has been surely laid, the goal is already within our grasp.
NEWTON B. DRURY

America came of God, without question, and we ought to dedicate ourselves to her service so that the goodness of America would make her eternal. . . . And if we live so that the people of the world want to be like us, want to be like what we are instead of what we have, then America will be safe and the world will be safe.
ULYSSES G. DUBACH

I hope the day will never come when the American nation will be the champion of the status quo. Once that happens, we shall have forfeited, and rightly forfeited, the support of the unsatisfied, of those who are the victims of inevitable imperfections, of those who, young in years or spirit, believe that they can make a better world and of those who dream dreams and want to make their dreams come true.
JOHN FOSTER DULLES

In a world where so much seems to be hidden by the smoke of falsity and moral degeneration, we Americans must grasp firmly the ideals which have made this country great. We must reaffirm the basic human values that have guided our forefathers. A revival of old-fashioned patriotism and a grateful acknowledgment of what our country has done for us would be good for all our souls.
MANTON S. EDDY

American working men are principals in the three-member team of capital, management, labor. Never

have they regarded themselves as a servile class that could attain freedom only through destruction of the industrial economy.
**DWIGHT D. EISENHOWER**

Every gathering of Americans—whether a few on the porch of a crossroads store or massed thousands in a great stadium—is the possessor of a potentially immeasurable influence on the future.
**DWIGHT D. EISENHOWER**

I don't think the United States needs superpatriots. We need patriotism, honestly practiced by all of us, and we don't need these people that are more patriotic than you or anyone else.
**DWIGHT D. EISENHOWER**

Men of widely divergent views in our own country live in peace together because they share certain common aspirations which are more important than their differences. . . . The common responsibility of all Americans is to become effective, helpful participants in a way of life that blends and harmonizes the fiercely competitive demands of the individual and society.
**DWIGHT D. EISENHOWER**

Whatever America hopes to bring to pass in the world must first happen in the heart of America. More than escape from death, it is a way of life. More than a haven for the weary, it is a hope for the brave.
**DWIGHT D. EISENHOWER**

When American life is most American it is apt to be most theatrical.
**RALPH ELLISON**

America is another name for opportunity.
**RALPH WALDO EMERSON**

Every ship that comes to America got its chart from Columbus.
**RALPH WALDO EMERSON**

In America nature is autocratic, saying, "I am not arguing, I am telling you."
**ERIK H. ERIKSON**

America is so vast that almost everything said about it is likely to be true, and the opposite is probably equally true.
**JAMES T. FARRELL**

The superiority of the American system is eloquently proved by the pressure of people who want to crash our borders.
**WILLIAM FEATHER**

As I steamed into New York this month, exactly 20 years after first landing in America, the thought uppermost in my mind after visiting Europe was this: How mightily the United States has progressed in wealth and power, and how Europe has failed to keep step. America has exhibited qualities of a strong, industrious, generous-hearted, enthusiastic youth. Europe has exhibited signs of age. . . . America, the Youth, has not been eaten up with jealousies and bitterness and strife. Europe, the veteran, has.
**B. C. FORBES**

Is America becoming decadent? Do we no longer regard our promises and pledges as sacred? . . . We promised to make peace with Germany only in conjunction with the Allies; but we brought forward a separate peace, demanding for ourselves all the advantages of the Treaty of Versailles but rejecting all the responsibilities embodied in the Treaty. It was America's President who induced Europe to form a League of Nations; and then America was the first country that refused to joint it. . . . If these

are not the symptoms of national decadency, what are they?
B. C. FORBES

The British have their own conception of what constitutes the typical American. He must have a flavor of the Wild West about him. He must do spectacular things. He must not be punctilious about dignity, decorum and other refinements characteristic of the real British gentleman. The Yankee pictured by the Briton must be a bustler. If he is occasionally flagrantly indiscreet in speech and action, then he is so much more surely stamped the genuine article. The most typical American the British ever set their eyes on was, in their judgment, Theodore Roosevelt.
B. C. FORBES

We pride ourselves on having become the big brother among the nations. We have the greatest national wealth. We have the greatest industries, the greatest power plants, the greatest mines. We have the greatest buildings. We have the greatest international banking houses. We have the greatest population of intelligent, educated, skilled citizens. Our place in the world is unrivaled, unchallenged, and unquestioned.

Well, how are we using our greatness? Are we utilizing our unmatched power, our unparalleled influence, as befits the strongest member of the family?
B. C. FORBES

What would you call America's most priceless asset? Surely not its limitless natural resources, not its matchless national wealth, not its unequalled store of gold, not its giant factories, not its surpassing railroads, not its unprecedented volume of cheap power. Is not its most priceless asset the character of its people, their indomitable self-confidence, their transcendent vision, their sleepless initiative and, perhaps above all, their inherent, irrepressible optimism?
B. C. FORBES

Blaming the U.S. for most of their problems is usually food for bursts of applause among our allies, and ever more frequently within the Third World. . . . But where do they put what's nearest and dearest to them—their money? Here. In the last year and a half oversea-ers have invested more money in the U.S. than ever before; more, for the first time, than Americans have invested abroad. So, too, their cash stash in U.S. stocks, bonds and Treasuries soars. The French send the Socialists to power and their money to New York.
MALCOLM FORBES

Rightly, we constantly berate ourselves—mostly everybody else but me and thee—about the things wrong in our country. . . . Something has to account, though, for this country's ongoing greatness, innate and actual. And I think the Conference Board's latest survey has put a finger on that something—four out of five Americans are satisfied with their jobs, one-third of those very satisfied. It's not surprising that job satisfaction climbs with earnings, but more significant is the fact that such satisfaction climbs with age [with] 86% of those 55 and over happy at what they're doing. . . .
MALCOLM FORBES

The Johnson Administration may have messed up a lot of major programs, according to which party you support . . . but I don't think too many thinking Americans will fault the President and the First Lady for their consistent, determined support of parks, our wilderness areas and some unspoiled, unbelievably attractive American scenery. [Johnson] has proposed a National Trails system, with four trails to start with. . . .

I don't know if you have ever taken a walk in the country or . . . joined contemporary neighboring adventurers on hikes. If you did, you know what a wondrous thing it is for mind as well as muscle.
MALCOLM FORBES

For some of us it seems like yesterday when Ike was in the White House, the U.S. Senate censured Joe McCarthy, and the Supreme Court unanimously ruled that racial segregation in public school was unconstitutional.
MALCOLM FORBES

It's hard to put your finger on just what it was about Dwight Eisenhower that gave him his unique place in the hearts of his countrymen. War hero? Not really. He never personally led a charge up any San Juan hills [or] Deweyed any enemy fleets at Manila Bay. A spectacular, dramatic, colorful President and Presidency? No one would so describe the Eisenhower years. . . . No, it wasn't any of the obvious Pedestal things. It wasn't his Greatness with a capital G; rather it was his goodness without the capital G; the compelling decency of the man; the unconscious yet visible guidance by his conscience.
MALCOLM FORBES

Our country is still young and its potential is still enormous. We should remember, as we look toward the future, that the more fully we believe in and achieve freedom and equal opportunity—not simply for ourselves but for others—the greater our accomplishments as a nation will be.
HENRY FORD II

We Americans say that the Constitution made the nation. Well, the Constitution is a great document and we never would have been a nation without it, but it took more than that to make the nation. Rather it was our forefathers and foremothers, who made the Constitution and then made it work. The government they constructed did get great things out of them, but it was not the government primarily that put the great things into them. What put the great things into them was their home life, their religion, their sense of personal responsibility to Almighty God, their devotion to education, their love of liberty, their personal character.
HARRY EMERSON FOSDICK, D.D.

We get twitted now and then on how we made this country. Well, we took the whole business, of course. It's not just that corner that we took away from Mexico. When we got it all together, we got a very shapely country—the best continental cut in all the world, between the two oceans and in the right temperature zone.
ROBERT FROST

Talleyrand once said to the first Napoleon that the United States is a giant without bones. Since that time our gristle has been rapidly hardening.
JAMES A. GARFIELD

Make no mistake about it. The first man who will walk on the moon has already been born. I hope in America.
GEN. JAMES GAVIN, 1958

When the white man came, we had the land and they had the Bibles. Now they have the land and we have the Bibles.
CHIEF DAN GEORGE

In America an hour is 40 minutes.
GERMAN SAYING

The greatness of the United States is due simply to this fact: Under the principle of individual liberty, human incentive has been given its widest scope.
CRAWFORD H. GREENEWALT

Every citizen of this country, whether he pounds nails, raises corn, designs rockets or writes poetry, should be taught to know and love his American heritage; to use the language well; to understand the physical universe, and to enjoy the arts. The dollars

he gains in the absence of enlightenment like this will be earned in drudgery and spent in ignorance.
**CALVIN E. GROSS**

It is as if all America were but a giant workshop, over the entrance of which is the blazing inscription, "No admission here, except on business."
**F. J. GRUND (1837)**

No citizen of this nation is worthy of the name unless he bears unswerving loyalty to the system under which he lives, the system that gives him more benefits than any other system yet devised by man. Loyalty leaves room to change the system when need be, but only under the ground rules by which we Americans live.
**JOHN A. HANNAH**

Ideals are the incentive payment of practical men. The opportunity to strive for them is the currency that has enriched America through the centuries.
**ROBERT E. HANNEGAN**

The American economic story, despite defects and drawbacks and dreams turned nightmares, is such a good and strong and persuasive story that it needs no attempt to conceal or gloss over blemishes and imperfections. It can stand on its own with its virtues and deficiencies fully displayed. Like Cromwell's face, the U.S. economy is best portrayed warts and all.
**HERBERT HARRIS**

You can't appreciate home until you've left it, money till it's spent, your wife till she's joined a woman's club, nor Old Glory till you see it hanging on a broomstick on the shanty of a consul in a foreign town.
**O. HENRY**

Every U.S. citizen owes allegiance to our nation. Some Americans consider that anything less than high treason is allegiance.
**CULLEN HIGHTOWER**

You cannot gauge the intelligence of an American by talking with him; you must work with him. The American polishes and refines his way of doing things—even the most common-place—the way the French of the 17th century polished their maxims.
**ERIC HOFFER**

In the homes of America are born the children of America, and from them go out into American life American men and women. They go out with the stamp of these homes upon them and only as these homes are what they should be, will they be what they should be.
**JOSIAH G. HOLLAND**

If America is to be run by the people, it is the people who must think. And we do not need to put on sackcloth and ashes to think. Nor should our minds work like a sundial which records only sunshine. Our thinking must square against some lessons of history, some principles of government and morals, if we would preserve the rights and dignity of men to which this nation is dedicated.
**HERBERT HOOVER**

It is those moral and spiritual qualities which rise alone in free men, which will fulfill the meaning of the word American. And with them will come centuries of further greatness to our country.
**HERBERT HOOVER**

The priceless treasure of boyhood is his endless enthusiasm, his high store of idealism, his affections and his hopes. When we preserve these, we have made men. We have made citizens and we have made Americans.
**HERBERT HOOVER**

We [the Government] are here not as masters but as servants, we are not here to glory in power, but to attest our loyalty to the commands and restrictions laid down by our sovereign, the people of the United

States, in whose name and by whose will we exercise our brief authority.
CHARLES EVANS HUGHES

The thing that impresses me most about this country is its hopefulness. It is this which distinguishes it from Europe, where there is hopeless depression and fear.
ALDOUS HUXLEY

I tremble for my country when I reflect that God is just.
THOMAS JEFFERSON

If some period be not fixed, either by the Constitution or by practice, to the services of the First Magistrate, his office, though nominally elective, will, in fact, be for life, and that will soon degenerate into an inheritance.
THOMAS JEFFERSON

The policy of the American government is to leave their citizens free, neither restraining nor aiding them in their pursuits.
THOMAS JEFFERSON

It is a very dangerous doctrine to consider the [Supreme Court] judges as the ultimate arbiters of all constitutional questions. It is one which would place us under the despotism of an oligarchy.
THOMAS JEFFERSON

Science and time and necessity have propelled us, the United States, to be the general store for the world, dealers in everything. Most of all, merchants for a better way of life.
LADY BIRD JOHNSON

Rome endured as long as there were Romans. America will endure as long as we remain American in spirit and in thought.
DAVID STARR JORDAN

The earlier days of the republic went into the acquisition of money and the provision for material things is now finding an outlet in the espousal of art. Now America has the leisure and the culture to foster beauty.
FRITZ KREISLER

America is a tune. It must be sung together.
GERALD S. LEE

Abandon your animosities and make your sons Americans!
ROBERT E. LEE

I have been up to see the [Confederate] Congress, and they do not seem to be able to do anything except to eat peanuts and chew tobacco, while my army is starving.
ROBERT E. LEE (1865)

Intellectually I know that America is no better than any other country; emotionally I know she is better than every other country.
SINCLAIR LEWIS

The abundant life of which we have heard so much recently does not come to those who have all obstacles removed from their paths by others. It develops from within and is rooted in strong mental and moral fiber. To look to government to supply all material safeguards is to sound the doom of the great American tradition. If America is to go forward, we must develop in our colleges ideals of courage, industry, and independence.
WILLIAM MATHER LEWIS

The great social adventure of America is no longer the conquest of the wilderness but the absorption of fifty different peoples.
WALTER LIPPMANN

If a man is going to be an American at all let him be so without any qualifying adjectives; and if he is going to be something else let him drop the word American from his personal description.
HENRY CABOT LODGE

In the mighty and almost limitless potential of American industry—the brilliance and rugged determination of its leaders; the skill, energy and patriotism of its workers—there has been welded an almost impregnable defense against the evil designs of any who would threaten the security of the American continent. It is indeed the most forceful and convincing argument yet evolved to restrain the irresponsibility of those who would recklessly bring down upon the good and peace-loving peoples of all the nations of the earth the disaster of total war.
DOUGLAS MACARTHUR

The map of America is a map of endlessness, of opening out, of forever and ever. No man's face would make you think of it but his hope might, his courage might.
ARCHIBALD MACLEISH

Americanism is not an accident of birth, but an achievement in terms of worth. Government does not create Americanism, but Americanism creates Government. Americanism is not a race, but a vision, a hope and an ideal.
LOUIS I. MANN

No political dreamer was ever wild enough to think of breaking down the lines which separate the States and compounding the American people into one common mass.
JOHN MARSHALL

America must remain, at any cost, the custodian of freedom, human dignity and economic security.
The United States must be strong, so that no nation may dare attack.
LOUIS B. MAYER

Education is the indispensable means by which the ideas of the men who founded the American Republic can be disseminated and perpetuated. Only through education can the people be kept from becoming greedy and ignorant, from degenerating into a populace incapable of self-government. It is only by education, religion, and morality that the people can save themselves from becoming a willing instrument of their own debasement and ruin. The American Republic will endure only as long as the ideas of the men who founded it continue dominant.
DANIEL L. MARSH

America's love has never been equalled in human history. She turns her cheek seventy times seven. She fights only to defend her family. But when she has defeated her enemies she binds their wounds, feeds their children, pays their bills and hands forth billions of dollars to restore them to an honorable place among the nations of the world.
EMMETT MCLOUGHLIN

America is the only country ever founded on the printed word.
MARSHALL MCLUHAN

American youth attributes much more importance to arriving at driver's-license age than at voting age.
MARSHALL MCLUHAN

The most fearful phenomenon of these midcentury years is not the atom bomb; atomic energy does have its constructive possibilities.... The most fearful event of these times is the colossal expansion of the government of the United States and the

constant increase of executive power within the government.
**WHEELER MCMILLEN**

Those tragic comedians, the Chamber of Commerce red hunters, the Women's Christian Temperance Union smellers, the censors of books, the Klan regulators, the Methodist prowlers, the Baptist guardians of sacred vessels—we have the national mentality of a police lieutenant.
**H. L. MENCKEN**

Things on the whole are faster in America; people don't *stand for election,* they *run for office.* If a person says he's sick, it doesn't mean regurgitating, it means ill. *Mad* means angry, not insane. Don't ask for the left-luggage; it's called a *checkroom.*
**JESSICA MITFORD**

To be a good American means to understand the simple principles on which our nation was founded, to observe them in our daily life and to fight for them.
**NEWBOLD MORRIS**

So Columbus said, somebody show me the sunset and somebody did and he set sail for it. And he discovered America and they put him in jail for it. And the fetters gave him welts. And they named America after somebody else.
**OGDEN NASH**

Wilderness to the people of America is a spiritual necessity, an antidote to the high pressure of modern life, a means of regaining serenity and equilibrium.
**SIGURD F. OLSON**

Never, I say, had a country so many openings to happiness as this. . . . Her cause was good. Her principles just and liberal. Her temper serene and firm. . . . The remembrance then of what is past, if it operates rightly must inspire her with the most laudable of an ambition, that of adding to the fair fame she began with. The world has seen her great adversity. . . . Let then, the world see that she can bear prosperity; and that her honest virtue in time of peace is equal to the bravest virtue in time of war.
**THOMAS PAINE**

Double—no, triple—our troubles and we'd still be better off than any other people on earth.
**RONALD REAGAN**

**A Primer of American Self-Government**

1. Understand, honor and preserve the Constitution of the United States.
2. Keep forever separate and distinct the legislative, executive and judicial functions of government.
3. Remember that government belongs to the people, is inherently inefficient, and that its activities should be limited to those which government alone can perform.
4. Be vigilant for freedom of speech, freedom of worship, and freedom of action.
5. Cherish the system of Free Enterprise which made America great.
6. Respect thrift and economy, and beware of debt.
7. Above all, let us be scrupulous in keeping our word and in respecting the rights of others.

**PHILIP D. REED**

The four cornerstones of character on which the structure of this nation was built are: Initiative, Imagination, Individuality and Independence.
**CAPT. EDWARD V. RICKENBACKER**

The world position which our country holds today is due to the wide vision of the statesmen who founded these United States and to the daring and indomitable persistence of the great industrial leaders, together with the myriads of men who with faith in their leadership have co-operated to rear

the marvelous industrial structure of which our country is justly so proud.
JOHN D. ROCKEFELLER, JR.

It's a great country, but you can't live in it for nothing.
WILL ROGERS

Everything is un-American that tends either to government by a plutocracy or government by a mob. To divide along the lines of section or caste or creed is un-American. All privileges based on wealth, and all enmity to honest men merely because they are wealthy, are un-American—both of them equally so. The things that will destroy America are prosperity-at-any-price, peace-at-any-price, safety-first instead of duty-first, the love of soft living and the get-rich-quick theory of life.
THEODORE ROOSEVELT

I wish all Americans would realize that American politics is world politics.
THEODORE ROOSEVELT

America remained a land of promise for lovers of freedom. Even Byron, at a moment when he was disgusted with Napoleon for not committing suicide, wrote an eloquent stanza in praise of Washington.
BERTRAND RUSSELL

Always the path of American destiny has been into the unknown. Always there arose enough reserves of strength, balances of sanity, portions of wisdom to carry the nation through to a fresh start with ever-renewing vitality.
CARL SANDBURG

If I added to their pride of America, I am happy.
CARL SANDBURG

Not often in the story of mankind does a man arrive on earth who is both steel and velvet, who is as hard as rock and soft as drifting fog, who holds in his heart and mind the paradox of terrible storm and peace unspeakable and perfect.
CARL SANDBURG (ON LINCOLN)

Americans still believe they are cut out to be successful—in everything: love, love-making, luck, luck-giving, money-making, sense-making, cancer-avoiding, clothes-wearing, car-driving, and so on.
WILLIAM SAROYAN

One of the main differences between our American form of republic and other forms of government is the freedom of the individual to choose and exercise his means to earn his livelihood. Time has proved that our system of private enterprise, making a team of labor, investment of savings and management, with the minimum of state and Federal Government interference generates the greatest number of opportunities for individuals to earn a decent living.
FRED G. SINGER

We have a glorious future within our grasp. The American people have learned a lot in the past twenty-five years about how to make our country the kind of land in which everyone can live in dignity, comfort and personal contentment, if he so wishes.
CHARLES R. SLIGH, JR.

The nations of the world look to the people of this country for leadership. They have seen our youth in action. They have seen their courage and their strength. Off the battlefield they have seen and admired the human kindness and the tolerance of the men who went overseas for us and for them. May we stand firm in our conviction that America has achieved a way of life that we can all cherish—and cherishing, strive ever to guard and improve.
GEORGE A. SLOAN

Six things we individual Americans can never afford are: Intolerance, indolence, injustice, indifference, intemperance and ingratitude. Whenever any of these enter, they lead to deterioration, defeat and disaster. Any nation given to them inevitably falls.
**J. RICHARD SNEED**

It took thrift and savings, together with tremendous character and vision, to make our nation what it is today. And it will take thrift and savings, together with constant ingenuity and stamina, to conserve our remaining resources to enable us to continue to be a great nation.
**JOHN W. SNYDER**

In the United States there is more room where nobody is than where anybody is. That is what makes America what it is.
**GERTRUDE STEIN**

Our forefathers gave us a system of government which has produced greater liberties and higher living standards than ever before experienced in the history of the world. As citizens it is our duty and our responsibility to do our utmost to protect that system and to provide moral leadership for the rest of the world.
**GEORGE E. STRINGFELLOW**

The New Dealers, labor politicians and Socialists have tried to take advantage of the natural American instinct for charity to forward their plans to socialize the furnishing of the necessities of life to all. If the Government gives free medical care to everybody, why not free food, clothing and housing?
**ROBERT A. TAFT**

The reason American cities are prosperous is that there is no place for people to sit down.
**ALFRED J. TALLEY**

In America one of the first things done in a new State is to make the post go there; in the forests of Michigan there is no cabin so isolated, no valley so wild, but that letters and newspapers arrive at least once a week.
**ALEXIS DE TOCQUEVILLE**

Of all the countries in the world, America is that in which the spread of ideas and of human industry is the most continual and most rapid.
**ALEXIS DE TOCQUEVILLE**

The worst country to be poor in is America.
**ARNOLD TOYNBEE**

There are many humorous things in the world; among them, the white man's notion that he is less savage than the other savages.
**MARK TWAIN**

The United States is the richest, and, both actually and potentially, the most powerful state on the globe. She has much to give to the world; indeed, to her hands is chiefly entrusted the shaping of the future. If democracy in the broadest and truest sense is to survive, it will be mainly because of her guardianship.
**LORD TWEEDSMUIR**

Teach our children the wholesome ideals of America today—and the threat of vicious Communism will be dead tomorrow.
**MARTIN VANBEE**

I know that all things considered, the United States of America, with all of its abuses of democracy and of liberty itself, is still the garden spot of the world, where peace, co-operation and constructive effort can and should prevail always and the cause of a higher Christian civilization advanced.
**GEORGE M. VERITY**

If we mean to support the liberty and independence which have cost us so much blood and treasure to establish, we must drive far away the demon of party spirit and local reproach.
**GEORGE WASHINGTON**

God grants liberty only to those who love it and are always ready to guard and defend it. Let our object be our country. And, by the blessing of God, may that country itself become a vast and splendid monument, not of oppression and terror, but of wisdom, of peace, and of liberty, upon which the world may gaze with admiration forever!
**DANIEL WEBSTER**

It's becoming increasingly difficult to reach the down-trodden masses in America, a comrade wrote to his superior. In the spring they're forever polishing their cars. In the summer they take vacations. In the fall they go to the world series and football games. And in the winter you can't get them away from their television sets. Please give me suggestions on how to let them know how oppressed they are.
**DEXTER WILLIAMS**

Our way of living together in America is a strong but delicate fabric. It is made up of many threads. It has been woven over many centuries by the patience and sacrifice of countless liberty-loving men and women. It serves as a cloak for the protection of poor and rich, of black and white, of Jew and Gentile, of foreign and native born. Let us not tear it asunder. For no man knows, once it is destroyed, where or when man will find its protective warmth again.
**WENDELL WILLKIE**

The interesting and inspiring thing about America is that she asks nothing for herself except what she has a right to ask for humanity itself.
**WOODROW WILSON**

We want the spirit of America to be efficient; we want American character to be efficient; we want American character to display itself in what I may, perhaps, be allowed to call spiritual efficiency—clear disinterested thinking and fearless action along the right lines of thought.
**WOODROW WILSON**

That which is to be most desired in America is oneness and not sameness. Sameness is the worst thing that could happen to the people of this country. To make all people the same would lower their quality, but oneness would raise it.
**RABBI STEPHEN S. WISE**

## *Ancestors*

Genealogy: An account of one's descent from an ancestor who did not particularly care to trace his own.
**AMBROSE BIERCE**

A man's ancestry is a positive property to him.
**EDWARD BULWER-LYTTON**

People will not look forward to posterity, who never look backward to their ancestors.
**EDMUND BURKE**

I'd rather have an inch of dog than miles of pedigree.
**DANA BURNET**

There are many kinds of conceit, but the chief one is to let people know what a very ancient and gifted family one descends from.
**BENVENUTO CELLINI**

To forget one's ancestors is to be a brook without a source, a tree without a root.
**CHINESE PROVERB**

Man is descended from a hairy-tailed quadruped, probably arboreal in his habits.
**CHARLES DARWIN**

Genealogy: A perverse preoccupation of those who seek to demonstrate that their forebears were better people than they are.
**SYDNEY J. HARRIS**

Every man is his own ancestor, and every man his own heir. He devises his own future, and he inherits his own past.
**H. F. HEDGE**

Many a family tree needs trimming.
**KIN HUBBARD**

If you would civilize a man, begin with his grandmother.
**VICTOR HUGO**

The proper time to influence the character of a child is about a hundred years before he is born.
**WILLIAM RALPH INGE**

I don't know who my grandfather was; I am much more concerned to know what his grandson will be.
**ABRAHAM LINCOLN**

We pay for the mistakes of our ancestors, and it seems only fair that they should leave us the money to pay with.
**DONALD MARQUIS**

It is indeed a desirable thing to be well descended, but the glory belongs to our ancestors.
**PLUTARCH**

Our ancestors are very good kind of folks, but they are the last people I should choose to have a visiting acquaintance with.
**RICHARD B. SHERIDAN**

Whoever serves his country well has no need of ancestors.
**VOLTAIRE**

## *Anger*

The angry man always thinks he can do more than he can.
**ALBERTANO OF BRESCIA**

Meanness is incurable; it cannot be cured by old age, or by anything else.
**ARISTOTLE**

Consider how much more you often suffer from your anger and grief, than from those very things for which you are angry and grieved.
**MARCUS AURELIUS ANTONINUS**

When thou art above measure angry, bethink thee how momentary a man's life is.
**MARCUS AURELIUS ANTONINUS**

How much more grievous are the consequences of anger than the causes of it.
**MARCUS AURELIUS ANTONINUS**

The most complete revenge is not to imitate the aggressor.
**MARCUS AURELIUS ANTONINUS**

Anger represents a certain power, when a great mind, prevented from executing its own generous desires, is moved by it.
**PIETRO ARETINO**

Angry men are blind and foolish, for reason at such time takes flight and, in her absence; wrath plun-

ders all the riches of the intellect, while the judgment remains the prisoner of its own pride.
PIETRO ARETINO

It is easy to fly into a passion—anybody can do that—but to be angry with the right person to the right extent and at the right time and with the right object and in the right way—that is not easy, and it is not everyone who can do it.
ARISTOTLE

A man that studieth revenge keeps his own wounds green.
FRANCIS BACON

Rage can only with difficulty, and never entirely, be brought under the domination of the intelligence, and therefore is not susceptible to any arguments whatsoever.
JAMES BALDWIN

A man that does not know how to be angry does not know how to be good.
HENRY WARD BEECHER

Never forget what a man has said to you when he was angry. If he has charged you with anything, you had better look it up.
HENRY WARD BEECHER

There is another man within me that's angry with me.
SIR THOMAS BROWNE

When one is in a good sound rage, it is astonishing how calm one can be.
EDWARD BULWER-LYTTON

He that wrestles with us strengthens our nerves and sharpens our skill. Our antagonist is our helper.
EDMUND BURKE

Human anger is a higher thing than what is called divine discontent. For you must be angry with something; but you can be discontented with everything.
G. K. CHESTERTON

If you are patient in one moment of anger, you will escape a hundred days of sorrow.
CHINESE PROVERB

A man is about as big as the things that make him angry.
WINSTON CHURCHILL

Anger is the most impotent of passions. It effects nothing it goes about, and hurts the one who is possessed by it more than the one against whom it is directed.
LORD CLARENDON

I know of no more disagreeable situation than to be left feeling generally angry without anybody in particular to be angry at.
FRANK MOORE COLBY

When anger rises, think of the consequences.
CONFUCIUS

It is the growling man who lives a dog's life.
COLEMAN COX

Conflict is the gadfly of thought. It stirs us to observation and memory. It instigates to invention. It shocks us out of sheeplike passivity, and sets us at noting and contriving.
JOHN DEWEY

I've learned that if you want to get even with someone at camp, you rub their underwear with poison ivy.
11-YEAR-OLD'S DISCOVERY

We boil at different degrees.
**RALPH WALDO EMERSON**

He is a fool who cannot be angry; but he is a wise man who will not.
**ENGLISH PROVERB**

If you do not wish to be prone to anger, do not feed the habit; give it nothing which may tend to its increase. At first, keep quiet and count the days when you were not angry: I used to be angry every day, then every other day: next, every two, then every three days! and if you succeed in passing thirty days, sacrifice to the gods in thanksgiving.
**EPICTETUS**

Whenever you are angry, be assured that it is not only a present evil, but that you have increased a habit.
**EPICTETUS**

Keeping score of old scores and scars, getting even and one-upping, always make you less than you are.
**MALCOLM FORBES**

It doesn't take much of a rule to measure a mean man.
**MALCOLM FORBES**

Meanness demeans the demeaner far more than the demeaned.
**MALCOLM FORBES**

Anger is never without a reason, but seldom with a good one.
**BENJAMIN FRANKLIN**

A string of reproaches against other people leads one to suspect the existence of a string of self-reproaches with the same content.
**SIGMUND FREUD**

Act nothing in furious passion. It's putting to sea in a storm.
**THOMAS FULLER**

A man in a passion rides a horse that runs away with him.
**THOMAS FULLER**

The best answer to anger is silence.
**GERMAN PROVERB**

When a man is wrong and won't admit it, he always gets angry.
**THOMAS C. HALIBURTON**

Anger is never without an argument, but seldom with a good one.
**LORD HALIFAX**

He who curbs his wrath merits forgiveness for his sins.
**HEBREW PROVERB**

Getting even with somebody is no way to get ahead of anybody.
**CULLEN HIGHTOWER**

Anger is a prelude to courage.
**ERIC HOFFER**

Reproach is infinite, and knows no end
So voluble a weapon is the tongue;
Wounded, we wound; and neither side can fail
For every man has equal strength to rail.
**HOMER**

Anger is a short madness.
**HORACE**

Righteous indignation: Your own wrath as opposed to the shocking bad temper of others.
ELBERT HUBBARD

A grouch escapes so many little annoyances that it almost pays to be one.
KIN HUBBARD

Anger may be foolish and absurd, and one may be irritated when in the wrong; but a man never feels outraged unless in some respect he is at bottom right.
VICTOR HUGO

When angry, count ten before you speak; if very angry, 100.
THOMAS JEFFERSON

Life is but short; no time can be afforded but for the indulgence of real sorrow, or contests upon questions seriously momentous. Let us not throw away any of our days upon useless resentment, or contend who shall hold out longest in stubborn malignity. It is best not to be angry; and best, in the next place, to be quickly reconciled.
SAMUEL JOHNSON

Anger is really disappointed hope.
ERICA JONG

Revenge is always the weak pleasure of a little and narrow mind.
JUVENAL

Men must either be caressed or else annihilated; they will revenge themselves for small injuries, but cannot do so for great ones; the injury therefore that we do to a man must be such that we need not fear his vengeance.
NICCOLÒ MACHIAVELLI

The size of a man can be measured by the size of the thing that makes him angry.
J. KENFIELD MORLEY

No man can think clearly when his fists are clenched.
GEORGE JEAN NATHAN

All anger is not sinful, because some degree of it, and on some occasions, is inevitable. But it becomes sinful and contradicts the rule of Scripture when it is conceived upon slight and inadequate provocation, and when it continues long.
WILLIAM PALEY

Every stroke our fury strikes is sure to hit ourselves at last.
WILLIAM PENN

Reprove not, in their wrath, excited men; good counsel comes all out of season then; but when their fury is appeased and past, they will perceive their faults, and mend at last. When he is cool and calm, then utter it.
JOHN RANDOLPH

Mean spirits under disappointment, like small beer in a thunderstorm, always turn sour.
JOHN RANDOLPH

Anger, if not restrained, is frequently more hurtful to us than the injury that provokes it.
SENECA

The greatest remedy for anger is delay.
SENECA

Wise men ne'er sit and wail their loss, but cheerily seek how to redress their harms.
WILLIAM SHAKESPEARE

A good man and a wise man may, at times, be angry with the world, and at times grieved for it; but no man was ever discontented with the world if he did his duty in it.
**ROBERT SOUTHEY**

An angry man is again angry with himself when he returns to reason.
**PUBLILIUS SYRUS**

It becomes no man to nurse despair, but, in the teeth of clenched antagonisms, to follow up the worthiest till he die.
**ALFRED, LORD TENNYSON**

When angry, count four, when very angry, swear.
**MARK TWAIN**

Keep cool; anger is not argument.
**DANIEL WEBSTER**

There is something among men more capable of shaking despotic power than lightning, whirlwind, or earthquake; that is the threatened indignation of the whole civilized world.
**DANIEL WEBSTER**

Moral indignation is jealousy with a halo.
**H. G. WELLS**

## *Animals*

Is it not wonderful that the love of the animal parent should be so violent while it lasts and that it should last no longer than is necessary for the preservation of the young?
**JOSEPH ADDISON**

Never try to teach a pig to think. It doesn't work and it annoys the pig.
**ANONYMOUS**

The reason dogs have so many friends is because they wag their tails and not their tongues.
**ANONYMOUS**

In seeking honey expect the sting of bees.
**ARABIAN PROVERB**

The dog was created especially for children. He is the god of frolic.
**HENRY WARD BEECHER**

Animals are not brethren, they are not underlings; they are other nations, caught with ourselves in the net of life and time.
**HENRY BESTON**

A dog is the only thing on earth that loves you more than he loves himself.
**JOSH BILLINGS**

Each outcry of the hunted hare
A fiber from the brain doth tear.
**WILLIAM BLAKE**

Dogs come when they're called; cats take a message and get back to you.
**MARY BLY**

Before you kick the dog, find out the name of its master.
**RAY E. BROWN**

All animals except man know that the principal business of life is to enjoy it.
**SAMUEL BUTLER**

Never look for birds of this year in the nest of the last.
MIGUEL DE CERVANTES

Dogs look up to you, cats look down on you. Give me a pig. He just looks you in the eye and treats you as an equal.
WINSTON CHURCHILL

Elephants suffer from too much patience. Their exhibitions of it may seem superb—such power and such restraint, combined, are noble—but a quality carried to excess defeats itself.
CLARENCE DAY

Animals are such agreeable friends; they ask no questions, they pass no criticisms.
GEORGE ELIOT

Consider the mosquito—he sings at his work and he keeps everlastingly at it. The only way to stop him is to kill him.
J. T. FISHER

The Latin proverb *homo homini lupus*—man is a wolf to man—is a libel on the wolf, which is gentle to other wolves.
GEOFFREY GORER

It is not the bee's touching on the flowers that gathers the honey, but her abiding for a time upon them, and drawing out the sweet.
JOSEPH HALL

The dinosaur's eloquent lesson is that if some bigness is good, an over-abundance of bigness is not necessarily better.
ERIC A. JOHNSTON

There's an old cliche, "Sick as a dog." After you have seen as many sick dogs as I have, you realize it's more truth than cliche. A dog who hurts can't reason that he has felt bad before and recovered to chase cats. He can't comfort himself that this too will pass. He doesn't even care whether the doctor, the nurse or the other patients think he's a coward. He's sick as a dog.
JAMES R. KINNEY

The toad beneath the harrow knows
Exactly where each tooth point goes.
RUDYARD KIPLING

I prefer drawing to talking. Drawing is faster, and allows less room for lies.
LE CORBUSIER

To understand what the outside of an aquarium looks like, it's better not to be a fish.
ANDRÉ MALRAUX

Bees aren't as busy as we think they are: They just can't buzz any slower.
ABE MARTIN

When I play with my cat, who knows but that she regards me more as a plaything than I do her?
MICHEL DE MONTAIGNE

The trouble with a kitten is
That
Eventually it becomes a
Cat.
OGDEN NASH

One who is too wise an observer of the business of others, like one who is too curious in observing the labor of bees, will often be stung for his curiosity.
ALEXANDER POPE

The use of butterflies is to adorn the world and delight the eyes of men, to brighten the country-

side, serving like so many golden spangles to decorate the fields.
JOHN RAY

There is one respect in which brutes show real wisdom when compared with us—I mean their quiet, placid enjoyment of the present moment.
ARTHUR SCHOPENHAUER

Don't make the mistake of treating your dogs like humans, or they'll treat you like dogs.
MARTHA SCOTT

Some people say that cats are sneaky, evil and cruel. True, and they have many other fine qualities as well.
MISSY SIZICK

A sparrow fluttering about the church is an antagonist which the most profound theologian in Europe is wholly unable to overcome.
SYDNEY SMITH

When a dog runs at you, whistle for him.
HENRY DAVID THOREAU

It does not do to leave a live dragon out of your calculations, if you live near him.
J.R.R. TOLKIEN

My favorite animal is the mule. He has a lot more horse sense than a horse. He knows when to stop eating. And he knows when to stop working.
HARRY S TRUMAN

If you pick up a starving dog and make him prosperous, he will not bite you. This is the principal difference between a dog and a man.
MARK TWAIN

Of all God's creatures there is only one that cannot be made the slave of the lash. That one is the cat.

If man could be crossed with the cat, it would improve man, but it would deteriorate the cat.
MARK TWAIN

We hope that, when the insects take over the world, they will remember with gratitude how we took them along on all our picnics.
BILL VAUGHAN

In the history of the world the prize has not gone to those species which specialized in methods of violence, or even in defensive armor. In fact, nature began with producing animals encased in hard shells for defense against the ill of life. But smaller animals, without external armor, warm-blooded, sensitive, alert, have cleared those monsters off the face of the earth.
ALFRED NORTH WHITEHEAD

## *Appearance*

Half the work that is done in this world is to make things appear what they are not.
E. R. BEADLE

Keeping your clothes well pressed will keep you from looking hard pressed.
COLEMAN COX

Beware, so long as you live, of judging men by their outward appearance.
JEAN DE LA FONTAINE

Looking the part helps get the chance to fill it. But if you fill the part, it matters not if you look it.
MALCOLM FORBES

More often than not, things and people are as they appear.
MALCOLM FORBES

Things are not always what they seem; the first appearance deceives many; the intelligence of few perceives what has been carefully hidden in the recesses of the mind.
**PHAEDRUS**

The time men spend in trying to impress others they could spend in doing the things by which others would be impressed.
**FRANK ROMER**

We do not see things as they are, we see things as we are.
**TALMUDIC SAYING**

One man is more concerned with the impression he makes on the rest of mankind, another with the impression the rest of mankind makes on him.
**ARTHUR SCHOPENHAUER**

The world is governed more by appearances than by realities, so that it is fully as necessary to seem to know something as to know it.
**DANIEL WEBSTER**

## *Architecture*

A good architect can improve the looks of an old house merely by discussing the cost of a new one.
**ANONYMOUS**

Architect: One who drafts a plan of your house, and plans a draft of your money.
**AMBROSE BIERCE**

Architecture is inhabited sculpture.
**CONSTANTIN BRANCUSI**

Architecture is the alphabet of giants; it is the largest set of symbols ever made to meet the eyes of men. A tower stands up like a sort of simplified statue, of much more than heroic size.
**G. K. CHESTERTON**

We shape our buildings; thereafter they shape us.
**WINSTON CHURCHILL**

The brevity of human life gives a melancholy to the profession of the architect.
**RALPH WALDO EMERSON**

I call architecture petrified music. Really there is something in this: The tone of mind produced by architecture approaches the effect of music.
**JOHANN WOLFGANG VON GOETHE**

The worst of a modern stylish mansion is that it has no place for ghosts.
**OLIVER WENDELL HOLMES**

Small rooms or dwellings discipline the mind; large ones weaken it.
**LEONARDO DA VINCI**

Of all the forms of visible otherworldliness, the Gothic is at once the most logical and the most beautiful. It reaches up magnificently—and a good half of it is palpably worthless.
**H. L. MENCKEN**

A chair is a very difficult object. A skyscraper is almost easier. That is why Chippendale is famous.
**LUDWIG MIES VAN DER ROHE**

In architecture the pride of man, his triumph over gravitation, his will to power, assume visible form. Architecture is a sort of oratory of power by means of form.
**FRIEDRICH WILHELM NIETZSCHE**

Any jackass can kick down a barn but it takes a good carpenter to build one.
SAM RAYBURN

The surroundings householders crave are glorified autobiographies ghost-written by willing architects and interior designers who, like their clients, want to show off.
T. H. ROBSJOHN-GIBBINGS

When we build, let us think that we build forever. Let it not be for present delight, nor for present use alone; let it be such work as our descendants will thank us for, and let us think, as we lay stone on stone, that a time is to come when those stones will be held sacred because our hands have touched them, and that men will say as they look upon the labor and wrought substance of them, See! this our fathers did for us.
JOHN RUSKIN

No architecture is so haughty as that which is simple.
JOHN RUSKIN

Always design a thing by considering it in its next larger context—a chair in a room, a room in a house, a house in an environment, an environment in a city plan.
ELIEL SAARINEN

The ancient Romans built their greatest masterpieces of architecture, their amphitheaters, for wild beasts to fight in.
VOLTAIRE

A doctor can bury his mistakes but an architect can only advise his client to plant vines.
FRANK LLOYD WRIGHT

## *Art*

If you practice an art, be proud of it and make it proud of you. . . . It may break your heart, but it will fill your heart before it breaks it; it will make you a person in your own right.
MAXWELL ANDERSON

Art is simply a right method of doing things. The test of the artist does not lie in the will with which he goes to work, but in the excellence of the work he produces.
THOMAS AQUINAS

I don't want people who want to dance. I want people who have to dance.
GEORGE BALANCHINE

The creative person is both more primitive and more cultivated, more destructive and more constructive, a lot madder and a lot saner, than the average person.
FRANK BARRON

Buy Old Masters. They fetch a much better price than old mistresses.
LORD BEAVERBROOK

Artists who have won fame are often embarrassed by it; thus their first works are often their best.
LUDWIG VAN BEETHOVEN

I wonder whether art has a higher function than to make me feel, appreciate, and enjoy natural objects for their art value. So, as I walk in the garden, I look at the flowers and shrubs and trees and discover in them an exquisiteness of contour, a vitality of edge or a vigor of spring as well as an infinite variety of color that no artifact I have seen in the last 60 years can rival.
BERNARD BERENSON

Art can never exist without naked beauty displayed.
WILLIAM BLAKE

The artist has never been a dictator, since he understands better than anybody else the variations in human personality.
HEYWOOD BROUN

An artist conscientiously moves in a direction which for some good reason he takes, putting one work in front of the other with the hope he'll arrive before death overtakes him.
JOHN CAGE

In every photographer there is something of a stroller.
HENRI CARTIER-BRESSON

Religion and art spring from the same root and are close kin. Economics and art are strangers.
WILLA CATHER

I suppose Gauguin would not approve of his own imitators, for he said, "In art one is a revolutionary or a plagiarist." Remembering the old schools and traditions, we might answer that the great artists have been the plagiarists.
G. K. CHESTERTON

Art is a mirror not because it is the same as the object, but because it is different. A mirror selects much as art selects; it gives the light of flames, but not their heat; the color of flowers, but not their fragrance; the faces of women, but not their voices; the proportions of stockbrokers, but not their solidity.
G. K. CHESTERTON

Art, like morality, consists of drawing the line somewhere.
G. K. CHESTERTON

Artistic temperament is a disease that afflicts amateurs.
G. K. CHESTERTON

Nothing sublimely artistic has ever arisen out of mere art, any more than anything essentially reasonable has ever arisen out of the pure reason. There must always be a rich moral soil for any great aesthetic growth.
G. K. CHESTERTON

The dignity of the artist lies in his duty of keeping awake the sense of wonder in the world. In this long vigil he often has to vary his methods of stimulation; but in this long vigil he is also himself striving against a continual tendency to sleep.
G. K. CHESTERTON

An artist carries on throughout his life a mysterious, uninterrupted conversation with his public.
MAURICE CHEVALIER

An artist cannot speak about his art any more than a plant can discuss horticulture.
JEAN COCTEAU

Art produces ugly things which frequently become beautiful with time. Fashion, on the other hand, produces beautiful things which always become ugly with time.
JEAN COCTEAU

There has never been a boy painter, nor can there be. The art requires a long apprenticeship, being mechanical as well as intellectual.
JOHN CONSTABLE

Creativity is inventing, experimenting, growing, taking risks, breaking rules, making mistakes, and having fun.
MARY LOU COOK

Art imitates nature as well as it can, as a pupil follows his master; thus it is sort of a grandchild of God.
DANTE

If I had my life to live over again, I would have made a rule to read some poetry and listen to some music at least once a week; for perhaps the parts of my brain now atrophied would have thus been kept active through use. The loss of these tastes is a loss of happiness, and may possibly be injurious to the intellect, and more probably to the moral character, by enfeebling the emotional part of our nature.
CHARLES DARWIN

The principle underlying all art is of a purely religious nature.
VINCENT D'INDY

Art is the most frenzied orgy man is capable of.
JEAN DUBUFFET

If a man have a genius for painting, poetry, music, architecture, or philosophy, he makes a bad husband, and an ill provider.
RALPH WALDO EMERSON

Nature is everything a man is born to, and art is the difference he makes in it.
JOHN ERSKINE

The aim of every artist is to arrest motion, which is life, by artificial means and hold it fixed so that a hundred years later, when a stranger looks at it, it moves again since it is life.
WILLIAM FAULKNER

The stamping out of the artist is one of the blind goals of every civilization. When a civilization becomes so standardized that the individual can no longer make an imprint on it, then that civilization is dying. The mass mind has taken over and another set of national glories is heading for history's scrap heap.
ELIE FAURE

Having once found the intensity of art, nothing else that can happen in life can ever again seem as important as the creative process.
F. SCOTT FITZGERALD

You're always believing ahead of your evidence. What was the evidence I could write a poem? I just believed it. The most creative thing in us is to believe a thing in.
ROBERT FROST

An artist cannot get along without a public; and when the public is absent, what does he do? He invents it, and turning his back on his age, he looks toward the future for what the present denies.
ANDRÉ GIDE

Art is a collaboration between God and the artist, and the less the artist does the better.
ANDRÉ GIDE

A man should hear a little music, read a little poetry, and see a fine picture every day of his life, in order that worldly cares may not obliterate the sense of the beautiful which God has implanted in the human soul.
JOHANN WOLFGANG VON GOETHE

All men are creative but few are artists.
PAUL GOODMAN

No artist is ahead of his time. He is his time. It's just that the others are behind the time.
MARTHA GRAHAM

The body is your instrument in dance, but your art is outside that creature, the body. I don't leap and jump any more. I look at young dancers and am envious, more aware of what glories the body contains. But sensitivity is not made dull by age.
MARTHA GRAHAM

The liberal arts inform and enlighten the independent citizen of a democracy in the use of his own resources. . . . They enlarge his capacity for self-knowledge and expand his opportunities for self-improvement . . . . They are the wellsprings of a free society.
A. WHITNEY GRISWOLD

The idea of a Christian art is a contradiction in terms.
ERNST HAECKEL

There is a field where all wonderful perfections of microscope and telescope fail, all exquisite niceties of weights and measures, as well as that which is behind them, the keen and driving power of the mind. No facts however indubitably detected, no effort of reason however magnificently maintained, can prove that Bach's music is beautiful.
EDITH HAMILTON

We are all, it seems, saving ourselves for the senior prom. But many of us forget that somewhere along the way we must learn to dance.
ALAN HARRINGTON

I think most of the people involved in any art always secretly wonder whether they are there because they're good or there because they're lucky.
KATHARINE HEPBURN

Comic-strip artists do not make good husbands, and God knows they do not make good comic strips.
DON HEROLD

The genuine artist is as much a dissatisfied person as the revolutionary, yet how diametrically opposed are the products each distills from his dissatisfaction.
ERIC HOFFER

I think it is owing to the good sense of the English that they have not painted better.
WILLIAM HOGARTH

Great art is an instant arrested in eternity.
JAMES GIBBONS HUNEKER

If it were not for the intellectual snobs who pay—in solid cash—the tribute which philistinism owes to culture, the arts would perish with their starving practitioners. Let us thank heaven for hypocrisy.
ALDOUS HUXLEY

We tend to think and feel in terms of the art we like; and if the art we like is bad then our thinking and feeling will be bad. And if the thinking and feeling of most of the individuals composing a society is bad, is not that society in danger?
ALDOUS HUXLEY

Art does not reproduce the visible; rather, it makes visible.
PAUL KLEE

Where the spirit does not work with the hand there is no art.
LEONARDO DA VINCI

I am the most curious of all to see what will be the next thing that I will do.
JACQUES LIPCHITZ

Art for art's sake makes no more sense than gin for gin's sake.
SOMERSET MAUGHAM

Society profits from every useful invention and from all the beneficent creative activities of individuals. The more good things others produce the more there is for us to share. The world profited more from Christopher Columbus' discovery than he did. The world has profited more from the inventions of Thomas A. Edison than he did. We are all beneficiaries of the achievements of the creative and business genius or talents of others.
GEORGE W. MAXEY

Arts and sciences are not cast in a mould, but are found and perfected by degrees, by often handling and polishing.
MICHEL DE MONTAIGNE

The artist isn't particularly keen on getting a thing done, as you call it. He gets his pleasure out of doing it, playing with it, fooling with it, if you like. The mere completion of it is an incident.
WILLIAM MCFEE

The artist has a special task and duty: the task of reminding men of their humanity and the promise of their creativity.
LEWIS MUMFORD

It is better to create than to be learned; creating is the true essence of life.
REINHOLD NIEBUHR

Nothing is more useful to man than those arts which have no utility.
OVID

I'm a joker who has understood his epoch and has extracted all he possibly could from the stupidity, greed and vanity of his contemporaries.
PABLO PICASSO

We all know art is not truth. Art is a lie to make us realize the truth.
PABLO PICASSO

Every child is an artist. The problem is how to remain an artist once he grows up.
PABLO PICASSO

Thanks to art, instead of seeing a single world, our own, we see it multiply until we have before us as many worlds as there are original artists.
MARCEL PROUST

Art is always the index of social vitality, the moving finger that records the destiny of a civilization. A wise statesman should keep an anxious eye on this graph, for it is more significant than a decline in exports or a fall in the value of a nation's currency.
HERBERT READ

A room hung with pictures is a room hung with thoughts.
SIR JOSHUA REYNOLDS

You desire a popular art? Begin by having a people whose minds are liberated, a people not crushed by misery and ceaseless toil, not brutalized by every superstition and every fanaticism, a people master of itself, and victor in the fight that is being waged today.
ROMAIN ROLLAND

Artists—by definition innocent—don't steal. But they do borrow without giving back.
NED ROREM

For me, painting is a way to forget life. It is a cry in the night, a strangled laugh.
GEORGES ROUAULT

Life without industry is guilt, industry without art is brutality.
**John Ruskin**

An artist is a dreamer consenting to dream of the actual world.
**George Santayana**

I don't think it's very useful to open wide the door for young artists; the ones who break down the door are more interesting.
**Paul Schrader**

Dance is the only art of which we ourselves are the stuff of which it is made.
**Ted Shawn**

The plastic arts are gross arts, dealing joyously with gross material facts. They call, in their servants, for a robust stomach and a great power of endurance, and while they will flourish in the scullery or on a dunghill, they fade at a breath from the drawing room.
**Paul Sickert**

Art is like a border of flowers along the course of civilization.
**Lincoln Steffens**

He who has learned to love an art or science has wisely laid up riches against the day of riches.
**Robert Louis Stevenson**

Try to make the work experience you select as fully as possible your own channel of a distinctive creative effort, where you are at once making a contribution derived from your talents, and by so doing are enriching the productive life of society—in business, art, education, social work, at home, or in some other of a thousand outlets.
**Ordway Tead**

Art is the only way to run away without leaving home.
**Twyla Tharp**

Art is a human activity consisting in this, that one man consciously, by means of certain external signs, hands on to others feelings he has lived through, and that other people are infected by these feelings, and also experience them.
**Leo Tolstoy**

Can it be possible that the painters make John the Baptist a Spaniard in Madrid and an Irishman in Dublin?
**Mark Twain**

Most important, novelty and creativity are unrecognizable unless they emerge from order.
**Ross A. Webber**

Beautiful forms and compositions are not made by chance, nor can they ever, in any material, be made at small expense. A composition for cheapness and not excellence of workmanship is the most frequent and certain cause of the rapid decay and entire destruction of arts and manufactures.
**Josiah Wedgwood**

An artist's career always begins tomorrow.
**James McNeill Whistler**

No great artist ever sees things as they really are. If he did he would cease to be an artist.
**Oscar Wilde**

Lying, a telling of beautiful untrue things, this is the proper aim of art.
**Oscar Wilde**

## Attitude

Without constancy there is neither love, friendship, nor virtue in the world.
**JOSEPH ADDISON**

Neutrality is no favorite with Providence, for we are so formed that it is scarcely possible for us to stand neutral in our hearts, although we may deem it prudent to appear so in our actions.
**CHARLES CALEB COLTON**

A good man it is not mine to see. Could I see a man possessed of constancy that would satisfy me.
**CONFUCIUS**

Go outdoors and get rid of nerves.
**FRANK CRANE**

A little learning is a dangerous thing, but a little patronage more so.
**CHARLES DICKENS**

The long span of the bridge of your life is supported by countless cables called habits, attitudes, and desires. What you do in life depends upon what you are and what you want. What you get from life depends upon how much you want it—how much you are willing to work and plan and co-operate and use your resources. The long span of the bridge of your life is supported by countless cables that you are spinning now, and that is why today is such an important day. Make the cables strong!
**L. G. ELLIOTT**

Coolness and absence of heat and haste indicate fine qualities.
**RALPH WALDO EMERSON**

Obstinacy in opinions holds the dogmatist in the chains of error, without hope of emancipation.
**JOHN C. GRANVILLE**

The greatest revolution of our generation is the discovery that human beings, by changing the inner attitudes of their minds, can change the outer aspects of their lives.
**WILLIAM JAMES**

If once the people become inattentive to the public affairs, you and I and Congress and Assemblies, Judges and Governors, shall all become wolves.
**THOMAS JEFFERSON**

Science may have found a cure for most evils; but it has found no remedy for the worst of them all—the apathy of human beings.
**HELEN KELLER**

Neutrality, as a lasting principle, is an evidence of weakness.
**LOUIS KOSSUTH**

Obstinacy is the strength of the weak. Firmness founded upon principle, upon truth and right, order and law, duty and generosity, is the obstinacy of sages.
**JOHANN LAVATER**

Your living is determined not so much by what life brings to you as by the attitude you bring to life; not so much by what happens to you as by the way your mind looks at what happens. Circumstances and situations do color life but you have been given the mind to choose what the color shall be.
**JOHN HOMER MILLER**

A man's greatest enemies are his own apathy and stubbornness.
**FRANK TYGER**

The people with whom you work reflect your own attitude. If you are suspicious, unfriendly and condescending, you will find these unlovely traits echoed all about you. But if you are on your best behavior, you will bring out the best in the persons with whom you are going to spend most of your waking hours.
BEATRICE VINCENT

Pluck takes us into a difficulty; nerve brings us out of it.
GEORGE JOHN WHYTE-MELVILLE

Nothing can stop the man with the right mental attitude from achieving his goal; nothing on earth can help the man with the wrong mental attitude.
W. W. ZIEGE

# B

## Banking

Business and life are like a bank account—you can't take out more than you put in.
**WILLIAM FEATHER**

A bank is a place where they lend you an umbrella in fair weather and ask for it back again when it begins to rain.
**ROBERT FROST**

Banking may well be a career from which no man really recovers.
**JOHN KENNETH GALBRAITH**

The federal [bank deposit] insurance scheme has worked up to now simply and solely because there have been very few bank failures. The next time we have a pestilence of them it will come to grief quickly enough, and if the good banks escape ruin with the bad ones it will be only because the taxpayer foots the bill.
**H. L. MENCKEN (1936)**

For a country, everything will be lost when the jobs of an economist and a banker become highly respected professions.
**BARON DE MONTESQUIEU**

Stay out of banks. You may never get as rich as you could with other people's money and some luck, but the tradeoff is sleeping at night.
**OLD SOUTHERN SAYING**

There was the South Ozone National Bank looking as though it had been waiting for me.
**WILLIE SUTTON**

## Beauty

Beauty: The adjustment of all parts proportionately so that one cannot add or subtract or change without impairing the harmony of the whole.
**LEON BATTISTA ALBERTI**

Beauty is one of the rare things that do not lead to doubt of God.
**JEAN ANOUILH**

Beauty is a greater recommendation than any letter of introduction.
**ARISTOTLE**

Beauty is only skin deep, and the world is full of thin-skinned people.
**RICHARD ARMOUR**

There is no excellent beauty that hath not some strangeness in the proportion.
**FRANCIS BACON**

Beauty: The power by which a woman charms a lover and terrifies a husband.
**AMBROSE BIERCE**

If you get simple beauty and nought else, you get about the best God invents.
**ROBERT BROWNING**

Where does beauty begin and where does it end? It ends where the artist begins.
**JOHN CAGE**

The love of beauty in its multiple forms is the noblest gift of the human cerebrum.
**ALEXIS CARREL**

Those who contemplate the beauty of the earth find reserves of strength that will endure as long as life lasts.
**RACHEL CARSON**

Beauty in a good woman is like fire at a distance or a sharp sword; the one does not burn, or the other wound, those who come not too close.
**MIGUEL DE CERVANTES**

It is the beautiful bird that gets caged.
**CHINESE PROVERB**

I shall never get used to not being the most beautiful woman in the room. It was an intoxication to sweep in and know every man had turned his head. It kept me in form.
**LADY RANDOLPH CHURCHILL**

There is in true beauty, as in courage, somewhat which narrow souls cannot dare to admire.
**WILLIAM CONGREVE**

Zest is the secret of all beauty. There is no beauty that is attractive without it.
**CHRISTIAN DIOR**

It seems to me we can never give up longing and wishing while we are thoroughly alive. There are certain things we feel to be beautiful and good, and we must hunger after them.
**GEORGE ELIOT**

Some thoughts always find us young, and keep us so. Such a thought is the love of the universal and eternal beauty.
**RALPH WALDO EMERSON**

Things are pretty, graceful, rich, elegant, handsome, but until they speak to the imagination, not yet beautiful.
**RALPH WALDO EMERSON**

Though we travel the world over to find the beautiful, we must carry it with us or we will find it not.
**RALPH WALDO EMERSON**

Without grace, beauty is an unbaited hook.
**FRENCH PROVERB**

When I am working on a problem, I never think about beauty. I think only about how to solve the problem. But when I have finished, if the solution is not beautiful, I know it is wrong.
**BUCKMINSTER FULLER**

Beauty and folly are generally companions.
**BALTASAR GRACIÁN**

Every day look at a beautiful picture, read a beautiful poem, listen to beautiful music, and, if possible, say some reasonable thing.
**JOHANN WOLFGANG VON GOETHE**

The beautiful is a phenomenon which is never apparent of itself, but is reflected in a thousand different works of the creator.
**JOHANN WOLFGANG VON GOETHE**

The soul that sees beauty may sometimes walk alone.
**JOHANN WOLFGANG VON GOETHE**

Ugliness creates bitterness. Ugliness is an eroding force on the people of our land. We are all here to try to change that.
**LADY BIRD JOHNSON**

The beautiful! It is beauty seen with the eye of the soul.
**JOSEPH JOUBERT**

The autumn of the beautiful is beautiful.
**LATIN PROVERB**

The task of man is not to discover new worlds, but to discover his own world in terms of human comprehension and beauty.
**ARCHIBALD MACLEISH**

Charisma means looking like everyone else.
**MARSHALL MCLUHAN**

Beauty is an ecstasy; it is as simple as hunger. There is really nothing to be said about it.
**SOMERSET MAUGHAM**

No one ever called me pretty when I was a little girl.
**MARILYN MONROE**

You may not, cannot, appropriate beauty. It is the wealth of the eye, and a cat may gaze upon a king.
**THEODORE PARKER**

There is always the possibility of beauty where there is an unsealed human eye; of music where there is an unstopped human ear; and of inspiration where there is a receptive human spirit.
**CHARLES HENRY PARKHURST, D.D.**

Beauty and wisdom are seldom found together.
**PETRONIUS**

Beauty is rather a light that plays over the symmetry of things than that symmetry itself.
**PLOTINUS**

That pleasure which is at once the most pure, the most elevating and the most intense, is derived, I maintain, from the contemplation of the beautiful.
**EDGAR ALLAN POE**

Remember that the most beautiful things in the world are the most useless: peacocks and lilies, for instance.
**JOHN RUSKIN**

To live with beauty is not only to give oneself a joy, it is to have the power of beauty at one's call. A man's life would be in a deep and manly way purified and sweetened if each day he could gain a little of the inspiration that poets fuse into their verse and have it share his visions for that day. The wise poet was right who advised us, daily to see a beautiful picture, daily to read a beautiful poem. He was right, he was practical.
**MARTIN W. SAMPSON**

Outstanding beauty, like outstanding gifts of any kind, tends to get in the way of normal emotional development and thus of that particular success in life which we call happiness.
**MILTON SAPERSTEIN**

Beauty is but a vain and doubtful good;
A shining gloss that fadeth suddenly;
A flower that dies when first it 'gins to bud,
A brittle glass that's broken presently.
**WILLIAM SHAKESPEARE**

Those who skim over the surface in a hit-or-miss fashion not only forfeit the best returns on their efforts, but are ever barred from the keen pleasure of seeing beauty in the results of their labor.
**RODERICK STEVENS**

A beauty is a woman you notice; a charmer is one who notices you.
ADLAI STEVENSON

There are women who have an indefinable charm in their faces which makes them beautiful to their intimates, but a cold stranger who tried to reason the matter out and find this beauty would fail.
MARK TWAIN

Industry is the root of all ugliness.
OSCAR WILDE

## *Beginning*

Affairs are easier of entrance than exit; and it is but common prudence to see our way out before we venture in.
AESOP

Begin: To have commenced is half the deed. Half yet remains; Begin again on this and thou wilt finish all.
AUSONIUS

Initiative is to success what a lighted match is to a candle.
ORLANDO A. BATTISTA

What the carburetor, sparkplug and self-starter are to an automobile, initiative, private enterprise and executive ability are to industry as a whole, including the wage earner, wage payer, wage spender and wage saver, i. e. , the investor. If the sparkplug and self-starter get out of commission, the car will come to a standstill.
WILLIAM J. H. BOETCKER

He who commences many things finishes but few.
H. G. BOHN

The beginnings of all things are small.
CICERO

America, in the eyes of the world, typifies above all else this quality of initiative. The greatest successes are nearly all the fruit of initiative. Why do we hold in such high esteem the achievements of the Wright brothers? Because they were illustrious examples of initiative and tenacity. And ideas are born of initiative, the children of men and women of initiative. Advancement is applied initiative. Don't imitate. Initiate.
B. C. FORBES

Are you in earnest? Seize this very minute. What you can do, or dream you can do, begin it. Begin it and the work will be completed.
JOHANN WOLFGANG VON GOETHE

Doing for people what they can and ought to do for themselves is a dangerous experiment. In the last analysis, the welfare of the workers depends upon their own initiative. Whatever is done under the guise of philanthropy or social morality which in any way lessens initiative is the greatest crime that can be committed against the toilers. Let social busybodies and professional public morals experts in their fads reflect upon the perils they rashly invite under this pretense of social welfare.
SAMUEL GOMPERS

Dare to be wise; begin! He who postpones the hour of living rightly is like the rustic who waits for the river to run out before he crosses.
HORACE

Initiative consists of doing the right thing without being told.
IRVING MACK

The beginnings of all things are weak and tender. We must therefore be clear-sighted in the begin-

nings, for, as in their budding we discern not the danger, so in their full growth we perceive not the remedy.
MICHEL DE MONTAIGNE

The last thing one knows—is what to put first.
BLAISE PASCAL

The only joy in the world is to begin.
CESARE PAVESE

When the ancients said a work well begun was half done, they meant to impress the importance of always endeavoring to make a good beginning.
POLYBIUS

While we ponder when to begin it becomes too late to do.
QUINTILIAN

In our complex world, there cannot be fruitful initiative without government, but unfortunately, there can be government without initiative.
BERTRAND RUSSELL

The difference between getting somewhere and nowhere is the courage to make an early start. The fellow who sits still and does just what he is told will never be told to do big things.
CHARLES M. SCHWAB

To do anything in this world worth doing, we must not stand back shivering and thinking of the cold and danger, but jump in, and scramble through as well as we can.
SYDNEY SMITH

Better it is to the right conduct of life to consider what will be the end of a thing, than what is the beginning of it; for what promises fair at first, may prove ill, and what seems at first a disadvantage, may prove very advantageous.
WILLIAM V. WELLS

## *Beliefs*

It's a wonderful feeling when you discover some evidence to support your beliefs.
ANONYMOUS

Much bending breaks the bow; much unbending the mind.
FRANCIS BACON

Confronted with the impossibility of remaining faithful to one's beliefs, and the equal impossibility of becoming free of them, one can be driven to the most inhuman excesses.
JAMES BALDWIN

When you want to believe in something, you also have to believe in everything that's necessary for believing in it.
UGO BETTI

No man is happy without a delusion of some kind. Delusions are as necessary to our happiness as realities.
CHRISTIAN BOVÉE

No more important duty can be urged upon those who are entering the great theater of life than simple loyalty to their best convictions.
EDWIN H. CHAPIN

Dogma does not mean the absence of thought, but the end of thought.
G. K. CHESTERTON

An unaspiring person believes according to what he achieves. An aspiring person achieves according to what he believes.
SRI CHINMOY

When is a man actually sick? He is sick only when his mind is empty of belief and his life is empty of promise.
SRI CHINMOY

This is the lesson: Never give in . . . never, never, never, never . . . in nothing, great or small, large or petty—never give in except to convictions of honor or good taste.
WINSTON CHURCHILL

All the strength and force of man comes from his faith in things unseen. He who believes is strong; he who doubts is weak. Strong convictions precede great actions.
JAMES FREEMAN CLARKE

Believe only half of what you see and nothing that you hear.
DINAH MULOCK CRAIK

Unless the man who works in an office is able to sell himself and his ideas, unless he has the power to convince others of the soundness of his convictions, he can never achieve his goal. He may have the best ideas in the world, he may have plans which would revolutionize entire industries. But unless he can persuade others that his ideas are good, he will never get the chance to put them into effect. Stripped of non-essentials, all business activity is a sales battle. And everyone in business must be a salesman.
ROBERT E. M. COWIE

A firm belief attracts facts. They come out iv' holes in th' ground an' cracks in th' wall to support belief, but they run away fr'm doubt.
FINLEY PETER DUNNE

All business proceeds on beliefs, or judgments of probabilities, and not on certainties.
CHARLES W. ELIOT

As long as our civilization is essentially one of property, of fences, of exclusiveness, it will be mocked by delusions.
RALPH WALDO EMERSON

I have found that the greatest help in meeting any problem with decency and self-respect and whatever courage is demanded, is to know where you yourself stand. That is, to have in words what you believe and are acting from.
WILLIAM FAULKNER

There are three fields in which all human beings are credulous: money, matrimony and medicine.
MORRIS FISHBEIN

At 18 our convictions are hills from which we look; at 45 they are caves in which we hide.
F. SCOTT FITZGERALD

A big league baseball manager declares that he would have the public feel extremely doubtful early in the season regarding the chances of his team to win the championship. Cocksureness, he implies, could not fail to have a bad effect upon his players, whereas public skepticism acted upon them as a challenge. There is wisdom in this for business concerns. The man who is smugly confident that he has arrived is ripe for the return trip. A measure of self-confidence is an asset when you are battling your way to the top. But cocksureness is not an asset but

a liability. It tends to dull the edge of effort. Also, it breeds arrogance that is distasteful.
**B. C. FORBES**

Believe in yourself, your neighbors, your work, your ultimate attainment of more complete happiness. It is only the farmer who faithfully plants seeds in the Spring, who reaps a harvest in the Autumn.
**B. C. FORBES**

The men who succeed best in public life are those who take the risk of standing by their own convictions.
**JAMES A. GARFIELD**

Whether you believe you can do a thing or not, you are right.
**HENRY FORD**

A supremely religious man or woman is one who believes deeply and consistently in the veracity of his highest experiences. He has his hours in the cellar... but he believes in the truth of the hours he spends upstairs.
**HARRY EMERSON FOSDICK, D.D.**

Devout believers are safeguarded in a high degree against the risk of certain neurotic illnesses; their acceptance of the universal neurosis spares them the task of building a personal one.
**SIGMUND FREUD**

We cannot tell some people what it is we believe, partly because they are too stupid to understand, partly because we are too proudly vague to explain.
**ROBERT FROST**

The practical effect of a belief is the real test of its soundness.
**J. A. FROUDE**

The will to believe is perhaps the most powerful but certainly the most dangerous human attribute.
**JOHN P. GRIER**

As soon as we cease to pry about at random, we shall come to rely upon accredited bodies of authoritative dogma; and as soon as we come to rely upon accredited bodies of authoritative dogma, not only are the days of our liberty over, but we have lost the password that has hitherto opened to us the gates of success as well.
**LEARNED HAND**

He that believes all, misseth; he that believes nothing, hits not.
**GEORGE HERBERT**

Men are tattooed with their special beliefs like so many South Sea Islanders; but a real human heart with divine love in it beats with the same glow under all the patterns of all earth's thousand tribes.
**OLIVER WENDELL HOLMES**

Nothing can be more unphilosophical than to be positive or dogmatical on any subject. When men are the most sure and arrogant, they are commonly the most mistaken and have then given reins to passion without that proper deliberation and suspense which alone can secure them from the grossest absurdities.
**DAVID HUME**

Disbelief in futurity loosens in a great measure the ties of morality, and may be for that reason pernicious to the peace of civil society.
**DAVID HUME**

Too few have the courage of my convictions.
**ROBERT M. HUTCHINS**

Be not afraid of life. Believe that life is worth living, and your belief will help create the fact.
**WILLIAM JAMES**

In the matter of belief, we are all extreme conservatives.
**WILLIAM JAMES**

Every man who attacks my belief diminishes in some degree my confidence in it, and therefore makes me uneasy; and I am angry with him who makes me uneasy.
**SAMUEL JOHNSON**

Assertion is not argument; to contradict the statement of an opponent is not proof that you are correct.
**SAMUEL JOHNSON**

The things a man believes most profoundly are rarely on the surface of his mind or tongue. Newly acquired notions—decisions based on expediency, the fashionable ideas of the moment—are right on top of the pile, ready to be displayed in bright after-dinner conversation. But the ideas that make up a man's philosophy of life are somewhere way down below.
**ERIC A. JOHNSTON**

Convictions are the mainsprings of action, the driving powers of life. What a man lives are his convictions.
**FRANCIS C. KELLEY**

Credulity is the man's weakness, but the child's strength.
**CHARLES LAMB**

Believe that you have it, and you have it.
**LATIN PROVERB**

Some like to understand what they believe in. Others like to believe in what they understand.
**STANISLAUS LEC**

With most people, unbelief in one thing is founded upon blind belief in another.
**GEORG CHRISTOPH LICHTENBERG**

First there is a time when we believe everything, then for a little while we believe with discrimination, then we believe nothing whatever, and then we believe everything again—and, moreover, give reasons why we believe.
**GEORG CHRISTOPH LICHTENBERG**

That which you vividly imagine, sincerely believe, ardently desire and enthusiastically act upon will inevitably come to pass.
**WILLIAM R. LUCAS**

Man is so inconsistent a creature that it is impossible to reason from his beliefs to his conduct, or from one part of his belief to another.
**THOMAS B. MACAULAY**

I wish I was as sure of anything as he is of everything.
**THOMAS B. MACAULAY**

Any man worth his salt will stick up for what he believes right, but it takes a slightly bigger man to acknowledge instantly and without reservation that he is in error.
**GEN. PEYTON C. MARCH**

Nothing is so firmly believed as what we least know.
**MICHEL DE MONTAIGNE**

Convictions are more dangerous enemies of truth than lies.
**FRIEDRICH WILHELM NIETZSCHE**

When you affirm big, believe big, and pray big, big things happen.
**NORMAN VINCENT PEALE**

I prefer credulity to skepticism and cynicism, for there is more promise in almost anything than in nothing at all.
**RALPH BARTON PERRY**

The man who believes he can do it is probably right, and so is the man who believes he can't.
**LAURENCE J. PETER**

Remember that what you believe will depend very much upon what you are.
**NOAH PORTER**

It is desire that engenders belief; if we fail as a rule to take this into account, it is because most of the desires that create beliefs end only with our own life.
**MARCEL PROUST**

The nobility of a human being is strictly independent of that of his convictions.
**JEAN ROSTAND**

Emphatic and reiterated assertion, especially during childhood, produces in most people a belief so firm as to have a hold even over the unconscious.
**BERTRAND RUSSELL**

Man is a credulous animal, and must believe in something; in the absence of good grounds for belief, he will be satisfied with bad ones.
**BERTRAND RUSSELL**

As the essence of courage is to stake one's life on a possibility, so the essence of faith is to believe that the possibility exists.
**WILLIAM SALTER**

People who feel themselves to be exiles in this world are mightily inclined to believe themselves citizens of another.
**GEORGE SANTAYANA**

What a man believes may be ascertained, not from his creed, but from the assumptions on which he habitually acts.
**GEORGE BERNARD SHAW**

He who is surety is never sure himself. Take advice, and never be security for more than you are quite willing to lose. Remember the word of the wise man: He that is surety for a stranger shall smart for it; and he that hateth suretyship is sure.
**CHARLES H. SPURGEON**

Our affections and beliefs are wiser than we; the best that is in us is better than we can understand; for it is grounded beyond experience, and guides us, blindfold but safe, from one age on to another.
**ROBERT LOUIS STEVENSON**

To have integrity the individual cannot merely be a weathervane turning briskly with every doctrinal wind that blows. He must possess key loyalties and key convictions which can serve as a basis of judgment and a standard of action.
**JOHN STUDEBAKER**

Follow your honest convictions and be strong.
**WILLIAM MAKEPEACE THACKERAY**

When the human race has once acquired a superstition nothing short of death is ever likely to remove it.
**MARK TWAIN**

In religion and politics, people's beliefs and convictions are in almost every case gotten at second hand, and without examination.
MARK TWAIN

Things that I felt absolutely sure of but a few years ago, I do not believe now; and this thought makes me see more clearly how foolish it would be to expect all men to agree with me.
F. D. VAN AMBURGH

They can conquer who believe they can.
VIRGIL

When I was young I was sure of everything; in a few years, having been mistaken a thousand times, I was not half so sure of most things as I was before; at present, I am hardly sure of anything but what God has revealed to me.
JOHN WESLEY

As one may bring himself to believe almost anything he is inclined to believe, it makes all the difference whether we begin or end with the inquiry, "What is truth?"
RICHARD WHATELY

Believe things, rather than man.
BENJAMIN WHICHCOTE

Do not attempt to do a thing unless you are sure of yourself; but do not relinquish it simply because someone else is not sure of you.
STEWART E. WHITE

## *Best*

All I want of the world is very little. I only want the best of everything, and there is so little of that.
MICHAEL ARLEN

Do what you know best; if you're a runner, run, if you're a bell, ring.
IGNAS BERNSTEIN

Be true to the best you know. This is your high ideal. If you do your best, you cannot do more. Do your best every day and your life will gradually expand into satisfying fullness. Cultivate the habit of doing one thing at a time with quiet deliberateness. Always allow yourself a sufficient margin of time in which to do your work well. Frequently examine your working methods to discover and eliminate unnecessary tension. Aim at poise, repose, and self-control. The relaxed worker accomplishes most.
H. W. DRESSER

There is only one real failure in life that is possible, and that is, not to be true to the best one knows.
JOHN FARRAR

If you do the best you can, you will find, nine times out of ten, that you have done as well as or better than anyone else.
WILLIAM FEATHER

The man who has done his level best, and who is conscious that he has done his best, is a success, even though the world may write him down a failure.
B. C. FORBES

The best is good enough.
GERMAN PROVERB

When the best things are not possible, the best may be made of those that are.
RICHARD HOOKER

I do the very best I know how—the very best I can; and mean to keep doing so until the end. If the end brings me out all right, what is said against me won't amount to anything. If the end brings me out

wrong, ten angels swearing I was right would make no difference.
**ABRAHAM LINCOLN**

I have simply tried to do what seemed best each day, as each day came.
**ABRAHAM LINCOLN**

When we have done our best, we should wait the result in peace.
**JOHN LUBBOCK**

It is a funny thing about life—if you refuse to accept anything but the best you very often get it.
**SOMERSET MAUGHAM**

Life's greatest adventure is in doing one's level best.
**ARTHUR E. MORGAN**

It is one's duty to make the most of the best that is in him.
**DUNCAN STUART**

All is for the best in the best of possible worlds.
**VOLTAIRE**

## *Bible*

The Bible, whatever else it may be—divine or human—is the greatest compilation of noble thoughts and deeds ever brought together and, as such, the greatest single instrument for popular education ever devised.
**ARTHUR BRYANT**

In all my perplexities and distresses, the Bible has never failed to give me light and strength.
**ROBERT E. LEE**

The Bible is a book about life: it is about kings, peasants, housewives, soldiers, servants. Every man is in the Bible. Your life is mirrored there and so is mine.
**ALBERT J. PENNER**

I thoroughly believe in a university education for both men and women, but I believe a knowledge of the Bible without a college course is more valuable than a college course without the Bible.
**WILLIAM LYON PHELPS**

All scripture is given by inspiration of God, and is profitable for doctrine, for reproof, for correction, for instruction in righteousness: that the man of God may be perfect, thoroughly furnished unto all good works.
**II TIMOTHY 3:16-17**

Adam was but human—this explains it all. He did not want the apple for the apple's sake, he wanted it only because it was forbidden. The mistake was in not forbidding the serpent; then he would have eaten the serpent.
**MARK TWAIN**

The Bible is a book of faith, and a book of doctrine and a book of morals, and a book of religion, of special revelation from God. But it is also a book which teaches man his own individual responsibility, his own dignity and his equality with his fellow-man.
**DANIEL WEBSTER**

## *Blame*

When a man points a finger at someone else, he should remember that three of his fingers are pointing at himself.
**ANONYMOUS**

Henry Ward Beecher, so the story goes, was once asked by a young preacher how he could keep his congregation wide awake and attentive during his sermons. Beecher replied that he always had a man watch for sleepers, with instructions, as soon as he saw anyone start nodding or dozing, to hasten to the pulpit and wake up the preacher. Aren't you and I usually less sensible? Would we not be inclined to have the watcher wake up not ourselves but the fellows caught sleeping? In other words, aren't we disposed always to blame others?
**B. C. FORBES**

How we love to blame others for our misfortunes! Almost every individual who has lost money in stock speculation has on the tip of his tongue an explanation which he trots out to show that it wasn't his own fault at all. . . . Hardly one loser has the manliness to say frankly, "I was wrong."
**B. C. FORBES**

When it's your own fault, things hurt worse than when someone else is to blame.
**MALCOLM FORBES**

Accepting blame when it's not really due sometimes makes the point better.
**MALCOLM FORBES**

If something goes wrong, it is more important to talk about who is going to fix it, than who is to blame.
**FRANCIS J. GABLE**

The search for someone to blame is always successful.
**ROBERT HALF**

It is criminal to steal a purse, daring to steal a fortune, a mark of greatness to steal a crown. The blame diminishes as the guilt increases.
**JOHANN FRIEDRICH VON SCHILLER**

People are always blaming their circumstances for what they are. I don't believe in circumstances. The people who get on in this world are they who get up and look for the circumstances they want, and, if they can't find them, make them.
**GEORGE BERNARD SHAW**

## *Blessings*

If one should give me a dish of sand, and tell me there were particles of iron in it, I might look for them with my eyes, and search for them with my clumsy fingers, and be unable to detect them; but let me take a magnet and sweep through it, and how would it draw to itself the almost invisible particles by the mere power of attraction! The unthinkful heart, like my finger in the sand, discovers no mercies; but let the thankful heart sweep through the day, and as the magnet finds the iron, so it will find, in every hour, some heavenly blessings.
**HENRY WARD BEECHER**

A patient, humble temper gathers blessings that are marred by the peevish and overlooked by the aspiring.
**EDWIN H. CHAPIN**

Certain of our blessings can never change. The important things of life will not perish. In whatever brave new world emerges from this chaos, homes will be created, good deeds will be done and sacrifices will be made. God will be reverently worshipped in many a church and chapel. Hospital, libraries and colleges will be organized and endowed. The greatest things will endure—faith, hope and love, and the moral nature in man.
**CLAUDE M. FUESS**

Take, I pray thee, my blessing that is brought to thee; because God hath dealt graciously with me, and because I have enough.
**GENESIS 33:11**

Reflect that life, like every other blessing, derives its value from its use alone.
**SAMUEL JOHNSON**

The private and personal blessings we enjoy, the blessings of immunity, safeguard, liberty and integrity, deserve the thanksgiving of a whole life.
**JEREMY TAYLOR**

Blessings we enjoy daily; and for the most of them, because they be so common, most men forget to pay their praise.
**IZAAK WALTON**

## *Boasting*

Exaggeration is a blood relation to falsehood and nearly as blamable.
**HOSEA BALLOU**

We exaggerate misfortune and happiness alike. We are never either so wretched or so happy as we say we are.
**HONORÉ DE BALZAC**

Falsehood often lurks upon the tongue of him, who, by self-praise, seeks to enhance his value in the eyes of others.
**JAMES GORDON BENNETT**

Some persons are exaggerators by temperament. They do not mean untruth, but their feelings are strong, and their imaginations vivid, so that their statements are largely discounted by those of calm judgment and cooler temperament. They do not realize that we always weaken what we exaggerate.
**TRYON EDWARDS**

He was like a cock who thought the sun had risen to hear him crow.
**GEORGE ELIOT**

Every ass loves to hear himself bray.
**THOMAS FULLER**

An exaggeration is a truth that has lost its temper.
**KAHLIL GIBRAN**

There is nothing quite so dead as a self-centered man—a man who holds himself up as a self-made success, and measures himself by himself and is pleased with the result.
**WESLEY G. HUBER, D. D.**

We always weaken whatever we exaggerate.
**JEAN FRANÇOIS DE LAHARPE**

The man who has not anything to boast of but his illustrious ancestors is like a potato—the only good belonging to him is underground.
**THOMAS OVERBURY**

What is the use of acquiring one's heart's desire if one cannot handle and gloat over it, show it to one's friends and gather an anthology of envy and admiration?
**DOROTHY SAYERS**

A man has the right to toot his own horn to his heart's content, so long as he stays in his own home, keeps the windows closed and does not make himself obnoxious to his neighbors.
**TIORIO**

The time is undoubtedly coming when it will be a confession of inferiority to overstate or distort the merits and special uses of any commodity, just as any boaster is self-branded a lightweight rather than a man of parts.
**Harvey W. Wiley**

When boasting ends, there dignity begins.
**Young**

## *Body*

No one hates his body.
**St. Augustine**

The human body is an energy system which is never a complete structure; never static; is in perpetual self-construction and self-destruction; we destroy it in order to make it new.
**Norman O. Brown**

Body and mind, like man and wife, do not always agree to die together.
**Charles Caleb Colton**

Know ye not that ye are the temple of God, and that the Spirit of God dwelleth in you? If any man defile the temple of God, him shall God destroy; for the temple of God is holy, which temple ye are.
**I Corinthians 3:16-17**

I live in company with a body, a silent companion, exacting and eternal. He it is who notes that individuality which is the seal of the weakness of our race. My soul has wings, but the brutal jailer is strict.
**Eugene Delacroix**

Body: A thing of shreds and patches, borrowed unequally from good and bad ancestors and a misfit from the start.
**Ralph Waldo Emerson**

The human body is the magazine of inventions, the patent office, where are the models from which every hint is taken. All the tools and engines on earth are only extensions of its limbs and senses.
**Ralph Waldo Emerson**

Our theological Church, as we know, has scorned and vilified the body till it has seemed almost a reproach and a shame to have one, yet at the same time has credited it with the power to drag the soul to perdition.
**Eliza Farnham**

The human body is made up of some four hundred muscles, evolved through centuries of physical activity. Unless these are used, they will deteriorate. The business executive should look for ways of using his muscles, naturally, each day. Instead of always using his desk bells, he should occasionally do an office errand himself. He might, with profit, walk one way or part way to his office instead of riding; or walk up or down a flight or two of stairs instead of invariably using the elevator. He should cultivate muscle hunger.
**Eugene Lyman Fisk**

Animals, we have been told, are taught by their organs. Yes, I would add, and so are men, but men have this further advantage that they can also teach their organs in return.
**Johann Wolfgang von Goethe**

Our body is a well-set clock, which keeps good time, but if it be too much or indiscreetly tampered with, the alarm runs out before the hour.
**Joseph Hall**

The human body was designed to walk, run or stop; it wasn't built for coasting.
**Cullen Hightower**

Nature gave men two ends—one to sit on and one to think with. Ever since then man's success or failure has been dependent on the one he used most.
**GEORGE R. KIRKPATRICK**

The body of man is a machine which winds its own springs.
**J. O. DE LA METTRIE**

It is so much more difficult to live with one's body than with one's soul. One's body is so much more exacting: What it won't have it won't have, and nothing can make bitter into sweet.
**D. H. LAWRENCE**

Our own physical body possesses a wisdom which we who inhabit the body lack. We give it orders which make no sense.
**HENRY MILLER**

A feeble body weakens the mind.
**JEAN-JACQUES ROUSSEAU**

What is more important in life than our bodies or in the world than what we look like?
**GEORGE SANTAYANA**

He will be the slave of many masters who is his body's slave.
**SENECA**

'Tis not enough to help the feeble up, but to support him after.
**WILLIAM SHAKESPEARE**

Stomach: A slave that must accept everything that is given to it, but which avenges wrongs as slyly as does the slave.
**EMILE SOUVESTER**

The authority of any governing institution must stop at its citizen's skin.
**GLORIA STEINEM**

Every man is the builder of a temple, called his body, to the god he worships, after a style peculiarly his own, nor can he get off by hammering marble instead. We are all sculptors and painters, and our material is our own flesh and blood and bones.
**HENRY DAVID THOREAU**

Whose property is my body? Probably mine. I so regard it. If I experiment with it, who must be answerable? I, not the State. If I choose injudiciously, does the State die? Oh, no.
**MARK TWAIN**

Body: A cell state in which every cell is a citizen.
**RUDOLF VIRCHOW**

How many people ever consider that the lack of certain qualities—such as balance, common sense, tranquility—affect the physical state of the human body?. . . Did you ever hear of people being sick because they hated someone? This is not uncommon.
**BISHOP WESTCOTT**

If anything is sacred the human body is sacred.
**WALT WHITMAN**

## *Boldness*

We make way for the man who boldly pushes past us.
**CHRISTIAN BOVÉE**

Boldness becomes rarer, the higher the rank.
**KARL VON CLAUSEWITZ**

Every man is bold when his whole fortune is at stake.
DIONYSUS OF HALICARNASSUS

Whatever you do, or dream you can do, begin it. Boldness has genius, power and magic in it.
JOHANN WOLFGANG VON GOETHE

Put a grain of boldness in everything you do.
BALTASAR GRACIÁN

It is better by a noble boldness to run the risk of being subject to half of the evils we anticipate, than to remain in cowardly listlessness for fear of what may happen.
HERODOTUS

A decent boldness ever meets with friends.
HOMER

There are some things one can only achieve by a deliberate leap in the opposite direction. One has to go abroad in order to find the home one has lost.
FRANZ KAFKA

In great straits and when hope is small, the boldest counsels are the safest.
LIVY

By audacity, great fears are concealed.
LUCAN

Both fortune and love befriend the bold.
OVID

Only the bold get to the top.
PUBLILIUS SYRUS

## *Books*

That is a good book which opened with expectation and closed with profit.
AMOS BRONSON ALCOTT

Book: A garden carried in a pocket.
ARABIAN PROVERB

For several days after my first book was published I carried it about in my pocket, and took surreptitious peeps at it to make sure the ink had not faded.
JAMES M. BARRIE

He that loveth a book will never want a faithful friend, a wholesome counselor, a cheerful companion, an effectual comforter. By study, by reading, by thinking, one may innocently divert and pleasantly entertain himself, as in all weathers, as in all fortunes.
BARROW

Books are the compass and telescopes and sextants and charts which other men have prepared to help us navigate the dangerous seas of human life.
JESSE LEE BENNETT

Diary: A daily record of that part of one's life which he can relate to himself without blushing.
AMBROSE BIERCE

Biography is, or should be, the yeast, the ferment, of the human spirit, which should stir and rouse it to the highest sense of its own achievement and its own power.
GAMALIEL BRADFORD

A book may be compared to your neighbor: if it be good, it cannot last too long; if bad, you cannot get rid of it too early.
HENRY BROOKE

As sources of ideas, professors simply cannot compete with books. Books can be found to fit almost every need, temper or interest. Books can be read when you are in the mood; they do not have to be taken in periodic doses. Books are both more personal and more impersonal than professors. Books have an inner confidence which individuals seldom show. . . . They are infinitely diverse. They can be found to express every point of view; if you want a different point of view, you can read a different book.
William G. Carleton

All that mankind has done, thought, gained or been: it is lying as in magic preservation in the pages of books.
Thomas Carlyle

The true university of these days is a collection of books.
Thomas Carlyle

Biography is the most universally pleasant and profitable of all reading.
Thomas Carlyle

The most valuable book we can read, about countries we have visited, is that which recalls to us something that we did notice, but did not notice that we noticed.
G. K. Chesterton

Books are true levelers. They give to all, who will faithfully use them, the society, the spiritual presence, of the best and greatest of our race.
William Ellery Channing

To add a library to a house is to give that house a soul.
Cicero

Other relaxations are peculiar to certain times, places and stages of life, but the study of letters is the nourishment of our youth, and the joy of our old age. They throw an additional splendor on prosperity, and are the resource and consolation of adversity; they delight at home, and are no embarrassment abroad; in short, they are company to us at night, our fellow travelers on a journey, and attendants in our rural recesses.
Cicero

Many books require no thought from those who read them, and for a very simple reason—they made no such demand upon those who wrote them.
Charles Caleb Colton

Autobiography is an obituary in serial form with the last installment missing.
Quentin Crisp

*Sartor Resartus* is simply unreadable, and for me that always sort of spoils a book.
Will Cuppy

The world of books is the most remarkable creation of man. Nothing else that he builds ever lasts. Monuments fall, nations perish, civilizations grow old and die out, and after an era of darkness new races build others. But in the world of books are volumes that have seen this happen again and again and yet live on, still young, still as fresh as the day they were written, still telling men's hearts of the hearts of men centuries dead.
Clarence Day

Don't join the book burners. Don't think you are going to conceal faults by concealing evidence that they ever existed. Don't be afraid to go in your library and read every book.
Dwight D. Eisenhower

When I get a little money, I buy books; if any is left, I buy food and clothes.
DESIDERIUS ERASMUS

There is no reader so parochial as the one who reads none but this morning's books. Books are not rolls, to be devoured only when they are hot and fresh. A good book retains its interior heat and will warm a generation yet unborn.
CLIFTON FADIMAN

Over the years, I've evolved a somewhat heretical but time- and mind-saving approach to books, articles, editorials that deal with weighty matters. More often than not, by beginning at the end and contemplating the conclusions, one can determine if it's worth going through the whole to get there.
MALCOLM FORBES

A dollar put into a book and a book mastered might change the whole course of a boy's life. It might easily be the beginning of the development of leadership that would carry the boy far in service to his fellow men.
HENRY FORD

I suggest that the only books that influence us are those for which we are ready, and which have gone a little farther down our particular path than we have yet got ourselves.
E. M. FORSTER

A man's life is made by the hours when great ideas lay hold upon him. And, except by way of living persons, there is no channel down which great ideas come oftener into human lives than by way of books.
HARRY EMERSON FOSDICK, D.D.

Never lend books, for no one ever returns them; the only books I have in my library are books that other folk have lent to me.
ANATOLE FRANCE

Thou mayest as well expect to grow stronger by always eating, as wiser by always reading. Too much overcharges Nature, and turns more into disease than nourishment. 'Tis thought and digestion which make books serviceable, and give health and vigor to the mind.
THOMAS FULLER

I don't think anyone should write his autobiography until after he's dead.
SAMUEL GOLDWYN

Autobiography is an unrivaled vehicle for telling the truth about other people.
PHILIP GUEDALLA

Were I to pray for a taste which should stand me in good stead under every variety of circumstances and be a source of happiness and a cheerfulness to me during life and a shield against its ills, however things might go amiss and the world frown upon me, it would be a taste for reading.
SIR JOHN HERSCHEL

It is those books which a man possesses but does not read which constitute the most suspicious evidence against him.
VICTOR HUGO

To be well informed, one must read quickly a great number of merely instructive books. To be cultivated, one must read slowly and with a lingering appreciation the comparatively few books that have been written by men who lived, thought, and felt with style.
ALDOUS HUXLEY

Books are never out of humour; never envious or jealous, they answer all questions with readiness; . . . they teach us how to live and how to die; they dispel melancholy by their mirth, and amuse by their

wit; they prepare the soul to suffer everything and desire nothing; they introduce us to ourselves.
Holbrook Jackson

The worst thing about new books is that they keep us from reading the old ones.
Joseph Joubert

A book is a mirror: If an ass peers into it, you can't expect an apostle to look out.
Georg Christoph Lichtenberg

The things I want to know are in books; my best friend is the man who'll get me a book I ain't read.
Abraham Lincoln

In science, read by preference the newest works; in literature, the oldest. The classics are always modern.
Edward Bulwer-Lytton

I would rather be a poor man in a garret with plenty of books than a king who did not love reading.
Thomas B. Macaulay

The walls of books around him, dense with the past, formed a kind of insulation against the present world and its disasters.
Ross MacDonald

A good book is the precious lifeblood of a master spirit, embalmed and treasured up on purpose to life beyond life.
John Milton

A book ought to be like a man or a woman, with some individual character in it, though eccentric, yet its own; with some blood in its veins and speculation in its eyes and a way and will of its own.
John Mitchell

A book is the only place where you can examine a fragile thought without breaking it, or explore an explosive idea without fear that it will go off in your face.
Edward P. Morgan

What is the virtue and service of a book? Only to help me live less gingerly and shabbily.
Christopher Morley

Books worth reading once are worth reading twice; and what is most important of all, the masterpieces of literature are worth reading a thousand times.
John Morley

A dose of poison can do its work but once, but a bad book can go on poisoning minds for generations.
W. John Murray

We take up a book at one time, and see nothing in it; at another, it is full of weighty remarks and precious thoughts.
Cardinal John Henry Newman

Just the knowledge that a good book is awaiting one at the end of a long day makes that day happier.
Kathleen Norris

Books are the open avenues down which, like kings coming to be crowned, great ideas and inspirations move to the abbey of man's soul. There are some people still left who understand perfectly what Fenelon meant when he said, "If the crowns of all the kingdoms of the empire were laid down at my feet in exchange for my books and my love of reading, I would spurn them all."
Ernest Dressel North

If minds are truly alive they will seek out books, for books are the human race recounting its memorable experiences, confronting its problems, searching for

solutions, drawing the blueprints of its futures. To read books is one way of growing along with one's fellows-in-growth.
HARRY A. OVERSTREET

The books which help you most are those which make you think the most. The hardest way of learning is by easy reading. But a great book that comes from a great thinker—it is a ship of thought, deep-freighted with truth and with beauty.
THEODORE PARKER

To desire to have many books, and never use them, is like the child that will have a candle burning by him all the while he is sleeping.
HENRY PEACHAM

Books come at my call and return when I desire them; they are never out of humor and they answer all my questions with readiness. Some present in review before me the events of past ages; others reveal to me the secrets of Nature. These teach me how to live, and those how to die; these dispel my melancholy by their mirth, and amuse me by their sallies of wit. Some there are who prepare my soul to suffer everything, to desire nothing, and to become thoroughly acquainted with itself. In a word, they open the door to all the arts and sciences.
PETRARCH

I hate books, for they only teach people to talk about what they do not understand.
JEAN-JACQUES ROUSSEAU

It is a pity, in my opinion, that no prize exists for the writer who best refrains from adding to the world's bad books.
WILLIAM SAROYAN

Any book which is at all important should be reread immediately.
ARTHUR SCHOPENHAUER

Books are good enough in their own way, but they are a mighty bloodless substitute for living.
ROBERT LOUIS STEVENSON

A great book should leave you with many experiences, and slightly exhausted at the end. You live several lives while reading it.
WILLIAM STYRON

I've given my memoirs far more thought than any of my marriages. You can't divorce a book.
GLORIA SWANSON

A truly good book is something as wildly natural and primitive, mysterious and marvelous, ambrosial and fertile as a fungus or a lichen.
HENRY DAVID THOREAU

The habit of reading is the only one I know in which there is no alloy. It lasts when all other pleasures fade. It will be there to support you when all other resources are gone. It will be present to you when the energies of your body have fallen away from you. It will make your hours pleasant to you as long as you live.
ANTHONY TROLLOPE

It is with the reading of books the same as with looking at pictures; one must, without doubt, without hesitations, with assurance, admire what is beautiful.
VINCENT VAN GOGH

I keep to old books, for they teach me something; from the new I learn very little.
VOLTAIRE

Only when one has lost all curiosity about the future has one reached the age to write an autobiography.
EVELYN WAUGH

I was never allowed to read the popular American children's books of my day because, as my mother said, the children spoke bad English without the author's knowing it.
**Edith Wharton**

## Boredom

It is indifference which is the cause of most of our unhappiness. Indifference to religion, to the happiness of others, and to the precious gift of freedom, and the wide liberty that is the inheritance of all in a free land.

Are we our Brother's Keeper? We certainly are! If we had no regard for others' feelings or fortune, we would grow cold and indifferent to life itself. Bound up with selfishness, we could not hope for the success that could easily be ours.
**George Matthew Adams**

A dull ax never loves grindstones.
**Henry Ward Beecher**

A bore is a person who talks when you wish him to listen.
**Ambrose Bierce**

Alienation is practiced by whole groups and classes of people. We may all bore one another to death this way, and the young, who are the most self-conscious about their alienation, can be the most boring of all.
**John Corry**

Nobody has any right to find life uninteresting or unrewarding who sees within the sphere of his own activity a wrong he can help to remedy, or within himself an evil he can hope to overcome.
**Charles W. Eliot**

Each man reserves to himself alone the right of being tedious.
**Ralph Waldo Emerson**

Some of the biggest bores I've ever known are men who have been highly successful in business, particularly self-made heads of big companies. Before the first olive has settled into the first martini, they pour the stories of their lives into the nearest and sometimes the remotest ears capturable. . . .

These men have indeed paid the price of success. To rise to the top of a big company often takes a totality of effort, concentration and dedication. Others, too, have to pay part of the price. Wife and children are out of mind even when in sight. . . .
**Malcolm Forbes**

A bore: Someone who persists in holding to his own views after we have enlightened him with ours.
**Malcolm Forbes**

Drudgery is as necessary to call out the treasures of the mind as harrowing and planting those of the earth.
**Margaret Fuller**

Desire is half of life; indifference is half of death.
**Kahlil Gibran**

When people are bored, it is primarily with their own selves that they are bored.
**Eric Hoffer**

The most destructive criticism is indifference.
**Edgar Watson Howe**

Highly educated bores are by far the worst; they know so much, in such fiendish detail, to be boring about.
**Louis Kronenberger**

We are raising a generation that has a woefully small stock of ideas and interests and emotions. It must be amused at all costs but it has little skill in amusing itself. It pays some of its members to do what the majority can no longer do for themselves. It is this inner poverty that makes for the worst kind of boredom.
ROBERT J. MCCRACKEN

Indifference is the invincible giant of the world.
OUIDA

A bore is a fellow talker who can change the topic of conversation to his subject faster than you can change it back to yours.
LAURENCE J. PETER

The biggest bore is the person who is bored by everyone and everything.
FRANK TYGER

## *Bravery*

I count him braver who overcomes his desires than him who conquers his enemies; for the hardest victory is the victory over self.
ARISTOTLE

The world has a way of giving what is demanded of it. If you are frightened and look for failure and poverty, you will get them, no matter how hard you may try to succeed. Lack of faith in yourself, in what life will do for you, cuts you off from the good things of the world. Expect victory and you make victory. Nowhere is this truer than in business life, where bravery and faith bring both material and spiritual rewards.
PRESTON BRADLEY

It is a brave act of valor to despise death; but where life is more terrible than death, it is then the truest valor to dare to live.
SIR THOMAS BROWNE

True valor lies in the middle, between cowardice and rashness.
MIGUEL DE CERVANTES

Bravery: A cheap and vulgar quality, of which the brightest instances are frequently found in the lowest savages.
PAUL CHATFIELD

Each man is a hero and an oracle to somebody.
RALPH WALDO EMERSON

There is a fine line between bravery and stupidity. If you get away with it you are brave. If you don't, you are stupid.
FRANCISCO T. ESCARIO

Some have been thought brave because they were afraid to run away.
THOMAS FULLER

All brave men love; for he only is brave who has affections to fight for, whether in the daily battle of life, or in physical contests.
NATHANIEL HAWTHORNE

My advice to you, if you should ever be in a hold-up, is to line up with the cowards and save your bravery for an occasion when it may be of some benefit to you.
O. HENRY

What excites and interests the looker-on at life, what the romances and the statues celebrate, and the grim civic monuments remind us of, is the everlasting battle of the powers of light with those of

darkness; with heroism reduced to its bare chance, yet ever and anon snatching victory from the jaws of death.
WILLIAM JAMES

Heroism, the Caucasian mountaineers say, is endurance for one moment more.
GEORGE F. KENNAN

It is the surmounting of difficulties that makes heroes.
LOUIS KOSSUTH

Physical bravery is an animal instinct; moral bravery is a much higher and truer courage.
WENDELL PHILLIPS

Greatness, in the last analysis, is largely bravery—courage in escaping from old ideas and old standards and respectable ways of doing things. This is one of the chief elements in what we vaguely call capacity. If you do not dare to differ from your associates and teachers you will never be great or your life sublime. You may be the happier as a result, or you may be miserable. Each of us is great insofar as we perceive and act on the infinite possibilities which lie undiscovered and unrecognized about us.
JAMES HARVEY ROBINSON

Love of fame, fear of disgrace, schemes for advancement; desire to make life comfortable and pleasant, and the urge to humiliate others are often at the root of the valor that men hold in such high esteem.
FRANÇOIS DE LA ROCHEFOUCAULD

Valor is a gift. Those having it never know for sure whether they have it till the test comes. And those having it in one test never know for sure if they have it when the next test comes.
CARL SANDBURG

Bravery escapes more dangers than cowardice.
JOSEPH SEGUR

Valor grows by daring, fear by holding back.
PUBLILIUS SYRUS

They are sure to be esteemed bravest who, having the clearest sense of both the pains and pleasures of life, do not on that account shrink from danger.
THUCYDIDES

Except a person be part coward, it is not a compliment to say he is brave.
MARK TWAIN

I do not like heroes; they make too much noise in the world. The more radiant their glory, the more odious they are.
VOLTAIRE

## *Britain*

The extremes of opulence and of want are more remarkable, and more constantly obvious, in [Great Britain] than in any other place that I ever saw.
JOHN QUINCY ADAMS

Englishman: A man who has never been able to tell a lie about others and who is never willing to face the truth about himself.
MICHAEL ARLEN

I think the British have the distinction above all other nations of being able to put new wine into old bottles without bursting them.
CLEMENT R. ATTLEE

The English winter—ending in July, to recommence in August.
LORD BYRON

By nationalism I mean a general recognition of the right of all nations to be national. I find it more confusing to call this patriotism, because patriotism, when it was rammed down my throat in the old jingo days, always meant that the British empire had a right to do everything and nobody else had a right to do anything.
G. K. CHESTERTON

It is a curious fact about British Islanders, who hate drill and have not been invaded for nearly a thousand years, that as danger comes nearer and grows they become progressively less nervous; when it is imminent they are fierce, when it is mortal they are fearless.
WINSTON CHURCHILL

The lowest and vilest alleys of London do not present a more dreadful record of sin than does the smiling and beautiful countryside.
SIR ARTHUR CONAN DOYLE

An Anglo-Saxon, Hinnissy, is a German that's forgot who was his parents.
FINLEY PETER DUNNE

No one can be as calculatedly rude as the British, which amazes Americans, who do not understand studied insult and can only offer abuse as a substitute.
PAUL GALLICO

The difference between the vanity of a Frenchman and an Englishman is this: The one thinks everything right that is French, while the other thinks everything wrong that is not English.
WILLIAM HAZLITT

A blaspheming Frenchman is a spectacle more pleasing to the Lord than a praying Englishman.
HEINRICH HEINE

In dealing with Englishmen you can be sure of one thing only, that the logical solution will not be adopted.
WILLIAM RALPH INGE

An Englishman is never so natural as when he's holding his tongue.
HENRY JAMES

If an earthquake were to engulf England tomorrow, the English would manage to meet and dine somewhere among the rubble, just to celebrate the event.
DOUGLAS WILLIAM JERROLD

Oats: a grain, which in England is generally given to horses, but in Scotland supports the people.
SAMUEL JOHNSON

When a man is tired of London, he is tired of life, for there is in London all that life can afford.
SAMUEL JOHNSON

In the dark days and darker nights when England stood alone—and most men save Englishmen despaired of England's life—he [Churchill] mobilized the English language and sent it into battle.
JOHN F. KENNEDY

If England was what England seems,
An' not the England of our dreams,
But only putty, brass and paint,
'Ow quick we'd chuck her!
But she ain't!
RUDYARD KIPLING

We know no spectacle so ridiculous as the British public in one of its periodic fits of morality.
THOMAS B. MACAULAY

I'm leaving because the weather is too good. I hate London when it's not raining.
GROUCHO MARX

The English are proud; the French are vain.
**JEAN-JACQUES ROUSSEAU**

England is the paradise of individuality, eccentricity, heresy, anomalies, hobbies and humors.
**GEORGE SANTAYANA**

Englishmen will never be slaves; they are free to do whatever the government and public opinion allow them to do.
**GEORGE BERNARD SHAW**

There is nothing so bad or so good that you will not find Englishmen doing it; but you will never find an Englishman in the wrong. He does everything on principle.
**GEORGE BERNARD SHAW**

What two ideas are more inseparable than beer and Britannia?
**SYDNEY SMITH**

What a pity it is that we have no amusements in England but vice and religion.
**SYDNEY SMITH**

How hard it is to make an Englishman acknowledge that he is happy.
**WILLIAM MAKEPEACE THACKERAY**

We are now so badly deteriorated that three Frenchmen can evidently beat one Englishman.
**HORACE WALPOLE**

If one could only teach the English how to talk and the Irish how to listen, society would be quite civilized.
**OSCAR WILDE**

England has 42 religions and only two sauces.
**VOLTAIRE**

## *Budget*

A balanced budget cannot be,
Amend the process as you will.
The dripping snouts within the trough
Will not forgo the tasty swill.
**ART BUCK**

The budget should be balanced, the Treasury should be refilled, public debt should be reduced, the arrogance of officialdom should be tempered and controlled, and the assistance to foreign lands should be curtailed lest Rome become bankrupt.
**CICERO (63 B.C.)**

A budget tells us what we can't afford, but it doesn't keep us from buying it.
**WILLIAM FEATHER**

It's discouraging how hard it is for a President to slice away large chunks of a $305 billion budget.
**GERALD FORD**

Budgets are not merely affairs of arithmetic, but in a thousand ways go to the root of prosperity of individuals, the relation of classes and the strength of kingdoms.
**WILLIAM E. GLADSTONE**

The budget is a mythical bean bag. Congress votes mythical beans into it, and then tries to reach in and pull real beans out.
**WILL ROGERS**

## *Bureaucracy*

Bureaucracies are designed to perform public business. But as soon as a bureaucracy is established, it

develops an autonomous spiritual life and comes to regard the public as its enemy.
BROOKS ATKINSON

The perfect bureaucrat everywhere is the man who manages to make no decisions and escape all responsibility.
BROOKS ATKINSON

Bureaucracy is a giant mechanism operated by pygmies.
HONORÉ DE BALZAC

Bureaucracy is the death of any achievement.
ALBERT EINSTEIN

One of the enduring truths of the nation's capital is that bureaucrats survive.
GERALD FORD

There is something about a bureaucrat that does not like a poem.
GORE VIDAL

## *Business*

There should be no age limits placed upon ambition, alertness, creativeness, or in fact on anything that may mark the mental or spiritual progress of any human being. . . . There is an old saying, Nothing ventured nothing gained. Obviously true, but on the other hand, even though many of our ventures come to no profitable end, the very fact that we ventured should be to our credit. People who stand still, or just watch from the sidelines of life, only partly live. To venture, and only to get fun out of it, has a constructive angle to it. Keep venturing and you'll never grow dull!
GEORGE MATTHEW ADAMS

We are all manufacturers—making good, making trouble or making excuses.
H. V. ADOLT

The person who minds nobody's business but his own is probably a millionaire.
ANONYMOUS

Professionals are people who can do their job when they don't feel like it. Amateurs are people who can't do their job when they do feel like it.
ANONYMOUS

The true worth of a man is to be measured by the objects he pursues.
MARCUS AURELIUS ANTONINUS

Business or toil is merely utilitarian. It is necessary, but does not enrich or ennoble a human life.
ARISTOTLE

Business is religion, and religion is business. The man who does not make a business of his religion has a religious life of no force, and the man who does not make a religion of his business has a business life of no character.
MALTBIE BABCOCK

In all negotiations of difficulty, a man may not look to sow and reap at once; but must prepare business, and so ripen it by degrees.
FRANCIS BACON

Business is really more agreeable than pleasure; it interests the whole mind, the aggregate nature of man more continuously, and more deeply. But it does not look as if it did.
WALTER BAGEHOT

Our problem in money-making or government affairs is how to remain properly venturesome and experimental without making fools of ourselves.
BERNARD M. BARUCH

There is too much emphasis on the alleged need for more purchasing power. What the country needs is stable purchasing power. Increased wages, higher pensions, more unemployment insurance, all are of no avail if the purchasing power of money falls faster.
BERNARD M. BARUCH

To prosper soundly in business, you must satisfy not only your customers, but you must lay yourself out to satisfy also the men who make your product and the men who sell it.
HARRY BASSETT

Corporation: An ingenious device for obtaining individual profit without individual responsibility.
AMBROSE BIERCE

If your business keeps you so busy that you have no time for anything else, there must be something wrong, either with you or with your business.
WILLIAM J. H. BOETCKER

**Ten Points**

1. You cannot bring about prosperity by discouraging thrift.
2. You cannot strengthen the weak by weakening the strong.
3. You cannot help small men by tearing down big men.
4. You cannot help the poor by destroying the rich.
5. You cannot lift the wage-earner by pulling down the wage-payer.
6. You cannot keep out of trouble by spending more than your income.
7. You cannot further the brotherhood of man by inciting class hatred.
8. You cannot establish sound security on borrowed money.
9. You cannot build character and courage by taking away a man's initiative and independence.
10. You cannot help men permanently by doing for them what they could and should do for themselves.

WILLIAM J. H. BOETCKER

Life is too short to be unhappy in business. If business were not a part of the joy of living, we might almost say that we have no right to live, because it is a pretty poor man who cannot get into the line for which he is fitted.
GEORGE L. BROWN

The humanities of business in this age have become more important than the techniques of business. Each business and industry has to sweep the public misunderstandings and the false notions off its own front walk. Thus will a pathway be cleared for popular appreciation of the important rôle of business in our freedom and in our way of life.
HARRY A. BULLIS

All purchases are born of dissatisfaction. No purchase of any product anywhere—impulse or deliberation—is ever made unless the purchaser is first dissatisfied in his present state.
WILLIAM M. BRYNGELSON

I like business because it is competitive, because it rewards deeds rather than words. I like business because it compels earnestness and does not permit me to neglect today's task while thinking about tomorrow. I like business because it undertakes to please, not reform; because it is honestly selfish, thereby avoiding hypocrisy and sentimentality. I like business because it promptly penalizes mistakes, shiftlessness and inefficiency, while rewarding

well those who give it the best they have in them. Lastly, I like business because each day is a fresh adventure.
R. H. CABELL

Business may not be the noblest pursuit, but it is true that men are bringing to it some of the qualities that actuate the explorer, scientist, artist: the zest, the open-mindedness, with which the scientific investigator explores some field of pure research.
EARNEST ELMO CALKINS

One of the great weaknesses of the American executive has been his indifference to those who misrepresent Business. The average man is too busily at work to reply to those who malign Business. He seems to accept the misrepresentation, libel and calumny as one of the necessary evils of Business, and silently submits until finally the undenied lies grow into general beliefs, with the result that both the public in general and Business in particular suffer.
CHARLES E. CARPENTER

The hardest thing to find is the independent business man who knows how to get all the factors working together, and who can so organize them that he can pay the bills out of the receipts. That everlasting problem spoils a good many business enterprises. I think I could run almost any business if somebody would pay the bills. I talk to a great many radical clubs. They say that capital exploits labor, that all the capitalist does is to hire some labor, underpay it, sell it at a high price and pocket the difference. Sometimes I say to them, "Now, if that is all there is to do, why don't some of you do that and make money yourself? The reason you don't is because you can't." If there are one hundred radicals present, I am pretty safe in saying that there isn't one man among them who can hire any kind of labor, pay the current wages, and get a product that he can sell for enough to pay the wages.
THOMAS NIXON CARVER

Business is always a struggle. There are always obstacles and competitors. There is never an open road, except the wide road that leads to failure. Every great success has always been achieved by fight. Every winner has scars. . . . The men who succeed are the efficient few. They are the few who have the ambition and will-power to develop themselves.
HERBERT N. CASSON

The best mental effort in the game of business is concentrated on the major problem of securing the consumer's dollar before the other fellow gets it.
STUART CHASE

The American business man cannot consider his work done when he views the income balance in black at the end of an accounting period. It is necessary for him to trace the social incidence of the figures that appear in his statement and prove to the general public that his management has not only been profitable in the accounting sense but salutary in terms of popular benefits.
COLBY M. CHESTER

Few people do business well who do nothing else.
LORD CHESTERFIELD

Some see private enterprise as a predatory target to be shot, others as a cow to be milked, but few are those who see it as a sturdy horse pulling the wagon.
WINSTON CHURCHILL

My precept to all who build, is, that the owner should be an ornament to the house, and not the house to the owner.
CICERO

Modern business requires that its salesmen be business men in the best sense of the word—men who know the ins and outs of the product or service they are selling . . . men who can make an intelligent and

effective presentation . . . and most of all, men who have the modern concept of service to the customer.
HUGH W. COBURN

Business will be better or worse.
CALVIN COOLIDGE

No enterprise can exist for itself alone. It ministers to some great need, it performs some great service, not for itself, but for others; or failing therein, it ceases to be profitable and ceases to exist.
CALVIN COOLIDGE

The business of America is business.
CALVIN COOLIDGE

This country has achieved its commercial and financial supremacy under a regime of private ownership. It conquered the wilderness, built our railroads, our factories, our public utilities, gave us the telegraph, the telephone, the electric light, the automobile, the airplane, the radio and a higher standard of living for all the people than obtains anywhere else in the world. No great invention ever came from a government-owned industry.
GEORGE B. CORTELYOU

All of the things now enjoyed by civilization have been created by some man and sold by another man before anybody really enjoyed the benefits of them.
JAMES G. DALY

It may never come, but I fancy that no man who has sympathy for the human race does not wish that sometime those who labor should have the whole product of their toil. Probably it will never come, but I wish that the time might come when men who work in the industries would own the industries.
CLARENCE DARROW

If it is not in the interest of the public it is not in the interest of business.
JOSEPH H. DEFREES

Things that are bad for business are bad for the people who work for business.
THOMAS E. DEWEY

There ought to be more scrupulous honesty in big business men than in any other human relation. For big business requires teamwork on a gigantic scale.
HENRY L. DOHERTY

Never shrink from doing anything which your business calls you to do. The man who is above his business may one day find his business above him.
JOHN DREW

The only things that evolve by themselves in an organization are disorder, friction and malperformance.
PETER DRUCKER

My greatest strength as a consultant is to be ignorant and ask a few questions.
PETER DRUCKER

The crossroads of trade are the meeting place of ideas, the attrition ground of rival customs and beliefs; diversities beget conflict, comparison, thought; superstitions cancel one another, and reason begins.
WILL DURANT

Men cannot for long live hopefully unless they are embarked upon some great unifying enterprise—one for which they may pledge their lives, their fortunes and their honor.
C. A. DYKSTRA

My son has said to me that if you want to participate actively with businessmen today, keep your hair

cut, stand straight and don't talk about the past.
**Tycoon Cyrus Eaton (at 84)**

There is far more danger in a public monopoly than there is in a private monopoly, for when government goes into business it can always shift its losses to the taxpayer. The Government never really goes into business, for it never makes ends meet, and that is the first requisite of business. It just mixes a little business with a lot of politics, and no one ever gets a chance to find out what is actually going on.
**Thomas A. Edison**

Commerce is a game of skill, which every man can not play, which few men can play well. The right merchant is one who has the just average of faculties we call commonsense; a man of strong affinity for facts, who makes up his decision on what he has seen. He is thoroughly persuaded of the truths of arithmetic. There is always a reason, in the man, for his good or bad fortune; and so, in making money. Men talk as if there were some magic about this, and believe in magic, in all parts of life. He knows that all goes on the old road, pound for pound, cent for cent—for every effect a perfect cause—and that good luck is another name for tenacity of purpose.
**Ralph Waldo Emerson**

Big business can't prosper without small business to supply its needs and buy its products. Labor can't prosper so long as capital lies idle. Capital can't prosper while labor is unemployed.
**DeWitt M. Emery**

You cannot stop speculation . . . in anything by process of law. Just as long as the value of property fluctuates, men will buy and sell with a hope of profit. There will always be speculation of some kind. If you throw it out of an organized exchange, you throw it out into the street.
**Henry C. Emery**

Whether we wish to begin a program of job simplification, or to improve the economic outlook of our people we must first be sure that the atmosphere is right. New ideas do not thrive in an atmosphere of suspicion, jealousy, fear or antagonism.
**Melvin J. Evans**

Business demands faith, compels earnestness, requires courage, is honestly selfish, is penalized for mistakes, and is the essence of life.
**William Feather**

Advertising and salesmanship are time-savers in the promotion of products. They are essential tools in meeting competition. At the foundation of every successful business, however, is a product which thoroughly satisfies a real need on the part of the buyer, and from which he profits and knows that he profits.
**William Feather**

That man is but of the lower part of the world who is not brought up to business and affairs.
**Owen Feltham**

To make one's own estate concentric with the public estate is to realize the conception of the church, the conception of the university, the conception of an essential democracy, and the conception of a business system that will really work.
**Michel J. T. Ferguson**

The first mark of good business is the ability to deliver. To deliver its product or service on time and in the condition which the client was led to expect. This dedication to provision and quality gives rise to corporate reliability. It makes friends and, in the end, is the reason why solvent companies remain solvent.
**Michel J. T. Ferguson**

There is nothing so useful to man in general, nor so beneficial to particular societies and individuals,

as trade. This is that alma mater, at whose plentiful breast all mankind are nourished.
HENRY FIELDING

You cannot afford to make the mistake of thinking you cannot be replaced. And your employer cannot afford to have a man around that he cannot afford to do without.
FRANK IRVING FLETCHER

A big business man was telling Henry Ford about a coach driver of super-expertness with his whip. The driver was telling how he could flick a fly off his horse's ear with his whip—and, a fly alighting just then, he promptly did so. Next he spied a grasshopper beside the road, and he flicked it off with equal dexterity. A little further along the road the passenger noticed an insect on a bush, and nudged the driver to get him.

Not on your life, replied the master of the whip. That there insect is a hornet sitting on his nest with an organization behind him. I leave him alone.
B. C. FORBES

I have known not a few men who, after reaching the summits of business success, found themselves miserable on attaining retirement age. They were so exclusively engrossed in their day-to-day affairs that they had no time for friend-making. . . . They may flatter themselves that their unrelaxing concentration on business constitutes patriotism of the highest order. They may tell themselves that the existing emergency will pass, and that they can then adopt different, more sociable, more friendly habits. [But] such a day is little likely to come for such individuals.
B. C. FORBES

Lord Northcliffe [British press magnate] once told me that he had discovered in America a tendency to install and worship system to such an extent that so much time was spent on system that little time was left for rounding up business to keep the system going. Is it not so with conferences? Isn't the legitimate purpose of conferences being lost sight of? Just how far should businessmen go in spending hours in conferences with their colleagues and shut out, meanwhile, all communication with those from whom they derive their business? Executives cannot make a business pay by taking in one another's washing.
B. C. FORBES

When you delve deep enough, you find that practically every great fortune and great enterprise in America have sprung from the courageous enterprise of some individual. It was Commodore Vanderbilt's enterprise in switching first from running a ferryboat to running other ships, and then, when he was well along in years, his enterprise in switching into railroading, that created what was to become one of the most notable fortunes in the history of the world.
B. C. FORBES

The world seems to have forgotten that, finally, business must be settled almost wholly by barter. Certainly, American bankers, investment bankers and promoters overlooked this basic fact when they joyfully proceeded to lend hundreds of millions and even billions to almost every foreign country on the face of the earth after the World War and before the collapse of our speculative boom. They never stopped to ask how the overseas borrowers could settle the colossal sums advanced to them. . . . The world had drifted too far away from the A.B.C. truth that trade and commerce must necessarily represent barter.
B. C. FORBES

Economists' unanimity that bad business is ahead is the most reassuring news possible. It's very unlikely that this will be the one time they're right.
MALCOLM FORBES

Speculator: One who bought stocks that went down.
MALCOLM FORBES

Notwithstanding all the megamerging in recent years and the ongoing giantness of the likes of General Motors, small businesses continue overwhelmingly to be America's biggest business. They make up 99.8% of the U.S.' business concerns. Over three-quarters of the dollar volume generated by construction and wholesaling comes from small businesses; they provide nearly half of the volume generated by the service industries, and account for 43% of our gross national product. And of the projected 3 million new jobs that will have been created by the end of this year, two-thirds will be in companies with fewer than 100 employees.
MALCOLM FORBES (1986)

Anyone who says businessmen deal only in facts, not fiction, has never read old five-year projections.
MALCOLM FORBES

When reading forecasts tied to percent rates of this and that, it's well to keep in mind that extending them too far into the future—no matter that they have been valid for several years past—is to presume a continuity of circumstances that never holds for any great length of time. . . . How about the not-so-long-ago projections for the continuing growth of utilities? Or natural gas, gasoline and oil consumption? Forecasts that run way out are invariably way off.
MALCOLM FORBES

In business, there's such a thing as an invaluable person, but no such thing as an indispensable one.
MALCOLM FORBES

U.S. Steel. It's probably hard for the younger generation to realize what a giant in every way, shape and form United States Steel once was in our economy. The fabled ogre of corporate folklore is now sick and tired, more likely to be pitied than pilloried. Since Ben Fairless' day, Big Steel has fumbled from one costly wrong decision to another, been heard when silence would have been wiser, been silent when speaking up would have been in order; spent wads for what were often the wrong new facilities and saved when salvation lay in modernizing. Sure it's still big. But it's sad to see the giant in such need of succor.
MALCOLM FORBES (1971)

Business is never so healthy as when, like a chicken, it must do a certain amount of scratching for what it gets.
HENRY FORD

Let all your things have their places; let each part of your business have its time.
BENJAMIN FRANKLIN

No nation was ever ruined by trade.
BENJAMIN FRANKLIN

The first mistake in public business is the going into it.
BENJAMIN FRANKLIN

Those who are surly and imperious to their inferiors are generally humble, flattering and cringing to their superiors.
THOMAS FULLER

Business is the salt of life.
THOMAS FULLER

If you would but exchange places with the other fellow, how much more you could appreciate your own position.
VICTOR E. GARDNER

Unless a business can stay in the black over the long term, averaging the bad years with good, it cannot sustain itself. A manager may have laudable social intentions of providing security for his employees, better products at lower prices for his customers. But if he cannot keep the business going in realizing these intentions he is defeated before he begins.
PAUL GARRETT

All our institutions rest upon business. Without it we should not have schools, colleges, churches, parks, playgrounds, pavements, books, libraries, art, music, or anything else that we value.
CASSIUS E. GATES

The meek shall inherit the earth, but not the mineral rights.
J. PAUL GETTY

As you cherish the things most worthwhile in your family life, cherish the things most worthwhile in your company.
WILLIAM B. GIVEN, JR.

Adequate distribution of goods makes, unmakes—or remakes—all capital values!
KENNETH GOODE

The only power corporations have, whether they be large or small, is the right to stand in the market place and cry their wares. If the customers find those wares good, they will buy and the corporations will prosper. If they do not, the proprietor will soon be sitting on the curbstone, whether we are talking about a large manufacturer or a roadside market.
CRAWFORD H. GREENEWALT

It is the customer, and the customer alone, who casts the vote that determines how big any company should be. . . . The regulations laid down by the consuming public are far more potent and far less flexible than any code of law, merely through the exercise of the natural forces of trade.
CRAWFORD H. GREENEWALT

A "tired businessman" is one whose business is usually not a successful one.
JOSEPH R. GRUNDY

Delegating work works, provided the one delegating works too.
ROBERT HALF

The more people who own little businesses of their own, the safer our country will be, and the better off its cities and towns; for the people who have a stake in their country and their community are its best citizens.
JOHN HANCOCK

What is a committee? A group of the unwilling, picked from the unfit, to do the unnecessary.
RICHARD HARKNESS

I have found [public relations] to be the craft of arranging truths so that people will like you. Public-relations specialists make flower arrangements of the facts, placing them so that the wilted and less attractive petals are hidden by the sturdy blooms.
ALAN HARRINGTON

The most sensible people to be met with in society are men of business and of the world, who argue from what they see and know, instead of spinning cobweb distinctions of what things ought to be.
WILLIAM HAZLITT

Who likes not his business, his business likes not him.
WILLIAM HAZLITT

It is probably safe to say that the best brains of the nation are to be found in industry. This is partly because industry can afford to pay the highest prices for talent, and also because of the training men receive in that field. That this fact is not more apparent is due in part to the reluctance of business men to reveal their accomplishments to the public, and also because they have directed their energies in the past almost exclusively to production problems.
**RALPH HENDERSHOT**

A company's business would increase 50% if you cleared the conference room of chairs.
**W. F. HENEGHAN**

The are more goods bought by the heart then by the head.
**GEORGE HENNING**

Pleasing ware is half sold.
**GEORGE HERBERT**

Great business turns on a little pin.
**GEORGE HERBERT**

All men's gains are the fruit of venturing.
**HERODOTUS**

A man is likely to mind his own business when it is worth minding. When it is not, he takes his mind off his own meaningless affairs by minding other people's business.
**ERIC HOFFER**

If we are to have a stabilized market demand, selling pressure should be maintained . . . perhaps increased . . . at the first sign of a decline in business. I know of no single way business managers can do more to stabilize market demand than through greater stabilization of sales and advertising expenditures.
**PAUL G. HOFFMAN**

One of the eternal conflicts out of which life is made up is that between the efforts of every man to get the most he can for his services and that of society disguised under the name of capital to get his services for the least possible return.
**OLIVER WENDELL HOLMES**

In thousands of years there has been no advance in public morals, in philosophy, in religion or in politics, but the advance in business has been the greatest miracle the world has ever known.
**EDGAR WATSON HOWE**

If we devote our time disparaging the products of our business rivals, we hurt business generally, reduce confidence, and increase discontent.
**EDWARD N. HURLEY**

Most business problems require common sense rather than legal reference. They require good judgment and honesty of purpose rather than reference to the courts.
**EDWARD N. HURLEY**

In the takeover business, if you want a friend, you buy a dog.
**CARL ICAHN**

Commerce is the great civilizer. We exchange ideas when we exchange fabrics.
**ROBERT G. INGERSOLL**

He who will not apply himself to business, eventually discovers that he means to get his bread by cheating, stealing, or begging, or else is wholly void of reason.
**ISCHOMACHUS**

No one fouls his hands in his own business.
**ITALIAN PROVERB**

I do not believe you can do today's job with yesterday's methods and be in business tomorrow.
**NELSON JACKSON**

Agriculture, manufactures, commerce and navigation, the four pillars of our prosperity, are most thriving when left most free to individual enterprise.
**THOMAS JEFFERSON**

When speculation has done its worst, two and two still make four.
**SAMUEL JOHNSON**

Morale is faith in the man at the top.
**ALBERT S. JOHNSTONE**

Whoever said, If it ain't broke, don't fix it, probably never heard of preventative maintenance.
**STEVEN KASPER**

Industry prospers when it offers people articles which they want more than they want anything they now have. The fact is that people never buy what they need. They buy what they want.
**CHARLES F. KETTERING**

To venture causes anxiety, but not to venture is to lose one's self... and to venture in the highest sense is precisely to become conscious of one's self.
**SÖREN KIERKEGAARD**

Men who pay whole-hearted attention to business, who train themselves, who develop every power to the full, are favored by the ill-training of the average man. Despite our boasted institutions of learning, most men are only half-educated, have no clear purpose in life or little real ambition, and are not honest in the highest meaning of the word. The only wonder is that well-trained, honest, ambitious, creative men do not forge to the front more rapidly.
**DARWIN P. KINGSLEY**

A. T. Stewart started life with a dollar and fifty cents. This merchant prince began by calling at the doors of houses in order to sell needles, thread and buttons. He soon found the people did not want them, and his small stock was thrown back on his hands. Then he said wisely, "I'll not buy any more of these goods, but I'll go and ask people what they do want." Thereafter he studied the needs and desires of people, found out just what they most wanted, endeavored to meet those wants, and became the greatest business man of his time.
**GRENVILLE KLEISER**

A big corporation is more or less blamed for being big; it is only big because it gives service. If it doesn't give service, it gets small faster than it grew big.
**WILLIAM S. KNUDSEN**

The one who keeps the stars in their place can keep us in our place. There is no depression for good deeds, and that is all that business consists of, and that is our real business.
**HENRY N. KOST**

The morale of an organization is not built from the bottom up; it filters from the top down.
**PETER B. KYNE**

### A Business Man's Prayer

Help me, O Lord, to remember that three feet make one yard, sixteen ounces one pound, four quarts one gallon and sixty minutes one hour. Help me to do business on the square. Make me sympathetic with the fellow who has broken in the struggle. Keep me from taking an unfair advantage of the weak, or from selling my self-respect for a profit. Blind my eyes to the petty faults of others, but reveal to me my own. Deafen my ears to the rustle of unholy skirts, and help me to live, day by day, in such a way that I shall be able to look across the table at my wife, who has been such a blessing to me, and have nothing to conceal.

And when comes the sound of low music, the scent of sweet flowers, and the crunch of footsteps on the gravel, make the ceremony short, and the epitaph simple—Here lies a man . . . one who was of service to others.

A. A. LARSEN

People will buy anything that's *one to a customer.*

SINCLAIR LEWIS

There is no better ballast for keeping the mind steady on its keel, and saving it from all risk of crankiness, than business.

JAMES RUSSELL LOWELL

Your market has a free choice, and only by supplying what the market wants, and not by your efforts to impose your merchandise, will you get your maximum share of the market's potential.

WALTER H. LOWY

Business more than any other occupation is a continual dealing with the future; it is a continual calculation, an instinctive exercise in foresight.

HENRY R. LUCE

The trade-unionist has the same limitation imposed upon him as the capitalist. He cannot advance his interests at the expense of society.

RAMSAY MACDONALD

All too much of the wage structure has been based on the time workers put in, rather than upon the product put out. The consumer dollar has no interest in how much time it buys—only in the character and quality of the product itself.

WHEELER MCMILLEN

No man will ever be a big executive who feels that he must, either openly or under cover, follow up every order he gives and see that it is done—nor will he ever develop a capable assistant.

JOHN LEE MAHIN

Be methodical if you would succeed in business, or in anything. Have a work for every moment, and mind the moment's work. Whatever your calling, master all its bearings and details, its principles, instruments and applications. Method is essential if you would get through your work easily and with economy of time.

WILLIAM MATTHEWS

Business is a combination of war and sport.

ANDRÉ MAUROIS

If the spirit of business adventure is killed, this country will cease to hold the foremost position in the world.

ANDREW W. MELLON

Morale is when your hands and feet keep on working when your head says it can't be done.

BENJAMIN MORRELL

It takes more than Capital to swing business. You've got to have the A.I.D. degree to get by—Advertising, Initiative and Dynamics.

REN MULFORD, JR.

A ship, to run a straight course, can have but one pilot and one steering wheel. The same applies to the successful operation of a business. There cannot be a steering wheel at every seat in an organization.

JULES ORMONT

Public relations, in this country, is the art of adapting big business to a democracy so that the people have confidence that they are being well served and

at the same time the business has freedom to serve them well.
**ARTHUR W. PAGE**

It is very sad for a man to make himself servant to a single thing; his manhood all taken out of him by the hydraulic pressure of excessive business.
**THEODORE PARKER**

A self-contained nation is a backward nation, with large numbers of people either permanently out of work, or very poorly paid in purchasing power. A nation which trades freely with all the world, selling to others those commodities which it can best produce, and buying from others those commodities which others can best produce, is by far the best conditioned nation for all practical purposes.
**WALTER PARKER**

Leaving business at the office sounds like a good rule, but it is one that can easily be carried too far because, to my mind, a man who intends to make a success should be collecting ideas and tips, and mapping out programs during every waking hour. Dismissing business after office hours has a nice sound, but I have found that often the business does not come back after the recess!
**JOHN HENRY PATTERSON**

We do not say that a man who takes no interest in public affairs is a man who minds his own business. We say he has no business being here at all.
**PERICLES**

Business is like a man rowing a boat upstream. He has no choice; he must go ahead or he will go back.
**LEWIS E. PIERSON**

Adoption and continuation of policies that incorporate a maximum of forward thinking should be the most vital single consideration of all executives.
**CHARLES PRESBREY**

Seest thou a man diligent in his business? He shall stand before kings; he shall not stand before mean men.
**PROVERBS 22:29**

The next generation of businessmen will be articulate, knowing what they believe and entering joyously into the battle of ideas, or there will be no business as we have known it heretofore.
**CLARENCE B. RANDALL**

Public relations work is generally considered to be a relatively new development. Actually, the principles involved are as old as the ages. The 9th Verse of the 14th Chapter of First Corinthians reads: "Except ye utter by the tongue words easy to be understood, how shall it be known what is spoken? For ye shall speak into the air." With the Bible as our authority, how can we public relations people fail?
**CLIFFORD B. REEVES**

Commerce tends to wear off those prejudices which maintain destruction and animosity between nations. It softens and polishes the manners of men. It unites them by one of the strongest of all ties—the desire of supplying their mutual wants. It disposes them to peace by establishing in every state an order of citizens bound by their interest to be the guardians of public tranquility.
**FREDERICK W. ROBERTSON**

A man who is at the top is a man who has the habit of getting to the bottom.
**JOSEPH E. ROGERS**

If you can build a business up big enough, it's respectable.
**WILL ROGERS**

You never get a second chance to make a good first impression.
**WILL ROGERS**

Even if you're on the right track you'll get run over if you just sit there.
WILL ROGERS

Every business should have its biographer—not after its head is dead but to show that he's very much alive.
FRANK ROMER

When we control business in the public interest we are also bound to encourage it in the public interest or it will be a bad thing for everybody and worst of all for those on whose behalf the control is nominally exercised.
THEODORE ROOSEVELT

We demand that big business give people a square deal; in return we must insist that when anyone engaged in big business honestly endeavors to do right, he shall himself be given a square deal.
THEODORE ROOSEVELT

The most important difference between business and academia is this: In business everything is dog eat dog. In academia it's just the reverse.
E. JOHN ROSENWALD, JR.

**Rules for Business Success**

1. Carefully examine every detail of the business.
2. Be prompt.
3. Take time to consider and then decide quickly.
4. Dare to go forward.
5. Bear your trouble patiently.
6. Maintain your integrity as a sacred thing.
7. Never tell business lies.
8. Make no useless acquaintances.
9. Never try to appear something more than you are.
10. Pay your debts promptly.
11. Learn how to risk your money at the right time.
12. Shun strong liquor.
13. Employ your time well.
14. Do not reckon on chance.
15. Be polite to everyone.
16. Never be discouraged.
17. Work hard and you will succeed.

MEYER ROTHSCHILD

He should be the owner of the land who rubs it between his hands every spring.
RUSSIAN PEASANT SAYING

A man who cannot mind his own business is not to be trusted with the king's.
GEORGE SAVILE (LORD HALIFAX)

He who thinks his place below him, will certainly be below his place.
GEORGE SAVILE (LORD HALIFAX)

There are almost four million small businesses in the United States. No planning with reference to pensions or wages or other major problems can afford to ignore the interests of this great group. If these interests are long ignored, our economic collapse is inevitable.
CHARLES W. SAWYER

Keeping a little ahead of conditions is one of the secrets of business; the trailer seldom goes far.
CHARLES M. SCHWAB

Business is a great game. I play it very hard and in as sportsmanlike a way as I know how, and I feel that at the end of the day I have got the fullest reward. I am an enthusiast in business. Besides ambition, business demands courage, judgment, imagination and organizing ability. But it has no use for self-satisfaction or for mental laziness—the first crime in the list.
**H. GORDON SELFRIDGE**

Get the confidence of the public and you will have no difficulty in getting their patronage. Inspire your whole force with the right spirit of service; encourage every sign of the true spirit. So display and advertise wares that customers shall buy with understanding. Treat them as guests when they come and when they go, whether or not they buy. Give them all that can be given fairly, on the principle that to him that giveth shall be given. Remember always that the recollection of quality remains long after the price is forgotten. Then your business will prosper by a natural process.
**H. GORDON SELFRIDGE**

People of the same trade seldom meet together for merriment and diversion, but the conversation ends in a conspiracy against the public.
**ADAM SMITH**

Consumption is the sole end and purpose of all production, and the interest of the producer ought to be attended to, only so far as it may be necessary for promoting that of the consumer.
**ADAM SMITH**

A dinner lubricates business.
**BARON STOWELL**

To succeed, a business must occupy a field of public usefulness by producing a good article at the lowest price consistent with fair treatment of all those concerned with its production, distribution and consumption.
**WALTER C. TEAGLE**

A jack-of-all-trades is king of none.
**P. K. THOMAJAN**

I have since learned that trade curses everything it handles; and though you trade in messages from heaven, the whole curse of trade attaches to the business.
**HENRY DAVID THOREAU**

What recommends commerce to me is its enterprise and bravery. It does not clasp its hands and pray to Jupiter.
**HENRY DAVID THOREAU**

I think that there is nothing, not even crime, more opposed to poetry, to philosophy, ay, to life itself than this incessant business.
**HENRY DAVID THOREAU**

In democracies, nothing is more great or more brilliant than commerce: It attracts the attention of the public and fills the imagination of the multitude; all energetic passions are directed towards it.
**ALEXIS DE TOCQUEVILLE**

Always tell yourself: The difference between running a business and ruining a business is *i*.
**FRANK TYGER**

A businessman is a hybrid between a dancer and a calculator.
**PAUL VALÉRY**

No legitimate business man ever got started on the road to permanent success by any other means than that of hard, intelligent work, coupled with an earned credit, plus character.
**F. D. VAN AMBURGH**

The most successful business man is the man who holds onto the old just as long as it is good and grabs the new just as soon as it is better.
ROBERT P. VANDERPOEL

All business sagacity reduces itself in the last analysis to a judicious use of sabotage.
THORSTEIN VEBLEN

I think I have learned, in some degree at least, to disregard the old maxim, "Do not get others to do what you can do yourself." My motto on the other hand is, "Do not do that which others can do as well."
BOOKER T. WASHINGTON

With the proper flow of commerce across the borders of all countries it is unnecessary for soldiers to march across those borders.
THOMAS J. WATSON

There is always room at the top.
DANIEL WEBSTER

Call on a business man only at business times, and on business; transact your business, and go about your business, in order to give him time to finish his business.
DUKE OF WELLINGTON

My own business always bores me to death; I prefer other people's.
OSCAR WILDE

The manufacturer who waits in the woods for the world to beat a path to his door is a great optimist. But the manufacturer who shows his mousetraps to the world keeps the smoke coming out of his chimney.
O. B. WINTERS

When two men in a business always agree, one of them is unnecessary.
WILLIAM WRIGLEY, JR.

In modern business it is not the crook who is to be feared most, it is the honest man who doesn't know what he is doing.
OWEN D. YOUNG

Markets as well as mobs respond to human emotions; markets as well as mobs can be inflamed to their own destruction.
OWEN D. YOUNG

When Hector was a pup and I was a boy, Pan American was the greatest thing, the greatest company in the brand-new air transportation industry. . . .
As seems to happen so frequently to people and businesses, success over the decades led to complacency and ultimately to red ink. From the longtime pinnacle when Pan Am was virtually writing the book, the procedures and the international air agreements that were dutifully passed. . . . Pan Am's affluence and influence have declined now to the point where it is receiving the wrong end of the stick, unfair treatment, the back of the hand.
MALCOLM FORBES (1976)

## *Busy*

Every man is worth just as much as the things he busies himself with.
MARCUS AURELIUS ANTONINUS

Whoever admits that he is too busy to improve his methods has acknowledged himself to be at the end of his rope. And that is always the saddest predicament which anyone can get into.
J. OGDEN ARMOUR

It is an undoubted truth that the less one has to do the less time one finds to do it in. One yawns, one procrastinates, one can do it when one will, and, therefore, one seldom does it at all; whereas, those who have a great deal of business must buckle to it; and then they always find time enough to do it.
**LORD CHESTERFIELD**

Who is more busy than he who hath least to do!
**JOHN CLARKE**

None are so busy as the fool and the knave.
**JOHN DRYDEN**

The busiest men have the most leisure.
**ENGLISH PROVERB**

The happiest people are those who are too busy to notice whether they are or not.
**WILLIAM FEATHER**

The busy man has few idle visitors; to the boiling pot the flies come not.
**BENJAMIN FRANKLIN**

Don't let yourself say or even think "I am busy," "I haven't time," "I am tired." That makes you feel busier or more rushed or more tired than you actually are.
**WILLIAM B. GIVEN, JR.**

The more we do, the more we can do; the more busy we are, the more leisure we have.
**WILLIAM HAZLITT**

The majority prove their worth by keeping busy. A busy life is the nearest thing to a purposeful life.
**ERIC HOFFER**

Occupation is the necessary basis of all enjoyment.
**LEIGH HUNT**

The busier we are, the more acutely we feel that we live.
**IMMANUEL KANT**

No thoroughly occupied man was ever yet very miserable.
**LETITIA E. LANDON**

A man who is very busy seldom changes his opinions.
**FRIEDRICH WILHELM NIETZSCHE**

You can't be asleep in business—at the ends of the arms of Morpheus are the hands of the receiver.
**FRANK ROMER**

Be busy in trading, receiving, and giving, for life is too good to be wasted in living.
**JOHN STERLING**

Extreme busyness, whether at school or college, kirk or market, is a symptom of deficient vitality; and a faculty for idleness implies a catholic appetite and a strong sense of personal identity.
**ROBERT LOUIS STEVENSON**

Many are idly busy. Domitian was busy, but then it was in catching flies.
**JEREMY TAYLOR**

It is not enough to be busy; so are the ants. The question is: What are we busy about?
**HENRY DAVID THOREAU**

## Canada

Canada has never been a melting pot; more like a tossed salad.
ARNOLD EDINBOROUGH

## Capitalism

Capitalism and communism stand at opposite poles. Their essential difference is this: The communist, seeing the rich man and his fine home, says: "No man should have so much." The capitalist, seeing the same thing, says: "All men should have as much."
PHELPS ADAMS

There is room in the world for both capitalism and communism and all gradations of them, provided only that neither system set upon pursuing an aggressively imperialistic course.
RALPH J. BUNCHE

It is just as illogical to suggest abolishing capitalism because it hasn't abolished poverty as it would be to suggest abolishing the churches because the churches haven't abolished sin.
C. DONALD DALLAS

Capitalism is the only system in the world founded on credit and character.
HUBERT EATON

The issue is the performance of Capitalism against the promises of Communism.
PAUL G. HOFFMAN

And the word is capitalism. We are too mealy-mouthed. We fear the word capitalism is unpopular. So we talk about the free enterprise system and run to cover in the folds of the flag and talk about the American Way of Life.
ERIC A. JOHNSTON

There can be no freedom of the individual, no democracy, without the capital system, the profit system, the private enterprise system. These are, in the end, inseparable. Those who would destroy freedom have only first to destroy the hope of gain, the profit of enterprise and risk-taking, the hope of accumulating capital, the hope to save something for one's old age and for one's children. For a community of men without property, and without the hope of getting it by honest effort, is a community of slaves of a despotic State.
RUSSELL C. LEFFINGWELL

American capitalism has been both overpraised and overindicted. It is neither the Plumed Knight nor the monstrous Robber Baron.
MAX LERNER

The capitalistic system is the oldest system in the world, and any system that has weathered the gales and chances of thousands of years must have something in it that is sound and true. We believe in the right of a man to himself, to his own property, to his own destiny, and we believe the government exists as the umpire in the game, not to come down and take the bat, but to see that the other fellows play the game according to the principles of fairness and justice.
NICHOLAS LONGWORTH

The record of the last century has been impressive. The problem for the future is to keep our capitalism dynamic—continue to raise living standards and yet to reduce, as much as possible, the human costs as reflected in insecurity and instability.
W. WALTER WILLIAMS

## Career

One of the greatest pleasures to be derived from wealth in any form is the delight inherent in choosing the proper vocational program for one's life. The child who has toys that will amuse him in all kinds of weather is enjoying the luxuries of life. The man who selects the proper vocation in life has all the luxuries that life can provide.
LLOYD E. BOUGHAM

Let a man practice the profession which he best knows.
CICERO

Each man has his own vocation. The talent is the call.
RALPH WALDO EMERSON

Every industrious man, in every lawful calling, is a useful man. And one principal reason why men are so often useless is that they neglect their own profession or calling, and divide and shift their attention among a multiplicity of objects and pursuits.
RALPH WALDO EMERSON

Nothing, not even sheer ability, can make up for the dedication required for a successful business career.
RAY EPPERT

Think not of yourself as the architect of your career but as the sculptor. Expect to have to do a lot of hard hammering and chiselling and scraping and polishing.
B. C. FORBES

It is a poor and disgraceful thing not to be able to reply, with some degree of certainty, to the simple questions, "What will you be? What will you do?"
JOHN FOSTER

Everyone has a vocation by which he earns his living, but he also has a vocation in an older sense of the word—the vocation to use his powers and live his life well.
RICHARD W. LIVINGSTONE

A decent man is not responsible for the vice or absurdity of his profession; and he ought not on that account refuse to pursue it; it is the custom of the country, there is money to be got by it, a man must live in the world and make the best of it, such as it is.
MICHEL DE MONTAIGNE

If a man has any brains at all, let him hold on to his calling, and, in the grand sweep of things, his turn will come at last.
WILLIAM MCCUNE

A career, like a business, must be budgeted. When it is necessary, the budget can be adjusted to meet changing conditions. A life that hasn't a definite plan is likely to become driftwood.
DAVID SARNOFF

The test of a vocation is the love of the drudgery it involves.
LOGAN PEARSALL SMITH

Only those who decline to scramble up the career ladder are interesting as human beings. Nothing is more boring than a man with a career.
ALEKSANDR SOLZHENITSYN

Man is called to nothing in this world. He has no destiny, no function, no vocation, any more than a plant or a dumb brute.
**Max Stirner**

To find a career to which you are adapted by nature, and then to work hard at it, is about as near to a formula for success and happiness as the world provides. One of the fortunate aspects of this formula is that, granted the right career has been found, the hard work takes care of itself. Then hard work is not hard work at all.
**Mark Sullivan**

Every profession does imply a trust for the service of the public.
**Benjamin Whichcote**

## *Cars*

Traffic is the lifestream of the 20th century. It is the sign of success and prosperity. After all, what is a pedestrian? He is a man who has two cars—one being driven by his wife, the other by one of his children.
**Robert Bradbury**

Trees sent Joyce Kilmer, but nothing quite sends most Americans like the smell of a new car interior and the soul-satisfying sound of shutting a new car door. There are few among us who don't find that sound as exciting as any bar of music. There are few among us who do not put a new chariot's aroma on a par with the perfume of the loveliest blooms. It's a deep yearning for both of these that, at this time of year, drives so many to the nearest auto showroom. Call it what you want, or call for the psychiatrist, but it's a powerful fact of American life.
**Malcolm Forbes**

Our national flower is the concrete cloverleaf.
**Lewis Mumford**

If you stay in Beverly Hills too long you become a Mercedes.
**Robert Redford**

The only way to solve the traffic problems of the country is to pass a law that only paid-for cars are allowed to use the highways.
**Will Rogers**

## *Chance*

We cannot bear to regard ourselves simply as playthings of blind chance; we cannot admit to feeling ourselves abandoned.
**Ugo Betti**

All of life is happen-stance,
A maze of drive and hope and chance;
For starters, why were we conceived?
For endings, what's to be believed?
**Art Buck**

The urge to gamble is so universal and its practice so pleasurable that I assume it must be evil.
**Heywood Broun**

He who distrusts the security of chance takes more pains to effect the safety which results from labor. To find what you seek in the road of life, the best proverb of all is that which says: "Leave no stone unturned."
**Edward Bulwer-Lytton**

There is no such thing as chance or accident; the words merely signify our ignorance of some real and immediate cause.
**Adam Clarke**

Those who trust to chance must abide by the results of chance. They have no legitimate complaint against anyone but themselves.
**CALVIN COOLIDGE**

I returned, and saw under the sun, that the race is not to the swift, nor the battle to the strong, neither yet riches to men of understanding, nor yet favour to men of skill; but time and chance happeneth to them all.
**ECCLESIASTES 9:11**

There is nothing in life so irrational, that good sense and chance may not set it to rights; nothing so rational, that folly and chance may not utterly confound it.
**JOHANN WOLFGANG VON GOETHE**

Chance has something to say in everything, even how to write a good letter.
**BALTASAR GRACIÁN**

He neither fears his fate too much or his deserts are small that puts it not unto the touch to win or lose it all.
**JAMES GRAHAM**

When you bet on a sure thing—hedge!
**ROBERT HALF**

Be not too presumptuously sure in any business; for things of this world depend on such a train of unseen chances that if it were in man's hands to set the tables, still he would not be certain to win the game.
**LORD HERBERT**

We all have to learn, in one way or another, that neither men nor boys get second chances in this world. We all get new chances to the end of our lives, but not second chances in the same set of circumstances; and the great difference between one person and another is how he takes hold and uses his first chance, and how he takes his fall if it is scored against him.
**THOMAS HUGHES**

You will never stub your toe standing still. The faster you go, the more chance there is of stubbing your toe, but the more chance you have of getting somewhere.
**CHARLES F. KETTERING**

I figure you have the same chance of winning the lottery whether you play or not.
**FRAN LEBOWITZ**

What chance has made yours is not really yours.
**LUCILIUS**

Unless a man has trained himself for his chance, the chance will only make him ridiculous. A great occasion is worth to a man exactly what his antecedents have enabled him to make of it.
**WILLIAM MATTHEWS**

Remember the Three Princes of Serendip who went out looking for treasure? They didn't find what they were looking for, but they kept finding things just as valuable. That's serendipity, and our business [drugs] is full of it.
**GEORGE MERCK**

In the field of observation chance only favors minds which are prepared.
**LOUIS PASTEUR**

In great affairs we ought to apply ourselves less to creating chances than to profiting from those that offer.
**FRANÇOIS DE LA ROCHEFOUCAULD**

There are no chances so unlucky from which clever people are not able to reap some advantage; and

none so lucky that the foolish are not able to turn them to their own disadvantage.
FRANÇOIS DE LA ROCHEFOUCAULD

Why not go out on a limb? Isn't that where the fruit is?
FRANK SCULLY

The roulette table pays nobody except him that keeps it. Nevertheless, a passion for gambling is common, though a passion for keeping roulette tables is unknown.
GEORGE BERNARD SHAW

When we count on chance in lieu of law and labor, we weaken our healthy attitudes toward work, our fellow men and our God.
RALPH W. SOCKMAN

We are in the world like men playing at tables; the chance is not in our power, but to pay it is; and when it is fallen, we must manage it as we can.
JEREMY TAYLOR

What can be more foolish than to think that all this rare fabric of heaven and earth could come by chance, when all the skill of art is not able to make an oyster!
JEREMY TAYLOR

Chance does nothing that has not been prepared beforehand.
ALEXIS DE TOCQUEVILLE

Necessity is the mother of taking chances.
MARK TWAIN

Chance is a word devoid of sense, nothing can exist without a cause.
VOLTAIRE

Gambling is the child of avarice, the brother of iniquity, and the father of mischief.
GEORGE WASHINGTON

## *Change*

All great changes are irksome to the human mind, especially those which are attended with great dangers and uncertain effects.
JOHN QUINCY ADAMS

He who reforms himself, has done much toward reforming others; and one reason why the world is not reformed, is, because each would have others make a beginning, and never thinks of himself doing it.
THOMAS ADAMS

Nothing that is not a real crime makes a man appear so contemptible and little in the eyes of the world as inconstancy.
JOSEPH ADDISON

Change is no modern invention. It is as old as time and as unlikely to disappear. It has always to be counted on as of the essence of human experience.
JAMES ROWLAND ANGELL

Things do change. The only question is that since things are deteriorating so quickly, will society and man's habits change quickly enough?
ISAAC ASIMOV

All things change, and you yourself are constantly wasting away. So also is the universe.
MARCUS AURELIUS ANTONINUS

Every so often we hear people clamor for a change. Let's change the Constitution, change the form of Government, change everything for better or worse

except to change the only thing that needs changing first: The human heart and our standard of success and human values.
**WILLIAM J. H. BOETCKER**

Consider how hard it is to change yourself and you'll understand what little chance you have of trying to change others.
**JACOB M. BRAUDE**

Part of human nature resents change, loves equilibrium, while another part welcomes novelty, loves the excitement of disequilibrium. There is no formula for the resolution of this tug-of-war, but it is obvious that absolute surrender to either of them invites disaster.
**J. BARTLET BREBNER**

I can think of few important movements for reform in which success was won by any method other than an energetic minority presenting the indifferent majority with a fait accompli, which was then accepted.
**VERA BRITTAIN**

To know what one can have and to do with it, being prepared for no more, is the basis of equilibrium.
**PEARL S. BUCK**

Change is inevitable, except from a vending machine.
**BUMPER STICKER**

Today is not yesterday. We ourselves change. How can our works and thoughts, if they are always to be the fittest, continue always the same? Change, indeed, is painful, yet ever needful; and if memory has its force and worth, so also has hope.
**THOMAS CARLYLE**

Every reform, however necessary, will by weak minds be carried to an excess, that itself will need reforming.
**SAMUEL TAYLOR COLERIDGE**

There is nothing wrong with change, if it is in the right direction.
**WINSTON CHURCHILL**

Reform is a . . . cathartic which our political quacks recommend to others, but will not take themselves; it is admired by all who cannot effect it, and abused by all who can.
**CHARLES CALEB COLTON**

We ought not to be overanxious to encourage innovation, for an old system must ever have two advantages over a new one; it is established and it is understood.
**CHARLES CALEB COLTON**

Change is inevitable in a progressive country. Change is constant.
**BENJAMIN DISRAELI**

A man who has reformed himself has contributed his full share towards the reformation of his neighbor.
**NORMAN DOUGLAS**

But innovation is more than a new method. It is a new view of the universe, as one of risk rather than of chance or of certainty. It is a new view of man's role in the universe; he creates order by taking risks. And this means that innovation, rather than being an assertion of human power, is an acceptance of human responsibility.
**PETER DRUCKER**

We are reformers in spring and summer. In autumn and winter we stand by the old. Reformers in the morning, conservatives at night. Reform is affirma-

tive; conservatism, negative. Conservatism goes for comfort; reform for truth.
RALPH WALDO EMERSON

Change, not habit, is what gets most of us down; habit is the stabilizer of human society, change accounts for its progress.
WILLIAM FEATHER

Elders always lament change—and the young cannot wait for it.
MALCOLM FORBES

Christians are supposed not merely to endure change, nor even to profit by it, but to cause it.
HARRY EMERSON FOSDICK, D.D.

You have to stop in order to change direction
ERICH FROMM

There is nothing more tragic in life than the utter impossibility of changing what you have done.
JOHN GALSWORTHY

There is danger in reckless change, but greater danger in blind conservatism.
HENRY GEORGE

All change is not growth; as all movement is not forward.
ELLEN GLASGOW

Let no one be ashamed to say yes today if yesterday he said no.
Or to say no today if yesterday he said yes. For that is life.
Never to have changed—what a pitiable thing of which to boast!
JOHANN WOLFGANG VON GOETHE

Give us the fortitude to endure the things which cannot be changed, and the courage to change the things which should be changed, and the wisdom to know one from the other.
BISHOP OLIVER J. HART

Every man is a reformer until reform tramps on his toes.
EDGAR WATSON HOWE

The path of least resistance is what makes rivers run crooked.
ELBERT HUBBARD

To reform a man, you must begin with his grandmother.
VICTOR HUGO

Great innovations should not be forced on slender majorities.
THOMAS JEFFERSON

There is a certain relief in change, even though it be from bad to worse; as I have found in traveling in a stage coach, that it is often a comfort to shift one's position and be bruised in a new place.
WASHINGTON IRVING

Long customs are not easily broken: He that attempts to change the course of his own life very often labors in vain; and how shall we do for others, what we are seldom able to do for ourselves?
SAMUEL JOHNSON

Such is the state of life that none are happy but by the anticipation of change. The change itself is nothing; when we have made it the next wish is to change again.
SAMUEL JOHNSON

To men pressed by their wants all change is ever welcome.
BEN JONSON

The world hates change, yet it is the only thing that has brought progress.
CHARLES F. KETTERING

All things are changed, and we change with them.
LOTHAIR I

The most effective way to cope with change is to help create it.
L. W. LYNETT

Who does more earnestly long for a change than he who is uneasy in his present circumstances? And who run to create confusions with so desperate a boldness as those who have nothing to lose, hope to gain by them?
SIR THOMAS MORE

The art of living does not consist in preserving and clinging to a particular mood of happiness, but in allowing happiness to change its form without being disappointed by the change, for happiness, like a child, must be allowed to grow up.
CHARLES L. MORGAN

Have no fear of change as such and, on the other hand, no liking for it merely for its own sake.
ROBERT MOSES

We must drop the idea that change comes slowly. It does ordinarily—in part because we think it does. Today changes must come fast; and we must adjust our mental habits, so that we can accept comfortably the idea of stopping one thing and beginning another overnight. We must discard the idea that past routine, past ways of doing things, are probably the best ways. On the contrary, we must assume that there is probably a better way to do almost everything. We must stop assuming that a thing which has never been done before probably cannot be done at all.
DONALD M. NELSON

If we are all the heirs both of time and of eternity, what is our destiny? Change is stamped on our occupations, our ambitions and desires, yet the hunger of eternity is in our hearts. That contrast, that paradox of life, may become either a blessing or a curse.
JAMES Z. NETTINGA

Grant me the serenity to accept the things I cannot change, the courage to change the things I can and the wisdom to know the difference.
REINHOLD NIEBUHR

I have always believed that it's important to show a new look periodically. Predictability can lead to failure.
T. BOONE PICKENS

The only thing constant in life is change.
FRANÇOIS DE LA ROCHEFOUCAULD

A little and a little, collected together, become a great deal; the heap in the barn consists of single grains, and drop and drop make the inundation.
SA'DI

Our economy has the tremendous advantage of possessing three and a half million business enterprises outside of agriculture and about six million business enterprises in agriculture . . . nearly ten million places where innovations may be authorized. . . . No regimented economy can hope to compete in dynamic drive with an economy which possesses nearly ten million independent centers of initiative.
SUMNER H. SLICHTER

There is nothing in this world constant but inconstancy.
JONATHAN SWIFT

It will always do to change for the better.
JAMES THOMSON

**Another Tack**

When you suspect you're going wrong,
Or lack the strength to move along
With placid poise among your peers,
Because of haunting doubts or fears:
It's time for you to shift your pack,
And steer upon another tack!

When wind and waves assail your ship,
And anchors from the bottom slip;
When clouds of mist obscure your sun,
And foaming waters madly run:
It's time for you to change your plan
And make a port while yet you can!

When men laugh at your woeful plight,
And seek your old repute to blight;
When all the world bestows a frown,
While you are sliding swiftly down:
It's time for you to show your grit.
And let the scoffers know you're fit!

When Failure opes your luckless door,
And struts across the creaking floor;
When Fortune flees and leaves you bare,
And former friends but coldly stare:
It's time for you to take a tack,
And show the world you're coming back!
LILBURN HARWOOD TOWNSEND

There is great work to be done. The foundations of the new world must be laid by those who have the courage to change the old; by those whose arteries are still soft and clear, whose minds are still active, and hearts still generous.
EARL WARREN

Few things are more striking than the fact that while the best are nearly powerless to effect changes, the worst are so potent.
GEORGE F. WATTS

An individual is more apt to change, perhaps, than all the world around him.
DANIEL WEBSTER

If you want to make enemies, try to change something.
WOODROW WILSON

There are no permanent changes because change itself is permanent. It behooves the industrialist to research and the investor to be vigilant.
RALPH L. WOODS

## *Character*

We often pray for purity, unselfishness, for the highest qualities of character, and forget that these things cannot be given, but must be earned.
LYMAN ABBOTT

Good character is that quality which makes one dependable whether being watched or not, which makes one truthful when it is to one's advantage to be a little less than truthful, which makes one courageous when faced with great obstacles, which endows one with the firmness of wise self-discipline.
ARTHUR S. ADAMS

Everyone knows that weeds eat out the life of the garden and of the productive fields. The gardener and farmer alike each has to keep the weeding process alive.

It's like that in the building and developing of character. No one knows our own faults and tendencies better than we do ourselves, so that it is up to each

one of us to keep the weeds out, and to keep all growth vigorous and fruitful.
GEORGE MATTHEW ADAMS

Among the sentiments of most powerful operation upon the human heart, and most highly honorable to the human character, are those of veneration for our forefathers and of love for our posterity.
JOHN QUINCY ADAMS

I never knew an early-rising, hard-working, prudent man, careful of his earnings and strictly honest, who complained of hard luck. A good character, good habits and iron industry are impregnable to the assaults of all ill-luck that fools ever dreamed.
JOSEPH ADDISON

Wherever man goes to dwell, his character goes with him.
AFRICAN PROVERB

The dearest to me are those of best character.
ARABIAN PROVERB

Character is that which reveals moral purpose, exposing the class of things a man chooses or avoids.
ARISTOTLE

Don't mistake personality for character.
WILMA ASKINAS

A character standard is far more important than ever a gold standard. The success of all economic systems is still dependent upon both righteous leaders and righteous people. In the last analysis, our national future depends upon our national character—that is, whether it is spiritually or materially minded.
ROGER W. BABSON

Courtesy, kindness, sincerity, truthfulness, thoughtfulness and good manners translated into behavior reflect one's true character.
HARRY F. BANKS

Character is a diamond that scratches every other stone.
CYRUS A. BARTOL

A man's ledger does not tell what he is, or what he is worth. Count what is in man, not what is on him, if you would know what he is worth—whether rich or poor.
HENRY WARD BEECHER

Good taste is better than bad taste, but bad taste is better than no taste.
ARNOLD BENNETT

Your greatness is measured by your kindness—
Your education and intellect by your modesty—
Your ignorance is betrayed by your suspicions and prejudices—
Your real caliber is measured by the consideration and tolerance you have for others.
WILLIAM J. H. BOETCKER

Some day, in years to come, you will be wrestling with the great temptation, or trembling under the great sorrow of your life. But the real struggle is here, now, in these quiet weeks. Now it is being decided whether, in the day of your supreme sorrow or temptation, you shall miserably fail or gloriously conquer. Character cannot be made except by a steady, long-continued process.
PHILLIPS BROOKS

Temperament we are born with, character we have to make; and that not in the grand moments . . . but in the daily, quiet paths of pilgrimage.
BALDWIN BROWN

It is fortunate to be of high birth, but it is no less to be of such character that people do not care to know whether you are or are not.
JEAN DE LA BRUYÈRE

It is an old saying, and one of fearful and fathomless import, that we are forming characters for eternity. Forming characters? Whose? Our own or others? Both—and in that momentous act lies the peril and responsibility of our existence.
ELIHU BURRITT

Character is formed, not by laws, commands, and decrees, but by quiet influence, unconscious suggestion and personal guidance.
MARION L. BURTON

Every man's work, whether it be literature or music or pictures or anything else, is always a portrait of himself, and the more he tries to conceal himself the more clearly will his character appear in spite of him.
SAMUEL BUTLER

Every human being is intended to have a character of his own; to be what no other is, and to do what no other can do.
WILLIAM ELLERY CHANNING

Every man is a volume, if you know how to read him.
WILLIAM ELLERY CHANNING

We never know a greater character unless there is in ourselves something congenial to it.
WILLIAM ELLERY CHANNING

In men of the highest character and noblest genius there is to be found an insatiable desire for honor, command, power, and glory.
CICERO

Before you are five and twenty you must establish a character that will serve you all your life.
LORD COLLINGWOOD

No man knows his true character until he has run out of gas, purchased something on the installment plan and raised an adolescent.
MARCELENE COX

Faced with crisis, the man of character falls back on himself.
CHARLES DE GAULLE

Characters never change. Opinions alter; characters are only developed.
BENJAMIN DISRAELI

Simplicity, honesty and sincerity are qualities that give character to people and to things produced by people.
WILLIAM FEATHER

Genuine good taste consists in saying much in few words, in choosing among our thoughts, in having order and arrangement in what we say, and in speaking with composure.
FRANÇOIS FÉNELON

You can easily judge the character of others by how they treat those who can do nothing for them or to them.
MALCOLM FORBES

Character is not made in a crisis—it is only exhibited.
ROBERT FREEMAN

You cannot dream yourself into a character; you must hammer and forge one for yourself.
J. A. FROUDE

Good taste is the modesty of the mind; that is why it cannot be either imitated or acquired.
EMILE DE GIRARDIN

It's only by the hard blows of adverse fortune that character is tooled.
ARNOLD GLASOW

A talent can be cultivated in tranquility; a character only in the rushing stream of life.
JOHANN WOLFGANG VON GOETHE

Nothing tells more about the character of a man than the things he makes fun of.
JOHANN WOLFGANG VON GOETHE

Talents are best nurtured in solitude; character is best formed in the stormy billows of the world.
JOHANN WOLFGANG VON GOETHE

People seldom improve when they have no other model but themselves to copy after.
OLIVER GOLDSMITH

You can cultivate taste, as you can the intellect. Full understanding whets the appetite and desire, and, later, sharpens the enjoyment of possession.
BALTASAR GRACIÁN

Fame is a vapor, popularity an accident, riches take wings. Only one thing endures, and that is character.
HORACE GREELEY

In judging character, too often we mistake rigidity for morality.
JOHN P. GRIER

How you react when the joke's on you can reveal your character.
ROBERT HALF

Character is the real foundation of all worthwhile success.
JOHN HAYS HAMMOND

A good name is seldom regained. When character is gone, all is gone, and one of the richest jewels of life is lost forever.
JOEL HAWES

Character is destiny.
HERACLITUS

We the people give our nation its character—and character flaws.
CULLEN HIGHTOWER

Character is power; it makes friends, draws patronage and support, and opens a sure way to wealth, honor and happiness.
JOHN HOWE

Only what we have wrought into our character during life can we take way with us.
ALEXANDER VON HUMBOLDT

The character that needs law to mend it is hardly worth the tinkering.
DOUGLAS WILLIAM JERROLD

Every man has three characters—that which he exhibits, that which he has, and that which he thinks he has.
ALPHONSE KARR

Men are not to be judged by their looks, habits, and appearances; but by the character of their lives and conversations, and by their works. It is better to be praised by one's own works than by the words of another.
ROGER L'ESTRANGE

You can never have a greater or a less dominion than over yourself.
LEONARDO DA VINCI

Underneath this flabby exterior is an enormous lack of character.
OSCAR LEVANT

Personality can open doors, but only character can keep them open.
ELMER G. LETERMAN

You cannot build character and courage by taking away man's initiative and independence.
ABRAHAM LINCOLN

The measure of a man's real character is what he would do if he knew he would never be found out.
THOMAS B. MACAULAY

The experience of the ages that are past, the hopes of the ages that are yet to come, unite their voices in an appeal to us; they implore us to think more of the character of our people than of its vast numbers; to look upon our vast natural resources, not as tempters to ostentation and pride, but as means to be converted, by the refining alchemy of education, into mental and spiritual treasures—and thus give to the world the example of a nation whose wisdom increases with its prosperity, and whose virtues are equal to its power.
HORACE MANN

Get to know two things about a man—how he earns his money and how he spends it—and you have the clue to his character, for you have a searchlight that shows up the inmost recesses of his soul. You know all you need to know about his standards, his motives, his driving desires, his real religion.
ROBERT J. MCCRACKEN

The goods of Fortune, even such as they really are, still need taste to enjoy them. It is the enjoying not the possessing, that makes us happy.
MICHELANGELO

A man's reputation is the opinion people have of him; his character is what he really is.
JACK MINER

If I take care of my character, my reputation will take care of itself.
DWIGHT MOODY

**The Man You Are**

It isn't the man that you might have been
Had the chance been yours again,
Nor the prize you wanted but didn't win
That weighs in the measure of men.
No futile "if" or poltroon "because"
Can rowel your stock to par.
The world cares naught for what never was—
It judges by what you are.

It isn't the man that you hope to be,
If fortune and fate are kind,
That the chill, keen eyes of the world will see
In weighing your will and mind.
The years ahead are a chartless sea,
And tomorrow's a world away;
It isn't the man that you'd like to be,
But the man that you are today.

There's little worth in the phantom praise
Of a time that may never dawn,
And less in a vain regret for days
And deeds long buried and gone.
There's little time on this busy earth
To argue the why and how.
The game is yours if you prove your worth,
And prove it here and now!
TED OLSEN

Character development is the great, if not the sole, aim of education.
WILLIAM O'SHEA

The force, the mass of character, mind, heart or soul that a man can put into any work is the most important factor in that work.
A. P. PEABODY

The highest of characters is his who is as ready to pardon the moral errors of mankind as if he were every day guilty of them himself; and as cautious of committing a fault as if he never forgave one.
PLINY THE YOUNGER

The real judges of your character aren't your neighbors, your relatives, or even the people you play bridge with. The folks who really know you are the waiters and clerks.
KATHERINE PIPER

The character we exhibit in the latter half of our life need not necessarily be, though it often is, our original character, developed further, dried up, exaggerated, or diminished. It can be its exact opposite, like a suit worn inside out.
MARCEL PROUST

It is sometimes frightening to observe the success which comes even to the outlaw with a polished technique, and we find ourselves doubting the validity of the virtues we have been taught. But I believe we must reckon with character in the end, for it is as potent a force in world conflict as it is in our own domestic affairs. It strikes the last blow in any battle.
PHILIP D. REED

We cannot easily discover our real character from a friend. He is a mirror, on which the warmth of our breath impedes the clearness of the reflection.
JEAN PAUL RICHTER

There is a kind of revolution of so general a character that it changes the tastes as well as the fortunes of the world.
FRANÇOIS DE LA ROCHEFOUCAULD

The most important thing for a young man is to establish a credit—a reputation, character.
JOHN D. ROCKEFELLER

I care not what others think of what I do, but I care very much about what I think of what I do: That is character!
THEODORE ROOSEVELT

Character is the foundation stone upon which one must build to win respect. Just as no worthy building can be erected on a weak foundation, so no lasting reputation worthy of respect can be built on a weak character. Without character, all effort to attain dignity is superficial, and results are sure to be disappointing.
R. C. SAMSEL

Men best show their character in trifles, where they are not on guard. It is in insignificant matters, and in the simplest habits, that we often see the boundless egotism which pays no regard to the feelings of others, and denies nothing to itself.
ARTHUR SCHOPENHAUER

To wilful men, the injuries that they themselves procure must be their schoolmasters.
WILLIAM SHAKESPEARE

Our success in war and peace depends not on luck, or rhetoric, or the intervention of mythical gods; it depends on human character and modern scientific creations, and on respect for the meaning and methods of science. . . . It is not luck but logic which in the present and future will win—the careful and log-

ical consideration of what effects come from specific causes, what are the natural reasons behind events, what are the processes required to adapt nature to the material and spiritual advantages of mankind.
**HARLOW SHAPLEY**

It seems that the analysis of character is the highest human entertainment. And literature does it, unlike gossip, without mentioning names.
**ISAAC BASHEVIS SINGER**

To be worth anything, character must be capable of standing firm upon its feet in the world of daily work, temptation and trial.
**SAMUEL SMILES**

A man has no more character than he can command in a time of crisis.
**RALPH W. SOCKMAN**

Not education, but character is man's greatest need—and man's greatest safeguard.
**HERBERT SPENCER**

Society asks of most men more than sheer intellect ability—it demands also moral hardiness, self-discipline, a competitive spirit and other qualities that in more old-fashioned terms we might simply call character.
**JULIUS ADAMS STRATTON**

Fame is what you have taken, character is what you give. When to this truth you awaken, then you begin to live.
**BAYARD TAYLOR**

Nature has written a letter of credit upon some men's faces that is honored wherever presented. You cannot help trusting such men. Their very presence gives confidence. There is promise to pay in their faces which gives confidence and you prefer it to another man's endorsement. Character is credit.
**WILLIAM MAKEPEACE THACKERAY**

The character of a generation is moulded by personal character.
**BROOKE FOSS WESTCOTT**

Character and personal force are the only investments that are worth anything.
**WALT WHITMAN**

The noblest contribution which any man can make for the benefit of posterity, is that of character. The richest bequest which any man can leave to the youth of his native land, is that of a shining, spotless example.
**ROBERT C. WINTHROP**

A man is the part he plays among his fellows. He is not isolated; he cannot be. His life is made up of the relations he bears to others—is made or marred by those relations, guided by them, judged by them, expressed in them. There is nothing else upon which he can spend his spirit—nothing else that we can see. It is by these he gets his spiritual growth; it is by these we see his character revealed, his purpose, his gifts. A few (men) act as those who have mastered the secrets of a serious art, with deliberate subordination of themselves to the great end and motive of the play. These have found themselves, and have all the ease of a perfect adjustment.
**WOODROW WILSON**

Character is a by-product; it is produced in the great manufacture of daily duty
**WOODROW WILSON**

## Charity

Charity brings to life again those who are spiritually dead.
THOMAS AQUINAS

Charity makes no decrease in property.
ARABIAN PROVERB

The unfortunate need people who will be kind to them; the prosperous need people to be kind to.
ARISTOTLE

It is heaven upon earth to have a man's mind move in charity, rest in providence and turn upon the poles of truth.
FRANCIS BACON

The best thing to give to your enemy is forgiveness; to an opponent, tolerance; to a friend, your heart; to your child, a good example; to a father, deference; to your mother, conduct that will make her proud of you; to yourself, respect; to all men, charity.
LORD BALFOUR

The charities of life are scattered everywhere, enameling the vales of human beings as the flowers paint the meadows. They are not the fruit of study, nor the privilege of refinement, but a natural instinct.
GEORGE BANCROFT

In necessary things, unity; in doubtful things, liberty; in all things, charity.
RICHARD BAXTER

The spirit of the world has four kinds of spirits diametrically opposed to charity—resentment, aversion, jealousy, and indifference.
JACQUES BOSSUET

Having leveled my palace, don't erect a hovel and complacently admire your own charity in giving me that for a home.
EMILY BRONTË

Did universal charity prevail, earth would be a heaven and hell a fable.
CHARLES CALEB COLTON

Public charities and benevolent associations for the gratuitous relief of every species of distress, are peculiar to Christianity; no other system of civil or religious policy has originated them; they form its highest praise and characteristic feature.
CHARLES CALEB COLTON

And though I have the gift of prophecy, and understand all mysteries, and all knowledge; and though I have all faith, so that I could remove mountains, and have not charity, I am nothing.
I CORINTHIANS 13:2

Though I speak with the tongues of men and of angels, and have not charity, I am as sounding brass, or a tinkling cymbal.
I CORINTHIANS 13:1

He who has no charity deserves no mercy.
ENGLISH PROVERB

Be charitable in your thoughts, in your speech and in your actions. Be charitable in your judgments, in your attitudes and in your prayers. Think charitably of your friends, your neighbors, your relatives and even your enemies. And if there be those whom you can help in a material way, do so in a quiet, friendly, neighborly way, as if it were the most common and everyday experience for you. Tongues of men and angels, gifts of prophecy and all mysteries and all knowledge are as nothing without charity.
CARDINAL HAYES

Bounty always receives part of its value from the manner in which it is bestowed.
**SAMUEL JOHNSON**

You are much surer that you are doing good when you pay money to those who work, as the recompense of their labors, than when you give money merely in charity.
**SAMUEL JOHNSON**

Be charitable and indulgent to everyone but yourself.
**JOSEPH JOUBERT**

He is truly great who hath a great charity.
**THOMAS À KEMPIS**

Every good act is charity. Your smiling in your brother's face, is charity; an exhortation of your fellowman to virtuous deeds, is equal to alms-giving; your putting a wanderer in the right road, is charity; your assisting the blind, is charity; your removing stones, and thorns, and other obstructions from the road, is charity; your giving water to the thirsty, is charity. A man's true wealth hereafter, is the good he does in this world to his fellow-man. "When he dies, people will say, What property has he left behind him?" But the angels will ask, "What good deeds has he sent before him?"
**MAHOMET**

Charity... is kind, it is not easily provok'd, it thinks no evil, it believes all things, hopes all things.
**COTTON MATHER**

They should be first among all, who contribute most to the good of all.
**GIUSEPPI MAZZINI**

The soldier who dies to save his brothers reaches the highest of all degrees of charity, and this is the virtue of a single act of charity: It cancels a whole lifetime of sin.
**CARDINAL MERCIER**

As for charity, it is a matter in which the immediate effect on the persons directly concerned, and the ultimate consequence to the general good, are apt to be at complete war with one another.
**JOHN STUART MILL**

The charitable give out at the door, and God puts in at the window.
**JOHN RAY**

Charity is injurious unless it helps the recipient to become independent of it.
**JOHN D. ROCKEFELLER, JR.**

Charity begins at hame, but shouldna end there.
**SCOTTISH PROVERB**

Our true acquisitions lie only in our charities, we get only as we give.
**WILLIAM SIMMS**

You have not lived a perfect day, even though you have earned your money, unless you have done something for someone who will never be able to repay you.
**RUTH SMELTZER**

That charity is bad which takes from independence its proper pride, and from mendicity its proper shame.
**ROBERT SOUTHEY**

While actions are always to be judged by the immutable standard of right and wrong, and judgments we pass upon men must be qualified by considerations of age, country, station and other accidental circumstances; and it will then be found

that he who is most charitable in his judgment is generally the least unjust.
**ROBERT SOUTHEY**

Charity is to will and do what is just and right in every transaction.
**EMANUEL SWEDENBORG**

He who has never denied himself for the sake of giving, has but glanced at the joys of charity.
**ANNE SWETCHINE**

People that trust wholly to others' charity, and without industry of their own, will always be poor.
**WILLIAM J. TEMPLE**

The eyes of America are on the future; but what use is that if those eyes are blinded? Unless we build our social structure to-day upon a more permanent foundation than the past it will not last beyond the lifetime of those who founded it. Charity, the realization of our brotherhood in God, is the only enduring foundation.
**ROBERT E. WOODS, D.D.**

## *Cheerfulness*

The cheerful live longest in years, and afterwards in our regard. Cheerfulness is the offshoot of goodness.
**CHRISTIAN BOVÉE**

I am glad I am an optimist. The pessimist is half-licked before he starts. . . . The optimist may not understand, or if he understands he may not agree with, prevailing ideas; but he believes, yes, knows, that in the long run and in due course there will prevail whatever is right and best.
**THOMAS A. BUCKNER**

Youth must be optimistic. Optimism is essential to achievement and it is also the foundation of courage and of true progress.
**NICHOLAS MURRAY BUTLER**

The optimist says we live in the best of all possible worlds; the pessimist fears this is true.
**JAMES BRANCH CABELL**

Wondrous is the strength of cheerfulness, and its power of endurance—the cheerful man will do more in the same time, will do it better, will persevere in it longer, than the sad or sullen.
**THOMAS CARLYLE**

Most of the troubles of humanity are imaginary and should be laughed out of court. It is folly to cross a bridge until you come to it, or to bid the Devil good-morning until you meet him—perfect folly. All is well until the stroke falls, and even then, nine times out of ten, it is not so bad as anticipated. A wise man is the confirmed optimist.
**ANDREW CARNEGIE**

Humanity never produces optimists till it has ceased to produce happy men.
**G. K. CHESTERTON**

You will find yourself refreshed by the presence of cheerful people. Why not make earnest effort to confer that pleasure on others? You will find half the battle is gained if you never allow yourself to say anything gloomy.
**LYDIA M. CHILD**

Do not trust to the cheering, for those very persons would shout as much if you and I were going to be hanged.
**OLIVER CROMWELL**

Optimism, unaccompanied by personal effort, is merely a state of mind and not fruitful.
EDWARD L. CURTIS

I feel an earnest and humble desire, and shall do till I die, to increase the stock of harmless cheerfulness.
CHARLES DICKENS

I have tried in my time to be a philosopher, but cheerfulness was always breaking in.
OLIVER EDWARDS

Exactness in little duties is a wonderful source of cheerfulness.
FREDERICK WILLIAM FABER

Promotion awaits the employee who radiates cheerfulness, not the employee who spreads gloom and dissatisfaction.

Doctors tell us that cheerfulness is an invaluable aid to health.

Cheerfulness is also an invaluable aid to promotion.
B. C. FORBES

When I dictated that headline ["Cultivate Cheerfulness"] to my secretary, she ejaculated: "Oh! You have already written on this subject."

I have, of that I am very well aware. But the importance of developing a cheerful attitude impresses me more and more with every passing decade. Life, in a sense, is mentally what you make it. I pity anyone who is chronically a grouch, pessimistic, discontented. A cheerful frame of mind is like church-going, largely a matter of habit; if you develop a morose attitude, the chances are that you will persist in it, just as if you get into the habit of going to church you continue to go....
B. C. FORBES (LAST EDITORIAL)

Nature intended you to be the fountain spring of cheerfulness and social life and not the monument of despair and melancholy.
ARTHUR HELPS

Many of the optimists in the world don't own a hundred dollars, and because of their optimism never will.
EDGAR WATSON HOWE

Optimism is a kind of heart stimulus—the digitalis of failure.
ELBERT HUBBARD

If you cheerfully bear your cross, it will bear you.
THOMAS À KEMPIS

The plainest sign of wisdom is continual cheerfulness; her state is like that of things in the regions above the moon, always clear and serene.
MICHEL DE MONTAIGNE

There is nothing more beautiful than cheerfulness in an old face.
JEAN PAUL RICHTER

To love all mankind, a cheerful state of being is required.
JEAN PAUL RICHTER

Cheerfulness is as natural to the heart of a man in strong health as color to his cheek; and wherever there is habitual gloom there must be either bad air, unwholesome food, improperly severe labor, or erring habits of life.
JOHN RUSKIN

He who remains cheerful in spirit and sees only the good side of all things, who never allows himself to be spiritually downcast but keeps his head high and courage in his heart, he sets in motion those fine,

still powers, which make every step through life easier for him.
RALPH WALDO TRINE

There is no personal charm so great as the charm of a cheerful temperament. It is a great error to suppose this comes entirely by nature—it comes quite as much by culture.
HENRY VAN DYKE

The world of achievement has always belonged to the optimist.
J. HAROLD WILKENS

## *Children*

Blessed be childhood, which brings down something of heaven into the midst of our rough earthliness.
HENRI FRÉDÉRIC AMIEL

Her little girl was late arriving home from school, so the mother began to scold her:

"Why are you so late?"

"I had to help another girl. She was in trouble."

"What did you do to help her?"

"Oh, I sat down and helped her cry."

ANONYMOUS

Teenagers are people who express a burning desire to be different by dressing exactly alike.
ANONYMOUS

The easy way to teach children the value of money is to borrow from them.
ANONYMOUS

The life of children, as much as that of intemperate men, is wholly governed by their desires.
ARISTOTLE

Children have never been very good at listening to their elders, but they have never failed to imitate them.
JAMES BALDWIN

Badgered, snubbed and scolded on the one hand; petted, flattered and indulged on the other—it is astonishing how many children work their way up to an honest manhood in spite of parents and friends. Human nature has an element of great toughness in it.
HENRY WARD BEECHER

To bring up a child in the way he should go, travel that way yourself once in a while.
JOSH BILLINGS

Never lend your car to anyone to whom you have given birth.
ERMA BOMBECK

Men profess a total lack of ability to wash baby's face simply because they believe there's no great fun in the business, at either end of the sponge.
HEYWOOD BROUN

Children enjoy the present because they have neither a past nor a future.
JEAN DE LA BRUYÈRE

If we had paid no more attention to our plants than we have to our children, we would now be living in a jungle of weed.
LUTHER BURBANK

Baseball may be the nation's game
With throw and run and hit;
But first among the skills, it seems,
Is learning how to spit.
ART BUCK

How soon do we forget
What elders used to know:
That children should be raised,
Not left like weeds to grow.
**ART BUCK**

Human life is cheapened
By a careless, unplanned start:
It's like a bread-line ration
When it should be à la carte.
**ART BUCK**

Sing not of birthing joys,
Mourn not the totless knee;
For every child that's born
Makes each of us less free.
**ART BUCK**

Too many innocent children are victims of preventable diseases—like being born.
**ART BUCK**

Children feel the whiteness of the lily with a graphic and passionate clearness which we cannot give them at all. The only thing we can give them is information—the information that if you break the lily in two it won't grow again.
**G. K. CHESTERTON**

A child's life is like a piece of paper on which every passerby leaves a mark.
**CHINESE PROVERB**

When I was a child, I spake as a child, I understood as a child, I thought as a child: but when I became a man, I put away childish things.
**I CORINTHIANS 13:11**

If you have never been hated by a child, you have never been a parent.
**BETTE DAVIS**

Who takes a child by the hand takes the mother by the heart.
**DANISH PROVERB**

The intimation never wholly deserts us that there is, in the unformed activities of childhood and youth, the possibilities of a better life for the community as well as for individuals here and there. This dim sense is the ground of our abiding idealization of childhood.
**JOHN DEWEY**

My hair stands on end at the cost and charges of these boys. Why was I ever a father! Why was my father ever a father!
**CHARLES DICKENS**

Cleaning your house while your kids are still growing is like shoveling the walk before it stops snowing.
**PHYLLIS DILLER**

If you want to see what children can do, you must stop giving them things.
**NORMAN DOUGLAS**

I've learned that my daddy can say a lot of words that I can't.
**8-YEAR-OLD'S DISCOVERY**

There never was a child so lovely but that his mother was glad to get him asleep.
**RALPH WALDO EMERSON**

Children are poor men's riches.
**ENGLISH PROVERB**

Any man who hates children can't be all bad.
**W. C. FIELDS**

Upon our children—how they are taught—rests the fate—or fortune—of tomorrow's world.
**B. C. FORBES**

Re raising kids: Love, without discipline, isn't.
**MALCOLM FORBES**

Speaking of birthdays, our firstborn [recently] turned 2. As parents sometimes fondly do, we reminisced a bit about his early days on earth—the excitement, the wonder, the fears when we brought him home. His every squeak or squawk we were sure heralded some terrible crisis; I tested the warmth of formulas from dusk to dawn, it seemed. We were so germ-conscious my wife even sterilized the skin of the oranges before squeezing them. How firstborns ever survive their parents' attentions is beyond me. However, they do, and he did, and, in spite of our efforts, he turned out to be quite a good guy.
**MALCOLM FORBES**

The other evening around 10 p.m. we were finishing dinner in a fine, famed San Francisco restaurant, when a relatively young parental pair came in with youngsters—two girls about nine and seven, and a boy of about five or six. The boy had on long pants and a bow tie and the girls were dressed like you'd think middle teenagers might be—in high heels and so forth. It always seems to me such a waste, such a missing of the point . . . There's a time—all too brief as it too soon becomes apparent to parents—to be little; a time to be in between; and a time to be old. Let each have its season . . . Let the little be little.
**MALCOLM FORBES**

I've learned that it's easier to stay out of trouble than to get out of trouble.
**14-YEAR OLD'S DISCOVERY**

I've learned that if your teenager doesn't think you're a real embarrassment and a hard-nosed bore, you're probably not doing your job.
**44-YEAR OLD'S DISCOVERY**

There were giants in the earth in those days; and also after that, when the sons of God came in unto the daughters of men, and they bare children to them, the same became mighty men which were of old, men of renown.
**GENESIS 6:4**

Children, love one another, and if that is not possible—at least try to put up with one another.
**JOHANN WOLFGANG VON GOETHE**

Before puberty the child's personality has not yet formed, and it is easier to guide its life and make it acquire specific habits of order, discipline, and work: after puberty the personality develops impetuously, and all extraneous intervention becomes odious, tyrannical, insufferable.
**ANTONIO GRAMSCI**

We try to make our children become more like us, instead of trying to become more like them—with the result that we pick up none of their good traits, and they pick up most of our bad ones.
**SYDNEY J. HARRIS**

Do not handicap your children by making their lives easy.
**ROBERT A. HEINLEIN**

The first service a child doth his father is to make him foolish.
**GEORGE HERBERT**

Adolescence is the period of life when we first become obsessed with trying to prove we are not a child—an obsession that can last a lifetime.
**CULLEN HIGHTOWER**

Every adult should be an expert on teenagers, after spending life's seven longest years being one.
CULLEN HIGHTOWER

The antidote for crime should be administered in childhood, by the parents. The problem is not fundamentally that of the improper child so much as it is that of the improper home.
JUSTICE JOHN W. HILL

Pretty much all the honest truthtelling there is in the world is done by children.
OLIVER WENDELL HOLMES

**Bill of Rights for Boys**

1. Like everybody else, a boy has a right to the pursuit of happiness.
2. He has a right to play so that he may stretch the imagination and prove his prowess and skill.
3. He has a right to the constructive joys of adventure, and the thrill that are a part of an open life.
4. He has a right to affection and friendship.
5. He has a right to the sense of security in belonging to some group.
6. He has a right to health protections that will make him an inch taller than his dad.
7. He has a right to the education and training that will amplify his own natural bents.
8. He has a right to accept the obligations of citizenship in a democracy—perhaps the greatest right a boy, or anyone else, can have.

HERBERT HOOVER

The glory of the nation rests in the character of her men. And character comes from boyhood. Thus every boy is a challenge to his elders. It is for them that we must win the war—it is for them that we must make a just and lasting peace. For the world of tomorrow, about which all of us are dreaming and planning, will be carried forward by the boys of today.
HERBERT HOOVER

All persons who bear the blessed title of parent have the personal responsibility to see that their children are growing up fully appreciative of the rights of God and their fellowmen.
J. EDGAR HOOVER

Juvenile delinquency can be prevented. It is not a scourge which rules with an inevitable necessity. One of the best weapons with which to attack this malady is religious training. The young boy and girl trained in the teachings of the Bible have a moral reliance which serves as a compass for everyday living. They know the difference between right and wrong, good and evil. They are able to conquer the temptations of life.
J. EDGAR HOOVER

We like little children, because they tear out as soon as they get what they want.
KIN HUBBARD

Being a good psychoanalyst has the same disadvantage as being a good parent: The children desert one as they grow up.
MORTON HUNT

Children are remarkable for their intelligence and ardor, for their curiosity, their intolerance of shams, the clarity and ruthlessness of their vision.
ALDOUS HUXLEY

Blessed be the hand that prepares a pleasure for a child, for there is no saying when and where it may bloom forth.
DOUGLAS WILLIAM JERROLD

You teach your daughters the diameters of the planets, and wonder when they have done that they do not delight in your company.
SAMUEL JOHNSON

Boys are the building blocks of a nation. The man who gives a boy a helping hand is therefore building sound foundations for the future.
PAUL MARTIN

Nothing you do for children is ever wasted. They seem not to notice us, hovering, averting our eyes, and they seldom offer thanks, but what we do for them is never wasted.
GARRISON KEILLOR

Our greatest obligation to our children is to prepare them to understand and to deal effectively with the world in which they will live and not with the world we have known or the world we would prefer to have.
GRAYSON KIRK

In the final analysis it is not what you do for your children but what you have taught them to do for themselves that will make them successful human beings.
ANN LANDERS

Only two kids enjoy high school. One is the captain of the football team. The other is his girlfriend.
LETTER TO ANN LANDERS

The secret of dealing successfully with a child is not to be its parent.
MELL LAZARUS

Ask your child what he wants for dinner only if he's buying.
FRAN LEBOWITZ

Children make the most desirable opponents in Scrabble, as they are both easy to beat and fun to cheat.
FRAN LEBOWITZ

Remember that as a teenager you are in the last stage of your life when you will be happy to hear the phone is for you.
FRAN LEBOWITZ

The challenge of the midcentury is to find—for our own children and, through international cooperation, for the children of the world—the means by which they can be helped to develop their fullest powers for creative living. Only in this way can we help to build the kind of world in which an enduring peace, with freedom and justice for all, will be achieved.
KATHARINE F. LENROOT

A child is a person who is going to carry on what you have started . . . the fate of humanity is in his hands.
ABRAHAM LINCOLN

Lending money to your children is comparable to a bank lending money to a Third World country: You never get the interest back, let alone the principal.
J. L. LONG

As we look to the future we realize that the child is the key to peace. How he grows, the personality he develops, the attitude he acquires, the knowledge and the experience he has—all determine how successfully he will live with others in this rapidly shrinking world.
LYDIA ANN LYNDE

She discovered with great delight that one does not love one's children just because they are one's chil-

dren but because of the friendship formed while raising them.
**GABRIEL GARCÍA MÁRQUEZ**

When their children fail to charm others, few parents can stay neutral.
**MIGNON MCLAUGHLIN**

Childhood is the kingdom where nobody dies.
**EDNA ST. VINCENT MILLAY**

The best way to keep children at home is to make the home atmosphere pleasant, and let the air out of the tires.
**DOROTHY PARKER**

The elements of instruction should be presented to the mind in childhood, but not with any compulsion.
**PLATO**

Children's children are the crown of old men; and the glory of children are their fathers.
**PROVERBS 17:6**

Train up a child in the way he should go: and when he is old, he will not depart from it.
**PROVERBS 22:6**

A child may have too much of his mother's blessing.
**JOHN RAY**

The conscience of children is formed by the influences that surround them; their notions of good and evil are the result of the moral atmosphere they breathe.
**JEAN PAUL RICHTER**

The words that a father speaks to his children in the privacy of home are not heard by the world, but, as in whispering galleries, they are clearly heard at the end, and by posterity.
**JEAN PAUL RICHTER**

For unflagging interest and enjoyment, a household of children, if things go reasonably well, certainly makes all other forms of success and achievement lose their importance by comparison.
**THEODORE ROOSEVELT**

The first thing a child should learn is how to endure. It is what he will have most need to know.
**JEAN-JACQUES ROUSSEAU**

How pleasant it is for a father to sit at his child's board. It is like an aged man reclining under the shadow of an oak which he has planted.
**SIR WALTER SCOTT**

A child hasn't a grown-up person's appetite for affection. A little of it goes a long way with them; and they like a good imitation of it better than the real thing, as every nurse knows.
**GEORGE BERNARD SHAW**

I've learned that when you put a June bug down a girl's dress, she goes crazy.
**6-YEAR-OLD'S DISCOVERY**

I've learned that if you spread the peas out on your plate, it looks like you ate more.
**6-YEAR-OLD'S DISCOVERY**

I've learned that you can't hide a piece of broccoli in a glass of milk.
**7-YEAR-OLD'S DISCOVERY**

It sometimes happens, even in the best of families, that a baby is born. This is not necessarily a cause

for alarm. The important thing is to keep your wits about you and borrow some money.
ELINOR GOULDING SMITH

What is more enchanting than the voices of young people when you can't hear what they say?
LOGAN PEARSALL SMITH

I do not love him because he is good, but because he is my little child.
RABINDRANATH TAGORE

If you wish to study men you must not neglect to mix with the society of children.
JESSE TORREY

I've learned that people without children always know just how you should raise yours.
29-YEAR-OLD'S DISCOVERY

Children begin by loving their parents. After a time they judge them. Rarely, if ever, do they forgive them.
OSCAR WILDE

I am convinced that, except in a few extraordinary cases, one form or another of an unhappy childhood is essential to the formation of exceptional gifts.
THORNTON WILDER

## *Choice*

There is no better measure of a person than what he does when he is absolutely free to choose.
WILMA ASKINAS

If we choose to be no more than clods of clay, then we shall be used as clods of clay for braver feet to tread on.
MARIE CORELLI

More errors arise from inhibited indecision than from impulsive behavior.
MORRIS L. ERNST

Indecision is debilitating; it feeds upon itself; it is, one might almost say, habit-forming. Not only that, but it is contagious; it transmits itself to others. . . . Business is dependent upon action. It cannot go forward by hesitation. Those in executive positions must fortify themselves with facts and accept responsibility for decisions based upon them. Often greater risk is involved in postponement than making a wrong decision.
HARRY A. HOPF

Very few live by choice. Every man is placed in his present condition by causes which acted without his foresight, and with which he did not always willingly cooperate; and therefore you will rarely meet one who does not think the lot of his neighbor better than his own.
SAMUEL JOHNSON

The measure of choosing well, is, whether a man likes and finds good in what he has chosen.
CHARLES LAMB

There is no good in arguing with the inevitable. The only argument available with an east wind is to put on your overcoat.
JAMES RUSSELL LOWELL

There is absolutely no inevitability as long as there is a willingness to contemplate what is happening.
MARSHALL MCLUHAN

You seldom get what you go after unless you know in advance what you want. Indecision has often given an advantage to the other fellow because he did his thinking beforehand.
MAURICE SWITZER

Choose always the way that seems the best, however rough it may be; custom will soon render it easy and agreeable.
**PYTHAGORAS**

My own view of history is that human beings do have genuine freedom to make choices. Our destiny is not predetermined for us; we determine it for ourselves.
**ARNOLD TOYNBEE**

The moment a question comes to your mind, see yourself mentally taking hold of it and disposing of it. In that moment is your choice made. Thus you learn to take the path to the right. Thus you learn to become the decider and not the vacillator. Thus you build character.
**H. VAN ANDERSON**

I don't think suicide is so terrible. Some rainy winter Sundays when there's a little boredom, you should always carry a gun. Not to shoot yourself, but to know exactly that you're always making a choice.
**LINA WERTMULLER**

Between two evils I always pick the one I never tried before.
**MAE WEST**

The more decisions that you are forced to make alone, the more you are aware of your freedom to choose.
**THORNTON WILDER**

## *Christianity*

Christ had something to say about economics. He said, "Lay not up your treasures on earth, but lay them up in heaven." Today, because we have laid up no treasure in heaven, we are in danger of losing what we have laid up on earth. Unless we rebuild God in our hearts we will never rebuild and reconstruct the world.
**HUMPHREY BEEVER, D.D.**

Scriptures: The sacred books of our holy religion, as distinguished from the false and profane writings on which all other faiths are based.
**AMBROSE BIERCE**

Emphasis on educational and vocational rehabilitation must not be allowed to overshadow the profound need that will exist for spiritual reorientation. Inevitably there will exist, to a considerable degree, psychological maladjustments manifested in disillusionment, resentment toward civilians, depression, and a sense of guilt. Spiritual therapy available in the resources of the Christian faith can accomplish most in overcoming these problems.
**JOHN S. BONNELL, D.D.**

No man or woman has achieved an effective personality who is not self-disciplined. Such discipline must not be an end in itself, but must be directed to the development of resolute Christian character.
**JOHN S. BONNELL, D.D.**

Independent of its connection with human destiny hereafter, the fate of republican government is indissolubly bound up with the fate of the Christian religion, and a people who reject its holy faith will find themselves the slaves of their own evil passions and of arbitrary power.
**LEWIS CASS**

A Christian is perpetually balanced between a Christian ideal of loving his enemies, a pagan ideal of punishing his enemies, and a chivalric ideal of only fighting his enemies fairly.
**G. K. CHESTERTON**

He who begins by loving Christianity better than truth will proceed by loving his own sect better than Christianity and end in loving himself better than all.
**SAMUEL TAYLOR COLERIDGE**

I cannot think that any man could ever tower upward into a very great philosopher unless he should begin or end with Christianity. A great man may, by a rare possibility, be an infidel. An intellect of the highest order must build on Christianity.
**THOMAS DE QUINCEY**

Remove the Christian Sabbath and the entire cathedral of our religion will ultimately crash into ruins. Take away the observance of the Sabbath and all the pillars of civilization will crumble and the human soul will atrophy and wither and men will degenerate into barbarians and beasts.
**HAROLD C. DEWINDT**

Some morning it is likely that the headlines of the world will scream forth the news that New York has been bombed. As tragic as this will be, it will nevertheless accomplish the deep unity that Christians should have. It is a sad commentary that our brotherhood, which exists by Christian love, is only truly cemented by Christian suffering.
**JAMES P. DE WOLFE, D.D.**

No one is without Christianity, if we agree on what we mean by the word. It is every individual's individual code of behavior by means of which he makes himself a better human being than his nature wants to be, if he followed his nature only.
**WILLIAM FAULKNER**

Christianity is no holiday parade. It sometimes means warfare, and first, last and always it means discipline. No religion has any integrity unless born of sacrifice.
**FREDERIC S. FLEMING**

A religion which does not enrich and enlarge life here and now, which denies rewards for worthiness this side of the grave, is not worthwhile, has not and should not have an irresistible appeal to a normally minded human being. Such was totally different from the brand of religion Christ enunciated, I am profoundly convinced. The Old Country concentrated mainly on the Old Testament. The New Testament fits better into the New World and the new day. It offers life more abundant, joy, peace, hope, unfailing and unstinted rewards here below.
**B. C. FORBES**

Before Christmas I was tempted to write this editorial but resisted for fear it would be misinterpreted. Despite all the plausible and applauded company programs against gift getting and giving by those who do business with one another, and despite Internal Revenue's ceiling on the value of presents, I still like the custom.... Across my desk come wonderful calendars, occasionally ashtrays, and other office-usable things. I don't feel bribed. I don't feel bought. I feel thought of. And I like it.
**MALCOLM FORBES**

He who shall introduce into public affairs the principles of primitive Christianity will change the face of the world.
**BENJAMIN FRANKLIN**

There is neither Jew nor Greek, there is neither bond nor free, there is neither male nor female: for ye are all one in Christ Jesus. And if ye be Christ's, then are ye Abraham's seed, and heirs according to the promise.
**GALATIANS 3:28-29**

It is a serious misunderstanding of Christ's and t he apostles' injunctions to aim at establishing and building up the Kingdom of God by political means. The only forces which this Kingdom knows are

religious and moral forces, and it rests on a basis of freedom.
**ADOLPH HARNACK**

Without true Christian principles, conservatism is a political philosophy of selfishness and liberalism is one of greed.
**THOMAS C. JEFFERY**

Christianity, as it cannot too strongly be stated, is not committed to any political system or form of government.
**RAYMOND C. KNOX**

The Christian faith is not one of cold intellect; rather it is full of love, grace and humanity. It has the strength and compassion with which Christ was able to change the course of human life from evil to good, from selfishness to service, from despair to faith in the highest.
**WILLIAM T. MANNING, D.D.**

We must acknowledge that there is such a thing as the pleasures of sin—temptation would not be so strong if this were not true. The answer is to make our love of God stronger than all temptation, and in that way to lead the good Christian life.
**PETER MARSHALL**

Christ didn't waste His time-trying to change the social order. Christ spent all His time fighting sin. Therefore it behooves the witnesses of Christ to say that we do not have to abolish capitalism and establish socialism or communism, that sin can flourish under those systems as well. Christianity is not opposed to any social order, but to sin.
**JOHN H. MCCOMB, D.D.**

It is true that we have not deliberately or wholly abandoned the Christian element in our tradition, but does that element count with us as it once did? Is the moral tone of the nation—its politics, its business life, its literature, its theatre, its movies, its radio networks, its television stations—Christian?
**ROBERT J. MCCRACKEN**

The Sermon on the Mount does not provide humanity with a complete guide to personal, social and economic problems. It sets forth spiritual attitudes, moral principles of universal validity, such as "Love your enemies," "Whatsoever ye would that men should do to you, do ye even so to them," and it leaves to Christians the task—the admittedly difficult task—of applying them in any given situation.
**ROBERT J. MCCRACKEN**

The ideas of man's inalienable rights of human dignity, freedom and democracy are direct products of the Christian way of life. The Christian religion is the tree upon which these fruits have grown. Christian propaganda must go on if the new world is to be righteous.
**RALPH S. MEADOWCROFT**

The service of the Christian religion and my own faith in essential Christianity would not be diminished one iota if it should in some way be discovered that no such individual as Jesus existed.
**ROBERT A. MILLIKAN**

We should seek to emulate Christ's virtue, and seek inspiration from His teachings. When we put these virtues into practical use, and lend a helping hand to our neighbor, then we will begin to appreciate Jesus' true stature as the perfect man, and we will help ourselves by imitating Him.
**PAUL NEWTON OTTO**

The Christian religion teaches me two points—that there is a God whom men can know, and that their nature is so corrupt that they are unworthy of Him.
**BLAISE PASCAL**

A lot of people today are afraid to give a real demonstration of their Christian faith. They want God's power, they believe in Christian morals and ethics but they conceal the fact. If our society is disintegrating, it is because we haven't enough forthright believers.
NORMAN VINCENT PEALE

Christianity is like electricity. It cannot enter a person unless it can pass through.
RICHARD C. RAINES

The true Christian is the true citizen, lofty of purpose, resolute in endeavor, ready for a hero's deeds, but never looking down on his task because it is cast in the day of small things; scornful of baseness, awake to his own duties as well as to his rights, following the higher law with reverence, and in this world doing all that in his power lies, so that when death comes he may feel that mankind is in some degree better because he lived.
THEODORE ROOSEVELT

The fundamental defect of Christian ethics consists in the fact that it labels certain classes of acts sins and others virtues on grounds that have nothing to do with their social consequences.
BERTRAND RUSSELL

The church may have seen its duty imperfectly, for it is made up of fallible human beings, but when all is said it has been the one power through nearly two thousand years which has stood for peace, for brotherhood, for the cause of the poor and distressed.
ERNEST F. SCOTT, D.D.

The world is rapidly being divided into two camps, the comradeship of anti-Christ and the brotherhood of Christ. The lines between these two are being drawn. How long the battle will be we know not; whether swords will have to be unsheathed we know not; whether blood will have to be shed we know not; whether it will be an armed conflict we know not. But in a conflict between truth and darkness, truth cannot lose.
BISHOP FULTON J. SHEEN

Empires built on force will always be destroyed. Those built on trust in Christ will remain.
JOSEPH R. SIZOO, D.D.

The Christian in whatever weather and under whatever skies, commits his life to God, is humble in spirit and is sure that God will vindicate those who trust Him. He frees himself in days of uncertainty from overanxious fear.
G. MORRIS SMITH, D.D.

America needs a great revival of religion, but it must be inspired by faith rather than fear. We do not come to Christ merely by trying to get away from the Kremlin, nor do we get to heaven simply by trying to escape from hell.
RALPH W. SOCKMAN

When the dictators and the opportunists are gone, the cross will still stand before us and something in us will say, "That is the real thing."
RALPH W. SOCKMAN

City folk need not feel sorry for themselves or be pessimistic about the soil in which Christianity is planted to live and bear fruit. The Christian faith was made for contest, and its best fruits are always produced out of the harsh soil of difficulty and danger.
THEODORE C. SPEERS, D.D.

Christianity is the good man's text; his life, the illustration.
JOSEPH P. THOMPSON

The task and triumph of Christianity is to make men and nations true and just and upright in all

their dealings, and to bring all law, as well as all conduct, into subjection and conformity to the law of God.
**Henry Van Dyke**

The trouble with some of us is that we have been inoculated with small doses of Christianity which keep us from catching the real thing.
**Leslie D. Weatherhead**

## Church

I have no objections to churches so long as they do not interfere with God's work.
**Brooks Atkinson**

Business checks up on itself frequently to be sure that it still is headed for its original goals. Is there not need for a similar check-up on the part of the church?
**Bruce Barton**

But if at the Church they would give us some ale,
And a pleasant fire our souls to regale,
We'd sing and we'd pray all the live-long day,
And never once wish from the Church to stray.
**William Blake**

Church by all means on Sunday. But what is the use of church if at the very center of life a man defrauds his neighbor and insults God by poor craftsmanship?
**Dwight D. Eisenhower**

The church of tomorrow must be universal. It cannot belong to a particular class, race or nation, but must transcend all such barriers so the brotherhood of man may be extended among us.
**Ralph S. Meadowcroft**

A war fitness conference some time ago declared that the highest form of recreation is to go to church. The word recreation should be written re-creation. More real rest can be gained from an hour and a quarter of worship under these circumstances than by eighteen holes of golf.
**Norman Vincent Peale**

The British churchgoer prefers a severe preacher because he thinks a few home truths will do his neighbors no harm.
**George Bernard Shaw**

The pulpit will not fulfill its function by merely thundering "Thou shalt nots." The church, together with the home, the school and all community agencies must provide constructive and creative activities for parents as well as for youth.
**Ralph W. Sockman**

We need the fellowship of the godly to safeguard our fellowship with the ungodly. This is the high function of the church. It calls its members to enter into social and civic movements. But it seeks to fill its members with such moral courage and spiritual power that they become part of the world's solution.
**Ralph W. Sockman**

## Cities

A great city is not to be confounded with a populous one.
**Aristotle**

The only real advantage of New York is that all its inhabitants ascend to heaven right after their deaths, having served their full term in hell right on Manhattan Island.
**Barnard (College) Bulletin**

The more I observed Washington, the more frequently I visited it, and the more people I interviewed there, the more I understood how prophetic L'Enfant was when he laid it out as a city that goes around in circles.
**JOHN MASON BROWN**

Miami Beach is where neon goes to die.
**LENNY BRUCE**

If you would be known, and not know, vegetate in a village; if you would know, and not be known, live in a city.
**CHARLES CALEB COLTON**

Like a city in dreams, the great white capital stretches along the placid river from Georgetown to the west to Anacostia on the east. It is a city of temporaries, a city of just-arriveds and only-visitings, built on the shifting sands of politics, filled with people passing through.
**ALLEN DRURY**

A great city—a great solitude.
**ENGLISH PROVERB**

Almost every time I leave New York and visit one of our smaller cities, one of my strongest impressions is that those who live in such communities enjoy a more tranquil life and form closer and deeper friendships than those of us buried among the millions of strangers who crowd our metropolitan cities. Visits to such places nearly always have a reassuring, inspiring effect. They cause one to feel that this nation is solidly built, that friendliness and neighborliness still abound, that the hearthstone still means much, that the life lived by the great body of the American people is sane, sensible, rational.
**B. C. FORBES**

What the small town may have contributed in the past is one side of the coin; the other side is urbanism and the greatest opportunity in the history of man to reach his full potential. Where the small town kept him prisoner, urbanism gives him freedom of choice—choice of education, choice of profession, choice of marriage.
**PHILIP HAUSER**

If you are lucky enough to have lived in Paris as a young man, then wherever you go for the rest of your life, it stays with you, for Paris is a moveable feast.
**ERNEST HEMINGWAY**

Washington is a city of Southern efficiency and Northern charm.
**JOHN F. KENNEDY**

To start with, there's [New York's] alien accent. "Tree" is the number between two and four. "Jeintz" is the name of the New York professional football team. A "fit" is a bottle measuring seven ounces less than a quart.
**FLETCHER KNEBEL**

When you leave New York, you are astonished at how clean the rest of the world is. Clean is not enough.
**FRAN LEBOWITZ**

To say the least, a town life makes one more tolerant and liberal in one's judgment of others.
**HENRY WADSWORTH LONGFELLOW**

New York attracts the most talented people in the world in the arts and professions. It also attracts them in other fields. Even the bums are talented.
**EDMUND LOVE**

He speaks English with the flawless imperfection of a New Yorker.
**GILBERT MILLSTEIN**

All cities are mad, but the madness is gallant. All cities are beautiful, but the beauty is grim.
CHRISTOPHER MORLEY

New York is the perfect model of a city, not the model of a perfect city.
LEWIS MUMFORD

A sample of the country does the city good; a sample of the city does the country good.
JOSEPH ROUX

Boston is a moral and intellectual nursery busy applying first principles to trifles.
GEORGE SANTAYANA

City life: millions of people being lonesome together.
HENRY DAVID THOREAU

New York is to the nation what the white church spire is to the village—the visible symbol of aspiration and faith, the white plume saying the way is up!
E. B. WHITE

## *Civilization*

The origin of civilization is man's determination to do nothing for himself which he can get done for him.
H. C. BAILEY

Civilization exists precisely so that there may be no masses but rather men alert enough never to constitute masses.
GEORGES BERNANOS

In the whole history of law and order the longest step forward was taken by primitive man when, as if by common consent, the tribe sat down in a circle and allowed only one man to speak at a time.
CURTIS BOK

Civilization . . . is like a river that flows sometimes slowly, sometimes fast, sometimes over a cataract, but always one way, toward the sea. It can well flood and drown out a whole countryside, and the further it runs, the bigger it grows, the more disastrous are its floods. But the nations are learning not only to rebuild their towns but to build fences along the whole course. They are beginning to study flood control, economic and social.
JOYCE CARY

Look back along the endless corridors of time and you will see that four things have built civilization: the spirit of religion, the spirit of creative art, the spirit of research and the spirit of business enterprise.
NEIL CAROTHERS

There is nothing more fragile than civilization.
HAVELOCK ELLIS

The true test of civilization is, not the census nor the size of cities, nor the crops—no, but the kind of man the country turns out.
RALPH WALDO EMERSON

Man was not intended by nature to live in communities and be civilized.
EPICURUS

A period of high civilization is one in which thoughts fly freely from mind to mind, from one country to another—yes, from the past into the present.
GILBERT HIGHET

After our ages-long journey from savagery to civility, let's hope we haven't bought a round-trip ticket.
CULLEN HIGHTOWER

You can't say that civilization don't advance, for in every war they kill you a new way.
**WILL ROGERS**

If we are to preserve civilization, we must first remain civilized.
**LOUIS ST. LAURENT**

Unless man has the wit and the grit to build his civilization on something better than material power, it is surely idle to talk of plans for a stable peace.
**FRANCIS B. SAYRE**

The central question is whether the wonderfully diverse and gifted assemblage of human beings on this earth really knows how to run a civilization.
**ADLAI STEVENSON**

No task is as difficult as striving to become a civilized person. But the lasting happiness which comes with that attempt makes the effort seem small indeed as compared with the value to be gained.
**LELAND P. STEWART**

In a living civilization there is always an element of unrest, for sensitiveness to ideas means curiosity, adventure, change. Civilized order survives on its merits and is transformed by its power of recognizing its imperfections.
**ALFRED NORTH WHITEHEAD**

## *Class*

Snobs talk as if they had begotten their own ancestors.
**HERBERT AGAR**

No state will be well administered unless the middle class holds sway.
**ARISTOTLE**

Aristocrats: Fellows that wear downy hats and clean shirts—guilty of education and suspected of bank accounts.
**AMBROSE BIERCE**

The true policy of a government is to make use of aristocracy, but under the forms and in the spirit of democracy.
**NAPOLEON BONAPARTE**

When the interval between the intellectual classes and the practical classes is too great, the former will possess no influence, the latter will reap no benefit.
**HENRY THOMAS BUCKLE**

The aristocracy of feudal parchment has passed away with a mighty rushing, and now, by a natural course, we arrive at aristocracy of the money-bag.
**THOMAS CARLYLE**

Aristocracy is an atmosphere; it is sometimes a healthy atmosphere; but it is very hard to say when it becomes an unhealthy atmosphere. You can prove that a man is not the son of a king, or that he is not the delegate of a definite number of people. But you cannot prove that a man is not a gentleman.
**G. K. CHESTERTON**

I know it was the fashion in Victorian times to say that England was represented by its great middle class and not by its aristocracy. That was the artfulness of its aristocracy. Never did a governing class govern so completely, by saying it did not govern at all.
**G. K. CHESTERTON**

The English political aristocracy will probably continue to reign. If they were regarded as a living aristocracy their energy and arrogance might irritate people into unrest or destruction. But as they are

presented to us as a dying aristocracy, we do not mind how long they take to die.
G. K. CHESTERTON

Aristocracy: What is left over from rich ancestors after the money is gone.
JOHN CIARDI

Aristocracy: A combination of many powerful men, for the purpose of maintaining their own particular interests. It is consequently a concentration of all the most effective parts of a community for a given end, hence its energy, efficiency and success.
JAMES FENIMORE COOPER

English history is aristocracy with the doors open. Who has courage and faculty, let him come in.
RALPH WALDO EMERSON

An intelligent class can scarce ever be, as a class, vicious, and never, as a class, indolent. The excited mental activity operates as a counterpoise to the stimulus of sense and appetite.
EDWARD EVERETT

Which class is happiest, the rich, the middle class or the poor? A very successful executive of a large organization touches upon this vital subject in a long letter to all his salesmen. He uses as his text a passage from Robinson Crusoe which included this: "My Father bid me observe it, and I should always find that the calamities of life were shared among the upper and lower part of mankind; but that the middle station had the fewest disasters, and were not exposed to so many vicissitudes as the higher or lower part of mankind."
B. C. FORBES

I distrust great men. . . . I believe in aristocracy, though. Its members are to be found in all nations and classes, and all through the ages, and there is a secret understanding between them when they meet. . . . They are sensitive for others as well as for themselves, they are considerate without being fussy, their pluck is not swankiness but the power to endure and they can take a joke.
E. M. FORSTER

Let him who expects one class of society to prosper in the highest degree, while the other is in distress, try whether one side of his face can smile while the other is pinched.
THOMAS FULLER

Americans are the only people in the world known to me whose status anxiety prompts them to advertise their college and university affiliations in the rear window of their automobiles.
PAUL FUSSELL

There is a natural aristocracy among men. The grounds of this are virtue and talent.
THOMAS JEFFERSON

The price of that upward mobility of which we have—as a people—for so long been so proud has become too high.
MARYA MANNES

I believe it to be most true that it seldom happens that men rise from low condition to high rank without employing either force or fraud.
NICCOLÒ MACHIAVELLI

In America we have an upper crust and a lower crust, but it's what's between—the middle class—that gives the real flavor.
VIRGINIA L. MCCLEARY

There is something to be said for government by a great aristocracy which has furnished leaders for the nation in peace and war for generations; even a democrat like myself must admit this.
THEODORE ROOSEVELT

We have inherited new difficulties because we have inherited more privileges.
ABRAM SACHAR

A Status symbol is an instrument you clash when you want someone to know you are there.
WILLIAM SANSOM

The servant problem has long been a staple of female conversation among those who could afford the problem, but never have so many talked about so few.
*TIME* MAGAZINE

The blunting effects of slavery upon the slaveholder's moral perceptions are known and conceded the world over; and a privileged class, an aristocracy, is but a band of slaveholders under another name.
MARK TWAIN

## *Common Sense*

A little common sense, goodwill, and a tiny dose of unselfishness could make this goodly earth into an earthly paradise.
RICHARD ALDINGTON

Common sense is the measure of the possible.
HENRI FRÉDÉRIC AMIEL

If a man can have only one kind of sense, let him have common sense. If he has that and uncommon sense, too, he is not far from genius.
HENRY WARD BEECHER

Commonsense in an uncommon degree is what the world calls wisdom.
SAMUEL TAYLOR COLERIDGE

Common sense is perhaps the most equally divided, but surely the most underemployed talent in the world.
CHRISTIANE COLLANGE

Common sense is genius dressed in its working clothes.
RALPH WALDO EMERSON

Society is always taken by surprise at any new example of common sense.
RALPH WALDO EMERSON

The common people of America display a quality of good common sense which is heartening to anyone who believes in the democratic process.
GEORGE GALLUP

Common sense is compelled to make its way without the enthusiasm of anyone; all admit it grudgingly.
EDGAR WATSON HOWE

Most business problems require common sense rather than legal reference. They require good judgment and honesty of purpose rather than reference to the courts.
EDWARD N. HURLEY

It is a thousand times better to have commonsense without education than to have education without commonsense.
ROBERT G. INGERSOLL

I read, I study, I examine, I listen, I reflect and out of all this I try to form an idea into which I put as much common sense as I can.
MARQUIS DE LAFAYETTE

Commonsense and good nature will do a lot to make the pilgrimage of life not too difficult.
SOMERSET MAUGHAM

The English have better sense than any other nation—and they are fools.
**METTERNICH**

Commonsense does not ask an impossible chess-board, but takes the one before it and plays the game.
**WENDELL PHILLIPS**

Common sense is the favorite daughter of reason.
**HENRY WHEELER SHAW (JOSH BILLINGS)**

Common sense is the knack of seeing things as they are, and doing things as they ought to be done.
**HARRIET BEECHER STOWE**

To act with common sense, according to the moment, is the best wisdom; and the best philosophy is to do one's duties, to take the world as it comes, submit respectfully to one's lot, bless the goodness what has given us so much happiness with it, whatever it is.
**HORACE WALPOLE**

## *Communism*

The criterion by which these people judge their action is a simple one. If in any part of the world the Communist Party, by no matter what means, is in power, that is democracy. If anywhere the Communists fail, then, however fair the conditions, it is regarded as Fascism.
**CLEMENT R. ATTLEE**

The only solution for the problem of Communism is pure, unadulterated Americanism.
**WILLIAM J. H. BOETCKER**

In five years, we've built a television network. The Russians have built a radar network.
**VANNEVAR BUSH**

Russia is not interested in European recovery because only in a starving country is it possible to impose communism on a people.
**CAMILLE CHAUTEMPS**

At the person-to-person level we shall always beat them [the Communists] because at that level we have something to give that they cannot match. We have the fundamental proposition of our Revolution to give: that man is the child of Nature's God; that he carries within him a spark that links him with the universe and differentiates him from the animals. . . . By practical person-to-person democracy we can teach the world to see in every individual that individual spark which gives to the principles of freedom a godlike validity.
**RUSSELL W. DAVENPORT**

I hate communism for its materialism. I hate it for its intolerance, because tolerance and not material gain is surely the hallmark of civilization. But it is not enough to say that we hate communism. We have to recognize that those who hold that creed hold it with a fervor that is almost a religion. If we are to defeat them we must therefore believe just as fervently in our faith and in ourselves.
**ANTHONY EDEN**

From behind the Iron Curtain, there are signs that tyranny is in trouble and reminders that its structure is as brittle as its surface is hard.
**DWIGHT D. EISENHOWER (1954)**

What is a Communist? One who hath yearnings
For equal division of unequal earnings.
Idler or bungler, or both, he is willing
To fork out his copper, and pocket your shilling.
**EBENEZER ELLIOTT**

Communism is obsessed with a hatred of ways of life other than its own and is afraid that unless these are swept away they will eventually overcome it.
**CYRIL FORSTER GARBETT, D.D.**

Communism possesses a language which every people can understand. Its elements are hunger, envy, and death.
**HEINRICH HEINE**

In a very real sense, today's contest between freedom and despotism is a contest between the American assembly line and the Communist party line.
**PAUL G. HOFFMAN**

If every American faced the reality of what the fulfillment of the Communist objectives means to him, he would be inspired to work harder to protect and preserve the individual liberty and freedom which is a part and parcel of our American Way of Life.
**J. EDGAR HOOVER**

Within our country the real peril lies not in what the Communists are capable of doing to us, but in what, through fear and hysteria, we are likely to do to ourselves in meeting the threat.
**J. HOWARD MCGRATH**

Communist: A fellow who has given up all hope of becoming a capitalist.
**ORVILLE REED**

The contrast between the Russian and American expansion in the modern world is one of direct opposites. The Russians sell an idea, above all their idea of the revolution and the logical state. Then, having penetrated with their idea, they follow to consolidate with their techniques, cold, brutal and bloody. But the Americans bring their techniques first, the logistics and mechanics of their system, and they leave its mothering, begetting idea to follow naturally behind.
**THEODORE H. WHITE**

Some people seem to think that there is a great difference between socialism and communism. But Karl Marx used the two words as synonyms. The best definition of a communist I have heard is that a communist is a socialist in a hurry.
**CHARLES E. WILSON**

We have slain a large [Soviet] dragon, but now we must live in a jungle filled with a bewildering variety of poisonous snakes, and in many ways the dragon was easier to keep track of.
**R. JAMES WOOLSEY, C.I.A. HEAD**

The Communist way to get the capital is to lock the doors, draw the blinds and put the screws to its people.
**SHIGERU YOSHIDA**

The principal lesson Soviet economic planning has to teach us is how it should not be done.
**T. ZAVALANI**

## *Competition*

There is a tendency among some businesses to criticize and belittle their competitors. This is a bad procedure. Praise them. Learn from them. There are times when you can co-operate with them to their advantage and to yours! Speak well of them and they will speak well of you. You can't destroy good ideas. Take advantage of them.
**GEORGE MATTHEW ADAMS**

The need and the desire to serve have always been and always will be a major motivating force of business. Neighbor competes with neighbor, and pretty

ruggedly, too, but nearly always to the end of giving the consumer more and better products, superior service, higher value. This is the American tradition. The fact that it has built the highest standard of living the world has ever known is evidence, to me at least, that there is something more than a dream of profits behind the progress we have achieved and hope to achieve in the future.
**JERVIS J. BABB**

Does anyone believe for one moment that the progress we have made would have been possible under bureaucratic control of any government. This country was founded upon the principle of the regulation of private effort, of making rules for the game, and under that system alone can we look for the same success in the future which has been ours in the past. Our position today is the direct result of the free play among our people of private competitive effort.
**ROGER W. BABSON**

The law of the jungle is no longer valid, if it ever was. We all believe in stiff and healthy competition and many of us have learned that it does nobody any good to destroy his competitor. If we did not have competition we would have to invent its equivalent. But we are also understanding with increasing realism that the well-being of worker and employer, of manufacturer and consumer, of economic and political life, are all bound up together.
**ERWIN D. CANHAM**

By competition the total amount of supply is increased, and by increase of the supply a competition in the sale ensues, and this enables the consumer to buy at lower rates. Of all human powers operating on the affairs of mankind, none is greater than that of competition.
**HENRY CLAY**

No amount of artificial protection can permanently maintain an obsolete product, an inferior process or a moribund organization against competitors which are based on scientifically improved products or methods.
**KARL T. COMPTON**

A man comes to measure his greatness by the regrets, envies and hatreds of his competitors.
**RALPH WALDO EMERSON**

We find the instinct to shut out competition deep-rooted even among banks and corporations, among corner grocers and haberdasheries, among peanut vendors and shoeshine boys—and even among young ladies in search of a husband.
**JAMES A. FARLEY**

Competition is the keen cutting edge of business, always shaving away at costs.
**HENRY FORD**

Competition whose motive is merely to compete, to drive some other fellow out, never carries very far. The competitor to be feared is one who never bothers about you at all, but goes on making his own business better all the time. Businesses that grow by development and improvement do not die. But when a business ceases to be creative, when it believes it has reached perfection and needs to do nothing but produce—no improvement, no development—it is done.
**HENRY FORD**

When a business firm attempts to mold its whole policy to meet the prices of its competitor that business is entering a labyrinth, the center of which is the chamber of despair. Highest quality never can be given nor obtained at the lowest prices. If a price must be sacrificed, quality must be sacrificed. If quality is sacrificed society is not truly served.
**H. T. GARVEY**

Save possibly in education effects, cooperation can produce no general results that competition will not produce.
HENRY GEORGE

Without the spur of competition we'd loaf out our life.
ARNOLD GLASOW

Striving to outdo one's companions on the golf course and tennis court or in the swimming pool constitutes several socially acceptable forms of suicide.
GEORGE GRIFFITH

Don't knock your competitors. By boosting others you will boost yourself. A little competition is a good thing and severe competition is a blessing. Thank God for competition.
JACOB KINDLEBERGER

In business, the competition will bite you if you keep running; if you stand still, they will swallow you.
SEMON KNUDSEN

Today's competitiveness, so much imposed from without, is exhausting, not exhilarating; is unending—a part of one's social life, one's solitude, one's sleep, one's sleeplessness.
LOUIS KRONENBERGER

Nobody talks more of free enterprise and competition and the best man winning than the man who inherited his father's store or farm.
C. WRIGHT MILLS

I don't like to lose, and that isn't so much because it is just a football game, but because defeat means the failure to reach your objective. I don't want a football player who doesn't take defeat to heart, who laughs it off with the thought, "Oh, well, there's another Saturday." The trouble in American life today, in business as well as in sports, is that too many people are afraid of competition. The result is that in some circles people have come to sneer at success if it costs hard work and training and sacrifice.
KNUTE ROCKNE

You cannot do away with the competitive system so long as trademarks remain to distinguish one product from another. You cannot cut out large-scale manufacture so long as there are established brands which breed consumer confidence and thus make mass production not only possible and profitable, but also economical.
PHILIP SALISBURY

The idea of imposing restrictions on a free economy to assure freedom of competition is like breaking a man's leg to make him run faster.
MORRIS R. SAYRE

Whenever I may be tempted to slack up and let the business run for awhile on its own impetus, I picture my competitor sitting at a desk in his opposition house, thinking and thinking with the most devilish intensity and clearness, and I ask myself what I can do to be prepared for his next brilliant move.
H. GORDON SELFRIDGE

Our Creator has put in us hungers that this earth cannot satisfy. We cannot be completely self-contained on earth. Physical sense cannot give us a full life, nor can knowledge alone. No life is full unless it is linked to something that goes on after we are dead. . . . If we have nothing more to live for than just to get ahead in a competitive system, then democracy will go down before other philosophies.
RALPH W. SOCKMAN

Competition, as the life of trade, surely is a tremendous spur to progress. Is it not the pursued man or business that advances through persistent effort to

keep ahead? The constant striving to maintain leadership ever involves new ways and means of accomplishing more efficiently and thus it is the "pursued is the progressive man." Put your pursuers on the payroll.
W. D. TOLAND

## Conduct

The ability to have our own way, and at the same time convince others they are having their own way, is a rare thing among men. Among women, it is as common as eyebrows.
THOMAS BAILEY ALDRICH

Conduct is three-fourths of our life and its largest concern.
MATTHEW ARNOLD

My son Hannibal will be a great general, because of all my soldiers he best knows how to obey.
HAMILCAR BARCA

Every man is valued in this world as he shows by his conduct that he wishes to be valued.
JEAN DE LA BRUYÈRE

Fundamentally, the force that rules the world is conduct, whether it be moral or immoral. If it is moral, at least there may be hope for the world. If immoral, there is not only no hope, but no prospect of anything but destruction of all that has been accomplished during the last 5,000 years.
NICHOLAS MURRAY BUTLER

Behave toward everyone as if receiving a great guest.
CONFUCIUS

History teaches us that men and nations behave wisely once they have exhausted all other alternatives.
ABBA EBAN

If we conducted ourselves as sensibly in good times as we do in hard times, we could acquire a competence.
WILLIAM FEATHER

Confront improper conduct, not by retaliation, but by example.
JOHN FOSTER

Watch your step when you immediately know the one way to do anything. Nine times out of ten, there are several better ways.
WILLIAM B. GIVEN, JR.

Behavior is a mirror, in which everyone shows his image.
JOHANN WOLFGANG VON GOETHE

Treat people as if they were what they ought to be and you help them to become what they are capable of being.
JOHANN WOLFGANG VON GOETHE

Be so that thy conduct can become law universal.
IMMANUEL KANT

There is always a right and a wrong way, and the wrong way always seems the more reasonable.
GEORGE MOORE

The big things of life are never done by a fussy man. Poise is one of the earmarks of mental strength.
PRESTON NOLAN

The virtue of man ought to be measured, not by his extraordinary exertions, but by his everyday conduct.
**BLAISE PASCAL**

The man who obeys is nearly always better than the man who commands.
**ERNEST RENAN**

Why did the children put beans in their ears when the one thing we told the children they must not do was put beans in their ears?
**CARL SANDBURG**

That man may safely venture on his way, who is so guided that he cannot stay.
**SIR WALTER SCOTT**

Either I will find a way, or I will make one.
**SIR PHILIP SIDNEY**

When man learns to understand and control his own behavior as well as he is learning to understand and control the behavior of crop plants and domestic animals, he may be justified in believing that he has become civilized.
**E. C. STAKMAN**

Depend not on fortune, but on conduct.
**PUBLILIUS SYRUS**

Poise is a big factor in a man's success. If I were a young man just starting out, I would talk things over with myself as a friend. I would set out to develop poise—for it can be developed. A man should learn to stand, what to do with his hands, what to do with his feet, look his man straight in the eye, dress well and look well and know he looks well. By dressing well I don't mean expensively, but neatly and in taste.
**F. EDSON WHITE**

The world is made better by every man improving his own conduct; and no reform is accomplished wholesale.
**WILLIAM ALLEN WHITE**

Have you not learn'd great lessons from those who rejected you and braced themselves against you or who treated you with contempt or disputed the passage with you?
**WALT WHITMAN**

## *Confidence*

Confidence is the foundation for all business relations. The degree of confidence a man has in others, and the degree of confidence others have in him, determines a man's standing in the commercial and industrial world.
**WILLIAM J. H. BOETCKER**

True prosperity is the result of well placed confidence in ourselves and our fellow man.
**BENJAMIN BURT**

A true man never frets about his place in the world, but just slides into it by the gravitation of his nature, and swings there as easily as a star.
**EDWIN H. CHAPIN**

Confidence is that feeling by which the mind embarks in great and honorable courses with a sure hope and trust in itself.
**CICERO**

Life is not easy for any of us. But what of that? We must have perseverance and, above all, confidence in ourselves. We must believe that we are gifted for something, and that this thing, at whatever cost, must be attained.
**MARIE CURIE**

It is not so much our friends' help that helps as the confidence of their help.
EPICURUS

He can inspire a group only if he himself is filled with confidence and hope of success.
FLOYD V. FILSON

We hear a good deal about business confidence, which means confidence of business in itself, in its government, and in its capacity for expansion. But confidence is only another way of saying that people believe each other, keep their promises, pay their debts, and regard their duty to society. As long as business observes these rules, it will have the confidence of the community and it will be safe from all of the irresponsible attacks of its enemies.
WILL H. HAYS

Skill and confidence are an unconquered army.
GEORGE HERBERT

Fortunate is the person who has developed the self-control to steer a straight course toward his objective in life, without being swayed from his purpose by either commendation or condemnation.
NAPOLEON HILL

We should place confidence in our employee. Confidence is the foundation of friendship. If we give it, we will receive it. Any person in a managerial position, from supervisor to president, who feels that his employee is basically not as good as he is and who suspects his employee is always trying to put something over on him, lacks the necessary qualities for human leadership—to say nothing of human friendship.
HARRY E. HUMPHREYS, JR.

In returning and rest shall ye be saved; in quietness and in confidence shall be your strength.
ISAIAH 30:15

I have seen boys on my baseball team go into slumps and never come out of them, and I have seen others snap right out and come back better than ever. I guess more players lick themselves than are ever licked by an opposing team. The first thing any man has to know is how to handle himself. Training counts. You can't win any game unless you are ready to win.
CONNIE MACK

Confidence is a plant of slow growth in an aged bosom.
WILLIAM PITT

Calm self-confidence is as far from conceit as the desire to earn a decent living is remote from greed.
CHANNING POLLOCK

It is surely one of nature's jokes that she so often gives an abundance of self-confidence to those who are not analytical and withholds even a smidgen of it from those who are.
PATRICIA PUMPHREY

Calm self-confidence is as far from conceit as the desire to earn a decent living is remote from greed.
CHANNING POLLOCK

Confidence and enthusiasm are the greatest sales producers in any kind of economy. Have confidence in your products and the house backing them, have enthusiasm for your job, call on your trade regularly and consistently, treat your trade courteously, and you will find that your customers will not have to be sold—they will be glad to buy.
O. B. SMITH

To do anything in this world worth doing, we must not stand back shivering and thinking of the cold and danger, but jump in, and scramble through as well as we can.
SYDNEY SMITH

Have confidence that if you have done a little thing well, you can do a bigger thing well, too.
JOSEPH STOREY

Confidence is a thing not to be produced by compulsion. Men cannot be forced into trust.
DANIEL WEBSTER

## *Congress*

You can't use tact with a Congressman. A Congressman is a hog. You must take a stick and hit him on the snout.
HENRY ADAMS

A completely planned national economy would be found to lead to a complete change in our form of government and of the relationship of the individual to the ruling power. The decisions to be taken, not in regulating, but in running what we have hitherto considered our private lives and business would require a swiftness and a unanimity which cannot be had from Congress.
JAMES TRUSLOW ADAMS

I have accepted a seat in the House of Representatives, and thereby have consented to my own ruin, to your ruin, and to the ruin of our children. I give you this warning that you may prepare your mind for your fate.
JOHN ADAMS

At last our Congress felt the heat
And stopped the regal stratagem
That many laws they laid upon us
Did not apply to them.
ART BUCK

In starting on a spending spree,
The Congress all too frequently
Can't make its way from A to B
Without a genuflect to Z.
ART BUCK

To lie to Congress is a crime
That generates much fuss,
But it's hallowed passage rite
When Congress lies to us.
ART BUCK

Make the Congressional Record a genuine record. Adopt a resolution . . . that specified the elimination of the abortion, the Appendix, that bulks large with constituent twaddle that never entered into [congressional] deliberations in the first place. Secondly, and of equal importance, state that the Record shall be a faithful translation of what was said, and shall be tampered with by no one between the time [it] was said and its appearance in print.
MALCOLM FORBES

The cause of that stunning 1994 election reversing Congressional parties' power? Why, of course—the gripes of wrath!
FRED HILLEGAS

Poverty passes from one generation to the next. Extravagance passes from one Congress to the next.
CULLEN HIGHTOWER

We may not imagine how our lives could be more frustrating and complex—but Congress can.
CULLEN HIGHTOWER

It is much easier in many ways for me—and for other Presidents, I think, who felt the same way—when Congress is not in town.
JOHN F. KENNEDY

Think of what would happen to us in America if there were no humorists; life would be one long Congressional Record.
**THOMAS L. MASSON**

Is there really someone who, searching for a group of wise and sensitive people to regulate him for his own good, would choose that group of people who constitute the membership of both houses of Congress?
**ROBERT NOZICK**

In a body [like Congress] where there are more than one hundred talking lawyers, you can make no calculation upon the termination of any debate, and frequently the more trifling the subject the more animated and protracted the discussion.
**FRANKLIN PIERCE**

The passion for office among members of Congress is very great if not absolutely disreputable, and greatly embarrasses the operation of the government. They create offices by their own votes and then seek to fill them themselves.
**JAMES K. POLK**

There are two periods when Congress does no business: One is before the holidays, and the other after.
**GEORGE D. PRENTICE**

The way to judge a good comedy is by how long it will last and have people talk about it. Now Congress has turned out some that have lived for years and people are still laughing about them.
**WILL ROGERS**

Congress does from a third to a half of what I think is the minimum that it ought to do, and I am profoundly grateful that I get as much.
**THEODORE ROOSEVELT**

The debates of that great assembly are frequently vague and perplexed, seeming to be dragged rather than to march to the intended goal. Something of this sort must, I think, always happen in public democratic assemblies.
**ALEXIS DE TOCQUEVILLE**

It could probably be shown by facts and figures that there is no distinctively native American criminal class except Congress.
**MARK TWAIN**

Suppose you were an idiot. And suppose that you were a member of Congress. But I repeat myself.
**MARK TWAIN**

Whiskey is carried into [congressional] committee rooms in demijohns and carried out in demagogues.
**MARK TWAIN**

Sure the people are stupid: The human race is stupid. Sure Congress is an inefficient instrument of government. But the people are not stupid enough to abandon representative government for any other kind, including government by the guy who knows.
**BERNARD DE VOTO**

I believe that if we introduced the Lord's Prayer here, senators would propose a large number of amendments to it.
**HENRY B. WILSON**

## Conscience

Conscience: A small, still voice that makes minority reports.
**FRANKLIN P. ADAMS**

Everyone in daily life carries such a heavy, mixed burden on his own conscience that he is reluctant to penalize those who have been caught.
**BROOKS ATKINSON**

It is an accepted law of ethics that punishment in the Court of Conscience, unlike that in Courts of Law, lessens with each repeated and unrebuked offense.
**JOSEPH S. AUERBACH**

Spend your time in nothing which you know must be repeated of; in nothing on which you might not pray for the blessing of God; in nothing which you could not review with a quiet conscience on your dying bed; in nothing which you might not safely and properly be found doing if death should surprise you in the act.
**RICHARD BAXTER**

A disciplined conscience is a man's best friend. It may not be his most amiable, but it is his most faithful monitor.
**HENRY WARD BEECHER**

Reason often makes mistakes, but conscience never does.
**JOSH BILLINGS**

Wisdom and beauty are the twin arches of that invisible bridge which leads from the individual conscience—ever rebellious against its destiny—to man's collective conscience, ever in search of general progress.
**JAIME TORRES BODET**

When it was seen that many of the wicked seemed quite untroubled by evil conscience . . . then the idea of future suffering was advanced.
**LEWIS BROWNE**

A quiet conscience makes one so serene.
**LORD BYRON**

It is far more important to me to preserve an unblemished conscience than to compass any object however great.
**WILLIAM ELLERY CHANNING**

A man that will enjoy a quiet conscience must lead a quiet life.
**LORD CHESTERFIELD**

He who sacrifices his conscience to ambition burns a picture to obtain the ashes.
**CHINESE PROVERB**

Whatever is done without ostentation, and without the people being witnesses of it, is, in my opinion, most praiseworthy: not that the public eye should be entirely avoided, for good actions desire to be placed in the light; but notwithstanding this, the greatest theater for virtue is conscience.
**CICERO**

Conscience is the root of all true courage; if a man would be brave let him obey his conscience.
**JAMES FREEMAN CLARKE**

The truth is not so much that man has conscience as that conscience has man.
**ISAAC DORNER**

A magazine editor recently asked me to sit down on my 40th birthday and write an article on the most important things I had learned in my first 40 years. I told him that the chief thing I had learned was that the copybook maxims are true, but that too many people forget this once they go out into the heat and hustle and bustle of the battle of life and only realize their truth once one foot is beginning

to slip into the grave. The man who has won millions at the cost of his conscience is a failure.
**B. C. FORBES**

A quiet conscience sleeps in thunder.
**THOMAS FULLER**

Conscience is a coward, and those faults it has not strength to prevent, it seldom has justice enough to accuse.
**OLIVER GOLDSMITH**

Conscience admonishes as a friend before punishing us as a judge.
**STANISLAUS LESZCYNSKI**

If your conscience won't stop you, pray for cold feet.
**ELMER G. LETERMAN**

The Anglo-Saxon conscience doesn't keep you from doing what you shouldn't, it just keeps you from enjoying it.
**SALVADOR DE MADARIAGA**

Conscience is the inner voice that warns us that someone may be looking.
**H. L. MENCKEN**

Whence do I get my rules of conduct? I find them in my heart. Whatever I feel to be good is good. Whatever I feel to be evil is evil. Conscience is the best of casuists.
**JEAN-JACQUES ROUSSEAU**

The foundation of the true joy is in the conscience.
**SENECA**

Whoever attempts to suppress liberty of conscience finishes some day by wishing for the Inquisition.
**JULES SIMON**

There is no witness so terrible—no accuser so powerful as conscience which dwells within us.
**SOPHOCLES**

Conscience is God's presence in Man.
**EMANUEL SWEDENBORG**

It is truly enough said that a corporation has no conscience; but a corporation of conscientious men is a corporation with a conscience.
**HENRY DAVID THOREAU**

A clean and sensitive conscience, a steadfast and scrupulous integrity in small things as well as great, is the most valuable of all possessions, to a nation as to an individual.
**HENRY VAN DYKE**

Conscience is that which hurts when everything else feels so good.
**GEORGE VAVOULIS**

Labor to keep alive that little spark of celestial fire, called conscience.
**GEORGE WASHINGTON**

If a dog will not come to you after he has looked you in the face, you ought to go home and examine your conscience.
**WOODROW WILSON**

## *Contentment*

Contentment is a pearl of great price, and whoever procures it at the expense of ten thousand desires makes a wise and a happy purchase.
**BALGUY**

If a man has come to that point where he is so content that he says; I do not want to know any more,

or do any more or be any more, he is in a state in which he ought to be changed into a mummy.
HENRY WARD BEECHER

Contentment is not happiness. An oyster may be contented.
CHRISTIAN BOVÉE

One who is contented with what he has done will never become famous for what he will do. He has laid down to die, and the grass is already growing over him.
CHRISTIAN BOVÉE

I am content with what I have, little be it, or much.
JOHN BUNYAN

It is not being out at heels that makes a man discontented, it is being out at heart. To be contented is to be good friends with yourself.
BLISS CARMAN

Intelligent discontent is the mainspring of civilization.
EUGENE V. DEBS

All our discontents spring from the want of thankfulness for what we have.
DANIEL DEFOE

Contentment gives a crown where fortune hath denied it.
JOHN FORD

Let thy discontents be thy secrets; if the world knows them 'twill despise thee and increase them.
BENJAMIN FRANKLIN

Content makes poor men rich; discontent makes rich men poor.
BENJAMIN FRANKLIN

Who is rich? He that is content. Who is that? Nobody.
BENJAMIN FRANKLIN

Contentment does not consist in heaping up more fuel, but in taking away some fire.
THOMAS FULLER

**Nine requisites for contented living:**

Health enough to make work a pleasure. Wealth enough to support your needs. Strength to battle with difficulties and overcome them. Grace enough to confess your sins and forsake them. Patience enough to toil until some good is accomplished. Charity enough to see some good in your neighbor. Love enough to move you to be useful and helpful to others. Faith enough to make real the things of God. Hope enough to remove all anxious fears concerning the future.
JOHANN WOLFGANG VON GOETHE

There are two kinds of discontent in this world; the discontent that works, and the discontent that wrings its hands. The first gets what it wants, and the second loses what it has. There's no cure for the first but success; and there's no cure at all for the second.
GORDON GRAHAM

All the discontented people I know are trying to be something they are not, to do something they cannot do.
DAVID GRAYSON

Moral stimulation is good but moral complacency is the most dangerous habit of mind we can develop, and that danger is serious and ever-present.
JOSEPH C. GREW

We shall be made truly wise if we be made content; content, too, not only with what we can understand, but content with what we do not understand—the

habit of mind which theologians call, and rightly, faith in God.
CHARLES KINGSLEY

It is right to be contented with what we have, never with what we are.
JAMES MACKINTOSH

Contentment preserves one from catching cold. Has a woman who knew that she was well dressed ever caught a cold? No, not even when she had scarcely a rag on her back.
FRIEDRICH WILHELM NIETZSCHE

If you are content, you have enough to live comfortably.
PLAUTUS

When we cannot find contentment in ourselves, it is useless to seek it elsewhere.
FRANÇOIS DE LA ROCHEFOUCAULD

The great menace to the life of an industry is industrial self-complacency.
DAVID SARNOFF

When a man is discontented with himself, it has one advantage . . . that it puts him into an excellent frame of mind for making a bargain.
LAURENCE STERNE

If the principles of contentment are not within us, the height of station and worldly grandeur will as soon add a cubit to a man's stature as to his happiness.
LAURENCE STERNE

Complacency is the enemy of progress.
DAVE STUTMAN

## Contracts

A verbal contract isn't worth the paper it's written on.
SAMUEL GOLDWYN

The value of all things contracted for is measurable by the appetite of the contractors, and there the just value is that which they be contented to give.
THOMAS HOBBES

Man is an animal that makes bargains; no other animal does this—one dog does not change a bone with another.
ADAM SMITH

When management and labor fail to resolve their differences through collective bargaining, they often nettle what is already an impatient public. And an impatient public may at any time decide that labor and management may have too much liberty. . . . One form it could take is compulsory arbitration. That would mean . . . wage-fixing. It would mean price-fixing. It would be the antithesis of collective bargaining.
HERMAN W. STEINKRAUS

## Cooperation

One hand cannot applaud alone.
ARABIAN PROVERB

We are born for co-operation, as are the feet, the hands, the eye-lids and the upper and lower jaws.
MARCUS AURELIUS ANTONINUS

A team is a mutual protection society formed to guarantee that no one person can be held to blame for a botched committee job that one man could have performed satisfactorily.
RUSSELL BAKER

Great discoveries and improvements invariably involve the co-operation of many minds. I may be given credit for having blazed the trail but when I look at the subsequent developments I feel the credit is due to others rather than to myself.
ALEXANDER GRAHAM BELL

What a different world this would be if our thinking workers and working thinkers, be they wage earners or wage payers, would realize that: Truth, justice, honesty and loyalty plus confidence, goodwill and harmony, will ever be the only possible stepping stones for a greater and better world. For only with such corner stones will mutually advantageous co-operation be made possible.
WILLIAM J. H. BOETCKER

You can employ men and hire hands to work for you, but you must win their hearts to have them work with you.
WILLIAM J. H. BOETCKER

To commit the execution of a purpose to one who disapproves of the plan of it is to employ but one-third of the man; his heart and his head are against you, you have commanded only his hands.
CHARLES CALEB COLTON

No matter how much work a man can do, no matter how engaging his personality may be, he will not advance far in business if he cannot work through others.
JOHN CRAIG

The simple virtues of willingness, readiness, alertness and courtesy will carry a man farther than mere smartness.
RANDALL THOMAS DAVIDSON

It is a prime objective of civilized society to raise the plane of living of all people, not to some single type, level or standard, but according to their respective needs and preferences, in such ways as will make for harmonious relations within and among nations. If nations will devote to this objective even a sizable fraction of the intelligence, human energies and material resources that total war brings forth, progressive success can be confidently expected.
JOSEPH S. DAVIS

Compromise is but the sacrifice of one right or good in the hope of retaining another—too often ending in the loss of both.
TRYON EDWARDS

If we are to build and maintain the strength required to cope with the problems of this age, we must cooperate one with the other, every section with all others, each group with its neighbors. This means domestic unity. . . . Unity does not imply rigid conformity to every doctrine or position of a particular political figure. But it does require a common devotion to the cardinal principles of our free system, shared knowledge and understanding of our own capacities and opportunities and a common determination to cooperate unreservedly in striving toward our truly important goals. This type of unity is the true source of our great energy—our spiritual, intellectual, material and creative energy.
DWIGHT D. EISENHOWER

The world must learn to work together, or finally it will not work at all.
DWIGHT D. EISENHOWER

Getting along with others is the essence of getting ahead, success being linked with cooperation.
WILLIAM FEATHER

Back of ninety-nine out of one hundred assertions that a thing cannot be done is nothing but the unwillingness to do it.
WILLIAM FEATHER

Community rivalry is, of course, an excellent and helpful thing, but you will grant, I think, that it has its limits of usefulness and that there is greater wisdom in sectional cooperation to promote larger welfare.
**EDWARD A. FILENE**

No society of nations, no people within a nation, no family can benefit through mutual aid unless good will exceeds ill will; unless the spirit of co-operation surpasses antagonism; unless we all see and act as though the other man's welfare determines our own welfare.
**HENRY FORD II**

Coming together is a beginning; keeping together is progress; working together is success.
**HENRY FORD**

Our common future is badly served when the eloquence of out attacks on the other fellow exceeds the energy with which we co-operate with them.
**CLARENCE FRANCIS**

If thou art a master, sometimes be blind; if a servant, sometimes be deaf.
**THOMAS FULLER**

Ninety per cent of the art of living consists of getting on with people one cannot stand.
**SAMUEL GOLDWYN**

The point that most needs to be borne in mind is that the welfare of every business is dependent upon cooperation and teamwork on the part of its personnel. Proper cooperation cannot be secured between groups of men who are constantly quarreling among themselves over petty grievances.
**CHARLES GOW**

The greatest ability in business is to get along with others and influence their actions. A chip on the shoulder is too heavy a piece of baggage to carry through life.
**JOHN HANCOCK**

The great problems of the age, international, national and corporate, have to do with the relationships of people. One must be skilled in getting along with others. But this skill must rest upon some such foundation as this: Technical competence; broad intellectual outlook; high sense of honor—moral and spiritual values; attention to the public interest; understanding and appreciation of human relationships.
**ROBERT N. HILKERT**

Never cut what you can untie.
**JOSEPH JOUBERT**

Men should bear with each other. There lives not the man who may not be cut up, aye, lashed to pieces, on his weakest side.
**JOHN KEATS**

If there is any such thing as a wise compromise, it is not likely to be reached by a refusal to think.
**JOSEPH WOOD KRUTCH**

Utmost decency, in all our dealings with the *other fellow,* is the greatest need of the hour. Isn't he just you and me? Besides, being the proper thing, in the long run, it pays handsome dividends.
**ALBERT B. LORD**

It is evident that many great and useful objects can be attained in this world only by cooperation.
**THOMAS B. MACAULAY**

Where the willingness is great, the difficulties cannot be great.
**NICCOLÒ MACHIAVELLI**

Two men working as a team will produce more than three men working as individuals.
**CHARLES P. MCCORMICK**

The true interest of Americans is mutual interest. The doctrines that put race against race, group against group, class against class and worker against employer all are false doctrines. They are preached only by assassins of progress who are economic parasites or political pirates. We want to recreate an America in which their falsehoods cannot prevail, where the energies of men and women shall be devoted to constructive efforts.
**WHEELER MCMILLEN**

To get along you must go along.
**SAM RAYBURN**

I have long been profoundly convinced that in the very nature of things, employers and employees are partners, not enemies; that their interests are common, not opposed; that in the long run the success of each is dependent upon the success of the other.
**JOHN D. ROCKEFELLER, JR.**

There is a point, of course, where a man must take the isolated peak and break with all his associates for clear principle; but until that time comes he must work, if he would be of use, with men as they are. As long as the good in them overbalances the evil, let him work with them for the best that can be obtained.
**THEODORE ROOSEVELT**

The races of mankind would perish did they cease to aid each other. From the time that the mother binds the child's head till the moment that some kind assistant wipes the brow of the dying, we cannot exist without mutual help.
**SIR WALTER SCOTT**

In a balanced organization, working towards a common objective, there is success.
**T. L. SCRUTTON**

Nothing less than a sense of divine co-operation can sustain us in the long pull of restoring the world to the orderly procedures of life.
**RALPH W. SOCKMAN**

Protestant, Roman Catholic and Jewish leaders should set one example to the world by getting together in conference and co-operation instead of resorting to controversy and conflict.
**RALPH W. SOCKMAN**

We cannot be independent of the kindly give-and-take spirit of cooperation in our work.
**RODERICK STEVENS**

From the beginning of our history the country has been afflicted with compromise. It is by compromise that human rights have been abandoned. I insist that this shall cease. The country needs repose after all its trials; it deserves repose. And repose can only be found in everlasting principles.
**CHARLES SUMNER**

You might as well fall flat on your face as lean over too far backward.
**JAMES THURBER**

Vital to every operation is cooperation.
**FRANK TYGER**

One of the most important trips a man can make is that involved in meeting the other fellow halfway.
**BRUCE VAN HORN**

Co-operation is spelled with two letters—WE.
GEORGE M. VERITY

## Country

If I can in any way contribute to the diversion or improvement of the country in which I live, I shall leave it, when I am summoned out of it, with the secret satisfaction of thinking that I have not lived in vain.
JOSEPH ADDISON

Citizenship comes first today in our crowded world. . . . No man can enjoy the privileges of education and thereafter with a clear conscience break his contract with society. To respect that contract is to be mature, to strengthen it is to be a good citizen, to do more than your share under it is to be noble.
ISAIAH BOWMAN

Laws have their proper place, but the responsibility of worthy citizenship is a personal one. We each have a separate and individual share in eradicating social evils and in refusing to perpetuate practices odious to a free nation.
HERBERT BROWNELL, JR.

When I am abroad, I always make it a rule never to criticize or attack the government of my own country. I make up for lost time when I come home.
WINSTON CHURCHILL

The big ideas in this world cannot survive unless they come to life in the individual citizen. It is what each man does in responding to his convictions that provides the forward thrust for any great movement.
NORMAN COUSINS

Of the whole sum of human life no small part is that which consists of a man's relations to his country, and his feelings concerning it.
WILLIAM E. GLADSTONE

A citizen has a complex duty. He ought to learn to express his opinions and to make up his own mind on the principal public issues. He ought never to miss the ballot box. And when he casts his vote for somebody, he should weigh that somebody in the scale of morals—which includes intellectual integrity.
HERBERT HOOVER

There is no such thing as a little country. The greatness of a people is no more determined by their number than the greatness of a man is determined by his height.
VICTOR HUGO

Every country should realize that its turn at world domination, domination because its rights coincided more or less with the character or progress of the epoch, must terminate with the change brought about by this progress.
JUAN RAMÓN JIMÉNEZ

Where the very safety of the country depends upon the resolution to be taken, no considerations of justice or injustice, humanity or cruelty, nor of glory or of shame, should be allowed to prevail. But putting all other considerations aside, the only question should be: What course will save the life and liberty of the country?
NICCOLÒ MACHIAVELLI

The best way to teach our young people the meaning of our democratic freedoms is to demonstrate, by our own example, that we have mastered the three R's of citizenship—Rights, Respect and Responsibilities.
EARL JAMES MCGRATH

Fix your eyes upon the greatness of your country as you have it before you day by day... and when you feel her great, remember that her greatness was won by men with courage, with knowledge of their duty and with a sense of honor in action, who, even if they failed in some venture, would not think of depriving their country of their powers but laid them at her feet as their fairest offering.
**PERICLES**

Some men go in for big game hunting or Old Masters or postage stamps, but my hobby happens to be my country.
**SAMUEL B. PETTENGILL**

The accent of a man's native country dwells in his mind and in his heart as well as in his speech.
**FRANÇOIS DE LA ROCHEFOUCAULD**

The man who loves other countries as much as his own stands on a level with the man who loves other women as much as he loves his own wife.
**THEODORE ROOSEVELT**

It is sweet to serve one's country by deeds, and it is not absurd to serve her by words.
**SALLUST**

It is right to prefer one's own country to others, because we are children and citizens before we can be travellers or philosophers.
**GEORGE SANTAYANA**

The proper means of increasing the love we bear to our native country is to reside some time in a foreign one.
**WILLIAM SHENSTONE**

I have no relish for the country; it is a kind of healthy grave.
**SYDNEY SMITH**

The best kind of citizen and the solidest kind of enterprise is one that can look the whole world in the face.
**M. E. TRACY**

Whoever serves his country well has no need of ancestors.
**VOLTAIRE**

Let our object be our country, our whole country, and nothing but our country. And, by the blessing of God, may that country itself become a vast and splendid monument, not of oppression and terror, but of wisdom, of peace and of liberty, upon which the world may gaze with admiration forever!
**DANIEL WEBSTER**

Nothing will ruin the country if the people themselves will undertake its safety; and nothing can save it if they leave that safety in any hands but their own.
**DANIEL WEBSTER**

## *Courage*

Courage and perseverance have a magical talisman, before which difficulties disappear and obstacles vanish into air.
**JOHN QUINCY ADAMS**

Courage that grows from constitution often forsakes a man when he has occasion for it; courage which arises from a sense of duty acts in a uniform manner.
**JOSEPH ADDISON**

It is easy to be brave from a safe distance.
**AESOP**

Often the test of courage is not to die but to live.
VITTORIO ALFIERI

Whether you be man or woman you will never do anything in this world without courage. It is the greatest quality of the mind next to honor.
JAMES LANE ALLEN

Until the day of his death, no man can be sure of his courage.
JEAN ANOUILH

Pay as little attention to discouragement as possible. Plough ahead as a steamer does, rough or smooth—rain or shine. To carry your cargo and make your port is the point.
MALTBIE BABCOCK

Courage: The lovely virtue—the rib of Himself that God sent down to His children.
JAMES M. BARRIE

Courage is a special kind of knowledge: the knowledge of how to fear what ought to be feared and how not to fear what ought not to be feared.
DAVID BEN-GURION

Courage is like love; it must have hope for nourishment.
NAPOLEON BONAPARTE

It is an error to suppose that courage means courage in everything. Most people are brave only in the dangers to which they accustom themselves, either in imagination or practice.
EDWARD BULWER-LYTTON

The paradox of courage is that a man must be a little careless of his life even in order to keep it.
G. K. CHESTERTON

Courage is the first of human qualities because it is the quality which guarantees all the others.
WINSTON CHURCHILL

Courage is what it takes to stand up and speak; courage is also what it takes to sit down and listen.
WINSTON CHURCHILL

Physical courage, which despises all danger, will make a man brave in one way; and moral courage, which despises all opinion, will make a man brave in another.
CHARLES CALEB COLTON

Every man of courage is a man of his word.
PIERRE CORNEILLE

My message to you is: Be courageous! I have lived a long time. I have seen history repeat itself again and again. I have seen many depressions in business. Always America has come out stronger and more prosperous. Be as brave as your fathers before you. Have faith! Go forward.
THOMAS EDISON'S LAST PUBLIC MESSAGE

A great part of courage is having done the thing before.
RALPH WALDO EMERSON

Courage consists in equality to the problem before us.
RALPH WALDO EMERSON

The courage of the tiger is one, and of the horse another.
RALPH WALDO EMERSON

Whatever you do, you need courage. Whatever course you decide upon, there is always someone to tell you you are wrong. There are always difficulties arising which tempt you to believe that your critics

are right. To map out a course of action and follow it to an end, requires some of the same courage which a soldier needs. Peace has its victories, but it takes brave men to win them.
**RALPH WALDO EMERSON**

And have you not received faculties which will enable you to bear all that happens to you? Have you not received greatness of spirit? Have you not received courage? Have you not received endurance?
**EPICTETUS**

Courage is worth nothing if the gods withhold their aid.
**EURIPIDES**

Courage is the supreme virtue, because it is the guarantor of every other virtue.
**BERGEN EVANS**

Courage is a virtue only so far as it is directed to produce.
**FRANÇOIS FÉNELON**

It takes courage to live—courage and strength and hope and humor. And courage and strength and hope and humor have to be bought and paid for with pain and work and prayers and tears.
**JEROME P. FLEISHMAN**

It is pleasant to be transferred from an office where one is afraid of a sergeant-major into an office where one can intimidate generals, and perhaps this is why history is so attractive to the more timid among us.
**E. M. FORSTER**

The rarest courage is the courage of thought.
**ANATOLE FRANCE**

In doubtful matters courage may do much; in desperate, patience.
**THOMAS FULLER**

Moral courage is a virtue of higher cast and nobler origin than physical. It springs from a consciousness of virtue and renders a man, in the pursuit or defense of right, superior to the fear of reproach, opposition in contempt.
**SAMUEL GOODRICH**

Like love, courage is no joking matter. If it yields once, it will have to yield again, and again. The same difficulty will have to be conquered later on, and it would have been better to get it over with.
**BALTASAR GRACIÁN**

Without courage, wisdom bears no fruit.
**BALTASAR GRACIÁN**

It is courage the world needs, not infallibility... courage is always the surest wisdom.
**WILFRED T. GRENFELL**

Life only demands from you the strength you possess. Only one feat is possible—not to have run away.
**DAG HAMMARSKJÖLD**

Courage is grace under pressure.
**ERNEST HEMINGWAY**

Someone has said that the "p" is silent in the word luck, but it belongs there nevertheless. Investigation usually turns up the fact that the lucky fellow is the plucky fellow who has been burning midnight oil and taking defeat after defeat with a smile.
**JAMES B. HILL**

Nothing is too high for the daring of mortals; we storm heaven itself in our folly.
**HORACE**

Anger is a prelude to courage.
**ERIC HOFFER**

The first step in handling anything is gaining the ability to face it.
**L. RON HUBBARD**

Courage without conscience is a wild beast.
**RALPH INGERSOLL**

One man with courage makes a majority.
**ANDREW JACKSON**

Timid men prefer the calm of despotism to the boisterous sea of liberty.
**THOMAS JEFFERSON**

Courage is a quality so necessary for maintaining virtue that it is always respected, even when it is associated with vice.
**SAMUEL JOHNSON**

Only be thou strong and very courageous, that thou mayest observe to do according to all the law, which Moses my servant commanded thee: turn not from it to the right hand or to the left, that thou mayest prosper whithersoever thou goest.
**JOSHUA 1:7**

Have I not commanded thee? Be strong and of good courage; be not afraid, neither be thou dismayed: for the Lord thy God is with thee whithersoever thou goest.
**JOSHUA 1:9**

Failure is only postponed success as long as courage coaches ambition. The habit of persistence is the habit of victory.
**HERBERT KAUFMAN**

Hope awakens courage. He who can implant courage in the human soul is the best physician.
**KARL LUDWIG VON KNEBEL**

If we as Americans show the same courage and common sense that motivated the men who sat at Philadelphia and gave us the Declaration of Independence and later the Constitution of the United States, there is no domestic problem we cannot solve and there is no foreign foe we need ever fear.
**WILLIAM F. KNOWLAND**

Courage is not simply one of the virtues, but the form of every virtue at the testing point.
**C. S. LEWIS**

Pugnacity is a form of courage, but a very bad form.
**SINCLAIR LEWIS**

It's easy to be courageous when you have no choice.
**MICHAEL MAGGIO**

The world is not perishing for the want of clever or talented or well-meaning men. It is perishing for the want of men of courage and resolution who, in devotion to the cause of right and truth, can rise above personal feeling and private ambition.
**ROBERT J. MCCRACKEN**

Courage is the most common and vulgar of the virtues.
**HERMAN MELVILLE**

The strongest, most generous and proudest of all virtues is courage.
**MICHEL DE MONTAIGNE**

Courage conquers all things.
**OVID**

Courage in danger is half the battle.
**PLAUTUS**

The only security is courage.
**FRANÇOIS DE LA ROCHEFOUCAULD**

Courage is sometimes frail as hope is frail: a fragile shoot between two stones that grows brave toward the sun though warmth and brightness fail, striving and faith the only strength it knows.
**FRANCES RODMAN**

Don't foul, don't flinch—hit the line hard.
**THEODORE ROOSEVELT**

Far better it is to dare mighty things, to win glorious triumphs, even though checkered by failure, than to take rank with those poor spirits who neither enjoy much nor suffer much, because they live in the gray twilight that knows not victory nor defeat.
**THEODORE ROOSEVELT**

Personal courage is really a very subordinate virtue—a virtue, indeed, in which we are surpassed by the lower animals; or else you would not hear people say, "as brave as a lion."
**ARTHUR SCHOPENHAUER**

The will to do, the soul to dare.
**SIR WALTER SCOTT**

Courage leads starward, fear toward death.
**SENECA**

There is nothing in the world so much admired as a man who knows how to bear unhappiness with courage.
**SENECA**

The most sublime courage I have ever witnessed has been among that class too poor to know they possessed it, and too humble for the world to discover it.
**GEORGE BERNARD SHAW**

I would define true courage to be a perfect sensibility of the measure of danger, and a mental willingness to endure it.
**WILLIAM TECUMSEH SHERMAN**

Who bravely dares must sometimes risk a fall.
**TOBIAS GEORGE SMOLLETT**

The test of tolerance comes when we are in a majority; the test of courage comes when we are in a minority.
**RALPH W. SOCKMAN**

Let the man who has to make his fortune in life remember this maxim: Attacking is the only secret. Dare and the world always yields; or if it beats you sometimes, dare it again and it will succumb.
**WILLIAM MAKEPEACE THACKERAY**

Courage, it would seem, is nothing less than the power to overcome danger, misfortune, fear, injustice, while continuing to affirm inwardly that life with all its sorrows is good; that everything is meaningful even if in a sense beyond our understanding; and that there is always tomorrow.
**DOROTHY THOMPSON**

Success is never final and Failure never fatal. It's courage that counts.
**GEORGE F. TILTON**

Courage is resistance to fear, mastery of fear—not absence of fear. Except a creature be part coward it is not a compliment to say it is brave; it is merely a loose missapplication of the word.
**MARK TWAIN**

It is curious that physical courage should be so common in the world, and moral courage so rare.
**MARK TWAIN**

True courage is not the brutal force of vulgar heroes, but the firm resolve of virtue and reason.
**ALFRED NORTH WHITEHEAD**

Only as a grand gesture of defeat will men creep into the arms of the state and seek refuge in its power rather than their own courage.
**HENRY M. WRISTON**

Why should we honor those that die upon the field of battle? A man may show as reckless a courage in entering into the abyss of himself.
**WILLIAM BUTLER YEATS**

It takes vision and courage to create—it takes faith and courage to prove.
**OWEN D. YOUNG**

## *Criticism*

It is folly for an eminent person to think of escaping censure, and a weakness to be affected by it. All the illustrious persons of antiquity, and indeed of every age, have passed through this fiery persecution. There is no defense against reproach but obscurity; it is a kind of concomitant to greatness.
**JOSEPH ADDISON**

It is ridiculous for any man to criticize the works of another who has not distinguished himself by his own performance.
**JOSEPH ADDISON**

You cannot raise a man up by calling him down.
**WILLIAM J. H. BOETCKER**

The pleasure of criticism deprives us of that of being deeply moved by beautiful things.
**JEAN DE LA BRUYÈRE**

The legitimate aim of criticism is to direct attention to the excellent. The bad will dig its own grave, and the imperfect may safely be left to that final neglect from which no amount of present undeserved popularity can rescue it.
**CHRISTIAN BOVÉE**

Any fool can criticize, condemn and complain—and most fools do.
**DALE CARNEGIE**

Censure is often useful, praise often deceitful.
**WINSTON CHURCHILL**

I criticize by creation, not by finding fault.
**CICERO**

It has been shrewdly said that when men abuse us, we should suspect ourselves, and when they praise us, them. It is a rare instance of virtue to despise censure which we do not deserve, and still more rare to despise praise, which we do. But that integrity that lives only on opinion would starve without it.
**CHARLES CALEB COLTON**

The chronic knocker gets more discomfort from his continual criticism than do all of the people that he is raving against.
**CHARLES J. DENNIS**

It is much easier to be critical than to be correct.
**BENJAMIN DISRAELI**

Most of our censure of others is only oblique praise of self, uttered to show the wisdom and superiority of the speaker.
**TRYON EDWARDS**

As to people saying a few idle words about us, we must not mind that any more than the old church steeple minds the rooks cawing about it.
GEORGE ELIOT

Criticism should not be querulous and wasting, all knife and rootpuller, but guiding, instructive, inspiring.
RALPH WALDO EMERSON

We are told we should always speak well of the dead. But wouldn't that sometimes be hypocrisy? The writer did not hesitate to criticize [American Woolen Co. head] William M. Wood during his life and now feels that his tragic death, by suicide, contains a lesson for at least a few of America's large employers.

When infirmity overtook him, he [attempted] works of repentance, but it was too late. . . . The writer knows that too many men of vast affairs are blind to the realities, the worthwhile things of life, and do not acquire a correct perspective until they feel themselves slipping toward the grave.
B. C. FORBES

There are no exceptions to the rule that everybody likes to be an exception to the rule.
MALCOLM FORBES

I like people to come back and tell me what I did wrong. That's the kindest thing you can do.
LILLIAN GISH

Many receive a criticism and think it is fine; think they got their money's worth; think well of the teacher for it, and then go on with their work just the same as before. That is the reason much of the wisdom of Plato is still locked up in the pages of Plato.
ROBERT HENRI

We are 90% alike, all we peoples, and 10% different. The trouble is that we forget the 90% and remember the 10% when we criticize others.
SIR CHARLES HIGHAM

To avoid criticism do nothing, say nothing, be nothing.
ELBERT HUBBARD

It is harder to avoid censure than to gain applause, for this may be done by one great or wise action in an age; but to escape censure a man must pass his whole life without saying or doing one ill or foolish thing.
DAVID HUME

A tart temper never mellows with age; and a sharp tongue is the only edged tool that grows keener with constant use.
WASHINGTON IRVING

I find the pain of little censure, even when it is unfounded, is more acute than the pleasure of much praise.
THOMAS JEFFERSON

Criticism is a study by which men grow important and formidable at very small expense.
SAMUEL JOHNSON

It behooves the minor critic, who hunts for blemishes, to be a little distrustful of his own sagacity.
JUNIUS

You do ill if you praise, but worse if you censure, when you do not rightly understand.
LEONARDO DA VINCI

Some critics are like chimneysweepers; they put out the fire below, and frighten the swallows from their nests above; they scrape a long time in the chimney,

cover themselves with soot, and bring nothing away but a bag of cinders, and then sing from the top of the house as if they had built it.
HENRY WADSWORTH LONGFELLOW

I have never found, in a long experience of politics, that criticism is ever inhibited by ignorance.
HAROLD MACMILLAN

It is our job to extol the benefits of our way of life rather than the weakness of other systems. If we do not do this we may find that we have done by default what others seek to do by design.
WILLIAM B. MCKESSON

There are two kinds of dramatic critics; destructive and constructive. I am a destructive. There are two kinds of guns: Krupp and pop.
GEORGE JEAN NATHAN

When men speak ill of thee, live so as nobody may believe them.
PLATO

It is a thing of no great difficulty to raise objections against another man's oration—nay, it is very easy; but to produce a better in its place is a work extremely troublesome.
PLUTARCH

It is not the critic who counts, nor the man who points out how the strong man stumbles or where the doers of deeds could have done better.
THEODORE ROOSEVELT

Stones and sticks are thrown only at fruit-bearing trees.
SA'DI

Show yourself more human than critical and your pleasure will increase.
DOMENICO SCARLATTI

I have yet to find the man, however exalted his station, who did not do better work and put forth greater effort under a spirit of approval than under a spirit of criticism.
CHARLES M. SCHWAB, STEEL MAGNATE

Pay no attention to what the critics say; there has never been a statue erected to a critic.
JEAN SIBELIUS

He who would acquire fame must not show himself afraid of censure. The dread of censure is the death of genius.
WILLIAM SIMMS

Neither praise nor blame is the object of true criticism. Justly to discriminate, firmly to establish, wisely to prescribe and honestly to award—these are the true aims and duties of criticism.
WILLIAM SIMMS

I know of no manner of speaking so offensive as that of giving praise, and closing it with an exception.
RICHARD STEELE

Censure is the tax a man pays to the public for being eminent.
JONATHAN SWIFT

I have ever held that the rod with which popular fancy invests criticism is properly the rod of divination: a hazel switch for the discovery of buried treasure, not a birch twig for the castigation of offenders.
ARTHUR SYMONS

You do not get a man's most effective criticism until you provoke him. Severe truth is expressed with some bitterness.
HENRY DAVID THOREAU

Criticism is the child and handmaid of reflection. It works by censure and censure implies a standard.
RICHARD G. WHITE

Has anybody ever seen a dramatic critic in the daytime? Of course not. They come out after dark, up to no good.
P. G. WODEHOUSE

## Culture

Every man's ability may be strengthened or increased by culture.
SIR JOHN JOSEPH CALDWELL ABBOTT

Culture looks beyond machinery, culture hates hatred; culture has one great passion—the passion for sweetness and light.
MATTHEW ARNOLD

Culture, the acquainting ourselves with the best that has been known and said in the world.
MATTHEW ARNOLD

The acquiring of culture is the developing of an avid hunger for knowledge and beauty.
JESSE LEE BENNETT

A man should be just cultured enough to be able to look like suspicion on culture, at first, not second hand.
SAMUEL BUTLER

Many men absorbed in business show such a rare quality of culture that we are surprised at it. The reason invariably is partly because hard work and even the weariness it leaves carry a nobility with them, but also because there is no room in such lives for inferior mental occupation.
ERNEST DIMNET

The boundaries of culture and rainfall never follow survey lines.
J. FRANK DOBIE

The most distinctive mark of a cultured mind is the ability to take another's point of view; to put one's self in another's place, and see life and its problems from a point of view different from one's own. To be willing to test a new idea; to be able to live on the edge of difference in all matters intellectually; to examine without heat the burning question of the day; to have imaginative sympathy, openness and flexibility of mind, steadiness and poise of feeling, cool calmness of judgment, is to have culture.
ARTHUR H. R. FAIRCHILD

For corporations to be bedfellows with the arts is good business for both. The architecture that houses a company is a more visible statement than the president's in the annual report. Ditto interiors, particularly of offices and sometimes, dramatically, in plants. For solvent businesses, support of community cultural undertakings in music, drama, dance creates great goodwill. Also, the existence of such activities is often important to the executives and their families that companies want to keep or attract to keep.
MALCOLM FORBES

I do not want my house to be walled in on all sides and my windows to be stuffed. I want the cultures of all lands to be blown about my house as freely as possible. But I refuse to be blown off my feet by any.
MAHATMA GANDHI

Culture is simply the hospitality of the intellect. Your mind is open to new ideas and larger views; when they enter, you know how to receive them, and to entertain, to be entertained, and take what they have to offer without allowing them to dominate you.
THOMAS KETTLE

Culture is the sum of all the forms of art, of love and of thought, which, in the course of centuries, have enabled man to be less enslaved.
ANDRÉ MALRAUX

Culture is not just an ornament; it is the expression of a nation's character, and at the same time it is a powerful instrument to mould character. The end of culture is right living.
SOMERSET MAUGHAM

Culture is what is left after everything we have learned has been forgotten. It consists of a deepened understanding, a breadth of outlook, an unbiased approach and a heart that has deep sympathy and strength of courage.
G. BROMLEY OXNAM

Culture, in the deeper issues, is no smooth, placid, academic thing. It is no carefully arranged system of rules and theories. It is the passionate and imaginative instinct for things that are distinguished, heroic and rare. It is the subtilizing and deepening of the human spirit in presence of the final mystery.
JOHN COWPER POWYS

## *Curiosity*

Curiosity is always rebuked as one of the restless weaknesses of humanity, but I am inclined to think that most people are not inquisitive enough. They have not what I call clean curiosity—a mere appetite for the truth. They cannot be interested and disinterested too.
G. K. CHESTERTON

Curiosity is free-wheeling intelligence. It endows the people who have it with a generosity in argument and a serenity in their own mode of life which spring from the cheerful willingness to let life take the forms it will.
ALISTAIR COOKE

There are two ways to interest a man or arouse his curiosity. One is to tell him something that he didn't know. The other is to remind him of something he has forgotten.
A. E. N. GRAY

Curiosity is one of the most permanent and certain characteristics of a vigorous intellect.
SAMUEL JOHNSON

Friendly concern is often simple curiosity.
BARON MCKAY

Satisfaction of one's curiosity is one of the greatest sources of happiness in life.
LINUS PAULING

One of the secrets of life is to keep our intellectual curiosity acute.
WILLIAM LYON PHELPS

There are different kinds of curiosity; one of interest, which causes us to learn that which would be useful to us; and the other of pride, which springs from a desire to know that of which others are ignorant.
FRANÇOIS DE LA ROCHEFOUCAULD

Life was meant to be lived, and curiosity must be kept alive. One must never, for whatever reason, turn his back on life.
ELEANOR ROOSEVELT

Curiosity is looking over other people's affairs and overlooking our own.
HERMAN L. WAYLAND

## Cynicism

A cynic is a blackguard whose faulty vision sees things as they are, not as they ought to be. Hence the custom among the Scythians of plucking out a cynic's eyes to improve his vision.
AMBROSE BIERCE

The cynic never grows up, but commits intellectual suicide.
CHARLES REYNOLDS BROWN

Cynics build no bridges; they make no discoveries; no gaps are spanned by them. Cynics may pride themselves in being realistic in their approach, but progress and the onward march of Christian civilization demand an inspiration and motivation that cynicism never affords. If we want progress we must take the forward look.
PAUL L. MCKAY, D.D.

Cynics and critics wake us up. Kindness often covers up the truth and allows us to sleep on in our ignorance.
WILFRED A. PETERSON

All seems infected that the infected spy, as all looks yellow to the jaundiced eye.
ALEXANDER POPE

The power of accurate observation is commonly called cynicism by those who have not got it.
GEORGE BERNARD SHAW

The only deadly sin I know is cynicism.
HENRY STIMSON

The cynic makes fun of all earnestness; he makes fun of everything and everyone who feels that something can be done. . . . But in his heart of hearts he knows that he is a defeated man and that his cynicism is merely an expression of the fact that he has lost courage and is beaten.
GEORGE E. VINCENT

A cynic is a man who knows the price of everything and the value of nothing.
OSCAR WILDE

# D

## Day

A cloudy day, or a little sunshine, have as great an influence on many constitutions as the most real blessings or misfortunes.
JOSEPH ADDISON

It's more difficult getting up early in the morning when you're wearing silk pajamas.
EDDIE ARCARO

In the morning let this thought be present: I am rising to a man's work.
MARCUS AURELIUS ANTONINUS

Live not one's life as though one had a thousand years, but live each day as the last.
MARCUS AURELIUS ANTONINUS

Each golden sunrise ushers in new opportunities for those who retain faith in themselves, and keep their chins up. No one has ever seen a cock crow with its head down. Courage to start and willingness to keep everlastingly at it are the requisites for success. Meet the sunrise with confidence. Fill every golden minute with right thinking and worthwhile endeavor. Do this and there will be joy for you in each golden sunset.
ALONZO NEWTON BENN

One of the illusions is that the present hour is not the critical, decisive hour. Write it in your heart that every day is the best day of the year.
RALPH WALDO EMERSON

To be seeing the world made new every morning, as if it were the morning of the first day, and then to make the most of it for the individual soul, as if it were the last day—is the daily curriculum of the mind's desire.
JOHN H. FINLEY

Early rising maketh a man whole in body, wholer in soul and richer in goods.
JOHN FITZHERBERT

One ought at least to hear a little melody every day, read a fine poem, see a good picture, and, if possible make a few sensible remarks.
JOHANN WOLFGANG VON GOETHE

Those that dare lose a day are dangerously prodigal; those that dare misspend it, desperate.
BISHOP JOSEPH HALL

Walter B. Pitkin has written a book on Life Begins at Forty. I rise to offer a substitute, Mr. Pitkin, Life Begins Each Morning. Whether one is twenty, forty or sixty; whether one has succeeded, failed or just muddled along; whether yesterday was full of sun or storm, or one of those dull days with no weather at all, Life Begins Each Morning! . . . Each night of life is a wall between to-day and the past. Each morning is the open door to a new world—new vistas, new aims, new tryings.
LEIGH MITCHELL HODGES

The dullest observer must be sensible of the order and serenity prevalent in those households where the occasional exercise of a beautiful form of worship in the morning gives, as it were, the keynote

to every temper for the day, and attunes every spirit to harmony.
WASHINGTON IRVING

The happiest part of a man's life is that which he passes lying awake in bed in the morning.
SAMUEL JOHNSON

Thou shalt ever joy at eventide if thou spend the day fruitfully.
THOMAS À KEMPIS

You do well to have visions of a better life than of every day, but it is the life of every day from which the elements of a better life must come.
MAURICE MAETERLINCK

**The Good New Day**

None but the futile mourn the past,
Or waste their hours in vain berating;
Each day is richer than the last;
There are new worlds to conquer waiting!

Though somber sunsets lend a wan
Regret to pleasant days gone from us,
The pilgrim stars go wheeling on,
And dawns bring new demesnes of promise!

The path that yesterday we trod
Was bright with blossom, sweet with clover;
Yet there must be a richer sod
Where the horizon trail dips over.

Onward and upward, mile on mile;
Deaf to the jibes, the mocker's chorus;
Facing each hazard with a smile—
Till a new world lies wide before us!

There is no going back. Why bind
Your swift pace with a phantom fetter?
Forget the good old days behind.
Go on—and make the new ones better!
TED OLSEN

The clean tongue, the clear head, and the bright eye are birthrights of each day.
SIR WILLIAM OSLER

Your morning thoughts may determine your conduct for the day. Optimistic thoughts will make your day bright and productive, while pessimistic thinking will make it dull and wasteful. Face each day cheerfully, smilingly and courageously, and it will naturally follow that your work will be a real pleasure and progress will be a delightful accomplishment.
WILLIAM M. PECK

Sunday is the day people go quietly mad, one way or another.
WILLIAM SAROYAN

One should count each day a separate life.
SENECA

There is nothing more universally commended than a fine day; the reason is, that people can commend it without envy.
WILLIAM SHENSTONE

When you rise in the morning, form a resolution to make the day a happy one to a fellow-creature.
SYDNEY SMITH

One golden day redeems a weary year.
CELIA THAXTER

Only that day dawns to which we are awake.
HENRY DAVID THOREAU

When you say good morning to the rabbi, say good morning also to the rabbi's wife.
YIDDISH PROVERB

## Death

The fence around a cemetery is foolish, for those inside can't come out and those outside don't want to get in.
**ARTHUR BRISBANE**

At death, those heirs
That seem the saddest,
Behind their masks
May be the gladdest.
**ART BUCK**

Nature, in her wily way,
Provides for our terminal care;
It's quaintly called eternal rest,
And all of us get the same share.
**ART BUCK**

To live in hearts we leave behind is not to die.
**CLYDE CAMPBELL**

No one could ever meet death for his country without the hope of immortality.
**CICERO**

I never wanted to see anybody die, but there are a few obituary notices I have read with pleasure.
**CLARENCE DARROW**

One must wait until the evening to see how splendid the day was; one cannot judge life until death.
**CHARLES DE GAULLE**

Worldly faces never look so worldly as at a funeral.
**GEORGE ELIOT**

True, you can't take it with you, but then, that's not the place where it comes in handy.
**BRENDAN FRANCIS**

We have long had death and taxes as the two standards of inevitability. But there are those who believe that death is the preferable of the two.
**ERWIN N. GRISWOLD**

Fortunate people often have very favorable beginnings and very tragic endings. What matters isn't being applauded when you arrive—for that is common—but being missed when you leave.
**BALTASAR GRACIÁN**

Death is the penalty we all pay for the privilege of life.
**ROBERT HALF**

I hope and trust to meet you in Heaven, both white and black—both white and black.
**ANDREW JACKSON**

Only death reveals what a nothing the body of man is.
**JUVENAL**

To judge of the real importance of the individual, we should think of the effect his death would produce.
**FRANÇOIS-GASTON DE LEVIS**

If they do kill me, I shall never die another death.
**ABRAHAM LINCOLN**

Only those are fit to live who are not afraid to die.
**DOUGLAS MACARTHUR**

The days of our years are threescore years and ten; and if by reason of strength they be fourscore years, yet is their strength labor and sorrow; for it is soon cut off, and we fly away.
**PSALMS 90:10**

There's no reason to be the richest man in the cemetery. You can't do any business from there.
**COLONEL SANDERS**

The way to overcome the fear and unreality of death and the hereafter is to learn to live with eternal and invisible things here and now. If we live only for the pleasures of sense, of course we cannot take our satisfactions with us. But if we live for the things of the spirit, truth, goodness, love and their like, we shall be fitted for the life which survives the grave.
RALPH W. SOCKMAN

We can't always have things to please us,
Little Johnny has gone to Jesus.
SOUTHERN CEMETERY EPITAPH

When it's time to die, let us not discover that we have never lived.
HENRY DAVID THOREAU

Let us endeavor so to live that when we come to die even the undertaker will be sorry.
MARK TWAIN

Whoever has lived long enough to find out what life is, knows how deep a debt of gratitude we owe to Adam, the first great benefactor of our race. He brought death into the world.
MARK TWAIN

All say, How hard it is we have to die,—a strange complaint to come from the mouths of people who have had to live.
MARK TWAIN

My grandfather was cut down in the prime of his life. My grandmother used to say, "If he had been cut down 15 minutes earlier, he could have been resuscitated."
MARK TWAIN

I did not attend his funeral, but I wrote a nice letter saying I approved it.
MARK TWAIN

If we take eternity to mean not infinite temporal duration but timelessness, then eternal life belongs to those who live in the present.
LUDWIG WITTGENSTEIN

## *Debt*

Time is running out on the fiscal policies which were initiated when our national debt was a small fraction of what it is today and which may have been expedient during the war but in present circumstances involve dangers so great as to demand that no further compromise with sound fiscal practice be tolerated.
J. STEWART BAKER

"Out of debt, out of danger" is, like many other proverbs, full of wisdom; but the word danger does not sufficiently express all that the warning demands. For a state of debt and embarrassment is a state of positive misery, and the sufferer is as one haunted by an evil spirit, and his heart can know neither rest nor peace till it is cast out.
CHARLES BRIDGES

Reduce the deficit?
I wish we would.
I doubt we really will:
It hurts too good.
ART BUCK

There are but two ways of paying debt—increase of industry in raising income, increase of thrift in laying out.
THOMAS CARLYLE

Owing money has never concerned me so long as I know where it could be repaid.
COL. HENRY CROWN

Let us live in as small a circle as we will, we are either debtors or creditors before we have had time to look around.
JOHANN WOLFGANG VON GOETHE

Much misconstruction and bitterness are spared to him who thinks naturally upon what he owes to others, rather than on what he ought to expect from them.
ELISABETH GUIZOT

The American way is the way most law-abiding, tax-paying Americans live—in debt. Does this make a balanced budget un-American?
CULLEN HIGHTOWER

Blessed are the young, for they shall inherit the national debt.
HERBERT HOOVER

To preserve their independence, we must not let our rules load us with perpetual debt. We must make our election between economy and liberty, or profusion and servitude.
THOMAS JEFFERSON

Debt is the secret foe of thrift, as vice and idleness are its open foes. The debt-habit is the twin brother of poverty.
THEODORE T. MUNGER

Good times are when people make debts to pay in bad times.
ROBERT QUILLEN

The first step in debt is like the first step in falsehood, involving the necessity of going on in the same course, debt following debt, as lie follows lie.
SAMUEL SMILES

Debt is the slavery of the free.
PUBLILIUS SYRUS

If you want the time to pass quickly, just give your note for 90 days.
R. B. THOMAS

## *Deception*

The easiest person to deceive is oneself.
EDWARD BULWER-LYTTON

Deceivers are the most dangerous members of society. They trifle with the best affections of our nature, and violate the most sacred obligations.
GEORGE CRABBE

Beware lest any man spoil you through philosophy and vain deceit, after the tradition of men, after the rudiments of the world, and not after Christ.
COLOSSIANS 2:8

The easiest thing of all is to deceive one's self; for what a man wishes he generally believes to be true.
DEMOSTHENES

Every man takes care that his neighbor shall not cheat him. But a day comes when he begins to care that he does not cheat his neighbor. Then all goes well.
RALPH WALDO EMERSON

Better to be occasionally cheated than perpetually suspicious.
B. C. FORBES

It is in the ability to deceive oneself that the greatest talent is shown.
ANATOLE FRANCE

Cheat me in the price, but not in the goods.
**THOMAS FULLER**

The natural man has a difficult time getting along in the world. Half the people think he is a scoundrel because he is not a hypocrite.
**EDGAR WATSON HOWE**

No man was ever so much deceived by another, as by himself.
**LORD GREVILLE**

It is very noble hypocrisy not to talk of one's self.
**FRIEDRICH WILHELM NIETZSCHE**

It is more shameful to distrust your friends than it is to be deceived by them.
**FRANÇOIS DE LA ROCHEFOUCAULD**

We often shed tears that deceive ourselves after deceiving others.
**FRANÇOIS DE LA ROCHEFOUCAULD**

You are never so easily fooled as when trying to fool someone else.
**FRANÇOIS DE LA ROCHEFOUCAULD**

I hope you have not been leading a double life, pretending to be wicked, and being really good all the time. That would be hypocrisy.
**OSCAR WILDE**

## *Decisions*

The man who insists upon seeing with perfect clearness before he decides, never decides. Accept life, and you cannot accept regret.
**HENRI FRÉDÉRIC AMIEL**

While an open mind is priceless, it is priceless only when its owner has the courage to make a final decision which closes the mind for action after the process of viewing all sides of the question has been completed. Failure to make a decision after due consideration of all the facts will quickly brand a man as unfit for a position of responsibility. Not all of your decisions will be correct. None of us is perfect. But if you get into the habit of making decisions, experience will develop your judgment to a point where more and more of your decisions will be right. After all, it is better to be right 51% of the time and get something done, than it is to get nothing done because you fear to reach a decision.
**H. W. ANDREWS**

When you come to a fork in the road—take it.
**YOGI BERRA**

When you approach a problem, strip yourself of preconceived opinions and prejudice, assemble and learn the facts of the situation, make the decision which seems to you to be the most honest, and then stick to it.
**CHESTER BOWLES**

Never make a decision yourself, if you don't have to. When one of your men asks you a question, ask him what is the answer. There is only one answer to many questions, and, therefore, this method answers many questions before they are asked. It not only develops your men, but also enables you to measure their ability.
**HENRY L. DOHERTY**

In many lines of work, it isn't how much you do that counts, but how much you do well and how often you decide right.
**WILLIAM FEATHER**

Nothing can be more destructive to vigor of action than protracted, anxious fluctuation, through reso-

lutions adopted, rejected, resumed, and suspended, and nothing causes a greater expense of feeling. A man without decision can never be said to belong to himself; he is as a wave of the sea, or a feather in the air which every breeze blows about as it listeth.
JOHN FOSTER

I have to be wrong a certain number of times in order to be right a certain number of times. However, in order to be either, I must first make a decision.
FRANK N. GIAMPIETRO

When possible make the decisions now, even if action is in the future. A reviewed decision usually is better than one reached at the last moment.
WILLIAM B. GIVEN, JR.

Decision is a sharp knife that cuts clean and straight; indecision, a dull one that hacks and tears and leaves ragged edges behind it.
GORDON GRAHAM

There is nothing more to be esteemed than a manly firmness and decision of character. I like a person who knows his own mind and sticks to it; who sees at once what, in given circumstances, is to be done, and does it.
WILLIAM HAZLITT

Deliberate with caution, but act with decision; and yield with graciousness or oppose with firmness.
CHARLES HOLE

Indecision is debilitating; it feeds upon itself; it is, one might almost say, habit-forming. Not only that, but it is contagious; it transmits itself to others. . . . Business is dependent upon action. It cannot go forward by hesitation. Those in executive positions must fortify themselves with facts and accept responsibility for decisions based upon them. Often greater risk is involved in postponement than in making a wrong decision.
HARRY A. HOPF

The percentage of mistakes in quick decisions is no greater than in long-drawn-out vacillations, and the effect of decisiveness itself makes things go and creates confidence.
ANNE O'HARE MCCORMICK

When, against one's will, one is high pressured into making a hurried decision, the best answer is always No, because No is more easily changed to Yes, than Yes is changed to No.
CHARLES E. NIELSON

An executive is a man who decides; sometimes he decides right, but always he decides.
JOHN HENRY PATTERSON

Quick decisions are unsafe decisions.
SOPHOCLES

## *Democracy*

I've never known a country to be starved into democracy.
SENATOR GEORGE D. AIKEN

Lincoln's reference to "government of the people, by the people, for the people" is a generally satisfactory definition of democracy. I say "generally" because when it comes to fair and workable details, democracy fails to completely meet the criteria enunciated by Lincoln by a rather wide margin.
SENATOR GEORGE D. AIKEN

If liberty and equality are chiefly to be found in democracy, they will be best attained when all persons alike share in government to the utmost.
**ARISTOTLE**

An informed people is one of the best guarantees of a continuing democracy.
**HARRY F. BANKS**

Aristocrat: A demokrat with hiz pockets filled.
**JOSH BILLINGS**

A man is judged by the company he keeps, and a company is judged by the men it keeps, and the people of Democratic nations are judged by the type and caliber of officers they elect.
**WILLIAM J. H. BOETCKER**

We cannot possibly reconcile the principle of democracy, *which means co-operation,* with the principle of governmental omniscience under which everyone waits for an order before doing anything. That way lies loss of freedom, and dictatorship.
**LEWIS H. BROWN**

Democracy is something we must always be working at. It is a process never finished, never ending. And each new height gained opens broader vistas for the future. Thus it has been as one looks back over the sweep of history; thus it must continue to be if democracy is to continue as a working tool in the hands of free men.
**EDMUND DE S. BRUNNER**

The democratic testament derives from Hamilton as well as from Jefferson. It has two main characteristics. The first is that the ordinary man believes in himself and in his ability, along with his fellows, to govern his country. It is when a people loses its self-confidence that it surrenders its soul to a dictator or an oligarchy. . . . The second is the belief, which is fundamental also in Christianity, of the worth of every human soul—the worth, not the equality.
**JOHN BUCHAN (LORD TWEEDSMUIR)**

Democracy, as I understand it, requires me to sacrifice myself for the masses, not to them. Who knows not that if you would save the people, you must often oppose them?
**JOHN C. CALHOUN**

Democratic living is not a station at which people arrive; it is a method of traveling.
**CLYDE CAMPBELL**

I am one of those people optimistic enough to believe in the future of democracy. No matter how widely we may have departed from the practice of democracy, no matter how many failures we may have had as a nation, it is a conviction to me that it is something too precious to make it a matter of any light moment that those things should be discarded.
**HARRY WOODBURN CHASE**

All real democracy is an attempt like that of a jolly hostess to bring the shy people out.
**G. K. CHESTERTON**

Democracy is the worst form of government except all others.
**WINSTON CHURCHILL**

The chief support of an autocracy is a standing army. The chief support of a democracy is an educated people.
**LOTUS D. COFFMAN**

Democracy needs more free speech, for even the speech of foolish people is valuable if it serves to guarantee the right of the wise to talk.
**DAVID CUSHMAN COYLE**

The moment our democracy ceases to respect God it will cease to respect your value as an individual. The moment it ceases to respect your value as an individual it ceases to be democracy.
THOMAS J. CURRAN

No democratic world will work as it should work until we recognize that we can only enjoy any right so long as we are prepared to discharge its equivalent duty. This applies just as much to states in their dealing with one another as to individuals within the states.
ANTHONY EDEN

How many of us are waiting for the opportunity to do some great thing for the betterment of our community, forgetting that the solution of the problem requires only the active intelligent fulfillment of individual civic duty. The only things which are wrong about our Government are the things which are wrong with you and me. Democracy is never a thing done; it is and always will be a goal to be achieved. It means action, not passive acquiescence in things as they are; it requires alertness to duty, a dynamic faith, a willingness to give for the good of all. It can live only as a result of loyalty and devotion to its principles expressed by daily deeds.
DOUGLAS L. EDMONDS

Democracy is a way of life. Democracy is sincerity, friendliness, courage and tolerance. If your life and mine do not exemplify these characteristics, we do not have the right to call ourselves full-fledged citizens of the world's greatest democracy.
MELVIN J. EVANS

Wipe out college—the Electoral College, that is. It's not merely that the constitutional provisions for it are anachronistic, but its continued existence is downright dangerous to our democratic system. It's not merely that Presidents can be and have been elected who have lost the popular vote, but its existence forces Presidential candidates to emphasize issues . . . not necessarily of national importance . . .
From all I've read, studied and thought about the matter, I can't find one good reason why the President and Vice President shouldn't be elected by popular vote.
MALCOLM FORBES

Two cheers for democracy: one because it admits variety and two because it permits criticism. Two cheers are quite enough: There is no occasion to give three.
E. M. FORSTER

Democracy is based upon the conviction that there are extraordinary possibilities in ordinary people.
HARRY EMERSON FOSDICK, D.D.

We can advance and develop democracy but little faster than we can advance and develop the average level of intelligence and knowledge within the democracy. That is the problem that confronts modern educators.
SAMUEL GOMPERS

The only thing wrong with democratic process is the failure to use it.
SEYMOUR GRAUBARD

Democracy has survived because time and again it has proved, under stress, its ability to harmonize and make productive, in every sphere of thought and action, the individual and the social instincts innate in man. In these respects it has demonstrated its superiority over all other political philosophies. All try to draw the line between the opportunities and responsibilities of the individual and those of society, but none draws it so subtly in accordance with reality as democracy.
A. WHITNEY GRISWOLD

Economic nationalism is a tenacious and potent enemy of world order. To combat this foe, world citizens must become more active.... To secure better legislation, the best informed citizens should be the most vocal in their own communities in demanding that measures of dubious sectional short-run benefit give way to policies better calculated to advance the interests of a free, democratic world civilization with material abundance for all of Adam's children.
ROBERT L. GULICK, JR.

A democracy has not get a body of definite opinion for the expression of which it seeks delegates; it is an assembly of human beings earnestly seeking guidance from those of whose sympathies it is sure.
J. B. S. HALDANE

Democracy is ever eager for rapid progress, and the only progress which can be rapid is progress down hill.
SIR JAMES JEANS

Democracy is not static. It is a way of living, and its growth in our society depends upon the opportunity of working together in areas of common interest, each taking responsibilities commensurate with ability.
EARL M. KATZ

Democracy has the only approach to human relationships that can make for a free flow of life forces.
FRANK KINGDON

Democracy is threatened by the inertia of good people, by the selfishness of most people, and by the evil designs of a few people.
STANLEY KING

Democracy and religion stand or fall together. Where democracy has been destroyed, religion has been doomed. Where religion has been trampled down, democracy has ceased to exist.... Tyrants have come and have had their day and then have passed while religion has survived them all.
HERBERT H. LEHMAN

In this and like communities public sentiment is everything. With public sentiment nothing can fail; without it nothing can succeed; consequently he who moulds public sentiment goes deeper than he who enacts statutes and decisions. He makes statutes and decisions possible or impossible to be executed.
ABRAHAM LINCOLN

Public sentiment is everything. With public sentiment, nothing can fail. Without it, nothing can succeed.
ABRAHAM LINCOLN

In a democracy, the opposition is not only tolerated as constitutional, but must be maintained because it is indispensable.
WALTER LIPPMANN

Democracy is never a thing done. Democracy is always something that a nation must be doing. What is necessary now is one thing and one thing only... that democracy become again democracy in action, not democracy accomplished and piled up in goods and gold.
ARCHIBALD MACLEISH

Democracy is eternal and human. It dignifies the human being; it respects humanity.
THOMAS MANN

The experience of a century and a half has demonstrated that our system of free government functions best when the maximum degree of information is made available to our people. In fact, free and candid discussion of vexing problems is the

bedrock of democracy and it may be our surest safeguard for peace.
BRIEN MCMAHON

Democracy is the art of running the circus from the monkey cage.
H. L. MENCKEN

Democracy is the theory that the common people know what they want, and deserve to get it good and hard.
H. L. MENCKEN

The antithesis of democracy is class dictatorship, whether by groups of bankers, investors, managers, politicians, lawyers or union members. Over a considerable part of the world the unspeakable doctrine is being preached that the ideal of a democratic State is a snare and a delusion. A politician if he denies the existence of the essentials of democracy and denies it in such a way as to create class feeling, is not working in the interest of democracy even though he protests to the high heavens that that is his objective.
RAYMOND E. MOLEY

We have forgotten in America that a democracy is the most difficult kind of government to maintain. It is the hardest kind of government under which to live. It is hardest to maintain because of the widespread political corruption to which it so easily lends itself. Our drift today toward complete totalitarian bureaucracy is one that threatens immediately the very freedoms for which our own boys are dying.
ERNEST R. PALEN, D.D.

We don't need democratization of privilege. What we need is the self-discipline of democracy.
THOMAS I. PARKINSON

In our democracy we must have a partnership of labor, of business and of government.
CHARLES H. PERCY

Democracy does not contain any force which will check the constant tendency to put more and more on the public payroll. The state is like a hive of bees in which the drones display, multiply and starve the workers so the idlers will consume the food and the workers will perish.
PLATO

That businessmen should from time to time direct candid criticism toward our Government is only understandable but salutary in a free democracy.
CLARENCE B. RANDALL

The real strength of democracy is that anyone who is not specifically against it must ultimately be for it, while communism suffers from the great tactical liability that anyone who is not specifically for it is eventually forced to oppose it.
EDWIN O. REICHAUER

In seeking a definition of democracy this one satisfies me best: democracy is a political expression of deeply felt religion. We are fallible. We certainly haven't attained perfection. But we can strive for it and the virtue is in the striving.
CARLOS P. ROMULO

The goal of a great democracy should be fulfillment, not ease. It should be adequacy, not serenity.
ABRAM SACHAR

For democracy to survive, every person must realize that mere insistence on his rights alone will be of little avail, that a recognition of one's obligations is imperative—and that one of the most important obligations is that of respecting the rights of others.
I. DAVID SATLOW

If you want to raise a crop for one year, plant corn. If you want to raise a crop for decades, plant trees. If you want to raise a crop for centuries, raise men.

If you want to plant a crop for eternities, raise democracies.
CARL A. SCHENK

Autocracies may survive for intermittent periods with populations of "yes men," but democracies need a perennially renewed supply of "know men."
ROBERT GORDON SPROUL

Many Americans cannot define democracy; like the schoolboy who when asked to define an elephant confessed he was unable to do so, but insisted he would recognize an elephant when he saw one.
ADLAI STEVENSON

The democratic ideal is contradictory to both tyranny and ignorance. Men must be free not only to think, to speak and to worship, but to build within themselves, through education, a preparedness for their later years. Not every man can be a leader, but every man, however limited his natural capacities, can improve in the direction of better choices for himself and his children. If our education is good, then by educating all the people we give every person a better chance.
GEORGE D. STODDARD

The real danger of democracy is, that the classes which have the power under it will assume all the rights and reject all the duties—that is, that they will use the political power to plunder those-who-have.
WILLIAM GRAHAM SUMNER

Sooner or later a democracy which is to survive has to be able to rely upon that enlargement of vision and purpose of those individuals who compose it, which means that their craving for devotion and self-sacrifice is satisfied in a democratic society on a nobler level, and with a finer recognition of the value of individual personality than is true of a national purpose of a totalitarian state under a dictator.
ORDWAY TEAD

Each generation must win democracy for itself. Many young persons wish they might have lived in the historic and courageous time of George Washington, for example, when there were victories to be made and real history written. On the contrary, there are just as big problems today, and every opportunity for development.
FRANK THAYER

One of the distinguishing characteristics of a democratic period is the taste that all men have for easy success and present enjoyment. This occurs in the pursuits of the intellect as well as in others.
ALEXIS DE TOCQUEVILLE

The progress of democracy seems irresistible, because it is the most uniform, the most ancient and the most permanent tendency which is to be found in history.
ALEXIS DE TOCQUEVILLE

When Benjamin Franklin was asked after a session of the Constitutional Convention, "What kind of a government have you given us?" he replied, "A democracy, if you can keep it." Our republic is founded on the principle that it will continue only as long as the people keep democracy alive.

From Lexington to Korea, American youth have fought to preserve democracy. With each political campaign, the people who vote keep democracy alive. Each citizen who participates in community affairs is keeping democracy alive. Every act of mercy and helpfulness, every word spoken for freedom, keeps the democratic spirit alive.

Democracy is maintained by passing it on from one generation to another in the school, in place of worship, in the home. At every stage, it must be strengthened. Let us therefore resolve to give to

our successors a stronger republic than was passed on to us.
THOMAS A. WATSON

I cannot too often repeat that Democracy is a word the real gist of which still sleeps, quite unawakened, notwithstanding the resonance and the many angry tempests out of which its syllables have come, from pen or tongue. It is a great word, whose history, I suppose, remains unwritten because that history has yet to be enacted.
WALT WHITMAN

## *Desires*

Though we seem grieved at the shortness of life in general, we are wishing every period of it at an end. The minor longs to be at age, then to be a man of business, then to make up an estate, then to arrive at honors, then to retire.
JOSEPH ADDISON

If things do not turn out as we wish, we should wish for them as they turn out.
ARISTOTLE

We should aim rather at leveling down our desires than leveling up our means.
ARISTOTLE

When a man's desires are boundless, his labors are endless. They will set him a task he can never go through, and cut him out work he can never finish. The satisfaction he seeks is always absent, and the happiness he aims at is ever at a distance.
BALGUY

Before I started on my trip around the world, someone gave me one of the most valuable hints I have ever had. It consists merely in shutting your eyes when you are in the midst of a great moment, or close to some marvel of time or space, and convincing yourself that you are at home again with the experience over and past; and what would you wish most to have examined or done if you could turn time and space back again.
WILLIAM BEEBE

The greatest provocations of lust are from our apparell.
ROBERT BURTON

Better to return and make a net, than to go down to the stream and merely wish for fish.
CHINESE PROVERB

One great difference between a wise man and a fool is, the former only wishes for what he may possibly obtain; the latter desires impossibilities.
DEMOCRITUS

When electricity was invented people became discontent with oil lamps. And so our missionaries employ this sound business principle: Show the people something better and they'll want it.
HORACE W. B. DONEGAN, D.D.

You can get what you desire and in just the measure of that desire.
THOMAS DREIER

Moderate desires constitute a character fitted to acquire all the good which the world can yield. He who has this character is prepared, in whatever situation he is, therewith to be content; has learned the science of being happy; and possesses the alchemic stone which changes every metal into gold.
TIMOTHY DWIGHT

It seems to me we can never give up longing and wishing while we are thoroughly alive. There are

certain things we feel to be beautiful and good, and we must hunger after them.
GEORGE ELIOT

Beware of what you want—for you will get it.
RALPH WALDO EMERSON

There are three wants which can never be satisfied: that of the rich, who want something more; that of the sick, who want something different; and that of the traveler, who says, Anywhere but here.
RALPH WALDO EMERSON

We'd all like to be taken for what we'd like to be.
MALCOLM FORBES

If your desires be endless, your cares and fears will be so too.
THOMAS FULLER

Most of us have a pretty clear idea of the world we want. What we lack is an understanding of how to go about getting it.
HUGH GIBSON

Beware of wishing for anything in youth, because you will get it in middle age.
JOHANN WOLFGANG VON GOETHE

Happy the man who early learns the wide chasm that lies between his wishes and his powers!
JOHANN WOLFGANG VON GOETHE

I respect the man who knows distinctly what he wishes. The greater part of all the mischief in the world arises from the fact that men do not sufficiently understand how to build a tower, and spend no more labor on the foundation than would be necessary to erect a hut.
JOHANN WOLFGANG VON GOETHE

Sometimes a man devotes all his life to the development of one part of his body... his wishbone.
ALLEN GRAY

A successful man is one who can lay a firm foundation with the bricks that others throw at him.
SIDNEY GREENBERG

By annihilating the desires, you annihilate the mind. Every man without passions has within him no principle of action, nor motive to act.
CLAUDE-ADRIEN HELVÉTIUS

He begins to die that quits his desires.
GEORGE HERBERT

Appetite, with an opinion of attaining, is called hope; the same without such opinion, despair.
THOMAS HOBBES

Now that fate has brought me what so long I so desired, it is too late, I am too tired.
LAURENCE HOPE

Besides the pleasure derived from acquired knowledge, there lurks in the mind of man, and tinged with a shade of sadness, an unsatisfactory longing for something beyond the present—a striving toward regions yet unknown and unopened.
KARL WILHELM VON HUMBOLDT

The reason why folks are always wishing for what they don't have is that there's nothing else to wish for.
HOUGHTON LINE

Ours is a world where people don't know what they want and are willing to go through hell to get it.
DONALD MARQUIS

Lord, grant that I may always desire more than I can accomplish.
MICHELANGELO

I have learned to seek my happiness by limiting my desires, rather than attempting to satisfy them.
JOHN STUART MILL

There is a vast difference in some instances between what we really need and that which we think we must have, and the realization of this truth will greatly lessen the seeming discomfort in doing without.
WILLIAM M. PECK

Wants awaken intellect. To gratify them disciplines intellect. The keener the want, the lustier the growth.
WENDELL PHILLIPS

Any refusal to recognize reality, for any reason whatever, has disastrous consequences. There are no evil thoughts except one: the refusal to think. Don't ignore your own desires. . . . Don't sacrifice them. Examine their cause. There is a limit to how much you should have to bear.
AYN RAND

We don't know what we want, but we are ready to bite somebody to get it.
WILL ROGERS

It is not the man who has little, but he who desires more, that is poor.
SENECA

As long as I have a want, I have a reason for living. Satisfaction is death.
GEORGE BERNARD SHAW

It is foolish to be ambitious for things one does not really want—or for things one cannot have.
GUISEPPE SILVA

The earnestness of your desire will indicate the distance you are likely to travel.
CLARK C. STOCKFORD

Too many young people itch for what they want without scratching for it.
TOM D. TAYLOR

The only limitless thing I know of is human want. Civilization itself is nothing more than the creation of wants, followed by methods of satisfying those wants. At the moment we had better give consideration to the fact that we may not be creating enough stuff to satisfy the wants this education has inspired.
JAMES SHELBY THOMAS

We make ourselves rich by making our wants few.
HENRY DAVID THOREAU

Wishes cost nothing unless you want them to come true.
FRANK TYGER

Human society is based on want. Life is based on want. Wild-eyed visionaries may dream of a world without need. Cloud-cuckoo-land. It can't be done.
H. G. WELLS

In this world there are only two tragedies: One is not getting what one wants, and the second is getting it.
OSCAR WILDE

The fewer the desires, the more peace.
WOODROW WILSON

The problem of abolishing want is not a problem in division, as the politicians so often aver; it is a problem in multiplication.
**HENRY M. WRISTON**

## Destiny

Thy lot or portion of life is seeking after thee; therefore be at rest from seeking after it.
**ALI IBN-ALI-TALIB**

How true it is that our destinies are decided by nothings and that a small imprudence helped by some insignificant accident, as an acorn is fertilized by a drop of rain, may raise the trees on which perhaps we and others shall be crucified.
**HENRI FRÉDÉRIC AMIEL**

Love nothing but that which comes to you woven in the pattern of your destiny.
**MARCUS AURELIUS ANTONINUS**

Destiny: A tyrant's authority for crime and a fool's excuse for failure.
**AMBROSE BIERCE**

The law of harvest is to reap more than you sow. Sow an act, and you reap a habit; sow a habit, and you reap a character; sow a character and you reap a destiny.
**GEORGE D. BOARDMAN**

A word, a look, an accent, may affect the destiny not only of individuals, but of nations. He is a bold man who calls anything a trifle.
**ANDREW CARNEGIE**

It is a mistake to look too far ahead. Only one link of the chain of destiny can be handled at a time.
**WINSTON CHURCHILL**

Every man carries with him the world in which he must live.
**F. MARION CRAWFORD**

How easy 'tis, when
Destiny proves kind,
With full-spread sails to run before the wind!
**JOHN DRYDEN**

We have an obligation to other people, to our neighbor and to our country. But the man who stops there has lost the purpose of his life below. Please bear in mind we are not created for time, but for eternity. God is the sure Tax-Gatherer. Yet how many refuse to pay tribute to Him.
**THOMAS LESTER GRAHAM, D.D.**

Blaming destiny is a poor out for those who don't reach desired destinations.
**MALCOLM FORBES**

Failure or success seem to have been allotted to men by their stars. But they retain the power of wriggling, of fighting with their star or against it, and in the whole universe the only really interesting movement is this wriggle.
**E. M. FORSTER**

He that is born to be hanged shall never be drowned.
**FRENCH PROVERB**

We sow our thoughts, and we reap our action; we sow our actions, and we reap our habits; we sow our habits and we reap our characters; we sow our characters and we reap our destiny.
**CHARLES A. HALL**

We are not permitted to choose the frame of our destiny. But what we put into it is ours.
**DAG HAMMARSKJÖLD**

Men heap together the mistakes of their lives, and create a monster they call Destiny.
JOHN OLIVER HOBBES

Lots of folks confuse bad management with destiny.
KIN HUBBARD

We still have it in our power to rise above the fears, imagined and real, and to shoulder the great burdens which destiny has placed upon us, not for our country alone, but for the benefit of all the world. That is the only destiny worthy of America.
HELEN KELLER

'Tis all a chequerboard of nights and days
Where Destiny with men for pieces plays:
Hither and thither moves, and mates, and slays,
And one by one back in the closet lays.
OMAR KHAYYAM

It's odd to think we might have been
Sun, moon and stars unto each other;
Only I turned down one little street
As you went up another.
FANNY HEASLIP LEA

No wind favors him who has no destined port.
MICHEL DE MONTAIGNE

Most of the critical things in life, which become the starting points of human destiny, are little things.
R. SMITH

Let us follow our destiny, ebb and flow. Whatever may happen, we master fortune by accepting it.
VIRGIL

Man's destiny lies half within himself, half without. To advance in either half at the expense of the other is literally insane.
PHILIP WYLIE

## *Difficulties*

The difficult tasks to be performed are not the ones that mean physical and mental labor, but the ones that you dislike, or the ones that you do not love. There are unpleasant angles to nearly every important job to be done in this world, but there must be an over-all love for doing each, else precious time and effort are uselessly wasted. I shall never forget noting a sign above a construction job that read: Builder of Difficult Foundations. That man must have loved that calling, else he would not have made a point of advertising the fact!
GEORGE MATTHEW ADAMS

No great advance has ever been made in science, politics, or religion, without controversy.
LYMAN BEECHER

You can't fly a kite unless you go against the wind and have a weight to keep it from turning somersault. The same with man. No man will succeed unless he is ready to face and overcome difficulties and is prepared to assume responsibilities.
WILLIAM J. H. BOETCKER

The difficulties and struggles of today are but the price we must pay for the accomplishments and victories of tomorrow.
WILLIAM J. H. BOETCKER

There are two ways of meeting difficulties: you alter the difficulties, or you alter yourself to meet them.
PHYLLIS BOTTOME

If you would only recognize that life is hard, things would be so much easier for you.
LOUIS D. BRANDEIS

They wrong man greatly who say he is to be seduced by ease. Difficulty, abnegation, martyrdom, death are the allurements that act on the heart of man.
**THOMAS CARLYLE**

The weak sinews become strong by their conflict with difficulties.
**EDWIN H. CHAPIN**

Every difficulty slurred over will be a ghost to disturb your repose later on.
**FRÉDÉRIC CHOPIN**

A fool often fails because he thinks what is difficult is easy, and a wise man because he thinks what is easy is difficult.
**JOHN CHURTON COLLINS**

Many of life's noblest enterprises might never have been undertaken if all the difficulties and defects could be foreseen.
**THEODORE L. CUYLER**

No one is useless in this world who lightens the burdens of it for another.
**CHARLES DICKENS**

Life has no smooth road for any of us, and in the bracing atmosphere of a high aim the very roughness stimulates the climber to steadier steps, till the legend, over the steep ways to the stars, fulfills itself.
**WILLIAM C. DOANE**

Difficulties exist to be surmounted.
**RALPH WALDO EMERSON**

Difficulties are things that show what men are.
**EPICTETUS**

What ought one to say then as each hardship comes? I was practising for this, I was training for this.
**EPICTETUS**

Unless a man has been kicked around a little, you can't really depend upon him to amount to anything.
**WILLIAM FEATHER**

The greatest difficulties lie where we are not looking for them.
**JOHANN WOLFGANG VON GOETHE**

When I hear somebody sigh that Life is hard, I am always tempted to ask, Compared to what?
**SYDNEY J. HARRIS**

Nothing is difficult, it is only we who are indolent.
**BENJAMIN R. HAYDON**

A man's worst difficulties begin when he is able to do as he likes.
**THOMAS H. HUXLEY**

Is not this the fast that I have chosen? to break the bands of wickedness, to undo the heavy burdens, and to let the oppressed go free, and that ye break every yoke?
**ISAIAH 58:6**

Life affords no higher pleasure than that of surmounting difficulties, passing from one step of success to another, forming new wishes and seeing them gratified. He that labors in any great or laudable undertaking has his fatigues first supported by hope and afterward rewarded by joy.
**SAMUEL JOHNSON**

If at times our actions seem to have made life difficult for others, it is only because history has made life difficult for us all.
**JOHN F. KENNEDY**

Much of truth is found upon the battlefield of controversy, and it is kept alive by sharp exchanges.
LAWRENCE A. KIMPTON

It is surmounting difficulties that makes heroes.
LOUIS KOSSUTH

No man ever sank under the burden of the day. It is when to-morrow's burden is added to the burden of to-day that the weight is more than a man can bear.
GEORGE MACDONALD

The difficulties, hardships and trials of life, the obstacles one encounters on the road to fortune are positive blessings. They knit the muscles more firmly, and teach self-reliance. Peril is the element in which power is developed.
WILLIAM MATTHEWS

It cannot be too often repeated that it is not helps, but obstacles, not facilities, but difficulties that make men.
WILLIAM MATTHEWS

There is no learned man but will confess he hath much profited by reading controversies; his senses awakened, his judgment sharpened, and the truth which he holds more firmly established. In logic they teach that contraries laid together more evidently appear; and controversy being permitted, falsehood will appear more false, and truth more true.
JOHN MILTON

Undertake something that is difficult; it will do you good. Unless you try to do something beyond what you have already mastered, you will never grow.
RONALD E. OSBORN

Burdens become light when cheerfully borne.
OVID

The individual who knows the score about life sees difficulties as opportunities.
NORMAN VINCENT PEALE

Accustom yourself to master and overcome things of difficulty; for if you observe, the left hand for want of practice is insignificant, and not adapted to general business, yet it holds the bridle better than the right, from constant use.
PLINY

The easy way is efficacious and speedy—the hard way arduous and long. But as the clock ticks, the easy way becomes harder and the hard way becomes easier. And as the calendar records the years, it becomes increasingly evident that the easy way rests hazardously upon shifting sands, whereas the hard way builds solidly a foundation of confidence that cannot be swept away.
DANIEL RAND

That which renders life burdensome to us, generally arises from the abuse of it.
JEAN-JACQUES ROUSSEAU

The most savage controversies are those about matters as to which there is no good evidence either way.
BERTRAND RUSSELL

It is not the burden but the overburden that kills the beast.
SPANISH PROVERB

If the way which, as I have shown, leads hither seems very difficult, it can nevertheless be found. It must indeed be difficult, since it is so seldom discovered; for if salvation lay ready to hand and could be discovered without great labor, how could it be possible that it should be neglected almost by everybody? But all noble things are as difficult as they are rare.
BARUCH SPINOZA

Many men owe the grandeur of their lives to their tremendous difficulties.
CHARLES H. SPURGEON

I sit on a man's back, choking him and making him carry me, and yet assure others that I am very sorry for him and wish to ease his lot by all possible means—except by getting off his back.
LEO TOLSTOY

Real difficulties can be overcome; it is only the imaginary ones that are unconquerable.
THEODORE N. VAIL

Take heart again; put your dismal fears away. One day, who knows? Even these hardships will be grand things to look back on.
VIRGIL

What is difficulty? Only a word indicating the degree of strength requisite for accomplishing particular objects; a mere notice of the necessity for exertion; a bugbear to children and fools; only a mere stimulus to men.
SAMUEL WARREN

It is a good rule to face difficulties at the time they arise and not allow them to increase unacknowledged.
EDWARD W. ZIEGLER

## *Dignity*

There is a proper dignity and proportion to be observed in the performance of every act of life.
MARCUS AURELIUS ANTONINUS

The sum of behavior is to retain a man's own dignity, without intruding upon the liberty of others.
FRANCIS BACON

The dignity of man is vindicated as much by the thinker and poet as by the statesman and soldier.
JAMES BRYANT CONANT

Nothing is more destructive of human dignity than a rule which imposes a mute and blind obedience.
ANTHONY EDEN

It is more offensive to outshine in dignity than in personal attractions.
BALTASAR GRACIÁN

There is a healthful hardiness about real dignity that never dreads contact and communion with others, however humble.
WASHINGTON IRVING

True dignity is never gained by place, and never lost when honors are withdrawn.
PHILIP MASSINGER

Let none presume to wear an undeserved dignity.
WILLIAM SHAKESPEARE

No race can prosper until it learns that there is as much dignity in tilling a field as in writing a poem.
BOOKER T. WASHINGTON

It is base and unworthy to live below the dignity of our nature.
BENJAMIN WHICHCOTE

Dignity is often a veil between us and the real truth of things.
EDWIN P. WHIPPLE

True dignity abides with him only, who, in the silent hour of inward thought, can still suspect, and still revere himself, in lowliness of heart.
WILLIAM WORDSWORTH

## Disagreement

The people to fear are not those who disagree with you, but those who disagree with you and are too cowardly to let you know.
NAPOLEON BONAPARTE

The great mind knows the power of gentleness, only tries force because persuasion fails.
ROBERT BROWNING

No man lives without jostling and being jostled; in all ways he has to elbow himself through the world, giving and receiving offense.
THOMAS CARLYLE

People generally quarrel because they cannot argue.
G. K. CHESTERTON

Two things, well considered, would prevent many personal and international quarrels; first, to have it well ascertained whether we are not disputing about terms rather than things, and second, to examine whether that on which we differ is worth contending for.
CHARLES CALEB COLTON

The effects of opposition are wonderful. There are men who rise refreshed on hearing of a threat—men to whom a crisis which intimidates and paralyzes the majority, comes graceful and beloved as a bride!
RALPH WALDO EMERSON

The worthless and offensive members of society, whose existence is a social pest, invariably think themselves the most ill-used people alive, and never get over their astonishment at the ingratitude and selfishness of their contemporaries.
RALPH WALDO EMERSON

In theory it is easy to convince an ignorant person; in actual life, men not only object to offer themselves to be convinced, but hate the man who has convinced them.
EPICTETUS

He who has learned to disagree without being disagreeable has discovered the most valuable secret of a diplomat.
ROBERT ESTABROOK

The last sound on the worthless earth will be two human beings trying to launch a homemade spaceship and already quarreling about where they are going next.
WILLIAM FAULKNER

In the course of my observation, the disputing, contradicting and confuting people are generally unfortunate in their affairs. They get victory sometimes, but they never get good will, which would be of more use to them.
BENJAMIN FRANKLIN

Convincing yourself does not win an argument.
ROBERT HALF

We may convince others by our arguments, but we can only persuade them by their own.
JOSEPH JOUBERT

No one can give faith unless he has faith. It is the persuaded who persuade.
JOSEPH JOUBERT

What occasions the greater part of the world's quarrels? Simply this: Two minds meet and do not understand each other in time enough to prevent any shock of surprise at the conduct of either party.
JOHN KEATS

Business today consists in persuading crowds.
**GERALD S. LEE**

Persuasion, kind, unassuming persuasion, should be adopted to influence the conduct of men. The opposite course would be a reversal of human nature, which is God's decree and can never be reversed.
**ABRAHAM LINCOLN**

Men are more ready to offend one who desires to be beloved than one who wishes to be feared.
**NICCOLÒ MACHIAVELLI**

A certain amount of opposition is a great help to a man; it is what he wants and must have to be good for anything. Hardship and opposition are the native soil of manhood and self-reliance.
**JOHN NEAL**

Before you try to convince anyone else be sure you are convinced, and if you cannot convince yourself, drop the subject.
**JOHN HENRY PATTERSON**

Take the course opposite to custom and you will almost always do well.
**JEAN-JACQUES ROUSSEAU**

Opposition inflames the enthusiast, never converts him.
**JOHANN FRIEDRICH VON SCHILLER**

A long dispute means that both parties are wrong.
**VOLTAIRE**

To constitute a dispute there must be two parties. To understand it well, both parties and all the circumstances must be fully heard; and to accommodate the differences, temper and mutual forbearance are requisite.
**GEORGE WASHINGTON**

Weak arguments are often thrust before my path; but although they are most unsubstantial, it is not easy to destroy them. There is not a more difficult feat known than to cut through a cushion with a sword.
**RICHARD WHATELY**

## *Discipline*

Hold yourself responsible for a higher standard than anybody else expects of you. Never excuse yourself. Never pity yourself. Be a hard master to yourself—and be linient to everybody else.
**HENRY WARD BEECHER**

The discipline which corrects the baseness of worldly passions, fortifies the heart with virtuous principles, enlightens the mind with useful knowledge, furnishes it with enjoyment from within itself is of more consequence to real felicity than all the provisions we can make of the goods of fortune.
**PAXTON BLAIR**

We must accept the disciplines of democracy as well as its freedoms. And those disciplines must come from ourselves, they must be reflections of our own attitudes. Discipline from without flourishes when discipline from within grows weak.
**HARRY WOODBURN CHASE**

The most we can get out of life is its discipline for ourselves, and its usefulness for others.
**TRYON EDWARDS**

Only the man who can impose discipline on himself is fit to discipline others or can impose discipline on others.
**WILLIAM FEATHER**

If we don't discipline ourselves the world will do it for us.
**WILLIAM FEATHER**

No horse gets anywhere until he is harnessed. No steam or gas ever drives anything until it is confined. No Niagara is ever turned into light and power until it is tunneled. No life ever grows great until it is focused, dedicated, disciplined.
**HARRY EMERSON FOSDICK, D.D.**

Life is tons of discipline.
**ROBERT FROST**

Discipline without freedom is tyranny. Freedom without discipline is chaos.
**CULLEN HIGHTOWER**

Man must be disciplined, for he is by nature raw and wild.
**IMMANUEL KANT**

I've never known a man worth his salt who in the long run, deep down in his heart, didn't appreciate the grind, the discipline. . . . I firmly believe that any man's finest hour—this greatest fulfillment to all he holds dear—is that moment when he has worked his heart out in a good cause and lies exhausted on the field of battle victorious.
**VINCE LOMBARDI**

With the worship of God must go denial of self. These are the two wings for flight. Pride of any kind will be rooted out, and also desire for power over others. Not until it is rooted out can the economic potentials be developed properly and made available for all. Love of God and love of the brethren are the true preparation and discipline for life.
**BERNARD C. NEWMAN, D.D.**

A stern discipline pervades all nature, which is a little cruel that it may be very kind.
**EDMUND SPENSER**

## *Discoveries*

Greater even than the greatest discovery is to keep open the way to future discovery.
**JOHN JACOB ABEL**

In olden times the pillory and the whipping-post were among the gentler forms of encouragement awaiting the inventor. Today we hail with enthusiasm a scientific discovery, and stand ready to make a stock company of it.
**THOMAS BAILEY ALDRICH**

A great discovery is a fact whose appearance in science gives rise to shining ideas, whose light dispels many obscurities and shows us new paths.
**CLAUDE BERNARD**

Where we cannot invent, we may at least improve; we may give somewhat of novelty to that which was old; condensation to that which was diffuse, perspicuity to that which was obscure, and currency to that which was recondite.
**CHARLES CALEB COLTON**

I am more of a sponge than an inventor. I absorb ideas from every source. I take half-matured schemes for mechanical development and make them practical. I am a sort of a middleman between the long-haired and impractical inventor and the hard-headed business man who measures all things in terms of dollars and cents. My principal business is giving commercial value to the brilliant but misdirected ideas of others.
**THOMAS EDISON**

There's a better way to do it. Find it!
**THOMAS EDISON**

The intellect has little to do on the road to discovery. There comes a leap in consciousness, call it intuition or what you will, and the solution comes to you and you don't know how or why. All great discoveries are made in this way.
**ALBERT EINSTEIN**

Things don't turn up in this world until somebody turns them up.
**JAMES A. GARFIELD**

When all the mountains in the world have been scaled, when the poles hold no more secrets, when the last acre of the last continent has been traversed, when, in short, everything on our planet is known and catalogued, the way will still be open for discovery. The world will never be conquered so long as the zest for conquest, for adventure, is in men's hearts.
**MAURICE HERZOG**

New discoveries in science . . . will continue to create a thousand new frontiers for those who still would adventure.
**HERBERT HOOVER**

I do not much wish well to discoveries, for I am always afraid they will end in conquest and robbery.
**SAMUEL JOHNSON**

An inventor is an engineer who doesn't take his education too seriously.
**CHARLES F. KETTERING**

When the Norsemen discovered America, they had no compass. Yet the compass had been invented by the Chinese thousands of years before. When, however, Mme. Curie discovered radium, the knowledge of her achievement was spread throughout the world as rapidly as cables and wires could carry it. Mme. Curie's work could have been of no value to the world if her discovery had been known to her alone.
**IVY L. LEE**

No man ever made a great discovery without the exercise of the imagination.
**GEORGE HENRY LEWES**

It is chiefly upon the lay citizen, informed about science but not its practitioner, that the country must depend in determining the use to which science is put, in resolving the many public policy questions that scientific discoveries constantly force upon us.
**DAVID E. LILIENTHAL**

Nearly every great discovery in science has come as the result of providing a new question rather than a new answer.
**PAUL A. MEGLITSCH**

People don't give a hoot about who made the original whatzit. They want to know who makes the best one.
**HOWARD W. NEWTON**

Invention, strictly speaking, is little more than a new combination of those images which have been previously gathered and deposited in the memory. Nothing can be made of nothing; he who has laid up no materials can produce no combinations.
**SIR JOSHUA REYNOLDS**

The greatest inventions were produced in the times of ignorance, [such] as the use of the compass, gunpowder and printing.
**JONATHAN SWIFT**

We are called the nation of inventors. And we are. We could still claim that title and wear its loftiest

honors if we had stopped with the first thing we ever invented, which was human liberty.
MARK TWAIN

Name the greatest of all inventors. Accident.
MARK TWAIN

Discoveries are often made by not following instructions; by going off the main road; by trying the untried.
FRANK TYGER

Scientific discovery consists in the interpretation for our own convenience of a system of existence which has been made with no eye to our convenience at all.
NORBERT WIENER

Benjamin Franklin may have discovered electricity, but it was the man who invented the meter who made the money.
EARL WILSON

## *Dishonesty*

Dishonesty is a forsaking of permanent for temporary advantage.
CHRISTIAN BOVÉE

To admire nothing is the motto which men of the world always affect. They think it vulgar to wonder or be enthusiastic. They have so much corruption and charlatanism, that they think the credit of all high policies must be delusive.
SAMUEL BRYDGES

Corrupt influence is itself the perennial spring of all prodigality, and of all disorder; it loads us more than millions of debt; takes away vigor from our arms, wisdom from our councils, and every shadow of authority and credit from the most venerable parts of our constitution.
EDMUND BURKE

I have known a vast quantity of nonsense talked about bad men not looking you in the face. Don't trust that conventional idea. Dishonesty will stare honesty out of countenance, any day in the week, if there is anything to be got by it.
CHARLES DICKENS

Shower on him every blessing, drown him in a sea of happiness, give him economic prosperity such that he should have nothing else to do but sleep, eat cakes, and busy himself with the continuation of the species, and even then, out of sheer ingratitude, sheer spite, man would play you some nasty trick.
FYODOR DOSTOYEVSKY

Many corporate managements and a lot of security analysts have reacted with much fuming and even more fumbling to the Texas Gulf Sulphur decision and the SEC's actions against trading on inside information.

I don't know why everyone is in such a hot sweat over these two things. The one had been illegal—and damned well properly so—for over 30 years. . . .

The initial reaction of some managements that these actions meant they could no longer talk to any publications or analysts was—is—asinine. Such sour silliness is quite the reverse of what was intended.
MALCOLM FORBES

That which is won ill, will never wear well, for there is a curse that attends it which will waste it. The same corrupt dispositions which incline men to sinful ways of getting, will incline them to the like sinful ways of spending.
MATTHEW HENRY

Dishonesty, cowardice and duplicity are never impulsive.
**GEORGE KNIGHT**

Men are so simple and yield so readily to the wants of the moment that he who will trick will always find another who will suffer himself to be tricked.
**NICCOLÒ MACHIAVELLI**

Our first duty is to war against dishonesty... war against it in public life, and... war against it in business life. Corruption in every form is the arch enemy of this Republic, the arch enemy of free institutions and of government by the people, an even more dangerous enemy than the open lawlessness of violence, because it works in hidden and furtive fashion.
**THEODORE ROOSEVELT**

Money dishonestly acquired is never worth its cost, while a good conscience never costs as much as it is worth.
**J. P. SENN**

## *Doctors*

The boat I always wanted is in my dentist's driveway.
**ANONYMOUS**

Never go to a doctor whose office plants have died.
**ERMA BOMBECK**

A good doctor's beyond price. And bills accordingly.
**MALCOLM FORBES**

## *Doing*

Don't just do something, stand there.
**DEAN ACHESON**

I have also thought about calling a conference, since a conference is a gathering of important people, who, singly, can do nothing, but together can decide that nothing can be done.
**FRED ALLEN**

One must learn by doing the thing, for though you think you know it, you have no certainty until you try.
**ARISTOTLE**

Doing little things well is a step toward doing big things better.
**HARRY F. BANKS**

If you have something to do that is worthwhile doing, don't talk about it, but do it. After you have done it, your friends and enemies will talk about it.
**GEORGE W. BLOUNT**

Nobody is capable of doing well at everything. On the other hand, everybody can do at least one thing much better than he can anything else.
**ROSS BYRON**

Everywhere in life the true question is, not what we have gained, but what we do.
**THOMAS CARLYLE**

Men do less than they ought, unless they do all that they can.
**THOMAS CARLYLE**

What one does easily, one does well.
**ANDREW CARNEGIE**

The key to whatever success I enjoy today is: Don't ask. Do.
**VIKKI CARR**

The shortest way to do many things is to do only one thing at a time.
RICHARD CECIL

Whatever is worth doing at all is worth doing well.
LORD CHESTERFIELD

Do as you would be done by, is the surest method of pleasing.
LORD CHESTERFIELD

If a thing is worth doing, it is worth doing badly.
G. K. CHESTERTON

Never do anything standing that you can do sitting, or anything sitting that you can do lying down.
CHINESE PROVERB

It's not enough that we do our best; sometimes we have to do what's required.
WINSTON CHURCHILL

One never notices what has been done; one can only see what remains to be done.
MARIE CURIE

The fact is, that to do anything in the world worth doing, we must not stand back shivering and thinking of the cold and danger, but jump in and scramble through as well as we can.
RICHARD CUSHING

When I go into my garden with a spade, and dig a bed, I feel such an exhilaration and health that I discover that I have been defrauding myself all this time in letting others do for me what I should have done with my own hands.
RALPH WALDO EMERSON

When looking back, usually I'm more sorry for the things I didn't do than for the things I shouldn't have done.
MALCOLM FORBES

Well done is better than well said.
BENJAMIN FRANKLIN

A man can do what he ought to do; and when he says he cannot, it is because he will not.
J. A. FROUDE

If you listen to the neverdo's, it's never done.
DAVID LLOYD GEORGE

How many years must a man do nothing, before he can at all know what is to be done and how to do it!
JOHANN WOLFGANG VON GOETHE

I am only one, but still I am one. I cannot do everything, but still I can do something and because I cannot do everything, I will not refuse to do the something that I can do.
EDWARD E. HALE

You have not done enough, you have never done enough, so long as it is still possible that you have something to contribute.
DAG HAMMARSKJÖLD

The shortest answer is doing.
GEORGE HERBERT

Now is no time to think of what you do not have. Think of what you can do with what there is.
ERNEST HEMINGWAY

It is not a question how much a man knows, but what use he makes of what he knows; not a ques-

tion of what he has acquired, and how he has been trained, but of what he is, and what he can do.
JOSIAH G. HOLLAND

The greatest thing in the world is for a man to be able to do something well, and say nothing about it.
EDGAR WATSON HOWE

The world is moving so fast now-a-days that the man who says it can't be done is generally interrupted by someone doing it.
ELBERT HUBBARD

For if any be a hearer of the word, and not a doer, he is like a man beholding his natural face in a glass: for he beholdeth himself, and goeth his way, and straightaway forgetteth what manner of man he was.
JAMES 1:23-24

Everybody ought to do at least two things each day that he hates to do, just for practice.
WILLIAM JAMES

In the dim background of our mind, we know what we ought to be doing, but somehow we cannot start. Every moment, we expect the spell to break, but it continues, pulse after pulse, and we float with it.
WILLIAM JAMES

One of the greatest failings of today's executive is his inability to do what he's supposed to do.
MALCOLM KENT

Thank God every morning when you get up that you have something to do that day which must be done, whether you like it or not.
CHARLES KINGSLEY

What you do when you don't have to, determines what you will be when you can no longer help it.
RUDYARD KIPLING

It is by translating your fine sense of aspiration into actual daily deeds that you grow toward your ideal. Link your lofty thoughts to earnest, active effort, and good results will inevitably follow. The great things you intend to do some time must have a beginning if they are ever to be done, so begin to do something worthwhile today.
GRENVILLE KLEISER

You cannot help men permanently by doing for them what they could and should do for themselves.
ABRAHAM LINCOLN

Truth as old as the hills is bound up in the Latin proverb, "Necessity is the mother of invention." It is surprising what a man can do when he has to, and how little most men will do when they don't have to.
WALTER LINN

There is no pleasure in having nothing to do; the fun is having lots to do and not doing it.
MARY WILSON LITTLE

It takes less time to do a thing right than to explain why you did it wrong.
HENRY WADSWORTH LONGFELLOW

The question for each man to settle is not what he would do if he had means, time, influence and educational advantages, but what he will do with the things he has.
HAMILTON WRIGHT MABIE

So much one man can do that does both act and know.
ANDREW MARVELL

To do each day two things one dislikes is a precept I have followed scrupulously: Every day I have got up and I have gone to bed.
SOMERSET MAUGHAM

What ever fortune brings, don't be afraid of doing things.
**A. A. MILNE**

It is not only what we do, but also what we do not do, for which we are accountable.
**MOLIÈRE**

The world is divided into people who do things and people who get the credit. Try, if you can, to belong to the first class. There's far less competition.
**DWIGHT MORROW**

Many enjoy the shade . . . but few rake leaves.
**JACK MORTON**

There are so many things that we wish we had done yesterday, so few that we feel like doing today.
**MIGNON MCLAUGHLIN**

He was a wise man who said: "As I grow older I pay less attention to what men say. I just watch what they do."
**WILFRED A. PETERSON**

Where you are is of no moment, but only what you are doing there. It is not the place that ennobles you, but you the place, and this only by doing that which is great and noble.
**PETRARCH**

Thinking well is wise; planning well, wiser; doing well wisest and best of all.
**PERSIAN PROVERB**

So much to do, so little done.
**CECIL RHODES**

The time men spend in trying to impress others they could spend in doing the things by which others would be impressed.
**FRANK ROMER**

Do to others as you would have others do to you, inspires all men with that other maxim of natural goodness a great deal less perfect, but perhaps more useful: Do good to yourself with as little prejudice as you can to others.
**JEAN-JACQUES ROUSSEAU**

Doing is the great thing. For if, resolutely, people do what is right, in time they come to like doing it.
**JOHN RUSKIN**

I feel that the greatest reward for doing is the opportunity to do more.
**JONAS SALK**

Oh what men dare do! what men may do! what men daily do, not knowing what they do!
**WILLIAM SHAKESPEARE**

Some have an idea that the reason we in this country discard things so readily is because we have so much. The facts are exactly opposite—the reason we have so much is simply because we discard things so readily. We replace the old in return for something that will serve us better.
**ALFRED P. SLOAN, JR.**

It is the greatest of all mistakes to do nothing because you can only do a little. Do what you can.
**SYDNEY SMITH**

Better do a little well, than a great deal badly.
**SOCRATES**

The thing that counts is not what we could do but what we actually do.
**LEO L. SPEARS**

Nothing is done. Everything in the world remains to be done or done over.
**LINCOLN STEFFENS**

Make it a point to do something every day that you don't want to do. This is the golden rule for acquiring the habit of doing your duty without pain.
MARK TWAIN

Even doing nothing takes doing.
FRANK TYGER

Being able to do something well is one of life's great joys.
FRANK TYGER

If we could only make our hands move as actively as our tongues, what wonders we could accomplish! Almost everyone loves to hear his own voice. It is so easy, too! Yet if we could say less and do more for each other's good, not alone would every home be happier, but communities would be enriched thereby. Instead of criticism by speech, to show someone a better way to do a thing would be of much greater value.
JOHN WANAMAKER

Not merely what we do, but what we try to do and why, are the true interpreters of what we are.
C. H. WOODWARD

All may do what has by man been done.
EDWARD YOUNG

## *Doubt*

If we begin with certainties, we shall end in doubts; but if we begin with doubts, and are patient in them, we shall end in certainties.
FRANCIS BACON

Weary the path that does not challenge. Doubt is an incentive to truth and patient inquiry leadeth the way.
HOSEA BALLOU

Uncertainty and expectation are the joys of life. Security is an insipid thing, though the overtaking and possessing of a wish discovers the folly of the chase.
WILLIAM CONGREVE

For if the trumpet give an uncertain sound, who shall prepare himself to the battle?
I CORINTHIANS 14:8

Uncertain ways unsafest are, and doubt a greater mischief than despair.
JOHN DENHAM

Seeking to know is only too often learning to doubt.
ANTOINETTE DESHOULIÈRES

Doubt, indulged and cherished, is in danger of becoming denial; but if honest, and bent on thorough investigation, it may soon lead to full establishment in the truth.
TRYON EDWARDS

Uncertainty hurts business. It annoys individuals. Why keep the whole country, including business and individuals, in uncertainty over the extent of the tax burdens to be placed upon us? How many of those who voted for Calvin Coolidge imagined for a moment that he would do nothing to bring about tax relief before 1926?.... But if the Administration persists in opposing a special session then it will inevitably be 1926 before action is taken.... Coolidge and Congress should ease our minds and grease our activities by reforming and reducing taxation as soon as feasible after March 4.
B. C. FORBES

When young, you're shocked by the number of people who turn out to have feet of clay. Older, you're surprised by the number of people who don't.
MALCOLM FORBES

The believer is happy; the doubter is wise.
HUNGARIAN PROVERB

Doubts and jealousies often beget the facts they fear.
THOMAS JEFFERSON

The more uncertain I have felt about myself, the more there has grown up in me a feeling of kinship with all things.
CARL JUNG

Nothing will ever be attempted if all possible objections must be first overcome.
SAMUEL JOHNSON

Men become civilized not in proportion to their willingness to believe, but in proportion to their willingness to doubt.
H. L. MENCKEN

Doubts are more cruel than the worst of truths.
MOLIÈRE

Four be the things
I'd been better without:
Love, curiosity,
Freckles and doubt.
DOROTHY PARKER

He that is overcautious will accomplish little.
JOHANN FRIEDRICH VON SCHILLER

Our doubts are traitors and cause us to miss the good we oft might win by fearing to attempt.
WILLIAM SHAKESPEARE

One of the most devastating experiences in human life is disillusionment. Of course there are some illusions the disillusionment of which is healthy. It takes two things to bowl over a tree—a heavy wind outside and decay inside. Much of the moral wreckage is caused by inner cynicism—a disgust with life's futility, an inability to see sense in it. A person in that mood is an easy mark for the next high wind.
ART SISSON

Among the safe courses, the safest of all is to doubt.
SPANISH PROVERB

Open your mouth and purse cautiously, and your stock of wealth and reputation shall, at least in repute, be great.
JOHANN ZIMMERMANN

## *Dreams*

Wonder is the beginning of wisdom in learning from books as well as from nature. If you never ask yourself any questions about the meaning of a passage, you cannot expect the book to give you any insight you do not already possess.
MORTIMER ADLER

If there were dreams to sell, what would you buy!
THOMAS LOVELL BEDDOES

The mightiest works have been accomplished by men who have kept their ability to dream great dreams.
WALTER BOWIE

If I had influence with the good fairy who is supposed to preside over the christening of all children, I should ask that her gift to each child in the world be a sense of wonder so indestructible that it would last throughout life, as an unfailing antidote against boredom and disenchantments of later years, the sterile preoccupation with things that are artificial, the alienation from our sources of strength.
RACHEL CARSON

The world values the seer above all men, and has always done so. Nay, it values all men in proportion as they partake of the character of seers. The Elgin Marbles and a decision of John Marshall are valued for the same reason. What we feel in them is a painstaking submission to facts beyond the author's control, and to ideas imposed upon him by his vision.
**JOHN JAY CHAPMAN**

Dreams and beasts are two keys by which we find out the keys of our own nature.
**RALPH WALDO EMERSON**

Always dream and shoot higher than you know you can do. Don't bother just to be better than your contemporaries or predecessors. Try to be better than yourself.
**WILLIAM FAULKNER**

Living and dreaming are two different things—but you can't do one without the other.
**MALCOLM FORBES**

When you cease to dream you cease to live.
**MALCOLM FORBES**

Dreaming is an act of pure imagination, attesting in all men a creative power, which, if it were available in waking, would make every man a Dante or a Shakespeare.
**H. F. HEDGE**

We do not really feel grateful toward those who make our dreams come true; they ruin our dreams.
**ERIC HOFFER**

Anyone can complain, but to see precisely what is wrong is a gift; accurate diagnosis comes from a unique power of vision and indicates the likelihood of an equally unique capacity to remedy the fault.
**WILLIAM ERNEST HOCKING**

Hold fast to dreams, for if dreams die, life is a broken-winged bird that cannot fly.
**LANGSTON HUGHES**

We sometimes from dreams pick up some hint worth improving by… reflection.
**THOMAS JEFFERSON**

No man will be found in whose mind airy notions do not sometimes tyrannize him and thus force him to hope or fear beyond the limits of sober probability.
**SAMUEL JOHNSON**

The vision of things to be done may come a long time before the way of doing them becomes clear, but woe to him who distrusts the vision.
**JENKIN LLOYD JONES**

The greatest thing about man is his ability to transcend himself, his ancestry and his environment and to become what he dreams of being.
**TULLY C. KNOLES**

All men dream, but unequally. Those that dream at night in the dusty recesses of their minds awake the next day to find that their dreams were just vanity. But those who dream during the day with their eyes wide open are dangerous men; they act out their dreams to make them reality.
**T. E. LAWRENCE**

One half of the world must sweat and groan that the other half may dream.
**HENRY WADSWORTH LONGFELLOW**

I make beanstalks; I'm a builder, like yourself.
**EDNA ST. VINCENT MILLAY**

Dreamers and doers—the world generally divides men into those two general classifications, but the

world is often wrong. There are men who win the admiration and respect of their fellowmen. They are the men worth while. Dreaming is just another name for thinking, planning, devising—another way of saying that a man exercises his soul. A steadfast soul, holding steadily to a dream ideal, plus a sturdy will determined to succeed in any venture, can make any dream come true. Use your mind and your will. They work together for you beautifully if you'll only give them a chance.
B. N. MILLS

A society without dreams would be like an individual sleeper without dreams to fill his night; it would die.
TOM NAIRN

True vision is always twofold. It involves emotional comprehensions as well as physical perception.
ROSS PARMENTER

I have a feeling—as compelling as a religious conviction—that if industry will constantly pass on to the worker and the customer all the savings of labor-saving machinery and invention, rather than siphon them off into the pools of watered securities, it will by that process keep distribution and production in balance and go as far toward Utopia as our poor human natures will go or be driven.
SAMUEL B. PETTENGILL

Wonder is the feeling of a philosopher; and philosophy begins in wonder.
PLATO

Visionary people are visionary partly because of the very great many things they don't see.
BERKELEY RICE

Among all human constructions the only ones that avoid the dissolving hands of time are castles in the air.
FREDERICO DE ROBERTO

The fellow that can only see a week ahead is always the popular fellow, for he is looking with the crowd. But the one that can see years ahead, he has a telescope but he can't make anybody believe he has it.
WILL ROGERS

Keep your eyes on the stars, and your feet on the ground.
THEODORE ROOSEVELT

To build Utopias in defiance of scientific principles is only a fool's errand. If false hopes are momentarily good for morale, we must ultimately pay for such folly in episodes of disillusionment, cynicism and despair.
MERRYLE STANLEY RUKEYSER

A rock pile ceases to be a rock pile the moment a single man contemplates it, bearing within him the image of a cathedral.
ANTOINE DE SAINT-EXUPÉRY

Keep true to the dreams of thy youth.
JOHANN FRIEDRICH VON SCHILLER

You see things; and you say Why? But I dream things that never were; and I say Why not?
GEORGE BERNARD SHAW

Men never cling to their dreams with such tenacity as at the moment when they are losing faith in them, and know it, but do not dare yet to confess it to themselves.
WILLIAM GRAHAM SUMNER

Happy are those who dream dreams and are ready to pay the price to make them come true.
LEON J. SUENENS

Vision is the art of seeing things invisible.
JONATHAN SWIFT

I have learned this at least by my experiment: that if one advances confidently in the direction of his dreams, and endeavors to live the life which he has imagined, he will meet with a success unexpected in common hours.
HENRY DAVID THOREAU

If you have built castles in the air, your work need not be lost; there is where they should be. Now put foundations under them.
HENRY DAVID THOREAU

We grow great by dreams. All big men are dreamers. They see things in the soft haze of a spring day or in the red fire of a long winter's evening. Some of us let these great dreams die, but others nourish and protect them, nurse them through bad days till they bring them to the sunshine and light which come always to those who sincerely hope that their dreams will come true.
WOODROW WILSON

Dreams never hurt anybody if he keeps working right behind the dream to make as much of it come real as he can.
F. W. WOOLWORTH

## Duty

The reward of doing one duty is the power to do another.
RABBI BEN AZAI

The best security for people's doing their duty is that they should not know anything else to do.
WALTER BAGEHOT

All higher motives, ideals, conceptions, sentiments in a man are no account if they do not come forward to strengthen him for the better discharge of the duties which devolve upon him in the ordinary affairs of life.
HENRY WARD BEECHER

There is not a moment without some duty.
CICERO

Is duty a mere sport, or an employ? Life an entrusted talent or a toy?
SAMUEL TAYLOR COLERIDGE

Do your duty and leave the rest to the gods.
PIERRE CORNEILLE

Sufficient to each day are the duties to be done and the trials to be endured. God never built a Christian strong enough to carry today's duties and tomorrow's anxieties piled on the top of them.
THEODORE L. CUYLER

Shirking easily becomes a habit as difficult to throw off as the use of drugs and has ruined many men's chances for success.
HENRY L. DOHERTY

Never shrink from doing anything which your business calls you to do. The man who is above his business, may one day find his business above him.
SAMUEL DREW

Do not be duped by little duties. Do not be a chore man all your days.
SAMUEL SMITH DRURY

How many of us are waiting for the opportunity to do some great thing for the betterment of our community, forgetting that the solution of the problem requires only the active intelligent fulfillment of individual civic duty. The only things which are wrong about our Government are the things which are wrong with you and me. Democracy is never

a thing done; it is and always will be a goal to be achieved. It means action, not passive acquiescence in things as they are; it requires alertness to duty, a dynamic faith, a willingness to give for the good of all. It can live only as a result of loyalty and devotion to its principles expressed by daily deeds.
**DOUGLAS L. EDMONDS**

Where duty is plain delay is both foolish and hazardous; where it is not, delay may be both wisdom and safety.
**TRYON EDWARDS**

We must find our duties in what comes to us, not in what we imagine might have been.
**GEORGE ELIOT**

The reward of one duty done is the power to fulfill another.
**GEORGE ELIOT**

Duty is that mode of action on the part of the individual which constitutes the best possible application of his capacity to the general benefit.
**WILLIAM GODWIN**

Knowledge of our duties is the most essential part of the philosophy of life. If you escape duty you avoid action. The world demands results.
**GEORGE W. GOETHALS**

How can you come to know yourself? Never by thinking; always by doing. Try to do your duty, and you'll know right away what you amount to. And what is your duty? Whatever the day calls for.
**JOHANN WOLFGANG VON GOETHE**

How shall we learn to know ourselves? By reflection? Never; but only through action. Strive to do thy duty; then shalt thou know what is in thee.
**JOHANN WOLFGANG VON GOETHE**

I declare my belief that it is not your duty to do anything that is not to your own interest. Whenever it is unquestionably your duty to do a thing, then it will benefit you to perform that duty.
**EDGAR WATSON HOWE**

It is worthy of special remark that when we are not too anxious about happiness and unhappiness, but devote ourselves to the strict and unsparing performance of duty, then happiness comes of itself.
**KARL WILHELM VON HUMBOLDT**

Only aim to do your duty, and mankind will give you credit where you fail.
**THOMAS JEFFERSON**

Duty is the sublimest word in the language; you can never do more than your duty; you shall never wish to do less.
**ROBERT E. LEE**

New occasions teach new duties.
**JAMES RUSSELL LOWELL**

There is nothing in the universe that I fear, but that I shall not know all my duty, or shall fail to do it.
**MARY LYON**

One sound always comes to the ear that is open, it is the steady drumbeat of Duty. No music in it, perhaps—only a dry rub-a-dub. Ah, but that steady beat marks the time for the whole orchestra of earth and heaven! It says to you: Do your work—do the duty nearest you! Keep step to that drumbeat, and the dullest march is taking you home.
**GEORGE S. MERRIAM**

Where it is a duty to worship the sun it is pretty sure to be a crime to examine the laws of heat.
**JOHN MORLEY**

A duty dodged is like a debt unpaid; it is only deferred, and we must come back and settle the account at last.
**JOSEPH FORT NEWTON**

Abasement, degradation is simply the manner of life of the man who has refused to be what it is his duty to be.
**JOSÉ ORTEGA Y GASSET**

Who escapes a duty, avoids a gain.
**THEODORE PARKER**

Let us do our duty in our shop or our kitchen, in the market, the street, the office, the school, the home, just as faithfully as if we stood in the front rank of some great battle, and knew that victory for mankind depended on our bravery, strength, and skill. When we do that, the humblest of us will be serving in that great army which achieves the welfare of the world.
**THEODORE PARKER**

We ought to use the best means we can to be well informed of our duty.
**THOMAS B. REED**

Next to doing the right thing, the most important thing is to let people know you are doing the right thing.
**JOHN D. ROCKEFELLER**

A sense of duty is useful in work, but offensive in personal relations.
**BERTRAND RUSSELL**

It is not enough to be ready to go where duty calls. A man should stand around where he can hear the call!
**ROBERT LOUIS STEVENSON**

Do not keep away from the measure which has no limit, or from the task which has no end.
**RABBI TARPHON**

For many years I was self-appointed inspector of snowstorms and rainstorms, and did my duty faithfully.
**HENRY DAVID THOREAU**

Great trials seem to be a necessary preparation for great duties.
**JAMES THOMSON**

A man who neglects his duty as a citizen is not entitled to his rights as a citizen.
**TIORIO**

To persevere in one's duty and be silent is the best answer to calumny.
**GEORGE WASHINGTON**

The consideration that human happiness and moral duty are inseparably connected will always continue to prompt me to promote the former by inculcating the practice of the latter.
**GEORGE WASHINGTON**

There's life alone in duty done; and rest alone in striving.
**JOHN GREENLEAF WHITTIER**

Duty is what one expects from others.
**OSCAR WILDE**

It is just as hard to do your duty when men are sneering at you as when they are shooting at you.
**WOODROW WILSON**

# E

## Economy

Colleges don't teach economics properly. Unfortunately we learn little from the experience of the past. An economist must know, besides his subject, ethics, logic, philosophy, the humanities and sociology, in fact everything that is part of how we live and react to one another.
BERNARD M. BARUCH

A science of economics must be developed before a science of politics can be logically formulated. Essentially, economics is the science of determining whether the interests of human beings are harmonious or antagonistic. This must be known before a science of politics can be formulated to determine the proper functions of government.
CLAUDE-FRÉDÉRIC BASTIAT

Inflation is a form of hidden taxation which it is almost impossible to measure.
JOHN BECKLEY

Thrift and prosperity have gone hand in hand since Abraham's flocks grew and multiplied. Thrift is not, as many suppose, a self repression. It is self expression, the demonstration of a will and ability to raise one's self to a higher plane of living. No depression was ever caused by people having too much money in reserve. No human being ever became a social drifter through the practice of sensible thrift.
HARVEY A. BLODGETT

Economy is a distributive virtue, and consists not in saving but in selection. Parsimony requires no providence, no sagacity, no powers of combination, no comparison, no judgment.
EDMUND BURKE

Mere parsimony is not economy. . . . Expense, and great expense, may be an essential part in true economy. . . . Economy is a distributive virtue, and consists, not in saving, but in selection.
EDMUND BURKE

People who never had enough thrift and forethought to buy and pay for property in the first place seldom have enough to keep the property up after they have gained it in some other way.
THOMAS NIXON CARVER

Thrift is that habit of character that prompts one to work for what he gets, to earn what is paid him; to invest a part of his earnings; to spend wisely and well; to save, but not hoard.
ARTHUR CHAMBERLAIN

He who will not economize will have to agonize.
CONFUCIUS

After order and liberty, economy is one of the highest essentials of a free government. Economy is always a guarantee of peace.
CALVIN COOLIDGE

Inflation is repudiation.
CALVIN COOLIDGE

In all recorded history there has not been one economist who has had to worry about where his next meal would come from.
PETER DRUCKER

Everyone is always in favor of general economy and particular expenditure.
ANTHONY EDEN

Economy does not consist in saving the coal, but in using the time while it burns.
RALPH WALDO EMERSON

Economy has frequently nothing whatever to do with the amount of money being spent, but with the wisdom used in spending it.
HENRY FORD

Economists are economical, among other things, of ideas; most make those of their graduate days do for a lifetime.
JOHN KENNETH GALBRAITH

Economic independence doesn't set anyone free. Or it shouldn't, for the higher up you go, the more responsibilities become yours.
BERNARD F. GIMBEL

He that spareth in everything is an inexcusable niggard. He that spareth in nothing is an inexcusable madman. The mean is to spare in what is least necessary, and to lay out more liberally in what is most required.
LORD HALIFAX

Economy is going without something you do want in case you should, some day, want something which you probably won't want.
ANTHONY H. HAWKINS

If one could divine the nature of the economic forces in the world, one could foretell the future.
ROBERT HEILBRONER

Economic depression cannot be cured by legislative action or executive pronouncement. Economic wounds must be healed by the action of the cells of the economic body, the producers and consumers themselves.
HERBERT HOOVER

Once upon a time my opponents honored me as possessing the fabulous intellectual and economic power by which I created a worldwide depression all by myself.
HERBERT HOOVER

I place economy among the first and most important virtues, and public debt as the greatest of dangers to be feared. . . . To preserve our independence, we must not let our rulers load us with perpetual debt. . . . We must make our choice between economy and liberty or profusion and servitude. . . . If we run into such debts, we must be taxed in our meat and drink, in our necessities and our comforts, in our labors and in our amusements. . . . If we can prevent the Government from wasting the labors of the people, under the pretense of caring for them, they will be happy.
THOMAS JEFFERSON

Thrift is care and scruple in the spending of one's means. It is not a virtue and it requires neither skill nor talent.
IMMANUEL KANT

When business embarks on a rampage which does not help humanity to live and *grow*—when it pushes beyond this range of usefulness and overproduces human needs—or when it falls behind and outlives its usefulness—it runs into trouble of some kind. And when the business tree is crowded with these dead or dying branches, the tree as a whole begins to suffer. We run into a business depression or plunge into industrial war to shake the rotten branches down.
V. C. KITCHEN

No gain is so certain as that which proceeds for the economical use of what you already have.
LATIN PROVERB

There is deep intuitive wisdom in this American tolerance of economic variety and in our refusal to commit ourselves to any one social and economic system. It is recognition of the fact that life and truth are too varied and complex to be confined within the pattern of any single deliberately planned economic system.
ARTHUR E. MORGAN

Large enterprises make the few rich, but the majority prosper only through the carefulness and detail of thrift.
THEODORE T. MUNGER

I would rather have people laugh at my economies than weep for my extravagance.
KING OSCAR II OF SWEDEN

We must be strong; we must seek to preserve our economic health and assist world recovery; we must define our objectives in terms of reality rather than in terms so extended that our power for good is diffused and wasted. And if we do all these things, while we must indeed face the future with a clear view of its possible perils, we need not quail before it.
DEXTER PERKINS

No civilized country in the world has ever voluntarily adopted the extreme philosophies of either fascism or communism, unless the middle class was first liquidated by inflation.
HENNING W. PRENTIS, JR.

The uprisings of 1789 cost Louis XVI some prerogatives, but four years later a valueless currency cost him his head. Germany's inflation of the 1920s laid the foundation upon which Hitler built. Indeed, a runaway inflation is the goal of revolutionists. The maxim of that apostle of revolution, Lenin, was "Debauch the currency!"
EDGAR M. QUEENY

Economy is in itself a great source of revenue.
SENECA

Economy is too late at the bottom of the purse.
SENECA

Economy is the art of making the most of life. The love of economy is the root of all virtue.
GEORGE BERNARD SHAW

The regard one shows economy, is like that we show an old aunt, who is to leave us something at last.
WILLIAM SHENSTONE

The love of economy is the root of all virtue.
GEORGE BERNARD SHAW

Parsimony, and not industry, is the immediate cause of the increase of capital. But whatever industry might acquire, if parsimony did not save and store up, the capital would never be the greater.
ADAM SMITH

Individual thrift and responsibility for the future must be preserved if we are to be healthy and prosperous under any social system, whatever it is to be. No social planning can invent a substitute for the general principle of individual self-support. Two irresponsible persons added together do not make a happy home, nor do a thousand individual failures, however organized, make a successful community.
RALPH W. SOCKMAN

Economic growth is not only unncessary, but ruinous.
ALEKSANDR SOLZHENITSYN

Economy is half the battle of life; it is not so hard to earn money as to spend it well.
CHARLES H. SPURGEON

Economic development involves the production of more food, more clothing, and more mechanical power to lighten people's burdens. It involves a better use of the world's human and natural resources. Looked at in the large, economic development means the continuous improvement and utilization of the resources and productive capacities of a people for the benefit of the people. It applies to farms as well as to factories. It applies to intellectual advancement as well as physical health. It applies to habits of work and habits of leisure, to the saving of capital and to its provident investment.
WILLARD L. THROP

We are not to judge thrift solely by the test of saving or spending. If one spends what he should prudently save, that certainly is to be deplored. But if one saves what he should prudently spend, that is not necessarily to be commended. A wise balance between the two is the desired end.
OWEN D. YOUNG

## *Education*

Knowledge accumulates in universities, because the freshmen bring a little in and the seniors take none away.
ANONYMOUS

A teacher affects eternity: he can never tell where his influence stops.
HENRY ADAMS

They know enough who know how to learn.
HENRY ADAMS

Education makes a greater difference between man and man than nature has made between man and brute.
JOHN ADAMS

A true teacher defends his pupils against his own personal influence.
AMOS BRONSON ALCOTT

The man who knows not and knows that he knows not is a child—teach him.
ARABIAN PROVERB

All who have meditated on the art of governing mankind have been convinced that the fate of empires depends on the education of youth.
ARISTOTLE

The roots of education are bitter, but the fruit is sweet.
ARISTOTLE

Those who educate children well are more to be honored than parents, for these only gave life, those the art of living well.
ARISTOTLE

If your civilization is to be enriched, it must be relived by every single child. It is in the schoolroom—or mostly in the schoolroom—while assimilating little tidbits of what has been the experience of men before him, that the child first makes the acquaintance of the human person, of the spiritual being he is.
MAX ASCOLI

It takes most men five years to recover from a college education, and to learn that poetry is as vital to thinking as knowledge.
BROOKS ATKINSON

A professor is one who talks in someone else's sleep.
**W. H. AUDEN**

A schoolmaster should have an atmosphere of awe, and walk wonderingly, as if he was amazed at being himself.
**WALTER BAGEHOT**

The man who graduates to-day and stops learning tomorrow is uneducated the day after.
**NEWTON D. BAKER**

The fruits of the earth do not more obviously require labor and cultivation to prepare them for our use and subsistence, than our faculties demand instruction and regulation in order to qualify us to become upright and valuable members of society, useful to others, or happy ourselves.
**BARROW**

Teaching is not a lost art, but the regard for it is a lost tradition.
**JACQUES BARZUN**

The test and the use of man's education is that he finds pleasure in the exercise of his mind.
**JACQUES BARZUN**

A republican government is in a hundred points weaker than one that is autocratic; but in this one point it is the strongest that ever existed—it has educated a race of men that are men.
**HENRY WARD BEECHER**

Life is amazing; and the teacher had better prepare himself to be a medium for that amazement.
**EDWARD BLISHEN**

You should have education enough so that you won't have to look up to people; and then more education so that you will be wise enough not to look down on people.
**M. L. BOREN**

Let's break the lock-step process that is now the accepted pattern of most collegiate systems. It is important to have the student demonstrate that he has developed a degree of intellectual competence rather than that he has acquired a certain number of semester credits.
**DETLEV V. BRONK**

Prejudices, it is well known, are most difficult to eradicate from the heart whose soil has never been loosened or fertilized by education; they grow there, firm as weeds among stones.
**CHARLOTTE BRONTË**

Education makes a people easy to lead, but difficult to drive; easy to govern, but impossible to enslave.
**HENRY BROUGHAM**

Education is anything that we do for the purpose of taking advantage of the experience of some one else.
**LYMAN BRYSON**

All of the energy we devote to improving advanced education in the United States and all of the financial contributions we make are investments that very specifically and realistically return to us that stability and expansion of the economy which gives the American enterprise system the franchise it was first given many years ago.
**HARRY A. BULLIS**

The best teacher is the one who suggests rather than dogmatizes, and inspires his listener with the wish to teach himself.
**EDWARD BULWER-LYTTON**

**Education is the chief defense of nations.**

EDMUND BURKE

**The five evidences of education are as follows:**

1. Correctness and precision of speech.
2. Refined and gentle manners.
3. The power and habit of reflection.
4. The power of growth.
5. The possession of efficiency—the power to do.

NICHOLAS MURRAY BUTLER

The teaching of any science, for purposes of liberal education, without linking it with social progress and teaching its social significance, is a crime against the student mind. It is like teaching a child how to pronounce words but not what they mean.

VERNON CARTER

The most effective teacher will always be biased, for the chief force in teaching is confidence and enthusiasm.

JOYCE CARY

A true university can never rest upon the will of one man. A true university always rests upon the wills of many divergent-minded old men, who refuse to be disturbed, but who growl in their kennels.

JOHN JAY CHAPMAN

Man's knowledge of science has clearly outstripped his knowledge of man. Our only hope of making the atom servant rather than master lies in education, in a broad liberal education where each student within his capacity can free himself from trammels of dogmatic prejudice and apply his educational accoutrement to besetting social and human problems.

HARRY WOODBURN CHASE

Properly speaking, there is no such thing as education. Education is simply the soul of a society as it passes from one generation to another. Whatever the soul is like, it will have to be passed on somehow, consciously or unconsciously; and that transition may be called education.

G. K. CHESTERTON

Without education we are in a horrible and deadly danger of taking educated people seriously.

G. K. CHESTERTON

Public education is a great instrument of social change. Through it, if we so desire, we can make our country more nearly a democracy without classes. . . . Education is a social process, perhaps the most important process in determining the future of our country, it should command a far larger portion of our national income than it does today.

JAMES BRYANT CONANT

Examinations are formidable even to the best prepared, for the greatest fool may ask more than the wisest man can answer.

CHARLES CALEB COLTON

Better build schoolhouses for the boy than cells for the man.

ELIZA COOK

My education began with a set of blocks which had on them the Roman numerals and the letters of the alphabet. It is not yet finished.

CALVIN COOLIDGE

Fortunately or otherwise we live at a time when the average individual has to know several times as much in order to keep informed as he did only thirty or forty years ago. Being "educated" today requires not only more than a superficial knowledge of the arts and sciences, but a sense of inter-relationship such as is taught in few schools. Finally, being "educated" today, in terms of the larger needs, means

preparation for world citizenship; in short, education for survival.
NORMAN COUSINS

It makes little difference what the trade, business, or branch of learning, in mechanical labor, or intellectual effort, the educated man is always superior to the common laborer. One who is in the habit of applying his powers in the right way will carry system into any occupation, and it will help him as much to handle a rope as to write a poem.
F. MARION CRAWFORD

If these distracted times prove anything, they prove that the greatest illusion is reliance upon the security and permanence of material possessions. We must search for some other coin. And we will discover that the treasure-house of education has stood intact and unshaken in the storm. The man of cultivated life has founded his house upon a rock. You can never take away the magnificent mansion of his mind.
JOHN CUDAHY

The teaching profession is the only profession that has no definition for malpractice.
MERIMON CUNINGGIM

I still think that children learn more about life and conduct when an interesting man is given the run of this tongue, and is not chained to a syllabus which dictates everything, including the opening and closing of the classroom windows.
ROBERTSON DAVIES

A good education is usually harmful to a dancer. A good calf is better than a good head.
AGNES DE MILLE

Nature and education are somewhat similar. The latter transforms man, and in so doing creates a second nature.
DEMOCRITUS

The devotion of democracy to education is a familiar fact. The superficial explanation is that a government resting upon popular suffrage cannot be successful unless those who elect and who obey their governors are educated. Since a democratic society repudiates the principle of external authority, it must find a substitute in voluntary disposition and interest; these can be created only by education.
JOHN DEWEY

The college undergraduate is a lot of things—many of them as familiar, predictable and responsible as the bounce of a basketball, and others as startling (and occasionally as disastrous) as the bounce of a football.
JOHN SLOAN DICKEY

A school is a place through which you have to pass before entering life, but where the teaching proper does not prepare you for life.
ERNEST DIMNET

Children have to be educated, but they have also to be left to educate themselves.
ERNEST DIMNET

The most important aspect of freedom of speech is freedom to learn. All education is a continuous dialogue—questions and answer that pursue every problem to the horizon. That is the essence of academic freedom.
WILLIAM O. DOUGLAS

I wouldn't attach too much importance to these student riots. I remember when I was a student at the Sorbonne I used to go out and riot occasionally.
JOHN FOSTER DULLES

Sixty years ago I knew everything; now I know nothing; education is a progressive discovery of our own ignorance.
WILL DURANT

The great end of education is, to discipline rather than to furnish the mind; to train it to the use of its own powers, rather than fill it with the accumulations of others.
TYRON EDWARDS

Education is that which remains when one has forgotten everything he learned in school.
ALBERT EINSTEIN

Never regard study as a duty, but as the enviable opportunity to learn to know the liberating influence of beauty in the realm of the spirit for your own personal joy and to the profit of the community to which your later work belongs.
ALBERT EINSTEIN

Schools need not preach political doctrine to defend democracy. If they shape men capable of critical thought and trained in social attitudes, that is all that is necessary.
ALBERT EINSTEIN

Liberal education develops a sense of right, duty and honor; and more and more in the modern world, large business rests on rectitude and honor as well as on good judgment.
CHARLES W. ELIOT

That which we do not call education is more precious than that which we call so.
RALPH WALDO EMERSON

There is no teaching until the public is brought into the same state or principle in which you are; a transfusion takes place; he is you and you are he; then is a teaching, and by no unfriendly chance or bad company can he ever quite lose the benefit.
RALPH WALDO EMERSON

The things taught in schools and colleges are not an education, but the means of education.
RALPH WALDO EMERSON

The whole secret of the teacher's force lies in the conviction that men are convertible.
RALPH WALDO EMERSON

Don't despair of a student if he has one clear idea.
NATHANIEL EMMONS

Two delusions fostered by higher education are that what is taught corresponds to what is learned, and that it will somehow pay off in money.
WILLIAM FEATHER

Education is the process by which the individual relates himself to the universe, gives himself citizenship in the changing world, shares the race's mind and enfranchises his own soul.
JOHN H. FINLEY

Nations have recently been led to borrow billions for war; no nation has ever borrowed largely for education.
ABRAHAM FLEXNER

We can't take a slipshod and easygoing attitude toward education in this country. And by "we" I don't mean "somebody else," but I mean me and I mean you. It is the future of our country—yours and mine—which is at stake.
HENRY FORD II

Vitally important for a young man or woman is, first, to realize the value of education, and then to cultivate earnestly, aggressively, ceaselessly, the habit of self-education. Without fresh supplies of knowledge, the brain will not develop healthily and vigor-

ously any more than the body can be sustained without fresh supplies of food.
B. C. FORBES

It's the less-bright students who make teachers teach better.
MALCOLM FORBES

The whole art of teaching is only the art of awakening the natural curiosity of young minds for the purpose of satisfying it afterwards.
ANATOLE FRANCE

A Bible and a newspaper in every house, a good school in every district—all studied and appreciated as they merit—are the principal support of virtue, morality, and civil liberty.
BENJAMIN FRANKLIN

Education is the ability to listen to almost anything without losing your temper or your self-confidence.
ROBERT FROST

The ultimate goal of the educational system is to shift to the individual the burden of pursuing his own education.
JOHN W. GARDNER

Next in importance to freedom and justice is popular education, without which neither freedom nor justice can be permanently maintained.
JAMES A. GARFIELD

The best teacher is . . . the one who kindles an inner fire, arouses moral enthusiasm, inspires the student with a vision of what he may become and reveals the worth and permanency of moral and spiritual and cultural values.
HAROLD GARNETT

Every man who rises above the common level has received two educations: the first from his teachers; the second, more personal and important, from himself.
EDWARD GIBBON

The ability to think straight, some knowledge of the past, some vision of the future, some skill to do useful service, some urge to fit that service into the wellbeing of the community—these are the most vital things education must try to produce. If we can achieve them in the citizens of our land, then, given the right to knowledge and the free use thereof, we shall have brought to America the wisdom and the courage to match her destiny.
VIRGINIA C. GILDERSLEEVE

One of the chief objects of education should be to widen the windows through which we view the world.
ARNOLD GLASOW

Alas! how much there is in education, and in our social institutions, to prepare us and our children for insanity.
JOHANN WOLFGANG VON GOETHE

Good teaching is one-fourth preparation and three-fourths theatre.
GAIL GODWIN

If you feel that you have both feet planted on solid ground, then the university has failed you.
ROBERT GOHEEN

A college education is not a quantitative body of memorized knowledge salted away in a card file. It is a taste for knowledge, a taste for philosophy, if you will; a capacity to explore, to question, to perceive relationships, between fields of knowledge and experience.
A. WHITNEY GRISWOLD

The fiscal operations of government are strongly, though no doubt unintentionally, adverse to private education. They do not provide the positive support recommended by the President's Commission on Higher Education and urgently needed by the private institutions if they are in fact to survive.
A. WHITNEY GRISWOLD

Education is what remains when we have forgotten all that we have been taught.
LORD HALIFAX

Education has now become the chief problem of the world, its one holy cause. The nations that see this will survive, and those that fail to do so will slowly perish. . . . There must be re-education of the will and of the heart as well as of the intellect, and the ideals of service must supplant those of selfishness and greed.
G. STANLEY HALL

The great value of formal education is that it is designed to foreshorten human experience. It endeavors with ease and economy to bring each succeeding generation up to date with respect to the past and to make it at home in the world. In this sense, it prepares each generation for life.
VIRGIL M. HANCHER

Higher education must lead the march back to the fundamentals of human relationships, to the old discovery that is ever new, that man does not live by bread alone.
JOHN A. HANNAH

If Americans have had a paramount educational objective, it has not been the building of bigger and bigger intellects but rather the setting of men upon their own feet.
ROBERT HARRIS

It may be that we should stop putting so much emphasis in our own minds on the monetary value of a college education and put more emphasis on the intangible social and cultural values to be derived from learning. The time may be coming when we will have to start accepting the idea that education is life, not merely a preparation for it.
SEYMOUR E. HARRIS

The two basic processes of education are knowing and valuing.
ROBERT J. HAVIGHURST

It is better to be able neither to read nor write than to be able to do nothing else.
WILLIAM HAZLITT

An important personal quality for a teacher is that he care about humanity. If he doesn't, he is taking his pay illegally.
EDWARD C. HELWICK

A good education prepares a child to be a good employee and a good citizen—in that order, with the importance of the former never exceeding the importance of the latter.
CULLEN HIGHTOWER

Life is but one continual course of instruction. The hand of the parent writes on the heart of the child the first faint characters which time deepens into strength so that nothing can efface them.
ROWLAND HILL

Our world is a college, events are teachers, happiness is the graduating point, character is the diploma God gives man.
NEWELL DWIGHT HILLIS

A child's education should begin at least 100 years before he is born.
OLIVER WENDELL HOLMES

We need education in the obvious more than investigation of the obscure.
OLIVER WENDELL HOLMES

My idea of education is to unsettle the minds of the young and inflame their intellects.
ROBERT M. HUTCHINS

We no longer have the three Rs in this country. Instead, we have the six Rs—remedial reading, remedial 'riting and remedial 'rithmetic.
ROBERT M. HUTCHINS

When we listen to the radio, look at television and read the newspapers we wonder whether universal education has been the great boon that its supporters have always claimed it would be.
ROBERT M. HUTCHINS

I care not what subject is taught if only it be taught well.
THOMAS H. HUXLEY

Perhaps the most valuable result of all education is the ability to make yourself do the thing you have to do, whether you like it or not.
THOMAS H. HUXLEY

## Education

To be at home in all lands and all ages; to count Nature as a familiar acquaintance and Art an intimate friend; to gain a standard for the appreciation of other men's work and the criticism of one's own; to carry the keys of the world's library in one's pocket, and feel its resources behind one in whatever task he undertakes; to make hosts of friends among the men of one's own age who are the leaders in all walks of life; to lose oneself in general enthusiasms and co-operate with others for common ends. . . .
WILLIAM DE WITT HYDE

Colleges are places where pebbles are polished and diamonds are dimmed.
ROBERT G. INGERSOLL

Let no youth have any anxiety about the upshot of his education, whatever the line of it may be. If he keep faithfully busy each hour of the working-day, he may safely leave the result to itself. He can with perfect certainty count on waking up some fine morning to find himself one of the competent ones of his generation.
WILLIAM JAMES

The true purpose of education is to cherish and unfold the seed of immortality already sown within us; to develop, to their fullest extent, the capacities of every kind with which the God who made us has endowed us.
ANNA JAMESON

I know of no safe repository for the ultimate powers of society but the people themselves; and if we think them not enlightened enough to exercise their control with a wholesome discretion, the remedy is not to take it from them, but to increase their discretion by education.
THOMAS JEFFERSON

He that teaches us anything which we knew not before is undoubtedly to be reverenced as a master.
SAMUEL JOHNSON

To find out what we presently are and where we are going, we must know what we have been and what others have done; and this, because the humanities are at once the creation and the interpreters of the past, is the great purpose of humanistic scholarship.
HOWARD MUMFORD JONES

I am now past the craggy paths of study, and come to the flowery plains of honor and reputation.
BEN JONSON

One looks back with appreciation to the brilliant teachers, but with gratitude to those who touch our human feelings. The curriculum is so much necessary raw material, but warmth is the vital element for the growing plant and for the soul of a child.
CARL JUNG

There is nothing more inspiring than having a mind unfold before you. Let people teach who have a calling. It is never just a job.
ABRAHAM KAPLAN

I find the three major problems on a campus are sex for the students, athletics for the alumni, and parking for the faculty.
CLARK KERR

It is on the sound education of the people that the security and destiny of every nation chiefly rests.
LOUIS KOSSUTH

Give vocational training to the manually minded, and the children's courts of the future will have less to do.
LEWIS E. LAWES

The work that the schoolmaster is doing is inestimable in its consequence. He is laying the foundation of the careers of men who are to lead the next generation. He is also knocking all the best stuff out of a great number of them.
STEPHEN LEACOCK

Poor is the pupil who does not surpass his master.
LEONARDO DA VINCI

America's future walks through the doors of our schools every day.
MARY JEAN LETENDRE

Men, in teaching others, learn themselves.
THOMAS LODGE

Too much attention has been paid to making education attractive by smoothing the path as compared with inducing strenuous voluntary effort.
ABBOTT LOWELL

Nothing is lost upon a man who is bent upon growth; nothing wasted on one who is always preparing for his work and his life by keeping eyes, mind, and heart open to nature, men, books, experience. Such a man finds ministers to his education on all sides; everything co-operates with his passion for growth. And what he gathers serves him at unexpected moments in unforeseen ways.
HAMILTON WRIGHT MABIE

To know every detail, to gain an insight into each secret, to learn every method, to secure every kind of skill, are the prime necessities in every art, craft or business. No time is too long, no study too hard, no discipline too severe for the attainment of complete familiarity with one's work and complete ease and skill in the art of doing it. As a man values his working life, he must be willing to pay the highest price of success in it—the price which severe training exacts.
HAMILTON WRIGHT MABIE

Jails and prisons are the complement of schools; so many less as you have of the latter, so many more you must have of the former.
HORACE MANN

No man is worthy of the honored name of a statesman who does not include the highest practicable education of the people in all his plans of administration. He may have eloquence, he may have a knowledge of all history, diplomacy, jurisprudence; and by these he might claim, in other countries, the elevated rank of a statesman; but, unless he speaks, plans, labors, at all times and in all places, for the culture and edification of the whole people, he is not, he cannot be, an American statesman.
HORACE MANN

If you are to find rewarding satisfaction in your work, if your life is to be rich and purposeful and crowned with high achievement, it is important you continue to be a growing person. Education is a continuing process. It does not end with the termination of your schooling. Education continues from the beginning of life to the end of life, and balanced growth throughout one's entire life is important for every individual.
HENRY T. MASCHAL

The aim of education should be to convert the mind into a living fountain, and not a reservoir. That which is filled by merely pumping in, will be emptied by pumping out.
JOHN M. MASON

A man who knows a subject thoroughly, a man so soaked in it that he eats it, sleeps it and dreams it—this man can always teach it with success, no matter how little he knows of technical pedagogy.
H. L. MENCKEN

No young man is educated if he comes out of college with the cheap and false values of the common man.
H. L. MENCKEN

Education is no longer thought of as a preparation for adult life, but as a continuing process of growth and development from birth until death.
STEPHEN MITCHELL

Industry must fight just as passionately for educational freedom as it does for economic freedom because that which threatens educational freedom threatens all freedoms.
CHARLES F. MOORE, JR.

Just as education without humanity is the most dangerous thing in the world, so education in love, human understanding and cooperation is the greatest hope of the world.
JOY ELMER MORGAN

Intelligence plus experience creates ideas, and experimentation with that form of chemistry—the contact of ideas with events—is the field of adult education.
FELIX MORLEY

Higher education is booming in the U.S.; the Gross National Mind is mounting along with Gross National Product.
MALCOLM MUGGERIDGE

I was greatly influenced by one of my teachers. She had a zeal not so much for perfection as for steady betterment—she demanded not excellence so much as integrity.
EDWARD R. MURROW

I've learned that my teacher always calls on me the one time I don't know the answer.
9-YEAR-OLD'S DISCOVERY

No bubble is so iridescent or floats longer than that blown by the successful teacher.
SIR WILLIAM OSLER

I may safely predict that the education of the future will be inventive-minded. It will believe so profoundly in the high value of the inventive or creative spirit that it will set itself to develop that spirit by all means within its power.
HARRY A. OVERSTREET

Education is a debt due from the present to the future generations.
GEORGE PEABODY

Education is a method whereby one acquires a higher grade of prejudices.
LAURENCE J. PETER

Being educated means to prefer the best not only to the worst but to the second best.
WILLIAM LYON PHELPS

The direction in which education starts a man will determine his future life.
PLATO

Thank goodness I was never sent to school; it would have rubbed off some of the originality.
BEATRIX POTTER

The noblest exercise of the mind within doors . . . is study.
WILLIAM RAMSEY

Formal education is but an incident in the lifetime of an individual. Most of us who have given the subject any study have come to realize that education is a continuous process ending only when ambition comes to a halt.
COL. R. I. REES

The carefully fostered theory that schoolwork can be made easy and enjoyable breaks down as soon as anything, however trivial, has to be learned.
AGNES REPPLIER

There is nothing so stupid as an educated man, if you get him off the thing he was educated in.
WILL ROGERS

Education is either from nature, from man or from things. The developing of our faculties and organs is the education of nature; that of man is the application we learn to make of this very developing; and that of things is the experience we acquire in regard to the different objects by which we are affected. All that we have not at our birth, and that we stand in need of at the years of maturity, is the gift of education.
JEAN-JACQUES ROUSSEAU

Education is leading human souls to what is best, and making what is best out of them; and these two objects are always attainable together, and by the same means; the training which makes men happiest in themselves also makes them most serviceable to others.
JOHN RUSKIN

The entire object of true education is to make people not merely do the right thing, but enjoy the right things; not merely industrious, but to love industry; not merely learned, but to love knowledge; not merely pure, but to love purity; not merely just, but to hunger and thirst after justice.
JOHN RUSKIN

Men are born ignorant, not stupid; they are made stupid by education.
BERTRAND RUSSELL

In a society safe and worthy to be free, teaching which produces a willingness to lead, as well as a willingness to follow, must be given to all.
WILLIAM F. RUSSELL

The well-meaning people who talk of education as if it were a substance distributable by coupon in large or small quantities never exhibit any understanding of the truth that you cannot teach anybody anything that he does not want to learn.
GEORGE SAMPSON

The great difficulty in education is to get experience out of ideas.
GEORGE SANTAYANA

A well-educated population, trained by mental discipline and culture, and deeply imbued with the religious principle, is the strongest bulwark of a nation.
**DAVID SCOTT**

A man cannot leave a better legacy to the world than a well-educated family.
**THOMAS SCOTT**

My joy in learning is partly that it enables me to teach.
**SENECA**

Consideration is not merely a matter of emotional goodwill but of intellectual vigor and moral self-sacrifice. Wisdom must combine with sympathy. That is why consideration underlies the phrase "a scholar and a gentleman," which really sums up the ideal of the output of a college education.
**CHARLES SEYMOUR**

We haven't taken time to begin to learn about the world through which we are passing.... I predict that our liberal arts faculties will more and more be giving refresher courses to graduates and to non-graduates alike.... It is time that the word "commencement" be given a new educational content for the graduating classes of our great universities.
**CHARLES SEYMOUR**

Teachers should be held in the highest honor. They are the allies of legislators; they have agency in the prevention of crime; they aid in regulating the atmosphere, whose incessant action and pressure cause the life-blood to circulate, and to return pure and healthful to the heart of the nation.
**LYDIA SIGOURNEY**

Education is the biggest business in America. It has the largest number of owners, the most extensive and costly plant, and utilizes the most valuable raw material. It has the greatest number of operators. It employs our greatest investment in money and time, with the exception of national defense. Its product has the greatest influence on both America and the world.
**CHARLES R. SLIGH, JR.**

The future of civilization is, to a great extent, being written in the classrooms of the world.
**MILTON L. SMITH**

The individual who is best prepared for any occupation is the one whose intelligence has been so well trained that he is able to adapt himself to any situation and whose point of view has been so humanized by his education that he will be a good person in any job or calling.
**MORTIMER SMITH**

The real object of education is to give children resources that will endure as long as life endures; habits that time will ameliorate, not destroy; occupation that will render sickness tolerable, solitude pleasant, age venerable, life more dignified and useful.
**SYDNEY SMITH**

An educated man is one on whom nothing is lost.
**WENDELL SMITH**

The great aim of education is not knowledge but action.
**HERBERT SPENCER**

Education is not any more the pale flower, to be nurtured in cloistered seclusion, away from the crass world's bruising conflict for material gain. Today education is part of that conflict. It is the prerequisite for material gain. Nor can even the scholar withdraw into the academic life. The academic life is right out there now, trying to make a living in competition with all the other forms of life.
**FRANCIS W. SPRINGER**

I thought that the chief thing to be done in order to equal boys was to be learned and courageous. So I decided to study Greek and learn to manage a horse.
**ELIZABETH CADY STANTON**

The worst education which teaches self-denial is better than the best which teaches everything else and not that.
**JOHN STERLING**

Study to shew thyself approved unto God, a workman that needeth not to be ashamed, rightly dividing the word of truth. But shun profane and vain babblings: for they will increase unto more ungodliness.
**II TIMOTHY 2:15-16**

I like to instruct people. It is noble to teach oneself. It is still nobler to teach others, and less trouble.
**MARK TWAIN**

I never let my schooling interfere with my education.
**MARK TWAIN**

It used to take me all vacation to grow a new hide in place of the one they flogged off me during the school term.
**MARK TWAIN**

Training is everything. The peach was once a bitter almond; the cauliflower is nothing but a cabbage with a college education.
**MARK TWAIN**

To teach, to guide, to explain, to help, to nurture—these are life's noblest attainments.
**FRANK TYGER**

Education is an admirable thing, but it is well to remember from time to time that nothing that's worth knowing can be taught.
**OSCAR WILDE**

Education is the mother of leadership.
**WENDELL WILLKIE**

Education today, more than ever before, must see clearly the dual objectives: Educating for living and educating for making a living.
**JAMES MASON WOOD**

One good teacher in a lifetime may sometimes change a delinquent into a solid citizen.
**PHILIP WYLIE**

All true educators since the time of Socrates and Plato have agreed that the primary object of education is the attainment of inner harmony, or, to put it into more up-to-date language, the integration of the personality. Without such an integration learning is no more than a collection of scraps, and the accumulation of knowledge becomes a danger to mental health.
**SIR ALFRED ZIMMERN**

## *Effort*

How much easier our work would be if we put forth as much effort trying to improve the quality of it as most of us do trying to find excuses for not properly attending to it.
**GEORGE W. BALLENGER**

Freedom is not free. Shaping and preserving society necessarily involves personal commitment, costly risk and constant effort; the cultivation of civil liberty can be no more passive than the cultivation of a farm. A man can inherit the land on which he lives, he can even inherit the first crop of produce after he takes over from those who came before him. But then if he stops, everything stops and begins to crumble. Nothing grows, nothing ripe and rewarding comes to him, unless he plows,

plants and tends the soil and unless he keeps it fertile year after year with the chemistry of effort and forethought.
**Edmond Cahn**

There is no joy in getting by on your job—doing as little as you can. There is a lot of pleasure in doing more than you have to. "And whosoever shall compel you to go a mile, go with him twain," says the Bible, wisely.
**Norman Carlisle**

Know what thou canst work at, and work at it like a Hercules.
**Thomas Carlyle**

A man is relieved and gay when he has put his heart into his work and done his best.
**Ralph Waldo Emerson**

So with slight efforts, how should one obtain great results? It is foolish even to desire it.
**Euripides**

Virtue proceeds through effort.
**Euripides**

There's no ceiling on effort!
**Harvey C. Fruehauf**

Keep the faculty of effort alive in you by a little gratuitous exercise every day. That is, be systematically ascetic or heroic in little unnecessary points, do every day or two something for no other reason than that you would rather not do it, so that when the hour of dire need draws nigh, it may find you not unnerved and untrained to stand the test.
**William James**

Whether our efforts are, or not, favored by life, let us be able to say, when we come near to the great goal, I have done what I could.
**Louis Pasteur**

Man's capacities have never been measured. Nor are we to judge of what he can do by precedents, so little has been tried.
**Henry David Thoreau**

Whatever your work is, dignify it with your best thought and effort.
**Esther Baldwin York**

##  *Ego*

Egotist: A man of low taste, more interested in himself than in me.
**Ambrose Bierce**

The bigger a man's head gets, the easier it is to fill his shoes.
**Henry A. Courtney**

Ego trip: a journey to nowhere.
**Robert Half**

Our ego is our silent partner—too often with a controlling interest.
**Cullen Hightower**

Left-wingers are incapable of conspiring because they're all egomaniacs.
**Norman Mailer**

Knowledge that puffs up the possessor's mind is ever more of a pernicious kind.
**William Mather**

When any man is more stupidly vain and outrageously egotistic than his fellows, he will hide his hideousness in humanitarianism.
**GEORGE MOORE**

An egotist is not a man who thinks too much of himself; he is a man who thinks too little of other people.
**JOSEPH FORT NEWTON**

To men and women who want to do things, there is nothing quite so driving as the force of an imprisoned ego. . . . All genius comes from this class.
**MARY ROBERTS RINEHART**

The egoist does not tolerate egoism.
**JOSEPH ROUX**

Egotism is the anesthetic which nature gives us to deaden the pain of being a fool.
**HERBERT SHOFIELD**

If the egotist is weak, his egotism is worthless. If the egotist is strong, acute, full of distinctive character, his egotism is precious, and remains a possession of the race.
**ALEXANDER SMITH**

No one has learned the meaning of life until he has surrendered his ego to the service of his fellow men.
**BERAN WOLFE**

## *Emotions*

It may be true of all relationships, not only between fathers and sons, but between men and women. Nothing seems fixed. Everything is always changing. We seem to have very little control over our emotional life.
**SHERWOOD ANDERSON**

Sensitiveness is closely allied to egotism. Indeed, excessive sensitiveness is only another name for morbid self-consciousness. The cure for it is to make more of our objects, and less of ourselves.
**CHRISTIAN BOVÉE**

There is no fire like passion, there is no shark like hatred, there is no snare like folly, there is no torrent like greed.
**BUDDHA**

People hate those who make them feel their own inferiority.
**LORD CHESTERFIELD**

The tragedy of life is in what dies inside a man while he lives—the death of genuine feeling, the death of inspired response, the death of the awareness that makes it possible to feel the pain or the glory of other men in yourself.
**NORMAN COUSINS**

Are you not justified in feeling inferior, when you seek to cover it up with arrogance and insolence?
**MALCOLM FORBES**

The appearance of things change according to the emotions and thus we see magic and beauty in them, while the magic and beauty are really in ourselves.
**KAHLIL GIBRAN**

Laughter and tears are meant to turn the wheels of the same sensibility; one is windpower, and the other waterpowered, that is all.
**OLIVER WENDELL HOLMES**

Systems die—instincts remain.
**OLIVER WENDELL HOLMES**

The toxin of fatigue has been demonstrated; but the poisons generated by evil temper and emotional

excess over non-essentials have not yet been determined, although without a doubt they exist. Explosions of temper, emotional cyclones, and needless fear and panic over disease or misfortune that seldom materialize, are simply bad habits. By proper ventilation and illumination of the mind it is possible to cultivate tolerance, poise and real courage without being a bromide-taker.
Elie Metchnikoff

Our ideas are here today and gone tomorrow, whereas our feelings are always with us, and we recognize those who feel like us, and at once, by a sort of instinct.
George Moore

The active part of man consists of powerful instincts, some of which are gentle and continuous; others violent and short; some baser, some nobler, and all necessary.
F. W. Newman

When I cry, do you want the tears to run all the way or shall I stop halfway down?
Margaret O'Brien (age 6)

The acceptance of the truth that joy and sorrow, laughter and tears are not confined to any particular time, place or people, but are universally distributed, should make us more tolerant of and more interested in the lives of others.
William M. Peck

Our emotions are the driving powers of our lives. When we are aroused emotionally, unless we do something great and good, we are in danger of letting our emotions become perverted. William James used to tell the story of a Russian woman who sat weeping at the tragic fate of the hero in the opera while her coachman froze to death outside.
Earl Riney

No one can make you feel inferior without your consent.
Eleanor Roosevelt

The degree of one's emotion varies inversely with one's knowledge of the facts—the less you know the hotter you get.
Bertrand Russell

The advantage of the emotions is that they lead us astray.
Oscar Wilde

Swift instinct leaps; slow reason feebly climbs.
Edward Young

## *Employees*

For employee success, loyalty and integrity are equally as important as ability.
Harry F. Banks

An organization of employees whose only aim is to fight the employers is just as detrimental to the general welfare of our country as an organization of employers merely to fight the employees. Therefore, be it resolved: That employers and employees get together, understand each other, and then work together for the good of all.
William J. H. Boetcker

If you want to be respected, be respectable.
If you want to be liked, be likeable.
If you want to be loved, be lovable.
If you want to be employed, be employable.
William J. H. Boetcker

There is no way of making a business successful that can vie with the policy of promoting those who render exceptional service.
Andrew Carnegie

Plenty of men can do good work for a spurt and with immediate promotion in mind, but for promotion you want a man in whom good work has become a habit.
**HENRY L. DOHERTY**

Frank W. Woolworth once told me that the turning-point in his career did not come until he was thrown flat on his back by illness. He was sure that his business would go to pieces during his long, enforced absence. Instead, he discovered that he had in his employ men who could overcome difficulties when given power to exercise initiative. After that Woolworth left many problems and difficulties to be solved by subordinates and turned his attention to big things.
**B. C. FORBES**

H.P. Davison, who became the number one Morgan partner and was widely recognized as among the ablest bankers America ever produced, modestly explained to me how he went about qualifying for promotion. Briefly, he always taught whoever was immediately below him to do his (Davison's) work; next he learned all he could about the job immediately ahead. In this way, whenever changes became necessary, his supervisors found it easy to promote him. After he rose to the top he followed the same principle of teaching others how to pinch-hit for him, thus avoiding delay or dislocation should he be absent at any time.
**B. C. FORBES**

New Year, the season for changes in positions and advances in salaries, approaches. If you have in your employ some who deserve more salary, do not compel them to go through the unpleasant ordeal of asking a raise, but, rather, voluntarily increase their remuneration. A raise that comes from the boss without asking is worth a lot more than one that has to be gouged out of him. Is it not true that a great many employers who would not dream of overcharging their customers have no qualms whatever about underpaying their employees if the latter will submit without protest?
**B. C. FORBES**

All too often we say of a man doing a good job that he is indispensable. A flattering canard, as so many disillusioned and retired and fired have discovered when the world seems to keep on turning without them. In business, a man can come nearest to indispensability by being dispensable in his current job. How can a man move up to new responsibilities if he is the only one able to handle his present tasks? It matters not how small or large the job you now have, if you have trained no one to do it as well, you're not available; you've made your promotion difficult if not impossible.
**MALCOLM FORBES**

Never hire someone who knows less than you do about what he's (or she's) hired to do.
**MALCOLM FORBES**

When my father was outraged by some really bad violation of business ethics, he would brand it unconscionable. I think it is appropriate to use that word to describe the present situation whereby a corporate employee forfeits all equity of time and money in his company's pension plan should he leave voluntarily, be fired or the company go under.... That is not right. It is heartening to see President Nixon pushing legislation that will safeguard employees' contributions in cases of bankruptcy or the misuse of funds. I hope the measure ultimately will include some form of vested interest in benefits....
**MALCOLM FORBES (1970)**

I tell you, sir, the only safeguard of order and discipline in the modern world is a standardized worker with interchangeable parts. That would solve the entire problem of management.
**JEAN GIRAUDOUX**

When you hire people who are smarter than you are, you prove you are smarter than they are.
RICHARD GRANT

People work for people, not for companies. A worker's regard for his supervisor will affect his opinion of his employer. Production is related to attitude, so much so that an organization which disregards this human equation will not achieve as much as it could achieve.
GERARD R. GRIFFIN

We should place confidence in our employee. Confidence is the foundation of friendship. If we give it, we will receive it. Any person in a managerial position, from supervisor to president, who feels that his employee is basically not as good as he is and who suspects his employee is always trying to put something over on him, lacks the necessary qualities for human leadership—to say nothing of human friendship.
HARRY E. HUMPHREYS, JR.

When people are against profits they're against business; when they're against business, they're against employment; when they're against employment, it's not surprising that a large number of them are unemployed.
RICHARD J. NEEDHAM

I have never met a business man in my life who is not delighted to take on additional employees whenever the demand for his goods and services makes it possible for him to do so.
HENNING W. PRENTIS, JR.

You can employ men and hire hands to work *for* you, but you must win their hearts to have them work *with* you.
TIORIO

When a man has equipped himself by thought and study for a bigger job, it usually happens that promotion comes along even before it is expected.
PERCY G. WINNETT

## *Employers*

The employer generally gets the employees he deserves.
SIR WALTER BILBEY

A man who tries to make the workmen believe that their employers are their natural enemies is indeed the worst enemy of workmen. For the employees of yesterday are the employers of today, and the employees of today can and will partly be the employers of tomorrow.
WILLIAM J. H. BOETCKER

With a full century of contrary proof in our possession and despite our demonstrated capacity for cooperative teamwork, some among us seem to accept the shibboleth of an unbridgeable gap between those who hire and those who are employed. We miserably fail to challenge the lie that what is good for management is necessarily bad for labor; that for one side to profit, the other must be depressed. Such distorted doctrine is false and foreign to the American scene where common ideals and purpose permit us a common approach toward the common good.
DWIGHT D. EISENHOWER

Are soft-hearted people handicapped in business? You have heard a businessman say of someone else, "He's all right, but he's too soft-hearted. . . . "

To be soft-hearted may be handicapping, in a sense. But on the whole, a soft heart is to be preferred to a hard heart. Hard-hearted, severe, dominating giants sometimes manage to get further and to amass more money. But they get less genuine joy out of life. . . .

It is the hard-boiled employer, not the soft-hearted species, that incites most of our strikes and does most to endanger the harmonious progress of democracy.
**B. C. FORBES**

Many men who do creditable things refuse to let it be known. This is a mistake. While we all admire modesty, nevertheless there is a great national need to do everything possible to bring home to the rank and file of the people that all employers and all wealthy men are not grinding, mercenary, selfish skinflints, but that many of them take delight in doing helpful things for others . . . Shortcomings of employers are constantly paraded. Why not let the public become acquainted with the better side which most present-day employers possess?
**B. C. FORBES**

The man who gives me employment, which I must have or suffer, that man is my master, let me call him what I will.
**HENRY GEORGE**

If, traditionally, employers and employees "have blasted at each other," often without dignity and courtesy, could it not be that they were talking two separate dialects? Because capital and labor both have such important contributions to make to the public welfare, it is particularly important that they exhibit, through men of good will, their evolution from a historic precedent of "trading blasts" to a new enlightenment which comes only from "trading places."
**J. RICHARD SNEED**

## *Enemies*

In all differences consider that both you and your opponent or enemy are mortal, and that ere long your very memories will be extinguished.
**AUREL**

When you go to dig a grave for your enemy—dig two.
**CHINESE PROVERB**

Choose a friend. He will help you. Alas, he deserts you. Choose an enemy. He will fight against you. Lo, he corrects and perfects you.
**SRI CHINMOY**

I love my enemies for two reasons: They inspire me to recognize my weakness. They also inspire me to perfect my imperfect nature.
**SRI CHINMOY**

If appeasing our enemies is not the answer, neither is hating them. . . . Somewhere between the extremes of appeasement and hate there is a place for courage and strength to express themselves in magnanimity and charity, and this is the place we must find.
**A. WHITNEY GRISWOLD**

The enemy who forces you to retreat is himself afraid of you at that very moment.
**ANDRÉ MAUROIS**

Learning from one's enemies is the best way to love them, for it puts one into a grateful mood toward them.
**FRIEDRICH WILHELM NIETZSCHE**

Be sober, be vigilant, because your adversary the devil, as a roaring lion, walketh about seeking whom he may devour.
**I PETER 5:8**

Rejoice not when thine enemy falleth, and let not thy heart be glad when he stumbleth; Lest the Lord see it, and it displease him, and he turn away his wrath from him.
**PROVERBS 24:17–18**

It's easier to fight one's enemies than to get on with one's friends.
CARDINAL DE RETZ

One very important ingredient of success is a good, wide-awake, persistent, tireless enemy. An enemy to an ambitious man is like the rhinoceros bird to the rhinoceros. When the enemy comes the rhinoceros bird tells about it. When a successful man is making mistakes the enemy immediately calls attention and warns the man. Get for yourself a first class enemy, cultivate him as an enemy, and when you achieve success, thank him.
COL. FRANK B. SHUTTS

Your worst enemy is always a man of your own trade.
SPANISH PROVERB

In order to have an enemy, one must be somebody. One must be a force before he can be resisted by another force. A malicious enemy is better than a clumsy friend.
ANNE SWETCHINE

It takes your enemy and your friend, working together, to hurt you: the one to slander you, and the other to bring the news to you.
MARK TWAIN

The man that makes a character, makes foes.
YOUNG

## *Energy*

The difference between one man and another is not mere ability—it is energy.
THOMAS ARNOLD

Energy, like the Biblical grain of mustard seed, will move mountains.
HOSEA BALLOU

Energy is the only life, and is from the body; and reason is the bound or outward circumference of energy. Energy is eternal delight.
WILLIAM BLAKE

The longer I live, the more deeply I am convinced that that which makes the difference between one man and another—between the weak and the powerful, the great and the insignificant, is energy—invisible determination—a purpose once formed and then death or victory. This quality will do anything that has to be done in the world, and no talents, no circumstances, no opportunities, will make one a man without it.
SIR THOMAS BUXTON

The average person puts only 25% of his energy and ability into his work. The world takes off its hat to those who put in more than 50% of their capacity, and stands on its head for those few and far between souls who devote 100%.
ANDREW CARNEGIE

I guess I am not naturally energetic. I like to sit around and talk.
CALVIN COOLIDGE

Intelligence and the spirit of adventure can be combined to create new energies, and out of these energies may come exciting and rewarding new prospects.
NORMAN COUSINS

The world belongs to the energetic.
RALPH WALDO EMERSON

The real difference between men is energy. A strong will, a settled purpose, an invincible determi-

nation, can accomplish almost anything; and in this lies the distinction between great men and little men.
**THOMAS FULLER**

Energy will do anything that can be done in the world; and no talents, no circumstances, no opportunities will make a two-legged animal a man without it.
**JOHANN WOLFGANG VON GOETHE**

A man doesn't need brilliance or genius, all he needs is energy.
**ALBERT M. GREENFIELD**

Our energy is in proportion to the resistance it meets. We attempt nothing great but from a sense of the difficulties we have to encounter; we persevere in nothing great but from a pride in overcoming them.
**WILLIAM HAZLITT**

It takes wit and interest and energy to be happy. The pursuit of happiness is a great activity. One must be open and alive. It is the greatest feat man has to accomplish, and spirits must flow. There must be courage. There are no easy ruts to get into which lead to happiness. A man must become interesting to himself and must become actually expressive before he can be happy.
**ROBERT HENRI**

He also has energy who cannot be deprived of it.
**JOHANN LAVATER**

There is no genius in life like the genius of energy and industry.
**DONALD G. MITCHELL**

It is sad that my emotional dependence on the man I love should have killed so much of my energy and ability; there was certainly once a great deal of energy in me.
**SONYA TOLSTOY**

I found that the men and women who got to the top were those who did the jobs they had in hand, with everything they had of energy and enthusiasm and hard work.
**HARRY S TRUMAN**

## *Enjoyment*

That one who does not get fun and enjoyment out of every day in which he lives, needs to reorganize his life. And the sooner the better, for pure enjoyment throughout life has more to do with one's happiness and efficiency than almost any other single element.
**GEORGE MATTHEW ADAMS**

So many rules are antifun
They're like a poison pill:
In time the only sanctioned things
Will be what makes us ill.
**ART BUCK**

All of the animals except man know that the principal business of life is to enjoy it.
**SAMUEL BUTLER**

It is a beautiful and blessed world we live in, and while life lasts, to lose the enjoyment of it is a sin.
**A. W. CHAMBERS**

To enjoy and give enjoyment, without injury to yourself or others; this is true morality.
**NICOLAS CHAMFORT**

Let us not be too prodigal when we are young, nor too parsimonious when we are old. Otherwise we

shall fall into the common error of those, who, when they had the power to enjoy, had not the prudence to acquire; and when they had the prudence to acquire, had no longer the power to enjoy.
**CHARLES CALEB COLTON**

And also that every man should eat and drink, and enjoy the good of all his labor, it is the gift of God.
**ECCLESIASTES 3:13**

Enjoyment is not a goal, it is a feeling that accompanies important ongoing activity.
**PAUL GOODMAN**

The pessimist's fault is that he is not gay enough himself to realize that the only lasting fun in life comes from what we may contribute to it.
**WILFRED T. GRENFELL**

There is nothing like fun, is there? I haven't any myself, but I do like it in others.
**THOMAS C. HALIBURTON**

I sincerely believe we are given life to enjoy and make it more enjoyable for others. . . . The best way to do this is to get in the middle of it.
**HENRY L. HARRELL, SR.**

Taking fun as simply fun and earnestness in earnest shows how thoroughly thou none of the two discernest.
**PIET HEIN**

The circus is the only fun you can buy that's good for you.
**ERNEST HEMINGWAY**

My grandfather . . . used to say, "Don't get involved with frivolities."
**KATHARINE HEPBURN**

Fun is like life insurance: the older you get, the more it costs.
**KIN HUBBARD**

True enjoyment comes from activity of the mind and exercise of the body; the two are ever united.
**KARL WILHELM VON HUMBOLDT**

Restraint is the golden rule of enjoyment.
**LETITIA E. LANDON**

Man only plays when in the full meaning of the word he is a man, and he is only completely a man when he plays.
**JOHANN FRIEDRICH VON SCHILLER**

The test of an enjoyment is the remembrance which it leaves behind.
**LOGAN PEARSALL SMITH**

There are two things to aim at in life: first to get what you want; and after that, to enjoy it. Only the wisest of mankind achieve the second.
**LOGAN PEARSALL SMITH**

No enjoyment, however inconsiderable, is confined to the present moment. A man is the happier for life from having made once an agreeable tour, or lived for any length of time with pleasant people, or enjoyed any considerable interval of innocent pleasure.
**SYDNEY SMITH**

The secret of my vigor and activity is that I have managed to have a lot of fun.
**LOWELL THOMAS**

Never run after your own hat—others will be delighted to do it; why spoil their fun?
**MARK TWAIN**

Work consists of whatever a body is obliged to do, and play consists of whatever a body is not obliged to do.
MARK TWAIN

One of the principal features of my entertainment is that it contains so many things that don't have anything to do with it.
ARTEMUS WARD

## Enthusiasm

The worst bankrupt in the world is the man who has lost his enthusiasm. Let a man lose everything else in the world but his enthusiasm and he will come through again to success.
H. W. ARNOLD

Fires can't be made with dead embers, nor can enthusiasm be stirred by spiritless men. Enthusiasm in our daily work lightens effort and turns even labor into pleasant tasks.
STANLEY BALDWIN

From the glow of enthusiasm I let the melody escape. I pursue it. Breathless I catch up with it. It flies again, it disappears, it plunges into a chaos of diverse emotions. I catch it again, I seize it, I embrace it with delight. . . . I multiply it by modulations, and at last I triumph in the first theme. There is the whole symphony.
LUDWIG VAN BEETHOVEN

Nothing is so contagious as enthusiasm.
EDWARD BULWER-LYTTON

The prudent man may direct a state, but it is the enthusiast who regenerates it.
EDWARD BULWER-LYTTON

Every man is enthusiastic at times. One man has enthusiasm for thirty minutes, another man has it for thirty days, but it is the man who has it for thirty years who makes a success in life.
EDWARD B. BUTLER

Enthusiasm is the greatest asset in the world. It beats money and power and influence. It is no more or less than faith in action.
HENRY CHESTER

Enthusiasm is a virtue rarely to be met with in seasons of calm and unruffled prosperity.
THOMAS CHALMERS

No wild enthusiast ever yet could rest, till half mankind were, like himself, possest.
WILLIAM COWPER

When enthusiasm is inspired by reason; controlled by caution; sound in theory; practical in application; reflects confidence; spreads good cheer; raises morale; inspires associates; arouses loyalty, and laughs at adversity, it is beyond price.
COLEMAN COX

Every production of genius must be the production of enthusiasm.
BENJAMIN DISRAELI

There is a sort of human paste that when it comes near the fire of enthusiasm is only baked into harder shape.
GEORGE ELIOT

Experience and enthusiasm are two fine business attributes seldom found in one individual.
WILLIAM FEATHER

It's so much easier to be enthusiastic—especially when there are grounds for it.
MALCOLM FORBES

Enthusiasm is at the bottom of all progress. With it there is accomplishment. Without it there are only alibis.
HENRY FORD

What a man accomplishes in a day depends upon the way in which he approaches his tasks. When we accept tough jobs as a challenge to our ability and wade into them with joy and enthusiasm miracles can happen. When we do our work with a dynamic conquering spirit we get things done.
ARLAND GILBERT

A mother should give her children a superabundance of enthusiasm, that after they have lost all they are sure to lose on mixing with the world, enough may still remain to prompt and support them through great actions.
JULIUS C. HARE

Weakness, fear, melancholy, together with ignorance, are the true sources of superstition. Hope, pride, presumption, a warm indignation, together with ignorance, are the true sources of enthusiasm.
DAVID HUME

Enthusiasts soon understand each other.
WASHINGTON IRVING

Study the unusually successful people you know, and you will find them imbued with enthusiasm for their work which is contagious. Not only are they themselves excited about what they are doing, but they also get you excited.
PAUL W. IVEY

In science, as in common life, we frequently see that a novelty in system, or in practice, cannot be duly appreciated till time has sobered the enthusiasm of its advocates.
MAUD

Men are nothing until they are excited.
MICHEL DE MONTAIGNE

If you can't get enthusiastic about your work, it's time to get alarmed—something is wrong. Compete with yourself; set your teeth and dive into the job of breaking your own record. No one keeps up his enthusiasm automatically. Enthusiasm must be nourished with new actions, new aspirations, new efforts, new vision. It is one's own fault if his enthusiasm is gone; he has failed to feed it. If you want to turn hours into minutes, renew your enthusiasm.
PAPYRUS

The essential in this time of moral poverty is to create enthusiasm.
PABLO PICASSO

Enthusiasm is the best protection in any situation. Wholeheartedness is contagious. Give yourself, if you wish to get others.
DAVID SEABURY

It is energy—the central element of which is will—that produces the miracles of enthusiasm in all ages. Everywhere it is the mainspring of what is called force of character and the sustaining power of all great action.
SAMUEL SMILES

The language of excitement is at best picturesque merely. You must be calm before you can utter oracles.
HENRY DAVID THOREAU

Apathy can only be overcome by enthusiasm, and enthusiasm can only be aroused by two things: first, an ideal which takes the imagination by storm, and second, a definite intelligible plan for carrying that ideal into practice.
ARNOLD TOYNBEE

Let us recognize the beauty and power of true enthusiasm; and whatever we may do to enlighten ourselves or others, guard against checking or chilling a single earnest sentiment.
HENRY TUCKERMAN

National enthusiasm is the great nursery of genius.
HENRY TUCKERMAN

Enthusiasm is that temper of the mind in which the imagination has got the better of the judgment.
WILLIAM WARBURTON

## *Envy*

One reason why so many people are unhappy, not knowing why, is that they have burdened their minds with resentments. These evil thoughts pile right on top of happier and generous ones and smother them so that they never get expression. Resentments are a form of hate.... What a dearth of good will and co-operation there are among human beings and nations! What a world this would be if we all worked together, and as a popular diplomat recently expressed it—played together!
GEORGE MATTHEW ADAMS

Upon every hand we meet with those who have some secret resentment that is ever being nurtured within their hearts. They resent the success, or happiness of some one whom they think is less deserving than they are. They resent the just recognition that comes to others from work and long effort to excel. Or, they may resent being born poor—or resent the fact that they were even born!... Strive to excel, strive to achieve, where others have failed, and you will find no space within your mind to lodge resentment. Resentment is the child of selfishness, foolish envy, and inactivity.... Our life upon this earth is too valuable for resentment of any kind. There is so much to do, so much to learn—so little time in which to live and work it all out.
GEORGE MATTHEW ADAMS

Few men have the natural strength to honor a friend's success without envy.
AESCHYLUS

Envy ought to have no place allowed it in the heart of man; for the goods of this present world are so vile and low that they are beneath it, and those of the future world are so vast and exalted that they are above it.
CHARLES CALEB COLTON

Our very best friends have a tincture of jealousy even in their friendship; and when they hear us praised by others, will ascribe it to sinister and interested motives if they can.
CHARLES CALEB COLTON

A man shall never be enriched by envy.
THOMAS DREIER

Men are so constituted that every one undertakes what he sees another successful in, whether he has aptitude for it or not.
JOHANN WOLFGANG VON GOETHE

It is better to be envied than to be pitied.
HERODOTUS

The envious man grows lean at the success of his neighbor.
HORACE

Envy always implies conscious inferiority wherever it resides.
PLINY

There is more self-love than love in jealousy.
**FRANÇOIS DE LA ROCHEFOUCAULD**

The truest mark of being born with great qualities, is being born without envy.
**FRANÇOIS DE LA ROCHEFOUCAULD**

We love in others what we lack ourselves, and would be everything but what we are.
**RICHARD H. STODDARD**

Grudges get heavier, the longer they are carried.
**P. K. THOMAJAN**

The chief barrier to happiness is envy.
**FRANK TYGER**

No man is greatly jealous who is not in some measure guilty.
**BENJAMIN WHICHCOTE**

If we did but know how little some enjoy of the great things that they possess, there would not be much envy in the world.
**YOUNG**

## *Equality*

This world and life of ours are filled with inequalities. The worst possible use to make of this fact, however, is to allow resentments to possess us. All of us have imagined limitations, but we have also the privilege of pushing them aside, and spreading our lives out! We never know any of our limitations until we put ourselves to the test. There are always growing pains working within us.
**GEORGE MATTHEW ADAMS**

The defect of equality is that we only desire it with our superiors.
**HENRY BECQUE**

Being equal seems to me
The last thing one would want to be:
Without an aim above the norm,
What is the goal of human form?
**ART BUCK**

Whatever difference there may appear to be in men's fortunes, there is still a certain compensation of good and ill in all, that makes them equal.
**PIERRE CHARRON**

The doctrine of human equality reposes on this: that there is no man really clever who has not found that he is stupid. There is no big man who has not felt small. Some men never feel small; but these are the few men who are.
**G. K. CHESTERTON**

The English are no nearer than they were a hundred years ago to knowing what Jefferson really meant when he said that God had created all men equal.
**G. K. CHESTERTON**

America's unique contribution to the world will not be automation, or mass production, and perhaps not art, music or poetry. We have in America through education the opportunity to approach in reality the age-old ideal of a society of free and equal men. If we succeed, this will be our unique contribution to human history.
**ARTHUR F. COREY**

We hold these truths to be self-evident, that all men are created equal, that they are endowed by their creator with certain unalienable rights, that among these are life, liberty and the pursuit of happiness. That to secure these rights, Governments

are instituted among men, deriving their just powers from the consent of the governed. That whenever any form of government becomes destructive of these ends, it is the right of the people to alter or to abolish it, and to institute new Government, laying its foundation on such principles and organizing its powers in such form, as to them shall seem most likely to effect their safety and happiness.
DECLARATION OF INDEPENDENCE

Every Frenchman wants to enjoy one or more privileges; that's the way he shows his passion for equality.
CHARLES DE GAULLE

If by saying that all men are born free and equal, you mean that they are all equally born, it is true, but true in no other sense; birth, talent, labor, virtue, and providence, are forever making differences.
EUGENE EDWARDS

Some persons are always ready to level those above them down to themselves, while they are never willing to level those below them up to their own position. But he that is under the influence of true humility will avoid both these extremes. On the one hand, he will be willing that all should rise just so far as their diligence and worth of character entitle them to; and on the other hand, he will be willing that his superiors should be known and acknowledged in their place, and have rendered to them all the honors that are their due.
JONATHAN EDWARDS

Some will always be above others. Destroy the inequality today, and it will appear again tomorrow.
RALPH WALDO EMERSON

Men are by nature equal. It is vain, therefore, to treat them as if they were equal.
J. A. FROUDE

Let him who expects one class of society to prosper in the highest degree, while the other is in distress, try whether one side of his face can smile while the other is pinched.
THOMAS FULLER

We are all born equal—equally helpless and equally indebted to others for whatever our survival turns out to be worth.
CULLEN HIGHTOWER

The hole and the patch should be commensurate.
THOMAS JEFFERSON

There can never be human happiness in a society that imposes a rule of "equality" which disregards merit and rewards incompetence.
DAVID LAWRENCE

For the reason that we are equal before God, we are made equal before the law of this land. And when you have said that, you have summed up and tied with a bowknot the complete American doctrine of equality.
CLARENCE E. MANION

The good Lord sees your heart, not the braid on your jacket; before him we are all in our birthday suits, generals and common men alike.
THOMAS MANN

There are many in this old world of ours who hold that things break about even for all of us. I have observed for example that we all get the same amount of ice. The rich get it in the summertime and the poor get it in the winter.
BAT MASTERSON

The true interest of Americans is mutual interest. The doctrines that put race against race, group against group, class against class, and worker

against employer, all are false doctrines. They are preached only by assassins of progress who are economic parasites or political pirates. We want to recreate an America in which falsehood cannot prevail, where the energies of men and women shall be devoted to constructive efforts.
WHEELER MCMILLEN

**Resolution**

Whereas the Supreme Power of the universe has deemed it natural to create human beings of various colors, races, and creeds; and

Whereas in His sight they all are His equally beloved children;

Therefore be it resolved that there is no superior race or group of peoples and that all men are brothers of equal rank; and be it further resolved that we know this and believe it now and forever!
M. NEWMAN

Equality is one of the most consummate scoundrels that ever crept from the brain of a political juggler—a fellow who thrusts his hand into the pocket of honest industry or enterprising talent, and squanders their hard-earned profits on profligate idleness or indolent stupidity.
JAMES KIRKE PAULDING

Nations will rise and fall, but equality remains the ideal. The universal aim is to achieve respect for the entire human race, not for the dominant few.
CARLOS P. ROMULO

An earthquake achieves what the law promises but does not in practice maintain—the equality of all men.
IGNAZIO SILONE

It is an interesting question how far men would retain their relative rank if they were divested of their clothes.
HENRY DAVID THOREAU

They who say all men are equal speak an undoubted truth, if they mean that all have an equal right to liberty, to their property, and to their protection of the laws. But they are mistaken if they think men are equal in their station and employments, since they are not so by their talents.
VOLTAIRE

## *Errors*

An error is always the more dangerous in proportion to the degree of truth which it contains.
HENRI FRÉDÉRIC AMIEL

There is no such source of error as the pursuit of absolute truth.
SAMUEL BUTLER

An error is simply a failure to adjust immediately from a preconception to an actuality.
JOHN CAGE

The greatest mistake is to imagine that we never err.
THOMAS CARLYLE

Honest error is to be pitied, not ridiculed.
LORD CHESTERFIELD

It is human to err; and the only final and deadly error, among all our errors, is denying that we have ever erred.
G. K. CHESTERTON

Ignorance is a blank sheet on which we may write; but error is a scribbled one from which we must first erase.
CHARLES CALEB COLTON

It is almost as difficult to make a man unlearn his errors as his knowledge.
**CHARLES CALEB COLTON**

I beseech you, in the bowels of Christ, think it possible you may be mistaken.
**OLIVER CROMWELL**

The chief cause of human errors is to be found in prejudices picked up in childhood.
**RENÉ DESCARTES**

Man is made for error; it enters his mind naturally, and he discovers a few truths only with the greatest effort.
**FREDERICK THE GREAT**

An old error is always more popular than a new truth.
**GERMAN PROVERB**

It is not only our errors which ruin us, but our way of conducting ourselves after committing them.
**YVETTE GILBERT**

I hate all bungling like sin, but most of all bungling in state affairs, which produces nothing but mischief to thousands and millions.
**JOHANN WOLFGANG VON GOETHE**

While man's desires and aspirations stir he cannot choose but err.
**JOHANN WOLFGANG VON GOETHE**

To err is human, but when the eraser wears out ahead of the pencil, you're overdoing it.
**J. JENKINS**

Error is not a fault of our knowledge, but a mistake of our judgment giving assent to that which is not true.
**JOHN LOCKE**

Sometimes we may learn more from a man's errors than from his virtues.
**HENRY WADSWORTH LONGFELLOW**

We come to learn that it does not pay to grieve too much over our errors. Ordinarily we try to do the best we can.
**ROBERT L. MASSON**

The world always makes the assumption that the exposure of an error is identical with the discovery of the truth—that error and truth are simply opposite. They are nothing of the sort. What the world turns to, when it is cured of one error, is usually simply another error, and maybe one worse than the first one.
**H. L. MENCKEN**

The credit belongs to the man who is actually in the arena; whose face is marred with dust and sweat; who strives valiantly; who errs and may fall again and again, because there is no effort without error or shortcoming.
**THEODORE ROOSEVELT**

Errors to be dangerous must have a great deal of truth mingled with them. It is only from this alliance that they can ever obtain an extensive circulation. From pure extravagance, and genuine, unmingled falsehood, the world never has, and never can sustain any mischief.
**SYDNEY SMITH**

Men are apt to prefer a prosperous error to an afflicted truth.
**JEREMY TAYLOR**

To err is human—but it feels divine.
**MAE WEST**

If a man is in too big a hurry to give up an error he is liable to give up some truth with it, and in

accepting the argument of the other man he is sure to get some error with it. After I get hold of a truth I hate to lose it again, and I like to sift all the truth out before I give up an error.
**WILBUR WRIGHT**

The pain that others give passes away in their later kindness, but that of our own blunders, especially when they hurt our vanity, never passes away.
**WILLIAM BUTLER YEATS**

## *Evil*

Eighty percent of our criminals come from unsympathetic homes.
**HANS CHRISTIAN ANDERSEN**

Hell is more bearable than nothingness.
**PHILIP JAMES BAILEY**

There is no happiness in wickedness.
**EZRA TAFT BENSON**

The contagion of crime is like that of the plague. Criminals collected together corrupt each other. They are worse than ever when, at the termination of their punishment, they return to society.
**NAPOLEON BONAPARTE**

When bad men combine, the good must associate, else they will fall one by one, an unpitied sacrifice in a contemptible struggle.
**EDMUND BURKE**

Only one thing is worse than a devil and that is an educated devil.
**GEORGE A. BUTTERICK**

Man's problem in the last analysis is man himself. A man beset by evil within and from without can mobilize his spiritual resources to conquer that evil. Just so can the human race mobilize its moral and spiritual power to defeat the material power of evil that threatens it.
**RICHARD E. BYRD**

The religion of Hell is patriotism, and the government is an enlightened democracy.
**JAMES BRANCH CABELL**

Men's hearts ought not be set against one another, but set with one another, and all against evil only.
**THOMAS CARLYLE**

The old assumption of the approximate impossibility of war really rested on a similar assumption about the impossibility of evil—and especially of evil in high places.
**G. K. CHESTERTON**

Do not be afraid of evil. But be always cheerful in doing good. Evil will soon leave you, for evil is extremely jealous of good.
**SRI CHINMOY**

Evils in the journey of life are like the hills which alarm travelers on the road. Both appear great at a distance, but when we approach them we find they are far less insurmountable than we had conceived.
**CHARLES CALEB COLTON**

Evil, which is our companion all our days, is not to be treated as a foe. It is wrong to cocker vice, but we grow narrow and pithless if we are furtive about it, for this is at best a pretense, and the sage knows good and evil are kindred. The worst of men harm others, and the best injure themselves.
**EDWARD DAHLBERG**

You need not choose evil; but have only to fail to choose good, and you drift fast enough toward evil.

You do not need to say, "I will be bad," you have only to say, "I will not choose God's choice," and the choice of evil is already settled.
**W. J. DAWSON**

Because sentence against an evil work is not executed speedily, therefore the heart of the sons of men is fully set in them to do evil.
**ECCLESIASTES 8:11**

Preventives of evil are far better than remedies; cheaper and easier of application, and surer in result.
**TRYON EDWARDS**

One soweth and another reapeth is a verity that applies to evil as well as good.
**GEORGE ELIOT**

There is no sort of wrong deed of which a man can bear the punishment alone; you can't isolate yourself and say that the evil that is in you shall not spread. Men's lives are as thoroughly blended with each other as the air they breathe; evil spreads as necessarily as disease.
**GEORGE ELIOT**

The first lesson of history is that evil is good.
**RALPH WALDO EMERSON**

For we wrestle not against flesh and blood, but against principalities, against powers, against the rulers of the darkness of this world, against a spiritual wickedness in high places.
**EPHESIANS 6:12**

The gift of a bad man can bring no good.
**EURIPIDES**

Crime in the city streets is more than a political issue. It's a too rampant fact. . . . In Indianapolis they have come up with a most sensible, affordable approach to the problem. Policemen are assigned their police patrol cars for personal use after hours. They are encouraged to use the police car while taking the family shopping, to the movies, and everywhere one takes one's family. As a result, says the Police Chief's assistant, we may have as many as 400 cars on the street instead of 100 or so per shift. [And] the presence of the police car obviously indicates the proximity of policemen.
**MALCOLM FORBES**

How in heck are they handling their surplus population in Hell these days? Maybe by the time you and I are in the queue there won't be room for us.
**MALCOLM FORBES**

The usual choice is not between the good and the bad but between the bad and the worse.
**FRENCH PROVERB**

Don't let us make imaginary evils, when you know we have so many real ones to encounter.
**OLIVER GOLDSMITH**

One uncooperative employee can sabotage an entire organization because bad spirit is more contagious than good spirit.
**ROBERT HALF**

Wherever they burn books they will also, in the end, burn human beings.
**HEINRICH HEINE**

Seeing every life as sacred can be costly. It can cost you your malice, a price many of us are unwilling to pay.
**CULLEN HIGHTOWER**

At the present time in this country there is more danger that criminals will escape justice than that they will be subjected to tyranny.
OLIVER WENDELL HOLMES

It is only when men associate with the wicked with the desire and purpose of doing them good, that they can rely upon the protection of God to preserve them from contamination.
CHARLES HODGE

Knowest thou not this of old, since man was placed upon earth, That the triumphing of the wicked is short, and the joy of the hypocrite but for a moment?
JOB 20:4–5

Evil acts of the past are never rectified by evil acts of the present.
LYNDON JOHNSON

Combinations of wickedness would overwhelm the world, by the advantage which licentious principles afford, did not those who have long practised perfidy grow faithless to each other.
JOHNSON

Where secrecy or mystery begins, vice or roguery is not far off.
JOHNSON

No man ever became very wicked all at once.
JUVENAL

Never tell evil of a man if you do not know it for a certainty; and if you know it for a certainty, then ask yourself, "Why should I tell it?"
JOHANN LAVATER

Say what you will about the devil, he's a hustler!
ABE MARTIN

Crime rarely fails to make the headlines. How one wishes there were some way of featuring and dramatizing good living and high thinking.
ROBERT J. MCCRACKEN

Whoever takes it upon himself to establish a commonwealth and prescribe laws must presuppose all men naturally bad, and that they will yield to their innate evil passions as often as they can do so with safety.
NICCOLÒ MACHIAVELLI

Hell begins on the day when God grants us a clear vision of all that we might have achieved, of all the gifts which we have wasted, of all that we might have done which we did not do.
GIAN-CARLO MENOTTI

Human beings do not do all the evil of which they are capable.
HENRY DE MONTHERLANT

Even in politics, an evil action has evil consequences. That, I believe, is a law of nature as precise as any law of physics or chemistry.
JAWAHARLAL NEHRU

Real evils can be either cured or endured; it is only imaginary evils that make people anxiety-ridden for a lifetime.
EARL NIGHTINGALE

We sometimes learn more from the sight of evil than from an example of good; and it is well to accustom ourselves to profit by the evil which is so common, while that which is good is so rare.
BLAISE PASCAL

A good end cannot sanctify evil means, nor must we ever do evil that good may come of it.
WILLIAM PENN

It is not noble to return evil for evil, at no time ought we to do an injury to our neighbors.
**PLATO**

Fret not thyself because of evildoers, neither be thou envious against the workers of iniquity. For they shall soon be cut down like the grass, and wither as the green herb.
**PSALMS 37:1–2**

Evil is but the shadow that, in this world, always accompanies good. You may have a world without shadow, but it will be a world without light—a mere dim, twilight world. If you would deepen the intensity of the light, you must be content to bring into deeper blackness and more distinct and definite outline, the shade that accompanies it.
**FREDERICK W. ROBERTSON**

It is the law of our humanity that man must know good through evil. No great principle ever triumphed but through much evil. No man ever progressed to greatness and goodness but through great mistakes.
**FREDERICK W. ROBERTSON**

Philosophy triumphs easily over past evils and future evils; but present evils triumph over it.
**FRANÇOIS DE LA ROCHEFOUCAULD**

Never let a man imagine that he can pursue a good end by evil means, without sinning against his own soul. The evil effect on himself is certain.
**ROBERT SOUTHEY**

Let us always have in mind that every attempt in the history of the world to establish a loafer's paradise has wound up in a dictator's hell-hole.
**HAROLD E. STASSEN**

The wise man avoids evil by anticipating it.
**PUBLILIUS SYRUS**

There can be no such thing as a necessary evil. For, if a thing is really necessary, it cannot be an evil and if it is an evil, it is not necessary.
**TIORIO**

There is only one way to put an end to evil, and that is to do good for evil.
**LEO TOLSTOY**

An evil mind is a constant solace.
**HENDRIK WILHELM VAN LOON**

Between two evils, I always pick the one I never tried before.
**MAE WEST**

## *Example*

Example has more followers than reason. We unconsciously imitate what pleases us, and approximate to the characters we most admire. A generous habit of thought and action carries with it an incalculable influence.
**CHRISTIAN BOVÉE**

Be such a man, and live such a life, that if every man were such as you, and every life a life such as yours, this earth would be God's paradise.
**PHILLIPS BROOKS**

Example is the school of mankind, and they will learn at no other.
**EDMUND BURKE**

Go make thy garden as fair as thou canst,
Thou workest never alone;
And he whose plot is next to thine
May see it and mend his own.
**ROBERT COLLYER**

When you try to step into someone else's shoes, you'll find they are either too big or too small.
**SIMHA DINITZ**

Example is better than precept.
**ENGLISH PROVERB**

It is a trite but true definition that examples work more forcibly on the mind than precepts.
**HENRY FIELDING**

You can preach a better sermon with your life than with your lips.
**OLIVER GOLDSMITH**

If birds of a feather flock together, they don't learn enough.
**ROBERT HALF**

Every great example takes hold of us with the authority of a miracle, and says to us, "If ye had but faith, ye, also, could do the same things."
**JACOBI**

The first great gift we can bestow on others is a good example.
**THOMAS MORELL**

Example is contagious behavior.
**CHARLES READE**

Men trust their eyes rather than their ears; the road by precept is long and tedious, by example short and effectual.
**SENECA**

Example teaches better than precept. It is the best modeler of the character of men and women. To set a lofty example is the richest bequest a man can leave behind him.
**SAMUEL SMILES**

Few things are harder to put up with than the annoyance of a good example.
**MARK TWAIN**

## *Excellence*

He whose first emotion, on the view of an excellent work, is to undervalue or depreciate it, will never have one of his own to show.
**AIKIN**

Excellence is an art won by training and habituation. We do not act rightly because we have virtue or excellence, but we rather have those because we have acted rightly. We are what we repeatedly do. Excellence, then, is not an act but a habit.
**ARISTOTLE**

I did some excellent things indifferently, some bad things excellently. Both were praised. The latter loudest.
**ELIZABETH BARRETT BROWNING**

Men have various subjects in which they may excel, or at least would be thought to excel, and though they love to hear justice done to them where they know they excel, yet they are most and best flattered upon those points where they wish to excel and yet are doubtful whether they do or not.
**LORD CHESTERFIELD**

He who stops being better stops being good.
**OLIVER CROMWELL**

One that desires to excel should endeavor it in those things that are in themselves most excellent.
**EPICTETUS**

One fact stands out in bold relief in the history of man's attempts for betterment. That is that when

compulsion is used, only resentment is aroused, and the end is not gained. Only through moral suasion and appeal to man's reason can a movement succeed.
SAMUEL GOMPERS

The less justified a man is in claiming excellence for his own self, the more ready he is to claim all excellence for his nation, his religion, his race or his holy cause.
ERIC HOFFER

A fundamental principle of education should be to make the pupil realize the meaning of excellence, of the first-rate, and to send him out of school and college persuaded that it is his business to learn what is first-rate and to pursue it—not only in the job by which he earns his living but in all the great fields of life and, above all, in living itself.
RICHARD W. LIVINGSTONE

Not a change for the better in our human housekeeping has ever taken place that wise and good men have not opposed it.
JAMES RUSSELL LOWELL

Strive for excellence in your calling, but as a subsidiary to this: Do not fail to enrich your whole capital as man. To be a giant, and not a dwarf in your profession, you must always be growing. The man that has ceased to go up intellectually has begun to go down.
WILLIAM MATTHEWS

There is no excellency without difficulty.
OVID

History is likely to look upon these times as the people age, for never before have so much money, effort and creativity been committed for the specific purpose of human betterment.
WAYNE PENNINGTON

Excellence is never granted to man but as the reward of labor. It argues no small strength of mind to persevere in habits of industry without the pleasure of perceiving those advances, which, like the hand of a clock, whilst they make hourly approaches to their point, yet proceed so slowly as to escape observation.
SIR JOSHUA REYNOLDS

I tell you that as long as I can conceive something better than myself I cannot be easy unless I am striving to bring it into existence or clearing the way for it.
GEORGE BERNARD SHAW

First, always seek to excel yourself. Put yourself in competition with yourself each day. Each morning look back upon your work of yesterday and then try to beat it. Second, I ask you to look upon the whole of life as a vast university—the ideal university of the future whose students will spend a part of the time in learning what to do and how to do it and then a larger part in actually doing the things they learn to do.
CHARLES M. SHELDON

Our priceless heritage is the American way of life, and nothing is more typical of the average American than his constant search for something better. The everlasting demand for better homes, better automobiles, better schools . . . better everything . . . has gone hand in hand with our devotion to freedom.
JAMES H. SHIELDS

Each excellent thing, once learned, serves for a measure of all other knowledge.
SIR PHILIP SIDNEY

In seasons of tumult and discord bad men have most power; mental and moral excellence require peace and quietness.
TACITUS

Next to excellence is the appreciation of it.
**WILLIAM MAKEPEACE THACKERAY**

We succeed in enterprises which demand the positive qualities we possess, but we excel in those which can also make use of our defects.
**ALEXIS DE TOCQUEVILLE**

Everyone expects to go further than his father went; everyone expects to be better than he was born and every generation has one big impulse in its heart—to exceed all the other generations of the past in all the things that make life worth living.
**WILLIAM ALLEN WHITE**

## *Executives*

Good executives never put off until tomorrow what they can get someone else to do today.
**ANONYMOUS**

Very few big executives want to be surrounded by "yes" men. Their greatest weakness often is the fact that "yes" men build up around the executive a wall of fiction, when what the executive wants most of all is plain facts.
**BURTON BIGELOW**

A valuable executive must possess a willingness and ability to assume responsibility, a fair knowledge of his particular branch of business, and a nice understanding of business principles in general, also to be able to read and understand human nature. There is no phase of knowledge which anyone can safely dismiss as valueless.
**CHARLES CHENEY**

It is the social obligation of management to make certain that its executives are functioning at peak performance, both physically and psychologically. To keep top men from spinning, management must see that executives should: receive periodic medical checkups; receive periodic psychological evaluations; be given an adequate number of assistants of proper ability; have their time pressures reduced through improved selling; be given training in leadership.
**STANLEY G. DUESKY**

If you don't take it for granted that the other man will do his job, you're not an executive.
**WILLIAM FEATHER**

After visiting several of America's most fashionable playgrounds, I have reached the conclusion that men who work hard enjoy life most. The men at such places can be divided into two classes, first, busy men of affairs . . . and, second, rich loafers. I was impressed by the obvious enjoyment corporation heads and other important executives were deriving from their vacation activities. . . . The idle rich fellows, on the other hand, although indulging in exactly the same activities, palpably were bored.
**B. C. FORBES**

Do too many executives still indulge in the shortsighted habit of issuing orders without taking the slightest pains to explain to those responsible for carrying them out the whyfor and wherefor of the orders? Where employees come in daily and hourly contact with the public, surely it is important that care be taken to fit them to reply intelligently to courteous questions. "Because them are orders" isn't a satisfying reply—even less satisfactory to the management than to the public.
**B. C. FORBES**

It is a great mistake for presidents and other leading executives of organizations having branches throughout the country to chain themselves to their desks at headquarters and send out rigid instructions to those in charge of distant branches and offices. Because a man sits in a palatial office in New York or

Chicago or Philadelphia or Detroit and draws a big salary, it does not necessarily follow that he knows better than the man on the spot what ought to be done. . . . Paul, Caesar, Napoleon did not merely sit at home and issue long-range instructions.
B. C. FORBES

The more I move among workers and factories and other plants, the stronger I become convinced that it is advisable to have as [a company] president a practical man, preferably one who has risen from the very bottom of the ladder. Workmen, I find, have far more respect for such men than for collar-and-cuff executives knowing little or nothing about the different kinds of work which have to be done by the workers. Wherever circumstances call for placing a financier or lawyer or a papa's son at the head of a large organization, he should be made chairman or some other title, but not president.
B. C. FORBES

Whenever possible, I like to have the supreme head of a company show me over the works. It is extremely illuminating to note the attitude of workers towards their boss, and equally interesting to note the attitude towards the workers. It is tragic to notice how many chief executives of large concerns are absolutely unknown, even by sight, to the rank and file of their workers.
B. C. FORBES

An inadequate chief executive officer's time at the top is always too long no matter how short.
MALCOLM FORBES

Executives who get there and stay suggest solutions when they present the problems.
MALCOLM FORBES

Hopeless cases: Executives who assert themselves by saying No when they should say Yes.
MALCOLM FORBES

People are talking about the new "civilized" way to fire executives. You kick 'em upstairs. They're given a little, a liberal tithe, nothing to do, and a secretary to do it with. What a way to go!
MALCOLM FORBES

The top people of the biggest companies are, surprisingly, often the nicest ones in their company I'm not sure, though, if they got there because they were good guys or that they're now good guys because they can afford to be.
MALCOLM FORBES

An executive is one who makes an immediate decision and is sometimes right.
ELBERT HUBBARD

When you know men and you know how to handle men, you've licked the problem of running a business. The executive's job is to provide leadership, the kind of leadership that develops the best efforts of the men under him. He can't do that if he shuts himself up in his office. He has to get out and get acquainted with his men.
ROY W. MOORE

Executive ability is deciding quickly and getting somebody else to do the work.
JOHN G. POLLARD

The best executive is the one who has sense enough to pick good men to do what he wants done, and self-restraint enough to keep from meddling with them while they do it.
THEODORE ROOSEVELT

Even for the neurotic executive—as for everyone else—work has great therapeutic value; it is generally his last refuge, and deterioration there marks the final collapse of the man; his marriage, his

social life, and the outside interests—all have suffered beforehand.
RICHARD A. SMITH

## Expectations

What a pleasure life would be to live if everybody would try to do only half of what he expects others to do.
WILLIAM J. H. BOETCKER

The element of the unexpected and the unforeseeable is what gives some of its relish to life and saves us from falling into the mechanical thralldom of the logicians.
WINSTON CHURCHILL

A pint can't hold a quart. If it holds a pint, it is doing all that can be expected of it.
MARGARET DELAND

As long as there are postmen, life will have zest.
WILLIAM JAMES

We love to expect, and when expectation is either disappointed or gratified, we want to be again expecting.
SAMUEL JOHNSON

We are living in a period which all too readily scraps the old for the new.... As a nation, we are in danger of forgetting that the new is not true because it is novel, and that the old is not false because it is ancient.
JOSEPH P. KENNEDY

It must be remembered that there is nothing more difficult to plan, more doubtful of success, nor more dangerous to manage, than the creation of a new system. For the initiator has the enmity of all who would profit by the preservation of the old institutions and merely lukewarm defenders in those who would gain by the new ones.
NICCOLÒ MACHIAVELLI

Presumption is our natural and original malady. When I play with my cat, who knows if I am not a pastime to her more than she is to me.
MICHEL DE MONTAIGNE

One does not expect in this world; one hopes and pays carfares.
JOSEPHINE PRESTON PEABODY

I am I and you are you. I'm not in this world to live up to your expectations and you're not in this world to live up to mine. If we meet, it's beautiful, if not, it can't be helped.
FRITZ PERLS

There is nothing more miserable and foolish than anticipation.
SENECA

Oft expectation fails, and most oft there where most it promises.
WILLIAM SHAKESPEARE

We must expect everything and fear everything from time to time.
MARQUIS DE VAUVENARGUES

## Experience

Any one who has had a long life of experiences is worth listening to, worth emulating, and worth tying to as a friend. No one can have too much experience in any line of endeavor. We readily welcome to our group of friends that one who talks with the voice of experience and common sense.

We know that we are safe in his hands. He is not going to get us into trouble. Rather is he going to point out the pitfalls and mistakes that experience has taught him to avoid. There is no experience but what carries its lasting good for us along with it. And you don't have to discard experience. It's a coat for life! It never wears out
GEORGE MATTHEW ADAMS

Experience is the hardest kind of teacher. It gives you the test first and the lesson afterward.
ANONYMOUS

By experience we find out a short way by a long wandering.
ROGER ASCHAM

Experience is the comb that Nature gives us after we are bald.
BELGIAN PROVERB

Experience is very valuable. It keeps a man who makes the same mistake twice from admitting it the third time.
BROOK BENTON

A little experience often upsets a lot of theory.
SAMUEL PARKS CADMAN

Experience takes dreadfully high school-wages, but he teaches like no other.
THOMAS CARLYLE

Experience is the universal mother of sciences.
MIGUEL DE CERVANTES

There are but few proverbial sayings that are not true, for they are drawn from experience itself, which is the mother of all sciences.
MIGUEL DE CERVANTES

You cannot speak of ocean to a well-frog, the creature of a narrower sphere. You cannot speak of ice to a summer insect, the creature of a season.
CHUANG-TZU

If men could learn from history, what lessons it might teach us! But passion and party blind our eyes, and the light which experience gives us is a lantern on the stern which shines only on the waves behind us.
SAMUEL TAYLOR COLERIDGE

To most men experience is like the stern lights of a ship, which illuminate only the track it has passed.
SAMUEL TAYLOR COLERIDGE

A prudent person profits from personal experience, a wise one from the experience of others.
JOSEPH COLLINS

The trouble with experience is that by the time you have it you are too old to take advantage of it.
JIMMY CONNORS

Experience is the child of thought, and thought is the child of action. We cannot learn men from books.
BENJAMIN DISRAELI

The less you know how to do your work the harder it is to do.
HENRY L. DOHERTY

It takes a lot of time to get experience, and once you have it you ought to go on using it.
BENJAMIN M. DUGGAR

For Everything you have missed you have gained something else.
RALPH WALDO EMERSON

Experience seems to be the only thing of any value that's widely distributed.
WILLIAM FEATHER

I've learned that when a man with money meets a man with experience, the man with the experience ends up with the money and the man with the money ends up with the experience.
59-YEAR-OLD'S DISCOVERY

Life is a series of experiences, each one of which makes us bigger, even though sometimes it is hard to realize this. For the world was built to develop character, and we must learn that the setbacks and griefs which we endure help us in our marching onward.
HENRY FORD

You take all the experience and judgment of men over 50 out of the world and there wouldn't be enough left to run it.
HENRY FORD

An observant man, in all his intercourse with society and the world, constantly and unperceived marks on every person and thing the figure expressive of its value, and therefore, on meeting that person or thing, knows instantly what kind and degree of attention to give it. This is to make something of experience.
JOHN FOSTER

In the business world, everyone is paid in two coins: cash and experience. Take the experience first; the cash will come later.
HAROLD GENEEN

An M.B.A's first shock could be the realization that companies require experience before they hire a chief executive officer.
ROBERT HALF

I have but one lamp by which my feet are guided, and that is the lamp of experience. I know of no way of judging of the future by the past.
PATRICK HENRY

Experience is something I always think I have until I get more of it.
BURTON HILLIS

Experience is not what happens to a man. It is what a man does with what happens to him.
ALDOUS HUXLEY

To every problem there is already a solution, whether you know it or not. To every sum in mathematics there is already a correct answer, whether the mathematician has found it or not.

It should be encouraging to you to know that if you are now confronted by any kind of problem, personal or otherwise, there is a way to solve it, and you will find the way as rapidly and as surely as you apply to it the principles of divine truth.

It is possible to make each year bring with it a lasting gift to add to the fullness of experience, to be treasured up, savored, and remembered. They need not be startling, these gifts of the years; they may be things that lie within the reach of all.
GRENVILLE KLEISER

Experience is the worst teacher; it gives the test before presenting the lesson.
VERNON LAW

Experience does not err; only your judgements err by expecting from her what is not in her power.
LEONARDO DA VINCI

Growing up is, after all, only the understanding that one's unique and incredible experience is what every one shares.
DORIS LESSING

One thorn of experience is worth a whole wilderness of warning.
JAMES RUSSELL LOWELL

The story of any one man's real experience finds its startling parallel in that of every one of us.
JAMES RUSSELL LOWELL

Age should not have its faith lifted but rather teach the world to admire wrinkles as the etchings of experience and the firm lines of character.
RALPH BARTON PERRY

There are many arts among men, the knowledge of which is acquired bit by bit by experience. For it is experience that causeth our life to move forward by the skill we acquire, while want of experience subjects us to the effects of chance.
PLATO

Men are wise in proportion, not to their experience, but to their capacity for experience.
GEORGE BERNARD SHAW

Experience is a jewel, and it had need be so, for it is often purchased at an infinite rate.
WILLIAM SHAKESPEARE

The rules which experience suggests are better than those which theorists elaborate in their libraries.
RICHARD S. STORRS

All experience is an arch wherethro' gleams that untraveled world whose margins fade forever and forever as we move.
ALFRED, LORD TENNYSON

No man was ever so completely skilled in the conduct of life, as not to receive new information from age and experience.
TERENCE

We should be careful to get out of an experience all the wisdom that is in it—not like the cat that sits down on a hot stove lid. She will never sit down on a hot stove lid again—and that is well; but also she will never sit down on a cold one anymore.
MARK TWAIN

We ought not to look back unless it is to derive useful lessons from past errors, and for the purpose of profiting by dearly bought experience.
GEORGE WASHINGTON

Man really knows nothing save what he has learned by his own experience.
CHRISTOPH M. WIELAND

# F

## Facts

Facts, when combined with ideas, constitute the greatest force in the world. They are greater than armaments, greater than finance, greater than science, business and law because they constitute the common denominator of all of them.
CARL W. ACKERMAN

It is not the facts which guide the conduct of men, but their opinions about facts; which may be entirely wrong. We can only make them right by discussion.
SIR NORMAN ANGELL

Every man has a right to his opinion, but no man has a right to be wrong in his facts.
BERNARD M. BARUCH

Facts that are not frankly faced have a habit of stabbing us in the back.
SIR HAROLD BOWDEN

Within the span of human time
Recorded fact can be suspect;
So much is known that isn't true,
So much erased as incorrect.
ART BUCK

Facts are to the mind what food is to the body. On the due digestion of the former depend the strength and wisdom of the one, just as vigor and health depend on the other. The wisest in council, the ablest in debate, and the most agreeable companion in the commerce of human life, is that man who has assimilated to his understanding the greatest number of facts.
EDMUND BURKE

Let us keep our mouths shut and our pens dry until we know the facts.
A. J. CARLSON

The moment you step into the world of facts, you step into the world of limits. You can free things from alien or accidental laws, but not from the laws of their own nature.
G. K. CHESTERTON

Only feeble minds are paralyzed by facts.
ARTHUR C. CLARKE

Creative thinking will improve as we relate the new fact to the old and all facts to each other.
JOHN DEWEY

Facts are the basis of policies but they do not create policies; they are only the stuff of which policies are made. Here is where synthesis comes in to build up the facts into useful knowledge which is wisdom, and it is wisdom that alone gives meaning and direction to life.
HAROLD W. DODDS

Facts are the most important thing in business. Study facts and do more than is expected of you.
FREDERICK H. ECKER

Facts are God's arguments; we should be careful never to misunderstand or pervert them.
TRYON EDWARDS

In some small field each child should attain, within the limited range of its experience and observation, the power to draw a justly limited inference from observed facts.
CHARLES W. ELIOT

No facts are to me sacred; none are profane; I simply experiment, an endless seeker, with no past at my back.
RALPH WALDO EMERSON

Any fact is better established by two or three good testimonies than by a thousand arguments.
NATHANIEL EMMONS

Get the facts, or the facts will get you. And when you get 'em, get 'em right, or they will get you wrong.
THOMAS FULLER

Details often kill initiative, but there have been few successful men who weren't good at details. Don't ignore details. Lick them.
WILLIAM B. GIVEN, JR.

We live in a spelling bee culture where the demand is for factual accuracy and everybody overlooks the absence of art or meaning in what's said. Too many people sent letters to Nero telling him he was fingering his fiddle wrong. This passion for data is a way of avoiding coming to terms with things.
MARK HARRIS

Facts do not cease to exist because they are ignored.
ALDOUS HUXLEY

All the ancients used to say that the emperor should concern himself with general principles, but need not deal with the smaller details; however, failure to attend to details will end up endangering your greater virtues.
K'ANG-HSI

Facts mean nothing unless they are rightly understood, rightly related and rightly interpreted.
R. L. LONG

No fact is so simple that it is not harder to believe than to doubt at the first presentation. Equally, there is nothing so mighty or so marvelous that the wonder it evokes does not tend to diminish in time.
LUCRETIUS

All genuine progress results from finding new facts. No law can be passed to make an acre yield 300 bushels. God has already established the laws. It is for us to discover them, and to learn the facts by which we can obey them.
WHEELER MCMILLEN

Facts, as such, never settled anything. They are working tools only. It is the implications that can be drawn from facts that count, and to evaluate these requires wisdom and judgment that are unrelated to the computer approach to life.
CLARENCE B. RANDALL

To give great attention to details is one mark of the genius—to putter with trifles is not.
CHARLES B. ROGERS

We should keep so close to facts that we never have to remember the second time what we said the first time.
F. MARION SMITH

Never face facts; if you do, you'll never get up in the morning.
MARLO THOMAS

The brightest flashes in the world of thought are incomplete until they have been proved to have their counterparts in the world of fact.
JOHN TYNDALL

It is the individual citizen's understanding of facts that counts in a democracy. In totalitarian states, only a few people have to know the significance of facts. Here in America everyone has to know what facts mean.
**PAUL A. WAGNER**

He that has a spirit of detail will do better in life than many who figured beyond him in the university.
**DANIEL WEBSTER**

## *Failure*

Nothing resembles pride so much as discouragement.
**HENRI FRÉDÉRIC AMIEL**

The path to oblivion often goes through a triumphal arch.
**DON-AMINADO**

Whoever admits that he is too busy to improve his methods, has acknowledged himself to be at the end of his rope. And that is always the saddest predicament which any one can get into.
**J. OGDEN ARMOUR**

Failures either do not know what they want, or jib at the price.
**W. H. AUDEN**

One of the things I learned the hard way was it does not pay to get discouraged. Keeping busy and making optimism a way of life can restore your faith in yourself.
**LUCILLE BALL**

Discouragement is of all ages: In youth it is a presentiment, in old age a remembrance.
**HONORÉ DE BALZAC**

Power in the hand of lack of knowledge, inexperience and ego is a sure way to failure.
**HARRY F. BANKS**

Try as we may, none of us can be free of conflict and woe. Even the greatest men have had to accept disappointments as their daily bread.... The art of living lies less in eliminating our troubles than in growing with them. Man and society must grow together. Each individual's efforts to discipline himself must be matched by society's struggle to enforce the rules of law and of justice under the law.
**BERNARD M. BARUCH**

It is defeat that turns bone to flint, and gristle to muscle, and makes a man invincible, and forms those heroic natures that are now in ascendency in the world. Do not, then, be afraid of defeat. You are never so near to victory as when defeated in a good cause.
**HENRY WARD BEECHER**

Even the best of men get knocked down many times in a lifetime. Occasional knocks aren't anything to be afraid of. In fact, they make the game of life interesting; they are the hazard and bunkers and sandtraps that force us to keep our mind on the game and play our best.
**CLINTON E. BERNARD**

**Seven national crimes:**

1. I don't think.
2. I don't know.
3. I don't care.
4. I am too busy.
5. I leave well enough alone.
6. I have no time to read and find out.
7. I am not interested.

**WILLIAM J. H. BOETCKER**

Time after time . . . today's crisis shrinks to next week's footnote to a newly headline disaster.
HAL BORLAND

Those whom the gods would destroy they first call promising.
JAN CAREW

Don't take no for an answer, never submit to failure. Do not be fobbed off with mere personal success or acceptance. You will make all kinds of mistakes, but as long as you are generous and true, and also fierce, you cannot hurt the world or even seriously distress her. She was made to be wooed and won by youth.
WINSTON CHURCHILL

Our greatest glory is not in never falling, but in rising every time we fall.
CONFUCIUS

Try to do to others as you would have them do to you, and do not be discouraged if they fail sometimes. It is much better that they should fail than that you should.
CHARLES DICKENS

The disappointment of manhood succeeds the delusion of youth.
BENJAMIN DISRAELI

Giving up is the ultimate tragedy.
ROBERT J. DONOVAN

Sometimes a noble failure serves the world as faithfully as a distinguished success.
EDWARD DOWDEN

Failures inspire pity, seldom admiration. The streets of the City of Failure are paved with alibis—some of which are absolutely perfect.
HARRY A. EARNSHAW

Many of life's failures are people who did not realize how close they were to success when they gave up.
THOMAS EDISON

I'm proof against that word failure. I've seen behind it. The only failure a man ought to fear is failure in cleaving to the purpose he sees to be best.
GEORGE ELIOT

When a man is pushed, tormented, defeated, he has a chance to learn something; he has been put on his wits; on his manhood; he has gained the facts; learns his ignorance; is cured of the insanity of conceit; has got moderation and real skill.
RALPH WALDO EMERSON

Don't let life discourage you; everyone who got where he is had to begin where he was.
RICHARD L. EVANS

No man is a failure who enjoys life.
WILLIAM FEATHER

Never let us be discouraged with ourselves. It is not when we are conscious of our faults that we are the most wicked; on the contrary, we are less so.
FRANÇOIS FÉNELON

Failure is success if we learn from it.
MALCOLM FORBES

### How to Fail

Try too hard.
MALCOLM FORBES

One who fears failure limits his activities. Failure is only the opportunity more intelligently to begin again.
HENRY FORD

He that is good for making excuses, is seldom good for anything else.
**BENJAMIN FRANKLIN**

He's no failure. He's not dead yet.
**W. L. GEORGE**

Our greatest glory consists not in never failing, but in rising every time we fall.
**OLIVER GOLDSMITH**

An excuse's only virtue is to salve its maker's guilt.
**STANLEY GOLDSTEIN**

There is no such thing as a good excuse.
**JOHN P. GRIER**

There are five types of men who fail in life; the machine, the miser, the hermit, the snob and the brute.
**WALTER WILBER GRUBER**

It is only after an unknown number of unrecorded labors, after a host of noble hearts have succumbed in discouragement, convinced that their cause is lost; it is only then that the cause triumphs.
**FRANÇOIS GUIZOT**

The longer is the excuse, the less likely it's the truth.
**ROBERT HALF**

Why should anybody be interested in some old man who was a failure?
**ERNEST HEMINGWAY**

Don't make excuses—make good.
**ELBERT HUBBARD**

There is no failure except in no longer trying.
**ELBERT HUBBARD**

There is the greatest practical benefit in making a few failures early in life.
**THOMAS H. HUXLEY**

The greatest test of courage on earth is to bear defeat without losing heart.
**ROBERT G. INGERSOLL**

The saddest of all failures is that of a soul, with its capabilities and possibilities, failing of life everlasting, and entering on that night of death upon which no morning ever dawns.
**HERRICK JOHNSON**

The men who try to do something and fail are infinitely better than those who try nothing and succeed.
**LLOYD JONES**

Don't be discouraged by a failure. It can be a positive experience. Failure is, in a sense, the highway to success, inasmuch as every discovery of what is false leads us to seek earnestly after what is true, and every fresh experience points out some form of error which we shall afterwards carefully avoid.
**JOHN KEATS**

Failure is, in a sense, the highway to success, inasmuch as every discovery of what is false leads us to seek earnestly after what is true.
**JOHN KEATS**

The only time you don't want to fail is the last time you try.
**CHARLES F. KETTERING**

We have forty million reasons for failure, but not a single excuse.
**RUDYARD KIPLING**

Never give a man up until he has failed at something he likes.
**LEWIS E. LAWES**

Let no feeling of discouragement prey upon you, and in the end you're sure to succeed.
ABRAHAM LINCOLN

In great attempts, it is glorious even to fail.
CASSIUS LONGINUS

Because a fellow has failed once or twice, or a dozen times, you don't want to set him down as a failure till he's dead or loses his courage—and that's the same thing.
GEORGE HORACE LORIMER

The only failure which lacks dignity is the failure to try.
MALCOLM F. MACNEIL

Lack of will power and drive cause more failure than lack of imagination and ability.
DENNIS MAHONEY

One is wasting life force every time he talks of failure, of hard luck, of troubles and trials, of past errors and mistakes. Let him turn his back on the past and face the light.
ORISON S. MARDEN

Besides the practical knowledge which defeat offers, there are important personality profits to be taken. Defeat strips away false values and makes you realize what you really want. It stops you from chasing butterflies and puts you to work digging gold.
WILLIAM MOULTON MARSTON

The same disappointments in life will chasten and refine one man's spirit, embitter another's.
WILLIAM MATTHEWS

How far high failure overleaps the bounds of low success.
LEWIS MORRIS

What is defeat? Nothing but education; nothing but the first step to something better.
WENDELL PHILLIPS

Keep out of the suction caused by those who drift backwards.
E. K. PIPER

Failures are divided into two classes—those who thought and never did, and those who did and never thought.
JOHN CHARLES SALAK

I believe that one of the characteristics of the human race—possibly the one that is primarily responsible for its course of evolution—is that it has grown by creatively responding to failure.
GLEN T. SEABORG

It is a healthy symptom when a man is dissatisfied without being discouraged.
ROY L. SMITH

Formula for failure: Try to please everybody.
HERBERT BAYARD SWOPE

There are two kinds of failures: The man who will do nothing he is told, and the man who will do nothing else.
PERLE THOMPSON

What is called resignation is confirmed desperation.
HENRY DAVID THOREAU

To be successful, you've got to be willing to fail.
FRANK TYGER

Whatever we succeed in doing is a transformation of something we have failed to do. Thus, when we fail, it is only because we have given up.
PAUL VALÉRY

Watch a man with scrutiny when his will is crossed, and his desires disappointed. The quality of spirit he reveals at that time will determine the character of that man.
RICHARD T. WILLIAMS

Let's learn and label properly Disappointment and Discouragement for what they are—two completely different states of mind. Disappointment can be a spur to improvement that will contribute to success. But Discouragement is a mortal enemy that destroys courage and robs one of the will to fight.

It is not circumstance that causes Discouragement, but one's own reaction to that circumstance. Everyone must meet Disappointment, many times; it is simply a part of life. When it is met, we may resign ourselves to Discouragement and failure. Or we may recognize each Disappointment as an asset by which we can profit, and take new strength from a lesson learned.

The choice is ours, each time, to make.
JOHN M. WILSON

The girl who can't dance says the band can't play.
YIDDISH PROVERB

## *Faith*

Faith is kept alive in us, and gathers strength, more from practice than from speculations.
JOSEPH ADDISON

Without faith a man can do nothing. But faith can stifle all science.
HENRI FRÉDÉRIC AMIEL

Faith is the reservoir from which we draw power. It provides that extra push that helps one to carry on. Someone has said that herd men win battles but free men win wars, for free men can fight on in the face of possible defeat. This is true because free men are men of faith, and faith strengthens convictions and undergirds hopes.
CHARLES A. ANSPACH

Faith is to believe what we do not see; and the reward of this faith is to see what we believe.
ST. AUGUSTINE

Inflexible in faith, invincible in arms.
JAMES BEATTIE

Faith without works is like a bird without wings; though she may hop about on earth, she will never fly to heaven. But when both are joined together, then doth the soul mount up to her eternal rest.
FRANCIS BEAUMONT

Every tomorrow has two handles. We can take hold of it with the handle of anxiety or the handle of faith. We should live for the future, and yet should find our life in the fidelities of the present; the last is only the method of the first.
HENRY WARD BEECHER

There are many persons that smile on hearing talk of building a better world and say that the world cares nothing for that. These persons have lost faith in people and God because of their own mistakes.
JOHN S. BONNELL, D.D.

The world has a way of giving what is demanded of it. If you are frightened and look for failure and poverty, you will get them, no matter how hard you may try to succeed. Lack of faith in yourself, in what life will do for you, cuts you off from the good things of the world. Expect victory and you make victory. No where is this truer than in business life where bravery and faith bring both material and spiritual rewards.
PRESTON BRADLEY

Faith that the thing can be done is essential to any great achievement.
**THOMAS N. CARRUTHERS**

A man of courage is also full of faith.
**CICERO**

As ye have therefore received Christ Jesus the Lord, so walk ye in him: rooted and built up in him, and established in the faith, as ye have been taught, abounding therein with thanksgiving.
**COLOSSIANS 2:6–7**

Faith gives the courage to live and do. Scientists, with their disciplined thinking, like others, need a basis for the good life, for aspiration, for courage to do great deeds. They need a faith to live by. The hope of the world lies in those who have such faith and who use the methods of science to make their visions become real. Visions and hope and faith are not part of science. They are beyond the nature that science knows. Of such is the religion that gives meaning to life.
**ARTHUR H. COMPTON**

Faith is the great motive power, and no man realizes his full possibilities unless he has the deep conviction that life is eternally important and that his work well done is a part of an unending plan.
**CALVIN COOLIDGE**

There is much in the world to make us afraid. There is much more in our faith to make us unafraid.
**FREDERICK W. CROPP**

We need not be afraid of the future, for the future will be in our own hands. We shall need courage, energy and determination, but above all, we shall need faith—faith in ourselves, in our communities and in our country.
**THOMAS E. DEWEY**

Send the harmony of a Great Desire vibrating through every fiber of your being. Pray for a task that will call forth your faith, your courage, your perseverance, and your spirit of sacrifice. Keep your hands and your soul clean, and the conquering current will flow freely.
**THOMAS DREIER**

I have lived a long time, and I have seen history repeat itself again and again. I have seen many depressions in business. Always America has come out stronger and more prosperous. Be as brave as your fathers before you. Have faith. Go forward.
**THOMAS EDISON**

Faith is not trying to believe something regardless of the evidence; faith is daring to do something regardless of the consequences.
**SHERWOOD EDDY**

Faith and love are apt to be spasmodic in the best minds. Men live on the brink of mysteries and harmonies into which they never enter, and with their hand on the door-latch they die outside.
**RALPH WALDO EMERSON**

Sure! Heart's Desire will come true some day. But you must trust and, trusting, you must wait. You've but to vision to clear the brighter way, and see what isn't written on the slate. You must *believe* that happier, bigger things are coming toward you through the trying year. Your ears must hear the rustle of the wings of God's glad messengers, so dry your tears! Our trials are tests; our sorrows pave the way for fuller life when we have earned it so. Give rein to *faith* and hail the brighter day, and you shall come at last real joy to know.
**JEROME P. FLEISHMAN**

The business man who has faith is not very likely to go wrong. He is going to steer his ship of commerce through the troubled waters of misfortune, perhaps

even adversity, with a serenity born of the consciousness that nothing can harm him permanently so long as he sees clearly and acts wisely. There will be many hands eager to retard his progress. Slander will raise its ugly head from many little by-ways along his path. Ill health may come; the loss of loved ones; the crippling of his finances; the striking down of his most cherished hopes; and yet—the man who has Faith—who believes that right is right will triumph.
**JEROME P. FLEISHMAN**

It is going to be a long, hard haul; it will require patience, courage, faith that hangs on when hope fails, if we are to tame the rude barbarity of man, so that the atomic age becomes a blessing, not a curse. There never was such a day for the Christian gospel. God help us all in these years ahead to make that gospel live in men and nations!
**HARRY EMERSON FOSDICK, D.D.**

In the affairs of this world, men are saved, not by faith, but by the want of it.
**BENJAMIN FRANKLIN**

Only a person who has faith in himself can be faithful to others.
**ERICH FROMM**

Faith is positive, enriching life in the here and now. Doubt is negative, robbing life of glow and meaning. So though I do not understand immortality, I choose to believe.
**WEBB B. GARRISON**

Faith is the backbone of the social and the foundation of the commercial fabric; remove faith between man and man, and society and commerce fall to pieces. There is not a happy home on earth but stands on faith; our heads are pillowed on it, we sleep at night in its arms with greater security for the safety of our lives, peace, and prosperity than bolts and bars can give.
**THOMAS GUTHRIE**

But without faith it is impossible to please him: for he that cometh to God must believe that he is, and that he is a rewarder of them that diligently seek him.
**HEBREWS 11:6**

Absolute faith corrupts as absolutely as absolute power.
**ERIC HOFFER**

It's faith in something and enthusiasm for something that makes life worth looking at.
**OLIVER WENDELL HOLMES**

Associate with men of faith. This tends to be reciprocal. Your faith will communicate itself to them, and their faith to you. Do your work in a faith atmosphere, and you will work at a maximum advantage. You impress others by your own faith, and they will have faith in you only in the degree that you have faith in yourself.
**GRENVILLE KLEISER**

If we are to survive the Atomic Age, we must have something to live by, to live on, and to live for. We must stand aside from the world's conspiracy of fear and hate and grasp once more the great monosyllables of life: faith, hope, and love. Men must live by these if they live at all under the crushing weight of history.
**OTTO PAUL KRETZMANN**

You can change your faith without changing gods, and vice versa.
**STANISLAUS LEC**

He who keeps his faith only, cannot be discrowned.
**JAMES RUSSELL LOWELL**

The only faith that wears well and holds its color in all weather is that which is woven of conviction.
JAMES RUSSELL LOWELL

If we have no faith in ourselves and in the kind of future we can create together, we are fit only to follow, not to lead. Let us remember that the Bible contains two proverbs we cannot afford to forget. The first is "Man does not live by bread alone" and the second is "Where there is no vision, the people perish."
CHARLES LUCKMAN

Faith, like light, should always be simple and unbending; while love, like warmth, should beam forth on every side, and bend to every necessity of our brethren.
MARTIN LUTHER

If ye have faith as a grain of mustard seed, ye shall say unto the mountain, Remove hence to yonder place; and it shall remove; and nothing shall be impossible unto you.
MATTHEW 17:20

Faith marches at the head of the army of progress. It is found beside the most refined life, the freest government, the profoundest philosophy, the noblest poetry, the purest humanity.
THEODORE T. MUNGER

There is many a thing which the world calls disappointment, but there is no such word in the dictionary of faith.
JOHN NEWTON

Nothing in life is more wonderful than faith—the one great moving force which we can neither weigh in the balance nor test in the crucible.
SIR WILLIAM OSLER

I believe the intelligent and consistent practice of the Christian faith can solve any personal problem. This conviction is based on hundreds of modern people who have passed through our conference rooms in a church at the heart of New York City. People must be taught to realize that in faith they have a mechanism and power by which they can actually live victorious, happy and successful lives.
NORMAN VINCENT PEALE

Religious faith may very well be considered a science, for it responds invariably to certain formulae. Perform the technique of faith according to the laws which have been proved workable in human experience and you will always get a result of power.
NORMAN VINCENT PEALE

The errors of faith are better than the best thoughts of unbelief.
THOMAS RUSSELL

Faith is indispensable, and the world at times does not seem to have quite enough of it. It can and has accomplished what seems to be the impossible. Wars have been started and men and nations lost for the lack of it. Faith starts from the individual and builds men and nations. America was built by and on the faith of our ancestors.
CARL SANDBURG

Columbus found a world, and had no chart save one that Faith deciphered in the skies.
GEORGE SANTAYANA

In actual life, every great enterprise begins with and takes its first forward step in faith.
AUGUST WILHELM VON SCHLEGEL

No ray of sunlight is ever lost, but the green which it awakes into existence needs time to sprout, and it is

not always granted to the sower to see the harvest. All work that is worth anything is done in faith.
ALBERT SCHWEITZER

There are glimpses of heaven to us in every act, or thought, or word, that raises us above ourselves.
A. P. STANLEY

In the harsh face of life faith can read a bracing gospel.
ROBERT LOUIS STEVENSON

Faith is the root of all blessings. Believe, and you should be saved; believe, and you must needs be satisfied; believe, and you cannot but be comforted and happy.
JEREMY TAYLOR

Kind hearts are more than coronets,
And simple faith than Norman blood.
ALFRED, LORD TENNYSON

'Tis not the dying for a faith that's so hard; 'tis the living up to it that is difficult.
WILLIAM MAKEPEACE THACKERAY

The mason asks but a narrow shelf to spring his brick from; man requires only an infinitely narrower one to spring his arch of faith from.
HENRY DAVID THOREAU

Doubt is the disease of this inquisitive, restless age. It is the price we pay for our advanced intelligence and civilization—the dim night of our resplendent day. But as the most beautiful light is born of darkness, so the faith that springs from conflict is often the strongest and best.
R. TURNBULL

It was the schoolboy who said, "Faith is believing what you know ain't so."
MARK TWAIN

When my external environment is clouded in doubt and despair . . . when the tempests of destruction are making my dreams of success tremble like the topmost spar of a helpless ship—when the skies seem to hold the closing ruin of all my fondest hopes, my mind, superior amid the outrages of this material world, rests upon the solid, immovable foundation of Faith. There is nothing in myself, but all is in my Master.
F. D. VAN AMBURGH

Faith is raising the sail of our little boat until it is caught up in the soft winds above and picks up speed, not from anything within itself, but from the vast resources of the universe around us.
W. RALPH WARD, JR.

The greatest asset of a man, a business or a nation is faith.

The men who built this country and those who made it prosper during its darkest days were men whose faith in its future was unshakable.

Men of courage, they dared to go forward despite all hazards; men of vision, they always looked forward, never backward.

Christianity, the greatest institution humanity has ever known, was founded by twelve men, limited in education, limited in resources, but with an abundance of faith and divine leadership.

The vision essential to clear thinking; to common sense needed for wise decisions; the courage of conviction based on facts not fancies; and the constructive spirit of faith as opposed to the destructive forces of doubt will preserve our Christian ways of life.
THOMAS J. WATSON

Faith is the root of all good works; a root that produces nothing is dead.
DANIEL WILSON

It takes vision and courage to create—it takes faith and courage to prove.
OWEN D. YOUNG

## False

Thou shalt not get found out is not one of God's commandments; and no man can be saved by trying to keep it.
LEONARD BACON

Men walk almost always in the paths trodden by others, proceeding in their actions by imitation.
NICCOLO DI BERNARDO

If you can't imitate him, don't copy him.
YOGI BERRA

If I take refuge in ambiguity, I assure you that it's quite conscious.
KINGMAN BREWSTER, JR.

There is a false modesty, which is vanity; a false glory, which is levity; a false grandeur, which is meanness; a false virtue, which is hypocrisy; and a false wisdom, which is prudery.
JEAN DE LA BRUYÈRE

He who is false to the present duty breaks a thread in the loom, and you will see the effect when the weaving of a life-time is unraveled.
WILLIAM ELLERY CHANNING

Falsehood is never so successful as when she baits her hook with truth, and no opinions so fatally mislead us as those that are not wholly wrong, as no watches so effectively deceive the wearer as those that are sometimes right.
CHARLES CALEB COLTON

There are more fakers in business than in jail.
MALCOLM FORBES

It is astonishing what force, purity and wisdom it requires for a human being to keep clear of falsehoods.
MARGARET FULLER

The united voice of millions cannot lend the smallest foundation to falsehood.
OLIVER GOLDSMITH

False gods must be repudiated, but that is not all: The reasons for their existence must be sought beneath their masks.
ALEXANDER HERZEN

Very much of what we call the progress of today consists in getting rid of false ideas, false conceptions of things, and in taking a point of view that enables us to see the principles, ideas and things in right relation to each other.
WILLIAM D. HOARD

An imitator is a man who succeeds in being an imitation.
ELBERT HUBBARD

Almost all absurdity of conduct arises from the imitation of those we cannot resemble.
SAMUEL JOHNSON

No man ever yet became great by imitation.
SAMUEL JOHNSON

It is a poor wit who lives by borrowing the words, decisions, mien, inventions and actions of others.
JOHANN LAVATER

False conclusions which have been reasoned out are infinitely worse than blind impulse.
**HORACE MANN**

A great part of art consists in imitation. For the whole conduct of life is based on this: that what we admire in others we want to do ourselves.
**QUINTILIAN**

Man is an imitative creature.
**JOHANN FRIEDRICH VON SCHILLER**

Deep breaths are very helpful at shallow parties.
**BARBARA WALTERS**

Only the shallow know themselves.
**OSCAR WILDE**

## *Fame*

A celebrity is a person who works hard all his life to become well known, then wears dark glasses to avoid being recognized.
**FRED ALLEN**

I don't want to achieve immortality through my work. I want to achieve it through not dying.
**WOODY ALLEN**

Fame always brings loneliness. Success is as ice cold and lonely as the North Pole.
**VICKY BAUM**

Happy is the man who hath never known what it is to taste of fame—to have it is a purgatory, to want it is a hell.
**EDWARD BULWER-LYTTON**

Fame you get accustomed to, but if it ever takes possession of you, then quite clearly you're in dead trouble.
**RICHARD BURTON**

All hunt for fame, but most mistake the way.
**CHARLES CHURCHILL**

Worldly fame is but a breath of wind that blows now this way, and now that, and changes name as it changes in direction.
**DANTE**

What's fame, after all, me la-ad? 'Tis apt to be what some wan writes on ye'er tombstone.
**FINLEY PETER DUNNE**

The wise man thinks of fame just enough to avoid being despised.
**EPICURUS**

Millions long for immortality who do not know what to do with themselves on a rainy Sunday afternoon.
**SUSAN ERTZ**

It quite often happens. A man bounds into sudden success, becomes obsessed by vanity, builds or buys a palace—and then has to close up the palace. The latest example is Clarence Saunders, who founded the Piggly Wiggly stores, launched a company, gathered in a lot of money, started building a million-dollar home, tried to fight Wall Street at its own game of speculating in stocks, gloried in having cornered his stock, lost out, and now makes this announcement concerning his palace now under construction at Memphis: "I am going to nail up the place and lock the gates until I can make the money to complete it."
**B. C. FORBES**

Fame is but the breath of people, and that often unwholesome.
THOMAS FULLER

If all else fails, immortality can always be assured by spectacular error.
JOHN KENNETH GALBRAITH

Wood burns because it has the proper stuff in it; and a man becomes famous because he has the proper stuff in him.
JOHANN WOLFGANG VON GOETHE

Fame usually comes to those who are thinking about something else.
OLIVER WENDELL HOLMES

Glory is largely a theatrical concept. There is no striving for glory without a vivid awareness of an audience.
ERIC HOFFER

Surely there must be some place where the great minds of Shelley, Homer and Spinoza go after death. The denial of immortality does not square with intelligence. Adolph S. Ochs, shortly before his death, said that he believed that he was more than an animal and that he did not believe that this life is the end. Our bodies change and in the end crumble. It is a house of clay. But inside there is a spiritual duplicate. As we have borne the image of the earthly, so shall we bear the image of the heavenly.
MALCOLM JAMES MACLEOD, D.D.

I do not like the man who squanders life for fame.
MARTIAL

If fame is only to come after death, I am in no hurry for it.
MARTIAL

Immortality is not a gift, immortality is an achievement; and only those that strive mightily shall possess it.
EDGAR LEE MASTERS

Renown is a source of toil and sorrow; obscurity is a source of happiness.
JOHANN L. VON MOSHEIM

Fame has only the span of a day they say. But to live in the hearts of the people—that is worth something.
OUIDA

Mankind differ in their notions of happiness; but in my opinion he truly possesses it who lives in the anticipation of honest fame, and the glorious figure he shall make in the eyes of posterity.
PLINY THE YOUNGER

Those who desire fame are fond of praise and flattery, though it comes from their inferiors.
PLINY THE YOUNGER

True glory consists in doing what deserves to be written; in writing what deserves to be read; and in so living as to make the world happier and better for our living in it.
PLINY

Fame due to the achievements of the mind never perishes.
PROPERTIUS

The fame of men ought always to be estimated by the means used to acquire it.
FRANÇOIS DE LA ROCHEFOUCAULD

Fame: The beginning of the fall of greatness.
VASILY V. ROZANOV

How men long for celebrity! Some would willingly sacrifice their lives for fame, and not a few would rather be known by their crimes than not known at all.
JOHN SINCLAIR

Nothing is easier to avoid than publicity. If one genuinely doesn't want it, one doesn't get it.
C. P. SNOW

Fame and rest are utter opposites.
RICHARD STEELE

What we think of ourselves makes a difference in our lives, and belief in immortality gives us the highest values of ourselves. When we so believe, we achieve proportions greater than mere matter.
JESSE WILLIAM STITT

The desire for fame is the last weakness wise men put off.
TACITUS

The desire for glory clings even to the best men longer than any other passion.
TACITUS

Fame is what you have taken, character is what you give. When to this truth you awaken, then you begin to live.
BAYARD TAYLOR

Spring is a natural resurrection, an experience in immortality.
HENRY DAVID THOREAU

There is only one way to get ready for immortality, and that is to love this life and live it as bravely and faithfully and cheerfully as we can.
HENRY VAN DYKE

In fame's temple there is always to be found a niche for rich dunces, importunate scoundrels, or successful butchers of the human race.
JOHANN ZIMMERMANN

## *Family*

I find this same problem exists in all fathers and sons. There is something about the relationship that is pretty difficult to put your finger on. I think fathers realize this and have it on their minds a good deal more than the sons realize.
SHERWOOD ANDERSON

It is a truth universally acknowledged, that a single man in possession of a good fortune must be in want of a wife.
JANE AUSTEN

Wife and children are a kind of discipline of humanity.
FRANCIS BACON

Every man who is high up loves to think that he has done it all himself; and the wife smiles, and lets it go at that.
JAMES M. BARRIE

What value has a human life?
It's much twixt man and child and wife.
But just outside the kith and kin,
It's worth perhaps a cynic's grin.
ART BUCK

I don't care what you say, women make the best wives.
DAGWOOD BUMSTEAD

Take the word "family." Strike out the "m" for mother and the "y" for youth—and all you have left is "fail."
**OMAR BURLESON**

Some people seem compelled by unkind fate to parental servitude for life. There is no form of penal service worse than this.
**SAMUEL BUTLER**

Cautiously avoid speaking of the domestic affairs either of yourself, or of other people. Yours are nothing to them but tedious gossip; and theirs are nothing to you.
**LORD CHESTERFIELD**

Few fathers care much for their sons, or at least, most of them care more for their money. Of those who really love their sons, few know how to do it.
**LORD CHESTERFIELD**

Twenty thousand years ago the family was the social unit. Now the social unit has become the world, in which it may truthfully be said that each person's welfare affects that of every other.
**ARTHUR H. COMPTON**

The father who does not teach his son his duties is equally guilty with the son who neglects them.
**CONFUCIUS**

Heredity: the thing a child gets from the other side of the family.
**MARCELENE COX**

The graveyards are full of women whose houses were so spotless you could eat off the floor. Remember, the second wife always has a maid.
**HELOISE CRUISE**

There are times when parenthood seems nothing but feeding the mouth that bites you.
**PETER DE VRIES**

The parent's job year in and year out, here a little and there a little, is to build up a disposition of good sportsmanship, of taking one's medicine, of facing the music, of being reviled and reviling not. This sense of not always being right, of recognition that perhaps we've made a mistake, seems left out of some grown-up children.
**SAMUEL SMITH DRURY**

The thing that impresses me most about America is the way parents obey their children.
**DUKE OF WINDSOR**

Instruction in the art of parenting can and should be an integral part of the studies in all school classes, K through 12.
**JOSEPH L. FANT III**

It isn't success if it costs you the companionship and chumminess and love of your children. Very often, busy, wealthy men of momentous affairs discover too late that they have sacrificed the finest thing in life, the affection of their family. Let me relate an incident [containing] a priceless suggestion for many ultra-busy businessmen. Frank L. Baker, prominent public utility executive, told a friend that he was going to give his young son an unusual Christmas present: "I am going to write my boy a letter telling him I am going to give him an hour of my time every day." Alas, Mr. Baker died two weeks later.
**B. C. FORBES**

Occasionally we all inherit, or are given, or get something or some things that are too good to use for a variety of seemingly sound but really quite silly reasons—they're heirlooms or too rare or too expensive or too fragile or too pretty. The result is heirloom linen handed down from generation to generation that falls apart when some benighted heiress decides to air it.

While I'm glad that past generations saved some things we now enjoy, we are enjoying them by using them instead of carefully storing them for our kids—in turn to store. Unused beautiful things are a waste.
MALCOLM FORBES

A father is a banker provided by nature.
FRENCH PROVERB

I could not point to any need in childhood as strong as that for a father's protection.
SIGMUND FREUD

Husbands are like fires:
They go out when unattended.
ZSA ZSA GABOR

A good father lives so he is a credit to his children.
ARNOLD GLASOW

I chose my wife, as she did her wedding gown, for qualities that would wear well.
OLIVER GOLDSMITH

Only mothers can think of the future, because they give birth to it in their children.
MAXIM GORKY

A man must marry only a very pretty woman in case he should ever want some other man to take her off his hands.
SACHA GUITRY

Family is the most effective form of government.
ROBERT HALF

Family life is the source of the greatest human happiness. This happiness is the simplest and least costly kind, and it cannot be purchased with money. But it can be increased if we do two things: if we recognize and uphold the essential values of family life and if we get and keep control of the process of social change so as to make it give us what is needed to make family life perform its essential functions.
ROBERT J. HAVIGHURST

Features alone do not run in the blood; vices and virtues, genius and folly, are transmitted through the same sure but unseen channel.
WILLIAM HAZLITT

One father is more than a hundred schoolmasters.
GEORGE HERBERT

The most important thing a father can do for his children is to love their mother.
THEODORE HESBURGH

The antidote for crime should be administered in childhood, by the parents. The problem is not fundamentally that of the improper child so much as it is that of the improper home.
JUSTICE JOHN W. HILL

Heredity: An omnibus in which all our ancestors ride, and every now and then one of them puts his head out and embarrasses us.
OLIVER WENDELL HOLMES

All persons who bear the blessed title of parent have the personal responsibility to see that their children are growing up fully appreciative of the rights of God and their fellowmen.
J. EDGAR HOOVER

The great virtue of parents is a great dowry.
HORACE

When you consider what a chance women have to poison their husbands, it's a wonder there isn't more of it done.
**KIN HUBBARD**

I had rather be shut up in a very modest cottage, with my books, my family and a few old friends, dining on simple bacon, and letting the world roll on as it liked, than to occupy the most splendid post which any human power can give.
**THOMAS JEFFERSON**

The mother is a matchless beast.
**JAMES KELLY**

I regard no man as poor who has a godly mother.
**ABRAHAM LINCOLN**

Parents wonder why the streams are bitter, when they themselves have poisoned the fountain.
**JOHN LOCKE**

Woman knows what Man has too long forgotten, that the ultimate economic and spiritual unit of any civilization is still the family.
**CLARE BOOTHE LUCE**

The only mothers it is safe to forget on Mother's Day are the good ones.
**MIGNON MCLAUGHLIN**

With him for a sire and her for a dam,
What should I be but just what I am?
**EDNA ST. VINCENT MILLAY**

It is only reasonable to allow the administration of affairs to mothers before their children reach the age prescribed by law at which they themselves can be responsible. But that father would have reared them ill who could not hope that in their maturity they would have more wisdom and competence than his wife.
**MICHEL DE MONTAIGNE**

Children aren't happy with nothing to ignore,
And that's what parents were created for.
**OGDEN NASH**

Family: A unit composed not only of children, but of men, women, an occasional animal, and the common cold.
**OGDEN NASH**

Some mothers need happy children; others need unhappy ones—otherwise they cannot prove their maternal virtues.
**FRIEDRICH WILHELM NIETZSCHE**

The worst misfortune that can happen to an ordinary man is to have an extraordinary father.
**AUSTIN O'MALLEY**

Families can help their members to grow individually. The family is the place to learn and follow moral standards. It can teach such things as fair play, which leads to justice, temperance in opinion, speech and habits, which frees from excess; honesty and sincerity, which lead to a disciplined, balanced like.
**ANNE G. PANNELL**

Heredity is what sets the parents of a teenager wondering about each other.
**LAURENCE J. PETER**

Wife: One who will do anything for her husband except stop criticizing and trying to improve him.
**J. B. PRIESTLEY**

To procure life, to obtain a mate and to rear offspring: such is the real business of life.
**W. WINWOOD READE**

What a father says to his children is not heard by the world, but it will be heard by posterity.
**JEAN PAUL RICHTER**

If you would reform the world from its errors and vices, begin enlisting the mothers.
**CHARLES SIMMONS**

Mere family never made a man great.
**MIKHAIL SKOBELEFF**

Everything is ideal to its parent.
**SOPHOCLES**

There is so little difference between husbands you might as well keep the first.
**ADELA ROGERS ST. JOHN**

It is not only paying wages, and giving commands, that constitute a master of a family; but prudence, equal behavior, with a readiness to protect and cherish them, is what entitles man to that character in their very hearts and sentiments.
**RICHARD STEELE**

Blessed are the mothers of the earth. They combine the practical and spiritual into the workable way of human life.
**WILLIAM L. STINGER**

To be a parent without an assistant is hard work.
**WILLIAM J. TEMPLE**

As are families, so is society. If well ordered, well instructed, and well governed, they are the springs from which go forth the streams of national greatness and prosperity—of civil order and public happiness.
**HARRY B. THAYER**

As long as you [prospective parents] are in your right mind don't you ever pray for twins. Twins amount to a permanent riot. And there ain't no real difference between triplets and an insurrection.
**MARK TWAIN**

When I was a boy of fourteen, my father was so ignorant I could hardly stand to have the old man around. But when I got to be twenty-one, I was astonished at how much the old man had learned in seven years.
**MARK TWAIN**

In Biblical times, a man could have as many wives as he could afford. Just like today.
**ABIGAIL VAN BUREN**

All women become like their mothers. That is their tragedy. No man does. That's his.
**OSCAR WILDE**

Fathers should be neither seen nor heard. That is the only proper basis for family life.
**OSCAR WILDE**

## *Fate*

We make our fortunes and we call them fate.
**DAVID ALROY**

It is a singular fact that many men of action incline to the theory of fatalism, while the greater part of men of thought believe in a divine providence.
**HONORÉ DE BALZAC**

Fate is not the ruler, but the servant of Providence.
**EDWARD BULWER-LYTTON**

If you believe in fate, believe in it, a least, for your good.
**RALPH WALDO EMERSON**

Whatever limits us we call Fate.
**RALPH WALDO EMERSON**

Fate with impartial hand turns out the doom of high and low; her capacious urn is constantly shaking out the names of all mankind.
**HORACE**

The Moving Finger writes; and, having writ,
Moves on: nor all your
Piety nor Wit
Shall lure it back to cancel half a line,
Nor all your tears wash out a Word of it.
**OMAR KHAYYAM**

Granting our wish is one of Fate's saddest jokes.
**JAMES RUSSELL LOWELL**

It is the fate of the coconut husk to float, of the stone to sink.
**MALAY PROVERB**

Fate often puts all the material for happiness and prosperity into a man's hands just to see how miserable he can make himself with them.
**DONALD MARQUIS**

If fate means you to lose, give him a good fight anyhow.
**WILLIAM MCFEE**

Fate is something you believe in when things are not going well. When they are, you forget it.
**AUBREY MENEN**

Our wills and fates do so contrary run, that our devices still are overthrown; our thoughts are ours, their ends none of our own.
**WILLIAM SHAKESPEARE**

Dreadful is the mysterious power of fate; there is no deliverance from it by wealth or by war, by walled city or dark, seabeaten ships.
**SOPHOCLES**

I do not believe in that word Fate. It is the refuge of every self-confessed failure.
**ANDREW SOUTAR**

## *Faults*

When dealing with people, remember you are not dealing with creatures of logic, but with creatures of emotion, creatures bristling with prejudice and motivated by pride and vanity.
**DALE CARNEGIE**

Think of your own faults the first part of the night when you are awake, and of the faults of others the latter part of the night when you are asleep.
**CHINESE PROVERB**

To copy faults is want of sense.
**CHARLES CHURCHILL**

Then the presidents and princes sought to find occasion against Daniel concerning the kingdom; but they could find no occasion nor fault; for as much as he was faithful, neither was there any error or fault found in him.
**DANIEL 6:4**

Everybody loves to find fault, it gives a feeling of superiority.
**WILLIAM FEATHER**

We can often do more for other men by correcting our own faults than by trying to correct theirs.
FRANÇOIS FÉNELON

Whether the stone bumps the jug or the jug bumps the stone it is bad for the jug.
FOLK SAYING

If a friend tell thee a fault, imagine always that he telleth thee not the whole.
THOMAS FULLER

There is no reward for finding fault.
ARNOLD GLASOW

It is easier to discover a deficiency in individuals, in states, and in Providence, than to see their real import and value.
GEORG WILHELM HEGEL

When we try to avoid one fault, we are led to the opposite, unless we be very careful.
HORACE

I have long been disposed to judge men by their average. If it is reasonably high, I am charitable with faults that look pretty black.
EDGAR WATSON HOWE

To many people virtue consists chiefly in repenting faults, not in avoiding them.
GEORG CHRISTOPH LICHTENBERG

I have not hated the man, but his faults.
MARTIAL

It is not so much the being exempt from faults, as having overcome them, that is an advantage to us.
ALEXANDER POPE

I never yet heard man or woman much abused that I was not inclined to think the better of them, and to transfer the suspicion or dislike to the one who found pleasure in pointing out the defects of another.
JANE PORTER

Don't be a fault-finding grouch; when you feel like finding fault with somebody or something stop for a moment and think; there is very apt to be something wrong within yourself. Don't permit yourself to show temper, and always remember that when you are in the right you can afford to keep your temper, and when you are in the wrong you cannot afford to lose it.
J. J. REYNOLDS

Almost all our faults are more pardonable than the methods we resort to to hide them.
FRANÇOIS DE LA ROCHEFOUCAULD

If we had no faults, we should not take so much pleasure in noting those of others.
FRANÇOIS DE LA ROCHEFOUCAULD

In the intercourse of life, we please more by our faults than by our good qualities.
FRANÇOIS DE LA ROCHEFOUCAULD

Strange, how, as we become more knowledgeable, faults become more numerous as well as obvious.
CHARLES B. ROGERS

However good you may be you have faults; however dull you may be you can find out what some of them are, and however slight they may be you had better make some—not too painful, but patient efforts to get rid of them.
JOHN RUSKIN

You will find it less easy to uproot faults than to choke them by gaining virtues. Do not think of

your faults, still less of other's faults. In every person who comes near you look for what is good and strong; honor that; try to imitate it, and your faults will drop off like dead leaves when their time comes.
JOHN RUSKIN

Faultfinding without suggestions for improvement is a waste of time.
RALPH C. SMEDLEY

Don't tell your friends their social faults; they will cure the fault and never forgive you.
LOGAN PEARSALL SMITH

Always acknowledge a fault quite frankly. This will throw those in authority off their guard and give you an opportunity to commit more.
MARK TWAIN

It is easy to find fault, if one has that disposition. There was once a man who, not being able to find any other fault with his coal, complained that there were too many prehistoric toads in it.
MARK TWAIN

Whosoever does not know how to recognize the faults of great men is incapable of estimating their perfections.
VOLTAIRE

## *Fear*

Fear gives intelligence even to fools.
ANONYMOUS

Fear is an insidious virus. Given a breeding place in our minds, it will permeate the whole body of our work; it will eat away our spirit and block the forward path of our endeavors. Fear is the greatest enemy of progress. Progress moves ever on, and does not linger to consider microscopically the implications of each particular action. Only small and over-cautious minds see the shadows of lurking enemies and dangers everywhere, and shrink away from the increased efforts needed to overcome them. Fear is met and destroyed with courage. Again and again, when the struggle seems hopeless and all opportunity lost—some man or woman with a little more courage, a little more effort, brings victory.
JAMES F. BELL

The worst sorrows in life are not in its losses and misfortunes, but its fears.
ARTHUR CHRISTOPHER BENSON

The people to fear are not those who disagree with you, but those who disagree with you and are too cowardly to let you know.
NAPOLEON BONAPARTE

Half our fears are baseless; the other half discreditable.
CHRISTIAN BOVÉE

A panic is a sudden desertion of us, and a going over to the enemy of our imagination.
CHRISTIAN BOVÉE

The concessions of the weak are the concessions of fear.
EDMUND BURKE

The question for us is . . . whether our fears will feed on themselves until we throw away our freedom in a wild attempt to preserve it. There is a great threat from overseas. But the threat here at home is, for the moment, greater.
VANNEVAR BUSH

No power is strong enough to be lasting if it labors under the weight of fear.
CICERO

Freedom from fear simply cannot be attained by political fiat or international agreement. Fear is a personal emotion and it can be controlled or conquered only by individual persons.
**FRANKLIN P. COLE, D.D.**

A superior man is the one who is free from fear and anxieties.
**CONFUCIUS**

The way of a superior man is threefold. Virtuous, he is free from anxieties; wise, he is free from perplexities; bold, he is free from fear.
**CONFUCIUS**

Depression, gloom, pessimism, despair, discouragement, these slay ten human beings to every one murdered by typhoid, influenza, diabetes or pneumonia. If tuberculosis is the great white plague, fear is the great black plague. Be cheerful.
**FRANK CRANE**

The first and greatest commandment is, "Don't let them scare you."
**ELMER DAVIS**

If a man harbors any sort of fear, it percolates through all his thinking, damages his personality, makes him landlord to a ghost.
**LLOYD C. DOUGLAS**

It is our attitude toward events, not events themselves, which we can control. Nothing is by its own nature calamitous—even death is terrible only if we fear it.
**EPICTETUS**

A man who causes fear cannot be free from fear.
**EPICURUS**

Fear is an acid which is pumped into one's atmosphere. It causes mental, moral spiritual asphyxiation, and sometimes death; death to energy and all growth.
**HORACE FLETCHER**

Who bathes in worldly joys, swims in a world of fears.
**PHINEAS FLETCHER**

To tremble before anticipated evils, is to bemoan what thou hast never lost.
**JOHANN WOLFGANG VON GOETHE**

It is never safe to look into the future with eyes of fear.
**E. H. HARRIMAN**

The original of all great and lasting societies consisted not in the mutual good will men had toward each other, but in the mutual fear they had of each other.
**THOMAS HOBBES**

A good scare is worth more to a man than advice.
**EDGAR WATSON HOWE**

The great Big Black Things that have loomed against the horizon of my life, threatening to devour me, simply loomed and nothing more. The things that have really made me miss my train have always been sweet, soft, pretty, pleasant things of which I was not in the least afraid.
**ELBERT HUBBARD**

He knew no fear except the fear of doing wrong.
**ROBERT G. INGERSOLL**

Never take counsel of your fears.
**ANDREW JACKSON**

If fear is cultivated it will become stronger. If faith is cultivated it will achieve the mastery. We have a right to believe that faith is the stronger emotion because it is positive whereas fear is negative.
JOHN PAUL JONES

The only thing we have to fear on this planet is man.
CARL JUNG

I find no foeman in the road but fear; to doubt is failure and to dare success.
FREDERIC KNOWLES

It is better to have a right destroyed than to abandon it because of fear.
PHILIP MANN

What the world has to eradicate is fear and ignorance.
JAN MASARYK

Fear is like fire: If controlled it will help you; if uncontrolled, it will rise up and destroy you. Men's actions depend to a great extent upon fear. We do things either because we enjoy doing them or because we are afraid not to do them. This sort of fear has no relation to physical or moral courage. It is inspired by the knowledge that we are not adequately prepared to face the future and the events it may bring—poverty perhaps, or injury, or death.
JOHN F. MILBURN

The thing in the world I am most afraid of is fear.
MICHEL DE MONTAIGNE

He who is afraid of a thing gives it power over him.
MOORISH PROVERB

Fortunately for themselves and the world, nearly all men are cowards and dare not act on what they believe. Nearly all our disasters come of a few fools having the courage of their convictions.
COVENTRY PATMORE

It is their interest on earth, not their stake in eternity, that makes men cowards.
EDEN PHILLPOTTS

The fear of the Lord tendeth to life: and he that hath it shall abide satisfied; he shall not be visited with evil.
PROVERBS 19:23

God is our refuge and strength, a very present help in trouble. Therefore we will not we fear, though the earth be removed, and though the mountains be carried into the midst of the sea.
PSALMS 46:1–2

Present fears are less than horrible imaginings.
WILLIAM SHAKESPEARE

Things done well and with a care, exempt themselves from fear.
WILLIAM SHAKESPEARE

There is no fear without some hope, and no hope without some fear.
BARUCH SPINOZA

Fear fades when facts are faced.
FRANK TYGER

The reason we all like to think so well of others is that we are all afraid of ourselves. The basis of optimism is sheer terror.
OSCAR WILDE

Your fears can be overcome if you deal with them properly. Fear is an emotion. Emotions come wholly from within, and have only the strength we allow them. As human beings, we enjoy the possession of an intellect, and it is the intellect, not the emotions, that must be the supreme guiding force of our lives if we are to know any measure of happiness here.

Emotions are the color of life; we would be drab creatures indeed without them. But we must control those emotions or they will control us. This is particularly true of the emotion of fear, which if allowed free rein would reduce all of us to trembling shadows of men, for whom only death could bring release.
**JOHN M. WILSON**

## *Fight*

When the fight begins within himself, a man's worth something.
**ROBERT BROWNING**

Every act of rebelling expresses a nostalgia for innocence.
**ALBERT CAMUS**

A child's instinct is almost perfect in the matter of fighting. The child's hero is always the man or boy who defends himself suddenly and splendidly against aggression.
**G. K. CHESTERTON**

We should not forget that our tradition is one of protest and revolt, and it is stultifying to celebrate the rebels of the past . . . while we silence the rebels of the present.
**HENRY STEELE COMMAGER**

I purpose to fight it out on this line if it takes all summer.
**ULYSSES S. GRANT**

It isn't the size of the dog in the fight, but the size of the fight in the dog that counts.
**WOODY HAYES**

Fight! Be somebody! If you have lost confidence in yourself, make believe you are somebody else, somebody that's got brains, and act like him.
**SOL HESS**

A little rebellion is a medicine necessary for the sound health of government.
**THOMAS JEFFERSON**

## *Food*

Shake and shake
The catsup bottle,
None will come,
And then a lot'll.
**RICHARD ARMOUR**

Food: Part of the spiritual expression of the French, and I do not believe that they have ever heard of calories.
**BEVERLY BAXTER**

A gourmet can tell from the flavor whether a woodcock's leg is the one on which the bird is accustomed to roost.
**LUCIUS BEEBE**

Edible: Good to eat, and wholesome to digest, as a worm to a toad, a toad to a snake, a snake to a pig, a pig to a man, and a man to a worm.
**AMBROSE BIERCE**

I've been on a constant diet for the last two decades. I've lost a total of 789 pounds. By all accounts, I should be hanging from a charm bracelet.
**ERMA BOMBECK**

If what we already know were simply applied to all the agricultural land of the world and the problem of proper distribution were given consideration, the world could feed itself well.
**LOUIS BROMFIELD**

We are always giving foreign names to very native things. If there is a thing that reeks of the glorious tradition of the old English tavern, it is toasted cheese. But for some wild reason we call it Welsh rarebit. I believe that what we call Irish stew might more properly be called English stew, and that it is not particularly familiar in Ireland.
**G. K. CHESTERTON**

The more you eat, the less flavor; the less you eat, the more flavor.
**CHINESE PROVERB**

Whatever will satisfy hunger is good food.
**CHINESE PROVERB**

To eat is human; to digest, divine.
**CHARLES TOWNSEND COPELAND**

I've been on a diet for two weeks and all I've lost is two weeks.
**TOTIE FIELDS**

If you don't watch your figure, you'll have more figure to watch.
**MALCOLM FORBES**

Gourmet: Usually little more than a glutton festooned with charge cards.
**SYDNEY J. HARRIS**

Ye shall eat in plenty, and be satisfied, and praise the name of the Lord your God, that hath dealt wondrously with you; and my people shall never be ashamed.
**JOEL 2:26**

Not a deed would he do,
Not a word would he utter,
Till he's weighed its relation
To plain bread and butter.
**JAMES RUSSELL LOWELL**

Dieting: A system of starving yourself to death so you can live a little longer.
**JAN MURRAY**

Stomachs shouldn't be waist baskets.
**P. K. THOMAJAN**

Health food makes me sick.
**CALVIN TRILLIN**

The true Southern watermelon is a boon apart, and not to be mentioned with common things. It is chief of this world's luxuries, king by the grace of God over all the fruits of the earth. When one has tasted it, he knows what the angels eat. It was not a Southern watermelon that Eve took; we know it because she repented.
**MARK TWAIN**

When a poor man eats a chicken, one of them is sick.
**YIDDISH PROVERB**

## *Fools*

If a fool and his money are soon parted, why are there so many rich fools?
**ANONYMOUS**

There is a foolish corner in the brain of the wisest man.
**ARISTOTLE**

Only intuition can protect you from the most dangerous individual of all, the articulate incompetent.
**ROBERT BERNSTEIN**

Idiot: A member of a large and powerful tribe whose influence in human affairs has always been dominant and controlling.
**AMBROSE BIERCE**

Nature never makes any blunders; when she makes a fool she means it.
**JOSH BILLINGS**

Never play down the importance of incompetence in the organization. It has always been the seed of discontent, independence and successful entrepreneurship.
**WILLIAM BLISS**

Make it idiot-proof and someone will make a better idiot.
**BUMPER STICKER**

The greatest pleasure of a dog is that you may make a fool of yourself with him, and not only will he not scold you, but he will make a fool of himself, too.
**SAMUEL BUTLER**

Any fool can criticize, condemn, and complain—and most fools do.
**DALE CARNEGIE**

Young men think old men are fools, but old men know young men are fools.
**GEORGE CHAPMAN**

Gullibility is the key to all adventures. The greenhorn is the ultimate victor in everything; it is he that gets the most out of life.
**G. K. CHESTERTON**

Fool me once, shame on you; fool me twice, shame on me.
**CHINESE PROVERB**

It is the peculiar quality of a fool to perceive the faults of others and to forget his own.
**CICERO**

What the fool cannot learn, he laughs at, thinking that by his laughter he shows superiority instead of a latent idiocy.
**MARIE CORELLI**

To follow foolish precedents, and wink with both our eyes, is easier than to think.
**WILLIAM COWPER**

How to get taken: Spend most of your time making sure you're not.
**MALCOLM FORBES**

If 50 million people say a foolish thing, it is still a foolish thing.
**ANATOLE FRANCE**

Young people tell what they are doing, old people what they have done and fools what they wish to do.
**FRENCH PROVERB**

He who laughs at everything is as big a fool as he who weeps at everything.
**BALTASAR GRACIÁN**

Why fools are endowed by Nature with voices so much louder than sensible people possess is a mystery. It is a fact emphasized throughout history.
**HERTZLER**

The fool has set in his heart that he can get more money through the tiring of his muscle and the starvation of his brain—but he can't.
WILLIAM D. HOARD

He dares to be a fool, and that is the first step in the direction of wisdom.
JAMES GIBBONS HUNEKER

There are two kinds of fools. One says, "This is old, therefore it is good." The other says, "This is new, therefore it is better."
WILLIAM RALPH INGE

A fellow who is always declaring he's no fool usually has his suspicions.
WILSON MIZNER

An erudite fool is a greater fool than an ignorant fool.
MOLIÈRE

If fools and folly rule the world, the end of man in our time may come as a rude shock, but it will no longer come as a complete surprise.
ABDUL RAHMAN PAZHWAK

If you wish to avoid seeing a fool you must first break your mirror.
FRANÇOIS RABELAIS

Sometimes a fool has talent, but never judgment.
FRANÇOIS DE LA ROCHEFOUCAULD

Professing themselves to be wise, they became fools.
ROMANS 1:22

When we are born we cry that we are come to this great stage of fools.
WILLIAM SHAKESPEARE

Arguing with a fool proves there are two.
DORIS M. SMITH

When a fool has made up his mind the market has gone by.
SPANISH PROVERB

No man really becomes a fool until he stops asking questions.
CHARLES P. STEINMETZ

It is easy to fool yourself. It is more difficult to fool the people you work for. It is still more difficult to fool the people you work with. And it is almost impossible to fool the people who work under your direction.
HARRY B. THAYER

One's own incompetence is a difficult fact to accept.
TERRY M. TOWNSEND

That which the fool does in the end the wise man does in the beginning.
RICHARD TRENCH

July 4th: Statistics show that we lose more fools on this day than on all the other days of the year put together. This proves, by the number left in stock, that one Fourth of July per year is now inadequate, the country has grown so.
MARK TWAIN

Let us be thankful for the fools; but for them the rest of us could not succeed.
MARK TWAIN

A fool is his own informer.
YIDDISH PROVERB

Send a fool to close the shutters and he'll close them all over town.
YIDDISH PROVERB

## Forcefulness

Epithets are not arguments. Abuse does not persuade.
ROBERT G. INGERSOLL

Some degree of abuse is inseparable from the proper use of everything.
JAMES MADISON

Who overcomes by force, hath overcome but half his foe.
JOHN MILTON

Forces rule the world, and not opinion; but opinion is that which makes use of force.
BLAISE PASCAL

Forcefulness in the character of a chief executive is an invaluable quality.
ROBERT K. PATTERSON

## Forgiveness

God will forgive me; it's his line of business.
ANONYMOUS

Forgive many things in others; nothing in yourself.
AUSONIUS

They who forgive most, shall be most forgiven.
JOSIAH W. BAILEY

If men wound you with injuries, meet them with patience; hasty words rankle the wound, soft language dresses it, forgiveness cures it, and oblivion takes away the scar. It is more noble by silence to avoid an injury than by argument to overcome it.
FRANCIS BEAUMONT

Two persons cannot long be friends if they cannot forgive each other's little failings.
JEAN DE LA BRUYÈRE

He who forgives easily invites offense.
PIERRE CORNEILLE

If the people around you are spiteful and callous and will not hear you, fall down before them and beg their forgiveness; for in truth you are to blame for their not wanting to hear you.
FYODOR DOSTOYEVSKY

Let all bitterness, and wrath, and anger, and clamour, and evil speaking, be put away from you, with all malice; and be ye kind to one another, tenderhearted, forgiving one another, even as God for Christ's sake hath forgiven you.
EPHESIANS 4:31–32

The only unforgivable sin: Being unforgiving.
MALCOLM FORBES

He that cannot forgive others, breaks the bridge over which he must pass himself; for every man has need to be forgiven.
LORD HERBERT

The final test of a realistic Christian life is a forgiving heart. . . . The place where forgiveness begins is a troubled, anxious heart. You will never be able to forgive anybody until you yourself are deeply disturbed. To be able to forgive we must come down from the citadel of pride, from the stronghold of hate and anger, from the high place where all emotions that issue from one's sense of being wronged shout only for vengeance and retaliation.
JOHN HEUSS

One thing you will probably remember well is any time you forgive and forget.
FRANKLIN P. JONES

When a deep injury is done to us, we never recover until we forgive.
**ALAN PATON**

As freely as the firmament embraces the world, or the sun pours forth impartially his beams, so mercy must encircle both friend and foe.
**JOHANN FRIEDRICH VON SCHILLER**

Mercy is the twin sister of truth.
**GEORGE SEAVER**

How to forgive is something we have to learn, not as a duty or an obligation but as an experience akin to the experience of love; it must come into being spontaneously.
**THEODORE C. SPEERS, D.D.**

Always forgive your enemies, nothing annoys them so much.
**OSCAR WILDE**

Execute true judgment, and show mercy and compassions every man to his brother: and oppress not the widow, nor the fatherless, the stranger nor the poor; and let none of you imagine evil against his brother in your heart.
**ZECHARIAH 7:9–10**

## *Fortune*

Fortune is for all; judgment is theirs who have won it for themselves.
**AESCHYLUS**

If a man look sharply and attentively, he shall see Fortune; for though she is blind, she is not invisible.
**FRANCIS BACON**

It cannot be denied that outward accidents conduce much fortune, but chiefly, the mold of a man's fortune is in his hands.
**FRANCIS BACON**

The use we make of our fortune determines as to its sufficiency. A little is enough if used wisely, and too much if expended foolishly.
**CHRISTIAN BOVÉE**

There is nothing keeps longer than a middling fortune, and nothing melts away sooner than a great one. Poverty treads on the heels of great and unexpected riches.
**JEAN DE LA BRUYÈRE**

Fortune always leaves some door open in disasters whereby to come at a remedy.
**MIGUEL DE CERVANTES**

Fortune turns round like a millwheel, and he who was yesterday at the top, lies today at the bottom.
**MIGUEL DE CERVANTES**

The brave man carves out his fortune, and every man is the son of his own works.
**MIGUEL DE CERVANTES**

Man's life is ruled by fortune, not by wisdom.
**CICERO**

The wheel of fortune turns around incessantly, and who can say to himself, I shall today be uppermost.
**CONFUCIUS**

It is not Justice the servant of men, but accident, hazard, Fortune—the ally of patient Time—that holds an even and scrupulous balance.
**JOSEPH CONRAD**

No one is ever satisfied with his fortune or dissatisfied with his understanding.
ANTOINETTE DESHOULIÈRES

Fortune is an evil chain to the body, and vice to the soul.
EPICTETUS

Fortune favors the audacious.
DESIDERIUS ERASMUS

When fortune smiles, what need of friends?
EURIPIDES

He is a good man whom fortune makes better.
THOMAS FULLER

Fortune is ever seen accompanying industry.
OLIVER GOLDSMITH

Fortune often makes up for the eminence of office by the inferiority of the officeholder.
BALTASAR GRACIÁN

Fortune pays sometimes for the intensity of her favors by the shortness of their duration.
BALTASAR GRACIÁN

There sometimes wants only a stroke of fortune to discover numberless latent good or bad qualities, which would otherwise have been eternally concealed.
LORD GREVILLE

The greatest reverses of fortune are the most easily borne from a sort of dignity belonging to them.
WILLIAM HAZLITT

You never find people laboring to convince you that you may live very happily upon a plentiful fortune.
SAMUEL JOHNSON

I certainly think that it is better to be impetuous than cautious, for fortune is a woman, and it is necessary if you wish to master her, to conquer her by force.
NICCOLÒ MACHIAVELLI

Men may second fortune, but they cannot thwart her—They may weave her web, but they cannot break it.
NICCOLÒ MACHIAVELLI

Fortune gives many too much, but none enough.
MARTIAL

The tallest trees are most in the power of the winds, and ambitious men of the blasts of fortune.
WILLIAM PENN

Good fortune will elevate even petty minds, and give them the appearance of a certain greatness and stateliness, as from their high place they look down upon the world; but the truly noble and resolved spirit raises itself, and becomes more conspicuous in times of disaster and ill fortune.
PLUTARCH

I made my fortune by being able to spot a certain kind of man.
AYN RAND

Industry is fortune's right hand and frugality her left.
JOHN RAY

Fortunate people never correct themselves. They always fancy they are in the right as long as fortune supports their ill conduct.
FRANÇOIS DE LA ROCHEFOUCAULD

High fortune makes both our virtues and vices stand out as objects that are brought clearly to view by the light.
FRANÇOIS DE LA ROCHEFOUCAULD

It requires greater virtues to support good than bad fortune.
**FRANÇOIS DE LA ROCHEFOUCAULD**

The most brilliant fortunes are often not worth the littleness required to gain them.
**FRANÇOIS DE LA ROCHEFOUCAULD**

It requires a great deal of boldness and a great deal of caution to make a great fortune; and when you have got it, it requires ten times as much wit to keep it.
**MEYER ROTHSCHILD**

A great fortune is a great servitude.
**SENECA**

Happy is the man who can endure the highest and lowest fortune. He who has endured such vicissitudes with equanimity has deprived misfortune of its power.
**SENECA**

We are sure to get the better of fortune if we do but grapple with her.
**SENECA**

There is a tide in the affairs of men, which, taken at the flood, leads on to fortune; omitted, all the voyage of their life is bound in shallows and in miseries.
**WILLIAM SHAKESPEARE**

When fortune smiles,
I smile to think,
How quickly she will frown.
**ROBERT SOUTHWELL**

There is no fortune so good that you can find nothing in it to complain of.
**PUBLILIUS SYRUS**

This is the posture of fortune's slaves: one foot in the gravy, one foot in the grave.
**JAMES THURBER**

Whatever may happen, every kind of fortune is to be overcome by bearing it.
**VIRGIL**

One is never more on trial than in the moment of excessive good fortune.
**LEW WALLACE**

If Fortune calls, offer him a seat.
**YIDDISH PROVERB**

Many have been ruined by their fortune, and many have escaped ruin by the want of fortune. To obtain it the great have become little, and the little great.
**JOHANN ZIMMERMANN**

## *Free Enterprise*

Most of us in the United States believe strongly in free enterprise; but sometimes we forget that freedom and duty always go hand in hand, and that if the free do not accept social responsibility they will not remain free.
**JOHN FOSTER DULLES**

To the infantryman, his country's military might is only those buddies he can see, and the equipment they have at hand; likewise, to the wage-earner, free enterprise is primarily the way his boss treats him and those around him.
**MALCOLM FORBES**

The record seems to show that free enterprise is the only system of government in the world that is not

on trial. If it is on trial, why is America being called upon to save the world from economic chaos?
**WALTER S. GIFFORD**

We will endure . . . if we accept our obligation to maintain stability in our world by conserving the traditions and institutions of the past and encouraging the orderly forces of progress. Those of us who assume that the capitalist society can and must endure rally around these standards. We believe in property but know it can flourish only when innovation has free rein and new enterprises (with the personal rewards that must go with them) can emerge. We are devoted to the idea of equality . . . of opportunity to rise. We are committed to the idea of man's rationality and his ability to make free choices for his own betterment and that of society.
**LOUIS M. HACKER**

Our free enterprise system has supplied the incentive that has challenged every person to give his best in production and creation. Because the incentive has been attractive, we have become the greatest producing nation on earth. To any degree that the incentive to create and produce is restricted, we will be retarded in our progress to a better America.
**RALPH A. HAYWARD**

I think things that contribute to the destruction of our free-incentive system are wrong. A trend against that free-incentive system is wrong, and should only be temporarily engaged in, in the event that war or something of that kind requires it. Otherwise, it should be reduced.
**GEORGE HUMPHREY**

If business is going to continue to sell through the decades, it must also promote an understanding, of what made those products possible, what is necessary to a free market, and what our free market means to the individual liberty of each of us, to be certain that the freedoms under which this nation was born and brought to this point shall endure in the future . . . for America is the product of our freedoms.
**E. F. HUTTON**

Free enterprise is a rough and competitive game. It is a hell of a lot better than a government monopoly.
**RONALD REAGAN**

We must lift the level of understanding both at home and abroad of what the free enterprise system is, what it is not, and how it benefits the people who live under it. We must somehow get these elementary truths across, not only to the people of other lands but to millions here at home who do not understand it, if we are to generate a powerful demand and desire for its retention.
**PHILIP D. REED**

## *Freedom*

Posterity! You will never know how much it cost the present generation to preserve your freedom. I hope you will make good use of it.
**JOHN QUINCY ADAMS**

A dangerous fallacy is to repudiate freedom in favor of an unknown future. What else but our own sturdy reliance on freedom can explain the unexampled record this country has made? In a period scarcely twice my own lifetime, it has risen from nothingness to become the world's greatest power. It has become the ark of the covenant of freedom.
**BERNARD M. BARUCH**

The free man is not he who defies the rules . . . but he who, recognizing the compulsions inherent in his being, seeks rather to read, mark, learn, and inwardly digest each day's experience.
**BERNARD IDDINGS BELL, D.D.**

Freedom of press and freedom of speech: What a blessing for a country while in the hands of honest, patriotic men; what a curse if in the hands of designing demagogues.
**WILLIAM J. H. BOETCKER**

With the right of free speech goes the right of free silence, particularly when a citizen is challenged without the provision of procedure for a fair fight. And with it the duty, if we do speak, to speak not only freely but fully. There would be less and better talk if this duty were observed, for the difficulty is not so much with free speech as with free truth.
**CURTIS BOK**

Political freedom goes hand in hand with religious freedom. Wherever religion is free men can no longer be kept in chains. Religious freedom means liberty for all, with special favors to none.
**JOHN S. BONNELL, D.D.**

Without free speech no search for truth is possible; without free speech progress is checked and the nations no longer march forward toward the nobler life which the future holds for man. Better a thousandfold abuse of free speech than denial of free speech. The abuse dies in a day, but the denial stays the life of the people, and entombs the hope of the race.
**CHARLES BRADLAUGH**

Depend upon it that the lovers of freedom will be free.
**EDMUND BURKE**

The fifth freedom, the Freedom of Individual Enterprise, is the keystone of the arch on which the other Four Freedoms rest. This is what freedom means.
**NICHOLAS MURRAY BUTLER**

Human freedom is . . . an achievement by man, and, as it was gained by vigilance and struggle, it can be lost by indifference and supineness.
**HARRY F. BYRD**

The only freedom worth possessing is that which gives enlargement to a people's energy, intellect, and virtues. The savage makes his boast of freedom. But what is its worth? He is, indeed, free from what he calls the yoke of civil institutions. But other and worse chains bind him. The very privation of civil government is in effect a chain, for, by withholding protection from property it virtually shackles the arm of industry, and forbids exertion for the melioration of his lot. Progress, the growth of intelligence and power, is the end and boon of liberty; and, without this, a people may have the name, but want the substance and spirit of freedom.
**WILLIAM ELLERY CHANNING**

Safe popular freedom consists of four things: The diffusion of liberty, of intelligence, of property, and of conscientiousness, and cannot be compounded of any three out of the four.
**JOSEPH COOK**

Freedom is no heritage. Preservation of freedom is a fresh challenge and a fresh conquest for each generation. It is based on the religious concept of the dignity of man. The discovery that man is free is the greatest discovery of the ages.
**C. DONALD DALLAS**

The objectives of education and industry are identical. Both are interested in good citizenship, in serving society, in a better life—and both firmly believe in freedom.
**HERMAN L. DONOVAN**

The hope of freedom depends in real measure upon our strength, our heart, and our wisdom. We must be strong in arms. We must be strong in the source

of all our armament—our productivity. We all—workers and farmers, foremen and financiers, technicians and builders—all must produce, produce more and produce yet more. We must be strong, above all, in the spiritual resources upon which all else depends. We must be devoted with all our heart to the values we defend. We must know that each of these values and virtues applies with equal force at the ends of the earth and in our relations with our neighbor next door.
**DWIGHT D. EISENHOWER**

The supreme belief of our society is the dignity and freedom of the individual. To the respect of that dignity, to the defense of that freedom, all effort is pledged.
**DWIGHT D. EISENHOWER**

Freedom may come quickly in robes of peace or after ages of conflict and war, but come it will, and abide it will, so long as the principles by which it was acquired are held sacred.
**EDWARD EVERETT**

What's the very first step taken by every dictatorship since history has been recorded? The prohibition of free speech, the curbing and elimination of a free press. A perhaps unintended but insidious assault on the freedom of the press to probe, to inform, is the effort by the Department of Justice to subpoena journalists and force them to reveal sources of information. . . . The decision by a federal court upholding a journalist's right to protect his sources is immensely valuable to all. . . . To let rage and pique at the press, for good or bad reasons, lead to a curbing of enterprising reporting would be a disaster. . . .
**MALCOLM FORBES**

Without freedom of thought, there can be no such thing as wisdom; and no such thing as public liberty without freedom of speech; which is the right of every man as far as by it he does not hurt or control the right of another; and this is the only check it ought to suffer and the only bounds it ought to know. . . . Whoever would overthrow the liberty of a nation must begin by subduing the freedom of speech, a thing terrible to traitors.
**BENJAMIN FRANKLIN**

The measure of a democracy is the measure of the freedom of its humblest citizens.
**JOHN GALSWORTHY**

Freedom is not worth having if it does not connote freedom to err.
**MAHATMA GANDHI**

None are more hopelessly enslaved than those who falsely believe they are free.
**JOHANN WOLFGANG VON GOETHE**

Freedom for workers is in turn conditioned by freedom for enterprise.
**WILLIAM GREEN**

Freedom costs you a great deal.
**LILLIAN HELLMAN**

Perfect freedom is as necessary to the health and vigor of commerce as it is to the health and vigor of citizenship.
**PATRICK HENRY**

The basic test of freedom is perhaps less in what we are free to do than in what we are free not to do.
**ERIC HOFFER**

To some, freedom means the opportunity to do what they want to do; to most it means not to do what they don't want to do.
**ERIC HOFFER**

I wish I could tell you that as we enter the second half of this twentieth century the feeling for freedom is running high in these United States. Unfortunately, this is not so. We seem to be passing through a period in which there is altogether too much fear, suspicion and hate in the atmosphere.... We have no thought police here, but discussion, criticism and debate can be stifled by fear as well as by force. School teachers, government clerks and officials, and even businessmen, can be frightened out of their rights under the First Amendment as effectively as if that Amendment were repealed. Of all forms of tyranny over the mind of man, none is more terrible than fear—to be afraid of being one's self among one's neighbors.
**PAUL G. HOFFMAN**

If the free peoples of the world perform as I know they can perform, they will be able to reverse the classic Marxist slogan and say to the distressed and enslaved workers behind the Curtain: "Arise, you have nothing to lose but your chains."
**PAUL G. HOFFMAN**

Freedom of speech does not give a person the right to shout "Fire" in a crowded theater.
**OLIVER WENDELL HOLMES**

A splendid storehouse of integrity and freedom has been bequeathed to us by our forefathers. In this day of confusion, of peril to liberty, our high duty is to see that this storehouse is not robbed of its contents.
**HERBERT HOOVER**

A man who is willing to accept restriction and barriers and is not afraid of them is free. A man who does nothing but fight restrictions and barriers will usually be trapped.
**L. RON HUBBARD**

If business is going to continue to sell through the decades, it must also promote an understanding of what made those products possible, what is necessary to a free market, and what our free market means to the individual liberty of each of us, to be certain that the freedoms under which this nation was born and brought to this point shall endure in the future... for America is the product of our freedoms.
**E. F. HUTTON**

It is better for a man to go wrong in freedom than to go right in chains.
**THOMAS H. HUXLEY**

One should never put on one's best trousers to go out to fight for freedom.
**HENRIK IBSEN**

Freedom is a precious thing today. Those who have it cherish it; those who fear it, want to destroy it; and those who don't have it will still fight for it.
**HARVEY C. JACOBS**

Freedom of religion, freedom of the press, freedom of person under protection of habeas corpus; and trial by juries impartially selected, these principles form the bright constellation which has gone before us, and guided our steps through an age of revolution and reformation.
**THOMAS JEFFERSON**

In every country where man is free to think and to speak, difference of opinion will arise from difference of perception, and the imperfection of reason; but these differences, when permitted, as in this happy country, to purify themselves by free discussion, are but as passing clouds overspreading our land transiently, and leaving our horizon more bright and serene.
**THOMAS JEFFERSON**

If a nation expects to be ignorant and free, in a state of civilization, it expects what never was and never will be.
THOMAS JEFFERSON

Our greatest happiness does not depend on the condition of life in which chance has placed us, but is always the result of a good conscience, good health, occupation, and freedom in all just pursuits.
THOMAS JEFFERSON

It is well for us to remember that America is what it is today because alone of all the countries of the world, we have expanded under those Siamese twins, political and economic freedom.
W. ALTON JONES

Little by little, the nations whose people believe in freedom, but who are strong enough to repel aggression if necessary, are getting together, becoming more closely united. . . . Good neighbors, when menaced by gangsters, meet, agree on laws for protecting themselves from the lawless elements. To lead and show the way in this direction is America's greatest challenge.
ESTES KEFAUVER

People hardly ever make use of the freedom they have, for example, freedom of thought; instead they demand freedom of speech as a compensation.
SÖREN KIERKEGAARD

There are two freedoms, the false where one is free to do what he likes, and the true where he is free to do what he ought.
CHARLES KINGSLEY

The cause of freedom is identified with the destinies of humanity, and in whatever part of the world it gains ground by and by, it will be a common gain to all those who desire it.
LOUIS KOSSUTH

Shall any of us repine that it is our lot to live in perilous and sacrificial days? Rather I say we are glad that we live in this time of mortal struggle and are doing our share to put to flight the powers of darkness. Our children and grandchildren will be proud that this country saved freedom for itself by helping to preserve it for the world.
THOMAS W. LAMONT

Freedom is not what a man does, nor what he is permitted to do. Freedom is part of what a man is.
ROBERT LESSING

Freedom is the last, best hope of earth.
ABRAHAM LINCOLN

If destruction be our lot we must ourselves be its author and finisher. As a nation of free men we must live through all time, or die by suicide.
ABRAHAM LINCOLN

Those who deny freedom to others deserve it not for themselves, and, under a just God, cannot long retain it.
ABRAHAM LINCOLN

Freedom which has genuine meaning is more than a timeless abstraction, more than an absence of restraints. It is something shaped freshly in each generation wrestling with the conditions which, in that particular time, limit and extend freedom.
HELEN M. LYND

Real freedom comes from the mastery, through knowledge, of historic conditions and race character, which makes possible a free and intelligent use of experience for the purpose of progress.
HAMILTON WRIGHT MABIE

Many politicians lay it down as a self-evident proposition that no people ought to be free till they

are fit to use their freedom. The maxim is worthy of the fool in the old story, who resolved not to go into the water till he had learned to swim.
THOMAS B. MACAULAY

Free will is not the liberty to do whatever one likes, but the power of doing whatever one sees ought to be done, even in the very face of otherwise overwhelming impulse. There lies freedom, indeed.
GEORGE MACDONALD

Only those cities and countries that are free can achieve greatness. . . . In free countries we also see wealth increase more rapidly, both that which results from the culture of the soil and that which is produced by industry and art; for everybody gladly multiplies those things, and seeks to acquire those goods the possession of which he can tranquilly enjoy.
NICCOLÒ MACHIAVELLI

There are more instances of the abridgment of the freedom of the people by gradual and silent encroachments of those in power than by violent and sudden usurpation.
JAMES MADISON

The manner in which the hours of freedom are spent determines, no less than labor and war, the moral worth of a nation.
MAURICE MAETERLINCK

If a nation values anything more than freedom, it will lose its freedom; and the irony of it is that if it is comfort or money that it values more, it will lose that too.
SOMERSET MAUGHAM

No nation deserves freedom or can long retain it which does not win it for itself. Revolutions must be made by the people and for the people.
GIUSEPPI MAZZINI

Cementing the relationships of the free peoples is not a job for government or diplomats alone. A large responsibility rests upon all of us.
JOHN J. MCCLOY

There is no freedom for the weak.
GEORGE MEREDITH

A people may prefer a free government, but if from indolence, or carelessness, or cowardice, or want of public spirit, they are unequal to the exertions necessary for preserving it; if they will not fight for it when it is directly attacked; . . . if by momentary discouragement, or temporary panic, or a fit of enthusiasm for an individual, they can be induced to lay their liberties at the feet even of a great man, or trust him with powers which enable him to subvert their institutions—in all these cases they are more or less unfit for liberty; and even though it may be for their good to have had it even for a short time, they are unlikely long to enjoy it.
JOHN STUART MILL

The only freedom which deserves the name is that of pursuing our own good, in our own way, so long as we do not attempt to deprive others of theirs, or impede their efforts to obtain it.
JOHN STUART MILL

We are no more free agents than the queen of clubs when she victoriously takes prisoner the knave of hearts.
MARY WORTLEY MONTAGU

Countries are well cultivated, not as they are fertile, but as they are free.
BARON DE MONTESQUIEU

Those who expect to reap the blessing of freedom must undertake to support it.
THOMAS PAINE

Freedom is like a bag of sand. If there is a hole anywhere in the bag, all the sand will run out. If any group of our people are denied their rights, sooner or later all groups stand to lose their rights. All the freedom will run out.
ROBERT K. PATTERSON

No matter whose the lips that would speak, they must be free and ungagged. The community which dares not protect its humblest and most hated member in the free utterance of his opinions, no matter how false or hateful, is only a gang of slaves. If there is anything in the universe that can't stand discussion, let it crack.
WENDELL PHILLIPS

In order to improve the condition of mankind all men must be given the certainty of security through the exchange of safeguards, the assurance of prosperity through an exchange of resources, the reality of freedom through the free movement of information, persons and ideas.
ANTOINE PINAY

Eventually women will learn there's no such thing as freedom. Their husbands are just as fastened to the deck as they are. Men get onto a treadmill and never got off.
KATHERINE ANNE PORTER

Freedom is placed in jeopardy more by those who will not exercise it than by those who will not permit it. Indifference opens more gates to the enemy than does tyranny.
EDWIN MCNEILL POTEAT

We have come to world leadership because our people have had the opportunity to develop this nation under a government and a Constitution that gave them political freedom and encouraged initiative, enterprise, responsibility, industry and thrift. Freedom and achievement are not unrelated. This nation has become one of history's finest illustrations of how a people can enrich life and raise their whole level of economic well-being when they are given justice, liberty and incentive.
HERBERT V. PROCHNOW

To have freedom is only to have that which is absolutely necessary to enable us to be what we ought to be, and to possess what we ought to possess.
IBN RAHEL

Freedom without obligation is anarchy; freedom with obligation is democracy.
EARL RINEY

They say that freedom is a constant struggle, goes the old song. It is. It is also more than that. Freedom is the struggle. It is never achieved except in the effort to reach it.
WALLACE ROBERTS

We are told by some that we are slaves. If being a slave means doing only what we have to do, then must of us are in truth slaves, but he who does more than he is required to do becomes at once free. He is his own master. How often do we hear it said, "It was not my work." Too often we fix our minds almost entirely upon what we are going to get and give no thought at all as to what we are going to give in return.
A. W. ROBERTSON

The war for freedom will never really be won because the price of freedom is constant vigilance over ourselves and over our Government.
ELEANOR ROOSEVELT

Freedom is not now, any more than at any other time, something to be preserved; it is something to be created. Freedom cannot be protected; it can only be extended.
DAVID SMITH

Freedom must always be exercised under discipline, and post-war higher education will, I believe, rededicate itself to the high purpose of social and civic devotion to a unified, outgoing, outgiving, democratic America.
ROBERT GORDON SPROUL

Whoever will be free must make himself free. Freedom is no fairy gift to fall into a man's lap. What is freedom? To have the will to be responsible for one's self.
MAX STIRNER

Those who deny freedom to others deserve it not for themselves, and, under a just God, they cannot long retain it.
CHARLES SUMNER

In our country we have those three unspeakably precious things: freedom of speech, freedom of conscience, and the prudence never to practice either.
MARK TWAIN

Progress in America has resulted from the freedom of the individual to venture for himself and to assure the gains and take all the losses as they come.
ROBERT R. WASON

We should divest ourselves of any idea that if we do good work on our regular jobs, we do enough and that there is no need to concern ourselves about politics. We should make up our mind where we stand and why we stand there. We should base our position on deep principles—not on the happenings and personalities of the day. Of course, we should be active citizens. We should vote ourselves, and we should influence our families and as many others as possible to vote. We should be firmly confident that ours is the beneficial, the constructive way. The adherents of the various forms of socialism never tire in their efforts to make the State supreme. With the same zeal and with the weight of history on our side, we should become champions of personal freedom and the private way.
ERNEST T. WEIR

Freedom is an indivisible word. If we want to enjoy it, and fight for it, we must be prepared to extend it to everyone, whether they are rich or poor, whether they agree with us or not, no matter what their race or the color of their skin.
WENDELL WILLKIE

Freedom means that if you are a professor, you don't have to alter science or history as a bureaucrat prescribes. If you own a newspaper, you don't limit your editorial opinions to what an official censor approves. . . . If you think taxes are too high, you can vote against those officials you think responsible. And there is no limitation upon your inherent American right to criticize anybody, anywhere, at any time.
WENDELL WILLKIE

We must unleash the energies of men, but we must in our revolution save this free way of life, bring well-being to a larger and larger number of people.
WENDELL WILLKIE

Only free people can hold their purpose and their honor steady to a common end, and prefer the interests of mankind to any narrow interest of their own.
WOODROW WILSON

Freedom dies with every individual; it is not reborn with his successors; it must be achieved anew, generation by generation.
HENRY M. WRISTON

## *Friendship*

Nothing in this world appeases loneliness as does a flock of friends! You can select them at random, write to one, dine with one, visit one, or take your problems to one. There is always at least one who will understand, inspire, and give you the lift you may need at the time. Fortify yourself with a flock of friends!
GEORGE MATTHEW ADAMS

One friend in a lifetime is much; two are many; three are hardly possible.
HENRY ADAMS

The influence of each human being on others in this life is a kind of immortality.
JOHN QUINCY ADAMS

Friendship improves happiness, and abates misery, by doubling our joy, and dividing our grief.
JOSEPH ADDISON

A doubtful friend is worse than a certain enemy. Let a man be one or the other, and then we know how to meet him.
AESOP

Love is blind; friendship closes its eyes.
ANONYMOUS

The best way to knock the chip off someone's shoulder is to pat him on the back.
ANONYMOUS

Am I united with my friend in heart, what matters if our places be wide apart!
ANWAR-I-SUHEILI

A friend is known when needed.
ARABIAN PROVERB

I keep my friends as misers do their treasure, because, of all things granted us by wisdom, none is greater or better than friendship.
PIETRO ARETINO

Friends are an aid to the young, to guard them from error; to the elderly, to attend to their wants and to supplement their failing power of action; to those in the prime of life, to assist them to noble deeds.
ARISTOTLE

Wishing to be friends is quick work, but friendship is a slow-ripening fruit.
ARISTOTLE

A friend is one who sees through you and still enjoys the view.
WILMA ASKINAS

No receipt openeth the heart but a true friend, to whom you may impart griefs, joys, fears, hopes, suspicions, counsels, and whatsoever lieth upon the heart to oppress it, in a kind of civil shrift or confession.
FRANCIS BACON

The communicating of a man's self to his friend works two contrary effects; for it redoubleth joys, and cutteth griefs in half.
FRANCIS BACON

The worst solitude is to be destitute of sincere friendship.
FRANCIS BACON

Courtesy is really nothing more than a form of friendliness. It is amazing what a warming influence it can have on an otherwise dreary world. It

has been said that a rise of one degree Fahrenheit in the mean annual temperature of the globe would free both polar regions from their ice. It is thrilling to contemplate what frigidity might be dispelled in the world of human relations if people made just a little better effort to be friendly.
M. BARTOS

Every man should have a fair-sized cemetery in which to bury the faults of his friends.
HENRY WARD BEECHER

You will make more friends in a week by getting yourself interested in other people than you can in a year by trying to get other people interested in you.
ARNOLD BENNETT

Friendship: A ship big enough to carry two in fair weather, but only one in foul.
AMBROSE BIERCE

While your friend holds you affectionately by both your hands you are safe, for you can watch both his.
AMBROSE BIERCE

Friendship is a word the very sight of which in print can make the heart warm.
AUGUSTINE BIRRELL

Friendships are fragile things, and require as much care in handling as any other fragile and precious thing.
RANDOLPH S. BOURNE

Friendship is a strong and habitual inclination in two persons to promote the good happiness of one another.
EUSTACE BUDGELL

There is no man so friendless but what he can find a friend sincere enough to tell him disagreeable truths.
EDWARD BULWER-LYTTON

Friendship is like money, easier made than kept.
SAMUEL BUTLER

You can make more friends in two months by becoming really interested in other people, than you can in two years by trying to get other people interested in you.
DALE CARNEGIE

He is our friend who loves more than admires us, and would aid us in our great work.
WILLIAM ELLERY CHANNING

Real friendship is a slow grower and never thrives unless engrafted upon a stock of known and reciprocal merit.
LORD CHESTERFIELD

He who cannot in his own house entertain a guest, when abroad will find few to entertain him.
CHINESE PROVERB

There is only one thing worse than fighting with allies and that is fighting without them.
WINSTON CHURCHILL

A friend is, as it were, a second self.
CICERO

Friendship is the only thing in the world concerning the usefulness of which all mankind are agreed.
CICERO

No discord should arise between friends, but if it does, then our care should be that the friendship

appear to have burned out rather than to have been stamped out.
CICERO

To accept a favor from a friend is to confer one.
JOHN CHURTON COLLINS

Friendship that flows from the heart cannot be frozen by adversity, as the water that flows from the spring cannot congeal in winter.
JAMES FENIMORE COOPER

Nothing is more limiting than a closed circle of acquaintanceship where every avenue of conversation has been explored and social exchanges are fixed in a known routine.
ARCHIBALD J. CRONIN

We are each of us angels with only one wing, and we can only fly by embracing each other.
LUCIANO DE CRESCENZO

The stranger in the land who looks into ten thousand faces for some answering look and never finds it, is in cheering society as compared with him who passes ten averted faces daily, that were once the countenances of friends.
CHARLES DICKENS

Make a better friend of every man with whom you come in contact.
HENRY L. DOHERTY

Forsake not an old friend, for a new one does not compare with him.
ECCLESIASTICUS 9:10

I have friends in overalls whose friendship I would not swap for the favor of the kings of the world.
THOMAS EDISON

What do we live for, if it is not to make life less difficult for each other?
GEORGE ELIOT

A friend is a person before whom I may think aloud.
RALPH WALDO EMERSON

Friends should be like books, easy to find when you need them, but seldom used.
RALPH WALDO EMERSON

Go often to the house of thy friend, for weeds choke the unused path.
RALPH WALDO EMERSON

I am for frank explanations with friends in cases of affronts. They sometimes save a perishing friendship or place it on a firmer basis than before. But secret discontent must always end badly.
RALPH WALDO EMERSON

It is one of the blessings of old friends that you can afford to be stupid with them.
RALPH WALDO EMERSON

The only way to have a friend is to be one.
RALPH WALDO EMERSON

In prosperity it is very easy to find a friend; in adversity, nothing is so difficult.
EPICTETUS

It is a good thing to be rich, it is a good thing to be strong, but it is a better thing to be beloved of many friends.
EURIPIDES

To complain that life has no joys while there is a single creature whom we can relieve by our bounty, assist by our counsels, or enliven by our presence, is to lament the loss of that which we possess, and is

just as rational as to die of thirst with the cup in our hands.
**THOMAS FITZOSBORNE**

Who enters my house as a friend will never be too early, always too late.
**FLEMISH PROVERB**

A certain ultra-dignified gentleman of unusual prominence carried himself so stiffly that nobody felt free to call him by his first name. He quarreled with a friend of earlier days and from then on the two never spoke. The day the friend died an associate found the ultra-dignified gentleman staring through the window. When he came out of his reverie, he soliloquized with a sigh, "He was the last to call me John." Is any man really entitled to regard himself a success who has failed to inspire at least a goodly number of fellow mortals to greet him by his first name?
**B. C. FORBES**

The way to make a true friend is to be one. Friendship implies loyalty, esteem, cordiality, sympathy, affection, readiness to aid, to help, to stick, to fight for, if need be. The real friend is he or she who can share all our sorrows and double our joys Radiate friendship and it will return sevenfold.
**B. C. FORBES**

Nothing hurts more than the friendly letter that one never got around to writing.
**BRENDAN FRANCIS**

I sincerely believe that the word relationships is the key to the prospect of a decent world. It seems abundantly clear that every problem you will have—in your family, in your work, in our nation, or in this world—is essentially a matter of relationships, of interdependence.
**CLARENCE FRANCIS**

A brother may not be a friend, but a friend will always be a brother.
**BENJAMIN FRANKLIN**

Years and years of happiness only make us realize how lucky we are to have friends that have shared and made that happiness a reality.
**ROBERT E. FREDERICK**

The first condition under which we can know a man at all is, that he be in essentials something like ourselves.
**J. A. FROUDE**

He is my friend, that succoreth me, not he that pitieth me.
**THOMAS FULLER**

A true friend never gets in your way unless you happen to be going down.
**ARNOLD GLASOW**

So live that your friends can defend you, but never have to.
**ARNOLD GLASOW**

Tell me with whom thou art found, and I will tell thee who thou art.
**JOHANN WOLFGANG VON GOETHE**

A man is judged by his friends, for the wise and the foolish have never agreed.
**BALTASAR GRACIÁN**

The friend of my adversity I shall always cherish most. I can better trust those who helped to relieve the gloom of my dark hours than those who are so ready to enjoy with me the sunshine of my prosperity.
**ULYSSES S. GRANT**

Who ceases to be a friend never was one.
GREEK PROVERB

It is great to have friends when one is young, but indeed it is still more so when you are getting old. When we are young, friends are, like everything else, a matter of course. In the old days we know what it means to have them.
EDVARD GRIEG

I do not think anybody in the world had so many friends as I have had. However, I once had an enemy, a determined enemy, and I have been trying all day to remember his name.
EDWARD E. HALE

The making of friends who are real friends, is the best token we have of a man's success in life.
EDWARD E. HALE

In this job I am not worried about my enemies. I can take care of them. It is my friends who are giving me trouble.
WARREN G. HARDING

Make all men your well-wishers, and then—in the year's steady sifting—some of them will turn into friends; and friends are the sunshine of life.
JOHN HAY

When you are friendly you are automatically inviting, and unconsciously developing, potential business. . . . The odds are always with the friendly representative, all other things being equal; and in many instances friendliness can compensate when all other things are not precisely equal.
HENRY W. HAYES

Friendship with the evil is like the shadow in the morning, decreasing every hour, but friendship with the good is like the evening shadows, increasing till the sun of life sets.
JOHANN GOTTFRIED VON HERDER

The best things in life are never rationed. Friendship, loyalty, love do not require coupons.
GEORGE T. HEWITT

Strangers are what friends are made of.
CULLEN HIGHTOWER

Brotherhood doesn't come in a package. It is not a commodity to be taken down from the shelf with one hand—it is an accomplishment of soul-searching prayer, and perseverance. . . . The spontaneous feeling of brotherhood is a mark of human maturity.
OVETA CULP HOBBY

One thing everybody in the world wants and needs is friendliness.
WILLIAM E. HOLLER

The man or woman who treasures his friends is usually solid gold himself.
MARJORIE HOLMES

Don't flatter yourself that friendship authorizes you to say disagreeable things to your intimates. The nearer you come into relation with a person, the more necessary does tact and courtesy become. Except in cases of necessity, which are rare, leave your friend to learn unpleasant things from his enemies; they are ready enough to tell him.
OLIVER WENDELL HOLMES

Instead of loving your enemies, treat your friends a little better.
EDGAR WATSON HOWE

Choose thy friends like thy books, few but choice.
**JAMES HOWELL**

A friend is a person who knows all about you—and still likes you.
**ELBERT HUBBARD**

In order to have friends, you must first be one.
**ELBERT HUBBARD**

Blessed are they who have the gift of making friends, for it is one of God's best gifts. It involves many things, but above all, the power of going out of one's self, and appreciating whatever is noble and loving in another.
**THOMAS HUGHES**

The free conversation of a friend is what I would prefer to any environment.
**DAVID HUME**

### Magic Medicine

There's a heap o' consolation
In the handclasp o' a friend;
It can wipe out desolation,
An' bring heartaches to an end;
It can soothe a troubled spirit
Like no magic in the land;
Heaven? You are pretty near it—
When a good friend grips your hand!
There's a heap o' satisfaction
In a friendly shoulder pat;
It's a simple little action—
But a mighty one, at that!
When firm fingers grip your shoulder,
When you sort o' need a brace,
Makes you stronger, braver, bolder,
An' more fit to run the race!
When you're full o' worry pizen,
An' the world is lookin' drear,
There's a heap o' energizin'
In a little pill o' cheer!
When some little frets distress you,
They put nectar in your cup—
Little phrases like God bless you!
An' the other one, Cheer up!
**JAMES EDWARD HUNGERFORD**

There is an emanation from the heart in genuine hospitality which cannot be described, but is immediately felt and puts the stranger at once at his ease.
**WASHINGTON IRVING**

Make no man your friend before inquiring how he has used his former friends; for you must expect him to treat you as he has treated them. Be slow to give your friendship, but when you have given it, strive to make it lasting; for it is as reprehensible to make many changes in one's associates as to have no friends at all. Neither test your friends to your own injury nor be willing to forego a test of your companions.
**ISOCRATES**

I have never considered a difference of opinion in politics, in religion, in philosophy, as a cause for withdrawing from a friend.
**THOMAS JEFFERSON**

Never have a friend that's poorer than yourself.
**DOUGLAS WILLIAM JERROLD**

Friendship, like love, is destroyed by long absence, though it may be increased by short intermissions.
**SAMUEL JOHNSON**

If a man does not make new acquaintance as he advances through life, he will soon find himself left alone. A man, sir, should keep his friendship in constant repair.
**SAMUEL JOHNSON**

To those who have lived long together, everything heard and everything seen recalls some pleasure communicated, some benefit conferred, some petty quarrel or some slight endearment. Esteem of great powers, or amiable qualities newly discovered may embroider a day or a week, but a friendship of twenty years is interwoven with the texture of life.
SAMUEL JOHNSON

Friends are thieves of time.
LATIN PROVERB

Let us be brothers—or I'll cut your throat.
ECOUCHARD LEBRUN-PINDARE

There is only one thing better than making a new friend, and that is keeping an old one.
ELMER G. LETERMAN

If you would win a man to your cause, first convince him that you are his true friend. Therein is a drop of honey that catches his heart, which, say what he will, is the greatest highroad to his reason, and which when once gained, you will find but little trouble in convincing his judgment of the justice of your cause, if, indeed, that cause be really a just one. On the contrary, assume to dictate to his judgment, or to command his action, or to make him as one to be shunned or despised, and he will retreat within himself, close all the avenues to his head and heart; and though your cause be naked truth itself, transformed to the heaviest lance, harder than steel and sharper than steel can be made, and though you throw it with more than Herculean force and precision, you shall be no more able to pierce him than to penetrate the hard shell of a tortoise with a rye straw.
ABRAHAM LINCOLN

The better part of one's life consists of his friendships.
ABRAHAM LINCOLN

Platonic friendship: the interval between the introduction and the first kiss.
SOPHIE IRENE LOEB

Everyone must have felt that a cheerful friend is like a sunny day, which sheds its brightness on all around; and most of us can, as we choose, make of this world either a palace or a prison.
JOHN LUBBOCK

No small part of the cruelty, oppression, miscalculation, and general mismanagement of human relations is due to the fact that in our dealings with others we do not see them as persons at all, but only as specimens or representatives of some type or other. . . . We react to the sample instead of to the real person.
ROBERT J. MACIVER

In time of great anxiety we can draw power from our friends. We should at such times, however, avoid friends who sympathize too deeply, who give us pity rather than strength. Like so many unwise parents, such friends—well meaning, though they be—give set lessons in fear rather than in courage. It is said that Napoleon before one of his great battles used to invite his marshals to file past his tent, where he grasped their hands in silence. Certain friends, like Napoleon, can give us a sense of triumphing power.
D. LUPTON

I will destroy my enemies by converting them to friends.
MAIMONIDES

There is a world of difference between the mass gregariousness which has for so long been the admired hallmark of American friendliness and the real, deep, sustained emotions of friendship.
MARYA MANNES

There is a way of speaking of people which has the mystical power of calling forth friendship and love for them—originating in friendship and love itself.
HANS MARGOLIUS

The ability to form friendships, to make people believe in you and trust you is one of the few absolutely fundamental qualities of success. Selling, buying, negotiating are so much smoother and easier when the parties enjoy each other's confidence. The young man who can make friends quickly will find that he will glide instead of stumble through life.
JOHN J. MCGUIRK

He alone has lost the art to live who cannot win new friends.
S. WEIR MITCHELL

It is part of the business of life to be affable and pleasing to those whom either nature, chance or circumstance has made our companions.
SIR THOMAS MORE

God gives us our relatives; thank God we can choose our friends.
ETHEL MUMFORD

What are friends for if you don't use them?
FREDDIE MYERS

Love demands infinitely less than friendship.
GEORGE JEAN NATHAN

Sometimes we owe a friend to the lucky circumstance that we give him no cause for envy.
FRIEDRICH WILHELM NIETZSCHE

I love a hand that meets my own with a grasp that causes some sensation.
FRANCIS S. OSGOOD

Could we see when and where we are to meet again, we would be more tender when we bid our friends goodbye.
OUIDA

A true friend unbosoms freely, advises justly, assists readily, adventures boldly, takes all patiently, defends courageously, and continues a friend unchangeably.
WILLIAM PENN

There can be no friendship where there is no freedom. Friendship loves a free air, and will not be fenced up in straight and narrow enclosures.
WILLIAM PENN

You can always tell a real friend: When you've made a fool of yourself he doesn't feel you've done a permanent job.
LAURENCE J. PETER

If you conceal your secret from your friend, you deserve to lose him.
PORTUGUESE PROVERB

That friendship will not continue to the end which is begun for an end.
FRANCIS QUARLES

Let us never adopt the maxim, Rather lose our friend than our jest.
QUINTILIAN

In a letter to a friend the thought is often unimportant, and the feeling, if it be only a desire to entertain him, everything.
SIR WALTER RALEIGH

We learn our virtues from the friends who love us; our faults from the enemy who hates us. We cannot easily discover our real character from a friend. He

is a mirror, on which the warmth of our breath impedes the clearness of the reflection.
JEAN PAUL RICHTER

A true friend is the greatest of all blessings, and that which we take the least care of all to acquire.
FRANÇOIS DE LA ROCHEFOUCAULD

A friendship founded on business is a good deal better than a business founded on friendship.
JOHN D. ROCKEFELLER

Be kindly affectioned one to another with brotherly love; in honor preferring one another; not slothful in business; fervent in spirit; serving the Lord; rejoicing in hope; patient in tribulation; continuing instant in prayer.
ROMANS 12:10–12

Brotherhood is the very price and condition of man's survival.
CARLOS P. ROMULO

There should be no inferiors and no superiors for true world friendship.
CARLOS P. ROMULO

The only true solution of our political and social problems lies in cultivating everywhere the spirit of brotherhood, of fellow feeling and understanding between man and man, and the willingness to treat a man as a man.
THEODORE ROOSEVELT

Friendship is almost always the union of a part of one mind with a part of another; people are friends in spots.
GEORGE SANTAYANA

Every time I paint a portrait I lose a friend.
JOHN SINGER SARGENT

Humanity cannot go forward, civilization cannot advance, except as the philosophy of force is replaced by that of human brotherhood. These two never can be reconciled, for they are postulated on altogether different and profoundly conflicting appraisals of human values. Wherever the philosophy of force establishes domination, civilization as we know it ends.
FRANCIS B. SAYRE

Be friends with everybody. When you have friends you will know there is somebody who will stand by you. You know the old saying, that if you have a single enemy you will find him everywhere. It doesn't pay to make enemies. Lead the life that will make you kindly and friendly to every one about you, and you will be surprised what a happy life you will live.
CHARLES M. SCHWAB

If you have no friends to share or rejoice in your success in life—if you cannot look back to those to whom you owe gratitude, or forward to those to whom you ought to afford protection, still it is no less incumbent on you to move steadily in the path of duty; for your active exertions are due not only to society; but in humble gratitude to the Being who made you a member of it, with powers to serve yourself and others.
SIR WALTER SCOTT

Be a friend to yourself, and others will.
SCOTTISH PROVERB

Counsel your friend on all things, especially on those which respect yourself. His counsel may then be useful where your own self-love might impair your judgment.
SENECA

The only service a friend can really render is to keep up your courage by holding up to you a mirror in which you can see a noble image of yourself.
GEORGE BERNARD SHAW

The worst cliques are those which consist of one man.
**GEORGE BERNARD SHAW**

The best time to frame an answer to the letters of a friend is the moment you receive them; then the warmth of friendship and the intelligence received most forcibly cooperate.
**WILLIAM SHENSTONE**

Love and friendship are the discoveries of ourselves in others, and our delight in the recognition; and in men, as in books, we only know that, the parallel of which we have in ourselves.
**ALEXANDER SMITH**

I can't forgive my friends for dying; I don't find these vanishing acts of theirs at all amusing.
**LOGAN PEARSALL SMITH**

Life is the continuous adjustment of internal relations to external relations.
**HERBERT SPENCER**

There is wisdom in generosity, as in everything else. A friend to everybody is often a friend to nobody.
**CHARLES H. SPURGEON**

A friend is a present you give yourself.
**ROBERT LOUIS STEVENSON**

We are all travelers in the desert of life and the best we can find in our journey is an honest friend.
**ROBERT LOUIS STEVENSON**

The essence of true friendship is to make allowances for one another's little lapses.
**DAVID STOREY**

We inherit our relatives and our features and may not escape them; but we can select our clothing and our friends, and let us be careful that both fit us.
**VOLNEY STREAMER**

When we are old, our friends find it difficult to please us, and are less concerned whether we be pleased or not.
**JONATHAN SWIFT**

We would all rather be in the company of somebody we like than in the company of the most superior being of our acquaintance.
**FRANK SWINNERTON**

Unless you make allowances for your friend's foibles, you betray your own.
**PUBLILIUS SYRUS**

We die as often as we lose a friend.
**PUBLILIUS SYRUS**

Although I love my friend because he is worthy, yet he is not worthy if he can do me no good.
**JEREMY TAYLOR**

Friendship is the allay of our sorrows, the ease of our passions, the discharge of our oppressions, the sanctuary to our calamities, the counselor of our doubts, the clarity of our minds, the emission of our thoughts, the exercise and improvement of what we dedicate.
**JEREMY TAYLOR**

Friendship is never established as an understood relation. It is a miracle which requires constant proofs. It is an exercise of the purest imagination and of the rarest faith!
**HENRY DAVID THOREAU**

The most I can do for my friend is simply to be his friend.
HENRY DAVID THOREAU

John Adams and Thomas Jefferson were political enemies, but they became fast friends. And when they passed away on the same day, the last words of one of them was, "The country is safe. Jefferson still lives." And the last words of the other was, "John Adams will see that things go forward."
HARRY S TRUMAN

The holy passion of Friendship is of so sweet and enduring a nature that it will last through a whole lifetime, if not asked to lend money.
MARK TWAIN

Good friends are like shock absorbers. They help you take the lumps and bumps on the road of life.
FRANK TYGER

Friendship consists of a willing ear, an understanding heart and a helping hand.
FRANK TYGER

I want no men around me who have not the knack of making friends.
FRANK A. VANDERLIP

One discovers a friend by chance, and cannot but feel regret that 20 or 30 years of life may have been spent without the least knowledge of him.
CHARLES DUDLEY WARNER

Be not forward, but friendly and courteous; the first to salute, hear and answer; and be not pensive when it is time to converse.
GEORGE WASHINGTON

We cherish our friends not for their ability to amuse us but for ours to amuse them.
EVELYN WAUGH

Every organism requires an environment of friends, partly to shield it from violent changes, and partly to supply it with its wants.
ALFRED NORTH WHITEHEAD

An acquaintance that begins with a compliment is sure to develop into a real friendship.
OSCAR WILDE

Friendship is the only cement that will hold the world together.
WOODROW WILSON

The workingman must not lose sight of the fact that the principle of brotherhood is applicable to all men, regardless of capital or poverty.
JOHN LEWIS ZACKER, D.D.

## *Future*

The future you shall know when it has come; before then, forget it.
AESCHYLUS

Work for your future as if you are going to live forever, for your afterlife as if you are going to die tomorrow.
ARABIAN PROVERB

The future is like heaven—everyone exalts it but no one wants to go there now.
JAMES BALDWIN

We steal if we touch tomorrow. It is God's.
HENRY WARD BEECHER

The lives and happiness of our children, as far ahead as the mind can reach, depend on us today. If we

succeed, posterity looking back will record that this was indeed man's finest hour.
CARL A. BERENDSEN

Future: That period of time in which our affairs prosper, our friends are true and our happiness is assured.
AMBROSE BIERCE

Don't ever prophesy: for if you prophesy wrong, nobody will forget it; and if you prophesy right, nobody will remember it.
JOSH BILLINGS

You can never plan the future by the past.
EDMUND BURKE

Real generosity toward the future consists in giving all to what is present.
ALBERT CAMUS

God's tomorrow will be better than any yesterday you have ever known.
THOMAS A. CARRUTH

He who lives in the future lives in a featureless blank; he lives in impersonality; he lives in Nirvana. The past is democratic, because it is a people. The future is despotic, because it is a caprice. Every man is alone in his prediction, just as each man is alone in a dream.
G. K. CHESTERTON

If we open a quarrel between the past and the present, we shall find that we have lost the future.
WINSTON CHURCHILL

The empires of the future are the empires of the mind.
WINSTON CHURCHILL

There is no future in any job. The future lies in the man who holds the job.
GEORGE CRANE

The world is full of people whose notion of a satisfactory future is, in fact, a return to the idealized past.
ROBERTSON DAVIES

The future belongs to those who are virile, to whom it is a pleasure to live, to create, to whet their intelligence on that of the others.
SIR HENRI DETERDING

The hinge of the future is on the door of the present. Keep men of honor and integrity in places of trust and you will not fear the future.
MARTIN DE VRIES

To provide for the future is a part of one's responsibility in life; and the world has scant consideration for the man who neglects it.
HENRY L. DOHERTY

Everyone's future is, in reality, an urn full of unknown treasures from which all may draw unguessed prizes.
LORD DUNSANY

Neither a wise man nor a brave man lies down on the tracks of history to wait for the train of the future to run over him.
DWIGHT D. EISENHOWER

If a man carefully examine his thoughts he will be surprised to find how much he lives in the future. His well-being is always ahead. Such a creature is probably immortal.
RALPH WALDO EMERSON

The man least dependent upon the morrow goes to meet the morrow most cheerfully.
EPICURUS

The future that we study and plan for begins today.
CHESTER O. FISCHER

Nobody can really guarantee the future. The best we can do is size up the chances, calculate the risks involved, estimate our ability to deal with them and then make our plans with confidence.
HENRY FORD II

It is a poor and disgraceful thing not to be able to reply, with some degree of certainty, to the simple questions, "What will you be? What will you do?"
JOHN FOSTER

That man is prudent who neither hopes nor fears anything from the uncertain events of the future.
ANATOLE FRANCE

To pierce the curtain of the future, to give shape and visage to mysteries still in the womb of time, is the gift of the imagination. It requires poetic sensibilities with which judges are rarely endowed and which their education does not normally develop.
FELIX FRANKFURTER

The danger of the past was that men became slaves. The danger of the future is that men may become robots.
ERICH FROMM

Some new machinery with adequate powers must be created now if our fine phrases and noble sentiments are to have substance and meaning for our children.
JAMES WILLIAM FULBRIGHT

It is better to have a hen tomorrow than an egg today.
THOMAS FULLER

Very specific and personal misfortune awaits those who presume to believe that the future is revealed to them.
JOHN KENNETH GALBRAITH

There are admirable potentialities in every human being. Believe in your strength and your youth. Learn to repeat endlessly to yourself: It all depends on me.
ANDRÉ GIDE

We are always looking to the future; the present does not satisfy us. Our ideal, whatever it may be, lies further on.
EZRA GILLETT

Never before has the future so rapidly become the past.
ARNOLD GLASOW

The hours we pass with happy prospects in view are more pleasing than those crowded with fruition.
OLIVER GOLDSMITH

Somewhere among the youth of today are minds capable of discovering ways to world peace, ways to deeper and more fulfilling lives, ways to new appreciations of beauty in art or literature or music, just as there have been minds capable of splitting the atom. Ours is the task of breaking the thought barrier which keeps our young people from realizing their creative potentiality.
SAMUEL B. GOULD

It is a great deed to leave nothing for tomorrow.
BALTASAR GRACIÁN

When you arrive at your future, will you blame your past?
**ROBERT HALF**

All of us must rid ourselves of the illusion that we can buy our way out of the problems of today by mortgaging the future.
**EDWARD HEATH**

In a world of checks and balances, the most successful man often is the one who stores up credits for the future rather than the one who insists on a daily quota of praise, reward and compensation for all he gives or does. There may seem to be injustices and inequities as we go along in living, but very often, in looking back, hardships and heartaches have turned out to be disguised blessings, hardening us for a crisis or a job or a condition which otherwise we might have been unable to handle creditably.
**EDGAR PAUL HERMANN**

What the future holds for us, depends on what we hold for the future. Hard working todays make high-winning tomorrows.
**WILLIAM E. HOLLER**

The future always holds something for the man who keeps his faith in it.
**H. L. HOLLIS**

I do not pin my dreams for the future to my country or even to my race. I think it probable that civilization somehow will last as long as I care to look ahead.
**OLIVER WENDELL HOLMES**

I have always sought to guide the future—but it is very lonely sometimes trying to play God.
**OLIVER WENDELL HOLMES**

We are not such pygmies as we sometimes think. I believe we are actually giants, with potentialities far greater than we perceive. We use less than 10 per cent of our powers, we are told. Why not try to release another small percentage at least? Even one per cent of what we have would be 10 per cent added to what we use, and 10 per cent is a large margin of profit in any enterprise.
**GARDNER HUNTING**

Ye that say, today or tomorrow we will go into such a city, and continue there a year, and buy and sell, and make gain: Whereas ye know not what shall be on the morrow. For what is your life? It is even a vapour, that appeareth for a little time, and then vanisheth away.
**JAMES 4:13–14**

He who can see three days ahead will be rich for three thousand years.
**JAPANESE PROVERB**

For the industrious, thinking, right-living young man the future holds as many rewards as any period in our nation's history.
**WILLIAM M. JEFFERS**

I like the dreams of the future better than the history of the past.
**THOMAS JEFFERSON**

The future belongs to the things that can grow, whether it be a tree or democracy.
**KENNETH D. JOHNSON**

Cheer up! The worst is yet to come.
**PHILANDER JOHNSON**

The future is purchased by the present.
**SAMUEL JOHNSON**

The testimony of every scientist is that the frontiers that are opening out ahead of us now are far wider and more spectacular than any frontier of America in the past. Our horizons are not closed. We are going to write a greater development in America than has ever been conceived.
ERIC A. JOHNSTON

The future is not in the hands of fate but in ours.
JULES JUSSERAND

The great French Marshal Lyautey once asked his gardener to plant a tree. The gardener objected that the tree was slow-growing and would not reach maturity for 100 years. The marshal replied: "In that case, there is no time to lose, plant it this afternoon."
JOHN F. KENNEDY

I object to people running down the future. I am going to live the rest of my life there, and I'd like it to be a nice place.
CHARLES F. KETTERING

If we would quit studying history and go ahead and study the future, we would be much better off. The future course of your lives will be spent in the future and it ought to be what you think. If you want a good one, it will be good. If you want a bad one, it will be bad. It can be good or bad.
CHARLES F. KETTERING

The future can be anything we want it to be, providing we have the faith and that we realize that peace, no less than war, requires blood and sweat and tears.
CHARLES F. KETTERING

We work day after day, not to finish things; but to make the future better . . . because we will spend the rest of our lives there.
CHARLES F. KETTERING

The person of tomorrow must have ability to live with himself. This assures inner strength to do what is right in material and human relationships. Its fruits are peace of mind and serenity of being.
ROGER M. KEYES

Everything that looks to the future elevates human nature; for never is life so low or so little as when occupied with the present.
WALTER SAVAGE LANDOR

They gave each other a smile with a future in it.
RING LARDNER

The present is big with the future.
GOTTFRIED WILHELM LEIBNIZ

The best thing about the future is that it comes only one day at a time.
ABRAHAM LINCOLN

You can't escape the responsibility of tomorrow by evading it today.
ABRAHAM LINCOLN

Look not sorrowfully into the past; it comes not back again. Wisely improve the present; it is thine. Go forth to meet the shadowy future without fear, and with a manly heart.
HENRY WADSWORTH LONGFELLOW

Even if I knew that tomorrow the world would go to pieces, I would still plant my apple tree.
MARTIN LUTHER

Take therefore no thought for the morrow: for the morrow shall take thought for the things of itself. Sufficient unto the day is the evil thereof.
MATTHEW 6:34

The future not being born, my friend, we will abstain from baptizing it.
**GEORGE MEREDITH**

In a life well lived, each succeeding day becomes better than the last. Each day, each year, each experience does not stand alone; it cannot be separated from what has happened before or what may happen after. Yesterday determines today, and today helps determine tomorrow.
**JOHN HOMER MILLER**

We have come from somewhere and are going somewhere. The great architect of the universe never built a stairway that leads to nowhere.
**ROBERT A. MILLIKAN**

Tomorrow to fresh woods and pastures anew.
**JOHN MILTON**

The future is a great land; a man cannot go around it in a day; he cannot measure it with a bound; he cannot bind its harvests into a single sheaf. It is wider than vision, and has no end.
**DONALD G. MITCHELL**

I neither complain of the past, nor do I fear the future.
**MICHEL DE MONTAIGNE**

What I would like to do is chart the future, and help people adjust to it, but when I look ahead all is cloudy and confused. I am an optimist, however. Man will triumph, man and humanity, in spite of everything.
**FRED WARNER NEAL**

Humanity does not know where to go because no one is waiting for it: not even God.
**ANTONIO PORCHIA**

How narrow our souls become when absorbed in any present good or ill! It is only the thought of the future that makes them great.
**JEAN PAUL RICHTER**

As people used to be wrong about the motion of the sun, so they are still wrong about the motion of the future. The future stands still, it is we who move in infinite space.
**RAINER MARIA RILKE**

The only limit to our realization of tomorrow will be our doubts of today.
**FRANKLIN D. ROOSEVELT**

All the best things and treasures of this world are not to be produced by each generation for itself, but we are all intended, not to carve our work in snow that will melt, but each and all of us to be continually rolling a great white gathering snowball, higher and higher, larger and larger, along the Alps of human power.
**JOHN RUSKIN**

When we build . . . let it not be for present delights nor for present use alone. Let it be such work as our descendants will thank us for, and let us think . . . that a time is to come when these stones will be held sacred because our hands have touched them, and that men will say as they look upon the labor, and the wrought substance of them, See! This our fathers did for us!
**JOHN RUSKIN**

We must welcome the future, remembering that soon it will be the past, and we must respect the past, knowing that once it was all that was humanly possible.
**GEORGE SANTAYANA**

Fear not for the future, weep not for the past.
**PERCY BYSSHE SHELLEY**

Despite world unrest, the frontiers of the future lie invitingly before us. They stretch to fabulous horizons of scientific and technological discovery—all holding promise of contribution to the national welfare. But these frontiers of tomorrow call for bold enterprise—for optimism, for the united effort of industry, labor, agriculture and government. In the mounting miracles of science, in the rapid advances of technology, lie the foundations for almost countless new industries and for far swifter social progress. This promise of progress is daily taking more definite shape and clearer form, as it shakes free of the post-war mists.
EARL O. SHREVE

Live only for today, and you ruin tomorrow.
CHARLES SIMMONS

There will be selfishness and greed and corruption and narrowness and intolerance in the world tomorrow and tomorrow's tomorrow. But pray God we may have the courage and the wisdom and the vision to raise a definite standard that will appeal to the best that is in man, and then strive mightily toward that goal.
HAROLD E. STASSEN

If one listens to the faintest but constant suggestions of his genius, which are certainly true, he sees not to what extremes, or even insanity, it may lead him; and yet that way, as he grows more resolute and faithful, his road lies.
HENRY DAVID THOREAU

The trouble with our times is that the future is not what it used to be.
PAUL VALÉRY

I like men who have a future and women who have a past.
OSCAR WILDE

The past cannot be changed, the future is still in your power.
HUGH WHITE

I am not afraid of tomorrow, for I have seen yesterday and I love today.
WILLIAM ALLEN WHITE, ON HIS 70TH BIRTHDAY

# G

## Generations

I have to study politics and war so that my sons can study mathematics, commerce and agriculture, so their sons can study poetry, painting and music.
JOHN QUINCY ADAMS

It is the privilege of posterity to set matters right between those antagonists who, by their rivalry for greatness, divided a whole age.
JOSEPH ADDISON

It is always self-defeating to pretend to the style of a generation younger than your own; it simply erases your own experience in history.
RENATA ADLER

Tradition means handing on all that is of value to the next generation.
HENRY LEWIS BULLEN

Generations are as the days of toilsome mankind.... What the father has made, the son can make and enjoy but has also work of his own appointed him. Thus all things wax and roll onwards; arts, establishments, opinions; nothing is ever completed, but ever completing.
THOMAS CARLYLE

Twenty can't be expected to tolerate sixty in all things, and sixty gets bored stiff with twenty's eternal love affairs.
EMILY CARR

A generation is growing old which never had anything to say for itself except that it was young. It was the first generation that believed in progress and nothing else.
G. K. CHESTERTON (1921)

Only take heed to thyself, and keep thy souls diligently, lest thou forget the things which thine eyes have seen, and lest they depart from thy heart all the days of thy life: but teach them thy sons, and thy sons' sons.
DEUTERONOMY 4:9

One generation passeth away, and another generation cometh; but the earth abideth forever.
ECCLESIASTES 1:4

Most oldsters are fascinated by the Future, while the young love to look back to earlier days, especially their own.
MALCOLM FORBES

Recently I labeled the argument—that 18-year-olds were old enough to vote if they were old enough to fight—a perfect example of a non sequitur. This precipitated a spirited discussion by two of my sons at the dinner table; (said) our 15-year-old, Tim: "Pop, fellows at 18 today are a lot smarter than your generation was at 18, and for sure smarter than teenagers were when voting-age requirements were first set in law." His older brother Bob elucidated: "Maybe not smarter, but certainly better informed, more knowledgeable.... More guys in school and college have helped, but primarily the boob tube has done it."
MALCOLM FORBES

To young people everything looks permanent, established—and in their eyes everything should

be, needs to be changed. To older people everything seems to change, and in their view almost nothing should.
**MALCOLM FORBES**

It is the nature of man that no one learns from experience. The follies of the fathers are lost on their children; each generation has to commit its own.
**FREDERICK THE GREAT**

Older generations are living proof that younger generations can survive their lunacy.
**CULLEN HIGHTOWER**

It is mere childishness to expect men to believe as their fathers did; that is, if they have any minds of their own. The world is a whole generation older and wiser than when the father was of the son's age.
**OLIVER WENDELL HOLMES**

We may consider each generation as a separate nation, with a right, by the will of the majority, to bind themselves, but none to bind the succeeding generation, more than the inhabitants of another country.
**THOMAS JEFFERSON**

We have to hate our immediate predecessors to get free of their authority.
**D. H. LAWRENCE**

The new generation forgets the spectres that may have tormented the old.
**HALLDOR LAXNESS**

Few can be induced to labor exclusively for posterity. Posterity has done nothing for us.
**ABRAHAM LINCOLN**

Every generation revolts against its fathers and makes friends with its grandfathers.
**LEWIS MUMFORD**

The great truths of human life do not spring new born to each new generation. They derive from long experience. They are the gathered wisdom of the race. They are renewed in time of conflict and danger. If the times in which we are now living do not bring a fuller understanding of the great traditions of the Western European peoples and an almost Messianic desire to affirm them, we are not worthy of that heritage.
**FREDERICK OSBORN**

Every age and generation must be as free to act for itself in all cases as the ages and generations which preceded it. The vanity of governing beyond the grave is the most ridiculous and insolent of all tyrannies.
**THOMAS PAINE**

We are too careless of posterity, not considering that as they are so the next generation will be.
**WILLIAM PENN**

An extraordinary nation's destiny will always be guided not by the transient efforts of one or even of several extraordinary men of a given period, but by the persistent power of the nation's traditions.
**MICHAEL PUPIN**

Every generation, no matter how paltry its character, thinks itself much wiser than the one immediately preceding it, let alone those that are more remote.
**ARTHUR SCHOPENHAUER**

The man who sees two or three generations is like one who sits in the conjuror's booth at a fair, and sees the same tricks two or three times. They are meant to be seen only once.
**ARTHUR SCHOPENHAUER**

Tradition is not a fetish to be prayed to—but a useful record of experiences. Time should bring improvement—but not all old things are worthless.

We are served by both the moderns and the ancients. The balanced man is he who clings to the best in the old—and appropriates the desirable in the new.
**RICHARD STEELE**

Amongst democratic nations, each generation is a new people.
**ALEXIS DE TOCQUEVILLE**

I have had enough experience in all my years, and have read enough of the past, to know that advice to grandchildren is usually wasted. If the second and third generations could profit by the experience of the first generation, we would not be having some of the troubles we have today.
**HARRY S TRUMAN**

It is fortunate that each generation does not comprehend its own ignorance. We are thus enabled to call our ancestors barbarous.
**CHARLES DUDLEY WARNER**

Every one expects to go further than his father went; every one expects to be better than he was born and every generation has one big impulse in its heart—to exceed all the other generations of the past in all the things that make life worth living.
**WILLIAM ALLEN WHITE**

Each generation criticizes the unconscious assumptions made by its parents. It may assent to them, but it brings them out into the open.
**ALFRED NORTH WHITEHEAD**

## *Generosity*

Watch lest prosperity destroy generosity.
**HENRY WARD BEECHER**

We need to be just before we are generous, as we need shirts before ruffles.
**SÉBASTIEN CHAMFORT**

He who confers a favor should at once forget it, if he is not to show a sordid, ungenerous spirit. To remind a man of a kindness conferred on him, and talk of it, is little different from reproach.
**DEMOSTHENES**

The secret pleasure of a generous act is the great mind's bribe.
**JOHN DRYDEN**

Generous gestures yield the most when that isn't their purpose.
**MALCOLM FORBES**

Generosity is giving more than you can; pride is taking less than you need.
**KAHLIL GIBRAN**

True generosity is a duty as indispensably necessary as those imposed on us by law.
**OLIVER GOLDSMITH**

Of all virtues magnanimity is the rarest; there are a hundred persons of merit for one who willingly acknowledges it in another.
**WILLIAM HAZLITT**

I would rather be a beggar and spend my money like a king, than be a king and spend money like a beggar.
**ROBERT G. INGERSOLL**

The generous who is always just, and the just who is always generous, may, unannounced, approach the throne of heaven.
**JOHANN LAVATER**

Generosity during life is a very different thing from generosity in the hour of death; one proceeds from genuine liberality, and benevolence; the other from pride or fear, or from the fact that you cannot take your money with you to the other world.
MARTIAL

I would have a man generous to his country, his neighbors, his kindred, his friends, and most of all his poor friends. Not like some who are most lavish with those who are able to give most of them.
PLINY

Many men have been capable of doing a wise thing, more a cunning thing, but very few a generous thing.
ALEXANDER POPE

If you desire to be magnanimous, undertake nothing rashly, and fear nothing thou undertakest. Fear nothing but infamy; dare anything but injury, the measure of magnanimity is to be neither rash nor timorous.
FRANCIS QUARLES

What seems to be generously is often no more than disguised ambition, which overlooks a small interest in order to secure a great one.
FRANÇOIS DE LA ROCHEFOUCAULD

Mighty of heart, mighty of mind, magnanimous—to be this is indeed to be great in life.
JOHN RUSKIN

He who allows his day to pass by without practicing generosity and enjoying life's pleasure is like a blacksmith's bellows—he breathes but does not live.
SANSKRIT PROVERB

Never measure your generosity by what you give, but rather by what you have left.
BISHOP FULTON J. SHEEN

Humanity is the virtue of a woman, generosity of a man. The fair sex, who have commonly much more tenderness than ours, have seldom so much generosity.
ADAM SMITH

Almost always the most indigent are most generous.
KING STANISLAUS OF POLAND

He who gives what he would as readily throw away, gives without generosity; for the essence of generosity is in self-sacrifice.
HENRY J. TAYLOR

Favors cease to be favors when there are conditions attached to them.
THORNTON WILDER

## *Genius*

Doing easily what others find difficult is talent; doing what is impossible for talent is genius.
HENRI FRÉDÉRIC AMIEL

As diamond cuts diamond, and one hone smooths a second, all the parts of intellect are whetstones to each other; and genius, which is but the result of their mutual sharpening, is character too.
CYRUS A. BARTOL

Genius is childhood recalled at will.
CHARLES BAUDELAIRE

Improvement makes straight roads; but the crooked roads without improvement are the roads of genius.
WILLIAM BLAKE

Since when was genius found respectable?
**ELIZABETH BARRETT BROWNING**

Every man who observes vigilantly and resolves steadfastly grows unconsciously into genius.
**EDWARD BULWER-LYTTON**

Genius is patience.
**GEORGE DE BUFFON**

Genius is fostered by industry.
**CICERO**

Genius must have talent as its complement and implement, just as in like manner imagination must have fancy. In short, the higher intellectual powers can only act through a corresponding energy of the lower.
**SAMUEL TAYLOR COLERIDGE**

Times of general calamity and confusion have ever been productive of the greatest minds. The purest ore is produced from the hottest furnace, and the brightest thunderbolt is elicited from the darkest storm.
**CHARLES CALEB COLTON**

When the creations of a genius collide with the mind of a layman, and produce an empty sound, there is little doubt as to which is at fault.
**SALVADOR DALI**

Genius is the quality of the special spirit, whether in poetry or politics or science, which raises a man above a single locality or nation to influence the people of the world.
**CORNELIS W. DE KIEWIET**

Education, however indispensable in a cultivated age, produces nothing on the side of genius. When education ends, genius often begins.
**ISAAC DISRAELI**

Genius is one per cent inspiration and ninety-nine per cent perspiration.
**THOMAS EDISON**

Great geniuses have the shortest biographies.
**RALPH WALDO EMERSON**

There are geniuses in trade as well as in war, or the state, or letters; and the reason why this or that man is fortunate is not to be told. It lies in the man: that is all anybody can tell you about it.
**RALPH WALDO EMERSON**

When Nature has work to be done, she creates a genius to do it.
**RALPH WALDO EMERSON**

Genius is entitled to respect only when it promotes the peace and improves the happiness of mankind.
**LORD ESSEX**

The true genius that conducts a state is he, who doing nothing himself, causes everything to be done; he contrives, he invents, he foresees the future; he reflects on what is past; he distributes and proportions things; he makes early preparations; he incessantly arms himself to struggle against fortune, as a swimmer against a rapid stream of water; he is attentive night and day, that he may leave nothing to chance.
**FRANÇOIS FÉNELON**

One of the strongest characteristics of genius is the power of lighting its own fire.
**JOHN FOSTER**

The greatest genius will never be worth much if he pretends to draw exclusively from his own resources. What is genius but the faculty of seizing and turning to account everything that strikes us?
**JOHANN WOLFGANG VON GOETHE**

Genius is the capacity of evading hard work.
ELBERT HUBBARD

Genius may have its limitations, but stupidity is not thus handicapped.
ELBERT HUBBARD

Genius is initiative on fire.
HOLBROOK JACKSON

No estimate is more in danger of erroneous calculations than those by which a man computes the force of his own genius.
SAMUEL JOHNSON

The true genius is a mind of large general powers, accidentally determined to some particular direction.
SAMUEL JOHNSON

Men of lofty genius when they are doing the least work are most active.
LEONARDO DA VINCI

To make the common marvelous is the test of genius.
JAMES RUSSELL LOWELL

The highest genius is willingness and ability to do hard work. Any other conception of genius makes it a doubtful, if not a dangerous possession.
ROBERT S. MACARTHUR

Genius is eternal patience
MICHELANGELO

I do not despise genius—indeed, I wish I had a basketful of it instead of a brain, but yet, after a great deal of experience and observation, I have become convinced that industry is a better horse to ride than genius. It may never carry any one man as far as genius has carried individuals, but industry will carry thousands into comfort and even into celebrity, and this it does with absolute certainty; whereas genius often refuses to be tamed and managed, and often goes with wretched morals. If you are to wish for either, wish for industry.
JULIAN RALPH

If there be anything that can be called genius, it consists chiefly in ability to give that attention to a subject which keeps it steadily in the mind, till we have surveyed it accurately on all sides.
THOMAS REID

Genius is only a superior power of seeing.
JOHN RUSKIN

A genius can't be forced; nor can you make an ape an alderman.
THOMAS SOMERVILLE

In talking about a genius, you would not say that he lies; he sees realities with different eyes from ours.
CONSTANTIN STANISLAVSKI

Genius does not need a special language; it uses newly whatever tongue it finds.
EDMUND STEDMAN

When a true genius appears in the world, you may know him by this sign, that the dunces are all in confederacy against him.
JONATHAN SWIFT

No man ever followed his genius until it misled him.
HENRY DAVID THOREAU

The function of genius is not to give new answers, but to pose new questions which time and mediocrity can resolve.
H. R. TREVOR-ROPER

There's a fine line between eccentrics and geniuses. If you're a little ahead of your time, you're an eccentric, and if you're too late, you're a failure, but if you hit it right on the head, you're a genius.
**THOMAS J. WATSON, JR.**

## Giving

It is more blessed to give than to receive.
**ACTS 20:35**

Thank the Lord that you can give, instead of depending on others to give to you.
**ANONYMOUS**

Of all the varieties of virtue, liberality is the most beloved.
**ARISTOTLE**

He that will not give some portion of his ease, his blood, his wealth for others' good is a poor, frozen churl.
**JOANNA BAILLIE**

If you'll forget the things you give
And ne'er forget what your receive,
Quite soon you'll make a host of friends
Who'll gladly aid you to achieve.
**ALONZO NEWTON BENN**

Blessed are those who can give without remembering and take without forgetting.
**ELIZABETH BIBESCO**

You need more tact in the dangerous art of giving presents than in any other social action.
**WILLIAM BOLITHO**

It is an anomaly of modern life that many find giving to be a burden. Such persons have omitted a preliminary giving. If one first gives himself to the Lord, all other giving is easy.
**JOHN S. BONNELL, D.D.**

Examples are few of men ruined by giving. Men are heroes in spending, cravens in what they give.
**CHRISTIAN BOVÉE**

The giving is the hardest part; what does it cost to add a smile?
**JEAN DE LA BRUYÈRE**

A man there was, and they called him mad; the more he gave, the more he had.
**JOHN BUNYAN**

Getters generally don't get happiness; givers get it. You simply give to others a bit of yourself—a thoughtful act a helpful idea, a word of appreciation, a lift over a rough spot, a sense of understanding, a timely suggestion. You take something out of your mind, garnished in kindness out of your heart, and put it into the other fellow's mind and heart.
**CHARLES H. BURR**

We make a living by what we get, we make a life by what we give.
**WINSTON CHURCHILL**

No person was ever honored for what he received. Honor has been the reward for what he gave.
**CALVIN COOLIDGE**

It should be our purpose in life to see that each of us makes such a contribution as will enable us to say that we, individually and collectively, are a part of the answer to the world problem and not part of the problem itself.
**ANDREW CORDIER**

Every man shall give as he is able, according to the blessing of the Lord thy God which he hath given thee.
**DEUTERONOMY 16:17**

The Lord shall open unto you his good treasure, the heaven to give the rain unto thy land in his season, and to bless all the work of thine hand: and thou shall lend unto many nations, and thou shalt not borrow.
**DEUTERONOMY 28:12**

How painful to give a gift to any person of sensibility, or of equality! It is next worse to receiving one.
**RALPH WALDO EMERSON**

We do not quite forgive a giver. The hand that feeds us is in some danger of being bitten.
**RALPH WALDO EMERSON**

Everyone may bring his little stone to assist in the construction of a future pyramid.
**CAMILLE FLAMMARION**

"D'ye think I'm in business for my health?" How often have you heard that? Every time I hear it I conclude that the man doesn't know what he is in business for. What are we in business for? We are in business to benefit others. If we are not, then our business won't prosper permanently. All business is a matter of reciprocity, of giving something in exchange for something else. Unless we give, we cannot receive. And the man or concern that gives us most naturally gets most in return. He reaps most who serves most. The most notably successful businesses are those that have rendered signally valuable services to the people.
**B. C. FORBES**

Give naught, get same. Give much, get same.
**MALCOLM FORBES**

O Divine Master, grant that I may not so much seek to be consoled as to console; to be understood, as to understand, to be loved, as to love; for it is in giving that we receive, it is in pardoning that we are pardoned, and it is in dying that we are born to eternal life.
**ST. FRANCIS OF ASSISI**

He gives twice that gives soon, i.e., he will soon be called to give again.
**BENJAMIN FRANKLIN**

When thou makes presents, let them be of such things as will last long; to the end they may be in some sort immortal, and may frequently refresh the memory of the receiver.
**THOMAS FULLER**

It is better to give than to lend, and it costs about the same.
**SIR PHILIP GIBBS**

Two can give as cheap as one.
**ARNOLD GLASOW**

An idea would never be liberal: It must be vigorous, positive, and without loose ends so that it may fulfill its divine mission and be productive. The proper place for liberality is in the realm of the emotions.
**JOHANN WOLFGANG VON GOETHE**

Share weight and woe, for misfortune falls with double force on him that stands alone.
**BALTASAR GRACIÁN**

Giving people a little more than they expect is a good way to get back a lot more than you'd expect.
**ROBERT HALF**

Why you are born and why you are living depend entirely on what you are getting out of this world

and what you are giving to it. I cannot prove that this is a balance of mathematical perfection, but my own observation of life leads me to the conclusion that there is a very real relationship, both quantitatively and qualitatively, between what you contribute and what you get out of this world.
**OSCAR HAMMERSTEIN II**

For every action there is an equal and opposite reaction. If you want to receive a great deal, you first have to give a great deal. If each individual will give of himself to whomever he can, wherever he can, in any way that he can, in the long run he will be compensated in the exact proportion that he gives.
**RALPH A. HAYWARD**

If tempted by something that feels altruistic, examine your motives and root out that self-deception. Then, if you still want to do it, wallow in it!
**ROBERT A. HEINLEIN**

There is a gift that is almost a blow, and there is a kind word that is munificence; so much is there in the way of doing things.
**ARTHUR HELPS**

A gift much expected is paid, not given.
**GEORGE HERBERT**

He that is long a giving knows not how to give.
**GEORGE HERBERT**

Give, if thou canst, an alms; if not, afford, instead of that, a sweet and gentle word.
**ROBERT HERRICK**

They who give have all things; they who withhold have nothing.
**HINDU PROVERB**

One always receiving, never giving, is like the stagnant pool, in which whatever flows remains, whatever remains corrupts.
**JOHN A. JAMES**

Life cannot subsist in society but by reciprocal concessions.
**SAMUEL JOHNSON**

Let him who exhorts others to give, give himself.
**LATIN PROVERB**

Who gives a trifle meanly is meaner than the trifle.
**JOHANN LAVATER**

Give what you have. To someone it may be better than you dare to think.
**HENRY WADSWORTH LONGFELLOW**

The greatest grace of a gift, perhaps, is that it anticipates and admits of no return.
**HENRY WADSWORTH LONGFELLOW**

The gift without the giver is rare.
**JAMES RUSSELL LOWELL**

Give, and it shall be given unto you; good measure, pressed down, and shaken together, and running over, shall men give into your bosom. For with the same measure that ye mete withal it shall be measured to you again.
**LUKE 6:38**

The heart of the giver makes the gift dear and precious.
**MARTIN LUTHER**

Bring ye all the tithes into the storehouse, that there may be meat in mine house, and prove me now herewith, saith the Lord of hosts, if I will not open you the windows of heaven, and pour you out a

blessing, that there shall not be room enough to receive it.
**MALACHI 3:10**

Be ashamed to die until you have won some victory for humanity.
**HORACE MANN**

Whoever makes great presents expects great presents in return.
**MARTIAL**

If it is more blessed to give than to receive, then most of us are content to let the other fellow have the greater blessing.
**SHAILER MATTHEWS**

For too many giving is occasional, spasmodic, ill-proportioned. It depends on what is left over when other things have had their full share. Sometimes what it means is that only the small change lying in their pockets goes to the support of good and worthy causes.
**ROBERT J. MCCRACKEN**

We can give only what we have to give. We can write out a check for a good cause only if we have money in the bank to cover the check. And in like fashion we can give understanding only if we have understanding. We can give a contagious sense of the heights and depths of life only if we have earned, and have in our possession, a feeling of those heights and depths.
**BONARO W. OVERSTREET**

The gift derives its value from the rank of the giver.
**OVID**

Presents which our love for the donor has rendered precious are ever the most acceptable.
**OVID**

He who is not liberal with what he has, does but deceive himself when he thinks he would be liberal if he had more.
**WILLIAM S. PLUMER**

The weakest among us has a gift, however seemingly trivial, which is peculiar to him and which worthily used will be a gift also to his race.
**JOHN RUSKIN**

You must give some time to your fellow man. Even if it's a little thing, do something for those who have need of help, something for which you get no pay but the privilege of doing it. For remember, you don't live in a world all your own. Your brothers are here, too.
**ALBERT SCHWEITZER**

A benefit consists not in that which is done or given, but in the intention of the giver or doer.
**SENECA**

It is another's fault if he be ungrateful; but it is mine if I do not give. To find one thankful man, I will oblige a great many that are not so. I had rather never receive a kindness than never bestow one. Not to return a benefit is a great sin; but not to confer one is a greater.
**SENECA**

If there be any truer measure of a man than by what he does, it must be by what he gives.
**ROBERT SOUTH**

We are rich only through what we give: and poor only through what we refuse and keep.
**ANNE SWETCHINE**

He giveth twice that giveth quickly.
**RICHARD TAVERNER**

Trust not the horse, O Trojans. Be it what it may, I fear the Greeks when they offer gifts.
VIRGIL

He gives not best who gives most; but he gives most who gives best. If I cannot give bountifully, yet will I give freely, and what I want in my mind, I will supply in my heart.
ARTHUR WARWICK

No man who continues to add something to the material, intellectual and moral well-being of the place in which he lives is left long without proper reward.
BOOKER T. WASHINGTON

Sharing is the great and imperative need of our time. An unshared life is not living. He who shares does not lessen but greatens his life, especially if sharing be done not formally nor conventionally, but with such heartiness as springs out of an understanding of the meaning of the religion of sharing.
RABBI STEPHEN S. WISE

## *Goals*

In this life we get only those things for which we hunt, for which we strive, and for which we are willing to sacrifice. It is better to aim for something that you want—even though you miss it—than to get something that you didn't aim to get, and which you don't want! If we look long enough for what we want in life we are almost sure to find it, no matter what that objective may be.
GEORGE MATTHEW ADAMS

Whether zeal or moderation be the point we aim at, let us keep fire out of the one, and frost out of the other.
JOSEPH ADDISON

Far away there in the sunshine are my highest aspirations. I may not reach them, but I can look up and see their beauty, believe in them and try to follow where they lead.
LOUISA MAY ALCOTT

As you think, you travel; and as you love, you attract. You are today where your thoughts have brought you; you will be tomorrow where your thoughts take you. You cannot escape the result of your thoughts, but you can endure and learn, can accept and be glad. You will realize the vision (not the idle wish), of your heart, be it base or beautiful, or a mixture of both, for you will always gravitate towards that which you, secretly, most love. Into your hands will be placed the exact results of your thoughts; you will receive that which you earn; no more, no less. Whatever your present environment may be, you will fall, remain or rise with your thoughts, your vision, your ideal. You will become as small as your controlling desire; as great as your dominant aspiration.
JAMES LANE ALLEN

There is no shame in having fallen. Nor any shame in being born into a lowly estate. There is only shame in not struggling to rise. And also shame for not wishing to attain the better. Or not dreaming about it and praying for it.
SAMUEL AMALU

Every art and every inquiry, as well as every practical pursuit, seems to aim at some good, whereby it has been well said that the good is that at which all things aim.
ARISTOTLE

When an archer misses the mark he turns and looks for the fault within himself. Failure to hit the bull's-eye is never the fault of the target. To improve your aim improve yourself.
GILBERT ARLAND

Today's put-off objectives reduce tomorrow's achievements.
HARRY F. BANKS

The life of every man is a diary in which he means to write one story, and writes another, and his humblest hour is when he compares the volume as it is with what he vowed to make it.
JAMES M. BARRIE

By every part of our nature we clasp things above us, one after another, not for the sake of remaining where we take hold, but that we may go higher.
HENRY WARD BEECHER

If you don't know where you're going, you'll end up somewhere else.
YOGI BERRA

Many imagine that the higher you go, the easier the climbing. Don't be governed by that theory unless you have a soft place to fall back into.
J. L. BOGGUS

My ancestors wandered in the wilderness for 40 years because even in biblical times, men would not stop to ask directions.
ELAYNE BOOSLER

A man's reach should exceed his grasp, or what's heaven for?
ROBERT BROWNING

Our aspirations are our possibilities.
ROBERT BROWNING

What I aspired to be, and was not, comforts me.
ROBERT BROWNING

The fact is, nothing comes; at least, nothing good. All has to be fetched.
CHARLES BUXTON

Write down on paper your goal in life. With that down in black and white, we really can get somewhere. Few can define their goal, much less write it. You cannot find happiness until your goal is clear and in view.
ROSS BYRON

Personal liberty will prove a poor and shrunken thing incapable of satisfying our aspirations if it does not exact as its minimum requirement that there shall be the preservation of opportunity for the growth of personality.
BENJAMIN CARDOZO

If you cry "Forward" you must without fail make plain in what direction to go.
ANTON CHEKHOV

Heights were made to be looked at, not to be looked from.
G. K. CHESTERTON

New boots . . . big steps
CHINESE PROVERB

If you aspire to the highest place it is no disgrace to stop at the second, or even the third.
CICERO

If you wish to travel far and fast, travel light. Take off all your envies, jealousies, unforgiveness, selfishness and fears.
GLENN CLARK

We are told that there are no new frontiers to conquer, but this is the attitude of those who despair today, who despaired yesterday, and who will still be at it during the rest of their lives. We dare not follow such an attitude of mind. It has been well stated that the pioneer is a creature not of time but of spirit.
MYERS Y. COOPER

No one rises so high as he who knows not whither he is going.
OLIVER CROMWELL

Life has no smooth road for any of us; and in the bracing atmosphere of a high aim the very roughness stimulates the climber to steadier steps, till the legend, over steep ways to the stars, fulfills itself.
WILLIAM C. DOANE

What I am thinking and doing day by day is resistlessly shaping my future—a future in which there is no expiation except through my own better conduct. No one can save me. No one can live my life for me. If I am wise I shall begin today to build my own truer and better world from within.
H. W. DRESSER

Perfection of means and confusion of goals seem, in my opinion, to characterize our age.
ALBERT EINSTEIN

There is no sorrow I have thought more about than that—to love what is great, and try to reach it, and yet to fail.
GEORGE ELIOT

Hitch your wagon to a star. Let us not fag in paltry works which serve our pot and bag alone.
RALPH WALDO EMERSON

It's all right to aim high if you have plenty of ammunition.
HAWLEY R. EVERHART

In business, as in baseball, the prizes go most often to the organizations that pursue their objective hard and relentlessly every day of the year.
WILLIAM FEATHER

We should look to the end in all things.
JEAN DE LA FONTAINE

How foolish you would be to start on a journey without knowing where you wanted to go. Have you ever sat down and seriously drawn up a plan for your life? Have you ever deliberately mapped out where you want to go during your life's journey? Now, isn't your life infinitely more important to you than any journey you may take? Why, therefore, not devote the most earnest effort to plan your life, to set for yourself a goal? We are now at the New Year season. Isn't this a peculiarly appropriate time to look ahead, to indulge in solemn thinking, to formulate life plans, to lay down a definite course to follow?
B. C. FORBES

If you don't know what you want to do, it's harder to do it.
MALCOLM FORBES

When you catch what you're after, it's gone.
MALCOLM FORBES

Concentrate on finding your goal, then concentrate on reaching it.
COL. MICHAEL FRIEDSAM

He that would have fruit must climb the tree.
THOMAS FULLER

He who moves not forward goes backward.
JOHANN WOLFGANG VON GOETHE

Whatever you can do, or dream you can . . . begin it; boldness has genius, power and magic in it.
JOHANN WOLFGANG VON GOETHE

The trick in life is to decide what's your major aim—to be rich, a golf champion, world's best father, etc. Once that's settled, you can get on with the happy, orderly process of achieving it.
STANLEY GOLDSTEIN

The grand difficulty is so to feel the reality of both worlds as to give each its due place in our thoughts and feelings—to keep our mind's eye, and our heart's eye, ever fixed on the land of Promise, without looking away from the road along which we are to travel toward it.
JULIUS C. HARE

Concentrate your energies and work hard. Launch out in new experiments. Never be afraid to have the courage of your opinions. Fix the lines you want to travel along and keep on them. That's all.
A. C. W. HARMSWORTH

Aim at the sun, and you may not reach it; but your arrow will fly far higher than if aimed at an object on a level with yourself.
JOEL HAWES

Not failure, but low aim, is a crime.
ERNEST HOLMES

Work your way up or rust your way out.
HOLTON

The rung of a ladder was never meant to rest upon, but only to hold a man's foot long enough to enable him to put the other somewhat higher.
THOMAS H. HUXLEY

What we truly and earnestly aspire to be, that in some sense we are.
ANNA JAMESON

Beaten paths are for beaten men.
ERIC A. JOHNSTON

The world turns aside to let any man pass who knows whither he is going.
DAVID STARR JORDAN

If you don't know where you are going, every road will get you nowhere.
HENRY KISSINGER

Make the most of today. Translate your good intentions into actual deeds. Know that you can do what ought to be done. Improve your plans. Keep a definite goal of achievement constantly in view. Realize that work well and worthily done makes life truly worth living.
GRENVILLE KLEISER

The journey of a thousand miles begins with one step.
LAO-TZU

Unless you know where you are going, any road will take you there.
THEODORE LEVITT

You can't just go on being a good egg. You must either hatch or go bad!
C. S. LEWIS

Determine that the thing can and shall be done, and then we shall find the way.
ABRAHAM LINCOLN

We must ask where we are and whither we are tending.
ABRAHAM LINCOLN

**Ten Pointers**

1. Be yourself. Cultivates desirable qualities.
2. Be alert. Look for opportunities to express yourself.
3. Be positive. Determine your goal and the route to it.
4. Be systematic. Take one step at a time.
5. Be persistent. Hold to your course.

6. Be a worker. Work your brain more than your body.
7. Be a student. Know your job.
8. Be fair. Treat the other man as you would be treated.
9. Be temperate. Avoid excess in anything.
10. Be confident. Have faith that cannot be weakened.

EVERETT W. LORD

Not failure, but low aim is crime.
JAMES RUSSELL LOWELL

Truly there is a tide in the affairs of men; but there is no gulf-stream setting forever in one direction.
JAMES RUSSELL LOWELL

To get anywhere, strike out for somewhere, or you'll get nowhere.
MARTHA LUPTON

When you determine what you want, you have made the most important decision of your life. You have to know what you want in order to attain it.
DOUGLAS LURTON

Ambition is but the evil shadow of aspiration.
GEORGE MACDONALD

The strong man, the positive, decisive man who has a program and is determined to carry it out, cuts his way to his goal regardless of difficulties. It is the discouraged man who turns aside and takes a crooked path.
ORISON S. MARDEN

Aim for a star, and keep your sights high! With a heart full of faith within, your feet on the ground and your eyes in the sky.
HELEN LOWRIE MARSHALL

Discover what you want most of all in this world, and set yourself to work on it.
JOHN HOMER MILLER

Aim high! It is no harder on your gun to shoot the feathers off an eagle than to shoot the fur off a skunk.
TROY MOORE

The young have aspirations that never come to pass, the old have reminiscences of what never happened.
H. H. MUNRO

Many are stubborn in pursuit of the path they have chosen, few in pursuit of the goal.
FRIEDRICH WILHELM NIETZSCHE

You must have long-range goals to keep you from being frustrated by short-range failures.
CHARLES C. NOBLE

And in navigation, the more sights we take, the more likely we are to hit port.
HENRY OSBORN

Thy destiny is only that of man, but thy aspirations may be those of a god.
OVID

Laboring toward distant aims sets the mind in a higher key and puts us at our best.
CHARLES HENRY PARKHURST, D.D.

You must make a habit of thinking in terms of a defined objective.
JOHN HENRY PATTERSON

Some men give up their designs when they have almost reached the goal; while others, on the con-

trary, obtain a victory by exerting, at the last moment, more vigorous efforts than before.
**POLYBIUS**

When you awaken some morning and hear that somebody or other has been discovered, you can put it down as a fact that he discovered himself years ago—since which time he has been working, toiling and striving to make himself worthy of general discovery.
**JAMES WHITCOMB RILEY**

The successful man lengthens his stride when he discovers that the signpost has deceived him; the failure looks for a place to sit down.
**J. R. ROGERS**

Take the course opposite to custom and you will almost always do well.
**JEAN-JACQUES ROUSSEAU**

What signifies the ladder, provided one rise and attain the end?
**CHARLES SAINTE-BEUVE**

Three men were laying brick.

The first was asked: "What are you doing?"

He answered: "Laying some brick."

The second man was asked: "What are you working for?"

He answered: "Five dollars a day."

The third man was asked: "What are you doing?"

He answered: "I am helping to build a great cathedral."

Which man are you?
**CHARLES M. SCHWAB**

Many of us are like the little boy we met trudging along a country road with a cat-rifle over his shoulder. "What are you hunting, buddy?" we asked. "Dunno, sir, I ain't seen it yet."
**R. LEE SHARPE**

To drift is to be in hell, to be in heaven is to steer.
**GEORGE BERNARD SHAW**

Who shoots at the midday sun, though sure he shall never hit the mark, yet sure he is that he shall shoot higher than he who aims at a bush.
**SIR PHILIP SIDNEY**

There are two things to aim at in life: first, to get what you want; and, after that, to enjoy it. Only the wisest of mankind achieve the second.
**LOGAN PEARSALL SMITH**

It is not for man to rest in absolute contentment. He is born to hopes and aspirations.
**ROBERT SOUTHEY**

There will be selfishness and greed and corruption and narrowness and intolerance in the world tomorrow and tomorrow's tomorrow. But pray God we may have the courage and the wisdom and the vision to raise a definite standard that will appeal to the best that is in man, and then strive mightily toward that goal.
**HAROLD E. STASSEN**

The peculiar fascination which the speeding train has for us comes from the evident progress it is making toward its definite goal ahead.
**RODERICK STEVENS**

Every individual should have a purpose in life which is worthy of intense effort—and constantly work toward the definite goal ahead.
**RODERICK STEVENS**

An aim in life is the only fortune worth the finding.
ROBERT LOUIS STEVENSON

The man with the average mentality, but with control, with a definite goal, and a clear conception of how it can be gained, and above all, with the power of application and labor, wins in the end.
WILLIAM HOWARD TAFT

Did you ever hear of a man who had striven all his life faithfully and singly toward an object, and in no measure obtained it? If a man constantly aspires, is he not elevated? Did ever a man try heroism, magnanimity, truth, sincerity, and find that there was no advantage in them—that it was a vain endeavor?
HENRY DAVID THOREAU

In the long run you hit only what you aim at. Therefore, though you should fail immediately, you had better aim at something high.
HENRY DAVID THOREAU

Being easy-going when you have a goal to reach seldom makes the going easy.
FRANK TYGER

The first step, my son, which we make in this world, is the one on which depends the rest of our days.
VOLTAIRE

Within us all there are wells of thought and dynamos of energy which are not suspected until emergencies arise. Then oftentimes we find that it is comparatively simple to double or treble our former capacities and to amaze ourselves by the results achieved. Quotas, when set up for us by others, are challenges which goad us on to surpass ourselves. The outstanding leaders of every age are those who set up their own quotas and constantly exceed them.
THOMAS J. WATSON

One ship drives east and another west
While the self-same breezes blow:
'Tis the set of the sail and not the gale
That bids them where to go.
ELLA WHEELER WILCOX

We are all in the gutter, but some of us are looking at the stars.
OSCAR WILDE

Not doing more than the average is what keeps the average down.
WILLIAM WINANS

## God

God will provide the victuals, but He will not cook the dinner.
ANONYMOUS

Differences of opinion give me but little concern; but it is a real pleasure to be brought into communication with any one who is in earnest, and who really looks to God's will as his standard of right and wrong, and judges of actions according to their greater or less conformity.
THOMAS ARNOLD

They that deny a God destroy man's nobility; for certainly man is of kin to the beasts by his body; and, if he be not kin to God by his spirit, he is a base and ignoble creature.
FRANCIS BACON

The righteousness of God itself has slowly changed from being the surest of facts into being the highest among various high ideals; and is now at all events our very own affair. This is evident in our ability

now to hang it gaily out of the window and now to roll it up again, somewhat like a flag.
**KARL BARTH**

What you hide from God, don't show your neighbors.
**IGNAS BERNSTEIN**

What America needs is businessman—indeed all men and women—not so much on their knees but on their toes, reaching up ever higher and higher to bring the laws of God down into, and as a part of, the laws of man.
**LOUIS BINSTOCK**

*Think* in the name of Almighty God. We must first have a worldwide awakening of the public conscience, a spiritual revival, a moral regeneration, before there can be permanent peace and real economic recovery. To this end we do not need new laws, but a new spirit; we do not need a change of government, but a change of the human heart. There can be no peace, there will be no recovery without it. Therefore, with a change of heart, let's all make a new start.
**WILLIAM J. H. BOETCKER**

There are some who are naive enough to believe that the basic conflict between communism and democracy is economic in nature. They are utterly mistaken. The conflict is between the kingdom of militant atheism and the Kingdom of God. The Kingdom of God stands above all isms and will remain unshaken and unscathed, the harbinger of a new day.
**JOHN S. BONNELL, D.D.**

Hardship, unbelief, suffering and poverty have not stopped our soldiery from rendering their service to God and man. The Salvation Army is a great empire, an empire without a frontier made up of a tangle of races, tongues and colors such as never before in all history gathered together under one flag.
**GEN. EVANGELINE BOOTH**

Inscription in lobby of the S. F. Bowser & Co. office building, Fort Wayne, Ind.:

I acknowledge God's great help in all things, of which this splendid office is one. One which all our office employees can enjoy. God help us to be grateful.
**S. F. BOWSER**

Get the pattern of your life from God, then go about your work and be yourself.
**PHILLIPS BROOKS**

No man has come to true greatness who has not felt in some degree that his life belongs to his race, and that what God gives him He gives him for mankind.
**PHILLIPS BROOKS**

The greatest discovery in man's thinking is that the world is good. The universe has goodness at its heart and God is on the side of good. Existence is life with a moral core. If you believe that God is good and that He created a universe in which the devil can't win, then you can live in peace and happiness.
**F. HOWARD CALLAHAN**

When the peoples of a nation are filled with God's spirit and seek guidance they will have it; and, having it, they will select leaders who are like-minded and will direct them into God's paths.
**JOSEPH I. CHAPMAN, D.D.**

If there was not God, there would be no atheists.
**G. K. CHESTERTON**

Those thinkers who cannot believe in any gods often assert that the love of humanity would be in

itself sufficient for them; and so, perhaps, it would, if they had it.
**G. K. CHESTERTON**

I go walking, and the hills loom above me, range upon range, one against the other. I cannot tell where one begins and another leaves off. But when I talk with God He lifts me up where I can see clearly, where everything has a distinct contour.
**MADAME CHIANG KAI-SHEK**

I am ready to meet my Maker. Whether my Maker is prepared for the ordeal of meeting me is another matter.
**WINSTON CHURCHILL**

God has a plan of justice, mercy, truth, co-operation and brotherhood which will bring peace upon this earth. As we worship God these qualities become part of our nature and we become fit inhabitants of the world God created. Human beings should worship God not alone to show their allegiance and dependence upon their Creator, but to absorb from Him the essential qualities of a permanent civilization.
**ALLEN E. CLAXTON, D.D.**

. . . Right with God, we are right with the rest of the world. Right with God, capital and labor work in unity and harmony. Right with God, then husband and wife share and care together. Right with God, then children become the source of sustaining life. Right with God, I can take the proper attitude toward my lower self.
**CLINTON C. COX**

If you believe in the Lord, He will do half the work—but the last half. He helps those who help themselves.
**CYRUS H. K. CURTIS**

It is the easiest thing in the world to obey God when He commands us to do what we like, and to trust Him when the path is all sunshine. The real victory of faith is to trust God in the dark, and through the dark.
**THEODORE L. CUYLER**

Every one comes between men's souls and God, either as a brick wall or as a bridge. Either you are leading men to God or you are driving them away.
**CANON LINDSAY DEWAR, D.D.**

Whatever the place allotted to us by Providence, that for us is the post of honor and duty. God estimates us not by the position we are in, but by the way in which we fill it.
**TRYON EDWARDS**

God is subtle but not malicious.
**ALBERT EINSTEIN**

If a man's eye is on the Eternal, his intellect will grow.
**RALPH WALDO EMERSON**

Try first thyself,
And after call in God;
For the worker
God himself lends aid.
**EURIPIDES**

Man wrote the Bible, not God. God wrote the books of Sciences, and man figures them out.
**GARY A. FELDMAN**

It is going to be a long, hard haul: it will require patience, courage, faith that hangs on when hope fails, if we are to tame the rude barbarity of man, so that the atomic age becomes a blessing, not a curse. There never was such a day for the Christian gospel. God help us all in these years ahead to make

that gospel live in men and nations!
**HARRY EMERSON FOSDICK, D.D.**

God does not want us to do extraordinary things: He wants us to do ordinary things extraordinarily well.
**BISHOP GORE**

The word of God is the Christian soul's best weapon, and it is essential to have it with him always. In doubt it decides, in consultation it directs; in anxiety it reassures; in sorrow it comforts; in failure it encourages; in defense it protects; in offense it is mightier than the mighty.
**WILFRED T. GRENFELL**

And the Lord answered me, and said, Write the vision, and make it plain upon tables, that he may run that readeth it.
**HABAKKUK 2:2**

If the masses of men were one-half as faithful to God—and obedient to His commands—as a dog is faithful to his master—and obedient to his commands—we would have a far better world to live in than we yet have found.
**R. B. HARRIS**

The word of God is quick, and powerful, and sharper than any two edged sword, piercing even to the dividing asunder of soul and spirit, and of the joints and marrow, and is a discerner of the thoughts and intents of the heart.
**HEBREWS 4:12**

For God is not unrighteous to forget your work and labour of love, which ye have shewed toward his name, in that ye have ministered to the saints, and do minister.
**HEBREWS 6:10**

The people that walked in darkness have seen a great light; they that dwell in the shadow of death, upon them hath the light shined.
**ISAIAH 9:2**

Thou wilt keep him in perfect peace, whose mind is stayed on thee: because he trusteth in thee. Trust ye in the Lord forever: for in the Lord Jehovah is everlasting strength.
**ISAIAH 26:3–4**

How beautiful upon the mountains are the feet of him that bringeth good tidings, that publisheth peace; that bringeth good tidings of good, that publisheth salvation; that sayeth unto Zion, Thy God reigneth!
**ISAIAH 52:7**

But now, O Lord, thou art our father; we are the clay, and thou our potter; and we all are the work of thy hand.
**ISAIAH 64:8**

And other sheep I have, which are not of this fold: them also I must bring, and they shall hear my voice; and there shall be one fold, and one shepherd.
**JOHN 10:16**

Verily, verily, I say unto you, He that believeth on me, the works that I do shall he do also; and greater works than these shall he do; because I go unto my Father.
**JOHN 14:12**

When men reject the Good Shepherd they follow some glorified bellwether who will lead the flock back to the jungle of tribal hate and strife.
**IRVING PEAKE JOHNSON**

God is action, complete with mistakes, fumblings, persistence, agony. God is not the power that has

found eternal equilibrium, but the power that is forever breaking every equilibrium, forever searching for a higher one.
**NIKOS KAZANTZAKIS**

In doing one's work primarily for God, the fear of undue restriction is put, sooner or later, out of the question. He pays me and He pays me well. He pays me and He will not fail to pay me. He pays me not merely for the rule of thumb task, which is all that men recognize, but to everything else I bring to my job in the way of industry, good intentions and cheerfulness. If the Lord loveth a cheerful giver, as St. Paul says, we may depend upon it that He loveth a cheerful worker; and where we can cleave the way to His love there we find His endless generosity.
**BASIL KING**

The finger of God never leaves identical fingerprints.
**STANISLAUS LEC**

Men are not flattered by being shown that there has been a difference of purpose between the Almighty and them.
**ABRAHAM LINCOLN**

"I will" is no word for man. There is a far diviner one, "I ought." Bow passion to reason, reason to conscience, and conscience to God, and then be as resolute and determined as you choose.
**IAN MACLAREN**

Blessed are ye, when men shall revile you, and persecute you, and say all manner of evil against you, for my sake.
**MATTHEW 5:11**

Take heed that ye do not your alms before men, to be seen of them: otherwise ye have no reward of your Father which is in heaven.
**MATTHEW 6:1**

Take my yoke upon you, and learn of me; for I am meek and lowly in heart; and ye shall find rest unto your souls. For my yoke is easy, and my burden is light.
**MATTHEW 11:29–30**

It isn't more light we need, it isn't more truth, and it isn't more scientific data. It is more Christ, more courage, more spiritual insight to act on the light we have.
**BENJAMIN E. MAYS**

Unless for 1,900 years people have been combining in a vast conspiracy to talk claptrap and humbug, Christ can change and renew human nature, can solve the moral problems of existence. And the moral problems, not the political or the economic ones, are the prior and basic problems of existence.
**ROBERT J. MCCRACKEN**

The hope of the world lies in the possibility that the scientists may get through to Christ and let Him control man's use of nature. That the citizen and the politician may get through to Christ as the redeemer who proved that brotherhood is inevitable and that all who seek beauty and truth, all who pray and all holy and humble men of heart may let God pull them to their destiny, where in Christ they may become workers here and now for the eternal works of God.
**ELMORE M. MCKEE, D.D.**

God is in the details.
**LUDWIG MIES VAN DER ROHE**

God, I can push the grass apart
And lay my finger on Thy heart!
**EDNA ST. VINCENT MILLAY**

There is no portion of our time that is our time, and the rest God's; there is no portion of money that is our money, and the rest God's money. It is all

His; He made it all, gives it all, and He has simply trusted it to us for His service. A servant has two purses, the master's and his own, but we have only one.
ADOLPHE MONOD

God gave man an upright countenance to survey the heavens, and to look upward to the stars.
OVID

Man was supposed to associate with nature because God is in nature. He is in the city too, but He is harder to find. When this country was a rural nation, it was a powerful nation, but now that it is organized into big cities it has fallen prey to evil and corrupt gangs.
NORMAN VINCENT PEALE

To remember that one is God's child, His own, that no matter what one has done God loves, even to the end, with a love that never lets go—that is the word men and women need when wars, hot and cold, mass movements and mass production, sweep over and swamp the individual. All else but his assurance fails the man in dire need.
ALBERT PEEL, D.D.

God deals with us whether in sickness or in health, whether in prosperity or adversity, whether in good or in evil days, whether in life or in death, not according to our merit but according to His mercy and love.
ALBERT J. PENNER

God is an undiscourageable God, who has never grown tired, who will never grow tired. He has always preserved for Himself a remnant of those who will live and speak and work for Him. In this fact is our hope for better days to come. Because of this fact we may even dare to believe in things that appear impossible today—enduring peace, the triumph of righteousness and goodwill toward men.
ALBERT J. PENNER

Any man who wants to give up his own self-centeredness and put his life on God's side will be put to work and will be given the only reward that even the greatest saint receives, namely, fellowship with God, reconciliation with the Father.
JAMES A. PIKE

Trust in the Lord with all thine heart; and lean not unto thine own understanding. In all thy ways acknowledge Him, and He shall direct thy paths.
PROVERBS 3:5–6

The words of the Lord are pure words: as silver tried in a furnace of earth, purified seven times. Thou shalt keep them, O Lord, thou shalt preserve them from this generation for ever.
PSALMS 12:6–7

As for God, his way is perfect: the word of the Lord is tried. He is a buckler to all those that trust in him.
PSALMS 18:30

The Lord is my shepherd; I shall not want. He maketh me to lie down in green pastures: he leadeth me beside the still waters. He restoreth my soul: he leadeth me in the paths of righteousness for his name's sake.
PSALMS 23:1–3

The Lord is my light and my salvation; whom shall I fear? The Lord is the strength of my life; of whom shall I be afraid?
PSALMS 27:1

As the hart panteth after the water brooks, so panteth my soul after thee, O God. My soul thirsteth

for God, the living God: when shall I come and appear before God?
**Psalms 42:1–2**

Whom have I in heaven but thee? and there is none upon earth that I desire beside thee. My flesh and my heart faileth: but God is the strength of my heart, and my portion forever.
**Psalms 73:25–26**

All nations whom thou hast made shall come and worship before thee, O Lord; and shall glorify thy name. For thou art great, and doest wondrous things: thou are God alone.
**Psalms 86:8–10**

I will lift up mine eyes unto the hills, from whence cometh my help. My help cometh from the Lord, which made heaven and earth.
**Psalms 121:1–2**

Except the Lord build the house, they labor in vain who built it; except the Lord keep the city, the watchman waketh in vain.
**Psalms 127:1**

Blessed is everyone that feareth the Lord; that walketh in his ways. For thou shalt eat the labor of thine hands; happy shalt thou be, and it shall be well with thee.
**Psalms 128:1–2**

Whither shall I go from thy spirit? or whither shall I flee from thy presence? If I ascent into heaven, thou art there; if I make my bed in hell, behold thou art there.
**Psalms 139:7–8**

He delighteth not in the strength of a horse: he taketh not pleasure in the legs of a man. The Lord taketh pleasure in them that fear him, in those that hope in his mercy.
**Psalms 147:11–12**

The world is a kind of spiritual kindergarten where millions of bewildered infants are trying to spell God with the wrong blocks.
**Edwin Arlington Robinson**

We are tempted to use God when we ought to be used by God.
**Sherman S. Robinson**

O the depth of the riches both of the wisdom and knowledge of God! How unsearchable are his judgments, and his ways past finding out! For who has known the mind of the Lord or who has been his counsellor?
**Romans 11:33–34**

After we have recognized that we are all undeserving creatures who have received the love of God, who can but respond and show it in his own life?
**Edgar F. Romig**

Let never day nor night unhallow'd pass, but still remember what the Lord hath done.
**William Shakespeare**

If we had intellectual vigor enough to ascend from effects to causes, we would explain political, economical and social phenomena less by credit sheets, balance of trade and reparations than by our attitude towards God.
**Bishop Fulton J. Sheen**

Balance the bad news of life with the good news of Christ.
**Ralph W. Sockman**

Make Christ the head of the house and He will transform religion into life, the greed of competition into the grace of cooperation, possession into trusteeship and the family into the spiritual atom of the atomic age.
RALPH W. SOCKMAN

Take what you want, said God, take it—and pay for it.
SPANISH PROVERB

Christ, Who is God, sanctified labor by toiling as a carpenter. So too did Christ sanctify capital by calling laborers to work in His vineyard, paying them their just hire. Shareholder with labor, it is capital's duty also to preserve itself blessed by fostering human happiness and prosperity, for no man should be slave nor master to another, but each should be servant to God and helpmate to his neighbor.
CARDINAL FRANCIS JOSEPH SPELLMAN

God is our only hope. He alone will not fail us, for He came to abide in our midst as one of us, if we will but open our heats to receive Him. He came to glory in our glory, to suffer in our sufferings, and, in this hour of fears and tears God is no stranger to our lot. He is yoked to the same plough as are we!
CARDINAL FRANCIS JOSEPH SPELLMAN

It is by the goodness of God that in our country we have those three unspeakably precious things: freedom of speech, freedom of conscience, and the prudence never to practice either.
MARK TWAIN

The noblest motive is the public good.
VIRGIL

Only a life built into God's place can succeed. Half of our discouragements are due to the fact that we are not in tune with the infinite harmony of the Great Power. We should be helpers in building the city of God—a city that will endure when all earthly cities crumble to dust.
BISHOP HERBERT E. WELCH

Fear of God builds churches but love of God builds men.
LOUIS O. WILLIAMS

We need to understand that the world's evil is only the accumulation of evils in us. It is the search for God that is urgent and practical in human life.
PAUL AUSTIN WOLFE

If God lived on earth, people would break his windows.
YIDDISH PROVERB

## *Golden Rule*

Of yore, when gold was fiscal god,
We had a Golden Rule,
But that was when we
Worked to eat,
And did our stints in
Sunday School.
ART BUCK

Tsze-King asked, "Is there one word which may serve as a rule of practice for all one's life?"

The Master said, "Is not reciprocity such a word? What you do not want done to yourself, do not do to others."
CONFUCIUS

The Golden Rule is of no use to you whatever unless you realize that it is your move.
FRANK CRANE

Why should the Golden Rule be so difficult in business and foreign relation? The happily married treat

each other as they wish to be treated. They treat their children better than they wish to be treated themselves. Unless we do unto a friend as we do unto ourselves, we lose a friend. In an emergency we rush to the aid of our neighbor. Is it so great a step to realize that all people everywhere are neighbors?
**ARTHUR DUNN**

Slowly and painfully man is learning that he must do to others what he would have them do to him.
**ANTHONY EDEN**

Do you know any Belief or Faith with followers that doesn't start with the Golden Rule?
**MALCOLM FORBES**

To keep the Golden Rule we must put ourselves in other people's places, but to do that consists in and depends upon picturing ourselves in their places. If we had the imagination to do that there would be fewer families estranged by misunderstanding between the older and the younger generations, fewer bitter judgments would pass our lips, fewer racial, national and class prejudices would stain our lives.
**HARRY EMERSON FOSDICK, D.D.**

Commit the Golden Rule to memory—now commit it to life.
**EDWIN MARKHAM**

Three ideas stand out above all others in the influence they have exerted and are destined to exert upon the development of the human race: The idea of the Golden Rule; the idea of natural law; the idea of age-long growth or evolution.
**ROBERT A. MILLIKAN**

If the Golden Rule is to be preached at all in these modern days, when so much of our life is devoted to business, it must be preached specially in its application to the conduct of business.
**F. S. SCHENCK**

People think of the Golden Rule as something mild and innocuous, like a baby lamb. But when they suffer an infringement of it, they think they've been mauled by a panther.
**FRANCIS WREN**

## *Goodness*

Good nature is more agreeable in conversation than wit, and gives a certain air to the countenance which is more amiable than beauty.
**JOSEPH ADDISON**

Good has two meanings: it means that which is good absolutely and that which is good for somebody.
**ARISTOTLE**

Goodness is easier to recognize than to define.
**W. H. AUDEN**

Let goodness go with the doing.
**MARCUS AURELIUS ANTONINUS**

Let us put an end, once for all, to this discussion of what a good man should be—and be one.
**MARCUS AURELIUS ANTONINUS**

No longer talk at all about the kind of man a good man ought to be, but be such.
**MARCUS AURELIUS ANTONINUS**

You exist but as a part inherent in a greater whole. Do not live as though you had a thousand years before you. The common due impends; while you live, and while you may, be good.
**MARCUS AURELIUS ANTONINUS**

Amid life's quests, there seems but worthy one: to do men good.
**GAMALIEL BAILEY**

All is not evil in America, nor is the country hopeless. God is greater than Satan. The forces that make for good are greater than the forces that make for evil, but they must have human channels through which they can flow.
**GORDON H. BAKER**

Good nature is often a mere matter of health.
**HENRY WARD BEECHER**

It is the greatest good to the greatest number which is the measure of right and wrong.
**JEREMY BENTHAM**

To become a thoroughly good man is the best prescription for keeping a sound mind in a sound body.
**FRANCES BOWEN**

Good is good, but better carrieth it.
**H. G. BOHN**

Reason teaches us that what is good is good for something, and that what is good for nothing is not good at all.
**FRANCIS HERBERT BRADLEY**

There is no limit to the good a man can do if he doesn't care who gets the credit.
**JUDSON B. BRANCH**

No man or woman of the humblest sort can really be strong, gentle and good, without the world being better for it, without somebody being helped and comforted by the very existence of that goodness.
**PHILLIPS BROOKS**

How happy the station which every moment furnishes opportunities of doing good to thousands! How dangerous that which every moment exposes to the injuring of millions!
**JEAN DE LA BRUYÈRE**

Good order is the foundation of all good things.
**EDMUND BURKE**

Whatever mitigates the woes or increases the happiness of others—this is my criterion of goodness. And whatever injures society at large, or any individual in it—this is my measure of iniquity.
**ROBERT BURNS**

Men should not try to overstrain their goodness more than any other faculty.
**SAMUEL BUTLER**

He cannot long be good that knows not why he is good.
**RICHARD CAREW**

Goodness is always an asset. A man who is straight, friendly and useful may never be famous, but he is respected and liked by all who know him. He has laid a sound foundation for success and he will have a worthwhile life.
**HERBERT N. CASSON**

The best way to keep good acts in memory is to refresh them with new.
**MARCUS CATO**

Every year of my life I grow more convinced that it is wisest and best to fix our attention on the beautiful and the good, and dwell as little as possible on the evil and the false.
**RICHARD CECIL**

It is impossible for good or evil to last forever; and hence it follows that the evil having lasted so long, the good must be now nigh at hand.
**MIGUEL DE CERVANTES**

Goodness consists not in the outward things we do, but in the inward thing we are. To be good is the great thing.
EDWIN H. CHAPIN

They're only truly great who are truly good.
GEORGE CHAPMAN

While I can crawl upon this planet I think myself obliged to do what good I can, in my narrow domestic spheres, to my fellow creatures, and to wish them all the good I cannot do.
LORD CHESTERFIELD

If you pursue good with labor, the labor passes away but the good remains; if you pursue evil with pleasure, the pleasure passes away and the evil remains.
CICERO

In nothing do men approach so nearly to the gods as doing good to men.
CICERO

Inability to tell good from evil is the greatest worry of man's life.
CICERO

Goodness and greatness go not always together.
JOHN CLARKE

In life we shall find many men that are great, and some that are good, but very few men that are both great and good.
CHARLES CALEB COLTON

Let no man presume to think that he can devise any plan of extensive good, unalloyed and unadulterated with evil.
CHARLES CALEB COLTON

He who wishes to secure the good of others has already secured his own.
CONFUCIUS

When you see a good man, think of emulating him; when you see a bad man, examine your own heart.
CONFUCIUS

Little progress can be made by merely attempting to repress what is evil; our great hope lies in developing what is good.
CALVIN COOLIDGE

Doing good, disinterested good, is not our trade.
WILLIAM COWPER

He who stops being better stops being good.
OLIVER CROMWELL

There are six things that "keep us going:"

First, the instinct to live, which we apparently have no part in making or deciding about.

Second, group consciousness and the desire that we have to win the approbation of our fellows within the group.

Third, the various interests that we may find in life, such as religion or art or some such other branch of esthetics.

Fourth, in our climate the habit of work.

Fifth, the sheer joy of physical life that we find in hours of well-earned recreation after hard work—games, fishing, tramping the hills, a good book before an open fire.

Sixth, and most important, the general feeling that we have that there is some abstract goodness or rightness in the world with which we may cooperate in making the world a fine place for a splendid race of men, women and children to live in.
FRANK PARKER DAY

He is the wisest and happiest man, who, by constant attention of thought discovers the greatest opportunity of doing good, and breaks through every opposition that he may improve these opportunities.
**PHILIP DODDRIDGE**

The smallest good deed is better than the grandest good intention.
**DUGUET**

Between two evils, choose neither; between two goods, choose both.
**TRYON EDWARDS**

To be good, we must do good; and by doing good, we take a sure means of being good, as the use and exercise of the muscles increase their power.
**TRYON EDWARDS**

To have a free, peaceful and prosperous world we must be ever stronger . . . particularly in the spiritual things. . . . It is American belief in decency and justice and progress and the value of individual liberty because of the rights conferred on each of us by our Creator that will carry us through. . . . There must be something in the heart as well as in the head.
**DWIGHT D. EISENHOWER**

Nothing is so good as it seems beforehand.
**GEORGE ELIOT**

He is good that failed never.
**DAVID FERGUSSON**

A good man therefore is a standing lesson to us all.
**HENRY FIELDING**

Let no man be sorry he has done good, because others have done evil! If a man has acted right, he has done well, though alone; if wrong, the sanction of all mankind will not justify him.
**HENRY FIELDING**

It's so much easier to do good than to be good.
**B. C. FORBES**

Make no expense but to do good to others or yourself.
**BENJAMIN FRANKLIN**

No man is so good, but another may be as good as he.
**THOMAS FULLER**

The luxury of doing good surpasses every other personal enjoyment.
**JOHN GAY**

Experience has convinced me that there is a thousand times more goodness, wisdom, and love in the world than men imagine.
**GEHLES**

The Good, the True and the Beautiful! Alas, the Good is so often untrue, the True so often unbeautiful, the Beautiful so often not good.
**ISAAC GOLDBERG**

Learn the luxury of doing good.
**OLIVER GOLDSMITH**

Whatever mitigates the woes, or increases the happiness of others, is a just criterion of goodness; and whatever injures society at large, or any individual in it, is a criterion of iniquity.
**OLIVER GOLDSMITH**

Every person is responsible for all the good within the scope of his abilities, and for no more, and none can tell whose sphere is the largest.
**GAIL HAMILTON**

Good nature is the beauty of the mind, and like personal beauty, wins almost without anything

else—sometimes, indeed, in spite of positive deficiencies.
JONAS HANWAY

Goodness without wisdom always accomplishes evil.
ROBERT A. HEINLEIN

It's hard to see a halo when you're looking for horns.
CULLEN HIGHTOWER

We can do more good by being good than in any other way.
ROWLAND HILL

The power of a man is his present means to obtain some future apparent good.
THOMAS HOBBES

Whatsoever is the object of any man's appetite or desire, that is it which he for his part calleth good.
THOMAS HOBBES

Set about doing good to somebody. Put on your hat, and go and visit the sick and poor of your neighborhood; inquire into their circumstances, and minister to their wants. Seek out the desolate, and afflicted, and oppressed, and tell them of the consolations of religion. I have often tried this method, and have always found it the best medicine for a heavy heart.
HOWARD

Nature will not forgive those who fail to fulfill the law of their being. The law of human beings is wisdom and goodness, not unlimited acquisition.
ROBERT M. HUTCHINS

An inexhaustible good nature is one of the most precious gifts of heaven, spreading itself like oil over the troubled sea of thought, and keeping the mind smooth and equable in the roughest weather.
WASHINGTON IRVING

Goodness, if it is to be really goodness and not merely conventional behavior, must be freely acquired; it cannot be imposed from without by discipline and cannot be achieved by merely keeping the rules.
CYRIL E. M. JOAD

As I know more of mankind I expect less of them, and am ready to call a man a good man upon easier terms than I was formerly.
SAMUEL JOHNSON

I read in a book that a man called Christ went about doing good. It is very disconcerting to me that I am so easily satisfied with just going about.
TOYOHIKO KAGAWA

An action is essentially good if the motive of the agent be good, regardless of the consequences.
IMMANUEL KANT

Walking on water wasn't built in a day.
JACK KEROUAC

The greatest pleasure I know, is to do a good action by stealth, and have it found out by accident.
CHARLES LAMB

You are not very good if you are not better than your best friends imagine you to be.
JOHANN LAVATER

When I do good, I feel good. When I do bad, I feel bad. And that's my religion.
ABRAHAM LINCOLN

The smallest actual good is better than the most magnificent promise of impossibilities.
THOMAS B. MACAULAY

An act of goodness is of itself an act of happiness. No reward coming after the event can compare with the sweet reward that went with it.
MAURICE MAETERLINCK

A man who wishes to make a profession of goodness in everything must necessarily come to grief among so many who are not good.
NICCOLÒ MACHIAVELLI

A good man doubles the length of his existence; to have lived so as to look back with pleasure on our past life is to live twice.
MARTIAL

To try too hard to make people good is one way to make them worse. The only way to make them good is to be good, remembering well the beam and the mote.
GEORGE MCDONALD

Good, the more communicated, more abundant grows.
JOHN MILTON

Report followeth not all goodness, except difficulty and rarity be joined thereto.
MICHEL DE MONTAIGNE

On the whole, human beings want to be good, but not too good, and not quite all the time.
GEORGE ORWELL

The world is my country, all mankind are my brethren, and to do good is my religion.
THOMAS PAINE

The good that we take with us at the last call is the good that we do while here.
WILLIAM M. PECK

Be rather bountiful than expensive; do good with what thou hast, or it will do thee no good.
WILLIAM PENN

For so it is the will of God, that with doing good ye may put to silence the ignorance of foolish men.
I PETER 2:15

That state is best ordered when the wicked have no command, and the good have.
PITTACUS

Withhold not good from them to whom it is due, when it is in the power of thine hand to do it. Say not unto thy neighbor, Go, and come again, and tomorrow I will give, when then thou has it by thee.
PROVERBS 3:27–28

The backslider in heart shall be filled with his own ways: and a good man shall be satisfied from himself.
PROVERBS 14:14

The bad you hear about a man may not be true, but when people say something good about him, you can bet on it.
ROBERT QUILLEN

That is my good that does me good.
JOHN RAY

Do not wait for extraordinary circumstances to do good; try to use ordinary situations.
JEAN PAUL RICHTER

The sorrow of knowing that there is evil in the best is far out-balanced by the joy of discovering that there is good in the worst.
AUSTEN FOX RIGGS

No man deserves to be praised for his goodness unless he has strength of character to be wicked.

All other goodness is generally nothing but indolence or impotence of will.
**FRANÇOIS DE LA ROCHEFOUCAULD**

Nothing is rarer than true good nature; they who are reputed to have it are generally only pliant or weak.
**FRANÇOIS DE LA ROCHEFOUCAULD**

Nobody does good to men with impunity.
**AUGUSTE RODIN**

And we know that all things work together for good to them that love God, to them who are called according to His purpose.
**ROMANS 8:28**

I desire to see in this country the decent men strong and the strong men decent, and until we get that combination in pretty good shape, we are not going to be by any means as successful as we should be.
**THEODORE ROOSEVELT**

My intellect as well as my instincts lead me to the conclusion that men have a positive yearning to be good.
**ALBERT ROSENFELD**

He that does good to another does also good to himself.
**SENECA**

It is not goodness to be better than the worst.
**SENECA**

The largest part of goodness is the will to become good.
**SENECA**

We are members of one great body planted by nature in a mutual love, and fitted for a social life.
We must consider that we were born for the good of the whole.
**SENECA**

If to do were as easy as to know what were good to do, chapels had been churches, and poor men's cottages princes' palaces. It is a good divine that follows his own instructions; I can easier teach twenty what were good to be done, than be one of the twenty to follow mine own teaching.
**WILLIAM SHAKESPEARE**

In this earthly world . . . to do harm is often laudable, to do good sometime accounted dangerous folly.
**WILLIAM SHAKESPEARE**

Doing good is the only certainly happy action of a man's life.
**SIR PHILIP SIDNEY**

Johnson well says, "He who waits to do a great deal of good at once will never do anything." Life is made up of little things. It is very rarely that an occasion is offered for doing a great deal at once. True greatness consists in being great in little things.
**CHARLES SIMMONS**

You, yourself, have got to see that there is no just interpretation of life except in terms of life's best things. No pleasure philosophy, no sensuality, no place nor power, no material success can for a moment give such inner satisfaction as the sense of living for good purposes, for maintenance of integrity, for the preservation of self-approval.
**MINOT SIMONS, D.D.**

There is one postulate on which pessimists and optimists agree. Both their arguments assume it to be self-evident that life is good or bad according as it does or does not bring a surplus of agreeable feeling.
**HERBERT SPENCER**

There are two things that men should never weary of—goodness and humility.
**ROBERT LOUIS STEVENSON**

There is an idea abroad among moral people that they should make their neighbors good. One person I have to make good: Myself. But my duty to my neighbor is much more nearly expressed by saying that I have to make him happy if I may.
**ROBERT LOUIS STEVENSON**

There is so much good in the worst of us, and so much bad in the best of us, that it behooves all of us not to talk about the rest of us.
**ROBERT LOUIS STEVENSON**

What is the real relation between happiness and goodness? It is only within a few generations that men have found courage to say that there is none.
**WILLIAM GRAHAM SUMNER**

The world is good-natured to people who are good-natured.
**WILLIAM MAKEPEACE THACKERAY**

No one would remember the Good Samaritan if he'd only had good intentions; he had money, too.
**MARGARET THATCHER**

See that none render evil for evil unto any man, but ever follow that which is good, both among yourselves, and to all men.
**I THESSALONIANS 5:15**

You can't keep a good man down or a bad one up.
**P. K. THOMAJAN**

Goodness is the only investment which never fails.
**HENRY DAVID THOREAU**

If I repent of anything, it is very likely to be my good behavior.
**HENRY DAVID THOREAU**

There is little pleasure in the world that is true and sincere beside the pleasure of doing our duty and doing good.
**JOHN TILLOTSON**

When we have practiced good actions awhile, they become easy; when they are easy, we take pleasure in them; when they please us, we do them frequently; and then, by frequency of act, they grow into a habit.
**JOHN TILLOTSON**

To be good is noble. To tell people how to be good is even nobler and much less trouble.
**MARK TWAIN**

That is good which doth good.
**RALPH VENNING**

The only way to compel men to speak good of us is to do it.
**VOLTAIRE**

Do all the good you can, in all the ways you can, to all the souls you can, in every place you can, at all the times you can, with all the zeal you can, as long as ever you can.
**JOHN WESLEY**

A good man's life is all of a piece.
**BENJAMIN WHICHCOTE**

Some things must be good in themselves, else there could be no measure whereby to lay out good and evil.
**BENJAMIN WHICHCOTE**

If you pretend to be good, the world takes you very seriously. If you pretend to be bad, it doesn't. Such is the outstanding stupidity of optimism.
**OSCAR WILDE**

Have as much good nature as good sense since they generally are companions.
**WILLIAM WYCHERLEY**

## *Goodwill*

If we understand that the Lord has given us a doctrine of wholehearted, aggressive goodwill, even toward unfriendly people, we can save our world, even at a time when it was never more difficult to believe in ourselves and our fellowmen.
**LEE VAUGHN BARKER, D.D.**

The transcendent importance of love and goodwill in all human relations is shown by their mighty beneficent effect upon the individual and society.
**GEORGE D. BIRKHOFF**

But if you should take the bond of goodwill out of the universe no house or city could stand, nor would even the tillage of the fields abide. If that statement is not clear, then you may understand how great is the power of friendship and of concord from a consideration of the results of enmity and disagreement. For what house is so strong, or what state so enduring that it cannot be utterly overthrown by animosities and division?
**CICERO**

Goodwill is the mightiest practical force in the universe.
**CHARLES F. DOLE**

None of us can buy goodwill; we must earn it.
**WILLIAM FEATHER**

Goodwill is the one and only asset that competition cannot undersell or destroy.
**MARSHALL FIELD**

Employers, have you ever stopped to reckon what the goodwill of your workers is worth? . . . In most large concerns it would be worth more in dollars and cents to have the goodwill of the working force than of those on the outside. It has been repeatedly demonstrated that the average working force is capable of increasing its production 25% or more whenever the workers feel so inclined. Workers animated by ill will cannot possibly give results equal to those of workers animated by goodwill. The tragic fact appears to be that a tremendous number of working forces are not so animated. . . .
**B. C. FORBES**

To mobilize our strength for security in this age of crisis, we must establish so impregnable a moral position that everywhere men of goodwill may find in our objectives the fulfillment of their yearnings for peace, freedom and abundance.
**W. AVERELL HARRIMAN**

I have found it helpful to keep constantly in mind that there are really two entries to be made for every transaction—one in terms of immediate dollars and cents, the other in terms of goodwill.
**RALPH HITZ**

A great asset of any business is goodwill. This is a trite statement but, like so many self-evident truths, it seldom gets the careful consideration it deserves. Goodwill does not come through clarion advertising appeals, exhortations, protestations. Character, from which stems goodwill, is a quality of slow growth through performance.
**W. ALTON JONES**

Goodwill to others is constructive thought. It helps build us up. It is good for your body. It makes your

blood purer, your muscles stronger, and your whole form more symmetrical in shape. It is the real elixir of life. The more such thought you attract to you, the more life you will have.
**PRENTICE MULFORD**

The most precious thing anyone—man or store, anybody or anything—can have is the goodwill of others. It is something as fragile as an orchid. And as beautiful! As precious as a gold nugget—and as hard to find. As powerful as a great turbine—and as hard to build. As wonderful as youth—and as hard to keep.
**AMOS PARRISH**

The foundation of good human relations is friendliness and good will. The right conception of business, in my judgment, is a transaction—or a series of transactions—carried out in the spirit of friendliness. There are, I know, some people in all walks of life who are so cold-blooded in their attitude that dealings with them chill the blood. There is much more to business than the exchange of material values. We can do business, just as we can carry on all other aspects of our lives, in a wholesome and friendly attitude. When we do so, our days become brighter and happier, more meaningful and more worthwhile.
**CHARLES G. REIGNER**

Goodwill is no easy symbol of good wishes. It is an immeasurable and tremendous energy, the atomic energy of the spirit.
**ELEANOR B. STOCK**

Goodwill is the mightiest practical force in the universe.
**TALMUDIC SAYING**

Henceforth in me instill, O God, a sweet good will to all mankind.
**THEODORE TILTON**

Goodwill cannot be insured. The only way to retain it is to keep earning it.
**FRANK TYGER**

By helping one another in times of disaster, nations are strengthening the bonds of goodwill that will yet bring the peoples of earth together.
**WALTER VAN KIRK**

Goodwill for a business is built by good goods, service and truthful advertising.
**E. R. WAITE**

## *Gossip*

If we knew what will be said about us when we are gone, we would have been gone a long time ago.
**DON-AMINADO**

If we all said to people's faces what we say behind one another's backs, society would be impossible.
**HONORÉ DE BALZAC**

There are many who dare not kill themselves for fear of what the neighbors will say.
**CYRIL CONNOLLY**

If you are told that such an one speaks ill of you, make no defense against what was said, but answer, "He surely knew not my other faults, else he would not have mentioned these only!"
**EPICTETUS**

Talking things over has its place in an organization [but] so-called "conferences" are being grossly overdone. One executive stops at the desk of another to tell him, perhaps, about the wonderful score he made at golf on Saturday afternoon. This chin-chin immediately becomes a "conference," and neither the office boy nor the telephone operator must dis-

turb either gentleman. More idle gossip is indulged in at many business "conferences" these days than an old wives' sewing circle would be guilty of.
**B. C. Forbes**

I don't care what is written about me so long as it isn't true.
**Katharine Hepburn**

Shun the inquisitive, for you will be sure to find him leaky. Open ears do not keep conscientiously what has been intrusted to them, and a word once spoken flies, never to be recalled.
**Horace**

If you haven't got anything nice to say about anybody, come sit next to me.
**Alice Roosevelt Longworth**

So live that you wouldn't be ashamed to sell the family parrot to the town gossip.
**Will Rogers**

One's own vanities and humiliations I find a delicious subject for conversation. Things said of me behind my back I don't enjoy, and don't listen to them.
**Logan Pearsall Smith**

There is only one thing in the world worse than being talked about, and that is not being talked about.
**Oscar Wilde**

## *Government*

While all other sciences have advanced, that of government is at a standstill—little better understood, little better practiced now than three or four thousand years ago.
**John Adams**

A feeble government produces more factions than an oppressive one.
**Fisher Ames**

It gets harder and harder to support the government in the manner to which it has become accustomed.
**Anonymous**

Whatsoever moveth is stronger than that which is moved, and whatsoever governeth is stronger than that which is governed.
**St. Aristides**

It would seem that one of the most important things that our universities can teach their students is the importance of studying our form of government, the vital necessity of college men taking an interest in the government or public service, and devoting part of their lives to that important work. Only in this way can the people regain the reins of government, become again the masters of their government, and resume self-government according to its original constitutional ideals. The people, by parting with control over their local affairs to bureaus at Washington, in truth "Sell their birthright for a mess of pottage."
**Henry H. Atkinson**

When any of the four pillars of government—religion, justice, counsel, and treasure—are mainly shaken or weakened, men had need to pray for fair weather.
**Francis Bacon**

All government is a trust. Every branch of government is a trust, and immemorially acknowledged to be so.
**Jeremy Bentham**

At best, outside aid can provide only a margin over and above what people are doing for themselves. It can be the margin between failure and success, but

only when there is substantial local effort. And there can be such an effort only when a nation has a will to develop—when there is a drive within the country itself to improve the living standards of its people, and a government which reflects that drive.
EUGENE R. BLACK

The real problem with which modern government has to deal is how to protect the citizen against the encroachment upon his rights and liberties by his own government, how to save him from the repressive schemes born of the egotism of public office.
WILLIAM E. BORAH

A reform is a correction of abuses, a revolution is a transfer of power.
EDWARD BULWER-LYTTON

Of representative assemblies may not this good be said: that contending parties fight there, since fight they must, by petition [and] parliamentary eloquence, not by sword, bayonet and bursts of military cannon.
THOMAS CARLYLE

Socialism is the weakest of all bulwarks against Communism. Socialists lead people up the garden path to the brink of a precipice and then turn around and say, as they tumble over, "We are very sorry; we never meant to go so far."
WINSTON CHURCHILL

The administration of government, like a guardianship, ought to be directed to the good of those who confer, not of those who receive the trust.
CICERO

Government is a trust, and the officers of the government are trustees; and both the trust and the trustees are created for the benefit of the people.
HENRY CLAY

A government for the people must depend for its success on the intelligence, the morality, the justice, and the interest of the people themselves.
GROVER CLEVELAND

The only choice which Providence has graciously left to a vicious government is either to fall by the people if they become enlightened, or with them, if they are kept enslaved and ignorant.
SAMUEL TAYLOR COLERIDGE

There is good government when those who are near are happy, and when those who are far away desire to come.
CONFUCIUS

Governments are necessarily continuing concerns. They have to keep going in good times and in bad. They therefore need a wide margin of safety. If taxes and debt are made all the people can bear when times are good, there will be certain disaster when times are bad.
CALVIN COOLIDGE

You have to stand every day three or four hours of visitors. Nine-tenths of them want something they ought not to have. If you keep dead-still they will run down in three or four minutes. If you even cough or smile they will start up all over again.
CALVIN COOLIDGE

You can only govern men by serving them. The rule is without exception.
VICTOR COUSIN

No matter what the form of a government, there are in fact only two kinds of government possible. Under one system, the state is everything and the individual is an incident. Under that system, the individual is a subject, rather than a citizen. Under that system, the individual has no rights, though they may be termed such; he has only privileges.

Under that system, the state is the reservoir of all rights, all privileges, all powers. But this system our forefathers rejected. They declared that all just government derives its powers from the consent of the governed. They affirmed the dignity and the sanctity of the individual. . . . They elected a man-made state, not a state-made man.
FRANK M. DIXON

The state has but one face for me: that of the police. To my eyes, all of the state's ministries have this single face, and I cannot imagine the ministry of culture other than as the police of culture, with its prefect and commissioners.
JEAN DUBUFFET

Do I think republics are ungrateful? I do. That's why they continue to be republics.
FINLEY PETER DUNNE

There is far more danger in public than in private monopoly, for when Government goes into business it can always shift its losses to the taxpayers. Government never makes ends meet—and that is the first requisite of business.
THOMAS EDISON

I firmly believe that the army of persons who urge greater and greater centralization of authority and greater and greater dependence upon the Federal Treasury are really more dangerous to our form of government than any external threat that can possibly be arrayed against us.
DWIGHT D. EISENHOWER

There is a kind of dictatorship that can come about through a creeping paralysis of thought, readiness to accept paternalistic measures by government, and along with those measure comes a surrender of our own responsibilities and therefore a surrender of our own thought over our own lives and our own right to exercise the vote. The free system gives the right to every citizen to do something for himself. Because he has the right, the opportunity is always there.
DWIGHT D. EISENHOWER

The less government we have the better—the fewer laws and the less confided power. The antidote to this abuse of formal government is the influence of private character, the growth of the individual.
RALPH WALDO EMERSON

Local government is the foundation of democracy, if it fails, democracy will fail.
ROBERT W. FLACK

If the World War [I] demonstrated anything it was that government ownership is fraught with the gravest dangers and usually leads to disaster. Take Britain. The two problems which have caused the greatest trouble since the war ended have been transportation and coal. The government seized both industries when the war broke out. It got them into such a hopeless mess that it does not know how to turn. [In] coal, the government now realizes, it took hold of the tail of a wild animal and is afraid to let go.
B. C. FORBES

Civil Service has itself become such a spoils system that a fed-to-the-teeth-with-bureaucracy public threatens to support a return to the old one.

Once in a civil service job, one needs only to live to rise. It's near impossible to be fired for incompetence, indifference, woeful attendance, insubordination, or even being caught red-handed in the cookie jar . . .

When Congress passed the civil service act slightly more than 100 years ago after a disappointed job-seeker assassinated President Garfield, it surely didn't have in mind that its baby would turn into such an uncivil monster.
MALCOLM FORBES

Pundits often poke fun at President Johnson's tendency to grab the phone and personally issue an order or a request to someone 25 layers below the top. I guess though that in these instances Mr. Johnson's long years of experience in government taught him where the inaction begins to set in.

If Presidents have such trouble moving the federal bureaucracy, what chance is there for us mere citizens? It's a point to keep in mind next time we start to say, "Let's have the Government do it." That's often a way, it would seem, of making sure that whatever it is that should be done isn't.
MALCOLM FORBES

We want no dictatorship of physicists, as physicists. If our democracy is to realize its full promise, we want no dictatorship at all—of any species. What we want and need is the enlightened and active interest of all men of intelligence and goodwill in their government, and their participation in its function.
JEROME FRANK

Government is itself an art, one of the subtlest of the arts. It is neither business, nor technology, nor applied science. It is the art of making men live together in peace and with reasonable happiness.
FELIX FRANKFURTER

It is wonderful how preposterously the affairs of the world are managed. We assemble parliaments and councils to have the benefit of collected wisdom, but we necessarily have, at the same time, the inconvenience of their collected passions, prejudices and private interests: for regulating commerce an assembly of great men is the greatest fool on earth.
BENJAMIN FRANKLIN

If private business should be supervised in the public interest, government, when it assumes a business role, is in equal need of supervision.
JAMES A. FULTON

All free governments are managed by the combined wisdom and folly of the people.
JAMES A. GARFIELD

It is the duty of government to make it difficult for people to do wrong, easy to do right.
WILLIAM E. GLADSTONE

In framing a government which is to be administered by men over men, the great difficulty lies in this: You must first enable the government to control the governed, and in the next place oblige it to control itself.
ALEXANDER HAMILTON

Why has government been instituted at all? Because the passions of men will not conform to the dictates of reason and justice, without constraint.
ALEXANDER HAMILTON

All good government must begin in the home. It is useless to make good laws for bad people. Public sentiment is more than law.
H. R. HAWES

No free government, or the blessings of liberty can be preserved to any people but by a firm adherence to justice, moderation, temperance, frugality, and virtue, and by a frequent recurrence to fundamental principles.
PATRICK HENRY

If we fixed a hangnail the way our government fixes the economy, we'd slam a car door on it.
CULLEN HIGHTOWER

Believe, if you will, that there may have been faults in our industrial system, yet the fact remains that the welfare of the average man has not so far advanced under any other form of government, and that whatever evil exists will not be corrected by

delegating to government, with all its weaknesses, the authority to run and control all business and to control the daily lives and activities of laboring mankind. Nor will any existing waste and extravagance of government be eliminated or appreciably diminished until the average man realizes that the burden of paying its bills will, through direct or indirect taxation, ultimately fall upon him, his children or his children's children.
JAMES B. HILL

There is one thing better than good government, and that is government in which all the people have a part.
WALTER HINES

There are very few so foolish that they had not rather govern themselves than be governed by others.
THOMAS HOBBES

Along this road of spending, the government either takes over, which is Socialism, or dictates institutional and economic life, which is Fascism.
HERBERT HOOVER

The history of mankind is one long record of giving revolution another trial—and then limping back at last to sanity, safety and hard work!
EDGAR WATSON HOWE

Emergency does not create power. Emergency does not increase granted power or remove or diminish the restrictions imposed upon power granted or reserved. The Constitution was adopted in a period of grave emergency. Its grants of power to the Federal government and its limitations of the power of the states were determined in the light of emergency and they are not altered by emergency.
CHARLES EVANS HUGHES

The first lesson in civics is that efficient government should begin at home.
CHARLES EVANS HUGHES

Government can be bigger than any of the players on the field as a referee, but it has no right to become one of the players.
AUSTIN IGLEHEART

There are no necessary evils in government. Its evils exist only in its abuses. If it would confine itself to equal protection, and, as Heaven does its rain, shower its favors alike on the high and on the low, the rich and the poor, it would be an unqualified blessing.
ANDREW JACKSON

I think we have more machinery of government than is necessary, too many parasites living on the labor of the industrious.
THOMAS JEFFERSON

My reading of history convinces me that most bad government results from too much government.
THOMAS JEFFERSON

The persons and property of out citizens are entitled to the protection of our government in all places where they may lawfully go.
THOMAS JEFFERSON

The qualifications of self-government in society are not innate. They are the result of habit and long training, and for these they will require time and probably much suffering.
THOMAS JEFFERSON

Those who bear equally the burdens of government should equally participate of its benefits.
THOMAS JEFFERSON

The future holds little hope for any government where the present holds no hope for the people.
LYNDON JOHNSON

One of the things we have to be thankful for is that we don't get as much government as we pay for.
CHARLES F. KETTERING

As restrictions and prohibitions are multiplied the people grow poorer and poorer. When they are subjected to overmuch government, the land is thrown into confusion.
LAO-TZU

It has long been a grave question whether any government, not too strong for the liberties of its people, can be strong enough to maintain its existence in great emergencies.
ABRAHAM LINCOLN

Let the people know the truth and the country is safe.
ABRAHAM LINCOLN

No man is good enough to govern another man without that other man's consent.
ABRAHAM LINCOLN

Dictatorship is always merely an aria, never an opera.
EMIL LUDWIG

A popular government without popular information, or the means of acquiring it, is but a prologue to a farce or a tragedy, or perhaps both.
JAMES MADISON

If it was wise, manly, and patriotic for us to establish a free government, it is equally wise to attend to the necessary means of its preservation.
JAMES MONROE

If a man hears our system attacked, and doesn't understand it well enough to pick out the flaws and the phonies in the argument, he is a likely candidate for the pinks and reds.
CHARLES G. MORTIMER

Nationalization would seem to operate on the theory that a socialistic government can legislate unsuccessful people into prosperity by legislating successful people out of it.
CECIL PALMER

Governments, like clocks, go from the motion men give them, and as governments are made and moved by men, so by them they are ruined also. Therefore governments depend upon men rather then men upon governments.
WILLIAM PENN

No system of government was ever so ill devised that, under proper men, it wouldn't work well enough.
WILLIAM PENN

The punishment suffered by the wise who refuse to take part in the government, is to live under the government of bad men.
PLATO

To be governed is to be, at every operation, every transaction, noted, counted, registered, taxed, stamped, measured, numbered, assessed, licensed, authorized, admonished, prevented, forbidden, reformed, corrected, punished.
P. J. PROUDHON

Men well governed should seek after no other liberty, for there can be no greater liberty than a good government.
SIR WALTER RALEIGH

Millions of individuals making their own decisions in the marketplace will always allocate resources better than any centralized government planning process.
**RONALD REAGAN**

The opportunity and the necessity for the Government's service to its people cannot be confined within rigid limits. The Constitution sets no such bounds. It is a living, vital institution whose function is to guide and not to curb necessary governmental powers.
**STANLEY F. REED**

There are only two places where Socialism works—one is a beehive and the other is an ant hill.
**IAN STEWARD RICHARDSON**

Things in our country run in spite of government, not by aid of it.
**WILL ROGERS**

Industrial combination is not wrong in itself. The danger lies in taking government into partnership.
**FRANKLIN D. ROOSEVELT**

Under government ownership corruption can flourish just as rankly as under private ownership.
**THEODORE ROOSEVELT**

The major problem confronting the world today is: Shall the people govern or be governed?
**JOHN A. ROSS**

Government originated in the attempt to find a form of association that defends and protects the person and property of each with the common force of all.
**JEAN-JACQUES ROUSSEAU**

The institution of representative government to us seems an essential part of democracy, but the ancients never thought of it. Its immense merit was that it enabled a large constituency to exert indirect power, and thus made possible the distribution of political responsibility throughout the great states of modern times.
**BERTRAND RUSSELL**

An administration, like a machine, does not create. It carries on.
**ANTOINE DE SAINT-EXUPÉRY**

They that govern the most make the least noise.
**JOHN SELDEN**

A hated government does not long survive.
**SENECA**

They who govern most make the least noise.
**JOHN SIDDEN**

As soon as government management begins it upsets the natural equilibrium of industrial relations, and each interference only requires further bureaucratic control until the end is the tyranny of the totalitarian state.
**ADAM SMITH (1776)**

All socialism involves slavery.... That which fundamentally distinguishes the slave is that he labours under coercion to satisfy another's desires.
**HERBERT SPENCER**

I know now why confusion in government is not only tolerated but encouraged. I have learned. A confused people can make no clear demands.
**JOHN STEINBECK**

Deplorable as the quality of service is in many private enterprises, it's not worthy that government operations don't reflect any more inspired effort.
**JACK I. STRAUSS**

It is not the function of the State to make men happy. They must make themselves happy in their own way, and at their own risk. The functions of the State lie entirely in the conditions or chances under which the pursuit of happiness is carried on.
**WILLIAM GRAHAM SUMNER**

Parliaments, which were originally set up to limit the profligacy of the ruling powers, have by evolution become less apt to limit than to increase expenditures.
**ANDRÉ TARDIEU**

To commit violent and unjust acts, it is not enough for a government to have the will or even the power; the habits, ideas and passions of the time must lend themselves to their committal.
**ALEXIS DE TOCQUEVILLE**

The citizen who calls on government to supply him with security from cradle to grave, thereby encouraging government spending, is a danger to himself and his fellow citizens. If his pleas are successful, he can lose his freedom and gain no security in exchange.
**FRANCIS A. TRUSLOW**

It is beyond the vision or ability of any human being to foretell what will follow partial socialization of industry and a governmental supervision over practically all business. . . . I feel, however, that we can assume that we will never go back to the old order of things; that we will find that this is simply the first chapter of a new book and that no one can as yet foretell the trend of the chapters or acts that are to follow.
**GEORGE M. VERITY**

In general, the art of government consists of making as much money as possible from one class of citizens to give to the other.
**VOLTAIRE**

Government is not reason, it is not eloquence—it is force! Like fire it is a dangerous servant and a fearful master; never for a moment should it be left to irresponsible action.
**GEORGE WASHINGTON**

The habits of thinking in a free country should inspire caution in those intrusted with its administration to confine themselves within their respective constitutional spheres, avoiding in the exercise of the powers of one department, to encroach upon another.
**GEORGE WASHINGTON**

If war should sweep our commerce from the seas, another generation will restore it. If war exhausts our treasury, future industry will replenish it. If war desiccate and lay waste our fields, under new cultivation they will grow green again and ripen to future harvest. If the walls of yonder Capitol should fall and its decorations be covered by the dust of battle, all these can be rebuilt. But who shall reconstruct the fabric of a demolished government; who shall dwell in the well-proportioned columns of constitutional liberty; who shall frame together the skillful architecture which unites sovereignty with state's rights, individual security with prosperity?
**DANIEL WEBSTER**

The best security against revolution is in constant correction of abuses and the introduction of needed improvements. It is the neglect of timely repair that makes rebuilding necessary.
**RICHARD WHATELY**

The natural consequence of a planned destruction of the economic power of private corporations would be the transfer of that power to government. It would not actually be destroyed. We would simply have big government corporations. Today the people have recourse against monopoly and ineffi-

ciency in private business. . . . There is no recourse against government monopoly and inefficiency.
**CHARLES E. WILSON**

The history of liberty is the history of the limitations on the power of the government.
**WOODROW WILSON**

Government means politics, and interference by government carries with it always the implication of coercion. We may accept the expanding power of bureaucrats so long as we bask in their friendly smile. But it is a dangerous temptation. Today politics may be our friend and tomorrow we may be its victims.
**OWEN D. YOUNG**

The essential problem is how to govern a large-scale world with small-scale local minds.
**SIR ALFRED ZIMMERN**

## *Gratitude*

No duty is more urgent than that of returning thanks.
**ST. AMBROSE**

When people are made to feel secure and important and appreciated, it will no longer be necessary for them to whittle down others in order to seem bigger by comparison.
**VIRGINIA ARCASTLE**

Next to ingratitude, the most painful thing to bear is gratitude.
**HENRY WARD BEECHER**

I want to thank everybody who made this day necessary.
**YOGI BERRA**

Do you know what is more hard to bear than the reverses of fortune? It is the baseness, the hideous ingratitude of man.
**NAPOLEON BONAPARTE**

Some have meat and cannot eat,
Some cannot eat that want it;
But we have meat and we can eat
Sae let the Lord be thankit.
**ROBERT BURNS, *BLESSING***

Gratitude is not only the greatest of virtues, but the parent of all others.
**CICERO**

He is a man of sense who does not grieve for what he has not, but rejoices in what he has.
**EPICTETUS**

When I'm not thank'd at all, I'm thank'd enough.
I've done my duty, and I've done no more.
**HENRY FIELDING**

Gratitude: A lively sense of future benefit.
**FRENCH DEFINITION**

Best of all is it to preserve everything in a pure, still heart, and let there be for every pulse a thanksgiving, and for every breath a song.
**KONRAD VON GESNER**

There is one day that is ours. There is one day when all we Americans who are not self-made go back to the old home to eat saleratus biscuits and marvel how much nearer to the porch the old pump looks than it used to . . . Thanksgiving Day . . . is the one day that is purely American.
**O. HENRY**

Thanksgiving for a farmer, doth invite God to bestow a second benefit.
**ROBERT HERRICK**

The deepest principle in human nature is the craving to be appreciated.
WILLIAM JAMES

Gratitude is the fruit of great cultivation; you do not find it among gross people.
SAMUEL JOHNSON

Particular pains particular thanks do ask.
BEN JONSON

One can never pay in gratitude; one can only pay in kind somewhere else in life.
ANNE MORROW LINDBERGH

A man may be ungrateful, but the human race is not so.
JOHN MILTON

The worship most acceptable to God comes from a thankful and cheerful heart.
PLUTARCH

Gratitude, in most men, is only a strong and secret hope of greater favors.
FRANÇOIS DE LA ROCHEFOUCAULD

Two kinds of gratitude: The sudden kind we feel for what we take; the larger kind we feel for what we give.
EDWIN ARLINGTON ROBINSON

He who receives a benefit with gratitude repays the first installment on his debt.
SENECA

Let the man, who would be grateful, think of repaying a kindness, even while receiving it.
SENECA

The private and personal blessings we enjoy, the blessings of immunity, safeguard, liberty, and integrity, deserve the thanksgiving of a whole life.
JEREMY TAYLOR

. . . When we learn to give thanks, we are learning to concentrate not on the bad things, but on the good things in our lives.
AMY VANDERBILT

As bread is the staff of life, the simple sustenance of the body, so appreciation is the food of the soul.
PRISCILLA WAYNE

Gratitude is not only the memory but the homage of the heart—rendered to God for His goodness.
NATHANIEL P. WILLIS

## *Greatness*

Great men are the real men, in them nature has succeeded.
HENRI FRÉDÉRIC AMIEL

Lincoln was not great because he was born in a log cabin, but because he got out of it.
JAMES TRUSLOW ADAMS

A man's true greatness lies in the consciousness of an honest purpose in life, founded on a just estimate of himself and everything else, on frequent self-examinations, and a steady obedience to the rule which he knows to be right, without troubling himself about what others may think or say, or whether they do or do not that which he thinks and says and does.
MARCUS AURELIUS ANTONINUS

All rising to a great place is by a winding stair.
FRANCIS BACON

Great thoughts, like great deeds, need no trumpet.
**JAMES M. BAILEY**

Great men suffer hours of depression through introspection and self-doubt. That is why they are great. That is why you will find modesty and humility the characteristics of such men.
**BRUCE BARTON**

Man must realize his own unimportance before he can appreciate his importance.
**R. M. BAUMGARDY**

Not being always able to follow others exactly, nor attain to the excellence of those he imitates, a prudent man should always follow in the path trodden by great men and imitate those who are most excellent, so that if he does not attain to their greatness, at any rate he will get some tinge of it.
**NICCOLO DI BERNARDO**

Whatever action is performed by a great man, common men follow in his footsteps, and whatever standards he sets by exemplary acts, all the world pursues.
**BHAGAVAD GITA**

If you would be accounted great by your contemporaries, be not too much greater than they.
**AMBROSE BIERCE**

A really great man is known by three signs—generosity in the design, humanity in the execution, moderation in success.
**OTTO EDUARD BISMARCK**

All men who are really great can afford to be really human and to be shown so.
**GAMALIEL BRADFORD**

No man has come to true greatness who has not felt in some degree that his life belongs to his race, and that what God gives him He gives him for mankind.
**PHILLIPS BROOKS**

The true test of a great man—that, at least, which must secure his place among the highest order of great men—is, his having been in advance of his age.
**HENRY BROUGHAM**

A great man leaves clean work behind him, and requires no sweeper up of the chips.
**ELIZABETH BARRETT BROWNING**

The nearer we come to great men the more clearly we see that they are only men. They rarely seem great to their valets.
**JEAN DE LA BRUYÈRE**

Difficulty is the nurse of greatness.
**WILLIAM CULLEN BRYANT**

Seem not greater than thou art.
**SAMUEL BURTON**

To do great work a man must be very idle as well as very industrious.
**SAMUEL BUTLER**

Great minds discuss ideas, average minds discuss events, small minds discuss people.
**HUGH C. CAMERON**

All greatness is unconscious, or it is little and naught.
**THOMAS CARLYLE**

Great men never feel great; small men never feel small.
**CHINESE PROVERB**

There is a great man who makes every man feel small. But the really great man is the man who makes every man feel great.
CHINESE PROVERB

The price of greatness is responsibility.
WINSTON CHURCHILL

Great minds had rather deserve contemporaneous applause without obtaining it, than obtain without deserving it. If it follow them it is well, but they will not deviate to follow it.
CHARLES CALEB COLTON

In life we shall find many men that are great, and some that are good, but very few men that are both great and good.
CHARLES CALEB COLTON

Subtract from a great man all that he owes to opportunity and all that he owes to chance; all that he has gained by the wisdom of his friends and by the folly of his enemies; and our Brobdingnag will often become a Lilliputian.
CHARLES CALEB COLTON

There are three marks of a superior man: being virtuous, he is free from anxiety; being wise, he is free from perplexity; being brave, he is free from fear.
CONFUCIUS

From the little spark may burst a mighty flame.
DANTE

Anybody can be nobody, but it takes a man to be somebody.
EUGENE V. DEBS

A great man is one who can have power and not abuse it.
HENRY L. DOHERTY

Man is not merely a combination of appetites, instincts, passions and curiosity. Something more is needed to explain great human deeds, virtues, sacrifices, martyrdom. There is an element in the great mystics, the saints, the prophets, whose influence has been felt for centuries, which escapes mere intelligence.
LECOMTE DU NOÜY

Great men speak to us only so far as we have ears and souls to hear them; only so far as we have in us the roots, at least, of what which flowers out in them.
WILL DURANT

Great spirits have always found violent opposition from mediocrities.
ALBERT EINSTEIN

Half of the harm that is done in this world is due to people who want to feel important . . . they do not mean to do harm . . . they are absorbed in the endless struggle to think well of themselves.
T. S. ELIOT

Great men are more distinguished by range and extent than by originality.
RALPH WALDO EMERSON

Great men are they who see that spiritual is stronger than material force, that thoughts rule the world.
RALPH WALDO EMERSON

The great man is not convulsible or tormentable; events pass over him without much impression.
RALPH WALDO EMERSON

To be great is to be misunderstood.
RALPH WALDO EMERSON

I note the derogatory rumors concerning the use of alcoholic stimulants and lavish living. It is the penalty of greatness.
W. C. FIELDS

The best teachers of humanity are the lives of great men.
CHARLES H. FOWLER

To accomplish great things, we must not only act, but also dream, not only plan, but also believe.
ANATOLE FRANCE

It is a great mistake to think of being great without goodness; and I pronounce it as certain that there was never yet a truly great man that was not at the same time truly virtuous.
BENJAMIN FRANKLIN

True greatness is the most ready to recognize and most willing to obey those simple outward laws which have been sanctioned by the experience of mankind.
J. A. FROUDE

Great men sometimes lose the reins and lose their heads. This time, let us hope that they will retain them and that when victory is assured they will sit down and reckon what the future is going to be for their countries as well as for other lands.
DAVID LLOYD GEORGE

The truly great man is he who would master no one, and who would be mastered by none.
KAHLIL GIBRAN

It doesn't take great men to do things, but it is doing things that make men great.
ARNOLD GLASOW

One is never done with knowing the greatest men or the greatest works of art—they carry you on and on, and at the last you feel that you are only beginning.
T. R. GLOVER

In general, it is not very difficult for little minds to attain splendid situations. It is much more difficult for great minds to attain the place to which their merit fully entitles them.
BARON VON GRIMM

The glory of a people, and of an age, is always the work of a small number of great men, and disappears with them.
BARON VON GRIMM

Every individual has a place to fill in the world, and is important in some respect, whether he chooses to be so or not.
NATHANIEL HAWTHORNE

He who comes up to his own idea of greatness must always have had a very low standard of it in his mind.
WILLIAM HAZLITT

True greatness, first of all, is a thing of the heart. It is alive with robust and generous sympathies. It is neither behind its age nor too far before it. It is up with its age, and ahead of it only just so far as to be able to lead its march. It cannot slumber, for activity is a necessity of its existence. It is no reservoir, but a fountain.
ROSWELL D. HITCHCOCK

The world's idea of greatness has been that he is greatest who succeeds in using his fellow men for the furtherance of his own ends.
A. H. HOGE

As a madman is apt to think himself grown suddenly great, so he that grows suddenly great is apt to borrow a little from the madman.
**SAMUEL JOHNSON**

Those who cannot feel the littleness of great things in themselves are apt to overlook the greatness of little things in others.
**OKAKURA KUZO**

The causes which most disturbed or accelerated the normal progress of society in antiquity were the appearance of great men.
**W. E. H. LECKY**

There is no right without a parallel duty, no liberty without the supremacy of the law, no high destiny without earnest perseverance, no greatness without self-denial.
**LIEBER**

Lives of great men all remind us we can make our lives sublime!
**HENRY WADSWORTH LONGFELLOW**

It is the age that forms the man, not the man that forms the age. Great minds do indeed react on the society which has made them what they are, but they only pay with interest what they have received.
**THOMAS B. MACAULAY**

If any man seeks for greatness, let him forget greatness and ask for truth, and he will find both.
**HORACE MANN**

To feel themselves in the presence of true greatness, many men find it necessary only to be alone.
**THOMAS L. MASSON**

Lack of something to feel important about is almost the greatest tragedy a man may have.
**ARTHUR E. MORGAN**

Those who cannot feel the littleness of great things in themselves are apt to overlook the greatness of little things in others.
**KAKUZO OKAKURA**

Do little things now; so shall big things come to thee by and by asking to be done.
**PERSIAN PROVERB**

I go to seek a great perhaps.
**FRANÇOIS RABELAIS**

Greatness, in the last analysis, is largely bravery—courage in escaping from old ideas and old standards and respectable ways of doing things. This is one of the chief elements in what we vaguely call capacity. If you do not dare differ from your associates and teachers you will never be great or your life sublime. You may be the happier as a result, or you may be miserable. Each of us is great insofar as we perceive and act on the infinite possibilities which lie undiscovered and unrecognized about us.
**JAMES HARVEY ROBINSON**

Those who give too much attention to trifling things become generally incapable of great ones.
**FRANÇOIS DE LA ROCHEFOUCAULD**

It's great to be great, but it's greater to be human.
**WILL ROGERS**

Great men never make bad use of their superiority; they see it, and feel it, and are not less modest. The more they have, the more they know their own deficiencies.
**JEAN-JACQUES ROUSSEAU**

I fear uniformity. You cannot manufacture great men any more than you can manufacture gold.
**JOHN RUSKIN**

Let a man in a garret but burn with enough intensity, and he will set fire to the world.
ANTOINE DE SAINT-EXUPÉRY

The greatest man is he who chooses right with the most invincible resolution; who resists to sorest temptation from within and without; who bears the heaviest burdens cheerfully; who is calmest in storms, and most fearless under menaces and frowns; whose reliance on truth, on virtue, and on God is most unfaltering.
SENECA

There's hope a great man's memory may outlive his life half a year.
WILLIAM SHAKESPEARE

A desire for bigness has hurt many folks. Putting oneself in the limelight at the expense of others is a wrong idea of greatness. The secret of greatness rather than bigness is to acclimate oneself to one's place of service and be true to one's own convictions. A life of this kind of service will forever remain the measure of one's true greatness.
RICHARD W. SHELLY, JR.

Life is made up of little things. It is very rarely that an occasion is offered for doing a great deal at once. True greatness consists in being great in little things.
CHARLES SIMMONS

Great men are very apt to have great faults; and the faults appear the greater by their contrast with their excellencies.
GERALD J. SIMMONS

The career of a great man remains an enduring monument of human energy. The man dies and disappears, but his thoughts and acts survive and leave an indelible stamp upon his race.
SAMUEL SMILES

The great man is the man who does a thing for the first time.
ALEXANDER SMITH

What makes greatness is starting something that lives after you.
RALPH W. SOCKMAN

Greatness is a two-faced coin—and its reverse is humility.
MARGUERITE STEEN

If thou art rich, then show the greatness of thy fortune; or what is better, the greatness of thy soul, in the meekness of thy conversation; condescend to men of low estate, support the distressed, and patronize the neglected. Be great.
LAURENCE STERNE

To have read the greatest works of any great poet, to have beheld or heard the greatest works of any great painter or musician, is a possession added to the best things of life.
ALGERNON CHARLES SWINBURNE

Might I give counsel to any man, I would say to him, try to frequent the company of your betters. In books and in life, that is the most wholesome society; learn to admire rightly; the great pleasure of life is that. Note what great men admire.
WILLIAM MAKEPEACE THACKERAY

Greatness has always been a mark to aim at. . . . It is not only inspiring but imperative to think continually of those who were truly great. Soldiers on forgotten fields of battle, scientists in makeshift laboratories, stubborn idealists fighting to save a lost cause, teachers who would not be intimidated, tireless doctors, the anonymous army of dreamers and doers—all these by their very living fought for everyone. They sacrificed hours of ease for our casual comforts; they gave up safety for our security.

Glorifying the heroic spirit of man, they added to our stature.
**LOUIS UNTERMEYER**

Some things have not changed since the dawn of history, and bid fair to last out time itself. One of these things is the capacity for greatness in man—his capacity for being often the master of the event—and sometimes even more—the changer of the course of history itself. This capacity for greatness is a very precious gift, and we are under a danger in our day of stifling it.
**WILLIAM CLYDE DE VANE**

Great men undertake great things because they are great; fools, because they think them easy.
**MARQUIS DE VAUVENARGUES**

Men are often capable of greater things than they perform. They are sent into the world with bills of credit, and seldom draw to their full extent.
**HORACE WALPOLE**

When a man realizes his littleness, his greatness can appear.
**H. G. WELLS**

Every great man nowadays has his disciples, and it is always Judas who writes the biography.
**OSCAR WILDE**

None think the great unhappy but the great.
**EDWARD YOUNG**

## *Greed*

Avarice, in old age, is foolish; for what can be more absurd than to increase our provisions for the road the nearer we approach to our journey's end?
**CICERO**

Avarice hoards itself poor; charity gives itself rich.
**GERMAN PROVERB**

Is not dread of thirst when your well is full, the thirst that is unquenchable?
**KAHLIL GIBRAN**

Avarice, or the desire of gain, is a universal passion which operates at all times, at all places, and upon all persons.
**DAVID HUME**

There is no calamity greater than lavish desires
There is no greater guilt than discontentment
And there is no greater disaster than greed.
**LAO-TZU**

Anyone with more than 365 pairs of shoes is a pig.
**BARBARA MELSER LIEBERMAN**

Take heed, and beware of covetousness; for a man's life consisteth not in the abundance of the things which he possesseth.
**LUKE 12:15**

We're all born brave, trusting and greedy, and most of us remain greedy.
**MIGNON MCLAUGHLIN**

Those who are greedy of praise prove that they are poor in merit.
**PLUTARCH**

No leader can make a happy, humane, workable society out of a stubborn lot of individualists who are more conscious of their rights than of their responsibilities, who accept a low moral standard in business and family life, who want more than they need, and are motivated by fear and greed, some of them forcing their will through blocs of special

interests which are prejudicial to the welfare of the whole society.
SAMUEL M. SHOEMAKER, D.D.

Covetousness, by a greediness of getting more, deprives itself of the true end of getting; it loses the enjoyment of what it had got.
THOMAS SPRAT

Happy the man who has learned the cause of things and has put under his feet all fear, inexorable fate, and the noisy strife of the hell of greed.
VIRGIL

The avaricious man is like the barren sandy ground of the desert which sucks in all the rain and dew with greediness, but yields no fruitful herbs or plants for the benefit of others.
ZENO OF CITIUM

## *Growth*

The most fatal illusion is the settled point of view. Life is growth and motion; a fixed point of view kills anybody who has one.
BROOKS ATKINSON

To grow and know what one is growing towards—that is the source of all strength and confidence in life.
JAMES BAILLIE

Life is growth—a challenge of environment. If we cannot meet our everyday surroundings with equanimity and pleasure and grow each day in some useful direction, then this splendid balance of cosmic forces which we call life is on the road toward misfortune, misery and destruction. Therefore, health is the most precious of all things.
LUTHER BURBANK

Time ripens all things. No man's born wise.
MIGUEL DE CERVANTES

When he who ponders these things cries that all flesh is grass, science joins with faith, replying: Make green, then, in thy season, the place wherein thou growest.
GEORGE W. CORNER

A man's growth is seen in the successive choirs of his friends.
RALPH WALDO EMERSON

No great thing is created suddenly, any more than a bunch of grapes or a fig. If you tell me that you desire a fig, I answer you that there must be time. Let it first blossom, then bear fruit, then ripen.
EPICTETUS

You cannot force the growth of human life and civilization, any more than you can force these slow-growing trees. That is the economy of Almighty God, that all good growth is slow growth.
WILLIAM J. GAYNOR

Everybody wants to be somebody, but nobody wants to grow.
JOHANN WOLFGANG VON GOETHE

There is no royal road to anything. One thing at a time, and all things in succession. That which grows slowly endures.
JOSIAH G. HOLLAND

In the business of life, Man is the only product. And there is only one direction in which man can possibly develop if he is to make a better living or yield a bigger dividend to himself, to his race, to nature or to God. He must grow in knowledge, wisdom, kindliness and understanding.
V. C. KITCHEN

Just as we outgrow a pair of trousers, we outgrow acquaintances, libraries, principles, etc. at times before they're worn out and at times—and this is the worst of all—before we have new ones.
GEORG CHRISTOPH LICHTENBERG

We want our children to grow up to be such persons that ill-fortune, if they meet with it, will bring out strength in them, and that good fortune will not trip them up, but make them winners.
EDWARD SANDFORD MARTIN

Undertake something that is difficult; it will do you good. Unless you try to do something beyond what you have already mastered, you will never grow.
RONALD E. OSBORN

Our growth depends not on how many experiences we devour, but on how many we digest.
RALPH W. SOCKMAN

Great occasions do not make heroes or cowards; they simply unveil them to the eyes of men. Silently and imperceptibly, as we wake or sleep, we grow strong or we grow weak, and at last some crisis shows us what we have become.
BISHOP WESTCOTT

Only mushrooms can grow in the shadow of mighty trees, but shrubs need light in order to grow. If you recognize that your father is a tree, you should move away and out of his shadow.
CARL ZIMMERER

## *Guilt*

We cling to our bad feelings and beat ourselves with the past when what we should do is let go of it, like Peter did. Once you let go of guilt, then you go out and change the world.
JAMES CARROLL

Guilt is ever at a loss, and confusion waits upon it; while innocence and bold truth are always ready for expression.
WILLIAM CONGREVE

Guilt always hurries toward its complement, punishment; only there does its satisfaction lie.
LAWRENCE DURRELL

I've learned that the greater a person's sense of guilt, the greater his need to cast blame on others.
46-YEAR-OLD'S DISCOVERY

Shame is the social side of guilt.
JOHN P. GRIER

The human condition suffers from the fact that our sins and our guilt are cumulative; we may assuage, we forgive, but have no way to forget.
JOSHUA LEDERBERG

We have no choice but to be guilty. God is unthinkable if we are innocent.
ARCHIBALD MACLEISH

He who knows no guilt knows no fear.
PHILIP MASSINGER

# H

## Habits

We think according to nature; we speak according to rules; but we act according to custom.
FRANCIS BACON

Custom governs the world; it is the tyrant of our feelings and our manners and rules the world with the hand of a despot.
JOHN BARTLETT

You don't get anything clean without getting something else dirty.
CECIL BAXTER

Woe unto them that are tired of everything, for everything will certainly be tired of them.
G. K. CHESTERTON

The nature of man is always the same; it is their habits that separate them.
CONFUCIUS

Any man who leads the regular and temperate life, not swerving from it in the least degree where his nourishment is concerned, can be but little affected by other disorders or incidental mishaps. Whereas, on the other hand, I truly conclude that disorderly habits of living are those which are fatal.
CORNARO

Make good habits and they will make you.
PARKS COUSINS

The customs and fashions of men change like leaves on the bough, some of which go and others come.
DANTE

Any act often repealed soon forms a habit; and habit allowed, steadily gains in strength. At first it may be but as the spider's web, easily broken through, but if not resisted it soon binds us with chains of steel.
TRYON EDWARDS

Habit is either the best of servants or the worst of masters.
NATHANIEL EMMONS

A nail is driven out by another nail; habit is overcome by habit.
DESIDERIUS ERASMUS

Custom may lead a man into many errors, but it justifies none.
HENRY FIELDING

It is not from nature, but from education and habits, that our wants are chiefly derived.
HENRY FIELDING

Fatigue is no more praiseworthy than drunkenness; both are evidence of bad habits.
L. G. FREEMAN

We're worn into grooves by Time—by our habits. In the end, these grooves are going to show whether we've been second rate or champions, each in his way in dispatching the affairs of every day. By choosing our habits, we determine the grooves into which Time will wear us; and these are grooves that

enrich our lives and make for ease of mind, peace, happiness—achievement.
FRANK B. GILBERTH

If everyone sweeps before his own front door, then the street is clean.
JOHANN WOLFGANG VON GOETHE

The diligent fostering of a candid habit of mind, even in trifles, is a matter of high moment both to character and opinions.
JOHN S. HOWSON

Custom, then, is the great guide to human life.
DAVID HUME

No habit has any real hold on you other than the hold you have on it.
GARDNER HUNTING

We must make automatic and habitual, as early as possible, as many useful actions as we can. The more of the details of our daily life we can hand over to the effortless custody of automatism, the more our higher powers of mind will be set free for their own proper work.
WILLIAM JAMES

The chains of habit are too weak to be felt until they are too strong to be broken.
JOHNSON

Habit is a cable; we weave a thread of it each day, and at last we cannot break it.
HORACE MANN

The unfortunate thing about this world is that good habits are so much easier to give up them bad ones.
SOMERSET MAUGHAM

The despotism of custom is on the wane. We are not content to know that things are; we ask whether they ought to be.
JOHN STUART MILL

Small habits well pursued betimes may reach the dignity of crimes.
HANNAH MORE

Habits change into character.
OVID

There are habits, not only of drinking, swearing, and lying, but of every modification of action, speech, and thought. Man is a bundle of habits; in a word, there is not a quality or function, either of body or mind, which does not feel the influence of this great law of animated nature.
WILLIAM PALEY

The best way to stop a bad habit is never to begin it.
JAMES C. PENNEY

The fixity of a habit is generally in direct proportion to its absurdity.
MARCEL PROUST

A deep meaning often lies in old customs.
JOHANN FRIEDRICH VON SCHILLER

Better keep yourself clean and bright; you are the window through which you must see the world.
GEORGE BERNARD SHAW

Good habits, which bring our lower passions and appetites under automatic control, leave our natures free to explore the larger experiences of life. Too many of us divide and dissipate our energies in debating actions which should be taken for granted.
RALPH W. SOCKMAN

I take it to be a principal rule of life, not to be too much addicted to any one thing.
**TERENCE**

Habit is habit, and not to be flung out of the window by any man, but coaxed downstairs a step at a time.
**MARK TWAIN**

Nothing so needs reforming as other people's habits.
**MARK TWAIN**

The formation of right habits is essential to your permanent security. They diminish your chance of falling when assailed, and they augment your chance of recovery when overthrown.
**JOHN TYNDALL**

The secret of being tiresome is to tell everything.
**VOLTAIRE**

## *Happiness*

I have now reigned above 50 years in victory or peace, beloved by my subjects, dreaded by my enemies, respected by my allies. Riches and honors, power and pleasure, have awaited my call, nor does any earthly blessing seem to have been wanting to my felicity. In this situation I have diligently numbered the days of pure and genuine happiness that have fallen to my lot; they amount to 14. Oh man! place not thy confidence in this world.
**ABD-AL-RAHMAN**

If you have nothing else to do, look about you and see if there isn't something close at hand that you can improve! It may make you wealthy, though it is more likely that it will make you happy.
**GEORGE MATTHEW ADAMS**

A man should always consider how much he has more than he wants and how much more unhappy he might be than he really is.
**JOSEPH ADDISON**

Three grand essentials to happiness in this life are something to do, something to love and something to hope for.
**JOSEPH ADDISON**

We must dare to be happy, and dare to confess it, regarding ourselves always as the depositories, not as the authors of our own joy.
**HENRI FRÉDÉRIC AMIEL**

The happiness of your life depends upon the quality of your thoughts: therefore, guard accordingly, and take care that you entertain no notion unsuitable to virtue and reasonable nature.
**MARCUS AURELIUS ANTONINUS**

Real happiness is cheap enough, yet how dearly we pay for its counterfeit.
**HOSEA BALLOU**

Nothing comes easy that is done well.
**HARRY F. BANKS**

It is not in doing what you like, but in liking what you do that is the secret of happiness.
**JAMES M. BARRIE**

Those who bring sunshine to the lives of others cannot keep it from themselves.
**JAMES M. BARRIE**

Pleasure only starts once the worm has got into the fruit; to become delightful, happiness must be tainted with poison.
**GEORGES BATAILLE**

A man without mirth is like a wagon without springs, in which one is caused disagreeably to jolt by every pebble over which it turns.
HENRY WARD BEECHER

The bird of paradise alights only upon the hand that does not grasp.
JOHN BERRY

Don't mistake pleasure for happiness. They are a different breed of dogs.
JOSH BILLINGS

The happiest time in a man's life is when he is in hot pursuit of a dollar with a reasonable prospect of overtaking it.
JOSH BILLINGS

It is the paradox of life that the way to miss pleasure is to seek it first. The very first condition of lasting happiness is that a life should be full of purpose, aiming at something outside self. As a matter of experience, we find that true happiness comes in seeking other things, in the manifold activities of life, in the healthful outgoing of all human powers.
HUGO L. BLACK

Not only is there a right to be happy, there is a duty to be happy. So much sadness exists in the world that we are all under obligation to contribute as much joy as lies within our powers.
JOHN S. BONNELL, D.D.

I had always imagined paradise as a kind of library.
JORGE LUIS BORGES

Unhappiness indicates wrong thinking; just as ill health indicates a bad regimen.
PAUL BOURGET

Happiness is a resultant of the relative strengths of positive and negative feelings rather than an absolute amount of one or the other.
NORMAN BRADBURN

Happiness, whether in business or private life, leaves very little trace in history.
FERNAND BRAUDEL

Happiness quite unshared can scarcely be called happiness; it has no taste.
EMILY BRONTË

Money doesn't always bring happiness. People with ten million dollars are no happier than people with nine million dollars.
HOBART BROWN

No man, with a man's heart in him gets far on his way without some bitter, soul-searching disappointment. Happy is he who is brave enough to push on to another stage of the journey.
JOHN MASON BROWN

The only true happiness comes from squandering ourselves for a purpose.
JOHN MASON BROWN

Happiness and virtue rest upon each other; the best are not only the happiest, but the happiest are usually the best.
EDWARD BULWER-LYTTON

To be happy, you must learn to forget yourself.
EDWARD BULWER-LYTTON

There is work that is work and there is play that is play; there is play that is work and work that is play. And in only one of these lies happiness.
GELETT BURGESS

Happiness and misery depend not upon how high up or low down you are—they depend not upon these, but on the direction in which you are tending.
SAMUEL BUTLER

We have all sinned and come short of the glory of making ourselves as comfortable as we easily might have done.
SAMUEL BUTLER

All who would win joy, must share it; happiness was born a twin.
LORD BYRON

There comes forever something between us and what we deem our happiness.
LORD BYRON

The secret of happiness is renunciation.
ANDREW CARNEGIE

If money is all that a man makes, then he will be poor—poor in happiness, poor in all that makes life worth living.
HERBERT N. CASSON

The three grand essentials of happiness are: something to do, someone to love, and something to hope for.
ALEXANDER CHALMERS

It is with happiness as with watches: the less complicated, the less easily deranged.
SÉBASTIEN CHAMFORT

The office of government is not to confer happiness, but to give men opportunity to work out happiness for themselves.
WILLIAM ELLERY CHANNING

Happy is he who still loves something he loved in the nursery: He has not been broken in two by time; he is not two men, but one, and he has saved not only his soul but his life.
G. K. CHESTERTON

An effort made for the happiness of others lifts us above ourselves.
LYDIA M. CHILD

Happiness is someone to love, something to do, and something to hope for.
CHINESE PROVERB

One does not leave a convivial party before closing time.
WINSTON CHURCHILL

I do not understand what the man who is happy wants in order to be happier.
CICERO

A perverse temper and fretful disposition will make any state of life whatsoever unhappy.
CICERO

We communicate happiness to others not often by great acts of devotion and self-sacrifice, but by the absence of fault-finding and censure, by being ready to sympathize with their notions and feelings, instead of forcing them to sympathize with ours.
ADAM CLARKE

I have lived to know that the great secret of happiness is this: never suffer your energies to stagnate. The old adage of too many irons in the fire, conveys an abominable lie. You cannot have too many—poker, tongs and all—keep them all going.
ADAM CLARKE

Do not run after happiness, but seek to do good, and you will find that happiness will run after you. The day will dawn full of expectation, the night will fall full of repose. This world will seem a very good place, and the world to come a better place still.
JAMES FREEMAN CLARKE

It is misery enough to have once been happy.
JOHN CLARKE

Happiness is a hard thing because it is achieved only by making others happy.
STUART CLOETE

The happiness of life is made up of minute fractions—the little, soon forgotten charities of a kiss or smile, a kind look, a heart-felt compliment, and the countless infinitesimals of pleasurable and genial feeling.
SAMUEL TAYLOR COLERIDGE

There is this difference between happiness and wisdom: He that thinks himself the happiest man really is so; but he that thinks himself the wisest is generally the greatest fool.
CHARLES CALEB COLTON

Making an issue of little things is one of the surest ways to spoil happiness. One's personal pride is felt to be vitally injured by surrender, but there is no quality of human nature so nearly royal as the ability to yield gracefully. It shows small confidence in one's own nature to fear that compromise lessens self-control. To consider constantly the comfort and happiness of another is not a sign of weakness but of strength.
CHARLES CONRAD

When men are easy in themselves, they let others remain so.
ANTHONY A. COOPER (LORD SHAFTESBURY)

We never enjoy perfect happiness; our most fortunate successes are mingled with sadness; some anxieties always perplex the reality of our satisfaction.
PIERRE CORNEILLE

A life of ease is a difficult pursuit.
WILLIAM COWPER

When a bit of sunshine hits ye,
After passing of a cloud,
When a fit of laughter gits ye
An' ye'r spine is feelin' proud,
Don't forgit to up and fling it
At a soul that's feelin' blue,
For the mint that ye sling it
It's a boomerang to you.
CAPT. JACK CRAWFORD

Life is made up, not of great sacrifices or duties, but of little things, in which smiles and kindness, and small obligations given habitually, are what preserve the heart and secure comfort.
WILLIAM DAVY

External things and opportunities so abound in American life that, instead of nurturing the true source of happiness, we tend to make it a direct aim. So we end in looking for happiness in possession of the external—in money, a good time, somebody to lean on, and so on. We are impatient, hurried and fretful because we do not find happiness where we look for it.
JOHN DEWEY

Search for a single, inclusive good is doomed to failure. Such happiness as life is capable of comes from the full participation of all our powers in the endeavor to wrest from each changing situation of experience its own full and unique meaning.
JOHN DEWEY

Action may not always bring happiness; but there is no happiness without action.
**BENJAMIN DISRAELI**

If we are ever to enjoy life, now is the time—not tomorrow, nor next year, nor in some future life after we have died. The best preparation for a better life next year is a full, complete, harmonious, joyous life this year. Our beliefs in a rich future life are of little importance unless we coin them into a rich present life. Today should always be our most wonderful day.
**THOMAS DREIER**

There is much to be said in favor of an English woman who never got angry when she was having uncomfortable moments, but to prolong them beyond the strictly necessary tick of the clock seemed to her as idiotic as to take in the shape of punishment and pain what could, by a little dexterous manipulation, be turned into a pleasure. It is bad enough to be uncomfortable without also punishing one's self by getting angry at what makes one uncomfortable.
**THOMAS DREIER**

Half the world is on the wrong scent in the pursuant of happiness. They think it consists in having and getting, and in being served by others. On the contrary, it consists in giving, and in serving others.
**HENRY DRUMMOND**

Happy the man, and happy he alone, he, who can call today his own.
**JOHN DRYDEN**

Seek happiness for its own sake, and you will not find it; seek for duty, and happiness will follow as the shadow comes with the sunshine.
**TRYON EDWARDS**

Well-being and happiness never appeared to me as an absolute aim. I am even inclined to compare such moral aims to the ambitions of a pig.
**ALBERT EINSTEIN**

Whether happiness may come or not, one should try and prepare one's self to do without it.
**GEORGE ELIOT**

Don't be a cynic, and bewail and bemoan. Omit the negative propositions. Don't waste yourself in rejection, nor bark against the bad, but chant the beauty of the good. Set down nothing that will not help somebody.
**RALPH WALDO EMERSON**

Happiness is a perfume you cannot pour on others without getting a few drops on yourself.
**RALPH WALDO EMERSON**

The high prize of life, the crowning glory of a man is to be born with a bias to some pursuit which finds him in employment and happiness—whether it be to make baskets, or broadswords, or canals, or statues, or songs.
**RALPH WALDO EMERSON**

There is only one way to happiness, and that is cease worrying about things which are beyond the power of our will.
**EPICTETUS**

May we never let the things we can't have, or don't have, or shouldn't have, spoil our enjoyment of the things we do have and can have. As we value our happiness let us not forget it, for one of the greatest lessons in life is learning to be happy without the things we cannot or should not have.
**RICHARD L. EVANS**

To be happy is not the purpose of our being, but to deserve happiness.
**IMMANUEL FICHTE**

Much has been said about the relative value of happiness; but write it on your heart that happiness is the cheapest thing in the world—when we buy it for someone else.
**PAUL FLEMMING**

To be happy, one must have a good stomach and a bad heart.
**LE BOVIER DE FONTENELLE**

"A happy man or woman," said Robert Louis Stevenson, "is a better thing to find than a five-pound note. He or she is a radiating focus of good will and their entrance into a room is as though another candle has been lighted." Learn to be cheerful and you will come near being happy. Life's race can best be run with a light heart and a buoyant countenance. Cheerfulness will open a door when other keys fail.
**B. C. FORBES**

A hug's a happy thing while a shrug's so often destructive.
**MALCOLM FORBES**

Profit is a by-product of work; happiness is its chief product.
**HENRY FORD**

Anyone who starts out to chase happiness will find it running away from him. We get happiness by indirection.
**HARRY EMERSON FOSDICK, D.D.**

A single sunbeam is enough to drive away many shadows.
**ST. FRANCIS OF ASSISI**

Happiness consists more in small conveniences or pleasures that occur every day, than in great pieces of good fortune that happen but seldom to a man in the course of his life.
**BENJAMIN FRANKLIN**

Human felicity is produced not so much by great pieces of good fortune that seldom happen, as by little advantages that occur every day.
**BENJAMIN FRANKLIN**

In dealings between man and man, truth; sincerity and integrity are of the utmost importance to the felicity of life.
**BENJAMIN FRANKLIN**

There are two ways of being happy: We must either diminish our wants or augment our means—either may do—the result is the same and it is for each man to decide for himself and to do that which happens to be easier.
**BENJAMIN FRANKLIN**

Success is getting what you want, happiness is wanting what you get.
**DAVE GARDNER**

To attain happiness in another world we need only to believe something, while to secure it in this world we must do something.
**C. P. GILMAN**

We take greater pains to persuade others that we are happy, than in endeavoring to be so ourselves.
**OLIVER GOLDSMITH**

If I could drop dead right now, I'd be the happiest man alive.
**SAMUEL GOLDWYN**

Pleasures, riches, honor and joy are sure to have care, disgrace, adversity and affliction in their train. There is no pleasure without pain, no joy without sorrow. O the folly of expecting lasting felicity in a vale of tears, or a paradise in a ruined world.
**GOTTHOLD**

Happiness is a rebound from hard work. One of the follies of man is to assume that he can enjoy mere emotion. As well try to eat beauty. Happiness must be tricked. She loves to see men work. She loves sweat, weariness, self-sacrifice. She will not be found in the palaces, but lurking in cornfields and factories, and hovering over littered desks. She crowns the unconscious head of the busy child.
**DAVID GRAYSON**

All happiness depends on a leisurely breakfast.
**JOHN GUNTHER**

Happiness in this world, when it comes, comes incidentally. Make it the object of pursuit, and it leads us a wild-goose chase, and is never attained. Follow some other object, and very possibly we may find that we have caught happiness without dreaming of it.
**NATHANIEL HAWTHORNE**

Planning for happiness is rarely successful. Happiness just happens.
**ROBERT HALF**

When a millionaire is a million times more happy than the owner of a single dollar, folks will have a real kick coming.
**JOSH HARPER**

I do not know of any sure way of making others happy as being so one's self.
**ARTHUR HELPS**

He that talks much of his happiness summons grief.
**GEORGE HERBERT**

It's pretty hard to find what does bring happiness. Poverty and wealth have both failed.
**KIN HUBBARD**

Happiness is the overcoming of not unknown obstacles toward a known goal.
**L. RON HUBBARD**

The happiness of this life depends less on what befalls you than the way in which you take it.
**ELBERT HUBBARD**

One can endure sorrow alone, but it takes two to be glad.
**ELBERT HUBBARD**

The supreme happiness of life is the conviction of being loved for yourself, or more correctly, being loved in spite of yourself.
**VICTOR HUGO**

Human happiness seems to consist in three ingredients; action, pleasure and indolence. And though these ingredients ought to be mixed in different proportions, according to the disposition of the person, yet no one ingredient can be entirely wanting without destroying in some measure the relish of the whole composition.
**DAVID HUME**

The most unhappy of all men is he who believes himself to be so.
**DAVID HUME**

Where ambition ends happiness begins.
**HUNGARIAN PROVERB**

The action is best which procures the greatest happiness for the greatest numbers.
**FRANCIS HUTCHESON**

I can sympathize with people's pains, but not with their pleasures. There is something curiously boring about somebody else's happiness.
**ALDOUS HUXLEY**

Labor and trouble one can always get through alone, but it takes two to be glad.
**HENRIK IBSEN**

The happiest people seem to be those who have no particular reason for being so except that they are so.
**WILLIAM RALPH INGE**

The happy people are those who are producing something; the bored people are those who are consuming much and producing nothing.
**WILLIAM RALPH INGE**

Happiness is not a reward—it is a consequence. Suffering is not a punishment—it is a result.
**ROBERT G. INGERSOLL**

Happiness is the only good. The time to be happy is now. The place to be happy is here. The way to be happy is to make others so.
**ROBERT G. INGERSOLL**

Joy is spiritual prosperity. That motto above your desk—"Smile!" How did that ever get into so many business offices? Does a smile help business? Try it. Joy makes the face shine, and he that hath a merry heart hath a continual feast.
**W. C. ISETT**

The first thing to learn in intercourse with others is non-interference with their own particular ways of being happy, provided those ways do not assume to interfere by violence with ours.
**WILLIAM JAMES**

Happiness comes of the capacity to feel deeply, to enjoy simply, to think freely, to risk life, to be needed.
**STORM JAMESON**

It is neither wealth nor splendor, but tranquillity and occupation, which give happiness.
**THOMAS JEFFERSON**

Our greatest happiness does not depend on the condition of life in which chance has placed us, but is always the result of a good conscience, good health, occupation, and freedom in all just pursuits.
**THOMAS JEFFERSON**

Perfect happiness, I believe, was never intended by the Deity to be the lot of one of his creatures in this world; but that he has very much put in our power the nearness of our approaches to it is what I have steadfastly believed.
**THOMAS JEFFERSON**

Every period of life is obliged to borrow its happiness from time to come.
**SAMUEL JOHNSON**

Philosophers there are who try to make themselves believe that this life is happy; but they believe it only while they are saying it, and never yet produced conviction in a single mind.
**SAMUEL JOHNSON**

Happiness should always remain a bit incomplete. After all, dreams are boundless.
**ANATOLY KARPOV**

Those who are not looking for happiness are the most likely to find it, because those who are searching forget that the surest way to be happy is to seek happiness for others.
**MARTIN LUTHER KING, JR.**

God did not intend the human family to be wafted to heaven on flowery beds of ease.
**FRANK KNOX**

### A Creed

To be so strong that nothing can disturb your peace of mind; to talk health, happiness and prosperity; to make your friends feel that there is something in them; to look on the sunny side of everything; to think only of the best; to be just as enthusiastic about the success of others as you are about your own; to forget the mistakes of the past and profit by them; to wear a cheerful countenance and give a smile to everyone you meet; to be too large for worry, too noble for anger, too strong for fear, and too happy to permit the presence of trouble.
**CHRISTIAN D. LARSON**

The more we search for an alibi, the more we discover that unhappiness on earth is man-made.
**DAVID LAWRENCE**

Happiness is the supreme object of existence.
**J. GILCHRIST LAWSON**

Happiness is not something you experience, it's something you remember.
**OSCAR LEVANT**

A long happiness losses by its mere length.
**GEORG CHRISTOPH LICHTENBERG**

In this sad world of ours, sorrow comes to all, and it often comes with bitter agony. Perfect relief is not possible, except with time. You cannot now believe that you will ever feel better. But this is not true. You are sure to be happy again. Knowing this, truly believing it, will make you less miserable now.
**ABRAHAM LINCOLN**

Most people are about as happy as they make up their minds to be.
**ABRAHAM LINCOLN**

Man's rank is his power to uplift.
**GEORGE MACDONALD**

Happiness is not so much in having or sharing. We make a living by what we get, but we make a life by what we give.
**NORMAN MACEWAN**

Life finds its purpose and fulfillment in the expansion of happiness.
**MAHARISHI MAHESH YOGI**

Space plus whatever you feel equals more whatever you feel, marvelous for happiness, God save you otherwise.
**BERNARD MALAMUD**

There is a wonderful mythical law of nature that the three things we crave most in life—happiness, freedom and peace of mind—are always attained by giving them to someone else.
**GEN. PEYTON C. MARCH**

Mirth is God's medicine; everybody ought to bathe in it. Grim care, moroseness, anxiety—all the rust of life—ought be scoured off by the oil of mirth.
**ORISON S. MARDEN**

Talk happiness. The world is sad enough without your woe.
**ORISON S. MARDEN**

The days that make us happy make us wise.
**JOHN MASEFIELD**

The first recipe for happiness is: Avoid too lengthy meditations on the past.
**ANDRÉ MAUROIS**

We all crave happiness, and we have at hand the predisposing conditions which make it possible. Nevertheless, the fact remains that deliberately to pursue happiness is not the surest way of achieving it. Seek it for its own sake and I doubt whether you will find it. The man who sets out to be the gay Bohemian becomes a hopeless tragedian.
**ROBERT J. MCCRACKEN**

Every job has drudgery, whether it is in the home, in the professional school or in the office. The first secret of happiness is the recognition of this fundamental fact.
**M. C. MCINTOSH**

There is only one honest impulse at the bottom of Puritanism, and that is the impulse to punish the man with a superior capacity for happiness.
**H. L. MENCKEN**

Ask yourself whether you are happy, and you cease to be so.
**JOHN STUART MILL**

Unquestionably, it is possible to do without happiness; it is done involuntarily by nineteen-twentieths of mankind.
**JOHN STUART MILL**

I have no money, no resources, no hopes. I am the happiest man alive.
**HENRY MILLER**

Unbroken happiness is a bore: It should have ups and downs.
**MOLIÈRE**

False happiness renders men stern and proud, and that happiness is never communicated. True happiness renders them kind and sensible, and that happiness is always shared.
**BARON DE MONTESQUIEU**

If one only wished to be happy, this could be easily accomplished; but we wish to be happier than other people, and this is always difficult, for we believe others to be happier than they are.
**BARON DE MONTESQUIEU**

I believe the recipe for happiness to be just enough money to pay the monthly bills you acquire, a little surplus to give you confidence, a little too much work each day, enthusiasm for your work, a substantial share of good health, a couple of real friends, and a wife and children to share life's beauty with you.
**J. KENFIELD MORLEY**

The merchant enjoys the felicity both of this world and the next.
**MUHAMMAD**

There is only one way to achieve happiness on this terrestrial ball, and that is to have either a clear conscience, or none at all.
**OGDEN NASH**

Not what we have, but what we use, not what we see, but what we choose, these are the things that mar or bless the sum of human happiness.
**JOSEPH FORT NEWTON**

The most intelligent men, like the strongest, find their happiness where others would find only disaster: in the labyrinth, in being hard with themselves and with others, in effort; their delight is self-mastery; in them asceticism becomes second nature, a necessity, as instinct.
**FRIEDRICH WILHELM NIETZSCHE**

What is happiness?—The feeling that power increases—that resistance is overcome.
**FRIEDRICH WILHELM NIETZSCHE**

Happiness is the harvest of a quiet eye.
**AUSTIN O'MALLEY**

We are here not to get all we can out of life for ourselves, but to try to make the lives of others happier.
**SIR WILLIAM OSLER**

If you count the sunny and the cloudy days of the whole year, you will find that the sunshine predominates.
**OVID**

Happiness is a by-product of an effort to make someone else happy.
**GRETTA PALMER**

Let a man choose what condition he will, and let him accumulate around him all the goods and gratifications seemingly calculated to make him happy in it; if that man is left at any time without occupation or amusement, and reflects on what he is, the meagre, languid felicity of his present lot will not bear him up. He will turn necessarily to gloomy anticipations of the future; and unless his occupation calls him out of himself, he is inevitably wretched.
**BLAISE PASCAL**

The belief that youth is the happiest time of life is founded on a fallacy. The happiest person is the person who thinks the most interesting thoughts, and we grow happier as we grow older.
**WILLIAM LYON PHELPS**

He who is of a calm and happy nature will hardly feel the pressure of age, but to him who is of an opposite disposition youth and age are equally a burden.
**PLATO**

The man who makes everything that leads to happiness depend upon himself, and not upon other men, has adopted the very best plan for living happily. This is the man of moderation, the man of manly character and of wisdom.
**PLATO**

Do not speak of your happiness to one less fortunate than yourself.
**PLUTARCH**

The state of life is most happy where superfluities are not required and necessities are not wanting.
**PLUTARCH**

We rich men count our happiness to lie in the little superfluities, not in necessities.
**PLUTARCH**

Man's real life is happy, chiefly because he is ever expecting that it soon will be so.
**EDGAR ALLAN POE**

Happiness: A way-station between too little and too much.
**CHANNING POLLOCK**

False happiness is like false money; it passes for a time as well as the true, and serves some ordinary occasions; but when it is brought to the touch, we find the lightness and alloy, and feel the loss.
**ALEXANDER POPE**

Happiness is not perfected until it is shared.
**JANE PORTER**

Every being must desire happiness for himself.
**RICHARD PRICE**

No one's happiness but my own is in my power to achieve or to destroy.
**AYN RAND**

The influences that really make and mar human happiness are beyond the reach of the law. The law can keep neighbors from trespassing, but it cannot put neighborly courtesy and goodwill into their relations.
**WALTER RAUSCHENBUSCH**

Children and fools have merry lives.
**JOHN RAY**

Happiness is only a by-product of successful living.
**AUSTEN FOX RIGGS**

The happy people of this world are never free. It is only youth which really wants freedom, or those who have set up a defensive mechanism against life, since to live is also to suffer.... Surely to be happy is better than to be free; and to be kind to all, to like many and love a few, to be needed and wanted by those we love, is certainly the nearest we can come to happiness.
**MARY ROBERTS RINEHART**

Before desiring something passionately, one should inquire into the happiness of the man who possesses it.
**FRANÇOIS DE LA ROCHEFOUCAULD**

Happiness is dependent on the taste and not on things. It is by having what we like that we are made happy, not by having what others think desirable.
**FRANÇOIS DE LA ROCHEFOUCAULD**

No person is either so happy or so unhappy as he imagines.
**FRANÇOIS DE LA ROCHEFOUCAULD**

We are more interested in making others believe we are happy than in trying to be happy ourselves.
**FRANÇOIS DE LA ROCHEFOUCAULD**

We are never so happy or so unhappy as we think.
**FRANÇOIS DE LA ROCHEFOUCAULD**

The road to happiness lies in two simple principles: find what it is that interests you and that you can do well, and when you find it put your whole soul into it—every bit of energy and ambition and natural ability you have.
**JOHN D. ROCKEFELLER III**

Happiness comes only when we push our brains and hearts to the farthest reaches of which we are capable.
**LEO ROSTEN**

I must accept life unconditionally. Most people ask for happiness on condition. Happiness can only be felt if you don't set any condition.
**ARTUR RUBINSTEIN**

Happiness is not a station you arrive at, but a manner of traveling.
**MARGARET LEE RUNBECK**

God intends no man to live in this world without working, but it seems to me no less evident that He intends every man to be happy in his work.
**JOHN RUSKIN**

Contempt for happiness is usually contempt for other people's happiness, and is an elegant disguise for hatred of the human race.
**BERTRAND RUSSELL**

The good life, as I conceive it, is a happy life. I do not mean that if you are good you will be happy; I mean that if you are happy you will be good.
**BERTRAND RUSSELL**

I may have thought the road to a world of free and happy human beings shorter than it is proving to be, but I was not wrong in thinking that it is worthwhile to live with a view to bringing it nearer.
**BERTRAND RUSSELL**

If there were in the world today any large number of people who desired their own happiness more than they desired the unhappiness of others, we could have a paradise in a few years.
**BERTRAND RUSSELL**

Men who are unhappy, like men who sleep badly, are always proud of the fact.
**BERTRAND RUSSELL**

To be without some of the things you want is an indispensable part of happiness.
**BERTRAND RUSSELL**

Of all created comforts, God is the lender; you are the borrower, not the owner.
**WALTER R. RUTHERFORD**

I believe in the possibility of happiness, if one cultivates intuition and outlives the grosser passions, including optimism.
**GEORGE SANTAYANA**

The profoundest affinities are the most readily felt; they remain a background and standard for all happiness and if we trace them out we succeed.
**GEORGE SANTAYANA**

The great happiness of life, I find, after all, to consist in the regular discharge of some mechanical duty.
**JOHANN FRIEDRICH VON SCHILLER**

Man is never happy, but spends his whole life in striving after something which he thinks will make him so.
**ARTHUR SCHOPENHAUER**

My life has no purpose, no direction, no aim, no meaning, and yet I'm happy. I can't figure it out. What am I doing right?
**CHARLES M. SCHULZ**

Happiness? That's nothing more than good health and a poor memory.
**ALBERT SCHWEITZER**

Humanity is fortunate, because no man is unhappy except by his own fault.
**SENECA**

The true felicity of life is to be free from anxieties and pertubations; to understand and do our duties to God and man, and to enjoy the present without any serious dependence on the future.
**SENECA**

No man is happy but by comparison.
**THOMAS SHADWELL**

I had rather have a fool to make me merry than experience to make me sad.
**WILLIAM SHAKESPEARE**

We have no more right to consume happiness without producing it than to consume wealth without producing it.
**GEORGE BERNARD SHAW**

Happiness is not in our circumstances but in ourselves. It is not something we see, like a rainbow, or feel, like the heat of a fire. Happiness is something we are.
**JOHN B. SHEERIN**

What leads to unhappiness, is making pleasure the chief aim.
**WILLIAM SHENSTONE**

Most true happiness comes from one's inner life, from the disposition of the mind and soul. Admittedly, a good inner life is difficult to achieve, especially in these trying times. It takes reflection and contemplation and self-discipline.
**WILLIAM L. SHIRER**

What can be added to the happiness of a man who is in health, out of debt, and has a clear conscience?
ADAM SMITH

When a man is happy, every effort to express his happiness mars its completeness.
ALEXANDER SMITH

Mankind is always happier for having been happy; so that if you make them happy now you make them happy twenty years hence, by the memory of it.
SYDNEY SMITH

The pursuit of happiness is a most ridiculous phrase: If you pursue happiness you'll never find it.
C. P. SNOW

Like swimming, riding, writing or playing golf, happiness can be learned.
BORIS SOKOLOFF

It is with words as with sunbeams—the more they are condensed, the deeper they burn.
ROBERT SOUTHEY

Objects we ardently pursue bring little happiness when gained; most of our pleasures come from unexpected sources.
HERBERT SPENCER

Mirth to a prudent man should always be accidental. It should naturally arise out of the occasion, and the occasion seldom be laid for it.
RICHARD STEELE

To describe happiness is to diminish it.
STENDHAL

Positiveness is a most absurd foible. If you are in the right, it lessens your triumph; if in the wrong, it adds shame to your defeat.
LAURENCE STERNE

A happy man or woman is a better thing to find than a five-pound note. He or she is a radiating focus of goodwill; and their entrance into a room is as though another candle had been lighted.
ROBERT LOUIS STEVENSON

There is no duty we so much underrate as the duty of being happy. By being happy, we sow anonymous benefits upon the world, which remain unknown even to ourselves, or when they are disclosed, surprise nobody so much as the benefactor.
ROBERT LOUIS STEVENSON

Happiness is a dividend on a well-invested life.
DUNCAN STUART

The best advice on the art of being happy is about as easy to follow as advice to be well when one is sick.
ANNE SWETCHINE

If we take an examination of what is understood by happiness . . . we shall find all its properties . . . under this short definition, that it is a perpetual possession of being well deceived.
JONATHAN SWIFT

Life is long to the miserable, but short to the happy.
PUBLILIUS SYRUS

No man is happy unless he believes he is.
PUBLILIUS SYRUS

A man of meditation is happy, not for an hour or a day, but quite round the circle of all his years.
ISAAC TAYLOR

Happiness is in action, and every power is intended for action; human happiness, therefore, can only be complete as all the powers have their full and legitimate play.
DAVID THOMAS

What wisdom, what warning can prevail against gladness? There is no law so strong that a little gladness may not transgress.
HENRY DAVID THOREAU

No clear-thinking or clear-seeing man or woman can be an apostle of despair. He alone fails who gives up and lies down. To get up each morning with the resolve to be happy; to take anew this attitude of mind whenever the dark or doleful thought presents itself, or whenever the bogeyman stalks into our room or across our path, is to set our own conditions to the events of each day. To do this is to condition circumstances instead of being conditioned by them.
RALPH WALDO TRINE

Are you so unobservant as not to have found out that sanity and happiness are an impossible combination?
MARK TWAIN

Doing what you like is freedom. Liking what you do is happiness.
FRANK TYGER

Happiness comes and goes and is short on staying power.
FRANK TYGER

Happiness is more a state of health than of wealth.
FRANK TYGER

Many people have known happiness, but didn't know it when they had it.
FRANK TYGER

Mirth prolongeth life, and causeth health.
NICHOLAS UDALL

Someone has well said, "Success is a journey, not a destination." Happiness is to be found along the way, not at the end of the road, for then the journey is over and it is too late. Today, this hour, this minute is the day, the hour, the minute for each of us to sense the fact that life is good, with all of its trials and troubles, and perhaps more interesting because of them.
ROBERT R. UPDEGRAFF

You never see the stock called Happiness quoted on the exchange.
HENRY VAN DYKE

When I think of how much you have meant to me all these years, it is almost more than I can do sometimes to keep from telling you so.
VERMONT HUSBAND'S COMPLIMENT

I firmly believe, notwithstanding all our complaints, that almost every person upon earth tastes upon the totality more happiness than misery.
HORACE WALPOLE

Though reading and conversation may furnish us with many ideas of men and things, yet it is our own meditation must form our judgment.
ISAAC WATTS

There are three sureties of happiness: good habits, amiability and forbearance.
WELSH PROVERB

If only we'd stop trying to be happy we'd have a pretty good time.
EDITH WHARTON

Felicity, not fluency of language, is a merit.
EDWIN P. WHIPPLE

Doubly rich is the man still boyish enough to play, laugh and sing as he carries and emanates sunshine along a friendly road.
CHARLES R. WIERS

Rich bachelors should be heavily taxed. It is not fair that some men should be happier than others.
**OSCAR WILDE**

The Constitution of America only guarantees pursuit of happiness—you have to catch up with it yourself. Fortunately, happiness is something that depends not on position but on disposition, and life is what you make it.
**GILL ROBB WILSON**

Happiness is not the station we arrive at but the manner by which we arrive.
**OLIVER G. WILSON**

No life can be barren which hears the whisper of the wind in the branches, or the voice of the sea as it breaks upon the shore; and no soul can lack happiness looking up to the midnight stars.
**WILLIAM WINTER**

If you observe a really happy man, you will find him building a boat, writing a symphony, educating his son, growing double dahlias, or looking for dinosaur eggs in the Gobi desert. He will not be searching for happiness as if it were a collar button that had rolled under the radiator, striving for it as the goal itself. He will have become aware that he is happy in the course of living life twenty-four crowded hours of each day.
**BERAN WOLFE**

True happiness must arise from well-regulated affections, and an affection includes a duty.
**MARY WOLLSTONECRAFT**

Giving of yourself, learning to be tolerant, giving recognition and approval to others, remaining flexible enough to mature and learn—yields happiness, harmony, contentment and productivity. These are the qualities of a rich life, the bounteous harvest of getting along with people.
**JACK C. YEWELL**

For me, happiness came from prayer to a kindly God, faith in a kindly God, love for my fellow man, and doing the very best I could every day of my life. I had looked for happiness in fast living, but it was not there. I tried to find it in money, but it was not there, either. But when I placed myself in tune with what I believe to be fundamental truths of life, when I began to develop my limited ability, to rid my mind of all kinds of tangled thoughts, and fill it with zeal and courage and love, when I gave myself a chance by treating myself decently and sensibly I began to feel the stimulating, warm glow of happiness, and life for me began to flow like a stream between smooth banks.
**YOUNG**

## *Hate*

He who surpasses or subdues mankind must look down on the hate of those below.
**LORD BYRON**

Most men know what they hate, few what they love.
**CHARLES CALEB COLTON**

There are many that despise half the world; but if there be any that despise the whole of it, it is because the other half despises them.
**CHARLES CALEB COLTON**

We hate some persons because we do not know them; and we will not know them because we hate them.
**CHARLES CALEB COLTON**

It is better to give love. Hatred is a low and degrading emotion and is so poisonous that no man is

strong enough to use it safely. The hatred we think we are directing against some person or thing or system has a devilish way of turning back upon us. When we seek revenge we administer slow poison to ourselves. When we administer affection it is astonishing what magical results we obtain.
THOMAS DREIER

Whenever I hear a man or women express hatred for any race, I wonder just what it is in themselves they hate so much. You can always be sure of this: You cannot express hatred for anything or anybody unless you make use of the supply of hatred within yourself. The only hatred you can express is your own personal possession. To hate is to be enslaved by evil.
THOMAS DREIER

Hating people is like burning down your own house to get rid of a rat.
HARRY EMERSON FOSDICK, D.D.

Impotent hatred is the most horrible of all emotions; one should hate nobody whom one cannot destroy.
JOHANN WOLFGANG VON GOETHE

Like gluttony or drunkenness, hatred seems an agreeable vice when you practice it yourself, but disgusting when observed in others.
WILLIAM H. IRWIN

If a man say, I love God, and hateth his brother, he is a liar; for he that loveth not his brother whom he has seen, how can he love God whom he hath not seen?
I JOHN 4:20

You can't be beautiful and hate.
BESS MYERSON

He who despises himself nevertheless esteems himself as a self-despiser.
FRIEDRICH WILHELM NIETZSCHE

Hatreds are the cinders of affection.
SIR WALTER RALEIGH

It is only those who are despicable who fear being despised.
FRANÇOIS DE LA ROCHEFOUCAULD

It is human nature to hate him whom you have injured.
TACITUS

Despise not small things, either for evil or good, for a look may work thy ruin, or a word create thy wealth. A spark is a little thing, yet it may kindle the world.
M. T. TUPPER

I shall never permit myself to stoop so low as to hate any man.
BOOKER T. WASHINGTON

## *Health*

There is a limit to the best of health, disease is always a near neighbor.
AESCHYLUS

Ulcers aren't the result of what you eat. You get ulcers from what's eating you.
ANONYMOUS

He who has health has hope, and he who has hope has everything.
ARABIAN PROVERB

Everybody's heart is open, you know, when they have recently escaped from severe pain, or are recovering the blessing of health.
JANE AUSTEN

A healthy body is a guest-chamber for the soul; a sick body is a prison.
FRANCIS BACON

Protect your health. Without it you face a serious handicap for success and happiness.
HARRY F. BANKS

Gluttony is the source of all our infirmities and the fountain of all our diseases. As a lamp is choked by a superabundance of oil, and a fire extinguished by excess of fuel, so is the natural health of the body destroyed by intemperate diet.
MARION L. BURTON

I reckon being ill as one of the great pleasures of life, provided one is not too ill and is not obliged to work till one is better.
SAMUEL BUTLER

We sit at breakfast, we sit on the train on the way to work, we sit at work, we sit at lunch, we sit all afternoon, a hodgepodge of sagging livers, sinking gall bladders, drooping stomachs, compressed intestines, and squashed pelvic organs.
JOHN BUTTON, JR.

Fitness: If it came in a bottle, everybody would have a good body.
CHER

Gluttony is a great fault; but we do not necessarily dislike a glutton. We only dislike the glutton when he becomes a gourmet—that is, we only dislike him when he not only wants the best for himself, but knows what is best for other people.
G. K. CHESTERTON

The trouble about always trying to preserve the health of the body is that it is so difficult to do so without destroying the health of the mind.
G. K. CHESTERTON

My good health is due to a soup made of white doves. It is simply wonderful as a tonic.
MADAME CHIANG KAI-SHEK

Fitness is to the '90s what personal growth was to the '70s.
LARRY CHRISPYN

Never hurry; take plenty of exercise; always be cheerful, and take all the sleep you need, and you may expect to be well.
JAMES FREEMAN CLARKE

Faddists are continually proclaiming the value of exercise. Four people out of five are more in need of rest than exercise.
LOGAN CLENDENING

You don't get ulcers from what you eat, but from what's eating you.
ALBERT CLIFFE

Minor surgery is surgery someone else is having.
JOSEPH COOK

Sleep is the golden chain that ties health and our bodies together.
THOMAS DEKKER

The health of nations is more important than the wealth of nations.
WILL DURANT

Sickness comes on horseback and departs on foot.
DUTCH PROVERB

Those who do not find time for exercise will have to find time for illness.
**EARL OF DERBY**

Health and appetite impart the sweetness to sugar, bread and meat.
**RALPH WALDO EMERSON**

We forget ourselves and our destinies in health; and the chief use of temporary sickness is to remind us of these concerns.
**RALPH WALDO EMERSON**

Health is better than wealth.
**ENGLISH PROVERB**

### Mental Health Rules

1. HAVE A HOBBY: Acquire pursuits which absorb your interest; sports and nature are best.
2. DEVELOP A PHILOSOPHY: Adapt yourself to social and spiritual surroundings.
3. SHARE YOUR THOUGHTS: Cultivate companionship in thought and in feeling. Confide, confess, consult.
4. FACE YOUR FEARS: Analyze them; daylight dismisses ghosts.
5. BALANCE FANTASY WITH FACT: Dream but also do; wish but build; imagine but ever face reality.
6. BEWARE ALLURING ESCAPES: Alcohol, opiates and barbitals may prove faithless friends.
7. EXERCISE: Walk, swim, golf—muscles need activity.
8. LOVE, BUT LOVE WISELY: Sex is a flame which uncontrolled may scorch; properly guided, it will light the torch of eternity.
9. DON'T BECOME BNGULFED IN A WHIRLPOOL OF WORRIES: Call early for help. The doctor is ready for your rescue.
10. TRUST IN TIME: Be patient and hopeful time is a great therapist.

**JOSEPH FETTERMAN**

Acquire good physique and mental robustness which comes from fresh air, sound and plain food, constant and compelling attention to waste matter, proper and peaceful sleep, and concentration on true religion, ethics, art and literature.
**J. T. FISHER**

There is a certain state of health that does not allow us to understand everything; and perhaps illness shuts us off from certain truths; but health shuts us off just as effectively from others.
**ANDRÉ GIDE**

Don't worry about losing weight; you'll find it exactly where you lost it.
**ROBERT HALF**

It's rare that patients ask for a second opinion when they're happy with the first.
**ROBERT HALF**

To lose one's health renders science null, art inglorious, strength unavailing, wealth useless, and eloquence powerless.
**HEROPHILUS**

Keep a watch also upon the faults of the patients, which also make them lie about the taking of things prescribed.
**HIPPOCRATES**

The joy of feeling fit physically is reflected in a clearer and more useful mind. You may read and study forever, but you come to no more important truthful conclusions than these two: 1. Take care of your body (eat and exercise properly), and your mind will improve. 2. Work hard, and be polite and fair, and your condition in the world will improve. No pills, tablets, lotions, philosophies, will do as much for you as this simple formula I have outlined. The formula is not of my invention. Every

intelligent man of experience since time began has taught it as a natural fact.
**EDGAR WATSON HOWE**

Health is most worth while to conserve. I do not mean simply the abounding vigor of youth, with abundance of fresh air and exercise and with its reserves which seem to mock the warnings of elders. I mean, rather, the sustained and protected strength which is based on the conservation of physical resources and gives promise of a long life well lived. In our onward journey the ranks are rapidly thinned by the passing out of those who have had their brief stay and were soon done. When their notes matured they were unable to meet them. Nothing is sadder than these physical bankruptcies, which deprive men and women of opportunities when, with the capital of experience well invested, they should have the most ample returns.
**CHARLES EVANS HUGHES**

True enjoyment comes from activity of the mind and exercise of the body; the two are united.
**ALEXANDER VON HUMBOLDT**

Health is worth more than learning.
**THOMAS JEFFERSON**

Health is so necessary to all the duties, as well as pleasures of life, that the crime of squandering it is equal to the folly.
**SAMUEL JOHNSON**

To preserve health is a moral and religious duty, for health is the basis of all social virtues. We can no longer be useful when not well.
**SAMUEL JOHNSON**

One of the most difficult things to contend with in a hospital is the assumption on the part of the staff that because you have lost your gall bladder you have also lost your mind.
**JEAN KERR**

If you look like your passport photo, you're too ill to travel.
**WILL KOMMEN**

How sickness enlarges the dimensions of a man's self to himself! Supreme selfishness is inculcated upon him as his only duty.
**CHARLES LAMB**

What have I gained by health? Intolerable dullness. What by moderate meals? A total blank.
**CHARLES LAMB**

One out of four people in this country is mentally unbalanced. Think of your three closest friends; if they seem OK, then you're the one.
**ANN LANDERS**

To insure good health: Eat lightly, breathe deeply, live moderately, cultivate cheerfulness, and maintain an interest in life.
**WILLIAM LOUDEN**

Disease makes men more physical; it leaves them with nothing but body.
**THOMAS MANN**

It's no longer a question of staying healthy. It's a question of finding a sickness you like.
**JACKIE MASON**

A man in good health is always full of advice to the sick.
**MENANDER**

It is a religious duty to maintain health. Eating and drinking, sleeping and waking and exercise are not

outside the province of religion. They are as much a part of it as prayer and worship and daily work. They vitally affect temper and temperament and the way people look at the world. A healthy body makes for a healthy mind and a healthy soul. It is essential to the finest and fullest kind of life.
**ROBERT J. MCCRACKEN**

Mental health problems do not affect three or four out of every five persons, but one out of one.
**DR. KARL MENNINGER**

Health is a precious thing, and the only one, in truth, meriting that a man should lay out not only his time, sweat, labor and goods, but also life itself to obtain it.
**MICHEL DE MONTAIGNE**

The only way to get 30 minutes' uninterrupted rest in a hospital is to ring for a nurse.
**OLD SOUTHERN SAYING**

Without health, life is not life; it is only a state of langour and suffering—an image of death.
**FRANÇOIS RABELAIS**

No matter how busy you are you usually find time to see to it that your automobile is kept in repair. You would never think of starting out if your automobile brakes, motor or gears were not functioning properly. But, how about your body? Has it ever occurred to you that you should have it checked up at least once every year? How do you know whether or not your vital organs are functioning properly? The man who submits himself to his family doctor for regular examination will rarely need to worry about his health. His physician will advise the proper diet, exercise, recreation, etc. If his advice is followed much trouble may be averted; many serious conditions can be halted in their early stages.
**JOHN L. RICE**

Preserving health by too severe a rule is a wearisome malady.
**FRANÇOIS DE LA ROCHEFOUCAULD**

The diseases which destroy a man are no less natural than the instincts which preserve him.
**GEORGE SANTAYANA**

A minor operation is one that is done on someone else.
**RICHARD SELZER**

Hold fast then to this sound and wholesome rule of life; indulge the body only as far as is needful for health.
**SENECA**

It is part of the cure to wish to be cured.
**SENECA**

I enjoy convalescence. It is the part that makes the illness worthwhile.
**GEORGE BERNARD SHAW**

The sound body is the product of the sound mind.
**GEORGE BERNARD SHAW**

Use your health, even to the point of wearing it out. That is what it is for. Spend all you have before you die; and do not outlive yourself.
**GEORGE BERNARD SHAW**

He is remarkably well, considering that he has been remarkably well for so many years.
**LOGAN PEARSALL SMITH**

A man too busy to take care of his health is like a mechanic too busy to take care of his tools.
**SPANISH PROVERB**

If you would live in health, be old early.
**SPANISH PROVERB**

People who are always taking care of their health are like misers, who are hoarding up a treasure which they have never spirit enough to enjoy.
**LAURENCE STERNE**

The only way for a rich man to be healthy is by exercise and abstinence, to live as if he were poor.
**WILLIAM J. TEMPLE**

When we are well, we all have good advice for those who are ill.
**TERENCE**

Health is the vital principle of bliss.
**JAMES THOMSON**

Measure your health by your sympathy with morning and Spring.
**HENRY DAVID THOREAU**

Look to your health; and if you have it, praise God, and value it next to a good conscience, for health is the second blessing that we mortals are capable of—a blessing that money cannot buy.
**IZAAK WALTON**

## *Heart*

If one should give me a dish of sand, and tell me there were particles of iron in it, I might look for them with my eyes, and search for them with my clumsy fingers, and be unable to detect them; but let me take a magnet and sweep through it, and how would it draw to itself the almost invisible particles by the mere power of attraction. The unthankful heart, like my finger in the sand, discovers no mercies; but let the thankful heart sweep through the day, and as the magnet finds the iron, so it will find, in every hour, some heavenly blessings, only the iron in God's sand in gold!
**HENRY WARD BEECHER**

No man can tell whether he is rich or poor by turning to his ledger. It is the heart that makes a man rich. He is rich according to what he is, not according to what he has.
**HENRY WARD BEECHER**

There is a dew in one flower and not in another, because one opens in cup and takes it in, while the other closes itself, and the drops run off. God rains His goodness and mercy as widespread as the dew, and if we lack them, it is because we will not open our hearts to receive them.
**HENRY WARD BEECHER**

There are important cases in which the difference between half a heart and a whole heart makes just the difference between signal defeat and a splendid victory.
**A. H. K. BOYD**

If a good face is a letter of recommendation, a good heart is a letter of credit.
**EDWARD BULWER-LYTTON**

To judge human character rightly, a man may sometimes have very small experience, provided he has a very large heart.
**EDWARD BULWER-LYTTON**

Win hearts, and you have all men's hands and purses.
**BURLEIGH**

A loving heart is the beginning of all knowledge.
**THOMAS CARLYLE**

Contact with the world either breaks or hardens the heart.
**SÉBASTIEN CHAMFORT**

The heart of all problems, whether economic, political or social, is a human heart. The man comes first, then the plan.
**L. M. CHARLES-EDWARDS, D.D.**

If I keep a green bough in my heart, the singing bird will come.
**CHINESE PROVERB**

But as it is written, eye hath not seen, nor ear heard, neither have entered into the heart of man, the things which God hath prepared for them that love him.
**I CORINTHIANS 2:9**

Some hearts are hidden, some have not a heart.
**GEORGE GRABBE**

What a sober man has in his heart, a drunken man has on his lips.
**DANISH PROVERB**

The human heart, at whatever age, opens only to the heart that opens in the return.
**MARIE EDGEWORTH**

Beware what you set your heart upon. For it surely shall be yours.
**RALPH WALDO EMERSON**

No man can deliver the goods if his heart is heavier than the load.
**FRANK IRVING FLETCHER**

A good heart can no more be concealed than a bad one.
**MALCOLM FORBES**

At the heart of any good business is a chief executive officer with one.
**MALCOLM FORBES**

To measure the man, measure his heart.
**MALCOLM FORBES**

When the heart is afire, some sparks will fly out of the mouth.
**THOMAS FULLER**

Awake, my heart, and sing!
**PAUL GERHARDT**

A man not perfect, but of heart so high, and such heroic rage, that even his hopes became a part of earth's eternal heritage.
**RICHARD GILDER**

There is no exercise better for the heart than reaching down and lifting people up.
**JOHN ANDREW HOLMES**

Whatever comes from the heart carries the heat and color of its birthplace.
**OLIVER WENDELL HOLMES**

It is the inclination and tendency of the heart which finally determines the opinions of the mind.
**CHRISTOPH LUTHARDT**

It is better to go down on the great seas which human hearts were made to sail than to rot at the wharves in ignoble anchorage.
**HAMILTON WRIGHT MABIE**

The great man is he who does not lose his child's heart.
**MENCIUS**

And the heart that is soonest awake to the flowers is always the first to be touched by the thorns.
**SIR THOMAS MORE**

Because of the law of gravitation the apple falls to the ground. Because of the law of growth the acorn becomes a mighty oak. Because of the law of causation, a man is as he thinketh in his heart. Nothing can happen without its adequate cause.
DON CARLOS MUSSER

There are good hearts to serve men in palaces as in cottages.
ROBERT OWEN

No true manhood can be trained by a merely intellectual process. You cannot train men by the intellect alone; you must train them by the heart.
JOSEPH PARKER

No matter how widely you have travelled, you haven't seen the world if you have failed to look into the human hearts that inhabit it.
DONALD C. PEATTIE

Who shall ascend into the hill of the Lord? or who shall stand in his holy place? He that hath clean hands, and a pure heart.
PSALMS 24:3–4

With my whole heart have I sought thee: O let me not wander from thy commandments. Thy word have I hid in mine heart, that I might not sin against thee.
PSALMS 119:10–11

Want and wealth equally harden the human heart, as frost and fire are both alien to the human flesh. Famine and gluttony alike drive away nature from the heart of man.
THEODORE E. PARKER

A light heart lives long.
WILLIAM SHAKESPEARE

The heart has always the pardoning power.
ANNE SWETCHINE

The most unproductive, empty, fruitless fellow in the world is the man with a barren heart. Happiness can never reach him, for nothing good and lasting can lodge in his heart. It is solid as a billiard ball. Contrast this man with his barren heart with the human that plays the game of life fairly and honestly and is willing to make others happy by his own sacrifices.
F. D. VAN AMBURGH

All grand thoughts come from the heart.
MARQUIS DE VAUVENARGUES

What I am concerned about in this fast-moving world in a time of crises, both in foreign and domestic affairs, is not so much a program as a spirit of approach, not so much a mind as a heart. A program lives today and dies tomorrow. A mind, if it be open, may change with each new day, but the spirit and the heart are as unchanging as the tides.
OWEN D. YOUNG

## *Help*

One rooster can't help another scratch the same piece of ground.
AFRICAN PROVERB

A helping word to one in trouble is often like a switch on a railroad track—an inch between wreck and smoothrolling prosperity.
HENRY WARD BEECHER

When a person is down in the world, an ounce of help is better than a pound of preaching.
EDWARD BULWER-LYTTON

Drop the hammer and pick up the shovel.
J. A. DEVER

English has two great forgotten words: "helpmeet," which is much greater than "lover," and "loving-kindness," which is so much greater than "love."
LAWRENCE DURRELL

It is one of the most beautiful compensations of this life that no man can sincerely try to help another without helping himself.
RALPH WALDO EMERSON

One right and honest definition of business is mutual helpfulness.
WILLIAM FEATHER

He who says he never needs help, most does.
MALCOLM FORBES

Time and money spent in helping men to do more for themselves is far better than mere giving.
HENRY FORD

Three helping one another bear the burden of six.
GEORGE HERBERT

Help thy brother's boat across, and lo! thine own has reached the shore.
HINDU PROVERB

All the other pleasures of life seem to wear out, but the pleasure of helping others in distress never does.
JULIUS ROSENWALD

Every great man is always being helped by everybody; for his gift is to get good out of all things and all persons.
JOHN RUSKIN

The race of mankind would perish did they cease to aid each other. We cannot exist without mutual help. All therefore that need aid have a right to ask it from their fellow-men; and no one who has the power of granting can refuse it without guilt.
SIR WALTER SCOTT

Without the help of others, any one of us would die, naked and starved. Consider the bread upon our table, the clothes upon our backs, the luxuries that make life pleasant; how many men worked in sunlit fields, in dark mines, in the fierce heart of modern metal, and among the looms and wheels of countless factories, in order to create them for our use and enjoyment.
ALFRED E. SMITH

It is one of the beautiful compensations of this life that no one can sincerely try to help another without helping himself.
CHARLES DUDLEY WARNER

Whoever in trouble and sorrow needs your help, give it to him. Whoever in anxiety or fear needs your friendship, give it to him. It isn't important whether he likes you. It isn't important whether you approve of his conduct. It isn't important what his creed or nationality may be.
E. N. WEST, D.D.

## *History*

The historian must not try to know what is truth, if he values his honesty; for if he cares for his truths, he is certain to falsify his facts.
HENRY ADAMS

There is nothing that solidifies and strengthens a nation like reading of the nation's own history,

whether that history is recorded in books or embodied in customs, institutions and monuments.
JOSEPH ANDERSON

Two things we ought to learn from history: one, that we are not in ourselves superior to our fathers; another, that we are shamefully and monstrously inferior to them, if we do not advance beyond them.
THOMAS ARNOLD

History: An account mostly false, of events unimportant, which are brought about by rulers mostly knaves, and soldiers mostly fools.
AMBROSE BIERCE

A good writer of history is a guy who is suspicious.
JIM BISHOP

There are always some areas world history does not reach, zones of silence and undisturbed ignorance.
FERNAND BRAUDEL

When ancient opinions and rules of life are taken away, the loss cannot possibly be estimated. From that moment we have no compass to govern us, nor can we know distinctly to what port to steer.
EDMUND BURKE

The true past departs not; no truth or goodness realized by man ever dies, or can die; but all is still here, and, recognized or not, lives and works through endless change.
THOMAS CARLYLE

In spite of the recent triumphs of science, men haven't changed much in the last 2,000 years, and in consequence, we must still try to learn from history. History is ourselves.
KENNETH CLARK

If men could learn from history, what lessons it might teach us! But passion and party blind our eyes, and the light which experience gives us is a lantern on the stern which shines only on the waves behind us.
SAMUEL TAYLOR COLERIDGE

We shall not understand the history of men and other times unless we ourselves are alive to the requirements which that history satisfied.
BENEDETTO CROCE

In the long run I firmly believe only one answer can emerge. Always before, in world history, the frailty and weakness which the dictator has postulated in the masses of mankind has finally been uncovered in himself by the inexorable march of events, and the world as a whole has somehow managed to achieve, over the years, continually higher and nobler modes of thinking and of living.
HARVEY N. DAVIS

It was the best of times, it was the worst of times, it was the age of wisdom, it was the age of foolishness, it was the epoch of belief, it was the epoch of incredulity, it was the season of Light, it was the season of Darkness, it was the spring of hope, it was the winter of despair.
CHARLES DICKENS

The history of the past interests us only in so far as it illuminates the history of the present.
ERNEST DIMNET

I am ashamed to see what a shallow village tale our so-called history is.
RALPH WALDO EMERSON

History records the names of royal bastards, but cannot tell us the origin of wheat.
JEAN HENRI FABRE

Mankind's study of man occupies nearly the whole field of literature. The burden of history is what man has been; of law, what he does; of physiology, what he is; of ethics, what he ought to be; of revelation, what he shall be.
**GEORGE FINLAYSON**

History is more or less bunk.
**HENRY FORD**

History never looks like history when you are living through it. It always looks confusing and messy, and it always looks uncomfortable.
**JOHN W. GARDNER**

The world's history is a divine poem of which the history of every nation is a canto and every man a word. Its strains have been pealing along down the centuries, and though there have been mingled the discords of warring cannon and dying men, yet... there has been a divine melody running through the song which speaks of hope and halcyon days to come.
**JAMES A. GARFIELD**

History is indeed little more than the register of the crimes, follies and misfortunes of mankind.
**EDWARD GIBBON**

The reason history is by turns gripping, boring and threatening is that it is a play in which the characters make up their lines as they go along.
**JOHN P. GRIER**

The use of history is to tell us what we are, for at our birth we are nearly empty vesseis and we become what our tradition pours into us.
**LEARNED HAND**

A generation which ignores history has no past—and no future.
**ROBERT A. HEINLEIN**

When I want to understand what is happening today, I try to decide what will happen tomorrow; I look back; a page of history is worth a volume of logic.
**OLIVER WENDELL HOLMES**

The future of nations cannot be frozen... cannot be foreseen. It we are going to accomplish anything in our time we must approach our problem in the knowledge that there is nothing rigid or immutable in human affairs. History is a story of growth, decay and change. If no provision, no allowance is made for change by peaceful means, it will come anyway—and with violence.
**HERBERT HOOVER**

That men do not learn very much from the lessons of history is the most important of all the lessons history has to teach.
**ALDOUS HUXLEY**

Only the vanquished remember history.
**MARSHALL MCLUHAN**

The historian's first duties are sacrilege and the mocking of false gods. They are his indispensable instruments for establishing the truth.
**JULES MICHELET**

History shows that great economic and social forces flow like a tide over communities only half conscious of that which is befalling them. Wise statesmen foresee what time is thus bringing, and try to shape institutions and mold men's thoughts and purposes in accordance with the change that is silently coming on. The unwise are those who bring nothing constructive to the process, and who greatly imperil the future of mankind by leaving great questions to be fought out between ignorant change on one hand and ignorant opposition to change on the other.
**JOHN STUART MILL**

One age cannot be completely understood if all the others are not understood. The song of history can only be sung as a whole.
JOSÉ ORTEGA Y GASSET

The most durable foundations for hope for a better future for humanity seem to me to be found in history, literature and religion.
BLISS PERRY

To be ignorant of the lives of the most celebrated men of antiquity is to continue in a state of childhood all our days.
PLUTARCH

If anyone wants to understand the course of man on earth, he must consider the fact of the long pause, three million years on the level of savagery, ten thousand years on the level of dependence on the fruits of hand labor, and a hundred or a hundred and fifty years of sudden sharp rise. One hundred or 150 years is the time included in what we call progress in man's history.
E. PARMALEE PRENTICE

The talent of historians lies in their creating a true ensemble out of facts which are but half-true.
ERNEST RENAN

The meaning of history is never apparent to those who make it; a leader in any age or generation is no more than a man who sees somewhat beyond the end of his nose.
THOMAS SUGRUE

A knowledge of American history is not something to be taken in six easy doses like vitamin pills.
LEWIS P. TODD

The man who ventures to write contemporary history must expect to be attacked both for everything he has said and everything he has not said.
VOLTAIRE

History makes one shudder and laugh by turns.
HORACE WALPOLE

History is a race between education and catastrophe.
H. G. WELLS

All centuries are dangerous; it is the business of the future to be dangerous. It must be admitted that there is a degree of instability which is inconsistent with civilization. But, on the whole, the great ages have been the unstable ages.
ALFRED NORTH WHITEHEAD

## *Holidays*

Christmas itself may be called into question if carried so far it creates indigestion.
RALPH BERGENGREN

The gist of New Year's Day is: Try again.
FRANK CRANE

Let your holidays be associated with great public events, and they may be the life of patriotism as well as a source of relaxation and personal employment.
TRYON EDWARDS

Except for excess decoration, excess commercialism, excess editorializing, excess caroling, excess bibbling, and excess cheer, I heartily approve of the Christmas spirit.
WILLIAM FEATHER

The Christmas spirit brings home to us—or should bring home to us—the profound Biblical truth that it is more blessed to give than to receive. Anything which inspires unselfishness makes for our ennoblement. Christmas does that.

I am all for Christmas.

B. C. FORBES

School-returning young may feel their sadness at the end of holidays such as Christmas vacation is unmatched, understood except by their fellows. Wrong.... Even intolerant, ever-growling Pops actually rue the day that reopened schools give back to parents their home—empty. Where, now, the top-volume screams of unintelligible combos from every transistor, phono or TV? The awful quiet of meals without arguments about which unheard of tune is No. 11 or 7.... The holidays provide only a short glimpse, a fleeting suggestion of what's happenin', man.

MALCOLM FORBES

There's one post-Christmas chore I love—writing thank-you letters.... Lots of companies for many reasonable reasons, I guess, have a policy against sending even Christmas cards, never mind things, at Christmastime. But our clan gets a big kick out of opening the Warner-Lambert box containing an assortment of their wares; we argue over which of the boys is to get the Union Oil Co. necktie [and] all the holiday long we play the marvelous Christmas music sent by Goodyear.... None of these things means that Forbes or Forbeses have been had. But all of us like being thought of.

MALCOLM FORBES

It is the custom to sneer at the modern apartment house, television, big-city Christmas, with its commercial taint... office parties, artificial Christmas trees... but future generations in search of their lost Christmases may well remember its innocence; yes, and its beauty, too.

PAUL GALLICO

It's smart to do your holiday hinting early.

ARNOLD GLASOW

People are happier at Yuletime because they take the milk of human kindness out of the deep freeze.

ARNOLD GLASOW

The New Year is at the door.... I wish for the stupid a little understanding, and for the understanding a little poetry. I wish the most beautiful clothes for the ladies and much money for the men. I wish a heart for the rich and a little bread for the poor. But above all, I wish that we may blackguard each other as little as possible during the New Year.

HEINRICH HEINE

The first thing to turn green in the spring is the Christmas jewelry.

KIN HUBBARD

No one ever regarded the first of January with indifference. It is the nativity of our common Adam.

CHARLES LAMB

Merry Christmas, Nearly Everybody!

OGDEN NASH

After a Christmas comes a Lent.

JOHN RAY

If all the year were playing holidays, to sport would be as tedious as to work; but when they seldom come, the wished for come.

WILLIAM SHAKESPEARE

I stopped believing in Santa Claus when I was six. Mother took me to see him in a department store and he asked for my autograph.

SHIRLEY TEMPLE

As you get older, you get tired of doing the same things over and over again, so you think Christmas has changed. It hasn't. It's you who has changed.
HARRY S TRUMAN

## Home

By the time a family pays off the mortgage for a home in the suburbs, the home isn't home, and the suburbs aren't suburbs.
ANONYMOUS

The starting points of character and destiny in the young begin with home environment and outside associations.
HARRY F. BANKS

Many a man who pays rent all his life owns his own home; and many a family has successfully saved for a home only to find itself at last with nothing but a house.
BRUCE BARTON

Cooking: An art, a noble science; cooks are gentlemen.
RICHARD BURTON

Only the home can found a state.
JOSEPH COOK

Look well to the hearthstone; therein all hope for America lies.
CALVIN COOLIDGE

Home is the place where, when you have to go there, they have to take you in.
ROBERT FROST

A home is no home unless it contains food and fire for the mind as well as for the body. For human beings are not so constituted that they can live without expansion. If they do not get it in one way, they must in another, or perish.
MARGARET FULLER

The happiness of the domestic fireside is the first boon to Heaven; and it is well it is so, since it is that which is the lot of the mass of mankind.
THOMAS JEFFERSON

No worldly success can compensate for failure in the home.
DAVID O. MCKAY

The home is the basis of a righteous life and no other instrumentality can take its place nor fulfill its essential functions.
DAVID O. MCKAY

If this world affords true happiness, it is to be found in a home where love and confidence increase with the years, where the necessities of life come without severe strain, where luxuries enter only after their cost has been carefully considered.
A. EDWARD NEWTON

A man's home is his hassle.
RESTAURANT SIGN

I hate housework! You make the bed, you do the dishes—and six months later you have to start all over again.
JOAN RIVERS

Home is the one place in all this world where hearts are sure of each other. It is the place of confidence. It is the spot where expressions of tenderness gush out without any dread of ridicule.
FREDERICK W. ROBERTSON

It is impossible to win the great prizes of life without running risks, and the greatest of all prizes are those connected with the home. No father and mother can hope to escape sorrow and anxiety, and there are dreadful moments when death comes very near to those we love, even if for the time being it passes by. But life is a great adventure, and the worst of all fears is the fear of living. There are many forms of success, many forms of triumph. But there is no other success that in any shape or way approaches that which is open to most of the many men and women who have the right ideals. These are the men and women who see that it is the intimate and homely things that count most. They are the men and women who have the courage to strive for the happiness which comes only with labor and effort and self-sacrifice, and those whose joy in life springs in part from power of work and sense of duty.
**THEODORE ROOSEVELT**

Only that traveling is good which reveals to me the value of home and enables me to enjoy it better.
**HENRY DAVID THOREAU**

Our houses are such unwieldy property that we are often imprisoned rather than housed by them.
**HENRY DAVID THOREAU**

What a fool he must be who thinks that his El Dorado is anywhere but where he lives.
**HENRY DAVID THOREAU**

The home . . . is the lens through which we get our first look at marriage and all civic duties; it is the clinic where, by conversation and attitude, impressions are created with respect to sobriety and reverence; it is the school where lessons of truth or falsehood, honesty or deceit are learned; it is the mold which ultimately determines the structure of society.
**PERRY F. WEBB**

## *Honesty*

To believe all men honest would be folly. To believe none so, is something worse.
**JOHN QUINCY ADAMS**

Man's first care should be to avoid the reproaches of his own heart, and next to escape the censures of the world. If the last interfere with the first it should be entirely neglected. But if not, there cannot be a greater satisfaction to an honest mind than to see its own approbation seconded by the applauses of the public.
**JOSEPH ADDISON**

No man is really honest; none of us is above the influence of gain.
**ARISTOPHANES**

Aside from the strictly moral standpoint, honesty is—not only the best policy, but the only possible policy from the standpoint of business relations. The fulfillment of the pledged word is of equal necessity to the conduct of all business. If we expect and demand virtue and honor in others, the flame of both must burn brightly within ourselves and shed their light to illuminate the erstwhile dark corners of distrust and dishonesty. . . . The truthful answer rests for the most part within ourselves, for like begets like. Honesty begets honesty; trust, trust; and so on through the whole category of desirable practices that must govern and control the world's affairs.
**JAMES F. BELL**

How desperately difficult it is to be honest with oneself. It is much easier to be honest with other people.
**EDWARD F. BENSON**

Men must be honest with themselves before they can be honest with others. A man who is not honest with himself presents a hopeless case.
**WILLIAM J. H. BOETCKER**

Put a rogue in the lime-light and he will act like an honest man.
**NAPOLEON BONAPARTE**

The surest way to remain poor is to be an honest man.
**NAPOLEON BONAPARTE**

Hard workers are usually honest; industry lifts them above temptation.
**CHRISTIAN BOVÉE**

Make yourself an honest man, and then you may be sure there is one rascal less in the world.
**THOMAS CARLYLE**

Honesty: The ability to resist small temptations.
**JOHN CIARDI**

To be honest is nothing; the reputation of it is all.
**WILLIAM CONGREVE**

Ninety-eight out of 100 of the rich men in America are honest. That is why they are rich.
**RUSSELL HERMAN CONWELL**

There is no twilight zone of honesty in business—a thing is right or it's wrong— it's black or it's white.
**JOHN F. DODGE**

The best advice I can give to any young man or young woman upon graduation from school can be summed up in exactly eight words, and they are—be honest with yourself and tell the truth.
**JAMES A. FARLEY**

Honesty is the cornerstone of character. The honest man or woman seeks not merely to avoid criminal or illegal acts, but to be scrupulously fair, upright, fearless in both action and expression. Honesty pays dividends both in dollars and in peace of mind.
**B. C. FORBES**

Trickery and treachery are the practices of fools that have not wits enough to be honest.
**BENJAMIN FRANKLIN**

Nothing is quite honest that is not commercial, but not everything commercial is honest.
**ROBERT FROST**

He that resolves to deal with none but honest men must leave off dealing.
**THOMAS FULLER**

Honest men fear neither the light nor the dark.
**THOMAS FULLER**

If thou employest plain men, and canst find such as are commonly honest, they will work faithfully, and report fairly. Cunning men will, for their own credit, adventure without command; and from thy business derive credit to themselves.
**THOMAS FULLER**

If you pity rogues, you are no great friend to honest men.
**THOMAS FULLER**

Honesty of thought and speech and written word is a jewel, and they who curb prejudice and seek honorably to know and speak the truth are the only builders of a better life.
**JOHN GALSWORTHY**

When you cannot make pure goods and full weight, go to something else that is honest, even if it is breaking stone.
**JAMES GAMBLE**

The darkest hour in the history of any young man is when he sits down to study how to get money without honestly earning it.
**HORACE GREELEY**

Our great error is that we suppose mankind more honest than they are.
**ALEXANDER HAMILTON**

Every man should make up his mind that if he expects to succeed, he must give an honest return for the other man's dollar.
**E. H. HARRIMAN**

Honesty and wisdom are such a delightful pastime, at another person's expense!
**NATHANIEL HAWTHORNE**

Honesty is one part of eloquence. We persuade others by being in earnest ourselves.
**WILLIAM HAZLITT**

There is no well-defined boundary between honesty and dishonesty. The frontiers of one blend with the outside limits of the other, and he who attempts to tread this dangerous ground may be sometimes in one domain and sometimes in the other.
**O. HENRY**

No public man can be a little crooked. There is no such thing as a no-man's-land between honesty and dishonesty.
**HERBERT HOOVER**

Honesty is largely a matter of information, of knowing that dishonesty is a mistake.
**EDGAR WATSON HOWE**

It pays to be honest, but it's beginning to look like the rewards are falling far short of what it costs to live.
**KIN HUBBARD**

Honesty pays, but it don't seem to pay enough to suit a lot of people.
**KIN HUBBARD**

Let none of us delude himself by supposing that honesty is always the best policy. It is not.
**WILLIAM RALPH INGE**

Every man who expresses an honest thought is a soldier in the army of intellectual liberty.
**ROBERT G. INGERSOLL**

Those who praise anything I do and anything I say, they are not my good friends. Those who with honest opinion tell me my faults and my mistakes, they are my good friends.
**ISOCRATES**

I have not observed men's honesty to increase with their riches.
**THOMAS JEFFERSON**

Men are disposed to live honestly, if the means of doing so are open to them.
**THOMAS JEFFERSON**

He who freely praises what he means to purchase, and he who enumerates the faults of what he means to sell, may set up a partnership with honesty.
**JOHANN LAVATER**

The more honesty a man has, the less he affects the air of a saint.
**JOHANN LAVATER**

Honesty isn't any policy at all; it's a state of mind or it isn't honesty.
EUGENE L'HOTE

You don't have to preach honesty to men with creative purpose. Let a human being throw the engines of his soul into the making of something, and the instinct of workmanship will take care of his honesty.
WALTER LIPPMANN

Honesty is often in the wrong.
LUCAN

Honesty is a good thing, but it is not profitable to its possessor unless it is kept under control. If you are not honest at all everybody hates you, and if you are absolutely honest you get martyred.
DONALD MARQUIS

If honesty did not exist, we ought to invent it as the best means of getting rich.
HONORÉ DE MIRABEAU

An honest man is not accountable for the vice and folly of his trade, and therefore ought not to refuse the exercise of it. It is the custom of his country, and there is profit in it. We must live by the world, and such as we find it, so make use of it.
MICHEL DE MONTAIGNE

Honest men are the soft easy cushions on which knaves repose and fatten.
THOMAS OTWAY

The honest man must be a perpetual renegade, the life of an honest man a perpetual infidelity. For the man who wishes to remain faithful to truth must make himself perpetually unfaithful to all the continual, successive, indefatigable, renascent errors.
CHARLES PIERRE PÉGUY

No one can ask honestly or hopefully to be delivered from temptation unless he has himself honestly and firmly determined to do the best he can to keep out of it.
JOHN RUSKIN

Ay, sir; to be honest, as this world goes, is to be one man picked out of ten thousand.
WILLIAM SHAKESPEARE

I thank God I am as honest as any man living that is an old man no honester than I.
WILLIAM SHAKESPEARE

I am afraid we must make the world honest before we can honestly say to our children that honesty is the best policy.
GEORGE BERNARD SHAW

It's better to be quotable than to be honest.
TOM STOPPARD

I consider the most enviable of titles the character of an honest man.
GEORGE WASHINGTON

I hope I shall always possess firmness and virtue enough to maintain what I consider the most enviable of all titles, the character of an Honest Man.
GEORGE WASHINGTON

Honesty is the best policy, but he who is governed by that maxim is not an honest man.
RICHARD WHATELY

## *Honor*

Honor's a fine imaginary notion, that draws in raw and unexperienced men to real mischiefs.
JOSEPH ADDISON

The religious man fears, the man of honor scorns, to do an ill action.
JOSEPH ADDISON

The place should not honor the man, but the man the place.
AGESILAUS

There never was a person who did anything worth doing who did not receive more than he gave.
HENRY WARD BEECHER

Honor is like the eye, which cannot suffer the least injury without damage; it is a precious stone, the price of which is lessened by the least flaw.
JACQUES BOSSUET

No amount of ability is of the slightest avail without honor.
ANDREW CARNEGIE

Our inheritance of well-founded, slowly conceived codes of honor, morals and manners, the passionate convictions which so many hundreds of millions share together of the principles of freedom and justice, are far more precious to us than anything which scientific discoveries could bestow.
WINSTON CHURCHILL

No person was ever honored for what he received. Honor has been the reward for what he gave.
CALVIN COOLIDGE

All are not just because they do no wrong; but he who will not wrong me when he may, he is truly just.
RICHARD CUMBERLAND

The effective impact upon us of men of honor, rectitude and goodwill is to arouse kindred impulses within us. We begin to detect in ourselves undeveloped capacities. The touch of the heroic awakens in us the slumbering hero. Fellowship with a true servant of mankind calls into action our latent impulses to minister.
CHARLES MALCOLM DOUGLAS, D.D.

Honor is not a matter of any man's calling merely, but rather of his own actions in it.
JOHN S. DWIGHT

The louder he talked of his honor, the faster we counted our spoons.
RALPH WALDO EMERSON

I have a lantern. You steal my lantern. What, then, is your honor worth no more to you than the price of my lantern!
EPICTETUS

He that hath a trade hath an estate and he that hath a calling hath an office of profit and honor.
BENJAMIN FRANKLIN

Honors run into money.
FRENCH PROVERB

Still to our gains our chief respect is had; reward it is that makes us good or bad.
ROBERT HERRICK

Through our great good fortune, in our youth our hearts were touched with fire. It was given us to learn at the outset that life is a profound and passionate thing. While we are permitted to scorn nothing but indifference, and do not pretend to undervalue the worldly rewards of ambition, we have seen with our own eyes, beyond and above the gold fields, the snowy heights of honor, and it is for us to bear the report to those who come after us.
OLIVER WENDELL HOLMES

An honor prudently declined often returns with increased luster.
**LIVY**

The honor of a country depends much more on removing its faults than on boasting of its qualities.
**GIUSEPPI MAZZINI**

The difference between a moral man and a man of honor is that the latter regrets a discreditable act; even when it has worked and he has not been caught.
**H. L. MENCKEN**

You can be deprived of your money, your job and your home by someone else, but remember that no one can ever take away your honor.
**WILLIAM LYON PHELPS**

To honor with hymns and panegyrics those who are still alive is not safe; a man should run his course and make a fair ending, and then we will praise him; and let praise be given equally to women as well as men who have been distinguished in virtue.
**PLATO**

Let honor be to us as strong an obligation as necessity is to others.
**PLINY**

Honor is a chain with many links. It leads from the simplest transactions . . . on up to international treaties involving the lives of millions of people. If we want to stay civilized, then each of us has the job of keeping that chain unbroken. For staying civilized, in the last analysis, depends on making promises—and keeping them.
**PHILIP D. REED**

Men show no mercy and expect no mercy, when honor calls, or when they fight for their idols or their gods.
**JOHANN FRIEDRICH VON SCHILLER**

That nation is worthless that will not, with pleasure, venture all for its honor.
**JOHANN FRIEDRICH VON SCHILLER**

Mine honor is my life; both grow in one; take honor from me and my life is done.
**WILLIAM SHAKESPEARE**

The shortest and surest way to live with honor in the world, is to be in reality what we would appear to be; all human virtues increase and strengthen themselves by the practice and experience of them.
**SOCRATES**

The biggest reward for a thing well done is to have done it.
**VOLTAIRE**

Our country's honor calls upon us for a vigorous and manly exertion; and if we now shamefully fail, we shall become infamous to the whole world.
**GEORGE WASHINGTON**

Be honorable yourself if you wish to associate with honorable people.
**WELSH PROVERB**

There are only two stimulants to one's best efforts—the fear of punishment, and the hope of reward. When neither is present, one can hardly hope that salespeople will want to be trained or want to do a good job. When disappointment is not expressed that one hasn't done a better job, or when credit is withheld when one has done a good job, there is absolutely no incentive to put forth the best effort.
**JOHN M. WILSON**

## Hope

He who has health, has hope; and he who has hope, has everything.
**ARABIAN PROVERB**

How tight can life be without the space of hope?
**ARABIAN PROVERB**

Hope is a waking dream.
**ARISTOTLE**

Hope is a good breakfast, but it is a bad supper.
**FRANCIS BACON**

The illusions of hope are apt to close one's eyes to the painful truth.
**HARRY F. BANKS**

The sunrise never failed us yet.
**CELIA BAXTER**

Waitings which ripen hopes are not delays.
**EDWARD BENLOWES**

Hope! Thou nurse of young desire.
**ISAAC BICKERSTAFF**

Hope: Desire and expectation rolled into one.
**AMBROSE BIERCE**

The spiritual life is indeed a life of struggle; but it is also a life of well-grounded hope. Hope is grounded in freedom, and freedom is grounded in all the high purposes and powers of spirit, human and divine. The last word of spirit is Victory.
**EDGAR SHEFFIELD BRIGHTMAN**

Hope springs exulting on triumphant wing.
**ROBERT BURNS**

Man is, properly speaking, based upon hope; he has no other possession but hope; this world of his is emphatically the place of hope.
**THOMAS CARLYLE**

Do not anxiously hope for what is not yet to come; do not vainly regret what is already past.
**CHINESE PROVERB**

Hope is a vigorous principle; it is furnished with light and heat to advise and execute; it sets the head and heart to work, and animates a man to do his utmost. And thus, by perpetually pushing and assurance, it puts a difficulty out of countenance, and makes a seeming impossibility give way.
**JEREMY COLLIER**

Times of general calamity and confusion have never been productive of the greatest minds. The purest ore is produced from the hottest furnace, and the brightest thunderbolt is elicited from the darkest storms.
**CHARLES CALEB COLTON**

Hope! Of all ills that men endure,
The only cheap and universal cure.
**ABRAHAM COWLEY**

The birthplace of Christianity was the tomb. The birthplace of splendor is desolation. Spring is conceived in the dark womb of Winter. And light is inevitably the offspring of darkness. For four dreary years and more the world writhed under the cruel thumb of economic disaster. Many thought that happiness had forever fled the earth. All this heaviness of night is surely but the prelude to a better dawn. The voice of God and the voice of Nature proclaim that the best is yet to be—always, the best is yet to be.
**ROBERT CROMIE**

Old man exhausted by ordeal, detached from human deeds, feeling the approach of the eternal cold, but always watching in the shadows for a gleam of hope!
CHARLES DE GAULLE

Hope of ill gain is the beginning of loss.
DEMOCRITUS

Hope is the thing with feathers that perches in the soul.
EMILY DICKINSON

To help the young soul, to add energy, inspire hope, and blow the coals into a useful flame; to redeem defeat by new thought and firm action, this, though not easy, is the work of divine men.
RALPH WALDO EMERSON

We judge of man's wisdom by his hope.
RALPH WALDO EMERSON

A ship ought not to be held by one anchor, nor life by a single hope.
EPICTETUS

The men who build the future are those who know that greater things are yet to come, and that they themselves will help bring them about. Their minds are illumined by the blazing sun of hope. They never stop to doubt. They haven't time.
MELVIN J. EVANS

This wonder we find in hope, that she is both a flatterer and a true friend. How many would die did not hope sustain them; how many have died by hoping too much!
OWEN FELTHAM

One should . . . be able to see things as hopeless and yet be determined to make them otherwise.
F. SCOTT FITZGERALD

He that lives upon hope will die fasting.
BENJAMIN FRANKLIN

Great hopes make great men.
THOMAS FULLER

He that wants hope is the poorest man alive.
THOMAS FULLER

Hope is worth any money.
THOMAS FULLER

In old age the consolation of hope is reserved for the tenderness of parents, who commence a new life in their children, the faith of enthusiasts, who sing hallelujahs above the clouds; and the vanity of authors, who presume the immortality of their name and writings.
EDWARD GIBBON

Correction does much, but encouragement does more. Encouragement after censure is as the sun after a shower.
JOHANN WOLFGANG VON GOETHE

There are situations in which hope and fear run together, in which they mutually destroy one another, and lose themselves in dull indifference.
JOHANN WOLFGANG VON GOETHE

Hope is a great falsifier. Let good judgment keep her in check.
BALTASAR GRACIÁN

Hope is a pleasant acquaintance, but an unsafe friend, not the man for your banker, though he may do for a traveling companion.
THOMAS C. HALIBURTON

Hope is a feeling that life and work have a meaning. You either have it or you don't, regardless of the state of the world that surrounds you.
**VACLAV HAVEL**

As a general rule, Providence seldom vouchsafes to mortals any more than just that degree of encouragement which suffices to keep them at a reasonably full exertion of their powers.
**NATHANIEL HAWTHORNE**

Hope is the best possession. None are completely wretched but those who are without hope, and few are reduced so low as that.
**WILLIAM HAZLITT**

It is natural to man to indulge in the illusion of hope. We are apt to shut our eyes against a painful truth, till she transforms us into beasts.
**PATRICK HENRY**

It is the around-the-corner brand of hope that prompts people to action, while the distant hope acts as an opiate.
**ERIC HOFFER**

There is nothing so well known as that we should not expect something for nothing—but we all do, and call it Hope.
**EDGAR WATSON HOWE**

Parties who want milk should not seat themselves on a stool in the middle of a field in hope that the cow will back up to them.
**ELBERT HUBBARD**

Hope is the only universal liar who never loses his reputation for veracity.
**ROBERT G. INGERSOLL**

The man who lives only by hope will die with despair.
**ITALIAN PROVERB**

I steer my bark with hope in the head, leaving fear astern.
**THOMAS JEFFERSON**

Hope: A species of happiness, and perhaps the chief happiness which this world affords.
**SAMUEL JOHNSON**

The natural flights of the human mind are not from pleasure to pleasure, but from hope to hope.
**SAMUEL JOHNSON**

Whatever enlarges hope will also exalt courage.
**SAMUEL JOHNSON**

How disappointment tracks the steps of hope.
**LETITIA E. LANDON**

There is always hope for an individual who stops to do some serious thinking about life.
**KATHERINE LOGAN**

The setting of a great hope is like the setting of the sun. The brightness of our life is gone.
**HENRY WADSWORTH LONGFELLOW**

Everything that is done in the world is done by hope. No merchant or tradesman would set himself to work if he did not hope to reap benefit thereby.
**MARTIN LUTHER**

There is no medicine like hope, no incentive so great, no tonic so powerful as expectation of something tomorrow.
**ORISON S. MARDEN**

The only way, boss, to keep hope in the world, is to keep changing its population frequently.
**DONALD MARQUIS**

Hope is the worst of evils, for it prolongs the torment of man.
**FRIEDRICH WILHELM NIETZSCHE**

Strong hope is a much greater stimulant of life than any realized joy could be.
**FRIEDRICH WILHELM NIETZSCHE**

It is not the variegated colors, the cheerful sounds, and the warm breezes which enliven us so much in Spring; it is the quiet prophetic spirit of endless hope, a presentiment of many happy days, the anticipation of higher everlasting blossoms and fruits, and the secret sympathy with the world that is developing itself.
**MARTIN OPITZ**

A student never forgets an encouraging private word, when it is given with sincere respect and admiration.
**WILLIAM LYON PHELPS**

In this world of unequal things and irregularities we should follow the Master's advice. He went about encouraging. He wasn't a fault-finder. He was a faith finder—a finder of human power and of human excellence.
**KARL REILAND, D.D.**

Hope is the last thing that dies in man, and though it be exceedingly deceitful, yet it is of this good use to us, that while we are traveling through life it conducts us in an easier and more pleasant way to our journey's end.
**FRANÇOIS DE LA ROCHEFOUCAULD**

Of all the forces that make for a better world, none is so indispensable, none so powerful, as hope. Without hope men are only half alive. With hope they dream and think and work.
**CHARLES SAWYER**

Hope is brightest when it dawns from fears.
**SIR WALTER SCOTT**

The miserable hath no other medicine, but only hope.
**WILLIAM SHAKESPEARE**

True hope is swift, and flies with swallow's wings. Kings it makes gods, and meaner creatures kings.
**WILLIAM SHAKESPEARE**

Hope is a flatterer, but the most upright of all parasites; for she frequents the poor man's hut, as well as the palace of his superior.
**WILLIAM SHENSTONE**

Toil, feel, think hope; you will be sure to dream enough before you die, without arranging for it.
**JOHN STERLING**

Every heart that has beat strong and cheerfully has left a hopeful impulse behind it in the world, and bettered the tradition of mankind.
**ROBERT LOUIS STEVENSON**

Hope is the boy, a blind, head-long pleasant fellow, good to chase swallows with the salt; Faith is the grave, experienced, yet smiling man. Hope lives on ignorance; open-eyed Faith is built upon a knowledge of our life, of the tyranny of circumstance and the frailty of human nature.
**ROBERT LOUIS STEVENSON**

To travel hopefully is a better thing than to arrive.
**ROBERT LOUIS STEVENSON**

Hope knows not if fear speaks truth, nor fear whether hope be blind as she.
ALGERNON CHARLES SWINBURNE

Earth has no hopeless islands or continents.
DAVID SWING

The mighty hopes that make us men.
ALFRED, LORD TENNYSON

You believe that easily which you hope for earnestly.
TERENCE

Hope can always cope.
P. K. THOMAJAN

Hope ever tells us tomorrow will be better.
TIBULLUS

Hope deceives more men than cunning does.
MARQUIS DE VAUVENARGUES

When we have lost everything, including hope, life becomes a disgrace and death a duty.
VOLTAIRE

I believe that any man's life will be filled with constant and unexpected encouragement, if he makes up his mind to do his level best each day, and as nearly as possible reaching the high-water mark of pure and useful living.
BOOKER T. WASHINGTON

Hope never abandons you; you abandon it.
GEORGE WEINBERG

Hope, like faith, is nothing if it is not courageous; it is nothing if it is not ridiculous.
THORNTON WILDER

## *Human Nature*

Inconsistency with ourselves is the great weakness of human nature.
JOSEPH ADDISON

Today the most useful person in the world is the man or woman who knows how to get along with other people. Human relations is the most important science in the broad curriculum of living.
STANLEY C. ALLYN

I wonder if the human touch, which people have, is not one of the greatest assets that one can have. You meet some people, and immediately you feel their warmth of mind or heart. You read a book, sit before the performance of a fine actor, or read a poem—and there it is—something that streams into your consciousness. . . . Those who keep climbing higher, in their chosen work, all have this outstanding something. The nurse in the hospital, the man who delivers your mail, the clerk behind many a store counter, and the effective minister or public speaker. Without this human touch, hope has little on which to feed or thrive.
GEORGE MATTHEW ADAMS

Perhaps the most important lesson the world has learned in the past fifty years is that it is not true that human nature is unchangeable. Human nature, on the contrary, can be changed with the greatest ease and to the utmost possible extent. If in this lies huge potential danger, it also contains some of the brightest hopes that we have for the future of mankind.
BRUCE BLIVEN

Are you appalled at existing conditions? Don't waste your energy trying to *change conditions from without! Change the Human Heart from within.*
WILLIAM J. H. BOETCKER

There is no problem of human nature which is insoluble.
RALPH J. BUNCHE

It will generally be found that those who sneer habitually at human nature, and affect to despise it, are among its worst and least pleasant samples.
CHARLES DICKENS

"Honesty is the best policy," "A dollar saved is a dollar earned," "Look before you leap," "A bird in the hand is worth two in the bush," "The laborer is worthy of his hire," may be scoffed at by some intellectuals as trite copybook rules, but nonetheless they sum up the elementary experience of the race in creating and consuming wealth. . . . People may change their minds as often as their coats, and new sets of rules of conduct may be written every week, but the fact remains that human nature has not changed and does not change, that inherent human beliefs stay the same; the fundamental rules of human conduct continue to hold.
LAMMOT DU PONT

However exquisitely human nature may have been described by writers, the true practical system can be learned only in the world.
HENRY FIELDING

The people I respect most behave as if they were immortal and as if society was eternal. Both assumptions are false: both of them must be accepted as true if we are to go on eating and working and loving, and are to keep open a few breathing holes for the human spirit.
E. M. FORSTER

The people of this country have shown by the highest proofs human nature can give that wherever the path of duty and honor may lead, however steep and rugged it may be, they are ready to walk in it.
JAMES A. GARFIELD

The sacred rights of mankind are not to be rummaged for among old parchments or musty records. They are written, as with a sunbeam, in the whole volume of human nature, by the hand of the Divinity itself, and can never be erased or obscured by mortal power.
ALEXANDER HAMILTON

Human nature is the same on every side of the Atlantic, and will be alike influenced by the same causes. The time to guard against corruption and tyranny is before they shall have gotten hold of us. It is better to keep the wolf out of the fold than to trust to drawing his teeth and claws after he shall have entered.
THOMAS JEFFERSON

Men in general are too material and do not make enough human contacts. If we search for the fundamentals which actually motivate us we will find that they come under four headings: love, money, adventure and religion. It is to some of them that we always owe that big urge which pushes us onward. Men who crush these impulses and settle down to everyday routine are bound to sink into mediocrity. No man is a complete unit of himself; he needs the contact, the stimulus and the driving power which is generated by his contact with other men, their ideas, and constantly changing scenes.
EDWARD S. JORDAN

I believe in human dignity as the source of national purpose, human liberty as the source of national action, the human heart as the source of national compassion, and in the human mind as the source of our invention and our ideas.
JOHN F. KENNEDY

Human nature has a much greater genius for sameness than for originality.
JAMES RUSSELL LOWELL

No small part of the cruelty, oppression, miscalculation, and general mismanagement of human relations is due to the fact that in our dealings with others we do not see them as persons at all, but only as specimens or representatives of some type or other. . . . We react to the sample instead of to the real person.
ROBERT J. MACIVER

The world and the human condition are not essentially benign.
IVAN MORRIS

All my life people have been coming to me with plans to make over society and its institutions. Many of these plans have seemed to me good. Some have been excellent. All of them have had one fatal defect. They have assumed that human nature would behave in a certain way. If it would behave in that way these plans would work, but if human nature would behave in that way these plans would not be necessary, for in that case society and its institutions would reform themselves.
ELIHU ROOT

The human spirit is stronger than anything that can happen to it.
C. C. SCOTT

To feel much for others and little for ourselves; to restrain our selfishness and exercise our benevolent affections, constitute the perfection of human nature.
ADAM SMITH

## *Humanity*

Relations between the sexes are so complicated that the only way you can tell if members of the set are going together is if they are married. Then, almost certainly, they are not.
CLEVELAND AMORY

Human beings have never changed and they never will. They can blow up this planet or organize it in any way they like, but the real problems will remain what they have always been. You're handsome or you're ugly. You're bright or you're a fool. You've got some honor or you haven't.
JEAN ANOUILH

It is a profound truth that women as a sex are vain; it is also a profound truth that men as a sex are vain.
ARNOLD BENNETT

There will always be a battle between the sexes because men and women want different things. Men want women and women want men.
GEORGE BURNS

Wherever humanity has made that hardest of all starts and lifted itself out of mere brutality is a sacred spot.
WILLA CATHER

No one knows where he who invented the plow was born, nor where he died; yet he has done more for humanity than the whole race of heroes who have drenched the earth with blood and whose deeds have been handed down with a precision proportionate only to the mischief they wrought.
CHARLES CALEB COLTON

Men and women are two locked caskets, of which each contains the key to the other.
ISAK DINESEN

All humanity is one undivided and indivisible family, and each one of us is responsible for the misdeeds of all the others.
MAHATMA GANDHI

You must not lose faith in humanity. Humanity is an ocean; if a few drops of the ocean are dirty, the ocean does not become dirty.
MAHATMA GANDHI

Men and women should live next door and visit each other once in a while.
KATHARINE HEPBURN

The traveler's-eye view of men and women is not satisfying. A man might spend his life in trains and restaurants and know nothing of humanity at the end. To know, one must be an actor as well as a spectator.
ALDOUS HUXLEY

We are a nation of 20 million bathrooms, with a humanist in every tub.
MARY MCCARTHY

Every day sees humanity more victorious in the struggle with space and time.
GUGLIELMO MARCONI

There is a destiny that makes us brothers: None goes his way alone: All that we send into the lives of others comes back into our own.
EDWIN MARKHAM

The chief obstacle to the progress of the human race is the human race.
DONALD MARQUIS

Each of us brings with him an element, more or less important, of the life of humanity to come.
GIUSEPPE MAZZINI

Your first duties—first as regards importance—are, as I have already told you, towards humanity. You are men before you are either citizens or fathers. If you do not embrace the whole human family in your affection, if you do not bear witness to your belief in the unity of that family, consequent upon the unity of God . . . if, wheresoever a fellow creature suffers, or the dignity of human nature is violated by falsehood or tyranny—you are not ready, if able, to aid the unhappy, and do not feel called upon to combat, if able, for the redemption of the betrayed or oppressed—you violate your law of life, you comprehend not that religion which will be the guide and blessing of the future.
GIUSEPPI MAZZINI

The only way in which one can make endurable man's inhumanity to man, and man's destruction of his own environment, is to exemplify in your own lives man's humanity to man and man's reverence for the place in which he lives.
ALAN PATON

Buy ye are a chosen generation, a royal priesthood, an holy nation, a peculiar people; that you should shew forth the praises of him who hath called you out of darkness into his marvellous light.
I PETER 2:9

It's great to be great, but it's greater to be human.
WILL ROGERS

History down through the centuries has proved again and again that there can be but one outcome to a struggle for selfish power against forces fighting to protect and advance human rights. Those genuinely serving humanity always ultimately emerge triumphant. It is under their standards that the [Western] allies choose to throw in their lot for humanity's defense.
FRANCIS B. SAYRE

Human beings are the only animals of which I am thoroughly and cravenly afraid.
GEORGE BERNARD SHAW

The desire for the well-being of one's own nation can be—and must be—made compatible with the welfare of all humanity.
**LOUIS L. SNYDER**

I am a man, and whatever concerns humanity is of interest to me.
**TERENCE**

Man is not on the earth solely for his own happiness. He is there to realize great things for humanity.
**VINCENT VAN GOGH**

Provision for others is a fundamental responsibility of human life.
**WOODROW WILSON**

## *Humble*

A just and reasonable modesty does not only recommend eloquence, but sets off every great talent which a man can be possessed of; it heightens all the virtues which it accompanies; like the shades in paintings, it raises and rounds every figure and makes the colors more beautiful, though not so glaring as they would be without.
**JOSEPH ADDISON**

Modesty is the art of drawing attention to whatever it is you are being humble about.
**ANONYMOUS**

Modesty is hardly to be described as a virtue. It is a feeling rather than a disposition. It is a kind of fear of falling into disrepute.
**ARISTOTLE**

It is no great thing to be humble when you are brought low; but to be humble when you are praised is a great and rare attainment.
**ST. BERNARD**

The more humble a man is before God, the more he will be exalted; the more humble he is before man, the more he will get rode roughshod.
**JOSH BILLINGS**

The true way to be humble is not to stoop till you are smaller than yourself, but to stand at your real height against some higher nature that shall show you what the real smallness of your greatest greatness is.
**PHILLIPS BROOKS**

If my people, which are called by my name, shall humble themselves, and pray, and seek my face, and turn from their wicked ways; then will I hear from heaven, and will forgive their sin, and heal their land.
**II CHRONICLES 7:11**

Never be haughty to the humble; never be humble to the haughty.
**JEFFERSON DAVIS**

One must become as humble as the dust before he can discover truth.
**MAHATMA GANDHI**

The society which scorns excellence in plumbing because plumbing is a humble activity and tolerates shoddiness in philosophy because it is an exalted activity will have neither good plumbing nor good philosophy. Neither its pipes nor its theories will hold water.
**JOHN W. GARDNER**

Modesty is an ornament, but you go further without it.
**GERMAN PROVERB**

Modesty is of no use to a beggar.
**HOMER**

Modesty in human beings is praised because it is not a matter of nature, but of will.
**LACTANTIUS**

A fellow once came to me to ask for an appointment as a minister abroad. Finding he could not get that, he came down to some more modest position. Finally, he asked to be made a tide-waiter. When he saw he could not get that, he asked me for an old pair of trousers. It is sometimes well to be humble.
**ABRAHAM LINCOLN**

Don't be so humble, you're not that great.
**GOLDA MEIR**

A humble man can do great things with an uncommon perfection because he is no longer concerned about accidentals, like his own interests and his own reputation, and therefore he no longer needs to waste his efforts in defending them.
**THOMAS MERTON**

To be humble to superiors is a duty, to equals courtesy, to inferiors nobleness.
**SIR THOMAS MORE**

Few people are modest enough to be estimated at their true worth.
**MARQUIS DE VAUVENARGUES**

Modesty is what ails me. That's what kept me under.
**ARTEMUS WARD**

Strive not with your superiors in argument, but always submit your judgment to others with modesty.
**GEORGE WASHINGTON**

## *Humility*

There is something in humility which strangely exalts the heart.
**ST. AUGUSTINE**

Life is a long lesson in humility.
**JAMES M. BARRIE**

Lack of proper humility, which is the fundamental aspect of Christianity, is the reason many men fail to display the courage and foresight that comes through complete faith in God.
**ADAM W. BURNETT, D.D.**

Humility is not a weak and timid quality; it must be carefully distinguished from a groveling spirit.
**EDWIN H. CHAPIN**

The wise person possesses humility. He knows that his small island of knowledge is surrounded by a vast sea of the unknown.
**HAROLD C. CHASE**

By humility I mean not the abjectness of a base mind, but a prudent care not to overvalue ourselves.
**NATHANIEL CREW**

Some persons are always ready to level those above them down to themselves, while they are never willing to level those below them up to their own position. But he that is under the influence of true humility will avoid both these extremes. On the one hand, he will be willing that all should rise just so far as their diligence and worth of character entitle them to; and on the other hand, he will be willing that his superiors should be known and acknowledged in their place, and have rendered to them all the honors that are their due.
**JONATHAN EDWARDS**

True humility is not an object, groveling, self-despising spirit; it is but a right estimate of ourselves as God sees us.
TRYON EDWARDS

Humility is the most difficult of all virtues to achieve; nothing dies harder than the desire to think well of self.
T. S. ELIOT

It is useless to gather virtues without humility, for the spirit of the Lord delighteth to dwell in the hearts of the humble.
DESIDERIUS ERASMUS

There is no true holiness without humility.
THOMAS FULLER

Humility is not my forte, and whenever I dwell for any length of time on my own shortcomings, they gradually begin to seem mild, harmless, rather engaging little things, not at all like the staring defects in other people's characters.
MARGARET HALSEY

The fruits of humility are love and peace.
HEBREW PROVERB

Of all kinds of shame, the worst, surely, is being ashamed of frugality or poverty.
LIVY

Humility leads to strength and not to weakness. It is the highest form of self-respect to admit mistakes and to make amends for them.
JOHN J. MCCLOY

Sense shines with a double luster when it is set in humility. An able and yet humble man is a jewel worth a kingdom.
WILLIAM PENN

Humility is often only a feigned submission, of which we make use to render others submissive. It is an artifice of pride which abases in order to exalt itself.
FRANÇOIS DE LA ROCHEFOUCAULD

I believe that the first test of a truly great man is his humility.
JOHN RUSKIN

Humility is a virtue all preach, none practice, and yet everybody is content to hear.
JOHN SELDEN

The more things a man is ashamed of, the more respectable he is.
GEORGE BERNARD SHAW

Humility is to make a right estimate of oneself.
CHARLES H. SPURGEON

We come nearest to the great when we are great in humility.
RABINDRANATH TAGORE

We do not have to acquire humility. There is humility in us—only we humiliate ourselves before false gods.
SIMONE WEIL

## *Humor*

Men ought to find the difference between saltness and bitterness. Certainly, he that hath a satirical vein, as he maketh others afraid of his wit, so he had need be afraid of others' memory.
FRANCIS BACON

Humor is falling downstairs if you do it in the act of telling your wife not to.
**KENNETH BIRD**

All my humor is based upon destruction and despair. If the whole world were tranquil, without disease and violence, I'd be standing on the breadline right in back of J. Edgar Hoover.
**LENNY BRUCE**

Humor purges the blood, making the body young, lively, and fit for any manner of employment.
**ROBERT BURTON**

A sense of humor keen enough to show a man his own absurdities will keep him from the commission of all sins, or nearly all, save those worth committing.
**SAMUEL BUTLER**

True humor springs not more from the head than from the heart.
**THOMAS CARLYLE**

All good activities which encourage people to learn how to live with one another pleasantly and to develop a sense of humor improve living.
**LEONARD CARMICHAEL**

For health and the constant enjoyment of life, give me a keen and ever present sense of humor; it is the next best thing to an abiding faith in providence.
**GEORGE B. CHEEVER**

When once you have got hold of a vulgar joke, you may be certain that you have got hold of a subtle and spiritual idea.
**G. K. CHESTERTON**

Men will confess to treason, murder, arson, false teeth, or a wig. How many of them will own up to a lack of humor?
**FRANK MOORE COLBY**

Humor is by far the most significant activity of the human brain.
**EDWARD DE BONO**

The last man that makes a joke owns it.
**FINLEY PETER DUNNE**

A different of taste in jokes is a great strain upon the affections.
**GEORGE ELIOT**

An uncontrolled sense of humor is often costly in business.
**WILLIAM FEATHER**

Humor is an affirmation of dignity, a declaration of man's superiority to all that befalls him.
**ROMAIN GARY**

Advice is sometimes transmitted more successfully through a joke than grave teaching.
**BALTASAR GRACIÁN**

Gaiety that sweetens existence and makes it wholesome—a sense of humor, a zest of enjoyment—this is the accompaniment of courage which gives it a supreme value. Something of the high laughter of a Cyrano de Bergerac—the world needs it.
**HERBERT HICHEN**

There is certainly no defense against adverse fortune which is, on the whole, so effectual as an habitual sense of humor.
**THOMAS W. HIGGINSON**

A jest often decides matters of importance more effectively and happily than seriousness.
HORACE

Some of the best of men make their lives tolerable by the fantasy that the spiritual torments they have lived through, the cruelty of friends, of parents, or of children, the sickening loss of love, had really been quite funny at the time. Be fond of the man who jests at his scars, if you like; but never believe he is being on the level with you.
PAMELA HANSFORD JOHNSON

Humor, a good sense of it, is to Americans what manhood is to Spaniards, and we will go to great lengths to prove it. Experiments with laboratory rats have shown that, if one psychologist in the room laughs at something a rat does, all of the other psychologists will laugh equally. Nobody wants to be left holding the joke.
GARRISON KEILLOR

Good humor is a tonic for mind and body. It is the best antidote for anxiety and depression. It is a business asset. It attracts and keeps friends. It lightens human burdens. It is the direct route to serenity and contentment.
GRENVILLE KLEISER

The hallmark of American humor is its pose of illiteracy.
RONALD KNOX

Humor simultaneously wounds and heals, indicts and pardons, diminishes and enlarges; it constitutes inner growth at the expense of outer gain, and those who possess and honestly practice it make themselves more through a willingness to make themselves less.
LOUIS KRONENBERGER

Life's more amusing than we thought.
ANDREW LANG

I think a sense of humor is the emotional equivalent of a sense of realism. One should not take everything seriously, and everybody takes some things seriously.
MICHAEL MACCOBY

Sense of humor: A thread of illuminated intelligence that links two opposite ideas.
THOMAS L. MASSON

The sense of humor is the oil of life's engine. Without it, the machinery creaks and groans. No lot is so hard, no aspect of things is so grim, but it relaxes before a hearty laugh.
GEORGE S. MERRIAM

I could not tread these perilous paths in safety, if I did not keep a saving sense of humor.
LORD NELSON

Good humor is a philosophic state of mind; it seems to say to nature that we take her no more seriously than she takes us. I maintain that one should always talk of philosophy with a smile. We owe it to the Eternal to be virtuous; but we have the right to add to this tribute our irony as a sort of personal reprisal.
JOSEPH RENAN

Life does not cease to be funny when people die any more than it ceases to be serious when people laugh.
GEORGE BERNARD SHAW

Good humor is the best shield against the darts of satirical raillery.
CHARLES SIMMONS

Some people are commended for a giddy kind of good humor, which is no more a virtue than drunkenness.
RICHARD STEELE

Good humor is one of the best articles of dress one can wear in society.
WILLIAM MAKEPEACE THACKERAY

Humor is emotional chaos remembered in tranquility.
JAMES THURBER

Never say a humorous thing to a man who does not possess humor. He will always use it in evidence against you.
HERBERT BEERBOHM TREE

The humorous story is American, the comic story is English, the witty story is French. The humorous story depends for its effect upon the manner of the telling; the comic and the witty story upon the matter.
MARK TWAIN

Humor implies a sure conception of the beautiful, the majestic and the true, by whose light it surveys and shapes their opposites. It is a humane influence, softening with mirth the ragged inequalities of existence, prompting tolerant views of life, bridging over the space which separates the lofty from the lowly, the great from the humble.
EDWIN P. WHIPPLE

## *Hunger*

You may proclaim, good sirs, your fine philosophy.
But till you feed us, right and wrong can wait.
BERTOLT BRECHT

Talk to those who understand, and give food to those who are hungry.
CHINESE PROVERB

No soup is ever eaten as hot as it is cooked.
GERMAN PROVERB

Appetite: Something you always bring to another's table.
JEWISH PROVERB

Where necessity ends, curiosity begins; and no sooner are we supplied with everything that nature can demand than we sit down to contrive artificial appetites.
JOHNSON

The stomach begs and clamors, and listens to no precepts. And yet it is not an obdurate creditor; for it is dismissed with small payment if you give it only what you owe, and not as much as you can.
SENECA

Mankind—in far too many places—is hungry. We can and must help. For hunger is no ally of freedom. The economic machinery of the world is stalled and damaged as a result of the war. The machinery must be repaired and started again. We have tools and parts. We have what is just as important—the know-how. . . . We can supply that know-how and guidance to make effective the aid we provide. For this aid is in our tradition—a tradition rooted in freedom and progress.
JOHN W. SNYDER

Hungry is a mighty fine sauce.
SOUTHERN FOLK SAYING

Hunger: One of the few cravings that cannot be appeased with another solution.
IRWIN VAN GROVE

# I

## Ideals

The best and noblest lives are those which are set toward high ideals.
RENÉ ALEMERAS

The vision that you glorify in your mind, the ideal that you enthrone in your heart—this you will build your life by, this you will become.
JAMES LANE ALLEN

Your circumstances may be uncongenial, but they shall not long remain so if you but perceive an Ideal and strive to reach it. You can not travel within and stand still without.
JAMES LANE ALLEN

The ideal man bears the accidents of life with dignity and grace, making the best of the circumstances.
ARISTOTLE

To live in the presence of great truths and eternal laws, to be led by permanent ideals—that is what keeps a man patient when the world ignores him, and calm and unspoiled when the world praises him.
HONORÉ DE BALZAC

All higher motives, ideals, conceptions, sentiments in a man are of no account if they do not come forward to strengthen him for the better discharge of the duties which devolve upon him in the ordinary affairs of life.
HENRY WARD BEECHER

It is no good making a fortune if you do not know how to enjoy it. Higher material standards are no good if you do not know how to use them for a better life. Economic ideals must include the ideal of beauty as well as the ideal of plenty. We want new capital, far more capital than is being created today, but we want it not only to advance material well-being but because we want a better and more beautiful life for the citizens.
SIR BASIL BLACKETT

If you are not an idealist by the time you are 20, you don't have a heart, but if you are still an idealist by 30, you don't have a head.
RANDOLPH S. BOURNE

The ideal life is in our blood and never will be lost. Sad will be the day for any man when he becomes contented with the thoughts he is thinking and the deeds he is doing—where there is not forever beating at the doors of his soul some great desire to do something larger which he knows that he was meant and made to do.
PHILLIPS BROOKS

Idealism is fine; but as it approaches reality, the cost becomes prohibitive.
WILLIAM BUCKLEY

Heads are wisest when they are cool, and hearts are strongest when they beat in response to noble ideals.
RALPH J. BUNCHE

All human things do require to have an ideal in them; to have some soul in them.
THOMAS CARLYLE

We see facts with our eyes; we see ideas with our minds; we see ideals with our souls. Whatever we see with our souls is real and permanent and cannot be destroyed.
GLENN CLARK

The danger to America is not in the direction of the failure to maintain its economic position, but in the direction of the failure to maintain its ideals.
CALVIN COOLIDGE

There is no force so democratic as the force of an ideal.
CALVIN COOLIDGE

Each person has an ideal, a hope, a dream of some sort which represents his soul. In the long light of eternity this seed of the future is all that matters! We must find this seed no matter how small it is; we must give to it the warmth of love, the light of understanding and the water of encouragement. We must learn to deal with people as they are—not as we wish them to be. We must study the moral values which shape our thinking, arouse our emotions and guide our conduct. We must get acquainted with our inner stream and find out what's going on in our heads and hearts. We must put an end to blind, instinctive, sensory thought and feeling. We must take time to be human.
COLBY DORR DAM

We have a system which, though far from perfect, is strong with idealism. It gives elbow room for men of all races and all beliefs. It is vital and dynamic. And it works. We have the means of shaping the world in our pattern. If we do, freedom will be assured for all men. The decision is in the hands of this generation. It is a challenge to our political competence. For western civilization it is the greatest challenge of all time.
WILLIAM O. DOUGLAS

What the world needs to know at this juncture is that our nation remains steadfast to its historic ideals, and follows its traditional course of sharing the spiritual, intellectual and material fruits of our free society, in helping the captives to become free and helping the free to remain free, not merely in a technical sense, but free in the sense of genuine opportunity to pursue happiness, in the spirit of our Declaration of Independence.
JOHN FOSTER DULLES

We never reach our ideals, whether of mental or moral improvement, but the thought of them shows us our deficiencies, and spurs us on to higher and better things.
TRYON EDWARDS

An ideal is the only thing that has any real force. We have lost sight of our own ideal and its tremendous force and vigor. Somehow that must be recaptured. It must be passed on to generations to come, to make them believe in it; so that the energy in man which has its source in the ideal will not be lost.
HOMER FERGUSON

Our outer life and experiences are the out-picturing of our inner thoughts and ideals.
LOWELL FILLMORE

No nation can rise above the level of the ideals of its citizens.
BROOKS FLETCHER

Man can never come up to his ideal standard. It is the nature of the immortal spirit to raise that standard higher and higher as it goes from strength to strength, still upward and onward.
MARGARET FULLER

Idealism increases in direct proportion to one's distance from the problem.
JOHN GALSWORTHY

An ideal is the most practical thing in the world, for it is a force behind action that must be reckoned with by the frankest materialist.
EDWARD H. GRIGGS

Ideals are the world's masters.
JOSIAH G. HOLLAND

Words without actions are the assassins of idealism.
HERBERT HOOVER

Washington and Lincoln were both idealists, and idealism is one of the greatest forces in the world. It makes seeming impossibilities possible and succeeds where prudence fails. But unless the idealist is brave and has the courage to face the truth, his idealism creates nothing.
GRENVILLE KLEISER

Misguided idealism is as unproductive as unconcern.
A. DODDS KINARD

He who, having lost one ideal, refuses to give his heart and soul to another and nobler, is like a man who declines to build a house on the rock because the wind and rain have ruined his house on the sand.
CONSTANCE NADEN

I looked for great men, but all I found were the apes of their ideals.
FRIEDRICH WILHELM NIETZSCHE

The idealist is incorrigible: If he be thrown out of his heaven, he makes an ideal of his hell.
FRIEDRICH WILHELM NIETZSCHE

An idealist is one who, on noticing that a rose smells better than a cabbage, concludes that it will also make better soup.
H. L. MENCKEN

All men need something to poetize and idealize their life a little—something which they value for more than its use and which is a symbol of their emancipation from the mere materialism and drudgery of daily life.
THEODORE E. PARKER

Every man has, at times, in his mind the ideal of what he should be, but is not. In all men that seek to improve, it is better than the actual character.
THEODORE W. PARKER

Blessed is he who carries within himself a God, an ideal, and who obeys it.
LOUIS PASTEUR

To live in the presence of great truths and eternal laws, to be led by permanent ideals—that is what keeps a man patient when the world ignores him, and calm and unspoiled when the world praises him.
A. P. PEABODY

Let us show, not merely in great crises, but in every day affairs of life, qualities of practical intelligence, of hardihood and endurance, and above all, the power of devotion to a lofty ideal.
THEODORE ROOSEVELT

A man's ideal, like his horizon, is constantly receding from him as he advances toward it.
W. G. T. SHEDD

Ideals are like stars: You will not succeed in touching them with your hands, but like the seafaring man on the desert of waters, you choose them as your guides, and following them, you reach your destiny.
CARL SCHURZ

Nobody grows old by merely living a number of years; people grow old only by deserting their ideals.
SAMUEL ULLMAN

A large portion of human beings live not so much in themselves as in what their desire to be. They create an ideal character the perfections of which compensate in some degree for imperfections of their own.
EDWIN P. WHIPPLE

There are many forms of triumph, but there is no other success that in any shape or way approaches that which is open to the men and women who have the right ideals. These are the men and women who see that it is the intimate and homely things that count most. They are the men and women who have the courage to strive for the happiness which comes only with labor, effort and self-sacrifice, and only to those whose joy in life springs in part from power of work and sense of duty.
CHARLES R. WIERS

Every great man of business has got somewhere a touch of the idealist in him.
WOODROW WILSON

No art can conquer the people alone—the people are conquered by an ideal of life upheld by authority.
WILLIAM BUTLER YEATS

## *Ideas*

In the life of a nation ideas are not the only things of value. Sentiment also is of great value; and the way to foster sentiment in people, and to develop it in the young, is to have a well-recorded past and to be familiar with it. . . . A people that studies its own past and rejoices in the nation's proud memories is likely to be a patriotic people, the bulwark of law and the courageous champion of right in the hour of need.
JOSEPH ANDERSON

Theory without experience is sterile, practice without theory is blind.
GEORGE JAY ANYON

Let us think of quietly enlarging our stock of true and fresh ideas, and not, as soon as we get an idea or half an idea, be running out with it into the street, and trying to make it rule there. Our ideas will, in the end, shape the world all the better for maturing a little.
MATTHEW ARNOLD

Life is the application of noble and profound ideas to life.
MATTHEW ARNOLD

Every time a man puts a new idea across, he faces a dozen men who thought of it before he did. But they only thought of it.
OREN ARNOLD

It seems to me that the thing that makes the theater worthwhile is the fact that it attracts so many people with ideas who are constantly trying to share them with the public. Real art is illumination. It gives a man an idea he never had before or lights up ideas that were formless or only lurking in the shadows of his mind. It adds stature to life.
BROOKS ATKINSON

He that will not apply new remedies must expect new evils.
FRANCIS BACON

One of the greatest pains to human nature is the pain of a new idea.
WALTER BAGEHOT

Ideas are cosmopolitan. They have the liberty of the world. You have no right to take the sword and cross the bounds of other nations, and enforce on them laws or institutions they are unwilling to re-

ceive. But there is no limit to the sphere of ideas. Your thoughts and feelings, the whole world lies open to them, and you have the right to send them into any latitude, and to give them sweep around the earth, to the mind of every human being.
HENRY WARD BEECHER

The rewards in business go to the man who does something with an idea.
WILLIAM BENTON

Your most brilliant ideas come in a flash, but the flash comes only after a lot of hard work. Nobody gets a big idea when he is not relaxed and nobody gets a big idea when he is relaxed all of the time.
EDWARD BLAKESLEE

The more an idea is developed, the more concise becomes its expression; the more a tree is pruned, the better is the fruit.
ALFRED BOUGEART

A fresh mind keeps the body fresh. Take in the ideas of the day, drain off those of yesterday. As to the morrow, time enough to consider it when it becomes today.
EDWARD BULWER-LYTTON

If one cares about ideas, one wants to gather them from every available source and test them in every way possible.
MARY I. BUNTING

One of the most hazardous of human occupations is the transferring of an idea from one mind to another. It's hazardous because you presuppose the existence of a second mind.
CHRISTIAN BURCKEL

An idea must not be condemned for being a little shy and incoherent; all new ideas are shy when introduced first among our old ones. We should have patience and see whether the incoherency is likely to wear off or to wear on, in which latter case the sooner we get rid of them the better.
SAMUEL BUTLER

Money never starts an idea; it is the idea that starts the money.
WILLIAM J. CAMERON

The idea is in thyself. The impediment, too, is in thyself.
THOMAS CARLYLE

The ideas I stand for are not mine. I borrowed them from Socrates. I swiped them from Chesterfield. I stole them from Jesus. And I put them in a book. If you don't like their rules, whose would you use?
DALE CARNEGIE

Nothing can be proposed so wild or so absurd as not to find a party, and often a very large party, to espouse it.
WILLIAM CECIL

Ideas are the mightiest influence on earth. One great thought breathed into a man may regenerate him.
WILLIAM ELLERY CHANNING

The wise only possess ideas; the great part of mankind are possessed by them.
SAMUEL TAYLOR COLERIDGE

The philosopher contemplates ideas; the teacher energizes ideas; the student generates ideas.
LIONEL CROCKER

Ideas make their way in silence like the waters that, altering behind the rocks of the Alps, loosen them from the mountains upon which they rest.
JEAN D'AUBIGNÉ

Many blunder in business through inability or an unwillingness to adopt new ideas. I have seen many a success turn to failure also, because the thought which should be trained on big things is cluttered up with the burdensome detail of little things.
**PHILIP S. DELANEY**

Ideas are the roots of creation.
**ERNEST DIMNET**

Neither man nor nation can exist without a sublime idea.
**FYODOR DOSTOYEVSKY**

Although words exist for the most part for the transmission of ideas, there are some which produce such violent disturbance in our feelings that the role they play in the transmission of ideas is lost in the background.
**ALBERT EINSTEIN**

Think, listen and read for ideas. Don't be afraid to speak up freely and fully about your ideas. Be ready to give and take criticism on ideas. Share your knowledge with others, and be willing to take a share of their ideas if they are good. Keep an open mind until you have learned as much as possible, and then evaluate and make your decision.
**ARTHUR EISENSTADT**

Wise men put their trust in ideas and not in circumstances.
**RALPH WALDO EMERSON**

Ideas must work through the brains and the arms of good and brave men, or they are no better than dreams.
**RALPH WALDO EMERSON**

We don't need men with new ideas as much as we need men who will put energy behind the old ideas.
**WILLIAM FEATHER**

A good idea that is not shared with others will gradually fade away and bear no fruit, but when it is shared it lives forever because it is passed on from one person to another and grows as it goes.
**LOWELL FILLMORE**

The test of a first-rate intelligence is the ability to hold two opposed ideas in mind at the same time and still retain the ability to function. One should, for example, be able to see things as hopeless and yet be determined to make them otherwise.
**F. SCOTT FITZGERALD**

Edward H. Harriman, then undisputed ruler of several railway empires, remarked that he liked to drop into an executive's office and find him with his feet on the desk. The chances were, he reasoned, that the man was taking time off to do nothing but think. Is it your experience—it is mine—that ideas can be hatched much more freely when not immersed in routine duties? . . . The subconscious mind seems to function most fruitfully when one's nose is not on the grindstone.
**B. C. FORBES**

Now, ideas are the raw material of progress. Everything first takes shape in the form of an idea. But an idea by itself is worth nothing. An idea, like a machine, must have power applied to it before it can accomplish anything. The men who have won fame and fortune through having an idea are those who devoted every ounce of their strength and every dollar they could muster to putting it into operation. Ford had a big idea, but he had to sweat and suffer and sacrifice in order to make it work.
**B. C. FORBES**

Thought is, perhaps, the forerunner and even the mother of ideas, and ideas are the most powerful and the most useful things in the world.
**GEORGE GARDNER**

Most of us have a pretty clear idea of the world we want. What we lack is an understanding of how to go about getting it.
**HUGH GIBSON**

Oh, would that my mind could let fall its dead ideas, as the tree does its withered leaves!
**ANDRÉ GIDE**

Behind every advance of the human race is a germ of creation growing in the mind of some lone individual. An individual whose dreams waken him in the night while others lie contentedly asleep.
**CRAWFORD H. GREENEWALT**

You have a shilling. I have a shilling. We swap. You have my shilling and I have yours. We are no better off. But suppose you have an idea and I have an idea. We swap. Now you have two ideas and I have two ideas. We have increased our stock of ideas 100 per cent.
**A. S. GREGG**

It is not at all likely that anyone ever had a totally original idea. He may put together old ideas into a new combination, but the elements which made up the new combination were mostly acquired from other people. Without many borrowed ideas there would be no inventions, new movements or anything else that is classed as new.
**GEORGE GRIER**

Nothing is so corrupting as a great idea whose time is past.
**JOHN P. GRIER**

In the long run of history, the censor and the inquisitor have always lost. The only sure weapon against bad ideas is better ideas.
**WHITNEY GRISWOLD**

Daring ideas are like chessmen moved forward; they may be beaten, but they may start a winning game.
**JOHANN WOLFGANG VON GOETHE**

So many new ideas are at first strange and horrible though ultimately valuable that a very heavy responsibility rests upon those who would prevent their dissemination.
**J. B. S. HALDANE**

Only he is free whose efforts are called out by what seems to him a good of itself by the belief that he is impressing upon the stuff of this world some idea authentically his own.
**LEARNED HAND**

We must treat ideas somewhat as though they were baby fish. Throw thousands out into the waters. Only a handful will survive but that is plenty.
**ANNE HEYWOOD**

All the lost mines of Mexico, all the argosies that ever sailed from the Indies, all the gold and silver-laden ships of the treasure fleets of storied Spain, count no more value than a beggar's dole compared with the wealth that is today created every eight hours by modern business ideas.
**WORTHINGTON C. HOLMAN**

To develop imaginative powers, we must specialize in our own fields but be alert to new ideas from any source and continually seize and set down our inspirational flashes when they come to us. The longer our imagination retains the idea, the clearer and more attainable it becomes.
**CARL HOLMES**

Many ideas grow better when transplanted into another mind than in the one where they sprung up. That which was a weed in one becomes a flower in the other, and a flower again dwindles down to a mere weed by the same change. Healthy growths

may become poisonous by falling upon the wrong mental soil, and what seemed a nightshade in one mind unfolds as a morning-glory in the other.
OLIVER WENDELL HOLMES

Many ideas grow better when transplanted into another mind than in the one where they sprang up.
OLIVER WENDELL HOLMES

The Ultimate Good desired is better reached by free trade in ideas—the best test of truth is the power of the thought to get itself accepted in the competition of the market.
OLIVER WENDELL HOLMES

An idea that is not dangerous is unworthy of being called an idea at all.
ELBERT HUBBARD

There is one thing stronger than all the armies in the world, and that is an idea whose time has come.
VICTOR HUGO

A healthful hunger for a great idea is the beauty and blessedness of life.
JEAN INGELOW

An idea, to be suggestive, must come to the individual with the force of a revelation.
WILLIAM JAMES

Let me exhort everyone to do their utmost to think outside and beyond our present circle of ideas. For every idea gained is a hundred years of slavery remitted.
RICHARD JEFFERIES

That fellow seems to me to possess but one idea, and that a wrong one.
SAMUEL JOHNSON

Ideas lose themselves as quickly as quail, and one must wing them the minute they rise out of the grass—or they are gone.
THOMAS F. KENNEDY

So long as new ideas are created, sales will continue to reach new highs.
CHARLES F. KETTERING

In many ways ideas are more important than people—they are much more permanent.
CHARLES F. KETTERING

I could not sleep . . . when I got on a hunt for an idea, until I had caught it; and when I thought I had got it I was not satisfied until I had repeated it over and over again, until I had put it in language plain enough as I thought, for any boy I knew to comprehend. This was a kind of passion with me, and it has stuck by me.
ABRAHAM LINCOLN

To ask at what time a man has first any ideas is to ask when he begins to perceive; having ideas and perception being the same thing.
JOHN LOCKE

It is not in the power of the most exalted wit or enlarged understanding, by any quickness or variety of thought, to invent or frame one new simple idea.
JOHN LOCKE

The requisite of a natural resource is an idea. There are no known limits, therefore, to the multiplication of natural resources of the earth, and exhaustion of them is impossible.
JAMES C. MALIN

An idea isn't responsible for the people who believe in it.
DONALD MARQUIS

Men's ideas are the direct emanations of their material state. This is true in politics, law, morality, religion, etc.
**KARL MARX**

I am never so happy as when a new thought occurs to me and a new horizon gradually discovers itself before my eyes. When a fresh idea dawns upon me, I feel lifted up, apart from the world of men, into a strange atmosphere of the spirit. It is a new freedom. I feel aloof from the world, and for a moment I am independent of all my surroundings.
**SOMERSET MAUGHAM**

Three ideas stand out above all others in the influence they have exerted and are destined to exert upon the development of the human race: The idea of the Golden Rule; the idea of natural law; the idea of age-long growth or evolution.
**ROBERT A. MILLIKAN**

There are two things that have to happen before an idea catches on. One is that the idea should be good. The other is that it should fit in with the temper of the age. If it does not, even a good idea may well be passed by.
**JAWAHARLAL NEHRU**

Most ideas are step-by-step children of other ideas.
**A. F. OSBORN**

The all-round liberally educated man, from Palaeolithic times to the time when the earth shall become a cold cinder, will always be the same, namely, the man who follows his standards of truth and beauty, who employs his learning and observation, his reason, his expression, for purposes of production, that is, to add something of his own to the stock of the world's ideas.
**H. F. OSBORN**

To get your ideas across, use small words, big ideas and short sentences.
**JOHN HENRY PATTERSON**

Ideas go booming through the world louder than cannon. Thoughts are mightier than armies. Principles have achieved more victories than horsemen or chariots.
**W. M. PAXTON**

Mere words are cheap and plenty enough, but ideas that rouse and set multitudes thinking come as gold from the mines.
**A. OWEN PENNY**

I claim no superior intellect but do subscribe to a gut feeling which says: I am not afraid to intellectually test any idea contradictory to my own because from that direction truth will surely come if I do not now possess it.
**W. M. PEPPER**

A great idea is usually original to more than one discoverer. Great ideas come when the world needs them. They surround the world's ignorance and press for admission.
**AUSTIN PHELPS**

As there are misanthropists or haters of men, so also are there misologists, or haters of ideas.
**PLATO**

It is a thing of no great difficulty to raise objections against another man's oration—nay, it is a very easy matter; but to produce a better in its place is a work extremely troublesome.
**PLUTARCH**

The only thing that can overcome a persuasive idea is a better idea.
**THEODORE S. REPPLIER**

Ideas are a capital that bears interest only in the hands of talent.
**ANTOINE DE RIVAROL**

People will sit up and take notice of you if you will sit up and take notice of what makes them sit up and take notice.
**FRANK ROMER**

An idea a day will keep the sheriff away.
**DON E. ROSEMAN**

If an idea is good, then it can only be implemented by other people.
**PHYLLIS SEATON**

There are no hard times for good ideas.
**H. GORDON SELFRIDGE**

Getting an idea should be like sitting down on a pin; it should make you jump up and do something.
**E. L. SIMPSON**

All ideas share one thing in common; they need to be considered and tried.
**FRANK TYGER**

It must be remembered that the object of the world of ideas as a whole is not the portrayal of reality—that would be an utterly impossible task—but rather to provide us with an instrument for finding our way about in this world more easily.
**HANS VAIHINGER**

We are healthy only to the extent that our ideas are humane.
**KURT VONNEGUT**

If we would stick to our knitting and do all the things we know we should do in carrying out the full intent and purpose of all of our old, tried, and found-true ideas and methods, we wouldn't have very much time to be dreaming about the new idea that so many people seem to think will be the savior of business.
**E. V. WALSH**

Every breeze wafts intelligence from country to country, every wave rolls it and gives it forth, and all in turn receive it. There is a vast commerce of ideas, there are marts and exchanges for intellectual discoveries, and a wonderful fellowship of those individual intelligences which make up the minds and opinions of the age.
**DANIEL WEBSTER**

Human history is, in essence, a history of ideas.
**H. G. WELLS**

If you have had your attention directed to the novelties of thought in your own lifetime, you will have observed that almost all really new ideas have a certain aspect of foolishness when they are first produced, and almost any idea which jogs you out of your current abstractions may be better than nothing.
**ALFRED NORTH WHITEHEAD**

The value of an idea has nothing whatever to do with the sincerity of the man who expresses it.
**OSCAR WILDE**

All the really good ideas I ever had came to me while I was milking a cow.
**GRANT WOOD**

The power of an idea can be measured by the degree of resistance it attracts.
**DAVID YOHO**

## Idleness

An idle man is a kind of monster in the creation. All nature is busy about him; every animal he sees reproaches him.
JOSEPH ADDISON

It has been said that idleness is the parent of mischief which is very true; but mischief itself is merely an attempt to escape from the dreary vacuum of idleness.
GEORGE BARROW

If you are idle you are on the way to ruin, and there are few stopping places upon it. It is rather a precipice than a road.
HENRY WARD BEECHER

You see men of the most delicate frames engaged in active and professional pursuits who really have no time for idleness. Let them become idle—let them take care of themselves, let them think of their health—and they die! The rust rots the steel which use preserves.
EDWARD BULWER-LYTTON

Too much idleness, I have observed, fills up a man's time much more completely, and leaves him less his own master, than any sort of employment whatsoever.
EDMUND BURKE

There is no greater cause of melancholy than idleness.
ROBERT BURTON

Blessed is the man that has found his work. One monster there is in the world, the idle man.
THOMAS CARLYLE

He doth all things with sadness and with peevishness, slackness and excusation, with idleness and without good will.
GEOFFREY CHAUCER

From its very inaction, idleness ultimately becomes the most active cause of evil; as a palsy is more to be dreaded than a fever. The Turks have a proverb which says that the devil tempts all other men, but that idle men tempt the devil.
CHARLES CALEB COLTON

Do not allow idleness to deceive you; for while you give him today he steals tomorrow from you.
ALFRED CROWQUILL

I never remember feeling tired by work, though idleness exhausts me completely.
SIR ARTHUR CONAN DOYLE

An idle brain is the devil's workshop.
ENGLISH PROVERB

Nobody can think straight who does not work. Idleness warps the mind. Thinking without constructive action becomes a disease.
HENRY FORD

He that is busy is tempted by one devil; he that is idle, by a legion.
THOMAS FULLER

Determine never to be idle. No person will have occasion to complain of the want of time who never loses any. It is wonderful how much may be done if we are always doing.
THOMAS JEFFERSON

It is impossible to enjoy idling thoroughly unless one has plenty of work to do.
JEROME K. JEROME

Every man is, or hopes to be, an idler.
SAMUEL JOHNSON

There is no kind of idleness by which we are so easily seduced as that which dignifies itself by the appearance of business.
SAMUEL JOHNSON

To be idle and to be poor have always been reproaches, and therefore every man endeavors with his utmost care to hide his poverty from others, and his idleness from himself.
SAMUEL JOHNSON

Time is the one thing that can never be retrieved. One may lose and regain a friend; one may lose and regain money; opportunity once spurned may come again; but the hours that are lost in idleness can never be brought back to be used in gainful pursuits. Most careers are made or marred in the hours after supper.
C. R. LAWTON

Few women and fewer men have enough character to be idle.
EDWARD V. LUCAS

Certainly work is not always required of a man. There is such a thing as a sacred idleness—the cultivation of which is now fearfully neglected.
GEORGE MACDONALD

Idleness among children, as among men, is the root of all evil, and leads to no other evil more certain than ill temper.
HANNAH MORE

There is also an honest and necessary idleness whereby good men are made more apt and ready to do their labors and vocations whereunto they are called.
JOHN NORTHBROOKE

Of all our faults, the one that we excuse most easily is idleness.
FRANÇOIS DE LA ROCHEFOUCAULD

Better sit idle than work for nought.
SCOTTISH PROVERB

He is not only idle who does nothing, but he is idle who might be better employed.
SOCRATES

There is one piece of advice, in a life of study, which I think no one will object to: and that is, every now and then to be completely idle, to do nothing at all.
SYDNEY SMITH

Idleness is the key of beggary and the root of all evil.
CHARLES H. SPURGEON

Idleness is the burial of a living man.
JEREMY TAYLOR

Shun idleness. It is a rust that attaches itself to the most brilliant metals.
VOLTAIRE

## *Ignorance*

Prejudice and self-sufficiency naturally proceed from inexperience of the world, and ignorance of mankind.
JOSEPH ADDISON

To be ignorant of one's ignorance is the malady of the ignorant.
AMOS BRONSON ALCOTT

Beware of ignorance when in motion; look out for inexperience when in action, and beware of the majority when mentally poisoned with misinformation, for collective ignorance does not become wisdom.
WILLIAM J. H. BOETCKER

Behind every argument is someone's ignorance.
LOUIS D. BRANDEIS

Ignorance is not innocence but sin.
ROBERT BROWNING

If you think education is expensive, try ignorance.
BUMPER STICKER

The truest characters of ignorance are vanity, and pride and arrogance.
SAMUEL BUTLER

Ignorance is an enemy, even to its owner. Knowledge is a friend, even to its hater. Ignorance hates knowledge because it is too pure. Knowledge fears ignorance because it is too sure.
SRI CHINMOY

To be conscious that you are ignorant is a great step to knowledge.
BENJAMIN DISRAELI

It is the ignorant and childish part of mankind that is the fighting part.
RALPH WALDO EMERSON

A learned blockhead is a greater blockhead than an ignorant one.
BENJAMIN FRANKLIN

While all complain of our ignorance and error, everyone exempts himself.
JOSEPH GLANVILL

There is nothing more frightening than a bustling ignorance.
JOHANN WOLFGANG VON GOETHE

The recipe for perpetual ignorance is: Be satisfied with your opinions and content with your knowledge.
ELBERT HUBBARD

Ignorance, when voluntary, is criminal, and a man may be properly charged with that evil which he neglected or refused to learn how to prevent.
SAMUEL JOHNSON

A man must have a certain amount of intelligent ignorance to get anywhere.
CHARLES F. KETTERING

Nothing in all the world is more dangerous than sincere ignorance and conscientious stupidity.
MARTIN LUTHER KING, JR.

I hope that my children, at least, if not I myself, will see the day when ignorance of the primary laws and facts of science will be looked upon as a defect only second to ignorance of the primary laws of religion and morality.
CHARLES KINGSLEY

Ignorance is voluntary misfortune.
NICHOLAS LANG

To know one's ignorance is the best part of knowledge.
LAO-TZU

What we know here is very little, but what we are ignorant of is immense.
**PIERRE SIMON LAPLACE**

It is impossible to defeat an ignorant man by argument.
**WILLIAM MCADOO**

Half knowledge is worse than ignorance.
**THOMAS B. MACAULAY**

To admit ignorance is to exhibit wisdom.
**ASHLEY MONTAGU**

Better be unborn than untaught, for ignorance is the root of misfortune.
**PLATO**

Ignorance of all things is an evil neither terrible nor excessive, nor yet the greatest of all; but great cleverness and much learning, if they be accompanied by a bad training, are a much greater misfortune.
**PLATO**

There is a determinable difference between the apparent casualness of mastery and the carelessness of ignorance.
**CHARLES B. ROGERS**

The common curse of mankind—folly and ignorance.
**WILLIAM SHAKESPEARE**

There is no darkness—but ignorance.
**WILLIAM SHAKESPEARE**

Uncultivated minds are not full of wild flowers, like uncultivated fields. Villainous weeds grow in them and they are the haunt of toads.
**LOGAN PEARSALL SMITH**

He that does not know those things which are of use and necessity for him to know, is but an ignorant man, whatever he may know besides.
**JOHN TILLOTSON**

It is poverty in a rich man to despise the poor and ignorance in a wise man to despise the ignorant.
**CONSTANCE C. VIGIL**

Ignorance is not bliss—it is oblivion.
**PHILIP WYLIE**

## *Illusions*

Beware lest you lose the substance by grasping at the shadow.
**AESOP**

We [Americans] suffer primarily not from our weaknesses, but from our illusions. We are haunted, not by reality, but by images which we have put in the place of reality.
**DANIEL J. BOORSTIN**

We must select the illusion which appeals to our temperament, and embrace it with passion, if we want to be happy.
**CYRIL CONNOLLY**

Every age is fed on illusions, lest men should renounce life early and the human race come to an end.
**JOSEPH CONRAD**

What difference is there, do you think, between those in Plato's cave who can only marvel at the shadows and images of various objects, provided they are content and don't know what they miss,

and the philosopher who has emerged from the cave and sees the real things?
**DESIDERIUS ERASMUS**

The illusion that times that were are better than those that are, has probably pervaded all ages.
**HORACE GREELEY**

Illusion is always based on reality, for its strength depends upon its fit with the desires, fears and experiences of countless humans.
**JOHN P. GRIER**

Rob the average man of his illusion and you rob him of his happiness at one stroke.
**HENRIK IBSEN**

No man will be found in whose mind airy notions do not sometimes tyrannize, and force him to hope or fear beyond the limits of sober probability.
**SAMUEL JOHNSON**

It appears to me that almost any man may, like the spider, spin from his own inwards his own airy citadel.
**JOHN KEATS**

The most important part of our lives—our sensations, emotions, desire, aspirations—takes place in a universe of illusions which science can attenuate or destroy, but which it is powerless to enrich.
**JOSEPH WOOD KRUTCH**

The notion that as a man grows older his illusions leave him is not quite true. What is true is that his early illusions are supplanted by new, and to him, equally convincing illusions.
**GEORGE JEAN NATHAN**

Pray look better, sir. Those things yonder are no giants, but windmills.
**SANCHO PANZA TO DON QUIXOTE**

Our experience is composed rather of illusions lost than wisdom acquired.
**JOSEPH ROUX**

A man loses his illusions first, his teeth second, and his follies last.
**HELEN ROWLAND**

A hallucination is a fact, not an error; what is erroneous is a judgment based upon it.
**BERTRAND RUSSELL**

The eyes are not responsible when the mind does the seeing.
**PUBLILIUS SYRUS**

It isn't safe to sit in judgment upon another person's illusion when you are not on the inside. While you are thinking it is a dream, he may be knowing it is a planet.
**MARK TWAIN**

Don't part with your illusions. When they are gone you may still exist, but you have ceased to live.
**MARK TWAIN**

Illusion is the first of all pleasures.
**VOLTAIRE**

## *Imagination*

Far away in the sunshine are my highest inspirations. I may not reach them, but I can look up and see the beauty, believe in them and try to follow where they lead.
**LOUISA MAY ALCOTT**

The human race is governed by its imagination.
**NAPOLEON BONAPARTE**

I get the facts, I study them patiently, I apply imagination.
**BERNARD M. BARUCH**

Your imagination has much to do with your life. It pictures beauty, success, desired results. On the other hand, it brings into focus ugliness, distress, and failure. It is for you to decide how you want your imagination to serve you.
**PHILIP CONLEY**

Imagination is as good as many voyages—and how much cheaper.
**GEORGE WILLIAM CURTIS**

Every great advance in science has issued from a new audacity of imagination.
**JOHN DEWEY**

Originality does not consist of inventing a new language, but in expressing in the accepted language all possible new and personal thoughts.
**RENÉ DUMESNIL**

Imagination is more important than knowledge.
**ALBERT EINSTEIN**

One couldn't carry on life comfortably without a little blindness to the fact that everything has been said better than we can put it ourselves.
**GEORGE ELIOT**

Imagination is not a talent of some men, but is the health of every man.
**RALPH WALDO EMERSON**

The body travels more easily than the mind, and until we have limbered up our imagination we continue to think as though we had stayed home. We have not really budged a step until we take up residence in someone else's point of view.
**JOHN ERSKINE**

The man who will use his skill and constructive imagination to see how much he can give for a dollar, instead of how little he can give for a dollar, is bound to succeed.
**HENRY FORD**

Anybody can do anything that he imagines.
**HENRY FORD**

It is the starved imagination, not the well-nourished, that is afraid.
**E. M. FORSTER**

The very core of peace and love is imagination. All altruism springs from putting yourself in the other person's place.
**HARRY EMERSON FOSDICK, D.D.**

Imagination is the secret reservoir of the riches of the human race.
**MAUDE L. FRANDSEN**

Inspiration is and can only be the product of free men.
**HOWARD E. FRITZ**

He who has learning without imagination has feet but no wings.
**STANLEY GOLDSTEIN**

The one mistake which is committed habitually by people who have the gift of half-genius, is waiting for inspiration.
**PHILIP HAMERTON**

Originality is simply a pair of fresh eyes.
**THOMAS W. HIGGINSON**

A figment of the imagination is just a harmless illusion—unless you are a victim of it.
**CULLEN HIGHTOWER**

There are two worlds: the world that we can measure with line and rule, and the world that we feel with our hearts and imagination.
**LEIGH HUNT**

The principal mark of genius is not perfection but originality, the opening of new frontiers.
**ARTHUR KOESTLER**

One of the virtues of being very young is that you don't let the facts get in the way of your imagination.
**SAM LEVENSON**

No man ever made a great discovery without the exercise of the imagination.
**GEORGE HENRY LEWES**

Imagination, where it is truly creative, is a faculty, not a quality; its seat is in the higher reason, and it is efficient only as the servant of the will. Imagination, as too often understood, is mere fantasy—the image-making power, common to all who have the gift of dreams.
**JAMES RUSSELL LOWELL**

If you turn the imagination loose like a hunting dog, it will often return with the bird in its mouth.
**WILLIAM MAXWELL**

All good things which exist are the fruits of originality.
**JOHN STUART MILL**

Originality is the one thing which unoriginal minds cannot feel the use of.
**JOHN STUART MILL**

A strong imagination begetteth opportunity.
**MICHEL DE MONTAIGNE**

Man sees himself lodged here in the mud and filth of the world, nailed and fastened to the most lifeless and stagnant part of the universe, in the lowest story of the house, at the furthest distance from the vault of Heaven, with the vilest animals; and yet, in his imagination, he places himself above the circle of the moon, and brings Heaven under his feet.
**MICHEL DE MONTAIGNE**

The power of imagination makes us infinite.
**JOHN MUIR**

The great composer does not set to work because he is inspired, but becomes inspired because he is working. Beethoven, Wagner, Bach and Mozart settled down day after day to the job in hand with as much regularity as an accountant settles down each day to his figures. They didn't waste time waiting for inspiration.
**ERNEST NEWMAN**

Imagination disposes of everything; it creates beauty, justice, happiness, which is everything in this world.
**BLAISE PASCAL**

In proportion as our own mind is enlarged we discover a greater number of men of originality. Commonplace people see no difference between one man and another.
**BLAISE PASCAL**

It may well be doubted whether human ingenuity can construct an enigma of the kind which human ingenuity may not, by proper application, resolve.
**EDGAR ALLAN POE**

The world of reality has its limits; the world of imagination is boundless. Not being able to enlarge the one, let us contract the other; for it is from their difference that all the evils arise which render us unhappy.
JEAN-JACQUES ROUSSEAU

The virtue of the imagination is its reaching, by intuition and intensity, a more essential truth than is seen at the surface of things.
JOHN RUSKIN

A man to carry on a successful business must have imagination. He must see things as in a vision, a dream of the whole thing.
CHARLES M. SCHWAB

The greatest instrument of moral good is the imagination.
PERCY BYSSHE SHELLEY

He is indebted to his memory for his jests and to his imagination for his facts.
RICHARD B. SHERIDAN

Originality does not consist is saying what no one has ever said before, but in saying exactly what you think yourself.
JAMES STEPHENS

Men of great parts are often unfortunate in the management of public business because they are apt to go out of the common road by the quickness of their imagination.
JONATHAN SWIFT

Imagination lit every lamp in this country, produced every article we use, built every church, made every discovery, performed every act of kindness and progress, created more and better things for more people. It is the priceless ingredient for a better day.
HENRY J. TAYLOR

Limiting one's pursuits to one lone avenue without benefit of change or diversion can result in a form of vapidity which sometimes deadens imagination.
EDWIN G. UHL

The imagination imitates. It is the critical spirit that creates.
OSCAR WILDE

## *Impossible*

The word impossible is not in my dictionary.
NAPOLEON BONAPARTE

I have learned to use the world impossible with the greatest caution.
WERNHER VON BRAUN

To wonder at nothing when it happens, to consider nothing impossible before it has come to pass.
CICERO

When a distinguished but elderly scientist states that something is possible, he is almost certainly right. When he states that something is impossible, he is probably wrong.
ARTHUR C. CLARKE

To believe a business impossible is the way to make it so. How many feasible projects have miscarried through despondency, and been strangled in their birth by a cowardly imagination.
JEREMY COLLIER

Only he who can see the invisible can do the impossible.
**FRANK L. GAINES**

Never tell a young person that something can not be done. God may have been waiting for centuries for somebody ignorant enough of the impossible to do that thing.
**JOHN ANDREW HOLMES**

Nothing is impossible; there are ways that lead to everything, and if we had sufficient will we should always have sufficient means. It is often merely for an excuse that we say things are impossible.
**FRANÇOIS DE LA ROCHEFOUCAULD**

Few things are impossible in themselves: application to make them succeed fails us more often than the means.
**FRANÇOIS DE LA ROCHEFOUCAULD**

Man can believe the impossible, but man can never believe the improbable.
**OSCAR WILDE**

## *Improvement*

There isn't a plant or a business on earth that couldn't stand a few improvements—and be better for them. Someone is going to think of them. Why not beat the other fellow to it?
**ROGER W. BABSON**

Everything can be improved.
**C. W. BARRON**

To face tomorrow with the thought of using the methods of yesterday is to envision life at a standstill. To keep ahead, each one of us, no matter what our task, must search for new and better methods—for even that which we now do well must be done better tomorrow.
**JAMES F. BELL**

It is not the rich man's son that the young struggler for advancement has to fear in the race for life, nor his nephew, nor his cousin. Let him look out for the dark horse in the boy who begins by sweeping out the office.
**ANDREW CARNEGIE**

We know that man was created, not with an instinct for his own degradation, but imbued with the desire and the power for improvement to which, perchance, there may be no limit short of perfection even here in this life upon earth.
**ANDREW CARNEGIE**

Do not hold the delusion that your advancement is accomplished by crushing others.
**CICERO**

Where we cannot invent, we may at least improve; we may give somewhat of novelty to that which was old, condensation to that which was diffuse, perspicuity to that which was obscure, and currency to that which was recondite.
**CHARLES CALEB COLTON**

A man who truly wants to make the world better should start by improving himself and his attitudes.
**FRED DEARMOND**

Why are we so blind? That which we improve, we have; that which we hoard is not for ourselves.
**DOROTHÉE DELUZY**

Every man, however obscure, however far removed from the general recognition, is one of a group of men impressible for good, and impressible for evil, and it is in the nature of things that he cannot really

improve himself without in some degree improving other men.
CHARLES DICKENS

People never improve unless they look to some standard or example higher and better than themselves.
TRYON EDWARDS

Improvement of one's economic position is helped more by cool persistence than by hot enthusiasm.
WILLIAM FEATHER

Humanity may endure the loss of everything; all its possessions may be turned away without infringing its true dignity—all but the possibility of improvement.
IMMANUEL FICHTE

The most essential feature of man is his improvableness.
JOHN FISKE

Men, said the Devil, are good to their brothers; they don't want to mend their own ways, but each other's.
PIET HEIN

The opportunity for the average workman to rise to the management positions in industry was never better than it is today. These opportunities will continue to grow in the next decade. If the average intelligent and honest workman supplements his practical work experience with study of the general problems of business he will find privileged opportunities and promotion awaiting him.
HENRY H. HEIMANN

You will probably get a larger position than you expect when you begin to do larger things than your firm expects you to do.
GEORGE C. HOBBS

There is no advancement to him who stands trembling because he cannot see the end from the beginning.
E. J. KLEMME

Slumber not in the tents of your fathers. The world is advancing. Advance with it.
GIUSEPPE MAZZINI

We should scrutinize all attempts to improve our condition and make sure that they do not in reality do us harm.
PETER MEDEWAR

The hope, and not the fact, of advancement is the spur to industry.
HENRY J. TAYLOR

## *Independence*

There is often as much independence in not being led, as in not being driven.
TRYON EDWARDS

The greatest of all human benefits, that, at least, without which no other benefit can be truly enjoyed, is independence.
PARKE GODWIN

It's easy to be independent when you've got money. But to be independent when you haven't got a thing—that's the Lord's test.
MAHALIA JACKSON

Let all your views in life be directed to a solid, however moderate, independence; without it no man can be happy, nor even honest.
JUNIUS

Self-government, self-discipline, self-responsibility are the triple safeguards of the independence of man.
BERNICE MOORE

To be independent is the business of a few only; it is the privilege of the strong.
FRIEDRICH WILHELM NIETZSCHE

Independence is of more value than any gifts; and to receive gifts is to lose it.
SA'DI

A great step towards independence is a good-humored stomach.
SENECA

Independency may be found in comparative as well as in absolute abundance; I mean where a person contracts his desires within the limits of his fortune.
WILLIAM SHENSTONE

## *Individual*

We are afraid to put men to live and trade each on his own private stock of reason; because we suspect that this stock in each man is small, and that the individuals would do better to avail themselves of the general bank and capital of nations and of age.
EDMUND BURKE

Not armies, not nations, have advanced the race; but here and there, in the course of the ages, an individual has stood up and cast his shadow over the world.
EDWIN H. CHAPIN

Individuality is either the mark of genius or the reverse. Mediocrity finds safety in standardization.
FREDERICK E. CRANE

What counts in any system is the intelligence, self-control, conscience and energy of the individual.
CYRUS EATON

More than ever before, in our country, this is the age of the individual. Endowed with the accumulated knowledge of centuries, armed with all the instruments of modern science, he is still assured personal freedom and wide avenues of expression so that he may win for himself, his family and his country greater material comfort, ease and happiness; greater spiritual satisfaction and contentment.
DWIGHT D. EISENHOWER

Regardless of circumstances, each man lives in a world of his own making.
JOSEPHA MURRAY EMMS

No task is so humble that it does not offer an outlet for individuality.
WILLIAM FEATHER

One man can completely change the character of a country, and the industry of its people, by dropping a single seed in fertile soil.
JOHN C. GIFFORD

Every individual has a place to fill in the world, and is important in some respect, whether he chooses to be so or not.
NATHANIEL HAWTHORNE

God gave every man individuality of constitution and a chance for achieving individuality of character. He puts special instruments into every man's hands by which to make himself and achieve his mission.
JOSIAH G. HOLLAND

Be thankful not only that you are an individual but also that others are different. The world needs all

kinds, but it also needs to respect and use that individuality.
DONALD A. LAIRD

In proportion to the development of his individuality, each person becomes more valuable to others. There is a greater fullness of life about his own existence, and when there is more life in the units there is more in the mass which is composed of them.
JOHN STUART MILL

A people, it appears, may be progressive for a certain length of time, and then stop. When does it stop? When it ceases to possess individuality.... Whatever crushes individuality is despotism, by whatever name it may be called.
JOHN STUART MILL

It is an absolute perfection to know how to get the very most out of one's individuality.
MICHEL DE MONTAIGNE

Individuality is everywhere to be spaced and respected as the root of everything good.
JEAN PAUL RICHTER

How beautifully is it ordered, that as many thousands work for one, so must every individual bring his labor to make the whole. The highest is not to despise the lowest, nor the lowest to envy the highest; each must live in all and by all.
GEORGE A. SALA

We seem to want mass production, but we must remember that men are individuals not to be satisfactorily dealt with in masses, and the making of men is more important than the production of things.
RALPH W. SOCKMAN

It is said that if Noah's ark had had to be built by a company, they would not have laid the keel yet; and it may be so. What is many men's business is nobody's business. The greatest things are accomplished by individual men.
CHARLES H. SPURGEON

There will never be a really free and enlightened state until the state comes to recognize the individual as a higher and independent power, from which all its own power and authority are derived, and treats him accordingly.
HENRY DAVID THOREAU

All great questions of politics and economics come down in the last analysis to the decisions and actions of individual men and women. They are questions of human relations, and we ought always to think about them in terms of men and women—the individual human beings who are involved in them. If we can get human relations on a proper basis, the statistics, finance and all other complicated technical aspects of these questions will be easier to solve.
THOMAS J. WATSON

Most men are individuals no longer so far as their business, its activities, or its moralities are concerned. They are not units but fractions.
WOODROW WILSON

## *Industry*

In the ordinary business of life, industry can do anything which genius can do, and very many things which it cannot.
HENRY WARD BEECHER

The ascending spiral of greatness in America has risen because industry has produced wealth, which in turn has supported educational institutions, which in turn have supplied leadership to industry

in order that with each succeeding generation it might produce more wealth.
**WALLACE F. BENNETT**

Industry is not only the instrument of improvement, but the foundation of pleasure. He who is a stranger to it may possess, but cannot enjoy, for it is labor only which gives relish to pleasure. It is the indispensable condition of possessing a sound mind in a sound body, and is the appointed vehicle of every good to man.
**PAXTON BLAIR**

Dividing industry into big and little is artificial. Industry is both—that makes it Industry. Ninety-eight per cent of American industries employ less than 500 men each. Today's big industries were small within our lifetime, many of today's small industries will become big before our lifetime ends. Large industries make small industries necessary, and small industries make large ones possible. Wipe out large industries and you wipe out three-fourths of the small ones; wipe out the small ones and the large ones cannot go on. They work together. Each has a part in the nation's job.
**WILLIAM J. CAMERON**

There is one rule for industrialists and that is: Make the best quality of goods possible at the lowest cost possible, paying the highest wages possible.
**HENRY FORD**

It is worth remembering that output per man in this country has increased on the average about two per cent a year during this century. Mere continuation of this trend will mean a future full of better things for more people. But it is my own feeling that the tremendous gains which have been achieved by machine techniques may be substantially matched when we learn to make better use of ourselves as people.
**HENRY FORD**

Sloth makes all things difficult, but industry all things easy.
**BENJAMIN FRANKLIN**

Industry need not wish, and he that lives upon hopes will die fasting. There are no gains without pains. He that hath a trade hath an estate, and he that hath a calling hath an office of profit and honor; but then the trade must be worked at, and the calling followed, or neither the estate nor the office will enable us to pay our taxes. If we are industrious, we shall never starve; for at the workingman's house hunger looks in, but dares not enter. Nor will the bailiff or the constable enter, for industry pays debts, while idleness and neglect increase them.
**BENJAMIN FRANKLIN**

The way to wealth is as plain as the way to market. It depends chiefly on two words, industry and frugality; that is, waste neither time nor money, but make the best use of both. Without industry and frugality nothing will do; with them, everything.
**BENJAMIN FRANKLIN**

In every rank, both great and small, it is industry that supports us all.
**JOHN GAY**

To industry, nothing is impossible.
**LATIN PROVERB**

I do not despise genius—indeed, I wish I had a basketful of it. But yet, after a great deal of experience and observation, I have become convinced that industry is a better horse to ride than genius. It may never carry any man as far as genius has carried individuals, but industry—patient, steady, intelligent industry—will carry thousands into comfort, and even celebrity; and this it does with absolute certainty.
**WALTER LIPPMANN**

The decisive element in modern life is not political but industrial. Our prosperity as a nation depends not upon the Republicans or the Democrats but upon the maintenance of a specific type of industrial system. In the United States, as in Russia, the expression of the opinion of the people has less and less significance as the requirements of an impersonal industrial system become more and more dominant. The supreme social problem of the twentieth century centers around the question whether the value of individual human life can be maintained when the decision of the individual has ceased to have social significance.
**FRANCIS E. MILLER**

If you have genius, industry will improve it; if you have none, industry will supply its place.
**SIR JOSHUA REYNOLDS**

I am convinced that when confidence has been established amongst all nations of the world, the present capacity of industrial countries will not be sufficient to satisfy the demand.
**OSKAR SEMPELL**

National progress is the sum of individual industry, energy, and uprightness, as national decay is of individual idleness, selfishness, and vice.
**SAMUEL SMILES**

Industry has been regarded in the past as a way to make a living. I believe it is the great new realization of Business America that industry can be something far finer and bigger, a way to make a life.
**E. T. TRIGG**

A man who gives his children habits of industry provides for them better than by giving them a fortune.
**RICHARD WHATELY**

## *Insults*

A thick skin is a gift from God.
**KONRAD ADENAUER**

He who does not shield himself from vilification receives it.
**ARABIAN PROVERB**

Slander cannot destroy the man . . . when the flood recedes, the rock is there.
**CHINESE PROVERB**

There is nothing that people bear more impatiently, or forgive less, than contempt; and an injury is much sooner forgotten than an insult.
**LORD CHESTERFIELD**

An insult is either sustained or destroyed, not by the disposition of those who insult, but by the disposition of those who bear it.
**ST. JOHN CHRYSOSTOM**

He who permits himself to be insulted deserves the insult.
**PIERRE CORNEILLE**

The man that dares traduce, because he can with safety to himself, is not a man.
**WILLIAM COWPER**

It seldom pays to be rude. It never pays to be half rude.
**NORMAN DOUGLAS**

No one can be as calculatedly rude as the British, which amazes Americans, who do not understand studied insult and can only offer abuse as a substitute.
**PAUL GALLICO**

Some people would not hesitate to drive up to the gate of heaven and honk.
**JOHN ANDREW HOLMES**

The habit of sneering marks the egotist, the fool, or the knave, or all three.
**JOHANN LAVATER**

A sneer is often the sign of heartless malignity.
**JOHANN LAVATER**

There are two insults no human will endure: the assertion that he has no sense of humor and the doubly impertinent assertion that he has never known trouble.
**SINCLAIR LEWIS**

A sneer is the weapon of the weak. Like other weapons of the devil, it is always cunningly ready to our hand, and there is more poison in the handle than in the point.
**JAMES RUSSELL LOWELL**

The only graceful way to accept an insult is to ignore it; if you can't ignore it, top it; if you can't top it, laugh at it; if you can't laugh at it, it's probably deserved.
**RUSSELL LYNES**

I hold it to be a proof of great prudence for men to abstain from threats and insulting words toward anyone, for neither diminishes the strength of the enemy.
**NICCOLÒ MACHIAVELLI**

No one is safe from slander. The best way is to pay no attention to it, but live in innocence and let the world talk.
**MOLIÈRE**

Man is much more sensitive to the contempt of others than to self-contempt.
**FRIEDRICH WILHELM NIETZSCHE**

Who can refute a sneer?
**WILLIAM PALEY**

The poorest way to face life is to face it with a sneer.
**THEODORE ROOSEVELT**

Obscenity is whatever happens to shock some elderly and ignorant magistrate.
**BERTRAND RUSSELL**

Rudeness is better than any argument; it totally eclipses intellect.
**ARTHUR SCHOPENHAUER**

With most people there will be no harm in occasionally mixing a grain of disdain with your treatment of them; that will make them value your friendship all the more.
**ARTHUR SCHOPENHAUER**

Contempt is commonly taken by the young for an evidence of understanding; but it is neither difficult to acquire, nor meritorious when acquired. To discover the imperfections of others is penetration; to hate them for their faults is contempt. We may be clearsighted without being malevolent, and make use of the errors we discover, to learn caution, not to gratify satire.
**SYDNEY SMITH**

There is a principle which is a bar against all information, which is proof against all argument and which cannot fail to keep a man in everlasting ignorance. This principle is contempt prior to examination.
**HERBERT SPENCER**

Speak not injurious words, neither in jest nor earnest; scoff at none although they give occasion.
**GEORGE WASHINGTON**

## Intelligence

Cleverness is serviceable for everything, sufficient for nothing.
**HENRI FRÉDÉRIC AMIEL**

What is an intelligent man? A man who enters with ease and completeness into the spirit of things and the intention of persons, and who arrives at an end by the shortest route.
**HENRI FRÉDÉRIC AMIEL**

The brave, impetuous heart yields everywhere to the subtle, contriving head.
**MATTHEW ARNOLD**

As diamonds cut diamonds, and one hone smooths a second, all the parts of intellect are whetstones to each other; and genius, which is but the result of their mutual sharpening, is character, too.
**CYRUS A. BARTOL**

Unintelligent people always look for a scapegoat.
**ERNEST BEVIN**

The brain is not an organ to be relied upon.
**ALEXANDER BLOCK**

Business and action strengthen the brain, but too much study weakens it.
**H. G. BOHN**

Man's brain is, after all, the greatest natural resource.
**KARL BRANDT**

Animals feed; man eats. Only the man of intellect and judgment knows how to eat.
**ANTHELME BRILLAT-SAVARIN**

Talent, taste, wit, good sense are very different things but by no means incompatible. Between good sense and good taste there exists the same difference as between cause and effect, and between wit and talent there is the same proportion as between a whole and its parts.
**JEAN DE LA BRUYÈRE**

If brilliance is a human plus,
And lack thereof a minus,
Should we consider that unfair,
And seek to redesign us?
**ART BUCK**

The commerce of intellect loves distant shores. The small retail dealer trades only with his neighbor; when the great merchant trades he links the four quarters of the globe.
**EDWARD BULWER-LYTTON**

An intellectual is someone whose mind watches itself.
**ALBERT CAMUS**

The education of the intellect is a great business; but an unconsecrated intellect is the saddest sight on which the sun looks down.
**EDWIN CHADWICK**

Good sense is at the bottom of everything: virtue, genius, wit, talent and taste.
**J. J. DE CHENIER**

It is a curious paradox that precisely in proportion to our own intellectual weakness, will be our credulity as to the mysterious powers assumed by others.
**CHARLES CALEB COLTON**

I know this world is ruled by Infinite Intelligence. It required Infinite Intelligence to create it and it requires Infinite Intelligence to keep it on its course. Everything that surrounds us—everything that exists—proves that there are Infinite Laws behind it. There can be no denying this fact. It is mathematical in its precision.
**THOMAS EDISON**

Intellect annuls fate. So far as a man thinks he is free.
**RALPH WALDO EMERSON**

Cleverness is not wisdom.
**EURIPIDES**

Brains aren't everything, but they're important.
**WILLIAM FEATHER**

The man who puts $10,000 additional capital into an established business is pretty certain of increased returns; and in the same way, the man who puts additional capital into his brains—information, well directed thought and study of possibilities—will as surely—yes, more surely—get increased returns. There is no capital and no increase in capital safer than that.
**MARSHALL FIELD**

The fundamental qualities for good execution of a plan are, first, naturally, intelligence; then discernment and judgment, which enable one to recognize the best methods to attain it; then singleness of purpose; and, lastly, what is most essential of all, will—stubborn will. A leader is above all things an animator. His thought and faith must be communicated to those he leads. He and they must form as one at the moment of executing a plan. That is the essential condition of success.
**FERDINAND FOCH**

Nothing is useless to the man of sense; he turns everything to account.
**CHARLES FONTAINE**

The best buy by way of management is brains—at any price.
**MALCOLM FORBES**

One good head is better than a hundred strong hands.
**THOMAS FULLER**

The brilliant moves we occasionally make would not have been possible without the prior dumb ones.
**STANLEY GOLDSTEIN**

When you hire people who are smarter than you are, you prove you are smarter than they are.
**R. H. GRANT**

The brain is a mass of cranial nerve tissue, most of it in mint condition.
**ROBERT HALF**

To meet the great tasks that are before us, we require all our intelligence, and we must be sound and wholesome in mind. We must proceed in order. The price of anger is failure.
**ELWOOD HENDRICKS**

The most fertile soil does not necessarily produce the most abundant harvest. It is the use we make of our faculties which renders them valuable.
**THOMAS W. HIGGINSON**

A moment's insight is sometimes worth a life's experience.
**OLIVER WENDELL HOLMES**

There are one-story intellects, two-story intellects, and three-story intellects with skylights. All fact

collectors, who have no aim beyond their facts, are one-story men. Two-story men compare, reason, generalize, using the labors of fact collectors as well as their own. Three-story men idealize, imagine, predict; their best illumination comes from above, through the skylight.
OLIVER WENDELL HOLMES

A rather important contemporary problem: too many unintelligent intellectuals.
WALTER HOVING

It takes a clever man to turn cynic and a wise man to be clever enough not to.
FANNIE HURST

Democracy has not failed; the intelligence of the race has failed before the problems the race has raised.
ROBERT M. HUTCHINS

As the mind must govern the hands, so in every society the man of intelligence must direct the man of labor.
JOHNSON

The man who gets the most satisfactory results is not always the man with the most brilliant single mind, but rather the man who can best co-ordinate the brains and talents of his associates.
W. ALTON JONES

No one is mediocre who has good sense and good sentiments.
JOSEPH JOUBERT

The difference between intelligence and an education is this—that intelligence will make you a good living.
CHARLES F. KETTERING

We cannot consider people truly educated if they think of education only as the gathering of facts, data and information. The intelligent person is one who has learned how to choose wisely and therefore has a sense of values, a purpose in life and a sense of direction.
J. MARTIN KLOTSCHE

Not many men have both good fortune and good sense.
LEVY

The earth flourishes, or is overrun with noxious weeds and brambles, as we apply or withhold the cultivating hand. So fares it with the intellectual system of man.
HORACE MANN

There's no underestimating the intelligence of the American public.
H. L. MENCKEN

In order to acquire intellect one must need it. One loses it when it is no longer necessary.
FRIEDRICH WILHELM NIETZSCHE

In making our decisions, we must use the brains that God has given us. But we must also use our hearts which He also gave us.
FULTON OURSLER

Intelligence is the effort to do the best you can at your particular job; the quality that gives dignity to that job, whether it happens to be scrubbing a floor or running a corporation.
JAMES C. PENNEY

There is danger when a man throws his tongue into high gear before he gets his brain a-going.
C. C. PHELPS

It's a terrible shame if you're born the brightest guy in your class. If you're not, then you have to hustle—and that's good.
**HAL PRINCE**

I am clever; and make no scruple of declaring it; why should i?
**FRANÇOIS DE LA ROCHEFOUCAULD**

Intellectual blemishes, like facial ones, grow more prominent with age.
**FRANÇOIS DE LA ROCHEFOUCAULD**

It is great cleverness to know how to conceal one's cleverness.
**FRANÇOIS DE LA ROCHEFOUCAULD**

Work alone does not suffice—the effort must be intelligent.
**CHARLES B. ROGERS**

So far as I can remember, there is not one word in the Gospels in praise of intelligence.
**BERTRAND RUSSELL**

It is the mark of a truly intelligent person to be moved by statistics.
**GEORGE BERNARD SHAW**

It is only the constant exertion and working of our sensitive, intellectual, moral, and physical machinery that keeps us from rusting, and so becoming useless.
**CHARLES SIMMONS**

I have a sixth sense, but not the other five. If I wasn't making money, they'd put me away.
**RED SKELTON**

The march of intellect is proceeding at quick time; and if its progress be not accompanied by a corresponding improvement in morals and religion, the faster it proceeds, with the more violence will you be hurried down the road to ruin.
**ROBERT SOUTHEY**

I rejoice that intelligence rules, that there are thousands and tens of thousands of wide-awake men and women, rich in the understanding of life's meaning, plodding along, singing as they go, doing their work, whether it be uphill or down, with an invincible determination, a simple modesty and a cheerfulness that radiates joy and happiness to all within reach of their influence.
**LOUIS A. STREMPLE**

If you would take, you must first give, this is the beginning of intelligence.
**TAO-TE-KING**

In the world a man will often be reputed to be a man of sense, only because he is not a man of talent.
**HENRY J. TAYLOR**

I have long thought, that the different abilities of men, which we call wisdom or prudence for the conduct of public affairs or private life, grow directly out of that little grain of good sense which they bring with them into the world; and that the defect of it in men comes from some want in their conception or birth.
**WILLIAM J. TEMPLE**

All men see the same objects, but do not equally understand them. Intelligence is the tongue that discerns and tastes them.
**THOMAS TRAHERNE**

Intellect and industry are never incompatible. There is more wisdom, and will be more benefit, in combining them than scholars like to believe, or than the common world imagine; life has time enough for both, and its happiness will be increased by the union.
**S. TURNER**

I doubt not that in due time, when the arts are brought to perfection, some means will be found to give a sound head to a man who has none at all.
**VOLTAIRE**

A superior and commanding intellect, a truly great man—when Heaven vouchsafes so rare a gift—is not a temporary flame, burning for a while, and then expiring, giving place to eternal darkness. It is rather a spark of fervent heat, as well as radiant light, with power to enkindle the common mass of human mind; so that, when it glimmers in its own decay, and finally goes out in death, no night follows; but it leaves the world all light, all on fire, from the potent contact of its own spirit.
**DANIEL WEBSTER**

I use not only all the brains I have but all I can borrow.
**WOODROW WILSON**

Of plain, sound sense, life's current coin is made.
**EDWARD YOUNG**

# J

## Jobs

There may be luck in getting a good job, but there's no luck in keeping it.
J. OGDEN ARMOUR

I received a letter from a lad asking me for an easy berth. To this I replied: "You cannot be an editor; do not try the law; do not think of the ministry; let alone all ships and merchandise; abhor politics; don't practice medicine; be not a farmer or a soldier or a sailor; don't study, don't think. None of these are easy. O, my son, you have come into a hard world. I know of only one easy place in it, and that is the grave!"
HENRY WARD BEECHER

Do it the hard way! Think ahead of your job. Then nothing in the world can keep the job ahead from reaching out for you. Do it better than it need be done. Next time doing it will be child's play. Let no one or anything stand between you and the difficult task, let nothing deny you this rich chance to gain strength by adversity, confidence by mastery, success by deserving it. Do it better each time. Do it better than anyone else can do it. I know this sounds old-fashioned. It is, but it has built the world.
HARLOW H. CURTICE

For it is the willingness of people to give of themselves over and above the demands of the job that distinguishes the great from the merely adequate organization.
PETER DRUCKER

Unless we can and do constantly seek and find ways and means to do a better job; unless we accept the challenge of the changing times; we have no right to survive and we shall not survive.
CHESTER O. FISCHER

Had I not gone through the ordeal, in more than one country, of landing a job, I would he tempted to lose patience over the number of letters pouring in from fellows who want me or someone else to hand them a job on a silver platter with a guarantee that they will receive the wonderful promotion their talents warrant.... But a tragic number of young men and even older men have a notion that it is not up to them to prosecute the bettering process. They look to someone else to perform the trick for them.
B. C. FORBES

I ought to consider my job a blessing—not a curse.
THEODORE HUGGENVIK

Usually there are responsible jobs going begging because not enough men are willing to sweat enough to master the problems involved.
W. ALTON JONES

Unless the job means more than the pay it will never pay more.
H. BERTRAM LEWIS

Queer thing, but we always think every other man's job is easier than our own. And the better he does it, the easier it looks.
EDEN PHILLPOTTS

It is easier to do a job right than to explain why you didn't.
MARTIN VAN BUREN

## Joy

Joys are bubble-like; what makes them bursts them too.
**PHILIP JAMES BAILEY**

There are joys which long to be ours. God sends ten thousand truths, which come about us like birds seeking inlet; but we are shut up to them, and so they bring us nothing, but sit and sing awhile upon the roof, and then fly away.
**HENRY WARD BEECHER**

God send you joy, for sorrow will come fast enough.
**JOHN CLARKE**

There are souls in this world which have the gift of finding joy everywhere and of leaving it behind them when they go.
**FREDERICK WILLIAM FABER**

The wise man seeks little joys, knowing that life is long and that his quota of great joys is distinctly limited.
**WILLIAM FEATHER**

The greatest joy of a thinking man is to have searched the explored and to quietly revere the unexplored.
**JOHANN WOLFGANG VON GOETHE**

When you jump for joy, beware that no one moves the ground from beneath your feet.
**STANISLAUS LEC**

They that sow in tears shall reap in joy. He that goeth forth and weepeth, bearing precious seed, shall doubtless come again with rejoicing, bringing his sheaves with him.
**PSALMS 126:5–6**

A joy that's shared is a joy made double.
**JOHN RAY**

I wish you all the joy that you can wish.
**WILLIAM SHAKESPEARE**

Sometimes hath the brightest day a cloud; and after summer evermore succeeds barren winter, with his wrathful nipping cold: So care and joys abound, as seasons fleet.
**WILLIAM SHAKESPEARE**

There is the true joy of life; to be used by a purpose recognized by yourself as a mighty one; to be thoroughly worn out before being thrown on the scrap heap; to be a force of nature instead of a feverish, selfish little clod of ailments and grievances complaining that life will not devote itself to making you happy.
**GEORGE BERNARD SHAW**

When the power of imparting joy is equal to the will, the human soul requires no other heaven.
**PERCY BYSSHE SHELLEY**

The very society of joy redoubles it; so that, while it lights upon my friend, it rebounds upon myself, and the brighter his candle burns, the more easily will it light mine.
**ROBERT SOUTHEY**

Things in which we do not take joy are either a burden upon our minds to be got rid of at any cost; or they are useful, and therefore in temporary and partial relation to us, becoming burdensome when their utility is lost; or they are like wandering vagabonds, loitering for a moment on the outskirts of our recognition, and then passing on. A thing is only completely our own when it is a thing of joy to us.
**RABINDRANATH TAGORE**

"On with the dance, let joy be unconfined" is my motto, whether there's a dance to dance or any joy to unconfine.
**MARK TWAIN**

Joy is the life of man's life.
**BENJAMIN WHICHCOTE**

## Judgment

What we do not understand we have no right to judge.
**HENRI FRÉDÉRIC AMIEL**

A good way to judge people is by observing how they treat those who can do them absolutely no good.
**ANONYMOUS**

Property may be destroyed and money may lose its purchasing power; but, character, health, knowledge and good judgment will always be in demand under all conditions.
**ROGER W. BABSON**

Discretion of speech is more than eloquence.
**FRANCIS BACON**

Three things you can be judged by, your voice, your face and your disposition.
**IGNAS BERNSTEIN**

Discretion is the perfection of reason, and a guide to us in all the duties of life. It is only found in men of sound sense and understanding.
**JEAN DE LA BRUYÈRE**

I shall tell you a great secret, my friend. Do not wait for the last judgment, it takes place very day.
**ALBERT CAMUS**

He who has the judge for his father goes into court with an easy mind.
**MIGUEL DE CERVANTES**

Good and bad luck is a synonym in the great majority of instances, for good and bad judgment.
**JOHN CHATFIELD**

In order to judge of the inside of others, study your own; for men in general are very much alike, and though one has one prevailing passion, and another has another, yet their operations are much the same; and whatever engages or disgusts, pleases, or offends you in others will engage, disgust, please or offend others in you.
**LORD CHESTERFIELD**

Statistics are no substitute for judgment.
**HENRY CLAY**

Do not condemn the judgment of another because it differs from your own. You may both be wrong.
**DANDEMIS**

He that opposes his own judgment against the consent of the times ought to be backed with unanswerable truths; and he that has truth on his side is a fool as well as a coward if he is afraid to own it because of other men's opinions.
**DANIEL DEFOE**

Let us hear the conclusion of the whole matter: Fear God, and keep his commandments: for this is the whole duty of man. For God shall bring every work into judgment, with every secret thing, whether it be good, or whether it be evil.
**ECCLESIASTES 12:13–14**

Trust also your own judgement, for it is your most reliable counselor. A man's mind has sometimes a

way of telling him more then seven watchmen posted on a high tower.
**ECCLESIASTICUS**

As in walking it is your great care not to run your foot upon a nail, or to tread awry, and strain your leg; so let it be in all the affairs of human life, not to hurt your mind or offend your judgment. And this rule, if observed carefully in all your deportment, will be a mighty security to you in your undertakings.
**EPICTETUS**

Sound judgment, with discernment, is the best of seers.
**EURIPIDES**

Associate with men of judgment, for judgment is found in conversation, and we make another man's judgment ours by frequenting his company.
**THOMAS FULLER**

Great ability without discretion comes almost invariably to a tragic end.
**LÉON-MICHEL GAMBETTA**

At twenty years of age the will resigns; at thirty, the wit; and at forty, the judgment.
**BALTASAR GRACIÁN**

Sum up at night what thou hast done by day, and in the morning what thou hast to do; dress and undress thy soul; mark the decay or growth of it. If with thy watch, that too be down, then wind up both. Since thou shalt be most surely judged, make thine accounts agree.
**LORD HERBERT**

Learn to depend upon yourself by doing things in accordance with your own way of thinking. Make your judgment trustworthy by trusting it. Cultivate regular periods of silence and meditation. The best time to build judgment is in solitude, when you can think out things for yourself without the probability of interruption.
**GRENVILLE KLEISER**

Judgment of the people is often wiser than the wisest men.
**LOUIS KOSSUTH**

A business man's judgment is no better than his information.
**ROBERT P. LAMONT**

Heat and animosity, contest and conflict may sharpen the wits, although they rarely do; they never strengthen the understanding, clear the perspicacity, guide the judgment, or improve the heart.
**WALTER SAVAGE LANDOR**

Ye shall do no unrighteousness in judgment: thou shalt not respect the person of the poor, nor honour the person of the mighty: but in righteousness shalt thou judge thy neighbour.
**LEVITICUS 19:15**

We judge ourselves by what we feel capable of doing, while others judge us by what we have already done.
**HENRY WADSWORTH LONGFELLOW**

True scholarship consists in knowing not what things exist, but what they mean; it is not memory but judgment.
**JAMES RUSSELL LOWELL**

Judge not, that ye be not judged. For with what judgment ye judge, ye shall be judged: and with what measure ye mete, it shall be measured to you again.
**MATTHEW 7:1–2**

Often a dash of judgment is better than a flash of genius.
**HOWARD W. NEWTON**

It is not permitted to the most equitable of men to be a judge in his own cause.
**BLAISE PASCAL**

He that judges not well of the importance of his affairs, though he may be always busy, he must make but a small progress.
**WILLIAM PENN**

Knowledge is the treasure, but judgment is the treasurer of a wise man.
**WILLIAM PENN**

Middle age is when the best exercise is one of discretion.
**LAURENCE J. PETER**

Let us not therefore judge one another any more: but judge this rather, that no man put a stumbling-block or an occasion to fall in his brother's way.
**ROMANS 14:13**

Of all the intellectual faculties, judgment is the last to mature. A child under the age of 15 should confine its attention either to subjects like mathematics, in which errors of judgment are impossible, or to subjects in which they are not very dangerous, like languages, natural science, history, etc.
**ARTHUR SCHOPENHAUER**

A right judgment draws us a profit from all things we see.
**WILLIAM SHAKESPEARE**

While actions are always to be judged by the immutable standard of right and wrong, the judgment we pass upon men must be qualified by considerations of age, country, situation, and other incidental circumstances; and it will then be found, that he who is most charitable in his judgment, is generally the least unjust.
**ROBERT SOUTHEY**

How little do they see what really is, who frame their hasty judgment upon that which seems.
**ROBERT SOUTHEY**

We do not judge men by what they are in themselves, but by what they are relatively to us.
**ANNE SWETCHINE**

Good judgment (like wisdom) requires careful appraisal of all three sides of the decision cube. Only a human computer with five sensory inputs, electro-biochemical memory core, plus a volition-laden imagination can do this. Industry hasn't been able to produce a like system yet. It is called the Model 1 Homo Sapiens.
**W. SIDNEY TAYLOR**

No man was ever endowed with a judgment so correct and judicious in regulating his life but that circumstances, time and experience would teach him something new, and apprise him that of those things with which he thought himself the best acquainted he knew nothing; and that those ideas which in theory appeared the most advantageous, were found, when brought into practice, to be altogether inapplicable.
**TERENCE**

Your best hope for success is that your associates aren't as good at judging you as you are at judging them.
**FRANK TYGER**

Judge a man by his questions rather than his answers.
**VOLTAIRE**

Be discreet in all things, and so render it unnecessary to be mysterious about any.
**DUKE OF WELLINGTON**

I mistrust the judgment of every man in a case in which his own wishes are concerned.
**DUKE OF WELLINGTON**

One cool judgment is worth a thousand hasty councils. The thing to do is to supply light and not heat.
**WOODROW WILSON**

## Justice

In the same degree that we overrate ourselves, we shall underrate others; for injustice allowed at home is not likely to be correct abroad.
**WASHINGTON ALLSTON**

Every man loves justice at another man's expense.
**ANONYMOUS**

Justice is a certain rectitude of mind whereby a man does what he ought to do in the circumstances confronting him.
**THOMAS AQUINAS**

By the just we mean that which is lawful and that which is fair and equitable.
**ARISTOTLE**

The greatest injustices proceed from those who pursue excess, not by those who are driven by necessity.
**ARISTOTLE**

If we do not maintain justice, justice will not maintain us.
**FRANCIS BACON**

Above all do not ask that justice be just: It is just, because it is justice. The idea of a just justice could have originated only in the brain of an anarchist.
**HONORÉ DE BALZAC**

Somehow, our sense of justice never turns in its sleep till long after the sense of injustice in others has been thoroughly aroused.
**MAX BEERBOHM**

Justice! Custodian of the world! But since the world errs, justice must be custodian of the world's errors.
**UGO BETTI**

Justice: a commodity which in a more or less adulterated condition the State sells to the citizen as a reward for his allegiance, taxes and personal service.
**AMBROSE BIERCE**

Many slow and sly deceptions
Make the justice system skew;
Due process, when thus maneuvered,
Thwarts the justice that is due.
**ART BUCK**

There's no surer justice in the world than that which makes the rich thief hang the poor one.
**PEIRE CARDENAL**

Justice consists in doing no injury to men; decency in giving them no offence.
**CICERO**

The aim of justice is to give everyone his due.
**CICERO**

All are not just because they do no wrong; but he who will not wrong me when he may, he is truly just.
**RICHARD CUMBERLAND**

There is no such thing as justice—in or out of court.
**CLARENCE DARROW**

Justice is always violent to the party offending, for each man is innocent in his own eyes.
**DANIEL DEFOE**

It is not possible to found a lasting power upon injustice, perjury, and treachery.
**DEMOSTHENES**

America can continue to be the source of emotional and moral strength for the world on one condition. That condition is that this nation stays prosperous, progressive, civilized; that our program of justice moves progressively forward; that we continue to reduce the areas of injustice within our borders. The great challenge of the century is to find ways and means of extending a practical program of justice to the farthest reaches of the world.
**WILLIAM O. DOUGLAS**

I tell ye Hogan's r-right whin he says "Justice is blind." Blind she is, an' deef an' dumb an' has a wooden leg!
**FINLEY PETER DUNNE**

A man is a little thing while he works by and for himself; but when he gives voice to the rules of love and justice, he is godlike.
**RALPH WALDO EMERSON**

Just definitions either prevent or put an end to disputes.
**NATHANIEL EMMONS**

There is no such thing as justice in the abstract; it is merely a compact between men.
**EPICURUS**

Above all other things is justice. Success is a good thing; wealth is good also; honor is better, but justice excels them all.
**DAVID DUDLEY FIELD**

It is impossible to find twelve fair men in all the world.
**W. C. FIELDS**

Most everyone wants to do what's fair, right, and good, but knowing what is is often the tough part.
**MALCOLM FORBES**

Righteousness, or justice, is undoubtedly of all the virtues, the surest foundation on which to create and establish a new state. But there are two nobler virtues, industry and frugality, which tend more to increase the wealth, power and grandeur of the community, than all the others without them.
**BENJAMIN FRANKLIN**

Justice is as strictly due between neighbor nations as between neighbor citizens.
**BENJAMIN FRANKLIN**

Justice is a machine that, when someone has given it a starting push, rolls on of itself.
**JOHN GALSWORTHY**

We win justice quickest by rendering justice to the other party.
**MAHATMA GANDHI**

Justice delayed, is justice denied.
**WILLIAM E. GLADSTONE**

If we are to keep our democracy, there must be one commandment: Thou shalt not ration justice.
**LEARNED HAND**

The man who wears injustice by his side, though powerful millions followed him to war, combats against the odds—against high heaven.
**WILLIAM HAVARD**

We ought always to deal justly, not only with those who are just to us, but likewise to those who endeavor to injure us; and this, for fear lest by rendering them evil for evil, we should fall into the same vice.
**HIEROCLES**

If you study the history and records of the world, you must admit that the source of justice was the fear of injustice.
HORACE

Mankind are always found prodigal both of blood and treasure in the maintenance of public justice.
DAVID HUME

Justice should remove the bandage from her eyes long enough to distinguish between the vicious and the unfortunate.
ROBERT G. INGERSOLL

Thus saith the Lord: Execute ye justice and righteousness, and deliver the spoiled out of the hand of the oppressor: and do no wrong, do no violence to the stranger, the fatherless, nor the widow, neither shed innocent blood in this place.
JEREMIAH 22:3

To embarrass justice by a multiplicity of laws, or to hazard it by confidence in judges, are the opposite rocks on which all civil institutions have been wrecked, and between which legislative wisdom has never yet found an open passage.
JOHNSON

Justice is the constant desire and effort to render to every man his due.
JUSTINIAN

Justice: A decision in your favor.
HARRY KAUFMAN

Nobody is poor unless he stands in need of justice.
LACTANTIUS

Injustice is relatively easy to bear; what stings is justice.
H. L. MENCKEN

He hath shewed thee, O man, what is good; and what doth the Lord require of thee, but to do justly, and to love mercy, and to walk humbly with thy God?
MICAH 6:8

If mankind does not relinquish at once, and forever, its vain, mad and fatal dream of justice, the world will lapse into barbarism.
GEORGE MOORE

Force without justice is tyrannical; justice without force is impotent.
BLAISE PASCAL

Justice and power must be brought together, so that whatever is just may be powerful, and whatever is powerful may be just.
BLAISE PASCAL

Justice is the insurance we have on our lives, and obedience is the premium we pay for it.
WILLIAM PENN

To heal the breach between the rich and the poor, it is necessary to distinguish between justice and charity.
POPE PIUS X

Justice is a faculty that may be developed. This development is what constitutes the education of the human race.
P. J. PROUDHON

Justice is spontaneous respect, mutually guaranteed, for human dignity, in whatever person it may be compromised and under whatever circumstances, and to whatever risk its defense may expose us.
P. J. PROUDHON

No cause is hopeless if it is just. Errors, no matter how popular, carry the seeds of their own destruction.
JOHN W. SCOVILLE

Justice is conscience, not a personal conscience but a conscience of the whole of humanity. Those who clearly recognize the voice of their own conscience usually recognize also the voice of justice.
ALEKSANDR SOLZHENITSYN

There is a point at which even justice does injury.
SOPHOCLES

Justice remains the greatest power on earth. To that tremendous power alone will we submit.
HARRY S TRUMAN

The rain falls upon the just and the unjust alike; a thing which would not happen if I were superintending the rain's affairs. No, I would rain softly and sweetly on the just, but if I caught a sample of the unjust outdoors I would drown him.
MARK TWAIN

To withdraw ourselves from the law of the strong, we have found ourselves obliged to submit to justice. Justice or might, we must choose between these two masters.
MARQUIS DE VAUVENARGUES

It is better to risk saving a guilty man than to condemn an innocent one.
VOLTAIRE

Justice is the great interest of man on earth. It is a ligament which holds civilized beings and civilized nations together.
DANIEL WEBSTER

No government is respectable which is not just. Without unspotted purity of public faith, without sacred, public principle, fidelity and honor, no mere forms of government, no machinery of laws, can give dignity to political society.
DANIEL WEBSTER

Judging from the main portions of the history of the world, so far, justice is always in jeopardy.
WALT WHITMAN

One should always play fairly when one has the winning cards.
OSCAR WILDE

Has justice ever grown in the soil of absolute power? Has not justice always come from the . . . heart and spirit of men who resist power?
WOODROW WILSON

The nature of men and of organized society dictates the maintenance in every field of action of the highest and purest standards of justice and of right dealing. . . . By justice the lawyer generally means the prompt, fair, and open application of impartial rules; but we call ours a Christian civilization, and a Christian conception of justice must be much higher. It must include sympathy and helpfulness and a willingness to forego self-interest in order to promote the welfare, happiness, and contentment of others and of the community as a whole.
WOODROW WILSON

We need justice. We need toleration, honesty and moral courage. These are modern virtues without which we cannot hope to control the forces science has let loose among us.
I. A. R. WYLIE

# K

## Kindness

Courtesy is the shortest distance between two people.
ANONYMOUS

God is not kind to those who are not kind to others.
ARABIAN PROVERB

He who is devoid of kindness is devoid of grace.
ARABIAN PROVERB

If a man be gracious to strangers, it shows that he is a citizen of the world, and his heart is no island, cut off from other islands, but a continent that joins them.
FRANCIS BACON

Kindness is wisdom; there is none in life but needs it, and may learn.
GAMALIEL BAILEY

When you teach kindness to animals, you teach reverence for life in general. The youngster who is taught concern for animals will grow up being kind to his fellow man. It follows, too, that he will not become callous to widespread suffering in any form.
BERNARD BECK

We may scatter the seeds of courtesy and kindness about us at little expense. Some of them will fall on good ground, and grow up into benevolence in the minds of others, and all of them will bear fruit of happiness in the bosom whence they spring.
JEREMY BENTHAM

A man's greatness is measured by his kindness—
A man's education and intellect by his modesty—
A man's ignorance is betrayed by his suspicions and prejudices.
His real caliber is measured by the consideration and tolerance he has for others.
WILLIAM J. H. BOETCKER

Kindness is a language the dumb can speak and the deaf can hear and understand.
CHRISTIAN BOVÉE

He who sows courtesy reaps friendship, and he who plants kindness gathers love.
RICHARD BROOKS

Of all the virtues necessary to the completion of the perfect man, there is none to be more delicately implied and less ostentatiously vaunted than that of exquisite feeling or universal benevolence.
EDWARD BULWER-LYTTON

If you treat with courtesy your equal, who is privileged to resent an impertinence, how much more cautious should you be to your dependents, from whom you demand a respectful demeanor.
A. W. CHAMBERS

I often wonder why people do not make more of the marvelous power there is in kindness. It is the greatest lever to move the hearts of men that the world has ever known—greater by far than anything that mere ingenuity can devise or subtlety suggest. Kindness is the kingpin of success in life; it is the prime factor in overcoming friction and making the human machinery run smoothly.
ANDREW CHAPMAN

If I keep a green bough in my heart, the singing bird will come.
**CHINESE PROVERB**

He who acknowledges a kindness has it still, and he who has a grateful sense of it has requited it.
**CICERO**

I believe in courtesy, the ritual by which we avoid hurting other people's feelings by satisfying our own egos.
**KENNETH CLARK**

Kindness is lost that's bestowed on children and old folks.
**JOHN CLARKE**

The more courtesy, the more craft.
**JOHN CLARKE**

In all the affairs of life, social as well as political, courtesies of a small and trivial character are the ones which strike deepest in the grateful and appreciating heart.
**HENRY CLAY**

The more kindness we heap upon one who hates us, the more we arm him to betray us.
**PIERRE CORNEILLE**

Life is made up, not of great sacrifices or duties, but of little things, in which smiles and kindness, and small obligations given habitually, are what preserve the heart and secure comfort.
**SIR HUMPHRY DAVY**

Amiable people, though often subject to imposition in their contact with the world, yet radiate so much of sunshine that they are reflected in all appreciative hearts.
**DOROTHÉE DELUZY**

I wonder why it is that we are not all kinder to each other than we are. How much the world needs it! How easily it is done!
**HENRY DRUMMOND**

What do we live for if it is not to make life less difficult for each other?
**GEORGE ELIOT**

To adorn our characters by the charm of an amiable nature shows at once a lover of beauty and a lover of man.
**EPICTETUS**

Little self-denials, little honesties, little passing words of sympathy, little nameless acts of kindness, little silent victories over favorite temptations—these are the silent threads of gold which, when woven together, gleam out so brightly in the pattern of life that God approved.
**FREDERICK W. FARRAR**

The prudence of the best heads is often defeated by the tenderness of the best hearts.
**HENRY FIELDING**

Courtesy gives its owner a passport round the world. It transmutes aliens into trusting friends.
**JAMES THOMAS FIELDS**

Courtesy is doing that which nothing under the sun makes you do but human kindness. Courtesy springs from the heart; if the mind prompts the action, there is a reason; if there be a reason, it is not courtesy, for courtesy has no reason. Courtesy is good will, and good will is prompted by the heart full of love to be kind. Only the generous man is truly courteous. He gives freely without a thought of receiving anything in return.
**B. C. FORBES**

What one thing does the world need most today—apart, that is, from the all-inclusive thing we call righteousness? Aren't you inclined to agree that what this old world needs is just the art of being kind? Every time I visit a factory or any other large business concern, I find myself trying to diagnose whether the atmosphere is one of kindliness or the reverse. And somehow, if there is palpably lacking that spirit of kindness, the owners . . . have fallen short of achieving 24-carat success no matter how imposing the financial balance sheet may be.
**B. C. FORBES**

Contrary to the cliché, genuinely nice guys most often finish first or very near it.
**MALCOLM FORBES**

All doors are open to courtesy.
**THOMAS FULLER**

The old Quaker was right: "I expect to pass through life but once. If there is any kindness, or any good thing I can do to my fellow beings, let me do it now. I shall pass this way but once."
**W. C. GANNETT**

Kindness is the golden chain by which society is bound together.
**JOHANN WOLFGANG VON GOETHE**

Kind looks, kind words, kind acts, and warm handshakes—these are secondary means of grace when men are in trouble and are fighting their unseen battles.
**JOHN HALL**

A man may fight fiercely to hold his own in business; but he does not need to fight to get ahead of someone in the elevator, or up the car steps, or at the postoffice window. And no matter how strong competition is, business and personal courtesy make it easier and pleasanter for everybody.
**WILLIAM H. HAMBY**

Kindness is the beginning and the end of the law.
**HEBREW PROVERB**

Be kind and considerate to others, depending somewhat upon who they are.
**DON HEROLD**

One difference between savagery and civilization is a little courtesy.
There's no telling what a lot of courtesy would do.
**CULLEN HIGHTOWER**

A happy life is made up of little things in which smiles and small favors are given habitually. A gift sent, a letter written, a call made, a recommendation given, transportation provided, a cake made, a book lent, a check sent—things which are done without hesitation. Kindness isn't sacrifice so much as it is being considerate for the feelings of others, sharing happiness, the unselfish thought, the spontaneous and friendly act, forgetfulness of our own present interests.
**CARL HOLMES**

One kind word can warm three winter months.
**JAPANESE PROVERB**

To act from pure benevolence is not possible for finite beings. Human benevolence is mingled with vanity, interest or some other motive.
**SAMUEL JOHNSON**

A part of kindness consists in loving people more than they deserve.
**JOSEPH JOUBERT**

Beneficence is a duty; and he who frequently practices it, and sees his benevolent intentions realized comes, at length, really to love him to whom he has done good.
IMMANUEL KANT

Small kindnesses, small courtesies, small considerations, habitually practiced in our social intercourse, give a greater charm to the character than the display of great talent and accomplishments.
KELTY

The habit of being uniformly considerate toward others will bring increased happiness to you. As you put into practice the qualities of patience, punctuality, sincerity and solicitude, you will have a better opinion of the world about you.
GRENVILLE KLEISER

Kindness in ourselves is the honey that blunts the sting of unkindness in another.
WALTER SAVAGE LANDOR

I have three precious things which I hold fast and prize. The first is gentleness; the second is frugality; the third is humility, which keeps me from putting myself before others. Be gentle and you can be bold; be frugal and you can be liberal; avoid putting yourself before others and you can become a leader among men.
LAO-TZU

Kindness in words creates confidence, kindness in thinking creates profoundness, kindness in giving creates love.
LAO-TZU

Be kind; every man you meet is fighting a hard battle.
IAN MACLAREN

After years of living with the coldest realities I still believe that one reaps what one sows and that to sow kindness is the best of all investments.
JOSEPH W. MARTIN, JR.

Benevolence is one of the distinguishing characters of man.
MENCIUS

If you have not often felt the joy of doing a kind act, you have neglected much, and most of all yourself.
A. NEILEN

Grace is indeed required to turn a man into a saint; and he who doubts this does not know what either a man or a saint is.
BLAISE PASCAL

Kind words do not cost much. They never blister the tongue or lips. Mental trouble was never known to arise from such quarters. Though they do not cost much yet they accomplish much. They make other people good natured. They also produce their own image on men's souls, and a beautiful image it is.
BLAISE PASCAL

I expect to pass through life but once. If, therefore, there be any kindness I can show, or any good thing I can do to any fellow-being, let me do it now, and not defer or neglect it, as I shall not pass this way again.
WILLIAM PENN

Let me hear thy loving-kindness in the morning; for in thee do I trust: cause me to know the way wherein I should walk; for I lift up my soul unto thee.
PSALMS 143:8

The principle of liberty and equality, if coupled with mere selfishness, will make men only devils,

each trying to be independent that he may fight only for his own interest. And here is the need of religion and its power, to bring in the principle of benevolence and love to men.
**JOHN RANDOLPH**

The last, best fruit which comes to late perfection, even in the kindliest soul, is tenderness toward the hard, forbearance toward the unforbearing, warmth of heart toward the cold, philanthropy toward the misanthropic.
**JEAN PAUL RICHTER**

Grace is to the body what clear thinking is to the mind.
**FRANÇOIS DE LA ROCHEFOUCAULD**

We should only affect compassion, and carefully avoid having any.
**FRANÇOIS DE LA ROCHEFOUCAULD**

Gentle to others, to himself severe.
**SAMUEL ROGERS**

Human kindness has never weakened the stamina or softened the fiber of a free people. A nation does not have to be cruel to be tough.
**FRANKLIN D. ROOSEVELT**

Use a sweet tongue, courtesy, and gentleness, and thou mayst manage to guide an elephant with a hair.
**SA'DI**

Guard within yourself that treasure kindness. Know how to give without hesitation, how to lose without regret, how to acquire without meanness.
**GEORGE SAND**

Among the qualities of mind and heart which conduce to worldly success, there is one, the importance of which is more real, and which is generally underrated in our day. . . . It is courtesy.
**HERBERT SCHIFFER**

Kindness works simply and perseveringly; it produces no strained relations which prejudice its working; strained relations which already exist it relaxes. Mistrust and misunderstanding it puts to flight, and it strengthens itself by calling forth answering kindness. Hence it is the furthest reaching and the most effective of all forces.
**ALBERT SCHWEITZER**

I had rather never receive a kindness than never bestow one.
**SENECA**

Wherever there is a human being there is a chance for kindness.
**SENECA**

Consideration is not merely a matter of emotional goodwill but of intellectual vigor and moral self-sacrifice. Wisdom must combine with sympathy. That is why consideration underlies the phrase a scholar and a gentleman, which really sums up the ideal of the output of a college education.
**CHARLES SEYMOUR**

Dissembling courtesy! How fine this tyrant can trickle when she wounds!
**WILLIAM SHAKESPEARE**

In nature there's no blemish but the mind; none can be call'd deform'd but the unkind.
**WILLIAM SHAKESPEARE**

What would you have? Your gentleness shall force more than your force move us to gentleness.
**WILLIAM SHAKESPEARE**

Compassion is the fellow-feeling of the unsound.
**GEORGE BERNARD SHAW**

A churlish courtesy rarely comes but either for gain or falsehood.
**SIR PHILIP SIDNEY**

The only true source of politeness is consideration—that vigilant moral sense which never loses sight of the rights, the claims and the sensibilities of others.
**WILLIAM SIMMS**

You have not lived a perfect day, even though you have earned your money; unless you have done something for someone who will never be able to repay you.
**RUTH SMELTZER**

There never was any heart truly great and generous, that was not also tender and compassionate.
**ROBERT SOUTHEY**

The value of compassion cannot be over-emphasized. Anyone can criticize. It takes a true believer to be compassionate. No greater burden can be born by an individual than to know no one cares or understands.
**ARTHUR H. STAINBACK, D.D.**

That should be considered long which can be decided but once.
**PUBLILIUS SYRUS**

Kindness is very indigestible. It disagrees with very proud stomachs.
**WILLIAM MAKEPEACE THACKERAY**

Never lose a chance of saying a kind word. As Collingwood never saw a vacant place in his estate but he took an acorn out of his pocket and planted it, so deal with your compliments through life. An acorn costs nothing, but it may spread into a prodigious timber.
**WILLIAM MAKEPEACE THACKERAY**

Kindness is the one commodity of which you should spend more than you earn.
**T. N. TIEMEYER**

High station in life is earned by the gallantry with which appalling experiences are survived with grace.
**TENNESSEE WILLIAMS**

Nothing is ever lost by courtesy. It is the cheapest of the pleasures; costs nothing and conveys much. It pleases him who gives and him who receives, and thus, like mercy, is twice blessed.
**ERASTUS WIMAN**

The best portion of a good man's life is his little, nameless, unremembered acts of kindness and of love.
**WILLIAM WORDSWORTH**

All values in this world are more or less questionable, but the most important thing in life is human kindness.
**YEVGENY YEVTUSHENKO**

## *Knowledge*

I find that a great part of the information I have was acquired by looking up something and finding something else on the way.
**FRANKLIN P. ADAMS**

You are your greatest investment. The more you store in that mind of yours, the more you enrich your experience, the more people you meet, the more books you read, and the more places you visit, the greater is that investment in all that you are.

Everything that you add to your peace of mind, and to your outlook upon life, is added capital that no one but yourself can dissipate.
GEORGE MATTHEW ADAMS

Knowledge is free at the library. Just bring your own container
ANONYMOUS

People who think they know it all are especially annoying to those of us who do.
ANONYMOUS

Say what you mean, mean what you say, but don't say it mean.
ANONYMOUS

Real knowledge, like everything else of the highest value, is not to be obtained easily. It must be worked for, studied for, thought for, and, more than all, it must be prayed for.
THOMAS ARNOLD

What is all our knowledge worth? We do not even know what the weather will be tomorrow.
BERTHOLD AUERBACH

To wisdom belongs the intellectual apprehension of eternal things; to knowledge, the rational knowledge of temporal things.
ST. AUGUSTINE

Knowledge and human power are synonymous, since the ignorance of the cause frustrates the effect.
FRANCIS BACON

I am not young enough to know everything.
JAMES M. BARRIE

Every day increases the sheer weight of knowledge put into our hands, some new power control over natural processes. . . . Our age is being forcibly reminded that knowledge is no substitute for wisdom. Far and away the most important thing in human life is living it.
FRANK R. BARRY

Of true knowledge at any time, a good part is merely convenient, necessary indeed to the worker, but not to an understanding of his subject: One can judge a building without knowing where to buy the bricks; one can understand a violin sonata without knowing how to score for the instrument. The work may in fact be better understood without a knowledge of the details of its manufacture, for attention to these tends to distract from meaning and effect.
JACQUES BARZUN

Mediocre men often have the most acquired knowledge.
CLAUDE BERNARD

To the small part of ignorance that we arrange and classify we give the name knowledge.
AMBROSE BIERCE

The trouble with people is not that they don't know, but that they know so much that ain't so.
JOSH BILLINGS

It is right it should be so;
Man was made for joy and woe;
And when this we rightly know
Through the world we safely go.
WILLIAM BLAKE

The quest for knowledge and the application of that knowledge for man's benefit will not be denied.
ROGER M. BLOUGH

What a man knows should find expression in what he does. The chief value of superior knowledge is that it leads to a performing manhood.
CHRISTIAN BOVÉE

Most men believe that it would benefit them if they could get a little from those who have more. How much more would it benefit them if they would learn a little from those who know more.
WILLIAM J. H. BOETCKER

Some men have a peculiar ability to know and to learn; some men excel others by their ability to have and to earn; some excel in producing things, others in creating ideas. They need each other; one is helpless without the other. This world needs them all.
WILLIAM J. H. BOETCKER

Any kind of knowledge gives a certain amount of power. A knowledge of details has served in many a crisis. A knowledge of details has often caught an error before it became a catastrophe.
AIMEE BUCHANAN

Every branch of knowledge which a good man possesses, he may apply to some good purpose.
CLAUDIUS BUCHANAN

The dissemination of information is one of the corner-stones of modern civilization.
JOHN F. BUDD

Knowledge cannot be stolen from us. It cannot be bought or sold. We may be poor, and the sheriff may come and sell our furniture, or drive away our cow, or take our pet lamb, and leave us homeless and penniless; but he cannot lay the law's hand upon the jewelry of our minds.
ELIHU BURRITT

A little knowledge is a dangerous thing, but a little want of knowledge is also a dangerous thing.
SAMUEL BUTLER

One of the principal challenges of our world to the individual is that he must not only achieve a fairly high degree of specialization to make him a useful member of society, but at the same time achieve enough general knowledge to enable him to look with sympathy and understanding on what is going on about him.
OLIVER J. CALDWELL

If you don't realize there is always somebody who knows how to do something better than you, then you don't give proper respects for others' talents.
HORTENSE CANADY

I've learned one thing—people who know the least anyways seem to know it the loudest.
ANDY CAPP

In every object there is inexhaustible meaning; the eye sees in it what the eye brings means of seeing.
THOMAS CARLYLE

Knowledge conquered by labor becomes a possession—a property entirely our own. A greater vividness and permanency of impression is secured, and facts thus acquired become registered in the mind in a way that mere imparted information can never produce.
THOMAS CARLYLE

Knowledge is a comfortable and necessary retreat and shelter for us in an advanced age; and if we do not plant it while young, it will give us no shade when we grow old.
LORD CHESTERFIELD

Learning is acquired by reading books; but the much more necessary learning, the knowledge of the world, is only to be acquired by reading men, and studying all the various editions of them.
LORD CHESTERFIELD

There is hardly any place or any company where you may not gain knowledge, if you please; almost everybody knows some one thing, and is glad to talk about that one thing.
LORD CHESTERFIELD

Do not try to entrap others with your haughty knowledge. To your wide surprise, they will entrap you with their lengthy ignorance.
SRI CHINMOY

Knowledge is the only instrument of production that is not subject to diminishing returns.
J. M. CLARK

Pleasure is a shadow, wealth is vanity, and power a pageant; but knowledge is ecstatic in enjoyment, perennial in frame, unlimited in space and indefinite in duration.
DE WITT CLINTON

The worth and value of knowledge is in proportion to the worth and value of its object.
SAMUEL TAYLOR COLERIDGE

He that studies only men, will get the body of knowledge without the soul, and he that studies only books, the soul without the body. He that to what he sees, adds observation, and to what he reads, reflection, is on the right road to knowledge, provided that in scrutinizing the hearts of others, he neglects not his own.
CHARLES CALEB COLTON

To know what we know what we know, and that we do not know what we do not know, that is true knowledge.
CONFUCIUS

One part of knowledge consists in being ignorant of such things that are not worthy of being known.
CRATES

Each new development starts from something else. It does not come out of a blue sky. You make use of that which has already entered the mind. . . . That is the real reason for accumulating knowledge.
ROBERT P. CRAWFORD

Knowledge dwells in heads replete with thoughts of other men; wisdom in minds attentive to their own.
WILLIAM COWPER

A greater poverty than that caused by lack of money is the poverty of unawareness. Men and women go about the world unaware of the beauty, the goodness, the glories in it. Their souls are poor. It is better to have a poor pocketbook than to suffer from a poor soul.
THOMAS DREIER

Herein lies the tragedy of the age: not that men are poor—all men know something of poverty; not that men are wicked—who is good? Not that men are ignorant—what is truth? Nay, but that men know so little of men.
W. E. B. DU BOIS

Knowledge is the eye of desire and can become the pilot of the soul.
WILL DURANT

Knowledge—full, unfettered knowledge of its own heritage, of freedom's enemies, of the whole world of men and ideas—this knowledge is a free people's surest strength.
DWIGHT D. EISENHOWER

Through knowledge and understanding we will drive from the temple of freedom all who seek to establish over us thought control—whether they be agents of a foreign power or demagogues thirsty for personal power and public notice.
DWIGHT D. EISENHOWER

To each individual the world will take on a different connotation of meaning—the important lies in the desire to search for an answer.
**T. S. Eliot**

We know too much, and are convinced of too little.
**T. S. Eliot**

Where is the wisdom we have lost in knowledge?
**T. S. Eliot**

Knowledge is the antidote to fear.
**Ralph Waldo Emerson**

Men of vision caught glimpses of truth and beauty shining aloft like stars: and in these glimpses was a new hope for the unification of mankind through enlightenment.
**Sir Robert Falconer**

It is no good to try to stop knowledge from going forward. Ignorance is never better than knowledge.
**Enrico Fermi**

I know what I can know, and am not troubled about what I cannot know.
**Johann Fichte**

Experts kill me. Economic experts, that is. Corporations, foundations, publications and governments pay them by the bucketful, and they fill buckets with forecasts that change more frequently than white-collar workers do shirts. "What Lies Ahead" is the usual title. "What Lies" would often be more appropriate. If women's hemlines changed as rapidly as an economist's forecasts, the fashion people and the textile industry would be more profitable than any other. In fact, if all the country's economists were laid end to end, they still wouldn't reach a conclusion.
**Malcolm Forbes**

If you don't know, it's not always necessary to admit it.
**Malcolm Forbes**

Those who act as if they know more than their boss seldom do.
**Malcolm Forbes**

If money is your only hope for independence, you will never have it. The only real security that a man can have in this world is a reserve of knowledge, experience and ability.
**Henry Ford**

It is well for the heart to be naïve and for the mind not to be.
**Anatole France**

If a man empties his purse into his head, no one can take it away from him. An investment in knowledge always pays the best interest.
**Benjamin Franklin**

The saying that knowledge is power is not quite true. *Used* knowledge is power, and more than power. It is money, and service, and better living for our fellowmen, and a hundred other good things. But mere knowledge, left unused, has not power in it.
**Edward E. Free**

He that sips of many arts, drinks of none.
**Thomas Fuller**

If you have knowledge, let others light their candles at it.
**Margaret Fuller**

Knowledge is a treasure but practice is the key to it.
**Thomas Fuller**

'Tis not knowing much, but what is useful, that makes a wise man.
THOMAS FULLER

Knowledge doesn't pay—it is what you do with it.
ARNOLD GLASOW

Knowledge is more valuable than morals.
MAXIM GORKY

Knowledge and courage take turns at greatness.
BALTASAR GRACIÁN

Head knowledge is good, but heart knowledge is indispensable. The training of the hands and feet must be added to make a rounded education. We must all learn these days to become spiritual pioneers if we would save the world from chaos.
E. V. HAMMOND

Infinite toil would not enable you to sweep away a mist; but by ascending a little you may often look over it altogether.
ARTHUR HELPS

Who is so deaf or so blind as is he that willfully will neither hear nor see?
JOHN HEYWOOD

He is wise who knows the sources of knowledge—who knows who has written and where it is to be found.
A. A. HODGE

Every year we have to wager our salvation on some prophecy based on imperfect knowledge.
OLIVER WENDELL HOLMES

The best part of our knowledge is that which teaches us where knowledge leaves off and ignorance begins.
OLIVER WENDELL HOLMES

An expert is a man who knows just that much more about his subject than his associates. Most of us are nearer the top than we think. We fail to realize how easy it is, how necessary it is to learn that fraction more.
WILLIAM N. HUTCHINS

If a little knowledge is dangerous, where is the man who has so much as to be out of danger?
THOMAS H. HUXLEY

For since the beginning of the world men have not heard, nor perceived by the ear, neither hath the eye seen, O God, beside thee, what he hath prepared for him that waiteth for him.
ISAIAH 64:4

If you love knowledge, you will be a master of knowledge. What you have come to know, pursue by exercise; what you have not learned, seek to add to your knowledge, for it is as reprehensible to hear a profitable saying and not grasp it as to be offered a good gift by one's friends and not accept it. Believe that many precepts are better than much wealth, for wealth quickly fails us, but precepts abide through all time.
ISOCRATES

There is no substitute for accurate knowledge. Know yourself, know your business, know your men.
RANDALL JACOBS

It appeareth that however certain forms of government are better calculated than others to protect individuals in the free exercises of their natural rights . . . yet experience hath shown, that even under the best forms, those entrusted with power have, in time, and by slow operations, perverted it into tyranny, and it is believed that the most effectual means of preventing this, would be to illuminate, as far as practicable, the minds of the people at large.
THOMAS JEFFERSON

Man is fed with fables through life, and leaves it in the belief he knows something of what has been passing, when in truth he knows nothing but what has passed under his own eyes.
THOMAS JEFFERSON

See everything. Overlook a great deal, improve a little.
POPE JOHN XXIII

Knowledge always desires increase; it is like fire, which must first be kindled by some external agent, but which will afterwards propagate itself.
JOHNSON

Knowledge is of two kinds. We know a subject ourselves or we know where we can find information upon it.
JOHNSON

Having harvested all the knowledge and wisdom we can from our mistakes and failures, we should put them behind us and go ahead, for vain regretting interferes with the flow of power into our own personalities.
EDITH JOHNSON

A desire of knowledge is the natural feeling of mankind; and every human being whose mind is not debauched will be willing to give all that he has to get knowledge.
SAMUEL JOHNSON

All wish to possess knowledge, but few, comparatively speaking, are willing to pay the price.
JUVENAL

You keep your light so shining a little in front of the next.
RUDYARD KIPLING

A business man's judgment is no better than his information.
ROBERT P. LAMONT

Those who know do not tell; those who tell do not know.
LAO-TZU

Without going out of doors, one may know the whole world, without looking out the window, one may see the way of heaven. The further one travels, the less one may know. Thus it is that without moving you shall know, without looking you shall see, without doing you shall achieve.
LAO-TZU

The color of the object illuminated partakes of the color of that which illuminates it.
LEONARDO DA VINCI

The only people who achieve much are those who want knowledge so badly that they seek it while the conditions are still unfavorable. Favorable conditions never come.
C. S. LEWIS

You generally hear that what a man doesn't know doesn't hurt him, but in business what a man doesn't know does hurt.
E. S. LEWIS

Within the next few years—a decade perhaps—we should be in a position to unlock new knowledge about life and matter so great that wholly new concepts of human life will follow in the wake of this new knowledge.
DAVID E. LILIENTHAL

The improvement of the understanding is for two ends; first, our own increase of knowledge; secondly, to enable us to deliver that knowledge to others.
JOHN LOCKE

What we see depends mainly on what we look for.
JOHN LUBBOCK

It is not lawful or proper for you to know everything.
LUCAN

Knowledge is power only if a man knows what facts not to bother about.
ROBERT LYND

Man can never plumb the depths of his own being; his image is not to be discovered in the extent of the knowledge he acquires but in the questions he asks.
ANDRÉ MALRAUX

It is well when the wise and the learned discover new truths; but how much better to diffuse the truths already discovered amongst the multitudes. Every addition to true knowledge is an addition to human power; and while a philosopher is discovering one new truth, millions of truths may be propagated amongst the people. . . . The whole land must be watered with the streams of knowledge.
HORACE MANN

The mere lapse of years is not life. To eat, to drink and sleep; to be exposed to darkness and the light; to pace around in the mill of habit and turn thought into an instrument of trade—this is not life. Knowledge, truth, love, beauty, goodness, faith, alone can give vitality to the mechanism of existence.
JAMES MARTINEAU

Solitary reading will enable a man to stuff himself with information, but without conversation his mind will become like a pond without an outlet—a mass of unhealthy stag nature. It is not enough to harvest knowledge by study; the wind of talk must winnow it and blow away the chaff. Then will the clear, bright grains of wisdom be garnered, for our own use or that of others.
WILLIAM MATTHEWS

As the age of information demands the simultaneous use of all our faculties, we discover that we are most at leisure when we are most intensely involved.
MARSHALL MCLUHAN

The experience of a century and a half has demonstrated that our system of free government functions best when the maximum degree of information is made available to our people. In fact, free and candid discussion of vexing problems is the bedrock of democracy and it may be our surest safeguard for peace.
BRIEN MCMAHON

"Know thyself" is a good saying, but not in all situations. In many it is better to say "Know others."
MENANDER

Sin, guilt, neurosis—they are one and the same, the fruit of the tree of knowledge.
HENRY MILLER

Fullness of knowledge always and necessarily means some understanding of the depths of our ignorance, and that is always conducive to both humility and reverence.
ROBERT A. MILLIKAN

It is not so important to know everything as to know the exact value of everything, to appreciate what we learn and to arrange what we know.
HANNAH MORE

A well-educated America need not fear the economic future of this country. There are no boundaries, no frontiers, as long as we continue to educate all those who have the potential capacity to use such knowledge intelligently.
WALTER J. MURPHY

If I have seen farther than others, it is because I have stood on the shoulders of giants.
**SIR ISAAC NEWTON**

We don't see things as they are, we see things as we are.
**ANAÏS NIN**

The highest purpose of intellectual cultivation is to give a man a perfect knowledge and mastery of his own inner self.
**NOVALIS**

Is anyone educated in whom the powers of conscious reasoning are untrained or undeveloped, however great may be the store of accumulated knowledge?
**JOSEPH H. ODELL**

It is much better to know something about everything than to know everything about one thing.
**BLAISE PASCAL**

You can't see clearly if you insist on smoking up your glasses.
**AMOS PARRISH**

Thinking leads a man to knowledge. He may see and hear and read and learn whatever he pleases, and as much as he pleases; he will never know anything of it, except as he has thought it over. . . . By thinking he has made it the property of his own mind.
**JOHANN PESTALOZZI**

The cloak of naiveté was the uniform of our success: we didn't know it couldn't be done.
**MARK PETERS**

All knowledge that is divorced from justice must be called cunning.
**PLATO**

Yea, if thou criest after knowledge, and liftest up thy voice for understanding; if thou seekest her as silver, and searchest for her as for hid treasures: Then shalt thou understand the fear of the Lord, and find the knowledge of God.
**PROVERBS 2:3–5**

What harm is there in getting knowledge and learning, were it from a sot, a pot, a fool, a winter mitten or an old slipper.
**FRANÇOIS RABELAIS**

Whether you know the shape of a pebble or the structure of a solar system, the axioms remain the same: that it exists and that you know it.
**AYN RAND**

Try to put well in practice what you already know; and in so doing, you will in good time, discover the hidden things you now inquire about. Practice what you know, and it will help to make clear what now you do not know.
**REMBRANDT**

Useful knowledge is a great support for intuition.
**CHARLES B. ROGERS**

There is much pleasure to be gained from useless knowledge.
**BERTRAND RUSSELL**

Whoever acquires knowledge but does not practice it is as one who ploughs but does not sow.
**SA'DI**

Knowledge alone does not stop men from evil. The poor and the ignorant are not the greatest sinners. Man's mind may unfold, his intellect grow more keen, his understanding more profound, yet side by side with this may be a moral degeneration such as existed in pagan Greece and Rome.
**WILLIAM A. SCULLY, D.D.**

A grain of real knowledge, of genuine controllable conviction, will outweigh a bushel of adroitness; and to produce persuasion there is one golden principle of rhetoric not put down in the books—to understand what you are talking about.
JOHN SEELEY

It is better to have useless knowledge than to know nothing.
SENECA

Consultant: an ordinary guy more than 50 miles from home.
ERIC SEVAREID

The things most people want to know about are usually none of their business.
GEORGE BERNARD SHAW

We don't live in a world of reality, we live in a world of perceptions.
GERALD J. SIMMONS

Though an inheritance of acres may be bequeathed, an inheritance of knowledge and wisdom cannot. The wealthy man may pay others for doing his work for him, but it is impossible to get his thinking done for him by another, or to purchase any kind of self-culture.
SAMUEL SMILES

In all living there is a certain narrowness of application which leads to breadth and power. We have to concentrate on a thing in order to master it. Then we must be broad enough not to be narrowed by our specialties.
RALPH W. SOCKMAN

When a man's knowledge is not in order, the more of it he has the greater will be his confusion.
HERBERT SPENCER

The desire of knowledge, like the thirst of riches, increases ever with the acquisition of it.
LAURENCE STERNE

We can achieve the utmost in economies by engineering knowledge; we can conquer new fields by research; we can build plants and machines that shall stand among the wonders of the world; but unless we put the right man in the right place—unless we make it possible for our workers and executives alike to enjoy a sense of satisfaction in their jobs, our efforts will have been in vain.
EDWARD R. STETTINIUS

The average man on the street needs to know more science today than the teachers knew a generation ago, just to be able to read his newspapers and magazines intelligently. Music, art—those possessions formerly of the fortunate few—now belong to the people. Whatever field of subject matter you name—its content and significance for modern living has doubled, trebled . . . in recent years!
ALEXANDER J. STODDARD

We cannot hold a torch to light another's path without brightening our own.
BEN SWEETLAND

Knowledge comes by eyes always open and working hands, and there is no knowledge that is not power.
JEREMY TAYLOR

I said that an expert was a fella who was afraid to learn anything new because then he wouldn't be an expert anymore.
HARRY S TRUMAN

Information appears to stew out of me naturally, like the precious otter of roses out of the otter.
MARK TWAIN

Though completely armed with knowledge and endowed with power, we are blind and impotent in a world we have equipped and organized—a world of which we now fear the inextricable complexity.
PAUL VALÉRY

Any piece of knowledge I acquire today has a value at this moment exactly proportional to my skill to deal with it. Tomorrow, when I know more, I recall that piece of knowledge and use it better.
MARK VAN DOREN

It is the glorious prerogative of the empire of knowledge that what it gains it never loses. On the contrary, it increases by the multiple of its own power: all its ends become means; all its attainments help to new conquests.
DANIEL WEBSTER

In the scientific world I find just that disinterested devotion to great ends that I hope will spread at last through the entire range of human activity.
H. G. WELLS

There are two ways of spreading light: to be the candle or the mirror that reflects it.
EDITH WHARTON

There is a thing called knowledge of the world which people do not have until they are middle aged. It is something which cannot be taught to younger people because it is not logical and does not obey laws which are constant. It has no rules.
THEODORE H. WHITE

In the advance of civilization, it is new knowledge which paves the way, and the pavement is eternal.
W. R. WHITNEY

Real intelligence is a creative use of knowledge, not merely an accumulation of facts. The slow thinker who can finally come up with an idea of his own is more important to the world than a walking encyclopedia who hasn't learned how to use information productively.
D. KENNETH WINEBRENNER

# L

## Labor

Don't condescend to unskilled labor. Try it for half a day first.
**BROOKS ATKINSON**

Labor is one of the processes by which A acquires property for B.
**AMBROSE BIERCE**

Such hath it been—shall be—beneath the sun: The many still must labor for the one.
**LORD BYRON**

There is no more dreadful punishment than futile and hopeless labor.
**ALBERT CAMUS**

Labor is life; from the inmost heart of the worker rises his God-given force, the sacred celestial life-essence breathed into him by Almighty God.
**THOMAS CARLYLE**

The true epic of our times is not arms and the man, but tools and the man, an infinitely wider kind of epic.
**THOMAS CARLYLE**

Labor is discovered to be the grand conqueror, enriching and building up nations more surely than the proudest battles.
**WILLIAM ELLERY CHANNING**

When you put on your clothes, remember the weaver's labor; when you take your daily food, remember the husbandman's work.
**CHINESE PROVERB**

The strong man meets his crisis with the most practical tools at hand. They may not be the best tools but they are available, which is all-important. He would rather use them, such as they are, than do nothing.
**RAYMOND CLAPPER**

Therefore, my beloved brethren, be ye steadfast, immovable, always abounding in the work of the Lord, forasmuch as ye know that your labor is not in vain in the Lord.
**I CORINTHIANS 15:58**

No country in the world, so far as I know, has yet succeeded in carrying through a planned economy without compulsion of labor.
**STAFFORD CRIPPS**

Labor, even the most humble and the most obscure, if it is well done, tends to beautify and embellish the world.
**GABRIELLE D'ANNUNZIO**

The best investment is in the tools of one's own trade.
**BENJAMIN FRANKLIN**

Sweating, slums, the sense of semislavery in labor must go. We must cultivate a sense of manhood by treating men as men.
**DAVID LLOYD GEORGE**

Labor disgraces no man; unfortunately, you occasionally find men who disgrace labor.
ULYSSES S. GRANT

The dignity of labor depends not on what you do, but how you do it.
EDWIN OSGOOD GROVER

Take not from the mouth of labor the bread it has earned.
THOMAS JEFFERSON

Excellence, in any department, can now be attained only by the labor of a lifetime. It is not purchased at a lesser price.
JOHNSON

He that never labors may know the pains of idleness, but not the pleasures.
SAMUEL JOHNSON

Labor's face is wrinkled with the wind, and swarthy with the sun.
JOHNSON

Genius begins great works; labor alone finishes them.
JOSEPH JOUBERT

Without labor there is no rest, nor without fighting can the victory be won.
THOMAS À KEMPIS

As labor is the common burden of our race, so the effort of some to shift their share of the burden onto the shoulders of others is the great durable curse of the race.
ABRAHAM LINCOLN

Take the tools in hand and carve your own best life.
DOUGLAS LURTON

Labor is a pleasure in itself.
MARCUS MANILIUS

Labor is the divine law of our existence; repose is desertion and suicide.
GIUSEPPI MAZZINI

The man who has the will to undergo all labor may win to any good.
MENANDER

Labor is rest from the sorrows that greet us; from all the petty vexations that meet us; from the sin-promptings that assail us; from the world-sirens that lure us to ill.
FRANCIS S. OSGOOD

The lottery of honest labor, drawn by time, is the only one whose prizes are worth taking up and carrying home.
THEODORE W. PARKER

Put off thy cares with thy clothes; so shall thy rest strengthen thy labor, and so thy labor sweeten thy rest.
FRANCIS QUARLES

I have long been profoundly convinced that in the very nature of things, employers and employees are partners, not enemies; that their interests are common, not opposed; that in the long run the success of each is dependent upon the success of the other. If the labor movement will do its share in outlawing industrial warfare; substituting partnership therefor; if more men of broad vision and high purpose respond to the opportunity for constructive leadership which labor unionism offers, well may it be that the trade union movement will enjoy the glory and honor of ushering in industrial peace.
JOHN D. ROCKEFELLER, JR.

We are coming to see that there should be no stifling of labor by capital, or of capital by labor; and also that there should be no stifling of labor by labor, or of capital by capital.
**JOHN D. ROCKEFELLER, JR.**

Don't be misled into believing that somehow the world owes you a living. The boy who believes that his parents, or the government, or any one else owes him his livelihood and that he can collect it without labor will wake up one day and find himself working for another boy who did not have that belief and, therefore, earned the right to have others work for him.
**DAVID SARNOFF**

The progress of the industrial age rests on the greater diversification of labor and the use of more elaborate tools and machinery which have increased productivity—in other words, saved labor. . . . In our attempt to cure the social ills, we should not kill the goose that has laid the golden eggs. If our society is sick, it is for other reasons than the conquest by man of the forces of nature.
**JOHN W. SCOVILLE**

'Tis no sin for a man to labor in his vocation.
**WILLIAM SHAKESPEARE**

To travel hopefully is a better thing than to arrive, and the true success is to labor.
**ROBERT LOUIS STEVENSON**

There is no real wealth but the labor of man. Were the mountains of gold and the valleys of silver, the world would not be one grain of corn richer; not one comfort would be added to the human race.
**PERCY BYSSHE SHELLEY**

The labor and sweat of our brows is so far from being a curse, that without it our very bread would not be so great a blessing.
**JEREMY TAYLOR**

Ah, why should life all labor be?
**ALFRED, LORD TENNYSON**

The fruits of labor are the sweetest of all pleasures.
**MARQUIS DE VAUVENARGUES**

America has proved that it is practicable to elevate the mass of mankind—the laboring or lower class—to raise them to self-respect, to make them competent to act a part in the great right and the great duty of self-government; and she has proved that this may be done by education and the diffusion of knowledge. She holds out an example a thousand times more encouraging than ever was presented before to those nine-tenths of the human race who are born without hereditary fortune or hereditary rank.
**DANIEL WEBSTER**

Labor is the great producer of wealth; it moves all other causes.
**DANIEL WEBSTER**

If we go far enough back into basic economics, we are eventually reminded that the only known way of producing money initially is by labor; somebody has to work with his brains or his back, and that capital is nothing more than the accumulation of money which has been paid to reward a man for his labor.
**WALTER B. WRISTON**

## Language

Our language is a maze of quirks,
With meaning odd or gone:
If at the top are those well-off,
Are those below well-on?
ART BUCK

So many words are incorrect,
And others deemed too deft
That carried to the Sterile end
There'll be no language left.
ART BUCK

Language is the armory of the human mind, and at once contains the trophies of its past and the weapons of its future conquests.
SAMUEL TAYLOR COLERIDGE

Mastery of language affords remarkable power.
FRANTZ FANON

Command of English, spoken or written, ranks at the top in business. Our main product is words, so a knowledge of their meaning and spelling and pronunciation is imperative. If a man knows the language well, he can find out about all else.
WILLIAM FEATHER

Even though you speak fluent English, you still must be careful with it in England. For example, you may think the British like their beer sour, flat and warm. But ask them, and they will assure you that they like it bitter, still and served with a chill off.
JOHN P. GRIER

Language is the picture and counterpart of thought.
MARK HOPKINS

Language is by its very nature a communal thing; that is, it expresses never the exact thing but a compromise—that which is common to you, me and everybody.
THOMAS ERNEST HULME

In human relations a little language goes farther than a little of almost anything else. Whereas one language now often makes a wall, two can make a gate.
WALTER V. KAULFERS

Coarsening of language means coarsening of knowledge, and a language community that uses language in a coarsened way is a community of coarsened sensibility.
SIGMUND KOCH

Slang is a poor man's poetry.
JOHN MOORE

The art of translation lies less in knowing the other language than in knowing your own.
NED ROREM

England and America are two countries separated by the same language.
GEORGE BERNARD SHAW

Ours is a precarious language, as every writer knows, in which the merest shadow line often separates affirmation from negation, sense from nonsense, and one sex from the other.
JAMES THURBER

## Laughter

Laughter, while it lasts, slackens and unbraces the mind, weakens the faculties, and causes a kind of

remissness and dissolution in all the powers of the soul.
JOSEPH ADDISON

One should take good care not to grow too wise for so great a pleasure of life as laughter.
JOSEPH ADDISON

Laughter is a tranquilizer with no side effects.
ANONYMOUS

Among those whom I like or admire, I can find no common denominator, but among those whom I love, I can: All of them make me laugh.
W. H. AUDEN

You grow up the day you have your first real laugh—at yourself.
ETHEL BARRYMORE

Laughter is day, and sobriety is night; a smile is the twilight that hovers gently between both, more bewitching than either.
HENRY WARD BEECHER

Men will let you abuse them if only you will make them laugh.
HENRY WARD BEECHER

All laughter is a muscular rigidity spasmodically relieved by involuntary twitching.
ROBERT BENCHLEY

No man who has once heartily and wholly laughed can be altogether irreclaimably bad.
THOMAS CARLYLE

The man who cannot laugh is not only fit for treasons, stratagems and spoils, but his whole life is already a treason and a stratagem.
THOMAS CARLYLE

If you want to make people weep, you must weep yourself. If you want to make people laugh, your face must remain serious.
GIOVANNI CASANOVA

The most thoroughly wasted of all days is that on which one has not laughed.
SÉBASTIEN CHAMFORT

The person who can laugh with life has developed deep roots with confidence and faith—faith in oneself, in people and in the world, as contrasted to negative ideas with distrust and discouragement.
DEMOCRITUS

No man ever distinguished himself who could not bear to be laughed at.
MARIE EDGEWORTH

He is not laughed at that laughs at himself first.
THOMAS FULLER

Laugh to forget, but don't forget to laugh.
ARNOLD GLASOW

He who laughs at everything is as big a fool as he who weeps at everything.
BALTASAR GRACIÁN

With mirth and laughter, let old wrinkles come.
THOMAS HARDY

Few men, I believe, are much worth loving in whom there is not something well worth laughing at.
JULIUS C. HARE

Anyone who takes himself too seriously always runs the risk of looking ridiculous; anyone who can consistently laugh at himself does not.
VACLAV HAVEL

Man is the only animal that laughs and weeps; for he is the only animal that is struck by the difference between what things are and what they might have been.
WILLIAM HAZLITT

A man isn't poor if he can still laugh.
RAYMOND HITCHCOCK

There are three things which are real: God, human folly and laughter. The first two are beyond our comprehension, so we must do what we can with the third.
JOHN F. KENNEDY

A laugh is worth a hundred groans in any market.
CHARLES LAMB

With the fearful strain that is on me night and day, if I did not laugh I should die.
ABRAHAM LINCOLN

The freedom of any society varies proportionately with the volume of its laughter.
ZERO MOSTEL

Man alone suffers so excruciatingly in the world that he was compelled to invent laughter.
FRIEDRICH WILHELM NIETZSCHE

Sayings designed to raise a laugh are generally untrue and never complimentary. Laughter is never far removed from derision.
QUINTILIAN

We are in the world to laugh. In purgatory or in hell we shall no longer be able to do so. And in heaven it would not be proper.
JULES RENARD

I am forced to try to make myself laugh that I may not cry: For one or other I must do.
SAMUEL RICHARDSON

He was born with the gift of laughter and a sense that the world was mad.
RAFAEL SABATINI

The young man who has not wept is a savage, and the old man who will not laugh is a fool.
GEORGE SANTAYANA

The cause of laughter is simply the sudden perception of the incongruity between a concept and the real project.
ARTHUR SCHOPENHAUER

I've learned that if you laugh and drink soda pop at the same time, it will come out your nose.
7-YEAR-OLD'S DISCOVERY

I am convinced that there can be no regeneration of mankind until laughter is put down.
PERCY BYSSHE SHELLEY

I live in a constant endeavor to fence against the infirmities of ill health, and the other evils of life, by mirth; being firmly persuaded that every time a man smiles—but much more so, when he laughs—that it adds something to this Fragment of Life.
LAURENCE STERNE

A good laugh is sunshine in a house.
WILLIAM MAKEPEACE THACKERAY

Power, money, persuasion, supplication, persecution—these can lift a colossal humbug, push it a little, weaken it a little; but only laughter can blow it to rags and atoms at a blast. Against the assault of laughter nothing can stand.
MARK TWAIN

Learn to laugh with others, and most important, at yourself.
**FRANK TYGER**

To laugh with others is one of life's great pleasures. To be laughed at by others is one of life's great hurts.
**FRANK TYGER**

In laughter there is always a kind of joyousness that is incompatible with contempt or indignation.
**VOLTAIRE**

People who laugh actually live longer than those who don't laugh. Few persons realize that health actually varies according to the amount of laughter.
**JAMES J. WALSH**

Laughter is not a bad beginning for a friendship, and it is the best ending for one.
**OSCAR WILDE**

## *Laws*

Nobody has a more sacred obligation to obey the law than those who make the law.
**JEAN ANOUILH**

Laws are not invented; they grow out of circumstances.
**AZARIAS**

That law may be set down as good which is certain in meaning, just in precept, convenient in execution, agreeable to the form of government, and productive of virtue in those that live under it.
**FRANCIS BACON**

It usually takes a hundred years to make a law, and then, after it has done its work, it usually takes another hundred years to get rid of it.
**HENRY WARD BEECHER**

Laws and institutions are constantly tending to gravitate. Like clocks, they must be occasionally cleansed, and wound up, and set to true time.
**HENRY WARD BEECHER**

It is a very easy thing to devise good laws; the difficulty is to make them effective. The great mistake is that of looking upon men as virtuous, or thinking that they can be made so by laws; and consequently the greatest art of a politician is to render vices serviceable to the cause of virtue.
**LORD BOLINGBROKE**

Bad laws are the worst sort of tyranny.
**EDMUND BURKE**

There is but one law for all; namely the law which governs all law—the law of our Creator, the law of humanity, justice, equity; the law of nature and of nations.
**EDMUND BURKE**

The violation of some laws is a normal part of the behavior of every citizen.
**STUART CHASE**

If you have ten thousand regulations you destroy all respect for the law.
**WINSTON CHURCHILL**

The science of legislation is like that of medicine in one respect; viz.: that it is far more easy to point out what will do harm, than what will do good.
**CHARLES CALEB COLTON**

The victim of too severe a law is considered a martyr, rather than a criminal.
**Charles Caleb Colton**

Coolidge's Law: Anytime you don't want anything, you get it.
**Calvin Coolidge**

The liberty of a people consists in being governed by laws which they have made themselves, under whatsoever form it be of government; the liberty of a private man, in being master of his own time and actions, as far as may consist with the laws of God and of his country.
**Abraham Cowley**

If we could make a great bonfire of the thousands of laws we have in this country, and start all over again with only the Golden Rule and the Ten Commandments, I am sure we would get along much better.
**Coleman Cox**

Laws should be like clothes. They should be made to fit the people they are meant to serve.
**Clarence Darrow**

A year ago, if I had $100 in gold in my pocket, I was a law-abiding citizen; if I perchance had a pint of whiskey I was a criminal. Today, if I have the whiskey, I am a law-abiding citizen; but if I have the gold I am a criminal violating the law.
**L. J. Dickinson (Jan. 1934)**

As civilization progresses, we should improve our laws basically, not superficially. Many things that are lawful are highly immoral and some things which are moral are unlawful.
**Henry L. Doherty**

The law should be loved a little because it is felt to be just; feared a little because it is severe; hated a little because it is to a certain degree out of sympathy with the prevalent temper of the day; and respected because it is felt to be a necessity.
**Emile Fourget**

The law, in its majestic equality, forbids all men to sleep under bridges, to beg in the streets and to steal bread—the rich as well as the poor.
**Anatole France**

Every one of us, whatever our speculative opinions, knows better than he practices, and recognizes a better law than he obeys.
**J. A. Froude**

Our human laws are but the copies, more or less imperfect, of the eternal laws, so far as we can read them.
**J. A. Froude**

An unjust law is itself a species of violence. Arrest for its breach is more so.
**Mahatma Gandhi**

The more laws, the less justice.
**German proverb**

The Englishman walks before the law like a trained horse in a circus. He has the sense of legality in his bones, in his muscles.
**Maxim Gorky**

Four out of five potential litigants will settle their disputes the first day they come together, if you will put the idea of arbitration into their heads.
**Moses H. Grossman**

There is something monstrous in commands couched in invented and unfamiliar language; an

alien master is the worst of all. The language of the law must not be foreign to the ears of those who are to obey it.
**LEARNED HAND**

Our laws can be friendly to those who obey them, and too often useful to those who don't.
**CULLEN HIGHTOWER**

We always exempt ourselves from the common laws. When I was a boy and the dentist pulled out a second tooth, I thought to myself that I would grow a third if I needed it. Experience discouraged this prophecy.
**OLIVER WENDELL HOLMES, JR.**

There are not enough jails, not enough policemen, not enough law courts, to enforce a law not supported by the people.
**HUBERT H. HUMPHREY**

The execution of the laws is more important than the making of them.
**THOMAS JEFFERSON**

This book of the law shall not depart out of thy mouth; but thou shall mediate therein day and night, that thou mayest observe to do according to all that is written therein: for then thou shalt make thy way prosperous, and then thou shalt have good success.
**JOSHUA 1:8**

Society fails to recognize that the tension between the police and the judiciary has always been fundamental to our constitutional system. It is intentional and healthy and constitutes the real difference between a free society and a police state.
**NICHOLAS KATZENBACH**

Morality cannot be legislated, but behavior can be regulated. Judicial decrees may not change the heart, but they can restrain the heartless.
**MARTIN LUTHER KING, JR.**

Of all injustice, that is the greatest which goes under the name of law, and of all sorts of tyranny the forcing of the letter of the law against the equity, is the most insupportable.
**ROGER L'ESTRANGE**

Let every man remember that to violate the law is to trample on the blood of his father, and to tear the charter of his own and his children's liberty. Let reverence for the laws be breathed by every American mother to the lisping babe that prattles on her lap; let it be written in primers, spelling books, and almanacs; let it be preached from the pulpit; proclaimed in the legislative halls, and enforced in courts of justice. In short, let it become the political religion of the nation.
**ABRAHAM LINCOLN**

No man can be a competent legislator who does not add to an upright intention and a sound judgment a certain degree of knowledge of the subjects on which he is to legislate.
**JAMES MADISON**

The test, after all, is not whether a certain law is popular, but whether the law is based upon fundamental justice, fundamental decency and righteousness, fundamental morality and goodness. What we need is not law enforcement, but law observance. In a modern society there is no real freedom from law. There is only freedom in law.
**PETER MARSHALL**

The purpose of law is to prevent the strong always having their way.
**OVID**

You cannot legislate the human race into heaven.
**CHARLES HENRY PARKHURST, D.D.**

Statutes are mere milestone, telling how far yesterday's thought had traveled; and the talk of the sidewalk today is the law of the land. With us, law is nothing unless close behind it stands a warm, living public opinion.
**WENDELL PHILLIPS**

The law does not generate justice, the law is nothing but a declaration and application of what is already just.
**P. J. PROUDHON**

No man is above the law, and no man is below it; nor do we ask any man's permission when we require him to obey it.
**THEODORE ROOSEVELT**

The cornerstone of this Republic, as of all free government, is respect for and obedience to the law. Where we permit the law to be defied or evaded, whether by rich man or poor man, by black man or white, we are by just so much weakening the bonds of our civilization and increasing the chances of its overthrow, and of the substitution therefore of a system in which there shall be violent alternations of anarchy and tyranny.
**THEODORE ROOSEVELT**

It is to law alone that men owe justice and liberty. It is this salutary organ of the will of all which establishes in civil rights the natural equality between men. It is this celestial voice which dictates to each citizen the precepts of public reason, and teaches him to act according to the rules of his own judgment and not to behave inconsistently with himself. It is with this voice alone that political leaders should speak when they command.
**JEAN-JACQUES ROUSSEAU**

Government can easily exist without law, but law cannot exist without government.
**BERTRAND RUSSELL**

Revolt and terror pay a price. Order and law have a cost.
**CARL SANDBURG**

Living for our country entails respect for and compliance with its laws, whether we like them or not, knowing well that a majority of us can change them if we wish.
**DAVE E. SMALLEY**

When the state is most corrupt, then laws are most multiplied.
**TACITUS**

Laws are always unstable unless they are founded on the manners of a nation; and manners are the only durable and resisting power in a people.
**ALEXIS DE TOCQUEVILLE**

Laws are sand, customs are rock. Laws can be evaded and punishment escaped, but an openly transgressed custom brings sure punishment.
**MARK TWAIN**

A multitude of laws in a country is like a great number of physicians, a sign of weakness and malady.
**VOLTAIRE**

Every instance of a man's suffering the penalty of the law, is an instance of the failure of that penalty in effecting its purpose, which is to deter from transgression.
**RICHARD WHATELY**

## Lawyers

Lawsuit: A machine which you go into as a pig and come out of as a sausage.
AMBROSE BIERCE

Litigant: A person about to give up his skin for the hope of retaining his bones.
AMBROSE BIERCE

Torts are lawyers' happy hours
Like double gins and fizz;
Spelled backward tort is trot,
Straight to the bank, that is.
ART BUCK

If there were no bad people, there would be no good lawyers.
CHARLES DICKENS

God works wonders now and then:
Behold! A lawyer and an honest man!
BENJAMIN FRANKLIN

Lawyer: The only man in whom ignorance of the law is not punished.
ELBERT HUBBARD

Discourage litigation. Persuade your neighbor to compromise whenever you can. As a peacemaker the lawyer has a superior opportunity of being a good man. There will still be business enough.
ABRAHAM LINCOLN

Woe unto you also, ye lawyers! for ye lade men with burdens grievous to be borne, and ye yourselves touch not the burdens with one of your fingers.
LUKE 11:46

Woe unto you, lawyers! for he have taken away the key of knowledge: ye entered not in yourselves, and them that were entering in ye hindered.
LUKE 11:52

Lawyers are men who hire out their words and anger.
MARTIAL

The minute you read something you can't understand, you can almost be sure it was drawn up by a lawyer.
WILL ROGERS

I've learned that in a divorce, only the lawyers come out ahead.
37-YEAR-OLD'S DISCOVERY

The lawyers' truth is not Truth, but consistency or a consistent expediency.
HENRY DAVID THOREAU

## Laziness

By nature, man is lazy, working only under compulsion; and when he is strong he will always live, as far as he can, upon the labor or the property of the weak.
HENRY BROOKS ADAMS

It's a slow burg—I spent a couple of weeks there one day.
AMERICAN FOLK SAYING

Nothing ages like laziness.
EDWARD BULWER-LYTTON

Laziness grows on people; it begins in cobwebs and ends in iron chains. The more one has to do the more he is able to accomplish.
SIR THOMAS BUXTON

Sloth never arrived at the attainment of a good wish.
MIGUEL DE CERVANTES

The love of indolence is universal, or next to it.
SAMUEL TAYLOR COLERIDGE

A man with nothing to do does far more strenuous labor than any other form of work. To be enforced to be idle is terribly difficult and even a small proportion of your day wasted is worse than working many hours overtime. But my greatest pity is for the man who dodges a job he knows he should do. He is a shirker; and boy! what punishment he takes . . . from himself.
E. R. COLLCORD

Sloth, if it has prevented many crimes, has also smothered many virtues.
CHARLES CALEB COLTON

Indolence is the dry rot of even a good mind and a good character; the practical uselessness of both. It is the waste of what might be a happy and useful life.
TRYON EDWARDS

Laziness is the one common deficiency in mankind that blocks the establishment of a perfect world in which everyone leads a happy life.
WILLIAM FEATHER

The constructive loafer uses his mind during the act of loafing, but he does not try to control his mind. In other words, loafing is educated day-dreaming. I do not plead for more loafing. I defend a reasonable amount of honest loafing as a tonic that is good for the body, mind and spirit.
WILLIAM FEATHER

Sloth, like rush, consumes faster than labor wears, while the key often used is always right.
BENJAMIN FRANKLIN

Laziness is a secret ingredient that goes into failure. But it's only kept a secret from the person who fails.
ROBERT HALF

The slothful man is the beggar's brother.
JAMES KELLY

If ever this free people, if this Government itself is ever utterly demoralized, it will come from this incessant human wriggle and struggle for office, which is but a way to live without work.
ABRAHAM LINCOLN

Loafing needs no explanation and is its own excuse.
CHRISTOPHER MORLEY

We make a pretext of difficulty to excuse our sloth.
QUINTILIAN

Though you may have known clever men who were indolent, you never knew a great man who was so; and when I hear a young man spoken of as giving promise of great genius, the first question I ask about him always is, "Does he work?"
JOHN RUSKIN

If you ask me which is the real hereditary sin of human nature, do you imagine I shall answer pride, or luxury, or ambition, or egotism? No; I shall say indolence. Who conquers indolence will conquer all the rest. Indeed all good principles must stagnate without mental activity.
JOHANN ZIMMERMANN

## Leadership

Leadership is the initiation and direction of endeavor in the pursuit of consequence. Anything else is criticism from janitors.
ROYAL ALCOTT

Leadership involves remembering past mistakes, an analysis of todays' achievements, and a well-grounded imagination in visualizing the problem of the future.
STANLEY C. ALLYN

The most substantial glory of a country is in its virtuous great men. Its prosperity will depend on its docility to learn from their example.
FISHER AMES

When a fellow thinks he is putting it over on the boss, the boss is not thinking of putting him over others to boss.
C. K. ANDERSON

Conductors of great symphony orchestras do not play every musical instrument; yet through leadership the ultimate production is an expressive and unified combination of tones.
THOMAS D. BAILEY

The man who is worthy of being a leader of men will never complain about the stupidity of his helpers, the ingratitude of mankind nor the inappreciation of the public. These are all a part of the great game of life. To meet them and overcome them and not to go down before them in disgust, discouragement or defeat—that is the final proof of power.
WILLIAM J. H. BOETCKER

A leader is a dealer in hope.
NAPOLEON BONAPARTE

It is hard to look up to a leader who keeps his ear to the ground.
JAMES H. BOREN

Leadership of a world-economy is an experience of power which may blind the victor to the march of history.
FERNAND BRAUDEL

There are no warlike peoples—just warlike leaders.
RALPH J. BUNCHE

Trained and inspired leadership is needed in the troubled world of today. We live in uncertainty and fear. The times call for thinking and straight thinking—one of the goals of true education. Unfortunately, the world so clamors for action that men and women devote little time to thinking. Many believe in second-hand thinking. They find it easier to ascertain and adopt the thoughts of others than to think for themselves.
JAMES F. BYRNES

When we think we lead we most are led.
LORD BYRON

A symphony may be played by a hundred musicians responsive under the baton of a master conductor or by fifty thousand mechanics playing a blueprint score.
WILLIAM J. CAMERON

We are not altogether here to tolerate. We are here to resist, to control and vanquish withal.
THOMAS CARLYLE

As soon as a man climbs up to a high position, he must train his subordinates and trust them. They must relieve him of all small matters. He must be set free to think, to travel, to plan, to see important

customers, to make improvements, to do all the big jobs of Leadership.
HERBERT N. CASSON

Safety first has been the motto of the human race for half a million years; but it has never been the motto of leaders. A leader must face danger. He must take the risk and the blame, and the brunt of the storm.
HERBERT N. CASSON

While once it was the rank and file that cheered with all the partisan passions at their heights, today it is the party leaders who are cheering themselves; and all by themselves. The mob that is their audience is in one vast universal trance, thinking about something else.
G. K. CHESTERTON

A man who wants to lead the orchestra must turn his back on the crowd.
JAMES CROOK

Leaders of men are later remembered less for the usefulness of what they have achieved than for the sweep of their endeavors.
CHARLES DE GAULLE

Men are of no importance. What counts is who commands.
CHARLES DE GAULLE

I must follow the people. Am I not their leader?
BENJAMIN DISRAELI

A leader of men must make decisions quickly; be independent; act and stand firm; be a fighter; speak openly, plainly, frankly; make defeats his lessons; co-operate; co-ordinate; use the best of any alliances or allies; walk with active faith courageously toward danger or the unknown; create a staff; know, love and represent the best interests of his followers; be loyal, true, frank and faithful; reward loyalty; have a high, intelligent and worthy purpose and ideal. Do justice; love mercy; fear no man but fear only God.
JOHN W. DODGE

You do not lead by hitting people over the head—that's assault, not leadership.
DWIGHT D. EISENHOWER

A good man likes a hard boss. I don't mean a nagging boss or a grouchy boss. I mean a boss who insists on things being done right and on time; a boss who is watching things closely enough so that he knows a good job from a poor one. Nothing is more discouraging to a good man than a boss who is not on the job, and who does not know whether things are going well or badly.
WILLIAM FEATHER

It's often a good idea to let the other fellow believe he is running things whether he is or not.
WILLIAM FEATHER

Elected leaders who forget how they got there won't the next time.
MALCOLM FORBES

No one's a leader if there are no followers.
MALCOLM FORBES

The question "Who ought to be boss?" is like asking "Who ought to be the tenor in the quartet?" Obviously, the man who can sing tenor.
HENRY FORD

If you command wisely, you'll be obeyed cheerfully.
THOMAS FULLER

To-day a reader, to-morrow a leader.
W. FUSSELMAN

If the modern leader doesn't know the facts, he is in grave trouble, but rarely do the facts provide unqualified guidance.
JOHN W. GARDNER

Real leaders are ordinary people with extraordinary determinations.
JOHN SEAMAN GARNS

The higher men climb the longer their working day. And any young man with a streak of idleness in him may better make up his mind at the beginning that mediocrity will be his lot. Without immense, sustained effort he will not climb high. And even though fortune or chance were to lift him high, he would not stay there. For to keep at the top is harder almost than to get there. There are no office hours for leaders.
CARDINAL GIBBONS

If history repeat itself, when will we enjoy the leadership of another Washington or Lincoln?
ARNOLD GLASOW

The business world reaches out for and rewards leaders who can relegate and delegate.
ARNOLD GLASOW

Faith in the ability of a leader is of slight service unless it be united with faith in his justice.
GEORGE W. GOETHALS

Do the thing that is right even when the boss isn't looking because the boss isn't a criterion. The real boss is standing alongside you every moment of your life.
ALFRED P. HAAKE

Those who can command themselves command others.
WILLIAM HAZLITT

Just as the real basics of human nature do not change from one generation to another, so the real basics of human leadership do not change from one leader to another—from one field to the next—but remain always and everywhere the same.
WILLIAM E. HOLLER

There must appear a spiritual and moral leadership rising above economic and political situations. Governments in both their domestic and foreign policies appeal for popular support by promises of material gain. We cannot make peace by mere appeal to greed. We must give the peoples of the world something to live for as well as something to live on.
JOHN ANDREW HOLMES

He that entereth not by the door into the sheepfold, but climbeth up some other way, the same is a thief and a robber. But he that entereth in by the door is the shepherd of the sheep.
JOHN 10:1–2

The control man has secured over nature has far outrun his control over himself.
ERNEST JONES

I've got to follow them, I am their leader.
ALEXANDER LEDRU-ROLLIN

The final test of a leader is that he leaves behind him in other men the conviction and the will to carry on.
WALTER LIPPMANN

One of the most hopeful portents of the times does not appear in any index of rising commodity prices—car loadings—bank deposits—or business volume—though it actuates all of them. It is the human factor—the stamina, the resourcefulness, the daring of the men to whom business look for leadership.

If adversity put business leadership to rigorous test—it also provided a rigorous course of training. If it took off the fat—it toughened the spirit.
P. W. LITCHFIELD

A person under the firm persuasion that he can command resources virtually has them.
LIVY

There is nothing more difficult to take in hand, more perilous to conduct, or more uncertain in its success than to take the lead in the introduction of a new order of things.
NICCOLÒ MACHIAVELLI

Leadership is action, not position.
DONALD H. MCGANNON

The crux of leadership is that you must constantly stop to consider how your decisions will influence people.
MICHIGAN STATE POLICE MAXIM

He is the best leader who most fully understands the nature of things, so that his plans are not doomed to ultimate failure; who possesses an active, far-ranging imagination which can see many possibilities; who has a sense of values, so that among possibilities he is able to choose the most excellent; who has a sense of order, to give form, design and program to the values and purposes he selects; who has practical sense and judgment, and so uses the most feasible means to accomplish his ends; and who has the energy and enthusiasm to carry his plans persistently toward fruition.
ARTHUR E. MORGAN

Big shots are little shots who kept shooting.
CHRISTOPHER MORLEY

The character and qualifications of the leader are reflected in the men he selects, develops and gathers around him. Show me the leader and I will know his men. Show me the men and I will know their leader. Therefore, to have loyal, efficient employees—be a loyal and efficient employer.
ARTHUR W. NEWCOMB

Thou seekest disciples? Then thou seekest ciphers.
FRIEDRICH WILHELM NIETZSCHE

I wonder if there is anyone in the world who can really direct the affairs of the world, or of his country, with any assurance of the result his actions would have.
MONTAGU C. NORMAN

A great leader never sets himself above his followers except in carrying responsibilities.
JULES ORMONT

Leadership appears to be the art of getting others to want to do something you are convinced should be done.
VANCE PACKARD

In any series of elements to be controlled, a selected small fraction, in terms of numbers of elements, always accounts for a large fraction in terms of effect.
VILFREDO PARETO

The best leaders are those most interested in surrounding themselves with assistants and associates smarter than they are—being frank in admitting this—and willing to pay for such talents.
AMOS PARRISH

Planners do not understand that Civil Service examinations can not grade men in loyalty, vision, integrity, teamwork and tenacity, which rate even

higher than native ability as qualifications for industrial leadership.
EDGAR M. QUEENY

A leader has two important characteristics; first, he is going somewhere; second, he is able to persuade other people to go with him.
MAXIMILIEN FRANÇOIS ROBESPIERRE

It's a terrible thing to look over your shoulder when you are trying to lead—and find no one there.
FRANKLIN D. ROOSEVELT

People ask the difference between a leader and a loss. . . . The leader works in the open and the boss in covert. The leader leads and the boss drives.
THEODORE ROOSEVELT

It is nothing to give pension and cottage to the widow who has lost her son; it is nothing to give food and medicine to the workman who has broken his arm, or the decrepit woman wasting in sickness. But it is something to use your time and strength to war with the waywardness and thoughtlessness of mankind; to keep the erring workman in your service till you have made him an unerring one, and to direct your fellow-merchant to the opportunity which his judgment would have lost.
JOHN RUSKIN

In a society safe and worthy to be free, teaching which produces a willingness to lead, as well as a willingness to follow, must be given to all.
WILLIAM F. RUSSELL

We cannot all be masters.
WILLIAM SHAKESPEARE

The ability to keep a cool head in an emergency, maintain poise in the midst of excitement, and to refuse to be stampeded are true marks of leadership.
R. SHANNON

What you cannot enforce, do not command.
SOPHOCLES

Reason and judgment are the qualities of a leader.
TACITUS

A man is rich in proportion to the number of things which he can afford to let alone.
HENRY DAVID THOREAU

It is said that it is far more difficult to hold and maintain leadership (liberty) than it is to attain it. Success is a ruthless competitor for it flatters and nourishes our weaknesses and lulls us into complacency. We bask in the sunshine of accomplishment and lose the spirit of humility which helps us visualize all the factors which have contributed to our success. We are apt to forget that we are only one of a team, that in unity there is strength and that we are strong only as long as each unit in our organization functions with precision.
SAMUEL TILDEN

You will never be a leader unless you first learn to follow and be led.
TIORIO

Leadership is the ability to get men to do what they don't want to do and like it.
HARRY S TRUMAN

The right of commanding is no longer an advantage transmitted by nature; like an inheritance, it is the fruit of labors, the price of courage.
VOLTAIRE

I say no body of men are fit to make Presidents, judges and generals, unless they themselves supply the best specimens of the same; and that supplying one or two such specimens illuminates the whole body for a thousand years.
WALT WHITMAN

Produce great men, the rest follows.
WALT WHITMAN

Mankind needs the American type of leadership. Let it be not discredited by those who are out of sympathy with it, who don't understand it or are incompetent to administer it. In America, the demand for power to compel is a confession of incompetence to lead.
EUGENE E. WILSON

## *Learning*

I find that a great part of the information I have was acquired by looking up something and finding something else on the way.
FRANKLIN P. ADAMS

They know enough who know how to learn.
HENRY ADAMS

The truth of it is, learning, like traveling and all other methods of improvement, as if finishes good sense, so it makes a silly man ten thousand times more insufferable by supplying variety of matter to his impertinence, and giving him an opportunity of abounding in absurdities.
JOSEPH ADDISON

Learning is a treasury whose keys are queries.
ARABIAN PROVERB

Surely the worst of the evils are the evils of the learned, and surely the best of good is the good of the learned.
ARABIAN PROVERB

To think of learning as a preparation for something beyond learning is a defeat of the process. The most important attitude that can be formed is that of desire to go on learning.
DANIEL BELL

Some will never learn anything because they understand everything too soon.
THOMAS BLOUNT

If you want to earn more—learn more. If you want to get more out of the world you must put more into the world. For, after all, men will get no more out of life than they put into it.
WILLIAM J. H. BOETCKER

Most men believe that it would benefit them if they could get a little from those who have more. How much more would it benefit them if they would learn a little from those who know more.
WILLIAM J. H. BOETCKER

It is some compensation for great evils that they enforce great lessons.
CHRISTIAN BOVÉE

A little general learning has come to be a useful thing in a world where from its infrequency it has ceased to be dangerous.
W. C. BROWNELL

Never seem wiser or more learned than the company you are with. Treat your learning like a watch and keep it hidden. Do not pull it out to count the hours, but give the time when you are asked.
LORD CHESTERFIELD

The man who has ceased to learn ought not to be allowed to wander around loose in these dangerous days.
M. M. COADY

He who learns but does not think is lost, he who thinks but does not learn is in danger.
**CONFUCIUS**

We live, and we learn, as much by unconscious absorption and imitation as by systematic effort.
**LUELLA B. COOK**

Learning consists of ideas, and not of the noise that is made by the mouth.
**WILLIAM COBBETT**

Seeing much, suffering much and studying much, are the three pillars of learning.
**BENJAMIN DISRAELI**

It is the studying that you do after your school days that really counts. Otherwise, you know only that which everyone else knows.
**HENRY L. DOHERTY**

In every man there is something wherein I may learn of him, and in that I am his pupil.
**RALPH WALDO EMERSON**

Whoso neglects learning in his youth loses the past and is dead for the future.
**EURIPIDES**

As long as learning is connected with earning, as long as certain jobs can only be reached through exams, so long must we take the examination system seriously. If another ladder to employment was contrived, much so-called education would disappear, and no one would be a penny the stupider.
**E. M. FORSTER**

One of the reasons mature people stop learning is that they become less and less willing to risk failure.
**JOHN W. GARDNER**

We have an infinite amount to learn both from nature and from each other.
**JOHN GLENN**

Go to the place where the thing you wish to know is native; your best teacher is there. Where the thing you wish to know is so dominant that you must breathe its very atmosphere, there teaching is most thorough and learning is most easy. You acquire a language most readily in the country where it is spoken; you study mineralogy best among miners; and so with everything else.
**JOHANN WOLFGANG VON GOETHE**

We are all, it seems, saving ourselves for the Senior Prom. But many of us forget that somewhere along the way we must learn to dance.
**ALAN HARRINGTON**

One hour of learning and good works in this world is better than all the joys of the hereafter.
**HEBREW PROVERB**

To stay young requires unceasing cultivation of the ability to unlearn of falsehoods.
**ROBERT A. HEINLEIN**

The love of learning and the love of money rarely meet.
**GEORGE HERBERT**

The sweetest and most inoffensive path of life leads through the avenues of science and learning; and whoever can either remove any obstruction in this way, or open up any new prospect, ought, so far, to be esteemed a benefactor to mankind.
**DAVID HUME**

If there is one thing more than any other that characterizes the average American, it is his eagerness to learn almost anything at almost any age.
**HANS V. KALTENBORN**

The young man who has the combination of the learning of books with the learning which comes of doing things with the hands need not worry about getting along in the world today, or at any time.
WILLIAM S. KNUDSEN

He who devotes 16 hours a day to hard study may become as wise at 60 as he thought himself at 20.
MARY LITTLE

None of the things children are to learn should ever be made a burden to them, or imposed on them as a task. Whatever is so imposed presently becomes irksome; the mind takes an aversion to it, though before it were a thing of delight.
JOHN LOCKE

There is no easy method of learning difficult things. The method is to close the door, give out that you are not at home, and work.
JOSEPH DE MAISTRE

One pound of learning requires ten pounds of commonsense to apply it.
PERSIAN PROVERB

A wise man will hear, and will increase learning; and a man of understanding shall attain unto wise counsels.
PROVERBS 1:5

Learning makes the wise wiser and the fool more foolish.
JOHN RAY

No man is the wiser for his learning: It may administer matter to work in or objects to work upon; but wit and wisdom are born with a man.
JOHN SELDEN

Learning and liberty march hand in hand, or they do not march at all: the one is the condition of the other.
HARTLEY SHAWCROSS

The more we study, the more we discover our ignorance.
PERCY BYSSHE SHELLEY

Learning, like money, may be of so base a coin as to be utterly void of use; or, if sterling, may require good management to make it serve the purposes of sense or happiness.
WILLIAM SHENSTONE

If it is sensible for the child to make an effort to learn how to be an adult, then it is essential for the adult to learn how to be aged.
EDWARD STIEGLITZ

Learning is either a continuing thing or it is nothing.
FRANK TYGER

Anyone who stops learning is old, whether this happens at twenty or eighty. Anyone who keeps on learning not only remains young, but becomes constantly more valuable regardless of physical capacity.
HARVEY ULLMAN

The purpose of learning to employ every minute properly is to unclutter our hours, deliver us of feverish activity and earn us true leisure.
ROBERT R. UPDEGRAFF

The secondhandedness of the learned world is the secret of its mediocrity.
ALFRED NORTH WHITEHEAD

Have you learned lessons only of those who admired you, and were tender with you, and stood aside for you? Have you not learned great lessons

from those who rejected you, and braced themselves against you, or disputed the passage with you?
WALT WHITMAN

Learning makes a man fit company for himself.
YOUNG

Our task as we grow older in a rapidly advancing science, is to retain the capacity of joy in discoveries which correct older ideas, and to learn from our pupils as we teach them.
HANS ZINSSER

## *Leisure*

You can go to doctors until the last cow has been placed in its shed. You can journey the earth in search of peace of mind. You can experiment with a dozen theories, hoping for a relief from worries, or the problems which beset you, but unless you learn to relax you will end up disappointed. Tension is a killer! Just relax and note the immediate effect. One of peace and ease of mind. One in which every organ of the body joins. In relaxation there is unity of mind, body and spirit.
GEORGE MATTHEW ADAMS

I am never less at leisure than when at leisure, nor less alone than when I am alone.
SCIPIO AFRICANUS

Leisure may prove to be a curse rather than a blessing, unless education teaches a flippant world that leisure is not a synonym for entertainment.
WILLIAM J. BOGAN

Let the world have whatever sports and recreations please them best, provided they be followed with discretion.
RICHARD BURTON

All his subjects be very glad, I thank God, to be busy with the golf, for they take it for pastime; my heart is very glad for it.
CATHERINE OF ARAGON

'Tis easy to resign a toilsome place,
But not to manage leisure with a grace,
Absence of occupation is not rest,
A mind quite vacant is a mind distressed.
WILLIAM COWPER

Men cannot labor on always. They must have recreation.
ORVILLE DEWEY

Increased means and increased leisure are the two civilizers of man.
BENJAMIN DISRAELI

Don't expect to be paid a dollar an hour for your working hours when you then use your leisure hours as though they were not worth five cents a dozen.
HENRY L. DOHERTY

There's an irony in the arithmetic that shows we're demanding our leisure faster inasmuch as no peoples in human history have had so much time (or wealth) for leisure as we Americans.
HENRY DREYFUSS

The continual tendency toward shorter hours is certainly connected with the modern development of industry, for with the use of power, mechanical devices and quicker methods the amount of effort to do the world's work is constantly being reduced. This tendency must be beneficial to the human race, for its more leisure time, and contributes to the joy of life.
LAMMOT DU PONT

As manpower is replaced by other sources of energy the entire conception of recreation shifts. What we do with these new leisure hours will determine the value of our culture.
**MORRIS L. ERNST**

The man who works 52 weeks in the year does not do his best in any one week of the year, Daniel Guggenheim, onetime head of the greatest smelting and mining family in America, impressed upon me. Real recreation quickens aspiration. The true purpose of recreation is not merely to amuse, not merely to afford pleasure, not merely to kill time, but to increase our fitness, enhance our usefulness, spur achievement.
**B. C. FORBES**

Many concerns now make part or the whole of their dividends from by-products that formerly went to waste. How do we, as individuals, utilize our principal by-product? Our principal by-product is, of course, our leisure time. Many years of observation forces the conclusion that a man's success or failure in life is determined as much by how he acts during his leisure as by how he acts during his work hours. Tell me how a young man spends his evenings and I will tell you how he is likely to spend the latter part of his life.
**B. C. FORBES**

The true purpose of recreation should be not merely to amuse, not merely to afford pleasure, not merely to kill time, but to increase our fitness, enhance our usefulness, spur achievement. Any form of recreation that impairs either our physical or mental efficiency does not recreate. Real recreation quickens aspiration.
**B. C. FORBES**

Employ thy time well if thou meanest to gain leisure.
**BENJAMIN FRANKLIN**

Leisure is time for doing something useful, and this leisure the diligent man will obtain.
**BENJAMIN FRANKLIN**

Some relaxation is necessary to people of every degree; the head that thinks and the hand that labors must have some little time to recruit their diminished powers.
**BERNARD GILPIN**

Many people know how to work hard; many others know how to play well; but the rarest talent in the world is the ability to introduce elements of playfulness into work, and to put some constructive labor into our leisure.
**SYDNEY J. HARRIS**

The time to relax is when you don't have time for it.
**SYDNEY J. HARRIS**

There is room enough in human life to crowd almost every art and science in it. If we pass "no day without a line"—visit no place without the company of a book—we may with ease fill libraries or empty them of their contents. The more we do, the more busy we are, the more leisure we have.
**WILLIAM HAZLITT**

When I am in the country, I wish to vegetate like the country.
**WILLIAM HAZLITT**

If today's average American is confronted with an hour of leisure, he is likely to palpitate with panic. An hour with nothing to do! So he jumps into a dither and into a car, and starts driving off fiercely in pursuit of diversion.... I thank heaven I grew up in a small town, in a horse-and-buggy era, when we had, or made time to sit and think, and often just to sit.... We catch a train. We grab a bite a lunch. We contact a client. Everything has to be active and electric.... We need less leg action and

more acute observation as we go. Slow down the muscles and stir up the mind.
**DON HEROLD**

Leisure is the mother of philosophy.
**THOMAS HOBBES**

The right use of leisure is no doubt a harder problem than the right use of our working hours. The soul is dyed the color of its leisure thoughts. As a man thinketh in his heart so is he.
**DEAN INGE**

All intellectual improvement arises from leisure.
**SAMUEL JOHNSON**

You were intended not only to work, but to rest, laugh, play and have proper leisure and enjoyment. To develop an all-around personality you must have interest outside of your regular vocation that will serve to balance your business responsibilities.
**GRENVILLE KLEISER**

Every now and then go away, have a little relaxation, for when you come back to your work your judgment will be surer, since to remain constantly at work will cause you to lose power of judgment. Go some distance away, because then the work appears smaller, and more of it can be taken in at a glance, and lack of harmony and proportion is more readily seen.
**LEONARDO DA VINCI**

It is that unoccupied space which makes a room habitable, as it is our leisure hours which make life endurable.
**LIN YUTANG**

He that will make good use of any part of his life must allow a large part of it to recreation.
**JOHN LOCKE**

If the world were not so full of people, and most of them did not have to work so hard, there would be more time for them to get out and lie on the grass, and there would be more grass for them to lie on.
**DONALD MARQUIS**

Don't overorganize your free time. Use leisure time for spur-of-the-moment impulses.
**ALEXANDER REID MARTIN**

I would not exchange my leisure hours for all the wealth in the world.
**HONORÉ DE MIRABEAU**

They know but little of society who think we can bear to be always employed, either in duties or meditation, without relaxation.
**HANNAH MORE**

It's necessary to relax your muscles when you can. Relaxing your brain is fatal.
**STIRLING MOSS**

I would live all my life in nonchalance and insouciance, were it not for making a living, which is rather a nouciance.
**OGDEN NASH**

Recreation is not a secondary concern for a democracy. It is a primary concern, for the kind of recreation a people make for themselves determines the kind of people they become and the kind of society they build.
**HARRY A. OVERSTREET**

Make thy recreation servant to thy business, lest thou become a slave to thy recreation.
**FRANCIS QUARLES**

To be able to fill leisure intelligently is the last product of civilization.
**BERTRAND RUSSELL**

Who has more leisure than a worm?
SENECA

It is doing some service to humanity to amuse innocently; and they know very little of society who think we can bear to be always employed, either in duties or meditations, without any relaxation.
SIR PHILIP SIDNEY

Sit loosely in the saddle.
ROBERT LOUIS STEVENSON

Recreation is nothing but a change of work—an occupation for the hands by those who live by their brains, or for the brains by those who live by their hands.
DOROTHY THOMPSON

It would be glorious to see mankind at leisure for once. It is nothing but work, work, work.
HENRY DAVID THOREAU

What the banker sighs for, the meanest clown may have—leisure and a quiet mind.
HENRY DAVID THOREAU

Leisure for men of business, and business for men of leisure, would cure many complaints.
HESTHER THRALE

To be able to fill leisure intelligently is the last product of civilization.
ARNOLD TOYNBEE

We do not educate people for leisure because we are afraid of it and have not yet outgrown the Puritan ethic which states that hard work is the prince of virtues and the devil finds mischief for idle hands.
DAVID TRIBE

Life is work, rest, and recreation, and depending on that recreation is the story of one's success or failure.
F. D. VAN AMBURGH

The walking-stick serves the purpose of an advertisement that the bearer's hands are employed otherwise than in useful effort, and it therefore has utility as an evidence of leisure.
THORSTEIN VEBLEN

Americans are more skillful workers than players. The churches are realizing that people have to learn how to enjoy their free time. New interests in life can be developed during these leisure hours. New hobbies can be enjoyed. The solidarity of the family can be strengthened by common activities and interests of its members in the free hours.
C. EVERETT WAGNER

People who cannot find time for recreation are obliged sooner or later to find time for illness.
JOHN WANAMAKER

Be temperate in your work, but don't carry the patience over into your leisure hours.
MONTY WOOLLEY

Leisure is pain; take off our chariot wheels; how heavily we drag the load of life!
EDWARD YOUNG

## *Liberty*

If ye love wealth greater than liberty, the tranquility of servitude greater than the animating contest for freedom, go home from us in peace. Crouch down and lick the hand that feeds you, and may posterity forget that ye were once our countrymen.
SAMUEL ADAMS (TO TORIES)

A day, an hour, of virtuous liberty is worth a whole eternity in bondage.
JOSEPH ADDISON

Liberty of speech inviteth and provoketh liberty to be used again, and so bringeth much to a man's knowledge.
FRANCIS BACON

The most essential mental quality for a free people, whose liberty is to be progressive, permanent, and on a large scale, is much stupidity.
WALTER BAGEHOT

What a curious phenomenon it is that you can get men to die for the liberty of the world who will not make the little sacrifice that is needed to free themselves from their own individual bondage.
BRUCE BARTON

The real democratic American idea is not that every man shall be on a level with every other, but that every one shall have liberty, without hindrance, to be what God made him.
HENRY WARD BEECHER

Liberty is to the collective body, what health is to every individual body. Without health no pleasure can be tasted by man; without liberty, no happiness can be enjoyed by society.
LORD BOLINGBROKE

Experience should teach us to be most on our guard to protect liberty when the government's purposes are beneficent. Men born to freedom are naturally alert to repel invasion of their liberty by evil-minded rules. The greatest dangers to liberty lurk in insidious encroachment by men of zeal, well-meaning but without understanding.
LOUIS D. BRANDEIS

The hinge of fate has made this nation leader in the struggle for the oppressed wherever darkness has fallen and the light of liberty has gone out. . . . So live, therefore, and so perform your part that free men across the future years will look back and say, "Here was a generation that did not seek security, but looked for opportunity."
W. NORWOOD BRIGANCE

Liberty, too, must be limited in order to be possessed.
EDMUND BURKE

The people never give up their liberties but under some delusion.
EDMUND BURKE

The true danger is, when liberty is nibbled away, for expedience, and by parts.
EDMUND BURKE

The human race cannot go forward without liberty. If this be correct, then all people everywhere should strive for liberty. If they achieve liberty, they will get a chance to pursue happiness and perhaps will be able to develop toward the ultimate goal of creation.
RICHARD E. BYRD

Liberty is dangerous.
ALBERT CAMUS

Liberty—is one of the choicest gifts that heaven hath bestowed upon man, and exceeds in volume all the treasures which the earth contains within its bosom or the sea covers. Liberty, as well as honor, man ought to preserve at the hazard of his life, for without it, life is insupportable.
MIGUEL DE CERVANTES

It is the privilege and duty of the present generation to pass on to its successors, unimpaired, the

heritage of liberty bequeathed to it by the founders of the Republic.
GEORGE B. CORTELYOU

No matter what the form of the government, the liberty of a people consists in being governed by laws which they have themselves made.
ABRAHAM COWLEY

The condition upon which God hath given liberty to man is eternal vigilance.
JOHN PHILPOT CURRAN

Liberty is the most jealous and exacting mistress that can beguile the brain and soul of man. From him who will not give her all, she will have nothing. She knows that his pretended love serves but to betray. But when once the fierce heat of her quenchless, lustrous eyes has burned into the victim's heart, he will know no other smile but hers.
CLARENCE DARROW

The United States, as a first colony in modern history to win independence for itself, instinctively shares the aspirations for liberty of all dependent and colonial peoples. We want to help and not hinder the spread of liberty. . . . That is the spirit which animates us. And if we remain true to that spirit, we can face the future with confidence, knowing that we shall be in harmony with those moral forces which ultimately will prevail.
JOHN FOSTER DULLES

Liberty is a product of order.
WILL DURANT

If the choice is given to us of liberty or security, we must scorn the latter with the proper contempt of free man and the sound judgment of wise men who know that liberty and security are not incompatible in the lives of honest men.
JAMES A. FARLEY

To say that we stand for personal liberty is not enough; personal liberty by itself alone can be selfish, individualistic, irresponsible, not believing in anything, not committed to anything, license without loyalty.
HARRY EMERSON FOSDICK, D.D.

Liberty will not descend to a people, a people must raise themselves to liberty; it is a blessing that must be earned before it can be enjoyed.
BENJAMIN FRANKLIN

They that give up essential liberty to obtain a little temporary safety deserve neither liberty nor safety.
BENJAMIN FRANKLIN

Liberty is not merely a privilege to be conferred; it is a habit to be acquired.
DAVID LLOYD GEORGE

Some folks believe liberty is doing as they please, but with controls on others.
ARNOLD GLASOW

There is a price tag on human liberty. That price is the willingness to assume the responsibilities of being free men. Payment of this price is a personal matter with each of us. It is not something we can get others to pay for us. To let others carry the responsibilities of freedom and the work and worry that accompany them—while we share only in the benefits—may be a very human impulse, but it is likely to be fatal.
EUGENE HOLMAN

If you take a worm's eye view of the ills in American life and our foreign relations, you may worry that we are entering the decline and fall of the greatest nation in history.

If you take a bird's eye view you will see the increasing skills, growing productivity, and the expansion

of education and understanding, with improving health and growing strength all over our nation. And from whence came this strength? It lies in freedom of men's initiative and the rewards of their efforts. It comes from our devotion to liberty and religious faith. We will have no decline and fall of this nation, provided we stand guard against the evils which would weaken these forces.
**HERBERT HOOVER**

Liberty is a thing of the spirit—to be free to worship, to think, to hold opinions, and to speak without fear—free to challenge wrong and oppression with surety of justice.
**HERBERT HOOVER**

To those who think that liberty is a good thing, and that it may someday be possible for people to live in a society fit for free, fully human individuals, a thorough education in the nature of language, its uses and abuses, seems indispensable.
**ALDOUS HUXLEY**

What light is to the eyes—what air is to the lungs—what love is to the heart, liberty is to the soul of man. Without liberty, the brain is a dungeon, where the chained thoughts die with their pinions pressed against the hingeless doors.
**ROBERT G. INGERSOLL**

If ever there was a holy war, it was that which saved our liberties and gave us independence.
**THOMAS JEFFERSON**

The people are the only sure reliance for the preservation of our liberty.
**THOMAS JEFFERSON**

We are all agreed as to our own liberty. We would have as much of it as we can get; but we are not agreed as to the liberty of others. For in proportion as we take, others must lose.
**JOHNSON**

Let it be impressed upon your minds, let it be instilled into your children, that the liberty of the press is the palladium of all the civil, political, and religious rights.
**JUNIUS**

Liberty without learning is always in peril, and learning without liberty is always in vain.
**JOHN F. KENNEDY**

In the American colonies, the main problem of liberty has been solved, demonstrated and practiced in such a manner as not to leave much to be said by European institutions.
**MARQUIS DE LAFAYETTE**

Where ignorance thrives, there can be no liberty, nor can it live very long even when there is enlightenment without the help of virtue.
**MIRABEAU LAMAR**

The chief end of man, as I see it, is to find security, have liberty to express his abilities, enjoy the love of family and friends, and to secure recognition of his talents, to worship God in his own way, and to participate in a government that will protect him in his exercise of these liberties, and by education and training in the development of the arts and sciences, and the techniques of their application, help him to find his proper place in the scheme of things.
**E. S. LEWIS**

A useful definition of liberty is obtained only by seeking the principle of liberty in the main business of human life, that is to say, in the process by which men educate their responses and learn to control their environment.
**WALTER LIPPMANN**

In Europe, charters of liberty have been granted by power. America has set the example, and France has followed it, of charters of power granted by liberty.
JAMES MADISON

This incomparable land of ours, it is true, is blessed by nature with protective oceans and with superabundant resources. But these alone do not make a civilization. That is built by human beings, in our case by imaginative, venturesome, creative and hard-working individuals dedicated to liberty. They came from many older nations. They held high the ideals of a classless society, government by the consent of all, with political parties to channel opinion into national policy. This civilization and its political institutions are ours to cherish in mastery or meanly, bitterly to lose.
RAYMOND E. MOLEY

A nation may lose its liberties in a day and not miss them in a century.
BARON DE MONTESQUIEU

To do what we will, is natural liberty; to do what we may consistently with the interests of the community to which we belong, is civil liberty, the only liberty to be desired in a state of civil society.
WILLIAM PALEY

Though most people shy away from talk of liberty, fearing, amid the confused uses of the term, that whatever they hear will be somebody's propaganda, they all know at what point liberty begins. It is the point at which they resent being shoved about.
STANLEY PARGELLIS

There is no doubt that the real destroyer of the liberties of any people is he who spreads among them bounties, donations and largess.
PLUTARCH

False notions of liberty are strangely common. People talk of it as if it meant the liberty of doing whatever one likes—whereas the only liberty that a man, worthy of the name of man, ought to ask for, is to have all restrictions, inward and outward, removed that prevent his doing what he ought.
FREDERICK W. ROBERTSON

Liberty is not in any form of government. It is in the heart of free man, he carries it with him everywhere.
JEAN-JACQUES ROUSSEAU

True liberty is a positive force, regulated by law. False liberty is a negative force, a release from restraint.
PHILIP SCHAFF

A well-governed appetite is a great part of liberty.
SENECA

Liberty means responsibility. That is why most men dread it.
GEORGE BERNARD SHAW

Liberty is no heirloom. It requires the daily bread of self-denial, the salt of law and, above all, the backbone of acknowledging responsibility for our deeds.
BISHOP FULTON J. SHEEN

Liberty is the result of free individual action, energy and independence.
SAMUEL SMILES

If men use their liberty in such a way as to surrender their liberty, are they thereafter any the less slaves? If people by a plebiscite elect a man despot over them, do they remain free because the despotism was of their own making? Are the coercive edicts issued by him to be regarded as legitimate because they are the ultimate outcome of their own votes?
HERBERT SPENCER

There is no truth to be gathered from all history more certain, or more momentous, than this:

That civil liberty cannot long be separated from religious liberty without danger and, ultimately, without destruction of both.

Wherever religious liberty exists, it will, first or last, bring in and establish civil liberty.

Wherever the State establishes one Church, suppressing all others, the State Church will, first or last, become the engine of despotism, and overthrow, unless it be itself overthrown, every vestige of political right.

**JOSEPH STORY**

This is the first nation that organized government on the basis of universal liberty with a free Church and a free State. This meant much at the time; it means much now and will continue to be the beacon of light and guidance for ourselves and of other nations. All that is good and practical and wise in the new developments can best be worked out under our form of government without destroying any of the basic principles upon which it rests.

**OSCAR S. STRAUS**

Despotism may govern without faith, but Liberty cannot.

**ALEXIS DE TOCQUEVILLE**

Liberty, in my opinion, is the only orthodoxy within the limits of which art may express itself and flourish freely—liberty that is the best of all things in the life of man, if it is all one with wisdom and virtue.

**ARTURO TOSCANINI**

The contest for ages has been to rescue liberty from the grasp of executive power.

**DANIEL WEBSTER**

Liberty is the only thing you cannot have unless you are willing to give it to others.

**WALTER A. WHITE**

Liberty has never come from government. Liberty has always come from the subjects of it. The history of liberty is a history of resistance. The history of liberty is a history of limitations of governmental power, not the increase of it. When we resist . . . concentration of power we are resisting the powers of death, because concentration of power is what always precedes the destruction of human liberties.

**WOODROW WILSON**

There can be no liberty that isn't earned.

**ROBERT R. YOUNG**

## *Lies*

A liar will not be believed, even when he speaks the truth.

**AESOP**

The three greatest lies:

1. The check is in the mail.
2. I'll respect you as much tomorrow as I do tonight.
3. I'm from the government and I'm here to help you.

**ANONYMOUS**

It is better to say, "I don't know," than to lie about it.

**IGNAS BERNSTEIN**

At times it's difficult to tell
What generates the greatest woe:
The truths of us told by a friend,
Or the lies of us told by a foe.

**ART BUCK**

Chameleons change their hue,
Opossums feign demise;
But man invented words
And, thus, more varied lies.

**ART BUCK**

Delusions, errors and lies are like huge, gaudy vessels, the rafters of which are rotten and worm-eaten, and those who embark in them are fated to be shipwrecked.
**BUDDHA**

Any fool can tell the truth, but it requires a man of some sense to know how to lie well.
**SAMUEL BUTLER**

The best liar is he who makes the smallest amount of lying go the longest way.
**SAMUEL BUTLER**

Some of the most frantic lies on the face of life are told with modesty and restraint; for the simple reason that only modesty and restraint will save them.
**G. K. CHESTERTON**

There are a terrible lot of lies going around the world, and the worst of it is half of them are true.
**WINSTON CHURCHILL**

A lie leads a man from a grove into a jungle.
**MARCELENE COX**

A great lie is like a great fish on dry land; it may fret and fling, and make a frightful bother, but it cannot hurt you. You have only to keep still and it will die of itself.
**GEORGE CRABBE**

Lying to ourselves is more deeply ingrained than lying to others.
**FYODOR DOSTOYEVSKY**

Lie detectors may have some limited uses, but for sure one of them isn't in the corporate hiring process. For the CIA, the FBI, the military's super-secret areas, lie detectors may have some psychological value. As proof positive, for sure they are not.

According to a recent *New York Times* article, leading academic critics contend that lie detectors are lucky to be right 70% of the time and are often no better than chance. Pentagon officials stress that "no machine can detect a lie;" lie detectors can only detect stress, may well reflect fear, surprise or anger at the interrogation rather than guilt. . . .
**MALCOLM FORBES**

As hypocrisy is said to be the highest compliment to virtue, the art of lying is the strongest acknowledgment of the force of truth.
**WILLIAM HAZLITT**

We lie loudest when we lie to ourselves.
**ERIC HOFFER**

Sin has many tools, but a lie is the handle which fits them all.
**OLIVER WENDELL HOLMES**

You never need think you can turn over any falsehood without a terrible squirming and scattering of the horrid little population that dwells under it.
**OLIVER WENDELL HOLMES**

I detest the man who hides one thing in the depths of his heart and speaks forth another.
**HOMER**

Life is a system of half-truths and lies.
Opportunistic, convenient evasion.
**LANGSTON HUGHES**

It is more from carelessness about the truth than from intentional lying that there is so much falsehood in the world.
**SAMUEL JOHNSON**

If there were no falsehood in the world, there would be no doubt; if there were no doubt, there would be

no inquiry; if no inquiry, no wisdom, no knowledge, no genius.
WALTER SAVAGE LANDOR

Society can exist only on the basis that there is some amount of polished lying and that no one says exactly as he thinks.
LIN YUTANG

No man has a good enough memory to be a successful liar.
ABRAHAM LINCOLN

He was the consummate politician; he didn't lie, neither did he tell the truth.
JOHN LUNDBERG

The biggest liar in the world is They Say.
DOUGLAS MALLOCH

Lying is a hateful and accursed vice. We have no other tie upon one another, but our word. If we did but discover the horror and consequences of it, we should pursue it with fire and sword, and more justly than other crimes.
MICHEL DE MONTAIGNE

The most common sort of lie is that by which a man deceives himself: the deception of others is a relatively rare offense.
FRIEDRICH WILHELM NIETZSCHE

The visionary lies to himself; the liar only to others.
FRIEDRICH WILHELM NIETZSCHE

It is twice as hard to crush a half-truth as a whole lie.
AUSTIN O'MALLEY

With lies you may go ahead in the world—but you can never go back.
RUSSIAN PROVERB

A lie has always a certain amount of weight with those who wish to believe it.
E. W. RICE

People lie because they don't remember clear what they saw. People lie because they can't help making a good story better than it was the way it happened.
CARL SANDBURG

She deceiving,
I believing;
What need lovers wish for more?
SIR CHARLES SEDLEY

A lie is an abomination unto the Lord, and a very present help in time of trouble.
ADLAI STEVENSON

One man lies in his work, and gets a bad reputation; another in his manners, and enjoys a good one.
HENRY DAVID THOREAU

I was brought up in a clergyman's household so I am a first-class liar.
DAME SYBIL THORNDIKE

George Washington, as a boy, was ignorant of the commonest accomplishments of youth. He could not even lie.
MARK TWAIN

One of the most striking differences between a cat and a lie is that a cat has only nine lives.
MARK TWAIN

Falsehoods not only disagree with truths, but usually quarrel among themselves.
DANIEL WEBSTER

The only form of lying that is absolutely beyond reproach is lying for its own sake.
**OSCAR WILDE**

A half truth is a whole lie.
**YIDDISH PROVERB**

## *Life*

I believe one of the greatest ideas for the prolongation of a useful and happy life experience is to have a variety of interests. . . . One's interest in life itself is always augmented by many a hobby of interest that contributes to one's special bent or happiness. These interests relax the mind and lessen tension on the nervous system. Fishermen understand this. People with many interests live, not only longest, but happiest. People with interests are never bores!
**GEORGE MATTHEW ADAMS**

Interests are a stimulant that gives only good aftereffects. The more interests anyone has the happier he is sure to be. And when I say interests I do not mean details. Details are little robbers. Interests not only add to one's enjoyment, but they actually prolong one's life, as has been proved time and again. A person begins to waste away just so soon as his interests begin to die or take flight. Interests do more than anything to aid one into the more abundant life.
**GEORGE MATTHEW ADAMS**

It's what each of us sows, and how, that gives us character and prestige. Seeds of kindness, goodwill, and human understanding, planted in fertile soil, spring up into deathless friendships, big deeds of worth, and a memory that will not soon fade out. We are all sowers of seeds—and let us never forget it!
**GEORGE MATTHEW ADAMS**

Though we seem grieved at the shortness of life in general, we are wishing every period of it at an end. The minor longs to be at age, then to be a man of business, then to make up an estate, then to arrive at honors, then to retire.
**JOSEPH ADDISON**

We all live under the same sky, but we don't all have the same horizon.
**KONRAD ADENAUER**

The goal is the same: life itself; and the price is the same; life itself.
**JAMES AGEE**

Our bravest and best lessons are not learned through success, but through misadventure.
**AMOS BRONSON ALCOTT**

I like long walks, especially when they are taken by people who annoy me.
**FRED ALLEN**

It gives liberty and breadth to thought to learn to judge our own epoch from the point of view of universal history, history from the point of view of geological periods, geology from the point of view of astronomy. When the duration of a man's life or of a people's life appears to us as microscopic as that of a fly, and inversely the life of a gnat as infinite as that of a celestial body, with all its dust of nations, we feel ourselves at once very small, and very great; and we are able, as it were, to survey from the height of spheres our own existence and the little whirlwinds which agitate our little world.
**HENRI FRÉDÉRIC AMIEL**

It is not what he has, or even what he does which expresses the worth of a man, but what he is.
**HENRI FRÉDÉRIC AMIEL**

Life is an apprenticeship to constant renunciations, to the steady failure of our claims, our hopes, our powers, our liberty.
**HENRI FRÉDÉRIC AMIEL**

If you can't run with the big dogs, stay up on the porch.
**ANONYMOUS**

Life is like a grindstone: Whether it grinds you down or polishes you up depends on what you're made of.
**ANONYMOUS**

Have you noticed that life, real honest-to-goodness life, with murders and catastrophes and fabulous inheritances, happens almost exclusively in the newspapers?
**JEAN ANOUILH**

Life is a wonderful thing to talk about, or to read about in history books—but it is terrible when one has to live it.
**JEAN ANOUILH**

What comes with ease goes with ease.
**ARABIAN PROVERB**

Life is seldom as unendurable as, to judge by the facts, it ought to be.
**BROOKS ATKINSON**

What you are must always displease you, if you would attain to that which you are not.
**ST. AUGUSTINE**

Man ought to know that in the theater of human life, it is only for Gods and angels to be spectators.
**FRANCIS BACON**

One of the most detestable habits of Lilliputian minds is to find their own littleness in others.
**HONORÉ DE BALZAC**

We will often find compensation if we think more of what life has given us and less about what life has taken away.
**WILLIAM BARCLAY**

Life, if properly viewed in any aspect, is great, but mainly great when viewed in its relation to the world to come.
**ALBERT BARNES**

The life of every man is a diary in which he means to write one story, and writes another, and his humblest hour is when he compares the volume as it is with what he vowed to make it.
**JAMES M. BARRIE**

Sometimes when I consider what tremendous consequences come from little things—a chance word, a tap on the shoulder, or a penny dropped on a newsstand—I am tempted to think . . . there are no little things.
**BRUCE BARTON**

We didn't all come over on the same ship, but were all in the same boat.
**BERNARD M. BARUCH**

The sooner we come to understand that things can be done without our assistance, the sooner we reach our philosophy of life.
**ANDERSON M. BATEN**

The deeper men go into life, the deeper is their conviction that this life is not all. It is an unfinished symphony. A day may round out an insect's life, and a bird or a beast needs no tomorrow. Not so with him who knows that he is related to God and has felt the power of an endless life.
**HENRY WARD BEECHER**

"Life is too short to little be"
Are words Disraeli wrote—

Words that are full of meaning, quite,
Which all should fully note;
So let's not worry o'er small things
Nor brood o'er matters drear,
But strive to study and work hard
And there'll be naught to fear.
**ALONZO NEWTON BENN**

The most important preliminary to the task of arranging one's life so that one may live fully and comfortably within one's daily budget of 24 hours is the calm realization of the extreme difficulty of the task, of the sacrifices and the endless effort which it demands.
**ARNOLD BENNETT**

You can observe a lot by just watching.
**YOGI BERRA**

Who cares about great marks left behind? We have one life, rigidly defined. Just one. Our life. We have nothing else.
**UGO BETTI**

Life begets life. Energy creates energy. It is only by spending oneself that one becomes rich.
**SARAH BERNHARDT**

There is no man in any rank who is always at liberty to act as he would incline. In some quarter or other he is limited by circumstances.
**PAXTON BLAIR**

Before you can write a check, you must first make out a deposit slip; before you can draw money out of a bank, you must put money into a bank; before you are entitled to a living, you must give the world a life; if you want to make a first-class living, learn to give the world a first-class life.
**WILLIAM J. H. BOETCKER**

Unless the young man looks around for himself and uses his own powers of observation and proves the assertion to be the falsity that it is, he falls under the spell of the misguidance and succumbs to a life of drudgery.
**EDWARD W. BOK**

It is our relation to circumstances that determines their influence over us. The same wind that carries one vessel into port may blow another off shore.
**CHRISTIAN BOVÉE**

Life's more than a magazine in which we flip the pages and enjoy the pictures.
**RALPH BOYER**

Life is a game with many rules but no referee. One learns how to play it more by watching it than by consulting any book, including the holy book. Small wonder, then, that so many play dirty, that so few win, that so many lose.
**JOSEPH BRODSKY**

Life comes before literature, as the material always comes before the work. The hills are full of marble before the world blooms with statues.
**PHILLIPS BROOKS**

The man who has begun to live more seriously within begins to live more simply without.
**PHILLIPS BROOKS**

Life is a glass given to us to fill; a busy life is filling it with as much as it can hold; a hurried life has had more poured into it than it can contain.
**WILLIAM ADAMS BROWN**

The ladder of life is full of splinters, but they always prick the hardest when we're sliding down.
**WILLIAM L. BROWNELL**

For man there are only three important events: birth, life and death; but he is unaware of being born, he suffers when he dies, and he forgets to live.
JEAN DE LA BRUYÈRE

Most men employ the first part of life to make the rest miserable.
JEAN DE LA BRUYÈRE

In life, as in whist, hope nothing from the way cards may be dealt to you. Play the cards, whatever they be, to the best of your skill.
EDWARD BULWER-LYTTON

Man must be disappointed with the lesser things of life before he can comprehend the full value of the greater.
EDWARD BULWER-LYTTON

There are two lives to each of us, the life of our actions, and the life of our minds and hearts. History reveals men's deeds and their outward characters, but not themselves. There is a secret self that has its own life, unpenetrated and unguessed.
EDWARD BULWER-LYTTON

To find new things, take the path you took yesterday.
JOHN BURROUGHS

Life is like music, it must be composed by ear, feeling and instinct, not by rule. Nevertheless one had better know the rules, for they sometimes guide in doubtful cases, though not often.
SAMUEL BUTLER

Life is one long process of getting tired.
SAMUEL BUTLER

Life is the art of drawing sufficient conclusions from insufficient premises.
SAMUEL BUTLER

There is no life of a man, faithfully recorded, but it is a heroic poem of its sort, rhymed or unrhymed.
THOMAS CARLYLE

The first man gets the oyster, the second man gets the shell.
ANDREW CARNEGIE

The truly important things in life—love, beauty and one's own uniqueness—are constantly being overlooked.
PABLO CASALS

**Cast of Characters**

I Won't is a tramp,
I Can't is a quitter,
I Don't Know is lazy,
I Wish I Could is a wisher,
I Might is waking up,
I Will Try is on his feet,
I Can is on his way.
I Will is at work,
I Did is now the boss.
EARL CASSEL

There are only two or three human stories, and they go on repeating themselves as fiercely as if they had never happened before.
WILLA CATHER

When one door is shut, another opens.
MIGUEL DE CERVANTES

Events are only the shells of ideas; and often it is the fluent thought of ages that is crystallized in a moment by the stroke of a pen or the point of a bayonet.
EDWIN H. CHAPIN

Great merit, or great failings, will make you respected or despised; but trifles, little attentions,

mere nothings, either done or neglected, will make you either liked or disliked in the general run of the world.
**LORD CHESTERFIELD**

Man must sit in chair with mouth open for very long time before roast duck fly in.
**CHINESE PROVERB**

If you wish to travel far and fast, travel light. Take off all your envies, jealousies, unforgiveness, selfishness and fears.
**GLENN CLARK**

Despite some of the horrors and barbarisms of modern life which appall and grieve us, life in the twentieth century undeniably has—or has the potentiality of—such richness, joy and adventure as were unknown to our ancestors except in their dreams.
**ARTHUR H. COMPTON**

Life is really simple, but men insist on making it complicated.
**CONFUCIUS**

Those who break down the dikes will themselves be drowned in the inundation.
**CONFUCIUS**

If we think of life as a journey and consider it to be the opportunity for getting from where we are to where we want to be, we will have a working rule that provides us with both a purpose and expanding possibilities for our lives.
**FRED P. CORSON**

Variety is the very spice of life, that gives it all its flavor.
**WILLIAM COWPER**

When small men cast long shadows the sun is going down.
**VENITA CRAVENS**

I do not mean to expose my ideas to ingenious ridicule by maintaining that everything happens to every man for the best; but I will contend, that he who makes the best use of it, fulfills the part of a wise and good man.
**RICHARD CUMBERLAND**

A man who dares to waste one hour of life has not discovered the value of life.
**CHARLES DARWIN**

Life is made up, not of great sacrifices or duties, but of little things, in which smiles and kindnesses, and small obligations, given habitually, are what win and preserve the heart and secure comfort.
**SIR HUMPHRY DAVY**

The real world is not easy to live in. It is rough; it is slippery. Without the most clear-eyed adjustments we fall and get crushed. A man must stay sober; not always, but most of the time.
**CLARENCE DAY**

Life unexamined, is not worth living.
**DEMOCRITUS**

If I can stop one heart from breaking
I shall not live in vain.
If I can ease one life from aching, or cool one pain,
Or help one fainting robin into his nest again,
I shall not live in vain.
**EMILY DICKINSON**

To live is so startling it leaves time for little else.
**EMILY DICKINSON**

Life is too short to be little.
**BENJAMIN DISRAELI**

Man is not the creature of circumstances, circumstances are the creatures of man. We are free agents, and man is more powerful than matter.
**BENJAMIN DISRAELI**

All finite things have their roots in the infinite, and if you wish to understand life at all, you cannot tear out its context. And that context, astounding even to bodily eyes, is the heaven of stars and the incredible procession of the great galaxies.
**W. MACNEILE DIXON**

Be sure to find a place for intellectual and cultural interests outside your daily occupation. It is necessary that you do so if this business of living is not to turn to dust and ashes in your mouth. Moreover, do not overlook the claims of religion as the explanation of an otherwise unintelligible world. It is not the fast tempo of modern life that kills but the boredom, a lack of strong interest and failure to grow that destroy. It is the feeling that nothing is worth while that makes men ill and unhappy.
**HAROLD W. DODDS**

When the great finals come, each one will be asked five questions:

First: What did you accomplish in the world with the power that God gave you?

Second: How did you help your neighbor and what did you do for those in need?

Third: What did you do to serve God?

Fourth: What did you leave in the world that was worth while when you came from it?

Last: What did you bring into this new world which will be of use here?
**J. STANLEY DURKEE**

Resolved, to live with all my might while I do live. Resolved, never to lose one moment of time, to improve it in the most profitable way I possibly can. Resolved, never to do anything which I should despise or think meanly of in another. Resolved, never to do anything out of revenge. Resolved, never to do anything which I should be afraid to do if it were the last hour of my life.
**JONATHAN EDWARDS**

Strange is our situation here upon earth. Each of us comes for a short visit, not knowing why, yet sometimes seeming to divine a purpose.

From the standpoint of daily life, however, there is one thing we do know: that man is here for the sake of other men—above all for those upon whose smile and well-being our own happiness depends, and also for the countless unknown souls with whose fate we are connected by a bond of sympathy. Many times a day I realize how much my own outer and inner life is built upon the labors of my fellow men, both living and dead, and how earnestly I must exert myself in order to give in return as much as I have received. My peace of mind is often troubled by the depressing sense that I have borrowed too heavily from the work of other men.
**ALBERT EINSTEIN**

The man who regards his own life and that of his fellow-creatures as meaningless is not merely unfortunate, but almost disqualified for life.
**ALBERT EINSTEIN**

The most beautiful thing we can experience is the mysterious. It is the source of all art and science. He to whom this emotion is a stranger, who can no longer pause to wonder and stand rapt in awe, is as good as dead; his eyes are closed.
**ALBERT EINSTEIN**

Birth, and copulation, and death.
That's all the facts, when you come to brass tacks.
**T. S. ELIOT**

It is not half as important to burn the midnight oil as it is to be awake in the daytime.
**E. W. ELMORE**

Try to enjoy the great festival of life with other men!
**EPICTETUS**

We do not choose our own parts in life, and have nothing to do with those parts. Our duty is confined to playing them well.
**EPICTETUS**

I envy that man who passes through life safely, to the world and fame unknown.
**EURIPIDES**

For most men life is a search for a proper manila envelope in which to get themselves filed.
**CLIFTON FADIMAN**

The important thing is to know how to take all things quietly.
**MICHAEL FARADAY**

One way to get the most out of life is to look upon it as an adventure.
**WILLIAM FEATHER**

The secret of prolonging life consists in not shortening it.
**ERNST VON FEUCHTERSLEBEN**

A man with a surplus can control circumstances, but a man without a surplus is controlled by them, and often he has no opportunity to exercise judgment.
**HARVEY S. FIRESTONE**

Though I have been among paralytics, to me the worst physical affliction is blindness. But spiritual blindness is worse.
**FRANCIS F. FISHER, D.D.**

If the existence of human beings leads to nothing, what is all this comedy about?
**CAMILLE FLAMMARION**

That which is useless dies. Animals that fail to serve some useful purpose in the scheme of things slowly but surely become extinct. Let any part of the human body cease to perform its ordained function, and it withers—as when an arm is long kept in a sling. This same decree, that nothing useless is permitted to survive, runs through the industrial world. . . . Let any concern cease to render useful service, and in time it shrivels. True, certain individuals, firms . . . may for a time appear immune. But sooner or later they pay the penalty.
**B. C. FORBES**

I heard one Wheel describe another: "He's absolutely copeless."
**MALCOLM FORBES**

It's great to Arrive, but the trip's most always most of the fun.
**MALCOLM FORBES**

People who can't see without glasses should wear them.
**MALCOLM FORBES**

Since we had nothing to do with our Arrival and usually are not consulted about our Departure, what makes so many of us think we're entitled to so much while we're here?
**MALCOLM FORBES**

Things there are no solution to: Inflation, bureaucracy & dandruff.
**MALCOLM FORBES**

To live your life in the fear of losing it is to lose the point of life.
**MALCOLM FORBES**

Every human life involves an unfathomable mystery, for man is the riddle of the universe, and the riddle of man is his endowment with personal capacities. The stars are not so strange as the mind that studies them, analyzes their light, and measures their distance.
**HARRY EMERSON FOSDICK, D.D.**

One never finds life worth living. One always has to make it worth living.
**HARRY EMERSON FOSDICK, D.D.**

To find one's work in the world and do it honorably, to keep one's record clean so that nothing clandestine, furtive, surreptitious can ever leap out upon one from ambush and spoil one's life, to be able, therefore, unafraid to look the world in the face, to live honorably also with one's own soul because one keeps there no secret place like the bloody closet in Bluebeard's palace where the dead things hang, to walk life's journey unhaunted by the ghosts of people from whose ruin one has stolen pleasure, and so at last to be a gentleman, one, that is, who puts a little more into life than one takes out—gather up the significance of such character, forty years old, sixty years old, eighty years old—one may well celebrate the solid satisfactions of such a life.
**HARRY EMERSON FOSDICK, D.D.**

Life is for everybody, just as sunshine is for everybody. To assert that you live your own life is like asserting that the sun sends out special rays for your own private benefit.
**FRANC-NOHAIR**

It is good to collect things; it is better to take walks.
**ANATOLE FRANCE**

We do not know what to do with this short life, but we want another that will be eternal.
**ANATOLE FRANCE**

Dost thou love life? Then do not squander time, for that is the stuff life is made of.
**BENJAMIN FRANKLIN**

The eyes of other people are the eyes that ruin us. If all but myself were blind, I should want neither fine clothes, fine houses, nor fine furniture.
**BENJAMIN FRANKLIN**

Life is half spent before one knows what it is.
**FRENCH PROVERB**

People could up the faults of those who keep them waiting.
**FRENCH PROVERB**

Life as we find it is too hard for us; it entails too much pain, too many disappointments, impossible tasks. We cannot do without palliative remedies.
**SIGMUND FREUD**

There is more to life than increasing its speed.
**MAHATMA GANDHI**

No life is so hard that you can't make it easier by the way you take it.
**ELLEN GLASGOW**

In life, as in football, you won't go far unless you know where the goalposts are.
ARNOLD GLASOW

Mysteries are not necessarily miracles.
JOHANN WOLFGANG VON GOETHE

We must not hope to be mowers
And to gather the ripe gold ears,
Unless we have first been sowers,
And watered the furrows with tears.

It is not just as we take it,
This mystical world of ours:
Life's field will yield as we make it,
A harvest of thorns or of flowers.
JOHANN WOLFGANG VON GOETHE

Little things are great to little men.
OLIVER GOLDSMITH

You can preach a better sermon with your life than with your lips.
OLIVER GOLDSMITH

If I were to prescribe one process in the training of men which is fundamental to success in any direction, it would be thoroughgoing training in the habit of accurate observation. It is a habit which every one of us should be seeking ever more to perfect.
EUGENE G. GRACE

Every day is a little life, and our whole life is but a day repeated. Therefore live every day as if it would be the last. Those that dare lose a day, are dangerously prodigal; those that dare misspend it are desperate.
JOSEPH HALL

For all that has been, "Thanks." For all that will be, "Yes."
DAG HAMMARSKJÖLD

A warning is like an alarm clock: If you don't pay any heed to its ringing, some day it will go off and you won't hear it.
SYDNEY J. HARRIS

The art of life is to know how to enjoy a little and to endure much.
WILLIAM HAZLITT

Homework, root canals and deadlines are the important things in life, and only when we have these major dramas taken care of can we presume to look at the larger questions.
CYNTHIA HEIMEL

I'd like to know what this whole show is all about before it's out.
PIET HEIN

The human question is not how many can possibly survive within the system, but what kind of existence is possible for those who do survive.
FRANK HERBERT

A handful of good life is better than a bushel of learning.
GEORGE HERBERT

You cannot make a windmill go with a pair of bellows.
GEORGE HERBERT

That man lives twice who lives the first life well.
ROBERT HERRICK

Life is a mirror and will reflect back to the thinker what he thinks into it.
ERNEST HOLMES

Life is a fatal complaint, and an eminently contagious one.
OLIVER WENDELL HOLMES

Life is a romantic business. It is painting a picture, not doing a sum; but you have to make the romance, and it will come to the question how much fire you have in your belly.
OLIVER WENDELL HOLMES

With most men life is like backgammon—half skill and half luck.
OLIVER WENDELL HOLMES

He is always a slave who cannot live on little.
HORACE

Life is like a game of cards. Reliability is the ace, industry the king, politeness the queen, thrift the jack. Commonsense is playing to best advantage the cards you draw. And every day, as the game proceeds, you will find the ace, king, queen, jack in your hand and opportunity to use them.
EDGAR WATSON HOWE

What a folly it is to dread the thought of throwing away life at once, and yet have no regard to throwing it away by parcels and piecemeal?
JOHN HOWE

The secret of the man who is universally interesting is that he is universally interested.
WILLIAM DEAN HOWELLS

Bohemia: A good place in which to camp, but a very poor place in which to settle down.
ELBERT HUBBARD

Every knock is a boost.
ELBERT HUBBARD

Everything comes too late for those who only wait.
ELBERT HUBBARD

Fences are made for those who cannot fly.
ELBERT HUBBARD

I play it cool, and dig all jive, and that's the reason I stay alive.
LANGSTON HUGHES

Life, in all ranks and situations, is an outward occupation, an actual and active work.
KARL WILHELM VON HUMBOLDT

He is happy whose circumstances suit his temper; but he is more excellent who can suit his temper to any circumstances.
DAVID HUME

There is no medicine for a life that fled.
IBYCUS

Don't get up from the feast of life without paying for your share of it.
WILLIAM RALPH INGE

Most of us spend our lives as if we had another one in the bank.
BEN IRWIN

When thou passeth through the waters, I will be with thee; and through the rivers, they shall not overflow thee; when thou walkest through the fire, thou shall not be burned; neither shall the flames kindle upon thee.
ISAIAH 43:2

It's all right letting yourself go, as long as you can get yourself back.
MICK JAGGER

Behold also the ships, which though they be so great, and are driven by fierce winds, yet they are turned about with a very small helm, whithersoever the governor listeth.
JAMES 3:4

Live all you can; it's a mistake not to. It doesn't so much matter what you do in particular, so long as you have your life. If you haven't had that, what have you had?
HENRY JAMES

One can read when one is middle-aged or old; but one can mingle in the world with fresh perceptions only when one is young. The great thing is to be saturated with something—that is, in one way or another, with life. . . .
HENRY JAMES

Be not afraid of life. Believe that life is worth living, and your belief will help create the fact.
WILLIAM JAMES

The great use of life is to spend it for something that will outlast it.
WILLIAM JAMES

If this life be not a real fight, in which something is eternally gained for the universe by success, it is no better than a game of private theatricals from which one may withdraw at will.
WILLIAM JAMES

Human life is everywhere a state in which much is to be endured, and little to be enjoyed.
SAMUEL JOHNSON

It is happily and kindly provided that in every life there are certain pauses, and interruptions, which force consideration upon the careless, and seriousness upon the light; points of time where one course of action ends and another begins.
JOHNSON

Life is not long, and too much of it must not pass in idle deliberation on how it shall be spent.
JOHNSON

The main of life is composed of small incidents and petty occurrences; of wishes for objects not remote, and grief for disappointments of no fatal consequence. . . .
SAMUEL JOHNSON

Novelty is indeed necessary to preserve eagerness and alacrity; but art and nature have stores inexhaustible by human intellects, and every moment produces something new to him who has quickened his faculties by diligent observation.
JOHNSON

Be a life long or short, its completeness depends on what it was lived for.
DAVID STARR JORDAN

There is always some levity even in excellent minds; they have wings to rise, and also to stay.
JOSEPH JOUBERT

Welcome, O life! I go to encounter for the millionth time the reality of experience and to forge in the smithy of my soul the uncreated conscience of my race.
JAMES JOYCE

Life is either a daring adventure or nothing.
HELEN KELLER

We should not lose ourselves in vainglorious schemes for changing human nature all over the planet. Rather, we should learn to view ourselves

with a sense of proportion and Christian humility before the enormous complexity of the world in which it has been given us to live.
**GEORGE F. KENNAN**

There will always be a Frontier where there is an open mind and a willing hand.
**CHARLES F. KETTERING**

Life must be lived forwards, but can only be understood backwards.
**SÖREN KIERKEGAARD**

Repetition is the reality and the seriousness of life.
**SÖREN KIERKEGAARD**

When 'Omer smote 'is bloomin' lyre,
He'd 'eard men sing by land an' sea;
An' what he thought 'e might require,
'E went and took—the same as me!
**RUDYARD KIPLING**

You never know where bottom is until you plumb for it.
**FREDERICK LAING**

Life is what happens to us while we are making other plans.
**THOMAS LA MANCE**

Not many sounds in life, and I include all urban and rural sounds, exceed in interest a knock at the door.
**CHARLES LAMB**

The greatest thing in the world is a human life; the greatest work in the world is the helpful touch upon that life. The look, the word, the invisible atmosphere of the home and the church, the sights and sounds of all the busy days enter the supersensitive and retentive soul, and are woven into the life tissue.
**CHARLES LAMOUREUX**

Circumstances form the character, but like petrifying waters, they harden while they form.
**LETITIA E. LANDON**

I have warmed both my hands before the fire of life.
**WALTER SAVAGE LANDOR**

He alone is an acute observer, who can observe minutely without being observed.
**JOHANN LAVATER**

Life is like an echo. We get from it what we put in it and, just like an echo, it often gives us much more.
**BORIS LAUER-LEONARDI**

The great man presides over all his states of consciousness with obstinate rigor.
**LEONARDO DA VINCI**

It is good to have an end to journey towards, but it is the journey that matters, in the end.
**URSULA LE GUIN**

We never think of the main business of life till a vain repentance minds us of it at the wrong end.
**ROGER L'ESTRANGE**

A man watches his pear tree day after day, impatient for the ripening of the fruit. Let him attempt to force the process, and he may spoil both fruit and tree. But let him patiently wait, and the ripe fruit at length falls into his lap.
**ABRAHAM LINCOLN**

One realizes the full importance of time only when there is little of it left. Every man's greatest capital asset is his unexpired years of productive life.
**P. W. LITCHFIELD**

Consult the dead upon things that were, but the living only on things that are.
**HENRY WADSWORTH LONGFELLOW**

It has done me good to be somewhat parched by the heat and drenched by the rain of life.
**HENRY WADSWORTH LONGFELLOW**

The lowest ebb is the turn of the tide.
**HENRY WADSWORTH LONGFELLOW**

Circumstances are the rulers of the weak; they are but the instruments of the wise.
**SAMUEL LOVER**

The falling drops at last will wear the stone.
**LUCRETIUS**

Life is like a game of poker: If you don't put any in the pot, there won't be any to take out.
**MOMS MABLEY**

Nothing is interesting if you're not interested.
**HELEN MACINNES**

Life never becomes a habit to me. It's always a marvel.
**KATHERINE MANSFIELD**

We win half the battle when we make up our minds to take the world as we find it, including the thorns.
**ORISON S. MARDEN**

I have always had a dread of becoming a passenger in life.
**DENMARK'S QUEEN MARGRETE II**

You can live a lifetime and, at the end of it, know more about other people than you know about yourself. You learn to watch other people, but you never learn to watch yourself because you strive against loneliness.
**BERYL MARKHAM**

A good man doubles the length of his existence; to have lived so as to look back with pleasure on our past life is to live twice.
**MARTIAL**

The mere lapse of years is not life. To eat, to drink, and sleep; to be exposed to darkness and the light; to pace around in the mill of habit, and turn thought into an instrument of trade—this is not life. Knowledge, truth, love, beauty, goodness, faith, alone can give vitality to the mechanism of existence.
**JAMES MARTINEAU**

I must go down to the seas again,
To the lonely sea and the sky;
And all I ask is a tall ship
And a star to steer her by.
**JOHN MASEFIELD**

The life force is vigorous. The delight that accompanies it counter-balances all the pains and hardships that confront men.
**SOMERSET MAUGHAM**

The true purpose of life, aside from resisting oppression from without, each individual carries within himself, the responsibility of living nobly or ignobly.
**DAVID O. MCKAY**

Live your life each day as you would climb a mountain. An occasional glance toward the summit keeps the goal in mind, but many beautiful scenes are to be observed from each new vantage point. Climb slowly, steadily, enjoying each passing moment; and the view from the summit will serve as a fitting climax for the journey.
**HAROLD V. MELCHERT**

To know that which lies before us in daily life is the prime wisdom.
JOHN MILTON

To my embarrassment, I was born in bed with a lady.
WILSON MIZNER

There are three ingredients in the good life: learning, earning and yearning.
CHRISTOPHER MORLEY

There is only one success: To be able to spend your life in your own way.
CHRISTOPHER MORLEY

The great business of life is to be, to do, to do without and to depart.
JOHN MORLEY

We have employments assigned to us for every circumstance in life. When we are alone, we have our thoughts to watch; in the family, our tempers; and in company, our tongues.
HANNAH MORE

Not on one string are all life's jewels strung.
WILLIAM MORRIS

The best of life is always ahead, always further on.
WILLIAM MULOCK

The humanities and science are not in inherent conflict but have become separated in the twentieth century. Now their essential unity must be re-emphasized, so that twentieth-century multiplicity may become twentieth-century unity.
LEWIS MUMFORD

Life is the only art that we are required to practice without preparation, and without being allowed the preliminary trials, the failures and botches, that are essential for training.
LEWIS MUMFORD

It is a sad thing to begin life with low conceptions of it. It may not be possible for a young man to measure life; but it is possible to say, I am resolved to put life to its noblest and best use.
THEODORE T. MUNGER

In some measure all that comes after you is going to be influenced and determined by the kind of life you make in your business of living. When reviewed from such a height of vision, even the seemingly least important life gathers round it a glory which truly passes understanding.
LAURENCE I. NEALE, D.D.

Fear not that thy life shall come to an end, but rather fear that it shall never have a beginning.
CARDINAL JOHN HENRY NEWMAN

Nothing would be done at all if a man waited till he could do it so well that no one could find fault with it.
CARDINAL JOHN HENRY NEWMAN

The irrationality of a thing is no argument against its existence, rather a condition of it.
FRIEDRICH WILHELM NIETZSCHE

One must be thrust out of a finished cycle in life, and that leap is the most difficult to make—to part with one's faith, one's love, when one would prefer to renew the faith and recreate the passion.
ANAÏS NIN

Life is easier to take than you'd think; all that is necessary is to accept the impossible, do without the indispensable, and bear the intolerable.
KATHLEEN NORRIS

If you aren't living on the edge, you're taking up too much space.
**NURSING HOME RESIDENT**

Tell me what ticks you off, and I will tell you what makes you tick.
**LLOYD JOHN OGILVIE**

Keep your mouth shut and your eyes open.
**SAMUEL PALMER**

Carlyle was right when he said that this life is only a gleam of light between two eternities. And still some folks take it so hecticly and so seriously. What's all the hurry for, anyway?
**AMOS PARRISH**

The sensibility of man to trifles, and his insensibility to great things, indicates a strange inversion.
**BLAISE PASCAL**

A person with a hundred interests is twice as alive as one with only fifty and four times as alive as the man who has only twenty-five. What are you interested in? Are your interests confined to your food, your home, your business, your clothes, your immediate family? If you would be free from nervous tension and live a healthier life, widen your interests, broaden yourself. There is a rich world around you in books, paintings, music, sports, and most important, people.
**NORMAN VINCENT PEALE**

Justice is the insurance we have on our lives, and obedience is the premium we pay for it.
**WILLIAM PENN**

No pain, no palm; no thorns, no throne; no gall, no glory; no cross, no crown.
**WILLIAM PENN**

Sooner or later, a man, if he is wise, discovers that life is a mixture of good days and bad, victory and defeat, give and take.
**WILFRED A. PETERSON**

A well-ordered life is like climbing a tower; the view halfway up is better than the view from the base, and it steadily becomes finer as the horizon expands.
**WILLIAM LYON PHELPS**

Life, with all its sorrows, cares, perplexities and heart-breaks, is more interesting than bovine placidity, hence more desirable. The more interesting it is, the happier it is.
**WILLIAM LYON PHELPS**

Life is little more than a loan shark: It exacts a high rate of interest for the few pleasures it concedes.
**LUIGI PIRANDELLO**

We feel in one world, we think and name in another. Between the two we can set up a system of references, but we cannot fill the gap.
**MARCEL PROUST**

A thousand shall fall at thy side, and ten thousand at thy right hand; but it shall not come nigh thee.
**PSALMS 91:7**

Yea, the darkness hideth not from thee; but the night shinest as the day: the darkness and the light are both alike to thee.
**PSALMS 139:12**

The desire not to be anything is the desire not to be.
**AYN RAND**

As I grow to understand life less and less, I learn to love it more and more.
**JULES RENARD**

I don't understand life at all, but I don't say it is impossible that God may understand it a little.
**JULES RENARD**

1. Do more than exist, live.
2. Do more than touch, feel.
3. Do more than look, observe.
4. Do more than read, absorb.
5. Do more than hear, listen.
6. Do more than listen, understand.
7. Do more than think, ponder.
8. Do more than talk, say something.

**JOHN H. RHOADES**

You can either be squirrel food or the seed of a mighty tree.
**PAUL RICHEY**

Inspect the neighborhood of thy life; every shelf, every nook of thine abode.
**JEAN PAUL RICHTER**

A variety of nothing is better than a monotony of something.
**JEAN PAUL RICHTER**

Who is speaking of victory? To survive is everything.
**RAINER MARIA RILKE**

Life, like war, is a series of mistakes, and he is not the best Christian nor the best general who makes the fewest false steps. Poor mediocrity may secure that, but he is best who wins the most splendid victories by the retrieval of mistakes.
**FREDERICK W. ROBERTSON**

Were we to take as much pains to be what we ought, as we do to disguise what we are, we might appear like ourselves without being at the trouble of any disguise at all.
**FRANÇOIS DE LA ROCHEFOUCAULD**

I believe in the supreme worth of the individual and in his right to life, liberty and the pursuit of happiness.

I believe that every right implies a responsibility; every opportunity, an obligation; every possession, a duty.

I believe that the law was made for man and not man for the law; that government is the servant of the people and not their master.

I believe in the dignity of labor, whether with head or hand; that the world owes no man a living but that it owes every man an opportunity to make a living.

I believe that thrift is essential to well-ordered living and that economy is a prime requisite of a sound financial structure, whether in government, business or personal affairs.

I believe that truth and justice are fundamental to an enduring social order.

I believe in the sacredness of a promise, that a man's word should be as good as his bond; that character—not wealth or power or position—is of supreme worth.

I believe that the rendering of useful service is the common duty of mankind and that only in the purifying fire of sacrifice is the dross of selfishness consumed and the greatness of the human soul set free.

I believe in an all-wise and all-loving God, named by whatever name, and that the individual's highest fulfillment, greatest happiness and widest usefulness are to be found in living in harmony with His will.

I believe that love is the greatest thing in the world; that it alone can overcome hate; that right can and will triumph over might.
**JOHN D. ROCKEFELLER, JR.**

You have to accept whatever comes, and the only important thing is that you meet it with the best you have to give.
**ELEANOR ROOSEVELT**

One of man's finest qualities is described by the simple word "guts"—the ability to take it. If you have the discipline to stand fast when your body wants to run, if you can control your temper and remain cheerful in the face of monotony or disappointment, you have "guts" in the soldiering sense. This ability to take it must be trained—the training is hard, mental as well as physical. But once ingrained, you can face and flail the enemy as a soldier, and enjoy the challenges of life as a civilian.
**COL. JOHN S. ROOSMA**

I'm passionately involved in life: I love its change, its color, its movement. To be alive, to be able to see, to walk, to have houses, music, paintings—it's all a miracle.
**ARTUR RUBINSTEIN**

Life is a magic vase filled to the brim; so made that you cannot dip into it nor draw from it; but it overflows into the hand that drops treasures into it—drop in malice and it overflows hate; drop in charity and it overflows love.
**JOHN RUSKIN**

There is no cure for birth and death save to enjoy the interval.
**GEORGE SANTAYANA**

We cannot withdraw our cards from the game. Were we as silent and mute as stones, our very passivity would be an act.
**JEAN-PAUL SARTRE**

That which goeth up must needs come down; and that which is down must needs go up. But Brahma has ordained that the that that goeth up is seldom the same as the that that hath gone down.
**GAUTAMA SAYAMUNI**

Consciousness is the mere surface of our minds, of which, as of the earth, we do not know the inside, but only the crust.
**ARTHUR SCHOPENHAUER**

The first forty years of life give us the text; the next thirty supply the commentary on it.
**ARTHUR SCHOPENHAUER**

Life is a language in which certain truths are conveyed to us; if we could learn them in some other way, we should not live.
**ARTHUR SCHOPENHAUER**

Life is neither to be wept over nor to be laughed at but to be understood.
**ARTHUR SCHOPENHAUER**

Life to the great majority is only a constant struggle for mere existence, with the certainty of losing it at last.
**ARTHUR SCHOPENHAUER**

Not one of us knows what effect his life produces, and what he gives to others; that is hidden from us and must remain so, though we are often allowed to see some little fraction of it, so that we may not lose courage. The way in which power works is a mystery.
**ALBERT SCHWEITZER**

No man will work for your interests unless they are his.
**DAVID SEABURY**

I would so live as if I knew that I received my being only for the benefit of others.
**SENECA**

It is within the power of every man to live his life nobly, but of no man to live forever. Yet so many of us hope that life will go on forever, and so few aspire to live nobly.
**SENECA**

Levity of behavior is the bane of all that is good and virtuous.
**SENECA**

Life is neither a good nor an evil, but simply the scene of good and evil.
**SENECA**

Nothing is so false as human life, nothing so treacherous. God knows no one would have accepted it as a gift, if it had not been given without our knowledge.
**SENECA**

We should every night call ourselves to an account: What infirmity have I mastered today? What passions opposed? What temptation resisted? What virtue acquired? Our vices will abate of themselves if they be brought every day to the shrift.
**SENECA**

Man ought always to have something that he prefers to life; otherwise life itself will seem to him tiresome and void.
**JOHANN SEUME**

Life is a disease; and the only difference between one man and another is the stage of the disease at which he lives.
**GEORGE BERNARD SHAW**

People are always blaming their circumstances for what they are. I don't believe in circumstances. The people who get on in this world are the people who get up and look for the circumstances they want and, if they can't find them, make them.
**GEORGE BERNARD SHAW**

What is life, but a series of inspired follies?
**GEORGE BERNARD SHAW**

A ship in harbor is safe, but that is not what ships are built for.
**JOHN SHEDD**

Life is like a cash register, in that every thought, every deed, like every sale, is registered and recorded.
**BISHOP FULTON J. SHEEN**

I have been a wanderer among distant fields. I have sailed down mighty rivers.
**PERCY BYSSHE SHELLEY**

Life to me is like a beach covered with lots of pebbles, the faster we qualify ourselves to pick these pebbles the richer we will be.
**EVAN A. SHOLL**

You, yourself, have got to see that there is no just interpretation of life except in terms of life's best things. No pleasure philosophy, no sensuality, no place nor power, no material success can for a moment give such inner satisfaction as the sense of living for good purposes, for maintenance of integrity, for the preservation of self-approval.
**MINOT SIMONS, D.D.**

In making a living today, many no longer leave room for life.
**JOSEPH R. SIZOO, D.D.**

History makes some amends for the shortness of life.
**ROBERT SKELTON**

Trifles make up the happiness or the misery of mortal life.
**ALEXANDER SMITH**

There are such astonishing things to be told about men and women, and hardly a man or a woman to whom one dares to tell them.
**LOGAN PEARSALL SMITH**

If you choose to represent the various parts in life by holes upon a table, of different shapes—some circular, some triangular, some square, some oblong—and the persons acting these parts by bits of wood of similar shapes, we shall generally find that the triangular person has got into the square hole, the oblong into the triangular, and a square person has squeezed himself into the round hole. The officer and the office, the doer and the thing done, seldom fit so exactly that we can say they were almost made for each other.
**SYDNEY SMITH**

Life is currently described as one of four ways: as a journey, as a battle, as a pilgrimage, and as a race. Select your own metaphor, but the finishing necessity is all the same. For if life is a journey, it must be completed. If life is a battle, it must be finished. If life is a pilgrimage, it must be concluded. And if life is a race, it must be won.
**J. RICHARD SNEED**

One of the indisputable lessons of life is that we cannot get or keep anything for ourselves alone unless we also get it for others too.
**J. RICHARD SNEED**

A trifle is often pregnant with high importance; the prudent man neglects no circumstance.
**SOPHOCLES**

Let a salad-maker be a spendthrift for oil, a miser for vinegar, a statesman for salt, and a madman for mixing.
**SPANISH PROVERB**

Life is the continuous adjustment of external relations.
**HERBERT SPENCER**

Life often seems like a long shipwreck of which the debris are friendship, glory and love.
**MADAME DE STAËL**

To be what we are, and to become what we are capable of becoming, is the only end of life.
**ROBERT LOUIS STEVENSON**

We thank Thee for this place in which we dwell; for the love that unites us; for the peace accorded us this day; for the hope with which we expect the morrow; for the health, the work, the food, and the bright skies that make our lives delightful; for our friends in all parts of the earth, and our friendly helpers in this foreign isle. Give us courage and gaiety and the quiet mind. Spare to us our friends, soften to us our enemies. Bless us, if it may be, in all our innocent endeavors. If it may not, give us the strength to encounter that which is to come, that we be brave in peril, constant in tribulation, temperate in wrath, and in all changes of fortune, and down to the gates of death, loyal and loving one to another.
**ROBERT LOUIS STEVENSON**

Life is a gamble at terrible odds; if it was a bet you wouldn't take it.
**TOM STOPPARD**

Any spoke will lead an ant to the hub.
**REX STOUT**

You ought to know how to rise above the trivialities of life, in which most people are found drowning themselves.
D. T. SUZUKI

Life is a little like disease, with its crises and periods of quiescence, its daily improvements and setbacks. But unlike other diseases life is always mortal.
ITALO SVEVO

It matters not how long you live, but how well.
PUBLILIUS SYRUS

It matters not what you are thought to be, but what you are.
PUBLILIUS SYRUS

Life is given to us, we earn it by giving it.
RABINDRANATH TAGORE

The shell must break before the bird can fly.
ALFRED, LORD TENNYSON

The cost of a thing is that amount of life which must be exchanged for it.
HENRY DAVID THOREAU

I think to myself I must attend to my diet; I must get up earlier and take a morning walk; I must have done with luxuries and devote myself to my muse. So I dam up my stream, and my waters gather to a head. I am frightened with the thought.
HENRY DAVID THOREAU

Measure your health by your sympathy with morning and Spring. If there is no response in you to the awakening of nature, if the prospect of an early morning walk does not banish sleep, if the warble of the first bluebird does not thrill you, know that the morning and spring of your life are past. Thus you may feel your pulse.
HENRY DAVID THOREAU

To be always intending to live a new life, but never to find time to set about it; this is as if a man should put off eating and drinking and sleeping from one day and night to another, till he is starved and destroyed.
JOHN TILLOTSON

The first thing the first couple did after committing the first sin was to get dressed. Thus Adam and Eve started the world of fashion, and styles have been changing ever since.
*TIME* MAGAZINE

Remember that life is neither pain nor pleasure; it is serious business, to be entered upon with courage and in a spirit of self-sacrifice.
ALEXIS DE TOCQUEVILLE

The idea shared by many that life is a vale of tears is just as false as the idea shared by the great majority, the idea to which youth and health and riches incline you, that life is a place of entertainment.
LEO TOLSTOY

Every man is born to one possession which outvalues all his others—his last breath.
MARK TWAIN

Why is it that we rejoice at a birth and grieve at a funeral? It is because we are not the person involved.
MARK TWAIN

Accept every blind date you can get, even with a girl who wears jeans. Maybe you can talk her out of them.
ABIGAIL VAN BUREN

Be glad of life because it gives you the chance to love and to work and to play and to look at the stars.
HENRY VAN DYKE

Remember what you possess in the world will be found at the day of your death to belong to others, but what you are will be yours forever.
HENRY VAN DYKE

There is a life that is worth living now as it was worth living in the former days, and that is the honest life, the useful life, the unselfish life, cleansed by devotion to an ideal. There is a battle worth fighting now as it was worth fighting then, and that is the battle for justice and equality: to make our city and our state free in fact as well as in name; to break the rings that strangle real liberty, and to keep them broken; to cleanse, so far as in our power lies, the fountains of our national life from political, commercial, and social corruption; to teach our sons and daughters, by precept and example, the honor of serving such a country as America. That is work worthy of the finest manhood and womanhood.
HENRY VAN DYKE

Life resembles the banquet of Damocles; the sword is ever suspended.
VOLTAIRE

A man is simple when his chief care is the wish to be what he ought to be; that is, honestly and naturally human. We may compare existence to raw material. What it is matters less than what is made of it, as the value of a work of art lies in the flowering of a workman's skill. True life is possible in social conditions the most diverse, and with natural gifts the most unequal. It is not fortune or personal advantage, but our turning them to account, that constitutes the value of life. Fame adds no more than does length of days; quality is the thing.
CHARLES WAGNER

There is no power on earth that can neutralize the influence of a high, pure, simple and useful life.
BOOKER T. WASHINGTON

The theory that can absorb the greatest number of facts, and persist in doing so, generation after generation through all changes of opinion and detail, is the one that must rule all observation.
JOHN WEISS

Get all you can without hunting your soul, your body, or your neighbor. Save all you can, cutting off every needless expense. Give all you can. Be glad to give, and ready to distribute; laying up in store for yourselves a good foundation against the time to come, that you may attain eternal life.
JOHN WESLEY

Life has a way of overgrowing its achievements as well as its ruins.
EDITH WHARTON

### A Creed

I would be true,
For there are those who trust me;
I would be pure,
For there are those who care;
I would be strong,
For there is much to suffer;
I would be brave,
For there is much to dare;
I would be friend to all—
The foe—the friendless;
I would be giving,
And forget the gift;
I would be humble,
For I know my weakness;
I would look up—
And laugh—and love—and lift.
HOWARD A. WHEELER

The most urgent necessity in human life is to be able to face life victoriously. For many—the number is appalling—are living mentally, physically, morally and spiritually defeated.
FREDERICK A. WICKETT

Fashion is that by which the fantastic becomes for a moment universal.
**OSCAR WILDE**

Life is far too important a thing ever to talk seriously about.
**OSCAR WILDE**

One should absorb the color of life, but one should never remember its details.
**OSCAR WILDE**

There are few things easier than to live badly and die well.
**OSCAR WILDE**

When a man says he has exhausted life one always knows life has exhausted him.
**OSCAR WILDE**

Life is the acceptance of responsibilities or their evasion; it is a business of meeting obligations or avoiding them. To every man the choice is continually being offered, and by the manner of his choosing you may fairly measure him.
**BEN AMES WILLIAMS**

Life is an unanswered question, but let's still believe in the dignity and importance of the question.
**TENNESSEE WILLIAMS**

All things come to him who waits—provided he knows what he is waiting for.
**WOODROW WILSON**

Life is a school. There is something new to learn wherever we may be, wherever we go, wherever we turn.
**WALTER A. WITT**

Life is divided into three terms—that which was, which is, and which will be. Let us learn from the past to profit by the present, and from the present to live better for the future.
**WILLIAM WORDSWORTH**

The big work of man is neither masonry, manufacturing nor merchandising. It is life itself. Incidentally, there are bricks to be laid, wood to be shaped and goods to be sold; but these are only jots and tittles in the scheme of individual existence. The main thing is life itself.
**RICHARD WIGHTMAN**

Life is the greatest bargain: We get it for nothing.
**YIDDISH PROVERB**

Think naught a trifle, though it small appear; Small stands the mountain, moments make the year, and trifles life.
**EDWARD YOUNG**

Who does the best his circumstance allows, does well, acts nobly; angels could do no more.
**EDWARD YOUNG**

## *Listening*

What a different world this would be if people would listen to those who know more and not merely try to get something from those who have more.
**WILLIAM J. H. BOETCKER**

While the right to talk may be the beginning of freedom, the necessity of listening is what makes that right important.
**WILL C. CRAWFORD**

The secret of a good memory is attention, and attention to a subject depends upon our interest in

it. We rarely forget that which has made a deep impression on our minds.
TRYON EDWARDS

It's just a step from making a customer willing to hear what you have to say, to making him willing to miss what you have to say.
FRANK FARRINGTON

One often reads about the art of conversation—how it's dying or what's needed to make it flourish, or how rare good ones are. But wouldn't you agree that the infinitely more valuable rara avis is a good listener?
MALCOLM FORBES

The art of conversation lies in listening.
MALCOLM FORBES

Good listeners generally make more sales than good talkers.
B. C. HOLWICK

While the right to talk may be the beginning of freedom, the necessity of listening is what makes the right important.
WALTER LIPPMANN

A good listener is not only popular everywhere, but after a while he knows something.
WILSON MIZNER

One of the best ways to persuade others is with your ears—by listening to them.
DEAN RUSK

I think the one lesson I have learned is that there is no substitute for paying attention.
DIANE SAWYER

To re-create strength, rest. To re-create mind, repose. To re-create cheerfulness, hope in God, or change the object of attention to one more elevated and worthy of thought.
GERALD J. SIMMONS

When you talk, you repeat what you already know; when you listen, you often learn something.
JARED SPARKS

All wise men share one trait in common: the ability to listen.
FRANK TYGER

Hearing is one of the body's five senses. But listening is an art.
FRANK TYGER

The reason why we have two ears and only one mouth is that we may listen the more and talk the less.
ZENO OF CITIUM

## *Living*

It is so small a thing to have enjoyed the sun, to have lived light in the spring, to have loved, to have thought, to have done?
MATTHEW ARNOLD

It is not death that a man should fear, but he should fear never beginning to live.
MARCUS AURELIUS ANTONINUS

The art of living is more like wrestling than dancing.
MARCUS AURELIUS ANTONINUS

It matters not how long we live but how.
PHILIP JAMES BAILEY

A successful house anywhere is one where you sense immediately that the people who live in it are really involved in being alive.
**BENJAMIN BALDWIN**

To live is like to love—all reason is against it, and all healthy instinct is for it.
**SAMUEL BUTLER**

We all live in the past, because there is nothing else to live in. To live in the present is like proposing to sit on a pin. It is too minute, it is too slight a support, it is too uncomfortable a posture, and it is of necessity followed immediately by totally different experiences, analogous to those of jumping up with a yell.
**G. K. CHESTERTON**

To live long it is necessary to live slowly.
**CICERO**

I know I'm not dead, but am I alive?
**FRANK CONROY**

You will find men who want to be carried on the shoulders of others, who think that the world owes them a living. They don't seem to see that we must all lift together and pull together.
**HENRY FORD**

What is there to do with life but to live it to the full?
**ARNOLD GLASOW**

The art of living rightly is like all arts; it must be learned and practiced with incessant care.
**JOHANN WOLFGANG VON GOETHE**

Living is a thing you do—now or never. Which do you?
**PIET HEIN**

The trials of living and the pangs of disease make even the short span of life too long.
**HERODOTUS**

To live is to function. That is all there is in living.
**OLIVER WENDELL HOLMES**

He possesses dominion over himself, and is happy, who can every day say, "I have lived." Tomorrow the heavenly Father may either involve the world in dark clouds, or cheer it with clear sunshine; he will not, however, render ineffectual the things which have already taken place.
**HORACE**

I have ever judged of the religion of others by their lives. For it is in our lives, and not from our works, that our religion must be read.
**THOMAS JEFFERSON**

To improve the golden moments of opportunity and catch the good that is within our reach, is the great art of living.
**SAMUEL JOHNSON**

If we are to survive the Atomic Age, we must have something to live by, to live on, and to live for. We must stand aside from the world's conspiracy of fear and hate and grasp once more the great monosyllables of life: faith, hope and love. Men must live by these if they live at all under the crushing weight of history.
**OTTO PAUL KRETZMANN**

Having outlived so many of my contemporaries, I ought not to forget that I may be thought to have outlived myself.
**JAMES MADISON**

Live and let live is not enough; live and help live is not too much.
**ORION E. MADISON**

A man lives not only his personal life as an individual but also, consciously or unconsciously, the life of his epoch and his contemporaries.
**THOMAS MANN**

When a man begins to understand himself he begins to live. When he begins to live he begins to understand his fellow men.
**NORVIN G. MCGRANAHAN**

Our great problem of the new post-war age will be not how to produce, but how to use; not how to create, but how to co-operate; not how to maim and to kill, but how to live.
**ROBERT A. MILLIKAN**

The great and glorious masterpiece of men is to live to the point. All other things—to reign, to hoard, to build—are, at most, but inconsiderable props and appendages.
**MICHEL DE MONTAIGNE**

We can't all be clam diggers or painters or heroes. But we can learn to live, every one of us. Some folks have a way of making fun of people who love beauty. Why? Nothing contributes so much to living as a knowledge of beauty and a love of it. Beauty of color, beauty of movement, beauty of line, beauty of sound. Don't be ashamed to delight in colors; don't think it's unmanly to love color; don't think you are soft because music gets you. On the contrary, it is the appreciation of such things which takes you almost halfway to the knowledge of how to live.
**GROVER C. ORTH**

It is better to live on the short of a large circle, than to describe the whole circumference of a small circle.
**CHARLES HENRY PARKHURST, D.D.**

We're too disease-conscious. We read that one out of 3 dies of this, one out of 5 dies of that. We should accept the fact that one out of one dies of something—and get on with the business of living.
**HERBERT RATTNER**

No one grows old by living—only by losing interest in living.
**MARIE BEYNON RAY**

Life's greatest achievement is the continual remaking of yourself so that at last you know how to live.
**WINFRED RHODES**

It is silliness to live when to live is torment.
**WILLIAM SHAKESPEARE**

The way not to lead a monotonous life is to live for others.
**BISHOP FULTON J. SHEEN**

The men who start out with the notion that the world owes them a living generally find that the world pays its debt in the penitentiary or the poorhouse.
**WILLIAM GRAHAM SUMNER**

The mass of men lead lives of quiet desperation.
**HENRY DAVID THOREAU**

They lived long that have lived well.
**WOODROW WILSON**

Some people are so afraid to die that they never begin to live.
**HENRY VAN DYKE**

There appears to exist a greater desire to live long than to live well! Measure by man's desires, he cannot live long enough; measure by his good deeds,

and he has not lived long enough; measure by his evil deeds, and he has lived too long.
**JOHANN ZIMMERMANN**

## Loneliness

It would do the world good if every man in it would compel himself occasionally to be absolutely alone. Most of the world's progress has come out of such loneliness.
**BRUCE BARTON**

Columbus discovered no isle or key so lonely as himself.
**RALPH WALDO EMERSON**

Loneliness is something you can't walk away from.
**WILLIAM FEATHER**

If I'm such a legend, why am I so lonely?
**JUDY GARLAND**

To most people loneliness is a doom. Yet loneliness is the very thing which God has chosen to be one of the schools of training for His very own. It is the fire that sheds the dross and reveals the gold.
**BERNARD M. MARTIN**

We seek pitifully to convey to others the treasures of our heart, but they have not the power to accept them, and so we go lonely, side by side but not together, unable to know our fellows and unknown by them.
**SOMERSET MAUGHAM**

People are lonely because they build walls instead of bridges.
**JOSEPH FORT NEWTON**

## Love

We [Americans] cheerfully assume that in some mystic way love conquers all, that good outweighs evil in the just balances of the universe and that at the eleventh hour something gloriously triumphant will prevent the worst before it happens.
**BROOKS ATKINSON**

A false enchantment can all too easily last a lifetime.
**W. H. AUDEN**

A crowd is not company, and faces are but a gallery of pictures, and talk is but a tinkling cymbal, where there is no love.
**FRANCIS BACON**

Why should I be angry with a man for loving himself better than me?
**FRANCIS BACON**

It is as absurd to say that a man can't love one woman all the time as it is to say that a violinist needs several violins to play the same piece of music.
**HONORÉ DE BALZAC**

Love: Two minds without a single thought.
**PHILIP BARRY**

Love is the delightful interval between meeting a beautiful girl and discovering that she looks like a haddock.
**JOHN BARRYMORE**

Paper napkins never return from a laundry, nor love from a trip to the law courts.
**JOHN BARRYMORE**

Of all earthly music, that which reaches farthest into heaven is the beating of a truly loving heart.
**HENRY WARD BEECHER**

Love: A temporary insanity curable by marriage.
**AMBROSE BIERCE**

Adam invented love at first sight, one of the greatest labor-saving machines the world ever saw.
**JOSH BILLINGS**

True affection is a body of enigmas, mysteries and riddles, wherein two so become one that they both become two.
**SIR THOMAS BROWNE**

Love and friendship exclude each other.
**JEAN DE LA BRUYÈRE**

Of all discriminations—
Decry them as you will—
The ultimate is love:
Forever or until?
**ART BUCK**

To live is like to love—all reason is against it, and all healthy instinct is for it.
**SAMUEL BUTLER**

Like the measles, love is most dangerous when it comes late in life.
**LORD BYRON**

Man's love is of man's life a thing apart. 'Tis women's whole existence.
**LORD BYRON**

Anything will give up its secrets if you love it enough.
**GEORGE WASHINGTON CARVER**

Love means to love that which is unlovable, or it is no virtue at all.
**G. K. CHESTERTON**

Many a man has fallen in love with a girl in a light so dim he would not have chosen a suit by it.
**MAURICE CHEVALIER**

We should measure affection, not like youngsters by the ardor of its passion, but by its strength and constancy.
**CICERO**

All men, even the most surly, are influenced by affection.
**SAMUEL TAYLOR COLERIDGE**

A great many people fall in love with or feel attracted to a person who offers the least possibility of harmonious union.
**RUDOLF DRIEKURS**

Greater is he who acts from love than he who acts from fear.
**SIMEON BEN ELEAZAR**

The effect of the indulgence of human affection is a certain cordial exhilaration.
**RALPH WALDO EMERSON**

Love never looks for faults, and whenever it discovers them in others it throws over them the mantle of charity and performs the two-fold miracle of making itself more beautiful and the one in whom the fault is found more happy.
**EDWARD H. EMMETT**

Take spring when it comes, and rejoice. Take happiness when it comes, and rejoice. Take love when it comes, and rejoice.
**CARL EWALD**

Love and scandal are the best sweeteners of tea.
**HENRY FIELDING**

Every time we hold our tongues instead of returning the sharp retort, show patience with another's faults, show a little more love and kindness, we are helping to stock-pile more of these peace-bringing qualities in the world instead of armaments for war.
CONSTANCE FOSTER

Religion has done love a great service by making it a sin.
ANATOLE FRANCE

In love there is always one who kisses and one who offers the cheek.
FRENCH PROVERB

And think not you can guide the course of love. For love, if it finds you worthy, shall guide your course.
KAHLIL GIBRAN

Work is love made visible.
KAHLIL GIBRAN

Everywhere, we learn only from those whom we love.
JOHANN WOLFGANG VON GOETHE

We are shaped and fashioned by what we love.
JOHANN WOLFGANG VON GOETHE

Into the world of fears and hatreds we need to pour a double portion of the spirit of confidence in the power of love. Not peace at any price, but love at all cost. All our problems today resolve themselves into the problem of learning to live together.
CANON PETER GREEN

The porcupine, whom one must handle gloved, may be respected, but never loved.
ARTHUR GUITERMAN

The more you love, the more you can love—and the more intensely you love. Nor is there any limit on how many you can love. If a person had time enough, he could love all that majority who are decent and just.
ROBERT A. HEINLEIN

Love is what's left of a relationship after all the selfishness has been removed.
CULLEN HIGHTOWER

There is radicalism in all getting and conservatism in all keeping. Lovemaking is radical, while marriage is conservative.
ERIC HOFFER

We probably have a greater love for those we support than for those who support us. Our vanity carries more weight than our self-interest.
ERIC HOFFER

Love is clutched at in preference to the laborious process of changing from within.
KAREN HORNEY

Nothing is more dreadful than a cold, unimpassioned indulgence. And love infallibly becomes cold and unimpassioned when it is too lightly made.
ALDOUS HUXLEY

Good nature is the cheapest commodity in the world, and love is the only thing that will pay ten percent to both borrower and lender.
ROBERT G. INGERSOLL

Beloved, I wish above all things that thou mayest prosper and be in health, even as thy soul prospereth.
III JOHN 2

Beloved, let us love one another: for love is of God; and everyone that loveth is born of God,

and knoweth God. He that loveth not knoweth not God; for God is love.
**I JOHN 4:7–8**

A new commandment I give unto you, that ye love one another: as I have loved you, that ye also love one another.
**JOHN 13:34**

The feeling of friendship is like that of being comfortably filled with roast beef; love, like being enlivened with champagne.
**SAMUEL JOHNSON**

Just remember the world is not a playground but a schoolroom. Life is not a holiday but an education. One eternal lesson for us all: to teach us how better we should love.
**BARBARA JORDAN**

Love is a sport in which the hunter must contrive to have the quarry in pursuit.
**ALPHONSE KERR**

No time of life is so beautiful as the early days of love, when with every meeting, every glance, one fetches something new home to rejoice over.
**SÖREN KIERKEGAARD**

Love at first sight is easy to understand. It's when two people have been looking at each other for years that it becomes a miracle.
**SAM LEVENSON**

The bravest are the tenderest. The loving are the daring.
**HENRY WADSWORTH LONGFELLOW**

Talk not of wasted affection; affection never was wasted.
**HENRY WADSWORTH LONGFELLOW**

One man all by himself is nothing. Two people who belong together make a world.
**HANS MARGOLIUS**

Love is what happens to a man and a woman who don't know each other.
**SOMERSET MAUGHAM**

There is no way under the sun of making a man worthy of love, except by loving him.
**THOMAS MERTON**

Parrots, tortoises and redwoods,
Live a longer life than men do,
Men a longer life than dogs do,
Dogs a longer life than love does.
**EDNA ST. VINCENT MILLAY**

It is a fine seasoning for joy to think of those we love.
**MOLIÈRE**

To live without loving is not really to live.
**MOLIÈRE**

The quarrels of lovers are like summer storms. Everything is more beautiful when they have passed.
**SUZANNE NECKER**

Family life is too intimate to be preserved by the spirit of justice. It can only be sustained by a spirit of love which goes beyond justice. Justice requires that we carefully weigh rights and privileges and assure that each member of a community receives his due share. Love does not weigh rights and privileges too carefully because it prompts each to bear the burden of the other.
**REINHOLD NIEBUHR**

Our civilization demands love and justice more than any other civilization ever has. The whole

technical mechanics of our era demands that we live as brothers. When we try, we realize how stubborn we are in resistance to God. We may go down to perdition before we are willing to live as brothers. The way we maintain our self-respect is to hold someone else in contempt.
REINHOLD NIEBUHR

Happy is he who dares courageously to defend what he loves.
OVID

By the time you swear you're his,
Shivering and sighing,
And he vows his passion is
Infinite, undying—
One of you is lying.
DOROTHY PARKER

Those who love deeply never grow old; they may die of old age, but they die young.
A. W. PINERO

He whom love touches not walks in darkness.
PLATO

No disguise can long conceal love where it exists, or long feign it where it is lacking.
FRANÇOIS DE LA ROCHEFOUCAULD

There are two sorts of constancy in love; the one comes from the constant discovery in our beloved of new grounds for love, and the other from making it a point of honor to be constant.
FRANÇOIS DE LA ROCHEFOUCAULD

There is only one kind of love, but there are one thousand imitations.
FRANÇOIS DE LA ROCHEFOUCAULD

We are nearer loving those who hate us than those who love us more than we wish.
FRANÇOIS DE LA ROCHEFOUCAULD

We forgive so long as we love.
FRANÇOIS DE LA ROCHEFOUCAULD

I believe that love is the greatest thing in the world; that it alone can overcome hate; that right can and will triumph over might.
JOHN D. ROCKEFELLER, JR.

Love cannot exists as a duty; to tell a child that it ought to love its parents and its brother and sisters is utterly useless, if not worse.
BERTRAND RUSSELL

Perhaps love is the process of my leading you gently back to yourself.
ANTOINE DE SAINT-EXUPÉRY

Love doesn't have to be perfect. Even perfect, it is still the best thing there is, for the simple reason that it is the most common and constant truth of all, of all life, all law and order, the very thing which holds everything together, which permits everything to move along in time and be its wonderful or ordinary self.
WILLIAM SAROYAN

Something lingers in the human family that is from certain branches of the animal family. Total love, straight through to issue, to children, can be a killer, and no man who is killed by love is ever the same, or ever again a son. He is a father forever after.
WILLIAM SAROYAN

Loving can cost a lot, but not loving always costs more, and those who fear to love often find that want of love is an emptiness that robs the joy from life.
MERLE SHAIN

Loving someone means helping them to be more themselves, which can be different from being what you'd like them to be, although often they turn out the same.
**MERLE SHAIN**

All my life, affection has been showered upon me, and every forward step I have made has been taken in spite of it.
**GEORGE BERNARD SHAW**

The fickleness of the women I love is only equalled by the infernal constancy of the women who love me.
**GEORGE BERNARD SHAW**

Love rarely overtakes, it mostly comes to meet us.
**WILHELM STEKEL**

'Tis sweet to feel by what fine-spun threads our affections are drawn together.
**LAURENCE STERNE**

Out upon it, I have loved
Three whole days together;
And am like to love three more
If it proves fair weather.
**SIR JOHN SUCKLING**

When the satisfaction or the security of another person becomes as significant to one as one's own satisfaction or security, then a state of love exists.
**HARRY STACK SULLIVAN**

Fear less, hope more; eat less, chew more; whine less, breathe more; talk less, say more; hate less, love more; and all good things are yours.
**SWEDISH PROVERB**

We live in this world when we love it.
**RABINDRANATH TAGORE**

More and more clearly every day, out of biology, anthropology, sociology, history, economic analysis, psychological insight, plain human decency and common sense, the necessary mandate of survival that we shall love all our neighbors as we do ourselves, is being confirmed and reaffirmed.
**ORDWAY TEAD**

No one worth possessing
Can be quite possessed.
**SARA TEASDALE**

There is no remedy for love but to love more.
**HENRY DAVID THOREAU**

Praise is well, compliment is well, but affection—that is the last and most precious reward that any man can win, whether by character or achievement.
**MARK TWAIN**

The language of love is spoken with a look, a touch, a sigh, a kiss and sometimes a word.
**FRANK TYGER**

The chains of love are never so binding as when their links are made of gold.
**ROYAL TYLER**

The emotion, the ecstasy of love, we all want, but God spare us the responsibility.
**JESSAMYN WEST**

What we can do for another is the test of powers; what we can suffer for is the test of love.
**BISHOP WESTCOTT**

In love, one always begins by deceiving oneself, and one always ends by deceiving others; and that is what the world calls a romance.
**OSCAR WILDE**

There is a land of the living and a land of the dead and the bridge is love.
**THORNTON WILDER**

Love is an energy which exists of itself. It is its own value.
**THORNTON WILDER**

We live by admiration, hope and love.
**WILLIAM WORDSWORTH**

## *Loyalty*

There is one element that is worth its weight in gold and that is loyalty. It will cover a multitude of weaknesses.
**PHILIP D. ARMOUR**

Loyalty must arise spontaneously from the hearts of people who love their country and respect their government.
**HUGO L. BLACK**

When young we are faithful to individuals, when older we grow more loyal to situations and to types.
**CYRIL CONNOLLY**

Loyalty cannot be blueprinted. It cannot be produced on an assembly line. In fact, it cannot be manufactured at all, for its origin is the human heart—the center of self-respect and human dignity. It is a force which leaps into being only when conditions are exactly right for it—and it is a force very sensitive to betrayal.
**MAURICE R. FRANKS**

Loyalty is a major force making for unity in any life—even in the existence of a civilization. . . . It gives point and flavor, most of all meaning, to a life or a culture.
**HARMON M. GEHR**

Whose bread I eat, his song I sing.
**GERMAN SAYING**

The strength of a country or creed lies in the true sense of loyalty it can arouse in the hearts of its people.
**LOUIS C. GERSTEIN**

No citizen of this nation is worthy of the name unless he bears unswerving loyalty to the system under which he lives, the system that gives him more benefits than any other system yet devised by man. Loyalty leaves room to change the system when need be, but only under the ground rules by which we Americans live.
**JOHN A. HANNAH**

An ounce of loyalty is worth a pound of cleverness.
**ELBERT HUBBARD**

The integrated life is that in which God holds the reins. It has nothing of the narrow or restricted in it. It is a fullness of life within a larger purpose that brings order out of chaos. Instead of several loyalties in conflict there is one supreme loyalty in which all lesser loyalties find their proper places. Instead of disintegration there is a sense of unity.
**FRANK GLENN LANKARD**

How many things in the world deserve our loyalty? Very few indeed. I think one should be loyal to immortality, which is another word for life, a stronger word for it.
**BORIS PASTERNAK**

If vitality gives a man's perspectives color, if community bonds give them breadth, if awareness of

the land makes them realistic, a deep sense of loyalty gives them personal meaning and integrity.
**HARRY HUNTT RANSOM**

It goes far toward making a man faithful to let him understand that you think him so; and he that does but suspect I will deceive him, gives me a sort of right to do so.
**SENECA**

Think not those faithful who praise all thy words and actions, but those who kindly reprove thy faults.
**SOCRATES**

My kind of loyalty was loyalty to one's country, not to its institutions or its office-holders.
**MARK TWAIN**

Faithfulness is to the emotional life what consistency is to the life of the intellect—simply a confession of failure.
**OSCAR WILDE**

## *Luck*

I never knew an early-rising, hardworking, prudent man, careful of his earnings, and strictly honest, who complained of bad luck. A good character, good habits, and iron industry are impregnable to the assaults of all the ill-luck that fools ever dreamed of.
**JOSEPH ADDISON**

If you wait for luck to help you, you'll have often an empty stomach.
**IGNAS BERNSTEIN**

Good luck reaches farther than long arms.
**H. G. BOHN**

The public man needs but one patron, namely, the lucky moment.
**EDWARD BULWER-LYTTON**

A stout man's heart breaks bad luck.
**MIGUEL DE CERVANTES**

Good and bad luck is a synonym in the great majority of instances, for good and bad judgment.
**JOHN CHATFIELD**

What helps luck is a habit of watching for opportunities, of having a patient, but restless mind, of sacrificing one's ease or vanity, or uniting a love of detail to foresight, and of passing through hard times bravely and cheerfully.
**CHARLES VICTOR CHERBULIEZ**

I am a great believer in Luck. The harder I work the more of it I seem to have.
**COLEMAN COX**

There isn't any luck that enters into anything, unless it's poker or shooting dice, maybe. There is no luck to merchandising. There is no luck in going out and working from early in the morning to long after dinner. That is not luck, it's work.
**FRED W. FITCH**

Backboneless employees are too ready to attribute the success of others to luck. Luck is usually the fruit of intelligent application. The man who is intent on making the most of his opportunities is too busy to bother about luck.
**B. C. FORBES**

There is an old saying, The harder you try the luckier you get. I kind of like that definition of luck.
**GERALD FORD**

It never occurs to fools that merit and good fortune are closely united.
**JOHANN WOLFGANG VON GOETHE**

There are rules to luck, for to the wise not all is accident. Try, therefore, to help luck along. Some are satisfied to stand politely before the portals of Fortune and to await her bidding; better those who push forward, and who employ their enterprise, who on the wings of their worth and valor seek to embrace luck and effectively to gain her favor. And yet, properly seasoned, there is no other way to her but that of virtue and attentiveness; for none has more good luck, or more bad luck, than he has wisdom, or unwisdom.
**BALTASAR GRACIÁN**

Luck is an accident that happens to the competent.
**ALBERT M. GREENFIELD**

Some folk want their luck buttered.
**THOMAS HARDY**

Good luck beats early rising.
**IRISH PROVERB**

I am a great believer in luck, and I find the harder I work the more I have of it.
**STEPHEN LEACOCK**

Now and then there is a person born so unlucky that he runs into accidents that started out to happen to somebody else.
**DONALD MARQUIS**

Your luck is how you treat people.
**BRIDGET O'DONNELL**

Luck means the hardships and privations which you have not hesitated to endure, the long nights you have devoted to work. Luck means the appointments you have never failed to keep; the trains you have never failed to catch.
**MAX O'RELL**

Luck generally comes to those who look after it; and my notion is that it taps, once in a lifetime, at everybody's door, but if industry does not open it luck goes away.
**CHARLES H. SPURGEON**

Luck never gives; it only lends.
**SWEDISH PROVERB**

# M

## Man

It is not the oath that makes us believe the man, but the man the oath.
AESCHYLUS

If I could get my membership fee back, I'd resign from the human race.
FRED ALLEN

Our dependence outweighs our independence, for we are independent only in our desire, while we are dependent on our health, on nature, on society, on everything in us and outside us.
HENRI FRÉDÉRIC AMIEL

All mankind is divided into three classes: Those that are immovable, those that are movable, and those that move.
ARABIAN PROVERB

There is a cropping-time in the races of men, as in the fruits of the field; and sometimes, if the shock be good, there springs up for a time a succession of splendid men; and then comes a period of barrenness.
ARISTOTLE

It isn't the common man at all who is important; it's the uncommon man.
NANCY ASTOR

A rational nature admits of nothing which is not serviceable to the rest of mankind.
MARCUS AURELIUS ANTONINUS

Despise not any man, and do not spurn anything; for there is no man that has not his hour, nor is there anything that has not its place.
RABBI BEN AZAI

A crowd is not company, and faces are but a gallery of pictures.
FRANCIS BACON

What is an individual? Just a bit of life shot off from the one Life in the universe—just a bit of love and truth dropped on this globe, just as the globe itself was once a bit of light and heat dropped from the sun.
C. W. BARRON

The significance of man is that he is insignificant and aware of it.
CARL BECKER

Many men build as cathedrals are built—the part nearest the ground finished, but that part which soars toward heaven, the turrets and the spires, forever incomplete.
HENRY WARD BEECHER

The speciously clever people who have been running things and us, calling themselves benefactors, bidding all men admire their sagacity, telling the church to rise up and bless them, appear more and more in their true light, as poor ignorant souls who in a strange madness for power and money have overlooked the beauty and the worth of God's great common people.
BERNARD IDDINGS BELL, D.D.

No one goes there nowadays, it's too crowded.
YOGI BERRA

There is a book into which some of us are happily led to look, and to look again, and never tire of looking. It is the Book of Man. You may open that book whenever and wherever you find another human voice to answer yours, and another human hand to take in your own.
WALTER BESANT

I consider that we are all self-seeking, cruel and destructive beings, except perhaps briefly to those we wish to impress. I am no longer hurt or astonished.
CHARITY BLACKSTOCK

Nought can deform the human race
Like to the armour's iron brace.
WILLIAM BLAKE

In great matters men show themselves as they wish to be seen; in small matters, as they are.
GAMALIEL BRADFORD

He who walks in another's tracks leaves no footprints.
JOAN L. BRANNON

You first parents of the human race . . . who ruined yourselves for an apple, what might you not have done for a truffled turkey?
ANTHELME BRILLAT-SAVARIN

What a man is is the basis of what he dreams and thinks, accepts and rejects, feels and perceives.
JOHN MASON BROWN

Man seeks his own good at the whole world's cost.
ROBERT BROWNING

Let us not complain against men because of their rudeness, their ingratitude, their injustice, their arrogance, their love of self, their forgetfulness of others. They are so made. Such is their nature.
JEAN DE LA BRUYÈRE

Flocking birds not of a feather
Dissent at length when thrust together;
Which means that forced diversity
Creates its own adversity.
ART BUCK

People are much more alike inside than they are on the surface.
VERNE BURNETT

The world will only, in the end, follow those who have despised as well as served it.
SAMUEL BUTLER

In men whom men condemn as ill
I find so much of goodness still,
In men whom men pronounce divine
I found so much of sin and blot,
I do not dare to draw a line
Between the two, where God has not.
LORD BYRON

Show me the man you honor, and I will know what kind of a man you are, for it shows me what your ideal of manhood is, and what kind of a man you long to be.
THOMAS CARLYLE

The true epic of our times is not arms and the man, but tools and the man, and infinitely wider kind of epic.
THOMAS CARLYLE

There are only two or three human stories, and they go on repeating themselves as fiercely as if they had never happened before.
WILLA CATHER

Three things too much, and three too little are pernicious to man; to speak much, and know little; to

spend much, and have little; to presume much, and be worth little.
MIGUEL DE CERVANTES

A true man never frets about his place in the world, but just slides into it by the gravitation of his nature, and swings there as easily as a star.
EDWIN H. CHAPIN

Chins are exclusively a human feature, not to be found among the beasts. If they had chins, most animals would look like each other.
MALCOLM DE CHAZAL

In nature a repulsive caterpillar turns into a lovely butterfly. But with human beings a lovely butterfly turns into a repulsive caterpillar.
ANTON CHEKHOV

Man is what he believes.
ANTON CHEKHOV

You must look into people, as well as at them.
LORD CHESTERFIELD

Man is an exception, whatever else he is. If it is not true that a divine being fell, then we can only say that one of the animals went entirely off its head.
G. K. CHESTERTON

Men always talk about the most important things to perfect strangers. In the perfect stranger we perceive man himself; the image of God is not disguised by resemblances to an uncle or doubts of the wisdom of a mustache.
G. K. CHESTERTON

We must be united, we must be undaunted, we must be inflexible. Our qualities and deeds must burn and glow through the gloom of Europe until they become the veritable beacon of its salvation.
WINSTON CHURCHILL

It is not the place that maketh the person, but the person that maketh the place honorable.
CICERO

Our Christian civilization, as well as our political democracy, has developed through the inspiration of a high faith in man, the common man. He is the sovereign of the State, not because he is always wise, but because he and his fellow-citizens are the State.
FRANKLIN P. COLE, D.D.

It is not until we have passed through the furnace that we are made to know how much dross there is in our composition.
CHARLES CALEB COLTON

The Master was entirely free from four things: prejudice, foregone conclusions, obstinacy, and egoism.
CONFUCIUS

The superior man will watch over himself when he is alone. He examines his heart that there may be nothing wrong there, and that he may have no cause of dissatisfaction with himself.
CONFUCIUS

Unless above him he can erect himself, how poor a thing is man!
SAMUEL DANIEL

Limit to strength?
There is no limit to strength.
Limit to courage?
There is no limit to courage.
Limit to suffering?
There is no limit to suffering.
GABRIELLE D'ANNUNZIO

Man (doubtless) was not created to be an idle fellow; he was not set in this universal orchard to stand still as a tree.
THOMAS DEKKER

The best security for civilization is the dwelling, and upon properly appointed and becoming dwellings depends, more than anything else, the improvement of mankind.
**BENJAMIN DISRAELI**

The man who follows the crowd will never be followed by a crowd.
**RICHARD S. DONNELL**

Let us teach our children to study man as well as mathematics and to build cathedrals as well as power stations.
**DAVID ECCLES**

It is not a struggle merely of economic theories, or forms of government or of military power. At issue is the true nature of man. Either man is the creature whom the psalmist described as a little lower than the angels . . . or man is a soulless, animated machine to be enslaved, used and consumed by the state for its own glorification. It is, therefore, a struggle which goes to the roots of the human spirit, and its shadow falls across the long sweep of man's destiny.
**DWIGHT D. EISENHOWER**

I know and see too well, when not voluntarily blind, the speedy limits of persons called high and worthy.
**RALPH WALDO EMERSON**

A man is known by the books he reads, by the company he keeps, by the praise he gives, by his dress, by his tastes, by his distastes, by the stories he tells, by his gait, by the motion of his eye, by the look of his house, of his chamber; for nothing on earth is solitary, but everything hath affinities infinite.
**RALPH WALDO EMERSON**

A mob is a society of bodies, voluntarily bereaving themselves of reason, and traversing its work. The mob is man, voluntarily descending to the nature of the beast. Its fit hour of activity is night; its actions are insane, like its whole constitution.
**RALPH WALDO EMERSON**

We own to man higher succors than food and fire. We owe to man man.
**RALPH WALDO EMERSON**

The great scientific discoveries of the past hundred years have been as child's play compared with the titanic forces that will be released when man applies himself to the understanding and mastery of his own nature.
**MELVIN J. EVANS**

Seek those who find your road agreeable, your personality and mind stimulating, your philosophy acceptable, and your experience helpful. Let those who do not, seek their own kind.
**JEAN HENRI FABRE**

Omit a few of the most abstruse sciences, and mankind's study of man occupies nearly the whole field of literature. The burden of history is what man has been; of law, what he does; of physiology, what he is; of ethics, what he ought to be; of revelation, what he shall be.
**GEORGE FINLAYSON**

Man as a race does not know what his limits are, where his boundaries lie. The race has constantly surprised itself by discovering the limits are not limits but ways, that the ocean is not an obstacle but a highway, that the forest is not a dark and threatening barrier but a useful source of food, light and shelter.
**JOSEPH J. FIRERAUGH**

The difference between men and boys is the price of their toys.
**MALCOLM FORBES**

Nobody can make anybody be someone he or she doesn't want to be.
**MALCOLM FORBES**

We settle things by a majority vote, and the psychological effect of doing that is to create the impression that the majority is probably right. Of course, on any fine issue the majority is sure to be wrong. Think of taking a majority vote on the best music. Jazz would win over Chopin. Or on the best novel. Many cheap scribblers would win over Tolstoy. And any day a prizefight will get a bigger crowd, larger gate receipts and wider newspaper publicity than any new revelation of goodness, truth or beauty could hope to achieve in a century.
**HARRY EMERSON FOSDICK, D.D.**

Men are not against you; they're merely for themselves.
**GENE FOWLER**

Of all the ways of defining man, the worst is the one which makes him out to be a rational animal.
**ANATOLE FRANCE**

Mankind are very odd creatures: One half censure what they practice, the other half practice what they censure; the rest always say and do as they ought.
**BENJAMIN FRANKLIN**

Essential characteristics of a gentleman: The will to put himself in the place of others; the horror of forcing others into positions from which he would himself recoil; the power to do what seems to him to be right, without considering what others may say or think.
**JOHN GALSWORTHY**

I mean to make myself a man, and if I succeed in that, I shall succeed in everything else.
**JAMES A. GARFIELD**

Territory is but the body of a nation. The people who inhabit its hills and valleys are its soul, its spirit, its life.
**JAMES A. GARFIELD**

We do not need more men. We do not need more money. We do not need more materials. What we do need is something to give a man a new spirit.... The problem of today is the people of today. It is people that make the times and not the times that make people. The trouble is with man himself.
**PAUL GARRETT**

By keeping men off, you keep them on.
**JOHN GAY**

When everyone is somebody then no one's anybody.
**WILLIAM S. GILBERT**

Man is to be trained chiefly by studying and by knowing man.
**WILLIAM E. GLADSTONE**

Man is not born to solve the problem of the universe, but to find out what he has to do; and to restrain himself within the limits of his comprehension.
**JOHANN WOLFGANG VON GOETHE**

The master proves himself in recognizing his limitations.
**JOHANN WOLFGANG VON GOETHE**

Treat people as if they were what they ought to be and you help them become what they are capable of becoming.
**JOHANN WOLFGANG VON GOETHE**

What is a minority? The chosen heroes of this earth have been in a minority. There is not a social, political, or religious privilege that you enjoy today that was not bought for you by the blood and tears

and patient suffering of the minority. It is the minority that have stood in the van of every moral conflict, and achieved all that is noble in the history of the world.
JOHN B. GOUGH

Thousands of engineers can design bridges, calculate strains and stresses, and draw up specifications for machines, but the great engineer is the man who can tell whether the bridge or the machine should be built at all, where it should be built and when.
EUGENE G. GRACE

In the world men must be dealt with according to what they are, and not to what they ought to be; and the great art of life is to find out what they are, and act with them accordingly.
CHARLES C. F. GREVILLE

He had assembled all the materials out of which to make himself a man but had never troubled to put them together.
KNUT HAMSUN

The real gentleman is one who is gentle in everything, at least in everything that depends on himself—in carriage, temper, constructions, aims, desires. He is mild, calm, quiet, even temperate—not hasty in judgment, not exorbitant in ambition, not overbearing, not proud, not rapacious, not oppressive.
JULIUS C.HARE

The most insignificant people are the most apt to sneer at others. They are safe from reprisals, and have no hope of rising in their own esteem but by lowering their neighbors.
WILLIAM HAZLITT

All men are not slimy warthogs. Some men are silly giraffes, some woebegone puppies, some insecure frogs. But if one is not careful, those slimy warthogs will ruin it for all the others.
CYNTHIA HEIMEL

A gentleman is one who never hurts anyone's feelings unintentionally.
OLIVER HERFORD

A dissenting minority feels free only when it can impose its will on the majority; what it abominates most is the dissent of the majority.
ERIC HOFFER

A gentleman is one who is too brave to lie, too generous to cheat, and who takes his share of the world and lets other people have theirs.
PAUL G. HOFFMAN

The gentleman is solid mahogany; the fashionable man is only veneer.
JOSIAH G. HOLLAND

Of all the creatures that creep and breathe on earth, there is none more wretched than man.
HOMER

Recently, in my opinion, there has been too much talk about the Common Man. It has been dinned into us that this is the Century of the Common Man. The idea seems to be that the Common Man has come into his own at last. But I have never been able to find out who this is. In fact, most Americans will get mad and fight if you try calling them common. . . . I have never met a father and mother who did not want their children to grow up to be uncommon men and women. May it always be so. For the future of America rests not in mediocrity, but in the constant renewal of leadership in every phase of our national life.
HERBERT HOOVER

Government, religion, property, books, are nothing but the scaffolding to build men. Earth holds up to her master no fruit like the finished man.
**KARL WILHELM VON HUMBOLDT**

Men are very queer animals—a mix of horse-nervousness, ass-stubbornness and camel-malice.
**THOMAS H. HUXLEY**

Thoughtfulness for others, generosity, modesty and self-respect are the qualities which make a real gentleman or lady.
**THOMAS H. HUXLEY**

The real nature of man is originally good, but it becomes clouded by contact with earthly things and therefore needs purification before it can shine forth in its native clarity.
**I CHING**

If I am a gentleman and you are a gentleman, who will milk the cow?
**IRISH FOLK SAYING**

Who ever hears of fat men heading a riot?
**WASHINGTON IRVING**

Man, biologically considered, and whatever else he may be into the bargain, is the most formidable of all beasts of prey, and indeed, the only one who preys systematically on his own species.
**WILLIAM JAMES**

It takes all sorts of people to make a world.
**DOUGLAS WILLIAM JERROLD**

There is nothing too little for so little a creature as man. It is by studying little things that we attain the great knowledge of having as little misery and as much happiness as possible.
**JOHNSON**

I refuse to accept the idea that the "isness" of man's present nature makes him morally incapable of reaching up for the "oughtness" that forever confronts him.
**MARTIN LUTHER KING, JR.**

The instinctive feeling of a great people is often wiser than its wisest men.
**LOUIS KOSSUTH**

Most men live beyond women, but often clinging to them the while; most women live through men, but not necessarily in their behalf.
**LOUIS KRONENBERGER**

Instead of demanding only that the common man may be given an opportunity to become as uncommon as possible, we make his commonness a virtue, and even in the case of candidates for high office, we sometimes praise them for being nearly indistinguishable from the average man in the street.
**JOSEPH WOOD KRUTCH**

Mankind is a weaver who from the wrong side works on the carpet of time. The day will come when he will see the right side and understand the grandeur of the pattern he with his own hands has woven through the centuries, without seeing anything but a tangle of string.
**ALPHONSE DE LAMARTINE**

Real misanthropes are not found in solitude, but in the real world; since it is experience of life, and not philosophy, which produces real hatred of mankind.
**GIACOMO LEOPARDI**

The history of mankind seems like kite flying; sometimes, when the wind is favorable, we let go the string a little and the kite soars a little higher; sometimes the wind is too rough and we have to lower it a little, and sometimes it gets caught

among the tree branches; but to reach the upper strata of pure bliss—ah, perhaps never.
LIN YUTANG

Some must follow and some command, though all are made of clay.
HENRY WADSWORTH LONGFELLOW

Whatever you may be sure of, be sure of this, that you are dreadfully like other people.
JAMES RUSSELL LOWELL

There is no kind of bondage which life lays upon us that may not yield both sweetness and strength; and nothing reveals a man's character more fully than the spirit in which he bears his limitations.
HAMILTON WRIGHT MABIE

In respect to foresight and firmness, the people are more prudent, more stable, and have better judgement than princes.
NICCOLÒ MACHIAVELLI

Speaking generally, men are ungrateful, fickle, hypocritical, fearful of danger and covetous of gain.
NICCOLÒ MACHIAVELLI

This business of measuring yourself by others means, of course, that you are never away from others, that you move with the crowd.
MARYA MANNES

By a divine paradox, wherever there is one slave there are two. So in the wonderful reciprocities of being, we can never reach the higher levels until all our fellows ascend with us. There is no true liberty for the individual except as he finds it in the liberty of all. There is no true security for the individual except as he finds it in the security of all.
EDWIN MARKHAM

None goes his way alone. All that we send into the lives of others comes back into our own.
EDWIN MARKHAM

We cannot live only for ourselves. A thousand fibers connect us with our fellow-men; and along those fibers, as sympathetic threads, our actions run as causes, and they come back to us as effects.
HENRY MELVILLE

Nothing can lift the heart of man like manhood in a fellow man.
HERMAN MELVILLE

To live is not to live for one's self; let us help one another.
MENANDER

Human beings are not like sheep; and even sheep are not undistinguishably alike. A man cannot get a coat or a pair of boots to fit him, unless they are either made to his measure, or he has a whole warehouseful to choose from: and is it easier to fit him with a life than with a coat, or are human beings more like one another in their whole physical and spiritual conformation than in the shape of their feet? If it were only that people have diversities of taste, that is reason enough for not attempting to shape them all after one model.
JOHN STUART MILL

Mankind are greater gainers by suffering each other to live as seems good to themselves, than by compelling each other to live as seems good to the rest.
JOHN STUART MILL

The abdomen is the reason why man does not easily take himself for a god.
FRIEDRICH WILHELM NIETZSCHE

What we know of man today is limited precisely by the extent to which we have regarded him as a machine.
**FRIEDRICH WILHELM NIETZSCHE**

I require only three things of a man. He must be handsome, ruthless, and stupid.
**DOROTHY PARKER**

No man is so great as mankind.
**THEODORE E. PARKER**

The multitude which is not brought to act as unity, is confusion. That unity which has not its origin in the multitude is tyranny.
**BLAISE PASCAL**

Render unto Caesar the things which are Caesar's and unto God the things which are God's. One would like to add: Give unto man things which are man's; give man his freedom and personality, his rights and religion.
**POPE PIUS XII**

The noblest of all studies is the study of what man is and of what life he should live.
**PLATO**

The proper study of mankind is man.
**ALEXANDER POPE**

If you are black, if you are Puerto Rican or Hispanic, be proud of that. But don't let it become a problem. Let it become somebody else's problem.
**COLIN POWELL**

When I consider thy heavens, the work of thy fingers, the moon and the stars, which thou hast ordained; what is man, that thou art mindful of him? and the son of man, that thou visitest him?
**PSALMS 8:3–4**

Blessed is the man that feareth the Lord, that delighteth greatly in his commandments. His seed shall be mighty upon earth: the generations of the upright shall be blessed.
**PSALMS 112:1–2**

Put not your trust in princes, nor in the son of man, in whom there is no help. His breath goeth forth, he returneth to his earth; in that very day his thoughts perish.
**PSALMS 146:3–4**

A man who tries to surpass another may perhaps succeed in equaling if not actually surpassing him, but one who merely follows can never quite come up with him: a follower, necessarily, is always behind.
**QUINTILIAN**

Man is a paradoxical being—the constant glory and scandal of this world.
**SARVEPALLI RADHAKRISHNAN**

This is the age of the common man, they tell us—a title which any man may claim to the extent of such distinction as he has managed not to achieve.
**AYN RAND**

The reason why the race of man moves slowly is because it must move all together.
**THOMAS B. REED**

It is not the situation which makes the man, but the man who makes the situation. The slave may be a freeman. The monarch may be a slave. Situations are noble or ignoble, as we make them.
**FREDERICK W. ROBERTSON**

I believe that the ultimate object of all activities in a republic should be the development of the manhood of its citizens.
**JOHN D. ROCKEFELLER, JR.**

I never met a man I didn't like.
**WILL ROGERS**

Ants and savages put strangers to death.
**BERTRAND RUSSELL**

The tears of strangers are only water.
**RUSSIAN PROVERB**

The job of inhabiting the world may simply be too much for the human race at its present stage of development, in which case we shall muddle through to something or other—which could be anything from simple stupor to final disaster.
**WILLIAM SAROYAN**

Every man takes the limits of his own field of vision for the limits of the world.
**ARTHUR SCHOPENHAUER**

When a man has put a limit on what he will do, he has put a limit on what he can do.
**CHARLES M. SCHWAB**

Man has become a superman . . . because he not only disposes of innate, physical forces, but because he is in command . . . of latent forces in nature and because he can put them to his service. . . . But the essential fact we must surely all feel in our hearts . . . is that we are becoming inhuman in proportion as we become supermen.
**ALBERT SCHWEITZER**

Those who follow the banners of reason are like the well-disciplined battalions which, wearing a more sober uniform and making a less dazzling show than the light troops commanded by imagination, enjoy more safety, and even more honor, in the conflicts of human life.
**SIR WALTER SCOTT**

How beauteous mankind is! O brave new world that has such people in it.
**WILLIAM SHAKESPEARE**

Use every man after his desert, and who should escape whipping?
**WILLIAM SHAKESPEARE**

We must love men ere they will seem to us worthy of our love.
**WILLIAM SHAKESPEARE**

Man can climb to the highest summits, but he cannot dwell there long.
**GEORGE BERNARD SHAW**

If a man is worth knowing at all, he is worth knowing well.
**ALEXANDER SMITH**

You see, among men who are honored with the common appellation of gentleman, many contradictions to that character.
**RICHARD STEELE**

Generally speaking anybody is more interesting doing nothing than doing anything.
**GERTRUDE STEIN**

Man, unlike any other thing organic or inorganic in the universe grows beyond his work, walks up the stairs of his concepts, emerges ahead of his accomplishments.
**JOHN STEINBECK**

The world will commonly end by making men what it thinks them.
**HENRY J. TAYLOR**

They range from animals to gods. They pray for you and they prey on you. They are bears for pun-

ishment and brutes for revenge. They want to be Everyone, Everywhere, Everything. Their restlessness fills them with wonderings and spurs them into wanderings. They are creatures of moods and modes. They try to look different, but deep down underneath they are all alike. They are hero-worshippers and idol-destroyers. They are quick to take sides and quick to swing from side to side. They like individuals who can appraise and praise them. People must be taken as they are and still they want to be taken as they aren't. They have their ways and want to get away with them. They cry for the moon and wail for a place in the sun. They are happiest in the hurly-burly, giving and taking, making and losing, to the tune of a hurdy-gurdy. They try everything once and seldom stop to think twice. But they are blessed with nine lives and often strike twelve at eleventh hours. With people all things are possible; without them, all things are impossible. They must forever be felt and dealt with. To lose contact with them is to lose contact with life.
**P. K. Thomajan**

The trouble with the rat race is that even if you win, you're still a rat.
**Lily Tomlin**

Everyone is a moon and has a dark side which he never shows to anybody.
**Mark Twain**

Man seems to be a rickety poor sort of thing, any way you take him; a kind of British Museum of infirmities and inferiorities. He is always undergoing repairs. A machine that was as unreliable as he is would have no market.
**Mark Twain**

Man is only man at the surface. Remove his skin, dissect, and immediately you come to machinery.
**Paul Valéry**

There is a loftier ambition than merely to stand high in the world. It is to stoop down and lift mankind a little higher.
**Henry Van Dyke**

If we could all agree that the world belongs to God we would see the world as a co-operative fellowship. We of the human race are so bound together and so interdependent that it behooves us all to live for the good of the whole.
**W. Earl Waldrop, D.D.**

Nine-tenths of the people were created so you would want to be with the other tenth.
**Horace Walpole**

Be not curious to know the affairs of others, neither approach to those that speak in private.
**George Washington**

Sleep not when others speak, sit not when others stand, speak not when you should hold your peace, walk not when others stop.
**George Washington**

Man, considered not merely as an organized being, but as a rational agent and a member of society, is perhaps the most wonderfully contrived and to us the most interesting specimen of Divine wisdom that we have any knowledge of.
**Richard Whately**

The greatest want of the world is the want of men—men who will not be bought or sold; men who in their inmost souls are true and honest; men who do not fear to call sin by its right name; men whose conscience is as true to duty as the needle to the pole; men who will stand for the right though the heavens fall.
**E. B. White**

The true perfection of man lies, not in what man has, but in what man is.... Nothing should be able to harm a man but himself. Nothing should be able to rob a man at all. What a man really has is what is in him. What is outside of him should be a matter of no importance.
OSCAR WILDE

So great has been the endurance, so incredible the achievement, that, as long as the sun keeps a set course in heaven, it would be foolish to despair of the human race.
ERNEST L. WOODWARD

I weigh the man, not his title, 'tis not the king's stamp can make the metal better.
WILLIAM WYCHERLEY

Nature revolves, but man advances.
EDWARD YOUNG

## *Management*

Management, in the sense of employer, is merely the agent for the public, the stockholders and the employees. It is management's job to preserve the balance fairly between all these interests, that each may have his fair share without imperilling the continuity of the effort upon which the whole depends.
JAMES F. BELL

A new type of management is required in this new business era—one that realizes that responsibility begins rather than ends when goods reach the shipping platform. First of all, such management will concern itself primarily with the manufacture of customers rather than the manufacture of the product alone. Management must resort to logical analysis more than to precedent. A keen understanding of human beings will permit management to secure unusual results.
HOWARD E. BLOOD

Every person engaged in a given enterprise is called upon to perform a managerial function, or at least to perform a function that is directly serving the purpose of management.
DONALDSON BROWN

One cannot manage too many affairs: Like pumpkins in the water, one pops up while you try to hold down the other.
CHINESE PROVERB

So much of what we call management consists in making it difficult for people to work.
PETER DRUCKER

The men who can manage men, manage the men who manage only things, and the men who can manage money manage all.
WILL AND ARIEL DURANT

Management is the art of getting three men to do three men's work.
WILLIAM FEATHER

Managing the other fellow's business is a fascinating game. Trade unionists all over the country have pronounced ideas for the reform of Wall Street banks; and Wall Street bankers are not far behind in giving plans for the tremendous improvement of trade union policies. Wholesalers have schemes for improving the retailer; the retailer knows just what is wrong in the conduct of wholesale business—and we might go through a long list.... Yet for some reason the classes that ought to be helped keep on stubbornly clinging to their own method of running their affairs....
B. C. FORBES

Basically, the problem of management is to produce more goods and services for satisfying people's wants at prices more people can afford to pay.
PAUL GARRETT

Quality of management is all-important. After all, what is a company but people? If the people have character, imagination, drive, that's good enough for me.
**DONALD A. HERMAN**

Lots of folks confuse bad management with destiny.
**ELBERT HUBBARD**

In a great business there is nothing so fatal as cunning management.
**JUNIUS**

Man is the principal syllable in Management.
**C. T. MCKENZIE**

My general theory is that sound management is merely sound thinking coupled with effective execution. The problems of all businesses are essentially the same. Yet there is some justification for the man who insists that his business is different. It is different. Therefore, while the principles of management are undoubtedly the same throughout business, the applications differ of necessity, and it is in the application of principles which anyone can understand that management proves itself good or bad.
**HERMAN NELSON**

I am convinced that much better results can be obtained from operating organizations which are responsible to a competent private management and boards of direction which must show economical operation, adequate upkeep, good public relations, and a profit than can possibly be secured from a national bureaucratic or a local political organization which is responsible to a constantly changing, short-lived political administration without any financial responsibility as to the result.
**HENRY EARLE RIGGS**

Good management consists in showing average people how to do the work of superior people.
**JOHN D. ROCKEFELLER**

Take my assets—but leave me my organization and in five years I'll have it all back.
**ALFRED M. SLOAN**

Where there is unity there is always victory.
**PUBLILIUS SYRUS**

It is said that it is far more difficult to hold and maintain leadership (liberty) than it is to attain it. Success is a ruthless competitor for it flatters and nourishes our weaknesses and lulls us into complacency. We bask in the sunshine of accomplishment and lose the spirit of humility which helps us visualize all the factors which have contributed to our success. We are apt to forget that we are only one of a team, that in unity there is strength and that we are strong only as long as each unit in our organization functions with precision.
**SAMUEL TILDEN**

To keep an organization young and fit, don't hire anyone until everybody's so overworked they'll be glad to see the newcomer no matter where he sits.
**ROBERT TOWNSEND**

The primary purpose of good corporation management is to keep a company in business indefinitely. They must look ahead and plan for depression risks, competition, obsolescence, exhaustion of natural resources, population movements, fashion changes, and political attack. They must grow reserves against hard times, improve and lower the cost of their products, stabilize the security of their workers as much as possible, and make the public like and desire their company as a community and national asset.
**CHARLES E. WILSON**

## Manners

It pays to be obvious, especially if you have a reputation for subtlety.
Isaac Asimov

Polish doesn't change quartz into a diamond.
Wilma Askinas

When away from home always be like the kind of man you would care to take into your own home.
William J. H. Boetcker

There ought to be a system of manners in every nation which a well-formed mind would be disposed to relish. To make us love our country, our country ought to be lovely.
Edmund Burke

Good breeding differs, if at all, from high breeding only as it gracefully remembers the rights of others, rather than gracefully insists on its own rights.
Thomas Carlyle

Good breeding is the art of showing men, by external signs, the internal reward we have for them. It arises from good sense, improved by conversing with good company.
Marcus Cato

Gravity must be natural and simple; there must be urbanity and tenderness in it. A man must not formalize on everything. He who does so is a fool; and a grave fool is, perhaps, more injurious than a light fool.
William Cecil

A man can buy nothing in the market with gentility.
William Cecil

Good manners are, to particular societies, what good morals are to society in general: their cement and their security.
Lord Chesterfield

Gentility is what is left over from rich ancestors after the money is gone.
John Ciardi

How majestic is naturalness. I have never met a man whom I really considered a great man who was not always natural and simple. Affectation is inevitably the mark of one not sure of himself.
Charles G. Dawes

It is the privilege of any human work which is well done to invest the doer with a certain haughtiness.
Ralph Waldo Emerson

Manners are the happy ways of doing things; each one a stroke of genius or of love, now repeated and hardened into usage.
Ralph Waldo Emerson

People who stare deserve the looks they get.
Malcolm Forbes

Good breeding sums up in its instinctive attitude all the efforts a man has made towards perfection, aye, and all that his ancestors have made before him. It is unconscious, the simple acting out of a sound, wholesome nature.
C. Hanford Henderson

Of all the things you wear, your expression is the most important.
Janet Lane

Affectation is an awkward and forced imitation of what should be genuine and easy, wanting the beauty that accompanies what is natural.
**JOHN LOCKE**

As laws are necessary that good manners may be preserved, so good manners are necessary that laws may be maintained.
**NICCOLÒ MACHIAVELLI**

A highbrow is a person educated beyond his intelligence.
**BRANDER MATTHEWS**

Manner is everything with some people, and something with everybody.
**CONYERS MIDDLETON**

I hate to see men overdressed; a man ought to look like he's put together by accident, not added up on purpose.
**CHRISTOPHER MORLEY**

Nothing is less important than which fork you use. Etiquette is the science of living. It embraces everything. It is ethics. It is honor.
**EMILY POST**

Manners make often fortunes.
**JOHN RAY**

Affected simplicity is refined imposture.
**FRANÇOIS DE LA ROCHEFOUCAULD**

Gravity is a mysterious carriage of the body invented to conceal the want of mind.
**FRANÇOIS DE LA ROCHEFOUCAULD**

The qualities we have do not make us so ridiculous as those we affect to have.
**FRANÇOIS DE LA ROCHEFOUCAULD**

In this world we must either institute conventional forms of expression or else pretend that we have nothing to express; the choice lies between a mask and a figleaf.
**GEORGE SANTAYANA**

Gravity is the very essence of imposture; it not only mistakes other things, but is apt perpetually to mistake itself.
**LORD SHAFTESBURY**

The great secret is not having bad manners or good manners or any other particular sort of manners, but having the same manner for all human souls; in short, behaving as if you were in heaven, where there are no third-class carriages, and one soul is as good as another.
**GEORGE BERNARD SHAW**

The test of a man's or woman's breeding is how they behave in a quarrel.
**GEORGE BERNARD SHAW**

Laws are always unstable unless they are founded on the manners of a nation; and manners are the only durable and resisting power in a people.
**ALEXIS DE TOCQUEVILLE**

Let your countenance be pleasant, but in serious matters let it be somewhat grave.
**GEORGE WASHINGTON**

Most of the men of dignity, who awe or bore their more genial brethren, are simply men who possess the art of passing off their insensibility for wisdom, their dullness for depth, and of concealing imbecility of intellect under haughtiness of manner.
**EDWIN P. WHIPPLE**

The test of good manners is to be able to put up pleasantly with bad ones.
**WENDELL WILLKIE**

## Marriage

Anyone who marries for money earns every cent of it.
**ANONYMOUS**

If there's one thing better than marrying a millionaire, it's divorcing him.
**ANONYMOUS**

Marriage is our last, best chance to grow up.
**JOSEPH BARTH**

The curse which lies upon marriage is that too often the individuals are joined in their weakness rather than in their strength—each asking from the other instead of finding pleasure in giving.
**SIMONE DE BEAUVOIR**

Marriage: The state or condition of a community consisting of a master, a mistress and two slaves, making in all, two.
**AMBROSE BIERCE**

I've never thought about divorce. I've thought about murder, but never divorce.
**DR. JOYCE BROTHERS**

On the whole, I haven't found men unduly loath to say, "I love you." The real trick is to get them to say, "Will you marry me?"
**ILKA CHASE**

I never married because there was no need. I have three pets at home that serve the same purpose as a husband. I have a dog that growls every morning, a parrot that swears all the afternoon and a cat that comes home late at night.
**MARIE CORELLI**

Even hooligans marry, though they know that marriage is but for a little while. It is alimony that is forever.
**QUENTIN CRISP**

To keep a fire burning brightly there's one easy rule: Keep the logs together, near enough to keep warm and far enough apart for breathing room. Good fire, good marriage, same rule.
**MARNIE REED CROWEL**

Almost all married people fight, although many are ashamed to admit it. Actually, a marriage in which no quarreling at all takes place may well be one that is dead or dying from emotional undernourishment. If you care, you probably fight.
**FLORA DAVIS**

The reason husbands and wives do not understand each other is because they belong to different sexes.
**DOROTHY DIX**

The chain of marriage is so heavy that it takes two to bear it; sometimes three.
**ALEXANDRE DUMAS**

His designs were strictly honorable, as the phrase is: that is, to rob a lady of her fortune by way of marriage.
**HENRY FIELDING**

Any marriage that survives a big wedding can probably survive.
**MALCOLM FORBES**

One thing that previous practice doesn't always make perfect: Marriage.
**MALCOLM FORBES**

To switch lads and lassies from quickie ceremonies back to the catered works in to-be-worn-only-once

white dresses, the [wedding] garment producers have turned to sociology. Through statistics as carefully laid out as a bridal train, they are establishing a correlation showing a higher divorce rate for the informally gowned.... They may just have something there.... If a bride has sunk a hunk of savings into a dress she can't use again in a second wedding, she might think twice about having a second.
**MALCOLM FORBES**

Where there's marriage without love, there will be love without marriage.
**BENJAMIN FRANKLIN**

Love makes passion, but money makes marriage.
**FRENCH PROVERB**

A man in love is incomplete until he is married. Then he is finished.
**ZSA ZSA GABOR**

I am a marvelous housekeeper. Every time I leave a man I keep his house.
**ZSA ZSA GABOR**

The happiest time in anyone's life is just after the first divorce.
**JOHN KENNETH GALBRAITH**

Love is an ideal thing; marriage is a real thing. A confusion of the real with the ideal never goes unpunished.
**JOHANN WOLFGANG VON GOETHE**

No compass has ever been invented for the high seas of matrimony.
**HEINRICH HEINE**

Love-making is radical, while marriage is conservative.
**ERIC HOFFER**

All marriages are happy. It's the living together afterward that causes all the trouble.
**RAYMOND HULL**

Courtship brings out the best. Marriage brings out the rest.
**CULLEN HIGHTOWER**

Never get married while you are going to college; it's hard enough to get a start if a prospective employer finds you've already made one mistake.
**KIN HUBBARD**

Marriage has many pains, but celibacy has no pleasures.
**SAMUEL JOHNSON**

I've had an exciting life. I married for love and got a little money along with it.
**ROSE KENNEDY**

Being divorced is like being hit by a Mack truck. If you live through it, you start looking very carefully to the right and to the left.
**JEAN KERR**

Marriage: Like buying something you've been admiring for a long time in a shop window. You may love it when you get it home, but it doesn't always go with everything else in the house.
**JEAN KERR**

My whole working philosophy is that the only stable happiness for mankind is that it shall live married in blessed union to woman kind—intimacy, physical and psychical, between a man and his wife. I wish to add that my state of bliss is by no means perfect.
**D. H. LAWRENCE**

Always remember that the most important thing in marriage is not happiness, but stability.
**GABRIEL GARCÍA MÁRQUEZ**

I belong to Bridegrooms Anonymous. Whenever I feel like getting married, they send over a lady in a housecoat and hair curlers to burn my toast for me.
DICK MARTIN

For in the resurrection they neither marry, nor are given in marriage, but are as the angels of God in heaven.
MATTHEW 22:30

A bachelor's virtue depends upon his alertness; a married man's depends upon his wife's.
H. L. MENCKEN

Bachelors know more about women than married men. If they didn't, they'd be married too.
H. L. MENCKEN

Marriage is three parts love and seven parts forgiveness of sins.
LANGDON MITCHELL

Marriage: May be compared to a cage: the birds without despair to get in, and those within despair to get out:
MICHEL DE MONTAIGNE

The trouble with wedlock is that there's not enough wed and too much lock.
CHRISTOPHER MORLEY

Think of your ancestors and your posterity, and you will never marry.
ETHEL MUMFORD

Marriage is the alliance of two people, one who never remembers birthdays and the other who never forgets them.
OGDEN NASH

Marriage is a book of which the first chapter is written in poetry and the remaining chapters in prose.
BEVERLEY NICHOLS

The best friend is likely to acquire the best wife, because a good marriage is based on the talent for friendship.
FRIEDRICH WILHELM NIETZSCHE

Other people's marriages are a perpetual source of amazement.
PATRICK O'BRIAN

No woman marries for money; they are all clever enough, before marrying a millionaire, to fall in love with him.
CESARE PAVESE

A good marriage is that in which each appoints the other the guardian of his solitude, and shows him this confidence, the greatest in his power to bestow.
RAINER MARIA RILKE

We would have broken up except for the children. Who were the children? She and I.
MORT SAHL

By all means marry. If you get a good wife, you'll be happy. If you get a bad one, you'll become a philosopher.
SOCRATES

Marriage is popular because it combines the maximum of temptation with the maximum of opportunity.
GEORGE BERNARD SHAW

Chains do not hold a marriage together. It is threads, hundreds of tiny threads which sew people together through the years.
SIMONE SIGNORET

I am glad I am not a man, for if I were I should be obliged to marry a woman.
**MADAME DE STAËL**

What they do in heaven we are ignorant of; but what they do not do we are told expressly; they neither marry nor are given in marriage.
**JONATHAN SWIFT**

Take it from me, marriage isn't a word—it's a sentence.
**KING VIDOR**

Don't marry a man to reform him—that's what reform schools are for.
**MAE WEST**

Marriage is a great institution, but I'm not ready for an institution yet.
**MAE WEST**

Bigamy is having one wife too many. Monogamy is the same.
**OSCAR WILDE**

The very essence of romance is uncertainty. If I ever marry, I'll try to forget the fact.
**OSCAR WILDE**

## *Media*

What the mass media offers is not popular art, but entertainment which is intended to be consumed like food, forgotten, and replaced by a new dish.
**W. H. AUDEN**

The most important service rendered by the press is that of educating people to approach printed matter with distrust.
**SAMUEL BUTLER**

TV cassette players will take ever-bigger bites out of the regular TV-viewing audience, moviegoers, sports and other event-attending spectators. Cassette players are now the hottest thing on the entertainment scene since popcorn. . . . Movie cassettes are improving the margin of profit for more and more Hollywood hits that don't make it at the box office. And of course, there is the home video camera. . . . The only limitation is the viewer's time. And there, my friends, is the rub of the matter. With only one pair of eyes and a 24-hour day, tape-popping addicts have less and less time for going out to pay to see things.
**MALCOLM FORBES**

If television encouraged us to work as much as it encourages us to do everything else, we could better afford to buy more of everything it advertises.
**CULLEN HIGHTOWER**

People who complain our press is biased should note that during World War II the press was on our side—and we won!
**CULLEN HIGHTOWER**

Why is the press America's showcase for freedom? Because just about everything else has been regulated.
**CULLEN HIGHTOWER**

I find television very educating. Every time somebody turns on the set I go into the other room and read a book.
**GROUCHO MARX**

## *Medicine*

I am dying with the help of too many physicians.
**ALEXANDER THE GREAT**

You medical people will have more lives to answer for in the other world than even we generals.
**NAPOLEON BONAPARTE**

As long as men are liable to die and are desirous to live, a physician will be made fun of, but he will be well paid.
**JEAN DE LA BRUYÈRE**

Medicine is the only profession that labors incessantly to destroy the reason for its existence.
**JAMES BRYCE**

The whole imposing edifice of modern medicine is like the celebrated Tower of Pisa—slightly off balance.
**CHARLES, PRINCE OF WALES**

The most Mighty hath created medicines out of the earth, and a wise man will not abhor them.
**ECCLESIASTICUS 38:4**

At today's prices for medicines, doctors and hospitals—if the latter are available at any price—only millionaires can afford to be hurt or sick and pay for it. Very few people want socialized medicine in the U.S. But pressure for it is going to appear with the same hurricane force as the demand for pollution control if the medicine men and hospital operators don't take soon some Draconian measures . . . At the present rate of doctor fees and hospital costs under Medicare and Medicaid plans [taxpayers] are shovelling in billions with nothing but escalation in sight.
**MALCOLM FORBES (1970)**

A disease known is half cured.
**THOMAS FULLER**

The dignity of a physician requires that he should look healthy, and as plump as nature intended him to be; for the common crowd consider those who are not of this excellent bodily condition to be unable to take care of themselves.
**HIPPOCRATES**

A good laugh and a long sleep are the best cures in the doctor's book.
**IRISH PROVERB**

We have to ask ourselves whether medicine is to remain a humanitarian and respected profession or a new but depersonalized science in the service of prolonging life rather than diminishing suffering.
**ELIZABETH KUBLER-ROSS**

To live by medicine is to live horribly.
**LINNAEUS**

All interest in disease and death is only another expression of interest in life.
**THOMAS MANN**

The desire to take medicine is perhaps the greatest feature that distinguishes men from animals.
**SIR WILLIAM OSLER**

Medicine being a compendium of the successive and contradictory mistakes of medical practitioners, when we summon the wisest of them to our aid, the chances are that we may be relying on a scientific truth the error of which will be recognized in a few years' time.
**MARCEL PROUST**

By medicine life may be prolonged, yet death will seize the doctor too.
**WILLIAM SHAKESPEARE**

There is no better surgeon than one with many scars.
**SPANISH PROVERB**

Men who are occupied in the restoration of health to other men, by the joint exertion of skill and humanity, are above all the great of the earth. They even partake of divinity, since to preserve and renew is almost as noble as to create.
**VOLTAIRE**

## *Memory*

Not the power to remember, but its very opposite, the power to forget, is a necessary condition for our existence.
**SHOLEM ASCH**

God gave us our memories so that we might have roses in December.
**JAMES M. BARRIE**

Memories are like stones: Time and distance erode them like acid.
**UGO BETTI**

The charm, one might say the genius, of memory is that it is choosy, chancy and temperamental; it rejects the edifying cathedral and indelibly photographs the small boy outside, chewing a hunk of melon in the dust.
**ELIZABETH BOWEN**

How strange are the tricks of memory, which, often hazy as a dream about the most important events of a man's life, religiously preserve the merest trifles.
**RICHARD BURTON**

A friend who cannot at a pinch remember a thing or two that never happened is as bad as one who does not know how to forget.
**SAMUEL BUTLER**

Memory is often the attribute of stupidity; it generally belongs to heavy spirits whom it makes even heavier by the baggage it loads on them.
**FRANÇOIS DE CHÂTEAUBRIAND**

There are many books which we think we have read when we have not. There are, at least, many that we think we remember when we do not. An original picture was, perhaps, imprinted upon the brain, but it has changed with our own changing minds. We only remember our remembrance.
**G. K. CHESTERTON**

Memory is the treasury and guardian of all things.
**CICERO**

A good storyteller is a person who has a good memory and hopes other people haven't.
**IRVIN S. COBB**

The difference between false memories and true ones is the same as for jewels: It is always the false ones that look the most real, the most brilliant.
**SALVADOR DALI**

She is an excellent creature, but she can never remember which came first, the Greeks or the Romans.
**BENJAMIN DISRAELI**

Isn't it fortunate how selective our recollections usually are.
**MALCOLM FORBES**

We are so constituted that we believe the most incredible things, and once they are engraved upon the memory, woe to him that endeavor to erase them.
**JOHANN WOLFGANG VON GOETHE**

The things we remember best are those best forgotten.
**BALTASAR GRACIÁN**

Memory: A child walking along a seashore. You never can tell what small pebble it will pick up and store away among its treasured things.
PIERCE HARRIS

Memory is a net: One finds it full of fish when he takes it from the brook, but a dozen miles of water have run through it without sticking.
OLIVER WENDELL HOLMES

The one who thinks over his experiences most, and weaves them into systematic relations with each other, will be the one with the best memory.
WILLIAM JAMES

Of all the faculties of the human mind, that of memory is the first that suffers decay from age.
THOMAS JEFFERSON

It would add much to human happiness, if an art could be taught of forgetting all of which the remembrance is at once useless and afflictive, that the mind might perform its functions without encumbrance, and the past might no longer encroach upon the present.
SAMUEL JOHNSON

No man has a good enough memory to make a successful liar.
ABRAHAM LINCOLN

The heart's memory eliminates the bad and magnifies the good; and thanks to this artifice we manage to endurc the burdens of the past.
GABRIEL GARCÍA MÁRQUEZ

To be able to enjoy one's past life is to live twice.
MARTIAL

Memory presents to us not what we choose but what it pleases.
MICHEL DE MONTAIGNE

Nothing fixes a thing so intensely in the memory as the wish to forget it.
MICHEL DE MONTAIGNE

Memories may escape the action of the will, may sleep a long time, but when stirred by the right influence, though that influence be light as a shadow, they flash into full stature and life with everything in place.
JOHN MUIR

The sweetest memory is that which involves something one should not have done; the bitterest, that which involves something one should have done and did not do.
GEORGE JEAN NATHAN

A great memory does not make a mind, any more than a dictionary is a piece of literature.
CARDINAL JOHN HENRY NEWMAN

Many a man fails to become a thinker for the sole reason that his memory is too good.
FRIEDRICH WILHELM NIETZSCHE

A habit of debt is very injurious to the memory.
AUSTIN O'MALLEY

If you wish to forget something on the spot, make a note that this thing is to be remembered.
EDGAR ALLAN POE

What was hard to bear is sweet to remember.
PORTUGUESE PROVERB

The repressed memory is like a noisy intruder being thrown out of the concert hall. You can throw him out, but he will hang on the door and continue to disturb the concert.
THEODOR REIK

Memory is what tells a man that his wife's birthday was yesterday.
**MARIO ROCCO**

A man's memory may almost become the art of continually varying and misrepresenting his past, according to his interest in the present.
**GEORGE SANTAYANA**

Our memories are independent of our wills. It is not easy to forget.
**RICHARD B. SHERIDAN**

A man's real possession is his memory. In nothing else is he rich, in nothing else is he poor.
**ALEXANDER SMITH**

Everything remembered is dear, endearing, touching, precious. At least the past is safe—though we didn't know it at the time. We know it now.
**SUSAN SONTAG**

Oh better than the minting
Of a gold-crowned king
Is the safe-kept memory
Of a lovely thing.
**SARA TEASDALE**

Memory is a capricious and arbitrary creature. You never can tell what pebble she will pick up from the shore of life to keep among her treasures, or what inconspicuous flower of the field she will preserve as the symbol of thoughts that do often lie too deep for tears. . . . And yet I do not doubt that the most important things are always the best remembered.
**HENRY VAN DYKE**

Memory is the diary that we all carry about with us.
**OSCAR WILDE**

Life is all memory, except for the present moment that goes by you so quick you hardly catch it going.
**TENNESSEE WILLIAMS**

## *Merit*

A work of real merit finds favor at last.
**AMOS BRONSON ALCOTT**

Merit is never so conspicuous as when coupled with an obscure origin, just as the moon never appears so lustrous as when it emerges from a cloud.
**CHRISTIAN BOVÉE**

I am told so many ill things of a man, and I see so few in him, that I began to suspect he has a real but troublesome merit, as being likely too eclipse that of others.
**JEAN DE LA BRUYÈRE**

Assuredly men of merit are never lacking at any time, for those are the men who manage affairs, and it is the affairs that produce the men.
**CATHERINE THE GREAT**

We ought not to judge of men's merits by their qualifications, but by the use they make of them.
**PIERRE CHARRON**

Real merit of any kind cannot long be concealed; it will be discovered, and nothing can depreciate it but a man exhibiting it himself. It may not always be rewarded as it ought; but it will always be known.
**LORD CHESTERFIELD**

Speak of the moderns without contempt and of the ancients without idolatry; judge them all by their merits and not by their age.
**LORD CHESTERFIELD**

Towers are measured by their shadows, and men of merit by those who are envious of them.
CHINESE PROVERB

Contemporaries appreciate the man rather than the merit; but posterity will regard the merit rather than the man.
CHARLES CALEB COLTON

We can perceive the difference between ourselves and our inferiors, but when it comes to a question of the difference between us and our superiors we fail to appreciate merits of which we have no preconceptions.
JAMES FENIMORE COOPER

Never to reward any one equal to his merits; but always to insinuate that the reward was above it.
HENRY FIELDING

There is no merit where there is no trial; and till experience stamps the mark of strength, cowards may pass for heroes and faith for falsehood.
AARON HILL

It is of no consequence of what parents a man is born, so he be a man of merit.
HORACE

Merit, God knows, is very little rewarded.
CHARLES LAMB

Arrogance in persons of merit affronts us more than arrogance in those without merit. Merit itself is an affront.
FRIEDRICH WILHELM NIETZSCHE

If you wish your merit to be known, acknowledge that of other people.
ORIENTAL PROVERB

By merit, not favoritism, shall we attain our ends.
PLOUT

Charm strikes the sight, but merit wins the soul.
ALEXANDER POPE

The sufficiency of merit is to know that my merit is not sufficient.
FRANCIS QUARLES

There is a certain noble pride, through which merit shines brighter than through modesty.
JEAN PAUL RICHTER

Our merit gains us the esteem of the virtuous—our star that of the public.
FRANÇOIS DE LA ROCHEFOUCAULD

The test of extraordinary merit is to see those who envy it the most, yet are obliged to praise it.
FRANÇOIS DE LA ROCHEFOUCAULD

The world more frequently recompenses the appearance of merit, than merit itself.
FRANÇOIS DE LA ROCHEFOUCAULD

There is merit without elevation, but there is no elevation without some merit.
FRANÇOIS DE LA ROCHEFOUCAULD

We must not judge of a man's merits by his great qualities, but by the use he makes of them.
FRANÇOIS DE LA ROCHEFOUCAULD

True merit, like a river, the deeper it is, the less noise it makes.
GEORGE SAVILE (LORD HALIFAX)

# Mind

One reason why men and women lose their heads so often is that they use them so little! It is the same with everything. If we have anything that is valuable, it must be put to some sort of use. If a man's muscles are neglected, he soon has none, or rather none worth mentioning. The more the mind is used the more flexible it becomes, and the more it takes upon itself new interests.
GEORGE MATTHEW ADAMS

One of the most important but one of the most difficult things for a powerful mind is to be its own master.
JOSEPH ADDISON

A man's mind may be likened to a garden, which may be intelligently cultivated or allowed to run wild; but whether cultivated or neglected, it must and will bring forth. If no useful seeds are put into it, then an abundance of useless weed-seed will fall therein and will continue to produce its kind.
JAMES LANE ALLEN

A man's felicity consists not in the outward and visible blessing of fortune, but in the inward and unseen perfections and riches of the mind.
ANARCHARSIS

The whole object of education is, or should be, to develop mind. The mind should be a thing that works. It should be able to pass judgment on events as they arise, make decisions.
SHERWOOD ANDERSON

I keep the telephone of my mind open to peace, harmony, health, love and abundance. Then, whenever doubt, anxiety or fear try to call me, they keep getting a busy signal—and they'll soon forget my number.
EDITH ARMSTRONG

He who cannot contract the sight of his mind, as well as dilate it, wants a great talent in life.
FRANCIS BACON

Much bending breaks the bow; much unbending the mind.
FRANCIS BACON

Rocks have been shaken from their solid base, but what shall move a firm and dauntless mind?
JOANNA BAILLIE

There are but two powers in the world, the sword and the mind. In the long run the sword is always beaten by the mind.
NAPOLEON BONAPARTE

Measure your mind's height by the shade it casts.
ROBERT BROWNING

Few minds wear out; more rust out.
CHRISTIAN BOVÉE

Mind unemployed is mind unenjoyed.
CHRISTIAN BOVÉE

The human mind cannot create anything. It produces nothing until after having been fertilized by experience and meditation; its acquisitions are the germs of its production.
GEORGE DE BUFFON

A mind once cultivated will not lie fallow for half an hour.
EDWARD BULWER-LYTTON

I don't suffer from insanity: I enjoy every minute of it.
BUMPER STICKER

It is well for people who think to change their minds occasionally in order to keep them clean.

For those who do not think, it is best at least to rearrange their prejudices once in a while.
LUTHER BURBANK

No state can be more destitute than that of a person, who, when the delights of sense forsake him, has no pleasures of the mind.
JAMES BURGH

The march of the human mind is slow.
EDMUND BURKE

An open mind is all very well in its way, but it ought not to be so open that there is no keeping anything in or out of it. It should be capable of shutting its doors sometimes, or it may be found a little draughty.
SAMUEL BUTLER

A small mind is obstinate. A great mind can lead and be led.
ALEXANDER CANNON

It is the mind which does the work of the world, so that the more there is of mind, the more work will be accomplished.
WILLIAM ELLERY CHANNING

A weak mind is like a microscope, which magnifies trifling things but cannot receive great ones.
LORD CHESTERFIELD

Prepare yourself for the world, as athletes used to do for their exercises; oil your mind and your manners, to give them the necessary suppleness and flexibility; strength alone will not do.
LORD CHESTERFIELD

I am incurably convinced that the object of opening the mind, as of opening the mouth, is to shut it again on something solid.
G. K. CHESTERTON

There is but an inch of difference between the cushioned chamber and the padded cell.
G. K. CHESTERTON

The empires of the future are the empires of the mind.
WINSTON CHURCHILL

The proof of a well-trained mind is that it rejoices in which is good and grieves at the opposite.
CICERO

We cannot employ the mind to advantage when we are filled with excessive food and drink.
CICERO

Today the treacherous, unexplored areas of the world are not in continents or the seas; they are in the minds and hearts of men.
ALLEN E. CLAXTON, D.D.

The extreme limit of wisdom—that's what the public calls madness.
JEAN COCTEAU

If you would stand well with a great mind, leave him with a favorable impression of yourself; if with a little mind, leave him with a favorable opinion of himself.
SAMUEL TAYLOR COLERIDGE

Times of general calamity and confusion have ever been productive of the greatest minds. The purest ore is produced from the hottest furnace, and the brightest thunderbolt is elicited from the darkest storm.
CHARLES CALEB COLTON

The best cure for a sluggish mind is to disturb its routine.
WILLIAM H. DANFORTH

Of all the many earthly resources we have at our command it is only our minds and the associated unique processes that are truly infinite.
CRAIG DAY

Minds are like parachutes—they only function when open.
LORD THOMAS DEWAR

The human mind is not a deep-freeze for storage but a forge for production; it must be supplied with fuel, fired and properly shaped.
WILLIAM A. DONAGHY

There is nothing so elastic as the human mind. The more we are obliged to do, the more we are able to accomplish.
TRYON EDWARDS

A chief event of life is the day in which we have encountered a mind that startled us.
RALPH WALDO EMERSON

Nothing is at last sacred but the integrity of your own mind.
RALPH WALDO EMERSON

When the Master of the universe has points to carry in his government he impresses his will in the structure of minds.
RALPH WALDO EMERSON

We are making stupendous effort to extend the physical and economic life of the many. But of what high consequence is that extension unless the activity of the mind is also extended, unless we strive ever to live better, rather than simply to make a better living?
JOHN H. FINLEY

We do not have to visit a madhouse to find disordered minds; our planet is the mental institution of the universe.
JOHANN WOLFGANG VON GOETHE

A mind too vigorous and active, serves only to consume the body to which it is joined.
OLIVER GOLDSMITH

It is impossible to live without brains, either one's own or borrowed.
BALTASAR GRACIÁN

Each man has, each year, his moment of madness, when he ties a rope around his neck, hands the end to his worst enemy, and says "Pull."
JOHN P. GRIER

People are afraid to think, or they don't know how. They fail to realize that, while emotions can't be suppressed, the mind can be strengthened. All over the world people are seeking peace of mind, but there can be no peace of mind without strength of mind.
ERIC B. GUTKIND

The mind, like the body, is subject to be hurt by everything it taketh for a remedy.
LORD HALIFAX

On earth there is nothing great but man; in man there is nothing great but mind.
SIR WILLIAM HAMILTON

A great mind is one that can forget or look beyond itself.
WILLIAM HAZLITT

The resolved mind hath no cares.
GEORGE HERBERT

A mind becomes a detriment when it acquires more intelligence than its integrity can handle.
CULLEN HIGHTOWER

The only way some of us exercise our minds is by jumping to conclusions.
CULLEN HIGHTOWER

A vacant mind invites dangerous inmates, as a deserted mansion tempts wandering outcasts to enter and take up their abode in its desolate apartments.
HILLIARD

Just as a particular soil wants some one element to fertilize it, just as the body in some conditions has a kind of famine for one special food, so the mind has its wants, which do not always call for what is best, but which know themselves and are as peremptory as the salt-sick sailor's call for a lemon or raw potato.
OLIVER WENDELL HOLMES

Insanity is hereditary. You get it from your children.
LILLIAM HOLSTEIN

Riches, honors and pleasure are the sweets which destroy the mind's appetite for heavenly food; poverty, disgrace and pain are the bitters which restore it.
GEORGE HORNE

The mind may undoubtedly affect the body; but the body also affects the mind. There is a reaction between them; and by lessening it on either side, you diminish the pain on both.
LEIGH HUNT

Great minds have purposes, others have wishes.
WASHINGTON IRVING

The inlet of a man's mind is what he learns; the outlet is what he accomplishes. If his mind is not fed by a continued supply of new ideas which he puts to work with purpose, and if there is no outlet in action, his mind becomes stagnant. Such a mind is a danger to the individual who owns it and is useless to the community.
JEREMIAH W. JENKS

A merchant may, perhaps, be a man of an enlarged mind, but there is nothing in trade connected with an enlarged mind.
SAMUEL JOHNSON

A truly strong and sound mind is the mind that can equally embrace great things and small.
SAMUEL JOHNSON

There will always be a Frontier where there is an open mind and a willing hand.
CHARLES F. KETTERING

Whenever you look at a piece of work and you think the fellow was crazy, then you want to pay some attention to that. One of you is likely to be, and you had better find out which one it is. It makes an awful lot of difference.
CHARLES F. KETTERING

If we are to have free minds to help relieve the stress of disquietude among others, we must first free ourselves from it.
ARTHUR LEE KINSOLVING

They copied all they could copy,
But they couldn't copy my mind;
And I left them sweatin' and stealin',
A year and a half behind.
RUDYARD KIPLING

One of the paradoxical lessons of the nuclear age is that at the moment when we are acquiring an unparalleled command over nature, we are forced to realize as never before that the problems of sur-

vival will have to be solved above all in the minds of men. In this task the fate of the mammoth and the dinosaur may serve as a warning that brute strength does not always supply the mechanism in the struggle for survival.
HENRY KISSINGER

No business, no movement, no activity on the part of man or a group of men can become any greater than the thinking minds and consciousness of the people who are back of the movement.
H. SPENCER LEWIS

When he was expected to use his mind, he felt like a right-handed person who has to do something with his left.
GEORG CHRISTOPH LICHTENBERG

Our reliance in this country is on the inquiring, individual human mind. Our strength is founded there; our resilience, our ability to face an ever-changing future and to master it. We are not frozen into the backward-facing impotence of those societies, fixed in the rigidness of an official dogma, to which the future is the mirror of the past. We are free to make the future for ourselves.
ARCHIBALD MACLEISH

Only in a quiet mind is adequate perception of the world.
HANS MARGOLIUS

How can great minds be produced in a country where the test of great minds is agreeing in the opinion of small minds?
JOHN STUART MILL

The mind is its own place, and in itself can make a heaven of Hell, a hell of Heaven.
JOHN MILTON

The worth of the mind consisteth not in going high, but in marching orderly.
MICHEL DE MONTAIGNE

Read every day something no one else in reading. Think every day something no one else is thinking. It is bad for the mind to be always a part of a unanimity.
CHRISTOPHER MORLEY

The mind is like the stomach. It is not how much you put into it that counts, but how much it digests.
A. J. NOCK

It is sometimes better to boggle the mind than to mind the boggle.
CHARLES OMAN

Only fools and dead men don't change their minds. Fools won't. Dead men can't.
JOHN HENRY PATTERSON

The mind longs for what it has missed.
PETRONIUS

The success or failure of every business enterprise is traceable to one source, and one source only, namely, somebody's mind, for no one has yet invented a machine that can think.
HENNING W. PRENTIS, JR.

If a man be endowed with a generous mind, this is the best kind of nobility.
PLATO

The great business of man is to improve his mind, and govern his manners; all other projects and pursuits, whether in our power to compass or not, are only amusements.
PLINY

The richest soil, if uncultivated, produces the rankest weeds.
PLUTARCH

Our minds are like our stomachs; they are whetted by the change of their food, and variety supplies both with fresh appetite.
QUINTILIAN

The best minds are not in government. If they were, business would hire them away.
RONALD REAGAN

The mind is but barren soil; a soil which is soon exhausted, and will produce no crop, or only one, unless it be continually fertilized and enriched with foreign matter.
SIR JOSHUA REYNOLDS

Not the state of the body but the state of the mind and soul is the measure of the wellbeing of each of us.
WINFRED RHODES

Every human mind is a great slumbering power until awakened by keen desire and by definite resolution to do.
EDGAR F. ROBERTS

The mind grows narrow in proportion as the soul grows corrupt.
JEAN-JACQUES ROUSSEAU

You cannot fathom your mind. . . . The more you draw from it, the more clear and fruitful it will be.
GEORGE A. SALA

Anything that the human mind can conceive can be produced ultimately.
DAVID SARNOFF

Great minds are like eagles, and build their nest in some lofty solitude.
ARTHUR SCHOPENHAUER

A willing mind makes a light foot.
SCOTTISH PROVERB

A good mind is lord of a kingdom.
SENECA

A golden mind stoops not to show of dross.
WILLIAM SHAKESPEARE

It is the mind that makes the body rich.
WILLIAM SHAKESPEARE

There is no better sign of a brave mind than a hard hand.
WILLIAM SHAKESPEARE

It is a very fine thing to have an open mind. But it is a fine thing only if you have the ability to make a decision after considering all sides of a question.
JAMES E. SMITH

A light and trifling mind never takes in great ideas, and never accomplishes anything great or good.
WILLIAM SPRAGUE

Quiet minds cannot be perplexed or frightened but go on in fortune or misfortune at their own private pace, like a clock during a thunderstorm.
ROBERT LOUIS STEVENSON

For God hath not given us the spirit of fear; but of power, and of love, and of a sound mind.
II TIMOTHY 1:7

In our thinking we must preserve an open and enquiring mind, an ability to see things through the eyes of our opponents, a skill for understanding the motives and thoughts of those whom we oppose. Yet we must act in the light of the best knowledge and reason available to us at the moment.
CARLETON WASHBURNE

The mind's the standard of the man.
ISAAC WATTS

If we work marble, it will perish; if we work upon brass, time will efface it; if we rear temples, they will crumble into dust; but if we work upon immortal minds and instill into them just principles, we are then engraving upon tablets which no time will efface, but will brighten and brighten to all eternity.
DANIEL WEBSTER

Mind is the great lever of all things; human thought is the process by which human ends are answered.
DANIEL WEBSTER

The only man who can't change his mind is a man who hasn't got one.
EDWARD NOYES WESCOTT

An open mind is all very well in its way, but it ought not to be so open that there is no keeping anything in or out of it.
ALFRED NORTH WHITEHEAD

You had better be ready to change your mind when needed or your mind will change you. The way a man's mind runs is the way he is sure to go.
HENRY B. WILSON

## *Misfortune*

Better be wise by the misfortunes of others than by your own.
AESOP

There is no misfortune, but to bear it nobly is good fortune.
MARCUS AURELIUS ANTONINUS

Misfortune makes of certain souls a vast desert through which rings the voice of God.
HONORÉ DE BALZAC

The greatest misfortune of all is not to be able to bear misfortune.
BIAS

Accident: An inevitable occurrence due to the action of immutable natural laws.
AMBROSE BIERCE

Calamities are of two kinds: misfortune to ourselves and good fortune to others.
AMBROSE BIERCE

Heaven sends us misfortunes as a moral tonic.
MARGUERITE BLESSINGTON

Most of our misfortunes are more supportable than the comments of our friends upon them.
CHARLES CALEB COLTON

If a great man struggling with misfortunes is a noble object, a little man that despises them is no contemptible one.
WILLIAM COWPER

Misfortunes always come in by the door that has been left open for them.
**CZECH PROVERB**

I never did anything worth doing by accident, nor did any of my inventions come by accident; they came by work.
**THOMAS EDISON**

There is no calamity that right words will not begin to redress.
**RALPH WALDO EMERSON**

On the occasion of every accident that befalls you, remember to turn to yourself and inquire what power you have for turning it to use.
**EPICTETUS**

There is in the worst of fortune the best of chances for a happy change.
**EURIPIDES**

We should learn, by reflecting on the misfortunes of others, that there is nothing singular in those which befall ourselves.
**THOMAS FITZOSBORNE**

By struggling with misfortunes, we are sure to receive some wounds in the conflict; but a sure method to come off victorious is by running away.
**OLIVER GOLDSMITH**

The effect of great and inevitable misfortune is to elevate those souls which it does not deprive of all virtue.
**FRANÇOIS GUIZOT**

There is an ambush everywhere from the army of accidents; therefore the rider of life runs with loosened reins.
**HAFIZ**

Misfortune does not always wait on vice; nor is success the constant guest of virtue.
**WILLIAM HAVARD**

The rice grain suffers under the blow of the pestle. But admire its whiteness once the order is over. So it is with men and the world we live in. To be a man one must suffer the blows of misfortune.
**HO CHI MINH**

A calamity that affects everyone is only half a calamity.
**ITALIAN PROVERB**

When any calamity has been suffered, the first thing to be remembered, is, how much has been escaped.
**JOHNSON**

It costs a man only a little exertion to bring misfortune on himself.
**MENANDER**

We feel a kind of bittersweet pricking of malicious delight in contemplating the misfortunes of others.
**MICHEL DE MONTAIGNE**

If fortune turns against you, even jelly breaks your tooth.
**PERSIAN PROVERB**

Some people think that all the world should share their misfortunes, though they do not share in the sufferings of any one else.
**A. POINCELOT**

We can profit only by our own misfortunes and those of others. The former, though they may be the more beneficial, are also the more painful; let us turn, then, to the latter.
**POLYBIUS**

No accidents are so unlucky but that the wise may draw some advantage from them; nor are there any so lucky but that the foolish may turn them to their own prejudice.
FRANÇOIS DE LA ROCHEFOUCAULD

Calamity is virtue's opportunity.
SENECA

If all our misfortunes were laid in one common heap, whence everyone must take an equal portion, most people would be content to take their own and depart.
SOCRATES

It is well to learn caution by the misfortunes of others.
PUBLILIUS SYRUS

The wise man sees in the misfortunes of others what he should avoid.
PUBLILIUS SYRUS

In the lottery of life there are more prizes drawn than blanks, and to one misfortune there are fifty advantages. Despondency is the most unprofitable feeling a man can indulge in.
DE WITT TALMAGE

Life is thickly sown with thorns, and I know no other remedy than to pass quickly through them. The longer we dwell on our misfortunes, the greater is their power to harm us.
VOLTAIRE

Show not yourself glad at the misfortune of another, though he were your enemy.
GEORGE WASHINGTON

From fortune to misfortune is but a step; from misfortune to fortune is a long way.
YIDDISH PROVERB

## *Mistakes*

More people would learn from their mistakes if they weren't so busy denying that they made them.
ANONYMOUS

Positive: being mistaken at the top of one's voice.
AMBROSE BIERCE

It is only an error in judgment to make a mistake, but it shows infirmity of character to adhere to it when discovered.
CHRISTIAN BOVÉE

Wise men learn by other men's mistakes, fools by their own.
H. G. BROWN

Three-fourths of the mistakes a man makes are made because he does not really know the things he thinks he knows.
JAMES BRYCE

Everybody makes mistakes,
A fault we all must share;
But attitudes have changed with time:
Too few of us now care.
ART BUCK

Mistakes are costly and somebody must pay. The time to correct a mistake is before it is made. The causes of mistakes are, first, I didn't know; second, I didn't think; third, I didn't care.
HENRY H. BUCKLEY

Life is very interesting, if you make mistakes.
GEORGES CARPENTIER

I can pardon everybody's mistakes except my own.
MARCUS CATO

Half of our mistakes in life arise from feeling where we ought to think, and thinking where we ought to feel.
JOHN CHURTON COLLINS

A man who has committed a mistake and doesn't correct it is committing another mistake.
CONFUCIUS

Who has credit enough in this world to pay for his mistakes?
EDWARD DAHLBERG

He who makes no mistakes never makes anything.
ENGLISH PROVERB

Mistakes occur when a man is over-worked or over-confident.
WILLIAM FEATHER

Making mistakes is human. Repeating 'em is too.
MALCOLM FORBES

None mess up more often than the old—except the young.
MALCOLM FORBES

An honest mistake always favors the restaurant.
ROBERT HALF

Why is it that the more mistakes people make, the more paranoid they become about other people's mistakes?
ROBERT HALF

The greatest mistake you can make in life is to be continually fearing you will make one.
ELBERT HUBBARD

Why did Nature create man? Was it to show that she is big enough to make mistakes, or was it pure ignorance?
HOLBROOK JACKSON

When I make a mistake, it's a beaut.
FIORELLO LA GUARDIA

Mistakes are part of the dues one pays for a full life.
SOPHIA LOREN

People will listen a great deal more patiently when you explain your mistakes than when you explain your success.
WILBUR D. NESBIT

Mistakes remembered are not faults forgot.
B. H. NEWELL

To make no mistakes is not in the power of man; but from their errors and mistakes the wise and good learn wisdom for the future.
PLUTARCH

The fellow who never makes a mistake takes his orders from one who does.
HERBERT V. PROCHNOW

We learn from our mistakes, and the amount we learn is in direct proportion to the amount we suffer from having made the mistakes.
TOMMY PROTHRO, FOOTBALL COACH

Men must try and try again. They must suffer the consequences of their own mistakes and learn by their own failures and their own successes.
LAWSON PURDY

Other people's mistakes are inexcusable.
ROBERT SELF

Calamity, war, famine, plague, death, adversity, disease, injury do not necessarily produce repentance. We may become better in a calamity but it does not necessarily make us repent. The essence of repentance is that we cannot be repentant until we confront our own self-righteousness with God's righteousness.
**BISHOP FULTON J. SHEEN**

He who never made a mistake never made a discovery.
**SAMUEL SMILES**

I don't care what people say about me. I do care about my mistakes.
**SOCRATES**

I love to make a mistake. It is my only assurance that I cannot reasonably be expected to assume the responsibility of omniscience.
**REX STOUT**

Our mistakes won't irreparably damage our lives unless we let them. It is said that in making Persian rugs the artist stands before the rug while a group of boys stands behind to pull the thread after the artist starts it. If one of the boys makes a mistake, the artist adjusts the pattern accordingly so that when the rug is finished no one can tell where the mistake was made. The same kind of adjustment will take place in our lives if we will but let go of the mental thread of each mistake and let God weave it into a successful, orderly pattern.
**JAMES E. SWEANEY**

Learn from the mistakes of others—you can't live long enough to make them all yourself.
**MARTIN VANBEE**

None are more liable to mistakes than those who act only on second thoughts.
**MARQUIS DE VAUVENARGUES**

The sages do not consider that making no mistakes is a blessing. They believe, rather, that the great virtue of man lies in his ability to correct his mistakes and continually to make a new man of himself.
**WANG YANG-MING**

When you make a mistake, don't look back at it long. Take the reason of the thing into your mind, and then look forward. Mistakes are lessons of wisdom. The past cannot be changed. The future is yet in your power.
**HUGH WHITE**

Experience is simply the name we give our mistakes.
**OSCAR WILDE**

## *Moderation*

Moderation is the key of lasting enjoyment.
**HOSEA BALLOU**

I believe in moderation in all things, including moderation.
**J. F. CARTER**

Temperance keeps the senses clear and unembarrassed and makes them seize the object with more keenness and satisfaction. It appears with life in the face and decorum in the person; it gives you the command of your head, secures your health and preserves you in a condition for business.
**JEREMY COLLIER**

Fortify yourself with moderation; for this is an impregnable fortress.
**EPICTETUS**

The true boundary of man is moderation. When once we pass that pale, our guardian angel quits his charge of us.
**OWEN FELTHAM**

In moderating, not in satisfying desires, lies peace.
**REGINALD HEBER**

Moderation is commonly firm, and firmness is commonly successful.
**SAMUEL JOHNSON**

Let your moderation be known unto all men. The Lord is at hand. Be careful for nothing; but in every thing by prayer and supplication with thanksgiving let your requests be made known unto God.
**PHILIPPIANS 4:5–6**

The man who makes everything that leads to happiness depend upon himself, and not upon other men, has adopted the very best plan for living happily. This is the man of moderation, the man of manly character and of wisdom.
**PLATO**

Temperance and labor are the two best physicians of man; labor sharpens the appetite, and temperance prevents from indulging to excess.
**JEAN-JACQUES ROUSSEAU**

Everything that exceeds the bounds of moderation has an unstable foundation.
**SENECA**

Power exercised with violence has seldom been of long duration, but temper and moderation generally produce permanence in all things.
**SENECA**

## *Money*

Capital is to the progress of society what gas is to a car.
**JAMES TRUSLOW ADAMS**

A man who is furnished with arguments from the mint will convince his antagonist much sooner than one who draws them from reason and philosophy.
**JOSEPH ADDISON**

Increased borrowing must be matched by increased ability to repay. Otherwise we aren't expanding the economy, we're merely puffing it up.
**HENRY C. ALEXANDER**

If only God would give me some clear sign! Like making a deposit in my name in a Swiss bank account.
**WOODY ALLEN**

Anyone who says money doesn't buy happiness doesn't know where to shop.
**ANONYMOUS**

Just as soon as people make enough money to live comfortably, they want to live extravagantly.
**ANONYMOUS**

There are more important things in life than a little money, and one of them is a lot of money.
**ANONYMOUS**

There are more things in life to worry about than just money—how to get hold of it, for example.
**ANONYMOUS**

Money is a guarantee that we may have what we want in the future. Though we need nothing at the moment it insures the possibility of satisfying a new desire when it arises.
**ARISTOTLE**

No social system will bring us happiness, health and prosperity unless it is inspired by something greater than materialism.
**CLEMENT R. ATTLEE**

Dress not thy thoughts in too fine a raiment. And be not a man of superfluous words or superfluous deeds.
MARCUS AURELIUS ANTONINUS

More people should learn to tell their dollars where to go instead of asking them where they went.
ROGER W. BABSON

Money is like muck, not good unless spread.
FRANCIS BACON

It seems to be a law of American life that whatever enriches us anywhere except in the wallet inevitably becomes uneconomic.
RUSSELL BAKER

Money, it turned out, was exactly like sex; you thought of nothing else if you didn't have it and thought of other things if you did.
JAMES BALDWIN

Money is a terrible master but an excellent servant.
P. T. BARNUM

Increased wages, higher pensions, more unemployment insurance, all are of no avail if the purchasing power of money falls faster.
BERNARD M. BARUCH

Money: A dream, a piece of paper on which is imprinted in invisible ink the dream of all the things it will buy, all the trinkets and all the power over others.
DAVID T. BAZELON

A nickel ain't worth a dime anymore.
YOGI BERRA

Let us keep a firm grip upon our money, for without it the whole assembly of virtues are but as blades of grass.
BHARTRIHARI

Money: A blessing that is of no advantage excepting when we part with it. An evidence of culture and a passport to polite society.
AMBROSE BIERCE

The more men, generally speaking, will do for a Dollar when they make it, the more that Dollar will do for them when they spend it.
WILLIAM J. H. BOETCKER

What our country really needs most are those things which money cannot buy.
WILLIAM J. H. BOETCKER

When men are so busy making money that they have no time for anything else, then the day is not far off when they will have no money for anything else.
WILLIAM J. H. BOETCKER

Abstinence from enjoyment is the only source of capital.
THOMAS BRASSEY

Rule No. 1:
Never lose money.
Rule No. 2:
Never forget Rule No. 1.
WARREN BUFFETT

Equity money is dynamic and debt money is static.
EDMUND BURKE

Frugality is founded on the principle that all riches have limits.
EDMUND BURKE

Money is the symbol of duty. It is the sacrament of having done for mankind that which mankind wanted.
SAMUEL BUTLER

They say that knowledge is power. I used to think so, but I now know that they meant money. Every guinea is a philosopher's stone.
LORD BYRON

Money never starts an idea; it is the idea that starts the money.
WILLIAM J. CAMERON

Put all good eggs in one basket and then watch that basket.
ANDREW CARNEGIE

Money entails duties. How shall we get the money and forget the duties?
EDWARD CARPENTER

Never stand begging for that which you have the power to earn.
MIGUEL DE CERVANTES

To desire money is much nobler than to desire success. Desiring money may mean desiring to return to your country, or marry the woman you love, or ransom your father from brigands. But desiring success must mean that you take an abstract pleasure in the unbrotherly act of distancing and disgracing other men.
G. K. CHESTERTON

Anywhere in the world salt is good to eat; anywhere in the world money is good to use.
CHINESE PROVERB

Frugality includes all the other virtues.
CICERO

Nothing so cements and holds together all the parts of a society as faith or credit, which can never be kept up unless men are under some force or necessity of honestly paying what they owe to one another.
CICERO

It is a common observation that any fool can get money; but they are not wise that think so.
CHARLES CALEB COLTON

To cure us of our immoderate love of gain, we should seriously consider how many goods there are that money will not purchase, and these the best; and how many evils there are that money will not remedy, and these the worst.
CHARLES CALEB COLTON

There is no dignity quite so impressive and no independence quite so important as living within your means.
CALVIN COOLIDGE

The worldly, in a sense, elude living. Engrossment with the material deadens their sensitivity to purely emotional issues.
ANNE CRONE

Of hobbies there are many, many, kinds. For example, money-making. But money-making is not exactly a hobby, for it will scarcely carry a boy along in continuous joy, comfort and pleasure—to say nothing of a full-grown man. Money comes, not because it is ridden as a hobby, but because a real hobby is ridden so cleverly and carefully that it oozes out money on the side!
JOHN COTTON DANA

As a general rule, nobody has money who ought to have it.
BENJAMIN DISRAELI

When you come right down to it, almost any problem eventually becomes a financial problem.
FREDERIC G. DONNER

What's money? A man is a success if he gets up in the morning and gets to bed at night and in between does what he wants to do.
**BOB DYLAN**

A feast is made for laughter, and wine maketh merry; but money answereth all things.
**ECCLESIASTES 10:19**

Money, which represents the prose of life, and is hardly spoken of in parlors without apology, is, in its effects and laws, as beautiful as roses.
**RALPH WALDO EMERSON**

Spend, and God will send.
**ENGLISH PROVERB**

The entire essence of America is the hope to first make money—then make money with money—then make lots of money with lots of money.
**PAUL ERDMAN**

A peculiarity of capital is that it cannot be employed productively without benefiting the community in which it is used.
**WILLIAM FEATHER**

The petty economies of the rich are just as amazing as the silly extravagances of the poor.
**WILLIAM FEATHER**

Make money your God, and it will plague you like the devil.
**HENRY FIELDING**

Why shouldn't the American people take half my money from me? I took all of it from them.
**EDWARD A. FILENE**

A man with a surplus can control circumstances, but a man without a surplus is controlled by them, and often he has no opportunity to exercise judgment.
**HARVEY S. FIRESTONE**

Of all the icy blasts that blow on love, a request for money is the most chilling and havoc-wreaking.
**GUSTAVE FLAUBERT**

He is a wise man who seeks by every legitimate means to make all the money he can honestly, for money can do so many worthwhile things in this world, not merely for one's self but for others. But he is an unmitigated fool who imagines for a moment that it is more important to make the money than to make it honestly. One of the advantages of possessing money is that it facilitates one's independence and mental attitude. The man head over heels in debt is more slave than independent.
**B. C. FORBES**

How is this for meanness? John Jacob Astor, father of the present Vincent Astor, used to have a Fifth Avenue Hotel barber go to his house every day to shave him. He didn't tip the barber every day, but gave him 50 cents a week. But—and here is the rub—instead of paying the barber on the same day each week, he systematically paid the tip one day later each week. . . . In the course of six weeks he thus skinned the barber out of a week's tip! Imagine a man of Astor's wealth descending to such a contemptible dodge to save 10 cents a week!
**B. C. FORBES**

How many men I know who are earning dollars aplenty, but who are really earning little of what counts. They are so overwhelmingly engrossed in business that they get nothing from their dollars. The Juggernaut of dollar-making has crushed out of them every capacity for genuine enjoyment, every grace, every unselfish sentiment and instinct.
**B. C. FORBES**

All work and no play makes jack. With enough jack, Jack needn't be a dull boy.
**MALCOLM FORBES**

Why, just a couple of economic seasons ago, was idle cash considered an indication of bad management or lazy management? Because it meant that management didn't have this money out at work...

Now look. Presto! A new fashion! Cash is back in! Denigrating liquidity has dropped quicker than hemlines. A management is now saluted if it has some cash, some liquidity, doesn't have to go to the money market at huge interest rates to get the wherewithal to keep going and growing. Along with Ben Franklin, my father and your father would understand and applaud this new economic fashion ....
**MALCOLM FORBES**

The cure for materialism is to have enough for everybody and to share. When people are sure of having what they need they cease to think about it.
**HENRY FORD**

The highest use of capital is not to make more money, but to make money do more for the betterment of life.
**HENRY FORD**

Many persons think that by hoarding money they are gaining safety for themselves. If money is your only hope for independence, you will never have it. The only real security that a man can have in this world is a reserve of knowledge, experience and ability. Without these qualities, money is practically useless. The security even of money depends on knowledge, experience and ability. If productive ideas are displaced by destructive ideas, economic life suffers.
**HENRY FORD**

Money doesn't change men, it merely unmasks them. If a man is naturally selfish or arrogant or greedy, the money brings that out, that is all.
**HENRY FORD**

Money is like an arm or leg—use it or lose it.
**HENRY FORD**

The notion that tipping is optional and the amount discretionary is as quaint as the soul who might try it. Short of being angered to the point of fisticuffs or other forms of mayhem, if you last in a restaurant long enough to get the check, the basic rules are simple:

Fifteen percent of the bill for the waiter; another 5% of the bill for the captain, in the places where he makes the salad and generally works at the job; one dollar per bottle for the wine steward; and/or a buck for the bartender if he had made several drinks. [And don't think] you can walk out without tipping if you have been dissatisfied....

Gold is the most useless thing in the world. I am not interested in money but in the things of which money is merely a symbol.
**HENRY FORD**

Old men are always advising young men to save money. That is bad advice. Don't save every nickel. Invest in yourself. I never saved a dollar until I was forty years old.
**HENRY FORD**

Beware of little expenses; a small leak will sink a great ship.
**BENJAMIN FRANKLIN**

Creditors have better memories than debtors, and creditors are a superstitious set—great observers of set days and times.
**BENJAMIN FRANKLIN**

Great spenders are bad lenders.
**BENJAMIN FRANKLIN**

He that is of the opinion money will do everything may well be suspected of doing everything for money.
**BENJAMIN FRANKLIN**

Money never made a man happy yet, nor will it. There is nothing in its nature to produce happiness.
BENJAMIN FRANKLIN

Remember, that time is money. . . . Remember, that credit is money . . . Remember, that money is of the prolific, generating nature. . . . Remember, that six pounds a year is but a groat a day. . . . Remember this saying, "The good payer is lord of another man's purse." He that is known to pay punctually and exactly to the time he promises, may at any time, and on any occasion, raise all the money his friends can spare. . . . In short, the way to wealth, if you desire it, is as plain as the way to market. It depends chiefly on two words, industry and frugality; that is, waste neither time nor money, but make the best use of both.
BENJAMIN FRANKLIN

The use of money is all the advantage there is in having money.
BENJAMIN FRANKLIN

What maintains one vice would bring up two children.
BENJAMIN FRANKLIN

God makes, and apparel shapes: but 'tis money that finishes the man.
THOMAS FULLER

If anything is evident about people who manage money, it is that the task attracts a very low level of talent, one that is protected in its highly imperfect profession by the mystery that is thought to enfold the subject of economics in general and of money in particular.
JOHN KENNETH GALBRAITH

That the love of money is the root of all evil can, conceivably, be disputed. What is not in doubt is that the pursuit of money, or an enduring association with it, is capable of inducing not only bizarre but ripely perverse behavior.
JOHN KENNETH GALBRAITH

The most popular labor-saving device is still money.
PHYLLIS GEORGE

The man who tips a shilling every time he stops for petrol is giving away annually the cost of lubricating his car.
J. PAUL GETTY

Money is like love; it kills slowly and painfully the one who withholds it, and it enlivens the other who turns it upon his fellow man.
KAHLIL GIBRAN

Many people take no care of their money till they come nearly to the end of it, and others do just the same with their time.
JOHANN WOLFGANG VON GOETHE

If frugality were established in the state, if our expenses were laid out rather in the necessaries than the superfluities of life, there might be fewer wants, and even fewer pleasures, but infinitely more happiness.
OLIVER GOLDSMITH

To rail at money, to wax indignant against it, are silly. Money is nothing; its power is purely symbolical. Money is the sign of liberty. To curse money is to curse liberty—to curse life, which is nothing, if it be not free.
RÉMY DE GOURMONT

The darkest hour in any man's life is when he sits down to plan how to get money without earning it.
HORACE GREELEY

A treasure is to be valued for its own sake and not for what it will buy.
GRAHAM GREENE

A man may come to disaster through an ill-spent halfpenny.
CALOUSTE SARKIS GULBENKIAN

Money: What you'd get along beautifully without if only other people weren't so crazy about it.
MARGARET HARRIMAN

Men make counterfeit money; in many more cases, money makes counterfeit men.
SYDNEY J. HARRIS

I pity that man who wants a coat so cheap that the man or woman who produces the cloth shall starve in the process.
BENJAMIN HARRISON

It is often easier to assemble armies than it is to assemble army revenues.
BENJAMIN HARRISON

Money is life to us wretched mortals.
HESIOD

America has the world's best money. Every U.S. dollar is secured by the universal demand for it.
CULLEN HIGHTOWER

Money can be fickle, having a lasting relationship with a few and a brief fling with others, while just flirting with the rest of us.
CULLEN HIGHTOWER

Of all the incentives for work, money is the most popular—and the most unreliable.
CULLEN HIGHTOWER

Money spent on myself may be a millstone about my neck; money spent on others may give me wings like the angels.
ROSWELL D. HITCHCOCK

American business needs a lifting purpose greater than the struggle of materialism.
HERBERT HOOVER

Get money by fair means if you can; if not, get money.
HORACE

Get money first; virtue comes after.
HORACE

When a man says money can do anything, that settles it: he hasn't any.
EDGAR WATSON HOWE

He that hath money in his purse cannot want a head for his shoulders.
JAMES HOWELL

The safest way to double your money is to fold it over and put it in your pocket.
KIN HUBBARD

It's a terribly hard job to spend a billion dollars and get your money's worth.
GEORGE HUMPHREY

Money as money is nothing.
H. L. HUNT

Everything you gather is just one that you can lose.
ROBERT HUNTER

Money may be the husk of many things, but not the kernel. It brings you food, but not appetite; medicine, but not health; acquaintances, but not friends; servants, but not faithfulness; days of joy, but not peace or happiness.
HENRIK IBSEN

I would rather be a beggar and spend my money like a king, than be a king and spend money like a beggar.
**ROBERT G. INGERSOLL**

Women prefer men who have something tender about them—especially the legal kind.
**KAY INGRAM**

Getting money is like digging with a needle; spending it is like water soaking into sand.
**JAPANESE PROVERB**

Go into the street, and give one man a lecture on morality, and another a shilling, and see which will respect you most.
**SAMUEL JOHNSON**

Money and time are the heaviest burdens of life, and the unhappiest of all mortals are those who have more of either than they know how to use.
**SAMUEL JOHNSON**

Sir, no man but a blockhead ever wrote except for money.
**SAMUEL JOHNSON**

There are few ways in which a man can be more innocently employed than in getting money.
**SAMUEL JOHNSON**

You cannot take a whiff of "Free enterprise" or a "Way of life," and start a factory with it. To start a factory and provide jobs, you have to have money—capital.
**ERIC A. JOHNSTON**

The covetous man never has money; the prodigal will have none shortly.
**BEN JONSON**

It is where a man spends his money that shows where his heart lies.
**A. EDWIN KEIGWIN, D.D.**

There is no subtler, no surer means of overturning the existing basis of society than to debauch the currency. The process engages all the hidden forces of economic law on the side of destruction, and does it in a manner which not one man in a million is able to diagnose....
**JOHN MAYNARD KEYNES**

If you cannot make money on one dollar—if you do not coax one dollar to work hard for you, you won't know how to make money out of one hundred thousand dollars.
**E. S. KINNEAR**

All the money in the world is no use to a man or his country if he spends it as fast as he makes it. All he has left is his bills and the reputation for being a fool.
**RUDYARD KIPLING**

Rich or poor, it's good to have money.
**SID LANCE**

Making a lot of money is all right, provided you don't have to pay too much for it.
**ALBERT LASKER**

It is easy to be generous with other people's money.
**LATIN PROVERB**

People die, but money never does.
**PENELOPE LIVELY**

Love of money is the disease which makes men most groveling and pitiful.
**CASSIUS LONGINUS**

It's good to have money and the things that money can buy, but it's good, too, to check up once in a while and make sure that you haven't lost the things that money can't buy.
**GEORGE HORACE LORIMER**

I don't like money actually, but it quiets my nerves.
**JOE LOUIS**

For which of you, intending to build a tower, sitteth not down first, and counteth the cost, whether he have sufficient to finish it?
**LUKE 14:28**

But for money and the need of it, there would not be half the friendship in the world. It is powerful for good if divinely used. Give it plenty of air and it is sweet as the hawthorn; shut it up and it cankers and breeds worms.
**GEORGE MACDONALD**

I am not rich. I am a poor man with money, which is not the same thing.
**GABRIEL GARCÍA MÁRQUEZ**

The love for money is only one among many.
**ALFRED MARSHALL**

Money is like a sixth sense—and you can't make use of the other five without it.
**SOMERSET MAUGHAM**

Get to know two things about a man—how he earns his money and how he spends it—and you have the clue to his character, for you have a searchlight that shows up the inmost recesses of his soul. You know all you need to know about his standards, his motives, his driving desires, his real religion.
**ROBERT J. MCCRACKEN**

I do not prize the word cheap. It is not a word of inspiration. It is the badge of poverty, the signal of distress. Cheap merchandise means cheap men and cheap men mean a cheap country.
**WILLIAM MCKINLEY**

We cannot gamble with anything so sacred as money.
**WILLIAM MCKINLEY**

The chief value of money lies in the fact that one lives in a world in which it is overestimated.
**H. L. MENCKEN**

Much work is merely a way to make money; much leisure is merely a way to spend it.
**C. WRIGHT MILLS**

A man's treatment of money is the most decisive test of his character—how he makes it and how he spends it.
**JAMES MOFFATT**

The most substantial people are the most frugal, and make the least show, and live at the least expense.
**FRANCIS MOORE**

He who makes money pleases God.
**MUHAMMAD**

I'm living so far beyond my income that we may almost be said to be living apart.
**H. H. MUNRO**

A credit card is a money tool, not a supplement to money. The failure to make this distinction has supplemented many a poor soul right into bankruptcy.
**PAULA NELSON**

Society can transport money from rich to poor only in a leaky bucket.
**ARTHUR M. OKUN**

Money doesn't care who makes it.
**OLD RETAIL SAYING**

Never borrow money except for a primary residence, education, or emergency health problems.
OLD SOUTHERN SAYING

How to make the summer months pass quickly: Borrow money in June, make the note payable in three months, and fall will be here before you know it.
OLD SOUTHERN SAYING

After a certain point money is meaningless. It's the game that counts.
ARISTOTLE ONASSIS

Public money ought to be touched with the most scrupulous conscientiousness of honor. It is not the produce of riches only, but of the hard earnings of labor and poverty. It is drawn even from the bitterness of want and misery. Not a beggar passes, or perishes in the streets, whose mite is not in that mass.
THOMAS PAINE

I do everything for a reason. Most of the time the reason is money.
SUZY PARKER

The two most beautiful words in the English language are "Check enclosed."
DOROTHY PARKER

There is no stronger craving in the world than that of the rich for titles, except that of the titled for riches.
HESKETH PEARSON

Frugality is good, if liberality be joined with it. The first is leaving off superfluous expenses; the last bestowing them to the benefit of others that need. The first without the last begets covetousness; the last with the first begets prodigality. Both together make an excellent temper. Happy the place where that is found.
WILLIAM PENN

All money nowadays seems to be produced with a natural homing instinct for the Treasury.
PRINCE PHILIP

A financier is a pawnbroker with imagination.
A. W. PINERO

Men and women with time on their hands, and money in their pockets, will dress like peacocks and behave like sparrows.
J. H. PLUMB

Nothing is cheap which is superfluous, for what one does not need, is dear at a penny.
PLUTARCH

Money was made for the free-hearted and generous.
JOHN RAY

I finally know what distinguishes man from the beasts: financial worries.
JULES RENARD

There is a certain Buddhistic calm that comes from having . . . money in the bank.
TOM ROBBINS

I believe that the power to make money is a gift from God.
JOHN D. ROCKEFELLER

Why, money isn't everything to an Englishman. There are other considerations when he marries, for instance, fondness for the girl.
DOWAGER DUCHESS OF ROXBURGHE

When money speaks, the truth keeps silent.
RUSSIAN PROVERB

Finance: the art of passing currency from hand to hand until it finally disappears.
ROBERT W. SARNOFF

Money is human happiness in the abstract: he, then, who is no longer capable of enjoying human happiness in the concrete devotes himself utterly to money.
ARTHUR SCHOPENHAUER

Money is like sea-water: The more we drink the thirstier we become; and the same is true of fame.
ARTHUR SCHOPENHAUER

Money is an important success symbol in our culture. Successful people surround themselves with success symbols—positive, pragmatic and supportive examples of solid accomplishment.
WHITT N. SCHULTZ

Credit is like a looking glass, which, when once sullied by a breath, may be wiped clear again, but if once cracked can never be repaired.
SIR WALTER SCOTT

Ask thy purse what thou should spend.
SCOTTISH PROVERB

With parsimony a little is sufficient; without it nothing is sufficient; but frugality makes a poor man rich.
SENECA

In nature all is managed for the best with perfect frugality and just reserve, profuse to none, but bountiful to all; never employing on one thing more than enough, but with exact economy retrenching the superfluous, and adding force to what is principal in everything.
LORD SHAFTESBURY

Financiers live in a world of illusion. They count on something which they call the capital of the country, which has no existence.
GEORGE BERNARD SHAW

It happens a little unluckily that the persons who have the most infinite contempt of money are the same that have the strongest appetite for the pleasures it procures.
WILLIAM SHENSTONE

If each year slightly less capital is invested in industry, the time will eventually come when the amount of equipment per laborer and, in consequence, the productivity and the wages of labor are less than they otherwise would be.
SUMNER H. SLICHTER

Money and sex are forces too unruly for our reason; they can only be controlled by taboos which we tamper with at our peril.
LOGAN PEARSALL SMITH

The integrity of our money does not depend upon domestic convertibility. It depends upon the great productive power of the American economy and the competence with which we manage our fiscal and monetary affairs.
ALLAN SPROUL

Money has little value to its possessor unless it also has value to others.
LELAND STANFORD

Money is a stupid measure of achievement but unfortunately it is the only universal measure we have.
CHARLES P. STEINMETZ

Money alone is only a mean; it presupposes a man to use it. The rich man can go where he pleases, but perhaps please himself nowhere. He can buy a library or visit the whole world, but perhaps has neither patience to read nor intelligence to see.... The purse may be full and the heart empty. He may have gained the world and lost himself; and with all his wealth around him ... he may live as blank a life as any tattered ditcher.
ROBERT LOUIS STEVENSON

I like Paris. They don't talk so much of money, but more of sex.
**VERA STRAVINSKY**

The invectives against capital in the hands of those who have it are double-faced, and when turned about are nothing but demands for capital in the hands of those who have it not, in order that they may do with it just what those who have it are now doing with it.
**WILLIAM GRAHAM SUMNER**

A wise man should have money in his head, but not in his heart.
**JONATHAN SWIFT**

No man will take counsel, but every man will take money. Therefore, money is better than counsel.
**JONATHAN SWIFT**

The surest way to establish your credit is to work yourself into the position of not needing any.
**MAURICE SWITZER**

We are all dependent upon the investment of capital.
**WILLIAM HOWARD TAFT**

The philosophy which affects to teach us a contempt of money does not run very deep.
**HENRY J. TAYLOR**

It is difficult to begin without borrowing, but perhaps it is the most generous course thus to permit your fellowmen to have an interest in your enterprise.
**HENRY DAVID THOREAU**

Never steal more than you actually need, for the possession of surplus money leads to extravagance, foppish attire, frivolous thought.
**DALTON TRUMBO**

His money is twice tainted: 'taint yours and 'taint mine.
**MARK TWAIN**

I never write metropolis for seven cents because I can get the same price for city. I never write policeman because I can get the same money for cop.
**MARK TWAIN**

The more money an American accumulates, the less interesting he becomes.
**GORE VIDAL**

The contempt of money is no more a virtue than to wash one's hand is one; but one does not willingly shake hands with a man that never washes his.
**HORACE WALPOLE**

Let us be happy and live within our means, even if we have to borrow money to do it with.
**ARTEMUS WARD**

Credit has done a thousand times more to enrich mankind than all the gold mines in the world. It has exalted labor, stimulated manufacture and pushed commerce over every sea.
**DANIEL WEBSTER**

If you divorce capital from labor, capital is hoarded, and labor starves.
**DANIEL WEBSTER**

Get all you can, without hurting your soul, your body, or your neighbor. Save all you can, cutting off every needless expense. Give all you can.
**JOHN WESLEY**

That is suitable to a man, in point of ornamental expense, not which he can afford to have, but which he can afford to lose.
**RICHARD WHATELY**

There is obviously a wide psychological gap that needs to be bridged between the poles of capital and labor. I believe that profit-sharing is the spark that can bridge that gap—that can close the cir-

cuit—and re-energize our capitalistic system. At the root of most labor-management disputes in the nation is the issue of profits and their disposal. Profit-sharing, by attacking the labor-management problem at its basic point of contention, seems to be the only fundamental way to resolve it.
WALTER H. WHEELER, JR.

What a man does with his wealth depends upon his idea of happiness. Those who draw prizes in life are apt to spend tastelessly, if not viciously; not knowing that it requires as much talent to spend as to make.
EDWIN P. WHIPPLE

The great rule is not to talk about money with people who have much more or much less than you.
KATHARINE WHITEHORN

The way to stop financial joyriding is to arrest the chauffeur, not the automobile.
WOODROW WILSON

Money makes up in a measure all other wants in men.
WILLIAM WYCHERLEY

With money in your pocket, you are wise and you are handsome and you sing well too.
YIDDISH PROVERB

Many good qualities are not sufficient to balance a single want—the want of money.
JOHANN ZIMMERMANN

## *Months*

You never realize how short a month is until you pay alimony.
JOHN BARRYMORE

Now grimy April comes again, maketh bloom the fire-escapes, maketh silvers in the rain, maketh winter coats and capes suddenly all worn and shabby like the fur of winter bears.
STEPHEN VINCENT BENET

October is the fallen leaf, but it is also a wider horizon more clearly seen. It is the distant hills once more in sight, and the enduring constellations above them once again.
HAL BORLAND

The sweet calm sunshine of October, now warms the low spot; upon its grassy mold the purple oakleaf falls, the birchen bough drops its bright spoil like arrow-heads of gold.
WILLIAM CULLEN BRYANT

April is the cruellest month, breeding lilacs out of the dead land, mixing memory and desire, stirring dull roots with spring rain.
T. S. ELIOT

February sunshine is as exhilarating as an unexpected holiday.
WILLIAM FEATHER

Oh what is so rare as a full day's work in June!
WILLIAM FEATHER

About all March is good for is keeping February and April apart.
ARNOLD GLASOW

The bleak wind of March made her tremble and shiver.
THOMAS HOOD

Tossing his mane of snows in wildest eddies and tangles, lion-like March cometh in, hoarse with tempestuous breath.
WILLIAM DEAN HOWELLS

February, the shortest month in the year, is also the worst.
**ITALIAN PROVERB**

March is outside the door flaming some old desire as man turns uneasily from his fire.
**DAVID MCCORD**

It is not enough that yearly, down this hill, April comes like an idiot, babbling and strewing flowers.
**EDNA ST. VINCENT MILLAY**

Ye who fear death, remember April with its swords of jade on a thousand hills.
**JOHN RICHARD MORELAND**

Proud-pied April dressed in all his trim hath put a spirit of youth in everything.
**WILLIAM SHAKESPEARE**

We shall hear the rain and wind beat dark December.
**WILLIAM SHAKESPEARE**

Well-apparel'd April on the heel of limping winter treads.
**WILLIAM SHAKESPEARE**

What is this passing scene? A peevish April day!
**HENRY KIRKE WHITE**

We have had our summer evenings, now for October eves!
**HUMBERT WOLFE**

## *Morals*

Morality is a private and costly luxury.
**HENRY ADAMS**

A person may be qualified to do greater good to mankind and become more beneficial to the world, by morality without faith than by faith without morality.
**JOSEPH ADDISON**

Discourses on morality and reflection on human nature are the best means we can make use of to improve our minds, gain a true knowledge of ourselves, and recover our souls out of the vice, ignorance, and prejudice which naturally cleave to them.
**JOSEPH ADDISON**

Morality represents for everybody a thoroughly definite and ascertained idea: the idea of human conduct regulated in a certain manner.
**MATTHEW ARNOLD**

Never let your sense of morals prevent you from doing what is right.
**ISAAC ASIMOV**

Let us not fail to speak clearly, frankly and firmly. Let us put at the service of peace and freedom, side by side with our material forces as long as those are needed, the invincible moral forces which always animate free people aware of the righteousness of their cause.
**VINCENT AURIOL**

Never did we have so many investigations of people's conduct. Never was it so dangerous to walk our streets. Never was it so hazardous to drive a car on our public highways. Never were the lights of moral integrity burning so dimly in our fair country as at this very moment.
**GORDON H. BAKER**

A man that puts himself on the ground of moral principle, though the whole world be against him, is mightier than them all; for the orb of time becomes such a man's shield, and every step brings him

nearer to the hand of omnipotence. Take ground for truth, and justice, and rectitude, and piety, and fight well, and there can be no question as to the result. We are to feel that right is itself a host. Never be afraid of minorities, so that minorities are based on principles.
HENRY WARD BEECHER

Morality is character and conduct such as is required by the circle or community in which the man's life happens to be placed. It shows how much good men require of us.
HENRY WARD BEECHER

Moral: Conforming to a local and mutable standard of right; having the quality of general expediency.
AMBROSE BIERCE

The foundations of morality are like all other foundations: If you dig too much about them the superstructure will come tumbling down.
SAMUEL BUTLER

Morality is the custom of one's country and the current feeling of one's peers.
SAMUEL BUTLER

It is unquestionably possible for an incorruptible man to succeed in business. But his scruples are an embarrassment. He must make up in ability for what he lacks in moral obliquity.
JOHN CHAPMAN

A moral character is attached to autumnal scenes. The flowers fading like our hopes, the leaves falling like our years, the clouds fleeting like our illusions, the light diminishing like our intelligence, the sun growing colder like our affections, the rivers becoming frozen like our lives—all bear secret relations to our destinies.
FRANÇOIS DE CHÂTEAUBRIAND

As individuals find crime to be a dead-end street, so communities and nations are subject to the same psychology. The moral side of public opinion is traditionally lazy, but there is an indefinable point at which it can be and is aroused.
ALLEN E. CLAXTON, D.D.

Many men who spend an hour a day in physical exercises to keep fit refuse to spend an hour a week in the cultivation of their morals and their ethics. We have put so much stress on developing muscles and so little emphasis on developing our souls that our children are beginning to doubt if we have any souls at all.
ALLEN E. CLAXTON, D.D.

Distaste is more emphatic when expressed as moral disapproval. With most of us the moral counterblast is nothing more than the angry rendering of a yawn.
FRANK MOORE COLBY

There are two principles of established acceptance in morals; first, that self-interest is the mainspring of all our actions, and secondly, that utility is the test of their value.
CHARLES CALEB COLTON

Wisdom, compassion and courage—these are three universally recognized moral qualities of man. It matters not in what way men come to the exercise of these moral qualities, the result is one and the same. When a man understands the nature and use of these three moral qualities, he will then understand how to put in order his personal conduct and character; he will understand how to govern men. When a man understands how to govern men, he will then understand how to govern nations and empires.
CONFUCIUS

A moral, sensible and well-bred man will not affront me, and no other can.
WILLIAM COWPER

A state to prosper, must be built on foundations of a moral character, and this character is the principal element of its strength, and the only guaranty of its permanence and prosperity.
JABEZ L. M. CURRY

We are on the threshold of an age that will raise the standards of living of all men everywhere.
SAMUEL T. DANA

The highest possible stage in moral culture is when we recognize that we ought to control our thoughts.
CHARLES DARWIN

Economic and military power can be developed under the spur of laws and appropriations. But moral power does not derive from any act of Congress. It depends on the relations of a people to their God. It is the churches to which we must look to develop the resources for the great moral offensive that is required to make human rights secure, and to win a just and lasting peace.
JOHN FOSTER DULLES

The great task of the peace is to work morals into it. The only sort of peace that will be real is one in which everybody takes his share of responsibility. World organizations and conferences will be of no value unless there is improvement in the relation of men to men.
SIR FREDERICK EGGLESTON

There would be no perceptible influence on the morals of the race if Hell were quenched and Heaven burned.
CHARLES W. ELIOT

There can be no high civility without a deep morality.
RALPH WALDO EMERSON

If you think of standardization as the best that you know today, but which is to be improved tomorrow—you get somewhere.
HENRY FORD

The moral law is written on the tablets of eternity. For every false word or unrighteous deed, for cruelty and oppression, for lust or vanity, the price has to be paid at last.
J. A. FROUDE

What is moral is what you feel good after and what is immoral is what you feel bad after.
ERNEST HEMINGWAY

The continuing flood of immorality and crime accompanies an all-too-evident substitution of a secular, materialistic philosophy for the historic reliance upon divine guidance which has been a cornerstone of our democracy.
J. EDGAR HOOVER

In thousands of years there has been no advance in public morals, in philosophy, in religion or in politics, but the advance in business has been the greatest miracle the world has ever known.
WALLIS E. HOWE

When moral courage feels that it is in the right, there is no personal daring of which it is incapable.
LEIGH HUNT

Every act of every man is a moral act, to be tested by moral, and not by economic, criteria.
ROBERT M. HUTCHINS

Morality is always the product of terror; its chains and strait-waistcoats are fashioned by those who dare not trust others, because they do not dare to trust themselves, to walk in liberty.
ALDOUS HUXLEY

He who steadily observes those moral precepts in which all religions concur will never be questioned at the gates of heaven as to the dogmas in which they all differ.
THOMAS JEFFERSON

Two things fill the mind with ever new and increasing wonder and awe—the starry heavens above me, and the moral law within me.
IMMANUEL KANT

With intellectuals, moral thought is often less a tonic that quickens ethical action than a narcotic that deadens it.
LOUIS KRONENBERGER

Only by a spiritual renaissance can we mobilize the mightiest force in the world—moral force.
DAVID LAWRENCE

There is nothing so bad but it can masquerade as moral.
WALTER LIPPMANN

Every man has his moral backside, too, which he doesn't expose unnecessarily but keeps covered as long as possible by the trousers of decorum.
GEORG CHRISTOPH LICHTENBERG

We are a kind of chameleon, taking our hue—the hue of our moral character—from those who are about us.
JOHN LOCKE

The manner in which the hours of freedom are spent determines, no less than labor and war, the moral worth of a nation.
MAURICE MAETERLINCK

Why, a moral truth is a hollow tooth which must be propped with gold.
EDGAR LEE MASTERS

The foundations of the world will be shaky until the moral props are restored.
ANNE O'HARE MCCORMICK

The greatest danger that faces this country is the danger of moral lassitude—liberty turned to license, rights demanded and duties shirked, the moral sense deteriorating, the traditions and standards of the nation weakened, the spiritual forces within it losing ground.
ROBERT J. MCCRACKEN

Nothing is politically right which is morally wrong.
DANIEL O'CONNELL

When a teacher of the future comes to point out to the youth of America how the highest rewards of intellect and devotion can be gained, he may say to them, not by subtlety and intrigue; not by wire-pulling and demagoguery; not by the arts of popularity; not by skill and shiftiness in following expediency; but by being firm in devotion to the principles of manhood and the application of morals and the courage of righteousness in the public life of our country; by being a man without guile and without fear, without selfishness, and with devotion to duty, devotion to his country.
ELIHU ROOT

Without civic morality communities perish; without personal morality their survival has no value.
BERTRAND RUSSELL

Morality without religion is a tree without roots; a stream without any spring to feed it; a house built on the sand; a pleasant place to live in till the heavens grow dark, and the storm begins to beat.
JAMES B. SHAW

To have a respect for ourselves guides our morals; and to have a deference for others governs our manners.
LAURENCE STERNE

If thy morals make thee dreary, depend upon it they are wrong.
**ROBERT LOUIS STEVENSON**

You must regulate your life by the standards you admire when you are at your best.
**JOHN M. THOMAS**

It is not best when we use our morals on weekdays; it gets them out of repair for Sundays.
**MARK TWAIN**

No matter what theory of the origin of government you adopt, if you follow it out to its legitimate conclusions it will bring you face to face with the moral law.
**HENRY VAN DYKE**

Morality is religion in practice; religion is morality in principle.
**JOSEPH WARDLAW**

Moral indignation is jealousy with a halo.
**H. G. WELLS**

Morality is simply the attitude we adopt toward people whom we personally dislike.
**OSCAR WILDE**

No one ever heard of state freedom, much less did anyone ever hear of state morals. Freedom and morals are the exclusive possession of individuals.
**HENRY M. WRISTON**

## *Motives*

There is no such thing as any sort of motive that is in itself a bad one.
**JEREMY BENTHAM**

Motives are better than actions. Men drift into crime. Of evil they do more than they contemplate, and of good they contemplate more than they do.
**CHRISTIAN BOVÉE**

If there's a cause without attention,
Although it's hardly worth a hoot,
Someone will get a smart idea
And start a tax-free Institute.
**ART BUCK**

If a cause be good, the most violent attack of its enemies will not injure it so much as an injudicious defense of it by its friends.
**CHARLES CALEB COLTON**

There are six things that keep us going:

First, the instinct to live, which we apparently have no part in making or deciding about.

Second, group consciousness and the desire that we have to win the approbation of our fellows within the group.

Third, the various interests that we may find in life, such as religion or art or some such other branch of esthetics.

Fourth, in our climate the habit of work.

Fifth, the sheer joy of physical life that we find in hours of well-earned recreation after hard work—games, fishing, tramping the hills, a good book before an open fire.

Sixth, and most important, the general feeling that we have that there is some abstract goodness or rightness in the world with which we may cooperate in making the world a fine place for a splendid race of men, women and children to live in.
**FRANK PARKER DAY**

We must not inquire too curiously into motives. They are apt to become feeble in the utterance.
**GEORGE ELIOT**

Cause and effect, means and ends, seed and fruit cannot be severed; for the effect already blooms in the cause, the end preexists in the means, the fruit in the seed.
RALPH WALDO EMERSON

A good intention clothes itself with power.
RALPH WALDO EMERSON

Without push pull's useless.
MALCOLM FORBES

The biggest gap in the world is the gap between the justice of a cause and the motives of the people pushing it.
JOHN P. GRIER

It is man's motive that counts for righteousness, not his outer act alone.
BLANCHE HUNTSINGER

Though a good motive cannot sanction a bad action, a bad motive will always vitiate a good action. In common and trivial matters we may act without motive, but in momentous ones the most careful deliberation is wisdom.
WILLIAM JAY

Let the motive be in the deed and not in the event. Be not one whose motive for action is the hope of reward.
KRISHNA

Respectable men and women content with the good and easy living are missing some of the most important things in life. Unless you give yourself to some great cause you haven't even begun to live.
WILLIAM P. MERRILL, D.D.

We should often be ashamed of our very best actions, if the world only saw the motives which caused them.
FRANÇOIS DE LA ROCHEFOUCAULD

Beware of people with good intentions.
THEODORE ROOSEVELT

The leader for the time being, whoever he may be, is but an instrument, to be used until broken and then to be cast aside; and if he is worth his salt he will care no more when he is broken than a soldier cares when he is sent where his life is forfeit in order that the victory may be won. In the long fight for righteousness the watchword for all of us is spend and be spent. It is a little matter whether any one man fails or succeeds; but the cause shall not fail, for it is the cause of mankind.
THEODORE ROOSEVELT

Good intentions are very mortal and perishable things; like very mellow and choice fruit they are difficult to keep.
CHARLES SIMMONS

Whenever a husband or a wife is murdered by his or her spouse, you never have to look for a motive.
SOUTHERN SAYING

Right intention is to the actions of a man what the soul is to the body, or the root to the tree.
JEREMY TAYLOR

It is always with the best intentions that the worst work is done.
OSCAR WILDE

## *Music*

A good musical comedy consists largely of disorderly conduct occasionally interrupted by talk.
GEORGE ADE

Music is one of the greatest gifts of all. It asks nothing in return but that we listen.
ANONYMOUS

Psychologists have found that music does things to you whether you like it or not. Fast tempos invariably raise your pulse, respiration, and blood pressure; slow music lowers them.
**DORON K. ANTRIM**

A verbal art like poetry is reflective; it stops to think. Music is immediate; it goes on to become.
**W. H. AUDEN**

Whether the angels play only Bach in praising God I am not quite sure; I am sure, however, that *en famille* they play only Mozart.
**KARL BARTH**

If an opera cannot be played by an organ-grinder—as Puccini's and Verdi's melodies were played—then that opera is not going to achieve immortality.
**SIR THOMAS BEECHAM**

Give us, O give us the man who sings at his work! Be his occupation what it may, he is equal to any of those who follow the same pursuit in silent sullenness. He will do more in the same time . . . he will do it better . . . he will persevere longer. One is scarcely sensible to fatigue while he marches to music. The very stars are said to make harmony as they revolve in their spheres.
**THOMAS CARLYLE**

On the subject of singing, the frog school and the lark school disagree.
**CHINESE PROVERB**

Music is the only language in which you cannot say a mean or sarcastic thing.
**JOHN ERSKINE**

Give me the making of the songs of a nation and I care not who makes the laws.
**ANDREW FLETCHER**

There are three things I have always loved and never understood—art, music, and women.
**LE BOVIER DE FONTENELLE**

Bach almost persuades me to become a Christian.
**ROGER FRY**

The nation makes music—the composer only arranges it.
**MIKHAIL GLINKA**

I know only two tunes: One of them is "Yankee Doodle" and the other isn't.
**ULYSSES S. GRANT**

If cities were built by the sound of music, then some edifices would appear to be constructed by grave, solemn tones, others by light, fantastic airs.
**NATHANIEL HAWTHORNE**

I occasionally play works by contemporary composers, and for two reasons. First, to discourage the composer from writing any more, and second to remind myself how much I appreciate Beethoven.
**JASCHA HEIFETZ**

Music is only useful if it is good music, whether light or serious. Unless it provides one with some vital experience which no other art can convey, it is not only useless but a nuisance.
**CONSTANT LAMBERT**

I sometimes think that the most plaintive ditty has brought a fuller joy and of longer duration to its composer than the conquest of Persia to the Macedonian.
**WALTER SAVAGE LANDOR**

Music: An incitement to love.
**LATIN PROVERB**

I have no pleasure in any man who despises music. It is no invention of ours: It is a gift of God.
**MARTIN LUTHER**

Music is queer. Its power seems unrelated to the other affections of man, so that a person who is elsewhere perfectly commonplace may have for it an extreme and delicate sensitiveness.
**SOMERSET MAUGHAM**

If the king loves music, there is little wrong in the land.
**MENCIUS**

Opera in English is, in the main, just about as sensible as baseball in Italian.
**H. L. MENCKEN**

To play great music, you must keep your eyes on a distant star.
**YEHUDI MENUHIN**

I can hold a note as long as the Chase National Bank.
**ETHEL MERMAN**

Without music life would be a mistake.
**FRIEDRICH WILHELM NIETZSCHE**

One man with a dream, at pleasure,
Shall go forth and conquer a crown;
And three with a new song's measure,
Can trample an empire down.
**ARTHUR O'SHAUGHNESSY**

How wonderful opera would be if there were no singers.
**GIOACCHINO ROSSINI**

One can't judge Wagner's *Lohengrin* after a first hearing, and I certainly don't intend hearing it a second time.
**GIOACCHINO ROSSINI**

The notes I handle no better than many pianists. But the pauses between the notes—ah, that is where the art resides.
**ARTUR SCHNABEL**

Let a short Act of Parliament be passed, placing all the street musicians outside the protection of the law, so that any citizen may assail with stones, sticks, knives, pistols or bombs without incurring any penalties.
**GEORGE BERNARD SHAW**

Music is the brandy of the damned.
**GEORGE BERNARD SHAW**

I wish the government would put a tax on pianos for the incompetent.
**DAME EDITH SITWELL**

Music: The only cheap and unpunished rapture upon earth.
**SYDNEY SMITH**

Wagner's music is better than it sounds.
**MARK TWAIN**

One of the advantages of pure congregational singing is that you can join in the singing whether you have a voice or not. The disadvantage is that your neighbor can do the same.
**CHARLES DUDLEY WARNER**

An unalterable and unquestioned law of the musical world required that the German text of French operas sung by Swedish artists should be translated into Italian for the clearer understanding of English-speaking audiences.
**EDITH WHARTON**

I like Wagner's music better than any other music. It is so loud that one can talk the whole time without other people hearing what one says. That is a great advantage.
**OSCAR WILDE**

# N

## Names

Whatever you lend let it be your money, and not your name. Money you may get again, and, if not, you may contrive to do without it; name once lost you cannot get again, and, if you cannot contrive to do without it, you had better never have been born.
EDWARD BULWER-LYTTON

The inheritance of a distinguished and noble name is a proud inheritance to him who lives worthily of it.
CHARLES CALEB COLTON

Get them to call you by your first name. This works in business and industry as well as in politics. Do you suppose Governor Smith of New York would have rolled up a record-breaking vote had he not been "Al" to everyone . . . ? "Mr. Smith" would have had no pulling power as "Al" has. . . . Nobody talks about "Mr." Ford. To the home folks he is "Hen," and to the rest of us he is "Henry". . . . Roosevelt didn't invite being called "Teddy" even by his closest associates, but he was "Teddy" or "T.R." to us just the same, just as Lincoln was "Abe" in his day and generation.
B. C. FORBES

I don't remember anybody's name. How do you think the "dahling" thing started?
EVA GABOR

A man's name is not like a mantle which merely hangs about him, and which one perchance may safely twitch and pull, but a perfectly fitting garment, which, like the skin, has grown over him, at which one cannot rake and scrape without injuring the man himself.
JOHANN WOLFGANG VON GOETHE

The invisible thing called a Good Name is made up of the breath of numbers that speak well of you.
LORD HALIFAX

A good name, like good will, is got by many actions and lost by one.
LORD JEFFREY

## Nation

If nations could only get down to being good neighbors, the waste and wickedness of all hot and cold wars would be over. . . . The Good Neighbor idea, as it is being worked out on the Western Hemisphere, is one of the most intelligent human things ever attempted, and I pray that it may endure forever and be an object lesson for the entire world. I don't care what color a man's body may be, nor from what spot on this globe he may have been born; there isn't very much difference fundamentally between him and me. We are both human beings. He has his likes, and so do I, but we live in the same world, with the same sky above us. He can have his likes and dislikes. Even as you and I. If we all thought the same, ours would be a dull world. But we can be neighborly—be good neighbors.
GEORGE MATTHEW ADAMS

The state is the great fictitious entity by which everyone seeks to live at the expense of everyone else.
CLAUDE-FRÉDÉRIC BASTIAT

Caution and conservatism are expected of old age; but when the young men of a nation are possessed of such a spirit, when they are afraid of the noise and strife caused by the applications of the truth,

heaven save the land! Its funeral bell has already rung.
HENRY WARD BEECHER

The modern state no longer has anything but rights; it does not recognize duties any more.
GEORGES BERNANOS

A state without some means of change is without the means of its conservation.
EDMUND BURKE

By gnawing through a dyke, even a rat may drown a nation.
EDMUND BURKE

We are going down the road to Statism. Where we will wind up no one can tell, but if some of the new programs . . . should be adopted, there is danger that the individual—whether farmer, worker, manufacturer, lawyer or doctor—will soon be an economic slave pulling an oar in the galley of the state.
JAMES F. BYRNES

A thousand years scarce serve to form a state; an hour may lay it in the dust.
LORD BYRON

The whole history of the world is summed up in the fact that, when nations are strong, they are not always just, and when they wish to be just, they are often no longer strong.
WINSTON CHURCHILL

A nation's character is the sum of its splendid deeds, they constitute one common patrimony, the nation's inheritance. They awe foreign powers, they arouse and animate our own people.
HENRY CLAY

No nation ever had an army large enough to guarantee it against attack in time of peace or insure it victory in time of war.
CALVIN COOLIDGE

The nation which forgets its defenders will itself be forgotten.
CALVIN COOLIDGE

The greatest asset of any nation is the spirit of its people, and the greatest danger that can menace any nation is the breakdown of that spirit—the will to win and the courage to work.
GEORGE B. CORTELYOU

Individuals may form communities, but it is institutions alone that can create a nation.
BENJAMIN DISRAELI

Nationalism: An infantile disease. It is the measles of mankind.
ALBERT EINSTEIN

The state is made for man, no man for the state.
ALBERT EINSTEIN

Every actual state is corrupt. Good men must not obey the laws too well.
RALPH WALDO EMERSON

Nationalism and internationalism! Both must stand together or the human race will be utterly destroyed. We shall never be able to destroy nationalism and we shall never be able to live without internationalism.
LINUS R. FIKE

A great nation cannot abandon its responsibilities. Responsibilities abandoned today return as more acute crises tomorrow.
GERALD FORD

God grant not only the love of liberty but a thorough knowledge of the rights of man may pervade all the nations of the earth—so that a philosopher may set his foot anywhere on its surface and say, "This is my Country."
**BENJAMIN FRANKLIN**

We cannot too often tell ourselves that the real wealth of a nation—the only enduring, worthwhile wealth—is in the spiritual, mental and physical health of the citizens, and that in a democracy we are all trustees.
**SIR HERBERT GEPP**

The nationalist has a broad hatred and a narrow love.
**ANDRÉ GIDE**

Altogether, national hatred is something peculiar. You will always find it strongest and most violent where there is the lowest degree of culture.
**JOHANN WOLFGANG VON GOETHE**

A nation without dregs and malcontents is orderly, peaceful and pleasant, but perhaps without the seed of things to come.
**ERIC HOFFER**

A nation's greatness resides not in her material resources, but in her will, faith, intelligence, and moral forces.
**JAMES M. HOPPIN**

States are made up of a considerable number of the ignorant and foolish, a small proportion of genuine knaves, and a sprinkling of capable and honest men, by whose efforts the former are kept in a reasonable state of guidance and the latter of repression.
**THOMAS H. HUXLEY**

States, like men, have their growth, their manhood, their decrepitude and their decay.
**WALTER SAVAGE LANDOR**

A nation may be said to consist of its territory, its people and its laws. The territory is the only part which is of certain durability. Laws change, people die, the land remains.
**ABRAHAM LINCOLN**

The worth of a state, in the long run, is the worth of the individuals composing it.
**JOHN STUART MILL**

Nationalism: One of the effective ways in which the modern man escapes life's ethical problems.
**REINHOLD NIEBUHR**

Many people with different backgrounds, cultures, languages, and creeds combine to make a nation. But that nation is greater than the sum total of the individual skills and talents of its people. Something more grows out of their unity than can be calculated by adding the assets of individual contributions. That intangible additional quantity is often due to the differences which make the texture of the nation rich. Therefore, we must never wipe out or deride the differences amongst us—for where there is no difference, there is only indifference.
**LOUIS NIZER**

What makes a nation great is not primarily its great men, but the stature of its innumerable mediocre ones.
**JOSÉ ORTEGA Y GASSET**

Great nations write their autobiography in three manuscripts—the book of their deeds, the book of their words, and the book of their art.
**JOHN RUSKIN**

Every nation thinks its own madness normal and requisite; more passion and more fancy it calls folly, less it calls imbecility.
**GEORGE SANTAYANA**

Every nation ridicules other nations, and all are right.
ARTHUR SCHOPENHAUER

The rise of statism in our time is the natural result of the longing of godless, unchurched people for some kind of protection. When we lose to God we turn to what looks like the next most powerful thing, which is the state. How bad a choice that is, let Germany and Russia in recent years testify.
SAMUEL M. SHOEMAKER, D.D.

National progress is the sum of individual industry, energy, and uprightness, as national decay is of individual idleness, selfishness, and vice.
SAMUEL SMILES

For every nation that lives peaceably, there will be many others to grow hard and push their arrogance to extremes; the gods attend to these things slowly. But they attend to those who put off God and turn to madness.
SOPHOCLES

There will never be a really free and enlightened state until the state comes to recognize the individual as a higher and independent power, from which all its own power and authority are derived, and treats him accordingly.
HENRY DAVID THOREAU

Local assemblies of the people constitute the strength of free nations. Municipal institutions are to liberty what primary schools are to science: they bring it within the people's reach, and teach them how to use and enjoy it. A nation may establish a system of free government, but without the spirit of municipal institutions it cannot have the spirit of liberty.
ALEXIS DE TOCQUEVILLE

All nations have present, or past, or future reasons for thinking themselves incomparable.
PAUL VALÉRY

Nationalism has two fatal charms for its devotees: It presupposes local self-sufficiency, which is a pleasant and desirable condition, and it suggests, very subtly, a certain personal superiority by reason of one's belonging to a place which is definable and familiar, as against a place that is strange, remote.
E. B. WHITE

An individual is as superb as a nation when he has the qualities which make a superb nation.
WALT WHITMAN

## *Nature*

A cloudy day, or a little sunshine, have as great an influence on many constitutions as the most real blessings or misfortunes.
JOSEPH ADDISON

Farm: What a city man dreams of at 5 P.M., never at 5 A.M.
ANONYMOUS

The guy who wrote "A job well done never needs doing again" never weeded a garden.
ANONYMOUS

Nature is a hanging judge.
ANONYMOUS

A tree that affords thee shade, do not order it to be cut down.
ARABIAN PROVERB

Ride the tributaries to reach the sea.
ARABIAN PROVERB

The cult of nature is a form of patronage by people who have declared their materialistic independence

from nature and do not have to struggle with nature every day of their lives.
BROOKS ATKINSON

Thou hast existed as a part; thou shalt disappear into that which produced thee. This, too, nature wills. Pass then through this little space of time conformably to nature and end thy journey in content, just as the olive falls when it is ripe, thanking the tree on which it grew and blessing the nature that gave it birth.
MARCUS AURELIUS ANTONINUS

Unceasingly contemplate the generation of all things through change and accustom thyself to the thought that the nature of the universe delights above all in changing the things that exist and making new ones of the same pattern, for everything that exists is the seed of that which shall come out of it.
MARCUS AURELIUS ANTONINUS

Nature is a labyrinth in which the very haste you move with will make you lose your way.
FRANCIS BACON

There are three things which make a nation great and prosperous—a fertile soil, busy workshops, and easy conveyance for men and commodities.
FRANCIS BACON

When ages grow to civility and elegancy, men come to build stately sooner than to garden finely, as if gardening were the greater perfection.
FRANCIS BACON

Rain! whose soft architectural hands have power to cut stones and chisel to shapes of grandeur the very mountains.
HENRY WARD BEECHER

The three great elemental sounds in nature are the sound of rain, the sound of wind in a primeval wood, and the sound of outer ocean on a beach.
HENRY BESTON

There is no forgiveness in nature.
UGO BETTI

Nature is the most thrifty thing in the world; she never wastes anything; she undergoes change, but there's no annihilation—the essence remains.
THOMAS BINNEY

To see a World in a Grain of Sand
And a heaven in a Wild Flower,
Hold Infinity in the palm of your hand
And Eternity in an hour.
WILLIAM BLAKE

The ignorant man marvels at the exceptional; the wise man marvels at the common; the greatest wonder of all is the regularity of nature.
GEORGE D. BOARDMAN

Pray to God for a good harvest, but don't stop hoeing.
BOHEMIAN PROVERB

To cultivate a garden is to walk with God.
CHRISTIAN BOVÉE

There is something infinitely healing in the repeated refrains of nature—the assurance that dawn comes after night, and spring after the winter.
RACHEL CARSON

I love to think of nature as an unlimited broadcasting station, through which God speaks to us every hour, if we will only tune in.
GEORGE WASHINGTON CARVER

Cutting down a weed is not so good as uprooting it.
SELWYN G. CHAMPION

For us who live in cities Nature is not natural. Nature is supernatural. Just as monks watched and strove to get a glimpse of heaven, so we watch and strive to get a glimpse of earth. It is as if men had cake and wine every day but were sometimes allowed common bread.
G. K. CHESTERTON

Modern nature-worship is all upside down. Trees and fields ought to be ordinary things; terraces and temples ought to be extraordinary. I am on the side of the man who lives in the country and wants to go to London.
G. K. CHESTERTON

He who keeps the hills, burns the wood; he who keeps the streams drinks the water.
CHINESE PROVERB

The peony, though large, is useless; the date blossom, though small, yields fruit.
CHINESE PROVERB

The only stock I ever invested in always had four legs attached to it.
CONSERVATIVE FARMER

How things look on the outside of us depends on how things are on the inside of us. Stay close to the heart of nature and forget this troubled world. Remember, there is nothing wrong with nature; the trouble is in ourselves.
PARKS COUSINS

We talk of our mastery of nature, which sounds very grand; but the fact is we respectfully adapt ourselves, first, to her ways.
CLARENCE DAY

Complete adaptation to environment means death. The essential point in all response is the desire to control environment.
JOHN DEWEY

Nature gives to every time and season some beauties of its own; and from morning to night, as from the cradle to the grave, is but a succession of changes so gentle and easy that we can scarcely mark their progress.
CHARLES DICKENS

All the rivers run into the sea; yet the sea is not full; unto the place from whence the rivers come, thither they return again.
ECCLESIASTES 1:7

Surely there is something in the unruffled calm of nature that overawes our little anxieties and doubts: the sight of the deep-blue sky, and the clustering stars above, seem to impart a quiet to the mind.
JONATHAN EDWARDS

Farming looks mighty easy when your plow is a pencil, and you're a thousand miles from a corn field.
DWIGHT D. EISENHOWER

All men are poets at heart. They serve nature for bread, but her loveliness overcomes them sometimes.
RALPH WALDO EMERSON

The good rain, like a bad preacher, does not know when to leave off.
RALPH WALDO EMERSON

Nature is reckless of the individual. When she has points to carry, she carries them.
RALPH WALDO EMERSON

Sail! quoth the king; Hold! saith the wind.
ENGLISH PROVERB

Deep snow in winter; tall grain in summer.
**ESTONIAN PROVERB**

In the book of nature, where every emotional, mental and spiritual quality of humanity may find its correspondence and illustrations, flowers represent good affections. As the flower precedes the fruit, and gives notice of its coming, so good thoughts, affections and intentions precede and give promise of deeds in love to others.
**HOMER EVERETT**

I hope a start at getting some oil out of the enormous Alaska field isn't indefinitely mired in a bureaucratic morass as a result of our national concern for the ecology. This concern must not be so misguided, misdirected, misused that it serves to stop economic growth, to bankrupt companies, to stifle new development, new jobs, new horizons.

In fighting new pollution and stemming present pollution, exciting, sometimes costly means and methods exist and others will evolve. But blanket legislative naysaying to expanding power and energy sources is stupid, self-defeating.
**MALCOLM FORBES (1970)**

When a fissure off the California coast started pumping and dumping oil on the nearby towns and beaches, everybody started dumping on Union Oil. Matters weren't helped one iota by a manufactured quotation attributed to Union's president, Fred Hartley, alleging his amazement at the publicity for the loss of a few birds. . . .

Fred Hartley never said what the press reported, as the transcript and the Senate committee members definitely established. But I don't suppose the truth will ever catch up with the more colorful falsehood.
**MALCOLM FORBES**

Will this massive outcry [about pollution] continue long enough to have effective results? Will federal and state laws be enacted with effective enforcement clauses? Will people be concerned long enough to pay the bill through higher prices? Will towns tolerate lost jobs when it proves too costly to clean obsolete plants? . . .

I think so, but it sure won't be as easy as the present outcry and political oratory suggest. The answers to preserving a livable environment are not all simple, and some of the nuts now pushing simplistic cure-alls won't help bring about any lasting solutions.
**MALCOLM FORBES (1970)**

The winds and waves are always on the side of the ablest navigators.
**EDWARD GIBBON**

Nature knows no pause in progress and development, and attaches her curse on all inaction.
**JOHANN WOLFGANG VON GOETHE**

Nature goes on her way, and all that to us seems an exception is really according to order.
**JOHANN WOLFGANG VON GOETHE**

There is no trifling with nature; it is always true, grave, and severe; it is always in the light, and the faults and errors fall to our share. It defies incompetency, but reveals its secrets to the competent, the truthful, and the pure.
**JOHANN WOLFGANG VON GOETHE**

The ever-present phenomenon ceases to exist for our senses. It was a city dweller, or a prisoner, or a blind man suddenly given his sight, who first noted natural beauty.
**RÉMY DE GOURMONT**

Nature often lets us down when we most need her; let us turn to art.
**BALTASAR GRACIÁN**

He who thinks everything must be in bloom when the strawberries are in bloom doesn't know anything about apples.
GREEK PROVERB

We do not know, in most cases, how far social failure and success are due to heredity, and how far to environment. But environment is the easier of the two to improve.
J. B. S. HALDANE

I have come to see the nonsense of trying to describe fine scenery.
NATHANIEL HAWTHORNE

There are only three pleasures in life pure and lasting, and all derived from inanimate things—books, pictures and the face of nature.
WILLIAM HAZLITT

To the natural philosopher, there is no natural object unimportant or trifling. From the least of Nature's works he may learn the greatest lessons.
SIR JOHN HERSCHEL

A goose flies by a chart which the Royal Geographical Society could not improve.
OLIVER WENDELL HOLMES

Everyone goes to the forest; some go for a walk to be inspired, and others go to cut down the trees.
VLADIMIR HOROWITZ

Art may make a suite of clothes, but nature must produce a man.
DAVID HUME

There is perhaps no solitary sensation so exquisite as that of slumbering on the grass or hay, shaded from the hot sun by a tree, with the consciousness of a fresh but light air running through the wide atmosphere, and the sky stretching far overhead upon all sides.
LEIGH HUNT

"Nature" will not longer do the work unaided. Nature—if by that we mean blind and non-conscious forces—has, marvelously, produced man and consciousness; they must carry on the task to new results which she alone can never reach.
JULIAN HUXLEY

The chessboard is the world; the pieces are the phenomena of the universe; the rules of the game are what we call laws of nature.
THOMAS H. HUXLEY

Different people have different duties assigned them by Nature; Nature has given one the power or the desire to do this, the other that. Each bird must sing with his own throat.
HENRIK IBSEN

In nature there are neither rewards nor punishments; there are consequences.
ROBERT G. INGERSOLL

A man finds in the productions of nature an inexhaustible stock of material on which he can employ himself, without any temptations to envy or malevolence, and has always a certain prospect of discovering new reasons for adoring the sovereign author of the universe.
SAMUEL JOHNSON

Rain is good for vegetables, and for the animals who eat those vegetables, and for the animals who eat those animals.
SAMUEL JOHNSON

I want to be freed neither from human beings, nor from myself, nor from nature; for all these appear to me the greatest of miracles.
CARL JUNG

What is more gentle than a wind in summer?
JOHN KEATS

Nature uses as little as possible of anything.
JOHANNES KEPLER

And that invented bowl we call the sky,
Whereunder crawling coop't we live and die,
Raise not your hand to it for help—for it
Rolls impotently on as thou or I.
OMAR KHAYYAM

We listen too much to the telephone and too little to nature. The wind is one of my sounds. A lonely sound, perhaps, but soothing.
ANDRE KOSTELANETZ

Nature takes no account of even the most reasonable of human excuses.
JOSEPH WOOD KRUTCH

Nothing that is natural is disgraceful.
LATIN PROVERB

Nature is full of infinite causes that have never occurred in experience.
LEONARDO DA VINCI

And when ye reap the harvest of your land, thou shalt not wholly reap the corners of thy field, neither shalt thou gather the gleanings of thy harvest.
LEVITICUS 19:9

Into each life some rain must fall; some days must be dark and dreary.
HENRY WADSWORTH LONGFELLOW

There are times when minds need to turn to simple things. Perhaps for a few of these nights all of us might do well to leave the briefcases at the office and to read again the pages of the Bible, and to reread the Declaration of Independence and the Constitution of the United States. We might do well to stay home a few days and walk over the fields, or to stand in the shelter of the barn door and reflect upon the relentless and yet benevolent forces of Mother Nature. The laws of nature are relentless. They can never be disobeyed without exacting a penalty. Yet they are benevolent, for when they are understood and obeyed, nature yields up the abundance that blesses those who understand and obey.
WHEELER MCMILLEN

In those vernal seasons of the year when the air is calm and pleasant, it were an injury and sullenness against nature not to go out and see her riches, and partake in her rejoicing with heaven and earth.
JOHN MILTON

This grand show is eternal. It is always sunrise somewhere; the dew is never all dried at once; a shower is forever falling; vapor is ever rising. Eternal sunrise, eternal sunset, eternal dawn and gloaming, on sea and continents and islands, each in its turn, as the round earth rolls.
JOHN MUIR

Nature always favors the hidden flaw.
MURPHY'S THIRD LAW

Life in the country teaches one that the really stimulating things are the quiet, natural things, and the really wearisome things are the noisy, unnatural things. It is more exciting to stand still than to dance. Silence is more eloquent than speech. Water is more stimulating than wine. Fresh air is more intoxicating than cigarette smoke. Sunlight is more subtle than electric light. The scent of grass is more luxurious than the most expensive perfume. The slow,

simple observations of the peasant are more wise than the most sparkling epigrams of the latest wit.
**BEVERLEY NICHOLS**

We came unto the land whither thou sentest us, and surely it floweth with milk and honey, and this is the fruit of it.
**NUMBERS 13:27**

Nature has perfections, in order to show that she is the image of God; and defects, to show that she is only his image.
**BLAISE PASCAL**

Nature imitates herself. A grain thrown into good ground brings forth fruit; a principle thrown into a good mind brings forth fruit. Everything is created and conducted by the same Master—the root, the branch, the fruits—the principles, the consequences.
**BLAISE PASCAL**

It were happy if we studied nature more in natural things; and acted according to nature, whose rules are few, plain, and most reasonable.
**WILLIAM PENN**

We ought not to treat living creatures like shoes or household belongings, which when worn with use we throw away.
**PLUTARCH**

There be three things which are too wonderful for me, yea, four which I know not: The way of an eagle in the air; the way of a serpent upon a rock; the way of a ship in the midst of the sea; and the way of a man with a maid.
**PROVERBS 30:18–19**

The floods have lifted up, O Lord, the floods have lifted up their voice; the floods lift up their waves. The Lord on high is mightier than the noise of many waters, yea, than the mighty waves of the sea.
**PSALMS 93:3–4**

We cannot live without the earth or apart from it, and something is shriveled in a man's heart when he turns away from it and concerns himself only with the affairs of men.
**MARJORIE K. RAWLINGS**

Intense study of nature, her secrets and her glories, will humble the meanest spirit.
**CHARLES B. ROGERS**

In the range of inorganic nature. I doubt if any object can be found more perfectly beautiful than a fresh, deep snowdrift, seen under warm light.
**JOHN RUSKIN**

It is curious, pathetic almost, how deeply seated in the human heart is the liking for gardens and gardening.

The survival of the fittest is the ageless law of nature, but the fittest are rarely the strong. The fittest are those endowed with the qualifications for adaptation, the ability to accept the inevitable and conform to the unavoidable, to harmonize with existing or changing conditions.
**DAVE E. SMALLEY**

Nature never quite goes along with us. She is somber at weddings, sunny at funerals, and she frowns on ninety-nine out of a hundred picnics.
**ALEXANDER SMITH**

Whatever you are by nature, keep to it; never desert your own line of talent. Be what nature intended you for, and you will succeed; be anything else and you will be ten thousand times worse than nothing.
**SYDNEY SMITH**

The best fertilizer is the owner's footprint.
**SOUTH CAROLINA SAYING**

The trash and litter of nature disappears into the ground with the passing of each year, but man's litter has more permanence.
**JOHN STEINBECK**

Wide flush the fields; the softening air is balm; echo the mountains round; the forest smiles and every hear tis joy.
**JAMES THOMSON**

I felt a positive yearning toward one bush this afternoon. There was a match found for me at last. I fell in love with a shrub oak.
**HENRY DAVID THOREAU**

Nature cares nothing for our logic, our human logic; she has her own, which we do not recognize and do not acknowledge until we are crunched under its wheel.
**IVAN TURGENEV**

Where nature is concerned, familiarity breeds love and knowledge, not contempt.
**STEWART L. UDALL**

My father asserted that there was no better place to bring up a family than in a rural environment.... There's something about getting up at 5 A.M., feeding the stock and chickens, and milking a couple of cows before breakfast that gives you a life-long respect for the price of butter and eggs.
**WILLIAM VAUGHN**

Animals have these advantages over man: They have no theologians to instruct them, their funerals cost them nothing, and no one starts lawsuits over their wills.
**VOLTAIRE**

What a man needs in gardening is a cast-iron back, with a hinge in it.
**CHARLES DUDLEY WARNER**

In the history of the world the prize has not gone to those species which specialized in methods of violence, or even in defensive armor. In fact, nature began with producing animals encased in hard shells for defense against the ills of life. It also experimented in size. But smaller animals, without external armor, warm-blooded, sensitive, alert, have cleared those monsters off the face of the earth.
**ALFRED NORTH WHITEHEAD**

I think I could turn and live with the animals. They are so placid and self-contained. They do not sweat and whine about their condition. Not one is dissatisfied. Not one is demented with the mania of owning things. Not one is disrespectful or unhappy over the world.
**WALT WHITMAN**

The world is too much with us; late and soon, getting and spending we lay waste our powers. Little we see in nature that is ours.
**WILLIAM WORDSWORTH**

## *Necessity*

Make yourself necessary to somebody.
**RALPH WALDO EMERSON**

Where necessity ends, curiosity begins; and no sooner are we supplied with everything that nature can demand than we sit down to contrive artificial appetites.
**JOHNSON**

Necessity may render a doubtful act innocent, but it cannot make it praiseworthy.
**JOSEPH JOUBERT**

There is no contending with necessity, and we should be very tender how we censure those that submit to it. 'Tis one thing to be at liberty to do what we will, and another thing to be tied up to do what we must.
**ROGER L'ESTRANGE**

Necessity is the plea for every infringement of human freedom. It is the argument of tyrants; it is the creed of slaves.
**WILLIAM PITT**

Necessity is the constant scourge of the lower classes, ennui of the higher ones.
**ARTHUR SCHOPENHAUER**

"Necessity is the mother of invention" is a silly proverb. "Necessity is the mother of futile dodges" is much nearer the truth.
**ALFRED NORTH WHITEHEAD**

## *Neighbors*

The love of our neighbor hath its bounds in each man's love of himself.
**ST. AUGUSTINE**

We make our friends; we make our enemies; but God makes our next-door neighbor.
**G. K. CHESTERTON**

A good neighbor—a found treasure.
**CHINESE PROVERB**

No one is rich enough to do without a neighbor.
**DANISH PROVERB**

We can live without our friends, but not without our neighbors.
**THOMAS FULLER**

It is your interest that is at stake when your neighbor's wall is ablaze.
**HORACE**

How seldom we weigh our neighbor in the same balance with ourselves!
**THOMAS À KEMPIS**

Someone said of nations—but it might well have been said of individuals, too—that they require of their neighbors something sufficiently akin to be understood, something sufficiently different to provoke attention, and something sufficiently great to command admiration.
**PHOEBE LOW**

All social life, stability, progress, depend upon each man's confidence in his neighbor, a reliance upon him to do his duty.
**A. LAWRENCE LOWELL**

Live for thy neighbor if thou wouldst live for thyself.
**SENECA**

More and more clearly every day, out of biology, anthropology, sociology, history, economic analysis, psychological insight, plain human decency and common sense, the necessary mandate of survival—that we shall love all our neighbors as we do ourselves—is being confirmed and reaffirmed.
**ORDWAY TEAD**

A little among neighbors is worth more than riches in a wilderness.
**WELSH PROVERB**

We are made for one another, and each is to be a supply to his neighbor.
**BENJAMIN WHICHCOTE**

## News

The evil that men do lives on the front pages of greedy newspapers, but the good is oft interred apathetically inside.
BROOKS ATKINSON

Journalism is popular, but it is popular mainly as fiction. Life is one world, and life seen in the newspapers another.
G. K. CHESTERTON

The tabloid newspaper actually means to the typical American what the Bible is popularly supposed to have meant to the typical Pilgrim Father: a very present help in time of trouble, plus a means of keeping out of trouble via harmless, since vicarious, indulgence in the pomps and vanities of this wicked world.
E. E. CUMMINGS

Evil report carries faster than any applause.
BALTASAR GRACIÁN

News is the first rough draft of history.
PHILIP L. GRAHAM

Were it left to me to decide whether we should have a government without newspapers, or newspapers without a government, I should not hesitate to prefer the latter.
THOMAS JEFFERSON

A good newspaper, I suppose, is a nation talking to itself.
ARTHUR MILLER

A reporter is always concerned with tomorrow. There's nothing tangible of yesterday. All I can say I've done is agitate the air ten or fifteen minutes and then boom—it's gone.
EDWARD R. MURROW

I do not like to get the news, because there has never been an era when so many things have been going right for so many of the wrong persons.
OGDEN NASH

A newspaper column, like a fish, should be consumed when fresh; otherwise it is not only indigestible but unspeakable.
JAMES RESTON

To a philosopher all news, as it is called, is gossip, and those who edit and read it are old women over their tea.
HENRY DAVID THOREAU

News is what a chap who doesn't care much about anything wants to read. And it's only news until he's read it. After that it's dead.
EVELYN WAUGH

## No

"No" is always a door-closing word; "Yes" is a door-opening word.
THOMAS DREIER

A gilded "No" is more satisfactory than a dry "Yes."
BALTASAR GRACIÁN

The super-salesman neither permits his subconscious mind to broadcast negative thoughts nor gives expression to them through words, for the reason that he understands that like attracts like and negative suggestions attract negative action and negative decisions from prospective buyers.
NAPOLEON HILL

The man who has not learned to say "No" will be a weak if not a wretched man as long as he lives.
A. MACLAREN

So many of us know what we are against, but not what we are for—what we disbelieve, not what we believe. A negative life easily becomes neutral and futile.
JOSEPH FORT NEWTON

We should all be very careful when we say "No" to a suggested improvement or plan made by a subordinate. A "No" in most cases is final. We are usually more careful when we say "Yes" because we know that our "Yes" decisions will have to stand the test of performance or further approval. As a matter of fact, we should be more careful with our "No's" for the very reason that they do not have to stand the test of performance or further approval.
A. W. ROBERTSON

It is a great evil, as well as a misfortune, to be unable to utter a prompt and decided "No."
CHARLES SIMMONS

When we can say "No," not only to things that are wrong and sinful, but also to things pleasant, profitable, and good which would hinder and clog our grand duties and our chief work, we shall understand more fully what life is worth, and how to make the most of it.
CHARLES A. STODDARD

## *Nobility*

A noble man compares and estimates himself by an idea which is higher than himself, and a mean man, by one lower than himself.
HENRY WARD BEECHER

Those who think nobly are noble.
ISAAC BICKERSTAFF

A degenerate nobleman, or one that is proud of his birth, is like a turnip: there is nothing good of him but that which is underground.
SAMUEL BUTLER

Nobility of birth does not always insure a corresponding unity of mind; if it did, it would always act as a stimulus to noble actions; but it sometimes acts as a clog rather than a spur.
CHARLES CALEB COLTON

Every noble activity makes room for itself.
RALPH WALDO EMERSON

The essence of true nobility is neglect to self.
J. A. FROUDE

Be noble, and the nobleness that lies in other men, sleeping but never dead, will rise in majesty to meet thine own.
JAMES RUSSELL LOWELL

The noble soul has reverence for itself.
FRIEDRICH WILHELM NIETZSCHE

We need above all to learn again to believe in the possibility of nobility of spirit in ourselves.
EUGENE O'NEILL

If a man be endowed with a generous mind, this is the best kind of nobility.
PLATO

Do not think it wasted time to submit yourself to any influence that will bring upon you any noble feeling.
JOHN RUSKIN

We are all sculptors and painters, and our material is our own flesh and blood and bones. Any nobleness begins at once to refine a man's features, and any meanness or sensuality to imbrute them.
HENRY DAVID THOREAU

## *Nothing*

Doing nothing is the hardest work of all.
ANONYMOUS

To be nothing is the result of doing nothing.
HARRY F. BANKS

Nothing is really work unless you would rather be doing something else.
JAMES M. BARRIE

Sometimes one pays most for the things one gets for nothing.
ALBERT EINSTEIN

To whom nothing is given, of him nothing can be required.
HENRY FIELDING

If you expect nothing, you're apt to be surprised. You'll get it.
MALCOLM FORBES

Nothing is sometimes the right thing to say.
MALCOLM FORBES

The occupation most becoming to a civilized man is to do nothing.
THÉOPHILE GAUTIER

I have spent my life laboriously doing nothing.
HUGO GROTIUS

Some people have a perfect genius for doing nothing, and doing it assiduously.
THOMAS C. HALIBURTON

The way to be nothing is to do nothing.
EDGAR WATSON HOWE

## Obligations

Happy the man to whom heaven has given a morsel of bread without laying him under the obligation of thanking any other for it than heaven itself.
MIGUEL DE CERVANTES

Small obligations, given habitually, are what preserve the heart and secure comfort.
WILLIAM DAVY

It is well known to all great men, that by conferring an obligation they do not always procure a friend, but are certain of creating many enemies.
HENRY FIELDING

We are always much better pleased to see those whom we have obliged than those who have obliged us.
FRANÇOIS DE LA ROCHEFOUCAULD

The more obligations we accept that are self-imposed, the freer we are.
JOHN C. SCHROEDER

Most men remember obligations, but not often to be grateful; the proud are made sour by the remembrance and the vain silent.
WILLIAM SIMMS

To feel oppressed by obligation is only to prove that we are incapable of a proper sentiment of gratitude. To receive favors from the unworthy is to admit that our selfishness is superior to our pride.
WILLIAM SIMMS

We cannot always oblige, but we can always speak obligingly.
VOLTAIRE

## Obstacles

You can surmount the obstacles in your path if you are determined, courageous and hard-working. Never be fainthearted. Be resolute, but never bitter. Bitterness will serve only to warp your personality. Permit no one to dissuade you from pursuing the goals you set for yourselves. Do not fear to pioneer, to venture down new paths of endeavor. Demand and make good use of your rights, but never fail to discharge faithfully the obligations and responsibilities of good citizenship. Be good Americans.
RALPH J. BUNCHE

The block of granite which was an obstacle in the path of the weak, becomes a steppingstone in the path of the strong.
THOMAS CARLYLE

If you find a path with no obstacles, it probably doesn't lead anywhere.
FRANK A. CLARK

In a paradisal state without work or struggle in which there were no obstacles to overcome, there could be no thought because every motive for thought would have disappeared, neither any real contemplation, because active and poetic contemplation contains in itself a world of practical struggles and affections.
BENEDETTO CROCE

It is a hard rule of life, and I believe a healthy one, that no great plan is ever carried out without meeting and overcoming endless obstacles that come up to try the skill of man's hand, the quality of his courage, and the endurance of his faith.
**DONALD DOUGLAS**

Braving obstacles and hardships is nobler than retreat to tranquility. The butterfly that hovers around the lamp until it dies is more admirable than the mole that lives in the dark tunnel.
**KAHLIL GIBRAN**

It is interesting to notice how some minds seem almost to create themselves, springing up under every disadvantage and working their solitary but irresistible way through a thousand obstacles.
**WASHINGTON IRVING**

The worst obstructionist in any community is not the man who is opposed to doing anything, but the man who will not do what he can because he cannot do what he would like to do.
**J. L. LONG**

The greater the obstacle the more glory in overcoming it.
**MOLIÈRE**

Obstacles are those frightful things you see when you take your eyes off the goal.
**HANNAH MORE**

## *Opinions*

He who is master of all opinions can never be the bigot of any.
**WILLIAM R. ALGER**

Point of view must mean more than mere prejudice; it should express conclusions reached by that painful process known as thinking. And when new facts or factors are presented, free men should be as vigilant to change their viewpoints as to confirm them.
**A. MORTIMER ASTBURY**

Opinion is the main thing which does good or harm in the world. It is our false opinions of things which ruin us.
**MARCUS AURELIUS ANTONINUS**

So long as there are earnest believers in the world, they will always wish to punish opinions, even if their judgment tells them it is unwise and their conscience that it is wrong.
**WALTER BAGEHOT**

We should allow others' excellences, to preserve a modest opinion of our own.
**ISAAC BARROW**

Opinions that are well rooted should grow and change like a healthy tree.
**IRVING BATCHELLER**

Absurdity: A statement or belief manifestly inconsistent with one's own opinion.
**AMBROSE BIERCE**

The man who never alters his opinion is like standing water, and breeds reptiles of the mind.
**WILLIAM BLAKE**

If in the last few years you hadn't discarded a major opinion or acquired a new one, check your pulse. You may be dead.
**GELETT BURGESS**

One of the mistakes in the conduct of human life is to suppose that other men's opinion are to make us happy.
**RICHARD BURTON**

He that complies against his will, is of his own opinion still.
SAMUEL BUTLER

Popular opinion is the greatest lie in the world.
THOMAS CARLYLE

The world is governed much more by opinion than by laws. It is not the judgment of courts, but the moral judgment of individuals and masses of men which is the chief wall of defense around property and life. With the progress of society, this power of opinion is taking the place of wars.
WILLIAM ELLERY CHANNING

No liberal man would impute a charge of unsteadiness to another for having changed his opinion.
CICERO

Opinions, like showers, are generate in high places, but they invariably descend into lower ones, and ultimately flow down to the people, as rain unto the sea.
CHARLES CALEB COLTON

Some of our problems can no more be solved correctly by majority opinion than can a problem in arithmetic and there are few problems that cannot be solved according to what is just and right without resort to popular opinion.
HENRY L. DOHERTY

He that never changes his opinions, never corrects his mistakes, will never be wiser on the morrow than he is today.
TRYON EDWARDS

A man cannot utter two or three sentences without disclosing to intelligent ears precisely where he stands in life and thought, whether in the kingdom of the senses and the understanding, or in that of ideas and imagination, or in the realm of intuitions and duty.
RALPH WALDO EMERSON

Every man should periodically be compelled to listen to opinions which are infuriating to him. To hear nothing but what is pleasing to one is to make a pillow of the mind.
ST. JOHN ERVINE

Never think badly of anyone, not even if the words or conduct of the person in question give good grounds for doing so.
JOSEMARIA ESCRIVA

The most distinctive mark of a cultured mind is the ability to take another's point of view; to put one's self in another's place, and see life and its problems from a point of view different from one's own. To be willing to test a new idea; to be able to live on the edge of difference in all matters intellectually; to examine without heat the burning question of the day; to have imaginative sympathy, openness and flexibility of mind, steadiness and poise of feeling, cool calmness of judgment, is to have culture.
ARTHUR H. R. FAIRCHILD

Sometimes only a change of viewpoint is needed to convert a tiresome duty into an interesting opportunity.
ALBERTA FLANDERS

The bell of public opinion is today making the Morgan-Rockefeller-Vanderbilt class jump. Nor are the strongest of our corporations immune. The railroads have had to jump pretty lively, and certain gigantic industrial combinations are also being put through their paces.
B. C. FORBES

The free expression of opinion, as experience has taught us, is the safety-valve of passion. The noise of the rushing steam, when it escapes, alarms the timid; but it is the sign that we are safe. The concession of reasonable privilege anticipates the growth of furious appetite.
WILLIAM E. GLADSTONE

In two opposite opinions, if one be perfectly reasonable, the other can't be perfectly right.
**OLIVER GOLDSMITH**

Our opinion of people depends less upon what we see in them than in what they make us see in ourselves.
**SARAH GRAND**

I do not regret having braved public opinion, when I knew it was wrong and was sure it would be merciless.
**HORACE GREELEY**

The opinions of men who think are always growing and changing, like living children.
**PHILIP HAMERTON**

We are very much what others think of us. The reception our observations meet with gives us courage to proceed, or damps our efforts.
**WILLIAM HAZLITT**

The men of the past had convictions, while we moderns have only opinions.
**HEINRICH HEINE**

Every time you give another a piece of your mind, you add to your own vacuum.
**FENWICK L. HOLMES**

We should be eternally vigilant against attempts to check the expression of opinions that we loathe.
**OLIVER WENDELL HOLMES**

Honest differences of views and honest debate are not disunity. They are the vital process of policy-making among free men.
**HERBERT HOOVER**

Our institutions were not devised to bring about uniformity of opinion, if they had been we might well abandon hope. It is important to remember, as has well been said, the essential characteristic of true liberty is that under its shelter many different types of life and character and opinion and belief can develop unmolested and unobstructed.
**CHARLES EVANS HUGHES**

There is no greater mistake than the hasty conclusion that opinions are worthless because they are badly argued.
**THOMAS H. HUXLEY**

I tolerate with the utmost latitude the right of others to differ from me in opinion.
**THOMAS JEFFERSON**

In every country where man is free to think and to speak, difference of opinion will arise from difference of perception, and the imperfection of reason; but these differences, when permitted, as in this happy country, to purify themselves by free discussion, are but as passing clouds overspreading our land transiently, and leaving our horizon more bright and serene.
**THOMAS JEFFERSON**

The opinions of men are not the object of civil government, nor under its jurisdiction.
**THOMAS JEFFERSON**

As for the differences of opinion upon speculative questions, if we wait till they are reconciled, the action of human affairs must be suspended forever. But neither are we to look for perfection in any one man, nor for agreement among many.
**JUNIUS**

He who has no opinion of his own, but depends upon the opinion and taste of others, is a slave.
**FRIEDRICH KLOPSTOCK**

I shall adopt new views as fast as they shall appear to be true views.
ABRAHAM LINCOLN

It is the man who does not want to express an opinion whose opinion I want.
ABRAHAM LINCOLN

It is a golden rule that one should never judge men by their opinions, but rather by what their opinions make of them.
GEORG CHRISTOPH LICHTENBERG

New opinions are always suspected and usually opposed because they are not already common.
JOHN LOCKE

Reactionaries must be deprived of the right to voice their opinions; only the people have that right.
MAO TSE-TUNG

Men are never so good or so bad as their opinions.
JAMES MACKINTOSH

Opinions cannot survive if one has no chance to fight for them.
THOMAS MANN

In a discussion the difficulty lies, not in being able to defend your opinion, but to know it.
ANDRÉ MAUROIS

If all mankind minus one were of one opinion, and only one person were of the contrary opinion, mankind would be no more justified in silencing that one person, than he, if he had the power, would be justified in silencing mankind.
JOHN STUART MILL

To be absolutely certain about something, one must know everything or nothing about it.
OLIN MILLER

I look upon the too good opinion that man has of himself, as the nursing mother of all false opinions, both public and private.
MICHEL DE MONTAIGNE

I can complain because rose bushes have thorns or rejoice because thorn bushes have roses. It's all how you look at it.
J. KENFIELD MORLEY

Today's public opinion, though it may appear as light as air, may become tomorrow's legislation—for better or for worse.
EARL NEWSOM

Have no kowtowing respect for precedent. Do not allow the dictate of public opinion to hamper your efforts.
JOHN HENRY PATTERSON

There is, and always has been, one tremendous ruler of the human race—and that ruler is that combination of the opinions of all, the leveling up of universal sense which is called public sentiment. That is the ever-present regulator and police of humanity.
THOMAS B. REED

Man is a gregarious animal, and much more so in his mind than in his body. He may like to go alone for a walk, but he hates to stand alone in his opinions.
GEORGE SANTAYANA

Don't judge a man by his opinion of himself.
J. L. SCHNADIG

If you want to discover your true opinion of anybody, observe the impression made on you by the first sight of a letter from him.
**ARTHUR SCHOPENHAUER**

Opinion is something wherein I go about to give reasons why all the world should think as I think.
**JOHN SELDEN**

The circumstances of the world are so variable, that an irrevocable purpose or opinion is almost synonymous with a foolish one.
**W. H. SEWARD**

Wind puffs up empty bladders; opinion, fools.
**SOCRATES**

Private opinion creates public opinion. Public opinion overflows eventually into national behavior as things are arranged at present, and can make or mar the world. That is why private opinion, and private behavior, and private conversation are so terrifyingly important.
**JAN STRUTHER**

Extreme views are never just; something always turns up which disturbs the calculations founded on their data.
**TANCRED**

Public opinion is a weak tyrant compared with our own private opinion.
**HENRY DAVID THOREAU**

No one agrees with other people's opinions; they merely agree with their own opinions expressed by somebody else.
**SYDNEY TREMAYNE**

It is the difference of opinion that makes horse races.
**MARK TWAIN**

What others think of us would be of little moment did it not, when known, so deeply tinge what we think of ourselves.
**PAUL VALÉRY**

Those who never retract their opinions love themselves more than they love the truth.
**RALPH VENNING**

One can give a really unbiased opinion only about things that do not interest one, which is no doubt the reason an unbiased opinion is always valueless. The man who sees both sides of a question is a man who sees absolutely nothing.
**OSCAR WILDE**

All empty souls tend to extreme opinion. It is only in those who have built up a rich world of memories and habits of thought that extreme opinions affront the sense of probability. Propositions, for instance, which set all the truth upon one side can only enter rich minds to dislocate and strain, if they can enter at all, and sooner or later the mind expels them by instinct.
**WILLIAM BUTLER YEATS**

The whole world is learning that treaties, constitutions, ordinances and bonds are good only to the extent that they are made coincident with basic human relationships which have the approval of that sensitive, quick acting and dominant power, the public opinion of the world.
**OWEN D. YOUNG**

## *Opportunities*

Most of us never recognize opportunity until it goes to work in our competitor's business.
**P. L. ANDARR**

Four things come not back—the spoken word, the sped arrow, the past life, and the neglected opportunity.
ARABIAN PROVERB

No one wearies of benefits received.
MARCUS AURELIUS ANTONINUS

Opportunities do not come with their values stamped upon them. Every one must be challenged. A day, dawns, quite like other days; in it a single hour comes, quite like other hours; but in that day and in that hour the chance of a lifetime faces us. To face every opportunity of life thoughtfully and ask its meaning bravely and earnestly, is the only way to meet the supreme opportunities when they come, whether open-faced or disguised.
MALTBIE BABCOCK

Opportunities are greater to-day than ever before in history. Young people graduating from our schools have greater chances for health, happiness and prosperity than had the children of any previous generation. A little money will do more to-day in setting up a young man or woman in business than it would ever do heretofore. There is a greater demand today for people of character than at any time in the history of America. Industry, intelligence, imagination and persistence are great gold mines.
ROGER W. BABSON

A wise man will make more opportunities than he finds.
FRANCIS BACON

When one door closes another door opens; but we often look so long and so regretfully upon the closed door that we do not see the ones which open for us.
ALEXANDER GRAHAM BELL

I've never met a person, I don't care what his condition, in whom I could not see possibilities. I don't care how much a man may consider himself a failure, I believe in him, for he can change the thing that is wrong in his life anytime he is prepared and ready to do it. Whenever he develops the desire, he can take away from his life the thing that is defeating it. The capacity for reformation and change lies within.
PRESTON BRADLEY

Genius and great abilities are often wanting; sometimes, only opportunities. Some deserve praise for what they have done; others for what they would have done.
JEAN DE LA BRUYÈRE

There is nothing in the world really beneficial that does not lie within the reach of an informed understanding and a well-protected pursuit.
EDMUND BURKE

The lure of the distant and the difficult is deceptive. The great opportunity is where you are.
JOHN BURROUGHS

The sure way to miss success is to miss the opportunity.
VICTOR CHASLES

What helps luck is a habit of watching for opportunities, of having a patient, but restless mind, of sacrificing one's ease or vanity, of uniting a love of detail to foresight, and of passing through hard times bravely and cheerfully.
CHARLES VICTOR CHERBULIEZ

An optimist sees an opportunity in every calamity; a pessimist sees a calamity in every opportunity.
WINSTON CHURCHILL

If we are to achieve a victorious standard of living today we must look for the opportunity in every

difficulty instead of being paralyzed at the thought of the difficulty in every opportunity.
**WALTER E. COLE**

Every one has a fair turn to be as great as he pleases.
**JEREMY COLLIER**

Small opportunities are often the beginning of great enterprises.
**DEMOSTHENES**

The great secret of success in life is for a man to be ready when his opportunity comes.
**BENJAMIN DISRAELI**

Next to knowing when to seize an opportunity, the most important thing in life is to know when to forego an advantage.
**BENJAMIN DISRAELI**

There is a hook in every benefit, that sticks in his jaws that takes that benefit, and draws him whither the benefactor will.
**JOHN DONNE**

Great opportunities come to all, but many do not know they have met them. The only preparation to take advantage of them is single fidelity to watch what each day brings.
**ALBERT E. DUNNING**

When blocked or defeated in an enterprise I had much at heart, I always turned immediately to another field of work where progress looked possible, biding my time for a chance to resume the obstructed road.
**CHARLES W. ELIOT**

It's them as take advantage that get advantage i' this world.
**GEORGE ELIOT**

What is opportunity to the man who can't use it? An unfecundated egg, which the waves of time wash away into nonentity.
**GEORGE ELIOT**

No great man ever complains of want of opportunity.
**RALPH WALDO EMERSON**

The prizes go to those who meet emergencies successfully. And the way to meet emergencies is to do each daily task the best we can; to act as though the eye of opportunity were always upon us. In the hundred-yard race the winner doesn't cross the tape line a dozen strides ahead of the field. He wins by inches. So we find it in ordinary business life. The big things that come our way are seldom the result of long thought or careful planning, but rather they are the fruit of seed planted in the daily routine of our work.
**WILLIAM FEATHER**

If you were to visit a certain rural section of Vermont, you would be shown two farms only a few miles apart, and you would be told that a lad raised on one of the farms today occupies the most responsible position in the whole world, the Presidency of the United States. From the other farm, you would be told, there went forth another lad who is today the head of one of the leading railroads in the U.S. . . . Whenever I hear wild denunciations of this country and its institutions I cannot but feel that . . . no other country on earth offers such advantages and opportunities for children born in humble circumstances.
**B. C. FORBES**

The majority of America's colossal fortunes have been made by entering industries in their early stages and developing leadership in them. . . . Think of what opportunities the present and the future contain in such fields as ship-building and ship-owning, aircraft, electrical development, the oil industry, different branches of the automotive

industry, foreign trade, international banking, invention, the chemical industry, moving pictures, color photography, and, one night add, labor leadership.
**B. C. FORBES (1921)**

I think luck is the sense to recognize an opportunity and the ability to take advantage of it. Every one has bad breaks, but every one also has opportunities. The man who can smile at his breaks and grab his chances gets on.
**SAMUEL GOLDWYN**

If you want to succeed in the world you must make your own opportunities as you go on. The man who waits for some seventh wave to toss him on dry land will find that the seventh wave is a long time coming.
**JOHN B. GOUGH**

If it exists, it's possible.
**JOHN P. GRIER**

I do not want anybody to convince my son that some one will guarantee him a living. I want him rather to realize that there is plenty of opportunity in this country for him to achieve success, but whether he wins or loses depends entirely on his own character, perseverance, thrift, intelligence and capacity for hard work.
**MAJOR JOHN L. GRIFFITH**

The belief in the existence of opportunities to achieve economic equality has had a longer and more vital tradition in American history than has been the case anywhere else.
**LOUIS HACKER**

Most of us don't recognize opportunity until we see it working for a competitor.
**JAY HUENFELD**

We must dream of an aristocracy of achievement arising out of a democracy of opportunity.
**THOMAS JEFFERSON**

Many do with opportunities as children do at the seashore; they fill their little hands with sand, and then let the grains fall through, one by one, till all are gone.
**T. JONES**

We are confronted with insurmountable opportunities.
**WALT KELLY**

There is no security on this earth. Only opportunity.
**DOUGLAS MACARTHUR**

Injuries should be done all together, so that being, less tasted, they will give less offense. Benefits should be granted little by little, so that they may be better enjoyed.
**NICCOLÒ MACHIAVELLI**

A pessimist is one who makes difficulties of his opportunities; an optimist is one who makes opportunities of his difficulties.
**REGINALD B. MANSELL**

Ask, and it shall be given you; seek and ye shall find; knock, and it shall be opened unto you. For every one that asketh receiveth; and he that seeketh findeth; and to him that knocketh it shall be opened.
**MATTHEW 7:7–8**

Opportunity has hair in front but is bald behind.
**PHAEDRUS**

Vigilance in watching opportunity; tact and daring in seizing upon opportunity; force and persistence in crowding opportunity to its utmost possible

achievement—these are the martial virtues which must command success.
**AUSTIN PHELPS**

The important point is to be on the spot at the moment most favorable for gaining the desired advantage; and it will be found that of men who get what they want in this world, both those who seem to hasten and those who seem to lounge are always at the right place at the right time.
**DAVID GRAHAM PHILLIPS**

No man's abilities are so remarkably shining as not to stand in need of a proper opportunity.
**PLINY**

Opportunity rarely knocks until you are ready. And few people have ever been really ready without receiving opportunity's call.
**CHANNING POLLOCK**

In this world the one thing supremely worth having is the opportunity to do well and worthily a piece of work of vital consequence to the welfare of mankind.
**THEODORE ROOSEVELT**

To be a great man it is necessary to turn to account all opportunities.
**FRANÇOIS DE LA ROCHEFOUCAULD**

Opportunity is as scarce as oxygen; men fairly breathe it and do not know it.
**DOC SANE**

Opportunity has power over all things.
**SOPHOCLES**

Opportunity is the best captain of all endeavor.
**SOPHOCLES**

No man can make his opportunity. He can only make use of such opportunities as occur.
**FORREST P. SHERMAN**

The dead are living all around us, watching with eager anticipation how we will handle the opportunities they left in our hands when they died.
**THEODORE C. SPEERS, D.D.**

Opportunity is rare, and a wise man will never let it go by him.
**BAYARD TAYLOR**

I make the most of all that comes, and the least of all that goes.
**SARA TEASDALE**

It is less important to redistribute wealth than it is to redistribute opportunity.
**ARTHUR H. VANDENBERG**

America is the land of, and for, uncommon men not only because it affords free choice and opportunity for people to become expert in their chosen occupations, but also because it has mechanisms and incentives for providing the tools of production that the skilled must operate if their skill is to have full fruition in abundant production.
**ENDERS M. VOORHEES**

The man who works need never be a problem to anyone. Opportunities multiply as they are seized; they die when neglected. Life is a long line of opportunities. Wealth is not in making money, but in making the man while he is making money. Production, not destruction, leads to success.
**JOHN WICKER**

To every man his chance, to every man, regardless of his birth, his shining golden opportunity. To every man the right to live, to work, to be himself, and to become whatever thing his manhood and his vision can contribute to make him.
**THOMAS WOLFE**

## Order

The less of routine, the more of life.
AMOS BRONSON ALCOTT

Order means light and peace, inward liberty and free command over one's self; order is power.
HENRI FRÉDÉRIC AMIEL

Nothing is orderly till man takes hold of it. Everything in creation lies around loose.
HENRY WARD BEECHER

Every great man exhibits the talent of organization or construction, whether it be in a poem, a philosophical system, a policy, or a strategy. And without method there is no organization nor construction.
EDWARD BULWER-LYTTON

Good order is the foundation of all good things.
EDMUND BURKE

Method is like packing things in a box; a good packer will get in half as much again as a bad one.
WILLIAM CECIL

When liberty destroys order, the hunger for order will destroy liberty.
WILL DURANT

Have a time and place for everything, and do everything in its time and place, and you will not only accomplish more, but have far more leisure than those who are always hurrying, as if vainly attempting to overtake time that had been lost.
TRYON EDWARDS

Method will teach you to win time.
JOHANN WOLFGANG VON GOETHE

We are rational creatures: Our virtue and perfection is to love reason, or rather to love order.
NICHOLAS MALEBRANCHE

Order and simplification are the first steps toward the master of a subject. The actual enemy is the unknown.
THOMAS MANN

There is an easier, better and quicker way to do most everything, and now as never before, we must seek those easier, better, quicker ways and methods.
GUSTAV METZMAN

There is no course of life so weak and sottish as that which is managed by order, method and discipline.
MICHEL DE MONTAIGNE

Almost all men are intelligent. It is method that they lack.
F. W. NICHOL

Most of life is routine—dull and grubby, but routine is the momentum that keeps a man going. If you wait for inspiration you'll be standing on the corner after the parade is a mile down the street.
BEN NICHOLAS

After you've done a thing the same way for two years, look it over carefully. After five years, look at it with suspicion. And after ten years, throw it away and start all over.
ALFRED E. PERLMAN

Sameness is the mother of disgust, variety the cure.
PETRARCH

I'm working to improve my methods, and every hour I save is an hour added to my life.
AYN RAND

Mere lack of success does not discredit a method, for there are many things that determine and perpetuate our sanctified ways of doing things besides their success in reaching their proposed ends.
JAMES HARVEY ROBINSON

Order is the sanity of the mind, the health of the body, the peace of the city, the security of the state. As the beams to a house, as the bones to the microcosm of man, so is order to all things.
ROBERT SOUTHEY

There is no lostness like that which comes to a man when a perfect and certain pattern has dissolved about him.
JOHN STEINBECK

Methods are the masters of masters.
CHARLES MAURICE DE TALLEYRAND

It is remarkable how easily and insensibly we fall into a particular route, and make a beaten track for ourselves.
HENRY DAVID THOREAU

Routine is a ground to stand on, a wall to retreat to; we cannot draw on our boots without bracing ourselves against it.
HENRY DAVID THOREAU

The art of progress is to preserve order amid change and to preserve change amid order.
ALFRED NORTH WHITEHEAD

## *Organization*

The only institutions that last a long time, do good and useful work, and are profitable, are those that are, and have been, well organized. You get the feel of this immediately whenever you visit such a place.... In organization there is always strength. Especially is this true in regard to a well-organized human being. He doesn't waste his substance, but is forever improving his mind and giving and radiating confidence.... The organized person organizes his day as he does himself. Thus it is that he makes the most of his time and goes to his bed for the night perfectly relaxed for rest and renewal. How happy we can make our own lives, and the lives of those about us, merely by self-organization!
GEORGE MATTHEW ADAMS

Large organization is loose organization. Nay, it would be almost as true to say that organization is always disorganization.
G. K. CHESTERTON

The primary asset of any business is its organization.
WILLIAM FEATHER

The young man who addresses himself in stern earnest to organizing his life—his habits, his associations, his reading, his study, his work—stands far more chance of rising to a position affording him opportunity to exercise his organizing abilities than the fellow who dawdles along without chart or compass, without plan or purpose, without self-improvement and self-discipline.
B. C. FORBES

Organization is the art of getting men to respond like thoroughbreds. When you cluck to a thoroughbred, he gives you all of the speed and strength of heart and sinew he has in him. When you cluck to a jackass, he kicks.
C. R. HOUSE

The soul of the individual was established nineteen hundred years ago, while only today are we beginning to see beyond that into the soul world of organization. We are realizing that an organization is not merely a collection of individuals, but is a

super-individual with like qualities, only larger. It should be as much more powerful spiritually than a single individual, as it is more powerful materially than a single individual. Everywhere men are recognizing that organizations should have souls. The meaning of this is overwhelming when one considers that the term organization covers not only the multitude of business and social societies, but countries, nations, and even international associations.
**ALVA KONKLE**

We trained hard—but it seemed that every time we were beginning to form into teams, we would be reorganized. I was to learn later in life that we tend to meet any new situation by reorganizing; and what a wonderful method it can be for creating the illusion of progress while producing confusion, inefficiency and demoralization.
**PETRONIUS**

An architect's arch is a heap of stones until and unless it is organized and grouped around a keystone. The keystone holds the pattern together. So it is with life. Unless there is some keystone conviction by which experience is organized, the individual remains little more than a bundle of feelings.
**MARTIN H. SCHARLEMANN**

The secret of all victory lies in the organization of the nonobvious.
**OSWALD SPENGLER**

# P

## Passions

When you have found out the prevailing passion of any man, remember never to trust him where that passion is concerned.
**LORD CHESTERFIELD**

We are ne'er like angels till our passion dies.
**THOMAS DEKKER**

A man in a passion rides a wild horse.
**BENJAMIN FRANKLIN**

Passion, joined with power, produceth thunder and ruin.
**THOMAS FULLER**

The passions are the humors of the mind, and the least excess sickens our judgment. If the disease spreads to the mouth, your reputation will be in danger.
**BALTASAR GRACIÁN**

To rule self and subdue our passions is the more praiseworthy because so few know how to do it.
**FRANCESCO GUICCIARDINI**

Passions unguided are for the most part mere madness.
**THOMAS HOBBES**

Absence diminishes little passions and increases great ones, as wind extinguishes candles and fans a fire.
**FRANÇOIS DE LA ROCHEFOUCAULD**

If we resist our passions it is more from their weakness than from our strength.
**FRANÇOIS DE LA ROCHEFOUCAULD**

Three passions, simple but overwhelmingly strong, have governed my life: the longing for love, the search for knowledge, and unbearable pity for the suffering of mankind.
**BERTRAND RUSSELL**

The only difference between a caprice and a lifelong passion is that the caprice lasts a little longer.
**OSCAR WILDE**

## Past

Only one accomplishment is beyond both the power and the mercy of the Gods. They cannot make the past as though it had never been.
**AESCHYLUS**

Forget the past. No one becomes successful in the past.
**ANONYMOUS**

Man is a history-making creature who can neither repeat his past nor leave it behind.
**W. H. AUDEN**

The true picture of the past flits by. The past can be seized only as an image which flashes up at the instant when it can be recognized and is never seen again.
**WALTER BENJAMIN**

Many are always praising the bygone time, for it is natural that the old should extol the days of their youth; the weak, the time of their strength; the sick,

the season of their vigor; and the disappointed, the springtide of their hopes.
**CALEB BINGHAM**

One may return to the place of his birth,
He cannot go back to his youth.
**JOHN BURROUGHS**

God cannot alter the past, that is why he is obliged to connive at the existence of historians.
**SAMUEL BUTLER**

We cannot fling ourselves into the blank future; we can only call up images from the past. This being so, the important principle follows, that how many images we have largely depends on how much past we have.
**G. K. CHESTERTON**

To be ignorant of what occurred before you were born is to remain always a child.
**CICERO**

Study the past if you would divine the future.
**CONFUCIUS**

The past is the only dead thing that smells sweet.
**CYRIL CONNOLLY**

We are well advised to keep on nodding terms with the people we used to be, whether we find them attractive company or not. Otherwise they turn up unannounced and surprise us, hammering on the mind's door at 4 A.M. of a dark night and demand to know who deserted them, who betrayed them, who is going to make amends.
**JOAN DIDION**

The past always looks better than it was; it's only pleasant because it isn't here.
**FINLEY PETER DUNNE**

We are not free to use today, or to promise tomorrow, because we are already mortgaged to yesterday.
**RALPH WALDO EMERSON**

It is sadder to find the past again and find it inadequate to the present than it is to have it elude you and remain forever a harmonious conception of memory.
**F. SCOTT FITZGERALD**

When I reflect, as I frequently do, upon the felicity I have enjoyed, I sometimes say to myself, that, were the offer made me, I would engage to run again, from beginning to end, the same career of life. All I would ask, should be the privilege of an author, to correct in a second edition, certain errors of the first.
**BENJAMIN FRANKLIN**

Nostalgia combines regularly with manifest respectability to give credence to old error as opposed to new truth.
**JOHN KENNETH GALBRAITH**

It is delightful to transport one's self into the spirit of the past, to see how a wise man has thought before us, and to what a glorious height we have at last reached.
**JOHANN WOLFGANG VON GOETHE**

The past is a funeral gone by.
**EDMUND GOSSE**

The illusion that times that were are better than those that are, has probably pervaded all ages.
**HORACE GREELEY**

Human life may be regarded as a succession of frontispieces. The way to be satisfied is never to look back.
**WILLIAM HAZLITT**

It is just possible to imagine what past epochs included in their thinking, but not what they excluded.
**HUGO VON HOFMANNSTHAL**

Nothing impresses the mind with a deeper feeling of loneliness than to tread the silent and deserted scene of former flow and pageant.
**WASHINGTON IRVING**

Nothing changes more constantly than the past; for the past that influences our lives does not consist of what happened, but of what men believe happened.
**GERALD W. JOHNSTON**

No man correctly informed as to the past will be disposed to take a morose or desponding view of the present.
**THOMAS B. MACAULAY**

Those who compare the age in which their lot has fallen with a golden age which exists only in imagination may talk of degeneracy and decay, but no man who is correctly informed as to the past will be disposed to take a morose or desponding view of the present.
**THOMAS B. MACAULAY**

The past is a bucket of ashes, so live not in your yesterdays, nor just for tomorrow, but in the here and now. Keep moving and forget the post-mortems. And remember, no one can get the jump on the future.
**CARL SANDBURG**

It is foolish to try to live on past experience. It is very dangerous, if not a fatal habit, to judge ourselves to be safe because of something that we felt or did twenty years ago.
**CHARLES H. SPURGEON**

I said there was but one solitary thing about the past worth remembering and that was the fact that it is past—can't be restored.
**MARK TWAIN**

The past is only the present become invisible and mute; its memoried glances and its murmurs are infinitely precious.
**MARY WEBB**

The great achievements of the past were the adventures of the past. Only the adventurous can understand the greatness of the past.
**ALFRED NORTH WHITEHEAD**

Past: Our cradle, not our prison, and there is danger as well as appeal in its glamour. The past is for inspiration, not imitation, for continuation, not repetition.
**ISRAEL ZANGWILL**

## *Patience*

Patience is passion tamed.
**LYMAN ABBOTT**

The remedy of time is patience.
**ARABIAN PROVERB**

Patience is so like fortitude that she seems either her sister or her daughter.
**ARISTOTLE**

**Prayer of the Modern American:**

Dear God, I pray for patience
And I want it right now!
**OREN ARNOLD**

Patience is the companion of wisdom.
**ST. AUGUSTINE**

Patience is a minor form of despair, disguised as a virtue.
AMBROSE BIERCE

He who can wait for what he desires takes the course not to be exceedingly grieved if he fails of it; he, on the contrary, who labors after a thing too impatiently thinks the success when it comes is not a recompense equal to all the pains he has been at about it.
JEAN DE LA BRUYÈRE

No road is too long to the man who advances deliberately and without undue haste; and no honors are too distant for the man who prepares himself for them with patience.
JEAN DE LA BRUYÈRE

There is one form of hope which is never unwise, and which certainly does not diminish with the increase of knowledge. In that form it changes its name, and we call it patience.
EDWARD BULWER-LYTTON

It is not necessary for all men to be great in action. The greatest and sublimest power is often simple patience.
HORACE BUSHNELL

Impatience never commanded success.
EDWIN H. CHAPIN

For national leaders it is sometimes easier to fight than to talk. Impatient cries for total victory are usually more popular than the patient tolerance required of a people whose leaders are seeking peaceful change down the intricate paths of diplomacy.
HARLAN CLEVELAND

Patience is a necessary ingredient of genius.
BENJAMIN DISRAELI

By patience and determination, rather than by a harsh upsetting of tradition, we move toward our national goal. This is the way we get things done in America. One man tells another, does what he can, till the sum of these effort grows into a national aspiration. Then occurs our miracle of democracy.
NEWTON B. DRURY

Possess your soul with patience.
JOHN DRYDEN

A handful of patience is worth more than a bushel of brains.
DUTCH PROVERB

In prosperity, caution; in adversity, patience.
DUTCH PROVERB

Successful salesman, authors, executives and workmen of every sort need patience. The great liability of youth is not inexperience but impatience.
WILLIAM FEATHER

Whether it's marriage of business, patience is the first rule of success.
WILLIAM FEATHER

Patience and time do more than strength or passion.
JEAN DE LA FONTAINE

Have patience with all things, but chiefly have patience with yourself. Do not lose courage in considering your own imperfections, but instantly start remedying them—every day begin the task anew.
ST. FRANCIS DE SALES

Job was not so miserable in his sufferings as happy in his patience.
THOMAS FULLER

Patience is the virtue of an ass that trots beneath his burden, and is quiet.
**GEORGE GRANVILLE**

Cast not away therefore thy confidence, which has great recompense of reward. For ye have need of patience that, after ye have done the will of God, ye might receive the promise.
**HEBREWS 10:35–36**

Patience strengthens the spirit, sweetens the temper, stifles anger, extinguishes envy, subdues pride, bridles the tongue.
**GEORGE HORNE**

The sharpest sting of adversity it borrows from our own impatience.
**GEORGE HORNE**

He that has no patience has nothing at all.
**ITALIAN PROVERB**

My brethren, count it all joy when ye fall into divers temptations; Knowing this, that the trying of your faith worketh patience. But let patience have her perfect work, that ye may be perfect and entire, wanting nothing.
**JAMES 1:2–4**

The mental disease of the present generation is impatience of study, contempt of the great masters of ancient wisdom, and a disposition to rely wholly upon unassisted genius and natural sagacity.
**JOHNSON**

All men command patience, although few be willing to practice it.
**THOMAS À KEMPIS**

He surely is most in need of another's patience, who has none of his own.
**JOHANN LAVATER**

Endurance is the crowning quality, and patience all the passion of great hearts.
**JAMES RUSSELL LOWELL**

Genius is eternal patience.
**MICHELANGELO**

A man must learn to endure that patiently which he cannot avoid conveniently.
**MICHEL DE MONTAIGNE**

The general order of things that takes care of fleas and moles also takes care of men, if they will have the same patience that fleas and moles have, to leave it to itself.
**MICHEL DE MONTAIGNE**

He invites a new injury who bears the old patiently.
**FYNES MORYSON**

Patience is bitter, but its fruits are sweet.
**JEAN-JACQUES ROUSSEAU**

On the whole, it is patience which makes the final difference between those who succeed or fail in all things. All the greatest people have it in an infinite degree, and among the less, the patient weak ones always conquer the impatient strong.
**JOHN RUSKIN**

There's no music in rest, but there's the making of music in it. And people are always missing that part of the life melody, always talking of perseverance and courage and fortitude; but patience is the finest and worthiest part of fortitude, and the rarest, too.
**JOHN RUSKIN**

Have patience. All things are difficult before they become easy.
**SA'DI**

Only those who have the patience to do simple things perfectly will acquire the skill to do difficult things easily.
JOHANN FRIEDRICH VON SCHILLER

How poor are they who have not patience! What wound did ever heal but by degrees.
WILLIAM SHAKESPEARE

Have patience and the mulberry leaf will become satin.
SPANISH PROVERB

A wise man does not try to hurry history. Many wars have been avoided by patience, and many have been precipitated by reckless haste.
ADLAI STEVENSON

Patience is the art of hoping.
MARQUIS DE VAUVENARGUES

## *Patriotism*

I must avow to your majesty [King George III] I have no attachment but to my own country.
JOHN ADAMS

Patriotism is a lively sense of responsibility. Nationalism is a silly cock crowing on its own dunghill.
RICHARD ALDINGTON

Patriotism: The first resort of a scoundrel.
AMBROSE BIERCE

Patriotism takes the place of religion in France. In the service of *la patrie,* the doing of one's duty is elevated into the sphere of exalted emotion.
W. C. BROWNELL

What scoundrels we would be if we did for ourselves what we are ready to do for Italy.
CAMILLO BENSO DI CAVOUR

Patriotism is easy to understand in America. It means looking out for yourself by looking out for your country.
CALVIN COOLIDGE

Patriotic talk is no proof of patriotism. Anyone can wave a flag. The real patriot lives his patriotism in everything he does.
JOHN M. DEVINE

When a whole nation is roaring patriotism at the top of its voice, I am fain to explore the cleanness of its hands and the purity of its heart.
RALPH WALDO EMERSON

Patriotism is collective responsibility.
ARNOLD GLASOW

I want to caution that we must not confuse patriotism with blind endorsement of bad policies.
MARK O. HATFIELD

Every man who loves his country, or wishes well to the best interests of society, will show himself a decided friend not only of morality and the laws, but of religious institutions, and honorably bear his part in supporting them.
JOEL HAWES

What is patriotism but the love of the good things we ate in our childhood?
LIN YUTANG

You're not supposed to be so blind with patriotism that you can't face reality. Wrong is wrong, no matter who does it or who says it.
MALCOLM X

No man is worth his salt who is not ready at all times to risk his body, to risk his well-being, to risk his life, in a great cause.
THEODORE ROOSEVELT

Patriotism: Your conviction that this country is superior to all other countries because you were born in it.
GEORGE BERNARD SHAW

No other factor in history, not even religion, has produced so many wars as has the clash of national egotisms sanctified by the name of patriotism.
PRESERVED SMITH

True patriotism is not manifested in short, frenzied bursts of emotion. It is the tranquil, steady dedication of a lifetime.
ADLAI STEVENSON

In the beginning of a change, the patriot is a scarce man, and brave, and hated and scorned. When his cause succeeds, the timid join him, for then it costs nothing to be a patriot.
MARK TWAIN

A real patriot is the fellow who gets a parking ticket and rejoices that the system works.
BILL VAUGHAN

Guard against the postures of pretended patriotism.
GEORGE WASHINGTON

## *Peace*

Calmness of mind is one of the beautiful jewels of wisdom. It is the result of long and patient effort in self-control. Its presence is an indication of ripened experience and of a more than ordinary knowledge of the laws and operations of thought.
JAMES ALLEN

A time will come when the science of destruction shall bend before the arts of peace; when the genius which multiplies our powers, which creates new products, which diffuses comfort and happiness among the great mass of the people, shall occupy in the general estimation of mankind that rank which reason and common sense now assign to it.
FRANÇOIS ARAGO

It is more difficult to organize peace than to win a war; but the fruits of victory will be lost if the peace is not well organized.
ARISTOTLE

We face the necessity of solving our problems at home in ways which may offer guidance to millions abroad groping for their own solutions. We must find answers for pressing problems of world peace, for raising living standards, safeguarding individual liberty and bringing management and labor to an understanding of the united effort necessary to advance the common good. If we face these issues we will find answers which will benefit our own people and provide the world with the lead it is looking for. This is surely our mission in the world today, and our great challenge.
WILLIAM L. BATT

The lesson which wars and depressions have taught is that if we want peace, prosperity and happiness at home we must help to establish them abroad.
HUGO L. BLACK

Tranquil pleasures last the longest. We are not fitted to bear long the burdens of great joy.
CHRISTIAN BOVÉE

Peace is not the elimination of the causes of war. Rather it is a mastery of great human forces and the creation of an environment in which human aims may be pursued constructively.
JAMES H. CASE, JR.

If there is righteousness in the heart there will be beauty in the character. It there be beauty in the character, there will be harmony in the home. If there is harmony in the home, there will be order in the nation. When there is order in the nation, there will be peace in the world.
**CHINESE PROVERB**

Vast and fearsome as the human scene has become, personal contacts of the right people, in the right places, at the right time, may yet have a potent and valuable part to play in the cause of peace which is in our hearts.
**WINSTON CHURCHILL**

Peace rules the day where reason rules the mind.
**WILLIAM WILKIE COLLINS**

Peace is not a relationship of Nations. It is a condition of mind brought about by a serenity of soul. Lasting peace can come only to peaceful people.
**HORACE E. DE LISSER**

Above all other purposes, we must labor by every peaceful means to build a world order founded upon justice and righteousness. That kind of world will have peace. That kind of peace will be worth having. That is the crowning responsibility that our people have laid upon us. That is the crowning task to which we dedicate ourselves.
**THOMAS E. DEWEY**

Peace comes only from loving, from mutual self-sacrifice and self-forgetfulness. Few today have humility or wisdom enough to know the world's deep need of love. We are too much possessed by national and racial and cultural pride.
**HORACE W. B. DONEGAN, D.D.**

If a conference lasts a long time, it must end in peace; no one can keep on defying his enemies all day.
**ALFRED DUGGAN**

The search for peace has its high hope and its deep frustrations. But after the frustration, there is always renewed hope.... We believe that international peace is an attainable goal. That is the premise that underlies all of our planning. We propose never to desist, never to admit discouragement, but confidently and steadily so to act that peace becomes for us a sustaining principle of action. In that, we know we shall not be alone. That is not merely because we have treaties of alliance and bonds of expedience. It is because the spirit of peace is a magnet which draws together many men and many nations and makes of them a fellowship of loyal partners for peace.
**JOHN FOSTER DULLES**

The world will never have lasting peace so long as men reserve for war the finest human qualities. Peace, no less than war, requires idealism and self-sacrifice and a righteous and dynamic faith.
**JOHN FOSTER DULLES**

We must continue to hold fast to the conviction that the peoples and nations who are today not the masters of their own destinies shall become their own masters. If we do all of this, not belligerently, but wisely and soberly; if we remain ever watchful for a sign from the Soviet rulers that they realize that freedom is not something to be frightened by, but something to be accepted, then we may indeed, as these eventful coming months unfold, advance the hopes for peace of the world.
**JOHN FOSTER DULLES**

Serenity is complete self-abnegation and enormous understanding.
**ELEANORA DUSE**

The great task of the peace is to work morals into it. The only sort of peace that will be real is one in which everybody takes his share of responsibility. World organizations and conferences will be of no

value unless there is improvement in the relation of men to men.
**SIR FREDERICK EGGLESTON**

Peace does not dwell in outward things, but within the soul; we may preserve it in the midst of the bitterest pain, if our will remain firm and submissive. Peace in this life springs from acquiescence, not in an exemption from suffering.
**FRANÇOIS FÉNELON**

No one can get inner peace by pouncing on it, by vigorously willing to have it. Peace is a margin of power around our daily need. Peace is a consciousness of springs too deep for earthly droughts to dry up. Peace is an awareness of reserves from beyond ourselves, so that our power is not so much in us as through us.
**HARRY EMERSON FOSDICK, D.D.**

Universal peace will be realized, not because man will become better, but because a new order of things, a new science, new economic necessities, will impose peace.
**ANATOLE FRANCE**

You can legislate many conditions—but you cannot legislate harmony into the hearts of men. To attain industrial peace, we need more than by-laws and compulsory rules.
**CLARENCE FRANCIS**

Lord, make us instruments of Thy peace. Where there is hatred, let us sow love; where there is injury, pardon; where there is discord, union; where there is doubt, faith; where there is despair, hope; where there is darkness, light; where there is sadness, joy.
**ST. FRANCIS OF ASSISI**

The thing for which we prepare and which we earnestly expect usually comes upon us. Food is prepared to be eaten; clothing is made to be worn; munitions of war are produced to be used in warfare. Just as truly, preparations made for purposes of peace help to bring about the peaceful condition for which they are prepared.
**FRANCIS J. GABLE**

We look forward to the time when the Power of Love will replace the Love of Power. Then will our world know the blessings of Peace.
**WILLIAM E. GLADSTONE**

He is the happiest, be he king or peasant, who finds peace in his home.
**JOHANN WOLFGANG VON GOETHE**

Peace among the nations, like happiness for the individual, is not an end, but a by-product that usually comes when you live right.
**EDWARD H. GRIGGS**

No peace is good unless educators and the church are allowed to speak and unless they conduct themselves so that they will be listened to. Not only a military office of intelligence is needed but a spiritual and intellectual intelligence service as well.
**CARL J. HAMBRO, D.D.**

If our hours were all serene, we might probably take almost as little note of them as the dial does of those that are clouded.
**WILLIAM HAZLITT**

Peace is such a precious jewel that I would give anything for it but truth.
**MATTHEW HENRY**

Peace is a nursing mother to the land.
**HESIOD**

The first and fundamental law of nature is to seek peace and follow it.
**THOMAS HOBBES**

With intelligence and humility and dedication as our ammunition, we can wage the peace throughout the world with a strength beyond armies, destroying nothing except hate and greed and distrust.
PAUL G. HOFFMAN

Nothing gives one person so much advantage over another as to remain cool and unruffled under all circumstances.
THOMAS JEFFERSON

For I know the thoughts that I think toward you, saith the Lord, thoughts of peace, and not of evil, to give you an expected end. Then shall ye call upon me, and ye shall go and pray unto me, and I will hearken unto you.
JEREMIAH 29:11–12

We love peace, but not peace at any price. There is a peace more destructive of the manhood of living man, than war is destructive of his body. Chains are worse than bayonets.
DOUGLAS WILLIAM JERROLD

Peace I leave with you, my peace I give unto you: not as the world giveth, give I unto you. Let not your heart be troubled, neither let it be afraid.
JOHN 14:27

These things I have spoken unto you, that in me ye might have peace. In the world ye shall have tribulation: but be of good cheer; I have overcome the world.
JOHN 16:33

Beauty I have learned from the ugly, charity from the unkind and peace from the turmoil of the world.
FREDERICK WARD KATES

Great tranquility of heart is his who cares for neither praise nor blame.
THOMAS À KEMPIS

I am a man of peace. God knows how I love peace. But I hope I shall never be such a coward as to mistake oppression for peace.
LOUIS KOSSUTH

There is but one bond of peace that is both permanent and enriching: The increasing knowledge of the world in which experiment occurs.
WALTER LIPPMANN

You can't take a crash course in serenity.
SHIRLEY MACLAINE

To be at peace with self, to find company and nourishment in self—this would be the test of the free and productive psyche.
MARYA MANNES

Only in quiet waters do things mirror themselves undistorted. Only in a quiet mind is adequate perception of the world.
HANS MARGOLIUS

I am quite sure we can achieve peace, but for that the Western nations must be united and must work together. . . . This is why I do feel that organization of the Western defenses between the countries concerned is the cornerstone for strengthening the peace.
PIERRE MENDÈS-FRANCE

If you are yourself at peace, then there is at least some peace in the world. Then share your peace with everyone, and everyone will be at peace.
THOMAS MERTON

Much remains to conquer still; peace hath her victories no less renowned than war.
**John Milton**

No sacrifice short of the sacrifice of individual liberty, individual self-respect, and individual enterprise is too great a price to pay for permanent peace.
**Clark H. Minor**

Peace is not merely an absence of war. It is also a state of mind.
**Jawaharlal Nehru**

Let the world see that this nation can bear prosperity; and that her honest virtue in time of peace is equal to her bravest valor in time of war.
**Thomas Paine**

There can be no peace when there is not God in the hearts of men. When you drive the devil out of the human heart the stream of life will be sweet, happy and peaceful.
**Charles Clifford Peale, D.D.**

There will be no peace so long as God remains unseated at the conference table.
**William M. Peck**

Five great enemies to peace inhabit with us: viz., avarice, ambition, envy, anger and pride. If those enemies were to be banished, we should infallibly enjoy perpetual peace.
**Petrarch**

For peace, with justice and honor, is the fairest and most profitable of possessions, but with disgrace and shameful cowardice, it is the most infamous and harmful of all.
**Polybius**

If we have not peace within ourselves, it is in vain to seek it from outward sources.
**François de la Rochefoucauld**

If we are to build for lasting peace, we must abandon the nineteenth-century conception that the road to peace lies through a nicely poised balance of power. Again and again cold experience has taught us that no peace dependent upon a balance of power lasts. If we would build upon twentieth-century reality, we must throw the balance of power theory out of the window.
**Francis B. Sayre**

Unless man has the wit and the grit to build his civilization on something better than material power, it is surely idle to talk of plans for a stable peace.
**Francis B. Sayre**

A peace is of the nature of a conquest. For then both parties nobly are subdued, and neither party loses.
**William Shakespeare**

Peace is not merely a vacuum left by the ending of wars. It is the creation of two eternal principles, justice and freedom.
**James T. Shotwell**

Peace is not absence of war, it is a virtue, a state of mind, a disposition for benevolence, confidence, justice.
**Baruch Spinoza**

Go placidly amid the noise and the haste, and remember what peace there may be in silence. As far as possible without surrender be on good terms with all persons. You are a child of the universe no less than the trees and the stars.
**Adlai Stevenson**

The language of excitement is at best picturesque. You must be calm before you can utter oracles.
HENRY DAVID THOREAU

Prejudice, ignorance, bitterness and, above all, selfishness are the great obstacles to peace in people, groups and nations.
JOSEPH A. TYTHERIDGE, D.D.

Peace comes to us through love, understanding of our fellow men, faith. Peace does not include selfishness nor indifference. Peace is never wrapped at a counter for a price. It is earned by giving of ourselves. Our own earned peace will ignite peace in our family, in our community, city, state, country, and flow over the entire world.
ANNETTE VICTORIN

Peace is a militant state, which is not secured by wishful thinking.... If we are to be sure of our liberty, we must be ready to fight for it.
GEN. JONATHAN WAINWRIGHT

Nations have no existence apart from their people. If every person in the world loved peace, every nation would love peace. If all men refused to fight one another, nations could not fight one another.
J. SHERMAN WALLACE

You may think there is not much that any one person can do toward achieving world peace. Yet if every person who believed in the ideas in the Golden Rule, the Sermon on the Mount and the Ten Commandments would begin practicing them in his own small sphere, the combined effect would be world-shaking.
ALFRED A. WEINSTEIN

There is no kind of peace which may be purchased on the bargain counter.
CAREY WILLIAMS

Peace, if it ever exists, will not be based on the fear of war but on the love of peace.
HERMAN WOUK

If peace is to come, it must be peace within your own mind and heart. If hatred is to die, you must scotch it within yourself. If intelligence is to triumph, you must be intelligent. There is no other pathway, no other salvation.
HENRY M. WRISTON

## *Perfection*

Culture is properly described as the love of perfection; it is a study of perfection.
MATTHEW ARNOLD

The humorous man recognizes that absolute purity, absolute justice, absolute logic and perfection are beyond human achievement and that men have been able to live happily for thousands of years in a state of genial frailty.
BROOKS ATKINSON

If you expect perfection from people your whole life is a series of disappointments, grumblings and complaints. If, on the contrary, you pitch your expectations low, taking folks as the inefficient creatures which they are, you are frequently surprised by having them perform better than you had hoped.
BRUCE BARTON

Imperfection means perfection hid.
ROBERT BROWNING

Aim at perfection in everything, though in most things it is unattainable. However, they who aim at it, and persevere, will come much nearer to it than

those whose laziness and despondency make them give it up as unattainable.
LORD CHESTERFIELD

The gem cannot be polished without friction, nor man perfected without trials.
CHINESE PROVERB

To talk about the need for perfection in man is to talk about the need for another species. The essence of man is imperfection. Imperfection and blazing contradictions—between mixed good and evil, altruism and selfishness, co-operativeness and combativeness, optimism and fatalism, affirmation and negation.
NORMAN COUSINS

As natural selection works solely by and for the good of each being, all corporeal and mental endowments will tend to progress toward perfection.
CHARLES DARWIN

The feeling of having done a job well is rewarding; the feeling of having done it perfectly is fatal.
DONLEY FEDDERSEN

If you're looking for perfection, look in the mirror. If you find it there, expect it elsewhere.
MALCOLM FORBES

Do not lose courage in considering your own imperfections, but instantly set about remedying them.
ST. FRANCIS DE SALES

Perfectionism is a dangerous state of mind in an imperfect world. The best way is to forget doubts and set about the task in hand. . . . If you are doing your best, you will not have time to worry about failure.
ROBERT HILLYER

To arrive at perfection, a man should have very sincere friends or inveterate enemies; because he would be made sensible of his good or ill conduct, either by the censures of the one or the admonitions of the other.
DIOGENES LAERTIUS

If you are pleased at finding faults, you are displeased at finding perfections.
JOHANN LAVATER

A great deal of the joy of life consists in doing perfectly, or at least to the best of one's ability, everything which one attempts to do. There is a sense of satisfaction, a pride in surveying such a work, a work which is rounded, full, exact, complete in all its parts—which the superficial man, who leaves his work in a slovenly, slipshod, half-finished condition can never know. It is this conscientious completeness which turns work into art. The smallest thing, well done, becomes artistic.
WILLIAM MATTHEWS

Trifles make perfection and perfection is not trifle.
MICHELANGELO

I do not know what comfort other people find in considering the weakness of great men, but 'tis always a mortification to me to observe that there is no perfection in humanity.
SAMUEL MONTAGUE

Perfection does not exist; to understand it is the triumph of human intelligence; to expect to possess it is the most dangerous kind of madness.
ALFRED DE MUSSET

A man can do his best only by confidently seeking (and perpetually missing) an unattainable perfection.
RALPH BARTON PERRY

The closest to perfection a person ever comes is when he fills out a job application form.
**STANLEY J. RANDALL**

If we pretend to have reached either perfection or satisfaction, we have degraded ourselves and our work. God's work only may express that, but ours may never have that sentence written upon it, "Behold it was very good."
**JOHN RUSKIN**

No perfect thing is too small for eternal recollection.
**ARTHUR SYMONS**

Perfection is attained by slow degrees; it requires the hand of time.
**VOLTAIRE**

## *Perseverance*

Courage and perseverance have a magical talisman, before which difficulties disappear and obstacles vanish into air.
**JOHN QUINCY ADAMS**

Our delight in any particular study, art or science rises in proportion to the application which we bestow upon it. Thus, what was at first an exercise becomes at length an entertainment.
**JOSEPH ADDISON**

Perseverance is failing 19 times and succeeding the 20th.
**J. ANDREWS**

Everything yields to diligence.
**ANTIPHANES**

Diligence is the greatest of teachers.
**ARABIAN PROVERB**

God is with those who patiently persevere.
**ARABIAN PROVERB**

Vigilance is not only the price of liberty, but of success of any sort.
**HENRY WARD BEECHER**

Fate gave to man the courage of endurance.
**LUDWIG VAN BEETHOVEN**

Just keep on agoing—don't dare to stand still; for water a-flowing is what turns the mill. Just keep on aworking and happiness gain, for no one oft shirking does greatness attain.
**ALONZO NEWTON BENN**

All that I have accomplished, or expect or hope to accomplish, has been, and will be by that plodding, patient, persevering process of accretion which builds the ant heap particle by particle, thought by thought, fact by fact. If I was ever actuated by ambition its highest and warmest aspiration reached no further than the hope to set before the young men of any country an example in employing those invaluable fragments of time called odd moments.
**ELIHU BURRITT**

He whipped his horses withal, and put his shoulder to the wheel.
**ROBERT BURTON**

In commitment, we dash the hopes of a thousand potential selves.
**LORD BYRON**

It is not necessary to hope in order to undertake, nor to succeed in order to persevere.
**CHARLES THE BOLD**

Diligence is the mother of good fortune, and idleness, its opposite, never brought a man to the goal of any of his best wishes.
**MIGUEL DE CERVANTES**

This is no time for ease and comfort. It is the time to dare and endure.
**WINSTON CHURCHILL**

Diligence, as it avails in all things, is also of the utmost moment in pleading causes. Diligence is to be particularly cultivated by us; it is to be constantly exerted, it is capable of effecting almost everything.
**CICERO**

The expectations of life depend upon diligence; the mechanic that would perfect his work must first sharpen his tools.
**CONFUCIUS**

High, but not the highest intelligence, combined with the greatest degree of persistence, will achieve greater eminence than the highest degree of intelligence without somewhat less persistence.
**CATHERINE M. COX**

However small in proportion the benefit which follows individual attempts to do good, a great deal may be accomplished by perseverance, even in the midst of discouragements and disappointments.
**GEORGE CRABBE**

It is the common fate of the indolent to see their rights become a prey to the active. The condition upon which God hath given liberty to man is eternal vigilance.
**JOHN PHILPOT CURRAN**

I have begun several things many times, and I have often succeeded at last. I will sit down, but the time will come when you will hear me.
**BENJAMIN DISRAELI**

I have brought myself by long meditation to the conviction that a human being with a settled purpose must accomplish it, and that nothing can resist a will which will stake even existence upon its fulfillment.
**BENJAMIN DISRAELI**

Vacillating people seldom succeed. They seldom win the solid respect of their fellows. Successful men and women are very careful in reaching decisions and very persistent and determined in action thereafter.
**L. G. ELLIOTT**

A determination to succeed is the only way to succeed that I know anything about.
**WILLIAM FEATHER**

How you start is important, very important, but in the end it is how you finish that counts. It is easier to be a self-starter than a self-finisher. The victor in the race is not the one who dashes off swiftest but the one who leads at the finish. In the race for success, speed is less important than stamina. The sticker outlasts the sprinter in life's race. In America we breed many hares but not so many tortoises.
**B. C. FORBES**

When the worms are scarce, what does a hen do? Does she stop scratching? She does not. She scratches all the harder. A lot of businessmen have been showing less sense than a hen since orders became scarce. They have laid off salesmen; they have stopped or reduced their advertising; they have simply resigned themselves to inaction and, of course, to pessimism. If a hen knows enough to scratch all the harder when the worms are scarce, surely businessmen . . . ought to have gumption enough to scratch all the harder for business.
**B. C. FORBES**

In business, eternal vigilance is the price of liquidity.
**MORRIS FRANKLIN**

In the realm of ideas, everything depends on enthusiasm; in the real world, all rests on perseverance.
**JOHANN WOLFGANG VON GOETHE**

Whatever necessity lays upon thee, endure; whatever she commands, do.
**JOHANN WOLFGANG VON GOETHE**

Mediocrity obtains more with application than superiority without it.
**BALTASAR GRACIÁN**

That which we persist in doing becomes easier for us to do. Not that the nature of the thing is changed, but that our power to do is increased.
**HEBER J. GRANT**

For me, hard work represents the supreme luxury of life.
**ALBERT M. GREENFIELD**

The greatest things ever done on earth have been done little by little.
**THOMAS GUTHRIE**

Persistence is what makes the impossible possible, the possible likely, and the likely definite.
**ROBERT HALF**

Whoever perseveres will be crowned.
**JOHANN GOTTFRIED VON HERDER**

A determined soul will do more with a rusty monkey wrench than a loafer will accomplish with all the tools in a machine shop.
**RUPERT HUGHES**

He conquers who endures.
**ITALIAN PROVERB**

When we see ourselves in a situation which must be endured and gone through, it is best to make up our minds to it, meet it with firmness, and accommodate everything to it in the best way practicable. This lessens the evil; while fretting and fuming only serves to increase your own torments.
**THOMAS JEFFERSON**

Few things are impossible to diligence and skill.
**SAMUEL JOHNSON**

Great works are performed not by strength but by perseverance.
**SAMUEL JOHNSON**

All the performances of human art, at which we look with praise or wonder, are instances of the resistless force of perseverance.
**SAMUEL JOHNSON**

Failure is only postponed success as long as courage coaches ambition. The habit of persistence is the habit of victory.
**HERBERT KAUFMAN**

Keep on going, and the chances are that you will stumble on something, perhaps when you are least expecting it. I never heard of anyone ever stumbling on something sitting down.
**CHARLES F. KETTERING**

When you want a thing deeply, earnestly and intensely, this feeling of desire reinforces your will and arouses in you the determination to work for the desired object. When you have a distinct purpose in view, your work becomes of absorbing interest. You bend your best powers to it; you give it concentrated attention; you think of little else than

the realization of this purpose; your will is stimulated into unusual activity, and as a consequence you do your work with an increasing sense of power.
**GRENVILLE KLEISER**

Press on. Nothing in the world can take the place of persistence.
**RAY KROC**

Act with a determination not to be turned aside by thoughts of the past and fears of the future.
**ROBERT E. LEE**

To live is not to learn, but to apply.
**LEGOUVÉ**

Perseverance and audacity generally win.
**DOROTHÉE DELUZY**

Individual commitment to a group effort—that is what makes a team work, a company work, a society work, a civilization work.
**VINCE LOMBARDI**

As long as the day lasts, let's give it all we got.
**DAVID O. MCKAY**

It is not enough to begin; continuance is necessary. Mere enrollment will not make one a scholar; the pupil must continue in the school through the long course, until he masters every branch. Success depends upon staying power. The reason for failure in most cases is lack of perseverance.
**J. R. MILLER**

Until one is committed, there is hesitancy, the chance to draw back, always ineffectiveness. Concerning all acts of initiative (and creation), there is one elementary truth, the ignorance of which kills countless ideas and splendid plans. That the moment one definitely commits oneself, then providence moves, too. All sorts of things occur to help one that would never otherwise have occurred.
**WILLIAM H. MURRAY**

Genius is perseverance in disguise.
**MIKE NEWLIN**

He conquers who endures.
**PERSIUS**

Perseverance is more prevailing than violence; and many things which cannot be overcome when they are together, yield themselves up when taken little by little.
**PLUTARCH**

Let a man begin with an earnest "I ought," and if he perseveres, by God's grace he will end in the free blessedness of "I will." Let him force himself to abound in small acts of duty, and he will, by and by, find them the joyous habit of his soul.
**FREDERICK W. ROBERTSON**

Few things are impracticable in themselves; and it is for want of application, rather than of means, that men fail of success.
**FRANÇOIS DE LA ROCHEFOUCAULD**

Don't foul, don't flinch—hit the line hard.
**THEODORE ROOSEVELT**

When business is not all that it should be there is a temptation to sit back and say, "Well, what's the use! We've done everything possible to stir up a little business and there is nothing doing so what's the use of trying!" There is always a way. There was a way in and there is a way out. And success comes to the man who grits his teeth, squares his jaw, and says, "There is a way for me and, by jingo, I'll find it." The stagnator gathers green scum, finally dries up and leaves an unsightly hollow.
**CLIFFORD SLOAN**

By perseverance the snail reached the Ark.
**CHARLES H. SPURGEON**

'Tis known by the name of perseverance in a good cause, and obstinacy in a bad one.
**LAURENCE STERNE**

Servants be not so diligent as they were wont to be.
**JANE STONER**

There are two ways of attaining an important end-force and perseverance. Force falls to the lot only of the privileged few, but austere and sustained perseverance can be practised by the most insignificant.
**ANNE SWETCHINE**

Don't bother about genius. Don't worry about being clever. Trust to hard work, perseverance and determination. And the best motto for a long march is: Don't grumble. Plug on!
**SIR FREDERICK TREVES**

It's dogged as does it.
**ANTHONY TROLLOPE**

An ounce of application is worth a ton of abstraction.
**BOOKER T. WASHINGTON**

To presevere in one's duty and be silent, is the best answer to calumny.
**GEORGE WASHINGTON**

Even in social life, it is persistency which attracts confidence more than talents and accomplishments.
**EDWIN P. WHIPPLE**

Without perseverance talent is a barren bed.
**WELSH PROVERB**

It is not necessary to hope in order to act, nor to succeed in order to persevere.
**WILLIAM OF ORANGE**

## *Personality*

A man's nature is best perceived in privateness, for there is no affectation; in passion, for that putteth a man out of his precepts; and in a new case or experiment, for there custom leaveth him.
**FRANCIS BACON**

The Christian State proclaims human personality to be supreme; the servile State denies it. Every compromise with the infinite value of the human soul leads straight back to savagery and to the jungle.
**BALDWIN**

As the sun is best seen at his rising and setting, so men's native dispositions are clearest seen when they are children, and when they are dying.
**ROBERT BOYLE**

He that fancies himself very enlightened, because he sees the deficiencies of others, may be very ignorant, because he has not studied his own.
**EDWARD BULWER-LYTTON**

The development of desirable traits and characteristics—that intangible something which we style personality—is the chief work of the school.
**FRANK CODY**

The well-developed, well-patterned individual human being is, in a strictly scientific sense, the highest phenomenon of which we have any knowledge; and the variety of individual personalities is the world's highest richness.
**JULIAN HUXLEY**

An appealing personality is not something grafted on from without. It is not like a coat of paint applied to a building or cosmetics used on the face. It is expressed through the body, the mind, the heart and the spirit. Although some persons seem to have

been born with an exceptionally appealing personality, no one has a monopoly on it.
EDITH JOHNSON

Personality is a person among persons. There is no personality of one man on a desert island.
KILPATRICK

The search for a new personality is futile; what is fruitful is the human interest the old personality can take in new activities.
CESARE PAVESE

If I were asked to sum up in a single phrase the main purpose of individual life I would express it as the enlargement of personality. Unless an individual can transcend the limits of class, sex, race, age and creed, his personality remains of necessity to that extent incomplete.
F. W. PETHICK-LAWRENCE

Every person in the world may not become a personage. But every person may become a personality. The happiest people are those who think the most interesting thoughts. Interesting thoughts can live only in cultivated minds. Those who decide to use leisure as a means of mental development, who love good music, good books, good pictures, good plays at the theater, good company, good conversation—what are they? They are the happiest people in the world; and they are not only happy in themselves, they are the cause of happiness in others.
WILLIAM LYON PHELPS

The globe has been circumnavigated, but no man ever yet has; you may survey a kingdom and note the result in maps, but all the savants in the world could not produce a reliable map of the poorest human personality.
ALEXANDER SMITH

No theory of the universe can be satisfactory which does not adequately account for the phenomena of life, especially in that richest form which finds expression in human personality.
B. H. STREETER

Men have yet to learn the value of human personality. The fact that a person is white, or black, or yellow, of one race or another, of this religion or that—these things are not all-important. It is the human personality that should come first.
JOHN R. VAN SICKLE

## *Philanthropy*

To give away money is an easy matter, and in any man's power. But to decide to whom to give it, and how large and when, and for what purpose and how, is neither in every man's power—nor an easy matter. Hence it is that such excellence is rare, praiseworthy and noble.
ARISTOTLE

Giving away a fortune is taking Christianity too far.
CHARLOTTE BINGHAM

I tell thee, thou foolish philanthropist, that I grudge the dollar, the dime, the cent I give to such men as do not belong to me and to whom I do not belong.
RALPH WALDO EMERSON

Philanthropies and charities have a certain air of quackery.
RALPH WALDO EMERSON

Philanthropy is commendable but it must not cause the philanthropist to overlook the circumstances of economic injustice which make philanthropy necessary.
MARTIN LUTHER KING, JR.

In the United States, doing good has come to be, like patriotism, a favorite device of persons with something to sell.
H. L. MENCKEN

Money giving is a very good criterion, in a way, of a person's mental health. Generous people are rarely mentally ill people.
DR. KARL MENNINGER

I do not know how wicked American millionaires are, but as I travel about and see the results of their generosity in the form of hospitals, churches, public libraries, universities, parks, recreation grounds, art museums and theatres I wonder what on earth we should do without them.
WILLIAM LYON PHELPS

A good deal of philanthropy arises in general from mere vanity and love of distinction gilded over to others and to themselves with some show of benevolent sentiment.
SIR WALTER SCOTT

Philanthropy [has become] simply the refuge of people who wish to annoy their fellow creatures.
OSCAR WILDE

## *Philosophy*

Every one of us, unconsciously, works out a personal philosophy of life, by which we are guided, inspired, and corrected, as time goes on. It is this philosophy by which we measure out our days, and by which we advertise to all about us the man, or woman, that we are.... It takes but a brief time to scent the life philosophy of anyone. It is defined in the conversation, in the look of the eye, and in the general mien of the person. It has no hiding place. It's like the perfume of the flower—unseen, but known almost instantly. It is the possession of the successful, and the happy. And it can be greatly embellished by the absorption of ideas and experiences of the useful of this earth.
GEORGE MATTHEW ADAMS

Philosopher: A man up in a balloon, with his family and friends holding the ropes which confine him to earth and trying to haul him down.
LOUISA MAY ALCOTT

Philosophy is a route of many roads leading from nowhere to nothing.
AMBROSE BIERCE

Philosophy recovers itself when it ceases to be the device for dealing with the problems of philosophers and becomes the method, cultivated by philosophers, for dealing with the problems of men.
JOHN DEWEY

All philosophy lies in two words, sustain and abstain.
EPICTETUS

Philosophy can add to our happiness in no other manner but by diminishing our misery; it should not pretend to increase our present stock, but make us economists of what we are possessed of. Happy were we all born philosophers; all born with a talent of thus dissipating our own cares by spreading them upon all mankind.
OLIVER GOLDSMITH

The creative mind is the playful mind. Philosophy is the play and dance of ideas.
ERIC HOFFER

Philosophy should be an energy; it should find its aim and its effect in the amelioration of mankind.
VICTOR HUGO

Be a philosopher, but amid all your philosophy, be still a man.
**DAVID HUME**

A philosophy which speaks, even indirectly, only to philosophers is no philosophy at all; and I think the same is true if it speaks only to scientists, or only to jurists, or priests, or any other special class.
**ABRAHAM KAPLAN**

To make the most of dull hours, to make the best of dull people, to like a poor jest better than none. To wear a threadbare coat like a gentleman; to be outvoted with a smile, to hitch your wagon to the old horse if no star is handy—that is wholesome philosophy.
**BLISS PERRY**

Philosophy is the art of living.
**PLUTARCH**

All work is an act of philosophy.
**AYN RAND**

Philosophy triumphs easily over past, and over future evils, but present evils triumph over philosophy.
**FRANÇOIS DE LA ROCHEFOUCAULD**

We need fewer philosophies and more philosophers.
**FRANK ROMER**

When men comfort themselves with philosophy, 'tis not because they have got two or three sentences, but because they have digested those sentences, and made them their own: philosophy is nothing but discretion.
**JOHN SELDEN**

There was never yet a philosopher that could endure the toothache patiently.
**WILLIAM SHAKESPEARE**

The discovery of what is true and the practice of that which is good, are the two most important aims of philosophy.
**VOLTAIRE**

Philosophy may teach us to bear with equanimity the misfortunes of our neighbors.
**OSCAR WILDE**

## *Planning*

We can't cross a bridge until we come to it; but I always like to lay down a pontoon ahead of time.
**BERNARD M. BARUCH**

The method of the enterprising is to plan with audacity and execute with vigor.
**CHRISTIAN BOVÉE**

Make no little plans, they have no magic to stir men's blood. Make big plans, aim high in hope and work and let your watchword be order and your beacon beauty.
**DAVID BURNHAM**

The man who is prepared has his battle half fought.
**MIGUEL DE CERVANTES**

The executive of the future will be rated by his ability to anticipate his problems rather than to meet them as they come.
**HOWARD COONLEY**

Make your plans as fantastic as you like, because 25 years from now, they will seem mediocre. Make your plans ten times as great as you first planned, and 25 years from now you will wonder why you did not make them 50 times as great.
**HENRY CURTIS**

Plan ahead: It wasn't raining when Noah built the ark.
RICHARD CUSHING

If you don't have a plan of life, you'll never have order.
JOSEMARIA ESCRIVA

We [often] have fine theories, but, somehow, we are not always able to carry them out in this workaday world. A chief executive, for example, can draw up a perfect organization chart—and then he wonders why it doesn't function smoothly in practice. . . . If even a Tiffany watch cannot be guaranteed to keep correct time when put to the test of everyday wear and tear, must we not be prepared to make allowance for erring mortals? It is right that executives should draw up perfect plans on paper; but it is all wrong for them to expect their paper plans to work out to perfection in this imperfect world.
B. C. FORBES

By failing to prepare you are preparing to fail.
BENJAMIN FRANKLIN

Thousands of engineers can design bridges, calculate strains and stresses, and draw up specifications for machines, but the great engineer is the man who can tell whether the bridge or the machine should be built at all, where it should be built, and when.
EUGENE G. GRACE

You and I must not complain if our plans break down if we have done our part. That probably means that the plans of One who knows more than we do have succeeded.
EDWARD E. HALE

I try to have no plans the failure of which would greatly annoy me. Half the unhappiness in the world is due to the failure of plans which were never reasonable, and often impossible.
EDGAR WATSON HOWE

He who every morning plans the transactions of the day and follows out that plan carries a thread that will guide him through the labyrinth of the most busy life. The orderly arrangement of his time is like a ray of life which darts itself through all his occupations. But where no plan is laid, where the disposal of time is surrendered merely to the chance of incident, chaos will soon reign.
VICTOR HUGO

Expect only 5% of an intelligence report to be accurate. The trick of a good commander is to isolate the 5%.
DOUGLAS MACARTHUR

Most business men generally are so busy coping with immediate and piecemeal matters that there is a lamentable tendency to let the long run or future take care of itself. We often are so busy putting out fires, so to speak, that we find it difficult to do the planning that would prevent those fires from occurring in the first place. As a prominent educator has expressed it, Americans generally spend so much time on things that are urgent that we have none left to spend on those that are important.
GUSTAV METZMAN

The best preparation for tomorrow is to do today's work superbly well.
SIR WILLIAM OSLER

Perfection of planning is a symptom of decay. During a period of exciting discovery or progress, there is no time to plan the perfect headquarters. The time for that comes later, when all the important work has been done.
C. NORTHCOTE PARKINSON

Well arranged time is the surest mark of a well arranged mind.
**PITMAN**

I thatched my roof when the sun was shining, and now I am not afraid of the storm.
**GEORGE F. STIVERS**

An intelligent plan is the first step to success. The man who plans knows where he is going, knows what progress he is making and has a pretty good idea when he will arrive. Planning is the open road to your destination. If you don't know where you are going, how can you expect to get there?
**BASIL S. WALSH**

The will to win is worthless if you do not have the will to prepare.
**THANE YOST**

## *Please*

Flattery, if judiciously administered, is always acceptable.
**MARGUERITE BLESSINGTON**

If you will please people, you must please them in their own way.
**LORD CHESTERFIELD**

An appeaser is one who feeds a crocodile—hoping it will eat him last.
**WINSTON CHURCHILL**

He that can please nobody is not so much to be pitied as he that nobody can please.
**CHARLES CALEB COLTON**

He who cannot love must learn to flatter.
**JOHANN WOLFGANG VON GOETHE**

He who endeavors to please must appear pleased.
**SAMUEL JOHNSON**

We all live in the hope of pleasing somebody; and the pleasure of pleasing ought to be greatest, and always will be greatest, when our endeavors are exerted in consequence of our duty.
**SAMUEL JOHNSON**

We sometimes imagine we hate flattery, but we only hate the way we are flattered.
**FRANÇOIS DE LA ROCHEFOUCAULD**

Pleasant dealing in the ordinary business of life is the oil, the grease, if you please, for the wheels; it facilitates the performance of that business, and lengthens the life of the human machines that do the work of the world.
**WALTER R. RUTHERFORD**

What really flatters a man is that you think him worth flattering.
**GEORGE BERNARD SHAW**

Nothing is so great an instance of ill-manner as flattery. If you flatter all the company, you please none; if you flatter only one or two, you affront the rest.
**JONATHAN SWIFT**

'Tis an old maxim in the schools that flattery is the food of fools. Yet now and then your men of wit will condescend to take a bit.
**JONATHAN SWIFT**

Will you help to make today more pleasant for someone, or more miserable? If the former, your day too will be more pleasant; if the latter, it too will be miserable.
**JOHN W. VOGEL**

## Pleasure

A fool bolts pleasure, then complains of moral indigestion.
MINNA ANTRIM

It is not abstinence from pleasures that is best, but mastery over them without being worsted.
ARISTIPPUS

One half the world cannot understand the pleasures of the other.
JANE AUSTEN

The great pleasure in life is doing what people say you cannot do.
WALTER BAGEHOT

People seem to enjoy things more when they know a lot of other people have been left out on the pleasure.
RUSSELL BAKER

Pleasure is in itself a good; nay, even setting aside immunity from pain, the only good.
JEREMY BENTHAM

Abstainer: A weak person who yields to the temptation of denying himself a pleasure.
AMBROSE BIERCE

Despite high goals and saintly roles
With which man's past was fused,
It now seems clear a primal aim
Is just to be amused.
ART BUCK

Perhaps one has to be very old before one learns how to be amused rather than shocked.
PEARL S. BUCK

Pleasure's a sin, and sometimes sin's a pleasure.
LORD BYRON

I am advising you as a friend, as a man of the world, as one who would not have you old while you are young, but would have you to take all the pleasures that reason points out, and that decency warrants.
LORD CHESTERFIELD

Pleasure is a necessary reciprocal: no one feels, who does not at the same time give it. To be pleased, one must please. What pleases you in others, will in general please them in you.
LORD CHESTERFIELD

It is not a virtue, but a deceptive copy and imitation of virtue, when we are led to the performance of duty by pleasure as its recompense.
CICERO

Honor is a public enemy, and conscience a domestic, and he that would secure his pleasure, must pay a tribute to one and go halves with t'other.
WILLIAM CONGREVE

Pleasure admitted in undue degree, enslaves the will, nor leaves the judgment free.
WILLIAM COWPER

If once a man indulges himself in murder, very soon he comes to think very little of robbing, and from robbing he comes next to drinking and Sabbath breaking, and from that to incivility and procrastination.
THOMAS DE QUINCEY

Though a taste of pleasure may quicken the relish of life, an unrestrained indulgence leads to inevitable destruction.
ROBERT DODSLEY

We enjoy thoroughly only the pleasure that we give.
**Alexandre Dumas**

The pleasure of life is according to the man that lives it, and not according to the work or place.
**Ralph Waldo Emerson**

Pleasure is the first good. It is the beginning of every choice and every aversion. It is the absence of pain in the body and of troubles in the soul.
**Epicurus**

A man who knows how to mix pleasures with business is never entirely possessed by them; he either quits or resumes them at his will; and in the use he makes of them he rather finds a relaxation than a dangerous charm that might corrupt him.
**St. Evremond**

Business is always interfering with pleasure—but it makes other pleasures possible.
**William Feather**

We must always skim over pleasures. They are like marshy lands that we must travel nimbly, hardly daring to put down our feet.
**Le Bovier de Fontenelle**

Pleasure is the most real good in this life.
**Frederick the Great**

Choose such pleasures as recreate much and cost little.
**Richard Fuller**

The best pleasures of this world are not quite true.
**Johann Wolfgang von Goethe**

We have more days to live through than pleasures. Be slow in enjoyment, quick at work, for men see work ended with pleasure, pleasure ended with regret.
**Baltasar Gracián**

Who will in time present pleasure refrain, shall in time to come the more pleasure obtain.
**John Heywood**

Fresh air and innocence are good if you don't take too much of them—but I always remember that most of the achievements and pleasures of life are in bad air.
**Oliver Wendell Holmes**

Do not bite at the bait of pleasure till you know there is no hook beneath it.
**Thomas Jefferson**

Do not bite at the bait of pleasure till you know there is no hook beneath it.
**Thomas Jefferson**

The ugliest of trades have their moments of pleasure. If I were a grave digger, or even a hangman, there are some people I could work for with a good deal of enjoyment.
**Douglas William Jerrold**

The great source of pleasure is variety.
**Samuel Johnson**

The liberty of using harmless pleasure will not be disputed; but it is still to be examined what pleasures are harmless.
**Samuel Johnson**

Give me books, fruit, French wine and fine weather and a little music out of doors, played by someone I do not know. I admire lolling on a lawn by a water-lilied pond to eat white currants and see goldfish, and go to the fair in the evening if I'm good.
**John Keats**

I wasted my substance, I know I did, on riotous living, so I did, but there's nothing on record to show I did more than my betters have done.
**RUDYARD KIPLING**

Love of pleasure is the disease which makes men most despicable.
**CASSIUS LONGINUS**

You can't live on amusement. It is the froth on water—an inch deep and then the mud.
**GEORGE MACDONALD**

What we learn with pleasure we never forget.
**LOUIS MERCIER**

My chief study all my life has been to lighten misfortunes and multiply pleasures, as far as human nature can.
**MARY WORTLEY MONTAGU**

Scratching is one of nature's sweetest gratifications, and the one nearest to hand.
**MICHEL DE MONTAIGNE**

Ill-luck is, in nine cases out of ten, the result of taking pleasure first and duty second, instead of duty first and pleasure second.
**THEODORE T. MUNGER**

If one starts with the notion that anything a man does which gives him pleasure is probably sinful, it is only one step to think it is harmful and the next thing to do is to pass a law against it.
**WILLIAM B. OBER**

There is no such thing as pure pleasure; some anxiety always goes with it.
**OVID**

I omit much usual declamation upon the dignity and capacity of our nature, the superiority of the soul to the body, of the rational to the animal part of our constitutions; upon the worthiness, refinement, and delicacy of some satisfactions; and the meanness, grossness, and sensuality of others: because I hold pleasures differ in nothing but in continuance and intensity.
**WILLIAM PALEY**

A life merely of pleasure, or chiefly of pleasure, is always a poor and worthless life.
**THEODORE W. PARKER**

Amusement that is excessive and followed only for its own sake, allures and deceives us.
**BLAISE PASCAL**

The mind ought sometimes to be amused that it may the better return to thought and to itself.
**PHAEDRUS**

Amusement is the happiness of those who cannot think.
**ALEXANDER POPE**

Old age is a tyrant, which forbids the pleasures of youth on pain of death.
**FRANÇOIS DE LA ROCHEFOUCAULD**

I can think of nothing less pleasurable than a life devoted to pleasure.
**JOHN D. ROCKEFELLER, JR.**

I used often to go to America during Prohibition, and there was far more drunkenness there than before; the prohibition of pornography has much the same effect.
**BERTRAND RUSSELL**

There are two things to aim at in life: first, to get what you want; and after that, to enjoy it. Only the wisest of mankind achieve the second.
LOGAN PEARSALL SMITH

Indulge yourself in pleasures only in so far as they are necessary for the preservation of health.
BARUCH SPINOZA

Pleasure, when it is a man's chief purpose, disappoints itself; and the constant application to it palls the faculty of enjoying it.
RICHARD STEELE

No pleasure lasts long unless there is variety in it.
PUBLILIUS SYRUS

All the instances of pleasure have a sting in the tail.
JEREMY TAYLOR

That man is richest whose pleasures are the cheapest.
HENRY DAVID THOREAU

Pleasure has its time; so too, has wisdom. Make love in thy youth, and in old age attend to thy salvation.
VOLTAIRE

A cigarette is the perfect type of a perfect pleasure. It is exquisite, and it leaves one unsatisfied. What more can one want?
OSCAR WILDE

Pleasure is Nature's test, her sign of approval. When man is happy, he is in harmony with himself and with his environment.
OSCAR WILDE

Pleasure is the only thing to live for. Nothing ages like happiness.
OSCAR WILDE

Simple pleasures are the last refuge of the complex.
OSCAR WILDE

All the things I really like to do are either illegal, immoral or fattening.
ALEXANDER WOOLLCOTT

## *Poetry*

Poetry: The impish attempt to paint the color of the wind.
MAXWELL BODENHEIM

You don't have to suffer to be a poet. Adolescence is enough suffering for anyone.
JOHN CIARDI

Take a commonplace, clean and polish it, light it so that it produces the same effect of youth and freshness and spontaneity as it did originally, and you have done a poet's job.
JEAN COCTEAU

Poetry: A literary gift—chiefly because you can't sell it.
CYNIC'S CYCLOPAEDIA

Poetry is boned with ideas, nerved and blooded with emotions, and held together with the tough, delicate skin of words.
PAUL ENGLE

People who read me seem to be divided into four groups: Twenty-five percent like me for the right reasons; 25% like me for the wrong reasons; 25% hate me for the wrong reasons; 25% hate me for the right reasons. It's that last 25% that worries me.
ROBERT FROST

Poetry is the renewal of words, setting them free, and that's what a poet is doing: loosening the words.
**ROBERT FROST**

There's no money in poetry, but then there's no poetry in money either.
**ROBERT GRAVES**

Poetry is the shortest way of saying something. It lets us express a dime's worth of ideas, or a quarter's worth of emotion, with a nickel's worth of words.
**JOHN P. GRIER**

When power leads man to arrogance, poetry reminds him of his limitations. When power narrows the area of man's concern, poetry reminds him of the richness and diversity of his existence. When power corrupts, poetry cleanses.
**JOHN F. KENNEDY**

You will find poetry nowhere unless you bring some of it with you.
**JOSEPH JOUBERT**

Perhaps no person can be a poet, or can even enjoy poetry, without a certain unsoundness of the mind.
**THOMAS B. MACAULAY**

Publishing a volume of verse is like dropping a rose-petal down the Grand Canyon and waiting for the echo.
**DONALD MARQUIS**

Certainly Kipling has gifts; the fairy godmothers were all tipsy at his christening: What will be do with them?
**SOMERSET MAUGHAM**

Poetry: A comforting piece of fiction set to more or less lascivious music.
**H. L. MENCKEN**

It is easier to write a mediocre poem than to understand a good one.
**MICHEL DE MONTAIGNE**

In his youth, Wordsworth sympathized with the French Revolution, went to France, wrote good poetry and had a natural daughter. At this period, he was a bad man. Then he became good, abandoned his daughter, adopted correct principles and wrote bad poetry.
**BERTRAND RUSSELL**

Poets, we know, are very sensitive people, and in my observation, one of the things they are most sensitive about is cash.
**ROBERT PENN WARREN**

Meredith is a prose Browning, and so is Browning; he used poetry as a medium for writing in prose.
**OSCAR WILDE**

Poetry has never brought me in enough money to buy shoestrings.
**WILLIAM WORDSWORTH**

## *Politeness*

One of the greatest victories you can gain over a man is to beat him at politeness.
**JOSH BILLINGS**

There is no policy like politeness; and a good manner is the best thing in the world either to get a good name, or to supply the want of it.
**EDWARD BULWER-LYTTON**

Politeness is an inexpensive way of making friends.
**WILLIAM FEATHER**

New York and surrounding country have been experiencing the worst snowstorms in years. Curiously, they have brought out the best qualities in human nature. Ordinarily, on the streets and in country roads, each man, each driver, is out for himself and delights in scoring over others. But I have noticed, both in the city and in the country, an entirely different spirit since travel became extremely difficult, sometimes impossible. Wagon drivers and truck drivers have shown the greatest readiness to help out others. Politeness not ordinarily witnessed has been the rule rather than the exception. . . .
**B. C. FORBES**

Politeness is the result of good sense and good nature.
**OLIVER GOLDSMITH**

Politeness is the chief sign of culture.
**BALTASAR GRACIÁN**

Moving parts in contact require lubrication to avoid excessive wear. Honorifics and formal politeness provide lubrication where people rub together. Often, the very young, the untraveled, the naïve, the unsophisticated deplore these formalities as empty, meaningless, or dishonest, and scorn to use them. No matter how pure their motives, they thereby throw sand into the machinery that does not work too well at best.
**ROBERT A. HEINLEIN**

Politeness is fictitious benevolence.
**SAMUEL JOHNSON**

Tact, the kind of tact you should cultivate, is not a form of deception or make-believe, but a cultivated taste which gives fine perception in seeing and doing what is best under all circumstances. There is nothing which will so readily bring you into favor, or disarm an opponent, as the right use of tact.
**GRENVILLE KLEISER**

Politeness is not always the sign of wisdom, but the want of it always leaves room for the suspicion of folly.
**WALTER SAVAGE LANDOR**

Politeness has been well defined as benevolence in small things.
**THOMAS B. MACAULAY**

Be sure, when you think you are being extremely tactful, that you are not in reality running away from something you ought to face.
**FRANK MEDLICOTT**

The spirit of politeness is a desire to bring about by our words and manners, that others may be pleased with us and with themselves.
**BARON DE MONTESQUIEU**

Tact is the knack of making a point without making an enemy.
**HOWARD W. NEWTON**

Tact is the interpreter of all riddles, the surmounter of all difficulties, the remover of all obstacles.
**WILLIAM SCARGILL**

Politeness is better than logic. You can often persuade when you cannot convince.
**HENRY WHEELER SHAW (JOSH BILLINGS)**

A quick and sound judgment, good common sense, kind feeling, and an instinctive perception of character, in these are the elements of what is called tact, which has so much to do with acceptability and success in life.
**CHARLES SIMMONS**

Tact is one of the first mental virtues, the absence of which is often fatal to the best of talents; it supplies the place of many talents.
**WILLIAM SIMMS**

Politeness is good nature regulated by good sense.
**SYDNEY SMITH**

It's a pity so many of us persist in regarding politeness as being merely a superficial social grace instead of what it really is, namely one of the necessities of life. Quite apart from politeness for its own sake, and as a matter of plain justice, it is invaluable as a sort of cushion or buffer to hold off the jolt that would otherwise disrupt the harmony of things.
**ZEALANDIA**

Tact is the great ability to see other people as they think you see them.
**CARL ZUCKMAYER**

## *Politics*

Every politician, when he leaves office, ought to go straight to jail and serve his time.
**AMERICAN FOLK SAYING**

Vote for the man who promises least; he'll be the least disappointing.
**BERNARD M. BARUCH**

Alliance: In international politics, the union of two thieves who have their hands so deeply into each other's pocket that they cannot separately plunder a third.
**AMBROSE BIERCE**

Conservative: A statesman who is enamored of existing evils, as distinguished from the Liberal, who wishes too replace them with others.
**AMBROSE BIERCE**

Politics: A strife of interest masquerading as a contest of principles.
**AMBROSE BIERCE**

Politicians think that by stopping up the chimney they can stop its smoking. They try the experiment, they drive the smoke back, and there is more smoke than ever; but they do not see that their want of common sense has increased the evil they would have prevented.
**BORNE**

In politics, merit is rewarded by the possessor being raised, like a target, to a position to be fired at.
**CHRISTIAN BOVÉE**

Government is too big and important to be left to the politicians.
**CHESTER BOWLES**

Nowhere are prejudices more mistaken for truth, passion for reason and invective for documentation than in politics.
**JOHN MASON BROWN**

Forward is a mystic move
That every politician touts,
Although his goal is not too clear
Much less its whereabouts.
**ART BUCK**

In politics forget the truth,
The focus is to win;
It's not what's needed to be done,
It's how it's made to spin.
**ART BUCK**

More funds, more funds! the spenders cry,
Our present means won't get us by;
Nor can we cut the current cost—
Our re-election might be lost.
**ART BUCK**

Politics have changed of late,
Which leaves me piqued and sad:

No longer can I separate
The good lies from the bad.
**ART BUCK**

It is the misfortune of all miscellaneous political combinations, that with the purest motives of their more generous members are ever mixed the most sordid interests and the fiercest passions of mean confederates.
**EDWARD BULWER-LYTTON**

An honest politician is one who when he is bought will stay bought.
**SIMON CAMERON**

England, left to itself, returns naturally to sport and laughter, and a genial individualism known as minding one's own business. It knows and cares very little about politics; that is why it puts up with politicians.
**G. K. CHESTERTON**

Most politicians have no politics. They are made entirely by the circumstances of their career. Lincoln kept clear in his mind from first to last his pure theory of politics. He never compromised by an inch in the statement of his principles, even when he had to compromise in the application of them.
**G. K. CHESTERTON**

When [a politician] is in opposition, he is an expert on the means to some end; and when he is in office he is an expert on the obstacles to it. In short, when he is impotent he proves to us that the thing is easy; and when he is omnipotent he proves that it is impossible.
**G. K. CHESTERTON**

A politician thinks of the next election; a statement of the next generation. A politician looks for the success of his party; a statesman for that of his country. The statesman wishes to steer, while the politician is satisfied to drift.
**JAMES FREEMAN CLARKE**

This is quite a game, politics. There are no permanent enemies, and no permanent friends, only permanent interests.
**WILLIAM CLAY**

The country still has faith in the rule of the people it's going to elect next.
**THEODORE COOK**

I have come to the conclusion that politics are too serious a matter to be left to politicians.
**CHARLES DE GAULLE**

Since a politician never believes what he says, he is surprised when others believe him.
**CHARLES DE GAULLE**

To be a liberal one doesn't have to be a wastrel.
**PAUL H. DOUGLAS**

Political controls in the sense that we think of bureaus or departments of government can never operate to produce collaboration between groups in the inner wheels of our industrial organization. It must come from inner compulsions and desires.
**WILLIAM O. DOUGLAS**

The political machine triumphs because it is a united minority acting against a divided majority.
**WILL DURANT**

I despise all adjectives that try to describe people as liberal or conservative, rightist or leftist, as long as they stay in the useful part of the road.
**DWIGHT D. EISENHOWER**

I get weary of the European habit of taking our money, resenting any slight hint as to what they should do, and then assuming, in addition, full right to criticize us as bitterly as they may desire.
**DWIGHT D. EISENHOWER**

All conservatives are such from personal defects. They have been effiminated by position of nature, born halt and blind, through luxury of their parents, and can only, like invalids, act on the defensive.
**RALPH WALDO EMERSON**

Conservatism stands on man's confessed limitations; reform on his indisputable infinitude; conservatism on circumstance; liberalism on power; one goes to make an adroit member of the social frame; the other to postpone all things to the man himself.
**RALPH WALDO EMERSON**

Men are conservatives when they are least vigorous or when they are most luxurious—they are conservatives after dinner.
**RALPH WALDO EMERSON**

Accuse American businessmen of being responsible for radicalism and they would indignantly deny the accusation. Yet, in one fundamental sense, they are responsible. They are responsible in the sense that they have utterly neglected to take part in the work and the organization which precede the choosing of candidates for political office. Local political organizations all over the land are conducted and controlled, as a rule, by politicians. . . .
Businessmen have shirked such responsibilities, leaving an untrammeled field to others less capable of carrying on the administration of government.
**B. C. FORBES**

It is not a case of whether we want to wash our hands of Europe or want to help her to regain her feet. The troubles of Europe have been laid on our doorstep, so to speak, and will plague us, if we do nothing to cure them, whether we like it or not.
**B. C. FORBES**

At the very moment President Johnson announced meaningful new [Vietnam] peace efforts and his own unavailability for another term, people believed they had been eye-ear witnesses to an historic event. The immediate reactions were more emotional than analytical. The stock market soared. Political viciousness lessened overnight. Peace looked not only possible, but probable. Now, from the perspective of a month later, can reasoning men reasonably conclude that these initial reactions, this surging optimism, were justified?
I think so.
**MALCOLM FORBES**

It's clear that something must be done about the effectively disruptive tactics of anarchistic handfuls [at political rallies]. Handling the occasional heckler is a storied, valuable art in politics; but a militant group of grubs [have] announced their determination to rape the right of candidates to be heard and of citizens to hear. Far, far too often these stinky finkies succeeded. . . .
Free speech is the first requisite of freedom and a viable, functioning democracy. The exercise of it cannot be at the option of those who think the right to dissent includes the right to destroy.
**MALCOLM FORBES**

A liberal is a man too broadminded to take his own side in a quarrel.
**ROBERT FROST**

A politician is a person with whose politics you don't agree; if you agree with him, he is a statesman.
**DAVID LLOYD GEORGE**

Political economy is only the economy of human aggregates, and its laws are laws which we may

individually recognize. What is required for their elucidation is not long arrays of statistics nor the collocation of laboriously ascertained facts, but that sort of clear thinking which, keeping in mind the distinction between the part and the whole, seeks the relations of familiar things, and which is as possible for the unlearned as for the learned.
**HENRY GEORGE**

Some politicians leave pussyfoot prints on the sands of time.
**ARNOLD GLASOW**

Twist the dial during an election year and you hear someone twisting the truth.
**ARNOLD GLASOW**

What will it take to be classed as a radical 25 years from now?
**ARNOLD GLASOW**

A liberal is a man who is willing to spend somebody else's money.
**CARTER GLASS**

I hate all bungling as I do sin, but particularly bungling in politics, which leads to the misery and ruin of many thousands and millions of people.
**JOHANN WOLFGANG VON GOETHE**

Politics is an excellent career, unless you get caught.
**ROBERT HALF**

Some politicians give conniving a bad name.
**ROBERT HALF**

The end of all political effort must be the well-being of the individual in the life of safety and freedom.
**DAG HAMMARSKJÖLD**

Diplomacy is living in state.
**OLIVER HERFORD**

Presidents cannot always kick evil-minded persons out of the front door. Such persons are often selected by the electors to represent them.
**HERBERT HOOVER**

Of all kinds of credulity, the most obstinate is that of party-spirit; of men, who, being numbered, they know not why, in any party, resign the use of their own eyes and ears, and resolve to believe nothing that does not favor those whom they profess to follow.
**JOHNSON**

A newspaper reported that I spent $30,000 a year buying Paris clothes and that women hate me for it. I couldn't spend that much unless I wore sable underwear.
**JACQUELINE KENNEDY**

I am the one person who can truthfully say, I got my job through the *New York Times.*
**JOHN F. KENNEDY**

I personally have lived through ten presidential campaigns, but I must say the eleventh makes me feel like I lived through twenty-five.
**JOHN F. KENNEDY**

Politics is a jungle—torn between doing the right thing and staying in office.
**JOHN F. KENNEDY**

One blames politicians, not for inconsistency but for obstinacy. They are the interpreters, not the masters, of our fate. It is their job, in fact, to register the *fait accompli.*
**JOHN MAYNARD KEYNES**

Politicians are the same all over. They promise to build a bridge where there is no river.
NIKITA KHRUSHCHEV

What is conservatism? Is it not adherence to the old and tried, against the new and untried?
ABRAHAM LINCOLN

The justification of majority rule in politics is not to be found in its ethical superiority.
WALTER LIPPMANN

The politicians were talking themselves red, white and blue in the face.
CLARE BOOTHE LUCE

In America you can go on the air and kid the politicians, and the politicians can go on the air and kid the people.
GROUCHO MARX

Being in politics is like being a football coach; you have to be smart enough to understand the game, and dumb enough to think it's important.
EUGENE MCCARTHY

If experience teaches us anything at all, it teaches us this: that a good politician, under democracy, is quite as unthinkable as an honest burglar.
H. L. MENCKEN

A party of order or stability, and a party of progress or reform, are both necessary elements of a healthy state of political life.
JOHN STUART MILL

The proper memory for a politician is one that knows what to remember and what to forget.
JOHN MORLEY

Politics is the diversion of trivial men who, when they succeed at it, become important in the eyes of more trivial men.
GEORGE JEAN NATHAN

Great political questions stir the deepest nature of one-half the nation, but they pass far above and over the heads of the other half.
WENDELL PHILLIPS

Every time we have an election, we get in worse men and the country keeps right on going. Times have proven only one thing and that is you can't ruin this country even with politics.
WILL ROGERS

A radical is a man with both feet firmly planted—in the air.
FRANKLIN D. ROOSEVELT

The true friend of property, the true conservative, is he who insists that property shall be the servant, not the master of the commonwealth; who insists that the creature of man's making shall be the servant, not the master of the man who made it. The citizens of the U.S. must effectively control the commercial forces they have called into being.
THEODORE ROOSEVELT

The most successful politician is he who says what the people are thinking most often and in the loudest voice.
THEODORE ROOSEVELT

If one man offers you democracy and another offers you a bag of grain, at what stage of starvation do you prefer the grain to the vote?
BERTRAND RUSSELL

He knows nothing and thinks he knows everything. That points clearly to a political career.
GEORGE BERNARD SHAW

The question of questions for the politicians should ever be—"What type of social structure am I tending to produce?" But this is a question he never entertains.
**HERBERT SPENCER**

Politics is perhaps the only profession for which no preparation is thought necessary.
**ROBERT LOUIS STEVENSON**

If you allow a political catchword to go on and grow, you will awaken some day to find it standing over you, arbiter of your destiny, against which you are powerless.
**WILLIAM GRAHAM SUMNER**

I have come to the conclusion that the major part of the President is to increase the gate receipts of expositions and fairs and bring tourists into the town.
**WILLIAM HOWARD TAFT**

I am getting ready to see Stalin and Churchill and it is a chore. I have to take my tuxedo, tails, high hat, low hat, and hard hat.
**HARRY S TRUMAN**

There are no personal sympathies in politics.
**MARGARET THATCHER**

Political corruption is the toboggan to national disruption.
**JOHN A. WARD**

No political leader operates without courtiers who hound him—deciding what and whom he sees, providing him with the thoughts he thinks. I find the greatest use of all in talking to the courtiers of the candidate. You get a vision of America as it comes to him.
**THEODORE H. WHITE**

Every man who takes office in Washington either grows or swells, and when I give a man an office, I watch him carefully to see whether he is growing or swelling.
**WOODROW WILSON**

There is scarcely anything more harmless than political or party malice. It is best to leave it to itself. Opposition and contradiction are the only means of giving it life or duration.
**JOHN WITHERSPOON**

## *Poor*

Everything that poverty touches becomes frightful.
**NICOLAS BOILEAU**

Ignorance and poverty are the best condiments for the great feast of the world, but the inexperienced and poor are never invited to it.
**ANTHONY BURGESS**

One is weary of hearing about the omnipotence of money. I will say rather that, for a genuine man, it is not evil to be poor.
**THOMAS CARLYLE**

Thousands upon thousands are yearly brought into a state of real poverty by their great anxiety not to be thought poor.
**WILLIAM COBBETT**

In a country well governed, poverty is something to be ashamed of. In a country badly governed, wealth is something to be ashamed of.
**CONFUCIUS**

When I was growing up, our town was so poor our rainbows came in black and white.
**ROBERT D. COWAN**

For the poor shall never cease out of the land; therefore I command thee, saying, Thou shalt open thine hand wide unto thy brother, to thy poor, and to thy needy, in thy land.
**DEUTERONOMY 15:11**

One must be poor to know the luxury of giving.
**GEORGE ELIOT**

Poverty often deprives a man of all spirit and virtue, it is hard for an empty bag to stand upright.
**BENJAMIN FRANKLIN**

For every talent that poverty has stimulated it has blighted a hundred.
**JOHN W. GARDNER**

Poverty is uncomfortable; but nine times out of ten the best thing that can happen to a young man is to be tossed overboard and compelled to sink or swim.
**JAMES A. GARFIELD**

To be poor, and seem to be poor, is a certain way never to rise.
**OLIVER GOLDSMITH**

Only the poor can know all the disadvantages of poverty. Only the rich can know all the disadvantages of wealth.
**CULLEN HIGHTOWER**

Of all the advantages which come to any young man, I believe it to be demonstrably true that poverty is the greatest.
**JOSIAH G. HOLLAND**

Poverty urges us to do and suffer anything that we may escape from it, and so leads us away from virtue.
**HORACE**

Woe to them that decree unrighteous decrees, and which write grievousness that they have prescribed. To turn aside the needy from judgment, and to take away the right from the poor of my people, that widows may be their prey, and that they may rob the fatherless!
**ISAIAH 10:1–2**

A single solitary philosopher may be great, virtuous and happy in the depth of poverty, but not a whole people.
**ISELIN**

A decent provision for the poor is the true test of civilization.
**SAMUEL JOHNSON**

Poverty is a great enemy to human happiness; it certainly destroys liberty, and it makes some virtues impracticable, and others extremely difficult.
**SAMUEL JOHNSON**

He who knows how to be poor knows everything.
**JULES MICHELET**

Poverty is very terrible, and sometimes kills the very soul within us; but it is the north wind that lashes men into Vikings; it is the soft, luscious south wind which lulls them to lotus dreams.
**OUIDA**

That man is to be accounted poor, of whatever rank he be, and suffers the pains of poverty, whose expenses exceed his resources; and no man is, property speaking, poor, but he.
**WILLIAM PALEY**

We Athenians hold that it is not poverty that is disgraceful but the failure to struggle against it.
**PERICLES**

Poverty is not dishonorable in itself, but only when it comes from idleness, intemperance, extravagance, and folly.
**PLUTARCH**

There is that scattereth, and yet increaseth; and there is that withholdeth more than is meet, but it tendeth to poverty.
**PROVERBS 11:24**

Poverty is not disgrace to a man, but it is confoundedly inconvenient.
**SYDNEY SMITH**

The doctrine of thrift for the poor is dumb and cruel, like advising them to try and lift themselves by their bootstraps.
**NORMAN THOMAS**

I've never been poor, only broke. Being poor is a frame of mind. Being broke is only a temporary situation.
**MIKE TODD**

In the small town of Hannibal, Missouri, when I was a boy, everybody was poor, but didn't know it; and everybody was comfortable and did know it.
**MARK TWAIN**

There is only one class in the community that thinks more about money than the rich, and that is the poor. The poor can think of nothing else. That is the misery of being poor.
**OSCAR WILDE**

## *Possessions*

The older I grow the less do I care for possessions. I look upon what I have as only something that has been loaned to me and which will pass to others after I am gone. I have treasures that cannot be measured by monetary standards but by the arithmetic of love. My only concern is—will they be loved as I have loved them? . . . There is no thrill in this life that returns so much satisfaction as to give to someone else from one's store of love and enjoyment of beauty. Such wealth is spiritually accumulative. And its dividends are never passed, but endlessly grow greater!
**GEORGE MATTHEW ADAMS**

What a man has honestly acquired is absolutely his own, which he may freely give, but cannot be taken from him without his consent.
**SAMUEL ADAMS**

Do not imagine yourself to have what you have not; but take full account of the excellencies which you possess, and in gratitude remember how you would hanker after them, if you had them not. At the same time take care that in thus hugging them, you do not get into the habit of prizing them so much that without them you would be perturbed.
**MARCUS AURELIUS ANTONINUS**

Give thy mind more to what thou has than to what thou hast not.
**MARCUS AURELIUS ANTONINUS**

Why grab possessions like thieves, or divide them like socialists, when you can ignore them like wise men?
**NATALIE CLIFFORD BARNEY**

There is, of course, a difference between what a man seizes and what he really possesses.
**PEARL S. BUCK**

Thieves respect property. They merely wish the property to become their property that they may more perfectly respect it.
**G. K. CHESTERTON**

Our most valuable possessions are those which can be shared without lessening—those which, when shared, multiply. Our least valuable possessions, on the other hand, are those which, when divided, are diminished.
**WILLIAM H. DANFORTH**

Americans are uneasy with their possessions, guilty about power, all of which is difficult for Europeans to perceive because they themselves are so truly materialistic, so versed in the uses of power.
**JOAN DIDION**

Possessions, outward success, publicity, luxury—to me these have always been contemptible. I believe that a simple and unassuming manner of life is best for everyone, best both for the body and the mind.
**ALBERT EINSTEIN**

Some men are born to own; can animate all their possessions. Others cannot; Their owning is not graceful; seems to be a compromise of their character; they seem to steal their own dividends.
**RALPH WALDO EMERSON**

Mankind, by the perverse depravity of their nature, esteem that which they have most desired as of no value the moment it is possessed, and torment themselves with fruitless wishes for that which is beyond their reach.
**FRANÇOIS FÉNELON**

Our life on earth is, and ought to be, material and carnal. But we have not yet learned to manage our materialism and carnalism properly; they are still entangled with our desire for ownership.
**E. M. FORSTER**

What I possess I would gladly retain. Change amuses the mind, yet scarcely profits.
**JOHANN WOLFGANG VON GOETHE**

Possession hinders enjoyment. It merely gives you the right to keep things for or from others, and thus you gain more enemies than friends.
**BALTASAR GRACIÁN**

How sweet an emotion is possession! What charm is inherent in ownership! What a foundation for vanity, even for the greater quality of self-respect, lies in a little property!
**DAVID GRAYSON**

Nothing can be so perfect while we possess it as it will seem when remembered.
**OLIVER WENDELL HOLMES**

Many possessions, if they do not make a man better, are at least expected to make his children happier; and this pathetic hope is behind many exertions.
**KARL WILHELM VON HUMBOLDT**

The thief cometh not, but for to steal, and to kill, and to destroy; I am come that they might have life, and that they might have it more abundantly.
**JOHN 10:10**

Some luck lies in not getting what you thought you wanted but getting what you have, which once you have it you may be smart enough to see is what you would have wanted had you known.
**GARRISON KEILLOR**

He who possesses most must be most afraid of loss.
**LEONARDO DA VINCI**

Things may come to those who wait, but only the things left by those who hustle.
**ABRAHAM LINCOLN**

Sell that ye have, and give alms; provide yourselves bags which wax not old, a treasure in the heavens

that faileth not, where no thief approacheth, nor moth corrupteth.
**LUKE 12:33**

Two things are as big as the man who possesses them—neither bigger nor smaller. One is a minute, the other a dollar.
**CHANNING POLLOCK**

Our most valuable possessions are those which can be shared without lessening; those which when shared, multiply. Our least valuable possessions are those which when divided are diminished.
**HUGH PRATHER**

Every increased possession loads us with new weariness.
**JOHN RUSKIN**

Everything comes to us that belongs to us if we create the capacity to receive it.
**RABINDRANATH TAGORE**

Have a place for everything and keep the thing somewhere else; this is not advice, it is merely custom.
**MARK TWAIN**

That anyone should be able to make it the sole purpose of his life-work, to sink into the grave weighed down with a great material load of money and goods, seems explicable only as the product of a perverse imagination.
**MAX WEBER**

## *Power*

An honest private man often grows cruel and abandoned when converted into an absolute prince. Give a man power of doing what he pleases with impunity, you extinguish his fear, and consequently overturn in him one of the great pillars of morality.
**JOSEPH ADDISON**

Nothing is more gratifying to the mind of man than power or dominion.
**JOSEPH ADDISON**

The man whose authority is recent is always stern.
**AESCHYLUS**

The price of power is responsibility for the public good.
**WINTHROP W. ALDRICH**

I have yet to encounter that common myth of weak men, an insurmountable barrier.
**JAMES LANE ALLEN**

Where a man does his best with only moderate powers, he will have the advantage over negligent superiority.
**JANE AUSTEN**

It is a strange desire, to seek power, and to lose liberty; or to seek power over others, and to lose power over a man's self.
**FRANCIS BACON**

All human power is a compound of time and patience.
**HONORÉ DE BALZAC**

Power is not revealed by striking hard or often, but by striking true.
**HONORÉ DE BALZAC**

If any man is rich and powerful he comes under the law of God by which the higher branches must take the burnings of the sun, and shade those that are

lower; by which the tall trees must protect the weak plants beneath them.
**HENRY WARD BEECHER**

Power requires legitimacy, or else it is despotism.
**JACK BEHRMAN**

Power is built up only to fall, unless it rests on the one solid basis—the basis of the spirit. The continual struggle to preserve the moral basis of the nation's strength—through the arts, education and thought—is the strongest bulwark of national security.
**JAIME TORRES BODET**

I know of nothing sublime which is not some modification of power.
**EDMUND BURKE**

Power intoxicates men. When a man is intoxicated by alcohol he can recover, but when intoxicated by power he seldom recovers.
**JAMES F. BYRNES**

Immense power is acquired by assuring yourself in your secret reveries that you were born to control affairs.
**ANDREW CARNEGIE**

You philosophers are lucky men. You write on paper, which is patient. Unfortunate Empress that I am, I write on the susceptible skins of living beings.
**CATHERINE THE GREAT**

Those who seek power for personal ends eventually run afoul of popular opinion.
**CHINESE PROVERB**

Orators are most vehement when they have the weakest cause, as men get on horseback when they cannot walk.
**CICERO**

Ambition makes the same mistake concerning power, that avarice makes as to wealth. She begins by accumulating it as a means to happiness, and finishes by continuing to accumulate it as an end.
**CHARLES CALEB COLTON**

To know the pains of power, we must go to those who have it. To know its pleasures, we must go to those who are seeking it. The pains of power are real, its pleasures imaginary.
**CHARLES CALEB COLTON**

Law is but a heathen word for power.
**DANIEL DEFOE**

Next to the assumption of power is the responsibility of relinquishing it.
**BENJAMIN DISRAELI**

The depositary of power is always unpopular.
**BENJAMIN DISRAELI**

A great man is one who can have power and not abuse it.
**HENRY L. DOHERTY**

Men, such as they are, very naturally seek money or power; and power because it is as good as money.
**RALPH WALDO EMERSON**

The power which resides in him is new in nature, and none but he knows what that is which he can do, nor does he know until he has tried.
**RALPH WALDO EMERSON**

Any one entrusted with power will abuse it if not also animated with the love of truth and virtue, no matter whether he be a prince, or one of the people.
**JEAN DE LA FONTAINE**

Authority's for sharing only when the sharer is sure of his (or hers).
MALCOLM FORBES

Clout is something some seem to have—until they try exercising it.
MALCOLM FORBES

Those carried away by power are soon carried away.
MALCOLM FORBES

You can't build a triumphant soul on hunger. All the more reason, then, why we who are not hungry nor hopelessly overborne by circumstance should surmount life and carry off a victory in the face of it. And more than pluck is needed to do that, more than just a philosophy believed with the mind. An inner experience of power is needed far beyond ourselves.
HARRY EMERSON FOSDICK, D.D.

Power doesn't corrupt people; people corrupt power.
WILLIAM GADDIS

Power is not happiness. Security and peace are more to be desired than a man at which nations tremble.
WILLIAM GODWIN

Beware of dissipating your powers; strive constantly to concentrate them. Genius thinks it can do whatever it sees others doing, but it is sure to repent of every ill-judged outlay.
JOHANN WOLFGANG VON GOETHE

In the general course of human nature, a power over a man's subsistence amounts to a power over his will.
ALEXANDER HAMILTON

The admiration of power in others is as common to man as the love of it in himself; the one makes him a tyrant, the other a slave.
WILLIAM HAZLITT

It is a hard but good law of fate that as every evil, so every excessive power wears itself out.
JOHANN GOTTFRIED VON HERDER

Real power has fullness and variety. It is not narrow like lightning, but broad like light. The man who truly and worthily excels in any one line of endeavor might also, under a change of circumstances, have excelled in some other line. Power is a thing of solidity and wholeness.
ROSWELL D. HITCHCOCK

Responsibilities gravitate to the person who can shoulder them; power flows to the man who knows how.
ELBERT HUBBARD

Every great advance in natural knowledge has involved the absolute rejection of authority.
THOMAS H. HUXLEY

I have never been able to conceive how any rational being could propose happiness to himself from the exercise of power over others.
THOMAS JEFFERSON

The general story of mankind will evince that lawful and settled authority is very seldom resisted when it is well employed.
SAMUEL JOHNSON

The possession of power inevitably spoils the free use of reason.
IMMANUEL KANT

The power in which we must have faith if we would be well, is the creative and curative power which exists in every living thing.
JOHN HARVEY KELLOGG

I have two basic convictions: First, more harm has been done by weak persons than by wicked persons;

secondly, the problems of the world are caused by the weakness of goodness rather than by the strength of evil. It is evident that we have allowed technology to outstrip social controls. . . . Man must catch up with what he has created.
HARRY S. KENNEDY

You all have powers you never dreamed of. You can do things you never thought you could do. There are no limitations in what you can do except the limitations in your own mind as to what you cannot do. Don't think you cannot. Think you can.
DARWIN P. KINGSLEY

Nothing more impairs authority than a too frequent or indiscreet use of it. If thunder itself was to be continual, it would excite no more terror than the noise of a mill.
ALFRED KINGSTON

Power corrupts, but absolute power is really neat.
EX-NAVY SECRETARY JOHN LEHMAN

Nearly all men can stand adversity, but if you want to test a man's character, give him power.
ABRAHAM LINCOLN

The great question which, in all ages, has disturbed mankind, and brought on them the greatest part of those mischiefs, which have ruined cities, depopulated countries, and disordered the peace of the world, has been, not whether there be power in the world, not whence it came, but who should have it.
JOHN LOCKE

The highest proof of virtue is to prossess boundless power without abusing it.
THOMAS B. MACAULAY

He is free who knows how to keep in his own hands the power to decide, at each step, the course of his life, and who lives in a society which does not block the exercise of that power.
SALVADOR DE MADARIAGA

The only purpose for which power can be rightfully exercised over any member of a civilized community, against his will, is to prevent harm to others. His own good, either physical or moral, is not a sufficient warrant.
JOHN STUART MILL

The best test of a man is authority.
MONTENEGRAN PROVERB

It is necessary from the very nature of things that power should be a check to power.
BARON DE MONTESQUIEU

The culminating point of administration is to know well how much power, great or small, we ought to use in all circumstances.
BARON DE MONTESQUIEU

The power of the state is measured by the power that men surrender to it.
FELIX MORLEY

Life is an instinct for growth, for survival, for the accumulation of forces, for power.
FRIEDRICH WILHELM NIETZSCHE

What is evil?—Whatever springs from weakness.
FRIEDRICH WILHELM NIETZSCHE

What is good? Whatever augments the feeling of power, the will to power, power itself, in man.
FRIEDRICH WILHELM NIETZSCHE

If thou wouldst conquer thy weakness thou must not gratify it.
WILLIAM PENN

Unlimited power is worse for the average person than unlimited alcohol; and the resulting intoxication is more damaging for others. Very few have not deteriorated when given absolute dominion. It is worse for the governor than for the governed.
WILLIAM LYON PHELPS

It has been said that absolute power corrupts absolutely, but may it not be truer to say that to be absolutely powerful a man must first corrupt himself?
TERENCE RATTIGAN

How a minority, reaching majority, seizing authority, hates a minority.
LEONARD H. ROBBINS

I should say that [the Chinese], in the main, aim at enjoyment, while we, in the main, aim at power. We like power over our fellow men, and we like power over Nature.
BERTRAND RUSSELL

To be able to endure odium is the first art to be learned by those who aspire to power.
SENECA

The weak and insipid white wine makes at length excellent vinegar.
WILLIAM SHENSTONE

You cannot run away from a weakness. You must sometimes fight it out or perish; and if that be so, why not now, and where you stand?
ROBERT LOUIS STEVENSON

The cause of all these evils was the desire for power which greed and ambition inspire.
THUCYDIDES

Power, from the standpoint of experience, is merely the relation that exists between the expression of someone's will and the execution of that will by others.
LEO TOLSTOY

Since nothing is settled until it is settled right, no matter how unlimited power a man may have, unless he exercises it fairly and justly his actions will return to plague him.
FRANK A. VANDERLIP

The prevailin' weakness of most public men is to slop over. G. Washington . . . never slopt over!
ARTEMUS WARD

Nothing in the world is more haughty than a man of moderate capacity when once raised to power.
BARON WESSENBURG

Right and truth are greater than any power, and all power is limited by right.
BENJAMIN WHICHCOTE

We all have weaknesses. But I have figured that others have put up with mine so tolerably that I would be much less than fair not to make a reasonable discount for theirs.
WILLIAM ALLEN WHITE

Wherever there is a man who exercises authority, there is a man who resists authority.
OSCAR WILDE

As a matter of fact and experience, the more power is divided the more irresponsible it becomes.
WOODROW WILSON

## *Praise*

The high-minded man is fond of conferring benefits, but it shames him to receive them.
ARISTOTLE

Consider how many do not even know your name, and how many will soon forget it, and how those who now praise you will presently blame you.
MARCUS AURELIUS ANTONINUS

Applause is the echo of a platitude.
AMBROSE BIERCE

A man's inner nature is revealed by what he praises—a man is self-judged by what he says of others. Thus a man is judged by his standards, by what he considers the best. And you can't find a more crucial test. It reveals the soul.
HUGO L. BLACK

He who discommendeth others obliquely commendeth himself.
SIR THOMAS BROWNE

Praise is a debt we owe unto the virtue of others, and due unto our own from all whom malice hath not made mutes, or envy struck dumb.
SIR THOMAS BROWNE

It would be a kind of ferocity to reject indifferently all sorts of praise. One should be glad to have that which comes from good men who praise in sincerity things that are really praiseworthy.
JEAN DE LA BRUYÈRE

To dispense with ceremony is the most delicate mode of conferring a compliment.
EDWARD BULWER-LYTTON

A fulsome praise does go a long way. You don't need too much of that, because the first thing you know you begin to believe it, and that is bad.
ERSKINE CALDWELL

Compliments or congratulations are always kindly taken, and cost nothing but pen, ink, and paper. I consider them as draughts upon good breeding, where the exchange is always greatly is favor of the drawer.
LORD CHESTERFIELD

We all are imbued with the love of praise.
CICERO

There are two modes of establishing our reputation: to be praised by honest men, and to be abused by rogues. It is best, however, to secure the former, because it will invariably be accompanied by the latter.
CHARLES CALEB COLTON

The superior man does not mind being in office; all he minds about is whether he has qualities that entitle him to office. He does not mind failing to get recognition; he is too busy doing the things that entitle him to recognition.
CONFUCIUS

Whoever pays you more court than he is accustomed to pay, either intends to deceive you or finds you necessary to him.
JOHN COURTENAY

I love criticism just so long as it is unqualified praise.
NOEL COWARD

He wants worth who dares not praise a foe.
JOHN DRYDEN

Sweet praise is like perfume. It is fine if you don't swallow it.
DWIGHT D. EISENHOWER

We thirst for approbation, yet cannot forgive the approver.
RALPH WALDO EMERSON

Any fact is better established by two or three good testimonies, than by a thousand arguments.
**NATHANIEL EMMONS**

Spite of all modesty, a man must own a pleasure in the hearing of his praise.
**GEORGE FARQUHAR**

Most of us, swimming against tides of trouble the world knows nothing about, need only a bit of praise or encouragement—and we'll make the goal. Say "Thank you!" whenever you think of it. Say "Nice job!" to that workman who put extra effort into his task. Say "Atta boy!" to the fellow who is struggling through in the face of odds. You'll get a whale of a lot of joy out of life that way. And people will love you.
**JEROME P. FLEISHMAN**

They that value not praise will never do anything worthy of praise.
**THOMAS FULLER**

Applause is the only appreciated interruption.
**ARNOLD GLASOW**

Reprove privately, praise publicly.
**ARNOLD GLASOW**

The praises of others may be of use in teaching us not what we are, but what we ought to be.
**AUGUSTUS HARE**

What a person praises is perhaps a surer standard, even, than what he condemns, of his character, information and abilities. No wonder, then, that most people are so shy of praising anything.
**AUGUSTUS HARE**

There is no verbal vitamin more potent than praise.
**FREDERICK B. HARRIS**

For as the earth bringeth forth her bud, and as the garden causeth the things that are sown in it to spring forth; so the Lord God will cause righteousness and praise to spring forth before all the nations.
**ISAIAH 61:11**

Applause abates diligence.
**SAMUEL JOHNSON**

The applause of a single human being is of great consequence.
**SAMUEL JOHNSON**

He who praises everybody praises nobody.
**SAMUEL JOHNSON**

Praise, like gold diamonds, owes its value to its scarcity.
**SAMUEL JOHNSON**

Praise is sometimes a good thing for the diffident and despondent. It teaches them properly to rely on the kindness of others.
**LETITIA E. LANDON**

I should entertain a mean opinion of myself if all men, or the most part, praised and admired me; it would prove me to be somewhat like them.
**WALTER SAVAGE LANDOR**

Consider carefully before you say a hard word to a man, but never let a chance to say a good one go by. Praise judiciously bestowed is money invested.
**GEORGE HORACE LORIMER**

Praise is warming and desirable, what the human race lives on like bread. But praise is an earned thing. It has to be deserved like an honorary degree or a hug from a child. A compliment is manna, a free gift.
**PHYLLIS MCGINLEY**

He praises the big horse and rides the small one.
**MEXICAN PROVERB**

He who freely magnifies what hath been nobly done, and fears not to declares as freely what might be done better, gives ye the best covenant of his fidelity.
**JOHN MILTON**

I much prefer a compliment, insincere or not, to sincere criticism.
**PLAUTUS**

Those who are greedy of praise prove that they are poor in merit.
**PLUTARCH**

It is not he who searches for praise who finds it.
**ANTOINE DE RIVAROL**

I have yet to find a man, whatever his situation in life, who did not do better work and put forth greater effort under a spirit of approval than he ever would do under a spirit of criticism.
**CHARLES M. SCHWAB**

It is great happiness to be praised of them who are most praiseworthy.
**SIR PHILIP SIDNEY**

Among the smaller duties of life, I hardly know any one more important than that of not praising where praise is not due.
**SYDNEY SMITH**

Reprove thy friend privately, commend him publicly.
**SOLON**

I know of no manner of speaking so offensive as that of giving praise, and closing with an exception.
**RICHARD STEELE**

Whenever you commend, add your reasons for doing so; it is this which distinguishes the approbation of a man of sense from the flattery of sycophants and admiration of fools.
**RICHARD STEELE**

Praise is the daughter of present power.
**JONATHAN SWIFT**

In modern life nothing produces such an effect as a good platitude. It makes the whole world kind.
**OSCAR WILDE**

Women are never disarmed by compliments. Men always are. That is the difference between the two sexes.
**OSCAR WILDE**

Recognition for a job well done is high on the list of motivating influences for all people; more important in many instances than compensation itself. When someone is promoted, a promotion that everyone could see coming because of an excellent record, the entire department is stimulated. For it is clear, then, that promotions are based on merit. A promotion that seems to come out of the blue, which is always the case when no one knows what the next fellow is doing, causes nothing but resentment and a further weakening of the will to work.
**JOHN M. WILSON**

The sweetest of all sounds is praise.
**XENOPHON**

## *Prayer*

The minds of people are so cluttered up with everyday living these days that they don't, or won't, take time out for a little prayer—for mental cleansing,

just as they take a bath for physical outer cleansing. Both are necessary.
**JO ANN CARLSON**

Man offers himself to God. He stands before Him like the canvas before the painter or the marble before the sculptor. At the same time he asks for His grace, expresses his needs and those of his brothers in suffering. Such a type of prayer demands complete renovation. The modest, the ignorant, and the poor are more capable of this self-denial than the rich and the intellectual.
**ALEXIS CARREL**

Prayer is a force as real as terrestrial gravity. As a physician, I have seen men, after all other therapy had failed, lifted out of disease and melancholy by the serene effort of prayer. Only in prayer do we achieve that complete and harmonious assembly of body, mind and spirit which gives the frail human reed its unshakable strength.
**ALEXIS CARREL**

Prayer, like radium, is a luminous and self-generating form of energy.
**ALEXIS CARREL**

The most powerful form of energy one can generate is not mechanical, electronic or even atomic energy, but prayer energy.
**ALEXIS CARREL**

The influence of prayer on the human mind and body is as demonstrable as that of secreting glands. Its results can be measured in terms of increased physical buoyancy, greater intellectual vigor, moral stamina, and a deeper understanding of the realities underlying human relationship.
**ALEXIS CARREL**

If a pig could pray, it would pray for swill. What do you pray for?
**B. C. FORBES**

Men have prayed in prison, men have prayed in slums and concentration camps. It's only the middle classes who demand to pray in suitable surroundings.
**GRAHAM GREENE**

The spectacle of a nation praying is more awe-inspiring than the explosion of an atomic bomb. The force of prayer is greater than any possible combination of man-made or man-controlled powers because prayer is man's greatest means of tapping the infinite resources of God.
**J. EDGAR HOOVER**

Prayer does not change God, but changes him who prays.
**SÖREN KIERKEGAARD**

When we pray "Our Father," I am praying for you, you are praying for me. In fact, if men everywhere would only learn to pray aright, "Our Father," there would be no differences to settle. It would not be long before Communist, imperialist, capitalist and what have you would stop their cold war and start to live at peace with one another.
**ALBERT N. NEIBACKER, D.D.**

We are all weak, finite, simple human beings, standing in the need of prayer. None need it so much as those who think they are strong, those who know it not but are deluded by self-sufficiency.
**HAROLD COOKE PHILLIPS, D.D.**

Practise in life whatever you pray for, and God will give it to you more abundantly.
**PUSEY**

A generous prayer is never presented in vain; the petition may be refused, but the petitioner is always, I believe, rewarded by some gracious visitation.
ROBERT LOUIS STEVENSON

We believe that prayer works miracles, and that all prayers are answered. But the greatest miracle is that some of them are actually answered exactly as we ourselves wish them to be.
GLENN STEWART

We should not be discouraged if our prayers go unanswered; if some were, we most certainly would have grave reservations about the sanity of God.
J. K. STUART

More tears are shed over answered prayers than unanswered ones.
ST. THERESA OF AVILA

When the gods choose to punish us, they merely answer our prayers.
OSCAR WILDE

We don't thank God enough for much that He has given us. Our prayers are too often the beggar's prayer, the prayer that asks for something. We offer too few prayers of thanksgiving and of praise.
ROBERT E. WOODS, D.D.

## *Prejudice*

Nothing is harder to topple than a fact that supports a deeply held prejudice denied by its holder.
RUSSELL L. ACKOFF

We can get the new world we want, if we want it enough to abandon our prejudices, every day, everywhere. We can build this world if we practise now what we said we were fighting for.
GWEN BRISTOW

Even in an advanced stage of civilization, there is always a tendency to prefer those parts of literature which favor ancient prejudices, rather than those which oppose them; and in cases where this tendency is very strong, the only effect of great learning will be to supply the materials which may corroborate old errors and confirm old superstitions. In our time such instances are not uncommon; and we frequently meet with men whose erudition ministers to their ignorance, and who, the more they read the less they know.
HENRY THOMAS BUCKLE

Our prejudices are our mistresses; reason is at best our wife, very often needed but seldom minded.
LORD CHESTERFIELD

America owes most of its social prejudices to the exaggerated religious opinions of the different sects which were so instrumental in establishing the colonies.
JAMES FENIMORE COOPER

Prejudice, which sees what it pleases, cannot see what is plain.
A. DEVERE

He that is possessed with a prejudice is possessed with a devil.
TRYON EDWARDS

Too many of us vote for our prejudices instead of our desires.
WILLIAM FEATHER

An unprejudiced mind is probably the rarest thing in the world; to nonprejudice I attach the greatest value.
ANDRÉ GIDE

He who never leaves his country is full of prejudices.
**CARLO GOLDONI**

Prejudices are the principles of people we dislike.
**JOHN P. GRIER**

Dogs bark at a person whom they do not know.
**HERACLITUS**

A great number of people think they are thinking when they are merely rearranging their prejudices.
**WILLIAM JAMES**

The world is as large as the range of one's interests. A narrow-minded man has a narrow outlook. The walls of his world shut out the broader horizon of affairs. Prejudice can maintain walls that no invention can remove.
**JOSEPH JASTROW**

Beware prejudices. They are like rats, and men's minds are like traps; prejudices get in easily, but it is doubtful if they ever get out.
**FRANCIS JEFFREY**

One may no more live in the world without picking up the moral prejudices of the world than one will be able to go to hell without perspiring.
**H. L. MENCKEN**

A great many people think they are thinking when they are really rearranging their prejudices.
**EDWARD R. MURROW**

Everyone is a prisoner of his own experiences. No one can eliminate prejudices—just recognize them.
**EDWARD R. MURROW**

Prejudice is a mist, which in our journey through the world often dims the brightest and obscures the best of all the good and glorious objects that meet us on our way.
**LORD SHAFTESBURY**

We are chameleons, and our partialities and prejudices change places with an easy and blessed facility.
**MARK TWAIN**

Prejudice is not held against people because they have evil qualities. Evil qualities are imputed to people because prejudices are held against them.
**MARSHALL WINGFIELD**

## *Present*

Bad times, hard times—this is what people keep saying; but let us live well, and times shall be good. We are the times: Such as we are, such are the times.
**ST. AUGUSTINE**

Don't waste good thoughts on yesterday
Nor on days yet to come,
But think good thoughts on things at hand
And strive to make things hum;
For now, today, is full of hope and pleasures
  we'll soon taste
If we will concentrate on now
And precious time not waste.
**ALONZO NEWTON BENN**

It is difficult to live in the present, ridiculous to live in the future, and impossible to live in the past.
**JIM BISHOP**

Our grand business is not to see what lies dimly in the distance, but to do what lies clearly at hand.
**THOMAS CARLYLE**

Men spend their lives in anticipations, in determining to be vastly happy at some period when they

have time. But the present time has one advantage over every other—it is our own. Past opportunities are gone, future are not come. We may lay in a stock of pleasures, as we would lay in a stock of wine; but if we defer the tasting of them too long, we shall find that both are soured by age.
CHARLES CALEB COLTON

I hope the day will never come when the American nation will be the champion of the status quo. Once that happens, we shall have forfeited, and rightly forfeited, the support of the unsatisfied, of those who are the victims of inevitable imperfections, of those who, young in years or spirit, believe that they can make a better world and of those who dream dreams and want to make their dreams come true.
JOHN FOSTER DULLES

One of the illusions of life is that the present hour is not the critical, decisive hour. Write it on your heart that every day is the best day of the year.
RALPH WALDO EMERSON

This time, like all other times, is a very good one, if we but know what to do with it.
RALPH WALDO EMERSON

We cannot overstate our debt to the past, but the moment has the supreme claim.
RALPH WALDO EMERSON

Let us think only of spending the present day well. Then when tomorrow shall have come, it will be called today, and then we will think about it.
ST. FRANCIS DE SALES

Let us . . . quietly accept our times, with the firm conviction that just as much good can be done today as at any time in the past, provided only that we have the will and the way to do it.
ETIENNE GILSON

The secret of what life's all about
Was answered by the sages:
Life's about one day at a time
No matter what your age is.
ROBERT HALF

The present is burdened too much with the past. We have not time, in our earthly existence, to appreciate what is warm with life, and immediately around us.
NATHANIEL HAWTHORNE

It is common to overlook what is near by keeping the eye fixed on something remote. In the same manner present opportunities are neglected, and attainable good is slighted by minds busied in extensive ranges and intent upon future advantages.
JOHNSON

The road recedes as the traveler advances, leaving a continuous present.
RICHARD LE GALLIENNE

The dogmas of the quiet past are inadequate to the stormy present. . . . As our case is new, so we must think anew and act anew.
ABRAHAM LINCOLN

Take time to enjoy the present.
ALEXANDER REID MARTIN

Who controls the past controls the future; who controls the present controls the past.
GEORGE ORWELL

Banish the future. Live only for the hour and its allotted work. Think not of the amount to be accomplished, the difficulties to be overcome, or the end to be attained, but set earnestly at the little task at your elbow, letting that be sufficient for the day.
SIR WILLIAM OSLER

Let ancient times delight other folk, I rejoice that I was not born till now.
**OVID**

Let any man examine his thoughts, and he will find them ever occupied with the past or the future. We scarcely think at all of the present; or if we do, it is only to borrow the light which it gives for regulating the future. The present is never our object; the past and the present we use as means; the future only is our end. Thus, we never live, we only hope to live.
**BLAISE PASCAL**

Begin doing what you want to do now. We are not living in eternity. We have only this moment, sparkling like a star in our hand—and melting like a snowflake. Let us use it before it is too late.
**MARIE BEYNON RAY**

The pace of events is moving so fast that unless we can find some way to keep our sights on tomorrow, we cannot expect to be in touch with today.
**DEAN RUSK**

"Now" is the watchword of the wise.
**CHARLES H. SPURGEON**

You must live in the present, launch yourself on every wave, find your eternity in each moment.
**HENRY DAVID THOREAU**

He who governed the world before I was born shall take care of it likewise when I am dead. My part is to improve the present moment.
**JOHN WESLEY**

## *Pride*

Pride is a great urge to action; but remember, the pride must be on the part of the buyer. On the part of the seller, it is vanity.
**JAMES R. ADAMS**

Riches are apt to betray a man into arrogance.
**JOSEPH ADDISON**

Conceit is God's gift to little men.
**BRUCE BARTON**

A proud man is seldom a grateful man, for he never thinks he gets as much as he deserves.
**HENRY WARD BEECHER**

It is pride which plies the world with so much harshness and severity. We are as rigorous to offenses as if we had never offended.
**PAXTON BLAIR**

Some of the proudest and most arrogant people I have known were morons and paupers, while some of the most wonderful and humble were wealthy.
**F. HOWARD CALLAHAN**

If I had only one sermon to preach it would be a sermon against pride.
**G. K. CHESTERTON**

The disesteem and contempt of others is inseparable from pride. It is hardly possible to overvalue ourselves but by undervaluing our neighbors.
**LORD CLARENDON**

A great business success was probably never attained by chasing the dollar, but is due to pride in one's work—the pride that makes business an art.
**HENRY L. DOHERTY**

I've never any pity for conceited people, because I think they carry their comfort about with them.
GEORGE ELIOT

Every time I see an Erie Railroad engine bearing the name of its faithful driver a thrill goes through me, for I know that the man guiding it has won this rare honor by many years of the most loyal and efficient service. Who will argue that only public men and corporation heads are entitled to have their names emblazoned on the scroll of honor?

"All workmen care about is money," you say? Wrong. Workers are made of exactly the same stuff as generals or senators or presidents or governors or industrial leaders. It is just as fitting to honor the worthiest of our wage earners as it is to honor others.
B. C. FORBES

"I don't feel myself that I know it all, but I have enough conceit to be successful." That observation was made by a businessman in his 30s who was making notable headway, although his path bristled with difficulties. Business places no premiums on shrinking violets. Employers prefer men who have self-assurance, forcefulness, go-aheadness, men who know their jobs and know that they know it.
B. C. FORBES

A man given to pride is usually proud of the wrong thing.
HENRY FORD

Every man has a right to be conceited until he is successful.
BENJAMIN FRANKLIN

Don't push out, or to use a slang expression, don't be on the make. Don't play the braggart. Don't be conceited. Don't have bad manners. Don't be on the lookout for number one. Don't lose your temper.

Don't be resentful of slights. Don't get malicious satisfaction out of the sins of others.
FRANK S. GAVIN, D.D.

Conceit is the quicksand of success.
ARNOLD GLASOW

Pride is a deeply rooted ailment of the soul. The penalty is misery; the remedy lies in the sincere, life-long cultivation of humility, which means true self-evaluation and a proper perspective toward past, present and future.
ROBERT GORDIS

Nothing so obstinately stands in the way of all sorts of progress as pride of opinion; while nothing is so foolish and baseless.
JOSIAH G. HOLLAND

When men are most sure and arrogant they are commonly most mistaken, giving views to passion without that proper deliberation which alone can secure them from the grossest absurdities.
DAVID HUME

Every good thought that we have, and every good action that we perform, lays us open to pride, and thus exposes us to the various assaults of vanity and self-satisfaction.
WILLIAM LAW

Pride is a form of selfishness.
DAVID LAWRENCE

Whenever nature leaves a hole in a person's mind, she generally plasters it over with a thick coat of self-conceit.
HENRY WADSWORTH LONGFELLOW

Conceit is to nature what paint is to beauty; it is not only needless, but it impairs what it would improve.
ALEXANDER POPE

Conceit causes more conversation than wit.
**FRANÇOIS DE LA ROCHEFOUCAULD**

Nature has given us pride to spare us the pain of being conscious of our imperfections.
**FRANÇOIS DE LA ROCHEFOUCAULD**

Conceit may puff a man up, but can never prop him up.
**JOHN RUSKIN**

Pride is at the bottom of all great mistakes.
**JOHN RUSKIN**

Look out how you use proud words; when you let proud words go, it is not easy to call them back.
**CARL SANDBURG**

To knock a thing down, especially if it is cocked at an arrogant angle, is a deep delight to the blood.
**GEORGE SANTAYANA**

Pride may be allowed to this or that degree, else a man cannot keep up his dignity.
**JOHN SELDEN**

My pride fell with my fortunes.
**WILLIAM SHAKESPEARE**

Pride is a fruitful source of uneasiness. It keeps the mind in disquiet. Humility is the antidote to this evil.
**LYDIA SIGOURNEY**

If a proud man makes me keep my distance, the comfort is that he keeps his at the same time.
**JONATHAN SWIFT**

He that is proud of riches is a fool. For if he be exalted above his neighbors because he hath more gold, how much inferior is he to a gold mine.
**JEREMY TAYLOR**

We can believe almost anything if it be necessary to protect our pride.
**DOUGLAS A. THOM**

Undertake not to teach your equal in the art himself professes; it savors arrogancy.
**GEORGE WASHINGTON**

Take away the self-conceited, and there will be elbowroom in the world.
**BENJAMIN WHICHCOTE**

Remember, when the peacock struts his stuff he shows his backside to half the world.
**HERVE WIENER**

Early in life I had to choose between honest arrogance and hypocritical humility. I chose honest arrogance and have seen no occasion to change.
**FRANK LLOYD WRIGHT**

Conceit and confidence are both of them cheats. The first always imposes on itself; the second frequently deceives others.
**JOHANN ZIMMERMANN**

## *Principles*

Always vote for a principle, though you vote alone, and you may cherish the sweet reflection that your vote is never lost.
**JOHN QUINCY ADAMS**

He who floats with the current, who does not guide himself according to higher principles, who has no ideal, no convictions—such a man is a mere article of the world's furniture—a thing moved, instead of a living and moving being—an echo, not a voice.
**HENRI FRÉDÉRIC AMIEL**

You can dissolve everything in the world, even a great fortune, into atoms. And the fundamental principles which govern the handling of a few postage stamps and of millions of dollars are exactly the same. They are the common law of business, and the whole practice of commerce is founded on them. They are so simple that a fool can't learn them; so hard that a lazy man won't.
**PHILIP D. ARMOUR**

Do not consider anything for your interest which makes you break your word, quit your modesty or inclines you to any practice which will not bear the light or look the world in the face.
**MARCUS AURELIUS ANTONINUS**

In any assembly, the simplest way to stop the transacting of business and split the ranks is to appeal to a principle.
**JACQUES BARZUN**

Expedients are for an hour, but principles are for the ages. Just because the rains descend, and the winds blow, we cannot afford to build on the shifting sands.
**HENRY WARD BEECHER**

Great ideals and principles do not live from generation to generation just because they are right, nor even because they have been carefully legislated. Ideals and principles continue from generation to generation only when they are built into the hearts of the children as they grow up.
**GEORGE S. BENSON**

Many people are liberal in principle, reluctant in practice.
**JOHN M. BURGESS**

Our inheritance of well-founded, slowly conceived codes of honor, morals and manners, the passionate convictions which so many hundreds of millions share together of the principles of freedom and justice, are far more precious to us than anything which scientific discoveries could bestow.
**WINSTON CHURCHILL**

He who merely knows right principles is not equal to him who loves them.
**CONFUCIUS**

Men of principle are always bold, but those who are bold are not always men of principle.
**CONFUCIUS**

A precedent embalms a principle.
**BENJAMIN DISRAELI**

We have always found that, if our principles were right, the area over which they were applied did not matter. Size is only a matter of the multiplication table.
**HENRY FORD**

The principles we live by, in business and in social life, are the most important part of happiness. We need to be careful, upon achieving happiness, not to lose the virtues which have produced it.
**HARRY HARRISON**

So act that your principle of action might safely be made a law for the whole world.
**IMMANUEL KANT**

It's easy to have principles when you're rich. The important thing is to have principles when you're poor.
**RAY KROC**

Many men do not allow their principles to take root, but pull them up every now and then, as children do the flowers they have planted, to see if they are growing.
**HENRY WADSWORTH LONGFELLOW**

Principle—particularly moral principle—can never be a weathervane, spinning around this way and that with the shifting winds of expediency. Moral principle is a compass forever fixed and forever true—and that is as important in business as it is in the classroom.
EDWARD R. LYMAN

In vain do they talk of happiness who never subdued an impulse in obedience to a principle. He who never sacrificed a present to a future good, or a personal to a general one, can speak of happiness only as the blind speak of color.
HORACE MANN

One thing I certainly never was made for, and that is to put principles on and off at the dictation of a party, as a lackey changes his livery at his master's command.
HORACE MANN

The principles which men profess on any controverted subject are usually a very incomplete exponent of the opinions they really hold.
JOHN STUART MILL

I love the man that can smile in trouble, that can gather strength from distress, and grow brave by reflection. 'Tis the business of little minds to shrink, but he whose heart is firm, and whose conscience approves his conduct, will pursue his principles unto death.
THOMAS PAINE

There is a point, of course, where a man must take the isolated peak and break with all his associates for clear principle; but until that time comes he must work, if he would be of use, with men as they are. As long as the good in them overbalances the evil, let him work with them for the best that can be obtained.
THEODORE ROOSEVELT

Our principles are the springs of our actions; our actions, the springs of our happiness or misery. Too much care, therefore, cannot be taken in forming our principles.
PHILIP SKELTON

It is often easier to fight for a principle than to live up to it.
ADLAI STEVENSON

In life it is possible merely to throw a heap of stones together, but this pile is not beautiful. We pyramid to the heights only when we lay stone on stone according to a beautiful plan. If we have no faith in the principles with which we build life, we are defeated.
W. N. THOMAS, D.D.

Men with intellectual light alone may make advances without moral principle, but without that moral principle which gospel faith produces, permanent progress is impossible.
JAMES B. WALKER

## *Problems*

Nearly all our ills are the result of neglect in some way or other. And this truth may be said to apply to the ills of nations as well. Negligence is at the bottom of all decay. And decay always starts by showing little signs—or warnings. Then is the time to show interest and to be alert. There is nothing quite so easy as to neglect, and nothing quite so difficult as to repair that negligence. Negligence always carries a high price. It costs nothing to avoid it!
GEORGE MATTHEW ADAMS

A soul exasperated by its ills falls out with everything, with its friends and also with itself.
JOSEPH ADDISON

Those who do not complain are never pitied.
JANE AUSTEN

You can overcome anything if you don't bellyache.
BERNARD M. BARUCH

There is no problem of human nature which is insoluble.
RALPH J. BUNCHE

It is a general error to suppose the loudest complainers for the public to be the most anxious for the welfare.
EDMUND BURKE

If you think there's a solution, you're a part of the problem.
GEORGE CARLIN

In a free country there is much clamor with little suffering; in a despotic state there is little complaint but much suffering.
HIPPOLYTE CARNOT

Unless we are prepared to search our souls to discover what to say, and then how to say it effectively, we cannot expect to deal successfully with today's domestic and personal problems, not to mention those international issues on which our very lives depend.
EVERETT CASE

An unaspiring person always complaints. There is no end to his complaints. He bitterly complains even when the blessings of opportunity knock at his very door.
SRI CHINMOY

There are three modes of bearing the ills of life: by indifference, by philosophy, and by religion.
CHARLES CALEB COLTON

Nobody's problem is ideal. Nobody has things just as he would like them. The thing to do is to make a success with what material I have. It is sheer waste of time and soul-power to imagine what I would do if things were different. They are not different.
FRANK CRANE

Anyone who looks for the good can always find much for which to be grateful, or he can dwell on the present evil and wreck his composure. . . . There is always an answer for every problem.
LOUISE W. EGGLESTON

Before it can be solved, a problem must be clearly stated and defined.
WILLIAM FEATHER

Problems always appear big when incompetent men are working on them.
WILLIAM FEATHER

It's so much easier to suggest solutions when you don't know too much about the problem.
MALCOLM FORBES

When things are bad we take a bit of comfort in the thought that they could always be worse. And when they are, we find hope in the thought that things are so bad they have to get better.
MALCOLM FORBES

The reward for being a good problem solver is to be heaped with more and more difficult problems to solve!
BUCKMINSTER FULLER

Should one look through a red glass at a white lily, he would seem to see a red lily. But there would be no red lily. So it is with humanity's problems. They consist of false mental pictures.
M. D. GARBRICK

No one is more definite about the solution than the one who doesn't understand the problem.
ROBERT HALF

All problems become smaller if you don't dodge them but confront them. Touch a thistle timidly, and it pricks you; grasp it boldly, and its spines crumble.
WILLIAM F. HALSEY

There are people who always find a hair in their soup for the simple reason that when they sit down before it, they shake their heads until one falls in.
FRIEDRICH HEBBEL

Every age has its problem, by solving which, humanity is helped forward.
HEINRICH HEINE

Problems worthy of attack prove their worth by hitting back.
PIET HEIN

Problems are the price of progress: Don't bring me anything but trouble—good news weakens me.
CHARLES F. KETTERING

Meddling with another man's folly is always thankless work.
RUDYARD KIPLING

Who hath not known ill fortune, never knew himself, or his own virtue.
MALLETT

No matter how big and tough a problem may be, get rid of confusion by taking one little step towards solution. Do something. Then try again. At the worst so long as you don't do it the same way twice, you will eventually use up all the wrong ways of doing it and thus the next try will be the right one.
GEORGE F. NORDENHOLT

It's not the tragedies that kill us, it's the messes.
DOROTHY PARKER

Every man has a rainy corner in his life, from which bad weather besets him.
JEAN PAUL RICHTER

Suffer the ill and look for the good.
JAMES SANDFORD

If this nation is going to survive meaningfully, and then perhaps grow decently, it has got to begin to know and accept enormous deprivation.
WILLIAM SAROYAN

Whoever fails to turn aside the ills of life by prudent forethought must submit to the course of destiny.
JOHANN FRIEDRICH VON SCHILLER

We have no more right to put our discordant states of mind into the lives of those around us and rob them of their sunshine and brightness than we have to enter their houses and steal their silverware.
JULIA SETON

It will generally be found that men who are constantly lamenting their ill luck are only reaping the consequences of their own neglect, mismanagement, and improvidence, or want of application.
SAMUEL SMILES

A great part of this life consists of contemplating what we cannot cure.
ROBERT LOUIS STEVENSON

We may be pretty certain that persons whom all the world treats ill deserve the treatment they get. The

world is a looking glass, and gives back to every man the reflection of his own face.
WILLIAM MAKEPEACE THACKERAY

Conceal thy domestic ills.
THALES

The most important thing to do in solving a problem is to begin.
FRANK TYGER

## Procrastination

When duty calls me, I'm prepared
As though our goals were aimed and shared.
I draw my breath in, shoulders straight,
And quietly procrastinate.
ALISON W. BIRCH

"But" is a word that cools many a warm impulse, stifles many a kindly thought, puts a dead stop to many a brotherly deed. No one would ever love his neighbor as himself if he listened to all the buts that could be said.
EDWARD BULWER-LYTTON

By the street of By-and-By, one arrives at the house of Never.
MIGUEL DE CERVANTES

Postponement: the sincerest form of rejection.
ROBERT HALF

Sure bet: Anything delayed will get further delayed.
ROBERT HALF

There is no pleasure in having nothing to do; the fun is in having lots to do and not doing it.
MARY LITTLE

Putting off a hard thing makes it impossible.
GEORGE HORACE LORIMER

Procrastination is the art of keeping up with yesterday.
DONALD MARQUIS

While we are postponing, life speeds by.
SENECA

## Production

Unless each man produces more than he receives, increases his output, there will be less for him and all the others.
BERNARD M. BARUCH

Hating hard work can get to be such an obsession that you won't let it pile up.
H. C. BROWN

Produce, produce! Were it but the pitifulest, infinitesimal fraction of a product, produce it in God's name. 'Tis the utmost thou hast in thee? Out with it then! Up, up! Whatsoever thy hand findeth to do, do it with thy whole might.
THOMAS CARLYLE

It is not size that counts in business. Some companies with $500,000 capital net more profits than other companies with $5,000,000. Size is a handicap unless efficiency goes with it.
HERBERT N. CASSON

Efficiency is doing things—not wishing you could do them, dreaming about them, or wondering if you can do them.
FRANK CRANE

One of the most deeply rooted fallacies in the mind of the working man is the idea that to produce less per hour will benefit him, because it will make his work last longer. This is a complete misconception of the fundamental truth that the source of all wealth lies in increased production. The worker fails to understand that the raises in wages, the better job, the continued employment he wants, and the high standard of living he enjoys, all depend upon increasing the rate of production.
FRED C. CRAWFORD

There can be no economy where there is no efficiency.
BENJAMIN DISRAELI

Let every employer get this into his mind: Production resulting from long hours worked unwillingly cannot but be less satisfactory than production from shorter hours worked willingly. . . . A willing, cheerful worker, with his heart in his job, will turn out more work and more satisfactory work in 44 hours a week than an unwilling worker, dissatisfied with his conditions, will turn out in 54 hours. It is good business, therefore, for every employer to go as far as he possibly can in reaching a schedule agreeable to his people.
B. C. FORBES

As it is with an individual, so it is with a nation. One must produce to have, or one will become a have-not.
HENRY GEORGE

The best hope of raising our own standards lies in the progressive expansion of production both here and abroad and making sure that the gains of increased productivity are, in fact, applied to social advance.
CARTER GOODRICH

If you reward nonproduction, you get nonproduction. When you penalize production, you get nonproduction.
L. RON HUBBARD

The genius of America is production; and a large percentage of our productive enterprises are headed by men who have come up from the worker's bench.
WILLIAM S. KNUDSEN

Historically the phenomenal growth of capacity of the American economy has come from a relatively large increase in production per man-hour and a much smaller increase in the size of the labor force; it has taken place in spite of a 25% reduction in working hours over the past 50 years.
FRANK D. NEWBURY

There is not, never has been, and never will be any substitute for productive work. No amount of legislation, no amount of money, borrowed or coined, no economic prestidigitation, governmental or otherwise, can, as such, increase by one iota the wealth of a nation or the standard of living of a people. Existing wealth or property can be and is being redistributed by law, but new wealth can be created only by men and by the man-made machines they guide.
PHILIP D. REED

To contrive is nothing! To construct is something! To produce is everything!
CAPT. EDWARD V. RICKENBACKER

It is more than probable that the average man could, with no injury to his health, increase his efficiency fifty percent.
WALTER DILL SCOTT

The efficiency of most workers is beyond the control of the management and depends more than has been supposed upon the willingness of men to do their best.
SUMNER H. SLICHTER

Only in more production and in new production can the American standard of living be increased and the economy be sound.
ALFRED P. SLOAN, JR.

## *Profit*

What needs to be cultivated among men interested in social relationships whether as owner, manager or employee, producer or consumer, seller or buyer, partner or competitor, is self-control, refraining from unfair advantage, determination to give value as well as to take it; the appreciation that immediate gain is not the principal consideration; that one group can not continue to profit at the expense of another without eventual loss to both; that all classes of men are mutually dependent on the services of each other; that the best service yields the greatest profit.
PRESTON S. ARKWRIGHT

Higher prices are themselves inflation and not merely the result of it. They are accelerated and not stopped by taxation. . . . It isn't high prices that persuade the high cost and marginal producer to make the investment necessary to bring him into production. It is the promise of profit. High prices without profit merely requires more investment to support turnover and inventory.
BERNARD M. BARUCH

I don't want to do business with those who don't make a profit, because they can't give the best service.
LEE BRISTOL

If you mean to profit, learn to please.
WINSTON CHURCHILL

It is a socialist idea that making profits is a vice. I consider the real vice is making losses.
WINSTON CHURCHILL

Civilization and profits go hand in hand.
CALVIN COOLIDGE

When shallow critics denounce the profit motive inherent in our system of private enterprise, they ignore the fact that it is an economic support of every human right we possess and without it, all rights would disappear.
DWIGHT D. EISENHOWER

No matter what you may read about [A&P heir] Huntington Hartford and his uniquely successful efforts to get rid of the money his family once made selling you groceries, today the big Fooders as well as the little ones net a shamefully tiny profit on their whopping volume of business. As Winn-Dixie's Davis put it to a Forbes editor, "If a woman buys $10 worth of groceries in one of our stores and tips the bag boy a quarter, he's made more on the sale than we have. And we're the most profitable major chain."
MALCOLM FORBES

Several weeks of summer vacation in the Thirties I spent working at $15 a week in the Forbes office. . . . I worked in the mail cage, where envelopes were slit and subscription payments extracted. Dad used to come pounding down the office aisle and pause long enough to ask, "How much today?" Inevitably the answer was inadequate—except once. That day the controller said excitedly, "Mr. Forbes, the ledger shows a slight profit this month!" . . . My father turned to him and said, "Young man, I don't give

a damn what your books show. Do we have any money in the bank?"
**MALCOLM FORBES**

When profit is unshared, it's less likely to grow greater.
**MALCOLM FORBES**

Profit is the product of labor plus capital multiplied by management. You can hire the first two. The last must be inspired.
**FOST**

The profit system is simply a fair and just reward for effort, and it applies to every executive and every workman.
**ERNEST HERMANN**

Where profit is, loss is hidden near by.
**JAPANESE PROVERB**

If thou will receive profit, read with humility, simplicity and faith, and seek not at any time the fame of being learned.
**THOMAS À KEMPIS**

Profit is a must. There can be no security for any employee in any business that doesn't make money. There can be no growth for that business. There can be no opportunity for the individual to achieve his personal ambitions unless his company makes money.
**DUNCAN C. MENZIES**

The successful producer of an article sells it for more than it cost him to make, and that's his profit. But the customer buys it only because it is worth more to him than he pays for it, and that's his profit. No one can long make a profit producing anything unless the customer makes a profit using it.
**SAMUEL B. PETTENGILL**

Nothing contributes so much to the prosperity and happiness of a country as high profits.
**DAVID RICARDO**

Profit is the ignition system of our economic engine.
**CHARLES SAWYER**

No profit grows where is no pleasure taken; in brief, sir, study what you most affect.
**WILLIAM SHAKESPEARE**

## *Progress*

The measure of progress of civilization is the progress of the people.
**GEORGE BANCROFT**

The time of day I do not tell,
As some do, by the clock,
Or by the distant chiming bells
Set on some steeple rack,
But by the progress that I see
In what I have to do.
It's either Done O'clock to me,
Or only Half-Past Through.
**JOHN KENDRICK BANGS**

Action and reaction, ebb and flow, trial and error, change—this is the rhythm of our living. Out of our overconfidence, fear; out of our fear, clearer vision, fresh hope. And out of hope, progress.
**BRUCE BARTON**

We should so live and labor in our time that what came to us as seed may go to the next generation as blossom, and that which came to us as blossom may go to them as fruit. That is what we mean by progress.
**HENRY WARD BEECHER**

Occasionally worshippers of the past put obstructions in the way of progress by saying that we must be true to our fathers, but no church can long continue to live on its past. There is only one way that we can be true to our fathers and that is to carry on to completion the work they have so nobly begun.
JOHN S. BONNELL, D.D.

The grandest of all laws is the law of progressive development. Under it, in the wide sweep of things, men grow wiser as they grow older, and societies better.
CHRISTIAN BOVÉE

Progress is the law of life; man is not a man as yet.
ROBERT BROWNING

Nothing in progression can rest on its original plan. We might as well think of rocking a grown man in the cradle of an infant.
EDMUND BURKE

All progress is based upon the universal innate desire on the part of every organism to live beyond its income.
SAMUEL BUTLER

The whole story of human and personal progress is an unmitigated tale of denials today—denials of rest, denials or repose and comfort and ease and pleasure—that tomorrow may be richer.
JAMES CARROLL

Progress is the mother of problems.
G. K. CHESTERTON

We are either progressing or retrograding all the while; there is no such thing as remaining stationary in this life.
JAMES FREEMAN CLARKE

Little progress can be made by merely attempting to repress what is evil; our great hope lies in developing what is good.
CALVIN COOLIDGE

Unless man in the midst of all his modernism finds a middle ground upon which to adjust his differences, there can be no mutual progress, human liberty is sacrificed and talent and free-will suffer. Improvement of the standards of living of the whole people is paramount, if civilization is to escape world fanaticism.
ARNOLD W. CRAFT

Progress in every age results only from the fact that there are some men and women who refuse to believe that what they knew to be right cannot be done.
RUSSELL W. DAVENPORT

Progress is nothing but the victory of laughter over dogma.
BENJAMIN DECASSERES

The man who will neither play nor do business unless everything is just to his liking and notions, retards rather than contributes to progress.
HENRY L. DOHERTY

Social progress does not have to be bought at the price of individual freedom. Our founders and forebears showed us a better way. I refuse to believe that, in traveling that way, we have come to a dead end.
JOHN FOSTER DULLES

Restlessness and discontent are the first necessities of progress.
THOMAS EDISON

Progress in industry depends very largely on the enterprise of deep-thinking men, who are ahead of the times in their ideas.
SIR WILLIAM ELLIS

All our progress is an unfolding, like the vegetable bud. You have first an instinct, then an opinion, then a knowledge, as the plant has root, bud and fruit. Trust the instinct to the end, though you can render no reason.
RALPH WALDO EMERSON

Progress is the activity of today and the assurance of tomorrow.
RALPH WALDO EMERSON

No man is able to make progress when he is wavering between opposite things.
EPICTETUS

The way to get ahead is to start now. If you start now, you will know a lot next year that you don't know now and that you would not have known next year if you had waited.
WILLIAM FEATHER

Technical progress is the real hope for the future of the country; political reform cannot do anything for us. The engineer is engaged in a war of human liberation; his technique is different. The political reformer fights against ambition and initiative; the engineer is fighting against slavery. It is better for all to live well with a few rich than for all to live in slavery on a lower level.
GLENN FRANK

I am suffocated and lost when I have not the bright feeling of progression.
MARGARET FULLER

The highest function of conservation is to keep what progressiveness has accomplished.
R. H. FULTON

The progress is made by correcting the mistakes resulting from the making of progress.
CLAUDE GIBB

The concept of progress acts as a protective mechanism to shield us from the terrors of the future.
FRANK HERBERT

All progress and growth is a matter of change, but change must be growth within our social and government concepts if it should not destroy them.
HERBERT HOOVER

Anything that interferes with individual progress ultimately will retard group progress.
GEORGE H. HOUSTON

Progress comes from the intelligent use of experience.
ELBERT HUBBARD

There is no law of progress. Our future is in our own hands, to make or to mar. It will be an uphill fight to the end, and would we have it otherwise? Let no one suppose that evolution will ever exempt us from struggles. "You forget," said the Devil, with a chuckle, "that I have been evolving too."
DEAN INGE

The progress of the world depends upon the men who walk in the fresh furrows and through the rustling corn; upon those whose faces are radiant with the glare of furnace fires; upon the delvers in mines, and the workers in shops; upon those who give to the Winter air the ringing music of the axe; upon those who battle with the boisterous billows

of the sea; upon the inventors and discoverers; upon the brave thinkers.
ROBERT G. INGERSOLL

Unprogressiveness . . . is usually a function of wrong thinking rather than age, Inflexibility of mind and resistance to new ideas crop up among the young as well as the old. To progress, one must be mentally alert and striving for self-improvement.
ALBERT JOHNSON

You can't sit on the lid of progress. If you do, you will be blown to pieces.
HENRY J. KAISER

Great steps in human progress are made by things that don't work the way philosophy thought they should. If things always worked the way they should, you could write the history of the world from now on. But they don't, and it is those deviations from the normal that make human progress.
CHARLES F. KETTERING

The price of progress is trouble.
CHARLES F. KETTERING

Life does not stand still. Where there is no progress there is disintegration. Today a thousand doors of enterprise are open to you, inviting you to useful work. To live at this time is an inestimable privilege, and a sacred obligation devolves upon you to make right use of your opportunities. Today is the day in which to attempt and achieve something worth while.
GRENVILLE KLEISER

The moving van is a symbol of more than our restlessness, it is the most conclusive evidence possible of our progress.
LOUIS KRONENBERGER

The prudent, penniless beginner in the world labors for wages for a while, saves a surplus with which to buy tools or land for himself another while, and at length hires another new beginner to help him. This is the just and generous and prosperous system which opens the way to all, gives hope to all, and consequently energy, and progress, and improvement of conditions to all.
ABRAHAM LINCOLN

At every crossing on the road that leads to the future, each progressive spirit is opposed by a thousand appointed to guard the past.
MAURICE MAETERLINCK

The moment a man ceases to progress, to grow higher, wider and deeper, then his life becomes stagnant.
ORISON S. MARDEN

Progress consists largely of learning to apply laws and truths that have always existed.
JOHN ALLAN MAY

All genuine progress results from finding new facts. No law can be passed to make an acre yield three hundred bushels. God has already established the laws. It is four us to discover them, and to learn the facts by which we can obey them.
WHEELER MCMILLEN

Progress might have been all right once, but it's gone on too long.
OGDEN NASH

They keep saying you can't stop progress, but it's coming so fast the sewage plants can't keep up with it.
LESTER J. NORRIS

By a peculiar prerogative, not only each individual is making daily advances in the sciences, and may

make advances in morality (which is the science, by way of eminence, of living well and being happy), but all mankind together is making a continual progress in proportion as the universe grows older. So that the whole human race, during the course of so many ages, may be considered as one man who never ceases to live and learn.
**BLAISE PASCAL**

Great strides in human progress are being made by men who delve deeply into the imagination, then through the medium of hard work, bring fancy into reality.
**ROBERT K. PATTERSON**

If human progress had been merely a matter of leadership we should be in Utopia today.
**THOMAS B. REED**

Progress is not made by taking pride in our present standards but by critically examining these standards, hypothetically setting higher standards and attempting to achieve them.
**JUDA L. ROSENSTEIN**

The greater part of progress is the desire to progress.
**SENECA**

All progress is initiated by challenging current conceptions, and executed by supplanting existing institutions.
**GEORGE BERNARD SHAW**

Progress in the half-century ahead will continue to be the creation of mind rather than of hand; of stout hearts rather than stern measures.
**NORMAN G. SHIDLE**

The true law of the race is progress and development. Whenever civilization pauses in the march of conquest, it is overthrown by the barbarian.
**WILLIAM SIMMS**

Our vast progress in transportation, past and future, is only a symbol of the progress that is possible by constantly striving toward new horizons in every human activity. Who can say what new horizons lie before us if we can but maintain the initiative and develop the imagination to penetrate them—new economic horizons, new horizons in the art of government, new social horizons, new horizons expanding in all directions, to the end that greater degrees of well-being may be enjoyed by every one, everywhere.
**ALFRED P. SLOAN, JR.**

Progress is always the product of fresh thinking, and much of it thinking which to practical men bears the semblance of dreaming.
**ROBERT GORDON SPROU**

Complacency is the enemy of progress.
**DAVE STUTMAN**

Scientific progress is like mounting a ladder; each step upwards is followed by a brief pause while the body regains its balance, and we can no more disregard the steps which have gone before than we could cut away the lower part of the ladder.
**OLIVER G. SUTTON**

Those who believe that we have reached the limit of business progress and employment opportunity in this country are like the farmer who had two windmills and pulled one down because he was afraid there was not enough wind for both.
**MORRIS S. TREMAINE**

Progress is not created by contented people.
**FRANK TYGER**

Progressiveness is looking forward intelligently, looking within critically, and moving on incessantly.
**WALDO PONDRAY WARREN**

To-day's pioneers are building to-morrow's progress.
THOMAS J. WATSON

Whenever an individual or a business decides that success has been attained, progress stops.
THOMAS J. WATSON

Certainly it is true that the constant striving for something better—the price of progress—adds to the total of human happiness. It stimulates industry by creating new wants. It multiplies opportunities for the employment of brain and brawn. And it bridges the gaps between peaks of prosperity and helps take up the slack during times of reaction.
JOHN N. WILLYS

In all human activities, practically in all matters of business, times of stress and difficulty are seasons of opportunity when the seeds of progress are sown.
THOMAS F. WOODLOCK

## *Promises*

Every civilization rests on a set of promises. . . . If the promises are broken too often, the civilization dies, no matter how rich it may be, or how mechanically clever. Hope and faith depend on the promises; if hope and faith go, everything goes.
HERBERT AGAR

You cannot live on other people's promises, but if you promise others enough, you can live on your own.
MARK CAINE

A promise is an I.O.U.
ROBERT HALF

Great men, till they have gained their ends, are giants in their promises, but, those obtained, weak pygmies in their performance.
PHILIP MASSINGER

To breed an animal with the right to make promises—is not this the paradoxical problem nature has set herself with regard to man?
FRIEDRICH WILHELM NIETZSCHE

Magnificent promises are always to be suspected.
THEODORE W. PARKER

He who promises runs in debt.
TALMUD

Undertake not what you cannot perform, but be careful to keep your promise.
GEORGE WASHINGTON

## *Property*

People who never had enough thrift and forethought to buy and pay for property in the first place seldom have enough to keep property up after they have gained it in some other way.
THOMAS NIXON CARVER

Property is desirable as the ground work of moral independence, as a means of improving the faculties, and of doing good to others, and as the agent in all that distinguishes the civilized man from the savage.
JAMES FENIMORE COOPER

How can you trust people who are poor and own no property? . . . Inequality of property will exist as long as liberty exists.
ALEXANDER HAMILTON

Few rich men own their own property. The property owns them.
**ROBERT G. INGERSOLL**

There is a desire of property in the sanest and best men, which Nature seems to have implanted as conservative of her works, and which is necessary to encourage and keep alive the arts.
**WALTER SAVAGE LANDOR**

The strongest bond of human sympathy, outside of the family relation, should be one uniting all working people, of all nations, and tongues, and kindreds. Nor should this lead us to a war upon property, or the owners of property. Property is the fruit of labor; property is desirable; is a positive good in the world. That some should be rich shows that others may become rich and, hence, is just encouragement to industry and enterprise. Let not him who is houseless pull down the house of another, but let him labor diligently and build one for himself, thus, by example, assuring that his own shall be safe from violence when built.
**ABRAHAM LINCOLN**

Property is dear to men not only for the sensual pleasure it can afford, but also because it is the bulwark of all they hold dearest on earth, and above all else, because it is the safeguard of those they love most against misery and all physical distress.
**WILLIAM GRAHAM SUMNER**

The accumulation of property is no guarantee of the development of character, but the development of character, or of any other good whatever, is impossible without property.
**WILLIAM GRAHAM SUMNER**

## *Prosperity*

To rejoice in the prosperity of another is to partake of it.
**WILLIAM AUSTIN**

If prosperity is regarded as the reward of virtue, it will be regarded as the symptom of virtue.
**G. K. CHESTERTON**

In prosperity let us particularly avoid pride, disdain and arrogance.
**CICERO**

When prosperity comes, do not use all of it.
**CONFUCIUS**

Prosperity cannot be divorced from humanity.
**CALVIN COOLIDGE**

Prosperity is only an instrument to be used, not a deity to be worshipped.
**CALVIN COOLIDGE**

Everything in the world may be endured except continuing prosperity.
**JOHANN WOLFGANG VON GOETHE**

Few enjoyments are given from the open and liberal hand of nature; but by art, labor and industry we can extract them in great abundance. Hence, the ideas of property become necessary in all civil society.
**DAVID HUME**

Prosperity is too apt to prevent us from examining our conduct, but adversity leads us to think properly of our state, and so is most beneficial to us.
**JOHNSON**

The prosperity of a people is proportionate to the number of hands and minds usefully employed. To the community, sedition is a fever, corruption is a gangrene, and idleness is an atrophy. Whatever body or society wastes more than it acquires, must gradually decay, and every being that continues to be fed, and eases to labor, takes away something from the public stock.
JOHNSON

In adversity assume the countenance of prosperity, and in prosperity moderate the temper and desires.
LIVY

So long as a man enjoys prosperity, he cares not whether he is beloved.
LUCAN

The old thought that one cannot be rich except at the expense of his neighbor, must pass away. True prosperity adds to the richness of the whole world, such as that of the man who makes two trees grow where only one grew before. The parasitical belief in prosperity as coming by the sacrifices of others has no place in the mind that thinks true. My benefit is your benefit, your success is my success, should be the basis of all our wealth.
ANNE RIX MILTZ

I hold it to be our duty to see that the wage-worker, the small producer, the ordinary consumer, shall get their fair share of business prosperity. But it either is or ought to be evident to everyone that business has to prosper before anybody can get any benefit from it.
THEODORE ROOSEVELT

You cannot create prosperity by law. Sustained thrift, industry, application, intelligence, are the only things that ever do, or ever will, create prosperity. But you can very easily destroy prosperity by law.
THEODORE ROOSEVELT

Few of us can stand prosperity. Another man's, I mean.
MARK TWAIN

Prosperity is the surest breeder of insolence I know.
MARK TWAIN

Take care to be an economist in prosperity: there is no fear of your being one in adversity.
JOHANN ZIMMERMANN

## *Prudence*

Prudence is no doubt a valuable quality, but prudence which degenerates into timidity is very seldom the path to safety.
VISCOUNT CECIL

Judgement is not on all occasions required, but prudence is.
LORD CHESTERFIELD

It is a truth but too well known, that rashness attends youth, as prudence does old age.
CICERO

Prudence is the necessary ingredient in all the virtues, without which they degenerate into folly and excess.
JEREMY COLLIER

It is impossible to live pleasurably without living prudently, and honorably, and justly; or to live prudently, and honorably, and justly, without living pleasurably.
EPICURUS

Prudence is a presumption of the future, contracted from the experience of time past.
THOMAS HOBBES

Prudence is but experience, which equal time equally bestows on all men, in all things they equally apply themselves unto.
**THOMAS HOBBES**

No other protection is wanting, provided you are under the guidance of prudence.
**JUVENAL**

Who makes quick us of the moment is a genius of prudence.
**JOHANN LAVATER**

. . . I think there is some virtue in eagerness, whether its object prove true or false. How utterly dull would be a wholly prudent man. . . . !
**ALDO LEOPOLD**

The prudent, penniless beginner in the world labors for wages for a while, saves a surplus with which to buy tools or land for himself another while, and at length hires another new beginner to help him. This is the just, and generous and prosperous system which opens the way to all, gives hope to all, and consequently energy, and progress, and improvement of conditions to all.
**ABRAHAM LINCOLN**

Temper your enjoyments with prudence, lest there be written on your heart that fearful word "satiety."
**FRANCIS QUARLES**

To act coolly, intelligently and prudently in perilous circumstances is the test of a man and also a nation.
**ADLAI STEVENSON**

Where destiny blunders, human prudence will not avail.
**PUBLILIUS SYRUS**

Is not he imprudent, who, seeing the tide making toward him apace, will sleep till the sea overwhelms him?
**JOHN TILLOTSON**

Often the prudent, far from making their destinies, succumb to them; it is destiny which makes them prudent.
**VOLTAIRE**

## *Purpose*

He who wishes to fulfill his mission in the world must be a man of one idea, that is, of one great overmastering purpose, overshadowing all his aims, and guiding and controlling his entire life.
**JULIUS BATE**

What men want is not talent, it is purpose; in other words, not the power to achieve, but will to labor. I believe that labor judiciously and continuously applied becomes genius.
**EDWARD BULWER-LYTTON**

A man's life may stagnate as literally as water may stagnate, and just as motion and direction are the remedy for one, so purpose and activity are the remedy for the other.
**JOHN BURROUGHS**

Have a purpose in life, and having it, throw into your work such strength of mind and muscle as God has given you.
**THOMAS CARLYLE**

The man without a purpose is like a ship without a rudder—a wait, a nothing, a no man.
**THOMAS CARLYLE**

I have brought myself by long meditation to the conviction that a human being with a settled purpose must accomplish it, and that nothing can resist a will which will stake even existence upon its fulfillment.
**BENJAMIN DISRAELI**

After all, what do we ask of life, here or indeed hereafter, but leave to serve, to live, to commune with our fellowmen, and with ourselves, and from the lap of earth to look up into the face of God?
**MICHAEL FAIRLESS**

The purpose of life is to believe, to hope, and to strive.
**INDIRA GANDHI**

What our deepest self craves is not mere enjoyment, but some supreme purpose that will enlist all our powers and will give unity and direction to our life. We can never know the profoundest joy without a conviction that our life is significant—not a meaningless episode. The loftiest aim of human life is the ethical perfecting of mankind—the transfiguration of humanity.
**HENRY J. GOLDING**

Find a purpose in life so big it will challenge every capacity to be at your best.
**DAVID O. MCKAY**

A purpose is the eternal condition of success.
**THEODORE T. MUNGER**

Purpose is what gives life a meaning.
**CHARLES HENRY PARKHURST, D.D.**

All the world over it is true that a double-minded man is unstable in all his ways, like a wave on the streamlet, tossed hither and thither with every eddy of its tide. A determinate purpose in life and a steady adhesion to it through all disadvantages, are indispensable conditions of success.
**WILLIAM M. PUNSHON**

The goal of life is imminent in each moment, each thought, word, act, and does not have to be sought apart from these. It consists in no specific achievement, but the state of mind in which everything is done, the quality infused into existence. The function of man is not to attain an object, but to fulfill a purpose; not to accomplish but to be accomplished.
**S. E. STANTON**

There is one quality more important than know-how, and we cannot accuse the U.S. of any undue amount of it. This is know-how by which we determine not only how to accomplish our purposes, but what our purposes are to be.
**NORBERT WIENER**

## Qualities

The nobler sort of man emphasizes the good qualities in others, and does not accentuate the bad. The inferior does the reverse. . . . The nobler sort of man pays special attention to nine points. He is anxious to see clearly, to hear distinctly, to be kindly in his looks, respectful in his demeanor, conscientious in his speech, earnest in his affairs. When in doubt, he is careful to inquire; when in anger, he thinks of the consequences; when offered an opportunity for gain, he thinks only of his duty.
CONFUCIUS

I believe that for permanent survival, man must balance science with other qualities of life, qualities of body and spirit as well as those of mind—qualities he cannot develop when he lets mechanics and luxury insulate him too greatly from the earth to which he was born.
CHARLES A. LINDBERGH

A great man is made up of qualities that meet or make great occasions.
JAMES RUSSELL LOWELL

Credit to the fullest the good qualities to be found in others, even though they may far outshine your own.
WILLIAM M. PECK

Any man will usually get from other men just what he is expecting of them. If he is looking for friendship he will likely receive it. If his attitude is that of indifference, it will beget indifference. And if a man is looking for a fight he will in all likelihood be accommodated in that. Men can be stimulated to show off their good qualities to the leader who seems to think they have good qualities.
JOHN RICHELSEN

It is not enough to have great qualities; we must also have the management of them.
FRANÇOIS DE LA ROCHEFOUCAULD

A man has generally the good or ill qualities which he attributes to mankind.
WILLIAM SHENSTONE

To bring the best human qualities to anything like perfection, to fill them with the sweet juices of courtesy and charity, prosperity, or, at all events, a moderate amount of it, is required.
ALEXANDER SMITH

Personal deficiencies might be termed negative qualities and include unreliability, failure to cooperate, laziness, untidiness, trouble making, interference and dishonesty.
Positive qualities would include willingness, cheerfulness, courtesy, honesty, neatness, reliability and temperance.
Many fail in their work because they are unable to overcome one personal deficiency. Check up on yourself. Don't be afraid to put yourself under a microscope.
Eliminate your negative qualities. Develop your positive ones. You can't win with the check mark in the wrong place.
M. WINETTE

## Quality

Quality isn't something that can be argued into an article or promised into it. It must be put there. If it isn't put there, the finest sales talk in the world won't act as a substitute.
C. G. CAMPBELL

I have never known a concern to make a decided success that did not do good, honest work, and even in these days of fiercest competition, when everything would seem to be a matter of price, there lies still at the root of great business success the very much more important factor of quality. The effect of attention to quality, upon every man in the service, from the president of the concern down to the humblest laborer, cannot be overestimated.
ANDREW CARNEGIE

The surest foundation of a manufacturing concern is quality. After that, and a long way after, comes cost.
ANDREW CARNEGIE

Quality is never an accident; it is always the result of high intention, sincere effort, intelligent direction and skillful execution; it represents the wise choice of many alternatives, the cumulative experience of many masters of craftsmanship. Quality also marks the search for an ideal after necessity has been satisfied and mere usefulness achieved.
WILL A. FOSTER

High people, Sir, are the best: Take a hundred ladies of quality, you'll find them better wives, better mothers, more willing to sacrifice their own pleasures to their children, than a hundred other women.
SAMUEL JOHNSON

The civilization of a country consists in the quality of life that is lived there, and this quality shows plainest in the things that people choose to talk about when they talk together, and in the way they choose to talk about them.
A. J. NOCK

People forget how fast you did a job—but they remember how well you did it.
HOWARD W. NEWTON

No matter how small and unimportant what we are doing may seem, if we do it well, it may soon become the step that will lead us to better things.
CHANNING POLLOCK

If a thing is old, it is a sign that it was fit to live. Old families, old customs, old styles survive because they are fit to survive. The guarantee of continuity is quality. Submerge the good in a flood of the new, and the good will come back to join the good which the new brings with it. Old-fashioned hospitality, old-fashioned politeness, old-fashioned honor in business had qualities of survival. These will come back.
CAPT. EDWARD V. RICKENBACKER

Quality is never an accident; it is always the result of intelligent efforts.
JOHN RUSKIN

Professionalism means consistency of quality.
FRANK TYGER

## Questions

"Why" and "How" are words so important that they cannot be too often used.
NAPOLEON BONAPARTE

Charm is a way of getting the answer "Yes" without having asked any clear question.
ALBERT CAMUS

A prudent question is one-half of wisdom.
**FRANCIS BACON**

It's very flattering to ask others about matters they're little qualified to discuss.
**MALCOLM FORBES**

One who never asks either knows everything or nothing.
**MALCOLM FORBES**

The smart ones ask when they don't know. And, sometimes, when they do.
**MALCOLM FORBES**

It's easier to see both sides of a question than the answer.
**ARNOLD GLASOW**

Both sides of a question do not belong to the poor old question at all, but to the opposing views which bedevil it.
**HENRY S. HASKINS**

Some men see things as they are and ask, "Why?" I dream things that never were and ask, "Why not?"
**ROBERT F. KENNEDY**

I had six honest serving men—they taught me all I knew: Their names were Where and What and When—and Why and How and Who.
**RUDYARD KIPLING**

No man really becomes a fool until he stops asking questions.
**CHARLES P. STEINMETZ**

It is not every question that deserves an answer.
**PUBLILIUS SYRUS**

Questions are never indiscreet, answers sometimes are.
**OSCAR WILDE**

The riddle does not exist. If a question can be put at all, then it can also be answered.
**LUDWIG WITTGENSTEIN**

# R

## Reading

Reading maketh a full man; conference a ready man; and writing an exact man; and, therefore, if a man write little, he had need have a great memory; if he confer little, he had need have a present wit; and if he read little, he had need have much cunning, to seem to know that he doth not.
**FRANCIS BACON**

I read for three things; first, to know what the world has done the last twenty-four hours, and is about to do today; second, for the knowledge that I specially want in my work; and third, for what will bring my mind into a proper mood.
**HENRY WARD BEECHER**

It is well to read everything of something, and something of everything.
**HENRY BROUGHAM**

Official warnings pummel us
With printed cautions we're to heed:
This may seem apt and yet it's sad
When maybe half of us can't read.
**ART BUCK**

To read without reflecting is like eating without digesting.
**EDMUND BURKE**

I no sooner come into the library, but I bolt the door to me, excluding lust, avarice and all such vices, whose nurse is idleness, the mother of ignorance and melancholy herself, and in the very lap of eternity, amongst so many divine souls, I take my seat, with so lofty a spirit and sweet content that I pity all our great ones and rich men that know not this happiness.
**RICHARD BURTON**

Happy is he who has laid up in his youth, and held fast in all fortune, a genuine and passionate love for reading.
**RUFUS CHOATE**

A man may as well expect to grow stronger by always eating as wiser by always reading.
**JEREMY COLLYER**

Reading provides the only way I know of by which children can see the whole view of how people who are in earnest about it grow slowly but surely into the habit of right conduct.
**ANNIS DUFF**

We sometimes receive letters from businessmen who say they are too busy to read. The man who is too busy to read is never likely to lead. The executive who aspires to success must keep himself well informed. His reading must not be confined to the reports of his own business laid on his desk, or to strictly trade journals, or to newspaper headlines. He must study what is going on throughout his own country and throughout the world. He must not remain blind to financial, industrial, economic trends, evolutions, revolutions.
**B. C. FORBES**

If you can read and don't, you're dumb.
**MALCOLM FORBES**

Reading makes a full man, meditation a profound man, discourse a clear man.
**BENJAMIN FRANKLIN**

Let us read with method, and propose to ourselves an end to what our studies may point. The use of reading is to aid us in thinking.
**EDWARD GIBBON**

My early and invincible love of reading I would not exchange for all the riches of India.
**EDWARD GIBBON**

To teach people to read without teaching them not to believe everything they read is only to prepare them for a new slavery.
**JEAN GUEHENNO**

The book which you read from a sense of duty, or because for any reason you must, does not commonly make friends with you. It may happen that it will yield you an unexpected delight, but this will be in its own unentreated way and in spite of your good intentions.
**WILLIAM DEAN HOWELLS**

What sense of superiority it gives one to escape reading some book which everyone else is reading.
**ALICE JAMES**

One ought to read just as inclination takes him, for what he reads as a task will do him little good.
**JOHNSON**

I forget the greater part of what I read, but all the same it nourishes my mind.
**GEORG CHRISTOPH LICHTENBERG**

Have you ever rightly considered what the mere ability to read means? That it is the key which admits us to the whole world of thought and fancy and imagination? To the company of saint and sage, of the wisest and the wittiest at their wisest and wittiest moment? That it enables us to see with the keenest eyes, hear with the finest ears, and listen to the sweetest voices of all time? More than that, it annihilates time and space for us.
**JAMES RUSSELL LOWELL**

Resolve to edge in a little reading every day, if it is but a single sentence. If you gain fifteen minutes a day, it will make itself felt at the end of the year.
**HORACE MANN**

Read every day something no one else is reading. Think something no one else is thinking. It is bad for the mind to be always a part of unanimity.
**CHRISTOPHER MORLEY**

Much reading is an oppression of the mind, and extinguishes the natural candle, which is the reason of so many senseless scholars in the world.
**WILLIAM PENN**

Never write on a subject without first having read yourself full on it; and never read on a subject till you have thought yourself hungry on it.
**JEAN PAUL RICHTER**

Reading is to the mind what exercise is to the body.
**RICHARD STEELE**

One may as well be asleep as to read for anything but to improve his mind and morals, and regulate his conduct.
**LAURENCE STERNE**

My education was the liberty I had to read indiscriminately and all the time, with my eyes hanging out.
**DYLAN THOMAS**

The man who does not read good books has no advantage over the man who can't read them.
**MARK TWAIN**

My family can always tell when I'm well into a novel because the meals get very crummy.
**ANNE TYLER**

We live in an age that reads too much to be wise.
**OSCAR WILDE**

It is well to read up everything within reach about your business; this not only improves your knowledge, your usefulness and your fitness for more responsible work, but it invests your business with more interest, since you understand its functions, its basic principles, its place in the general scheme of things.
**DANIEL WILLARD**

## Reality

Some people are still unaware that reality contains unparalleled beauties. The fantastic and unexpected, the everchanging and renewing is nowhere so exemplified as in real life itself!
**BERENICE ABBOTT**

I have lived long enough to be battered by the realities of life and not too long to be downed by them.
**JOHN MASON BROWN**

The wise men of antiquity, when they wished to make the whole world peaceful and happy, first put their own States into proper order. Before putting their States into proper order, they regulated their own families. Before regulating their families, they regulated themselves. Before regulating themselves, they tried to be sincere in their thoughts. Before being sincere in their thoughts, they tried to see things exactly as they really were.
**CONFUCIUS**

Do people love truth? On the contrary, mankind has employed its subtlest ingenuity and intelligence in efforts to evade or conceal it. . . . Do human beings love justice? The sordid travesties in our courts year after year suggest that they love justice only for themselves. Do they love peace? Can anyone seriously ask the question? Do they love freedom? Only for those who share their views. Love of peace, freedom, justice, truth—this is a myth that has been created by the folk mind, and if the artist does not look behind the myth to the reality, he will indeed wander amid the phantoms which he creates.
**VARDIS FISHER**

There will always be another reality to make fiction of the truth we think we've arrived at.
**CHRISTOPHER FRY**

Few men have imagination enough for reality.
**JOHANN WOLFGANG VON GOETHE**

What we need most, is not so much to realize the idea as to idealize the real.
**FREDERICK HEDGE**

The greatest realities are physical and economic, all the subtleties of life come afterward.
**JOYCE CAROL OATES**

For the experienced to survive, reality must be considered.
**CHARLES B. RICHARDSON**

It is harder to kill a phantom than a reality.
**VIRGINIA WOOLF**

## Reason

"Theirs not to make reply, theirs not to reason why," may be a good enough motto for men who are on their way to be shot. But from such men expect no empires to be builded, no inventions made, no great discoveries brought to light.
**BRUCE BARTON**

If we would guide by the light of reason we must let our minds be bold.
**LOUIS D. BRANDEIS**

Logical behavior often comes dangerously near toppling over into the absurd.
**LOUISE CRISTINA**

He only employs his passion who can make no use of his reason.
**CICERO**

I am (thank God) constitutionally superior to reason.
**WILLIAM WILKIE COLLINS**

Free inquiry, if restrained within due bounds, and applied to proper subjects, is a most important privilege of the human mind; and if well conducted, is one of the greatest friends to truth. But when reason knows neither its office nor its limits, and when employed on subjects foreign to its jurisdiction, it then becomes a privilege dangerous to be exercised.
**JEAN D'AUBIGNÉ**

He that will not reason is a bigot; he that cannot reason is a fool; and he that dares not reason is a slave.
**SIR WILLIAM DRUMMOND**

Good sense and good nature are never separated; and good nature is the product of right reason.
**JOHN DRYDEN**

The crossroads of trade are the meeting place of ideas, the attrition ground of rival customs and beliefs; diversities beget conflict, comparison, thought; superstitions cancel one another, and reason begins.
**WILL DURANT**

We do not act because we know, but we know because we are called upon to act; the practical reason is the root of all reason.
**JOHANN FICHTE**

Neither great poverty nor great riches will hear reason.
**HENRY FIELDING**

So convenient a thing it is to be a reasonable creature, since it enables one to find or make a reason for everything one has a mind to do.
**BENJAMIN FRANKLIN**

They that will not be counselled, cannot be helped. If you do not hear reason she will rap you on the knuckles.
**BENJAMIN FRANKLIN**

Let us not dream that reason can ever be popular. Passions, emotions, may be made popular, but reason remains ever the property of the few.
**JOHANN WOLFGANG VON GOETHE**

Come now, and let us reason together, saith the Lord: though your sins be as scarlet, they shall be as white as snow; though they be red like crimson, they shall be as wool.
**ISAIAH 1:18**

Error of opinion may be tolerated where reason is left free to combat it.
**THOMAS JEFFERSON**

The life of sense begins by assuming that we can only fitfully live the life of reason.
LOUIS KRONENBERGER

Nothing under the sun is ever accidental.
GOTTHOLD LESSING

When I'm getting ready to reason with a man, I spend one-third of my time thinking about myself and what I am going to say—and two-thirds thinking about him and what he is going to say.
ABRAHAM LINCOLN

Human beings are the only creatures who are able to behave irrationally in the name of reason.
ASHLEY MONTAGU

He who establishes his argument by noise and command, shows that his reason is weak.
MICHEL DE MONTAIGNE

A man always has two reasons for doing anything. A good reason and a real reason.
J. P. MORGAN

We are generally better persuaded by the reasons we discover ourselves than by those given to us by others.
BLAISE PASCAL

Real life is, to most men, a long second-best, a perpetual compromise between the ideal and the possible; but the world of pure reason knows no compromise, no practical limitations, no barrier to the creative activity.
BERTRAND RUSSELL

The heart has reasons of which the reason has no knowledge.
GEORGE SANTAYANA

When a man has not a good reason for doing a thing, he has one good reason for letting it alone.
THOMAS SCOTT

The open mind never acts—when we have done our utmost to arrive at a reasonable conclusion, we still, when we can reason and investigate no more, must close our minds for the moment with a snap, and act dogmatically on our own conclusion. The man who wants to make an entirely reasonable will dies intestate.
GEORGE BERNARD SHAW

The man whom Heaven appoints to govern others, should himself first learn to bend his passions to the sway of reason.
JAMES THOMSON

Reason unites us, not only with our contemporaries, but with men who lived two thousand years before us, and with those who will live after us.
LEO TOLSTOY

How difficult it is to persuade a man to reason against his interest; though he is convinced that equity is against him.
JOHN TRUSLER

Until someone has lighted on the secret of making men's minds more accurate, all the progress that can be made in the discovery of truth will not prevent their reasoning falsely; and the further anyone attempts to speed them beyond the common notions, the more he will lay them open to error.
MARQUIS DE VAUVANARGUES

Reason, too late perhaps, may convince you of the folly of misspending time.
GEORGE WASHINGTON

Put fear out of your heart. This nation will survive, this state will prosper, the orderly business of life

will go forward if only men can speak in whatever way given them to utter what their hearts hold—by voice, by posted card, by letter or by press. Reason never has failed men. Only force and oppression have made the wrecks in the world.
**WILLIAM ALLEN WHITE**

I can stand brute force, but brute reason is quite unbearable. It is hitting below the intellect.
**OSCAR WILDE**

## *Religion*

If we make religion our business, God will make it our blessedness.
**H. G. J. ADAM**

There is not enough love, obviously, in our religious exercises; we try to buy ourselves into good relationship with God. We bow Him out of our lives in normal things and then think we can ingratiate ourselves by a few religious exercises on Sunday. The attitude seems to be: Lord, I'll do my part and you do Yours but let's not become too intimate in the process.
**WILLIAM WARD AYER, D.D.**

I have not been able to find a single useful institution which has not been founded either by an intensely religious man or by the son of a praying father or a praying mother. I have made the statement before the chambers of commerce of all the largest cities of the country and have asked them to bring forward a case that is an exception to this rule. Thus far, I have not heard of a single one.
**ROGER W. BABSON**

A man without religion or spiritual vision is like a captain who finds himself in the midst of an uncharted sea, without compass, rudder and steering wheel. He never knows where he is, which way he is going and where he is going to land.
**WILLIAM J. H. BOETCKER**

The Church alone can bring about the spiritual revival and the moral regeneration this world needs before there can be permanent peace and sound economic recovery, and to this end we do not need new laws but a new spirit.
**WILLIAM J. H. BOETCKER**

True religion is not a mere doctrine, something that can be taught, but is a way of life. A life in community with God. It must be experienced to be appreciated. A life of service. A living by giving and finding one's own happiness by bringing happiness into the lives of others.
**WILLIAM J. H. BOETCKER**

Religion is excellent stuff for keeping common people quiet.
**NAPOLEON BONAPARTE**

When Rome's youth became debased and enervated, when regard was lost for men's honor and women's purity, when the sanctity of the home was violated, when her literature became cynical and debased, her dominion ended. The moral life of any people rises or falls with the vitality or decay of its religious life.
**JOHN S. BONNELL, D.D.**

One of the hardest lessons we have to learn in this life, and one that many persons never learn, is to see the divine, the celestial, the pure, in the common, the near at hand—to see that heaven lies about us here in this world.
**JOHN BURROUGHS**

It is the test of a good religion whether you can make a joke about it.
**G. K. CHESTERTON**

Surely, life is more than eating and drinking, more than buying and selling, more than getting and spending, more than the cultivation of the mind and a healthy body. It is the widening of our horizon, the broadening of our vision, the reaching out to eternal realities, the discipline of self until we can truly say, "I live, yet not I but Christ liveth in me."
E. CLOWES CHORLEY, D.D.

The strength of a country is the strength of its religious convictions.
CALVIN COOLIDGE

Under our institutions the only way to perfect the Government is to perfect the individual citizen. It is necessary to reach the mind and soul of the individual. I know of no way that this can be done save through the influence of religion and education. By religion I do not mean fanaticism or bigotry; by education I do not mean the cant of the schools, but a broad and tolerant faith, loving thy neighbor as thyself, and a training and experience that enables the human mind to see into the heart of things.
CALVIN COOLIDGE

The future of religion is connected with the possibility of developing a faith in the possibilities of human experience and human relationships that will create a vital sense of the solidarity of human interests and inspire action to make that sense a reality.
JOHN DEWEY

The intellectual content of religions has always finally adapted itself to scientific and social conditions after they have become clear. . . . For this reason I do not think that those who are concerned about the future of a religious attitude should trouble themselves about the conflict of science with traditional doctrines.
JOHN DEWEY

The cosmic religious experience is the strongest and noblest driving force behind scientific research.
ALBERT EINSTEIN

The most beautiful thing we can experience is the mysterious. It is the source of all true art and science. He to whom the emotion is a stranger, who can no longer pause to wonder and stand wrapped in awe, is as good as dead; his eyes are closed. The insight into the mystery of life, coupled though it be with fear, has also given rise to religion. To know what is impenetrable to us really exists, manifesting itself as the highest wisdom and the most radiant beauty, which our dull faculties can comprehend only in their most primitive forms—this knowledge, this feeling is at the center of true religiousness.
ALBERT EINSTEIN

This is what I found out about religion: It gives you courage to make the decisions you must make in a crisis, and then the confidence to leave the result to a higher Power. Only by trust in God can a man carrying responsibility find repose.
DWIGHT D. EISENHOWER

What the church should be telling the worker is that the first demand religion makes on him is that he should be a good workman. If he is a carpenter he should be a competent carpenter. Church by all means on Sundays—but what is the use of church if at the very center of life a man defrauds his neighbor and insults God by poor craftsmanship.
DWIGHT D. EISENHOWER

Religion is as effectively destroyed by bigotry as by indifference.
RALPH WALDO EMERSON

The man without religion is as a ship without a rudder.
B. C. FORBES

We moderns with all our pride in our boasted civilization are back where that ancient world was when it first confronted Christ. We are desperately in need of salvation. It is a humiliating experience for an individual or a whole generation to have to acknowledge that it needs to be saved, but only a blind man can fail to see that that is our situation now.
HARRY EMERSON FOSDICK, D.D.

So when the crisis is upon you, remember that God, like a trainer of wrestlers, has matched you with a tough and stalwart antagonist—that you may prove a victor at the Great Games. Yet without toil or sweat this may not be.
EPICTETUS

What religion needs today is not more flying with God, or leaping with God, or jumping up and down with God, or going into spasms and convulsions and epileptic fits with God. What religion needs today is more walking with God.
MILO H. GATES, D.D.

The various modes of worship which prevailed in the Roman world were all considered by the people as equally true, by the philosophers as equally false, and by the magistrate as equally useful.
EDWARD GIBBON

**Fundamental Facts of Religion**

Man is condemned on account of his sins alone.

Salvation is the gift of God through grace alone.

Redemption is through the crucified Christ alone.

God's means of grace are effected through the Holy Spirit alone.

Justification before God by faith alone.

Authority through religion in the word of God alone.

The priesthood of believers exists through the risen Christ alone.

The brotherhood of believers is through the church alone.

The Christian life lives by love alone.

Liberty of conscience by truth alone.

WALTON H. GREEVER, D.D.

Why should a country worship another country's tin gods, when it has tin gods of its own?
JOHN P. GRIER

Religion is a disease, but it is a noble disease.
HERACLITUS

The very helpfulness of the world today is in itself a repudiation of that self-sufficient and self-confident view of life that the world in its progressive development has outgrown the need of religion. It is religion which gives the world what it most needs, a standard of right living, a cause to maintain and defend, a leader to follow and a law to obey.
JOHN GRIER HIBBEN

Religion must be used in furthering great works of justice and reform. It must be used to establish right relations between different groups of men, and thus to make a reality of brotherhood. It must be used to abolish poverty, the breeding ground of all misery and crime, by distributing equably among men the abundance of the soil. And it must be used to get rid of war and to establish enduring peace. Here is the supreme test of the effectiveness of religion.
JOHN HAYNES HOLMES

It often happens that I wake at night and begin to think about a serious problem and decide I must tell the Pope about it. Then I wake up completely and remember that I am the Pope.
POPE JOHN XXIII

It is pretty well demonstrated in the experience of the human race that man cannot attain his full

stature as a rightly fashioned person without the inspiration and guidance of religion. It makes one feel himself to be a citizen of an enlarged universe—a two storied world to which he belongs, the upper story as real as the basic material one.
RUFUS JONES

What church I go to on Sunday, what dogma of the Catholic Church I believe in, is my business; and whatever faith any other American has is his business.
JOHN F. KENNEDY

It has long been recognized that an education which does not provide for an intelligent understanding of religion is incomplete.
RAYMOND C. KNOX

If a man has peace with the universe, peace with his own soul and peace with his fellowmen, that man has religion.
J. WILLIAM LLOYD

The works of nature and the works of revelation display religion to mankind in characters so large and visible that those who are not quite blind may in them see and read the first principles and most necessary parts of it and from thence penetrate into those infinite depths filled with the treasures of wisdom and knowledge.
JOHN LOCKE

Here in our land, and in other lands, many have been drifting toward a religion which says much about rights but little about duties; a religion which thinks only about humanity and little about God; which lays great stress on service but little stress on faith; which puts all the emphasis on man and his power and very little on God and His power.
WILLIAM T. MANNING, D.D.

The Puritan hated bear-baiting, not because it gave pain to the bear, but because it gave pleasure to the spectators.
THOMAS B. MACAULAY

The objection to Puritans is not that they try to make us think as they do, but that they try to make us do as they think.
H. L. MENCKEN

There is a divinity that shapes our ends—but we can help by listening for Its voice.
KATHLEEN NORRIS

Men never do evil so completely and cheerfully as when they do it from a religious conviction.
BLAISE PASCAL

If thou wouldst preserve a sound body, use fasting and walking; if a healthful soul, fasting and praying. Walking exercises the body; praying exercises the soul; fasting cleanses both.
FRANCIS QUARLES

What the world craves today is a more spiritual and less formal religion. To the man or woman facing death, great conflict, the big problems of human life, the forms of religion are of minor concern, while the spirit of religion is a desperately needed source of inspiration, comfort and strength.
JOHN D. ROCKEFELLER, JR.

The function of a modern religion is to accumulate spiritual power in life and for life. We need that power all the time, but if it has not been accumulated it is not there when we need it most. In a world like this, particularly like the one at the present time, can anyone get along just as well without the inspirations of religion? He cannot. Religion keeps us up to the everlasting effort to attain the best life and best things in life.
MINOT SIMONS, D.D.

Habit must play a larger place in our religious life. We worship when we feel like it, we pray when we feel like it. We read the Bible when we feel like it. Leaving our religious exercises to the promptings of impulse, we become creatures of impulse rather than soldiers of Christ. An army made up of creatures of impulse would be only a mob. So is a church.
RALPH W. SOCKMAN

The test of our religion is whether it fits us to meet emergencies. A man has no more character than he can command in a time of crisis.
RALPH W. SOCKMAN

The gates of wisdom and truth are forever closed to those who are wise in their own conceits; they have always opened before the expectancy of the humble and the teachable. The great need of the religious soul is the capacity to be receptive. It is a matter of record that no generation of religious people throughout history has ever been lacking in the fellowship and leadership of men and women of rare intellectual power.
THEODORE C. SPEERS, D.D.

We have got to begin a vast reclamation project to revitalize religion for those to whom it means little or nothing. This can be done not by trying to persuade those outside the church to believe what we believe but by pointing out to them the presence of the unrecognized religion that already exists in their lives.
THEODORE C. SPEERS, D.D.

To live, mankind must recover its essential humanness and its innate divinity; men must recover their capacity for humility, sanity and integrity; soldier and civilians must see their hope in some other world than one completely dominated by the physical and chemical sciences.
GEORGE F. G. STANLEY

Religion is life and lifts you out of yourself. We must believe God is too big to fail.
SAMUEL H. SWEENEY

We have just enough religion to make us hate, but not enough to make us love one another.
JONATHAN SWIFT

Everything for which democracy stands is based on religious faith. Neither enlightened self-interest nor practical ethics can make an effective substitute.
ELBERT D. THOMAS

Few sinners are saved after the first 20 minutes of a sermon.
MARK TWAIN

We despise all reverences and all objects of reverence which are outside the pale of our list of sacred things. And yet, with strange inconsistency, we are shocked when other people despise and defile the things that are holy to us.
MARK TWAIN

Our business is not only with eternity but with time, to build up on earth the kingdom of God, to enable man to live worthily and not merely to die in hope.
LORD TWEEDSMUIR

In some respects the world is in the same situation that it was in after the fall of the Roman empire. There is an even greater need for a religious revival now because paganism has become sophisticated.
BARBARA WARD

While just government protects all in their religious rites, true religion affords government its surest support.
GEORGE WASHINGTON

Religion, properly understood, should be largely independent of seasons and places. Religion should

not surrender to control by alternations of climate. There is something lacking in a religion which the summertime can destroy.
PHILIP S. WATTERS, D.D.

There are few of us so blind as not to realize that unless the moral force of religious conviction impels, the goal of truth and lasting international co-operation cannot be attained; there are few of us who do not appreciate the vital truth of the words, "If God does not build the house, those who build it build in vain."
SUMNER WELLES

Science has made the world a great neighborhood, but religion must make it a great brotherhood.
LESTER A. WELLIVER

True religion is the life we live, not the creed we profess, and some day will be recognized by quality and quantity, and not by brand.
J. F. WRIGHT

As long as men and nations are aware of their divine origin, that human beings are a reflection of the source of all life, then it follows that it is the beholden duty of man to increase goodness, beauty, truth and peace in the world. But when men and nations deny the relationship of man to the divine, then the soil is fertile for the growth of hatred, injustice, strife and war.
JOSEPH ZEITLIN

A religion that serves today's needs and holds tomorrow's promise should not consist of dying forms and cold rituals, but of living hope and friendly righteousness. Justice, honor, and truth will be found where righteousness is found. If all people return to religion and find peace, the world will find peace.
WAYLAND ZWAYER, D.D.

## *Reputation*

A man's character is the reliability of himself. His reputation is the opinion others have formed of him. Character is in him; reputation is from other people.
HENRY WARD BEECHER

It is the penalty of fame that a man must ever keep rising. "Get a reputation, and then go to bed," is the absurdest of all maxims. "Keep up a reputation or go to bed," would be nearer the truth.
EDWIN H. CHAPIN

To disregard what the world thinks of us is not only arrogant but utterly shameless.
CICERO

The two most precious things this side the grave are our reputation and our life. But it is to be lamented that the most contemptible whisper may deprive us of the one, and the weakest weapon of the other. A wise man, therefore, will be more anxious to deserve a fair name than to possess it, and this will teach him so to live as not to be afraid to die.
COTTON

You can't build up a reputation on what you are going to do.
HENRY FORD

I have visited many countries, and have been in cities without number, yet never did I enter a town which could not produce ten or twelve little great men; all fancying themselves known to the rest of the world, and complimenting each other upon their extensive reputation.
OLIVER GOLDSMITH

A man's reputation is not in his own keeping. It lies at the mercy of the profligacy of others.
WILLIAM HAZLITT

How many people live on the reputation of the reputation they might have made!
**Oliver Wendell Holmes**

What people say behind your back is your standing in the community in which you live.
**Edgar Watson Howe**

We sometimes speak of winning reputation as though that were the final goal. The truth is contrary to this. Reputation is a reward, to be sure, but it is really the beginning, not the end of endeavor. It should not be the signal for a let down, but rather, a reminder that the standards which won recognition can never again be lowered. From him who gives much—much is forever after expected.
**Alvan Macauley**

It's a fine thing to have a finger pointed at one, and to hear people say, "That's the man."
**Persius**

Reputations are longer in the making than the losing.
**Paul von Ringelheim**

Whatever ignominy or disgrace we have incurred, it is almost always in our power to reestablish our reputation.
**François de la Rochefoucauld**

It is better to be nobly remembered than nobly born.
**John Ruskin**

How awful to reflect that what people say of us is true!
**Logan Pearsall Smith**

The way to gain a good reputation is to endeavor to be what you desire to appear.
**Socrates**

A fair reputation is a plant delicate in its nature, and by no means rapid in its growth. It will not shoot up in a night, like the gourd of the prophet, but like that gourd, it may perish in a night.
**Jeremy Taylor**

Associate yourself with men of good quality if you esteem your own reputation; for 'tis better to be alone than in bad company.
**George Washington**

## *Research*

Basic research is what I am doing when I don't know what I am doing.
**Wernher von Braun**

No research is ever quite complete. It is the glory of a good bit of work that it opens the way for something still better, and this repeatedly leads to its own eclipse.
**Mervin Gordon**

The best insurance policy for the future of an industry is research, which will help it to foresee future lines of development, to solve its immediate problems, and to improve and cheapen its products.
**Sir Harold Hartley**

Research is an organized method of trying to find out what you are going to do after you cannot do what you are doing now. It may also be said to be the method of keeping a customer reasonably dissatisfied with what he has. That means constant improvement and change so that the customer will be stimulated to desire the new product enough to buy it to replace the one he has.
**Charles F. Kettering**

Research is exemplified in the problem-solving mind as contrasted with the let-well-enough-alone mind. It is the composer mind instead of the fiddler mind. It is the tomorrow mind instead of the yesterday mind.
**CHARLES F. KETTERING**

Research . . . is nothing but a state of mind—a friendly, welcoming attitude toward change; going out to look for a change instead of waiting for it to come. Research, for practical men, is an effort to do things better. . . . The research state of mind can apply to anything—personal affairs or any kind of business, big or little.
**CHARLES F. KETTERING**

Research means that you don't know, but are willing to find out.
**CHARLES F. KETTERING**

Research is the reconnaissance party of industry, roving the unknown territories ahead independently, yet not without purpose, seeing for the first time what all the following world will see a few years hence.
**S. M. KINTER**

The common facts of today are the products of yesterday's research.
**DUNCAN MACDONALD**

Research teaches a man to admit he is wrong and to be proud of the fact that he does so, rather than try with all his energy to defend an unsound plan because he is afraid that admission of error is a confession of weakness when rather it is a sign of strength.
**H. E. STOCHER**

I salute the workers in physical research as the poets of today. It may be that they do not write in verse, but their communications are of such lively interest that they are on the front pages of our newspapers and command space in agricultural periodicals. They appeal to the imagination of us all. They contribute the warming glow of inspiration to industry, and when industry pulls their ideas down from the heavens to the earth and harnesses them for practical service, it, too, feels that it is an important actor, not only in the makings of things but on the larger stage of human spirit. There may be enough poetry in the whir of our machines so that our machine age will become immortal.
**OWEN D. YOUNG**

## *Resolution*

Irresolution on the schemes of life which offer themselves to our choice, and inconstancy in pursuing them, are the greatest causes of all our unhappiness.
**JOSEPH ADDISON**

Nothing relieves and ventilates the mind like a resolution.
**JOHN BURROUGHS**

There is no moment like the present. The man who will not execute his resolutions when they are fresh upon him can have no hope from them afterwards; they will be dissipated, lost, and perish in the hurry and scurry of the world, or sunk in the slough of indolence.
**MARIE EDGEWORTH**

He that resolves upon any great and good end, has, by that very resolution, scaled the chief barrier to it. He will find such resolution removing difficulties, searching out or making means, giving courage for despondency, and strength for weakness, and like the star to the wise men of old, ever guiding him nearer and nearer to perfection.
**TRYON EDWARDS**

Most good resolutions start too late and end too soon.
**ARNOLD GLASOW**

We can do anything we want to do if we stick to it long enough.
**HELEN KELLER**

No one would have crossed the ocean if he could have gotten off the ship in the storm.
**CHARLES F. KETTERING**

Good resolutions are a pleasant crop to sow. The seed springs up so readily, and the blossoms open so soon with such a brave show, especially at first. But when the time of flowers has passed, what as to the fruit?
**LUCAS MALET**

With irresolute finger he knocked at each one of the doorways of life, and abided in none.
**OWEN MEREDITH**

When nothing seems to help, I go and look at a stonecutter hammering away at his rock, perhaps a hundred times without as much as a crack showing in it. Yet, at the hundred and first blow it will split in two, and I know it was not that last blow that did it, but all that had gone before.
**JACOB A. RIIS**

Every human mind is a great slumbering power until awakened by keen desire and by definite resolution to do.
**EDGAR F. ROBERTS**

Be stirring as the time, be fire with fire, threaten the threatener, and outface the brow of bragging horror; so shall inferior eyes, that borrow their behaviors from the great, grow great by your example and put on the dauntless spirit of resolution.
**WILLIAM SHAKESPEARE**

Experience teacheth that resolution is a sole help in need.
**WILLIAM SHAKESPEARE**

See first that the design is wise and just; that ascertained, pursue it resolutely.
**WILLIAM SHAKESPEARE**

### A Morning Resolve

I will this day try to live a simple, sincere, and serene life; repelling promptly every thought of discontent, anxiety, discouragement, impurity, and self-seeking; cultivating cheerfulness, magnanimity, charity, and the habit of holy silence; exercising economy in expenditure, carefulness in conversation, diligence in appointed service, fidelity to every trust, and a childlike trust in God.
**JOHN H. VINCENT**

In no direction that we turn do we find ease or comfort. If we are honest and if we have the will to win we find only danger, hard work and iron resolution.
**WENDELL WILLKIE**

## *Respect*

Too often a sense of loyalty depends on admiration, and if we can't admire, it is difficult to be loyal.
**AIMEE BUCHANAN**

All true love is founded on esteem.
**GEORGE BUCKINGHAM**

Great souls are always loyally submissive, reverent to what is over them: only small mean souls are otherwise.
**THOMAS CARLYLE**

No nobler feeling than this, of admiration for one higher than himself, dwells in the breast of man. It

is to this hour, and at all hours, the vivifying influence in man's life.
THOMAS CARLYLE

In handling men, there are three feelings that a man must not possess—fear, dislike and contempt. If he is afraid of men he cannot handle them. Neither can he influence them in his favor if he dislikes or scorns them. He must neither cringe nor sneer. He must have both self-respect and respect for others.
HERBERT N. CASSON

Seek respect mainly from thyself, for it comes first from within.
STEVEN H. COOGLER

Having the courage to live within one's means is respectability.
BENJAMIN DISRAELI

Human affairs inspire in noble hearts only two feelings—admiration or pity.
ANATOLE FRANCE

The respect of those you respect is worth more than the applause of the multitude.
ARNOLD GLASOW

A flippant, frivolous man may ridicule others, may controvert them, scorn them; but he who has any respect for himself seems to have renounced the right of thinking meanly of others.
JOHANN WOLFGANG VON GOETHE

The way to procure insults is to submit to them. A man meets with no more respect than he exacts.
WILLIAM HAZLITT

Violence ever defeats its own ends. Where you cannot drive you can always persuade. A gentle word, a kind look, a good-natured smile can work wonders and accomplish miracles. There is a secret pride in every human heart that revolts at tyranny. You may order and drive an individual, but you cannot make him respect you.
WILLIAM HAZLITT

He that respects not is not respected.
GEORGE HERBERT

People who bite the hand that feeds them usually lick the boot that kicks them.
ERIC HOFFER

Respect a man, he will do the more.
JAMES HOWELL

Every man is to be respected as an absolute end in himself; and it is a crime against the dignity that belongs to him as a human being, to use him as a mere means for some external purpose.
IMMANUEL KANT

Things hard to come by are much esteemed.
LATIN PROVERB

Esteem has more engaging charms than friendship, or even love. It captivates hearts better, and never makes ingrates.
STANISLAUS LESZCYNSKI

We are usually mistaken in esteeming men too much; rarely in esteeming them too little.
STANISLAUS LESZCYNSKI

He that respects himself is safe from others; he wears a coat of mail that none can pierce.
HENRY WADSWORTH LONGFELLOW

Whose best and most fruitful gift was the power of admiration, which made it possible for me to learn.

Now, as in my youth, I am looking up to the truly great creations of the past, which I see high above my own and which alone deserve the name of greatness.
THOMAS MANN

We have so exalted a notion of the human soul that we cannot bear to be despised, or even not to be esteemed by it. Man, in fact, places all his happiness in this esteem.
BLAISE PASCAL

This is the final test of a gentleman; his respect for those who can be of no possible service to him.
WILLIAM LYON PHELPS

We as a people seem to be losing all sense of respect for ourselves and our fellow men, with the result that in a thoroughly intolerant attitude we hesitate not a minute to secure an organized minority, or even a majority, to attempt by resolution or law to impose our will on a large body of people in matters where no moral wrong is involved and where liberty is curtailed.
JOHN J. RASKOB

We always like those who admire us, but we do not always like those whom we admire.
FRANÇOIS DE LA ROCHEFOUCAULD

Only those who respect the personality of others can be of real use to them.
ALBERT SCHWEITZER

Reverence for life does not allow the scholar to live for his science alone, even if he is very useful to the community in so doing. Reverence for life does not permit the artist to exist only for his art, even if he gives inspiration to many by its means. Reverence for life refuses to let the businessman imagine that he fulfills all legitimate demands in the course of his business activities. Reverence for life demands for all that they should sacrifice a portion of their own lives for others.
ALBERT SCHWEITZER

Admiration is one of the most bewitching, enthusiastic passions of the mind; and every common moralist knows that it arises from novelty and surprise, the inseparable attendants of imposture.
WILLIAM WARBURTON

Nobody likes having salt rubbed into their wounds, even if it is the salt of the earth.
REBECCA WEST

When one has never heard a man's name in the course of one's life, it speaks volumes for him; he must be quite respectable.
OSCAR WILDE

## *Responsibility*

The price of power is responsibility for the public good.
WINTHROP W. ALDRICH

No individual raindrop ever considers itself responsible for the flood.
ANONYMOUS

He didn't get promoted,
Blamed it on his luck;
The office gossip was
He likes to pass the buck.
CECIL BAXTER

There has been in recent years excessive emphasis on a citizen's rights and inadequate stress upon his duties and responsibilities.
PAXTON BLAIR

Whoever claims a right for himself must respect the like right in another. Whoever wishes to assert his will as a member of a community must not only consent to obey the will of the community but bear his share in serving it. As he is to profit by the safety and prosperity the community provides, so he must seek its good and place his personal will at its disposal. Benefit and burden, power and responsibility go together.
JAMES BRYCE

When a man decides to do something he must go all the way, but he must take responsibility for what he does. He must know first why he is doing it and then he must proceed with his actions with no doubts or remorse.
CARLOS CASTANEDA

Responsibility is the possibility of opportunity culminating in inevitable fulfillment.
SRI CHINMOY

The price of greatness is responsibility.
WINSTON CHURCHILL

A power above all human responsibility ought to be above all human attainment.
CHARLES CALEB COLTON

When you find a man who knows his job and is willing to take responsibility, keep out of his way and don't bother him with unnecessary supervision. What you may think is co-operation is nothing but interference.
THOMAS DREIER

Never mind your happiness; do your duty.
WILL DURANT

Those who enjoy responsibility usually get it; those who merely like exercising authority usually lose it.
MALCOLM FORBES

The vast majority of persons of our race have a natural tendency to shrink from the responsibility of standing and acting alone.
FRANCIS GALTON

If one defines the term dropout to mean a person who has given up serious effort to meet his responsibilities, then every business office, government agency, golf club and university faculty would yield its quota.
JOHN GARDNER

I've never known of an instance in the history of our company where an executive unloaded responsibilities and duties on one lower in the ranks, that he did not find himself immediately loaded from above with greater responsibilities.
ARTHUR F. HALL

To let oneself be bound by a duty from the moment you see it approaching is part of the integrity that alone justifies responsibility.
DAG HAMMARSKJÖLD

Responsibility for the creation of the good world in which the good life may be realized, which the frustrated ages of the past loaded upon the gods, is now being assumed by man. The ideal of this modern drift is the realization of the full joy in living.
A. EUSTACE HAYDON

If you load responsibility on a man unworthy of it he will always betray himself.
AUGUST HECKSCHER

Responsibility walks hand in hand with capacity and power.
JOSIAH G. HOLLAND

Power flows to the man who knows how. Responsibilities gravitate to the person who can shoulder them.
ELBERT HUBBARD

Some people grow under responsibility, others merely swell.
CARL HUBBELL

Great businessmen often have the deepest sense of community responsibilities and the sort of realistic approach that helps bring about improvements in their cities.
YOUSUF KARSH

You can't escape the responsibility of tomorrow by evading it today.
ABRAHAM LINCOLN

Just how we fit into the plans of the Great Architect and how much He has assigned us to do, we do not know, but if we fail in our assignment it is pretty certain that part of the job will be left undone. But fit in we certainly do somehow, else we would not have a sense of our own responsibility. A purely materialistic philosophy is to me the height of unintelligence.
ROBERT A. MILLIKAN

Why did the Lord give us so much quickness unless it was to avoid responsibility?
OGDEN NASH

We are not put here on earth to play around. There is work to be done. There are responsibilities to be met. Humanity needs the abilities of every man and woman.
ALDEN PALMER

I believe that every right implies a responsibility; every opportunity, an obligation; every possession, a duty.
JOHN D. ROCKEFELLER

Every right has its responsibilities. Like the right itself, these responsibilities stem from no man-made law, but from the very nature of man and society. The security, progress and welfare of one group is measured finally in the security, progress and welfare of all mankind.
LEWIS SCHWELLENBACH

A man to be truly free must accept responsibilities. To be relieved of responsibility means to lose freedom and liberty. Thus it can come about that the real enemy of man can be the state.
C. T. A. SPARKS, D.D.

It is easy to dodge our responsibilities, but we cannot dodge the consequences of dodging our responsibilities.
SIR JOSIAH STAMP

With all its alluring promise that some one else will guarantee for the rainy day, social security can never replace the program that man's future welfare is, after all, a matter of individual responsibility.
HAROLD STONIER

We are all concerned, of course. But concern alone never solved a problem. Concern is useful only if converted to meaningful action. And, for the business executive, meaningful action today is interpreted as corporate responsibility.
THOMAS I. STORRS

Men who do things without being told draw the most wages.
EDWIN H. STUART

In your area of responsibility, if you do not control events, you are at the mercy of events.
HARLAND SVARE

The real freedom of any individual can always be measured by the amount of responsibility which he must assume for his own welfare and security.
ROBERT WELCH

Man is still responsible. He must turn the alloy of modern experience into the steel of mastery and character. His success lies not with the stars but with himself. He must carry on the fight of self-correction and discipline. He must fight mediocrity as sin and live against the imperative of life's highest ideal.
FRANK CURTIS WILLIAMS, D.D.

I feel the responsibility of the occasion. Responsibility is proportionate to opportunity.
WOODROW WILSON

There is a single reason why 99 out of 100 average business men never become leaders. That is their unwillingness to pay the price of responsibility. By the price of responsibility I mean hard driving, continual work . . . the courage to make decisions, to stand the gaff . . . the scourging honesty of never fooling yourself about yourself. You travel the road to leadership heavily laden. While the nine-to-five-o'clock worker takes his ease, you are toiling upward through the night. Laboriously you extend your mental frontiers. Any new effort, the psychologists say, wears a new groove in the brain. And the grooves that lead to the heights are not made between nine and five. They are burned in by midnight oil.
OWEN D. YOUNG

## *Rest*

Sleep is not always an unmixed blessing. It brings relief to the nerves and strength to the body, but it also brings cold sanity to shatter the flimsy emotional structures of the night before.
ERIC AMBLER

We sleep, but the loom of life never stops and the pattern which was weaving when the sun went down is weaving when it comes up tomorrow.
HENRY WARD BEECHER

The wagon rests in winter, the sled rests in summer, man never rests.
IGNAS BERNSTEIN

Rest and motion, unrelieved and unchecked, are equally destructive.
BENJAMIN CARDOZO

Rest is a fine medicine. Let your stomachs rest, ye dyspeptics; let your brain rest, you wearied and worried men of business; let your limbs rest, ye children of toil!
THOMAS CARLYLE

Sleep: The golden chain that ties health and our bodies together.
THOMAS DEKKER

He that can take rest is greater than he that can take cities.
BENJAMIN FRANKLIN

If you sleep till noon, you have no right to complain that the days are short.
THOMAS FULLER

God . . . authorizes us to take that rest and refreshment which are necessary to keeping up the strength of mind and body.
ST. JOHN BAPTISTE DE LA SALLE

Periods of wholesome laziness, after days of energetic effort, will wonderfully tone up the mind and body. It does not involve loss of time, since after a day of complete rest and quietness you will return to your regular occupation with renewed interest and vigor.
GRENVILLE KLEISER

There is nothing so insupportable to man as to be in entire repose; without passion, occupation, amusement, or application. Then it is that he feels his own nothingness, isolation, insignificance, dependent nature, powerlessness, emptiness. Immediately there issue from his soul ennui, sadness, chagrin, vexation, despair.
BLAISE PASCAL

Rest is the sweet sauce of labor.
PLUTARCH

If we could learn how to balance rest against effort, calmness against strain, quiet against turmoil, we would assure ourselves of joy in living and psychological health for life.
JOSEPHINE RATHBONE

Rest has cured more people than all the medicine in the world.
HAROLD J. REILLY

You can't be asleep in business—at the ends of the arms of Morpheus are the hands of the receiver.
FRANK ROMER

The best thing we have is sleep, of course, and what is sleep except the putting aside of everything tentative for another interval of final and everlasting truth? Sleep isn't dying, but it is certainly keeping in touch with it.
WILLIAM SAROYAN

Days of respite are golden days.
ROBERT SOUTH

A man who values a good night's rest will not lie down with enmity in his heart, if he can help it.
LAURENCE STERNE

Rest is valuable only so far as it is a contrast. Pursued as an end, it becomes a most pitiable condition.
DAVID SWING

When one begins to turn in bed it is time to turn out.
DUKE OF WELLINGTON

## *Riches*

The quest for riches darkens the sense of right and wrong.
ANTIPHANES

Great riches have sold more men than they have bought.
FRANCIS BACON

Riches are for spending, and spending for honor and good actions; therefore extraordinary expense must be limited by the worth of the occasion.
FRANCIS BACON

The prouder a man is, the more he thinks he deserves, and the more he thinks he deserves, the less he really does deserve.
HENRY WARD BEECHER

He hath riches sufficient, who hath enough to be charitable.
**SIR THOMAS BROWNE**

Let us not envy some men their accumulated riches; their burden would be too heavy for us; we could not sacrifice, as they do, health, quiet, honor and conscience, to obtain them: It is to pay so dear from them that the bargain is a loss.
**JEAN DE LA BRUYÈRE**

Riches should be admitted into our houses, but not into our hearts; we may take them into our possession, but not into our affections.
**PIERRE CHARRON**

A man seldom gets rich without ill-got gain; as a horse does not fatten without feeding in the night.
**CHINESE PROVERB**

The best way to realize the pleasure of feeling rich is to live in a smaller house than your means would entitle you to have.
**EDWARD CLARKE**

But this I say, He which soweth sparingly shall reap also sparingly, and he which soweth bountifully shall reap also bountifully.
**II CORINTHIANS 9:6**

Perhaps you will say a man is not young; I answer, he is rich; he is not gentle, handsome, witty, brave, good-humored, but he is rich, rich, rich, rich, rich—that one word contradicts everything you can say against him.
**HENRY FIELDING**

Americans are like a rich father who wishes he knew how to give his sons the hardships that made him rich.
**ROBERT FROST**

Riches are gotten with pain, kept with care and lost with grief.
**THOMAS FULLER**

The pleasures of the rich are bought with the tears of the poor.
**THOMAS FULLER**

I am indeed rich, since my income is superior to my expense and my expense is equal to my wishes.
**EDWARD GIBBON**

Come with us to the field, or go with our brothers to the sea and cast your net. For the land and the sea shall be bountiful to you even as to us.
**KAHLIL GIBRAN**

The riches we impart are the only wealth we shall always retain.
**MATTHEW HENRY**

There is a burden of care in getting riches; fear in keeping them; temptation in using them; guilt in abusing them, sorrow in losing them; and a burden of account at last to be given concerning them.
**MATTHEW HENRY**

Riches ennoble a man's circumstances, but not himself.
**IMMANUEL KANT**

Plenty and indigence depend upon the opinion every one has of them; and riches, like glory of health, have no more beauty or pleasure than their possessor is pleaded to lend them.
**MICHEL DE MONTAIGNE**

That plenty should produce either covetousness or prodigality is a perversion of providence; and yet the generality of men are the worse for their riches.
**WILLIAM PENN**

Riches are a cause of evil, not because, of themselves, they do any evil, but because they goad men on to evil.
**POSIDONIUS**

If thou art rich, thou art poor; for, like an ass, whose back with ingots bows, thou bearest thy heavy riches but a journey, and death unloads thee.
**WILLIAM SHAKESPEARE**

Those who obtain riches by labor, care, and watching, know their value. Those who impart them to sustain and extend knowledge, virtue, and religion, know their use. Those who lose them by accident or fraud know their vanity. And those who experience the difficulties and dangers of preserving them know their perplexities.
**CHARLES SIMMONS**

He that is proud of riches is a fool. For if he be exalted above his neighbors because he hath more gold, how much inferior is he to a gold mine.
**JEREMY TAYLOR**

Leisure and solitude are the best effect of riches, because they are the mother of thought. Both are avoided by most rich men, who seek company and business, which are signs of being weary of themselves.
**WILLIAM J. TEMPLE**

Worldly riches are like nuts; many clothes are torn getting them, many a tooth broke in cracking them, but never a belly filled with eating them.
**RALPH VENNING**

## *Right*

Never will God suffer the reward to be lost, of those who do right.
**ARABIAN PROVERB**

We have heard enough about being practical and efficient and prudent. We heard it preached through several decades that these things would save the world. I think that, with the salty taste of blood and sweat on our lips, we are learning that we had best talk once again about doing what is right.
**ELLIS ARNALL**

If any man is able to convince me and show me that I do not think or act right, I will gladly change; for I seek the truth, by which no man was ever injured. But he is injured who abides in his error and ignorance.
**MARCUS AURELIUS ANTONINUS**

Every man, at the bottom of his heart, wants to do right. But only he can do right who knows right; only he knows right who thinks right; only he thinks right who believes right. It takes an army of patriotic and order-obeying soldiers to win a war. But only by an army of public-spirited and law-abiding citizens can we hope to win the peace and maintain and remain a great nation.
**WILLIAM J. H. BOETCKER**

That can not be justice for one which results in an Injustice to others; that can not be Security for one which results in Insecurity to others; that cannot be Right for one which inflicts a Wrong upon others.
**WILLIAM J. H. BOETCKER**

The machine that works right is worth more money to you than the machine that works wrong; so is the man who thinks right worth more money to you than the man who thinks wrong.
**WILLIAM J. H. BOETCKER**

A man who lives right, and is right, has more power in his silence than another has by his words.
**PHILLIPS BROOKS**

From a worldly point of view there is no mistake so great as that of being always right.
**SAMUEL BUTLER**

Let a man try faithfully, manfully to be right, he will daily grow more and more right. It is at the bottom of the condition on which all men have to cultivate themselves.
**THOMAS CARLYLE**

There are two ways, one is right; the other is wrong. If your work is only about right, then it is wrong.
**GEORGE WASHINGTON CARVER**

It may make a difference to all eternity whether we do right or wrong today.
**JAMES FREEMAN CLARKE**

The superior man seeks what is right; the inferior one, what is profitable.
**CONFUCIUS**

To see what is right, and not do it, is want of courage, or of principle.
**CONFUCIUS**

Right actions for the future are the best apologies for wrong ones in the past.
**TRYON EDWARDS**

The last temptation is the greatest treason:
To do the right deed for the wrong reason.
**T. S. ELIOT**

Being right half the time beats being half right all the time.
**MALCOLM FORBES**

To be engaged in opposing wrong affords but a slender guarantee for being right.
**WILLIAM E. GLADSTONE**

It's easier to remember when you are right than when the other person was right.
**ROBERT HALF**

I am right and therefore shall not give up the contest.
**RUTHERFORD B. HAYES**

In a family argument, if it turns out you are right, apologize at once!
**ROBERT A. HEINLEIN**

It is not who is right, but what is right, that is of importance.
**THOMAS H. HUXLEY**

Right is the only ingredient that can make might lasting in our policy and conduct toward each other, toward minorities and disadvantaged men or people—yes, even toward our enemies.
**ROBERT H. JACKSON**

My principle is to do whatever is right, and leave consequences to him who has the disposal of them.
**THOMAS JEFFERSON**

Nothing can be truly great which is not right.
**JOHNSON**

The more people who believe something, the more apt it is to be wrong. The person who's right often has to stand alone.
**SÖREN KIERKEGAARD**

If both factions, or neither, shall abuse you, you will probably be about right. Beware of being assailed by one and praised by the other.
**ABRAHAM LINCOLN**

Let us have faith that right makes might; and in that faith let us dare to do our duty as we understand it.
ABRAHAM LINCOLN

Stand with anybody that stands right and part with him when he goes wrong.
ABRAHAM LINCOLN

Narrow minds think nothing right that is above their own capacity.
FRANÇOIS DE LA ROCHEFOUCAULD

Aggressive fighting for the right is the greatest sport in the world.
THEODORE ROOSEVELT

At times, although one is perfectly right, one's legs tremble; at other times, although one is completely in the wrong, birds sing in one's soul.
VASILY V. ROZANOV

What is rightly done stays with us, to support another right beyond, or higher up; whatever is wrongly done vanishes; and by the blank, betrays what we would have built above.
JOHN RUSKIN

No man has a right to do as he pleases, except when he pleases to do right.
CHARLES SIMMONS

Rightness expresses of actions what straightness does of lines; and there can no more be two kinds of right action than there can be two kinds of straight lines.
HERBERT SPENCER

If it be right to me, it is right.
MAX STIRNER

Always do right. This will gratify some people and astonish the rest.
MARK TWAIN

It is better to be old-fashioned and right than to be up-to-date and wrong.
TIORIO

## *Righteousness*

Sow to yourselves in righteousness, reap in mercy; break up your fallow ground; for it is time to seek the Lord, till he come and rain righteousness upon you.
HOSEA 10:12

Say ye to the righteous that it will be well with him: for they shall eat the fruits of their doings. Woe unto the wicked! it shall be ill with him: for the reward of his hands shall be given him.
ISAIAH 3:10–11

Woe unto him that buildeth his house by unrighteousness and his chambers by wrong: that useth his neighbor's service without wages, and giveth him not for his work.
JEREMIAH 22:13

Better is a little with righteousness than great revenues without right. A man's heart deviseth his way: but the Lord directeth his steps.
PROVERBS 16:8–9

When the righteous are in authority, the people rejoice; but when the wicked beareth rule, the people mourn.
PROVERBS 29:2

Who shall abide in thy tabernacle? Who shall dwell in thy holy hill? He that walketh uprightly, and

worketh righteousness, and speaketh the truth in his heart.
**PSALMS 15:1–2**

The righteous shall flourish like the palm tree: he shall grow like a cedar in Lebanon. Those that be planted in the house of the Lord shall flourish in the courts of our God.
**PSALMS 92:12–13**

I have fought the good fight, I have finished my course, I have kept the faith. Henceforth there is laid up for me a crown of righteousness, which the Lord, the righteous judge, shall give me at that day; and not to me only, but unto all them also that love his appearing.
**II TIMOTHY 4:7–8**

## *Rights*

So long as any number among us remains indifferent to the . . . rights of our fellow-citizens, or becomes emotionally unbalanced to the point of overriding such rights, they are striking not at our first, but at our last line of defense.
**FRANCIS BIDDLE**

Nations begin to dig their own graves when men talk more of human rights and less of human duties.
**WILLIAM J. H. BOETCKER**

In a democracy, society must recognize that the individual has rights which are guaranteed, and the individual must recognize that he has responsibilities which are not to be evaded.
**HARRY WOODBURN CHASE**

We need not concern ourselves much about rights of property if we faithfully observe the rights of persons.
**CALVIN COOLIDGE**

Men are entitled to equal rights—but to equal rights to unequal things.
**CHARLES JAMES FOX**

I am the inferior of any man whose rights I trample underfoot.
**HORACE GREELEY**

The true civilization is where every man gives to every other every right he claims for himself.
**ROBERT G. INGERSOLL**

No man has a natural right to commit aggression on the natural rights of another; and this is all from which the laws ought to restrain him.
**THOMAS JEFFERSON**

Majorities must recognize that minorities have rights which ought not to be extinguished and they must remember that history can be written as the record of the follies of the majority.
**LINDSAY ROGERS**

Every right has its responsibilities. Like the right itself, these responsibilities stem from no man-made law, but from the very nature of man and society. The security, progress and welfare of one group is measured finally in the security, progress and welfare of all mankind.
**LEWIS SCHWELLENBACH**

## *Rules*

When ancient opinions and rules of life are taken away, the loss cannot possibly be estimated. From that moment we have no compass to govern us, nor can we know distinctly to what port to steer.
**EDMUND BURKE**

"Honesty is the best policy," "A dollar saved is a dollar earned," "Look before you leap," "A bird in

the hand is worth two in the bush," "The laborer is worthy of his hire," may be scoffed at by some intellectuals as trite copybook rules, but nonetheless they sum up the elementary experience of the race in creating and consuming wealth. . . . People may change their minds as often as their coats, and new sets of rules of conduct may be written every week, but the fact remains that human nature has not changed and does not change, that inherent human beliefs stay the same; the fundamental rules of human conduct continue to hold.
LAMMOT DU PONT

He who rules must humor full as much as he commands.
GEORGE ELIOT

It is not enough that you form, and even follow the most excellent rules for conducting yourself in the world; you must, also, know when to deviate from them, and where lies the exception.
LORD GREVILLE

### Ten Commandments

1. Never put off till to-morrow what you can do to-day.
2. Never trouble another for what you can do yourself.
3. Never spend your money before you have earned it.
4. Never buy what you do not want because it is cheap.
5. Pride costs more than hunger, thirst and cold.
6. We seldom report of having eaten too little.
7. Nothing is troublesome that we do willingly.
8. How much pain evils have cost us that have never happened!
9. Take things always by the smooth handle.
10. When angry, count ten before you speak, if very angry, count a hundred.

THOMAS JEFFERSON

### Good Rules to Follow

Learn to get along with people.

Learn to exhibit more patience than any other man you know.

Learn to respect other men's ideas and opinions.

Learn to think problems through to the end.

Learn to try to put yourself in the other fellow's place.

Be democratic.

Be loyal.

Cultivate cheerfulness.

*Work.*

HARRY J. KLINGLER

In any given society the authority of man over man runs in inverse proportion to the intellectual development of that society.
P. J. PROUDHON

Rules of conduct, whatever they may be, are not sufficient to produce good results unless the ends sought are good.
BERTRAND RUSSELL

Anyone who studies the state of things which preceded the French Revolution will see that the tremendous catastrophe came about from so excessive a regulation of men's actions in all their details, and such an enormous drafting away of the products of their actions to maintain the regulating organization, that life was fast becoming impracticable. And if we ask what then made, and now makes, this error possible, we find it to be the political superstition that governmental power is subject to no restraints.
HERBERT SPENCER

The rules which experience suggests are better than those which theorists elaborate in their libraries.
RICHARD S. STORRS

## Rulers

Despotism or unlimited sovereignty is the same in a majority of a popular assembly, an aristocratic council, an oligarchical junta, and a single emperor.
JOHN QUINCY ADAMS

The strongest poison ever known
Came from Caesar's laurel crown.
WILLIAM BLAKE

Within the highest echelons
Of politician-carnivores,
A demagogue is one whose lies
Are more believable than yours.
ART BUCK

Only with a new ruler do you realize the value of the old.
BURMESE PROVERB

As the bird feels about the net that entangles it, so do men feel about those who rule them.
CHINESE PROVERB

The character of the ruler is like the wind, the people like the grass. In whatever direction the wind blows, the grass bends.
CONFUCIUS

Men tinged with sovereignty can easily feel that the king can do no wrong.
PAUL H. DOUGLAS

Nothing is more becoming a ruler than to despise no one, nor to be insolent, but to preside over all impartially.
EPICTETUS

Whosoever is king, thou shalt be his man.
THOMAS FULLER

Kings ought to shear, not skin their sheep.
ROBERT HERRICK

The obligation of the subjects to the sovereign is understood to last as long, but no longer, than the power lasteth by which he is able to protect them.
THOMAS HOBBES

He who knows should rule, and he who does not know should obey.
ITALIAN PROVERB

All despotism is bad; but the worst is that which works with the machinery of freedom.
JUNIUS

The secret of the demagogue is to make himself as stupid as his audience so they believe they are as clever as he.
KARL KRAUS

In the birth of societies it is the chiefs of states who give it its special character; and afterward it is this special character that forms the chiefs of state.
BARON DE MONTESQUIEU

To rule is not so much a question of the heavy hand as the firm seat.
JOSÉ ORTEGA Y GASSET

In every village there will arise some miscreant, to establish the most grinding tyranny by calling himself the people.
SIR ROBERT PEEL

In the kingdom of the blind, the one-eyed king can still goof up.
LAURENCE J. PETER

I never could believe that Providence had sent a few men into the world, ready booted and spurred to

ride, and millions ready saddled and bridled to be ridden.
**RICHARD RUMBOLD**

He that ruleth over men must be just, ruling in the fear of God. And he shall be as the light of the morning, when the sun riseth, even a morning without clouds: as the tender grass springing out of the earth by clear shining after rain.
**II SAMUEL 23:3–4**

They that govern make least noise, as they that row the barge do work and puff and sweat, while he that governs sits quietly at the stern, and scarce is seen to stir.
**JOHN SELDEN**

I will believe in the right of one man to govern a nation despotically when I find a man born into the world with boots and spurs, and a nation born with saddles on their backs.
**ALGERNON SIDNEY**

A tyrant is nothing but a slave turned inside out.
**HERBERT SPENCER**

When a claim is imposed—by dictation instead of arbitration—it means enslavement whether the demand is great or small.
**THUCYDIDES**

When the king retires at night his crown rests on a nail fastened to the wall. Why, on a nail, which is nothing but a common object? Why not on a minister's head? Because the minister might take himself seriously and believe he is the king. No such danger with a nail.
**ELIE WIESEL**

# S

## Salesmanship

There is no more fascinating business in this world than that of selling. Without salesmen there would be little progress made. Selling is behind every successful enterprise of whatever character. Even a country has to have its salesmen. Character is the salesman's stock in trade. It is he who must first sell himself. The product itself is secondary. . . . Truthfulness, enthusiasm, and patience are great assets to every salesman. Without them he could not go far. Courage and courtesy are essential equipment. Leave your prospective customer with a smile and he will welcome you on your next visit. Bear in mind to be always a sales*man!*

GEORGE MATTHEW ADAMS

A salesman minus enthusiasm is just a clerk.

HARRY F. BANKS

Good will plus good service brings sales success that no competition can possibly undersell.

HARRY F. BANKS

There is a creed that every salesman who succeeds lives up to. It is simple and brief—and it works. Here it is:

Believe first in what you sell.

Believe your prospect will profit by it.

Believe in the firm back of you.

GEORGE J. BARNES

Salesmanship starts when the customer says no.

GEORGE O. BOULE, JR.

All the world is a store, and all the people in it are salespeople. That is to say, every one of us human beings is trying to transfer an idea from his own head into some other brain. And that is the essence of salesmanship.

ARTHUR BRISBANE

Successful salesmanship is 90% preparation and 10% presentation.

BERTRAND R. CANFIELD

Unless the man who works in an office is able to sell himself and his ideas, unless he has the power to convince others of the soundness of his convictions, he can never achieve his goal. He may have the best ideas in the world, he may have plans which would revolutionize entire industries. But unless he can persuade others that his ideas are good, he will never get the chance to put them into effect. Stripped of non-essentials, all business activity is a sales battle. And everyone in business must be a salesman.

ROBERT E. M. COWIE

**Sales Formula**

1. Speak plain—interestingly, intelligently.
2. Explain—patiently, thoroughly.
3. Convince—facts, factors, figures.
4. Highlights—brief résumé of picture.
5. Close—income, appreciation, diversification, safety.

Our American civilization is no accident. It exists because it was founded securely upon the concept of human liberty. It exists because we have learned

to defend the rights of the individual and to respect the dignity of man.
**BENJAMIN F. FAIRLESS**

Once you have sold a customer, make sure he is satisfied with your goods. Stay with him until the goods are used up or worn out. Your product may be of such long life that you will never sell him again, but he will sell you and your product to his friends.
**WILLIAM FEATHER**

Here's a pointer culled from the careers of men who have attained notable success: Don't sit in your office during the hours prospects can be seen. Do your office work before or after the hours during which possible customers can be reached. This may mean adding an hour or two quite often to your day's work; but in times like this particularly, the securing of a satisfactory amount of business through the expenditure of an extra hour or two a day is not an unreasonable price to pay.
**B. C. FORBES**

I've learned that you never ask a tire salesman if you need new tires.
**44-YEAR-OLD'S DISCOVERY**

A salesman, like the storage battery in your car, is constantly discharging energy. Unless he is recharged at frequent intervals he soon runs dry. This is one of the greatest responsibilities of sales leadership.
**RICHARD GRANT**

To me, super salesmanship is not high pressure. It's living, 24 hours a day, the work you are in, and naturally extends to every one you contact.
**OTTO N. HAHN**

Salesmanship consists of transferring a conviction by a seller to a buyer.
**PAUL G. HOFFMAN**

Salesmen should bear in mind that more mature men who have reached a certain point in business buy rather than are sold. A real salesman does not attempt to sell his prospect but instead directs his efforts towards putting the prospect in a frame of mind so that he will be moved to action by a given set of facts.
**ROY HOWARD**

When a man is trying to sell you something, don't imagine he is that polite all the time.
**EDGAR WATSON HOWE**

If you were to list the one hundred most successful business organizations in America, I am sure you would find that the great majority of them are successful because they have employed unique or intensive sales methods.
**W. ALTON JONES**

I think that American salesmanship can be a weapon more powerful than the atomic bomb.
**HENRY J. KAISER**

Without salesmanship we could not sell anything. If we could not sell anything we might as well not make anything, because if we made things and couldn't sell them it would be as bad as if we sold things and couldn't make them.
**STEPHEN LEACOCK**

No matter what a man's vocation or avocation may be, the nature of his progress through life is largely dependent upon his ability to sell. And the most important things he has to sell are himself and his good qualities.
**FREDERICK W. NICHOL**

Happy salesmen not only multiply their volume of business and their income, they also multiply themselves.
**WALTER RUSSELL**

We are all salesmen every day of our lives. We are selling our ideas, our plans, our enthusiasms to those with whom we come in contact.
CHARLES M. SCHWAB

The salesman who thinks that his first duty is selling is absolutely wrong. Selling is only one of the two important things a salesman is supposed to do—and it is not the more important of the two. The salesman's first duty is to make friends for his house.
ELLSWORTH M. STATLER

If I were a salesman, I would double my possible calls, for some of the best business comes through an unexpected source. Where well-laid plans have failed persistent plugging has won.
F. D. VAN AMBURGH

The average American salesman keeps 33 men and women at work—33 people producing the product he sells—and is responsible for the livelihood of 130 people.
ROBERT A. WHITNEY

## *Satisfaction*

Be satisfied with your business, and learn to love what you were bred to.
MARCUS AURELIUS ANTONINUS

Forward as occasion offers. Never look round to see whether any shall note it.... Be satisfied with success in even the smallest matter, and think that even such a result is no trifle.
MARCUS AURELIUS ANTONINUS

Little minds find satisfaction for their feelings, good or bad, in little things.
HONORÉ DE BALZAC

Only man clogs his happiness with care, destroying what is, with thoughts of what may be.
JOHN DRYDEN

Show me a thoroughly satisfied man—and I will show you a failure.
THOMAS EDISON

Human life may be regarded as a succession of frontispieces. The way to be satisfied is never to look back.
WILLIAM HAZLITT

It is not futile sometimes to be dissatisfied with life. To be dissatisfied with the order of human affairs as they are, also means to start building a better world.
HANS MARGOLIUS

To be able to look back upon one's past life with satisfaction is to live twice.
MARTIAL

There have been a few moments when I have known complete satisfaction, but only a few. I have rarely been free from the disturbing realization that my playing might have been better.
JAN IGNACE PADEREWSKI

A man who is always satisfied with himself is seldom satisfied with others.
FRANÇOIS DE LA ROCHEFOUCAULD

There's no satisfaction in hanging a man who does not object to it.
GEORGE BERNARD SHAW

We can achieve the utmost in economies by engineering knowledge; we can conquer new fields by research; we can build plants and machines that shall stand among the wonders of the world; but unless we put the right man in the right place—

unless we make it possible for our workers and executives alike to enjoy a sense of satisfaction in their jobs, our efforts will have been in vain.
**EDWARD R. STETTINIUS, JR.**

We are never satisfied with our own.
**TERENCE**

Only madmen and fools are pleased with themselves; no wise man is good enough for his own satisfaction.
**BENJAMIN WHICHCOTE**

## *Science*

Machines are beneficial to the degree that they eliminate the need for labor, harmful to the degree that they eliminate the need for skill.
**W. H. AUDEN**

The aims of pure basic science, unlike those of applied science, are neither fast-flowing nor pragmatic. The quick harvest of applied science is the useable process, the medicine, the machine. The shy fruit of pure science is understanding.
**LINCOLN BARNETT**

A tool is but the extension of a man's hand and a machine is but a complex tool; and he that invents a machine augments the power of man and the well-being of mankind
**HENRY WARD BEECHER**

We owe a lot to Thomas Edison—if it wasn't for him, we'd be watching television by candlelight.
**MILTON BERLE**

Science increases our power in proportion as it lowers our pride.
**CLAUDE BERNARD**

Observatory: A place where astronomers conjecture away the guesses of their predecessors.
**AMBROSE BIERCE**

Science can give mankind a better standard of living, better health and a better mental life, if mankind in turn gives science the sympathy and support so essential to its progress.
**VANNEVAR BUSH**

The machine can free man or enslave him; it can make of this world something resembling a paradise or a purgatory. Men have it within their power to achieve a security hitherto dreamed of only by the philosophers, or they may go the way of the dinosaurs, actually disappearing from the earth because they fail to develop the social and political intelligence to adjust to the world where their mechanical intelligence has created.
**WILLIAM G. CARLETON**

That there is an evolution of one sort or another is now common ground among scientists. Whether or not that evolution is directed is another question.
**TEILHARD DE CHARDIN**

Man's knowledge of science has clearly outstripped his knowledge of man. Our only hope of making the atom servant rather than master lies in education, in a broad liberal education where each student within his capacity can free himself from trammels of dogmatic prejudice and apply his educational accoutrement of besetting social and human problems.
**HARRY WOODBURN CHASE**

An archeologist is the best husband any woman can have; the older she gets, the more interested he is in her.
**AGATHA CHRISTIE**

In their essence there can be no conflict between science and religion. Science is a reliable method of

finding truth. Religion is the search for a satisfying basis for life. . . . Yet a world that has science needs, as never before, the inspiration that religion has to offer. . . . Beyond the nature taught by science is the spirit that gives meaning to life.
ARTHUR H. COMPTON

Exhilarated by the eerie beauties and epochal discoveries of outer space, we ought nevertheless to remember that our home planet is undoubtedly one of the most beautiful and richly endowed in the universe. Anyway, it is our first order of business; space is a poor second. This much will remain evident to the pure and sane.
DAVID CORT

I look at the natural geological record as a history of the world imperfectly kept and written in a changing dialect; of this history we possess the last volume alone, relating only to two or three countries. Of this volume, only here and there a short chapter has been preserved; and of each page, only here and there a few lines.
CHARLES DARWIN

Daily it is forced home on the mind of the biologist that nothing, not even the wind that blows, is so unstable as the level of the crust of this earth.
CHARLES DARWIN

In television and books, humans are always threatened by aliens from outer space. But can one imagine a being intelligent enough to create the technology and method to travel light years to earth being stupid enough to kill the simple creatures that it found here?
EDGAR H. DAVIS

The social problems raised by science must be faced and solved by the social sciences and the humanities. . . . If, in the long run, science is going to continue to create rather than destroy, it must be supplemented by the knowledge and wisdom to be gained from the other branches of the curriculum. For it should not be forgotten that the sacred human rights which we fought Hitler to preserve, stem from the teachings of these subjects to which we confess allegiance, but which we rarely understand completely or follow sincerely.
HAROLD W. DODDS

We must not ask where science and technology are taking us, but rather how we can manage science and technology so that they can help us get where we want to go.
RENE DUBOS

Science has sometimes been said to be opposed to faith, and inconsistent with it. But all science, in fact, rests on a basis of faith, for it assumes the permanence and uniformity of natural laws—a thing which can never be demonstrated.
TRYON EDWARDS

The whole of science is nothing more than a refinement of everyday thinking.
ALBERT EINSTEIN

There are two great classes of men: the people and the scholars, the men of science. For the former, nothing exists but that which directly leads to action. It is for the latter to see beyond. They are the free artists who create the future and its history, the conscious architects of the world.
IMMANUEL FICHTE

The most famous self-made man in the world today is our own Edison. Talk with Mr. Edison and he will tell you he owes much if not most of his success to omnivorous reading. *Forbes* is one of his favorite publications. How closely he reads it can be gathered from a letter just received from him in which he asks the editor to forward a long analytical letter to the writer of a series of articles which

contained two figures Mr. Edison questions, and he wants to know exactly on what authority or investigation they were based. Both letters were the product of Mr. Edison and were signed by him.
B. C. FORBES

Thomas Edison reads not for entertainment but to increase his store of knowledge. He sucks in information as eagerly as the bee sucks honey from flowers. The whole world, so to speak, pours its wisdom into his mind. He regards it as a criminal waste of time to go through the slow and painful ordeal of ascertaining things for one's self if these same things have already been ascertained and made available by others. In Edison's mind knowledge is power.
B. C. FORBES

Scientists ofttimes have the greatest faith in a higher power. The more they dig into, establish facts and figures, the more they marvel about the mystery of it all.
MALCOLM FORBES

When those seven spacebound hearts in one explosive instant ceased their mortal beats, the sight stunned us all to a depth that hasn't been so plumbed since President Kennedy's assassination. After 56 successful manned flights, we'd come to marvel less at the wonder of it all; to be ever less aware of the enormity of the dangers, to take almost for granted the shuttle stage of the space age that our relatively tiny plant Earth is now into.

America's heart has gone out to the near and dear of the Seven. But we've in no way lost heart for the awesome challenge that we face.... Those deaths were not in vain.
MALCOLM FORBES (1986)

What an exciting super-tomorrow it will be! Americans are today making the greatest scientific developments in our history. That is a promise of new levels of employment, industrial activity and human happiness.
CLARENCE FRANCIS

It is a mistake to believe that science consists in nothing but conclusively proved propositions, and it is unjust to demand that it should. It is a demand made by those who feel a craving for authority in some form to replace the religious catechism by something else, even a scientific one.
SIGMUND FREUD

In questions of science, the authority of a thousand is not worth that humble reasoning of a single individual.
GALILEO GALILEI

Science is the knowledge of consequences, and dependence of one fact upon another.
THOMAS HOBBES

Science is a first-rate piece of furniture for a man's upper chamber, if he has common sense on the ground floor.
OLIVER WENDELL HOLMES

New discoveries in science... will continue to create a thousand new frontiers for those who would still adventure.
HERBERT HOOVER

One machine can do the work of fifty ordinary men. No machine can do the work of one extraordinary man.
ELBERT HUBBARD

Today, the atom, in the form of weapons, is the shield of our liberties and the bulwark of our freedoms. Tomorrow, in the form of peacetime power, the atom can remake this world closer to the heart's desire.
HENRY M. JACKSON

Ours is the age which is proud of machines that think, and suspicious of men who try to.
**HOWARD MUMFORD JONES**

We are just in the kindergarten of uncovering things; there is no downcurve in science.
**CHARLES F. KETTERING**

Science has always promised two things not necessarily related—an increase first in our powers, second in our happiness and wisdom; and we have come to realize that it is the first and less important of the two promises which it has kept most abundantly.
**JOSEPH WOOD KRUTCH**

Science itself is humanist in the sense that it doesn't discriminate between human beings, but it is also morally neutral. It is no better or worse than the ethos with and for which it is being used.
**MAX LERNER**

It is chiefly upon the lay citizen, informed about science but not its practitioner, that the country must depend in determining the use to which science is put, in resolving the many public policy questions that scientific discoveries constantly force upon us.
**DAVID E. LILIENTHAL**

While becoming nuclear giants we have remained ethical infants.
**CLIFFORD MCENTARFER**

A human being who is absolutely dependent upon his own muscles can just barely keep himself alive under favorable circumstances; and to raise himself above the animals he must in some way supplement his own feeble strength. Civilization came into existence because certain strong groups of people used the muscles of men and women of weaker groups for this purpose; if there were no machines to-day there would be no art, literature, science, leisure, or comfort for anyone without slavery.
**F. A. MERRICK**

If I have been able to see farther than others, it was because I stood on the shoulders of giants.
**SIR ISAAC NEWTON**

I have rarely seen the face of a mechanic in the action of creation which was not fine, never one which was not earnest and impressive.
**THOMAS NELSON PAGE**

Science belongs to no one country.
**LOUIS PASTEUR**

Take interest, I implore you, in those sacred dwellings which are designated by the expression term, laboratories. Demand that they be multiplied and advanced. These are the temples of the future, temples of well-being and happiness . . . where humanity grows greater, stronger, better.
**LOUIS PASTEUR**

Science seeks truth and discovers rightness. Religion seeks righteousness and discovers truth. Both have acquired knowledge of creative and destructive ways, and both point the same way of right living.
**WILLIAM G. PATTEN**

A new scientific truth does not triumph by convincing its opponents, but rather because its opponents die, and a new generation grows up that is familiar with it.
**MAX PLANCK**

The simplest schoolboy is now familiar with truths for which Archimedes would have sacrificed his life.
**ERNEST RENAN**

I like talking to engineers best. They build bridges, they're very precise, very disciplined, yet I find they have roving minds.
RALPH RICHARDSON

The work of science is to substitute facts for appearances and demonstrations for impressions.
JOHN RUSKIN

In art nothing worth doing can be done without genius; in science even a very moderate capacity can contribute to a supreme achievement.
BERTRAND RUSSELL

The technical progress of industry has been a reflection of our ability to apply increasingly accurate methods of measurement to material things. The art of measuring psychological human dimensions is relatively undeveloped. To all of the complexities of management we must bring to bear infinite patience and persistence, consistency and complete sincerity.
LOUIS RUTHENBURG

If we are to become the masters of science, not its slaves, we must learn to use its immense power to good purpose. The machine itself has neither mind nor soul nor moral sense. Only man has been endowed with these godlike attributes. Every age has its destined duty. Ours is to nurture an awareness of those divine attributes and a sense of responsibility in giving them expression.
DAVID SARNOFF

There are practically no new physical frontiers for the modern Davy Crocketts to explore. (But) the scientific frontiers of today are just as mysterious and challenging as were the geographical frontiers of 150 years ago. We have barely scratched the surface in our exploration of the wonders of God's universe.
CHARLES B. SHUMAN

The possibilities of modern technology are tremendous. If these possibilities can be realized, no one can doubt that we are on the threshold of gaining a far better standard of living than man has ever known. Never have the rewards of willingness to take a broad view of common interests been greater.
SUMNER H. SLICHTER

The greatest engineering is the engineering of men.
ROBERT LOUIS STEVENSON

Science has its being in a perpetual mental restlessness.
WILLIAM J. TEMPLE

Science moves, but slowly, slowly, creeping on from point to point.
ALFRED, LORD TENNYSON

Technology is now forcing upon us a standard of behavior that formerly was expected only of saints.
ARNOLD TOYNBEE

It was necessary for us to discover greater powers of destruction than our enemies. We did. But after every war we have followed through with a new rise in our standard of living by the application of war-taught knowledge for the benefit of the world. It will be the same with the atomic bomb principles.
THOMAS J. WATSON

Science . . . is a natural and integral part of man's whole life, an activity which, at base, is a blend of logic, intuition, art and belief. It has been refined into an instrument of great beauty and precision by the few, but this science of the few is merely the distillation of the experience of the many. As a natural social activity of man, science belongs to all men.
WARREN WEAVER

Civilization requires slaves. Human slavery is wrong, insecure and demoralizing. On mechanical

slavery, on the slavery of the machine, the future of the world depends.
**OSCAR WILDE**

Material science now has the clear possibility and promise of the systematic utilization of all the natural resources of the earth for the good of the whole human race.... Maintaining and improving the standard of living of all the peoples of the earth through increasing use of mechanical horsepower and the scientific approach is now one of the keys to peace in the world.
**CHARLES E. WILSON**

We Americans live in a scientific world. We use scientific and technological developments to reduce backbreaking labor, to gain shorter working hours and higher pay, to raise our living standards to the world's highest. That is why the scientist's job concerns everybody vitally. Today's pioneer does not wear a coonskin cap or shoulder a rifle. More likely he is wearing a laboratory apron and wielding a stirring rod. He continually finds new lands to explore in his test tubes. His hunting is done with the microscope. He seeks new horizons in the cyclotron.
**ROBERT E. WILSON**

## *Seasons*

Summer: The time of year that children slam the door they left open all winter.
**ANONYMOUS**

Ah, summer, what power you have to make us suffer and like it.
**RUSSELL BAKER**

Sweet daughter of a rough and stormy sire, hoar winter's blooming child, delightful spring.
**ANNA BARBAULD**

The quality of life, which in the ardour of spring was personal and sexual, becomes social in midsummer.
**HENRY BESTON**

Summer ends, and autumn comes, and he who would have it otherwise would have high tide always and a full moon every night.
**HAL BORLAND**

Autumn arrives early in the morning, but spring at the close of a winter day.
**ELIZABETH BOWEN**

Summer is a sailor in a rowboat and ice cream on your dress when you're four years old. Summer is a man with his coat off, wet sand between your toes, the smell of a garden an hour before moonrise. Oh, summer is silk itself, a giant geranium and music from a flute far away.
**MICHAEL BROWN**

June reared the bunch of flowers you carry from seeds of April's sowing.
**ROBERT BROWNING**

And the spring comes slowly up this way.
**ROBERT BURNS**

The tendinous part of the mind, so to speak, is more developed in winter; the fleshy, in summer. I should say winter has given the bone and sinew to literature, summer the tissues and blood.
**JOHN BURROUGHS**

In the midst of winter, I finally learned that there was in me an invincible summer.
**ALBERT CAMUS**

Spring is nature taking up its option on the world.
**JIMMY CANNON**

Everything holds its breath except spring. She bursts through as strong as ever.
**EMILY CARR**

Spring is sooner recognized by plants than by men.
**CHINESE PROVERB**

The spring comes slowly up this way.
**SAMUEL TAYLOR COLERIDGE**

Summer has set in with its usual severity.
**SAMUEL TAYLOR COLERIDGE**

Summer: The season of inferior sledding.
**ESKIMO PROVERB**

Alas, that spring should vanish with the rose!
**EDWARD FITZGERALD**

Summer, with its dog days, its vacations, its distractions, is over. We have had our holidays, our rest, our recreation. The fall season, with its new opportunities for effort, enterprise and achievement, is upon us. Let us rip off our coats and get down to business. We may have allowed pessimism to grip us during the summer months. We may even have allowed laziness to enter our bones. Now it is up to us to throw off both lassitude and pessimism. The time has come for action, for aggressiveness. . . .
**B. C. FORBES**

One cannot walk into an April day in a negative way. With spring, each man's plans and hopes result in new efforts, fresh actions.

All of which has a mighty important bearing on the economy. There are those of us who think that the psychology of man, each and together, has more impact on markets, business, services and building and all the fabric of an economy than all the more measurable statistical indices.
**MALCOLM FORBES**

Oh, the lovely fickleness of an April day.
**WILLIAM GIBSON**

I should like to enjoy this summer flower by flower, as if it were to be the last one for me.
**ANDRÉ GIDE**

Spring: Nature renewing its lease on life.
**ARNOLD GLASOW**

The only difference between April and March is that you expect it in March.
**ARNOLD GLASOW**

It is the Mayflower and our hope; the spring is come.
**EDWARD E. HALE**

It was one of the first of the spring days—one of the days that seemed to be promise and fulfillment in one.
**LUCRETIA PEABODY HALE**

Spring unlocks the flowers to paint the laughing soil.
**REGINALD HEBER**

Here is the ghost of a summer that lived for us.
Here is a promise of summer to be.
**WILLIAM E. HENLEY**

Every mile is two in winter.
**GEORGE HERBERT**

He that passeth a winter's day escapes an enemy.
**GEORGE HERBERT**

I saw old autumn in the misty morn stand shadowless like silence.
**THOMAS HOOD**

Summer treads on heels of spring.
**HORACE**

Summer afternoon, summer afternoon; to me those have always been the two most beautiful words in the English language.
**HENRY JAMES**

When a poet mentions the spring we know that the zephyrs are about to whisper, that the groves are to recover their verdure, the linnets to warble forth their notes of love, and the flocks and herds to frisk over vales painted with flowers.
**SAMUEL JOHNSON**

Season of mists and mellow fruitfulness.
**JOHN KEATS**

There is something of summer in the hum of insects.
**WALTER SAVAGE LANDOR**

The course of the seasons is a piece of clockwork, with a cuckoo to call when it is spring.
**GEORG CHRISTOPH LICHTENBERG**

If Spring came but once a century instead of once a year or burst forth with the sound of an earthquake and not in silence, what wonder and expectation there would be in all hearts to behold the miraculous change.
**HENRY WADSWORTH LONGFELLOW**

Magnificent autumn! He comes not like a pilgrim, clad in russet weeds; not like a hermit, clad in gray; but like a warrior with the stain of blood in his brazen mail.
**HENRY WADSWORTH LONGFELLOW**

Oh, the long and dreary winter! Oh, the cold and cruel winter!
**HENRY WADSWORTH LONGFELLOW**

It is the genius of the summer to restore to us the Golden Age when men lay lazily under the trees, and crimson-cheeked fruits fell all around them with a plump, so that they had not even to take the trouble to rise out of their lethargy in order to pick them.
**ROBERT LYND**

Winter air is one of the things that can be still without being stagnant. As a matter of fact, the stiller it is the more it seems to tingle with life.
**ROBERT LYND**

Autumn is the American season. In Europe the leaves turn yellow or brown, and fall. Here they take fire on the trees and hang there flaming. We think this frost-fire is a portent somehow: a promise that the continent has given us. Life, too, we think, is capable of taking fire in this country; of creating beauty never seen.
**ARCHIBALD MACLEISH**

Summer is drawn blinds in Louisiana, long winds in Wyoming, shades of elms and maples in New England.
**ARCHIBALD MACLEISH**

In those vernal seasons of the year when the air is calm and pleasant, it were an injury and sullenness against nature not to go out and see her riches, and partake in her rejoicing with heaven and earth.
**JOHN MILTON**

Interest in the changing seasons is a much happier state of mind than being hopelessly in love with spring.
**GEORGE SANTAYANA**

Rough winds do shake the darling buds of May.
And summer's lease hath all too short a date.
**WILLIAM SHAKESPEARE**

The teeming autumn, big with rich increase.
**WILLIAM SHAKESPEARE**

Winter tames man, woman and beast.
**WILLIAM SHAKESPEARE**

The day becomes more solemn and serene when noon is past: There is a harmony in autumn and a luster in its sky which through the summer is not heard or seen, as if it could not be, as if it had not been.
**PERCY BYSSHE SHELLEY**

Never speak to me about summer; summer has no charms for me. I look forward anxiously to the return of bad weather and blazing fires.
**SYDNEY SMITH**

How sad would be November if we had no knowledge of the spring!
**EDWIN TEALE**

Full knee-deep lies the winter snow, and the winter winds are wearily sighing.
**ALFRED, LORD TENNYSON**

Come, gentle Spring! ethereal Mildness! come.
**JAMES THOMSON**

Far-handed spring unbosoms every grace.
**JAMES THOMSON**

The first day of spring is one thing, and the first spring day is another. The difference between them is sometimes as great as a month.
**HENRY VAN DYKE**

Extreme cold when it first arrives seems to generate cheerfulness and sociability. For a few hours all life's dubious problems are dropped in favor of the clear and congenial task of keeping alive.
**E. B. WHITE**

The first day of spring was once the time for taking the young virgins into the fields, there in dalliance to set an example in fertility for Nature to follow. Now we just set the clock an hour ahead and change the oil in the crankcase.
**E. B. WHITE**

## *Secrets*

What right have we to pry into the secret of others? True or false, the take that is gabbled to us, what concern is it of ours?
**EDWARD BULWER-LYTTON**

A man's most open actions have a secret side to them.
**JOSEPH CONRAD**

Leaders in every walk of life act shortsightedly when they refuse to take suitable opportunity to afford the public a chance to get acquainted with them. Half this world's troubles spring from misunderstanding, from mistrust, from secrecy. The remedy lies in letting in the daylight, in allowing the public to know how our leaders won their way to the front, in bringing home to the rank and file that those at the top had to work hard and climb hard to get there. Quite a part of my time is devoted to the very purpose of trying to bring about a better understanding between the haves and the have-nots. . . .
**B. C. FORBES**

Three can keep a secret, if two of them are dead.
**BENJAMIN FRANKLIN**

Nothing is as burdensome as a secret.
**FRENCH PROVERB**

A secret is diluted by the square of the number of those who have heard it.
**ROBERT HALF**

No one ever keeps a secret so well as a child.
VICTOR HUGO

The truth about a man lies first and foremost in what he hides.
ANDRÉ MALRAUX

I will govern my life and thoughts as if the whole world were to see the one and to read the other, for what does it signify to make anything a secret to my neighbor, when to God, who is the searcher of our hearts, all our privacies are open?
SENECA

Secrecy is the soul of business.
SPANISH PROVERB

## Security

We will never have real safety and security for the wage earners unless we provide for safety and security for the wage payers and the wage savers, investors, and then, by all means, protection for both against reckless wasters and wage spenders.
WILLIAM J. H. BOETCKER

While employers and employees and the public unite to make for physical safety, let's all unite to make America safe industrially; let's make it safe for labor to invest its skill; let's make it safe for capital to invest its money; let's make it safe for initiative, energy and enterprises to invest its experience and executive ability; let's make it worthwhile for all.
WILLIAM J. H. BOETCKER

Security is a false god; begin making sacrifices to it and you are lost.
PAUL BOWLES

You are financially secure when you can afford anything you want and you don't want anything.
ART BUCK

There are safe and unsafe ways of doing nearly anything. The knowledge or the knack of doing things safely is gained by experience, properly directed.
RALPH BUDD

Too many people are thinking of security instead of opportunity. They seem more afraid of life than of death.
JAMES F. BYRNES

There is not much collective security in a flock of sheep on the way to the butcher.
WINSTON CHURCHILL

It's an old adage that the way to be safe is never to be secure.... Each one of us requires the spur of insecurity to force us to do our best.
HAROLD W. DODDS

The search for static security—in the law and elsewhere—is misguided. The fact is security can only be achieved through constant change, through discarding old ideas that have outlived their usefulness and adapting others to current facts.
WILLIAM O. DOUGLAS

We believe that our truly urgent need is to make our nation secure, our economy strong and our dollar sound. For every American this matter of the sound dollar is crucial. Without a sound dollar, every American family would face a renewal of inflation, an ever-increasing cost of living, the withering away of savings and life insurance policies.
DWIGHT D. EISENHOWER

Security isn't securities. It's knowing that someone cares whether you are or cease to be.
MALCOLM FORBES

The ultimate in futility is owning important jewelry. Insurers often insist on the wearing of paste replicas because necks with real rocks around 'em risk wringing.
MALCOLM FORBES

The farther we get away from the land, the greater our insecurity.
HENRY FORD

No government can guarantee security. It can only tax production, distribution and service and gradually crush the power to pay taxes. That settles nothing. It only uses up the gains of the past and postpones the developments of the future.
HENRY FORD

The psychic task which a person can and must set for himself is not to feel secure but to be able to tolerate insecurity.
ERICH FROMM

Security is the mother of danger and the grandmother of destruction.
THOMAS FULLER

Whoever created the name life insurance had to be the sales genius of all time.
ROBERT HALF

It is when we all play safe that we create a world of utmost insecurity.
DAG HAMMARSKJÖLD

Security is the priceless product of freedom. Only the strong can be secure, and only in freedom can men produce those material resources which can secure them from want at home and against aggression from abroad.
B. E. HUTCHINSON

Security is mostly a superstition. It does not exist in nature, nor do the children of men as a whole experience it. Avoiding danger is no safer in the long run than outright exposure. The fearful are caught as often as the bold. Faith alone defends.
HELEN KELLER

He who is firmly seated in authority soon learns to think security, and not progress, the highest lesson of statecraft.
JAMES RUSSELL LOWELL

As soon as a preoccupation with security begins to dominate human life, the scope of human life itself tends to be diminished.
GABRIEL MARCEL

By a divine paradox, wherever there is one slave there are two. So in the wonderful reciprocities of being, we can never reach the higher levels until all our fellows ascend with us. There is no true liberty for the individual except as he finds it in the liberty of all. There is no true security for the individual except as he finds it in the security of all.
EDWIN MARKHAM

The trouble with worrying so much about your security in the future is that you feel so insecure in the present.
HARLAN MILLER

The parent can train the natures of children to remain fast while their habits change through the years. We must have a citizenry which will by long inner training be able to feel secure in a storm. No parent can raise that kind of child till he is himself that kind of person.
H. CLAY MITCHELL, D.D.

The fire at the manufacturing plant was due to friction caused by a large inventory rubbing up against an insurance policy.
OLD SOUTHERN SAYING

Happiness has many roots, but none more important than security.
EDWARD R. STETTINIUS, JR.

The trouble with complete security is its drab monotony. A life without the impetus of work and struggle is only half a life, and most of us would settle down to complete inertia if we did not have to work to eat.
CID RICKETTS SUMNER

The desire for safety stands against every great and noble enterprise.
TACITUS

## Self

If somebody tells you you have ears like a donkey, pay no attention. But if two people tell you, buy yourself a saddle.
SHOLEM ALEICHEM

He who asks of life nothing but the improvement of his own nature . . . is less liable than anyone else to miss and waste life.
HENRI FRÉDÉRIC AMIEL

Every man must scratch his head with his own nails.
ARABIAN PROVERB

I count him braver who overcomes his desires than him who conquers his enemies; for the hardest victory is the victory over self.
ARISTOTLE

Never esteem anything as of advantage to thee that shall make thee break thy word or lose thy self-respect.
MARCUS AURELIUS ANTONINUS

Man must be arched and buttressed from within, else the temple will crumble to dust.
MARCUS AURELIUS ANTONINUS

Whatever task you undertake, do it with all your heart and soul. Always be courteous, never be discouraged. Beware of him who promises something for nothing. Do not blame anybody for your mistakes and failures. Do not look for approval except the consciousness of doing your best.
BERNARD M. BARUCH

To be ambitious for wealth, and yet always expecting to be poor; to be always doubting your ability to get what you long for, is like trying to reach east by traveling west. There is no philosophy which will help man to succeed when he is always doubting his ability to do so, and thus attracting failure. No matter how hard you work for success if your thought is saturated with the fear of failure, it will kill your efforts, neutralize you endeavors and make success impossible.
CHARLES BAUDOUIN

He's a self-made man,
Certainly no faker.
His only fault is
He worships his maker.
CECIL BAXTER

The world cannot deprive a man of his rectitude, the nobility of his soul or his belief in Almighty God; nor can the world give these riches to a man. Only within himself can he find them, these fragrant flowers of life.
LOUIS BEALE

A man's true estate of power and riches is to be in himself; not in his dwelling or position or external relations, but in his own essential character.
HENRY WARD BEECHER

A man without self-restraint is like a barrel without hoops, and tumbles to pieces.
HENRY WARD BEECHER

There is no one who cannot find a place for himself in our kind of world. Each of us has some unique capacity waiting for realization. Every person is valuable in his own existence—for himself alone. In our communities, in our circle of family and friends, each of us can bring to fruition these innate, God-given abilities.
GEORGE H. BENDER

No bird soars too high, if he soars on his own wings.
WILLIAM BLAKE

If you want to know how rich you really are, find out what would be left of you tomorrow if you should lose every dollar you own tonight.
WILLIAM J. H. BOETCKER

If you wish to succeed in managing and controlling others—Learn to manage and control yourself.
WILLIAM J. H. BOETCKER

Never mind what the "people" think of you! They may overestimate or underestimate you! Until they discover your real worth, your success depends mainly upon what you think of yourself and whether you believe in yourself. You can succeed if nobody else believes it; but you will never succeed if you don't believe in yourself.
WILLIAM J. H. BOETCKER

That you may retain your self-respect—it is better to displease the people by doing what you know is right, than to temporarily please them by doing what you know is wrong.
WILLIAM J. H. BOETCKER

He that is master of himself will soon be master of others.
H. G. BOHN

Self-distrust is the cause of most of our failures. In the assurance of strength, there is strength, and they are the weakest, however strong, who have no faith in themselves or their own powers.
CHRISTIAN BOVÉE

The right to be let alone is the most comprehensive of rights and the right most valued in civilized man.
LOUIS D. BRANDEIS

Get away from the crowd when you can. Keep yourself to yourself, if only for a few hours daily.
ARTHUR BRISBANE

Self-reliance and self-respect are about as valuable commodities as we can carry in our pack through life.
LUTHER BURBANK

Oh, wad some power the giftie gie us to see oursel's as ithers see us.
ROBERT BURNS

From self alone expect applause.
MARION L. BURTON

The world will always be governed by self-interest: we should not try to stop this: we should try and make the self-interest of cads a little more coincident with that of decent people.
SAMUEL BUTLER

Self-laudation abounds among the unpolished, but nothing can stamp a man more sharply as ill-bred.
CHARLES BUXTON

Let every man mind his own business.
**MIGUEL DE CERVANTES**

It is asked, how can the laboring man find time for self-culture? I answer, that an earnest purpose finds time, or makes it. It seizes on spare moments, and turns fragments to golden account. A man who follows his calling with industry and spirit, and uses his earnings economically, will always have some portion of the day at command. And it is astonishing how fruitful of improvement a short season becomes, when eagerly seized and faithfully used. It has often been observed, that those who have the most time at their disposal profit by it the least. A single hour in the day, steadily given to the study of some interesting subject, brings unexpected accumulations of knowledge.
**WILLIAM ELLERY CHANNING**

There is such a thing as honest pride and self-respect.
**EDWIN H. CHAPIN**

Our own self-love draws a thick veil between us and our faults.
**LORD CHESTERFIELD**

Those whom you can make like themselves better will, I promise you, like you very well.
**LORD CHESTERFIELD**

It is necessary to try to surpass one's self always; this occupation ought to last as long as life.
**QUEEN CHRISTINA**

Every man is the painter and the sculptor of his own life.
**ST. JOHN CHRYSOSTOM**

No external advantages can supply the place of self-reliance. The force of one's being, if it has any force, must come from within. No one can safely imitate another; nor by following in the footsteps of another can he ever gain distinction or enjoy prosperity.
**R. W. CLARK**

None of us has an identity except as part of our families, our friends, our society, our faith, our world. Connection with others validates our lives.
**HAROLD CLURMAN**

Be yourself. Ape no greatness. Be willing to pass for what you are.
**SAMUEL COLEY**

People who have nothing to do are quickly tired by their own company.
**JEREMY COLLIER**

A man's best friends are his ten fingers.
**ROBERT COLLYER**

We are all serving a self-sentence in the dungeon of self.
**CYRIL CONNOLLY**

It is difficult for men in high office to avoid the malady of self-delusion. They are always surrounded by worshippers. They are constantly, and for the most part sincerely, assured of their greatness.
**CALVIN COOLIDGE**

To be nobody-but-yourself—in a world which is doing its best, night and day, to make you everybody but yourself—means to fight the hardest battle which any human being can fight, and never stop fighting.
**E. E. CUMMINGS**

We never understand a thing so well, and make it our own, as when we have discovered it for ourselves.
**RENÉ DESCARTES**

At this critical period of our country, we must have a government of self-respect. As a people, we create that self-respect in our government. However, we must recognize that we are in a conflict which will be with us for at least a generation. Perhaps for fifty years to come. Let us face the simple fact: there is no gadget or device for victory. To think so is to delude ourselves. We cannot buy our way out nor appease our way out. Our moral strength is in ourselves, in our patience, in our courage, in our decision and in our resolution.
WILLIAM J. DONOVAN

Self government is no less essential to the development, growth, and happiness of the individual than to the nation.
WILLIAM H. DOUGLAS

Before a painter puts a brush to his canvas he sees his picture mentally. It is the mental concept that he externalizes with the help of paint and canvas. If you think of yourself in terms of a painting, what do you see? How do you appear to yourself? Is the picture one you think worth painting? You are what you think you are. You create yourself in the image you hold in your mind. What you are advertises what you think.
THOMAS DREIER

No one can live my life for me. If I am wise, I shall begin today to build my own truer and better world from within.
H. W. DRESSER

We can change our whole life and the attitude of people around us simply by changing ourselves.
RUDOLF DRIEKURS

Touchiness, when it becomes chronic, is a morbid condition of the inward disposition. It is self-love inflamed to the acute point.
SIR WILLIAM DRUMMOND

Self-defense is Nature's oldest law.
JOHN DRYDEN

A person who doubts himself is like a man who would enlist in the ranks of his enemies and bear arms against himself. He makes his failure certain by himself being the first person to be convicted of it.
ALEXANDRE DUMAS

This country was not built by men who relied on somebody else to take care of them. It was built by men who relied on themselves, who dared to shape their own lives, who had enough courage to blaze new trails—enough confidence in themselves to take the necessary risks.
J. OLLIE EDMUNDS

Whatever deprives a man of personal individual motive for self-improvement and robust exertion will not make him free, but on the contrary more servile and in the long run less intelligent, industrious and free, for freedom is a matter of character and will power.
CHARLES W. ELIOT

One's self-satisfaction is an untaxed kind of property which it is very unpleasant to find depreciated.
GEORGE ELIOT

There is a great deal of unmapped country within us.
GEORGE ELIOT

Men who know themselves are no longer fools; they stand on the threshold of the Door of Wisdom.
HAVELOCK ELLIS

All are needed by each one. Nothing is fair or good alone.
RALPH WALDO EMERSON

Do not spill thy soul in running hither and yon, grieving over the mistakes and the vices of others.

The one person whom it is most necessary to reform is yourself.
**RALPH WALDO EMERSON**

Make the most to yourself, for that is all there is to you.
**RALPH WALDO EMERSON**

There is a time in every man's education when he arrives at the conviction that envy is ignorance; that imitation is suicide; that he must take himself for better, for worse, as his portion; that though the wide universe is full of good, no kernel of nourishing corn can come to him but through his toil bestowed on that plot of ground which is given him to till. The power which resides in him is new in Nature, and none but he knows what that is which he can do, nor does he know until he has tried.
**RALPH WALDO EMERSON**

No man is free who is not master of himself.
**EPICTETUS**

Before an egg can grow into a chicken, it must first totally cease to be an egg. Each thing must lose its original identity before it can be something else. Therefore, before a thing is transformed into something else, it must come to a level of no-thingness.
**PERLE EPSTEIN**

Blow your own horn loud. If you succeed, people will forgive your noise; if you fail, they'll forget it.
**WILLIAM FEATHER**

Invest in yourself—if you have confidence in yourself.
**WILLIAM FEATHER**

It is better to rely on yourself than on your friends.
**WILLIAM FEATHER**

Self-restraint is feeling your oats without sowing them.
**SHANON FIFE**

Every individual is a king in the castle of his own mind. As king of his thoughts he can think those thoughts which will make him an unhappy and fearful monarch, or he can make his reign joyous and harmonious by listening to the Father within himself before making decisions.
**LOWELL FILLMORE**

Each of us is an impregnable fortress that can be laid waste only from within.
**TIMOTHY J. FLYNN**

### I Resolve for 1920

To sit down, all by myself and take a personal stock-taking once a month

To be no more charitable in viewing my own faults than I am in viewing the faults of others.

To face the facts candidly and courageously.

To address myself carefully, prayerfully, to remedying defects.

**B. C. FORBES**

What you have outside you counts less than what you have inside you.
**B. C. FORBES**

The man who is bigger than his job keeps cool. He does not lose his head, he refuses to become rattled, to fly off in a temper. The man who would control others must be able to control himself. There is something admirable, something inspiring, something soul-stirring about a man who displays coolness and courage under extremely trying circumstances. A good temper is not only a business asset. It is the secret of health. The longer you live, the

more you will learn that a disordered temper breeds a disordered body.
B. C. FORBES

Where you're from only matters in relation to where you are.
MALCOLM FORBES

The great trouble today is that there are too many people looking for someone else to do something for them. The solution of most of our troubles is to be found in everyone doing something for himself.
HENRY FORD

Rebellion against your handicaps gets you nowhere. Self-pity gets you nowhere. One must have the adventurous daring to accept oneself as a bundle of possibilities and undertake the most interesting game in the world—making the most of one's best.
HARRY EMERSON FOSDICK, D.D.

We reproach people for talking about themselves, but it is the subject they treat best.
ANATOLE FRANCE

He that falls in love with himself will have no rivals.
BENJAMIN FRANKLIN

If you would have a faithful servant and one that you like, serve yourself.
BENJAMIN FRANKLIN

What is best for people is what they do for themselves.
BENJAMIN FRANKLIN

A man is little the better for liking himself if nobody else likes him.
THOMAS FULLER

There is no dependence that can be sure but a dependence upon one's self.
JOHN GAY

Every man is two men; one is awake in the darkness, the other asleep in the light.
KAHLIL GIBRAN

You give but little when you give of your possessions. It is when you give of yourself that you truly give.
KAHLIL GIBRAN

You've no idea what a poor opinion I have of myself—and how little I deserve it.
WILLIAM S. GILBERT

A man capable of loving himself will be like a well-kept flower garden—productive and inspiring to others.
MARGUERETTE GILMORE

Whenever you are too selfishly looking out for your own interest, you have only one person working for you—yourself. When you help a dozen other people with their problems, you have a dozen people working with you.
WILLIAM B. GIVEN, JR.

He who is plenteously provided for from within needs but little from without.
JOHANN WOLFGANG VON GOETHE

Know thyself? If I knew myself, I'd run away.
JOHANN WOLFGANG VON GOETHE

Let everyone sweep in front of his own door and the whole world will be clean.
JOHANN WOLFGANG VON GOETHE

The best of all governments is that which teaches us to govern ourselves.
**JOHANN WOLFGANG VON GOETHE**

Whatever liberates our spirit without giving us self-control is disastrous.
**JOHANN WOLFGANG VON GOETHE**

The fortunate circumstances of our lives are generally found, at last, to be of our own producing.
**OLIVER GOLDSMITH**

He is great enough that is his own master.
**JOSEPH HALL**

Every person is responsible for all the good within the scope of his abilities, and for no more, and none can tell whose sphere is the largest.
**GAIL HAMILTON**

A self-made man may prefer a self-made name.
**LEARNED HAND**

Many men spend their lives in gazing at their own shadows, and so dwindle away into shadows thereof.
**AUGUSTUS HARE**

It's surprising how many persons go through life without ever recognizing that their feelings toward other people are largely determined by their feelings toward themselves, and if you're not comfortable within yourself, you can't be comfortable with others.
**SYDNEY J. HARRIS**

Ninety per cent of the world's woe comes from people not knowing themselves, their abilities, their frailties, and even their real virtues. Most of us go almost all the way through life as complete strangers to ourselves—so how can we know anyone else?
**SYDNEY J. HARRIS**

No man would, I think, exchange his existence with any other man, however fortunate. We had as lief not be, as not be ourselves.
**WILLIAM HAZLITT**

"I remain true to myself." Exactly. That is your misfortune. Would that, just once, you could be untrue to yourself.
**FRIEDRICH HEBBEL**

What happens to us is nothing. What happens in us is as inexhaustible and infinite as eternity through which we pass.
**JENO HECTAI**

Self-respect—that cornerstone of all virtue.
**SIR JOHN HERSCHEL**

Self-reliance can turn a salesman into a merchant; a politician into a statesman; an attorney into a jurist; an unknown youth into a great leader. All are to be tomorrow's big leaders—those who in solitude sit above the clang and dust of time, with the world's secret trembling on their lips.
**HILLIS**

It is not love of self but hatred of self which is at the root of the troubles that afflict our world.
**ERIC HOFFER**

What lies behind us and what lies before us are tiny matters compared with what lies within us.
**OLIVER WENDELL HOLMES**

There is no Sure Thing, but the surest is a good job well attended to, for steady promotion is almost certain; and no one can help you in holding a good job except Old Man You. Some say an active commercial club, an up-and-coming community, a good pastor, a reform administration at Washington, are necessary; others say a man is made by his wife or

mother, but Old Man You really does it, or doesn't do it; many teach what is called good sense, but only you may acquire it.
EDGAR WATSON HOWE

The average man plays to the gallery of his own self-esteem.
ELBERT HUBBARD

What others say of me matters little; what I myself say and do matters much.
ELBERT HUBBARD

Probably the most neglected friend you have is you.
L. RON HUBBARD

A man has to live with himself, and he should see to it that he always has good company.
CHARLES EVANS HUGHES

The strongest man in the world is he who stands most alone.
HENRIK IBSEN

Everyone gives himself credit for more brains than he has and less money.
ITALIAN PROVERB

I am of a sect by myself, as far as I know.
THOMAS JEFFERSON

Measure yourself by your best moments, not by your worst. We are too prone to judge ourselves by our moments of despondency and depression. We have all felt the desire, at times almost victorious desire, to get away from everything and retire into a cottage in the wilderness. But we don't do it, because we are better men and women than we think we are.
ROBERT JOHNSON

Every man is of importance to himself.
SAMUEL JOHNSON

Few men survey themselves with so much severity as not to admit prejudices in their own favor.
SAMUEL JOHNSON

Your levelers wish to level down as far as themselves, but they cannot bear leveling up to themselves.
SAMUEL JOHNSON

Our business in life is not to get ahead of others, but to get ahead of ourselves—to break our own records, to outstrip our yesterday by our today, to do our work with more force than ever before.
STEWART B. JOHNSON

Many persons wonder why they don't amount to more than they do, have good stuff in them, energetic, persevering, and have ample opportunities. It is all a case of trimming the useless branches and throwing the whole force of power into the development of something that counts.
WALTER J. JOHNSTON

I am only one; but I am still one. I cannot do everything, but still I can do something. I will not refuse to do the something I can do.
HELEN KELLER

Self-pity is our worst enemy, and if we yield to it, we can never do anything wise in the world.
HELEN KELLER

Every man who believes in himself, no matter who he be, stands on a higher level than the wobbler.
HERMANN KEYSERLING

Just as you are unconsciously influenced by outside advertisement, announcement, and appeal, so you can vitally influence your life from within by auto-

suggestion. The first thing each morning, and the last thing each night, suggest to yourself specific ideas that you wish to embody in your character and personality. Address such suggestions to yourself, silently or aloud, until they are deeply impressed upon your mind.
**GRENVILLE KLEISER**

Humility is a part of wisdom, and is most becoming in men. But let no one discourage self-reliance; it is, of all the rest, the greatest quality of true manliness.
**LOUIS KOSSUTH**

He who gains a victory over other men is strong; but he who gains a victory over himself is all powerful.
**LAO-TZU**

He who knows others is clever, but he who knows himself is enlightened.
**LAO-TZU**

Than self-restraint there is nothing better.
**LAO-TZU**

You come to understand yourself through understanding others. History is full of examples of philosophers and holy men who retired into the wilderness to ponder the mystery of self. But you can't learn to understand yourself by withdrawing to your mountaintop or A-bomb shelter. The self, by which we mean the personality, exists chiefly in the appreciation and esteem of your fellows.
**RICHARD LAKE**

A man's mind is the man himself.
**LATIN PROVERB**

He conquers who conquers himself.
**LATIN PROVERB**

Many will hate you if you love yourself.
**LATIN PROVERB**

Think wrongly, if you please; but in all cases think for yourself.
**LESSING**

When you are alone you are all your own.
**LEONARDO DA VINCI**

He who is in love with himself has at least this advantage—he won't encounter many rivals.
**GEORG CHRISTOPH LICHTENBERG**

What we do upon some great occasion will probably depend on what we already are; and what we are will be the result of previous years of self-discipline.
**H. P. LIDDON**

Every man has a property in his own person; this nobody has a right to but himself.
**JOHN LOCKE**

Truly, this world can get on without us, if we would but think so.
**HENRY WADSWORTH LONGFELLOW**

There is little that can withstand a man who can conquer himself.
**LOUIS XIV**

There is only one thing that will really train the human mind and that is the voluntary use of the mind by the man himself. You may aid him, you may guide him, you may suggest to him and, above all else, you may inspire him. But the only thing worth having is that which he gets by his own exertions, and what he gets is in direct proportion to what he puts into it.
**ALBERT L. LOWELL**

The greatest service we can perform for others is to help them to help themselves.
**HORACE MANN**

Self-respect is at the bottom of all good manners. They are the expression of discipline, of goodwill, of respect for other people's rights and comfort and feelings.
**Edgar S. Martin**

Follow your own path, no matter what people say.
**Karl Marx**

He that would govern others, first should be the master of himself.
**Philip Massinger**

There is no man so low down that the cure for his condition does not lie strictly within himself.
**Thomas L. Masson**

The difficulties, hardships, and trials of life, the obstacles one encounters on the road to fortune, are positive blessings. They knit the muscles more firmly, and teach self-reliance. Peril is the element in which power is developed.
**William Matthews**

When a man begins to understand himself he begins to live. When he begins to live he begins to understand his fellow men.
**Norvin G. McGranahan**

We often rebel against the strenuousness and chaos of our time. But historically it has always been in such time that man won his great inner victories.
**Elmore M. McKee, D.D.**

In the old days, everything was private. There were private houses and private parties and private yachts and private railroad cars and private everything. Now everything is public—even one's private life.
**Mrs. G. Alexander McKinlock**

"Know thyself" means this, that you get acquainted with what you know, and what you can do.
**Menander**

If you love men and they are unfriendly, look into your love; if you rule men and they are unruly, look into your wisdom; if you are courteous to them and they do not respond, look into your courtesy. If what you do is vain, always seek within.
**Mencius**

Excess of self-inflation, as self-deflation, is unwise and unworthy of a mature man.
**Henry G. Mendelson**

To know thyself must mean to know the malignancy of one's own instincts and to know as well one's power to deflect it.
**Dr. Karl Menninger**

He who reigns within himself, and rules passions, desires, and fears, is more than a king.
**John Milton**

Ofttimes nothing profits more than self-esteem, grounded on just and right well manag'd.
**John Milton**

The pious and just honoring of ourselves may be thought the fountainhead from whence every laudable and worthy enterprise issues forth.
**John Milton**

We are all mortals, and each is for himself.
**Molière**

I care not so much what I am in the opinion of others as what I am in my own; I would be rich of myself and not by borrowing.
**Michel de Montaigne**

Men throw themselves on foreign assistances to spare their own, which, after all, are the only certain and sufficient ones.
MICHEL DE MONTAIGNE

My library is my kingdom, and here I try to make my rule absolute—shutting off this single nook from wife, daughter and society. Elsewhere I have only a verbal authority, and vague. Unhappy is the man, in my opinion, who has no spot at home where he can be at home to himself—to court himself and hide away.
MICHEL DE MONTAIGNE

The great thing in the world is to know how to be sufficient unto oneself.
MICHEL DE MONTAIGNE

Lack of something to feel important about is almost the greatest tragedy a man may have.
ARTHUR E. MORGAN

What lies behind us and what lies before are tiny matters compared to what lies within us.
WILLIAM MORROW

He who reveals to me what is in me and helps me to externalize it in fuller terms of self-trust, is my real helper, for he assists me in the birth of those things which he knows are in me and in all men.
W. JOHN MURRAY

It is the mark of a superior man that, left to himself, he is able endlessly to amuse, interest and entertain himself out of his personal stock of meditations, ideas, criticisms, memories, philosophy, humor, and what not.
GEORGE JEAN NATHAN

Hardship and opposition are the native soil of manhood and self-reliance.
NEAL

Robinson had a servant even better than Friday: His name was Crusoe.
FRIEDRICH WILHELM NIETZSCHE

People work for self-expression. Even when they talk loudest about getting the money they are really most interested in doing a job skillfully, so that others will admire it and give them that inward glow of satisfaction which comes of achievement. From the painter, producing his masterpieces, to the truck driver, piloting his leviathan across city streets, the basic inward thought is: I am the best caballero in all Mexico.
HOWARD VINCENT O'BRIEN

Do you wish men to speak well of you? Then never speak well of yourself.
BLAISE PASCAL

We are more easily persuaded, in general, by the reasons we ourselves discover than by those which are given to us by others.
BLAISE PASCAL

We are only falsehood, duplicity, contradiction; we both conceal and disguise ourselves from ourselves.
BLAISE PASCAL

He who overcomes others is strong; but he who overcomes himself is mightier.
JOHN HENRY PATTERSON

It is easy to look down on others; to look down on ourselves is the difficulty.
LORD PETERBOROUGH

Whatever your lot may be, paddle your own canoe.
EDWARD P. PHILPOTS

When a man lives, he lives and does not see himself. . . . With different persons, he may be quite a different individual.
LUIGI PIRANDELLO

The cause of all the blunders committed by man arises from excessive self-love. He who intends to be a great man ought to love neither himself nor his own things, but only what is just, whether it happens to be done by himself or by another.
**PLATO**

The measure of a man is not determined by his show of outward strength or the volume of his voice or the thunder of his action. It is to be seen rather in terms of the strength of his inner self in terms of the nature and depth of his commitments the sincerity of his purpose and his willingness to continue growing up.
**GRADE E. POULARD**

One of the very best of all earthly possessions is self-possession.
**GEORGE D. PRENTICE**

Read not books alone, but men, and amongst them chiefly thyself. If thou find anything questionable there, use the commentary of a severe friend, rather than the gloss of a sweet-lipped flatterer; there is more profit in a distasteful truth than in deceitful sweetness.
**FRANCIS QUARLES**

Civilization is the progress of a society towards privacy. The savage's whole existence is public, ruled by the laws of his tribe. Civilization is the process of setting man free from men.
**AYN RAND**

We have always known that heedless self-interest was bad morals; we know now that it is bad economics.
**FRANKLIN D. ROOSEVELT**

As soon as any man says of the affairs of State, "What does it matter to me?" that State may be given up for lost.
**JEAN-JACQUES ROUSSEAU**

Keep cool and you command everybody.
**LOUIS LÉON DE SAINT-JUST**

There is but one virtue—the eternal sacrifice of self.
**GEORGE SAND**

Nobody, but nobody, is going to tell me I'm not the most. I am. I was the most when everybody else was struggling bitterly to become a little.
**WILLIAM SAROYAN**

We forfeit three-fourths of ourselves in order to be like other people.
**ARTHUR SCHOPENHAUER**

The world is governed by self-interest only.
**JOHANN FRIEDRICH VON SCHILLER**

Each of us needs time for mental self-renewal.
**WHITT N. SCHULTZ**

Teach self-denial and make its practice pleasure, and you can create for the world a destiny more sublime that ever issued from the brain of the wildest dreamer.
**SIR WALTER SCOTT**

A man is a lion for his own cause.
**SCOTTISH PROVERB**

Most powerful is he who has himself in his own power.
**SENECA**

We can be thankful to a friend for a few acres, or a little money; and yet for the freedom and command of the whole earth, and for the great benefits of our being, our life, health, and reason, we look upon ourselves as under no obligation.
**SENECA**

It is the hardest thing in the world to be a good thinker without being a good self examiner.
LORD SHAFTESBURY

It is impossible you should take true root but by the fair weather that you make yourself; it is needful that you frame the season for your own harvest.
WILLIAM SHAKESPEARE

Self-love is not so vile a sin as self-neglecting.
WILLIAM SHAKESPEARE

Self-denial is not a virtue, it is only the effect of prudence on rascality.
GEORGE BERNARD SHAW

Who will adhere to him that abandons himself?
SIR PHILIP SIDNEY

Self-approbation, when founded in truth and a good conscience, is a source of some of the purest joys known to man.
CHARLES SIMMONS

Some of us have turned our freedom into exploitation, our land into a dust bowl. We can't make a nation strong when it is held together by the rotten rope of self-interest. Too often we think of democracy only in terms of getting our rights.
JOSEPH R. SIZOO, D.D.

For want of self-restraint many men are engaged all their lives in fighting with difficulties of their own making, and rendering success impossible by their own cross-grained ungentleness.
SAMUEL SMILES

The worst counterfeit of tolerance is the sheer self-interest which argues that we want others to have a good time when in reality our real motive is that others may think well of us.
RALPH W. SOCKMAN

Know thyself.
SOCRATES

You can never expect too much of yourself in the matter of giving yourself to others.
THEODORE C. SPEERS, D.D.

In vain he seeketh others to suppress who hath not learned himself first to subdue.
EDMUND SPENSER

The greatest pride, or the greatest despondency, is the greatest ignorance of one's self.
BARUCH SPINOZA

It is hardly possible to suspect another without having in one's self the seeds of the baseness the other is accused of.
KING STANISLAUS OF POLAND

Such is the weakness of our nature, that when men are a little exalted in their condition they immediately conceive they have additional senses, and their capacities enlarged not only above other men, but above human comprehension itself.
RICHARD STEELE

To be honest, to be kind—to earn a little and spend a little less, to make upon the whole a family happier for his presence, to renounce when that shall be necessary and not be embittered, to keep a few friends, but these without capitulation—above all, on the same grim condition, to keep friends with himself—here is a task for all that a man has of fortitude and delicacy.
ROBERT LOUIS STEVENSON

Nothing is more to me than myself.
MAX STIRNER

He who would be well taken care of must take care of himself.
WILLIAM GRAHAM SUMNER

He conquers twice who conquers himself in victory.
PUBLILIUS SYRUS

Self-reverence, self-knowledge, self-control, these three alone lead life to sovereign power.
ALFRED, LORD TENNYSON

He who lives only to benefit himself confers on the world a benefit when he dies.
TERTULLIAN

The most difficult thing in life is to know yourself.
THALES

If a man does not keep pace with his companions, perhaps it is because he hears a different drummer. Let him step in the music which he hears, however measured or far away.
HENRY DAVID THOREAU

It is as hard to see oneself as to look backwards without turning around.
HENRY DAVID THOREAU

Not till we are lost, in other words, not till we have lost the world, do we begin to find ourselves, and realize where we are and the infinite extent of our relations.
HENRY DAVID THOREAU

In his private heart no man much respects himself.
MARK TWAIN

We do not deal much in facts when we are contemplating ourselves.
MARK TWAIN

We can secure other people's approval if we do right and try hard; but our own is worth a hundred of it, and no way has been found out of securing that.
MARK TWAIN

Every person is powered by a self-esteem engine.
FRANK TYGER

Self-appraisal will do more for you than self-praise will.
FRANK TYGER

The greatest obstacle to your success is probably you.
FRANK TYGER

It is not love we should have painted as blind, but self-love.
VOLTAIRE

Self-love is the instrument of our preservation; It resembles the provision for the reproduction of mankind: It is necessary, it gives us pleasure, and we must conceal it.
VOLTAIRE

No man is self-made who unmakes others.
STEPHEN VORIS

Would you hurt a man keenest, strike at his self-love.
LEW WALLACE

I set myself on fire and people come to watch me burn.
JOHN WESLEY

I don't like myself, I'm crazy about myself.
MAE WEST

Neither human applause nor human censure is to be taken as the best of truth; but either should set us upon testing ourselves.
RICHARD WHATELY

Though not always called upon to condemn ourselves, it is always safe to suspect ourselves.
RICHARD WHATELY

He that neither knows himself nor thinks he can learn of others is not fit for company.
BENJAMIN WHICHCOTE

Man is a wonder to himself; he can neither govern nor know himself.
BENJAMIN WHICHCOTE

When I give, I give myself.
WALT WHITMAN

Other people are quite dreadful. The only possible society is one's self.
OSCAR WILDE

Self-denial is simply a method by which man arrests his progress.
OSCAR WILDE

There is luxury in self-reproach. When we blame ourselves, we feel no one else has a right to blame us.
OSCAR WILDE

I'm a self-made man, but I think if I had it to do over again, I'd call in someone else.
ROLAND YOUNG

The more you speak of yourself, the more likely you are to lie.
JOHANN ZIMMERMANN

## *Selfishness*

I have been a selfish being all my life, in practice, though not in principle.
JANE AUSTEN

Be unselfish. That is the first and final commandment for those who would be useful, and happy in their usefulness. If you think of yourself only, you cannot develop because you are choking the source of development, which is spiritual expansion through thought for others.
CHARLES W. ELIOT

If I had the opportunity to say a final word to all the young people of America, it would be this: Don't think too much about yourself. Try to cultivate the habit of thinking of others; this will reward you. Selfishness always brings its own revenge. It cannot be escaped. Be unselfish. That is the first and final commandment for those who would be useful and happy in their usefulness.
CHARLES W. ELIOT

Selfishness can be a virtue. Selfishness is essential to survival, and without survival we cannot protect those whom we love more than ourselves.
DUKE ELLINGTON

Selfishness is the root and source of all natural and moral evils.
NATHANIEL EMMONS

If there is to be peace in the world, peace must be established first in every human heart. All the trouble in the world is due to selfishness. It always has been and always will be.
JOSEPH F. FLANNELLY

How much that the world calls selfishness is only generosity with narrow walls—a too exclusive solic-

itude to maintain a wife in luxury, or make one's children rich.
THOMAS W. HIGGINSON

The force of selfishness is as inevitable and as calculable as the force of gravitation.
GEORGE S. HILLARD

The malignity that never forgets or forgives is found only in base and ignoble natures, whose aims are selfish, and whose means are indirect, cowardly, and treacherous.
GEORGE S. HILLARD

The selfish spirit of commerce knows no country, and feels no passion or principle but that of gain.
THOMAS JEFFERSON

If all the people in this world, in which we live, were as selfish as a few of the people in this world, in which we live, there would be no world in which to live.
W. L. ORME

The principle of liberty and equality, if coupled with mere selfishness, will make men only devils, each trying to be independent that he may fight only for his own interest. And here is the need of religion and its power, to bring in the principle of benevolence and love to men.
JOHN RANDOLPH

No man can live happily who regards himself alone, who turns everything to his own advantage. Thou must live for another if thou wishest to live for thyself.
SENECA

Unselfish and noble actions are the most radiant pages in the biography of souls.
DAVID THOMAS

A man is called selfish, not for pursuing his own good, but for neglecting his neighbor's.
RICHARD WHATELY

Selfishness is not living as one wishes to live. It is asking others to live as one wishes to live.
OSCAR WILDE

## *Service*

Service makes men competent.
LYMAN ABBOTT

To give real service you must add something which cannot be bought or measured with money, and that is sincerity and integrity.
DONALD A. ADAMS

If things are not going well with you, begin your effort at correcting the situation by carefully examining the service you are rendering, and especially the spirit in which you are rendering it.
ROGER W. BABSON

I still hold the primitive belief that people who truly wish to benefit humanity do it for love and for free, and they tend to die lousy deaths in a world that doesn't deserve them.
CHARITY BLACKSTOCK

Our immediate future as Americans may depend upon the living we make, but the future of America depends upon the life we live and the services we render.
WILLIAM J. H. BOETCKER

The more you learn what to do with yourself, and the more you do for others, the more you will learn to enjoy the abundant life.
WILLIAM J. H. BOETCKER

The making of money, the accumulation of material power, is not all there is to living. Life is something more than these, and the man who misses this truth misses the greatest joy and satisfaction that can come into his life—service for others.
EDWARD W. BOK

Businesses planned for service are apt to succeed; businesses planned for profit are apt to fail.
NICHOLAS MURRAY BUTLER

The work an unknown good man has done is like a vein of water flowing hidden underground, secretly making the ground green.
THOMAS CARLYLE

Service to a just cause rewards the worker with more real happiness and satisfaction than any other venture of life.
CARRIE CHAPMAN CATT

Great industries are not built up by getting the best of someone else, but by giving goods and services that are worth more to your customers than the amount they pay you in return.
G. HEATH CLARK

It is not where you serve, but how you serve.
J. RUBIN CLARK

We should render a service to a friend to bind him closer to us, and to an enemy to make a friend of him.
CLEOBULUS

Under our institutions each individual is born to sovereignty. Whatever he may adopt as a means of livelihood, his real business is serving his country. He cannot hold himself above his fellow men. The greatest place of command is really the place of obedience, and the greatest place of honor is really the place of service.
CALVIN COOLIDGE

The vital force in business life is the honest desire to serve. Business, it is said, is the science of service. He profits most who serves best. At the very bottom of the wish to render service must be honesty of purpose, and, as I go along through life, I see more and more that honesty in word, thought, and work means success. It spells a life worth living and in business, clean success.
GEORGE EBERHARD

Only a life lived for others is a life worthwhile.
ALBERT EINSTEIN

There is one wish ruling over all mankind, and it is a wish which is never in any single instance granted—each man wishes to be his own master. It is a boy's beatific vision, and it remains the grown-up man's ruling passion to the last. But the fact is, life is a service; the only question is, whom will we serve?
FREDERICK WILLIAM FABER

To devote a portion of one's leisure to doing something for someone else is one of the highest forms of recreation.
GERALD B. FITZGERALD

To complain that life has no joys while there is a single creature whom we can relieve by our bounty, assist by our counsels, or enliven by our presence, is to lament the loss of that which we possess, and is just as rational as to die of thirst with the cup in our hands.
THOMAS FITZOSBORNE

This year I round out 50 years of newspaper and magazine work. My philosophy has undergone some, but not drastic, change. I feel that in the first half of his life a man should devote himself primar-

ily to making headway in the world. But, after having succeeded in providing reasonably for himself and his immediate dependents, I have come to feel more and more that there are other things in life besides moneymaking. One who has attained a competency should, I profoundly feel . . . allocate a large part of his time and vitality to benefiting his fellow men.
**B. C. FORBES (MAY 1944)**

Which is more worthwhile earning: a large fortune or the esteem and gratitude of the nation? This question is prompted anew by the death of ex-Secretary of the Interior [Franklin K.] Lane. He remained in public service, doing most noble work, until his means became absolutely exhausted, and he died before having had the opportunity to reaccumulate any bank account. . . . He died leaving no estate whatsoever. Is what he did leave more to be desired, more to be coveted, than a fortune reaching into six or seven figures?
**B. C. FORBES**

One of the most amazing things ever said on this earth is Jesus's statement: "He that is greatest among you shall be your servant." Nobody has one chance in a billion of being thought really great after a century has passed except those who have been the servants of all. That strange realist from Bethlehem knew that.
**HARRY EMERSON FOSDICK, D.D.**

The most significant social service is not rendered in and through public movements, but is rendered in and through private business and professions.
**GLENN FRANK**

When people are serving, life is no longer meaningless.
**JOHN W. GARDNER**

The true measure of a man is not the number of servants he has, but the number of people he serves.
**ARNOLD GLASOW**

Service is the rent that we pay for our room on earth.
**LORD HALIFAX**

Show me the business man or institution not guided by sentiment and service; by the idea that he profits most who serves best and I will show you a man or an outfit that is dead or dying.
**B. F. HARRIS**

Service without reward is punishment.
**GEORGE HERBERT**

He serves me most, who serves his country best.
**HOMER**

Any man who is physically able has no right to refuse service to his country.
**HERBERT HOOVER**

A big corporation is more or less blamed for being big, but it is only big because it gives service. If it doesn't give service, it gets small faster than it grew big.
**WILLIAM S. KNUDSEN**

Find out where you can render a service, and then render it. The rest is up to the Lord.
**S. S. KRESGE**

The life of a man consists not in seeing visions and in dreaming dreams, but in active charity and in willing service.
**HENRY WADSWORTH LONGFELLOW**

The conception of perfect service is constantly expanding and must be handled by broad and lib-

eral minded men who put equity and fairness above gain—who put a proper valuation upon a satisfied customer as an asset running into the thousands of dollars, and who love a job thoroughly well done and get a kick out of doing it.
ALVAN MACAULEY

The most infectiously joyous men and women are those who forget themselves in thinking about others and serving others. Happiness comes not by deliberately courting and wooing it but by giving oneself in self-effacing surrender to great values.
ROBERT J. MCCRACKEN

Respectable men and women content with the good and easy living are missing some of the most important things in life. Unless you give yourself to some great cause you haven't even begun to live.
WILLIAM P. MERRILL

The measure of a man is not the number of his servants but in the number of people whom he serves.
PAUL D. MOODY

Try to forget yourself in the service of others. For when we think too much of ourselves and our own interests, we easily become despondent. But when we work for others, our efforts return to bless us.
SIDNEY POWELL

The successful person is one who is able to take his talents and invest them in the business of living in a manner that leads to the accomplishment of a full life of service. . . . The medium of exchange is not the dollar but services rendered.
SOL ROTH

As soon as public service ceases to be the chief business of the citizens, and they would rather serve with their money than with their persons, the state is not far from its fall.
JEAN-JACQUES ROUSSEAU

One could of course say that a man's due is to be measured by his services to the community, but I cannot imagine how these services are to be estimated. Compare a baker and an opera singer. You could live without the opera singer, but not without the services of the baker. On this ground you might say that the baker performs a greater service; but no lover of music would agree.
BERTRAND RUSSELL

I don't know what your destiny will be, but one thing I know: the only ones among you who will be really happy are those who will have sought and found how to serve.
ALBERT SCHWEITZER

Whatever you have received more than others—in health, in talents, in ability, in success, in a pleasant childhood, in harmonious conditions of home life—all this you must not take to yourself as a matter of course. In gratitude for your good fortune, you must render in return some sacrifice of your own life for another life.
ALBERT SCHWEITZER

Today's business leader cannot justify his existence by profit statements alone. He must also render service to his local, national and world community.
DOROTHY SHAVER

A desire for bigness has hurt many folks. Putting oneself in the limelight at the expense of others is a wrong idea of greatness. The secret of greatness rather than bigness is to acclimate oneself to one's place of service and be true to one's own convictions. A life of this kind of service will forever remain the measure of one's true greatness.
RICHARD W. SHELLY, JR.

All the wild ideas of unbalanced agitators the world over in their ignorant and pitiable quest for happiness through revolution, confiscation of property,

and crime, cannot overthrow the eternal truth that the one route to happiness through property or government is over the broad and open highway of service. And service always means industry, thrift, respect for authority, and recognition of the rights of others.
WILLIAM G. SIBLEY

Have I done anything for society? I have then done more for myself. Let that question and truth be always present to thy mind, and work without cessation.
WILLIAM SIMMS

The world has never been so rich in helpers as it is today, and consequently never have there been people so happy and so blessed in their lives. Volunteers for human service seem to spring from the ground. It would be difficult to point out a more encouraging fact for the world's future.
MINOT SIMONS, D.D.

When we act upon the formula of giving service we seem to get what we want and we also get it for the other person, too. In the high art of serving others, workers sustain their morale, management keeps its customers, and the nation prospers. One of the indisputable lessons of life is that we cannot get or keep anything for ourselves alone unless we also get it for others, too.
J. RICHARD SNEED

A man should inure himself to voluntary labor, and not give up to indulgence and pleasure, as they beget no good constitution of body nor knowledge of mind.
SOCRATES

In the New Testament it is taught that willing and voluntary service to others is the highest duty and glory in human life.... The men of talent are constantly forced to serve the rest. They make the discoveries and inventions, order the battles, write the books, and produce the works of art. The benefit and enjoyment go to the whole. There are those who joyfully order their own lives so that they may serve the welfare of mankind.
WILLIAM GRAHAM SUMNER

And he gave it for his opinion, that whoever could make two ears of corn, or two blades of grass, to grow upon a spot of ground where only one grew before, would deserve better of mankind, and do more essential service to this country, than the whole race of politicians put together.
JONATHAN SWIFT

Life is a place of service, and in that service one has to suffer a great deal that is hard to bear, but more often to experience a great deal of joy. But that joy can be real only if people look upon their life as a service, and have a definite object in life outside themselves and their personal happiness.
LEO TOLSTOY

The sole meaning of life is to serve humanity.
LEO TOLSTOY

The vocation of every man and woman is to serve other people.
LEO TOLSTOY

No man who continues to add something to the material, intellectual and moral well-being of the place in which he lives is left long without proper reward.
BOOKER T. WASHINGTON

## *Sex*

Why did [God] give us genitals then if he wanted us to think clearly?
GRAHAM GREENE

We've only one virginity to lose,
And where we lost it there our hearts will be.
**RUDYARD KIPLING**

Whatever else can be said about sex, it cannot be called a dignified performance.
**HELEN LAWRENSON**

A promiscuous person is someone who is getting more sex than you are.
**VICTOR LOWNES**

About money and sex it is impossible to be truthful ever; one's ego is too involved.
**MALCOLM MUGGERIDGE**

Sex: Something that children never discuss in the presence of their elders.
**ARTHUR SOMERS ROCHE**

## *Silence*

He who is silent is forgotten; he who abstains is taken at his word; he who does not advance falls back; he who stops is overwhelmed, distanced, crushed; he who ceases to grow greater becomes smaller; he who leaves off, gives up; the stationary condition is the beginning of the end.
**HENRI FRÉDÉRIC AMIEL**

Most of us know how to say nothing; few of us know when.
**ANONYMOUS**

There is no wholly satisfactory substitute for brains, but silence does pretty well.
**ANONYMOUS**

Most men talk too much. Much of my success has been due to keeping my mouth shut.
**J. OGDEN ARMOUR**

Drawing on my fine command of language, I said nothing.
**ROBERT BENCHLEY**

A man who lives right, and is right, has more power in his silence than another has by his words.
**PHILLIPS BROOKS**

The main reason why silence is so efficacious an element of repute is, first, because of that magnification which proverbially belongs to the unknown; and, secondly, because silence provokes no man's envy, and wounds no man's self-love.
**EDWARD BULWER-LYTTON**

If we have not quiet in our minds, outward comfort will do no more for us than a golden slipper on a gouty foot.
**JOHN BUNYAN**

Thought works in silence; so does virtue. One might erect statues to silence.
**THOMAS CARLYLE**

Silence is the unbearable repartee.
**G. K. CHESTERTON**

Silence is a true friend that never betrays.
**CONFUCIUS**

One nice thing about silence is that it can't be repeated.
**GARY COOPER**

Nothing is often a good thing to say, and always a clever thing to say.
**WILL DURANT**

Blessed is the man who, having nothing to say, abstains from giving in words evidence of the fact.
**GEORGE ELIOT**

Silence is an answer to a wise man.
**EURIPIDES**

An educated man is one who knows a lot and says nothing about it.
**GRACIE FIELDS**

A judicious silence is always better than truth spoken without charity.
**ST. FRANCIS DE SALES**

Remember not only to say the right thing in the right place, but far more difficult still, to leave unsaid the wrong thing at the tempting moment.
**BENJAMIN FRANKLIN**

Silence makes no mistakes.
**FRENCH PROVERB**

Quiet persons are welcome everywhere.
**THOMAS FULLER**

Silence is one great art of conversation. He is not a fool who knows when to hold his tongue; and a person may gain credit for sense, eloquence, wit, who merely says nothing to lessen the opinion which others have of these qualities in themselves.
**WILLIAM HAZLITT**

All noise is waste. So cultivate quietness in your speech, in your thoughts, in your emotions. Speak habitually low. Wait for attention and then your low words will be charged with dynamite.
**ELBERT HUBBARD**

He who thinks much says but little in proportion to his thoughts. He selects that language which will convey his ideas in the most explicit and direct manner.
**WASHINGTON IRVING**

Just as the soil that has lain fallow produces a richer harvest, so it is with human beings—the bare and silent moments are those when the busy mind finds light and air. The thoughts that arise in these brief intervals, when one takes time to look up, are growing thoughts.
**MARISKA KARASZ**

Silence is a great peacemaker.
**HENRY WADSWORTH LONGFELLOW**

Do not the most moving moments of our lives find us without words?
**MARCEL MARCEAU**

It is an experiment worth trying to be alone and to be quiet for a brief period every day. Under city conditions it may be difficult to carry out, but most of us could do it if we tried. At any rate, we should moderate the pace at which we are living. If we remain at high gear, at top pressure, we are bound to suffer from fatigue and strain.
**ROBERT J. MCCRACKEN**

You have not converted a man because you have silenced him.
**JOHN MORLEY**

Never, never do great thoughts come to a man while he is discontented or fretful. There must be quiet in the temple of his soul before the windows of it will open for him to see out of them into the infinite. Quiet is what heavenly powers move in. It is in silence that the stars move on, and it is in quiet that our souls are visited from on high.
**WILLIAM MOUNTFORD**

A sage thing is timely silence, and better than any speech.
**PLUTARCH**

It is better either to be silent or to say things of more value than silence. Sooner throw a pearl at hazard than an idle or useless word; and do not say a little in many words but a great deal in a few.
PYTHAGORAS

A happy life must be to a great extent a quiet life, for it is only in an atmosphere of quiet that true joy can live.
BERTRAND RUSSELL

It is difficult to keep quiet if you have nothing to do.
ARTHUR SCHOPENHAUER

The silence, often of pure innocence, persuades where speaking fails.
WILLIAM SHAKESPEARE

Silence is the most perfect expression of scorn.
GEORGE BERNARD SHAW

Silence is one of the hardest arguments to refute.
MAURICE R. SHOCHATT

The world would be happier if men had the same capacity to be silent that they have to speak.
BARUCH SPINOZA

Let a fool hold his tongue and he will pass for a sage.
PUBLILIUS SYRUS

Silence is the universal refuge, the sequel to all dull discourses and all foolish acts, a balm to our every chagrin, as welcome after satiety as after disappointment.
HENRY DAVID THOREAU

Well-timed silence hath more eloquence than speech.
M. T. TUPPER

The true test of being comfortable with someone else is the ability to share silence.
FRANK TYGER

You can often profit from being at a loss for words.
FRANK TYGER

You can only improve on saying nothing by saying nothing often.
FRANK TYGER

## *Simplicity*

I have grown to believe: That the one thing worth aiming at is simplicity of heart and life; That one's relations with others should be direct, not diplomatic; That power leaves a bitter taste in the mouth; That meanness and hardness and coldness are the unforgivable sins; That conventionality is the mother of dreariness; That pleasure exists not in the virtue of material conditions, but in the joyful heart; That the world is a very interesting and beautiful place; That congenial labor is the secret of happiness.
ARTHUR CHRISTOPHER BENSON

Refined policy has ever been the parent of confusion, and ever will be so, as long as the world endures. Plain good intention, which is as easily discovered at the first view as fraud is surely detected at last, is of no mean force in the government of mankind. Genuine simplicity of heart is a healing and cementing principle.
EDMUND BURKE

Finding a way to live the simple life today is man's most complicated task.
HENRY A. COURTNEY

There is a master key to success with which no man can fail. Its name is simplicity. Simplicity, I mean,

in the sense of reducing to the simplest possible terms every problem that besets us. Whenever I have met a business proposition which, after taking thought, I could not reduce to simplicity, I have left it alone.
SIR HENRI DETERDING

Everything should be made as simple as possible, but not simpler.
ALBERT EINSTEIN

Possessions, outward success, publicity, luxury—to me these have always been contemptible. I believe that a simple and unassuming manner of life is best for every one, best both for the body and the mind.
ALBERT EINSTEIN

Nothing is more simple than greatness; indeed, to be simple is to be great.
RALPH WALDO EMERSON

The greatest results in life are usually attained by simple means and the exercise of ordinary qualities. These may for the most part be summed up in these two—commonsense and perseverance.
OWEN FELTHAM

Simplicity of character is the natural result of profound thought.
WILLIAM HAZLITT

In character, in manners, in style, in all things, the supreme excellence is simplicity.
HENRY WADSWORTH LONGFELLOW

The silence of the place was like a sleep, so full of rest it seemed.
HENRY WADSWORTH LONGFELLOW

Whenever two hypotheses cover the facts, use the simpler of the two.
WILLIAM OCKHAM

Beauty of style and harmony and grace and good rhythm depend on simplicity.
PLATO

There is nothing quite so complicated as simplicity.
CHARLES POORE

There is a certain majesty in simplicity which is far above all the quaintness of wit.
ALEXANDER POPE

A knowing simplicity is easily distinguished from the barrenness of ignorance.
CHARLES B. ROGERS

A childlike mind, in its simplicity, practices that science of good to which the wise may be blind.
JOHANN FRIEDRICH VON SCHILLER

Simplicity, of all things, is the hardest to be copied.
RICHARD STEELE

Seek simplicity, and distrust it.
ALFRED NORTH WHITEHEAD

## *Sincerity*

The essential element in personal magnetism is a consuming sincerity—an overwhelming faith in the importance of the work one has to do.
BRUCE BARTON

Earnestness is the devotion of all the faculties.
CHRISTIAN BOVÉE

Earnest people are often people who habitually look on the serious side of things that have no serious side.
VAN WYCK BROOKS

If life must not be taken too seriously, then so neither must death.
**SAMUEL BUTLER**

The one serious conviction that a man should have is that nothing is to be taken too seriously.
**SAMUEL BUTLER**

It is an article of faith in my creed to pick the man who does not take himself seriously, but does take his work seriously.
**MICHAEL C. CAHILL**

I should say sincerity, a deep, great, genuine sincerity is the first characteristic of all men in any way heroic.
**THOMAS CARLYLE**

The sincere alone can recognize sincerity.
**THOMAS CARLYLE**

A man in earnest finds means, or, if he cannot find, creates them.
**WILLIAM ELLERY CHANNING**

Even where there is talent, culture, knowledge, if there is not earnestness, it does not go to the root of things.
**JAMES FREEMAN CLARKE**

There is no substitute for thoroughgoing, ardent and sincere earnestness.
**CHARLES DICKENS**

Sincerity is no test of truth—no evidence of correctness of conduct. You may take poison sincerely believing it the needed medicine, but will it save your life?
**TRYON EDWARDS**

The first virtue of all really great men is that they are sincere. They eradicate hypocrisy from their hearts. They bravely unveil their weaknesses, their doubts, their defects. They are courageous. They boldly ride a-tilt against prejudices. No civil, moral nor immoral power overawes them. They love their fellow-men profoundly. They are generous. They allow their hearts to expand. They have compassion for all forms of suffering. Pity is the very foundation-stone of Genius.
**ANATOLE FRANCE**

Of all the evil spirits abroad at this hour in the world, insincerity is the most dangerous.
**J. A. FROUDE**

It is not so important to be serious as it is to be serious about the important things.
**ROBERT M. HUTCHINS**

It is an old and true maxim that a drop of honey catches more flies than a gallon of gall. So with men, if you would win a man to your cause, first convince him that you are his sincere friend.
**ABRAHAM LINCOLN**

Sincerity is impossible unless it pervades the whole being, and the pretense of it saps the very foundation of character.
**JAMES RUSSELL LOWELL**

Sincerity in society is like an iron girder in a house of cards.
**SOMERSET MAUGHAM**

Many who think that they are taking life seriously are actually only taking themselves seriously. Who takes himself seriously is overconscious of his rights; who takes life seriously is fully conscious of his obligations.
**JOSEPH T. O'CALLAHAN**

The great enemy of clear language is insincerity. When there is a gap between one's real and one's

declared aims, one turns, as it were, instinctively to long words and exhausted idioms, like a cuttlefish squirting out ink.
**GEORGE ORWELL**

This world is given as the prize for the men in earnest.
**FREDERICK W. ROBERTSON**

Solemnity is a device of the body to hide the faults of the mind.
**FRANÇOIS DE LA ROCHEFOUCAULD**

To be practical in life means to take everything seriously and nothing tragically.
**ARTHUR SCHNITZLER**

It is dangerous to be sincere unless you are also stupid.
**GEORGE BERNARD SHAW**

Be sincere. Be simple in words, manners, and gestures. Amuse as well as instruct. If you can make a man laugh, you can make him think and make him like and believe you.
**ALFRED E. SMITH**

He who is sincere has the easiest task in the world, for, truth being always consistent with itself, he is put to no trouble about his words and actions; it is like traveling on a plain road, which is sure to bring you to your journey's end better than byways in which many lose themselves.
**JOHN TILLOTSON**

Sincerity is to speak as we think, to do as we pretend and profess, to perform what we promise, and really to be what we would seem and appear to be.
**JOHN TILLOTSON**

We are apt to say that money talks, but it speaks a broken, poverty-stricken language. Hearts talk better, clearer and with wider intelligence.
**WILLIAM ALLEN WHITE**

A little sincerity is a dangerous thing, and a great deal of it is absolutely fatal.
**OSCAR WILDE**

## *Sins*

Indifferent acts are judged by their ends; sins are judged by themselves.
**ST. AUGUSTINE**

There is often a sin of omission as well as of commission.
**MARCUS AURELIUS ANTONINUS**

It is much easier to repent of sins that we have committed than to repent of those we intend to commit.
**JOSH BILLINGS**

The harlot's cry from street to street
Shall weave old England's winding sheet.
**WILLIAM BLAKE**

That which we call sin in others is experiment for us.
**RALPH WALDO EMERSON**

Men are not punished for their sins, but by them.
**ELBERT HUBBARD**

If we say that we have no sin, we deceive ourselves and the truth is not in us. If we confess our sins, he is faithful and just to forgive us our sins, and to cleanse us from all unrighteousness.
**I JOHN 1:8–9**

To have no sense of sin is to have no taste, and to have no taste is to be a loser at the end.
**MURRAY KEMPTON**

And Jesus answering said unto them, They that are whole need not a physician; but they that are sick. I came not to call the righteous, but sinners to repentance.
**LUKE 5:31–32**

There is nothing from without a man, that entering into him can defile him: but the things which come out of him, those are they that defile the man.
**MARK 7:15**

For if after they have escaped the pollutions of the world through the knowledge of the Lord and Savior Jesus Christ, they are again entangled therein, and overcome, the latter end is worse with them than the beginning.
**II PETER 2:20**

No peace was ever won from fate by subterfuge or agreement; no peace is ever in store for any of us, but that which we shall win by victory over shame or sin—victory over the sin that oppresses, as well as over that which corrupts.
**JOHN RUSKIN**

## *Smiles*

Something of a person's character may be discovered by observing how he smiles.
**CHRISTIAN BOVÉE**

If it's nothing more than a smile—give that away and keep on giving it.
**BETH BROWN**

Wear a smile and have friends; wear a scowl and have wrinkles. What do we live for if not to make the world less difficult for each other?
**GEORGE ELIOT**

Grin and bear it. You can lighten a problem's weight, if you brighten up and smile. There is more power to a punch delivered in high spirits than one delivered in low spirits.
**DOUGLAS FAIRBANKS**

One of the ceaseless wonders of the world: The power of a smile.
**MALCOLM FORBES**

No matter how much madder it may make you, get out of bed forcing a smile. You may not smile because you are cheerful; but if you will force yourself to smile, you'll end up laughing. You will be cheerful because you smile. Repeated experiments prove that when man assumes the facial expression of a given mental mood—any given mood—then that mental mood itself will follow.
**KENNETH GOODE**

Smile to yourself until you have warmed your own heart with the sunshine of your cheery countenance. Then go out—and radiate your smile.
**BRUNO HAGSPIEL**

None are homely who smile.
**ROBERT HALF**

We come into this world crying while all around us are smiling. May we so live that we go out of this world smiling while everybody around us is weeping.
**PERSIAN PROVERB**

Abolish lashing ambition. Stifle stinging jealousy. Wreck remorse's whip. Regret no yesterdays. Hobble feverish hurry. Trust serenely. Choke com-

plaints with commendation. Make "Smile and Push" your motto.
**CHRISTIAN F. REISNER, D.D.**

The robb'd that smiles steals something from the thief.
**WILLIAM SHAKESPEARE**

## Society

Slavery in all its forms, in all its degrees, is a violation of divine law, and a degradation of human nature.
**JACQUES PIERRE BRISSOT**

Society is a partnership in all science; a partnership in all art; a partnership in every virtue and in all perfection. As the ends of such a partnership cannot be obtained in many generations, it becomes a partnership not only between those who are living, but between those who are dead and those who are to be born.
**EDMUND BURKE**

Those who attempt to level never equalize. In all societies some description must be uppermost. The levellers, therefore, only change and pervert the natural order of things; they load the edifice of society by setting up in the air what the solidity of the structure requires to be on the ground.
**EDMUND BURKE**

This generation has learned all over again that there are great differences between a social order that is fundamentally bad and one that is essentially good.
**HARRY WOODBURN CHASE**

No one can accept responsibility in the world unless he takes it first on his own doorstep. So for us in industry I can see only one sure course to follow. Call it common sense, call it policy, call it anything you like. To my mind, industry must aim for, exist for and everlastingly operate for the good of the community. The community can't ride one track and business another. The two are inseparable, interactive and interdependent.
**CLEO F. CRAIG**

A man of a right spirit is not a man of narrow and private views, but is greatly interested and concerned for the good of the community to which he belongs, and particularly of the city or village in which he resides, and for the true welfare of the society of which he is a member.
**JONATHAN EDWARDS**

In this democracy there are no titles. Yet there is no land on the face of the earth where titles are more freely bestowed—or arrogated. If a man isn't known as Judge or Colonel or Doctor or Professor or General or Governor or Senator or Congressman or Ambassador or Secretary or Captain or Chief, then the chances are that he is described as some kind of a king. We have our Tobacco Kings, our Steel Kings, our Lumber Kings, our Chemical Kings, our Automobile Kings, our Coal Kings, our Traction Kings, and doubtless we will shortly have our Bootlegger Kings.
**B. C. FORBES**

Ultimately there can be no freedom for self unless it is vouchsafed for others; there can be no security where there is fear, and a democratic society presupposes confidence and candor in the relations of men with one another and eager collaboration for the larger ends of life instead of the pursuit of petty, selfish or vainglorious aims.
**FELIX FRANKFURTER**

Social progress makes the well-being of all more and more the business of each.
**HENRY GEORGE**

The law of society is, each for all, as well as all for each. No one can keep to himself the good he may do, any more than he can keep the bad.
HENRY GEORGE

Empty heads are fond of long titles.
GERMAN PROVERB

The wise sometimes condescend to accept of titles; but none but a fool would imagine them of any real importance. We ought to depend upon intrinsic merit, and not on the slender helps of a title.
OLIVER GOLDSMITH

The truth is, we can't afford not to become involved in social problems. It has got to be a cost of doing business—and it will be costly—so that your community will be worth doing business in and living in.
ELISHA GRAY II

The delicate balance between modesty and conceit is popularity.
ROBERT HALF

We ought to belong to society, to have our place in it, and yet be capable of a complete existence outside it.
PHILIP HAMERTON

Popularity disarms envy in well-disposed minds. Those are ever the most ready to do justice to others, who feel that the world has done them justice.
WILLIAM HAZLITT

Is life so dear, or peace so sweet, as to be purchased at the price of chains and slavery? Forbid it, Almighty God!
PATRICK HENRY

To perform well elites need tending and nurturing. They need attention, and would rather be persecuted than ignored. With the masses it is the other way around—like weeds, they thrive best when left alone.
ERIC HOFFER

I have no doubt that when the power of either capital or labor is extended in such a way as to attack the life of the community, those who seek their private interests at such cost are public enemies and should be dealt with as such.
OLIVER WENDELL HOLMES

It is a very curious fact that, with all our boasted free and equal superiority over the communities of the Old World, our people have the most enormous appetite for Old World titles of distinction.
OLIVER WENDELL HOLMES

He will always be a slave who does not know how to live upon a little.
HORACE

A state, in which the citizens are compelled or actuated by means of a dictator to obey even the best laws, might be a tranquil, peaceable, prosperous State; but it would always seem to me a multitude of well-cared-for slaves, rather than a nation of free and independent men with no restraint save such as was required to prevent any infringement on right.
KARL WILHELM VON HUMBOLDT

A community is like a ship; everyone ought to be prepared to take the helm.
HENRIK IBSEN

There are only two classes in society: those who get more than they earn, and those who earn more than they get.
HOLBROOK JACKSON

We are not only gregarious animals, liking to be in sight of our fellows, but we have an innate propen-

sity to get ourselves noticed, and noticed favorably, by our kind.
WILLIAM JAMES

It is an unfinished society that we offer the world—a society that is forever committed to change, to improvement and to growth, that will never stagnate in the certitude of ideology or the finalities of dogma.
ROBERT F. KENNEDY

Any society that takes away from those most capable and gives to the least will perish.
ABRAHAM LINCOLN

It is the age that forms the man, not the man that forms the age. Great minds do indeed react on the society which has made them what they are, but they only pay with interest what they have received.
THOMAS B. MACAULAY

It is not titles that honor men, but men that honor titles.
NICCOLÒ MACHIAVELLI

If men can be made to understand that society, with its rigid codes and stratifications, is in its confused infancy rather than in the apex of its development; if they can be made to understand that the conflicts and contradictions of society can only be resolved by scientific long-range planning—then we will succeed in maintaining what civilization we have and drive onward to greater culture.
A. M. MEERLOO

Whatever makes man a slave takes half his worth away.
ALEXANDER POPE

The social fabric of a well-established nation is tough stuff. It can be pulled around and stretched a considerable distance before it breaks. But when the final rupture comes, the damage done is beyond repair.
HENNING W. PRENTIS, JR.

A man is not a slave in being compelled to work against his will, but in being compelled to work without hope and without reward.
W. WINWOOD READE

That which happens to the soil when it ceases to be cultivated, happens to man himself when he foolishly forsakes society for solitude; the brambles grow up in his desert heart.
ANTOINE DE RIVAROL

All my life people have been coming to me with plans to make over society and its institutions. Many of these plans have seemed to me good. Some of them have been excellent. All of them have had one fatal defect. They have assumed that human nature would behave in a certain way. If it would behave in that way almost any one of these plans would work, but if human nature would behave in that way not any of the plans would be necessary, for in that case society and its institutions would naturally reform themselves to perfection.
ELIHU ROOT

Society is like the air; necessary to breathe, but insufficient to live on.
GEORGE SANTAYANA

The community in which each man acts like his neighbor is not yet a civilized community.
ARCHIBALD SAYCE

There are only two classes in good society in England: the equestrian classes and the neurotic classes.
GEORGE BERNARD SHAW

It is a tragedy when the mind, soul and heart are in slavery in a way of life which refuses to recognize that people have rights before God. It is a war which makes hate a badge of honor, slavery the keystone to prosperity. Not to resist would make one an accomplice to crime. Resistance was part of the program of Jesus. We must resist oppression and tyranny. We have to end it no matter what it costs.
**JOSEPH R. SIZOO, D.D.**

As are families, so is society. If well ordered, well instructed, and well governed, they are the springs from which go forth the streams of national greatness and prosperity—of civil order and public happiness.
**FRANK THAYER**

I have three chairs in my house; one for solitude, two for friendship and three for society.
**HENRY DAVID THOREAU**

High society is for those who have stopped working and no longer have anything important to do.
**WOODROW WILSON**

## *Solitude*

For the self-development of men and women it is absolutely necessary that they should be alone with themselves at least one hour each day—to get the blessings of solitude.
**WILLIAM J. H. BOETCKER**

It is easy in the world to live after the world's opinion—it is easy in solitude to live after your own; but the great man is he who, in the midst of the world, keeps with perfect sweetness the independence of solitude.
**RALPH WALDO EMERSON**

By all means use sometimes to be alone. Salute thyself; see what thy soul doth wear.
**GEORGE HERBERT**

Many have no happier moments than those that they pass in solitude, abandoned to their own imagination, which sometimes puts sceptres in their hands or miters on their heads, shifts the scene of pleasure with endless variety, bids all the forms of beauty sparkle before them, and gluts them with every change of visionary luxury.
**JOHNSON**

Solitude is as needful to the imagination as society is wholesome for the character.
**JAMES RUSSELL LOWELL**

The great omission in American life is solitude; not loneliness, for this is an alienation that thrives most in the midst of crowds, but that zone of time and space free from outside pressure which is the incubator of the spirit.
**MARYA MANNES**

There is no escape into that solitude in which a man can determine what is right and good for him rather than how others rate him.
**MARYA MANNES**

The heart beats louder and the soul hears quicker in silence and solitude.
**WENDELL PHILLIPS**

Solitude is not measured by the miles of space that intervene between a man and his fellows.
**HENRY DAVID THOREAU**

The way a man speaks lays bare the texture of his mind, the goodness of his heart, the inner pain or the sweet serenity that are his companions in solitude.
**HARRIET VAN HORNE**

## Sorrow

Resolve to be thyself; and know that he who finds himself, loses his misery.
MATTHEW ARNOLD

Regrets are as personal as fingerprints. Discarding what is vain or false, facing the facts that should truly disturb your conscience, is worth whatever time it takes or pain it may cause. It can pay to the future what you owe to the past.
MARGARET CULKIN BANNING

We have no right to ask when sorrow comes, "Why did this happen to me?" unless we ask the same question for every joy that comes our way.
PHILIP S. BERNSTEIN

Regret for time wasted can become a power for good in the time that remains.
ARTHUR BRISBANE

If there is a hell upon earth it is to be found in a melancholy man's heart.
ROBERT BURTON

Sorrow was made for man, not for beasts; yet if men encourage melancholy too much, they become no better than beasts.
MIGUEL DE CERVANTES

There is no greater sorrow than remembering happy times in the midst of misery.
DANTE

Waste no tears over the griefs of yesterday.
EURIPIDES

Make not a bosom friend of a melancholy sad soul: he goes always heavy loaded, and thou must bear half.
THOMAS FULLER

When sorrow is asleep, wake it not.
THOMAS FULLER

If we are more affected by the ruin of a palace than by the conflagration of a cottage, our humanity must have formed a very erroneous estimate of the miseries of human life.
EDWARD GIBBON

The capacity of sorrow belongs to our grandeur; and the loftiest of our race are those who have had the profoundest griefs because they have had the profoundest sympathies.
HENRY GILES

Regret for the things we did can be tempered by time; it is regret for the things we did not do that is inconsolable.
SYDNEY J. HARRIS

Life is made up of sobs, sniffles and smiles, with sniffles predominating.
O. HENRY

The miserable are very talkative.
HINDU PROVERB

There are a good many real miseries in life that one cannot help smiling at, but they are the smiles that make wrinkles and not dimples.
OLIVER WENDELL HOLMES

It is wrong to be sorry without ceasing.
HOMER

We live in a world which is full of misery and ignorance, and the plain duty of each and all of us is to try to make the little corner he can influence somewhat less miserable and somewhat less ignorant than it was before he entered it.
THOMAS H. HUXLEY

Thou shalt forget thy misery, and remember it as waters that pass away: and thine age shall be clearer than the noonday; thou shalt shine forth, thou shalt be as the morning.
**Job 11:16–17**

Sorrow is a kind of rust of the soul, which every new idea contributes in its passage to scour away.
**Samuel Johnson**

There is no wisdom in useless and hopeless sorrow.
**Samuel Johnson**

When you find yourself overcovered, as it were, by melancholy, the best way is to go out and do something kind to somebody or other.
**Keble**

Believe me, every man has his secret sorrows, which the world knows not; and oftentimes we call a man cold, when he is only sad.
**Henry Wadsworth Longfellow**

The first lesson of life is to burn our own smoke; that is, not to inflict on outsiders our personal sorrows and petty morbidness, not to keep thinking of ourselves as exceptional cases.
**James Russell Lowell**

I do believe there is many a tear in the heart that never reaches the eyes.
**Norman MacEwan**

Regret is an appalling waste of energy; you can't build on it; it's only good for wallowing in.
**Katherine Mansfield**

All men's miseries come from their inability to sit quiet and alone.
**Blaise Pascal**

It befalls us, as it does many in their mature years, to regret that blessed time when studies could have been more orderly, more intense, and more conclusive. For us it was not always that way.
**Pope Paul VI**

In such a season, golden, spacious, out already whispering of the end, there will often come to a man a certain solemn mood, a vein of not unpleasing melancholy, and for a little while he will see all life moving to a grave measure, an adagio for strings.
**J. B. Priestley**

Not a day passes over this earth, but men and women of no note do great deeds, speak great words and suffer noble sorrows.
**Charles Reed**

And God shall wipe away all tears from their eyes; and there shall be no more death, neither sorrow, nor crying, neither shall there be any more pain; for the former things are passed away.
**Revelation 21:4**

There are times when God asks nothing of his children except silence, patience, and tears.
**C. S. Robinson**

There's such a charm in melancholy I would not if I could be gay.
**Samuel Rogers**

Almost all of our sorrows spring out of our relations with other people.
**Arthur Schopenhauer**

What's gone and what's past help should be past grief.
**William Shakespeare**

If all men were to bring their miseries together in one place, most would be glad to take each his own home again rather than take a portion out of the common stock.
SOLON

Despondency is the most unprofitable feeling a man can indulge in.
DE WITT TALMADGE

Nature refuses to sympathize with our sorrow. She seems not to have provided for, but by a thousand contrivances against it. She has bevelled the margins of the eyelids that the tears may not overflow on the cheek.
HENRY DAVID THOREAU

Pure and complete sorrow is as impossible as pure and complete joy.
LEO TOLSTOY

Half of the secular unrest and dismal, profane sadness of modern society comes from the vain idea that every man is bound to be a critic of life.
HENRY VAN DYKE

'Tis impious in a good man to be sad.
EDWARD YOUNG

## 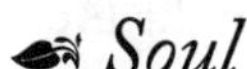 *Soul*

The athletic fool, to whom what heaven denied of soul, is well compensated in limbs.
JOHN ARMSTRONG

Such as are thy habitual thoughts, such also will be the character of thy soul—for the soul is dyed by the thoughts. Dye it then, with a continuous series of such thoughts as these—that where a man can live, there if he will he can also live well.
MARCUS AURELIUS ANTONINUS

There seems to be an unalterable contradiction between the human mind and its employments. How can a soul be a merchant? What relation to an immortal being have the price of linseed, the brokerage on hemp? Can an undying creature debit petty expenses and charge for carriage paid? The soul ties its shoes; the mind washes its hands in a basin. All is incongruous.
WALTER BAGEHOT

If my soul were not light, I would die.
JOANNA BAILLIE

Every human soul is of infinite value, eternal, free; no human being, therefore, is so placed as not to have within his reach, in himself and others, objects adequate to infinite endeavor.
LORD BALFOUR

Our bodies are where we stay; Our souls are what we are.
CECIL BAXTER

Even in the meanest sorts of labor, the whole soul of a man is composed into a kind of real harmony the instant he sets himself to work.
NORMAN CARLISLE

No iron chain, or outward force of any kind, could ever compel the soul of man to believe or disbelieve.
THOMAS CARLYLE

There is need of a sprightly and vigilant soul to discern and lay hold on favorable junctures.
PIERRE CHARRON

The soul would have no rainbow had the eyes no tears.
JOHN VANCE CHENEY

Laws just or unjust may govern men's actions. Tyrannies may restrain or regulate their words. The

machinery of propaganda may pack their minds with falsehood and deny them truth for many generations of time. But the soul of man thus held in trance or frozen in a long night can be awakened by a spark coming from God knows where and in a moment the whole structure of lies and oppression is on trial for its life.
**WINSTON CHURCHILL**

No man is free who is not master of his soul and controller of his spirit.
**THOMAS CROMBIE**

You will do the greatest service to the state if you shall raise, not the roofs of the houses, but the souls of the citizens: for it is better that great souls should dwell in small houses rather than for mean slaves to lurk in great houses.
**EPICTETUS**

I believe that man will not merely endure, he will prevail. He is immortal not because he alone among creatures has an inexhaustible voice, but because he has a soul.
**WILLIAM FAULKNER**

Man is so made that when anything fires his soul impossibilities vanish.
**JEAN DE LA FONTAINE**

Food may be essential as fuel for the body, but good food is fuel for the soul.
**MALCOLM FORBES**

I am fully convinced that the soul is indestructible, and that its activity will continue through eternity. It is like the sun, which, to our eyes, seems to set in night; but it has in reality only gone to diffuse its light elsewhere.
**JOHANN WOLFGANG VON GOETHE**

The real duty of man is not to extend his power or multiply his wealth beyond his needs, but to enrich and enjoy his imperishable possession: his soul.
**GILBERT HIGHET**

Governments know that the life of the world cannot be saved if the soul of the world is allowed to be lost.
**HERBERT HOOVER**

Corporations have no souls, so the legend runs. Granted. But those selected to manage their affairs must have to achieve success. Sometimes, however, they enter upon a mad scramble for material results, and lose them in consequence. Although a concern thus headed may seem to flourish for a brief spell and yield material dividends, it is certain to cease to do so, and must gradually decay. The proper executive is unquestionably he who adopts the Golden Rule as the keynote of his life; who buries self, when acting in a representative capacity, for he is sure so to conduct himself on all occasions as to reflect credit upon himself, and the concern by which he is engaged as well.
**FERDINAND W. LAFRENTZ**

Years may wrinkle the skin, but to give up interest wrinkles the soul.
**DOUGLAS MACARTHUR**

How shall the soul of a man be larger than the life he has lived?
**EDGAR LEE MASTERS**

What lies behind us and what lies before us are tiny matters compared to what lies within us.
**WILLIAM MORROW**

Never does a man know the force that is in him till some mighty affection or grief has humanized the soul.
**FREDERICK W. ROBERTSON**

The soul's maladies have their relapses like the body's. What we take for a cure is often just a momentary rally or a new form of the disease.
**FRANÇOIS DE LA ROCHEFOUCAULD**

It is not the eye that sees the beauty of the heaven, nor the ear that hears the sweetness of music or the glad tidings of a prosperous occurrence, but the soul, that perceives all the relishes of intellectual perfection.
**JEREMY TAYLOR**

Money is not required to buy one necessity of the soul.
**HENRY DAVID THOREAU**

It seems to me that the soul, when alone with itself and speaking to itself, uses only a small number of words, none of them extraordinary.
**PAUL VALÉRY**

## *Speaking*

Speak softly and sweetly. If your words are soft and sweet, they won't be as hard to swallow if you have to eat them.
**ANONYMOUS**

There is nothing wrong with having nothing to say—unless you insist on saying it.
**ANONYMOUS**

What is said is more important than who said it.
**ANONYMOUS**

Why is it that those who have something to say can't say it, while those who have nothing to say keep saying it?
**ANONYMOUS**

The voice is a second face.
**GERARD BAUER**

Loquacity: A disorder which renders the sufferer unable to curb his tongue when you wish to talk.
**AMBROSE BIERCE**

On speaking, first have something to say, second say it, third stop when you have said it, and finally give it an accurate title.
**JOHN SHAW BILLINGS**

To speak well supposes a habit of attention which shows itself in the thought; by language we learn to think and above all to develop thought.
**CARL VICTOR DE BONSTETTEN**

In order to speak short upon any subject, think long.
**H. H. BRACKENRIDGE**

I favor legal freedoms,
Such as that of speech.
But there's need of substance
Something more than screech.
**ART BUCK**

Brevity is very good, when we are, or are not, understood.
**SAMUEL BUTLER**

And as the he knew not what to say, he swore.
**LORD BYRON**

Speech is too often not the art of concealing thought, but of quite stifling and suspending thought, so that there is none to conceal.
**THOMAS CARLYLE**

Speech is the gift of all, but thought of few.
**CATO**

Little said is soon amended.
**MIGUEL DE CERVANTES**

Talk does not cook rice.
**CHINESE PROVERB**

If you don't say anything, you won't be called upon to repeat it.
**CALVIN COOLIDGE**

If you have anything of importance to tell me, for God's sake begin at the end.
**SARA J. DUNCAN**

Let thy speech be short, comprehending much in a few words.
**ECCLESIASTICUS**

Be not rash with thy mouth, and let not thine heart be hasty to utter any thing before God: for God is in heaven, and thou upon earth: therefore let thy words be few.
**ECCLESIASTES 5:2**

A man cannot speak but he judges and reveals himself. With his will, or against his will, he draws his portrait to the eye of others by every word. Every opinion reacts on him who utters it.
**RALPH WALDO EMERSON**

Better to slip with the foot than with the tongue.
**ENGLISH PROVERB**

The Lord said unto him, Who made man's mouth? or who maketh the dumb, or deaf, or the seeing, or the blind? have not I the Lord? Now therefore go, and I will be with thy mouth, and teach thee what thou shalt say.
**EXODUS 4:11–12**

If you say what you think, don't expect to hear only what you like.
**MALCOLM FORBES**

Speak not but what may benefit others or yourself; avoid trifling conversation.
**BENJAMIN FRANKLIN**

Think twice before you speak, or act once, and you will speak or act the more wisely for it.
**BENJAMIN FRANKLIN**

The true use of speech is not so much to express our wants as to conceal them.
**OLIVER GOLDSMITH**

Yes and No are soon said, but give much to think over.
**BALTASAR GRACIÁN**

There are three things to aim at in public speaking: first to get into your subject, then to get your subject into yourself, and lastly, to get your subject into your hearers.
**A. S. GREGG**

He who speaks the loudest is the least heard.
**ROBERT HALF**

Speak fitly, or be silent wisely.
**GEORGE HERBERT**

From listening comes wisdom, and from speaking repentance.
**ITALIAN PROVERB**

Half a brain is enough for him who says little.
**ITALIAN PROVERB**

And the tongue is a fire, a world of iniquity: so is the tongue among our members, that it defileth the

whole body, and setteth on fire the whole course of nature; and it is set on fire of hell.
JAMES 3:6

The tongue no man can tame; it is an unruly evil, full of deadly poison. Therewith we bless God, even the Father; and therewith curse we men, which are made after the similitude of God. Out of the same mouth proceedeth blessing and cursing.
JAMES 3:8–10

The tongue is more to be feared than the sword.
JAPANESE PROVERB

Speeches that are measured by the hour will die with the hour.
THOMAS JEFFERSON

Talking and eloquence are not the same: to speak, and to speak well are two things. A fool may talk, but a wise man speaks.
BEN JONSON

Speech is the mother, not the handmaid, of thought.
KARL KRAUS

He who sedulously attends, pointed asks, calmly speaks, cooly answers, and ceases when he has no more to say is in possession of some of the best requisites of man.
JOHANN LAVATER

Brevity: To say at once whatever is to be said.
GEORG CHRISTOPH LICHTENBERG

In times like the present, men should utter nothing for which they would not willingly be responsible through time and in eternity.
ABRAHAM LINCOLN

Blessed are they who have nothing to say, and who cannot be persuaded to say it.
JAMES RUSSELL LOWELL

Speech is civilization itself. The word—even the most contradictory word—preserves contact. It is silence which isolates.
THOMAS MANN

Not that which goeth into the mouth defileth a man; but that which cometh out of the mouth, this defileth a man.
MATTHEW 15:11

If nobody spoke unless he had something to say, the human race would very soon lose the use of speech.
SOMERSET MAUGHAM

If you keep your mouth shut you will never put your foot in it.
AUSTIN O'MALLEY

From men, man learns to speak, from the gods to keep silent.
PLUTARCH

Remember what Simonides said—that he never repented that he had held his tongue, but often that he had spoken.
PLUTARCH

Speaking much is a sign of vanity; for he that is lavish in words is a niggard in deed.
SIR WALTER RALEIGH

Speech is a picture of the mind.
JOHN RAY

It is but a poor eloquence which only shows that the orator can talk.
SIR JOSHUA REYNOLDS

A speech without a specific purpose is like a journey without a destination.
**RALPH C. SMEDLEY**

Whatever your grade or position, if you know how and when to speak, and when to remain silent, your chances of real success are proportionately increased.
**RALPH C. SMEDLEY**

It is not of so much consequence what you say, as how you say it. Memorable sentences are memorable on account of some single irradiating word.
**ALEXANDER SMITH**

There are three things that ought to be considered before some things are spoken: the manner, the place and the time.
**ROBERT SOUTHEY**

It is the first rule of oratory that a man must appear such as he would persuade others to be; and that can be accomplished only by the force of his life.
**JONATHAN SWIFT**

Nature, which gave us two eyes to see and two ears to hear, has given us but one tongue to speak.
**JONATHAN SWIFT**

Speech is the mirror of the soul; as a man speaks, so he is.
**PUBLILIUS SYRUS**

It usually takes more than three weeks to prepare a good impromptu speech.
**MARK TWAIN**

There is much to be said for not saying much.
**FRANK TYGER**

All pleasantry should be short; and it might even be as well were the serious short also.
**VOLTAIRE**

In a free and republican government, you cannot restrain the voice of the multitude. Every man will speak as he thinks, or, more properly, without thinking, and consequently will judge of effects without attending to their causes.
**GEORGE WASHINGTON**

Where all have the right to speak, some foolish speaking is done. But where, as in a dictatorship, all speak alike, little thinking is done.
**FRANK L. WEIL**

Preach not because you have to say something, but because you have something to say.
**RICHARD WHATELY**

Every man is born with the faculty of reason and the faculty of speech, but why should he be able to speak before he has anything to say?
**BENJAMIN WHICHCOTE**

I have always been among those who believed that the greatest freedom of speech was the greatest safety, because if a man is a fool the best thing to do is to encourage him to advertise the fact by speaking.
**WOODROW WILSON**

Never rise to speak till you have something to say; and when you have said it, cease.
**JOHN WITHERSPOON**

## *Spiritual*

It is the spirit of a person that hangs above him like a star in the sky. People identify him at once, and

join with him until there is formed a parade of men and women, thus inspired. No matter where you find this spirit working, whether in a person or an entire organization, you may know that Heaven has dropped a note of joy into the world!
George Matthew Adams

Of course the one who gains the most from the contest is the player himself, and no one can long be a player if he is a poor sport and fails to do his best. Let the game be tennis, golf, baseball, or football, or the bigger game called life, whatever it is we must do our best because it keeps up the spirit—and that's what we need more than anything else. And if I keep up my spirit, and by example help to pull my neighbor out of his slump then my life has not been a failure. I am a success!
Malcolm W. Bingay

What a different world this would be if the people of all nations would realize that we need, first of all, a worldwide awakening of the public conscience, a spiritual revival and a moral regeneration before we can have real political and industrial peace.
William J. H. Boetcker

Do you know what amazes me more than anything else—the impotence of force to organize anything? There are only two powers in the world—the spirit and the sword; and in the long run the sword will always be conquered by the spirit.
Napoleon Bonaparte

We must believe in a Being, a divine will, or in an intelligent purpose behind the world. And we must live as if the world had sense, not as if the world were meaningless. Cold, cynical people are not only unhappy, but are dead to the spiritual values that make life. Only the positive attitude in acts of kindness and peace will give the joyous life.
Charles Reynolds Brown

We are not human beings having a spiritual experience. We are spiritual beings having a human experience.
Teilhard de Chardin

The failure of our modern world, with its moral and ethical collapse, may be traced directly to our spiritual ignorance and moral disobedience. The ethical conditions under which we live are disgracefully unsanitary. It is futile to expect peace and goodwill on earth while our homes are infested with the germs of selfishness, irreverence and lust. The world-wide epidemic of hatred, cruelty, murder and war is the inevitable result of our moral and spiritual disobedience. We cannot break the laws of the universe with impunity.
Allen E. Claxton, D.D.

We do not need more national development, we need more spiritual development. We do not need more intellectual power, we need more spiritual power. We do not need more knowledge, we need more character. We do not need more law, we need more religion. We do not need more of the things that are seen, we need more of the things that are unseen.
Calvin Coolidge

The greatest asset of any nation is the spirit of its people, and the greatest danger that can menace any nation is the breakdown of that spirit—the will to win and the course to work.
George B. Cortelyou

Our problem is within ourselves. We have found the means to blow the world physically apart. Spiritually, we have yet to find the means to put together the world's broken pieces.
Thomas E. Dewey

It is the tragedy of things spiritual that they languish if unorganized, and are contaminated by the material needs of their organization.
WILL DURANT

A man of a right spirit is not a man of narrow and private views, but is greatly interested and concerned for the good of the community to which he belongs, and particularly of the city or village in which he resides, and for the true welfare of the society of which he is a member.
JONATHAN EDWARDS

The spirit of man is more important than mere physical strength, and the spiritual fiber of a nation than its wealth.
DWIGHT D. EISENHOWER

Great men are they who see that spiritual is stronger than any material force; that thoughts rule the world.
RALPH WALDO EMERSON

Material riches are proving inadequate and are depreciated. God's love is bestowing sufficient benefits on the nation and the world, but the benefits are not getting to the people. Something is intervening, and it is the greed of people. The only values that are everlasting are spiritual, and when we lose them we lose everything.
ANTHONY H. EVANS, D.D.

All earthly delights are sweeter in expectation than enjoyment; but all spiritual pleasures more in fruition than expectation.
OWEN FELTHAM

Brethren, if a man be overtaken in a fault, ye which are spiritual, restore such a one in the spirit of meekness, considering thyself, lest thou also be tempted.
GALATIANS 6:1

If wrinkles must be written upon our brows, let them not be written upon the heart. The spirit should not grow old.
JAMES A. GARFIELD

What they are pleased to term the spirit of the times is mostly the gentlemen's own spirit wherein the times are made to mirror.
JOHANN WOLFGANG VON GOETHE

A weak spirit does more harm than a weak body.
BALTASAR GRACIÁN

An obligation rests upon each one of us to analyze the intellectual problem of his time and to attempt to formulate his statement of its significance, for the impact of modern science affects the individual as well as society. Each one of us must answer to himself what place it will find in the mansions of his spirit.
HAYWARD KENISTON

The means by which we live have outdistanced the ends for which we live. Our scientific power has outrun our spiritual power. We have guided missiles and misguided men.
MARTIN LUTHER KING, JR.

The basic need of the world is spirituality. The issue between free people and Communism is not economic; . . . the issue is the preservation of the freedom of man as a living soul.
DOUGLAS MACARTHUR

The educated man is a man with certain subtle spiritual qualities which make him calm in adversity, happy when alone, just in his dealings, rational and sane in the fullest meaning of that word in all the affairs of life.
RAMSAY MACDONALD

How shortsighted we often are in dealing with what, in the final reckoning, are spiritual maladies. The poverty of our resources may be seen in the kind of remedies we propose—change of air, change of diet, a round of gaiety and merrymaking. They have all been tried and they all have their value. But for the deeper maladies of the soul, for the man who has lost his grip on God and on the meaning of life they are the merest quackery. People want something against which they can lean back and know that it will never give.
ROBERT J. MCCRACKEN

Not to be beloved and yet retained is the greatest injury to a gentle spirit.
JOHN MILTON

It is now evident to all men of spiritual discernment that healing of the world's woes will not come through this or that social or political theory; not through violent changes in government, but in the still small voice that speaks to the conscience and the heart.
ARTHUR J. MOORE, D.D.

If we want to utilize in the proper way and to the fullest extent the products of man's intellect, we must develop that part of man's being that is his heart and spirit.
FERDINAND PECORA

He that hath no rule over his own spirit is like a city that is broken down and without walls.
PROVERBS 25:28

One truth stands firm. All that happens in world history rests on something spiritual. If the spiritual is strong, it creates world history. If it is weak, it suffers world history.
ALBERT SCHWEITZER

Spiritual power is a force which history clearly teaches has been the greatest force in the development of men. Yet we have been merely playing with it and never have really studied it as we have the physical forces. Some day people will learn that material things do not bring happiness, and are of little use in making people creative and powerful. Then the scientists of the world will turn their laboratories over to the study of spiritual forces which have hardly been scratched.
CHARLES P. STEINMETZ

It is not likely that posterity will fall in love with us, but not impossible that it may respect or sympathize; so a man would rather leave behind him the portrait of his spirit than a portrait of his face.
ROBERT LOUIS STEVENSON

The miracle, or the power, that elevates the few is to be found in their industry, application, and perseverance under the promptings of a brave, determined spirit.
MARK TWAIN

It is the spiritual fight to better human conditions which brings serenity and peace within.
OSWALD G. VILLARD

He who has not the spirit of his age has all the misery of it.
VOLTAIRE

## *Sports*

God does not charge time spent fishing against a man's allotted life span.
AMERICAN INDIAN PROVERB

Nothing increases your golf score like witnesses.
ANONYMOUS

In America, it is sport that is the opiate of the masses.
**RUSSELL BAKER**

Playing snooker gives you firm hands and helps to build up character. It is the ideal recreation for dedicated nuns.
**ARCHBISHOP LUIGI BARBARITO**

Baseball: Almost the only place in life where a sacrifice is really appreciated.
**MARK BELTAIRE**

Academy: A modern school where football is taught.
**AMBROSE BIERCE**

We have not made cricket and football [soccer] professional because of any astonishing avarice or new vulgarity. We have made them professional because we would have them perfect. We have dedicated men to them as to some god of inhuman excellence. We care more for football than for the fun of playing football.
**G. K. CHESTERTON**

Golf has taught me there is a connection between pain and pleasure. Golf spelled backwards is flog.
**PHYLLIS DILLER**

A good sweat, with the blood pounding through my body, makes me feel alive, revitalized. I gain a sense of mastery and assurance. I feel good about myself. Then I can feel good about others.
**ARTHUR DOBRIN**

So you wish to conquer in the Olympic Games? But first mark the conditions and the consequences. You will have to put yourself under discipline; to eat by the rule, to avoid cakes and sweetmeats; to take exercise at the appointed hour whether you like it or not, in cold and heat; to abstain from cold drinks and wine at your will; in a word, to give yourself over to the trainer as to a physician.
**EPICTETUS**

I played golf some time ago with John D. Rockefeller. The other day, I played with Charles M. Schwab.... Both played exactly the same. Neither overreached [or] tried to do more than he was capable of.... Most golfers, like most businessmen, swat the ball with all their might and trust more or less to luck as to the result.... Now, both Rockefeller and Schwab hit a straight ball nine times out of ten. In fact, in the first 17 holes I played with Schwab, he didn't foozle a single shot. I could drive a ball 25 to 50 yards further than he, but quite often it flew wild. The result was that Schwab licked me decisively.
**B. C. FORBES**

The most indispensable item in any fisherman's equipment is his hat. This ancient relic preserves not only the memory of every trout he ever caught, but also the smell.
**COREY FORD**

Dwell not too long upon sports; for as they refresh a man that is weary, so they weary a man that is refreshed.
**THOMAS FULLER**

He who spends all his life in sport is like one who hears nothing but fringes and eats nothing but sauces.
**RICHARD FULLER**

The balls used in top class games are generally smaller than those used in others.
**PAUL FUSSELL**

Pro football is like nuclear warfare: There are no winners, only survivors.
FRANK GIFFORD

A golf course is the epitome of all that is purely transitory in the universe, a space not to dwell in, but to get over as quickly as possible.
JEAN GIRAUDOUX

Bullfighting is the only art in which the artist is in danger of death and in which the degree of brilliance in the performance is left to the fighter's honor.
ERNEST HEMINGWAY

Father always emphasized being a good sportsman. Lose as if you like it, and win as if you were used to it.
THOMAS HITCHCOCK

To brag little, to lose well,
To crow gently if in luck,
To pay up, to own up,
To shut up if beaten,
Are the virtues of a sportingman.
OLIVER WENDELL HOLMES

I have a lifetime contract. That means I can't be fired during the third quarter if we are ahead and moving the ball.
LOU HOLTZ

Anglers boast of the innocence of their pastime; yet it puts fellow-creatures to the torture. They pique themselves on their meditative faculties; and yet their only excuse is a want of thought.
LEIGH HUNT

Two things only the people anxiously desire, bread and the Circus games.
JUVENAL

Football today is far too much a sport for the few who can play it well; the rest of us, and too many of our children, get our exercise from climbing up the seats in stadiums, or from walking across the room to turn on our television sets.
JOHN F. KENNEDY

We are inclined to think that if we watch a football game or a baseball game, we have taken part in it.
JOHN F. KENNEDY

Tennis is a perfect combination of violent action taking place in an atmosphere of total tranquility.
BILLIE JEAN KING

Rodeoing is about the only sport you can't fix. You'd have to talk to the bulls and horses, and they wouldn't understand you.
BILL LINDERMAN

If you see a tennis player who looks as if he is working hard, then that means he isn't very good.
HELEN WILLS MOODY

The real test in golf and in life is not in keeping out of the rough, but in getting out after we are in.
JOHN H. MOORE

The genuine sportsman is not hidebound by seasons and opening dates. He loves his ground no less when it resounds with mating song, and when the shyness of wild creatures melts in the genial warmth of spring and the armistice of love.
ERIC H. PARTRIDGE

When he says "Sit down!" I don't even look for a chair.
PLAYER (ABOUT VINCE LOMBARDI)

Golf: A plague invented by the Calvinistic Scots as a punishment for man's sins.
JAMES RESTON

The man who goes up in a balloon does not feel as if he were ascending; he only sees the earth sinking deeper below him.
ARTHUR SCHOPENHAUER

When a man wants to murder a tiger he calls it sport; when a tiger wants to murder him, he calls it ferocity.
GEORGE BERNARD SHAW

I don't think I can take seriously any game that takes less than three days to reach its conclusion.
TOM STOPPARD

Most sorts of diversion in men, children and other animals are an imitation of fighting.
JONATHAN SWIFT

Ideally, the umpire should have the integrity of a Supreme Court justice, the physical agility of an acrobat, the endurance of Job and the imperturbability of Buddha.
*TIME* MAGAZINE

It was a charming August day, just the day that trout enjoy lying in cool, deep places, and moving their fins in quiet content, indifferent to the skimming fly or to the proffered sport of rod and reel.
CHARLES DUDLEY WARNER

## *Statesman*

True statesmanship is the art of changing a nation from what it is into what it ought to be.
WILLIAM R. ALGER

A disposition to preserve, and an ability to improve, taken together, would be my standard of a statesman.
EDMUND BURKE

The great difference between the real statesman and the pretender is, that the one sees into the future, while the other regards only the present; the one lives by the day, and acts on expedience; the other acts on enduring principles and for immortality.
EDMUND BURKE

A politician thinks of the next election; a statesman, of the next generation.
JAMES FREEMAN CLARKE

The three great ends for a statesman are, security to possessors, facility to acquirers, and liberty and hope to the people.
SAMUEL TAYLOR COLERIDGE

Statesmen stand out because politicians are as alike as peas.
ARNOLD GLASOW

If I had wished to raise up a race of statesmen higher than politicians, animated not by greed or selfishness, by policy or party, I would familiarize the boys of the land with the characters of the Bible.
JOHN HALL

A statesman is a politician who is held upright by equal pressure from all directions.
ERIC A. JOHNSTON

The art of statesmanship is to foresee the inevitable and to expedite its occurrence.
CHARLES MAURICE DE TALLEYRAND

A statesman is a politician who's been dead ten or 15 years.
HARRY S TRUMAN

## Stocks

Nothing tells in the long run like a good judgment, and no sound judgment can remain with the man whose mind is disturbed by the mercurial changes of the stock exchange. It places him under an influence akin to intoxication. What is not, he sees, and what he sees, is not.
**ANDREW CARNEGIE**

One of the funny things about the stock market is that every time one man buys, another sells, and both think they are astute.
**WILLIAM FEATHER**

Henry Ford has several times sneered at unproductive stockholders.... Well, now. Let's see. Who made Henry Ford's own automobile company possible? The stockholders who originally advanced money to him. Who makes it possible for you and me to be carried to and from business by train or street car? Stockholders.... Who made our vast telephone and telegraph service possible? Stockholders.... Were stockholders all over the country to withdraw their capital from the enterprises in which they are invested, there would be a panic... on a scale never before known.
**B. C. FORBES**

If I owned any of these Hot New Issues that have doubled, tripled, quintupled or umptupled within days and in some cases hours after they were issued, I most certainly would grab my fabulous windfall, thank my lucky stars and invest the money. It's utter nonsense to think any newly issued stock is really worth two, ten or 20 times the [offering] price.... A management so stupid as to sell shares [cheap], and an underwriter so obtuse as not to discern the real value, together would provide reason enough for a sensible man to get rid of his shares.
**MALCOLM FORBES**

Don't gamble! Take all your savings and buy some good stock and hold it till it goes up, then sell it. If it don't go up, don't buy it.
**WILL ROGERS**

Is it not odd that the only generous person I ever knew, who had money to be generous with, should be a stockbroker?
**PERCY BYSSHE SHELLEY**

Do not argue with the market, for it is like the weather: Though not always kind, it is always right.
**KENNETH E. WALDEN**

## Strength

Look well into thyself; there is a source of strength which will always spring up if thou wilt always look there.
**MARCUS AURELIUS ANTONINUS**

Men seem neither to understand their riches nor their strength. Of the former they believe greater things than they should; of the latter, less.
**FRANCIS BACON**

Greatness lies not in being strong, but in the right using of strength.
**HENRY WARD BEECHER**

Better to be a strong man with a weak point, than to be a weak man without a strong point. A diamond with a flaw is more valuable than a brick without a flaw.
**WILLIAM J. H. BOETCKER**

In the assurance of strength there is strength; and they are the weakest, however strong, who have no faith in themselves or their powers.
**CHRISTIAN BOVÉE**

I've never been one who thought the good Lord should make life easy; I've just asked Him to make me strong.
EVA BOWRING

The world abhors closeness, and all but admires extravagance; yet a slack hand shows weakness, and a tight hand strength.
SIR THOMAS BUXTON

Few men during their lifetime come anywhere near exhausting the resources dwelling within them. There are deep wells of strength that are never used.
RICHARD E. BYRD

The block of granite which is an obstacle in the pathway of the weak becomes a stepping-stone in the pathway of the strong.
THOMAS CARLYLE

Steel can be tempered and hardened, and so can men. In this world of struggle, which was not designed for softies, a man must be harder than what hits him. Yes, he must be diamond-hard. Then he'll not be fed up with his little personal troubles.
HERBERT N. CASSON

At times to think of one's outer helplessness is good, but to think always of one's inner strength is infinitely better.
SRI CHINMOY

All the strength and force of man comes from his faith in things unseen. He who believes is strong; he who doubts is weak. Strong convictions precede great actions.
JAMES FREEMAN CLARKE

For strength to bear is found in duty alone,
And he is blest indeed who learns to make
The joy of others cure his own heartache.
GALEN DRAKE

Live in terms of your strong points. Magnify them. Let your weaknesses shrivel up and die from lack of nourishment.
WILLIAM YOUNG ELLIOTT

The opinion of the strongest is always the best.
JEAN DE LA FONTAINE

The difference between towering and cowering is totally a matter of inner posture.
MALCOLM FORBES

Only a strong tree can stand alone.
ARNOLD GLASOW

There is nothing magnanimous in bearing misfortunes with fortitude, when the whole world is looking on.... He who, without friends to encourage or even without hope to alleviate his misfortunes, can behave with tranquility and indifference, is truly great.
OLIVER GOLDSMITH

These three things deplete man's strength: fear, travel and sin.
HEBREW PROVERB

A man's strength cannot always be judged by his strongest actions; in many instances he is judged by his weakness.
J. W. A. HENDERSON

Fortitude: That quality of mind which does not care what happens so long as it does not happen to us.
ELBERT HUBBARD

They that wait upon the Lord shall renew their strength; they shall mount up with wings as eagles; they shall run, and not be weary; and they shall walk, and not faint.
ISAIAH 40:31

Know how sublime a thing it is to suffer and be strong.
**HENRY WADSWORTH LONGFELLOW**

That cause is strong which has, not a multitude, but one strong man behind it.
**JAMES RUSSELL LOWELL**

A living being seeks, above all, to discharge its strength. Life is will to power.
**FREIDRICH WILHELM NIETZSCHE**

A man must be strong enough to mold the peculiarity of his imperfections into the perfection of his peculiarities.
**WALTER RATHENAU**

The more weakness, the more falsehood; strength goes straight.
**JEAN PAUL RICHTER**

Only strong natures can really be sweet ones; those that seem sweet are in general only weak, and may easily turn sour.
**FRANÇOIS DE LA ROCHEFOUCAULD**

Moderate exercise and toil, so far from prejudicing, strengthen and consolidate the body.
**RICHARD RUSH**

Anyone who proposes to do good must not expect people to roll stones out of his way, but must accept his lot calmly if they even roll a few more on it. A strength which becomes clearer and stronger through experiences of such obstacles is the only strength that can conquer them. Resistance is only a waste of strength.
**ALBERT SCHWEITZER**

He who has injured thee was either stronger or weaker than thee. If weaker, spare him; if stronger, spare thyself.
**SENECA**

Oh! it is excellent to have a giant's strength; but it is tyrannous to use it like a giant.
**WILLIAM SHAKESPEARE**

Whatever strengthens and purifies the affections, enlarges the imagination, and adds spirit to sense, is useful.
**PERCY BYSSHE SHELLEY**

Nothing is so strong as gentleness, and nothing is so gentle as real strength.
**RALPH W. SOCKMAN**

Whatever increases the strength and authority of your body over your mind, that is sin to you, however innocent it may be in itself.
**ROBERT SOUTHEY**

Strength alone knows conflict; weakness is below even defeat, and is born vanquished.
**ANNE SWETCHINE**

Although men are accused of not knowing their own weakness, yet perhaps few know their own strength. It is in men as in soils, where sometimes there is a vein of gold which the owner knows not of.
**JONATHAN SWIFT**

No rock so hard but that a little wave may beat admission in a thousand years.
**ALFRED, LORD TENNYSON**

The wayside of business is full of brilliant men who started out with a spurt, and lacked the stamina to finish. Their places were taken by patient and unshowy plodders who never knew when to quit.
**J. R. TODD**

## Study

Concentration is my motto—first honesty, then industry, then concentration.
ANDREW CARNEGIE

Get over the idea that only children should spend their time in study. Be a student so long as you still have something to learn, and this will mean all your life.
HENRY L. DOHERTY

It is the studying that you do after your school days that really counts. Otherwise you know only that which everyone else knows.
HENRY L. DOHERTY

Concentration is the secret of strength in politics, in war, in trade, in short in all management of human affairs.
RALPH WALDO EMERSON

As the gardener, by severe pruning, forces the sap of the tree into one or two vigorous limbs, so should you stop off your miscellaneous activity and concentrate your force on one or a few points.
RALPH WALDO EMERSON

Concentrate on your job and you will forget your other troubles.
WILLIAM FEATHER

The love of study, a passion which derives fresh vigor from enjoyment, supplies each day and hour with a perpetual source of independent and rational pleasure.
EDWARD GIBBON

The use of a thing is only a part of its significance. To know anything thoroughly, to have the full command of it in all its appliances, we must study it on its own account, independently of any special application.
JOHANN WOLFGANG VON GOETHE

I will study and get ready and someday my chance will come.
ABRAHAM LINCOLN

There is no easy method of learning difficult things. The method is to close the door, give out that you are not at home, and work.
JOSEPH DE MAISTRE

My definition of an educated person is one who can concentrate on one subject for more than 2 minutes.
ROBERT A. MILLIKAN

If the study to which you apply yourself has a tendency to weaken your affection, and to destroy your taste for those simple pleasures in which no alloy can possibly mix, then that study is certainly unlawful, that is to say, not befitting the human mind.
MARY SHELLEY

I care not what your education is, elaborate or nothing, what your mental calibre is, great or small, that man who concentrates all his energies of body, mind and soul in one direction is a tremendous man.
DE WITT TALMAGE

There is no business, no avocation whatever, which will not permit a man who has the inclination to give a little time every day to study.
DANIEL WYTTENBACH

## Stupidity

The good Lord set definite limits on man's wisdom, but set no limits on his stupidity—and that's just not fair!
KONRAD ADENAUER

Never ascribe to malice what can perfectly well be explained by stupidity.
ANONYMOUS

Obstinacy and vehemency in opinion are the surest proof of stupidity.
BERNARD BARTON

There's goat in all of us, a stupid, stubborn goat.
R. P. BLACKMUR

Rascality has limits; stupidity has not.
NAPOLEON BONAPARTE

There must always be some who are brighter and some who are stupider. The latter make up for it by being better workers.
BERTOLT BRECHT

Be kind to dumb animals; they are kind to dumb people.
BUMPER STICKER

The question now is: Can we understand our stupidity? This is a test of intellect, not of character.
JOHN KING FAIRBANK

The dumbest people I know are those who Know It All.
MALCOLM FORBES

There is no stupid work, there are only stupid people.
FRENCH PROVERB

The man who is clever and industrious is suited to high staff appointments; use can be made of a man who is stupid and lazy; the man who is clever and lazy is suited for the highest command, he has the nerve to deal with all situations; but the man who is stupid and industrious is a danger and must be dismissed immediately.
BARON VON HAMMERSTEIN-EQUOARD

Never underestimate the power of human stupidity.
ROBERT A. HEINLEIN

The hardest thing to cope with is not selfishness or vanity or deceitfulness, but sheer stupidity.
ERIC HOFFER

Genius may have its limitations, but stupidity is not thus handicapped.
ELBERT HUBBARD

It is so pleasant to come across people who are more stupid than ourselves. We love them at once for being so.
JEROME K. JEROME

He that reads and grows no wiser seldom suspects his own deficiency, but complains of hard words and obscure sentences, and asks why books are written which cannot be understood.
SAMUEL JOHNSON

Stupidity is an elemental force for which no earthquake is a match.
KARL KRAUS

To accuse another of having weak kidneys, lungs or heart is not a crime; on the contrary, saying he has a weak brain is a crime. To be considered stupid and to be told so is more painful than being called gluttonous, mendacious, violent, lascivious, lazy, cowardly; every weakness, every vice, has found its

defenders, its ennoblement and exaltation, but stupidity hasn't.
**PRIMO LEVI**

Nothing sways the stupid more than arguments they can't understand.
**CARDINAL DE RETZ**

The trouble with the world is that the stupid are cocksure and the intelligent full of doubt.
**BERTRAND RUSSELL**

Never forget this: There isn't any man who's stupid all the way around.
**EUGENE F. RYAN**

The gods themselves struggle in vain against stupidity.
**JOHANN FRIEDRICH VON SCHILLER**

Tell a man something is bad, and he's not at all sure he wants to give it up. Describe it as stupid, and he knows it's the better part of caution to listen.
**DAVID SEABURY**

Idleness is the stupidity of the body, and stupidity is the idleness of the mind.
**JOHANN SEUME**

The great mistake made by intelligent people is to refuse to believe that the world is as stupid as it is.
**MADAME DE TENCIN**

Strange as it may seem, no amount of learning can cure stupidity, and formal education positively fortifies it.
**STEPHEN VIZINCZEY**

There is no sin except stupidity.
**OSCAR WILDE**

Whenever a man does a thoroughly stupid thing it is always from the noblest motive.
**OSCAR WILDE**

## *Success*

No student ever attains very eminent success by simply doing what is required of him: it is the amount and excellence of what is over and above the required, that determines the greatness of ultimate distinction.
**CHARLES KENDALL ADAMS**

One of the greatest secrets of success and happiness is always to have something left over. It may be earnings that are set aside as an investment and for the proverbial rainy day, or it may be that energy of ours that we conserve rather than waste. He who sees in arguments and disputes their futility, and who retires to himself to work things out, is a wise man. It is wiser to think things out, rather than to fight them out. You don't get used up this way!
**GEORGE MATTHEW ADAMS**

There is no such thing as a self-made man. We are made up of thousands of others. Every one who has ever done a kind deed for us, or spoken one word of encouragement to us, has entered into the make-up of our character and of our thoughts, as well as our success.
**GEORGE MATTHEW ADAMS**

'Tis not in mortals to command success, but we'll do more, Sempronius, we'll deserve it.
**JOSEPH ADDISON**

We mount to heaven mostly on the ruins of our cherished schemes, finding our failures were successes.
**AMOS BRONSON ALCOTT**

Distinction is the consequence, never the object, of a great mind.
**WASHINGTON ALLSTON**

All men seek one goal: success or happiness. The only way to achieve true success is to express yourself completely in service to society. First, have a definite, clear, practical ideal—a goal, an objective. Second, have the necessary means to achieve your ends—wisdom, money, materials and methods. Third, adjust all your means to that end.
**ARISTOTLE**

1. Good men are not cheap.
2. Capital can do nothing without brains to direct it.
3. No general can fight his battles alone. He must depend upon his lieutenants, and his success depends upon his ability to secure the right man for the right place.
4. There is no such thing as luck.
5. Most men talk too much. Much of my success has been due to keeping my mouth shut.

**J. OGDEN ARMOUR**

Ambition, confidence, enthusiasm and success are produced by courage, faith, pride and hard work.
**HARRY F. BANKS**

For success, attitude is equally as important as ability.
**HARRY F. BANKS**

If at first you do succeed—try to hide your astonishment.
**HARRY F. BANKS**

To succeed, one must posses an effective combination of ability, ambition, courage, drive, hard work, integrity and loyalty.
**HARRY F. BANKS**

Success is the reward for accomplishment.
**HARRY F. BANKS**

Success is not a matter of desire, but the product of hard work.
**JACK BARRINGER**

Neither patents, processes nor secrets are any longer assurance of success. The men responsible for the financing of industry have come to recognize that scientific methods have largely leveled down the advantages between one product and another. There are no longer any secrets in business—at least not in the most successful business.
**BRUCE BARTON**

Recipe for success: Be polite, prepare yourself for whatever you are asked to do, keep yourself tidy, be cheerful, don't be envious, be honest with yourself so you will be honest with others, be helpful, interest yourself in your job, don't pity yourself, be quick to praise, be loyal to your friends, avoid prejudices, be independent, interest yourself in politics, and read the newspapers.
**BERNARD M. BARUCH**

There is a certain cowardice, a certain weakness, rather, among respectable folk. Only brigands are convinced—of what? That they must succeed. And so they do succeed.
**CHARLES BAUDELAIRE**

It is not the going out of port, but the coming in, that determines the success of a voyage.
**HENRY WARD BEECHER**

Success is full of promise till men get it; and then it is a last-year's nest from which the birds have flown.
**HENRY WARD BEECHER**

Man cannot be satisfied with mere success. He is concerned with the terms upon which success comes to him. And very often the terms seem more important than the success.
CHARLES A. BENNETT

The toughest thing about success is that you've got to keep on being a success. Talent is only a starting point in business. You've got to keep working that talent.
IRVING BERLIN

Success is the one unpardonable sin against one's fellows.
AMBROSE BIERCE

What is known as success assumes nearly as many aliases as there are those who seek it. Like love, it can come to commoners as well as courtiers. Like virtue, it is its own reward. Like the Holy Grail, it seldom appears to those who don't pursue it.
STEPHEN BIRMINGHAM

Mark, young man, the line you succeed in will be of your own finding. The Davids in life do not slay the Goliaths of difficulty and temptation in another's armor, even though it be the king's, but with their own self-made weapons, though they be nothing more formidable than a sling and a pebble.
G. E. BISHOP

Never mind what others do; do better than yourself, beat your own record from day to day, and you are a success.
WILLIAM J. H. BOETCKER

Success makes a fool seem wise.
H. G. BOHN

The victory of success is half won when one gains the habit of work.
SARAH BOLTON

In business the earning of profit is something more than an incident of success. It is an essential condition of success; because the continued absence of profit itself spells failure. But while loss spells failure, large profits do not connote success. Success must be sought in business also in excellence of performance; and in business, excellence of performance manifests itself, among other things, in the advancing of methods and processes; in the improvement of products; in more perfect organization, eliminating friction as well as waste; in bettering the condition of the workingmen, developing their faculties and promoting their happiness; and in the establishment of right relations with customers and with the community.
LOUIS D. BRANDEIS

A successful life is not an easy life. It is built upon strong qualities, sacrifice, endeavor, loyalty, integrity.
GRANT D. BRANDON

Success in any enterprise requires the right product, methods and men and each must complement the others.
JOSEPH BURGER

If I die prematurely, at any rate I shall be saved from being bored by my own success.
SAMUEL BUTLER

There are two great rules in life, the one general and the other particular. The first is that everyone can in the end get what he wants if he only tries. This is the general rule. The particular rule is that every individual is more or less of an exception to the general rule.
SAMUEL BUTLER

Experience shows that success is due less to ability than to zeal. The winner is he who gives himself to his work, body and soul.
CHARLES BUXTON

The road to success is not to be run upon by seven-leagued boots. Step by step, little by little, bit by bit—that is the way to wealth, that is the way to wisdom, that is the way to glory.
**CHARLES BUXTON**

Success in business implies optimism, mutual confidence, and fair play. A business man must hold a high opinion of the worth of what he has to sell and he must feel that he is a useful public servant.
**R. H. CABELL**

I believe the true road to preeminent success in any line is to make yourself master of that line.
**ANDREW CARNEGIE**

### Ten Success Rules

Put success before amusement.

Learn something every day.

Cut free from routine.

Concentrate on net profits.

Make your services known.

Never worry over trifles.

Shape your decisions quickly.

Acquire skill and technique.

Deserve loyalty and co-operation.

Value character above all.
**HERBERT N. CASSON**

True success is the only thing that you cannot have unless and until you have offered it to others.
**SRI CHINMOY**

By different methods different men excel, but where is he who can do all things well?
**CHARLES CHURCHILL**

Success is a journey—not a destination.
**H. TOM COLLARD**

The secret of success in life is known only to those who have not succeeded.
**JOHN CHURTON COLLINS**

To know a man, observe how he wins his object, rather than how he loses it; for when we fail, our pride supports; when we succeed, it betrays us.
**CHARLES CALEB COLTON**

The superior man makes the difficulty to be overcome his first interest; success comes only later.
**CONFUCIUS**

A long time ago a noted specialist said that his secret of success as a physician was keeping the patient's head cool and his feet warm. And it is just now becoming generally known that a hot head and cold feet are enough to bring disaster to even a well man.
**O. BYRON COOPER**

You do not succeed because you do not know what you want, or you don't want it intensely enough.
**FRANK CRANE**

Being called very, very difficult is the beginning of success. Until you're called very, very difficult you're really nobody at all.
**BETTE DAVIS**

Real success is not on the stage, but off the stage as a human being, and how you get along with your fellow men.
**SAMMY DAVIS, JR.**

Mediocrity requires aloofness to preserve its dignity.
**CHARLES G. DAWES**

Success has a great tendency to conceal and throw a veil over the evil deeds of men.
**DEMOSTHENES**

Set the course of your lives by the three stars—sincerity, courage, unselfishness. From these flow a host of other virtues. . . . He who follows them and does not seek success, will attain the highest type of success, that which lies in the esteem of those among whom he dwells.
MONROE E. DEUTSCH

Success is counted sweetest by those who ne'er succeed.
EMILY DICKINSON

I have begun several times many things, and I have often succeeded at last.
BENJAMIN DISRAELI

Success is the child of audacity.
BENJAMIN DISRAELI

There is a vast difference between success at twenty-five and success at sixty. At sixty, nobody envies you. Instead, everybody rejoices generously, sincerely, in your good fortune.
MARIE DRESSLER

Be awful nice to 'em goin' up, because you're gonna meet 'em all comin' down.
JIMMY DURANTE

The best augury of a man's success in his profession is that he thinks it is the finest in the world.
GEORGE ELIOT

Success is relative: It is what we can make of the mess we have made of things.
T. S. ELIOT

Great and dramatic changes have taken place in the world. Old values, old ways of thinking, have changed—to give way to new and pressing problems that tax all our optimism and purpose, and that call for the best we can contribute to the work of the world. But one fact stands out clear and challenging: The sound, basic principles of personal progress and success have not changed. They have been modified and accelerated in their operation—given new directions, perhaps—but still the greatest rewards go to those who can give most.
L. G. ELLIOTT

I look on that man as happy, who, when there is a question of success, looks into his work for a reply.
RALPH WALDO EMERSON

To laugh often and much: To win the respect of intelligent people and the affection of children, to earn the appreciation of honest critics and endure the betrayal of false friends; to appreciate beauty, to find the best in others, to leave the world a bit better whether by a healthy child, a garden patch, or a redeemed social condition; to know even one life has breathed easier because you lived. This is to have succeeded.
RALPH WALDO EMERSON

The line between failure and success is so fine that we scarcely know when we pass it—so fine that we often are on the line and do not know it.
RALPH WALDO EMERSON

The secret of success in society is a certain heartiness and sympathy. A man who is not happy in company, cannot find any word in his memory that will fit the occasion; all his information is a little impertinent. A man who is happy there, finds in every turn of the conversation occasions for the introduction of what he has to say. The favorites of society are able men, and of more spirit than wit, who have no uncomfortable egotism, but who exactly fill the hour and the company, contented and contenting.
RALPH WALDO EMERSON

Along with success comes a reputation for wisdom.
**EURIPIDES**

Deliver me from all evildoers that talk nothing but sickness and failure.

Grant me the companionship of men who think success and men who work for it.

Loan me associates who cheerfully face the problems of a day and try hard to overcome them.

Relieve me of all cynics and critics.

Give me good health and the strength to be of real service to the world, and I'll get all that's good for me, and will what's left to those who want it.
**WILLIAM FEATHER**

He that succeeds makes an important thing of the immediate task.
**WILLIAM FEATHER**

If at first you don't succeed try hard work.
**WILLIAM FEATHER**

Nobody succeeds in a big way except by risking failure.
**WILLIAM FEATHER**

Success seems to be largely a matter of hanging on after others have let go.
**WILLIAM FEATHER**

There isn't much thrill in success unless one has first been close to failure.
**WILLIAM FEATHER**

An executive cannot gradually dismiss details. Business is made up of details and I notice that the chief executive who dismisses them is quite likely to dismiss his business.

Success is the sum of detail. It might perhaps be pleasing to imagine oneself beyond details and engaged only in great things, but as I have often observed, if one attends only to great things and lets the little things pass the great things become little; that is, the business shrinks.

It is not possible for an executive to hold himself aloof from anything. No business, no matter what its size, can be called safe until it has been forced to learn economy and rigidly to measure values of men and materials.
**HARVEY S. FIRESTONE**

I have found that it is much easier to make a success in life than to make a success of one's life.
**G. W. FOLLIN**

Call the roll in your memory of conspicuously successful [business] giants and, if you know anything about their careers, you will be struck by the fact that almost every one of them encountered inordinate difficulties sufficient to crush all but the gamest of spirits. Edison went hungry many times before he became famous.
**B. C. FORBES**

For my part, I rather distrust men or concerns that rise up with the speed of rockets. Sudden rises are sometimes followed by equally sudden falls. I have most faith in the individual or enterprise that advances step by step. A mushroom can spring up in a day; an oak takes 50 years or more to reach maturity. Mushrooms don't last; oaks do. The real cause for an enormous number of business failures is premature over-expansion, attempting to gallop before learning to creep. Sudden successes often invite sudden reverses.
**B. C. FORBES**

Madame Curie didn't stumble upon radium by accident. She searched and experimented and sweated and suffered years before she found it. Success rarely is an accident.
**B. C. FORBES**

Success is finding, or making, that position which enables you to contribute to the world the very greatest services of which you are capable, through the diligent, persevering, resolute cultivation of all the faculties God has endowed you with, and doing it all with cheerfulness, scorning to allow difficulties or defeats to drive you to pessimism or despair. Success consists of being and doing, not simply accumulating. The businessman or business enterprise that aspires to win the highest recognition for success must distinguish himself or itself, not by the magnitude of the profits, but by the value of service performed.
**B. C. Forbes**

The fittest, not the richest, make the most enviable mark. Pampered sons of plutocrats may shine for a time in society, but not in the world of affairs and of service unless they rip off their coats and get to work early and stay late. To be born with a golden spoon in the mouth is more of a handicap than a help in attaining worthwhile success in this age.
**B. C. Forbes**

The very first task given Harvey D. Gibson on entering the Boston office of the American Express Co., when he left college, was to shoulder a couple of knapsacks—after he had finished sweeping the floor—and deliver bundles of canceled checks to local banks. The first bundle he delivered was from the Liberty National Bank of New York. Fifteen years later he became president of this same bank. Had he scorned to sweep the floor, as being beneath the dignity of a college-bred youth, is it likely that he would be where he is today?
**B. C. Forbes**

There is more genuine joy in climbing the hill of success, even though sweat may be spent and toes may be stubbed, than in aimlessly sliding down the path to failure. If a straight, honorable path has been chosen, the gaining of the summit yields lasting satisfaction. The morass of failure, if reached through laziness, indifference or other avoidable fault, yields nothing but ignominy and sorrow for self and family and friends.
**B. C. Forbes**

Nothing recedes like success.
**Bryan Forbes**

### How to Succeed

Try hard enough.
**Malcolm Forbes**

The only advice I can think of that's of any value to anybody that is eager to have success—whatever that means in life—is to do what turns you on. If you're not doing something that's got you all wrapped up, you just can't do it well. You're going to lay an egg.
**Malcolm Forbes (commencement address, 1988)**

You have to come up in the world before it's worthwhile for those worth less to put you down.
**Malcolm Forbes**

If there is any great secret of success in life, it lies in the ability to put yourself in the other person's place and to see things from his point of view—as well as your own.
**Henry Ford**

To be a success, devote three or four hours a day to being an executive and the rest of the time to thinking.
**Felix Frankfurter**

Success has ruin'd many a man.
**Benjamin Franklin**

### Trade

As we pay others, so we are paid,
Life gives us back just what we give;
And so, goodwill controls success,
But trade that we may truly live.
Sales may be made in money, yes,
But they are always made to men;
And so, goodwill controls success,
Bringing folks back to buy again.
He profits most whose every sale,
Creates a friend whose kindly thought
Serves to perpetuate the tale,
Of what and where and why he bought.

FURROW

No age or time of life, no position or circumstance, has a monopoly on success. Any age is the right age to start doing!

GERARD

Success is simple. Do what's right, the right way, at the right time.

ARNOLD GLASOW

Men are so constituted that every one undertakes what he sees another successful in, whether he has aptitude for it or not.

JOHANN WOLFGANG VON GOETHE

In spite of the fact that the ladder tapers to one-man rungs at the top, the roomiest part is farthest up.

CHARLES GOW

Success rarely brings satisfaction.

BALTASAR GRACIÁN

Take care to make things turn out well. Some people scruple more over pointing things in the right direction than over successfully reaching their goals. The disgrace of failure outweighs the diligence they showed. A winner is never asked for explanations.

BALTASAR GRACIÁN

Every man should make up his mind that if he expects to succeed, he must give an honest return for the other man's dollar.

E. H. HARRIMAN

It isn't what you make . . . it's what you do with what you make.

RALPH A. HAYWARD

The way to secure success is to be more anxious about obtaining than about deserving it.

WILLIAM HAZLITT

To do anything, to dig a hole in the ground, to plant a cabbage, to hit a mark, to move a shuttle, to work a pattern—in a word, to attempt to produce any effect, and to succeed, has something in it that gratifies the lover of power.

WILLIAM HAZLITT

All outward success, when it has value, is but the inevitable result of an inward success of full living, full play and enjoyment of one's faculties.

ROBERT HENRI

If well thou hast begun, go on; it is the end that crowns us, not the fight.

ROBERT HERRICK

### Foundation Stones

In building a firm foundation for Success, here are a few stones to remember:

1. The wisdom of preparation.
2. The value of confidence.
3. The worth of honesty.
4. The privilege of working.
5. The discipline of struggle.
6. The magnetism of character.
7. The radiance of health.

8. The forcefulness of simplicity.
9. The winsomeness of courtesy.
10. The attractiveness of modesty.
11. The inspiration of cleanliness.
12. The satisfaction of serving.
13. The power of suggestion.
14. The buoyancy of enthusiasm.
15. The advantage of initiative.
16. The virtue of patience.
17. The rewards of co-operation.
18. The fruitfulness of perseverance.
19. The sportsmanship of losing.
20. The joy of winning.

ROLLO C. HESTER

Failure can be bought on easy terms; success must be paid for in advance.

CULLEN HIGHTOWER

Success comes to those who become success conscious. Failure comes to those who indifferently allow themselves to become failure conscious.

NAPOLEON HILL

Success is good management in action.

WILLIAM E. HOLLER

Our definition of success is unorthodox. We claim that any man who is honest, fair, tolerant, kindly, charitable of others and well behaved is a success, no matter what his station in life.

JAY E. HOUSE

Every successful man I have heard of has done the best he could with conditions as he found them, and not waited until the next year for better.

EDGAR WATSON HOWE

If you succeed in life, you must do it in spite of the efforts of others to pull you down. There is nothing in the idea that people are willing to help those who help themselves. People are willing to help a man who can't help himself, but as soon as a man is able to help himself, and does it, they join in making his life as uncomfortable as possible.

EDGAR WATSON HOWE

No man ever knows the few joys of living without some sort of success to his credit. Of all the games worth a candle, success is first. The greatest punishment is to be despised by your neighbors, the world and members of your family.

EDGAR WATSON HOWE

The men of greatest usefulness are those who have a surplus; those who have only good will and love for their fellows cannot equal in well-doing those who have money and success to their credit.

EDGAR WATSON HOWE

Pray that success will not come any faster than you are able to endure it.

ELBERT HUBBARD

Sometimes the pilgrimage from rags to riches is a journey from rage to wretchedness.

R. M. HUBER

Success consists of a series of little daily victories.

LADDIE F. HUTAR

It is not enough to aim, you must hit.

ITALIAN PROVERB

The moral flabbiness born of the exclusive worship of the bitch-goddess *Success.* That—with the squalid cash interpretation put on the word success—is our national disease.

WILLIAM JAMES

Flash powder makes a more brilliant light than the arc lamp, but you can't use it to light your street corner because it doesn't last long enough. Stability is more essential to success than brilliancy.
RICHARD LLOYD JONES

Perhaps, for worldly success, we need virtues that makes us loved and faults that makes us feared.
JOSEPH JOUBERT

The secret of success of every man who has ever been successful lies in the fact that he formed the habit of doing those things that failures don't like to do.
A. JACKSON KING

Men who have attained things worth having in this world have worked while others idled, have persevered when others gave up in despair, have practiced early in life the valuable habits of self-denial, industry, and singleness of purpose. As a result, they enjoy in later life the success so often erroneously attributed to good luck.
GRENVILLE KLEISER

Succeed we must, at all cost—even if it means being a dead millionaire at fifty.
LOUIS KRONENBERGER

We gain nothing by being with such as ourselves; we encourage each other in mediocrity. I am always longing to be with men more excellent than myself.
CHARLES LAMB

Decision and determination are the engineer and fireman of our train to opportunity and success.
BURT LAWLOR

Success didn't spoil me; I've always been insufferable.
FRAN LEBOWITZ

The talent of success is nothing more than doing what you can do well and doing well whatever you do without thought of fame.
HENRY WADSWORTH LONGFELLOW

We do not meet with success except by reiterated efforts.
FRANÇOISE DE MAINTENON

If you would succeed in life, it is of first importance that your individuality, your independence, your determination be trained that you not be lost in the crowd.
ORISON S. MARDEN

The successful people are the ones who can think up stuff for the rest of the world to keep busy at.
DONALD MARQUIS

Success is the brand on the brow of the man who has aimed too low.
JOHN MASEFIELD

The common idea that success spoils people by making them vain, egotistic and self-complacent is erroneous; on the contrary, it makes them for the most part, humble, tolerant and kind. Failure makes people cruel and bitter.
SOMERSET MAUGHAM

Only a mediocre person is always at his best.
SOMERSET MAUGHAM

More than the bad, the good has always been the enemy of the best. Mediocrity and complacency are wholly more dangerous to idealism than the recognized bad things in life.
JAMES L. MCCONAUGHTY

The ability to form friendships, to make people believe in you and trust you is one of the few

absolutely fundamental qualities of success. Selling, buying, negotiating are so much smoother and easier when the parties enjoy each other's confidence. The young man who can make friends quickly will find that he will glide instead of stumble through life.
JOHN J. MCGUIRK

The young man who would succeed must identify his interests with those of his employer and exercise the same diligence in matters entrusted to him as he would in his own affairs. Back of all the gifts the candidate for success may possess must be a willing capacity for hard work. . . . Youth today is not considered a handicap in selecting men for responsible jobs, as it was twenty years ago. . . . In almost any field today in which a youngster has an intelligent interest, the road to the top is open as it never was before. But the one way to the top is by persistent, intelligent, hard work.
A. T. MERCIER

In order to succeed, at times you have to make something from nothing.
RUTH MICKLEBY-LAND

I've gone through life believing in the strength and competence of others; never in my own. Now, dazzled, I discovered that my capacities were real. It was like finding a fortune in the lining of an old coat.
JOAN MILLS

The gent who wakes up and finds himself a success hasn't been asleep.
WILSON MIZNER

I have always observed that to succeed in the world one should appear like a fool but be wise.
BARON DE MONTESQUIEU

In most things success depends on knowing how long it takes to succeed.
BARON DE MONTESQUIEU

Big shots are only little shots who keep shooting.
CHRISTOPHER MORLEY

There is only one success—to be able to spend your own life in your own way.
CHRISTOPHER MORLEY

I am inclined to put the zenith of success—the time of most consideration and public labor—as somewhere in the sixties, say from sixty-five to seventy.
W. ROBERTSON NICOLL

Nothing is so detrimental to quality as success.
J. M. K. NYKS

You can succeed in anything if you give somebody else the credit for doing it.
OLD SOUTHERN SAYING

Either attempt it not, or succeed.
OVID

The art of dealing with people is the foremost secret of successful men. A man's success in handling people is the very yardstick by which the outcome of his whole life's work is measured.
PAUL C. PACKER

Have success and there will always be fools to say that you have talent.
EDOUARD PAILLERON

These three things—work, will, success—fill human existences. Will opens the door to success, both brilliant and happy. Work passes these doors,

and at the end of the journey success comes in to crown one's efforts.
LOUIS PASTEUR

Life has not taught me to expect nothing, but she has taught me not to expect success to be the inevitable result of my endeavors.
ALAN PATON

Business is founded on vision and confidence; success on industry and cooperation.
JOHN HENRY PATTERSON

One never learns by success. Success is the plateau that one rests upon to take breath and look down from upon the straight and difficult path, but one does not climb upon a plateau.
JOSEPHINE PRESTON PEABODY

The man who lives for himself is a failure. Even if he gains much wealth, position or power he still is a failure. The man who lives for others has achieved true success. A rich man who consecrates his wealth and his position to the good of humanity is a success. A poor man who gives of his service and his sympathy to others has achieved true success even though material prosperity or outward honors never come to him.
NORMAN VINCENT PEALE

Success in business does not depend upon genius. Any young man of ordinary intelligence who is normally sound and not afraid to work should succeed in spite of obstacles and handicaps if he plays the game fairly and keeps everlastingly at it.
JAMES C. PENNEY

Success is dangerous. One begins to copy oneself, and to copy oneself is more dangerous than to copy others. It leads to sterility.
PABLO PICASSO

Nothing is so impudent as Success—unless it be those she favours.
JAMES ROBINSON PLANCHE

Success: A process of becoming who you already are.
FRANK POTTS

Rest satisfied with doing well, and leave others to talk of you as they please.
PYTHAGORAS

On the clarity of your ideas depends the scope of your success in any endeavor.
JAMES ROBERTSON

The art of putting into play mediocre qualities often begets more reputation than is achieved by true merit.
FRANÇOIS DE LA ROCHEFOUCAULD

If you want to succeed you should strike out on new paths rather than travel the worn paths of accepted success.
JOHN D. ROCKEFELLER

The most important single ingredient in the formula of success is knowing how to get along with people.
THEODORE ROOSEVELT

Unless a man has been taught what to do with success after getting it, the achievement of it must inevitably leave him prey to boredom.
BERTRAND RUSSELL

In my mind, talent plus knowledge, plus effort account for success.
GERTRUDE SAMUELS

The best place to succeed is where you are with what you have.
CHARLES M. SCHWAB

His head was turned by too great success.
**SENECA**

The conditions of conquest are always easy. We have but to toil awhile, endure awhile, believe always, and never turn back.
**SENECA**

Success does not consist in never making blunders, but in never making the same one the second time.
**HENRY WHEELER SHAW (JOSH BILLINGS)**

The difference between failure and success is doing a thing nearly right and doing it exactly right.
**EDWARD C. SIMMONS**

The great highroad of human welfare lies along the old highway of steadfast well-doing; and they who are the most persistent, and work in the true spirit, will invariably be the most successful. Success treads on the heels of every right effort.
**SAMUEL SMILES**

It is natural to every man to wish for distinction; and the praise of those who can confer honor by their praise, in spite of all false philosophy, is sweet to every human heart; but as eminence can be but the lot of a few, patience of obscurity is a duty which we owe not more to our own happiness than to the quiet of the world at large.
**SYDNEY SMITH**

Faith in your own powers and confidence in your individual methods are essential to success.
**RODERICK STEVENS**

One only gets to the top rung on the ladder by steadily climbing up one at a time, and suddenly all sorts of powers, all sort of abilities which you thought never belonged to you—suddenly become within your own possibility and you think, "Well, I'll have a go, too."
**MARGARET THATCHER**

The life without men praise and regard as successful is but one kind. Why should we exaggerate any one kind at the expense of the others?
**HENRY DAVID THOREAU**

Men are born to succeed—not to fail.
**HENRY DAVID THOREAU**

Success usually comes to those who are too busy to be looking for it.
**HENRY DAVID THOREAU**

If at first you do succeed, it can give you a false sense of importance.
**FRANK TYGER**

In achieving success, backbone is more important than wishbone.
**FRANK TYGER**

Most barriers to your success are man-made. And most often, you're the man who made them.
**FRANK TYGER**

Success comes to those who know it isn't coming to them and who go out to get it.
**FRANK TYGER**

Success is often just an idea away.
**FRANK TYGER**

Success won't just come to you. It has to be met at least halfway.
**FRANK TYGER**

The ladder of success doesn't care who climbs it.
**FRANK TYGER**

The road to success is usually off the beaten path.
FRANK TYGER

If I wanted to become a tramp, I would seek information and advice from the most successful tramp I could find. If I wanted to become a failure I would seek advice from men who have never succeeded. If I wanted to succeed in all things, I would look around me for those who are succeeding, and do as they have done.
JOSEPH MARSHALL WADE

One big reason why men do not develop greater abilities, greater sales strength, greater resourcefulness is because they use neither their abilities nor their opportunities. We don't need more strength or more ability or greater opportunity. What we need is to use what we have. Men fail and their families suffer deprivations when all the time these men have in their possession the same assets other men are utilizing to accumulate a fortune. . . . Life doesn't cheat. It doesn't pay in counterfeit coin. It doesn't lock up shop and go home when pay-day comes. It pays every man exactly what he has earned. The age-old law that a man gets what he earns hasn't been suspended! When we take that truth home and believe it, we've turned a big corner on the high road that runs straight through to success.
BASIL S. WALSH

I have learned that success is to be measured not so much by the position that one has reached in life as by the obstacles which he has overcome while trying to succeed.
BOOKER T. WASHINGTON

When a man does all he can, though it succeeds not well, blame not him that did it.
GEORGE WASHINGTON

Who never climbs as rarely falls.
JOHN GREENLEAF WHITTIER

The most urgent necessity in human life is to be able to face life victoriously. For many—the number is appalling—are living mentally, physically, morally and spiritually defeated.
FREDERICK A. WICKETT

Under normal periods, any man's success hinges about 5 percent on what others do for him and 95 percent on what he does, with emphasis on the does. The years that lie ahead will be no bed of roses for any business man. No matter how high the tide of prosperity may rise, no business man will share therein who does not gear himself and his business to a new tempo to meet changing conditions and the problems and difficulties that await our solution.
JAMES A. WORSHAM

## *Suffering*

Our real blessings often appear to us in the shape of pains, losses and disappointments; but let us have patience, and we soon shall see them in their proper figures.
JOSEPH ADDISON

Take heart. Suffering, when it climbs the highest, lasts but a little time.
AESCHYLUS

Suffering becomes beautiful when anyone bears great calamities with cheerfulness, not through insensibility but through greatness of mind.
ARISTOTLE

The wise man does not expose himself needlessly to danger, since there are few things for which he cares sufficiently; but he is willing, in great crises to give even his life—knowing that under certain conditions it is not worth while to live.
ARISTOTLE

Present suffering is not enjoyable, but life would be worth little without it. The difference between iron and steel is fire, but steel is worth all it costs.
MALTBIE BABCOCK

Never press a point too hard because a deep wound is hard to heal and usually leaves a scar.
DALE CARNEGIE

In a free country there is much clamor with little suffering; in a despotic state there is little complaint but much suffering.
CARUOT

The important thing is this: to be able at any moment to sacrifice what we are for what we could become.
CHARLES DU BOS

To make sacrifices in big things is easy, but to make sacrifices in little things is what we are seldom capable of.
JOHANN WOLFGANG VON GOETHE

All experience hath shown that mankind are more disposed to suffer, while evils are sufferable, than to right themselves by abolishing the forms to which they are accustomed.
THOMAS JEFFERSON

To suffer and to endure is the lot of humanity.
POPE LEO XIII

I do not believe that sheer suffering teaches. If suffering alone taught, all the world would be wise since everyone suffers. To suffering must be added mourning, understanding, patience, love, openness and the willingness to remain vulnerable.
ANNE MORROW LINDBERGH

It is not true that suffering ennobles the character; happiness does that sometimes, but suffering for the most part makes men petty and vindictive.
SOMERSET MAUGHAM

We must learn to suffer what we cannot evade; our life, like the harmony of the world, is composed of contrary things, and one part is no less necessary than the other.
MICHEL DE MONTAIGNE

Distrust all in whom the impulse to punish is powerful.
FRIEDRICH WILHELM NIETZSCHE

Every step forward is made at the cost of mental and physical pain to someone.
FRIEDRICH WILHELM NIETZSCHE

What really makes one indignant about suffering isn't the thing itself but the senselessness of it.
FRIEDRICH WILHELM NIETZSCHE

It stands to reason that where there's sacrifice, there's someone collecting sacrificial offerings. Where there is service, there is someone being served. The man who speaks to you of sacrifice speaks of slaves and masters. And intends to be master.
AYN RAND

He jests at scars that never felt a wound.
WILLIAM SHAKESPEARE

Count no mortal fortunate till he has departed this life free from pain.
SOPHOCLES

People generally do not appreciate what they do not suffer for. A thing is held to be cheap if it did not cost dearly. Honor is lightly worn if it was easily

attained. Inherited liberty is too often carelessly used until it is repossessed through sacrifices.
**FRED ROBERT TIFFANY, D.D.**

## *Superiority*

It has always been a crime to be above the crowd. That's the real reason why some men in public life are maligned, attacked and slandered, for they are beyond the reach of those who realize in their own heart that the greatness of others shows their own smallness, their own inferiority.
**WILLIAM J. H. BOETCKER**

Joe . . . was ignorant enough to feel superior to everything.
**JOHN CIARDI**

I love being superior to myself better than [to] my equals.
**SAMUEL TAYLOR COLERIDGE**

The superior man is slow in his words and earnest in his conduct.
**CONFUCIUS**

The way of a superior man is threefold: virtuous, he is free from anxieties; wise, he is free from perplexities; bold, he is free from fear.
**CONFUCIUS**

From above we can hear the crowd below growling and grumbling and taking it easy.
**ROBERT DOLLAR**

There is no such thing as human superiority.
**DWIGHT D. EISENHOWER**

Superiority is always detested.
**BALTASAR GRACIÁN**

People who look down on other people don't end up being looked up to.
**ROBERT HALF**

To be loved we must merit but little esteem; all superiority attracts awe and aversion.
**CLAUDE-ADRIEN HELVÉTIUS**

There was one who thought he was above me, and he was above me until he had that thought.
**ELBERT HUBBARD**

The superior man is the providence of the inferior. He is eyes for the blind, strength for the weak, and a shield for the defenseless. He stands erect by bending above the fallen. He rises by lifting others.
**ROBERT G. INGERSOLL**

The superior man is he who develops, in harmonious proportions, his moral, intellectual and physical nature.
**DOUGLAS WILLIAM JERROLD**

The superiority of some men is merely local. They are great because their associates are little.
**JOHNSON**

A man should live with his superiors as he does with his fire: not too near, lest he burn; nor too far off, lest he freeze.
**DIOGENES LAERTIUS**

I caught sight of a haze upon his face—of that mist which arises invariably from the blissful feeling that one is superior to others.
**GEORG CHRISTOPH LICHTENBERG**

The outstanding characteristic of the relationship between the subordinate and his superiors is his dependence upon them for the satisfaction of his needs.
**DOUGLAS MCGREGOR**

## Sympathy

We are living at a time when creeds and ideologies vary and clash. But the gospel of human sympathy is universal and eternal.
SAMUEL HOPKINS ADAMS

All calm inquiry conducted among those who have their main principles of judgment in common, leads, if not to an approximation of views, yet, at least, to an increase of sympathy.
THOMAS ARNOLD

Needs there groan a world in anguish just to teach us sympathy?
ROBERT BROWNING

Next to love sympathy is the divinest passion of the human heart.
EDMUND BURKE

I believe that order is better than chaos, creation better than destruction. I prefer gentleness to violence, forgiveness to vendetta: On the whole I think that knowledge is preferable to ignorance, and I am sure that human sympathy is more valuable than ideology.
KENNETH CLARK

The busy world sometimes forgets that we need sympathy in our happiness as well as in our sorrow.
C. HANFORD HENDERSON

Sympathy is never wasted except when you give it to yourself.
JOHN W. RAPER

Sympathy is a thing to be encouraged apart from humane considerations, because it supplies us with the materials for wisdom.
ROBERT LOUIS STEVENSON

One of the most poignant of all human experiences is empathy—the ability to feel what others feel when suffering from pain or loss.
LOUIS JOLYON WEST

# T

## Talent

The English instinctively admire any man who has no talent and is modest about it.
JAMES AGEE

To do easily what is difficult for others is the mark of talent.
HENRI FRÉDÉRIC AMIEL

Genius is the gold in the mine; talent is the miner that works and brings it out.
MARGUERITE BLESSINGTON

Everyone has talent at 25. The difficulty is to have it at 50.
EDGAR DEGAS

It always seemed to me a sort of clever stupidity only to have one sort of talent—like a carrier pigeon.
GEORGE ELIOT

Every natural power exhilarates; a true talent delights the possessor first.
RALPH WALDO EMERSON

Talent for talent's sake is a bauble and a show. Talent working with joy in the cause of universal truth lifts the possessor to new power as a benefactor.
RALPH WALDO EMERSON

No one respects a talent that is concealed.
DESIDERIUS ERASMUS

If a man can make typewriters better than anyone else, let us, in the name of common sense, keep him on the job of making typewriters.
WILLIAM FEATHER

Of all the young men in America only a few hundred can get into major league baseball, and of these only a handful in a decade can get into the Hall of Fame. So it goes in all human activity. Talent is screened, screened, screened. Some become multimillionaires and chairmen of the board, and some of us must be content to play baseball at company picnics or manage a credit union without pay.
WILLIAM FEATHER

Hide not your talents, they for use were made.
What's a sundial in the shade?
BENJAMIN FRANKLIN

If the power to do hard work is not talent, it is the best possible substitute for it.
JAMES A. GARFIELD

The man who cannot enjoy his own natural gifts in silence, and find his reward in the exercise of them, will generally find himself badly off.
JOHANN WOLFGANG VON GOETHE

Don't show off every day, or you'll stop surprising people. There must always be some novelty left over. The person who displays a little more of it each day keeps up expectations, and no one ever discovers the limits of his talent.
BALTASAR GRACIÁN

Talent does you no good unless it's recognized by someone else.
**ROBERT HALF**

Every man must at last accept himself for his portion, and learn to do his work with the tools and talents with which he has been endowed. That some are more richly endowed than others should cause no concern, for in the final analysis it may appear that the mighty oak is of less importance than the tiny violet which blooms in humble obscurity at its feet.
**CHARLES A. HAWLEY**

There must always be some advantage on one side or the other, and it is better that advantage should be had by talents than by chance.
**SAMUEL JOHNSON**

Talent is that which is in a man's power; genius is that in whose power a man is.
**JAMES RUSSELL LOWELL**

Each man has to seek out his own special aptitude for a higher life in the midst of the humble and inevitable reality of daily existence. Than this, there can be no nobler aim in life.
**MAURICE MAETERLINCK**

One well-cultivated talent, deepened and enlarged, is worth 100 shallow faculties. The first law of success in this day, when so many things are clamoring for attention, is concentration—to bend all the energies to one point, and to go directly to that point, looking neither to the right nor to the left.
**WILLIAM MATTHEWS**

If I have talent and intelligence, I shall get on; if not, it isn't worth pulling me out of the mud.
**MUSORGSKI**

Hidden talent counts for nothing.
**NERO**

As tools become rusty, so does the mind; a garden uncared for soon becomes smothered in weeds; a talent neglected withers and dies.
**ETHEL R. PAGE**

Nature has concealed at the bottom of our minds talents and abilities of which we are not aware.
**FRANÇOIS DE LA ROCHEFOUCAULD**

There are some bad qualities which make great talents.
**FRANÇOIS DE LA ROCHEFOUCAULD**

Shun no toil to make yourself remarkable by some one talent. Yet do not devote yourself to one branch exclusively. Strive to get clear notions about all. Give up no science entirely, for all science is one.
**SENECA**

Life's greatest gift is natural talent.
**P. K. THOMAJAN**

One of the greatest talents of all is the talent to recognize and to develop talent in others.
**FRANK TYGER**

If a man has a talent and cannot use it, he has failed. If he has a talent and uses only half of it, he has partly failed. If he has talent and learns somehow to use the whole of it, he has gloriously succeeded, and won a satisfaction and a triumph few men will ever know.
**THOMAS WOLFE**

The real tragedy of life is not in being limited to one talent, but in the failure to use the one talent.
**EDGAR W. WORK**

## Talk

Conversation: Something that starts the moment you put your foot through the television set.
ANONYMOUS

I think the first prerequisite to civilization is an ability to make polite conversation.
W. H. AUDEN

Anybody at all has the right to talk about himself—provided he knows how to be entertaining.
CHARLES BAUDELAIRE

Civilized people can talk about anything. For them no subject is taboo. . . . In civilized societies there will be no intellectual bogeys at sight of which great grownup babies are expected to hide their eyes.
CLIVE BELL

Conversation: A fair for the display of the minor mental commodities, each exhibitor being too intent upon the arrangement of his own wares to observe those of his neighbor.
AMBROSE BIERCE

Two great talkers will not travel far together.
GEORGE BORROW

The great gift of conversation lies less in displaying it ourselves than in drawing it out of others. He who leaves your company pleased with himself and his own cleverness is perfectly well pleased with you.
JEAN DE LA BRUYÈRE

Talkers will refrain from evil speaking when listeners refrain from evil hearing.
EDWARD BULWER-LYTTON

No mortal has a right to wag his tongue, much less to wag his pen, without saying something.
THOMAS CARLYLE

Talk that does not end in any kind of action is better suppressed altogether.
THOMAS CARLYLE

Eloquence is vehement simplicity.
RICHARD CECIL

A man does not know what he is saying until he knows what he is not saying.
G. K. CHESTERTON

Who thinks an inch, but talks a yard, needs a kick in the foot.
CHINESE PROVERB

He is an eloquent man who can treat humble subjects with delicacy, lofty things impressively, and moderate things temperately.
CICERO

Never close your lips to those to whom you have opened your heart.
CHARLES DICKENS

The art of conversation is to be prompt without being stubborn; to refute without argument, and to clothe great matters in a motley garb.
BENJAMIN DISRAELI

When the eyes say one thing and the tongue another, a practiced man relies on the language of the first.
RALPH WALDO EMERSON

Beware of the man who will not engage in idle conversation; he is planning to steal your walking stick or water your stock.
WILLIAM A. EMERSON, JR.

Those who talk loudly are rarely listened to.
MALCOLM FORBES

A man is seldom better than his conversation.
GERMAN PROVERB

Never speak of yourself to others; make them talk about themselves instead. Therein lies the whole art of pleasing. Everyone knows it and everyone forgets it.
EDMOND & JULES DE GONCOURT

Streams of oratory do not always come from mountains of thought.
CHARLES GRANT

Conversation: The slowest form of human communication.
DON HEROLD

The longer I live, the more I have come to value the gift of eloquence. Every American youth, if he desires for any purpose to get influence over his countrymen in an honorable way, will seek to become a good public speaker.
GEORGE F. HOAR

Talking is like playing on the harp; there is as much in laying the hands on the strings to stop their vibrations as in twanging them to bring our their music.
OLIVER WENDELL HOLMES

Writing or printing is like shooting with a rifle; you may hit your reader's mind or miss it. But talking is like playing at a mark with the pipe of an engine; if it is within reach, and you have time enough, you can't help hitting it.
OLIVER WENDELL HOLMES

Never explain—your friends don't need it, and your enemies won't believe you anyhow.
ELBERT HUBBARD

There are not enough bon mots in existence to provide any industrious conversationalist with a new stock for every occasion.
ALDOUS HUXLEY

The most valuable of talents is that of never using two words when one will do.
THOMAS JEFFERSON

The happiest conversation is that of which nothing is distinctly remembered, but a general effect of pleasing impression.
SAMUEL JOHNSON

A gossip is one who talks to you about others; a bore is one who talks to you about himself; and a brilliant conversationalist is one who talks to you about yourself.
LISA KIRK

Discreetly keep most of your radical opinions to yourself. When with people be a listener a large part of the time. Be considerate in every word and act, and resist the tendency to say clever things. The best evidence of your culture is the tone and temper of your conversation.
GRENVILLE KLEISER

A perfect conversation would run much less to brilliant sentences than to unfinished ones.
LOUIS KRONENBERGER

I attribute the little I know to my not having been ashamed to ask for information, and to my rule of conversing with all descriptions of men on those topics that form their own peculiar professions and pursuits.
**John Locke**

Men are never so likely to settle a question rightly as when they discuss it freely.
**Thomas B. Macaulay**

Conversation means being able to disagree and still continue the conversation.
**Dwight MacDonald**

The greatest troublemaker is one who talks too much.
**Dale W. McMillen**

No pleasure is fully delightful without communications, and no delight absolute except imparted.
**Michel de Montaigne**

Those who have few affairs to attend to are great talkers. The less men think, the more they talk.
**Baron de Montesquieu**

We Athenians . . . instead of looking on discussion as a stumbling block in the way of action, think of it as an indispensable preliminary to any wise action at all.
**Pericles**

And 'tis remarkable that they who talk most are those who have the least to say.
**Matthew Prior**

It is not what we learn in conversation that enriches us. It is the elation that comes of swift contact with tingling currents of thought.
**Agnes Repplier**

The reason why so few people are agreeable in conversation is that each is thinking more about what he intends to say than about what others are saying, and we never listen when we are eager to speak.
**François de La Rochefoucauld**

What a people talk about means something. What they don't talk about means something.
**William Saroyan**

I distrust the incommunicable; it is the source of all violence.
**Jean-Paul Sartre**

The pith of conversation does not consist in exhibiting your own superior knowledge on matters of small importance, but enlarging, improving and correcting information you possess, by the authority of others.
**Sir Walter Scott**

Conversation should be pleasant without scurrility, witty without affectation, free without indecency, learned without conceitedness, novel without falsehood.
**William Shakespeare**

Real communication is impossible without listening.
**Ralph C. Smedley**

It is the dread of something happening, something unknown and dreadful, that makes us do anything to keep the flicker of talk from dying out.
**Logan Pearsall Smith**

Talk is by far the most accessible of pleasures. It costs nothing in money, it is all profit, it completes our education, founds and fosters our friendships, and can be enjoyed at any age and in almost any state of health.
**Robert Louis Stevenson**

Remember, every time you open your mouth to talk, your mind walks out and parades up and down the words.
EDWIN H. STUART

Conversation is the image of the mind. As the man is, so is his talk.
PUBLILIUS SYRUS

Brisk talkers are usually slow thinkers. There is, indeed, no wild beast more to be dreaded than a communicative man having nothing to communicate. If you are civil to the voluble they will abuse your patience; if brusque, your character.
JONATHAN SWIFT

I was gratified to be able to answer promptly, and I did. I said I didn't know.
MARK TWAIN

People have to talk about something just to keep their voice boxes in working order, so they'll have good voice boxes in case there's ever anything really meaningful to say.
KURT VONNEGUT

Let your discourse with men of business always be short and comprehensive.
GEORGE WASHINGTON

My skepticism long ago led me to the belief that writers write for themselves and not for their readers, and that art has nothing to do with communication between person and person, but only between different parts of a person's mind.
REBECCA WEST

Conversation should touch everything but should concentrate itself on nothing.
OSCAR WILDE

There is only one thing in the world worse than being talked about and that is not being talked about.
OSCAR WILDE

It is an excellent rule to be observed in all discussions, that men should give soft words and hard arguments; that they should not so much strive to silence or vex, as to convince their opponents.
J. HAROLD WILKENS

The only birds that talk are parrots, and they don't fly very high.
WILBUR WRIGHT

Nothing makes a man hate a woman more than her constant conversation.
WILLIAM WYCHERLEY

## *Taxes*

Count the day when, turning on its axis, this earth imposes no additional taxes.
FRANKLIN P. ADAMS

An income tax form is like a laundry list—either way you lose your shirt.
FRED ALLEN

Our Founding Fathers objected to taxation without representation. They should see it today with representation.
ANONYMOUS

An economy breathes through its tax loopholes.
BARRY BRACEWELL-MILNES

Why does a small tax increase cost you two hundred dollars and a substantial tax cut save you thirty cents?
PEG BRACKEN

Like mothers, taxes are often misunderstood but seldom forgotten.
LORD BRAMWELL

The tax-exempt privilege is a feature always reflected in the market price of [municipal] bonds. The investor pays for it.
LOUIS D. BRANDEIS

There is just one thing I can promise you about the outer-space program: Your tax dollar will go further.
WERNHER VON BRAUN

Taxing is an easy business. Any projector can contrive new impositions; any bungler can add to the old; but is it altogether wise to have no other bounds to your impositions than the patience of those who are to bear them?
EDMUND BURKE

A citizen can hardly distinguish between a tax and a fine, except that a fine is generally much lighter.
G. K. CHESTERTON

The imposition of taxes has its limits. There is a maximum which cannot be transcended. Suppose the citizen to be taxed by the general government to the utmost extent of his ability, or a thing as much as it can possibly bear, and the state imposes a tax at the same time, which authority is to take it?
HENRY CLAY

The art of taxation consists in so plucking the goose as to obtain the largest possible amount of feathers with the smallest possible amount of hissing.
JEAN BAPTISTE COLBERT

The point to remember is what the government gives it must first take away.
JOHN S. COLEMAN

I do not believe that the government should ask social legislation in the guise of taxation. If we are to adopt socialism, it should be presented to the people of this country as socialism and not under the guise of a law to collect revenue.
CALVIN COOLIDGE

The only thing that hurts more than paying an income tax is not having to pay an income tax.
THOMAS R. DEWAR

The hardest thing in the world to understand is the income tax.
ALBERT EINSTEIN

April is the month when the green returns to the lawn, the trees and the Internal Revenue Service.
EVAN ESAR

It is easier to start taxes than to stop them. A tax an inch long can easily become a yard long. That has been the history of the income tax. Would not the sales tax be likely to have a similar history [in the U.S.]? . . . Canadian newspapers report that an increase in the sales tax threatens to drive the Mackenzie King administration out of office. Canada began with a sales tax of 2%. . . . Starting this month the tax is 6%. The burden, in other words, has already been increased 200% . . . What the U.S. needs is not new taxes, is not more taxes, but fewer and lower taxes.
B. C. FORBES

Friends and neighbors complain that taxes are indeed very heavy, and if those laid on by the government were the only ones we had to pay, we might the more easily discharge them; but we have many others, and much more grievous to some of us. We are taxed twice as much by our idleness, three times as much by our pride, and four times as much by our folly.
BENJAMIN FRANKLIN

April showers are taxpayer's tears.
**ARNOLD GLASOW**

Deficit: What you have left after paying your taxes.
**ARNOLD GLASOW**

When making out your income tax, it's better to give than to deceive.
**ARNOLD GLASOW**

I'm proud to be paying taxes to the U.S. The only thing is—I could be just as proud for half the money.
**ARTHUR GODFREY**

Man is not like other animals in the ways that are really significant: Animals have instincts, we have taxes.
**ERVING GOFFMAN**

We have long had death and taxes as the two standards of inevitability. But there are those who believe that death is the preferable of the two.
**ERWIN N. GRISWOLD**

The United States is the only country where it takes more brains to figure your tax than to earn the money to pay it.
**EDWARD J. GURNEY**

Anyone may so arrange his affairs that his taxes shall be low as possible; he is not bound to choose that pattern which will best pay the treasury; there is not even a patriotic duty to increase one's taxes.
**LEARNED HAND**

Taxes are not levied for the benefit of the taxed.
**ROBERT A. HEINLEIN**

An old-fashioned handshake is a good way to do business—unless the IRS demands a copy.
**CULLEN HIGHTOWER**

I like to pay taxes. With them I buy civilization.
**OLIVER WENDELL HOLMES**

That the government takes up to 50% of the profits from professional earnings or business transactions, while the individual takes all the risks, is intensely discouraging to initiative.
**HERBERT HOOVER**

The suppression of unnecessary offices, of useless establishments and expenses, enabled us to discontinue our internal taxes. These, covering our land with officers, and opening our doors to their intrusions, had already begun that process of domiciliary vexation which, once entered, is scarcely to be restrained from reaching, successively, every article of property and produce.
**THOMAS JEFFERSON**

Taxes grow without rain.
**JEWISH PROVERB**

In 1790, the nation which had fought a revolution against taxation without representation discovered that some of its citizens weren't much happier about taxation with representation.
**LYNDON JOHNSON**

The avoidance of taxes is the only intellectual pursuit that carries any reward.
**JOHN MAYNARD KEYNES**

And it came to pass in those days, that there went out a decree from Caesar Augustus, that all the world should be taxed.
**LUKE 2:1**

Man is a thinking animal, a talking animal, a toolmaking animal, a building animal, a political animal, a fantasizing animal. But in the twilight of a civilization he is chiefly a taxpaying animal.
**HUGH MACLENNAN**

If Einstein and the agents of the Internal Revenue Service cannot understand the Tax Code, then the ordinary taxpayers of the U.S. are entitled to a little help.
WARREN MAGNUSON

Unquestionably, there is progress. The average American now pays out almost as much in taxes alone as he formerly got in wages.
H. L. MENCKEN

Each citizen contributes to the revenues of the State a portion of his property in order that his tenure of the rest may be secure.
BARON DE MONTESQUIEU

Avoid falsehoods like the plague except in matters of taxation, which do not count, since here you are not lying to take someone else's goods, but to prevent your own from being unjustly seized.
GIOVANNI MORELLI

All money nowadays seems to be produced with a natural homing instinct for the Treasury.
PRINCE PHILIP

Where there is an income tax, the just man will pay more and the unjust less on the same income.
PLATO

Taxation and representation are inseparably united. God hath joined them; no British Parliament can put them asunder.
CHARLES PRATT (LORD CAMDEN)

Next to being shot at and missed, nothing is really quite as satisfying as an income tax refund.
F. J. RAYMOND

The taxpayer: Someone who works for the government but doesn't have to take a civil service examination.
RONALD REAGAN

The power to tax is the power to destroy only in the sense that those who have power can misuse it.
JUSTICE STANLEY F. REED

The income tax has made more liars out of the American people than golf has. Even when you make a tax form out on the level, you don't know when it's through if you are a crook or a martyr.
WILL ROGERS

When everybody has got money they cut taxes, and when they're broke they raise taxes. That's statesmanship of the highest order.
WILL ROGERS

Noah must have taken into the Ark two taxes, one male and one female. And did they multiply bountifully! Next to guinea pigs, taxes must have been the most prolific animals.
WILL ROGERS

The income tax has made liars out of more Americans than golf.
WILL ROGERS

Taxes are paid in the sweat of every man who labors. If those taxes are excessive, they are reflected in idle factories, tax-sold farms and in hordes of hungry people, tramping the streets and seeking jobs in vain.
FRANKLIN D. ROOSEVELT

Taxes are the death of taxidermy. The folks who used to be the backbones of our business—Vanderbilts, Astors, Goulds, Belmonts—still shoot a tiger now and then or catch a marlin or bag a wild turkey, but,

with the old estates gone, where would they find a place to hang them?
**ELMER ROWLAND**

The Tax Collector's letters are invariably mimeographed, and all they say is that you still haven't paid him.
**WILLIAM SAROYAN**

A government which robs Peter to pay Paul can always count on Paul's support.
**GEORGE BERNARD SHAW**

Nothing is more familiar in taxation than the imposition of a tax upon a class or upon individuals who enjoy no direct benefit from its expenditure, and who are not responsible for the condition to be remedied.
**JUSTICE HARLAN F. STONE**

To produce an income tax return that has any depth to it, any feeling, one must have Lived—and Suffered.
**FRANK SULLIVAN**

What is the difference between a taxidermist and a tax collector? The taxidermist takes only your skin.
**MARK TWAIN**

The thing generally raised on city land is taxes.
**CHARLES DUDLEY WARNER**

Every country in the world has its hands up to the elbows in the American taxpayer's pocket.
**KENNETH WHERRY**

## *Temper*

We must interpret a bad temper as the sign of an inferiority complex.
**ALFRED ADLER**

When a great merchant of Liverpool was asked by what means he had contrived to realize the large fortune he possessed, his reply was, "By one article alone, in which thou mayest deal too, if thou pleasant—it is civility."
**RICHARD BENTLEY**

Bad temper is its own scourge. Few things are more bitter than to feel bitter. A man's venom poisons himself more than his victim.
**CHARLES BUXTON**

Men who have had a great deal of experience learn not to lose their temper.
**CHARLES VICTOR CHERBULIEZ**

A man who cannot command his temper should not think of being a man of business.
**LORD CHESTERFIELD**

The difficult part of good temper consists in forbearance, and accommodation to the ill-humor of others.
**WILLIAM EMPSON**

Civility costs nothing.
**ENGLISH PROVERB**

Avoid letting temper block progress—keep cool.
**WILLIAM FEATHER**

There is perhaps no phenomenon which contains so much destructive feeling as moral indignation, which permits envy or hate to be acted out under the guise of virtue.
**ERICH FROMM**

Good temper is an estate for life.
**WILLIAM HAZLITT**

He who restrains his temper will have all his sins forgiven.
**HEBREW PROVERB**

More than half the difficulties of the world would be allayed or removed by the exhibition of good temper.
SIR ARTHUR HELPS

Civility is a charm that attracts the love of all men.
GEORGE HORNE

A tart temper never mellows with age, and a sharp tongue is the only edged tool that grows keener with constant use.
WASHINGTON IRVING

Good temper, like a sunny day, sheds a ray of brightness over everything; it is the sweetener of toil and the soother of disquietude!
WASHINGTON IRVING

He was so generally civil that nobody thanked him for it.
SAMUEL JOHNSON

The toxin of fatigue has been demonstrated; but the poisons generated by evil temper and emotional excess over non-essentials have not yet been determined, although without a doubt they exist. Explosions of temper, emotional cyclones, and needless fear and panic over disease or misfortune that seldom materialize, are simply bad habits. By proper ventilation and illumination of the mind it is possible to cultivate tolerance, poise and real courage without being a bromide-taker.
ELIE METCHNIKOFF

Civility costs nothing and buys everything.
MARY WORTLEY MONTAGU

The growth of wisdom may be gauged accurately by the decline of ill temper.
FRIEDRICH WILHELM NIETZSCHE

Don't hit at all if it is honorably possible to avoid hitting; but never hit soft.
THEODORE ROOSEVELT

Curses are like processions; they return to the place from which they came.
RUFFINI

Temper, if ungoverned, governs the whole man.
LORD SHAFTESBURY

A vigorous temper is not altogether an evil. Men who are easy as an old shoe are generally of little worth.
CHARLES H. SPURGEON

A show of temper is never a hit.
FRANK TYGER

When it comes down to pure ornamental cursing, the native American is gifted above the sons of men.
MARK TWAIN

Man is a rational animal who always loses his temper when he is called upon to act in accordance with the dictates of reason.
OSCAR WILDE

He owned and operated a ferocious temper.
THOMAS R. YBARRA

## *Temptation*

It is good to be without vices, but it is not good to be without temptations.
WALTER BAGEHOT

There is no memory with less satisfaction in it than the memory of some temptation we resisted.
JAMES BRANCH CABELL

Better shun the bait than struggle in the snare.
JOHN DRYDEN

Every moment of resistance to temptation is a victory.
FREDERICK WILLIAM FABER

Whoever yields to temptation debases himself with a debasement from which he can never rise. A man can be wronged and live; but the unrestricted, unchecked impulse to do wrong is the first and second death.
HORACE MANN

The devil never tempted a man whom he found judiciously employed.
CHARLES H. SPURGEON

Temptation rarely comes in working hours. It is in their leisure time that men are made or marred.
W. M. TAYLOR

I can resist anything except temptation.
OSCAR WILDE

The only way to get rid of a temptation is to yield to it.
OSCAR WILDE

## *Thinking*

If we would keep filling our minds with the picture of happy things ahead, many of the worries and anxieties, and perhaps ill health, would naturally melt away. . . . If we lived in the atmosphere of expectancy, so many of our petty problems would be no problems at all! Always expect the best. Then if you have to hurdle a few tough problems, you will have generated the strength and courage to do so. Successful businesses are forever planning and dreaming ahead. And so should we, as individuals. . . . Expect to discover the best in people and they will do the same for you. We must be constructive in our thoughts and our attitude toward life.
GEORGE MATTHEW ADAMS

What you think means more than anything else in your life. More than what you earn, more than where you live, more than your social position, and more than what anyone else may think about you.
GEORGE MATTHEW ADAMS

The ultimate value of life depends upon awareness and the power of contemplation rather than upon mere survival.
ARISTOTLE

The firefly only shines when on the wing; so it is with the mind; when we rest we darken.
PHILIP JAMES BAILEY

Some of the greatest thinking has been done by those who cared little for riches—Pasteur, Edison, Jane Addams—and who shall say that theirs was not the richer life? Today, the world knows the poetry of Shakespeare, the music of Wagner, the art of Rembrandt; but who knows even the names of the money barons of their day—or cares to know? If you want your name to live after you, you'll not give all your thought to money. But, whether you want to make money, or write a book, or build a bridge, or run a streetcar—or do anything else successfully—you'll do well to remember that in all the world there is no word more important than—"*Think!*"
EDWIN BAIRD

I think that I think; therefore, I think I am.
AMBROSE BIERCE

There is a sweet pleasure in contemplation; and when a man hath run through a set of vanities to

the declension of his age, he knows not what to do with himself if he cannot think.
**THOMAS BLOUNT**

All that we know we have absorbed from our own experiences, or rearranged in our minds from observing other people, or reasoned out either consciously or unconsciously from thought-data given by inheritance or gathered from our own previous trends of thinking in moments past. The way we are going to think tomorrow depends largely on what we are thinking today.
**DAVID LESLIE BROWN**

To most people nothing is more troublesome than the effort of thinking.
**JAMES BRYCE**

Never say, I don't think. The only thing that makes you a higher order of animal is the ability to think.
**HENRY H. BUCKLEY**

To read without reflecting is like eating without digesting.
**EDMUND BURKE**

All the problems of the world could be settled easily if men were only willing to think.
**NICHOLAS MURRAY BUTLER**

We get into the habit of living before acquiring the habit of thinking.
**ALBERT CAMUS**

Thinking, for many, is life's most painful activity. For the fortunate others, there's not much in life that approaches it.
**CARTH CATE**

Muddy water let stand will clear.
**CHINESE PROVERB**

As a man without forethought scarcely deserves the name of man, so forethought without reflection is but a metaphorical phrase for the instinct of a beast.
**SAMUEL TAYLOR COLERIDGE**

If you are not a thinking man, to what purpose are you a man at all?
**SAMUEL TAYLOR COLERIDGE**

Men of strong minds and who think for themselves, should not be discouraged on finding occasionally that some of their best ideas have been anticipated by former writers; they will neither anathematize others nor despair themselves. They will rather go on discovering things before discovered, until they are rewarded with a land hitherto unknown, an empire indisputably their own, both by right of conquest and of discovery.
**CHARLES CALEB COLTON**

Study without reflection is a waste of time; reflection without study is dangerous.
**CONFUCIUS**

What should I disparage my parts by thinking what to say? None but dull rogues think.
**WILLIAM CONGREVE**

The rich are too indolent, the poor too weak, to bear the insupportable fatigue of thinking.
**WILLIAM COWPER**

Creative thinking is today's most prized, profit-producing possession for any individual, corporation or country. It has the capacity to change you, your business and the world.
**ROBERT P. CRAWFORD**

To think is to differ.
**CLARENCE DARROW**

In order to improve the mind, we ought less to learn, than to contemplate.
**RENÉ DESCARTES**

The intellectual function of trouble is to lead men to think. . . . Depression is a small price to pay if it induces us to think about the cause of the disorder, confusion and insecurity which are the outstanding traits of our social life.
**JOHN DEWEY**

Some people study all their life, and at their death they have learned everything except to think.
**FRANÇOIS DOMERGUE**

The life each of us lives is the life within the limits of our own thinking. To have life more abundant, we must think in the limitless terms of abundance.
**THOMAS DREIER**

A wise man once observed that men will love you if you make them think they think, but will hate you if you make them think.
**HORACE C. DUDLEY**

The trouble with most people is that they think with their hopes or fears or wishes rather than with their minds.
**WILL DURANT**

You can't stop people from thinking—but you can start them.
**FRANK A. DUSCH**

Thinking is hard work.
**THOMAS EDISON**

The efficient man is the man who thinks for himself, and is capable of thinking hard and long.
**CHARLES W. ELIOT**

Character is higher than intellect. Thinking is the function. Living is the functionary.
**RALPH WALDO EMERSON**

Do not craze yourself with thinking, but go about your business anywhere. Life is not intellectual and critical, but sturdy.
**RALPH WALDO EMERSON**

The greatest difficulty is that men do not think enough of themselves, do not consider what it is that they are sacrificing when they follow in a herd, or when they cater for their establishment. . . . A man should learn to detect and foster that gleam of light which flashes across his mind from within far more than the luster of the whole firmament without. Yet he dismisses without notice his peculiar thought because it is peculiar. The time will come when he will postpone all acquired knowledge to this spontaneous wisdom, and will watch for this illumination more than those who watch for the morning.
**RALPH WALDO EMERSON**

Rule-of-thumb methods no longer suffice for either nation or individual. New formulas must be the product of thought, of hard, serious, sustained, clear-headed thinking. From office boy to statesman, the prizes are for those who most effectively exert their brains, who take deep, earnest, studious counsel of their minds, who stamp themselves as thinkers.
**B. C. FORBES**

It's more fun to arrive at a conclusion than to justify it.
**MALCOLM FORBES**

Pleasure is more in contemplation than in realization.
**MALCOLM FORBES**

A man who cannot think is not an educated man, however many college degrees he may have acquired.
**HENRY FORD**

Thinking is the hardest work there is—which is probably the reason why so few engage in it.
HENRY FORD

Indiscriminate use of the radio denies a man the opportunities for reflection and for satisfying those needs of withdrawal of which silent prayer is only one manifestation.
FELIX FRANKFURTER

The brain is a wonderful organ. It starts working the moment you get up and does not stop until you get into the office.
ROBERT FROST

Let no man imagine that he has no influence. Whoever he may be, and wherever he may be placed, the man who thinks becomes a light and a power.
HENRY GEORGE

Speaking or writing without thinking is like shooting without aiming.
ARNOLD GLASOW

People are afraid to think, or they don't know how. They fail to realize that, while emotions can't be suppressed, the mind can be strengthened. All over the world people are seeking peace of mind, but there can be no peace of mind without strength of mind.
ERIC B. GUTKIND

The real danger is not that machines will begin to think like men, but that men will begin to think like machines.
SYDNEY J. HARRIS

Deliberate with caution, but act with decision; and yield with graciousness, or oppose with firmness.
CHARLES HOLE

Most people think dramatically, not quantitatively.
OLIVER WENDELL HOLMES

A moment of thinking is an hour in words.
THOMAS HOOD

If America is to be run by the people, it is the people who must think. And we do not need to put on sackcloth and ashes to think. Nor should our minds work like a sundial which records only sunshine. Our thinking must square against some lessons of history, some principles of government and morals, if we would preserve the rights and dignity of men to which this nation is dedicated.
HERBERT HOOVER

Thinkers help other people to think, for they formulate what others are thinking. No person writes or thinks alone; thought is in the air but its expression is necessary to create a tangible spirit of the times.
ELBERT HUBBARD

You can lead a boy to college, but you cannot make him think.
ELBERT HUBBARD

It isn't what people think that is important, but the reason they think what they think.
EUGENE IONESCO

So long as you live and in whatever circumstances the kaleidoscope of life may place you, think for yourself and act in accordance with the conclusions of that thinking; avoid so far as possible drifting with the current of the mob or being too easily influenced by the outward manifestation of things. Take your own look beneath the surface and don't trust others to look for you. If you will follow this rule consistently, I am sure you will keep out of much trouble, will make the most out of your life

and, what is more, will contribute most of value to the community life.
FRANK B. JEWETT

Think of the ills from which you are exempt.
JOSEPH JOUBERT

Thinking is one thing no one has ever been able to tax.
CHARLES F. KETTERING

The brain has muscles for thinking as the legs have muscles for walking.
J. O. DE LA METTRIE

Today the world is the victim of propaganda because people are not intellectually competent. More than anything the United States needs effective citizens competent to do their own thinking.
WILLIAM MATHER LEWIS

History is full of examples of lonely thinkers who were belittled by the established figures of the time and who, it now turns out, were deservedly neglected.
LEON LIPSON

It is curious how tyrannical the habit of reading is, and what shifts we make to escape thinking. There is no bore we dread being left alone with so much as our own minds.
JAMES RUSSELL LOWELL

We think too small. Like the frog at the bottom of the well. He thinks the sky is only as big as the top of the well. If he surfaced, he would have an entirely different view.
MAO TSE-TUNG

A great thinker is seldom a disputant. He answers other men's arguments by stating the truth as he sees it.
DANIEL MARCH

Life would be poor without creative activity in great or little things. But a life would be also poor without the power to look quietly around, without the restful glance at other lives.
HANS MARGOLIUS

If you make people think they're thinking, they'll love you. If you really make them think, they'll hate you.
DONALD MARQUIS

It is curious shifts we make to escape thinking.
HERMAN MELVILLE

In this age the man who dares to think for himself and to act independently does a service to his race.
JOHN STUART MILL

You probably wouldn't worry about what people think of you if you could know how seldom they do.
OLIN MILLER

Analyzing what you haven't got as well as what you have is a necessary ingredient of a career.
GRACE MOORE

Nothing ages people like not thinking.
CHRISTOPHER MORLEY

Obvious thinking commonly leads to wrong judgments and wrong conclusions.
HUMPHREY B. NEIL

Many a man fails to become a thinker for the sole reason that his memory is too good.
FRIEDRICH WILHELM NIETZSCHE

Man is a reed, the most feeble thing in nature, but he is a thinking reed.
BLAISE PASCAL

Thinking is the talking of the soul with itself.
PLATO

My clearest recollection of a long-ago interview with Thomas Edison is of a single sentence that was painted or hung on a wall in his room. In effect, the sentence was: "It is remarkable to what lengths people will go to avoid thought." That is tragically true. Some of us think, more of us think we think, and most of us don't even think of thinking. The result is a somewhat cockeyed world.
CHANNING POLLOCK

It is the glory of God to conceal a thing; but the honour of kings is to search out a matter.
PROVERBS 25:2

There is no expedient to which a man will not resort to avoid the real labor of thinking.
SIR JOSHUA REYNOLDS

I believe that if you think about disaster, you will get it. Brood about death and you hasten your demise. Think positively and masterfully, with confidence and faith, and life becomes more secure, more fraught with action, richer in achievement and experience.
CAPT. EDWARD V. RICKENBACKER

I can give you a six-word formula for success: Think things through—then follow through.
CAPT. EDWARD V. RICKENBACKER

For I say, through the grace given unto me, to every man that is among you, not to think of himself more highly than he ought to think; but to think soberly, according as God hath dealt to every man the measure of faith.
ROMANS 12:3

Think as you work, for in the final analysis your worth to your company comes not only in solving problems but in anticipating them.
H. H. ROSS

Thinking is like loving and dying. Each of us must do it for himself.
JOSIAH ROYCE

The challenge to think systematically about large, ambiguous questions is inherently daunting, and is one that many businessmen—activists by nature—may be reluctant to take up. But if businessmen are to manage events, rather than be managed by them, there is no alternative.
WILLIAM SIMON RUKEYSER

Most people would die sooner than think; in fact, they do so.
BERTRAND RUSSELL

He who considers too much will perform little.
JOHANN FRIEDRICH VON SCHILLER

We may divide thinkers into those who think for themselves and those who think through others.
ARTHUR SCHOPENHAUER

It is the hardest thing in the world to be a good thinker without being a good self-examiner.
LORD SHAFTESBURY

There is nothing either good or bad but thinking makes it so.
WILLIAM SHAKESPEARE

Those who devise better methods of utilizing manpower, tools, machinery, materials and facilities are making real contributions toward our national security. Today, these ideas are a form of insurance for our national security; tomorrow, this same progressive thinking is insurance for our individual security—it is, in effect, job insurance.
**R. SHANNON**

Few people think more than two or three times a year. I have made an international reputation for myself by thinking once or twice a week.
**GEORGE BERNARD SHAW**

I never could find any man who could think for two minutes together.
**SYDNEY SMITH**

The only way in which one human being can properly attempt to influence another is by encouraging him to think for himself, instead of endeavoring to instill ready-made opinions into his head.
**LESLIE STEPHEN**

There are very few original thinkers in the world, or ever have been; the greatest part of those who are called philosophers, have adopted the opinions of some who went before them, and so having chosen their respective guides, they maintain with zeal what they have thus imbibed.
**DUGALD STEWART**

We learn to do neither by thinking nor by doing; we learn to do by thinking about what we are doing.
**GEORGE D. STODDARD**

Teach the young people how to think, not what to think.
**SIDNEY SUGARMAN**

Before you orgazine you ought to analyze and see what the elements of the business are.
**GERARD SWOPE**

Thinking, not growth, makes manhood. Accustom yourself, therefore, to thinking. Set yourself to understand whatever you see or read. To join thinking with reading is one of the first maxims, and one of the easiest operations.
**ISAAC TAYLOR**

What priming will do to a pump, information and a sincere, understanding talking to will do to an active, impressionable mind—get it started, provoke it to think.
**TIORIO**

Asking someone to think often seems to be cruel and inhuman punishment.
**FRANK TYGER**

They can because they think they can.
**VIRGIL**

This world is a comedy to those that think, a tragedy to those that feel.
**HORACE WALPOLE**

Are you willing to think? Consider carefully, for the answer to that question will largely determine your success or failure in life. If you would develop your judgment, use it. Exercise your power of judgment as often as you can, for the first rule of good judgment is practice. The functions of your mind, no less than the muscles of your body, receive their strength through repeated use.
**JOHN M. WILSON**

If the power of reflecting on the past, and darting the keen eye of contemplation into futurity, be the grand privilege of man, it must be granted that

some people enjoy this prerogative in a very limited degree.
**MARY WOLLSTONECRAFT**

Plain living and high thinking are no more.
**WILLIAM WORDSWORTH**

## *Thought*

Thought means life, since those who do not think do not live in any high or real sense. Thinking makes the man.
**AMOS BRONSON ALCOTT**

Our life is what our thoughts make it. A man will find that as he alters his thoughts toward things and other people, things and other people will alter towards him.
**JAMES ALLEN**

You are today where your thoughts have brought you. You will be tomorrow where your thoughts take you.
**JAMES LANE ALLEN**

Such as are thy habitual thoughts, such also will be the character of thy soul—for the soul is dyed by the thoughts. Dye it then, with a continuous series of such thoughts as these—that where a man can live, there if he will, he can also live well.
**MARCUS AURELIUS ANTONINUS**

The happiness of your life depends upon the quality of your thoughts.
**MARCUS AURELIUS ANTONINUS**

Our life is what our thoughts make it.
**MARCUS AURELIUS ANTONINUS**

A man would do well to carry a pencil in his pocket, and write down the thoughts of the moment. Those that come unsought for are commonly the most valuable, and should be secured, because they seldom return.
**FRANCIS BACON**

Thinking cannot be clear until it has had expression—we must write, or speak, or act our thoughts, or they will remain in half torpid form. Our feelings must have expression, or they will be as clouds, which, till they descend in rain, will never bring up fruit or flowers. So it is with all the inward feelings; expression gives them development—thought is the blossom; language is the opening bud; action the fruit behind it.
**HENRY WARD BEECHER**

Good thoughts and acts will soon improve the health and strength of man, for man was made to think and act according to God's plan; and plan God did that man should live a decent, honest life, enjoying health and happiness, the better with a wife.
**ALONZO NEWTON BENN**

Thoughts are the pinions of the soul,
And carry far when they're set free,
And if they're good, great good they'll do
And benefit both you and me;
So we should gladly do our share
Of worthwhile work and thinking, too;
And spread the thoughts of brotherhood—Think
thoughts that none have cause to rue.
**ALONZO NEWTON BENN**

Think like a man of action and act like a man of thought.
**HENRI BERGSON**

Example has more followers than reason. We unconsciously imitate what pleases us, and approximate to the characters we most admire. A generous habit of thought and action carries with it an incalculable influence.
**CHRISTIAN BOVÉE**

There is no less invention in aptly applying a thought found in a book, than in being the first author of the thought.
ROBERT BOYLE

## Thought

You say "I think" ten times a day
Or fifteen times, or twenty
And even more. Well, anyway
You sure repeat it plenty.
But pause and ponder half a wink
And start your brain-cells clinking;
"I think" you say, but do you Think
Or only Think you're thinking?

How often is the thing you've thought
Out of Yourself created
And not a dictum you've been taught
And simply imitated?
Into a reverie you sink
And like an owl you're blinking,
But do you actually Think,
Or only Think you're thinking?

"I think," you say—and ladle out
Some fusty old opinion
That probably was known about
In Pharaoh's dominion.
Do new ideas ever slink
Into your cranium's chinking?
I wonder—do you really think
Or only Think you're thinking?

Traditions, customs, fill your head
And some of them have virtue,
But most of them have long been dead
They fester there and hurt you.
Son, chuck that clutter in the drink,
Wake up—don't sit there blinking!
Wake up! And then perhaps you'll Think
And not just Think you're thinking!
BERTON BRALEY

Keep your thoughts right—for as you think, so you are. Thoughts are things, therefore, think only the things that will make the world better and you unashamed.
HENRY H. BUCKLEY

I still find each day too short for all the thoughts I want to think, all the walks I want to take, all the books I want to read, and all the friends I want to see. The longer I live, the more my mind dwells upon the beauty and the wonder of the world.
JOHN BURROUGHS

A thought once awakened does not again slumber.
THOMAS CARLYLE

The lightning spark of thought, generated or, say rather, heaven-kindled, in the solitary mind, awakens its express likeness in another mind, in a thousand other minds, and all blaze up together in combined fire.
THOMAS CARLYLE

True effort, in fact, as of a captive struggling to free himself: That is thought.
THOMAS CARLYLE

Secret study, silent thought, is, after all, the mightiest agent in human affairs.
WILLIAM ELLERY CHANNING

They who have read about everything are thought to understand everything, too, but it is not always so; reading furnishes the mind only with materials of knowledge; it is thinking that makes what we read ours. We are of the ruminating kind, and it is not enough to cram ourselves with a great load of collections—we must chew them over again.
WILLIAM ELLERY CHANNING

As soon as true thought has entered our mind, it gives a light which makes us see a crowd of other objects which we have never perceived before.
FRANÇOIS DE CHÂTEAUBRIAND

Silence and reserve suggest latent power. What some men think has more effect than what others say.
LORD CHESTERFIELD

Human foresight often leaves its proudest possessor only a choice of evils.
CHARLES CALEB COLTON

Mental pleasures never cloy; unlike those of the body, they are increased by reputation, approved by reflection, and strengthened by enjoyment.
CHARLES CALEB COLTON

Though the proportion of those who think be extremely small, yet every individual flatters himself that he is one of the number.
CHARLES CALEB COLTON

To dally much with subjects mean and low, proves that the mind is weak or makes it so.
WILLIAM COWPER

Our best friends and our worst enemies are our thoughts. A thought can do us more good than a doctor or a banker or a faithful friend. It can also do us more harm than a brick.
FRANK CRANE

Our thought is the key which unlocks the doors of the world.
SAMUEL MCC. CROTHERS

Our success or our failure is the result of our mental condition—our thoughts about people and about ourselves—our attitudes toward people and toward ourselves.
DAN CUSTER

Think all you speak, but speak not all you think. Thoughts are your own; your words are so no more.
PATRICK DELANY

It is impossible for men engaged in low and groveling pursuits to have noble and generous sentiments. A man's thought must always follow his employment.
DEMOSTHENES

Nurture your mind with great thoughts; to believe in the heroic makes heroes.
BENJAMIN DISRAELI

I'm sick to death of abstraction.
FRED DOOLEY

It is remarkable to what lengths people will go to avoid thought.
THOMAS EDISON

Thoughts lead on to purposes; purposes go forth in action; actions form habits; habits decide character; and character fixes our destiny.
TRYON EDWARDS

One couldn't carry on life comfortably without a little blindness to the fact that everything has been said better than we can put it ourselves.
GEORGE ELIOT

Our thoughts are often worse than we are.
GEORGE ELIOT

The gates of thought,—how slow and late they discover themselves! Yet when they appear, we see that they were always there, always open.
RALPH WALDO EMERSON

The last change in our point of view gives the whole world a pictorial air.
**RALPH WALDO EMERSON**

The revelation of thought takes man out of servitude into freedom.
**RALPH WALDO EMERSON**

Thought is the property of those only who can entertain it.
**RALPH WALDO EMERSON**

What is the hardest task in the world? To think.
**RALPH WALDO EMERSON**

We do not yet trust the unknown powers of thought. Whence came all these tools, inventions, books laws, parties, kingdoms? Out of the invisible world, through a few brains. The arts and institutions of men are created out of thought. The powers that make the capitalist are metaphysical, the force of method and force of will makes trade, and builds towns.
**RALPH WALDO EMERSON**

Men are not influenced by things, but by their thoughts about things.
**EPICTETUS**

Every definition is dangerous
**DESIDERIUS ERASMUS**

Second thoughts are ever wiser.
**EURIPIDES**

The one and only formative power given to man is thought. By his thinking he not only makes character, but body and affairs, for as he thinketh within himself, so is he.
**CHARLES FILLMORE**

Thought, not money, is the real business capital, and if you know absolutely that what you are doing is right, then you are bound to accomplish it in due season.
**HARVEY S. FIRESTONE**

Thought is the most precious, the most personal, and the most independent thing possessed by man. Its liberty cannot be attacked.
**CAMILLE FLAMMARION**

Thinkers perish, thoughts don't.
**MALCOLM FORBES**

To have thought far too little, we shall find in the review of life, among our capital faults.
**JOHN FOSTER**

By words we learn thoughts, and by thoughts we learn life.
**JEAN BAPTISTE GIRARD**

Keep a firm hand on the throttle of your train of thought.
**ARNOLD GLASOW**

For many things we can find substitutes, but there is not now, nor will there ever be, a substitute for creative thought.
**CRAWFORD H. GREENEWALT**

Thoughts . . . are like the soil of John Brown. They go marching on. They still live and make their influence powerfully felt when the paper on which they are printed is yellow and crumbling with age.
**WALTER DAN GRIFFITH**

In matters of conscience, first thoughts are best; in matters of prudence, last thoughts are best.
**ROBERT HALL**

The effort which I make the people are placed to call the fruit of genius. It is the fruit of labor and thought.
**ALEXANDER HAMILTON**

Have you not learned that not stocks or bonds or stately homes, or products of mill or field are our country? It is the splendid thought that is in our minds.
**BENJAMIN HARRISON**

Nothing is more unaccountable than the spell that often lurks in a spoken word. A thought may be present to the mind, and two minds conscious of the same thought, but as long as it remains unspoken their familiar talk flows quietly over the hidden idea.
**NATHANIEL HAWTHORNE**

Mark this well, ye proud men of action! Ye are, after all, nothing but unconscious instruments of the men of thought.
**HEINRICH HEINE**

Thought precedes action as lighting does thunder.
**HEINRICH HEINE**

We should lay up in our minds a store of goodly thoughts which will be a living treasure of knowledge always with us, and from which, at various times, and amidst all the shiftings of circumstances, we might be sure of drawing some comfort, guidance and sympathy.
**SIR ARTHUR HELPS**

Thus we build in the ice, thus we write on the waves of the sea; the roaring waves pass away, the ice melts, and away goes our palace, like our thoughts.
**JOHANN GOTTFRIED VON HERDER**

Nobody has ever thought out anything in a shower bath because it's too fast and too efficient.
**DON HEROLD**

The gratification of a thoughtless pleasure soon evaporates; the pleasure of a gratifying thought never ends.
**CULLEN HIGHTOWER**

A thought is often original, though you have uttered it a hundred times. It has come to you over a new route, by a new and express train of association.
**OLIVER WENDELL HOLMES**

A man is not idle because he is absorbed in thought. There is a visible labor and there is an invisible labor.
**VICTOR HUGO**

Certain thoughts are prayers. There are certain moments when, whatever be the attitude of the body, the soul is on its knees.
**VICTOR HUGO**

Single-mindedness is all very well in cows or baboons; in an animal claiming to belong to the same species as Shakespeare, it is simply disgraceful.
**ALDOUS HUXLEY**

After the ship has sunk, everyone knows how she might have been saved.
**ITALIAN PROVERB**

The glow of one warm thought is to me worth more than money.
**THOMAS JEFFERSON**

All that is good in man lies in youthful feeling and mature thought.
**JOSEPH JOUBERT**

Fully to understand a grand and beautiful thought requires, perhaps, as much time as to conceive it.
**JOSEPH JOUBERT**

When a nation gives birth to a man who is able to produce a great thought, another is born who is able to understand and admire it.
JOSEPH JOUBERT

The only means of strengthening one's intellect is to make up one's mind about nothing—to let the mind be a thoroughfare for all thoughts.
JOHN KEATS

Where all think alike, no one thinks very much.
WALTER LIPPMANN

The thoughts that come often unsought, and, as it were, drop into the mind, are commonly the most valuable of any we have, and therefore should be secured, because they seldom return again.
JOHN LOCKE

Heavy thoughts bring our physical maladies; when the soul is oppressed, so is the body.
MARTIN LUTHER

Our destiny changes with our thought; we shall become what we wish to become, do what we wish to do, when our habitual thought corresponds with our desire.
ORISON S. MARDEN

Who supplies another with a constructive thought has enriched him forever.
ALFRED A. MONTAPERT

It will be a shock to men when they realize that thoughts that were fast enough for today are not fast enough for tomorrow. But thinking tomorrow's thoughts today is one kind of future life.
CHRISTOPHER MORLEY

The functions of an executive are to create and enforce policies rather than to work out problems resulting from such policies.
LOUIS F. MUSIL

If we are not responsible for the thoughts that pass our doors, we are at least responsible for those we admit and entertain.
CHARLES B. NEWCOMB

If I have done the public any service, it is due to patient thought.
SIR ISAAC NEWTON

When we talk in company we lose our unique tone of voice, and this leads us to make statements which in no way correspond to our real thoughts.
FRIEDRICH WILHELM NIETZSCHE

There are two distinct classes of what are called thoughts: those that we produce in ourselves by reflection and the act of thinking and those that bolt into the mind of their own accord.
THOMAS PAINE

All of our dignity consists in thought. Let us endeavor then to think well; this is the principle of morality.
BLAISE PASCAL

Always remember to bound thy thoughts to the present occasion.
WILLIAM PENN

Clear therefore thy head, and rally, and manage thy thoughts rightly, and thou wilt save time, and see and do thy business well; for thy judgment will be distinct, thy mind free, and the faculties strong and regular.
WILLIAM PENN

Man being made a reasonable, and so a thinking creature, there is nothing more worthy of his being, than the right direction and employment of his thoughts; since upon this depends both his usefulness to the public, and his own present and future benefit in all respects.
**WILLIAM PENN**

Upon the whole matter, employ thy thoughts as thy business requires, and let that have place according to merit and urgency; giving every thing a review and due digestion, and thou wilt prevent many errors and vexations, as well as save much time to thy self in the course of thy life.
**WILLIAM PENN**

Thoughts, even more than overt acts, reveal character.
**WILLIAM S. PLUMER**

Thought is the first faculty of man; to express it is one of his first desires; to spread it, his dearest privilege.
**ABBÉ RAYNAL**

I have plenty of thoughts, but I'm going to keep them to myself for a while.
**L. MENDEL RIVERS**

Make yourselves nests of pleasant thoughts. None of us knows what fairy palaces we may build of beautiful thought—proof against all adversity. Bright fancies, satisfied memories, noble histories, faithful sayings, treasure houses of precious and restful thoughts, which care cannot disturb, nor pain make gloomy, nor poverty take away from us.
**JOHN RUSKIN**

The first essential character [of civilization], I should say, is forethought. This, I would say, is what distinguishes men from brutes and adults from children.
**BERTRAND RUSSELL**

Thoughts are but dreams till their effect be tried.
**WILLIAM SHAKESPEARE**

They only babble who practice not reflection. I shall think; and thought is silence.
**RICHARD SHERIDAN**

We can't always control what happens to us. But we can control what we think about what happens. . . . And what we are thinking is our life at any particular moment.
**NORMAN G. SHIDLE**

They are never alone that are accompanied with noble thoughts.
**SIR PHILIP SIDNEY**

You can see an awful lot by looking in a rear-view mirror.
**ROBERT SKELTON**

A thought may be very commendable as a thought, but I value it chiefly as a window through which I can obtain insight on the thinker.
**ALEXANDER SMITH**

A principle of policy once established, be it sound or unsound, is almost sure, through evolution, to exert an influence far beyond that created at the time of its original inception.
**ALFRED P. SLOAN, JR.**

Do not think that what your thoughts dwell upon is of no matter. Your thoughts are making you.
**BISHOP STEERE**

Every man has some peculiar train of thought which he falls back upon when he is alone. This, to a great degree, moulds the man.
**DUGALD STEWART**

We have only to change the point of view and the greatest action looks mean.
**WILLIAM MAKEPEACE THACKERAY**

Be a Columbus to whole new continents and worlds within you, opening new channels, not of trade, but of thought.
**HENRY DAVID THOREAU**

Each thought that is welcomed and recorded is a nest egg, by the side of which more will be laid.
**HENRY DAVID THOREAU**

Few things are brought to a successful issue by impetuous desire, but most by calm and prudent forethought.
**THUCYDIDES**

The point of aim for our vigilance to hold in view is to dwell upon the brightest parts in every prospect, to call off the thoughts when running upon disagreeable objects, and strive to be pleased with the present circumstances.
**ABRAHAM TUCKER**

A man is infinitely more complicated than his thoughts.
**PAUL VALÉRY**

The second, sober thought of the people is seldom wrong, and always efficient.
**MARTIN VAN BUREN**

When thought is too weak to be simply expressed, it's clear proof that it should be rejected.
**MARQUIS DE VAUVANARGUES**

The charm of a deed is its doing; the charm of a life is its living; the soul of the thing is the thought.
**EUGENE FITCH WARE**

His words span rivers and mountains, but his thoughts are still only six inches long.
**E. B. WHITE**

We need to cultivate fertility in thought as we have cultivated efficiency in administration.
**NORBERT WIENER**

All thought is immoral. Its very essence is destruction. If you think of anything you kill it. Nothing survives being thought of.
**OSCAR WILDE**

He that will not command his thoughts will soon lose the command of his actions.
**WOODROW WILSON**

## *Time*

Time wounds all heels.
**JANE ACE**

We cannot waste time. We can only waste ourselves.
**GEORGE MATTHEW ADAMS**

Time brings all things to pass.
**AESCHYLUS**

Every day has been so short, every hour so fleeting, every minute so filled with the life I love, that time for me has fled on too swift a wing.
**AGA KHAN III**

Don't think of how you're going to spend your time—use it.
**WILMA ASKINAS**

If time were the wicked sheriff in a horse opera, I'd pay for riding lessons and take his gun away.
**W. H. AUDEN**

Time is a sort of river of passing events, and strong is its current; no sooner is a thing brought to sight than it is swept by and another takes its place, and this too will be swept away.
MARCUS AURELIUS ANTONINUS

Time is the measure of business as money is of wares; and business is bought at a dear hand where there is small despatch.
FRANCIS BACON

To choose time is to save time.
FRANCIS BACON

Time is a dressmaker specializing in alterations.
FAITH BALDWIN

A sense of the value of time—that is, of the best way to divide one's time into one's various activities—is an essential preliminary to efficient work; it is the only method of avoiding hurry.
ARNOLD BENNETT

Killing time is the chief end of our society.
UGO BETTI

You will never find time for anything. If you want time, you must make it.
CHARLES BIXTON

Regret for time wasted can become a power for good in the time that remains, if we will only stop the waste and the idle, useless regretting.
ARTHUR BRISBANE

Those who make the worse use of their time most complain of its shortness.
JEAN DE LA BRUYÈRE

Punctuality is the stem virtue of men of business, and the graceful courtesy of prices.
EDWARD BULWER-LYTTON

The forty-four-hour week has no charm for me. I'm looking for a forty-hour day.
NICHOLAS MURRAY BUTLER

You will never find time for anything. If you want time you must make it.
CHARLES BUXTON

Time ripens all things; no man is born wise.
MIGUEL DE CERVANTES

Know the true value of time; snatch, seize and enjoy every moment of it. No idleness, no laziness, no procrastination.
LORD CHESTERFIELD

The laboring man and the artificer knows what every hour of his time is worth, and parts not with it but for the full value: they are only noblemen and gentlemen, who should know best how to use it, that think it only fit to be cast away; and their not knowing how to set a true value upon this, is the true cause of the wrong estimate they make of all other things.
LORD CLARENDON

Much may be done in those little shreds and patches of time which every day produces, and which most men throw away, but which nevertheless will make at the end of it no small deduction from the life of man.
CHARLES CALEB COLTON

We work not only to produce but to give value to time.
EUGÈNE DELACROIX

Time and happenings and the grace of God are the best solvers of puzzles. One must leave much to these, if he is not to worry himself into premature senility.
**ALEX DOW**

To every thing there is a season, and a time to every purpose under heaven: A time to be born, and a time to die; a time to plant, and a time to pluck up that which is planted; a time to kill, and a time to heal; a time to break down, and a time to build up; a time to weep, and a time to laugh; a time to mourn, and a time to dance.
**ECCLESIASTES 3:1–4**

There is time for everything.
**THOMAS EDISON**

Old and new make the warp and woof of every moment. There is no thread that is not a twist of these two strands.
**RALPH WALDO EMERSON**

Time is a file that wears and makes no noise.
**ENGLISH PROVERB**

One sees the past better than it was; one finds the present worse than it is; one hopes for a future happier than it will be.
**MADAME D'EPINAY**

If you never break a promise, if you always pay the money you owe exactly on the day it is due, nobody will know but that you are worth a billion. And you will be just as good a risk as a man worth a billion, for all that he could do would be to pay promptly on the due date.
**HAMILTON FISH**

Our forefathers were given to dawdling. They had lots of time—with much to spare. They went in for three-volume novels and two-hour sermons. They walked—and walked slowly, at that. They conversed by the hour and wrote yard-long letters. . . . Yesterday was the day of the leisurely sailing ship. Today is the day of the steam, oil and electric power ship. Tomorrow will be the day of the flying ship. All inspired by the quest for abbreviating space and saving time.
**B. C. FORBES**

Time mends all, ends all things earthly.
**B. C. FORBES**

Arriving for a luncheon or dinner engagement an hour late is almost as bad as arriving an hour early.
**MALCOLM FORBES**

Nothing is ever like it used to be.
**MALCOLM FORBES**

Unless you're serving time there's never enough of it.
**MALCOLM FORBES**

Do not squander time, for that is the stuff life is made of.
**BENJAMIN FRANKLIN**

It is familiarity with life that makes time speed quickly. When every day is a step in the unknown, as for children, the days are long with gathering of experience.
**GEORGE GISSING**

Believe me when I tell you that thrift of time will repay you in after life, with a usury of profit beyond your most sanguine dreams; and that waste of it will make you dwindle, alike in intellectual and moral stature, beyond your darkest reckoning.
**WILLIAM E. GLADSTONE**

Timing is everything. It is as important to know when as to know how.
**ARNOLD GLASOW**

One always has time enough if only one applies it well.
**JOHANN WOLFGANG VON GOETHE**

The right man is the one who seizes the moment.
**JOHANN WOLFGANG VON GOETHE**

God Himself chasteneth not with a rod but with time.
**BALTASAR GRACIÁN**

The real secret of how to use time is to pack it as you would a portmanteau, filling up the small spaces with small things.
**SIR HENRY HADDOW**

There's no such thing as not enough time if you're doing what you want to do.
**ROBERT HALF**

The wheels of nature are not meant to roll backward; everything presses on toward Eternity—from the birth of Time, an impetuous current has set in which bears all the sons of men toward that interminable ocean.
**ROBERT HALL**

Never a tear bedims the eye that time and patience will not dry.
**BRET HARTE**

As we advance in life, we acquire a keener sense of the value of time. Nothing else, indeed, seems of any consequence; and we become misers in this respect.
**WILLIAM HAZLITT**

Even as we speak, jealous time flees—seize this day, and put little faith in tomorrow.
**HORACE**

You'll find as you grow older that you weren't born such a very great while ago after all. The time shortens up.
**WILLIAM DEAN HOWELLS**

Short as life is, we make it still shorter by the careless waste of time.
**VICTOR HUGO**

One of the best lessons that anyone can learn in life is how to use time wisely. Consider what can be done in ten minutes. If you need a little mental relaxation, you can sit down with a friend and play a game of cards. If you need some physical recreation, you can engage in a few exercises that will help tone up you body. Perhaps you have a friend who for weeks or months has been looking for a letter. Then there may be among your acquaintances someone whose friendship you would value highly and whose counsel would be profitable. Learn to use ten minutes intelligently. It will pay you huge dividends.
**WILLIAM A. IRWIN**

No person will have occasion to complain of the want of time, who never loses any.
**THOMAS JEFFERSON**

An Italian philosopher said that time was his estate; an estate indeed which will produce nothing without cultivation, but will always abundantly repay the labors of industry, and generally satisfy the most extensive desires, if no part of it be suffered to lie in waste by negligence, to be overrun with noxious plants, or laid out for show rather than for use.
**JOHNSON**

Time is a fixed income and, as with any income, the real problem facing most of us is how to live successfully within our daily allotment.
**MARGARET B. JOHNSTONE**

Time, that aged nurse, rocked me to patience.
**JOHN KEATS**

Time stays long enough for anyone who will use it.
**LEONARDO DA VINCI**

Be avaricious of time; do not give any moment without receiving it in value; only allow hours to go from you with as much regret as you give to your gold; do not allow a single day to pass without increasing the treasure of your knowledge and virtue.
**LETOURNEUX**

My countrymen, one and all, think calmly and well upon this whole subject. Nothing valuable can be lost by taking time. . . . Intelligence, patriotism, Christianity and a firm reliance on Him who has never yet forsaken this favored land are still competent to adjust in the best way all our present difficulty. In your hands, my dissatisfied countrymen, are the momentous issues.
**ABRAHAM LINCOLN**

One realizes the full importance of time only when there is little of it left. Every man's greatest capital asset is his unexpired years of productive life.
**P. W. LITCHFIELD**

No minute lost
Comes ever back again.
Take heed and see
Ye nothing do in vain.
**LONDON CLOCK TOWER MOTTO**

The everyday cares and duties, which men call drudgery, are the weights and counterpoises of the clock of time, giving its pendulum a true vibration and its hands a regular motion; and when they cease to hang upon its wheels, the pendulum no longer swings, the hands no longer move, the clock stands still.
**HENRY WADSWORTH LONGFELLOW**

The thing we long for, that we are for one transcendent moment.
**JAMES RUSSELL LOWELL**

Lost, somewhere between sunrise and sunset, sixty golden minutes. Each set with sixty diamond seconds. No reward is offered, for they are gone forever.
**HORACE MANN**

Nothing inspires confidence in a business man sooner than punctuality, nor is there any habit which sooner saps his reputation than that of being always behind time.
**W. MATHEWS**

Time is a breedy creature: The minutes propagate hours, the hours beget days, the days raise huge families of months, and before we know it we are crowded out of this sweet life by mere surplus of time's offspring.
**CHRISTOPHER MORLEY**

In the city, time becomes visible.
**LEWIS MUMFORD**

The more sand has escaped from the hour glass of our life, the clearer we should see through it.
**JEAN PAUL**

Among the millions of nerve cells that clothe parts of the brain there runs a thread of time, the thread that has run through each succeeding wakeful hour of the individual's past life.
**WILDER G. PENFIELD**

Time cannot be influenced by mankind. It gives each of us a beginning, and an end. And this makes us question the significance of what comes between. But if you can create something time cannot erode, something which ignores the eccentricities of particular eras or moments, something truly timeless, this is a significant victory.
**FERDINAND PORSCHE**

The time which we have at our disposal every day is elastic; the passions that we feel expand it, those that we inspire contract it; and habit fills up the rest.
**MARCEL PROUST**

Time, which changes people, does not alter the image we have retained of them.
**MARCEL PROUST**

The man who wastes to-day lamenting yesterday will waste to-morrow lamenting to-day.
**PHILIP M. RASKIN**

Without the management of time, you will soon have nothing left to manage.
**WILLIAM D. REIFF**

Don't be fooled by the calendar. There are only as many days in the year as you make use of. One man gets only a week's value out of a year while another man gets a full year's value out of a week.
**CHARLES RICHARDS**

Permanence is a man-made fantasy smiled on by time.
**PAUL VON RINGELHEIM**

Nothing is a waste of time if you use the experience wisely.
**AUGUSTE RODIN**

God never imposes a duty without giving time to do it.
**JOHN RUSKIN**

Save time thinking you can do the other fellow's job better than he can—put it in doing your job better!
**HERBERT A. SCHOENFELD**

Part of our time is snatched from us, part is gently subtracted and part slides insensibly away.
**SENECA**

Time heals what reason cannot.
**SENECA**

Better three hours too soon, than one minute too late.
**WILLIAM SHAKESPEARE**

The end crowns all; and that old common arbitrator, time, will one day end it.
**WILLIAM SHAKESPEARE**

Take all the swift advantage of the hours.
**WILLIAM SHAKESPEARE**

Thus we play the fool with the time and the spirits of the wise sit in the clouds and mock us.
**WILLIAM SHAKESPEARE**

Everything we feel is made of Time. All the beauties of life are shaped by it.
**PETER SHAFFER**

Life is too short, and the time we waste in yawning can never be regained.
**STENDHAL**

It is later than you think.
**SUNDIAL INSCRIPTION**

There is, by God's grace, an immeasurable distance between late and too late.
**ANNE SWETCHINE**

During a very busy life I have often been asked, "How did you manage to do it all?" The answer is very simple: It is because I did everything promptly.
**SIR RICHARD TANGYE**

The time best employed is that which one wastes.
**CLAUDE TELLIER**

Time is the most valuable thing a man can spend.
**THEOPHRASTUS**

Waste of time is the most extravagant of all expense.
**THEOPHRASTUS**

Time is
Too slow for those who Wait,
Too swift for those who Fear,
Too long for those who Grieve;
Too short for those who Rejoice;
But for those who Love,
Time is Eternity.
**HENRY VAN DYKE**

Loss of time through sociability, idle talk, luxury, even more sleep than is necessary for health, six to at most eight hours, is worthy of absolute moral condemnation.
**MAX WEBER**

Time is a storm in which we are all lost.
**WILLIAM CARLOS WILLIAMS**

Many of us spend half our time wishing for things we could have if we didn't spend half our time wishing.
**ALEXANDER WOOLLCOTT**

## *Today*

Each day of your life, as soon as you open your eyes in the morning, you can square away for a happy and successful day. It's the mood and the purpose of the inception of each day that are the important facts in charting your course for the day. We can always square away for a fresh start, no matter what the past has been. It's today that is the paramount problem always. Yesterday is but history.
**GEORGE MATTHEW ADAMS**

Do today what should be done. Your tomorrow may never come.
**HARRY F. BANKS**

No matter what looms ahead, if you can eat today, enjoy the sunlight today, mix good cheer with friends today, enjoy it and bless God for it. Do not look back on happiness—or dream of it in the future. You are only sure of today; do not let yourself be cheated out of it.
**HENRY WARD BEECHER**

One today is worth two tomorrows; what I am to be, I am now becoming.
**BENJAMIN FRANKLIN**

Never regret yesterday. Life is in you today, and you make your tomorrow.
**L. RON HUBBARD**

Do today's duty, fight today's temptation; do not weaken and distract yourself by looking forward to things you cannot see, and could not understand if you saw them.
**CHARLES KINGSLEY**

I will utter what I believe today, if it should contradict all I said yesterday.
**WENDELL PHILLIPS**

Lay hold of today's task and you will not depend so much upon tomorrow's.
SENECA

The past, the present and the future are really one—they are today.
STOWE

Today is the pupil of yesterday.
PUBLILIUS SYRUS

Live for today. Multitudes of people have failed to live for today. They have spent their lives reaching for the future. What they have had within their grasp today they have missed entirely, because only the future has intrigued them . . . and the first thing they knew the future became the past. . . . Too late had they come to that realization, and when finally it dawned upon them, they realized that life upon this earth was very fleeting, and they realized the truth of the observation that "A thousand years are as but a day."
WILLIAM ALLEN WHITE

## *Tolerance*

Tolerance consists of seeing certain things with your heart instead of with your eyes.
ORLANDO A. BATTISTA

Toleration is good for all or it is good for none.
EDMUND BURKE

Intolerance has been the curse of every age and state.
S. DAVIES

Half the secret of getting along with people is consideration of their views; the other half is tolerance in one's own views.
DANIEL FROHMAN

Tolerance comes with age. I see no fault committed that I myself could not have committed at some time or other.
JOHANN WOLFGANG VON GOETHE

Intolerance is the Do Not Touch sign on something that cannot bear touching. We do not mind having our hair ruffled, but we will not tolerate any familiarity with the toupée that covers our baldness.
ERIC HOFFER

Nonconformists travel as a rule in bunches. You rarely find a nonconformist who goes it alone. And woe to him inside a nonconformist clique who does not conform with nonconformity.
ERIC HOFFER

The mind of a bigot is like the pupil of the eye; the more light you pour upon it, the more it will contract.
OLIVER WENDELL HOLMES

What is objectionable, what is dangerous about extremists is not that they are extreme, but that they are intolerant. The evil is not what they say about their cause, but what they say about their opponents.
ROBERT F. KENNEDY

I believe with all my heart that civilization has produced nothing finer than a man or woman who thinks and practices true tolerance. Some one has said that most of us don't think, we just occasionally rearrange our prejudices. And I suspect that even today, with all the progress we have made in liberal thought, the quality of true tolerance is as rare as the quality of mercy. That men of all creeds have fundamental common objectives is a fact one must learn by the process of education. How to work jointly toward these objectives must be learned by experience.
FRANK KNOX

Tolerance is the positive and cordial effort to understand another's beliefs, practices and habits without necessarily sharing or accepting them.
**JOSHUA L. LIEBMAN**

We are in favor of tolerance, but it is a very difficult thing to tolerate the intolerant and impossible to tolerate the intolerable.
**GEORGE D. PRENTICE**

Nothing is so difficult as to achieve results in this world if one is full of great tolerance and the milk of human kindness.
**CORINNE ROBINSON**

It is easy to be tolerant when you do not care.
**CLEMENT F. ROGERS**

It is not a merit to tolerate, but rather a crime to be intolerant.
**PERCY BYSSHE SHELLEY**

The resource of bigotry and intolerance, when convicted of error, is always the same; silenced by argument, it endeavors to silence by persecution, in old times by fire and sword, in modern days by the tongue.
**GERALD J. SIMMONS**

Toleration has never been the cause of civil war; while, on the contrary, persecution has covered the earth with blood and carnage.
**VOLTAIRE**

## *Travel*

Travel: Some good advice
From one who knows:
Take twice the cash
And half the clothes.
**ANONYMOUS**

Our gifts and attainments are not only to be light and warmth in our own dwellings, but are to shine through the window, into the dark night, to guide and cheer bewildered travelers on the road.
**HENRY WARD BEECHER**

I have wandered all my life, and I have also traveled; the difference between the two being this, that we wander for distraction, but we travel for fulfillment.
**HILAIRE BELLOC**

I sometimes think Thomas Cook should be numbered among the secular saints. He took travel from the privileged and gave it to the common people.
**ARCHBISHOP OF CANTERBURY**

The whole object of travel is not to set foot on foreign land; it is at last to set foot on one's own country as foreign land.
**G. K. CHESTERTON**

As a member of an escorted tour, you don't even have to know the Matterhorn isn't a tuba.
**TEMPLE FIELDING**

When we keep our noses very close to our own daily grind for a very long period, we are in danger of becoming, every now and again, pessimistic. The best cure I know of is to pack up and visit other parts of the country. You can't go very far wrong no matter which direction you take. Last year, for example, I was wonderfully braced up by a visit, first, to the southern part of the Pacific coast... where I climbed mountains to see staggering hydro-electric developments carried out there with daring enterprise and admirable courage.
**B. C. FORBES**

Astrology isn't something I'm into, but while awaiting [my ill-fated] trans-Atlantic balloon attempt, the *Los Angeles Times* Jan. 1, 1975 column on the

subject under my sign, Leo, advised: Find easier and faster forms of transportation.
MALCOLM FORBES

Traveling is one way of lengthening life, at least in appearance.
BENJAMIN FRANKLIN

Travel makes a wise man better but a fool worse.
THOMAS FULLER

Our object in traveling should be, not to gratify curiosity, and seek mere temporary amusement, but to learn, and to venerate, to improve the understanding and the heart.
GRESLEY

One of the pleasantest things in the world is going on a journey; but I like to go by myself.
WILLIAM HAZLITT

They change their clime, but not their mind, who rush across the sea.
HORACE

All travel has its advantages. If the traveler visits better countries, he may learn to improve his own; and if fortune carries him to worse, he may learn to enjoy his own.
JOHNSON

The use of traveling is to regulate imagination by reality, and, instead of thinking how things may be, to see them as they are.
JOHNSON

I have traveled more than anyone else, and I have noticed that even the angels speak English with an accent.
MARK TWAIN

## *Trouble*

A crowd of troubles passed him by
As he with courage waited;
He said, "Where do you troubles fly
When you are thus belated?"
"We go," they say, "to those who mope,
Who look on life dejected,
Who meekly say 'good-bye' to hope,
We go where we're expected."
FRANCIS J. ALLISON

The wise man does not expose himself needlessly to danger, since there are few things for which he cares sufficiently; but he is willing, in great crises, to give even his life—knowing that under certain conditions it is not worth while to live.
ARISTOTLE

Troubles are usually the brooms and shovels that smooth the road to a good man's fortune; and many a man curses the rain that falls upon his head, and knows not that it brings abundance to drive away hunger.
ST. BASIL

We are always in the forge, or on the anvil; by trials God is shaping us for higher things.
HENRY WARD BEECHER

This is the mark of a really admirable man: steadfastness in the face of trouble.
LUDWIG VAN BEETHOVEN

Many modern (so-called) Reformers are just as dangerous as the physician who makes a wrong diagnosis of a disease. They see the trouble from without and prescribe external remedies, while the cause of the trouble is within and needs internal treatment.
WILLIAM J. H. BOETCKER

Warning! Following are the names of the Seven Mischievous Misses who are responsible for most of our troubles: Miss Information, Miss Quotation, Miss Representation, Miss Interpretation, Miss Construction, Miss Conception, Miss Understanding. Don't listen to them! Beware!
WILLIAM J. H. BOETCKER

Nine-tenths of the serious controversies which arise in life result from misunderstandings; result from one man not knowing the facts which to the other man seem important, or otherwise failing to appreciate his point of view.
LOUIS D. BRANDEIS

There are nettles everywhere, but smooth, green grasses are more common still; the blue of heaven is larger than the cloud.
E. B. BROWNING

Half the trouble in the world arises from men trying to anticipate their time and season, and the other half from their trying to prolong them.
ARTHUR BRYANT

If you would not have affliction visit you twice, listen at once to what it teaches.
JAMES BURGH

The thorns which I have reap'd are of the tree I planted; they have torn me, and I bleed.
LORD BYRON

I have had a long, long life full of troubles, but there is one curious fact about them—nine-tenths of them never happened.
ANDREW CARNEGIE

The average man takes life as a trouble. He is in a chronic state of irritation at the whole performance. He does not learn to differentiate between troubles and difficulties, usually, until some real trouble bowls him over. He fusses about pin-pricks until a mule kicks him. Then he learns the difference.
HERBERT N. CASSON

It is pleasant to recall past troubles.
CICERO

If you see ten troubles coming down the road, you can be sure that nine will run into the ditch before they reach you and you have to battle with only one of them.
CALVIN COOLIDGE

Being oppressed . . . and sorry can be a way of life, just like any other.
JOHN CORRY

The cares of today are seldom those of tomorrow; and when we lie down at night we may safely say to most of our troubles, "Ye have done your worst, and we shall see you no more."
WILLIAM COWPER

This world has cares enough to plague us; but he who meditates on others' woe, shall, in that meditation, lose his own.
RICHARD CUMBERLAND

When you talk about your troubles, your ailments, your diseases, your hurts, you give longer life to what makes you unhappy. Talking about your grievances merely adds to those grievances. Give recognition only to what you desire. Think and talk only about the good things that add to your enjoyment of your work and life. If you don't talk about your grievances, you'll be delighted to find them disappearing quickly.
THOMAS DREIER

When I go to bed, I leave my troubles in my clothes.
DUTCH PROVERB

I returned, and considered all the oppressions that are done under the sun; and behold the tears of such as were oppressed, and they had no comforter; and on the side of their oppressors there was power; but they had no comforter.
**ECCLESIASTES 4:1**

The world is full of cactus, but we don't have to sit on it.
**WILL FOLEY**

Whenever calamity howlers shake their heads and impress upon you that this, that, and the next dire catastrophe is to befall this nation or the nations of the world—such as, for example, that exhaustion of the world's oil supply will bring all transportation and machinery to a standstill through lack of lubrication, or that exhaustion of the earth's stores of coal will make life unlivable in these cold climates—just smile and reply that the worst troubles of all are those that never happen [and] that you prefer not to cross shaky bridges until you come to them. . . .
**B. C. FORBES**

A danger foreseen is half avoided.
**THOMAS FULLER**

Most troubles arise from loafing when we should be working or talking when we should be listening.
**ARNOLD GLASOW**

Some folks think they're being friendly when they tell you their troubles.
**ARNOLD GLASOW**

The world is full of thorns and thistles. It's all in how you grasp them.
**ARNOLD GLASOW**

The best remedy for disturbances is to let them run their course, for so they quiet down.
**BALTASAR GRACIÁN**

Never bear more than one kind of trouble at a time. Some people bear three—all they have had, all they have now and all they expect to have.
**EDWARD E. HALE**

It is doubtful whether the oppressed ever fight for freedom. They fight for pride and power—power to oppress others.
**ERIC HOFFER**

As a man handles his troubles during the day, he goes to bed at night a General, Captain or Private.
**EDGAR WATSON HOWE**

He who would have no trouble in this world must not be born in it.
**ITALIAN PROVERB**

Men do not get up and do mischief, without there is someone in the head of it.
**ANDREW JACKSON**

A man used to vicissitudes is not easily dejected.
**SAMUEL JOHNSON**

Borrow trouble for yourself, if that's your nature, but don't lend it to your neighbors.
**RUDYARD KIPLING**

Man never fastened one end of a chain around the neck of his brother, that God did not fasten the other end around the neck of the oppressor.
**ALPHONSE DE LAMARTINE**

The happy and efficient people in this world are those who accept trouble as a normal detail of human life and resolve to capitalize it when it comes along. For trouble is the thing that strong men grow by. Met in the right way it is a sure-fire means of putting iron into the victim's will and making him a tougher man to down forever after.
**H. BERTRAM LEWIS**

Trouble is the next best thing to enjoyment; there is no fate in the world so horrible as to have no share in either its joy or sorrows.
HENRY WADSWORTH LONGFELLOW

A small trouble is like a pebble. Hold it too close to your eye and it fills the whole world and puts everything out of focus. Hold it at proper viewing distance and it can be examined and properly classified. Throw it at your feet and it can be seen in its true setting, just one more tiny bump on the pathway to eternity.
CELIA LUCE

Just because the river is quiet does not mean the crocodiles have left.
MALAY PROVERB

A good many gifted people would accomplish more in life if thorns grew on laurels, so they would be harder to rest upon.
RUSH MIDDLECOMBE

If you will call your troubles experiences, and remember that every experience develops some latent force within you, you will grow vigorous and happy, however adverse your circumstances may seem to be.
J. R. MILLER

It takes just as long to get out of any trouble as it took to get into it. And sometimes longer.
J. KENFIELD MORLEY

From winter, plague and pestilence, good Lord, deliver us!
THOMAS NASHE

If we survive danger it steels our courage more than anything else.
REINHOLD NIEBUHR

The harder the conflict, the more glorious the triumph. What we obtain too cheap, we esteem too lightly; 'tis dearness only that gives everything its value. I love the man that can smile in trouble, that can gather strength from distress, and grow brave by reflection. 'Tis the business of little minds to shrink; but he whose heart is firm, and whose conscience approves his conduct, will pursue his principles until death.
THOMAS PAINE

The best education in the world is that got by struggling to get a living.
WENDELL PHILLIPS

Our greatest troubles spring from something that is as admirable as it is dangerous . . . our impatience to better the lot of our fellows.
KARL POPPER

He who foresees calamities, suffers them twice over.
BEILBY PORTEOUS

He that passeth by, and meddleth with strife not belonging to him, is like one that taketh a dog by the ears.
PROVERBS 26:17

Though I walk in the midst of trouble, thou wilt revive me: thou shalt stretch forth thine hand against the wrath of mine enemies, and thy right hand shall save me.
PSALMS 138:7

It is only necessary to make war with five things: with the maladies of the body, the ignorances of the mind, with the passions of the body, with the seditions of the city, and the discords of families.
PYTHAGORAS

A bright day is easily clouded by a murky road.
CHARLES B. ROGERS

The wise man thinks about his troubles only when there is some purpose in doing so; at other times he thinks about other things.
BERTRAND RUSSELL

Danger and delight grow on one stalk.
SCOTTISH PROVERB

No evil is without its compensation. The less money, the less trouble; the less favor, the less envy. Even in those cases which put us out of wits, it is not the loss itself, but the estimate of the loss that troubles us.
SENECA

We are not here to play, to dream, to drift;
We have hard work to do and loads to lift;
Shun not the struggle—face it, 'tis God's gift.
LORD SHAFTESBURY

There is far too much talk about making life easy. It is all right to take the pain and bitterness out of struggle; but were you to take the struggle out, there would be no adequate chance for young Americans.
PAUL SHOUP

Most of the conflicts and disagreements among men result from misunderstanding.
RALPH C. SMEDLEY

Only those who get into scrapes with their eyes open can find a safe way out.
LOGAN PEARSALL SMITH

May you be a mail carrier and have sore feet.
SPANISH GYPSY CURSE

This is an age in which the struggle is for the minds of men; a struggle to create understanding and sympathy between peoples of different races, culture and history; a struggle in which all those who love freedom will do all they can to establish at least a powerful mental alliance amongst themselves against the forces of tyranny. Let us each—yourself and myself—all of us—work toward the goal that in the end we may live in peace and good will together.
PERCEY C. SPENDER

We must do what we can to reduce, not increase, tensions. We must do what we can to present only the facts as we know them, not as we imagine them to be. We must learn to live with crisis in an age which calls for cool heads and accurate appraisals.
PERCEY C. SPENDER

He is most free from danger, who, even when safe, is on his guard.
PUBLILIUS SYRUS

Let us not pray to be sheltered from dangers but to be fearless when facing them.
RABINDRANATH TAGORE

He who shares the afflictions of others will merit to behold the comforting of humanity.
TALMUDIC SAYING

If thou has a bundle of thorns in thy lot, there is no need to sit down on it.
JEREMY TAYLOR

In times of great stress, in times of depression, the public mind loses its balance and becomes the victim of the catchword.
SIR HENRY THORNTON

Everybody knows blue Monday. Sometimes we see red. Black looks are disconcerting. Often the weak-hearted show the white feather or a yellow streak. And that dark brown taste is not unknown. But if you want to keep in the pink of mental condition you mustn't let disturbing riots of color mess up your environment.
H. E. TOWNSEND

Temper is what gets most of us into trouble. Pride is what keeps us there.
**MARK TWAIN**

Never complain about your troubles; they are responsible for more than half of your income.
**ROBERT R. UPDEGRAFF**

If some great catastrophe is not announced every morning, we feel a certain void. Nothing in the paper today, we sigh.
**PAUL VALÉRY**

Trouble will come soon enough, and when he does come receive him as pleasantly as possible. Like the tax collector, he is a disagreeable chap to have in one's house, but the more amiably you greet him the sooner he will go away.
**ARTEMUS WARD**

Let your heart feel for the affliction and distress of every one.
**GEORGE WASHINGTON**

Humanity either makes, or breeds, or tolerates all its afflictions, great or small.
**H. G. WELLS**

He that can't endure the bad,
Will not live to see the good.
**YIDDISH PROVERB**

## *Trust*

Suspicion is far more apt to be wrong than right; oftener unjust than just. It is no friend to virtue, and always an enemy to happiness.
**HOSEA BALLOU**

A man is already of consequence in the world when it is known that we can implicitly rely upon him. Often I have known a man to be preferred in stations of honor and profit because he had this reputation: When he said he knew a thing, he knew it, and when he said he would do a thing, he did it.
**EDWARD BULWER-LYTTON**

The man who trusts men will make fewer mistakes than he who distrusts them.
**CAMILLO BENSO DI CAVOUR**

Suspicion is a thing very few people can entertain without letting the hypothesis turn, in their minds, into fact . . . only scientists can walk around and around a hypothesis without even beginning to confuse it with truth.
**DAVID CORT**

You may be deceived if you trust too much, but you will live in torment if you do not trust enough.
**FRANK CRANE**

There is one common safeguard in the nature of prudent men, which is a good security for all, but especially for democracies against despots. What do I mean? Mistrust. Keep this, hold to this; preserve this only, and you can never be injured.
**DEMOSTHENES**

What has not been examined impartially has not been well examined. Skepticism is therefore the first step toward truth.
**DENIS DIDEROT**

Man's life would be wretched and confined if it were to miss the candid intimacy developed by mutual trust and esteem.
**EDWIN DUMMER**

Skepticism is slow suicide.
**RALPH WALDO EMERSON**

It is a good maxim to trust a person entirely or not at all.
**HENRY FIELDING**

No virtue is more universally accepted as a test of good character than trustworthiness.
**HARRY EMERSON FOSDICK, D.D.**

Mistrust carries one much further than trust.
**GERMAN PROVERB**

The hundred-point man is one who is true to every trust; who keeps his word; who is loyal to the firm that employs him; who does not listen for insults nor look for slights; who carries a civil tongue in his head; who is polite to strangers without being fresh; who is considerate toward servants; who is moderate in his eating and drinking; who is willing to learn; who is cautious and yet courageous.
**ELBERT HUBBARD**

Blessed is the man that trusteth in the Lord, and whose hope the Lord is. For he shall be as a tree planted by the waters, and that spreadest out her roots by the river, and shall not see when heat cometh, but her leaf shall be green; and shall not be careful in the year of drought, neither shall cease from yielding fruit.
**JEREMIAH 17:7–8**

Suspicion is no less an enemy to virtue than to happiness. He that is already corrupt is naturally suspicious, and he that becomes suspicious will quickly be corrupt.
**JOHNSON**

Mistrust the man who finds everything good; the man who finds everything evil; and still more the man who is indifferent to everything.
**JOHANN LAVATER**

It is not the cares of today, but the cares of tomorrow that weigh a man down. For the needs of today we have corresponding strength given. For the morrow we are told to trust. It is not ours yet.
**GEORGE MACDONALD**

To be trusted is a greater compliment than to be loved.
**GEORGE MACDONALD**

A certain amount of distrust is wholesome, but not so much of others as of ourselves. Neither vanity nor conceit can exist in the same atmosphere with it.
**SUZANNE NECKER**

Do not let yourself be tainted with a barren skepticism.
**LOUIS PASTEUR**

No matter what your career may be, do not let yourselves become tainted by a deprecating and barren skepticism. Do not let yourselves be discouraged by the sadness of certain hours which pass over nations.
**LOUIS PASTEUR**

A feeling of distrust is always the last which a great mind acquires.
**JEAN BAPTISTE RACINE**

I have never accepted a bad check from anyone I did not trust.
**RON RASMUS**

The trust that we put in ourselves makes us feel trust in others.
**FRANÇOIS DE LA ROCHEFOUCAULD**

I think we may safely trust a good deal more than we do. We may waive just so much care of ourselves as we honestly bestow elsewhere.
**HENRY DAVID THOREAU**

We are always paid for our suspicion by finding what we suspect.
**HENRY DAVID THOREAU**

My father used to say: Never suspect people. It's better to be deceived or mistaken, which is only human, after all, than to be suspicious, which is common.
**STARK YOUNG**

## *Truth*

Truth is the discipline of the ascetic, the quest of the mystic, the faith of the simple, the ransom of the weak, the standard of the righteous, the doctrine of the meek, and the challenge of Nature. Together, all these constitute the Law of the Universe.
**JOHN HAY ALLISON**

Truth is the secret of eloquence and virtue, the basis of moral authority; it is the highest summit of art and of life.
**HENRI FRÉDÉRIC AMIEL**

If you want to annoy your neighbors, tell the truth about them.
**PIETRO ARETINO**

The search for truth is in one way hard and in another way easy, for it is evident that no one can master it fully or miss it wholly. But each adds a little to our knowledge of nature, and from all the facts assembled there arises a certain grandeur.
**ARISTOTLE**

We must hold fast to the austere but true doctrine as to what really governs politics and saves or destroys states. Having in mind things true, things elevated, things just, things pure, things amiable, things of good report; having these in mind, studying and loving these, is what saves states.
**MATTHEW ARNOLD**

Purity of soul cannot be lost without consent.
**ST. AUGUSTINE**

If it is not seemly, do it not; if it is not true, speak it not.
**MARCUS AURELIUS ANTONINUS**

If a man will begin with certainties, he will end with doubts; but if he will be content to begin with doubts, he will end in certainties.
**FRANCIS BACON**

Truth is the daughter of time, not of authority.
**FRANCIS BACON**

Power is not revealed by striking hard or often, but by striking true.
**HONORÉ DE BALZAC**

Any man can work when every stroke of his hand brings down the fruit rattling from the tree to the ground; but to labor in season and out of season, under every discouragement, by the power of truth . . . that requires a heroism which is transcendent.
**HENRY WARD BEECHER**

I believe that the time given to refutation in philosophy is usually time lost. Of the many attacks directed by many thinkers against each other, what

now remains? Nothing, or assuredly very little. That which counts and endures is the modicum of positive truth which each contributes. The true statement is, of itself, able to displace the erroneous idea, and becomes, without our having taken the trouble of refuting anyone, the best of refutations.
HENRI BERGSON

He that would make real progess in knowledge must dedicate his age as well as youth, the latter growth as well as the first fruits, at the altar of truth.
GEORGE BERKELEY

Truth is the cry of all, but the game of the few.
GEORGE BERKELEY

It is not moral to lie, but you don't always have to tell the truth.
IGNAS BERNSTEIN

As scarce as truth is, the supply has always been in excess of the demand.
JOSH BILLINGS

A truth that's told with bad intent
Beats all the lies you can invent.
WILLIAM BLAKE

Everything that is possible to be believed is an image of the truth.
WILLIAM BLAKE

Truth can never be told so as to be understood and not be believed.
WILLIAM BLAKE

There are those who so dislike the nude that they find something indecent in the naked truth.
FRANCIS HERBERT BRADLEY

The stream of time sweeps away errors, and leaves the truth for the inheritance of humanity.
GEORG BRANDES

We anticipate a time when the love of truth shall have come up to our love of liberty, and men shall be cordially tolerant and earnest believers both at once.
PHILLIPS BROOKS

Truth never hurts the teller.
ROBERT BROWNING

The exact contrary of what is generally believed is often the truth.
JEAN DE LA BRUYÈRE

Truth is a gem that is found at a great depth; whilst on the surface of the world all things are weighed by the false scale of custom.
LORD BYRON

Free and fair discussion will ever be found the firmest friend to truth.
G. CAMPBELL

Can there be a more horrible object in existence than an eloquent man not speaking the truth?
THOMAS CARLYLE

We must make the truth as simple, as persuasive, as impelling, and as interesting as the lie often seems to be. The truth can never enslave, it can never mesmerize. The truth is always within us. We do not awaken to an external fact, but to an eternal birthright which is the innermost of realities. Let us, then, recapture our thinking by getting back to first principles. When once we see the meaning of God, and man's relationship to Him, nothing can ever enslave our thinking again.
ERWIN D. CANHAM

I have discovered the art of fooling diplomats; I speak the truth and they never believe me.
CAMILLO BENSO DI CAVOUR

Truth will rise above falsehood as oil above water.
MIGUEL DE CERVANTES

We live in the present, we dream of the future and we learn eternal truths from the past.
MADAME CHIANG KAI-SHEK

Men occasionally stumble over the truth, but most of them pick themselves up and hurry off as if nothing had happened.
WINSTON CHURCHILL

Science is but a mere heap of facts, not a gold chain of truths, if we refuse to link it to the throne of God.
F. P. COBBE

To all new truths, or renovation of old truths, it must be as in the ark between the destroyed and the about-to-be renovated world. The raven must be sent out before the dove, and ominous controversy must precede peace and the olive wreath.
SAMUEL TAYLOR COLERIDGE

We must not let go manifest truths because we cannot answer all questions about them.
JEREMY COLLIER

Truth is the object of philosophy, but not always of philosophers.
JOHN CHURTON COLLINS

The interests of society often render it expedient not to utter the whole truth, the interests of science never: for in this field we have much more to fear from the deficiency of truth than from its abundance.
CHARLES CALEB COLTON

The statement has truth but not quite enough to be true.
FRANCIS M. CORNFORD

The pursuit of truth shall set you free—even if you never catch up with it.
CLARENCE DARROW

The love of truth is the stimulus to all noble conversation. This is the root of all the charities. The tree which springs from it may have a thousand branches, but they will all bear a golden and generous fruitage.
ORVILLE DEWEY

Frank and explicit: That is the right line to take when you wish to conceal your mind and confuse the minds of others.
BENJAMIN DISRAELI

There is no wisdom like frankness.
BENJAMIN DISRAELI

Time is precious but truth is more precious than time.
BENJAMIN DISRAELI

Truth is never to be expected from authors whose understanding is warped with enthusiasm.
JOHN DRYDEN

Personal magnetism is a mixture of rugged Honesty, pulsating Energy, and self-organized Intelligence. I believe, absolutely, that truth is the strongest and most powerful weapon a man can use, whether he is fighting for a reform or fighting for a sale.
ARTHUR DUNN

Accuracy is the twin brother of honesty; inaccuracy is a near kin to falsehood.
TRYON EDWARDS

Keep true, never be ashamed of doing right; decide on what you think is right, and stick to it.
GEORGE ELIOT

Every violation of truth is not only a sort of suicide in the liar, but is a stab at the health of human society.
RALPH WALDO EMERSON

God offers to every mind its choice between truth and repose. Take which you please—you can never have both.
RALPH WALDO EMERSON

Some men's words I remember so well that I must often use them to express my thought. Yes, because I perceive that we have heard the same truth, but they have heard it better.
RALPH WALDO EMERSON

The greatest homage we can pay to truth is to use it.
RALPH WALDO EMERSON

The highest compact we can make with our fellow is: Let there be truth between us two forevermore.
RALPH WALDO EMERSON

We are of different opinions at different hours but we always may be said to be at heart on the side of truth.
RALPH WALDO EMERSON

Truth travels down from the heights of philosophy to the humblest walks of life, and up from the simplest perceptions of an awakened intellect to the discoveries which almost change the face of the world. At every stage of its progress it is genial, luminous, creative.
EDWARD EVERETT

If we want to possess poise and to be capable of clear thinking, it is essential, first of all, to rise above the confusion of conflicting rumors and diverse opinions and listen to the eternal verities which God has given to men for their guidance and preservation.
LEON MERLE FLANDERS, D.D.

The search for truth is, as it always has been, the noblest expression of the human spirit. Man's insatiable desire for knowledge about himself, about his environment and the forces by which he is surrounded, gives life its meaning and purpose, and clothes it with final dignity. . . . And yet we know, deep in our hearts, that knowledge is not enough. . . . Unless we can anchor our knowledge to moral purposes, the ultimate result will be dust and ashes—dust and ashes that will bury the hopes and monuments of men beyond recovery.
RAYMOND B. FOSDICK

A man who seeks truth and loves it must be reckoned precious to any human society.
FREDERICK THE GREAT

The greatest and noblest pleasure which men can have in this world is to discover new truths; and the next is to shake off old prejudices.
FREDERICK THE GREAT

There is nothing certain but the unforeseen.
J. A. FROUDE

Truth is the nursing mother of genius. No man can be absolutely true to himself, eschewing cant, compromise, servile imitation, and complaisance without becoming original.
MARGARET FULLER

Beware of telling an improbable truth.
THOMAS FULLER

An exaggeration is a truth that has lost its temper.
KAHLIL GIBRAN

Truth is a deep kindness that teaches us to be content in our everyday life and share with the people the same happiness.
KAHLIL GIBRAN

Truth must be repeated again and again, because error is constantly being preached round about.
JOHANN WOLFGANG VON GOETHE

I don't want any yesmen around me. I want everyone to tell me the truth—even though it costs him his job.
SAMUEL GOLDWYN

It is as hard to tell the truth as to hide it.
BALTASAR GRACIÁN

The sense of ultimate truth is the intellectual counterpart of the esthetic sense of perfect beauty, or the moral sense of perfect good.
LORD HALIFAX

The greatest truths are the simplest; and so are the greatest men.
JULIUS C. HARE

The question is not whether a doctrine is beautiful but whether it is true. When we wish to go to a place, we do not ask whether the road leads through a pretty country, but whether it is the right road.
JULIUS C. HARE

In the long run, digging for truth has always proved not only more interesting but more profitable than digging for gold.
GEORGE R. HARRISON

Science is teaching man to know and reverence truth, and to believe that only as far as he knows and loves it can he live worthily on earth and vindicate the dignity of his spirit.
MOSES HARVEY

No man can, for any considerable time, wear one face to himself, and another to the multitude, without finally getting bewildered as to which is the true one.
NATHANIEL HAWTHORNE

The best test of truth is the power of the thought to get itself accepted in the competition of the market.
OLIVER WENDELL HOLMES

The longing for certainty and repose is in every human mind. But certainty is generally illusion and repose is not the destiny of man.
OLIVER WENDELL HOLMES

Truth is tough. It will not break, like a bubble, at a touch; nay, you may kick it about all day, like a football, and it will be round and full at evening.
OLIVER WENDELL HOLMES

Truth, when not sought after, rarely comes to light.
OLIVER WENDELL HOLMES

The search for truth is really a lot of good fun.
VERNON HOWARD

We must be truthful and fair in the ordinary affairs of life before we can be truthful and fair in patriotism and religion.
EDGAR WATSON HOWE

History has its truth; and so has legend hers.
VICTOR HUGO

Nothing great in science has ever been done by men, whatever their powers, in whom the divine afflatus of the truth-seeker was wanting.
THOMAS H. HUXLEY

There is no alleviation for the sufferings of mankind except veracity of thought and action, and the resolute facing of the world as it is.
THOMAS H. HUXLEY

The spirit of truth and the spirit of freedom—they are the pillars of society.
HENRIK IBSEN

If people are not being told the truth about their problems, the majority not only may, but invariably must, make the wrong judgments.
RALPH INGERSOLL

The ultimate test of what a truth means is the conduct it dictates or inspires.
WILLIAM JAMES

There is no worse lie than a truth misunderstood by those who hear it.
WILLIAM JAMES

We have to live today by what truth we can get today and be ready tomorrow to call it falsehood.
WILLIAM JAMES

Any truth is only true up to a certain point. When one oversteps the mark, it becomes a non-truth.
SÖREN KIERKEGAARD

Be sure of the foundation of your life. Know why you live as you do. Be ready to give a reason for it. Do not, in such a matter as life, build an opinion or custom on what you guess is true. Make it a matter of certainty and science.
THOMAS STARR KING

A presumed monopoly on truth obstructs negotiation and accommodation. Good results may be given up in the quest for ever-elusive ideal solutions.
HENRY KISSINGER

Let your desire for truth transcend all minor considerations. Ignorance is invariably confident. The man of knowledge learns to realize his own needs. Be honest and severe in your self-appraisal. Learn the art of learning, and you are well on the way to achievement. True greatness is reflective, not assertive.
GRENVILLE KLEISER

The real truths are those that can be invented.
KARL KRAUS

Not the truth of which one supposes himself possessed, but the effort he has made to arrive at truth, makes the worth of the man. For not by the possession, but by the investigation, of truth are his powers expanded. Possession makes us easy, indolent, proud. If God held all Truth shut in his right hand, and in his left nothing but the everrestless instinct for truth, and should say to me, Choose! I should bow humbly to his *left* hand, and say, "Father, give."
LESSING

The trouble with too many people is they believe the realm of truth always lies within their vision.
ABRAHAM LINCOLN

True opinions can prevail only if the facts to which they refer are known; if they are not known, false ideas are just as effective as true ones, if not a little more effective.
WALTER LIPPMANN

Truth is often eclipsed but never extinguished.
LIVY

It is one thing to show a man that he is in error, and another to put him in possession of truth.
JOHN LOCKE

Let us then be what we are, and speak what we think, and in all things keep ourselves loyal to truth.
HENRY WADSWORTH LONGFELLOW

Great truths are portions of the soul of man.
JAMES RUSSELL LOWELL

Peace if possible, but truth at any rate.
**MARTIN LUTHER**

There is no wisdom save in truth. Truth is everlasting, but our ideas about truth are changeable. Only a little of the first fruits of wisdom, only a few fragments of the boundless heights, breadths and depths of truth, have I been able to gather.
**MARTIN LUTHER**

And in the end, through the long ages of our quest for light, it will be found that truth is still mightier than the sword. For out of the welter of human carnage and human sorrow and human weal the indestructible thing that will always live is a sound idea.
**DOUGLAS MACARTHUR**

Let us labor for that larger comprehension of truth, and that more thorough repudiation of error, which shall make the history of mankind a series of ascending developments.
**HORACE MANN**

You need not tell all the truth, unless to those who have a right to know it all. But let all you tell be truth.
**HORACE MANN**

The most plausible reasons may be advanced for acts of a questionable, nature, but if we know in our hearts what is right, we will not long be deceived by the merely plausible. It is our great task today, first to perceive the truth, then to present it so boldly and sincerely that it will reach and find response in the hearts of all.
**JOYCE MAYHEW**

Not the violent conflict between parts of the truth, but the quiet suppression of half of it, is the formidable evil; there is always hope when people are forced to listen to both sides; it is when they attend to only one that errors harden into prejudices, and truth itself ceases to have the effect of truth, by being exaggerated into falsehood.
**JOHN STUART MILL**

All truth is safe and nothing else is safe; and he who keeps back the truth, or withholds it from men, from motives of expediency, is either a coward or a criminal or both.
**MAX MULLER**

The meaning, the value, the truth of life can be learned only by an actual performance of its duties, and truth can be learned and the soul saved in no other way.
**THEODORE T. MUNGER**

Truth is not a crystal one can put in one's pocket, but an infinite fluid into which one falls headlong.
**ROBERT MUSIL**

In the mountains of truth you never climb in vain.
**FRIEDRICH WILHELM NIETZSCHE**

Nobody dies nowadays of fatal truths: there are too many antidotes to them.
**FRIEDRICH WILHELM NIETZSCHE**

Truth has many shells. Each is the truth, but each represents a different aspect, depending on the bias, self-interest, or other psychological coloration which remains on the surface. As one after another shell is removed, the picture of truth changes. Only if one can reach the core, hidden beneath the protective covering, does one feel he knows the bare truth.
**LOUIS NIZER**

Truth lives in the cellar: error on the doorstep.
**AUSTIN O'MALLEY**

The man who moves, humbly, in the direction of truth comes closer to it than the partisan who

claims to have the truth assembled within the framework of some streamlined ideology.
**OSCAR OSTLUND**

Clocks will go as they are set; but man, irregular man, is never constant, never certain.
**THOMAS OTWAY**

Falsehood is in a hurry; it may be at any moment detected and punished; truth is calm, serene; its judgment cometh out of the chambers of eternity.
**JOSEPH PARKER**

We know truth, not only by reason, but also by the heart, and it is from this last that we know first principles; and reason, which has nothing to do with it, tries in vain to combat them. The skeptics who desire truth alone labor in vain.
**BLAISE PASCAL**

In every generation there has to be some fool who will speak the truth as he sees it.
**BORIS PASTERNAK**

Painful truths should be delivered in the softest terms, and expressed no farther than is necessary to produce their due effect.
**JAMES GATES PERCIVAL**

For he that will love life, and see good days, let him refrain his tongue from evil, and his lips that they speak no guile.
**I PETER 3:10**

There are certain times when most people are in a disposition of being informed, and 'tis incredible what a vast good a little truth might do, spoken in such seasons.
**ALEXANDER POPE**

Don't argue with the truth.
**PAUL A. POTTER**

Let not mercy and truth foresake thee: bind them about thy neck; write them upon the table of thine heart: so shalt thou find favour and good understanding in the sight of God and man.
**PROVERBS 3:3–4**

O send out thy light and thy truth: let them lead me; let them bring me unto thy holy hill, and to thy tabernacles.
**PSALMS 43:3**

Tell the truth and shame the Devil.
**FRANÇOIS RABELAIS**

Some persons profit by lying convincingly; I, by telling the truth unconvincingly. It is not so difficult as you might suppose, for in this world, where actually nothing is commonplace, people believe only in the commonplace, that which they are accustomed to see.
**ROBERT L. RIPLEY**

It is not the number of books you read, nor the variety of sermons you hear, nor the amount of religious conversation in which you mix, but it is the frequency and earnestness with which you meditate on these things till the truth in them becomes your own and part of your being, that ensures your growth.
**FREDERICK W. ROBERTSON**

There is no power on earth more formidable than the truth.
**MARGARET LEE RUNBECK**

Truth is so hard to tell, it sometimes needs fiction to make it plausible.
**DAGOBERT D. RUNES**

When a man tells you that he knows the exact truth about anything you are safe in inferring that he is an inexact man.
**BERTRAND RUSSELL**

It is a great advantage for a system of philosophy to be substantially true.
GEORGE SANTAYANA

There is hardly any man so strict as not to vary a little from truth when he is to make an excuse.
GEORGE SAVILE (LORD HALIFAX)

This above all, to thine own self be true, and it must follow, as the night the day, thou canst not then be false to any man.
WILLIAM SHAKESPEARE

As scarce as truth is, the supply has always been in excess of the demand.
HENRY WHEELER SHAW (JOSH BILLINGS)

My way of joking is to tell the truth; it's the funniest joke in the world.
GEORGE BERNARD SHAW

Weigh not so much what men assert, as what they prove. Truth is simple and naked, and needs not invention to apparel her comeliness.
SIR PHILIP SIDNEY

It is the calling of great men, not so much to preach new truths, as to rescue from oblivion those old truths which it is our wisdom to remember and our weakness to forget.
SYDNEY SMITH

Do we know that truth is life and falsehood spiritual death? Do we know that beauty is joy and ugliness sin? Do we know that justice is the condition of well-being and happiness, while injustice of any kind is defeat? In a universe of uncertainties these values alone are certain. They give order and design to living.
SYDNEY BRUCE SNOW, D.D.

As long as we can keep our international relations in the realm of conference rather than open conflict, we are giving truth more time to vindicate itself. And what we ourselves need is more faith in the power of truth.
RALPH W. SOCKMAN

The priceless heritage of the free and independent interchange of thought is not to be kept without ceaseless vigilance. Only by guarding the truth itself can we guard the greatest of all our liberties—the right to proclaim the truth. On that liberty rests the destiny of millions.
LORD SOUTHWOOD

He who would distinguish the true from the false must have an adequate idea of what is true and false.
BARUCH SPINOZA

We must never throw away a bushel of truth because it happens to contain a few grains of chaff.
DEAN STANLEY

Fear is not in the habit of speaking truth; when perfect sincerity is expected, perfect freedom must be allowed; nor has anyone who is apt to be angry when he hears the truth any cause to wonder that he does not hear it.
TACITUS

A cliche is a truth one doesn't believe.
BERNARD TAPER

It takes two to speak the truth—one to speak and another to hear.
HENRY DAVID THOREAU

Study to show thyself approved unto God, a workman that needeth not to be ashamed, rightly dividing the word of truth.
II TIMOTHY 3:15

There is no philosopher in the world so great but he believes a million things on the faith of other people and accepts a great many more truths than he demonstrates.
ALEXIS DE TOCQUEVILLE

Most writers regard truth as their most valuable possession, and therefore are most economical in it use.
MARK TWAIN

When in doubt, tell the truth.
MARK TWAIN

If a man never contradicts himself, it is because he never says anything.
MIGUEL DE UNAMUNO

There is no conflict between the Old and the New; the conflict is between the False and the True.
HENRY VAN DYKE

There are truths which are not for all men, nor for all occasions.
VOLTAIRE

In all science error precedes the truth, and it is better it should go first than last.
HORACE WALPOLE

Associate yourself with men of good quality, if you esteem your reputation. Be not apt to relate news, if you know not the truth thereof. Speak no evil of the absent, for it is unjust. Undertake not what you cannot perform, but be careful to keep your promise. There is but one straight course, and that is to seek truth, and pursue it steadily. Nothing but harmony, honesty, industry and frugality are necessary to make us a great and happy nation.
GEORGE WASHINGTON

At a distance from the theater of action, truth is not always related without embellishment.
GEORGE WASHINGTON

Truth will ultimately prevail where there are plans taken to bring it to light.
GEORGE WASHINGTON

As one may bring himself to believe almost anything he is inclined to believe, it makes all the difference whether we begin or end with the inquiry, "What is truth?"
RICHARD WHATELY

Every one wishes to have truth on his side, but it is not every one that sincerely wishes to be on the side of truth.
RICHARD WHATELY

Do not attempt to do a thing unless you are sure of yourself; but do not relinquish it simply because someone else is not sure of you.
STEWART E. WHITE

It is more important that a proposition be interesting than that it be true.
ALFRED NORTH WHITEHEAD

Do I contradict myself? Very well, then, I contradict myself; (I am large. I contain multitudes).
WALT WHITMAN

A thing is not necessarily true because a man dies for it.
OSCAR WILDE

A truth ceases to be true when more than one person believes in it.
OSCAR WILDE

It is perfectly monstrous the way people go about nowadays saying things against one, behind one's back, that are absolutely and entirely true.
OSCAR WILDE

All cruel people describe themselves as paragons of frankness.
TENNESSEE WILLIAMS

## *Trying*

God lends a helping hand to the man who tries hard.
AESCHYLUS

Man can have but what he strives for.
ARABIAN PROVERB

There is a calculated risk in everything. There has been a calculated risk in every stage of American development. The nation was built by men who took risks—pioneers who were not afraid of the wilderness, business men who were not afraid of failure, scientists who were not afraid of the truth, thinkers who were not afraid of progress, dreamers who were not afraid of action.
BROOKS ATKINSON

Experiment is folly when experience shows the way.
ROGER W. BABSON

As plants take hold, not for the sake of staying, but only that they may climb higher, so it is with men. By every part of our nature we clasp things above us, one after another, not for the sake of remaining where we take hold, but that we may go higher.
HENRY WARD BEECHER

Striving for excellence motivates you; striving for perfection is demoralizing.
HARRIET BRAIKER

You don't get hits by trying hard. You try easy.
GEORGE BRETT

'Tis not what man does which exalts him, but what man would do!
ROBERT BROWNING

The journey of a thousand miles starts with a single step.
CHINESE PROVERB

Any life truly lived is a risky business, and if one puts up too many fences against the risks one ends by shutting out life itself.
KENNETH S. DAVIS

All life is an experiment. The more experiments you make the better.
RALPH WALDO EMERSON

Venture nothing, and life is less than it should be.
MALCOLM FORBES

Don't be afraid to take a big step if one is indicated. You can't cross a chasm in two small jumps.
DAVID LLOYD GEORGE

Experiments don't fail. When you try something new, you either learn that it is worthwhile for you or that it does not work for you, and thus save future time by not trying it again.
STANLEY GOLDSTEIN

To get profit without risk, experience without danger, and reward without work, is as impossible as it is to live without being born.
A. P. GOUTHEV

I will spit on my hands and take better hold.
JOHN HEYWOOD

Until you try, you don't know what you can't do.
**HENRY JAMES**

Nothing will ever be attempted, if all possible objections must first be overcome.
**SAMUEL JOHNSON**

Keep on going and the chances are that you will stumble on something, perhaps when you are least expecting it. I have never heard of anyone stumbling on something sitting down.
**CHARLES F. KETTERING**

During the first period of a man's life the greatest danger is: not to take the risk. When once the risk has really been taken, then the greatest danger is to risk too much.
**SÖREN KIERKEGAARD**

Without risk, faith is an impossibility.
**SÖREN KIERKEGAARD**

Many a man never fails because he never tries.
**NORMAN MACEWAN**

To be alive at all involves some risk.
**HAROLD MACMILLAN**

If I have not attained, I have striven.
**OWEN MEREDITH**

Every noble acquisition is attended with its risks; he who fears to encounter the one must not expect to obtain the other.
**PIETRO METASTASIO**

Either do not attempt at all, or go through with it.
**OVID**

Contrary to the commonly accepted belief, it is the risk element in our capitalistic system which produces an economy of security. Risk brings out the ingenuity and resourcefulness which insure the success of enough ventures to keep the economy growing and secure.
**ROBERT RAWLS**

Trying is the touchstone to accomplishment.
**PAUL VON RINGELHEIM**

Whatever course you have chosen for yourself, it will not be a chore but an adventure if you bring to it a sense of the glory of striving—if your sights are set far above the merely secure and mediocre.
**DAVID SARNOFF**

I never heard of a person stumbling on something sitting down.
**WHITT N. SCHULTZ**

The attempt and not the deed confounds us.
**WILLIAM SHAKESPEARE**

A failure is not always a mistake; it may simply be the best one can do under the circumstances. The real mistake is to stop trying.
**B. F. SKINNER**

For want of a block, man will stumble at a straw.
**JONATHAN SWIFT**

No mistake or failure is as bad as to stop and not try again.
**JOHN WANAMAKER**

## *Tyranny*

It is far easier to act under conditions of tyranny than to think.
**HANNAH ARENDT**

A tyrant is the worst disease, and the cause of all others.
**WILLIAM BLAKE**

No totalitarians, no wars, no fears, famines or perils of any kind can really break a man's spirit until he breaks it himself by surrendering. Tyranny has many dread powers, but not the power to rule the spirit.
**EDGAR SHEFFIELD BRIGHTMAN**

Many of the greatest tyrants on the records of history have begun their reigns in the fairest manner. But this unnatural power corrupts both the heart and the understanding.
**EDMUND BURKE**

Tyrants forego all respect for humanity in proportion as they are sunk beneath it. Taught to believe themselves of a different species, they really become so, lose their participation with their kind, and in mimicking the god dwindle into the brute.
**WILLIAM HAZLITT**

There is bound to be a certain amount of trouble running any country. If you are president the trouble happens to you, but if you are a tyrant you can arrange things so that most of the trouble happens to other people.
**DONALD MARQUIS**

The harshest tyranny is that which acts under the protection of legality and the banner of justice.
**BARON DE MONTESQUIEU**

It is time to fear when tyrants seem to kiss.
**WILLIAM SHAKESPEARE**

# U

## Understanding

The eye of the understanding is like the eye of the sense; for as you may see great objects through small crannies or holes, so you may see great axioms of nature through small and contemptible instances.
**FRANCIS BACON**

Men are admitted into heaven not because they have curbed or governed their passions, but because they have cultivated their understandings.
**WILLIAM BLAKE**

The thing most people want is genuine understanding. If you can understand the feelings and moods of another person, you have something fine to offer.
**PAUL BROCK**

He who calls in the aid of an equal understanding doubles his own; and he who profits of a superior understanding raises his powers to a level with the height of the superior understanding he unites with.
**EDMUND BURKE**

We are lonely even in the milling crowds of a city, where we may only be recognized as customers for goods and services. Our personalities are weakened and starved by the impersonal life in a city. That is why there is so much wreckage in a city. Our families answer this need to some degree, but not completely. And so, in the last analysis it is only God who can give us the comfort of utter understanding.
**LYMAN V. CADY, D.D.**

Be not disturbed at being misunderstood; be disturbed rather at not being understanding.
**CHINESE PROVERB**

Brethren, be not children in understanding: howbeit in malice be ye children, but in understanding be men.
**I CORINTHIANS 14:20**

Nothing in life is to be feared. It is only to be understood.
**MARIE CURIE**

What better way is there to make men love one another than to make men understand one another. True charity comes only with clarity—just as mercy is but justice that understands. Surely the root of all evil is the inability to see clearly that which is.
**WILL DURANT**

There exists a passion for comprehension, just as there exists a passion for music. That passion is rather common in children, but gets lost in most people later on. Without this passion there would be neither mathematics nor natural science.
**ALBERT EINSTEIN**

If you want understanding try giving some.
**MALCOLM FORBES**

When you don't understand, it's sometimes easier to look like you do.
**MALCOLM FORBES**

"With all thy getting, get understanding," is the banner under which these *Forbes* editorials have appeared since the first issue of the publication. We have no illusions about what great wealth can do and what it cannot do. We believe in the worthwhileness of striving by all worthy means to attain success and to attain wealth. Simply because we are

convinced that no amount of money is worth the sacrifice of one's better instincts, of one's self-respect—of one's soul, if you wish—simply because we are convinced that riches not gained legitimately and decently are not worth having. . . .
**B. C. FORBES**

To understand and to be understood makes our happiness on earth.
**GERMAN PROVERB**

The great need today in every phase of our social, economical and political life is understanding. It has always been so, but today the need is even greater.
**CHARLES R. HOOK**

In the deep, unwritten wisdom of life there are many things to be learned that cannot be taught. We never know them by hearing them spoken, but we grow into them by experience and recognize them through understanding. Understanding is a great experience in itself, but it does not come through instruction.
**ANTHONY HOPE**

Understanding is more comprehensive than intellect because it intuits truths that cautious intellect can get sight of but never embrace—like a sea-gazer who never plunges in. When we understand, we have left intellect on the shore and don't need it and its crabbed analyses.
**DAVID S. JONES**

The great art of learning is to understand but little at a time.
**JOHN LOCKE**

There are three kinds of brains: One understands of itself, another can be taught to understand, and the third can neither understand of itself or be taught to understand.
**NICCOLÒ MACHIAVELLI**

True fortitude of understanding consists in not suffering what we do know to be disturbed by what we do not know.
**WILLIAM PALEY**

Thoughts are wonderful things, that they can bring two people, so far apart, into harmony and understanding for even a little while.
**ERNEST PYLE**

If you wish to please people, you must begin by understanding them.
**CHARLES READE**

A man of understanding finds less difficulty in submitting to a wrong-headed fellow, than in attempting to set him right.
**FRANÇOIS DE LA ROCHEFOUCAULD**

The ways to knowledge are multitudinous—the way to understanding is devious.
**CHARLES B. ROGERS**

Each of us is a little lonely, deep inside, and cries to be understood.
**LEO ROSTEN**

Our greatest opportunities for advancing productivity and improving living standards are to be found in the field of human relationships. Having achieved a better understanding of each other and their common responsibility to consumers and investors, both management and labor should do all in their power to educate the American public to understanding of the simple economic facts that underlie our industrial and business relationships.
**LOUIS RUTHENBURG**

No one really understands the grief or joy of another. We always imagine that we are approaching some other, but our lines of travel are actually parallel.
**FRANZ SCHUBERT**

It is the great destiny of human science, not to ease man's labors or prolong his life, noble as those ends may be nor to serve the ends of power, but to enable man to walk upright without fear in a world which he at length will understand and which is his home.
**PAUL B. SEARS**

Most men take least notice of what is plain, as if that were of no use; but puzzle their thoughts, and lose themselves in those vast depths and abysses which no human understanding can fathom.
**SHERLOCK**

When the heart is won, the understanding is easily convinced.
**CHARLES SIMMONS**

Depend on this one fact: The future of mankind, peace, progress and prosperity must be finally determined by the extent to which men can be brought to a state of common and honest understanding.
**RALPH C. SMEDLEY**

Understanding comes through communication, and through understanding we find the way to peace.
**RALPH C. SMEDLEY**

To fulfill the hopes of democracy in our American adventure we must attempt to understand one another better, must try to avoid all unnecessary clash of personalities, and develop calmly, before situations arise, suitable techniques for the handling of our differences. No opinion at variance with ours should ever be permitted to threaten our basic human relationship with anyone.
**J. RICHARD SNEED**

I have tried sedulously not to laugh at the acts of man, nor to lament them, nor to detest them, but to understand them.
**BARUCH SPINOZA**

I know no evil so great as the abuse of the understanding, and yet there is no one vice more common.
**RICHARD STEELE**

Unless we give part of ourselves away, unless we can live with other people and understand them and help them, we are missing the most essential part of our own human lives.
**HAROLD TAYLOR**

My intimate contact with those great producing organizations and the men in them has given me great confidence in the machinery and the spirit now available for the building of a proper world. I do not mean that our industrial system is as good as it should be, but if I am looking for intelligent and unselfish understanding of our problems, and a generous approach to their solution, I shall seek it among the makers and builders with far more confidence than among the talkers, the manipulators and the vote seekers.
**WALTER TEAGUE**

We shall see but little if we require to understand what we see. How few things can a man measure with the tape of his understanding.
**HENRY DAVID THOREAU**

The man who can put himself in the place of other men, who can understand the workings of their minds, need never worry about what the future has in store for him.
**OWEN D. YOUNG**

## *Usefulness*

Nothing in this world is so good as usefulness. It binds your fellow creatures to you, and you to them; it tends to the improvement of your own character

and gives you a real importance in society, much beyond what any artificial station can bestow.
B. C. BRODIE

Everyone knows the usefulness of the useful, but no one knows the usefulness of the useless.
CHUANG-TZU

All the good things of the world are no further good to us than as they are of use; and of all we may heap up we enjoy only as much as we can use, and no more.
DANIEL DEFOE

One principal reason why men are so often useless is, that they divide and shift their attention among a multiplicity of objects and pursuits.
NATHANIEL EMMONS

Whatever you have, you must either use or lose.
HENRY FORD

A useless life is only an early death.
JOHANN WOLFGANG VON GOETHE

The practical man is the adventurer, the investigator, the believer in research, the asker of questions, the man who refuses to believe that perfection has been attained.... There is no thrill or joy in merely doing that which any one can do.... It is always safe to assume, not that the old way is wrong, but that there may be a better way.
HENRY R. HARROWER

What praise is implied in the simple epithet useful! What reproach in the contrary.
DAVID HUME

A barking dog is often more useful than a sleeping lion.
WASHINGTON IRVING

We must make automatic and habitual, as early as possible, as many useful actions as we can.... The more of the details of our daily life we can hand over to the effortless custody of automatism, the more our higher powers of mind will be set free for their own proper work.
WILLIAM JAMES

Take two workers in an organization. One limits his giving by wages he is paid. He insists on being paid instantly for what he does. That shows he is a man of limited imagination and intelligence. The other is a natural giver. His philosophy of life compels him to make himself useful. He knows that if he takes care of other people's problems they will be forced to take care of him to protect their own interests. The more a man gives of himself to his work, the more he will get out of it, both in wages and satisfaction.
J. T. MACKEY

Success can corrupt, usefulness can only exalt.
DIMITRI MITROPOLOUS

When no new thoughts fill the mind—when no horizons beckon—when life is in the past, not in the future—you are on the way to uselessness.
FREDERICK K. STAMM

It is not paradox to say that in our most theoretical moods we may be nearest to our most practical applications.
ALFRED NORTH WHITEHEAD

Any use of a human being in which less is demanded of him and less is attributed to him than his full status is a degradation and a waste.
NORBERT WIENER

# V

## Vacations

A vacation is a sunburn at premium prices.
HAL CHADWICKE

Vacations for wage earners have proved both popular with workers and profitable for employers. Unfortunately, the majority of large employers have not yet followed the example set by a number of progressive corporations. I don't know of a single company that has abandoned vacations for wage earners after having tried the experiment. But I do know many that are delighted with the fruits they have gathered. Under some of the plans vacations with pay must be earned by good behavior, punctuality, etc. . . . The best results have come where the treatment has been regarded as most liberal.
B. C. FORBES

The average vacation is one-tenth playing—nine-tenths paying.
ARNOLD GLASOW

The longing to get away from it all never was so great as in our present time of tension and trouble. We want something to lift us out of the mess into which much of life seems to have fallen.
GLENN STEWART

Vacation is that time when you wish you had something to do while doing nothing.
FRANK TYGER

A vacation is what you take when you can no longer take what you've been taking.
EARL WILSON

## Values

One of the great arts in living is to learn the art of accurately appraising values. Everything that we think, that we earn, that we have given to us, that in any way touches our consciousness, has its own value. These values are apt to change with the mood, with time, or because of circumstances. We cannot safely tie to any material value. The values of all material possessions change continually, sometimes over night. Nothing of this nature has any permanent set value. The real values are those that stay by you, give you happiness and enrich you. They are the human values.
GEORGE MATTHEW ADAMS

He, whose first emotion on the view of an excellent production is to undervalue it, will never have one of his own to show.
JOHN AIKEN

Look beneath the surface; let not the several quality of a thing nor its worth escape thee.
MARCUS AURELIUS ANTONINUS

Nothing of worth or weight can be achieved with half a mind, with a faint heart and with lame endeavor.
ISAAC BARROW

I know it is more agreeable to walk upon carpets than to lie upon dungeon floors; I know it is pleasant to have all the comforts and luxuries of civilization; but he who cares only for these things is worth no more than a butterfly contented and thoughtless

upon a morning flower; and who ever thought of rearing a tombstone to a last-summer's butterfly?
**HENRY WARD BEECHER**

Every man is valued in this world as he shows by his conduct that he wishes to be valued.
**JEAN DE LA BRUYÈRE**

Men are valued, not for what they are, but for what they seem to be.
**EDWARD BULWER-LYTTON**

In a world where so much seems to be hidden by the smoke of falsity and moral degeneration, we Americans must grasp firmly the ideals which have made this country great. We must reaffirm the basic human values that have guided our forefathers. A revival of old-fashioned patriotism and a grateful acknowledgment of what our country has done for us would be good for all our souls.
**MANTON S. EDDY**

Sometimes one pays most for the things one gets for nothing.
**ALBERT EINSTEIN**

Try not to become a man of success, but rather a man of value.
**ALBERT EINSTEIN**

One's real worth is never a quantifiable thing.
**MALCOLM FORBES**

Victory is sweetest when you've known defeat.

Ability will never catch up with the demand for it.

You pay for everything, even including speaking your mind (with or without one).

Too many people overvalue what they are not and undervalue what they are.
**MALCOLM FORBES**

There is too much stress today on material things. I try to teach my children not so much the value of cents, but a sense of values.
**MORRIS FRANKLIN**

The worthless usually live long.
**BALTASAR GRACIÁN**

The function of values is to give us the illusion of purpose in life.
**JOHN P. GRIER**

A true measure of your worth includes all the benefits others have gained from your success.
**CULLEN HIGHTOWER**

A man's worth is what he is divided by what he thinks he is.
**ERIC HOFFER**

We cannot define God or any of the real values of life. What is the vague thing called forth that is worth living and dying for? Beauty, truth, friendship, love, creation—these are the great values of life. We can't prove them, or explain them, yet they are the most stable things in our lives.
**JESSE HERMAN HOLMES**

Obsolescence is a factor which says that the new thing I bring you is worth more than the unused value of the old thing.
**CHARLES F. KETTERING**

Cultivate fine taste and discrimination in your choice of things. Get a right idea of values. Material possessions that you do not need and cannot use may be only an encumbrance. Let your guiding rule be not how much but how good. A thing you do not want is dear at any price. Avoid surplusage. Choose things that express your own individuality. You must possess your things or they will possess

you. Look for quality rather than quantity. Unnecessary possessions bring unnecessary care and responsibility. Excess is waste. Have an occasional stock-taking and eliminate unsparingly.
**GRENVILLE KLEISER**

Today's value system considers holding on to one's money as important as holding on to one's sanity.
**JAMES A. KNIGHT**

Civilization ceases when we no longer respect and no longer put into their correct places the fundamental values, such as work, family and country; such as the individual, honor and religion.
**R. P. LEBRET**

Today we are afraid of simple words like goodness and mercy and kindness. We don't believe in the good old words because we don't believe in the good old values anymore.
**LIN YUTANG**

It is difficult to make a man miserable while he feels he is worthy of himself and claims kindred to the great God who made him.
**ABRAHAM LINCOLN**

Sometimes great life-changing values come to us in brief moments of contact with high-potential personalities.
**WALTER MACPEEK**

Minds are cluttered from the age of six with the values of others—values which bear little relation to their own private capacities, needs and desires.
**MARYA MANNES**

Man's chief purpose . . . is the creation and preservation of values; that is what gives meaning to our civilization, and the participation in this is what gives significance, ultimately, to the individual human life.
**LEWIS MUMFORD**

The greatest gains and values are farthest from being appreciated. We easily come to doubt if they exist. We soon forget them. They are the highest reality.
**HENRY DAVID THOREAU**

There is no readier way for a man to bring his own worth into question than by endeavoring to detract from the worth of other men.
**JOHN TILLOTSON**

A sentimentalist is a man who sees an absurd value in everything and doesn't know the market price of a single thing.
**OSCAR WILDE**

## *Vanity*

An ostentatious man will rather relate a blunder or an absurdity he has committed, than be debarred from talking of his own dear person.
**JOSEPH ADDISON**

Vanity is a mortgage that must be deducted from the value of a man.
**OTTO EDUARD BISMARCK**

Don't you feel disgusted when you see some fellow strutting along with the air of a peacock? Doesn't the pompous gentleman cause you to laugh—or swear? Isn't vanity the essence of childishness? I have been trying to analyze in my own mind whether more or fewer of our so-called big men are obsessed with pride today than 20 years ago. I believe that more of our leaders are now democratic, approachable, likeable fellows than was the case in the earlier years of this century. . . . The press and the people have abundantly brought it home to the rich that their riches do not entitle them to any special deference or homage. . . .
**B. C. FORBES**

I have seldom seen much ostentation and much learning met together.
**JOSEPH HALL**

Vanity is truly the motive-power that moves humanity, and it is flattery that greases the wheels.
**JEROME K. JEROME**

Nothing so soothes our vanity as a display of greater vanity in others; it makes us vain, in fact, of our modesty.
**LOUIS KRONENBERGER**

When you are disposed to be vain of your mental acquirements, look up to those who are more accomplished than yourself, that you may be fired with emulation; but when you feel dissatisfied with your circumstances, look down on those beneath you, that you may learn contentment.
**HANNAH MORE**

He who denies his own vanity usually has it in so brutal a form that he must shut his eyes in order to avoid despising himself.
**FRIEDRICH WILHELM NIETZSCHE**

One will not go far wrong if one attributes extreme actions to vanity, average ones to habit and petty ones to fear.
**FRIEDRICH WILHELM NIETZSCHE**

There are no grades of vanity, there are only grades of ability in concealing it.
**MARK TWAIN**

It is curious how vanity helps the successful man and wrecks the failure.
**OSCAR WILDE**

The surest cure for vanity is loneliness.
**THOMAS WOLFE**

## *Violence*

Violence is the last refuge of the incompetent.
**ISAAC ASIMOV**

Violence is just when kindness is vain.
**PIERRE CORNEILLE**

Violent excitement exhausts the mind and leaves it withered and sterile.
**FRANÇOIS FÉNELON**

Can you understand why the Congress, most states and most cities refuse to pass legislation requiring the registration and licensing of any and all guns? For the life of me, I can't. We must register our cars and be licensed to drive. In many places we must get licenses for dogs and even bicycles. Being required to register firearms and show the competence and capacity to handle them hardly seems unreasonable, hardly seems an infringement of freedom.
What is it that blocks such legislation? Why do they block it? How are they able to block it?
**MALCOLM FORBES**

Violence ever defeats its own ends. Where you cannot drive you can always persuade. A gentle word, a kind look, a good-natured smile can work wonders and accomplish miracles. There is a secret pride in every human heart that revolts at tyranny. You may order and drive an individual, but you cannot make him respect you.
**WILLIAM HAZLITT**

What a vast difference there is between the barbarism that precedes culture and the barbarism that follows it.
**FRIEDRICH HEBBEL**

It is bad enough to persevere in barbarism; it is worse to relapse into it; but worst of all is consciously to seek it out.
**AUREL KOLNAI**

Nothing good ever comes of violence.
**MARTIN LUTHER**

Salvation and justice are not to be found in revolution, but in evolution through concord. Violence has ever achieved only destruction, not construction; the kindling of passions, not their pacification; the accumulation of hate and destruction, not the reconciliation of the contending parties; and it has reduced men and parties to the difficult task of building slowly after sad experience on the ruins of discord.
**POPE PIUS XII**

If you injure your neighbor, better not do it by halves.
**GEORGE BERNARD SHAW**

## *Virtue*

When we live habitually with the wicked, we become necessarily their victims or their disciples; on the contrary, when we associate with the virtuous we form ourselves in imitation of their virtues, or at least lose, every day, something of our faults.
**AGAPET**

There is virtue in country houses, in gardens and orchards, in fields, streams and groves, in rustic recreations and plain manners, that neither cities nor universities enjoy.
**AMOS BRONSON ALCOTT**

If we can implant in our people the Christian virtues which we sum up in the world character, and, at the same time, give them a knowledge of the line which should be drawn between voluntary action and governmental compulsion in a democracy, and of what can be accomplished within the stern laws of economics, we will enable them to retain their freedom, and at the same time, make them worthy to be free.
**WINTHROP W. ALDRICH**

There are some jobs in which it is impossible for a man to be virtuous.
**ARISTOTLE**

I'm as pure as the driven slush.
**TALLULAH BANKHEAD**

Only have enough of little virtues and common fidelities, and you need not mourn because you are neither a hero nor a saint.
**HENRY WARD BEECHER**

It is a very easy thing to devise good laws; the difficulty is to make them effective. The great mistake is that of looking on all men as virtuous, or thinking that they can be made so by laws; and consequently the greatest art of a politician is to render vices serviceable to the cause of virtue.
**LORD BOLINGBROKE**

The virtues which keep this world sweet and the faithfulness which keeps it steadfast are chiefly those of the average man. The danger of the two-talent man is that he will be content with mediocrity.
**W. RUSSELL BOWIE**

It is easier to enrich ourselves with a thousand virtues, than to correct ourselves of a single fault.
**JEAN DE LA BRUYÈRE**

For most men, and most circumstances, pleasure—tangible material prosperity in this world—is the safest test of virtue. Progress has ever been through the pleasures rather than through the extreme sharp

virtues, and the most virtuous have leaned to excess rather than to ascetism.
SAMUEL BUTLER

Virtue, as such, naturally procures considerable advantages to the virtuous.
JOSEPH BUTLER

Ethical living is the indispensable condition of all that is most worthwhile in the world.
ERNEST CALDECOTT

I have always thought it would be easier to redeem a man steeped in vice and crime than a greedy, narrow-minded, pitiless merchant.
ALBERT CAMUS

We are all exceptional cases. Each man insists on being innocent, even if it means accusing the whole human race, and heaven.
ALBERT CAMUS

Virtue is like health: the harmony of the whole man.
THOMAS CARLYLE

What is virtue? Reason in practice.
J. J. DE CHENIER

The door to virtue is heavy and hard to push.
CHINESE PROVERB

The more virtuous any man is, the less easily does he suspect others to be vicious.
CICERO

Virtue and decency are so nearly related that it is difficult to separate them from each other but in our imagination.
CICERO

Virtue is its own reward.
CICERO

Cannot our ethical system be taught upon a non-sectarian basis in all schools, squaring it up with the sciences to the end that our boys and girls, when they emerge, are not ripe fruit for the disbelieving skeptics and the intellectual exhibitionists?
ANDREW V. CLEMENTS

He that has energy enough to root out a vice, should go further, and try to plant a virtue in its place, otherwise he will have his labor to renew. A strong soil that has produced weeds may be made to produce wheat.
CHARLES CALEB COLTON

He that is good will infallibly become better, and he that is bad will as certainly become worse, for vice, virtue and time are three things that never stand still.
CHARLES CALEB COLTON

Nothing more completely baffles one who is full of tricks and duplicity than straightforward and simple integrity in another.
CHARLES CALEB COLTON

Sincerity and truth are the basis of every virtue.
CONFUCIUS

Blessings ever wait on virtuous deeds, and though a late, a sure reward succeeds.
WILLIAM CONGREVE

What is virtue? It is to hold yourself to your fullest development as a person and as a responsible member of the human community.
ARTHUR DOBRIN

Man is not merely a combination of appetites, instincts, passions and curiosity. Something more is needed to explain great human deeds, virtues, sacrifices, martyrdom. There is an element in the great

mystics, the saints, the prophets, whose influence has been felt for centuries, which escapes mere intelligence.
LECOMTE DU NOÜY

A little integrity is better than any career.
RALPH WALDO EMERSON

The only reward of virtue is virtue.
RALPH WALDO EMERSON

If virtue promises happiness, prosperity and peace, then progress in virtue is progress in each of these; for to whatever point the perfection of anything brings us, progress is always an approach toward it.
EPICTETUS

The soul that companies with virtue is like an ever-flowing source. It is a pure, clear, and wholesome draught, sweet, rich and generous of its store, that injures not, neither destroys.
EPICTETUS

When grown people speak of the innocence of children, they don't really know what they mean. Pressed, they will go a step further and say, "Well, ignorance then." The child is neither. There is no crime which a boy of 11 has not envisaged long ago. His only innocence is, he may not yet be old enough to desire the fruits of it. His ignorance is, he does not know how to commit it.
WILLIAM FAULKNER

Integrity begins with a person being willing to be honest with himself.
CORT R. FLINT

Compliment others on the virtues they have; and they're not half as pleased as being complimented for the ones they don't have.
MALCOLM FORBES

You're fortunate when you can afford to be virtuous.
MALCOLM FORBES

What is called virtue in the common sense of the word has nothing to do with this or that man's prosperity, or even happiness.
J. A. FROUDE

Want of prudence is too frequently the want of virtue.
OLIVER GOLDSMITH

Never put much confidence in such as put no confidence in others. A man prone to suspect evil is mostly looking in his neighbor for what he sees in himself. As to the pure all things are pure, even so to the impure all things are impure.
JULIUS C. HARE

If we want more brotherhood and goodwill, more intelligence, more clear thinking, more honesty and sincerity, more tolerance and human understanding we must concentrate upon cultivating these qualities within ourselves. There is a natural progression in social advancement from the individual spirit to the family, to the community, to the nation and to the world at large. The line of progress can move in no other direction. There is no substitute for personal integrity.
HOWARD W. HINTZ, D.D.

Becky Sharp's acute remark that it is not difficult to be virtuous on ten thousand a year has its applications to nations; and it is futile to expect a hungry and squalid population to be anything but violent and gross.
THOMAS H. HUXLEY

There can be no final truth in ethics any more than in physics, until the last man has had his experience and said his say.
WILLIAM JAMES

There is a natural aristocracy among men. The grounds for this are virtue and talents.
THOMAS JEFFERSON

Integrity without knowledge is weak and useless, and knowledge without integrity is dangerous and dreadful.
SAMUEL JOHNSON

Let them call it mischief; when it is past and prospered, it will be virtue.
BEN JONSON

Wisdom is knowing what to do next, virtue is doing it.
DAVID STARR JORDAN

Virtue by calculation is the virtue of vice.
JOSEPH JOUBERT

Integrity is praised, and starves.
JUVENAL

Courage, energy and patience are the virtues which appeal to my heart.
FRITZ KREISLER

I have three precious things which I hold fast and prize. The first is gentleness; the second is frugality; the third is humility, which keeps me from putting myself before others. Be gentle and you can be bold; be frugal and you can be liberal; avoid putting yourself before others and you can become a leader among men.
LAO-TZU

What do I owe to my times, to my country, to my neighbors, to my friends? Such are the questions which a virtuous man ought often to ask himself.
JOHANN LAVATER

The morals of men are more governed by their pursuits than by their opinions. A type of virtue is first formed by circumstances, and men afterwards make it the model upon which their theories are framed.
W. E. H. LECKY

Deliberate virtue is never worth much: The virtue of feeling or habit is the thing.
GEORG CHRISTOPH LICHTENBERG

Virtue is everywhere that which is thought praiseworthy; and nothing else but that which has the allowance of public esteem is called virtue.
JOHN LOCKE

A man can be as truly a saint in a factory as in a monastery, and there is as much need of him in the one as in the other.
ROBERT J. MCCRACKEN

Most men admire virtue, who follow not her lore.
JOHN MILTON

Industry, economy, honesty and kindness form a quartet of virtue that will never be improved upon.
JAMES OLIVER

When we are planning for posterity, we ought to remember that virtue is not hereditary.
THOMAS PAINE

In all things preserve integrity; and the consciousness of thine own uprightness will alleviate the toil of business.
WILLIAM PALEY

A large part of virtue consists in good habits.
WILLIAM PALEY

The strength of a man's virtue must not be measured by his occasional efforts, but by his ordinary life.
BLAISE PASCAL

We are apt to love praise, but not to deserve it. But if we would deserve it, we must love virtue more than that.
**William Penn**

Whatsoever things are true, whatsoever things are honest, whatsoever things are just, whatsoever things are pure, whatsoever things are lovely, whatsoever things are of good report; if there be any virtue, and if there be any praise, think on these things.
**Philippians 4:8**

Virtue, though she gets her beginning from nature, yet receives her finishing touches from learning.
**Quintilian**

If self-knowledge is the road to virtue, so is virtue still more the road to self-knowledge.
**Jean Paul Richter**

If vanity does not entirely overthrow the virtues, at least it makes them all totter.
**François de La Rochefoucauld**

Some people with great virtues are disagreeable, while others with great vices are delightful.
**François de La Rochefoucauld**

We need greater virtues to sustain good than evil fortune.
**François de La Rochefoucauld**

What we take for virtue is often nothing but an assemblage of different actions, and of different interests, that fortune or our industry knows how to arrange.
**François de La Rochefoucauld**

A man need not extol his virtues, nor comment on his failings; his friends know the former, and his enemies will search out the latter.
**Charles B. Rogers**

A virtue and a muscle are alike. If neither of them is exercised they get weak and flabby.
**Richard L. Rooney**

Though conditions have grown puzzling in their complexity, though changes have been vast, yet we may remain absolutely sure of one thing; that now as ever in the past, and as it will ever be in the future, there can be no substitute for elemental virtues, for the elemental qualities to which we allude when we speak of a man, not only as a good man, but as emphatically a man. We can build up the standard of individual citizenship and individual well-being, we can raise the national standard and make it what it can and shall be made, only by each of us steadfastly keeping in mind that there can be no substitute for the world-old commonplace qualities of truth, justice, and courage, thrift, industry, common sense and genuine sympathy with the fellow feelings of others.
**Theodore Roosevelt**

No virtue is safe that is not enthusiastic.
**John Seeley**

Nature does not bestow virtue; to be good is an art.
**Seneca**

To be ambitious of true honor, of the true glory and perfection of our natures, is the very principle and incentive of virtue.
**Sir Philip Sidney**

Integrity is the first step to true greatness. Men love to praise, but are slow to practice it.
**Charles Simmons**

The man who cannot believe in himself cannot believe in anything else. The basis of all integrity and character is whatever faith we have in our own integrity.
**Roy L. Smith**

The shortest and surest way to live with honor in the world is to be in reality what we would appear to be; and if we observe, we shall find that all human virtues increase and strengthen themselves by the practice and experience of them.
**SOCRATES**

We live in a war of two antagonistic ethical philosophies, the ethical policy taught in the books and schools, and the success policy.
**WILLIAM GRAHAM SUMNER**

The wicked are wicked, no doubt, and they go astray and they fall, and they come by their deserts; but who can tell the mischief which the very virtuous do?
**WILLIAM MAKEPEACE THACKERAY**

Virtue has never been as respectable as money.
**MARK TWAIN**

Good company and good discourse are the sinews of virtue.
**IZAAK WALTON**

Few men have virtue to withstand the highest bidder.
**GEORGE WASHINGTON**

High ethical standards bring about efficient business methods.
**WATTS**

The pure are not fortune's favorites.
**WELSH PROVERB**

Virtue has its own reward, but no sale at the box office.
**MAE WEST**

One should seek virtue for its own sake and not from hope or fear, or any external motive. It is in virtue that happiness consists, for virtue is the state of mind which tends to make the whole of life harmonious.
**ZENO OF CITIUM**

## *Voting*

Always vote for a principle, though you vote alone, and you may cherish the sweet reflection that your vote is never lost.
**JOHN QUINCY ADAMS**

If the people are to be the final tribunal then they must vote for what is right rather than according to their own selfish interests, else we are treading the path of danger.
**HENRY L. DOHERTY**

Our American heritage is threatened as much by our own indifference as it is by the most unscrupulous office or by the most powerful foreign threat. The future of this republic is in the hands of the American voter.
**DWIGHT D. EISENHOWER**

A lot of voters always cast their ballot for the candidate who seems to them to be one of the people. That means he must have the same superstitions, the same unbalanced prejudices, and the same lack of understanding of public finances that are characteristic of the majority. A better choice would be a candidate who has a closer understanding and a better education than the majority. Too much voting is based on affability rather than on ability.
**WILLIAM FEATHER**

People vote their resentment, not their appreciation. The average man does not vote for anything, but against something.
**WILLIAM BENNETT MUNRO**

Bad officials are elected by good citizens who do not vote.
**GEORGE JEAN NATHAN**

## Wages

The big salaries in business always go to those who have what it takes to get things done. That is true not only of those executives who guide the destinies of a business, but it is true of those upon whom those executives must depend for results.
J. C. ASPLEY

A fair day's-wage for a fair day's-work: it is as just a demand as governed men ever made of governing. It is the everlasting right of man.
THOMAS CARLYLE

Always remember that there is a law of compensation which operates just as infallibly as gravitation, and that victory goes at last where it ought to, and that this is just as true of individuals as of nations.
WILLIAM FEATHER

Note to salary setters: Pay your people the least possible and you'll get from them the same.
MALCOLM FORBES

Of course, it is not the employer who pays wages. He only handles the money. It is the product that pays wages and it is the management that arranges the production so that the product may pay the wages.
HENRY FORD

I've noticed two things about men who get big salaries. They are almost invariably men who, in conversation or in conference, are adaptable. They quickly get the other fellow's view. They are more eager to do this than to express their own ideas. Also, they state their own point of view convincingly.
JOHN HALLOCK

A day's pay for a day's work is more than adequate when both the work and the pay are appreciated as much as they are expected.
CULLEN HIGHTOWER

There's always somebody who is paid too much and taxed too little—and it's always somebody else.
CULLEN HIGHTOWER

The ideal income is a thousand dollars a day—and expenses.
PIERRE LORILLARD

Anybody who has any doubt about the resourcefulness or the ingenuity of a plumber never got a bill from one.
GEORGE MEANY

One of labor's long-range objectives is to achieve in every basic industry a guaranteed annual wage so that the consumers of this country can have a sustained income month in and month out, because only on that basis can we sustain an economy of full employment and full production and full distribution.
WALTER P. REUTHER

Even Noah got no salary for the first six months—partly on account of the weather and partly because he was learning navigation.
MARK TWAIN

## War

The leaders of the French Revolution excited the poor against the rich; this made the rich poor, but it never made the poor rich.
**FISHER AMES**

The demonstration that war, however victorious, spells ruin, has results alike disastrous and incalculable, produces a political and social chaos whose end no man can see—all this is too plain, too inescapable, not to make the desire to avoid it a genuine one. The explanation is that popular thought does not grasp the relation between policies which seem on the surface legitimate or advantageous, and the final effect as a cause of war and chaos.
**SIR NORMAN ANGELL**

If you think old soldiers just fade away, try getting into your old army uniform.
**ANONYMOUS**

War would end if the dead could return.
**BALDWIN**

Why does civilization keep on receding? Each war, even if won, is a fresh defeat to our intelligence.
**SARAH BERNHARDT**

I am convinced that the best service a retired general can perform is to turn in his tongue along with his suit, and to mothball his opinions.
**GEN. OMAR NELSON BRADLEY**

The flint of war routinely sparks,
No steel need ever strike it.
To arms! is nature's hearty cry;
We fight because we like it.
**ART BUCK**

I wonder what our world would be like if men always had sacrificed as freely to prevent wars as to win them.
**FRANK A. CLARK**

The army is a good book in which to study human life. One learns there to put his hand to everything. The most delicate and rich are forced to see poverty and live with it; to understand distress; and to know how rapid and great are the revolutions and changes of life.
**ALFRED DE VIGNY**

There are plenty of reasons for hope. There need be no war with Russia, and those who would fight her now, on the theory that we had better do it and get it over with, are lightheaded promoters of world destruction.
**HAROLD W. DODDS**

There is one extremely simple method of bringing an end to what is called the cold war—observe the Charter of the U.N.; refrain from the use of force or the threat of force in international relations and from the support and direction of subversion against the institutions of other countries.
**JOHN FOSTER DULLES**

We love to succor the distressed. But how different our attitude is when we are implored to extend the benefit of our influence to help prevent distress and disaster among other nations. Were Germany to be plunged into anarchy or Bolshevism and her people overtaken by hunger and other calamities we would doubtless rush in, as we rushed into Russia, and feed the hungry. . . . But we keep on refusing to have anything to do with the effort to establish firmly an international organization having for its object the prevention of war and all its attendant horrors.
**B. C. FORBES**

A little while ago I visited Omaha Beach for the second time in my life. In the intervening 26 years, nearly 20,000 tides had come and gone and little remains visible of the greatest military landing in man's history of endless warring. What's to be seen is mostly in a superb museum and a panoramic cemetery. The cemetery memorializes with dignity and grandeur the event and the dead, and moves one deeply.

Before they die less precipitously and/or in lesser purpose, Americans who can should visit World War II's Normandy Beach. Such seeing and remembering helps a man's perspective.

**MALCOLM FORBES**

Bringing Home The Boys has been a top objective of Americans ever since we first sent some of them overseas decades ago. At the close of World War I the phrase flowered, though I'll bet it was used in connection with the Spanish American War. Probably even before that, when Americans stormed the forts outside Mexico City in 1847. Thank God we're doing so again from Vietnam. But the Return of Americans shouldn't be confined to battle zones. We are neither wanted, nor needed, nor should we be in large numbers in such places as Germany, Korea, Thailand, Okinawa, Japan, the Philippines, Turkey, Spain and so on, ad nauseam.

**MALCOLM FORBES**

It is a damned sight easier to start wars than to end them. This truth has been stated for as long and as often as it has been ignored. High time and thank God, we are at least moving toward de-escalation in Vietnam. The road to extrication will be long, painful, bitter. But it must be trod. We are so bogged down in Vietnam that we cannot respond effectively anywhere else in the world to a military power play except through atomic bombardment.

**MALCOLM FORBES**

Memorably marking D-Day has significant additional consequence because of the stark contrast to the impact of a later conflict—Vietnam. World War II, as did World War I 25 years earlier, united the country with a fervor and totality unequalled before (including 1776) or since. Vietnam eventually divided this nation as nothing since the Civil War. Those deep, deep scars have been slow to heal.... So it's important that the vast majority of Americans who have clear memories only of Vietnam be reminded that there were times, and will be times, when this country will react with awesome unanimity to a challenge to our being....

**MALCOLM FORBES**

Remember, it hasn't gone away—the 4,500-mile bitterly disputed border between Russia and China... When we are eyeballing with Russia on the Middle East or Indochina... we must remember the growing tension-increasing absorption with China...

**MALCOLM FORBES (1970)**

The Vietnam War Memorial is as impressive in its starkness as the stark reality of death was for those whose names it holds. With rare exception, facing death's not easy. A war for a cause that unites a nation in a fight essential for its survival and principles is one thing.... But to fight and die in a police action that rent the home front, when hundreds of one's peers were applauded for fleeing the country... that's another matter. It's long past time that those who lived through it, as well as those who died in it, get the deep though belated thanks of their countrymen and the caring they merit.

**MALCOLM FORBES**

Wars almost never end the way starters had in mind.

**MALCOLM FORBES**

There never was a good war or a bad peace.

**BENJAMIN FRANKLIN**

There can be no profit in the making or selling of things to be destroyed in war. Men may think that they have such profit, but in the end the profit will turn out to be a loss.
ALEXANDER HAMILTON

It is the blood of the soldier that makes the general great.
ITALIAN PROVERB

None but an armed nation can dispense with a standing army.
THOMAS JEFFERSON

Outlawing all atomic weapons would be a magnificent gesture. However, it should be remembered that Gettysburg had a local ordinance forbidding the discharge of firearms.
HOMER D. KING

How is the world ruled and how do wars start? Diplomats tell lies to journalists and then believe what they read.
KARL KRAUS

There is no such thing as an inevitable war. If war comes, it will be from failure of human wisdom.
BONAR LAW

My dear [General] McClelland: If you don't want to use the Army I should like to borrow it for a while.
ABRAHAM LINCOLN

I know war as few other men now living know it, and nothing to me is more revolting. I have long advocated its complete abolition, as its very destructiveness on both friend and foe has rendered it useless as a method of settling international disputes.
DOUGLAS MACARTHUR

One ought never to allow a disorder to take place in order to avoid war, for war is not thereby avoided, but only deferred to your disadvantage.
NICCOLÒ MACHIAVELLI

Of all the evils to public liberty, war is perhaps the most to be dreaded, because it comprises and develops every other. War is the patent of armies; from these proceed debts and taxes. And armies, and debts, and taxes, are the known instruments for bringing the many under the dominion of the few. In war, too, the discretionary power of the executive is extended; its influence in dealing out offices, honors, and emoluments is multiplied; and all the means of seducing the minds are added to those of subduing the force of the people! No nation could preserve its freedom in the midst of continual warfare.
JAMES MADISON

War is only a cowardly escape from the problems of peace.
THOMAS MANN

The instruments of war can be manufactured . . . human blood cannot be; and the lack of just one pint could mean the life of an American serviceman.
GEORGE C. MARSHALL

Always remember that a soldier's pack is lighter than a slave's chains.
DAVID O. MCKAY

All of us who grew up before World War II are immigrants in time, immigrants from an earlier world, living in an age essentially different from anything we knew before.
MARGARET MEAD

War will disappear, like the dinosaur, when changes in world conditions have destroyed its survival value.
ROBERT A. MILLIKAN

War hath no fury like a noncombatant.
**Charles Edward Montague**

Social problems can no longer be solved by class warfare any more than international problems can be solved by wars between nations. Warfare is negative and will sooner or later lead to destruction, while goodwill and co-operation are positive and supply the only safe basis for building a better future.
**J. Nansen**

The world cannot continue to wage war like physical giants and to seek peace like intellectual pygmies.
**Basil O'Connor**

You can no more win a war than you can win an earthquake.
**Jeannette Rankin**

No international Eighteenth Amendment will get rid of war or the instruments of war until civilization finds a way for accomplishing what war has done in the past. Simply to prohibit war is not going to get rid of it. Wars must be anticipated and the causes got rid of by a readiness to accept peaceful means of settlement.
**James T. Shotwell**

In the eyes of the people, the general who wins a battle has made no mistakes.
**Voltaire**

War is partially the result of the greed of men, of imperialistic ambitions, the desire to reach out and possess what others possess. We have seen the hatred of one people for another, notably the persecution of the Jews. Such hatred, however, as well as the cruelty and unkindness that may exist below the veneer of our civilization, are transitory.
**Alfred Grant Walton, D.D.**

It was necessary for us to discover greater powers of destruction than our enemies. We did. But after every war we have followed through with a new rise in our standard of living by the application of war-taught knowledge for the benefit of the world. It will be the same with the atomic bomb principles.
**Thomas J. Watson**

As long as war is looked upon as wicked, it will always have its fascination. When it is looked upon as vulgar, it will cease to be popular.
**Oscar Wilde**

## *Waste*

An extravagance is anything you buy that is of no earthly use to your wife.
**Franklin P. Adams**

Next to the dog, the wastebasket is man's best friend.
**Anonymous**

The road of excess leads to the palace of wisdom; for we never know what is enough until we know what is more than enough.
**William Blake**

I suppose that one reason why the road to ruin is broad, is to accommodate the great amount of travel in that direction.
**Josh Billings**

What is taken from the fortune, also, may haply be so much lifted from the soul. The greatness of a loss, as the proverb suggests, is determinable, not so much by what we have lost, as by what we have left.
**Christian Bovée**

The excesses of our youth are drafts upon our old age.
**Charles Caleb Colton**

The injury of prodigality leads to this, that he that will not economize will have to agonize.
**CONFUCIUS**

We never seem to know what anything means until we have lost it. The full significance of these words, property, ease, health—the wealth of meaning that lies in epithets, parent, child, friend, we never know until they are taken away; till in place of the bright, visible being, comes the awful and desolate shadow where nothing is—where we stretch out our hands in vain, and strain our eyes upon dark and dismal vacuity.
**ORVILLE DEWEY**

From time waste there can be no salvage. It is the easiest of all waste and the hardest to correct because it does not litter the floor.
**HENRY FORD**

The government in business may waste time and money without rendering service. In the end the public pays in taxes. The corporation cannot waste or it will fall. It cannot make unfair rulings or give high-handed, expensive service, for there are not enough people willing to accept inferior service to make a volume of business that will pay dividends.
**HENRY FORD**

Many people take no care of their money till they come nearly to the end of it, and others do just the same with their time.
**JOHANN WOLFGANG VON GOETHE**

Excesses are essentially gestures. It is easy to be extremely cruel, magnanimous, humble or self-sacrificing when we see ourselves as actors in a performance.
**ERIC HOFFER**

Man's chief difference from the brutes lies in the exuberant excess of his subjective propensities.

Prune his extravagance, sober him, and you undo him.
**WILLIAM JAMES**

By eating what is sufficient man is enabled to work; he is hindered from working and becomes heavy, idle, and stupid if he takes too much. As to bodily distempers occasioned by excess, there is no end of them.
**T. JONES**

He who is the cause of another's advancement is thereby the cause of his own ruin.
**NICCOLÒ MACHIAVELLI**

Losses are comparative, imagination only makes them of any moment.
**BLAISE PASCAL**

In life it is more necessary to lose than to gain. A seed will only germinate if it dies. One has to live without getting tired, one must look forward and feed on one's living reserves, which oblivion no less than memory produces.
**BORIS PASTERNAK**

Spend and be free, but make no waste.
**JOHN RAY**

No hour is to be considered a waste which teaches one what not to do.
**CHARLES B. ROGERS**

Why shouldn't things be largely absurd, futile and transitory? They are so; and we are so, and they and we go very well together.
**GEORGE SANTAYANA**

Wasted time means wasted lives.
**R. SHANNON**

Hundreds would never have known want if they had not at first known waste.
CHARLES H. SPURGEON

Benjamin Franklin went through life an altered man because he once paid too dearly for a penny whistle. My concern springs usually from a deeper source, to wit, from having bought a whistle when I did not want one.
ROBERT LOUIS STEVENSON

We are forced to measure each moment partly in and of itself, for if everything is justified solely by the future, life becomes rather futile.
MALCOLM R. SUTHERLAND, JR.

I hold this to be the rule of life: Too much of anything is bad.
TERENCE

Too much of a good thing can be wonderful.
MAE WEST

## *Wealth*

There is a growing sentiment in America that regular saving should be ignored—that the government will take care of people and give them security when they get beyond a certain age or become old and unable to work, but it must be borne in mind that the people who earn and do save, take care of the government! Were it not for the thrifty and the willing workers, the government would be in a bad way.
GEORGE MATTHEW ADAMS

Our price system is made up of many different kinds of prices—wage rates, interest rates, rents, stock market quotations, commodity prices, wholesale prices, retail prices, charges for professional services, and many others. All of these prices are continually fluctuating in response to underlying conditions of supply and demand, and in so doing they direct every phase of economic activity. . . . The price mechanism is probably the only possible device yet conceived which can weld the personal and individually determined preferences, desires, and ambitions of men into a social order. . . . Under a regime of governmentally fixed prices the continuance of democratic institutions is impossible. . . . A government undertaking delicate price dictation . . . could tolerate no criticism.
WINTHROP W. ALDRICH

Another advantage of being rich is that all your faults are called eccentricities.
ANONYMOUS

There are two things needed in these days; first, for rich men to find out how poor men live; and, second, for poor men to know how rich men work.
E. ATKINSON

More people should learn to tell their dollars where to go instead of asking them where they went.
ROGER W. BABSON

Be not penny-wise; riches have wings; sometimes they fly away of themselves, and sometimes they must be set flying to bring in more.
FRANCIS BACON

If all the gold in the world were melted down into a solid cube it would be about the size of an eight-room house. If a man got possession of all that gold—billions of dollars worth, he could not buy a friend, character, peace of mind, clear conscience, or a sense of eternity.
CHARLES F. BANNING

Save for gold, jewels, works of art, perhaps good agricultural land, and a very few other things, there ain't no such animal as a permanent investment.
BERNARD M. BARUCH

The true way to gain much, is never to desire to gain too much. He is not rich that possesses much, but he that covets no more; and he is not poor that enjoys little, but he that wants too much.
**FRANCIS BEAUMONT**

If any man is rich and powerful he comes under the law of God by which the higher branches must take the burnings of the sun, and shade those that are lower; by which the tall trees must protect the weak plants beneath them.
**HENRY WARD BEECHER**

In this world it is not what we take up, but what we give up, that makes us rich.
**HENRY WARD BEECHER**

Very few men acquire wealth in such a manner as to receive pleasure from it.
**HENRY WARD BEECHER**

The ascending spiral of greatness in America has risen because industry has produced wealth, which in turn has supported educational institutions, which in turn have supplied leadership to industry in order that with each succeeding generation it might produced more wealth.
**WALLACE F. BENNETT**

The best condition in life is not to be so rich as to be envied nor so poor as to be damned.
**JOSH BILLINGS**

If you want to know how rich you really are, find out what would be left of you tomorrow if you should lose every dollar you own tonight?
**WILLIAM J. H. BOETCKER**

The more you learn what to do with yourself, and the more you do for others, the more you will learn to enjoy the abundant life.
**WILLIAM J. H. BOETCKER**

If the majority of people of a country, no matter how great its natural resources, organize and conspire to get more out and put less in, to do less and get more, how long will, how long can it last?
**WILLIAM J. H. BOETCKER**

Misers are neither relations, nor friends, nor citizens, nor Christians, nor perhaps even human beings.
**JEAN DE LA BRUYÈRE**

We all covet wealth, but not its perils.
**JEAN DE LA BRUYÈRE**

If your capacity to acquire has outstripped your capacity to enjoy, you are on the way to the scrap-heap.
**GLEN BUCK**

Save a part of your income and begin now, for the man with a surplus controls circumstances and the man without a surplus is controlled by circumstances.
**HENRY H. BUCKLEY**

If we command our wealth, we shall be rich and free; if our wealth commands us, we are poor indeed.
**EDMUND BURKE**

For anything worth having one must pay the price; and the price is always work, patience, love, self-sacrifice—no paper currency, no promises to pay, but the goal of real service.
**JOHN BURROUGHS**

By whatever basis human desires are classified, the promise of an abundant life covers virtually all. To the spiritual it suggests escape from futility; to the sensuous it calls up visions of luxury; to the defeated it is a dream of success. To the idle it pledges ease; to the weary, rest; to the frightened it means safety; to the anxious, security; and to the improvident it conjures inexhaustible resources. Persuade a man

that you can give him the thing he most desires and you will be his hero; offer him justification for his failures and he will be your disciple; assure him a boundless supply of loaves and fishes and he will seek to make you king.
SAMUEL PARKS CADMAN

The wealth of man is the number of things which he loves and blesses, which he is loved and blessed by.
THOMAS CARLYLE

At the end, the acquisition of wealth is ignoble in the extreme. I assume that you save and long for wealth only as a means of enabling you the better to do some good in your day and generation.
ANDREW CARNEGIE

Surplus wealth is a sacred trust which its possessor is bound to administer in his lifetime for the good of the community.
ANDREW CARNEGIE

The day is not far distant when the man who dies leaving behind him millions of available wealth, which was free for him to administer during life, will pass away unwept, unhonored, and unsung, no matter to what uses he leaves the dross which he cannot take with him.
ANDREW CARNEGIE

The gratification of wealth is not found in mere possession or in lavish expenditure, but in its wise application.
MIGUEL DE CERVANTES

I knew once a very covetous, sordid fellow who used to say, "Take care of the pence, for the pounds will take care of themselves."
LORD CHESTERFIELD

Nothing is more fallacious than wealth. Today it is for thee, tomorrow it is against thee. It arms the eyes of the envious everywhere. It is a hostile comrade, a domestic enemy.
ST. JOHN CHRYSOSTOM

It is difficult to set bounds to the price unless you first set bounds to the wish.
CICERO

There is enough for all. The earth is a generous mother; she will provide in plentiful abundance food for all her children if they will but cultivate her soil in justice and in peace.
BOURKE COCKRAN

He that will not permit his wealth to do any good to others while he is living, prevents it from doing any good to himself when he is dead; and by an egotism that is suicidal and has a double edge, cuts himself off from the truest pleasure here and the highest happiness hereafter.
CHARLES CALEB COLTON

It is much better to have your gold in the hand than in the heart.
CHARLES CALEB COLTON

Many speak the truth when they say that they despise riches, but they mean the riches possessed by other men.
CHARLES CALEB COLTON

Our wealth is often a snare to ourselves and always a temptation to others.
CHARLES CALEB COLTON

That which we acquire with the most difficulty we retain the longest; as those who have earned a fortune are usually more careful of it than those who have inherited one.
CHARLES CALEB COLTON

Money is power. Every good man and woman ought to strive for power, to do good with it when obtained. I say, get rich, get rich!
RUSSELL HERMAN CONWELL

To acquire wealth is difficult, to preserve it more difficult, but to spend it wisely most difficult of all.
EDWARD DAY

The secret point of money and power in America is neither the things that money can buy nor power for power's sake but absolute personal freedom, mobility, privacy.
JOAN DIDION

A billion dollars here, a billion dollars there, and pretty soon you're talking about real money.
EVERETT DIRKSEN

All heiresses are beautiful.
JOHN DRYDEN

Each man also to whom God hath given riches and wealth, and hath given him power to eat thereof, and to take his portion, and to rejoice in his labor; this is the gift of God. For he shall not much remember the days of his life; because God answereth him in the joy of his heart.
ECCLESIASTES 5:19–20

If rich men would remember that shrouds have no pockets, they would, while living, share their wealth with their children, and give for the good of others, and so know the highest pleasure wealth can give.
TRYON EDWARDS

It requires a great deal of boldness and a great deal of caution to make a great fortune, and when you have got it, it requires ten times as much wit to keep it.
RALPH WALDO EMERSON

Wealth brings with it its own checks and balances. The basis of political economy is noninterference. The only safe rule is found in the self-adjusting meter of demand and supply. Open the doors of opportunity to talent and virtue and they will do themselves justice, and property will not be in bad hands. In a free and just commonwealth, property rushes from the idle and imbecile to the industrious, brave and persevering.
RALPH WALDO EMERSON

Bare-faced covetousness was the moving spirit of civilization from the first dawn to the present day; wealth, and again wealth, and for the third time wealth; wealth, not of society, but of the puny individual, was its only and final aim.
FRIEDRICH ENGELS

Poor men seek meat for their stomachs, rich men stomachs for their meat.
ENGLISH PROVERB

Lampis the shipowner, on being asked how he acquired his great wealth, replied, "My great wealth was acquired with no difficulty, but my small wealth, my first gains, with much labor."
EPICTETUS

When the anger of the gods is incurred, wealth or power only bring more devastating punishment.
EURIPIDES

They shall cast their silver in the streets, and their gold shall be removed: their silver and their gold shall not be able to deliver them in the day of the wrath of the Lord: they shall not satisfy their souls, neither fill their bowels: because it is the stumbling block of their iniquity.
EZEKIEL 7:19

Let me tell you about the very rich. They are different from you and me. They possess and enjoy early,

and it does something to them, makes them soft where we are trustful, in a way that, unless you were born rich, it is very difficult to understand.
**F. SCOTT FITZGERALD**

Are your desires purely selfish? Do your tastes run to a grand home, automobiles, fine clothes, an abundance of amusements, and so forth? If so, look around you at people who have such things in superabundance. Are they any happier, do you think, than you are? Are they any better morally? Are they any stronger physically? Are they better liked by their friends than you are by your friends? . . . Carnegie said, "Millionaires rarely smile." This is substantially true.
**B. C. FORBES**

A nation's economic salvation does not lie in the amount of money its rich inhabitants can squander recklessly. A nation's economic salvation lies in the amount of money its inhabitants can save and invest after providing themselves with all the necessaries and all the reasonable comforts of life.
**B. C. FORBES**

A young financial writer once brought ridicule upon himself by stating that a certain company had nothing to commend it except excellent earnings. Well, there are companies whose earnings are excellent but whose stocks I would never recommend. In selecting investments, I attach prime importance to the men behind them. I'd rather buy brains and character than earnings. Earnings can be good one year and poor the next. But if you put your money into securities run by men combining conspicuous brains and unimpeachable character, the likelihood is that the financial results will prove satisfactory.
**B. C. FORBES**

If the United States is to produce a nation of investors—as we must if we are to gain financial world-leadership—it is imperative that boards of directors be so constituted as to adequately represent the interests and inspire the complete confidence of investors of moderate substance.
**B. C. FORBES**

Remember, diamonds are only lumps of coal that stuck to their jobs.
**B. C. FORBES**

In all the thrashing about that results from our dwindling gold reserves, it's about time that this country and other countries get some perspective on the situation.

The day this country is out of the stuff, that day gold becomes what it's worth as a metal and no longer will have much significance as a monetary measurement.

It isn't the gold we have that makes this nation rich. It's what we make, our knowhow, our productivity. So long as this country produces more and better, the world will continue to want what we make.
**MALCOLM FORBES**

Investor: One who bought stocks that went up.
**MALCOLM FORBES**

In transactions of trade it is not to be supposed that, as in gaming, what one party gains the other must necessarily lose. The gain to each may be equal. If A. has more corn than he can consume, but wants cattle; and B. has more cattle, but wants corn; exchange is gain to each; thereby the common stock of comforts in life is increased.
**BENJAMIN FRANKLIN**

To be thrown upon one's own resources is to be cast into the very lap of fortune; for our faculties then undergo a development and display an energy of which they were previously unsusceptible.
**BENJAMIN FRANKLIN**

Wherever desirable superfluities are imported, industry is excited, and thereby plenty is produced. Were only necessaries permitted to be purchased, men would work no more than was necessary for that purpose.
BENJAMIN FRANKLIN

He is not fit for riches who is afraid to use them.
THOMAS FULLER

Let me gain by you, and no matter whether you love me or not.
THOMAS FULLER

There are good reasons why men possessed of money, like men earlier favored with noble birth and great title, imagine that the awe and admiration that wealth inspires derive from their own wisdom or personalities. The contrast between their view of themselves, as so enhanced, and the frequently ridiculous or depraved reality, has ever been a source of wonder or amusement.
JOHN KENNETH GALBRAITH

Wealth is a means to an end, not the end itself. As a synonym for health and happiness, it has had a fair trial and failed dismally.
JOHN GALSWORTHY

He who by an exertion of mind or body, adds to the aggregate of enjoyable wealth, increases the sum of human knowledge, or gives to human life higher elevation or greater fullness—he is, in the larger meaning of the words, a producer, a working man, a laborer, and is honestly earning honest wages.
HENRY GEORGE

I have no complex about wealth. I have worked hard for my money, producing things people need. I believe that the able industrial leader who creates wealth and employment is more worthy of historical notice than politicians or soldiers.
J. PAUL GETTY

I am indeed rich, since my income is superior to my expense, and my expense is equal to my wishes.
EDWARD GIBBON

Hereditary wealth is in reality a premium paid to idleness.
WILLIAM GODWIN

One is led astray alike by sympathy and coldness, by praise and by blame.
JOHANN WOLFGANG VON GOETHE

His greatest riches—ignorance of wealth.
OLIVER GOLDSMITH

Ill fares the land
To hastening ills a prey
When wealth accumulates
But men decay.
OLIVER GOLDSMITH

The jests of the rich are ever successful.
OLIVER GOLDSMITH

If you want to hear about the power and glory of wealth, ask a man who's seeking it. But if you want to learn of wealth's burdens and difficulties, ask a man who's been wealthy a long time.
STANLEY GOLDSTEIN

As we look at the oppressed lands we are forced to the conclusion that many of the evils which confront them, and indeed us, today derive directly from man's service to Mammon. The creation of godless ideals, the setting up of wealth, power and personal success as the chief aims of life, has contributed more than any other single factor to pre-

cipitate the moral economic crisis with which these lands are faced today and which at present is even overshadowing and threatening the demoralization of our own country.
WILLIAM T. GREEN, D.D.

Consider your ways. Ye have sown much, and bring in little; ye eat, but ye have not enough; ye drink, but ye are not filled with drink; ye clothe you, but there is none warm; and he that earneth wages earneth wages to put into a bag with holes.
HAGGAI 1:6

Rich people should consider that they are only trustees for what they posses, and should show their wealth to be more in doing good than merely in having it.
JOSEPH HALL

Sometimes the best gain is to lose.
HERBERT

I wish I were either rich enough or poor enough to do a lot of things that are impossible in my present comfortable circumstances.
DON HEROLD

Wealth is not of necessity a curse, nor poverty a blessing. Wholesome and easy abundance is better than either extreme; better for our manhood that we have enough for daily comfort; enough for culture, for hospitality, for Christian charity. More than this may or may not be a blessing. Certainly it can be a blessing only by being accepted as a trust.
RAYMOND HITCHCOCK

Man is a luxury-loving animal. Take away play, fancies and luxuries and you will turn a man into a dull, sluggish creature, barely energetic enough to obtain a bare subsistence.
ERIC HOFFER

High descent and meritorious deeds, unless united to wealth, are as useless as seaweed.
HORACE

When I caution you against becoming a miser, I do not therefore advise you to become a prodigal or a spendthrift.
HORACE

To acquire wealth is not easy, yet to keep it is even more difficult. . . . It is said that wealth is like a viper which is harmless if a man know how to take hold of it; but, if he does not, it will twine around his hand and bite him.
FRANK K. HOUSTON

Every gain made by individuals or societies is almost instantly taken for granted. The luminous ceiling toward which we raise our longing eyes becomes, when we have climbed to the next floor, a stretch of disregarded linoleum beneath our feet.
ALDOUS HUXLEY

No man is any the worse off because another acquires wealth by trade, or by the exercise of a profession; on the contrary, he cannot have acquired his wealth except by benefiting others to the extent of what they considered to be its value.
THOMAS H. HUXLEY

Speculation is the romance of trade, and casts contempt upon all its sober realities. It renders the stock-jobber a magician, and the exchange a region of enchantment.
WASHINGTON IRVING

In the practical as in the theoretic life, the man whose acquisitions stick is the man who is always achieving and advancing, whilst his neighbors, spending most of their time in relearning what they once knew but have forgotten, simply hold their own.
WILLIAM JAMES

How many toil to lay up riches which they never enjoy.
WILLIAM JAY

. . . he that getteth riches, and not by right, shall leave them in the midst of his days, and at his end shall be a fool.
JEREMIAH 17:11

They spend their days in wealth, and in a moment go down to the grave. Therefore they say unto God, Depart from us; for we desire not the knowledge of thy ways. What is the Almighty that we should serve him?
JOB 21:13–15

If we fasten our attention on what we have, rather than on what we lack, a very little wealth is sufficient.
FRANCIS JOHNSON

A man who both spends and saves money is the happiest man, because he has both enjoyments.
SAMUEL JOHNSON

Few enterprises of great labor or hazard would be undertaken if we had not the power of magnifying the advantages we expect from them.
SAMUEL JOHNSON

It is better to live rich than to die rich.
SAMUEL JOHNSON

We do not commonly find men of superior sense amongst those of the highest fortune.
JUVENAL

A speculator is one who runs risks of which he is aware, and an investor is one who runs risks of which he is unaware.
JOHN MAYNARD KEYNES

There is just as much honey in the flowers this year as there ever was. The soil will produce abundantly when fertilized well with elbow grease and good sense.
JACOB KINDLEBERGER

Savings represent much more than mere money value. They are the proof that the saver is worth something in himself. Any fool can waste; any fool can muddle; but it takes something more of a man to save and the more he saves the more of a man he makes of himself. Waste and extravagance unsettle a man's mind for every crisis; thrift, which means some form of self-restraint, steadies it.
RUDYARD KIPLING

No gain is so certain as that which proceeds from the economical use of what you already have.
LATIN PROVERB

Never say you know a man until you have divided an inheritance with him.
JOHANN LAVATER

He who wishes to be rich in a day will be hanged in a year.
LEONARDO DA VINCI

One's strongest asset is simultaneously his point of strongest vulnerability.
HARRY LEVINSON

That some should be rich, shows that others may become rich, and hence is just encouragement to industry and enterprise.
ABRAHAM LINCOLN

If the wealth of this country were distributed, 90 percent would be destroyed by the act of distribution. The resulting starvation and anarchy would destroy the rest in less than thirty days.
JAMES F. LINCOLN

I've been more bossed by my fortune than it has been bossed by me.
**JOHN P. LIPPETT**

Never buy at the bottom, and always sell too soon.
**JESSE L. LIVERMORE**

Wealth may be an excellent thing, for it means power, leisure and liberty.
**JAMES RUSSELL LOWELL**

Wealth is the smallest thing on earth, the least gift that God has bestowed on mankind.
**MARTIN LUTHER**

There are many things in which one gains and the other loses; but if it is essential to any transaction that only one side shall gain, the thing is not of God.
**GEORGE MACDONALD**

A son can bear with equanimity the loss of his father, but the loss of his inheritance may drive him to despair.
**NICCOLÒ MACHIAVELLI**

Luxury makes a man so soft that it is hard to please him, and easy to trouble him; so that his pleasures at last become his burden. Luxury is a nice master, hard to be pleased.
**MACKENZIE**

When a man tells you he got rich through hard work, ask him: "Whose?"
**DONALD MARQUIS**

Spend some time alone and learn to develop your personal resources.
**ALEXANDER REID MARTIN**

For whosoever hath, to him shall be given, and he shall have more abundance; but whosoever hath not, from him shall be taken away even that he hath.
**MATTHEW 13:12**

God must love the rich or he wouldn't divide so much among so few of them.
**H. L. MENCKEN**

The most valuable of human possessions, next to a superior and disdainful air, is the reputation of being well-to-do. Nothing else so neatly eases one's way through life, especially in democratic countries.
**H. L. MENCKEN**

In investing money, the amount of interest you want should depend on whether you want to eat well or sleep well.
**J. KENFIELD MORLEY**

A man's true wealth is the good he does in this world.
**MUHAMMAD**

The habit of saving is itself an education; it fosters every virtue, teaches self-denial, cultivates the sense of order, trains to forethought, and so broadens the mind.
**THEODORE T. MUNGER**

The Government can destroy wealth but it cannot create wealth, which is the product of labor and management working with creation.
**ALFALFA BILL MURRAY**

I don't mind their having a lot of money,
And I don't care how they employ it,
But I do think they damn well ought to admit they enjoy it.
**OGDEN NASH**

Every man has his price. This is not true. But for every man there exists a bait which he cannot resist swallowing.
**FRIEDRICH WILHELM NIETZSCHE**

Although wealth may not bring happiness, the immediate prospect of it provides a wonderfully close imitation.
**PATRICK O'BRIAN**

Why is it no one ever sent me yet
One perfect limousine, do you suppose?
Ah no, it's always just my luck to get
One perfect rose.
**DOROTHY PARKER**

You may not have saved a lot of money in your life, but if you have saved a lot of heartaches for other folks, you are a pretty rich man.
**SETH PARKER**

Those who condemn wealth are those who have none and see no chance of getting it.
**WILLIAM PENN PATRICK**

Every luxury must be paid for, and everything is a luxury, starting with being in the world.
**CESARE PAVESE**

Luxury is the first, second and third cause of the ruin of republics. It is the vampire which soothes us into a fatal slumber while it sucks the life-blood of our veins.
**PAYSON**

There is no sound basis upon which it may be assumed that all poor men are godly and all rich men are evil, no more than it could be assumed that all rich men are good and all poor men are bad.
**NORMAN VINCENT PEALE**

Get place and wealth, if possible with grace; if not, by any means get wealth and place.
**ALEXANDER POPE**

To whom can riches give repute, or trust, content, or pleasure, but the good and the just?
**ALEXANDER POPE**

He that oppresseth the poor to increase his riches, and he that giveth to the rich, shall surely come to want.
**PROVERBS 22:16**

They that trust in their wealth, and boast themselves in the multitude of their riches; none of them can by any means redeem his brother, nor give to God a ransom for him.
**PSALMS 49:6–7**

Be not thou afraid when one is made rich, when the glory of his house is increased; for when he dieth he shall carry nothing away: his glory shall not descend after him.
**PSALMS 49:16–17**

Thou hast caused men to ride over our heads; we went through fire and through water: but thou broughtest us out into a wealthy place.
**PSALMS 66:12**

As there is no worldly gain without some loss, so there is no worldly loss without some gain. If thou hast lost thy wealth, thou hast lost some trouble with it. If thou art degraded from thy honor, thou art likewise freed from the stroke of envy. If sickness hath blurred thy beauty, it hath delivered thee from pride. Set the allowance against the loss and thou shalt find no loss great. He loses little or nothing who reserves himself.
**FRANCIS QUARLES**

If you count all your assets you always show a profit.
**ROBERT QUILLEN**

To save something each month develops self-control. This power frees one from fear and gives abiding courage.
**SAMUEL REYBURN**

Be not concerned if thou findest thyself in possession of unexpected wealth; Allah will provide an unexpected use for it.
**JAMES J. ROCHE**

Well, yes, you could say we have independent means.
**JOHN D. ROCKEFELLER III**

Probably the greatest harm done by vast wealth is the harm that we of moderate means do to ourselves when we let the vices of envy and hatred enter deep into our own natures.
**THEODORE ROOSEVELT**

It takes a great deal of boldness mixed with a vast deal of caution to acquire a great fortune; but then it takes ten times as much wit to keep it after you have got it as it took you to make it.
**MEYER ROTHSCHILD**

A fool and her money are soon courted.
**HELEN ROWLAND**

Why is one man richer than another? Because he is more industrious, more persevering and more sagacious.
**JOHN RUSKIN**

By doing good with his money, a man, as it were, stamps the image of God upon it, and makes it pass current for the merchandise of heaven.
**J. RUTLEDGE**

The surplus wealth we have gained to some extent at least belongs to our fellow beings; we are only the temporary custodians of our fortunes, and let us be careful that no just complaint can be made against our stewardship.
**JACOB H. SCHIFF**

Look at a gown of gold, and you will at least get a sleeve of it.
**SIR WALTER SCOTT**

A great fortune is a great slavery.
**SENECA**

A miser grows rich by seeming poor; an extravagant man grows poor by seeming rich.
**WILLIAM SHAKESPEARE**

Abundance consists not alone in material possession, but in an uncovetous spirit.
**CHARLES M. SHELDON**

Wealth is not only what you have but it is also what you are.
**STERLING W. SILL**

Wealth is a dangerous inheritance, unless the inheritor is trained to active benevolence.
**CHARLES SIMMONS**

The real price of everything is the toil and trouble of acquiring it.
**ADAM SMITH**

Whatever a person saves from his revenue he adds to his capital, and either employs it himself in maintaining an additional number of productive hands, or enables some person to do so . . . for a share of profits. As the capital of an individual can be increased only by what he saves . . . so the capital of a society can be increased only in the same manner.
**ADAM SMITH**

Solvency is entirely a matter of temperament and not of income.
**LOGAN PEARSALL SMITH**

After buying into the Consols, I read Seneca "On the Contempt of Wealth." What intolerable nonsense!
**SYDNEY SMITH**

If a rich man is proud of his wealth, he should not be praised until it is known how he employs it.
**SOCRATES**

Luxury, today, is solitude and silence.
**PAUL-HENRI SPAAK**

We shall have better business when everyone realizes that while it pays to invest money in their industries and develop natural resources, it pays still higher dividends to improve mankind and develop human resources.
**H. E. STEINER**

Earn a little, and spend a little—less.
**JOHN STEVENSON**

Just as war is waged with the blood of others, fortunes are made with other people's money.
**ANDRE SUARES**

Being rich is having money; being wealth is having time.
**STEPHEN SWID**

The miser is as much in want of what he has as of what he has not.
**PUBLILIUS SYRUS**

There is no gain so certain as that which arises from sparing what you have.
**PUBLILIUS SYRUS**

There must be a reason why some people can afford to live well. They must have worked for it. I only feel angry when I see waste. When I see people throwing away things we could see.
**MOTHER TERESA**

A man is rich in proportion to the number of things which he can afford to let alone.
**HENRY DAVID THOREAU**

Most of the luxuries, and many of the so-called comforts of life are not only indispensible, but positive hindrances to the elevation of mankind.
**HENRY DAVID THOREAU**

Superfluous wealth can buy superfluities only.
**HENRY DAVID THOREAU**

Charge them that are rich in this world, that they be not highminded, nor trust in uncertain riches, but in the living God, who giveth us richly all things to enjoy.
**I TIMOTHY 6:17**

What is most important for democracy is not that great fortunes should not exist, but that great fortunes should not remain in the same hands. In that way they do not form a class.
**ALEXIS DE TOCQUEVILLE**

I think that the reason why we Americans seem to be so addicted to trying to get rich suddenly is merely because the opportunity to make promising efforts in that direction has offered itself to us with a frequency out of all proportion to the European experience.
**MARK TWAIN**

There are two times in a man's life when he should not speculate: when he can't afford it, and when he can.
**MARK TWAIN**

Enough is often too much in our material world, but seldom enough in our material world.
**ROBERT L. UPSHUR**

He had so much money that he could afford to look poor.
**EDGAR WALLACE**

Get all you can without hurting your soul, your body, or your neighbor. Save all you can, cutting off every needless expense. Give all you can. Be glad to give, and ready to distribute; laying up in store for yourselves a good foundation against the time to come, that you may attain eternal life.
**JOHN WESLEY**

Make all you can, save all you can, give all you can.
**JOHN WESLEY**

No man is rich enough to buy back his past.
**OSCAR WILDE**

Natural resources of the world are distributed unequally among different countries and so is the population of the world. Distribution of resources is imperfectly related to the distribution of population, and trade between countries is the principal door to progress for all. It is peculiarly true of trade that the whole is greater than the sum of its parts.
**JOHN G. WINANT**

You can never be too rich or too thin.
**DUCHESS OF WINDSOR**

If a man successful in business expends a part of his income in things of no real use, while the poor employed by him pass through difficulties in getting the necessaries of life, this requires his serious attention.
**JOHN WOOLMAN**

Rich man down and poor man up—they are still not even.
**YIDDISH PROVERB**

I have about concluded that wealth is a state of mind, and that anyone can acquire a wealthy state of mind by thinking rich thoughts.
**EDWARD YOUNG**

Much learning shows how little mortals know; much wealth, how little worldlings enjoy.
**EDWARD YOUNG**

## *Weather*

What dreadful hot weather we have! It keeps me in a continual state of inelegance.
**JANE AUSTEN**

What men call gallantry, and gods adultery,
Is much more common where the climate's sultry.
**LORD BYRON**

For the man sound in body and serene in mind there is no such thing as bad weather; every sky has its beauty, and storms which whip the blood do but make it pulse more vigorously.
**GEORGE GISSING**

Weather in towns is like a skylark in a counting-house—out of place and in the way.
**JEROME K. JEROME**

Climate has much to do with cheerfulness, but nourishing food, a good digestion, and good health much more.
**ALEXANDER RHODES**

Sunshine is delicious, rain is refreshing, wind braces up, snow is exhilarating; there is no such thing as bad weather, only different kinds of good weather.
JOHN RUSKIN

Weather is a literary specialty, and no untrained hand can turn out a good article on it.
MARK TWAIN

Beautiful snow! It can do nothing wrong.
JOHN WHITTAKER WATSON

A hard, dull bitterness of cold.
JOHN GREENLEAF WHITTIER

Whenever people talk to me about the weather, I always feel certain that they mean something else.
OSCAR WILDE

## *Will*

For purposes of action nothing is more useful than narrowness of thought combined with energy of will.
HENRI FRÉDÉRIC AMIEL

Lack of will power and drive cause more failures than lack of intelligence and ability.
HARRY F. BANKS

I think it rather fine, this necessity for the tense bracing of the will before anything worth doing can be done. I rather like it myself. I feel it is to be the chief thing that differentiates me from the cat by the fire.
ARNOLD BENNETT

Will is the master of the world. Those who want something, those who know what they want, even those who want nothing, but want it badly, govern the world.
FERDINAND BRUNETIÈRE

Great souls have wills; feeble ones have only wishes.
CHINESE PROVERB

There is no power in man greater to effect anything than a will determined to exert its utmost force.
RICHARD CUMBERLAND

Let not thy will roar when thy power can be whisper.
THOMAS FULLER

If we will it, it is no dream.
THEODORE HERZL

People do not lack strength; they lack will.
VICTOR HUGO

In the moral world there is nothing impossible if we can bring a thorough will to do it. Man can do everything with himself, but he must not attempt to do too much with others.
KARL WILHELM VON HUMBOLDT

Will is character in action.
WILLIAM MCDOUGALL

Nothing is impossible to the man who can will.
HONORÉ DE MIRABEAU

If we need of a strong will in order to do good, it is still more necessary for us in order not to do evil.
THOMAS MOLE

We cannot be held to what is beyond our strength and means; for at times the accomplishment and execution may not be in our power, and indeed there is nothing really in our own power except the will: on this are necessarily based and founded all the principles that regulate the duty of man.
MICHEL DE MONTAIGNE

Lack of will power has caused more failure than lack of intelligence or ability.
FLOWER A. NEWHOUSE

Will opens the door to success, both brilliant and happy.
LOUIS PASTEUR

Work usually follows will.
LOUIS PASTEUR

We have more power than will; and it is only to exculpate ourselves that we often say that things are impracticable.
FRANÇOIS DE LA ROCHEFOUCAULD

Every man stamps his value on himself. The price we challenge for ourselves is given us by others. Man is made great or little by his own will.
JOHANN FRIEDRICH VON SCHILLER

The will is the strong blind man who carries on his shoulders the lame man who can see.
ARTHUR SCHOPENHAUER

To will and not to do when there is opportunity, is in reality not to will; and to love what is good and not to do it, when it is possible, is in reality not to love it.
EMANUEL SWEDENBORG

## *Winning*

There are hundreds who can stand failure to one who can stand success; the good loser is far more common than the good winner.
FRANKLIN P. ADAMS

Anybody can win unless there happens to be a second entry.
GEORGE ADE

Victories that are easy are cheap. Those only are worth having which come as the result of hard work.
HENRY WARD BEECHER

Be it jewel or toy, not the prize gives the joy, but the striving to win the prize.
EDWARD BULWER-LYTTON

Know ye not that they which run in a race run all, but that one receiveth the prize? So run, that ye may obtain.
I CORINTHIANS 9:24

A winner must first know what losing's like.
MALCOLM FORBES

After the fact, our hearts always go out to the fallen Goliaths. Yet we invariably root for their Davids. Until they're winners.
MALCOLM FORBES

If you've had a good time playing the game, you're a winner even if you lose.
MALCOLM FORBES

Pursue not a victory too far. He hath conquered well that hath made his enemy fly; thou mayest beat him to a desperate resistance, which may ruin thee.
HERBERT

The game is the thing. The wins and losses are not the thing. One loses every time one wins, for he then has no game.
L. RON HUBBARD

The man who wins may have been counted out several times, but he didn't hear the referee.
H. E. JANSEN

Spurts don't count. The final score makes no mention of a splendid start if the finish proves that you were an also ran.
**HERBERT KAUFMAN**

You can't expect to win unless you know why you lose.
**BENJAMIN LIPSON**

Winning isn't everything, but wanting to win is.
**VINCE LOMBARDI**

I have seen boys on my baseball team go into slumps and never come out of them, and I have seen others snap right out and come back better than ever. I guess more players lick themselves than are ever licked by an opposing team. The first thing any man has to know is how to handle himself. Training counts. You can't win any game unless you are ready to win.
**CONNIE MACK**

Nothing is ever gained by winning an argument and losing a customer.
**C. F. NORTON**

**Ten Commandments for Victory**

1. Obey orders always, honestly, cheerfully and conscientiously!
2. Do your duty on time all the time!
3. Practice self-control and self-denial always!
4. Be considerate of others; be willing to give before you take!
5. Be neat and clean in person as well as in speech!
6. Don't find fault, lest you find time for little else!
7. Whatever you do, do it just a little bit better than anyone else!
8. Resolve to win, always on the alert for Victory!
9. Be true to yourself, your comrades, your God and your country!
10. Be faithful and dependable, ever mindful of your sacred privilege in serving America!

**MAJ. MANFRED PAKAS**

When it comes to winning, you need the skill and the will.
**FRANK TYGER**

## *Wisdom*

We cannot advance without new experiments in living, but no wise man tries every day what he has proved wrong the day before.
**JAMES TRUSLOW ADAMS**

Wisdom consists in rising superior both to madness and to common sense, and is lending oneself to the universal illusion without becoming its dupe.
**HENRI FRÉDÉRIC AMIEL**

Wisdom is divided into two parts: (a) having a great deal to say, and (b) not saying it.
**ANONYMOUS**

Keep the gold and keep the silver, but give us wisdom.
**ARABIAN PROVERB**

Wise men, though all laws were abolished, would lead the same life.
**ARISTOPHANES**

A prudent question is one-half of wisdom.
**FRANCIS BACON**

Nothing doth more hurt in a state than that cunning men pass for wise.
**FRANCIS BACON**

If your luck is good, you get credit for wisdom.
**IGNAS BERNSTEIN**

The wise man hits first, then hollers help.
**IGNAS BERNSTEIN**

Aphorism: Predigested wisdom.
**AMBROSE BIERCE**

Wisdom is special knowledge in excess of all that is known.
**AMBROSE BIERCE**

The price of wisdom is eternal thought.
**FRANK BIRCH**

He who is virtuous is wise; and he who is wise is good; and he who is good is happy.
**BOETHIUS**

True wisdom lies in gathering the precious things out of each day as it goes by.
**E. S. BOUTON**

Mixing one's wines may be a mistake, but old and new wisdom mix admirably.
**BERTOLT BRECHT**

As a solid rock is not shaken by a strong gale, so wise persons remain unaffected by praise or censure.
**BUDDHA**

There is a courageous wisdom; there is also a false reptile prudence, the result, not of caution, but of fear.
**EDMUND BURKE**

A man doesn't begin to attain wisdom until he recognizes he is no longer indispensable.
**RICHARD E. BYRD**

A man begins cutting his wisdom teeth the first time he bites off more than he can chew.
**HERB CAEN**

Great men are the commissioned guides of mankind, who rule their fellows because they are wiser.
**THOMAS CARLYLE**

Wise men learn more from fools than fools from the wise.
**CATO**

True wisdom comes from the overcoming of suffering and sin. All true wisdom is therefore touched with sadness.
**WHITTAKER CHAMBERS**

Be wiser than other people if you can; but do not tell them so.
**LORD CHESTERFIELD**

Wise people may say what they will, but one passion is never cured by another.
**LORD CHESTERFIELD**

It is better to speak wisdom foolishly, like the saints, rather than to speak folly wisely, like the dons.
**G. K. CHESTERTON**

A single conversation across the table with a wise man is worth a month's study of books.
**CHINESE PROVERB**

The chief aim of wisdom is to enable one to bear with the stupidity of the ignorant.
**WINSTON CHURCHILL**

He that sympathizes in all the happiness of others, perhaps himself enjoys the safest happiness; and he

that is warned by the folly of others has perhaps attained the soundest wisdom.
CHARLES CALEB COLTON

There is this difference between happiness and wisdom, that he that thinks himself the happiest man, really is so; but he that thinks himself the wisest, is generally the greatest fool.
CHARLES CALEB COLTON

Any fool can carry on, but only the wise man knows how to shorten sail.
JOSEPH CONRAD

Knowledge comes, but wisdom lingers. It may not be difficult to store up in the mind a vast quantity of facts within a comparatively short time, but the ability to form judgments requires the severe discipline of hard work and the tempering heat of experience and maturity.
CALVIN COOLIDGE

Knowledge is proud that he has learned so much; wisdom is humble that he knows no more.
WILLIAM COWPER

The height of human wisdom is to bring our tempers down to our circumstances, and to make a calm within, under the weight of the greatest storm without.
DANIEL DEFOE

When we know how to read our own hearts, we acquire wisdom of the hearts of others.
DENIS DIDEROT

All of us encounter, at least once in our life, some individual who utters words that make us think forever. There are men whose phrases are oracles; who condense in a sentence the secrets of life; who blurt out an aphorism that forms a character, or illustrates an existence.
BENJAMIN DISRAELI

The wisdom of the wise and the experience of ages may be preserved by quotation.
BENJAMIN DISRAELI

All wisdom may be reduced to two words—wait and hope.
ALEXANDRE DUMAS

Science gives us knowledge, but only philosophy can give us wisdom.
WILL DURANT

For God giveth to a man that is good in his sight wisdom, and knowledge, and joy: but to the sinner he giveth travail, to gather and to heap up, that he may give to him that is good before God.
ECCLESIASTES 2:26

For wisdom is a defence, and money is a defence: but the excellency of knowledge is, that wisdom giveth life to them that have it.
ECCLESIASTES 7:12

The words of wise men are heard in quiet more than the cry of him that ruleth among fools. Wisdom is better than weapons of war; but one sinner destroyeth much good.
ECCLESIASTES 9:17–18

The words of the wise are as goads, and as nails fastened by the masters of assemblies, which are given from one shepherd. And further, by these, my son, be admonished: of making many books there is no end; and much study is a weariness of the flesh.
ECCLESIASTES 12:11–12

Wisdom is like electricity. There is no permanently wise man, but men capable of wisdom, who, being put into certain company, or other favorable conditions, become wise for a while, as glasses being rubbed acquire electric power for a while.
RALPH WALDO EMERSON

Wisdom will never let us stand with any man on an unfriendly footing. We refuse sympathy and intimacy with people, as if we waited for some better sympathy or intimacy to come. But whence and when: Tomorrow will be like today. Life wastes itself while we are preparing to live.
RALPH WALDO EMERSON

The two powers which in my opinion constitute a wise man are those of bearing and forbearing.
EPICTETUS

Wisdom is knowing when to speak your mind and when to mind your speech.
EVANGEL

Stoicism is the wisdom of madness and cynicism the madness of wisdom.
BERGEN EVANS

Speakers have been showering us with pearls of wisdom for centuries, and if all of their valuable advice were laid end to end, it would still be just as good as new. Very little of it has ever been used.
BENJAMIN F. FAIRLESS

He who hesitates is sometimes wise.
MALCOLM FORBES

Once in a while there's wisdom in recognizing that the Boss is.
MALCOLM FORBES

It is human nature to think wisely and act foolishly.
ANATOLE FRANCE

When you assemble a number of men to have the advantage of their joint wisdom, you inevitably assemble with those men all their prejudices, their passions, their errors of opinion, their local interests and their selfish views.
BENJAMIN FRANKLIN

A wise man will make tools of what comes to hand.
THOMAS FULLER

The fool wanders, the wise man travels.
THOMAS FULLER

Wisdom in a poor man is a diamond set in lead.
THOMAS FULLER

Wisdom, itself, is often an abstraction associated not with fact or reality, but with the man who asserts it and the manner of its assertion.
JOHN KENNETH GALBRAITH

The man who questions opinion is wise; the man who quarrels with facts is a fool.
FRANK A. GARBUTT

Keep me away from the wisdom which does not cry, the philosophy which does not laugh and the greatest which does not bow before children.
KAHLIL GIBRAN

Wisdom ceases to be wisdom when it becomes too proud to weep, too grave to laugh, and too self-ful to seek other than itself.
KAHLIL GIBRAN

The true greatness and the true happiness of a country consist in wisdom; in that enlarged and comprehensive wisdom which includes education,

knowledge, religion, virtue, freedom, with every influence which advances and every institution which supports them.
**HENRY GILES**

To comprehend a man's life, it is necessary to know not merely what he does, but also what he purposely leaves undone. There is a limit to the work that can be got out of a human body or a human brain, and he is a wise man who wastes no energy on pursuits for which he is not fitted; and he is still wiser who, from among the things that he can do well, chooses and resolutely follows the best.
**WILLIAM E. GLADSTONE**

All truly wise thoughts have been thought already thousands of times; but to make them truly ours, we must think them over again honestly till they take firm root in our personal experience.
**JOHANN WOLFGANG VON GOETHE**

The mind is found most acute and most uneasy in the morning. Uneasiness is, indeed, a species of sagacity—a passive sagacity. Fools are never uneasy.
**JOHANN WOLFGANG VON GOETHE**

Wisdom makes but a slow defense against trouble, though at last a sure one.
**OLIVER GOLDSMITH**

No mistakes, no experience; no experience, no wisdom.
**STANLEY GOLDSTEIN**

A wise man gets more out of his enemies than a fool gets out of his friends.
**BALTASAR GRACIÁN**

Knowledge without wisdom is double folly.
**BALTASAR GRACIÁN**

The sage has one advantage: He is immortal. If this is not his century, many others will be.
**BALTASAR GRACIÁN**

The intellect of the wise is like glass: It admits the light of heaven and reflects it.
**AUGUSTUS HARE**

The wise know the value of riches, but the rich do not know the pleasures of wisdom.
**HEBREW PROVERB**

Ninety percent of all human wisdom is the ability to mind your own business.
**ROBERT A. HEINLEIN**

Where wisdom is called for, force is of little use.
**HERODOTUS**

Knowledge can be communicated, but not wisdom. One can find it, live it, be fortified by it, do wonders through it, but one cannot communicate and teach it.
**HERMANN HESSE**

Such is the nature of men that howsoever they may acknowledge many others to be more witty, or more eloquent, or more learned, yet they will hardly believe there may be many so wise as themselves.
**THOMAS HOBBES**

It is the folly of the world, constantly, which confounds its wisdom.
**OLIVER WENDELL HOLMES**

It is the province of knowledge to speak, and it is the privilege of wisdom to listen.
**OLIVER WENDELL HOLMES**

How prone to doubt, how cautious are the wise!
**HOMER**

Those unacquainted with the world take pleasure in intimacy with great men; those who are wiser fear the consequences.
**HORACE**

A man must not think he can save himself the trouble of being a sensible man and a gentleman by going to his lawyer, any more than he can get himself a sound constitution by going to his doctor.
**EDGAR WATSON HOWE**

True wisdom is to know what is best worth knowing, and to do what is best worth doing.
**EDWARD PORTER HUMPHREY**

Wisdom denotes the pursuing of the best ends by the best means.
**FRANCIS HUTCHESON**

Nature will not forgive those who fail to fulfill the law of their being. The law of human beings is wisdom and goodness, not unlimited acquisition.
**ROBERT M. HUTCHINS**

He is great who can do what he wishes; he is wise who wishes to do what he can.
**AUGUST IFFLAND**

The wisdom of the wise is an uncommon degree of common sense.
**WILLIAM RALPH INGE**

If any of you lack wisdom, let him ask of God, that giveth to all men liberally, and upbraideth not: and it shall be given him.
**JAMES 1:5**

The art of being wise is the art of knowing what to overlook.
**WILLIAM JAMES**

Knowledge without wisdom is a load of books on the back of an ass.
**JAPANESE PROVERB**

The wise men are ashamed, they are dismayed and taken: lo, they have rejected the word of the Lord; and what wisdom is in them?
**JEREMIAH 8:9**

Thus saith the Lord, Let not the wise man glory in his wisdom, neither let the mighty man glory in his might, let not the rich man glory in his riches: But let him that glorieth glory in this, that he understandeth and knoweth me, that I am the Lord which exercise loving-kindness, judgment, and righteousness in the earth: for in these things I delight, saith the Lord.
**JEREMIAH 9:23–4**

He hath made the earth by his power, he hath established the world by his wisdom, and hath stretched out the heaven by his understanding.
**JEREMIAH 51:15**

Whence then cometh wisdom? and where is the place of understanding? Seeing it is hid from the eyes of all living, and kept close from the fowls of the air.
**JOB 23:20–21**

Very few men are wise by their own counsel, or learned by their own teaching; for he that was only taught by himself had a fool as his master.
**BEN JONSON**

Maxims are to the intellect what laws are to actions: They do not enlighten, but guide and direct, and though themselves blind, are protecting.
**JOSEPH JOUBERT**

It is a maxim received in life that, in general, we can determine more wisely for others than for ourselves. The reason of it is so clear in argument that it hardly wants the confirming of experience.
JUNIUS

The first point of wisdom is to discern that which is false; the second to know that which is true.
LACTANTIUS

Make wisdom your provision for the journey from youth to old age, for it is a more certain support than all other possessions.
DIOGENES LAERTIUS

The proverbial wisdom of the populace at gates, on roads, and in markets, instructs him who studies man more fully than a thousand rules ostentatiously arranged.
JOHANN LAVATER

It may serve as a comfort to us, in all our calamities and afflictions, that he that loses anything and gets wisdom by it is a gainer by the loss.
ROGER L'ESTRANGE

There are people who think that everything one does with a serious face is sensible.
GEORG CHRISTOPH LICHTENBERG

I do not think much of a man who is not wiser today than he was yesterday.
ABRAHAM LINCOLN

It requires wisdom to understand wisdom; the music is nothing if the audience is deaf.
WALTER LIPPMANN

The wise are neither young nor old—their physical age tells us nothing, any more than the generality of men can be divided between age and youth on the basis of their knowledge. The wise are always young in will and energy and old in experience and reflection.
FRANCES R. LISCHNER

Proverbs are in the world of thought what gold coin is in the world of business—great value in small compass, and equally current among all people. Sometimes the proverb may be false, the coin counterfeit, but in both cases the false proves the value of the true.
DANIEL MARCH

Be wise; soar not too high to fall, but stoop to rise.
PHILIP MASSINGER

If one's life reaches to or beyond 70, one must have acquired some wisdom along the way or be intellectually dead or a damned fool.
DOROTHY MCCALL

To know that which before us lies in daily life is the prime wisdom.
JOHN MILTON

What is strength without a double share of wisdom? Strength's not made to rule, but to subserve, where wisdom bears command.
JOHN MILTON

A wise man sees as much as he ought, not as much as he can.
MICHEL DE MONTAIGNE

We can be knowledgeable with other men's knowledge, but we cannot be wise with other men's wisdom.
MICHEL DE MONTAIGNE

Wisdom comes not from experience but from meditating on experience and assimilating it.
JOY ELMER MORGAN

Knowledge comes by taking things apart: analysis. But wisdom comes by putting things together.
**JOHN A. MORRISON**

Life is given for wisdom, and yet we are not wise; for goodness, and we are not good; for overcoming evil, and evil remains; for patience and sympathy and love, and yet we are fretful and hard and weak and selfish. We are keyed not to attainment, but to the struggle toward it.
**THEODORE T. MUNGER**

The growth of wisdom may be gauged accurately by the decline of ill temper.
**FRIEDRICH WILHELM NIETZSCHE**

The fellowship of country roads is a goodly one, and in that fellowship one can find lifelong comrades, passing acquaintances, and a wisdom that can be gained, perhaps, in no other way. It is the wisdom of fields and woods, compounded by the observing eye and the understanding heart; and it is a wisdom that does not grow old, that lasts until a man's hiking days are done, and then it brightens many a fireside hour.
**ARTHUR WALLACE PEACH**

He who is taught to live upon little owes more to his father's wisdom than he who has a great deal left him does to his father's care.
**WILLIAM PENN**

The wise man will want to be ever with him who is better than himself.
**PLATO**

The wisest have the most authority.
**PLATO**

Every man, however wise, needs the advice of some sagacious friend in the affairs of life.
**PLAUTUS**

He is happy in his wisdom who has learned at another's expense.
**PLAUTUS**

Wisdom is the principal thing; therefore get wisdom: and with all thy getting get understanding. Exalt her, and she shall promote thee: she shall bring thee to honour, when thou dost embrace her.
**PROVERBS 4:7–8**

Through wisdom is an house builded; and by understanding it is established: and by knowledge shall the chambers be filled with all precious and pleasant riches.
**PROVERBS 24:3–4**

The fear of the Lord is the beginning of wisdom: a good understanding have all they that do his commandments: his praise endureth forever.
**PSALMS 111–10**

Wisdom thoroughly learned, will never be forgotten.
**PYTHAGORAS**

Be wisely worldly, but not worldly wise.
**FRANCIS QUARLES**

The constancy of sages is nothing but the art of locking up their agitation in their hearts.
**FRANÇOIS DE LA ROCHEFOUCAULD**

Wisdom is to the mind what health is to the body.
**FRANÇOIS DE LA ROCHEFOUCAULD**

Nine-tenths of wisdom consists in being wise in time.
**THEODORE ROOSEVELT**

The difference between a wise guy and a wise man is plenty!
**GALEN STAR ROSS**

Good people are good because they've come to wisdom through failure.
WILLIAM SAROYAN

Fools are aye fond o' flittin' and wise men o' sittin'.
SCOTTISH PROVERB

Precepts or maxims are of great weight; and a few useful ones at hand do more toward a happy life than whole volumes that we know not where to find.
SENECA

Wisdom does not show itself so much in precept as in life—in firmness of mind and a mastery of appetite. It teaches us to do as well as to talk; and to make our words and actions all of a color.
SENECA

Wisely and slow; they stumble that run fast.
WILLIAM SHAKESPEARE

Wisdom makes but a slow defense against trouble, though at last a sure one.
OLIVER SMITH

Much wisdom often goes with fewer words.
SOPHOCLES

Wisdom outweighs any wealth.
SOPHOCLES

The wise man must remember that while he is a descendant of the past, he is a parent of the future.
HERBERT SPENCER

Wisdom is the right use of knowledge. To know is not to be wise. Many men know a great deal, and are all the greater fools for it. There is no fool so great a fool as a knowing fool. But to know how to use knowledge is to have wisdom.
CHARLES H. SPURGEON

It is sometimes wise to forget who we are.
PUBLILIUS SYRUS

A man's wisdom is his best friend; folly his worst enemy.
WILLIAM J. TEMPLE

Immortal gods! How much does one man excel another! What a difference there is between a wise man and a fool.
TERENCE

Colors fade, temples crumble, empires fall, but wise words endure.
DAME SYBIL THORNDIKE

A man never reaches that dizzy height of wisdom that he can no longer be led by the nose.
MARK TWAIN

He is a hard man who is only just, and a sad one who is only wise.
VOLTAIRE

Citizens may be born free; they are not born wise. Therefore, the business of liberal education in a democracy is to make free men wise.
F. CHAMPION WARD

Wisdom is the power that enables us to use knowledge for the benefit of ourselves and others.
THOMAS J. WATSON

Perhaps wisdom is to be found in people who have suffered greatly but have surmounted it.
LOUIS JOLYON WEST

Wisdom is oftimes nearer when we stoop than when we soar.
WILLIAM WORDSWORTH

## Wit

Wit is a treacherous dart. It is perhaps the only weapon with which it is possible to stab oneself in one's own back.
GEOFFREY BOCCA

Better the fragrant herb of wit and a little cream of affability than all the pretty cups in the world.
VAN WYCK BROOKS

Repartee is what you wish you'd said.
HEYWOOD BROUN

If you have wit, use it to please and not to hurt: you may shine like the sun in the temperate zones without scorching.
LORD CHESTERFIELD

Impropriety is the soul of wit.
SOMERSET MAUGHAM

Brevity is the soul of lingerie.
DOROTHY PARKER

As empty vessels make the loudest sound, so they that have the least wit are the greatest blabbers.
PLATO

He that would pun would pick a pocket.
ALEXANDER POPE

## Women

You can never trust a woman; she may be true to you.
DOUGLAS AINSLIE

Never play cards with a man called Doc. Never eat in a place called Mom's. Never sleep with a woman whose troubles are worse than your own.
NELSON ALGREN

A youthful figure is what you get when you ask a woman her age.
ANONYMOUS

The first time Adam had a chance, he laid the blame on women.
NANCY ASTOR

A woman, especially if she have the misfortune of knowing anything, should conceal it as well as she can.
JANE AUSTEN

It is the good girls who keep the diaries; the bad girls never have the time.
TALLULAH BANKHEAD

The trouble with life is that there are so many beautiful women—and so little time.
JOHN BARRYMORE

The way to fight a woman is with your hat. Grab it and run.
JOHN BARRYMORE

Most women are not so young as they painted.
MAX BEERBOHM

Empty wine bottles have a bad opinion of women.
AMBROSE BIERCE

Women would be more charming if one could fall into her arms without falling into her hands.
AMBROSE BIERCE

Behind almost every woman you ever heard of stands a man who let her down.
NAOMI BLIVEN

The trouble with some women is that they get all excited about nothing—and then marry him.
CHER

Being a woman is a terribly difficult trade, since it consists principally of dealing with men.
JOSEPH CONRAD

The average man is more interested in a woman who is interested in him than he is in a woman with beautiful legs.
MARLENE DIETRICH

Man is not the enemy here, but the fellow victim. The real enemy is women's denigration of themselves.
BETTY FRIEDAN

Contrary to popular belief, English women do not wear tweed nightgowns.
HERMIONE GINGOLD

There is only one proper way to wear a beautiful dress: to forget you are wearing it.
MADAME DE GIRARDIN

A faithful woman looks to the spring, a good book, perfume, earthquakes, and divine revelation for the experience others find in a lover. They deceive their husbands, so to speak, with the entire world, men excepted.
JEAN GIRAUDOUX

The low regard in which women hold themselves is not necessarily their fault, but it is surely one of their gravest problems.
JOHN P. GRIER

There is nothing like a ticker tape except a woman—nothing that promises, hour after hour, day after day, such sudden developments; nothing that disappoints so often or occasionally fulfils with such unbelievable, passionate magnificence.
WALTER K. GUTMAN

The hardest years in a woman's life are those between 10 and 70.
HELEN HAYES (AT 83)

A man is in general better pleased when he has a good dinner upon his table, than when his wife talks Greek.
SAMUEL JOHNSON

The colonel's lady and Judy O'Grady are sisters under their skins.
RUDYARD KIPLING

All one's life as a young woman one is on show, a focus of attention, people notice you. You set yourself up to being noticed and admired. And then, not expecting it, you become middle-aged and anonymous.
DORIS LESSING

I'm furious about the Women's Liberationists. They keep getting up on soapboxes and proclaiming that women are brighter than men. That's true, but it should be kept very quiet or it ruins the whole racket.
ANITA LOOS

It isn't that gentlemen really prefer blondes, it's just that we look dumber.
ANITA LOOS

But if God had wanted us to think with our wombs, why did he give us a brain?
CLARE BOOTHE LUCE

Our bodies are shaped to bear children, and our lives are a working out of the processes of creation. All our ambitions and intelligence are beside that great elemental point.
**PHYLLIS MCGINLEY**

Women's liberation is just a lot of foolishness. It's the men who are discriminated against. They can't bear children. And no one's likely to do anything about that.
**GOLDA MEIR**

No matter how happily a woman may be married, it always pleases her to discover that there is a nice man who wishes she were not.
**H. L. MENCKEN**

The allurement that women hold out to men is precisely the allurement that Cape Hatteras holds out to sailors: They are enormously dangerous and hence enormously fascinating.
**H. L. MENCKEN**

A kiss can be a comma, a question mark or an exclamation point. That's basic spelling that every woman ought to know.
**MISTINGUETTE**

I don't mind living in a man's world as long as I can be a woman in it.
**MARILYN MONROE**

Dancing is wonderful training for girls; it's the first place you learn to guess what a man is going to do before he does it.
**CHRISTOPHER MORLEY**

People in the U.S. used to think that if girls were good at sports their sexuality would be affected. Being feminine meant being a cheerleader, not an athlete. The image of women is changing now. You don't have to be pretty for people to come and see you play.
**MARTINA NAVRATILOVA**

Woman was God's second mistake.
**FRIEDRICH WILHELM NIETZSCHE**

If women didn't exist, all the money in the world would have no meaning.
**ARISTOTLE ONASSIS**

When the candles are out, all women are fair.
**PLUTARCH**

The charms of a passing woman are usually in direct relation to the speed of her passing.
**MARCEL PROUST**

Who can find a virtuous woman? for her price is far above rubies. The heart of her husband doth safely trust in her, so that he shall have no need of spoil. She will do him good and not evil all the days of her life.
**PROVERBS 31:10–12**

I never expected to see the day when girls would get sunburned in the places they now do.
**WILL ROGERS**

Any woman who has a great deal to offer the world is in trouble.
**HAZEL SCOTT**

No man is a match for a woman, except with a poker and a hobnailed pair of boots—and not always even then.
**GEORGE BERNARD SHAW**

Think what cowards men would be if they had to bear children. Women are altogether a superior species.
**GEORGE BERNARD SHAW**

The best class of women from the New World have done much to change the face of London society. In a word, they have brought the grit and 'go' of a new race to bear on our rusty if cherished institutions. They have made us more modern in our ways and more up-do-date in our opinions; they have taught us how to manage the mere man, and how to rule our own houses and keep our own money. In a word, they opened our eyes to women's rights long before we ever heard of a Suffragette demonstration.
LETTER TO THE *TATLER*, 1910

I'm 65 and I guess that puts me in the geriatrics. But if there were 15 months in the year, I'd only be 48. That's the trouble with us. We number everything. Take women, for example. I think they deserve to have more than 12 years between the ages of 28 and 40.
JAMES THURBER

From birth to age 18, a girl needs good parents, from 18 to 35 she needs good looks, from 35 to 55 she needs a good personality, and from 55 on she needs cash.
SOPHIE TUCKER

After all these years, I see that I was wrong about Eve in the beginning; it is better to live outside the Garden with her than inside it without her.
MARK TWAIN'S ADAM

Every man has a secret ambition: To outsmart horses, fish and women.
MARK TWAIN

My advice to girls: first, don't smoke—to excess; second, don't drink—to excess; third, don't marry—to excess.
MARK TWAIN

The Queen is most anxious to enlist everyone who can speak or write to join in checking this mad, wicked folly of Women's Rights, with all its attendant horrors on which her poor, feeble sex is bent, forgetting every sense of womanly feeling and propriety.
QUEEN VICTORIA

Man cannot degrade woman without himself falling into degradation; he cannot elevate her without at the same time elevating himself.
ALEXANDER WALKER

One should never trust a woman who tells one her real age. A woman who would tell that would tell anything.
OSCAR WILDE

I have bursts of being a lady, but it doesn't last long.
SHELLEY WINTERS

## *Words*

Ideas in the mind are the transcript of the world, words are the transcript of ideas; and writing and printing are the transcript of words.
JOSEPH ADDISON

When you have spoken the word, it reigns over you. When it is unspoken you reign over it.
ARABIAN PROVERB

Words once printed assume a life of their own.
WILMA ASKINAS

Vocabulary is an index to a civilization, and ours is a disturbed one. That's why so many of the new words deal with war, violence, drugs, racism, and not so many with peace and prosperity.
CLARENCE BARNHART

The best way to keep one's word is not to give it.
NAPOLEON BONAPARTE

"Speak English," said the Eaglet. "I don't know the meaning of half these long words, and what's more, I don't believe you do either."
LEWIS CARROLL

Short words are best and the old words when short are best of all.
WINSTON CHURCHILL

Oh, the comfort, the inexpressible comfort, of feeling safe with a person, having neither to weigh thoughts nor measure words, but pouring them all right out, just as they are, chaff and grain together; certain that a faithful hand will take and sift them, keep what is worth keeping, and with the breath of kindness blow the rest away.
REX COLE

For one word a man is often deemed to be wise, and for one word he is often deemed to be foolish. We should be careful indeed what we say.
CONFUCIUS

Words are the voice of the heart.
CONFUCIUS

There is never enough time to say our last word—the last word of our love, of our desire, faith, remorse, submission, revolt.
JOSEPH CONRAD

The secret things belong to the Lord our God: but those things which are revealed belong unto us and to our children forever, that we may do all the words of his law.
DEUTERONOMY 29:29

Although words exist for the most part for the transmission of ideas, there are some which produce such violent disturbance in our feelings that the role they play in the transmission of ideas is lost in the background.
ALBERT EINSTEIN

Because his wife is of such a delicate nature, a man avoids using certain words all through his married life, and then one day he picks up a bestseller she is reading and finds five of the words in the first chapter.
WILLIAM FEATHER

The power of words is immense. A well-chosen word has often sufficed to stop a flying army, to change defeat into victory, and to save an empire.
EMILE DE GIRARDIN

Nothing is more unaccountable than the spell that often lurks in a spoken word. A thought may be present to the mind, and two minds conscious of the same thought, but as long as it remains unspoken their familiar talk flows quietly over the hidden idea.
NATHANIEL HAWTHORNE

Sticks and stones can break your bones, but words can make your blood boil.
CULLEN HIGHTOWER

Language rarely lies. It can reveal the insincerity of a writer's claims simply through a grating adjective or an inflated phrase. We come upon a frenzy of words and suspect it hides a paucity of feeling.
IRVING HOWE

Words, like eyeglasses, blur everything that they do not make more clear.
JOSEPH JOUBERT

Words are the most powerful drug used by mankind.
RUDYARD KIPLING

We should have a great many fewer disputes in the world if words were taken for what they are, the signs of our ideas only, and not for things themselves.
**JOHN LOCKE**

But I say unto you, That every idle word that men shall speak, they shall give account thereof in the day of judgement.
**MATTHEW 12:36**

The world is satisfied with words, few care to dive beneath the surface.
**BLAISE PASCAL**

If a civil word or two will render a man happy, he must be a wretch indeed who will not tell them to him.
**WILLIAM PENN**

In words as fashions the same rule will hold,
Alike fantastic if too new or old;
Be not the first by whom the new are tried
Nor yet the last to lay the old aside.
**ALEXANDER POPE**

Let the words of my mouth, and the meditation of my heart, be acceptable in they sight, O Lord, my strength and my redeemer.
**PSALMS 19:14**

What you keep by you, you may change and mend; but words, once spoken, can never be recalled.
**WENTWORTH ROSCOMMON**

Words are loaded pistols.
**JEAN-PAUL SARTRE**

A word too much always defeats its purpose.
**ARTHUR SCHOPENHAUER**

Words are often seen hunting for an idea, but ideas are never seen hunting for words.
**HENRY WHEELER SHAW (JOSH BILLINGS)**

Such as thy words are, such will thine affections be esteemed; and such as thine affections, will be thy deeds; and such as thy deeds will be thy life.
**SOCRATES**

A powerful agent is the right word. Whenever we come upon one of those intensely right words in a book or a newspaper the resulting effect is physical as well as spiritual, and electrically prompt.
**MARK TWAIN**

He'd be a much nicer fellow if he had a good swear now and then.
**JOHN TYNDALL**

If your foot slips, you may recover your balance, but if your tongue slips, you cannot recall your words.
**MARTIN VANBEE**

One great use of words is to hide our thoughts.
**VOLTAIRE**

## *Work*

Without rest, a man cannot work; without work, the rest does not give you any benefit.
**ABKHASIAN PROVERB**

People do not get tired out from working where work is intelligently handled. Work, if it is interesting, is a stimulant. It's worry and a lack of interest in what one does that tire and discourage. Every one of us should have our pet interests—as many as we can handle efficiently and happily. Our interests should never be allowed to lag or get cold so that all enthusiasm is spent. Each day can be one of

triumph if you keep up to your interests—feeding them as they feed you!
GEORGE MATTHEW ADAMS

Most of the trades, professions, and ways of living among mankind, take their original either from the love of the pleasure, or the fear of want. The former, when it becomes too violent, degenerates into luxury, and the latter into avarice.
JOSEPH ADDISON

Work only tires a woman, but it ruins a man.
AFRICAN PROVERB

A work of real merit finds favor at last.
AMOS BRONSON ALCOTT

We can't think in terms of men alone, any more than we can of machines alone, or money alone. It takes all three. We need a growing population—men; we need a developing technology—machines; we need thrift and savings to provide the capital so that the machines may serve the men.
HENRY C. ALEXANDER

If you feel that you are indispensable, put your finger in a glass of water, withdraw it, and note the hole you have left.
ANONYMOUS

He works and blows the coals, and has plenty of other irons in the fire.
ARISTOPHANES

Love work.
Turn a deaf ear to slander.
Be considerate in correcting others.
Do not be taken up by trifles.
Do not resent plain speaking.
Meet offenders half-way.
Be thorough in thought.
Have an open mind.
Do your duty without grumbling.
MARCUS AURELIUS ANTONINUS

They are happy men whose natures sort with their vocations.
FRANCIS BACON

The superstition that all our hours of work are a minus quantity in the happiness of life, and all the hours of idleness are plus ones, is a most ludicrous and pernicious doctrine, and its greatest support comes from our not taking sufficient trouble, not making a real effort, to make work as near pleasure as it can be.
LORD BALFOUR

It is necessary to work, if not from inclination, at least from despair. Everything considered, work is less boring than amusing oneself.
CHARLES BAUDELAIRE

I received a letter from a lad asking me for an easy berth. To this I replied: "You cannot be an editor; do not try the law: do not think of the ministry; let alone all ships and merchandise; abhor politics; don't practice medicine; be not a farmer or a soldier or a sailor; don't study, don't think. None of these are easy. O, my son, you have come into a hard world. I know of only one easy place in it, and that is the grave!"
HENRY WARD BEECHER

If we would have anything of benefit, we must earn it, and earning it become shrewd, inventive, ingenious, active, enterprising.
HENRY WARD BEECHER

No fine work can be done without concentration and self-sacrifice and toil and doubt.
MAX BEERBOHM

Anyone can do any amount of work, provided it isn't the work he is supposed to be doing at that moment.
ROBERT BENCHLEY

Less shirk means less irk in work!
ALONZO NEWTON BENN

Men are more important than tools. If you don't believe so, put a good tool into the hands of a poor workman.
JOHN J. BERNET

Men divide themselves into four classes: (1) Those who never do what they are told—always less; (2) those who will do what they are told—but no more; (3) those who will do things without being told: (4) those who will inspire others and make them do things. It's up to you.
WILLIAM J. H. BOETCKER

No man can make good during working hours who does the wrong thing outside of working hours.
WILLIAM J. H. BOETCKER

You can employ men and hire hands to work for you, but you will have to win their hearts to have them work with you.
WILLIAM J. H. BOETCKER

The true wealth of a state consists in the number of its inhabitants, in their toil and industry.
NAPOLEON BONAPARTE

**The six laws of work are:**

1. A man must drive his energy, not be driven by it.
2. A man must be master of his hours and days, not their servant.
3. The way to push things through to a finish effectively must be learned.
4. A man must earnestly want.
5. Never permit failure to become a habit.
6. Learn to adust yourself to the conditions you have to endure, but make a point of trying to alter or correct conditions so that they are most favorable to you.

WILLIAM FREDERICK BOOK

The noblest workers of this world bequeath us nothing so great as the image of themselves. Their task, be it ever so glorious, is historical and transient, but the majesty of their spirit is essential and eternal.
GEORGE BROWN

There are only two ways of getting on in this world; by one's own industry or by the weakness of others.
JEAN DE LA BRUYÈRE

I find in life that most affairs that require serious handling are distasteful. For this reason, I have always believed that the successful man has the hardest battle with himself rather than with the other fellow. To bring one's self to a frame of mind and to the proper energy to accomplish things that require plain hard work continuously is the one big battle that everyone has. When this battle is won for all time, then everything is easy.
THOMAS A. BUCKNER

If your work is work to you and you don't see beyond that work and see the pleasure in work and the pleasure in service, look out; you are in danger of standing in your present station for a long, long time.
MILAN R. BUMP

Employment, which Galen calls nature's physician, is so essential to human happiness that indolence is justly considered as the mother of misery.
BURTON

Work with some men is as besetting a sin as idleness with others.
SAMUEL BUTLER

I never work hard when I am working; I only work hard when I am not working.
IRVING CAESAR

It is an article of faith in my creed to pick the man who does not take himself seriously, but does take his work seriously.
MICHAEL C. CAHILL

Nature has made occupation a necessity to us; society makes it a duty; habit makes it a pleasure.
CAPELLE

All work, even cotton-spinning is noble; work is alone noble.
THOMAS CARLYLE

Blessed is he who has found his work; let him ask no other blessedness.
THOMAS CARLYLE

Even in the meanest sorts of labor, the whole soul of a man is composed into a kind of real harmony the instant he sets himself to work.
THOMAS CARLYLE

He that will not work according to his faculty, let him perish according to his necessity: There is no law juster than that.
THOMAS CARLYLE

Oh, give us the man who sings at his work.
THOMAS CARLYLE

The glory of a workman, still more of a master-workman, that he does his work well, ought to be his most precious possession; like the honor of a soldier, dearer to him than life.
THOMAS CARLYLE

There is a perennial nobleness and even sacredness in work.
THOMAS CARLYLE

Work is a grand cure for all the maladies and miseries that ever beset mankind—honest work, which you intend getting done.
THOMAS CARLYLE

Set me a task in which I can put something of my very self, and it is a task no longer; it is joy; it is art.
BLISS CARMAN

It marks a big step in a man's development when he comes to realize that other men can be called in to help him do a better job than he can do alone.
ANDREW CARNEGIE

I hold that a man had better be dead than alive when his work is done.
ALICE CARY

It is an undoubted truth that the less one has to do the less time one finds to do it in. One yawns, one procrastinates, one can do it when one will, and, therefore, one seldom does it at all; whereas those who have a great deal of business must (to use a vulgar expression) buckle to it; and then they always find time enough to do it in.
LORD CHESTERFIELD

This one makes a net;
This one stands and wishes.
Would you like to bet
Which one gets the fishes?
CHINESE RHYME

Let every man practice the art that he knows best.
CICERO

**What Kind of a Chap Are You?**

Are you one of the chaps who can take his raps
And still not hit the floor;
Who'll stick by the gun till his task is done
And then look 'round for more?
Do you grin at your work or sulk and shirk
When the job seems hard to do;
Are you there with the grit to do your bit;
Can the boss depend on you?
If your conscience clear, with nothing to fear
As you punch the clock each night;
When you leave the job, do your pulses throb
With the thought of a task done right?
Is it pleasure or dread when you pillow your head
And think of the coming day;
Do you breathe a prayer for strength to bear
Does your job mean simply play?
Just pause a bit and see if you fit
In the class that's pictured here—
For it's never too late to clean the slate
And start on a record clear.
FRANK A. COLLINS

A windmill is eternally at work to accomplish one end, although it shifts with every variation of the weathercock, and assumes ten different positions in a day.
CHARLES CALEB COLTON

All one's work might have been better done; but this is a sort of reflection a worker must put aside courageously if he doesn't mean every one of his conceptions to remain forever a private vision, an evanescent reverie.
JOSEPH CONRAD

A man is a worker. If he is not that he is nothing.
JOSEPH CONRAD

All growth depends upon activity. There is no development physically or intellectually without effort, and effort means work. Work is not a curse; it is the prerogative of intelligence, the only means to manhood, and the measure of civilization.
CALVIN COOLIDGE

The man who builds a factory builds a temple; the man who works there worships there; and to each is due not scorn and blame but reverence and praise.
CALVIN COOLIDGE

No matter how much work a man can do, no matter how engaging his personality may be, he will not advance far in business if he cannot work through others.
JOHN CRAIG

To make a man happy, fill his hands with work, his heart with affection, his mind with purpose, his memory with useful knowledge, his future with hope, and his stomach with food. The devil never enters a man except one of these rooms be vacant. Cast him out and sweep and garnish the room, and he will return with seven other devils. The only way to be rid of him is to fill the room and take down your "To Let" sign.
FREDERICK E. CRANE

It's the men behind who make the man ahead.
MERLE CROWELL

The more help a man has in his garden, the less it belongs to him.
WILLIAM H. DAVIES

We would rather have one man or woman working with us than three merely working for us.
J. DABNEY DAY

The workers are the saviors of society, the redeemers of the race.
**Eugene V. Debs**

Nothing is really work unless you would rather be doing something else.
**Chub De Wolfe**

My idea of the real aristocrat is the master workman, no matter what his line of work may be.
**Henry L. Doherty**

When you find a man who knows his job and is willing to take responsibility, keep out of his way and don't bother him with unnecessary supervision. What you may think is cooperation is nothing but interference.
**Thomas Dreier**

Work is hard if you're paid to do it, and it's pleasure if you pay to be allowed to do it.
**Finley Peter Dunne**

Whatsoever thy hand findeth to do, do it with thy might; for there is no work, nor device, nor knowledge, nor wisdom, in the grave, whither thou goest.
**Ecclesiastes 9:10**

If I were to suggest a general rule for happiness, I would say "Work a little harder; work a little longer; work!"
**Frederick H. Ecker**

I am wondering what would have happened to me if some fluent talker had converted me to the theory of the eight-hour day and convinced me that it was not fair to my fellow workers to put forth my best efforts in my work. I am glad that the eight-hour day had not been invented when I was a young man. If my life had been made up of eight-hour days I do not believe I could have accomplished a great deal. This country would not amount to as much as it does if the young men of fifty years ago had been afraid that they might earn more than they were paid for.
**Thomas Edison**

How do I work? I grope.
**Albert Einstein**

Many times a day I realize how my own outer and inner life is built upon the labors of my fellow men, both living and dead, and how earnestly I must exert myself in return as much as I have received.
**Albert Einstein**

A man is relieved and gay when he has put his heart into his work and done his best; what he has said or done otherwise shall give him no peace.
**Ralph Waldo Emerson**

The shoemaker makes a good shoe because he makes nothing else.
**Ralph Waldo Emerson**

The sum of wisdom is that time is never lost that is devoted to work.
**Ralph Waldo Emerson**

Elbow grease is the best polish.
**English proverb**

I therefore, the prisoner of the Lord, beseech you that ye walk worthy of the vocation wherewith ye are called, with all lowliness and meekness, with long-suffering, forbearing one another in love.
**Ephesians 4:1–2**

Let him that stole steal no more: but rather let him labor, working with his hands the thing which is good, that he may have to give to him that needeth.
**Ephesians 4:28**

One of the saddest things is that the only thing a man can do for eight hours a day, day after day, is work. You can't eat eight hours a day nor drink for eight hours a day nor make love for eight hours.
**WILLIAM FAULKNER**

How people try to avoid work and how well some of them succeed!
**WILLIAM FEATHER**

It's not the increasing competition; it's going back to real work that most of us complain about.
**WILLIAM FEATHER**

The right man can make a good job out of any job.
**WILLIAM FEATHER**

Whether we like it or not, we must work, and we must accept employment at the best terms we can get.
**WILLIAM FEATHER**

Work is the best method devised for killing time.
**WILLIAM FEATHER**

Here below is not the land of happiness; it is only the land of toil; and every joy which comes to us is only to strengthen us for some greater labor that is to succeed.
**IMMANUEL FICHTE**

Conditions never get so bad in this country but that a man who works can get business.
**LAWRENCE P. FISHER**

Failures are few among people who have found a work they like enough to do it well. You invest money in your work; invest love in it too. Like your work. Like the materials and the tools with which you work. Like the people with whom you work. Like the place where you work. It pays well.
**CLARENCE E. FLYNN**

Genius is often a short way of spelling hard work. Poverty, obscurity, struggle and ambition formed the foundation for many careers of transcendent achievement. Few marks are made in the world's history by eight-hour-day men. . . . Sir Joshua Reynolds had but one maxim for success: "Work, work, work." Is not rigid and continuous training necessary for the making of strong athletes? Hard work is not fatal to real success. *Vouloir c'est pouvoir.*
**B. C. FORBES**

Has your work become very easy? Do you find you can do it with little effort? Has it ceased to impose any strain or fatigue upon you? Do you no longer feel loss of vitality after a long spell of it? Can you now do it as easy as water rolls off a duck's back? If so, look out! Do some stock-taking. Examine your output. . . . Work done with little effort is likely to yield little result. Every job can be done excellently or indifferently. Excellence necessitates effort—hard, sustained, concentrated effort.
**B. C. FORBES**

J. P. Morgan, then past 70, was asked by the son of an eminent father why he [Morgan] didn't retire. "When did your father retire?"asked Mr. Morgan, without looking up from his desk. "In 1902." "When did he die?" "Oh, at the end of 1904." "Huh!" snapped Mr. Morgan, "If he had kept on working he would have been alive still."

Work is God's best medicine. It is God's medicine for man.
**B. C. FORBES**

Ugliness, squalor are breeding grounds for revolution. Beauty is conducive to tranquillity, happiness. Beautifying of homes and places of worship began with the dawn of civilization. Beautifying of workplaces is only in its infancy. Yet, since men normally spend more than half of their waking hours at work, surely it is important that adequate attention be devoted to elevating their working environment,

whether office or factory, foundry or machine shop, mine or warehouse. Beautiful surroundings subtly encourage beautiful living. Drab surroundings, bad air, bad light, evoke bad reactions.
B. C. FORBES

When the snow and the ice were inches deep at home I was able to journey southwards where there was no snow and plenty of sunshine. How I revelled in my leisure during the first few days. . . . Gradually, however, my zest for play subsided. Even golf began to savor of monotony and work. By the end of two weeks I was eager to return to the daily grind. I found, too, that men and women who had nothing to do . . . were a rather dissatisfied, peevish lot. Work, even too much work, is preferable to too much play. Play can become harder work than work.
B. C. FORBES

Whimpering never kept a leaking vessel from foundering. Vigorously manning the pumps has. Get busy with your head and hands, not your chin.
B. C. FORBES

In these striking times there's an understandable tendency on the part of those struck to deplore with vehemence the ready availability of unemployment insurance for workers not working. In fact, only a fraction of those collecting unemployment compensation are strikers. And only a small percentage of those collecting unemployment compensation are unwilling to work. In these times of wide and widening unemployment—reaching near to 5 million at the moment—it shouldn't take much thought to make one glad unemployment insurance is as substantial and of as long duration as it is.
MALCOLM FORBES (1971)

If you have a job without any aggravations, you don't have a job.
MALCOLM FORBES

The hardest work of all: Doing nothing.
MALCOLM FORBES

When the joy of the job's gone, when it's no fun trying anymore, quit before you're fired.
MALCOLM FORBES

When those with ability at their job get to thinking they can't be done without, they're already on their way out.
MALCOLM FORBES

Working at what you enjoy is far more important than what you're working at.
MALCOLM FORBES

Life is work, and everything you do is so much more experience. Sometimes you work for wages, sometimes not, but what does anybody make but a living? And whatever you have you must either use or lose.
HENRY FORD

Nobody can think straight who does not work. Idleness warps the mind. Thinking without constructive action becomes a disease.
HENRY FORD

The object of living is work, experience, happiness. There is joy in work. All that money can do is buy us some one else's work in exchange for our own. There is no happiness except in the realization that we have accomplished something.
HENRY FORD

There are two ways of making yourself stand out from the crowd. One is by having a job so big you can go home before the bell rings if you want to. The other is by finding so much to do that you must stay after the others have gone. The one who enjoys the former once took advantage of the latter.
HENRY FORD

There are two things needed in these days; first for rich men to find out how poor men live; and second, for poor men to know how rich men work.
JOHN FOSTER

I early found that when I worked for myself alone, myself alone worked for me; but when I worked for others also, others worked also for me.
BENJAMIN FRANKLIN

It's all very well in practice, but it will never work in theory.
FRENCH MANAGEMENT SAYING

Work has a greater effect than any other technique of living in the direction of binding the individual more closely to reality; in his work, at least, he is securely attached to a part of reality, the human community.
SIGMUND FREUD

The delusive idea that men merely toil and work for the sake of preserving their bodies, and procuring for themselves bread, houses, clothes, is degrading and not to be encouraged. The true origin of man's activity and creativeness lies in his unceasing impulse to embody outside himself the divine and spiritual element within.
FRIEDRICH FROEBEL

Your work is really important. Even the smallest job has such a definite place it might be likened to a piece in a jigsaw puzzle; the puzzle would not be complete without it.
FRANCIS J. GABLE

But let every man prove his own work, and then shall he have rejoicing in himself alone, and not in another.
GALATIANS 6:4

Unemployment is rarely considered desirable except by those who have not experienced it.
JOHN KENNETH GALBRAITH

Employment is nature's physician, and is essential to human happiness.
GALEN

My grandfather once told me that there are two kinds of people: those who do the work and those who take the credit. He told me to try to be in the first group; there was much less competition there.
INDIRA GANDHI

He who by any exertion of mind or body adds to the aggregate of enjoyable wealth, increases the sum of human knowledge or gives to human life higher elevation or greater fullness—he is, in the larger meaning of the words, a producer, a workingman, a laborer, and is honestly earning honest wages.
HENRY GEORGE

You work that you may keep pace with the earth and the soul of the earth. For to be idle is to become a stranger unto the seasons, and to step out of life's procession, that marches in majesty and proud submission towards the infinite.
KAHLIL GIBRAN

Man must work. That is certain as the sun. But he may work grudgingly or he many work gratefully; he may work as a man, or he may work as a machine. There is no work so rude, that he may not exalt it; no work so impassive, that he may not breathe a soul into it; no work so dull that he may not enliven it.
HENRY GILES

It's getting so people don't want to work with their hands . . . or their head.
ARNOLD GLASOW

To set the world on fire, warm up to your job.
**ARNOLD GLASOW**

Most people work the greater part of their time for a mere living; and the little freedom which remains to them so troubles them that they use every means of getting rid of it.
**JOHANN WOLFGANG VON GOETHE**

When work is a pleasure, life is a joy. When work is duty, life is slavery.
**MAXIM GORKY**

Choose an occupation in which you can win praise. Most things depend upon the satisfaction of others. Esteem is to perfection what the breeze is to flowers: breath and life.
**BALTASAR GRACIÁN**

Quit while you're ahead. All the best gamblers do.
**BALTASAR GRACIÁN**

Work is the price that is paid for reputation.
**BALTASAR GRACIÁN**

It must be obvious to those who take the time to look at human life that its greatest values lie not in getting things, but in doing them, in doing them together, in all working toward a common aim, in the experience of comradeship, of warmhearted 100 percent human life.
**W. T. GRANT**

With labor and management working together in common cause—and not against each other—we can build and produce and prosper, and defeat any threat, from whatever source, against our own security and the peace of the world.
**WILLIAM GREEN**

For me, hard work represents the supreme luxury of life.
**ALBERT M. GREENFIELD**

A man is never astonished that he doesn't know what another does, but he is surprised at the gross ignorance of the other in not knowing he does.
**THOMAS C. HALIBURTON**

Work is uninspiring, unappreciated and underpaid—unless you're out of it.
**ROBERT HALF**

Work is a great blessing; after evil came into the world, it was given as an antidote, not as a punishing.
**ARTHUR S. HARDY**

Have you ever noticed that it is generally the same people who talk about the need for incentive to make a man work successfully, who resent the idea of incentive to make a man think successfully?
**SYDNEY J. HARRIS**

He who does nothing renders himself incapable of doing any thing; but while we are executing any work, we are preparing and qualifying ourselves to undertake another.
**WILLIAM HAZLITT**

The only time some people work like a horse is when the boss rides them.
**GABRIEL HEATTER**

A man at work at his trade is the equal of the most learned doctor.
**HEBREW PROVERB**

One's lifework, I have learned, grows with the working and the living. Do it as if your life

depended on it, and the first thing you know, you'll have made a life out of it.
**THERESA HELBURN**

He that labors and thrives spins gold.
**GEORGE HERBERT**

Work is the greatest thing in the world, so we should always save some of it for tomorrow.
**DON HEROLD**

They must hunger in frost that will not work in heat.
**JOHN HEYWOOD**

Do not waste a minute—not a second—in trying to demonstrate to others the merits of your performance. If your work does not vindicate itself, you cannot vindicate it.
**THOMAS W. HIGGINSON**

In our nation there are two classes of nobility: the law-abiding workers and the law-abiding employers who sustain each other.
**CULLEN HIGHTOWER**

Incentives are spurs that goad a man to do what he doesn't particularly like, to get something he does particularly want. They are rewards he voluntarily strives for.
**PAUL G. HOFFMAN**

It is by work that man carves his way to that measure of power which will fit him for his destiny.
**JOSIAH G. HOLLAND**

A day's impact is better than a month of dead pull.
**OLIVER WENDELL HOLMES**

Nothing worthwhile comes easily. Half effort does not produce half results. It produces no results.
Work, continuous work and hard work, is the only way to accomplish results that last.
**HAMILTON HOLT**

Light is the task where many share the toil.
**HOMER**

There is only one thing for a man to do who is married to a woman who enjoys spending money, and that is to enjoy earning it.
**EDGAR WATSON HOWE**

He was in love with his work, and he felt the enthusiasm for it which nothing but the work we can do well inspires in us.
**WILLIAM DEAN HOWELLS**

We work to become, not to acquire.
**ELBERT HUBBARD**

The person who studiously avoids work usually works far harder than the man who pleasantly confronts it and does it. Men who cannot work are not happy men.
**L. RON HUBBARD**

You may know for a certainty that if your work is becoming uninteresting, so are you; for work is an inanimate thing and can be made lively and interesting only by injecting yourself into it. Your job is only as big as you are.
**GEORGE C. HUBBS**

I believe in work, hard work and long hours of work. Men do not break down from overwork, but from worry and dissipation.
**CHARLES EVANS HUGHES**

Like every man of sense and good feeling, I abominate work.
**ALDOUS HUXLEY**

The dole is utterly demoralizing; its chief effect is to turn the unemployed into the unemployable.
**DEAN INGE**

If you want to leave your footprints on the sands of time, be sure you're wearing work shoes.
**ITALIAN PROVERB**

Nothing is so fatiguing as the eternal hanging on of an uncompleted task.
**WILLIAM JAMES**

Occupation was one of the pleasures of paradise, and we cannot be happy without it.
**ANNA JAMESON**

Never fear the want of business. A man who qualifies himself well for his calling, never fails of employment.
**THOMAS JEFFERSON**

I like work, it fascinates me. I can sit and look at it for hours. I love to keep it by me: the idea of getting rid of it nearly breaks my heart.
**JEROME K. JEROME**

The ugliest of trades have their moments of pleasure. If I were a grave-digger, or even a hangman, there are some people I could work for with a great deal of enjoyment.
**DOUGLAS WILLIAM JERROLD**

The man who works for the gold in the job rather than for the money in the pay envelope, is the fellow who gets on.
**JOSEPH FRENCH JOHNSON**

In business, as most of it is constituted today, a man becomes valuable only as he recognizes the relation of his work to that of all his associates. One worker more or less makes little difference to most big organizations, and any man may be replaced. It is the cumulative effort that counts.
**W. ALTON JONES**

Amateurs hope; professionals work.
**GARSON KANIN**

People who decide they came to earth to work, who make work their personal philosophy, are kept very busy.
**CONSTANTINE KARAMANLIS**

My share of the work of the world may be limited, but the fact that it is work makes it precious. Darwin could work only half an hour at a time; but in many diligent half-hours he laid anew the foundations of philosophy. Green, the historian, tells us that the world is moved not only by the mighty shoves of the heroes, but also by the aggregate of the tiny pushes of each honest worker.
**H. KELLOGG**

There has never been any 30-hour week for men who had anything to do.
**CHARLES F. KETTERING**

The only worthwhile things that have come to us in this life have come through work that was almost always hard, and often bitter. We believe that this has always been true of mankind and that it will always be true. We believe not in how little work, but how much; not in how few hours, but how many. America must not grow soft!
**JACOB KINDLEBERGER**

Being forced to work, and forced to do your best, will breed in you temperance and self-control, diligence and strength of will, cheerfulness and content, and a hundred virtues which the idle never know.
**CHARLES KINGSLEY**

Thank God every morning when you get up that you have something to do that day which must be done, whether you like it or not. Being forced to work, and forced to do your best, will breed in you temperance and self-control, diligence and strength of will, cheerfulness and content, and a hundred virtues which the idle never know.
**CHARLES KINGSLEY**

More men have died from overwork than the importance of the word justifies.
**RUDYARD KIPLING**

Be grateful for the joy of life. Be glad for the privilege of work. Be thankful for the opportunity to give and serve. Good work is the great character-builder, the sweetener of life, the maker of destiny. Let the spirit of your work be right, and whether your task be great or small you will then have the satisfaction of knowing it is worth while.
**GRENVILLE KLEISER**

There is honor in labor. Work is the medicine of the soul. It is more: it is your very life, without which you would amount to little.
**GRENVILLE KLEISER**

For the last third of life there remains only work. It alone is always stimulating, rejuvenating, exciting and satisfying.
**KATHE KOLLWITZ**

If you are poor, work. If you are burdened with seemingly unfair responsibilities, work. If you are happy, work. Idleness gives room for doubts and fears. If disappointments come, keep right on working. If sorrow overwhelms you and loved ones seem not true, work. If health is threatened, work. When faith falters and reason fails, just work. When dreams are shattered and hope seems dead, work. Work as if your life were in peril. It really is. No matter what ails you, work. Work faithfully—work with faith. Work is the greatest remedy available for both mental and physical afflictions.
**KORSAREN**

The only way to eliminate unemployment is to eliminate unemployment benefits.
**PHILIP LARKIN**

To industry nothing is impossible.
**LATIN PROVERB**

Needed more than ever is a better understanding of incentives to production. When the price control officials take due account of the need for preserving incentives—and when the Congress also takes this into consideration in the making of tax rates—there will be a better chance to restrain all groups and curb inflationary trends.
**DAVID LAWRENCE**

God sells us all things at the price of labor.
**LEONARDO DA VINCI**

In the democratic way of life it is not "the best things in life are free," but rather "the best things in life are worth working for!"
**RUTH M. LEVERTON**

If ever this free people, if this government itself is ever utterly demoralized, it will come from this human wiggle and struggle for office—that is, a way to live without work.
**ABRAHAM LINCOLN**

If you intend to go to work, there is no better place than right where you are; if you do not intend to go to work, you cannot get along anywhere. Squirming and crawling about from place to place can do no good.
**ABRAHAM LINCOLN**

The strongest bond of human sympathy, outside the family relation, should be one uniting all working people, of all nations, and tongues, and kindreds. Nor should this lead to a war upon property, or the owners of property. Property is the fruit of labor; property is desirable; is a positive good in the world. That some should be rich shows that others may become rich, and hence, is just encouragement to industry and enterprise. Let not him who is houseless pull down the house of another, but let him labor diligently and build one for himself, thus by example assuring that his own shall be safe from violence when built.
**ABRAHAM LINCOLN**

A people, secure in their jobs, taking pride in their work, and sure of just recognition, will help our society grow to new heights. If all industry should adopt an incentive system, the standard of living of all peoples would be quadrupled; friction between labor and management would disappear, and the satisfaction of all workers would be greatly enhanced.
**JAMES F. LINCOLN**

No man is born into the world whose work is not born with him. There is always work, and tools to work with, for those who will, and blessed are the horny hands of toil. The busy world shoves angrily aside the man who stands with arms akimbo until occasion tells him what to do; and he who waits to have his task marked out shall die and leave his errand unfulfilled.
**JAMES RUSSELL LOWELL**

In the final analysis, there is no other solution to a man's problems but the day's honest work, the day's honest decisions, the day's generous utterance, and the day's good deed.
**CLARE BOOTHE LUCE**

The highest genius is willingness and ability to do hard work. Any other conception of genius makes it a doubtful, if not a dangerous, possession.
**ROBERT S. MACARTHUR**

Work is a dull thing; you cannot get away from that. The only agreeable existence is one of idleness, and that is not, unfortunately, always compatible with continuing to exist at all.
**ROSE MACAULAY**

Find something you love to do and you'll never have to work a day in your life.
**HARVEY MACKAY**

We thoroughly enjoy the work of a man only if the enjoyment of his work can be applied with respect and love for the man.
**HANS MARGOLIUS**

No human pursuit achieves dignity unless it can be called work, and when you can experience a physical loneliness for the tools of your trade, you see that the other things—the experiments, the irrelevant vocations, the vanities you used to hold—were false to you.
**BERYL MARKHAM**

He worked like hell in the country so he could live in the city, where he worked like hell so he could live in the country.
**DONALD MARQUIS**

Work is the true elixir of life. The busiest man is the happiest man. Excellence in any art or profession is attained only by hard and persistent work. Never believe that you are perfect. When a man imagines, even after years of striving, that he has attained perfection, his decline begins.
**SIR THEODORE MARTIN (92)**

The only liberty an inferior man really cherishes is the liberty to quit work, stretch out in the sun, and scratch himself.
**H. L. Mencken**

There comes a point in any organization where too much supervision means that supervisors spend too much time writing memorandums to one another, making needless telephone calls to one another, and the like, with no more productive work being accomplished in the aggregate, and possibly even less. We must strike the correct balance between too much supervision, and too little supervision.
**Gustav Metzman**

The bad workmen who form the majority of the operatives in many branches of industry are decidedly of the opinion that bad workmen ought to receive the same wages as good.
**John Stuart Mill**

Let us go forth and resolutely dare with sweat of brow to toil our little day.
**John Milton**

The more I work, the more I want to work.
**Joan Miró**

Often our work seems insignificant and unimportant when we compare ourselves with the immensity of time and the universe, but God gave us our moment on earth to be used in the best possible way.
**J. V. Moldenhawer, D.D.**

Elbow grease; the kind that won't soil a shirt.
**Garry Moore**

Give me love and work—these two only.
**William Morris**

It takes a highly intellectual individual to enjoy leisure. . . . Most of us had better count on working. What a man really wants is creative challenge with sufficient skills to bring him within the reach of success so that he may have the expanding joy of achievement. . . . Few people overwork; plenty overeat, overworry, overdrink. . . . Few realize real joy and happiness of conquest. The basis of mental health for the average adult is more work, provided the work is not mere drudgery.
**Fay B. Nash**

People forget how fast you did a job—but they remember how well you did it.
**Howard W. Newton**

Though a little one, the master-word (work) looms large in meaning. It is the open sesame to every mortal, the great equalizer in the world, the true philosopher's stone which transmutes all the base metal of humanity into goal.
**Sir William Osler**

A great factory with the machinery all working and revolving with absolute and rhythmic regularity and with the men all driven by one impulse, and moving in unison as though a constituent part of the mighty machine, is one of the most inspiring examples of directed force that the world knows. I have rarely seen the face of a mechanic in the action of creation which was not fine, never one which was not earnest and impressive.
**Thomas Nelson Page**

He who would do some great things in this short life must apply himself to work with such a concentration of force as, to idle spectators who live only to amuse themselves, looks like insanity.
**Francis Parkman**

I never knew a man escape failures, in either mind or body, who worked seven days in a week.
**SIR ROBERT PEEL**

But make not more business necessary than is so; and rather lessen than augment work for thyself.
**WILLIAM PENN**

Nor yet be overeager in pursuit of any thing; for the mercurial too often happen to leave judgment behind them, and sometimes make work for repentance.
**WILLIAM PENN**

. . . Human society is not a machine, and it must not be made such, even in the economic field. . . . Access to employment [shall not be] made to depend on registration in certain parties or in organizations which deal with the distribution of employment. . . . It is necessary that humanity turn its gaze toward the action of God . . . to aid and redeem mankind from all its ills.
**POPE PIUS XII**

We must infer that all things are produced more plentifully and easily and of a better quality when one man does one thing which is natural to him and does it at the right time, and leaves other things.
**PLATO**

There is a singing ecstasy in good work.
**CHANNING POLLOCK**

What I still ask for daily—for life as long as I have work to do, and work as long as I have life.
**REYNOLDS PRICE**

Some are bent with toil, and some get crooked trying to avoid it.
**HERBERT V. PROCHNOW**

I see no virtues where I smell no sweat.
**FRANCIS QUARLES**

Whatever you do, if you do it hard enough you'll enjoy it. The important thing is to work and work hard.
**DAVID ROCKEFELLER**

When work goes out of style we may expect to see civilization totter and fall.
**JOHN D. ROCKEFELLER**

Extend pity to no man because he has to work. If he is worth his salt, he will work. I envy the man who has work worth doing and does it well. There never has been devised, and there never will be devised, any law which will enable a man to succeed save by the exercise of those qualities which have always been the prerequisites of success, the qualities of hard work, of keen intelligence, of unflinching will.
**THEODORE ROOSEVELT**

Far and away the best prize that life offers is the chance to work hard at work worth doing.
**THEODORE ROOSEVELT**

The world is moved not only by the mighty shoves of the heroes, but also by the aggregate of the tiny pushes of each honest worker.
**FRANK C. ROSS**

In order that people may be happy in their work, these three things are needed: They must be fit for it. They must not do too much of it. And they must have a sense of success in it.
**JOHN RUSKIN**

The highest reward for a person's toil is not what he gets for it, but what he becomes by it.
**JOHN RUSKIN**

The moment a man can really do his work, he becomes speechless about it; all words are idle to him; all theories. Does a bird need to theorize about building its nest, or boast of it when built? All good work is essentially done that way; without hesitation; without difficulty; without boasting.
**JOHN RUSKIN**

There is rough work to be done, and rough men must do it; there is gentle work to be done, and gentlemen must do it.
**JOHN RUSKIN**

Though you may have known clever men who were indolent, you never knew a great man who was so; and when I hear a young man spoken of as giving promise of great genius, the first question I ask about him always is, "Does he work?"
**JOHN RUSKIN**

Work is of two kinds: first, altering the position of matter at or near the earth's surface relatively to other such matter; second, telling other people to do so. The first kind is unpleasant and ill paid; the second is pleasant and highly paid.
**BERTRAND RUSSELL**

The Lord recompense thy work, and a full reward be given thee of the Lord God of Israel, under whose wings thou art come to trust.
**RUTH 4:12**

We are not here to play, to dream, to drift;
We have hard work to do and loads to lift;
Shun not the struggle—face it,
'tis God's gift.
**LORD SHAFTESBURY**

The terrible newly imported American doctrine that everyone ought to do something.
**OSBERT SITWELL**

I am suggesting to you the simple idea that people work harder and smarter if they find their work satisfying and know that it is appreciated.
**ROBERT F. SIX**

Those who have most to do, and are willing to work, will find the most time.
**SAMUEL SMILES**

The one who doesn't pull his weight is not asked to pull, while the one who does, pulls for two.
**ALEXANDR SOLZHENITSYN**

Without labor nothing prospers.
**SOPHOCLES**

The true craftsman has a light in his eye that money can't buy.
**HAL STEBBINS**

If a man love the labor of any trade, apart from any question of success or fame, the gods have called him.
**ROBERT LOUIS STEVENSON**

There is no boon in nature. All the blessings we enjoy are the fruits of labor, toil, self-denial, and study.
**WILLIAM GRAHAM SUMNER**

The only method by which people can be supported is out of the effort of those who are earning their own way. We must not create a deterrent to hard work.
**ROBERT A. TAFT**

Do not keep away from the measure which has no limit, or from the task which has no end.
**RABBI TARPHON**

The day is short, and the work is great, and the laborers are sluggish and the reward is much, and the Master of the house is urgent.
**RABBI TARPHON**

Whatsoever we beg of God, let us also work for it.
**JEREMY TAYLOR**

Know them which labor among you . . . esteem them very highly in love for their work's sake.
**I THESSALONIANS 5:12**

For even when we were with you, this we commanded you, that if any would not work, neither should he eat.
**II THESSALONIANS 3:10**

Good for the body is the work of the body, good for the soul is the work of the soul, and good for either the work of the other.
**HENRY DAVID THOREAU**

Next to us is not the workman whom we have hired, with whom we love so well to talk, but the workman whose work we are.
**HENRY DAVID THOREAU**

Among a democratic people, where there is no hereditary wealth, every man works to earn a living, or is born of parents who have worked. The notion of labor is therefore presented to the mind, on every side, as the necessary, natural, and honest condition.
**ALEXIS DE TOCQUEVILLE**

I do not like work even when someone else does it.
**MARK TWAIN**

Let us be grateful to Adam our benefactor. He cut us out of the blessing of idleness and won for us the curse of labor.
**MARK TWAIN**

The law of work does seem utterly unfair—but there it is, and nothing can change it; the higher the pay in enjoyment the worker gets out of it, the higher shall be his pay in money also.
**MARK TWAIN**

When you like your work, every day is a holiday.
**FRANK TYGER**

It is easier to do a job right than to explain why you didn't.
**MARTIN VAN BUREN**

Work is often the father of pleasure.
**VOLTAIRE**

Work spares us from three great evils: boredom, vice and need.
**VOLTAIRE**

My destiny is solitude, and my life is work.
**RICHARD WAGNER**

Accepting government aid is like taking drugs—pleasant at first, habit-forming later, damning at last.
**WILLIAM W. WARD**

Employment gives health, sobriety, and morals. Constant employment and well-paid labor produce, in a country like ours, general prosperity, content and cheerfulness.
**DANIEL WEBSTER**

Even the strongest personality will regress and eventually may disintegrate if there is no incentive (other than threat of punishment) for the work he does. When there is no feeling to accomplishment, children fail to develop properly and old people rapidly decline.
**JOSEPH WHITNEY**

The man who works need never be a problem to anyone. Opportunities multiply as they are seized; they die when neglected. Life is a long line of opportunities. Wealth is not in making money, but in making the man while he is making money. Production, not destruction, leads to success.
JOHN WICKER

Work is the curse of the drinking classes.
OSCAR WILDE

Work is the refuge of people who have nothing better to do.
OSCAR WILDE

It is better to lay your life upon the altar of worthy endeavor than to luxuriate and perish as a weed.
ALBERT L. WILLIAMS

Much of the present difficulty in industrial relations arises from the fact that too many employers as well as too many legislators take the Labor Leader more seriously than he deserves to be taken, while taking the ordinary, everyday, middle-of-the-road wage-earner less seriously than he deserves to be taken.
WHITING WILLIAMS

Work only a half a day. It makes no difference which half—the first 12 hours or the last 12 hours.
KEMMONS WILSON

Never try to work a man who will work you to death trying to work him.
ROBERT LEWIS WILSON

No task, rightly done, is truly private. It is part of the world's work.
WOODROW WILSON

We would rather have one man or woman working with us than three merely working for us.
F. W. WOOLWORTH

Because I helped to wind the clock, I come to hear it strike.
WILLIAM BUTLER YEATS

Sorrow's best antidote is employment.
YOUNG

## *World*

Had I been present at the Creation, I would have given some useful hints for the better ordering of the Universe.
ALPHONSO THE LEARNED

I hear noise but see no grinding.
ARABIAN PROVERB

Remember, you can't drain the ocean with a teaspoon.
IGNAS BERNSTEIN

The earth is, like our own skin, fated to carry the scars of ancient wounds.
FERNAND BRAUDEL

Our sun is one of 100 billion stars in our galaxy. Our galaxy is one of the billions of galaxies populating the universe. It would be the height of presumption to think that we are the only living things within that enormous immensity.
WERNHER VON BRAUN

If we find life in outer space
I hope we don't romance it;
We can't afford the extra aid,
Much less the cost of transit.
ART BUCK

The biggest problem in the world could have been solved when it was small.
WITTER BYNNER

The world is a thing that a man must learn to despise, and even to neglect, before he can learn to reverence it, and work in it and for it.
THOMAS CARLYLE

This world, after all our science and sciences, is still a miracle, wonderful, inscrutable, magical and more, to whosoever will think of it.
THOMAS CARLYLE

The task for us now, if we are to survive, is to build the earth.
TEILHARD DE CHARDIN

The real trouble with this world of ours is not that it is an unreasonable one. The trouble is that it is nearly reasonable, but not quite.
G. K. CHESTERTON

Every blade of grass has its spot on earth whence it draws its life, its strength; and so is man rooted to the land from which he draws his faith together with his life.
JOSEPH CONRAD

Most people are quiet in the world, and live in it tentatively, as if it were not their own.
E. L. DOCTOROW

The world has forgotten, in its concern with Left and Right, that there is an Above and Below.
GALEN DRAKE

The World is a great mirror. It reflects back to you what you are. If you are loving, if you are friendly, if you are helpful, the World will prove loving and friendly and helpful to you. The World is what you are.
THOMAS DREIER

The free world has need that its foreign policies should fairly measure the realities of the world in which we live. There are certain principles to which we hold: the sanctity of treaties, good faith between nations, the interdependence of peoples from which no country, however powerful, can altogether escape.
ANTHONY EDEN

Here is the world, sound as a nut, perfect, not the smallest piece of chaos left, never a stitch nor an end, nor a mark of haste, or botching, or a second thought; but the theory of the world is a thing of shreds and patches.
RALPH WALDO EMERSON

God has made no one absolute. The rich depend on the poor, as well as the poor on the rich. The world is but a magnificent building; all the stones are gradually cemented together. No one subsists by himself.
OWEN FELTHAM

I am satisfied with, and stand firm as a rock on the belief that all that happens in God's world is for the best, but what is merely germ, what blossom and what fruit I do not know.
JOHANN FICHTE

The world is a book and he who stays at home reads only one page.
M. K. FRELINGHUYSEN

The world is so filled with interesting things to do that the longest human life could not exhaust more than a small fraction of them.
FRANK GAINES

You can't shut out the world without shutting yourself in.
ARNOLD GLASOW

I do not have to make over the universe; I have only to do my job, great or small, and to look often at the trees and the hills and the sky, and be friendly with all men.
**DAVID GRAYSON**

By our efforts to resolve differences between nations by peaceful means, by the help we have given others to regain their strength, by the determination with which we have fulfilled our obligations under the United Nations Charter, we have established our position on a firm moral foundation. . . . Our faith that we can succeed is justified. For the first time in history, the most powerful nation in the world is dedicated to peace and in partnership with other nations is mobilizing its moral force and its resources for world security.
**W. AVERELL HARRIMAN**

To him who looks upon the world rationally, the world in its turn presents a rational aspect. The relation is mutual.
**GEORG WILHELM HEGEL**

Maybe this world is another planet's hell.
**ALDOUS HUXLEY**

This may not be the best of all possible worlds, but to say that it is the worst is mere petulant nonsense.
**THOMAS H. HUXLEY**

Admiration for ourselves and our institutions is too often measured by our contempt and dislike for foreigners.
**WILLIAM RALPH INGE**

Man will never be entirely willing to give up this world for the next nor the next world for this.
**WILLIAM RALPH INGE**

All the people like us are We,
And everyone else is They.
And They live over the sea,
While We live over the way.
But—would you believe it?—
They look upon We
As only a sort of They.
**RUDYARD KIPLING**

Half the world wants to be like Thoreau worrying about the noise of traffic on the way up to Boston; the other half use up their lives being part of that noise. I like the second half.
**FRANZ KLINE**

Sometimes, when one person is missing, the whole world seems depopulated.
**ALPHONSE DE LAMARTINE**

When the world is destroyed, it will be destroyed not by its madmen but by the sanity of its experts and the superior ignorance of its bureaucrats.
**JOHN LE CARRÉ**

Not for himself, but for the world he lives.
**LUCAN**

What can we do to prevent a mad ruler, or a desperate one, from destroying civilization by pressing a button? Most persons agree that force-against-force to keep the peace is a futile policy. Happily, today a better plan is already at work. This is the program of collective security through the United Nations. More than any other organization in history, the U.N. symbolizes the collective conscience of mankind.
**CHARLES W. MAYO**

The more noise a man or a motor makes the less power there is available.
**W. R. MCGEARY**

It is ridiculous ever to forget that you and your business are each implanted in the society of the moment.... We cannot ignore the world of our time. We had better understand it.
J. IRWIN MILLER

There is very definitely something that each of us can do to help strengthen the United Nations. If enough of us will do it, the results can be decisive. Each of us... in his own home... in his own community can help to develop public interest, understanding and support for what the United Nations is trying to do. Once an informed and enlightened public interest is aroused, no government on the face of the earth—I don't care what its form may be—can be indifferent to its pressure. National policies are the sum total of the informed public thinking of citizens.
ANGUS S. MITCHELL

The universe is full of magical things, patiently waiting for our wits to grow sharper.
EDEN PHILLPOTTS

Noise is manufactured in the city, just as goods are manufactured. The city is the place where noise is kept in stock, completely detached from the object from which it came.
MAX PICARD

It is with narrow-souled people as with narrow-necked bottles; the less they have in it, the more noise they make in pouring it out.
ALEXANDER POPE

The [British] attitude to foreigners is like their attitude to dogs: Dogs are neither human nor British, but so long as you keep them under control, give them their exercise, feed them, pat them, you will find their wild emotions are amusing, and their characters interesting.
V. S. PRITCHETT

O Lord, how manifold are thy works! In wisdom hast thou made them all: the earth is full of thy riches.
PSALMS 104:24

When you look at the world in a narrow way, how narrow it seems! When you look at it in a mean way, how mean it is! When you look at it selfishly, how selfish it is! But when you look at it in a broad, generous, friendly spirit, what wonderful people you find in it.
HORACE RUTLEDGE

The universe, as far as we can observe it, is a wonderful and immense engine.... If we dramatize its life and conceive its spirit, we are filled with wonder, terror and amusement, so magnificent is the spirit.
GEORGE SANTAYANA

The whole world and every human being in it is everybody's business.
WILLIAM SAROYAN

The world as it is has been humanly made and must be humanly remade.
MINOT SIMONS, D. D.

This is a good world. We need not approve of all the items in it, nor of all the individuals in it; but the world itself—which is more than its parts or individuals; which has a soul, a spirit, a fundamental relation to each of us deeper than all other relations—is a friendly world.
JAN CHRISTIAAN SMUTS

Once you kick the world, and the world and you will live together at a reasonably good understanding.
JONATHAN SWIFT

The world is a looking glass and gives back to every man the reflection of his own face. Frown at it and

it will in turn look sourly upon you; laugh at it and with it and it is a jolly kind companion.
WILLIAM MAKEPEACE THACKERAY

If the world is cold, make it your business to build fires.
HORACE TRAUBEL

A federation of all humanity, together with a sufficient measure of social justice to ensure health, education and a rough equality of opportunity, would mean such a release and increase of human energy as to open a new phase in human history.
H. G. WELLS

## Worry

No one can work and achieve efficiently with a pack of worries on his back. People who enjoy life and radiate their happiness fear nothing. Fear never has led, and never will lead, a man victoriously in any phase of life. . . . A cheerful frame of mind, reenforced by relaxation, which in itself banishes fatigue, is the medicine that puts all Ghosts of Fear on the run! So, get fun out of what you do—and you will do much, and be glad that you are alive.
GEORGE MATTHEW ADAMS

There's many a pessimist who got that way by financing an optimist.
ANONYMOUS

Worry is rust upon the blade.
HENRY WARD BEECHER

Worry is evidence of an ill-controlled brain; it is merely a stupid waste of time in unpleasantness. If men and women practiced mental calisthenics as they do physical calisthenics, they would purge their brains of this foolishness.
ARNOLD BENNETT

There are people who are always anticipating trouble, and in this way they manage to enjoy many sorrows that never really happen to them.
JOSH BILLINGS

Anxiety is the poison of human life, the parent of many sins and of more miseries. In a world where everything is doubtful, and where we may be disappointed, and be blessed in disappointment, why this restless stir and commotion of mind? Can it alter the cause, or unravel the mystery of human events?
PAXTON BLAIR

The man of regular life and rational mind never despairs.
CHARLOTTE BRONTË

Better be despised for too anxious apprehensions, than ruined by too confident security.
EDMUND BURKE

A friend of mine tells me that a Beethoven symphony can solve for him a problem of conduct. I've no doubt that it does so simply by giving him a sense of the tragedy and the greatness of human destiny, which makes his personal anxieties seem small, which throws them into a new proportion.
JOYCE CARY

Sing away sorrow, cast away care.
MIGUEL DE CERVANTES

Do not lie in a ditch and say, God help me; use the lawful tools He hath lent thee.
GEORGE CHAPMAN

Nobody should ever look anxious except those who have no anxiety.
BENJAMIN DISRAELI

The hearts of men are chilled by the threat of the cold war and by the touch of a still icier pessimism

which is blood brother to despair. Men who are without faith and, therefore, cannot hope, are inclined to yield to the pressure of circumstances and events and give up their liberties, seeking security and warmth in peace at any price and in freedom from molestation.
**THOMAS A. DONNELLAN, D.D.**

As a cure for worrying, work is better than whiskey.
**THOMAS EDISON**

What we call despair is often the painful eagerness of unfed hope.
**GEORGE ELIOT**

When one seeks assurance, there's none from those who respond, "Now, don't you worry about a thing." If you weren't worried, you wouldn't have asked. If you are concerned, it's nice to know that those you query are, too. I'll take a worrier any day over a platitudinous reassurer.
**MALCOLM FORBES**

Do not anticipate trouble, or worry about what may never happen. Keep in the sunlight.
**BENJAMIN FRANKLIN**

Industry pays debts, despair increases them.
**BENJAMIN FRANKLIN**

You'll break the worry habit the day you decide you can meet and master the worst that can happen to you.
**ARNOLD GLASOW**

Worry compounds the futility of being trapped on a dead-end street. Thinking opens new avenues.
**CULLEN HIGHTOWER**

Worry is interest paid on trouble before it becomes due.
**WILLIAM RALPH INGE**

We care what happens to people only in proportion as we know what people are.
**HENRY JAMES**

Pessimism leads to weakness; optimism to power.
**WILLIAM JAMES**

There is little peace or comfort in life if we are always anxious as to future events. He that worries himself with the dread of possible contingences will never be at rest.
**JOHNSON**

Life is too short for mean anxieties.
**CHARLES KINGSLEY**

It is certainly wrong to despair; and if despair is wrong hope is right.
**JOHN LUBBOCK**

The mere apprehension of a coming evil has put many into a situation of the utmost danger.
**LUCAN**

A pessimist is one who makes difficulties of his opportunities; an optimist is one who makes opportunities of his difficulties.
**REGINALD B. MANSELL**

Worry affects the circulation, the heart, the glands, the whole nervous system, and profoundly affects the health. I have never known a man who died from overwork, but many who died from doubt.
**CHARLES W. MAYO**

One of the wisest men in Des Moines tells me that he has kept track of the 50 principal things he's

worried in the last ten years, jotting 'em down at the bottom of the pages in his diary in green ink. He finds that not one of them actually happened; but they bothered him just as much as if they had.
**HARLAN MILLER**

Anxiety is love's greatest killer. It makes one feel as you might when a drowning man holds on to you. You want to save him, but you know he will strangle you in his panic.
**ANAÏS NIN**

Agitation prevents rebellion, keeps the peace, and secures progress. Every step she gains is gained forever. Muskets are the weapons of animals. Agitation is the atmosphere of the brains.
**WENDELL PHILLIPS**

A pound of worry won't pay an ounce of debt.
**JOHN RAY**

Worry is a thin stream of fear trickling through the mind. If encouraged, it cuts a channel into which all other thoughts are drained.
**ARTHUR SOMERS ROCHE**

A job becomes work only when you worry about it.
**JOSEPHINE SCHAEFER**

The mind that is anxious about the future is miserable.
**SENECA**

Care's an enemy of life.
**WILLIAM SHAKESPEARE**

Sweet recreation barred, what doth ensue but moody and dull melancholy, kinsman to grim and comfortless despair.
**WILLIAM SHAKESPEARE**

A pessimist is a man who thinks everybody as nasty as himself, and hates them for it.
**GEORGE BERNARD SHAW**

Our cares are the mothers not only of our charities and virtues, but of our best joys, and most cheering and enduring pleasures.
**WILLIAM SIMMS**

In being realistic we do not always have to be pessimistic. Christ never blinked his eyes at bad things. But he never became so obsessed with human evil that he lost faith in man.
**RALPH W. SOCKMAN**

Worry, whatever its source, weakens, takes away courage, and shortens life.
**JOHN LANCASTER SPALDING**

There is no sadder sight than a young pessimist.
**MARK TWAIN**

Despair not only aggravates our misery but our weakness.
**MARQUIS DE VAUVENARGUES**

Peace of mind: The contentment of the man who is too busy to worry by day, and too sleepy to worry at night.
**WOODROW WILSON**

## *Writing*

Hush little bright line,
Don't you cry,
You'll be a cliché
By and by.
**FRED ALLEN**

Walter Scott has no business to write novels, especially good ones. He has fame and profit enough as a poet, and should not be taking the bread out of other people's mouths.
JANE AUSTEN

Fiction is not a dream. Nor is it guesswork. It is imagining based on facts, and the facts must be accurate or the work of imagining will not stand up.
MARGARET CULKIN BANNING

I don't know if Bacon wrote the works of Shakespeare, but if he did not, he missed the opportunity of his life.
JAMES M. BARRIE

A curious thing about written literature: It is about four thousand years old, but we have no way of knowing whether four thousand years constitutes senility or the maiden blush of youth.
JOHN BARTH

By its very looseness, by its way of evoking rather than defining, suggesting rather than saying, English is a magnificent vehicle for emotional poetry.
MAX BEERBOHM

A writer is in the broadest sense a spokesman of his community. Through him that community comes to know its heart. Without such knowledge, how long can it survive?
SAUL BELLOW

Novel: a short story padded.
AMBROSE BIERCE

About the most originality that any writer can hope to achieve honestly is to steal with good judgment.
JOSH BILLINGS

What is conceived well is expressed clearly, and the words to say it will arrive with ease.
NICOLAS BOILEAU

A novelist is stuck with his youth. We spend it without paying much attention to how it will work out as material; nevertheless, we must draw on whatever was there for the rest of our lives.
VANCE BOURJAILLY

Writers seldom choose as friends those self-contained characters who are never in trouble, never unhappy or ill, never make mistakes, and always count their change when it is handed to them.
CATHERINE DRINKER BOWEN

It is by sitting down to write every morning that one becomes a writer. Those who do not do this remain amateurs.
GERALD BRENAN

One of the pleasures of reading old letters is the knowledge that they need no answer.
LORD BYRON

There is a great discovery still to be made in literature—that of paying literary men by the quantity they do not write.
THOMAS CARLYLE

A letter shows the man it is written to as well as the man it is written by.
LORD CHESTERFIELD

Next to doing things that deserve to be written, nothing gets a man more credit, or gives him more pleasure than to write things that deserve to be read.
LORD CHESTERFIELD

Everyone seems to assume that the unscrupulous parts of journalism will be the frivolous or jocular

parts. This is against all ethical experience. Jokes are generally honest. Complete solemnity is almost always dishonest. The writer of the snippet merely refers to a frivolous and fugitive fact in a frivolous and fugitive way. The writer of the leading article has to write about a fact he has known for 20 minutes as though he has studied it for 20 years.
**G. K. CHESTERTON**

French novels were written for adults, and confined to adults. English novels were thrown open to schoolgirls—and cut down for them. In Paris the baby was forbidden to read the man's literature; in London the man was often compelled to read the baby's. Both conditions can be described as liberty.
**G. K. CHESTERTON**

The best time for planning a book is while you're doing the dishes.
**AGATHA CHRISTIE**

As in political, so in literary action, a man wins friends for himself mostly by the passion of his prejudices.
**JOSEPH CONRAD**

In America only the successful writer is important, in France all writers are important, in England no writer is important, in Australia you have to explain what a writer is.
**GEOFFREY COTTERELL**

An editor should tell the author his writing is better than it is. Not a lot better, a little better.
**T. S. ELIOT**

Someone said: "The dead writers are remote from us because we know so much more than they did." Precisely, and they are what we know.
**T. S. ELIOT**

Henry James was one of the nicest old ladies I ever met.
**WILLIAM FAULKNER**

You should approach Joyce's *Ulysses* as the illiterate Baptist preacher approaches the Old Testament: with faith.
**WILLIAM FAULKNER**

The ideal view for daily writing, hour on hour, is the blank brick wall of a cold-storage warehouse. Failing this, a stretch of sky will do, cloudless if possible.
**EDNA FERBER**

May the founder of *Forbes* make a confession? The motive underlying the creation of Forbes was the furthering of better understanding between employers and employees, between the strong and the weak, between the high and the low, between the rich and the poor, between the haves and the have-nots. It was foreseen years ago that, unless those who ruled were understandingly interpreted to those ruled, unless those who ruled could be induced to treat more humanely those whom they rule . . . this country would be in danger of suffering political and social upheavals. . . .
**B. C. FORBES**

It ticks me no end when people get ticked off at those of us who comment audibly and in print on events and problems. That's what we're paid for.

Why clutter up your mind with a bunch of facts that might inhibit the solve-ability of us who must express an opinion? After all, all the world cries out for a solution to its problems, and we supply them right and left. Come to think of it, it's we who should be giving our deplorers and detractors the blast; because 99% of the time they don't do as we say.
**MALCOLM FORBES**

Personal & Confidential. Letters so marked should be. When the contents are only printed matter, though, the minifrauder succeeds in sowing ill will & ire.
**MALCOLM FORBES**

Putting pen to paper lights more fire than matches ever will.
**MALCOLM FORBES**

Real writers—that is, capital "W" Writers—rarely make much money. Their biggest reward is the occasional reader's response. . . . Commentators-in-print voicing big fat opinions—you might call us small "w" writers—get considerably more feedback than Writers. The letters I personally find most flattering are not the very rare ones that speak well of my editorials, but the occasional reader who wants to know who writes them. I always happily assume the letter-writers is implying that the editorials are so good that I couldn't have written them myself.
**MALCOLM FORBES**

I suppose I am a born novelist, for the things I imagine are more vital and vivid to me than the things I remember.
**ELLEN GLASGOW**

Nothing you write, if you hope to be any good, will ever come out as you had first hoped.
**LILLIAN HELLMAN**

All modern American literature comes from one book by Mark Twain called *Huckleberry Finn.*
**ERNEST HEMINGWAY**

Nothing comes easily. My work smells of sweat.
**ERIC HOFFER**

No poems can live long or please that are written by water-drinkers.
**HORACE**

It takes a great deal of history to produce a little literature.
**HENRY JAMES**

In all pointed sentences, some degree of accuracy must be sacrificed to conciseness.
**SAMUEL JOHNSON**

The only end of writing is to enable readers better to enjoy life or better to endure it.
**SAMUEL JOHNSON**

Your manuscript is both good and original, but the part that is good is not original, and the part that is original is not good.
**SAMUEL JOHNSON**

One must never judge the writer by the man; but one may fairly judge the man by the writer.
**LOUIS KRONENBERGER**

Some things can only be said in fiction, but that doesn't mean they aren't true.
**AARON LATHAM**

Writing is not hard. Just get paper and pencil, sit down and write it as it occurs to you. The writing is easy—it's the occurring that's hard.
**STEPHEN LEACOCK**

Looking back, I imagine I was always writing. Twaddle it was too. But far better write twaddle or anything, anything, than nothing at all.
**KATHERINE MANSFIELD**

If you want to get rich from writing, write the sort of thing that's read by persons who move their lips when they're reading to themselves.
DONALD MARQUIS

There are three rules for writing a novel. Unfortunately, no one knows what they are.
SOMERSET MAUGHAM

In literature as in love, we are astonished at what is chosen by others.
ANDRÉ MAUROIS

Most clear writing is a sign that there is no exploration going on. Clear prose indicates the absence of thought.
MARSHALL MCLUHAN

Writing is the hardest way of earning a living, with the possible exception of wrestling alligators.
OLIN MILLER

The sinister thing about writing is that it starts off seeming so easy and ends up being so hard.
L. RUST MILLS

An author is a fool who, not content with having bored those who have lived with him, insists on boring future generations.
BARON DE MONTESQUIEU

When I stepped from hard manual work to writing, I just stepped from one kind of hard work to another.
SEAN O'CASEY

To write well consists of continuously making small erosions, wearing away grammar in its established form, current norms of language. It is an act of permanent rebellion and subversion against social environs.
JOSÉ ORTEGA Y GASSETT

Asking a working writer what he thinks about critics is like asking a lamppost what it feels about dogs.
JOHN OSBORNE

I have made this a rather long letter because I haven't had time to make it shorter.
BLAISE PASCAL

If, at the close of business each evening, I myself can understand what I've written, I feel the day hasn't been totally wasted.
S. J. PERELMAN

To me, writing is a horseback ride into heaven and hell and back. I am grateful if I can crawl back alive.
THOMAS SANCHEZ

I became a writer because during several of the most important years of my life, writing seemed to me to be the most unreal, unattractive, and unecessary idea ever imposed upon the human race.
WILLIAM SAROYAN

Writing, when properly managed, is but a different name for conversation.
LAURENCE STERNE

With 60 staring me in the face, I have developed inflammation of the sentence structure and a definite hardening of the paragraphs.
JAMES THURBER

Adam was the only man who, when he said a good thing, knew that nobody had said it before him.
MARK TWAIN

I was sorry to hear my name mentioned as one of the great authors, because they have a sad habit of dying off. Chaucer is dead, so is Milton, so is Shakespeare, and I am not feeling very well myself.
MARK TWAIN

My own luck has been curious all my literary life; I could never tell a lie that anyone would doubt, nor a truth that anyone would believe.
**MARK TWAIN**

Whenever the literary German dives into a sentence, that is the last you are going to see of him until he emerges on the other side of his Atlantic with his verb in his mouth.
**MARK TWAIN**

Mark Twain was so good with crowds that he became, in competition with singers and dancers and actors and acrobats, one of the most popular performers of his time. It is so unusual, and so psychologically unlikely, too, for a great writer to be a great performer, too. . . .
**KURT VONNEGUT**

I am persuaded that foolish writers and foolish readers are created for each other; and that fortune provides readers as she does mates for ugly women.
**HORACE WALPOLE**

Journalism justifies its own existence by the great Darwinian principle of the survival of the vulgarist.
**OSCAR WILDE**

The way Bernard Shaw believes in himself is very refreshing in these atheistic days when so many believe in no God at all.
**ISRAEL ZANGWILL**

## *Wrong*

A wrong-doer is often a man that has left something undone, not always he that has done something.
**MARCUS AURELIUS ANTONINUS**

The surest method against scandal is live it down in well-doing.
**HERMANN BOERHAAVE**

Those who cause divisions, in order to injure other people; are in fact preparing pitfalls for their own ruin.
**CHINESE PROVERB**

It is better to do the wrong thing that to do nothing.
**WINSTON CHURCHILL**

Faults of the head are punished in this world: those of the heart in another; but as most of our vices are compound, so is their punishment.
**CHARLES CALEB COLTON**

I have never been hurt by anything I didn't say.
**CALVIN COOLIDGE**

Never put a man in the wrong. He will hold it against you forever.
**WILL DURANT**

A man in the wrong may more easily be convinced than one half right.
**RALPH WALDO EMERSON**

His heart was a great as the world, but there was no room in it to hold the memory of a wrong.
**RALPH WALDO EMERSON**

Hoarding one's hurts hurts only the hoarder.
**MALCOLM FORBES**

Sin lies in hurting other people unnecessarily. All other sins are invented nonsense.
**ROBERT A. HEINLEIN**

It is better to suffer wrong than to do it, and happier to be sometimes cheated than not to trust.
SAMUEL JOHNSON

Never do a wrong thing to make a friend or to keep one.
ROBERT E. LEE

It has ever been my experience that folks who have no vices have very few virtues.
ABRAHAM LINCOLN

The worst-tempered people I've ever met were people who knew they were wrong.
WILSON MIZNER

Believe nothing against another but on good authority; and never report what may hurt another, unless it be a greater hurt to some other to conceal it.
WILLIAM PENN

A man should never be ashamed to own he has been in the wrong, which is but saying in other words, that he is wiser today than he was yesterday.
ALEXANDER POPE

When our vices quit us we flatter ourselves with the belief that it is we who quit them.
FRANÇOIS DE LA ROCHEFOUCAULD

What once were vices are now manners.
SENECA

He who injured you was either stronger or weaker. If he was weaker, spare him; if he was stronger, spare yourself.
SENECA

To persist in doing wrong extenuates not the wrong, but makes it much more heavy.
WILLIAM SHAKESPEARE

The best remedy for an injury is to forget it.
PUBLILIUS SYRUS

He who commits a wrong will himself inevitably see the writing on the wall, though the world may not count him guilty.
MARTIN TUPPER

It's often wrong to do the thing you have a right to do.
FRANK TYGER

The individual who cultivates grievances, and who is perpetually exacting explanations of his assumed wrongs, can only be ignored, and left to the education of time and of development.... One does not argue or contend with the foul miasma that settles over stagnant water; one leaves it and climbs to a higher region, where the air is pure and the sunshine fair.
LILLIAN WHITING

# Y

## Youth

Youth is easily deceived because it is quick to hope.
**ARISTOTLE**

Youth loves honor and victory more than money.
**ARISTOTLE**

Youth has the resilience to absorb disaster and weave it into the pattern of its life, no mater how anguishing the thorn that penetrates its flesh.
**SHOLEM ASCH**

Young men are fitter to invent than to judge; fitter for execution than for counsel; and fitter for new projects than for settled business.
**FRANCIS BACON**

When young men are beginning life, the most important period, it is often said, is that in which their habits are formed. That is a very important period. But the period in which the ideas of the young are formed and adopted is more important still. For the ideal with which you go forward to measure things determines the nature, so far as you are concerned, of everything you meet.
**HENRY WARD BEECHER**

Affection is certain deformity. By forming themselves on fantastic models, the young begin with being ridiculous and often end in being vicious.
**HUGH BLAIR**

Youth is young life plus curiosity minus understanding.
**ANTHONY BROOKS**

The youth of today and the youth of tomorrow will be accorded an almost unequaled opportunity for great accomplishment and for human service.
**NICHOLAS MURRAY BUTLER**

My supply of Scotch caution never has been small; but I was apparently something of a daredevil now and then to the manufacturing fathers of Pittsburgh. They were old and I was young, which made all the difference.
**ANDREW CARNEGIE**

Young men are apt to think themselves wise enough, as drunken men are apt to think themselves sober enough.
**LORD CHESTERFIELD**

Youth is always too serious, and just now it is too serious about frivolity.
**G. K. CHESTERTON**

Elderly people and those in authority cannot always be relied upon to take enlightened and comprehending views of what they call the indiscretions of youth.
**WINSTON CHURCHILL**

I remember my youth and the feeling that will never come back any more—the feeling that I could last forever, outlast the sea, the earth, and all men.
**JOSEPH CONRAD**

A boy who isn't handicapped is handicapped.
**E. L. CORD**

The young always have the same problem—how to rebel and conform at the same time. They have now

solved this by defying their parents and copying one another.
**QUENTIN CRISP**

If I had the opportunity to say a fine word to all the young people of America, it would be this: Don't think too much about yourselves. Try to cultivate the habit of thinking of others; this will reward you. Nourish your minds by good reading, constant reading. Discover what your lifework is, work in which you can do most good, in which you can be happiest. Be unafraid in all things when you know you are in the right.
**CHARLES W. ELIOT**

Tell me how a young man spends his evenings and I will tell you how far he is likely to go in the world. The popular notion is that a youth's progress depends upon how he acts during his working hours. It doesn't. It depends far more upon how he utilizes his leisure.... If he spends it in harmless idleness, he is likely to be kept on the payroll, but that will be about all. If he diligently utilizes his own time... to fit himself for more responsible duties, then the greater responsibilities—and greater rewards—are almost certain to come to him.
**B. C. FORBES**

I thoroughly agree with the famed Shaw observation that Youth is such a wonderful thing; what a crime that it is wasted on children. Just look at the present crop: Topped by hair so shaggy it would embarrass a shaggy dog. Dressed in gear that varies from Beatnik Boutique to Edwardian Mod. Expressing doubts that everything we tell them is necessarily so.

Reported in a recent *New York Times* piece was a passage describing today's youth as loving luxury, hating authority, being bored, ill-mannered, and lacking respect for adults. That observation was ascribed to 4th century B.C. philosopher Socrates.
**MALCOLM FORBES (1966)**

This is a youth-oriented society, and the joke is on them because youth is a disease from which we all recover.
**DOROTHY FULDHEIM**

I leave everything to the young men. You've got to give youthful men authority and responsibility if you're going to build up an organization. Otherwise you'll always be the boss yourself and you won't leave anything behind you.
**A. P. GIANNINI (70)**

You're immature if you can't accept reality or responsibility.
**ARNOLD GLASOW**

Girls we love for what they are; young men for what they promise to be.
**JOHANN WOLFGANG VON GOETHE**

The destiny of any nation, at any given time, depends on the opinions of its young men under five-and-twenty.
**JOHANN WOLFGANG VON GOETHE**

You are only young once, but you can be immature forever.
**JOHN P. GRIER**

Immaturity can last a lifetime.
**ROBERT HALF**

Young man: Be honest; train yourself for useful work; love God.
**MILTON S. HERSHEY**

I would not waste the springtime of my youth in idle dalliance; I would plant rich seeds to blossom in my manhood, and bear fruit when I am old.
**HILLHOUSE**

A compilation of what outstanding people said or wrote at the age of 20 would make a collection of asinine pronouncements.
**ERIC HOFFER**

If a society is to preserve stability and a degree of continuity, it must know how to keep its adolescents from imposing their tastes, attitudes, values and fantasies on everyday life.
**ERIC HOFFER**

It is the malady of our age that the young are so busy teaching us that they have no time left to learn.
**ERIC HOFFER**

Youth is a frightening age . . . so many problems; so little wisdom to solve them.
**WALTER HOVING**

Every young man should aim at independence and should prepare himself for a vocation; above all, he should so manage his life that the steps of his progress are taken without improper aids; that he calls no one master, that he does not win or deserve the reputation of being a tool of others, and that if called to public service he may assume its duties with the satisfaction of knowing that he is free to rise to the height of his opportunity.
**CHARLES EVANS HUGHES**

Develop in youth the devotion to home interests and home affairs, to community interests and community affairs that led the founding fathers to establish a nation of communities upon this continent, dedicated to a decent, free life of equal opportunity under God, and consecrated to the principle that the State exists as an instrument for serving the individual, not for enslaving him. So instructed, American youth can be trusted.
**JOSEPH P. KENNEDY**

Hard are life's early steps; and but that youth is buoyant, confident and strong in hope, men would behold its threshold and despair.
**LETITIA E. LANDON**

When I was young I looked like Al Capone, but I lacked his compassion.
**OSCAR LEVANT**

So long as a man still has inspiration and the will to go on, he still exemplifies youth.
**MAURICE J. LEWI**

When we are out of sympathy with the young, then I think our work in this world is over.
**GEORGE MACDONALD**

The much-sought prize of eternal youth is just arrested development.
**EDGAR LEE MASTERS**

Youth is the opportunity to do something and to become somebody.
**THEODORE T. MUNGER**

The surest way to corrupt a young man is to teach him to esteem more highly those who think alike than those who think differently.
**FRIEDRICH WILHELM NIETZSCHE**

Youth is not a time of life; it is a state of mind. People grow old only by deserting their ideals and by outgrowing the consciousness of youth. Years wrinkle the skin, but to give up enthusiasm wrinkles the soul. . . . You are as old as your doubt; your fear; your despair. The way to keep young is to keep your faith young. Keep your self-confidence young. Keep your hope young.
**LUELLA F. PHELAN**

Not once have I sighed for childhood and youth again.
WALTER B. PITKIN

Like its politicians and its wars, society has the teenagers it deserves.
J. B. PRIESTLEY

Consider what heavy responsibility lies upon you in your youth, to determine, among realities, by what you will be delighted, and, among imaginations, by whose you will be led.
JOHN RUSKIN

To the young I should offer two maxims: Don't accept superficial solutions of difficult problems. It is better to do a little good than much harm. I should not offer anything more specific; every young person should decide on his or her own credo.
BERTRAND RUSSELL

My suggestion to ambitious young men would be to conserve and develop their physical and mental strength, cram their heads with all the useful knowledge they can, and work, work, work—not simply for their own advancement but to get worthwhile things done.
EDWARD G. SEUBERT

The real problem in the years ahead is one of making the most efficient use of all our national resources—and not the least of these resources is our intelligent youth.
GEORGE A. SLOAN

There is nothing that you can have when you are old that can replace being young and having nothing.
MARY WALLACE SMITH

All sorts of allowances are made for the illusions of youth; and none, or almost none, for the disenchantments of age.
ROBERT LOUIS STEVENSON

The best rules to form a young man are: to talk a little, to hear much, to reflect alone upon what has passed in company, to distrust one's own opinions, and value others' that deserve it.
WILLIAM J. TEMPLE

Life would be infinitely happier if we could only be born at the age of 80 and gradually approach 18.
MARK TWAIN

There is no trade or employment but the young man following it may become a hero.
WALT WHITMAN

Youth is a circumstance you can't do anything about. The trick is to grow up without getting old.
FRANK LLOYD WRIGHT

When you are dissatisfied and would like to go back to youth, think of algebra.
GENE YASENAK

A young man of pleasure is a man of pains.
YOUNG

# Z

## Zeal

There is no place in a fanatic's head where reason can enter.
NAPOLEON BONAPARTE

The greatest dangers to liberty lurk in insidious encroachment by men of zeal, well meaning but without understanding.
LOUIS D. BRANDEIS

Zeal without knowledge is like fire without a grate to contain it; like a sword without a hilt to wield it by; like a high-bred horse without a bridle to guide him. It speaks without thinking, acts without planning, seeks to accomplish a good end without the adoption of becoming means.
JULIUS BATE

Experience shows that success is due less to ability than to zeal. The winner is he who gives himself to his work body and soul.
CHARLES BUXTON

A fanatic is one who can't change his mind and won't change the subject.
WINSTON CHURCHILL

The fanatic is incorruptible: If he kills for an idea, he can just as well get himself killed for one; in either case, tyrant or martyr, he is a monster.
E. M. CIORAN

Zeal without knowledge is sister of folly.
JOHN DAVIES

A fanatic is a man that does what he thinks the Lord would if He knew all the facts.
FINLEY PETER DUNNE

Zeal is fit only for wise men, but is found mostly in fools.
THOMAS FULLER

Zeal without knowledge is fire without light.
THOMAS FULLER

Political extremism involves two prime ingredients: an excessively simple diagnosis of the world's ills and a conviction that there are identifiable villains back of it all.
JOHN W. GARDNER

I do not love a man who is zealous for nothing.
OLIVER GOLDSMITH

Defoe says that there were a hundred thousand country fellows in his time ready to fight to the death against popery, without knowing whether popery was a man or a horse.
WILLIAM HAZLITT

If there is anything more dangerous to the life of the mind than having no independent commitment to ideas, it is having an excess of commitment to some special and constricted idea.
RICHARD HOFSTADTER

At least two-thirds of our miseries spring from human stupidity, human malice and those great motivators and justifiers of malice and stupidity:

idealism, dogmatism and proselytizing zeal on behalf of religious or political ideas.
ALDOUS HUXLEY

In the fevered state of our country, no good can ever result from any attempt to set one of these fiery zealots to rights, either in fact or in principle. They are determined as to the facts they will believe and the opinions on which they will act.
THOMAS JEFFERSON

Zeal is very blind, or badly regulated, when it encroaches upon the rights of others.
QUESNEL

Fanaticism consists in redoubling your efforts when you have forgotten your aim.
GEORGE SANTAYANA

Zeal for the public good is the characteristic of a man of honor and a gentleman, and must take place of pleasures, profits, and all other private gratifications. Whoever wants this motive, is an open enemy, or an inglorious neuter to mankind, in proportion to the misapplied advantages with which nature and fortune have blessed him.
RICHARD STEELE

Nothing spoils human nature more than false zeal. The good nature of a heathen is more God-like than the furious zeal of a Christian.
BENJAMIN WHICHCOTE

An infallible method of making fanatics is to persuade before you instruct.
VOLTAIRE

# INDEX